OUR FIREMEN

A HISTORY OF THE
NEW YORK FIRE DEPARTMENTS

Volunteer and Paid

OUR FIREMEN.

A.E. COSTELLO
AUTHOR and PUBLISHER.

OUR FIREMEN

A HISTORY

OF THE

New York Fire Departments

≫ VOLUNTEER AND PAID ≪

By

Augustine E. Costello

First published in 1887.

CHRONOLOGICAL, HISTORICAL, STATISTICAL, AND BIOGRAPHICAL PORTRAITS OF THE MOST
FAMOUS FIREMEN, AND SKETCHES OF THEIR DEEDS OF SELF-SACRIFICE AND INTREPIDITY
• A RECORD OF GALLANT ACHIEVEMENTS • AN ILLUSTRATED HISTORY OF THE OLD
HAND ENGINE OF THE PAST AND THE STEAM ENGINE OF THE PRESENT •
INSURANCE, ITS BENEFICENCE AND IMPORTANCE • GREAT FIRES OF
THE METROPOLIS FOR TWO CENTURIES • THE ARCHITECTURAL
GROWTH OF THE EMPIRE CITY • MECHANICAL DEVICES
• FIRE ZOUAVES • THE CHARITABLE FUND •
MEMORABLE TARGET COMPANIES, ETC.

KNICKERBOCKER
PRESS

NEW YORK

OUR FIREMEN
A HISTORY OF THE NEW YORK FIRE DEPARTMENTS
Volunteer and Paid

Published by
KNICKERBOCKER PRESS
276 Fifth Avenue
New York, NY 10001

Copyright © 1997 by Knickerbocker Press

First published in 1887 by A.E. Costello.

ISBN 1-57715-013-9

MANUFACTURED IN THE UNITED STATES OF AMERICA.

Our Firemen.

When the red sheet winds and whirls,
 In the coil of frightful death,
When the bannered smoke unfurls,
 And the hot walls drink our breath;
When the far-off crowd appears,
 Choking in the demon glare,
And some helpless form appears,
 In that furnace of despair;
"Save! Oh! Save!" the people cry;
 But who plucks the human brand?
Who will do the deed or die?
 'Tis a Fireman of the land!
Then give them Honor, give them Fame,
 A health to hands that fight
 the flame.
 —Eliza Cook.

This Book is Dedicated to

Our Firemen.

IF PROMETHEUS WAS WORTHY OF THE WRATH OF HEAVEN FOR KINDLING
THE FIRST FIRE UPON EARTH, HOW OUGHT ALL THE GODS TO HONOR THE MEN
WHO MAKE IT THEIR PROFESSIONAL BUSINESS TO PUT IT OUT.

John G. Saxe.

HISTORY OF THE FIRE DEPARTMENTS OF THE CITY OF NEW YORK, to be worthy of the subject, should embrace the most important and interesting episodes of the municipal government. So intimate were these departments connected with, and so closely are they still related to, all that is most worthy of mention in the history of the city, that the story of the Fire Departments is, to a great extent, the story of the rise, progress, and development of the City of New York.

Our Firemen, Volunteer and Paid, have left imperishable names and cherished memories which are dear to our citizens.

The recital of their self-sacrificing deeds must recall whatever is sublime in fidelity to duty and the faithful performance of a sacred public trust. No body of men could have been imbued with a more praiseworthy and unselfish desire to protect life and property. The Fire Departments, from the beginning, have been composed of men, who, at the call of duty, have abandoned their business, the social circle, or the comfortable surroundings of the family, when called upon to do battle with the flames. Their ardor and enthusiasm have borne them into hardships and dangers from which men made of stuff less stern would have shrunk in dismay. Not so they; the more imminent the danger —the greater the difficulty—the more dauntless their courage and the more their intrepidity verged on recklessness. Through fire and smoke, and amid the crash of falling walls, Our Firemen, impelled by an inspiring sense of duty, have ever remained valiantly at their post and faced death with the unflinching fortitude of true soldiers. The life of a Fireman, it is almost superfluous to say, is one of constant hardship and danger. He jeopardizes his life that others may live. He sacrifices his personal and domestic comfort that the safety and happiness of his fellow citizens may be assured. In a word, the duties of a Fireman are so exacting, so full of menace to life and limb, and so much depends upon his exertions in moments of panic and peril, that every man in the Department may be said to have the attributes of a hero.

The debt of gratitude our citizens owe these brave men can never be fully repaid. The men who "went before," who were legislated out of unpaid office by the Act of March 30, 1865, are passing away. The Paid Department has attained the highest efficiency possible. Could then a better time than the present be chosen for publishing a history of their methods and their appliances from 1648 to date? No work worthy of the subject—a monument to both Old and New—exists. The lives saved, the property protected, the suffering and the catastrophes averted, cannot be estimated by the imperfect and meagre statistics to be found in the archives of the Department.

The writer has made an earnest, if not a successful, effort, to do justice to the achievements and fame of our New York Firemen. The importance of the subject has made it difficult of treatment, and has called for an expenditure of money which in any other book would be considered reckless extravagance. The engravings (over six hundred and fifty in number) are certainly not without merit, and all bear the stamp of originality. Major D. E. Cronin's well-known artistic ability has largely contributed to the embellishment of these pages. Credit in this line is also due to Mr. Louis Oram. As to the literary style of the book, the writer cannot undertake to be his own critic. No attempt has been made to depart from a plain, straightforward statement of facts. Fine writing is not aimed at; like beauty, the story of Our Firemen needs no extraneous adornment. The writer, however, has the satisfaction of knowing that no pains have been spared to make this history complete and accurate in every detail and department.

The history of Insurance Matters, the Fire Engine, and the Architectural Growth of the City has been compiled from the most trustworthy sources, and will doubtless lend an additional interest to the work.

The chapters devoted to biography are, perhaps, the most interesting of any in the book. They treat of men whose lives have been devoted to fire service—human salamanders, in a sense—who braved the devouring element, with all its attending dangers, and performed duties the most laborious, in the interest of humanity and philanthrophy. That the names and records of others (equally brave and zealous firemen) have been omitted is no fault of the author. The line had to be drawn somewhere, or else there would be no limit to the number of pages. While it is true that the names of men whose services are entitled to honorable recognition in a work of this description have been unavoidably excluded, not from any unworthy motive, but because of the exigencies of space, it cannot be said that those who have been mentioned are not entitled to all the praise bestowed upon them. Above all things, accuracy of statement has been aimed at. For the first time the history of the various fire companies has been compiled and published. This, it need hardly be said, was no easy task. Owing to the large number of companies, length of service, and varied experiences, it was impossible to do strict justice to all by publishing their history with that fullness of detail to which, no doubt, they are properly entitled. Much that is interesting and important has been left unsaid; but what has been printed is in the main correct. To insure so desirable an end, proofs of each company have been submitted for revision to firemen who were cognizant of the facts. The same plan has been adopted with respect to other leading departments or features of the book. By this means a number of firemen have been actively employed in the editing of this book.

Much, it is true, had to be sacrificed that would make very interesting reading; but brevity has its virtues also. The admonition of Judas Maccabœus to the ambassadors has had its application in the writing of this book:

"Speak, and be brief,
Waste not the time in useless rhetoric.
Words are not things."

Some old firemen, or other critics, may, perhaps, say that the book contains a vast amount of local history not specially appertaining to fire matters; for instance, the chapters on Architecture, the Water Supply of the City, Improvement and Growth of the Metropolis, Fire Insurance, etc. It is, however, the opinion of the writer, that all these subjects, apart from their great interest to the public generally, and New Yorkers particularly, are intimately connected with the history of the rise, progress, and development of the Fire Departments of this city. They are not mere " side shows;" they are part and parcel of the story of Our Firemen—as essential as the character of Hamlet himself to the play which bears his name—and without which this history would be incomplete and unsatisfactory.

This book has grown to such stalwart proportions, past all calculation, in fact, that the writer has been urged to issue it in two volumes. This, however, he considered ill advised. Experience teaches that one big volume, even if it is high-priced, will command a larger sale than the same work divided into two volumes, and made cheap at that. It is useless to say here what labor and money have been expended to make this volume worthy of the cause and the subject. It will suffice that the book is now in the hands of the public.

A large portion of the Extra Library Edition is already disposed of. This fact is one that naturally brings joy to the heart of the writer and the endorsers, and demonstrates the great popularity of OUR FIREMEN. The uniform price of the Extra Library Edition is:

FULL TURKEY MOROCCO, GILT EDGES, $10.

This edition (sold in this city only), will be printed on fine calendered paper, and will, it is hoped, be an artistic and a literary triumph.

Other prices of the book are:

HALF TURKEY MOROCCO, MARBLE EDGES, $8.   ENGLISH CLOTH, PLAIN EDGES, $6.

Our leading citizens and business men will be afforded an opportunity to become subscribers to the Extra Edition; the names so recorded forming, as it were, a Roll of Honor. The great popularity of OUR FIREMEN, apart from the merits of the book, or the objects of publication, will, doubtless, find a ready sale for this and many other editions. At all events, the publisher intends to act well his part in doing all in his power to make the book a business success. That, after all, is the main object, regarded from an everyday point of view.

The writer takes pride—pardonable, he hopes—in drawing attention to the fact that this book is published under the most favorable auspices. Not alone has he received the endorsement and approval of the various fire organizations of this city, and the hearty support and co-operation of leading Firemen, but the book is also published under the sanction of contract with the Trustees of the Relief Fund of the Paid Fire Department (the Fire Commissioners), and the Board of Directors of the Volunteer Firemen's Association.

COPY OF CERTIFICATE FROM THE TRUSTEES OF THE FIREMEN'S RELIEF FUND (FIRE COMMISSIONERS):

HEADQUARTERS

Fire Department City of New York,

155 & 157 MERCER STREET,

HENRY D. PURROY, RICHARD CROKER, ELWARD SMITH, } Commissioners. *New York, December 16th 1885.*

"THIS IS TO CERTIFY, *That the Trustees of the Relief Fund, Fire Department, City of New York, have consented to the publication of a history of the Department, by Mr. Augustine E. Costello,* * * * * * * * *in the preparation of which Mr. Costello has been given access to the records of this Department.*"

Trustees of the Relief Fund, { Henry D. Purroy
Richard Croker
Edward Smith.

December 16, 1885.

AUGUSTINE E. COSTELLO, ESQR.

DEAR SIR: I have the honor to transmit to you herewith Certificate signed by the Trustees of the Relief Fund of this Department, concerning the publication of a history of the Department, etc., by you.

Very Respectfully,

Carl Jussen
Secretary

CERTIFICATE, BOARD OF DIRECTORS OF THE VOLUNTEER FIREMEN'S
ASSOCIATION:

HEADQUARTERS
Volunteer Firemen's Association

Of the City of New York.

143 East Eighth Street, bet. Broadway and 4th Ave.

New York, Deer 15ᵗʰ 1886.

Board of Directors in regular session. Mr. John J. Blair, chairman, presiding, and two-thirds of the Board present ; it was

Resolved, That the Board, on behalf, and in the name of "The Volunteer Firemen's Association of the City of New York," fully endorse and recognize the book, "OUR FIREMEN," as a work peculiarly thorough and complete. In fact, a work, as a history of the Fire Department, that is well worthy of the subject. We regard the volume as immensely superior to any of the kind ever published.

*   *   *   *   *   *   *   *   *   *   *

Resolved, That we heartily recommend the book to the perusal of the general public—firemen and citizens alike—as well worthy of their attention.   *   *   *   *   *

Resolved, That the volume, "OUR FIREMEN," is the *only* publication of the kind having the endorsement of our organization,   *   *   *   *   *   *   *   *

William E. Bishop.
Financial Secretary

Countersigned
John Decker
President.
James S. Ferris
1st Vice President

AUGUSTINE E. COSTELLO,
Author and Publisher "OUR FIREMEN."

FROM GEORGE W. ANDERSON, PRESIDENT VETERAN FIREMEN'S ASSOCIATION:

Veteran Firemen's Association,
OF THE CITY OF NEW YORK.
53 East Tenth Street

New York, December 10 1886

Mr A. E. Costello
Dear Sir

Realizing, and appreciating the magnitude of the task you have accomplished in the publication of the book "Our Firemen", we desire to place on record our hearty approval and endorsement of the same. You can rest assured that our earnest efforts to promote the interest of the enterprise will be sincerely extended,

Very truly Yours
Geo W Anderson.
Prest Vet Firemens Assn.

ENDORSEMENT FURNISHED BY EX-FIRE COMMISSIONER AND PRESENT POLICE JUSTICE JOHN J. GORMAN, PRESIDENT EXEMPT FIREMEN'S BENEVOLENT FUND:

OFFICE BOARD OF TRUSTEES EXEMPT FIREMEN'S BENEVOLENT FUND,
NO. 174 CANAL STREET,
NEW YORK, January 27, 1887.

MR. AUGUSTINE E. COSTELLO,
Author and Publisher "OUR FIREMEN."

MY DEAR SIR : It is with very great pleasure, that I, on behalf of the Board of Trustees of the Exempt Firemen's Benevolent Fund of the City of New York, hereby endorse your book, "OUR FIREMEN"; a book, I am free to say, of great research, historical merit, and remarkable accuracy. For the first time a history of the Fire Department of this city has been written. Your book, "OUR FIREMEN," is worthy the name and the subject. I commend its perusal to all, and hope that it will meet with public favor, as it is undoubtedly deserving of popular success.

I am, very truly yours,

John J Gorman

President, Exempt Firemen's Benevolent Fund.

ENDORSEMENT OF WILLIAM M. RANDELL, SECRETARY OF THE FIRE PATROL COMMITTEE, NEW YORK BOARD OF FIRE UNDERWRITERS:

NEW YORK BOARD OF FIRE UNDERWRITERS,
FIRE PATROL COMMITTEE,
No. 115 Broadway, February 1, 1887.

A. E. COSTELLO.

MY DEAR SIR: I have had the pleasure of perusing some of the advance sheets of your new book, "OUR FIREMEN," and I desire to express my appreciation of it.

I unhesitatingly endorse the book, and recommend it as well worthy of public favor.

It is historic, full of information, and highly interesting, and recalls many reminiscenses of fire life, and of our city's growth and prosperity.

Wishing you much success, I am, very truly yours.

Wm M. Randell

A. C. HENDRICK, TREASURER,
NEW HAVEN, CONN.

GEO. A. STEERE, PRESIDENT,
PROVIDENCE, R. I

HENRY A. HILLS, SECRETARY,
CINCINNATI O.

National Association of Fire Engineers. Office of Secretary

Cincinnati, O., Feby 9th 1887

Augustine E. Costello Esq
Author and Publisher of "Our Firemen"
My Dear Sir:—

Naturally the National Association of Fire Engineers take great interest in the success of your book "Our Firemen", Knowing as we all do of its great merit and thoroughness in dealing with the complicated and diversified subject of which it treats, We have been long looking for such a book, and now we have got it we mean to show our appreciation by practical efforts in forwarding the interests of the book.

"Our Firemen" I have no doubt will command a very large sale.

With best wishes I am
Yours Very Truly
Henry A. Hills Secretary
National Association of
Fire Engineers —

The publisher begs leave to say that no DONATIONS will be accepted. His desire is that the book should sell on its merits.

It would be the height of ingratitude if the writer did not make suitable acknowledgments to the friends and collaborators who have so largely assisted in the compilation of this book. The thanks of the undersigned are due to Mr. George B. Taylor, of the New York *Times*, who has an intimate knowledge of fire matters. Mr. James Clancy, of the New York *Herald*, has also rendered signal service. The warmest thanks of the writer are likewise due to the Fire Commissioners, Secretary Carl Jussen, William M. Randell, William B. Dunley, W. P. Allen, E. B. Child, Hon. Charles P. Daly, Judge John J. Gorman, and others, for many kind offices rendered. Acknowledgments for courtesy shown are also due to Arnett C. Smith, No. 14 Fulton Street, and to Charles E. Van Glahn, No. 546 Fifth Avenue, who possess very fine collections of relics of the Old Volunteer Department.

Augustine E. Costello

MARCH, 1887.

CONTENTS.

CHAPTER VII.

CHAPTER VIII.

CHAPTER IX.

CHAPTER X.

CHAPTER XI.

CHAPTER XII.

CHAPTER XIII.

CHAPTER XIV.

CHAPTER XXVIII.

CHAPTER XXIX.

CHAPTER XXX.

CHAPTER XXXI.

CHAPTER XXXII.

CHAPTER XXXIII.

CONTENTS.

CHAPTER XLI.

Organization and Incorporation of the Fund.—The First Beginnings.—Quaint and Strange Methods Adopted to Create a Fund.—Names of the Early Officers.—Legislation Looking to the Creation of a Charitable Fund and its Distribution.—The Beneficiaries.—The Amount of Money Received each Year.—Revenue Derived from Annual Balls.—A Tax of Two Per Cent. License Fees Exacted from Insurance Agents.—The Metropolitan Fair.—Firemen's Monument.—Fire Commissioners.

CHAPTER XLII.

(Eleventh N. Y. S. V.)—Brave Deeds that have Gone into History.—The Firemen Gallantly Respond to President Lincoln's Appeal for Men.—Formation of the First Regiment of Fire Zouaves.—On to Washington.—Death of Colonel Ellsworth.— Colonel Farnham Taken from the Field in a Dying Condition.—Captain Jack Wildey. —Colonel Leoser.—Lieutenant Divver.—The Second Regiment of Fire Zouaves.— Their Valiant Services in the Field.

CHAPTER XLIII.

House in Fulton Street.—Old Building.—Site of Fireman's Hall.—Mercer Street Headquarters.—Laying of the Corner Stone.—Imposing Ceremonies.—Speech by Thomas Franklin.

CHAPTER XLIV.

Some of the Brilliant Annual Entertainments of the Old Department.—Wealth, Fashion, and Beauty at the Terpsichorean Entertainments.—All for Charity.—Organizations that were Concurrent with the Fire Companies.—Target Practice.—The Gulick Guards and Others.—Chowder Parties.—What the Old Boys did with Themselves after their Disbandment.

CHAPTER XLV.

Their Headquarters and Association Rooms.—The Association of Exempt Firemen.— New York Firemen's Association.—Volunteer Firemen's Association.—Veteran Firemen's Association.—A Noble Charity.—Reception Tendered to the Old Guard.— Volunteer Firemen's Sons' Association.

CHAPTER XLVI.

George Washington an Active Fireman.—His Great Interest in Fire Matters.—The Growth and Progress of the City.—Some Quaint Fire Ordinances.—Fires and Fire Bugs.—Life Saving Firemen.—Gallant and Devoted.—Brave Men; Honest Men. —We may not Look upon their Like again.

PAID DEPARTMENT.

CHAPTER LIV.

The Great Benevolent Society.—Blest Offspring of Modern Civilization.—The Friend of the Poor, the Guardian of the Helpless, the Protector of Home, the Safeguard of Honorable Competence.

CHAPTER LV.

Its Origin, Growth, and Development.—Fire Apparatus in Use before the Christian Era.— The Force Pump.—The Invention of Fire Engines.—Application of the Air Chamber.— Introduction of Leather Hose.—Newsham's and Simpkin's Inventions.—Ericsson's Portable Steam Engine, Etc., Etc.

CHAPTER LVI.

First Habitations Occupied by White Settlers on Manhattan Island.—Primitive Structures. Dutch Architecture.—Some Important Buildings Erected about the Beginning of the Present Century.—More Recent Improvements.—The Great Expansion of the City.— Fire-Proof Buildings.—Churches, Public Edifices, Flats, and Private Dwellings.

CHAPTER LVII.

Improved new Engine Houses.—Description of the new Headquarters' Building.—A Fine Edifice.—The Fire Marshal.—Knowing Horses and Dogs.—Life in the Engine House.— Getting Quickly to a Fire.—Running Risks.—St. George's Flats.

CHAPTER LVIII.

Some Heads of Departments Throughout the Country.—Big Cities with Distinguished Fire Chiefs.—Men who have Risen through Merit.—Their Experiences and Responsibilities.

LIST OF ILLUSTRATIONS.

VOLUNTEER DEPARTMENT.

PAID DEPARTMENT.

Our Firemen:

History of the New York Fire Departments.

CHAPTER I.

GENESIS OF FIRE EXTINGUISHING.

1609—1664.—Manhattan Island as seen by the discoverer, Henry Hudson.—"A Rugged Fragment of Creation." — Primitive Fire Apparatus. — Quaint Customs. — Dutch Architecture. — First Fire Ordinance (1648).—Fire Wardens and Surveyors of Buildings.—The Reign of the Knickerbockers.

IN considering the history of the Fire Departments of New York City some degree of attention must necessarily be given to a variety of subjects calculated to illustrate the growth and rapid development of the city. And what a wonderful story that is! What a bewildering panorama it reveals! What changes have to be noted, what pregnant events dwelt upon, and what a wonderful tale of progress is to be unfolded! What alterations, moreover, have occurred in the locality now occupied by the city of New York since the ship of the discoverer first entered its quiet waters, or even since the burgomasters and schepens of New Amsterdam surrendered the infant metropolis to its English captors. The cluster of trading houses and rude huts of those days has expanded into the first city of the United States and the third largest in the world, containing over one million and a half of inhabitants, and untold wealth. But marvelous as is this material progress, it is not a whit more so than the story of the New York firemen. This gallant band of citizens has been and still continues to be, the protectors and defenders of the city in all its varied stages—from infancy to manhood. Such changes as have been effected from time to time in the organization of the departments have been brought about to conform to pressing public requirements and to keep pace with the times. Hence it became necessary, at successive periods, to pass a number of municipal ordinances regulating the force and defining their duty. These ordinances contain a pretty comprehensive history of the doings and operations of the firemen of our city.

It is also a noteworthy circumstance that the New World, even in its youth, should have shown its parent how best to guard against the dreadful ravages of fire, and how most scientifically to fight the flames which had been the terror of the Old World.

Europe, with its ages of civilization, and with all its inventive talent, had conceived nothing like the New York Fire Departments. No transatlantic city could show so devoted a band of men as our old Volunteers; and to-day our new department stands unrivaled for efficiency. The fame of the paid department has crossed the seas. One of the first sights which visitors to our shores are anxious to see is a fire engine house. An exhibition drill is to them some-

LANDING OF HENRY HUDSON.

From back of Hudson Hose Co., No. 1. Original in rooms of Volunteer Association, Eighth Street.

thing to be remembered in after years. But the volunteers were the pioneers of the glory of the Fire Department of New York. It is not too much to say that they built up the present admirable system. They, at least, largely and directly contributed to the perfection of its organization.

Our early firemen were drawn from all ranks in life—the greater part from the most influential classes. Each man felt he had a stake in the city, and readily volunteered his services. Many of them were individually the makers of our history. As a body, they have written one of the most remarkable pages in the history of the country. A volume devoted to these gallant fellows ought, therefore, to be a very interesting one.

As we have already intimated, we cannot touch a single company of the fire department, or the briefest period of the annals of that company, without finding ourselves face to face with some interesting bit of the history of New York. The histories of New York are all excellent in their way, but not one, we presume to say, has dealt with its people as this history does. We have walked into the people's houses, so to speak, and have become intimate with them as no ordinary historian, who views men and manners afar off, has yet thought of doing. The result of our industry, of our new departure, appears in every page. The Fire Department is co-existent with the first Dutch settlement. It makes us acquainted with the British colonists; it carries us into revolutionary times; we are borne along in the telling of its story to those piping times of peace when the only enemy that menaced the Empire City was the fire fiend or the importation of disease; it brings us up to the stirring political times that for thirty years preceded the rebellion, and then it launches us into those years, red with the blood of contending brothers, and wherein

OLDEST VIEW OF NEW AMSTERDAM. FROM THE BESCHRYRINGHE VAN VIRGINIA, 1651.
From Drawing in possession of W. M. Randell, Office of Board of Fire Underwriters.

those gallant firemen have played a conspicuous part. The experience of the firemen has been of use to the architect and the merchant. Nearly every improvement in the way of building has been the suggestion of men who have seen the evil effects of old methods and styles. They have given a fillip to the inventiveness of the practical engineer, and have helped to improve, in various ways, the useful arts. Thus, it will be seen, that no one who is ambitious to write a true history of the Fire Department can fail of writing a history of New York City, with all that the name implies.

What, then, would Henry Hudson, the intrepid navigator, when he landed on these shores, have thought of such a story, had the enchanted wand of some wizard transformed the primeval beauties of Manhattan Island into the panoramic picture which it presents to-day, with its vast population, its commercial enterprises, and teeming business life. Surely, the adventurous skipper of the "Vlie-boat" or "Half Moon" would have thought it impossible that in the period of two and three-quarters of a century such a metamorphosis could have taken place. Well may we believe that he lingered with enthusiastic delight along the picturesque shores of the harbor and the bay, the magnificence of the scenery being such as to cause him rapturously to exclaim, "It is as beautiful a land as the foot of man can tread upon!"

The site of New York originally presented only a wild and rough aspect, covered with a thick forest, its beach broken and sandy, or rocky and full of inlets forming marshes. These irregularities of surface rendered it all the more undesirable for building purposes. The early colonists made but little effort to overcome or remove those rude obstacles of nature in the path of civilized life.

"A more forbidding spot of earth," remarks a local historian, "on which to erect a great city has seldom been seen than was presented in the original ground plan of the city of New York; and in rearing a city on such a foundation the builders have combined the arts of the stonecutters of ancient Petræa and the amphibious labors of the founders of Venice and St. Petersburg."

Sudden acclivities and projecting crags were originally intermingled with ponds and marshes. In some parts the tide penetrated nearly to the middle of

AN INDIAN VILLAGE OF THE MANHATTANS.
Prior to the occupation by the Dutch.

the island; and in others were fresh water ponds, elevated considerably above tidewater. Midway between the Hudson and East Rivers was a pond of fresh water, which was discharged by a brook running southeastwardly to the East River, through a vast swamp or estuary—the tract now reaching from Pearl Street on the west to Catharine Street on the east, and extending up nearly to Chatham Street. To the west of this swamp was another of less extent, separated from the former by a ridge, upon which Pearl Street runs. This, in after years, was long known as Beekman's swamp. To the west of the fresh pond was a valley of wet land reaching down to the Hudson, and ending in a marsh, a region now traversed by Canal Street. Beyond this belt of fresh water and marshes, that almost insulated the part below them, there lay to the northeastward a fine tract of arable land and extensive meadows, the south-eastern angle of which was known for many years as Corlaer's Hook, so called after an early proprietor. Farther up, on the eastern side, the land was more broken and rocky, swelling into eminences, with intervening swamps and morasses. The west side of the island was less varied in its natural features. The shore of the Hudson for a distance of three or four miles was low, and intersected by bays and estuaries.

As seen by the early navigators, this rugged fragment of creation was clothed in its primeval forests. The land thus discovered was not altogether an uninhabited waste. Scattered and enfeebled bands of the great family of the Mohegans were found along the banks of the Hudson. In character, habits, and pursuits, the human tenants of these wilds were but one remove from their irrational associates of the wilderness.

Adrian Block and his companions, whose ship was destroyed by fire, suffered great hardships on the island in the winter of 1613. They erected four huts near the southern point of the island, or about the present site of No. 39 Broadway. These were the first human habitations constructed by Europeans on the Island of Manhattan.

Ten years later, the dwellers, who had increased in numbers, built themselves huts, and, for the common protection, constructed a fort, which they made in the form of a regular square, with four bastions. Those who could not find room within the fort built houses under the walls, and they formed the first street. This they called Hoogh Straat, now Pearl Street. Presently rude cottages began to cluster about the block house, and in good time the incipient metropolis assumed the title of New Amsterdam, while the whole territory of Hudson's River was called New Netherland. During the directorship of Peter Minuet (1624-33) the whole island of Manhattan was

PETER STUYVESANT AND BURGOMASTERS.

purchased from the Indians for a sum about equal to twenty-four dollars. As the rigorous winter season demanded a plentiful supply of fuel, the dry and inflammable nature of the huts—for houses they can scarcely be called—often gave rise to very destructive and alarming conflagrations. As early as the year 1628, it is recorded that some of the property of the colonists had been destroyed by fire. The experience of this, their first fire, was not lost upon them, for we find that in this year, "the making of brick, lime, and potash, was now begun, and grist and saw mills were built."

"On this island of Manhattan," says the Rev. Isaac Jogues, "and in its environs, there may well be four or five hundred men of different sects and nations; the Director-General told me that there were persons of eighteen different languages; they are settled here and there on the river, above and below, as the beauty and conveniences of the spot invited each to settle; some mechanics, however, who ply their trades, are ranged under the fort; all the others were exposed to the incursions of the natives, who, in the year 1643, while I was there, actually killed some two score Hollanders, and burnt many houses and barns full of wheat.''

After the conclusion, on the part of the authorities, to build a city tavern, in the year 1642, its site was selected close to the shore, south of the road to the ferry. The building was of considerable dimensions and cost; and this place was chosen for its situation, as giving a good appearance to the town from the harbor. The building was erected near high water mark, on the present northwest corner of Pearl Street and Coenties Alley. After the organization of the city magistracy, in 1653, this building was ceded to the city for the purpose of a city hall, and was used as such until the year 1699. Its principal use was for the sittings of the burgomasters and schepens, and for the prison. The chamber occupied for the sitting of the magistrates was on the southeast corner of the second story, the prison chamber being in the rear, on the other side of the house, facing a yard which extended to ''Hoogh Straat'' (Pearl Street). Upon the roof was a cupola, in which was hung a bell, in the year 1656, which was rung for the assembling of the magistrates, and also on occasions of the publication of proclamations, the proclamations being read in front of the hall.

More permanent and substantial improvements were inaugurated by Governor Stuyvesant. He had been director of the company's colony at Curaçoa, where he lost a leg in an unsuccessful attack on the Portuguese island of Saint Martin. Being obliged to return to Holland for surgical aid, the directors, in recognition of his '' Roman courage,'' sent him to New Netherland as '' redresser-general'' of all abuses. He arrived in New Amsterdam in the middle of May, 1647, and found the colony in a ''low condition.'' The aspect of city affairs was certainly not attractive. Fences were straggling, the public ways crooked, and many of the houses, which were chiefly built of wood and thatched with straw, encroached on the lines of the streets.

To remedy these defects stringent ordinances were passed, and ''surveyors of buildings'' were appointed (July 25, 1647) to regulate the erection of new houses ''within or around the city of New Amsterdam.'' Citizens were obliged to see to the sweeping of their chimneys, while the abolishment of wooden chimneys and thatched roofs was decreed.

These are the names of the surveyors of buildings: His Excellency, Lubert van Duicklargen, the Equipage-master; Paulus Leendersen Vandiegrist, and the Secretary, Cornelis Van Teinhoven. These officials were ''authorized and empowered to condemn all improprieties and disorder in buildings, fences, palisades, posts, and rails.'' Persons designing to build, plant, or settle, within or about the city of New Amsterdam, were warned, ''that nothing shall be done or undertaken without the knowledge, consent, and examination of the aforesaid surveyors of buildings, in the penalty of twenty-five carolus guilders; and also of having whatever they may have put up removed.''

Fires were of frequent occurrence. The inflammable materials of which the houses were composed, and the insufficient means of extinguishing the flames, led to great anxiety and insecurity, and a corresponding vigilance, or what was deemed vigilance, in the prevention of fire. As the houses of the New Amsterdamers were mostly confined to the southern point of the island, the settlement was well supplied with water with which to do battle in case of emergency. Besides being within easy reach of the waters of the bay, the East and the

North Rivers, a stream " deep enough for market boats " to ascend flowed in from the bay through the center of the present Broad Street as far as Exchange Place.   Also, there was generally to be found a well or cistern in the garden of each house.   But this abundant supply of water was about as practical a factor in the extinguishment of fire as were the " oceans of water " to the thirsty mariners, who, nevertheless, had " not a drop to drink."   This paradox will be understood when it is stated that it was a difficult matter for the so-called fire-

The eminent Burghers, Manheers, Tenbroek and Hardenbroeck disputing about the plan of the City of New Amsterdam. The one insisting that they should run out docks and wharfs, and the other that it should be cut up and intersected by canals, after the manner of Old Amsterdam. The dispute ended in high words without coming to any conclusion on a subject of so much interest to posterity, and was the cause of much bad feeling between the parties and their descendants ever after.

(From an old print.)

men of this primitive era to utilize these natural sources of supply, and still more difficult of accomplishment to transport the water in sufficient quantities to the scene of the conflagration. The water had to be carried by hand, and " in such emergencies," remarks the Hon. Charles P. Daly, " we may imagine the scene of confusion that must have ensued when tubs, pails, or other means of carrying water, had to be hastily improvised to stay the progress of a fire."

This state of affairs was not destined to last long. It was the first period of fire organization. Other and more potent methods were, however, soon to be inaugurated. In order to introduce these methods the city fathers of those days, after due deliberation, and as a result of their combined official wisdom, signed the doom of wooden chimneys and thatched roofs, while four fire wardens were appointed to enforce the ordinance. This was the first step in the right direction; other plans were under consideration, and their adoption followed in good time. But as it took a very long while to set the wheels of Dutch official machinery in motion, reforms of every kind were slow and uncertain, and the easygoing burghers were content with one progressive measure at a time. Hence it came to pass that the year 1648 was a memorable one in the annals of New Amsterdam, for it was then that the first fire ordinance was passed. Houses, or log cabins, had been run up with an entire disregard to the alarming possibilities of the ravages of fire. These rude dwellings were, it would seem, specially constructed with a view to their speedily becoming a prey to the devouring element. Wooden chimneys and thatched roofs were certainly not designed to stay the fury of the flames. These naturally inflammable materials were subjected to a double process of seasoning, namely, to heat within and the rays of the sun without. Hence, a spark ignited them and a flame destroyed. It was in this year, then (1648), that a system of fire police was first established, the immediate cause of which was the happening of fires in two places. The preamble to this ordinance declares that " it had come to the knowledge of his excellency, the Director-General, that certain careless persons were in the habit of neglecting to clean their chimneys by sweeping, and of paying no attention to their fires, whereby lately fires have occurred in two houses." Mention is made of the fact that the danger of fire is greater as the number of houses increases, particularly as the majority of the houses were built of wood and covered with reeds, while some of the houses, it is pointed out, had wooden chimneys, " which is very dangerous." Therefore it is declared to be advisable and highly necessary to look closely into the matter.

From this time forth it is ordered no wooden or platted chimneys shall be permitted to be built in any houses between the Fort and the Fresh Water, but that those already standing shall be suffered to remain during the good pleasure of the fire wardens. To the end that the foregoing may be duly observed, the following persons were appointed fire wardens : From the Council, the Commissary Adrian Keyser; and from the Commonalty, Thomas Hall, Martin Krieger, and George Woolsey. They, in their turn, it is stipulated, shall visit all the houses in the city, between the Fort and the Fresh Water, and shall inspect the chimneys whether they be kept clean by sweeping, and as often as any shall be discovered to be foul they shall condemn them, and the owners shall immediately, without any gainsaying, pay the fine of three guilders for each chimney thus condemned—to be appropriated to the maintenance of fire ladders, hooks, and buckets, which shall be provided and procured the first opportunity. And in case the houses of any person shall be burned, or be on fire, either through his own negligence or his own fire, he shall be mulcted in the penalty of twenty-five guilders, to be appropriated as aforesaid.

The appointment of these fire wardens may be regarded as the initiatory effort to establish a system of protection against fire. They are the first fire functionaries, and as such it is interesting to learn something about them beyond their names. Martin Krieger was the proprietor of a famous tavern opposite the Bowling Green. At a later period, when the city was incorporated and a municipal government formed, he was a member of Governor Stuyvesant's council, and from this time until the capture of the city by the British he filled many important offices. Thomas Hall was an Englishman. Having been captured by the Dutch and paroled, he took up his residence among his friendly captors, and in time became a man of wealth, filling many public offices. He owned a large farm in the vicinity of Spruce and Beekman Streets. This farm in later years passed into the hands of William Beekman, the ancestor of the Beekman family. Adrian Keyser was officially connected with the Dutch West India Company, by whom the New Netherlands was founded. He was afterwards a member of the Executive Council. George Woolsey, like Thomas Hall, was an Englishman. He came out as the agent of Isaac Allerton, a leading Dutch trader. The descendants of these men are to this day honored residents of this city.

NEW YORK (MANHATTAN), 1656.

A survey of the town was begun in 1654 and completed in 1656. The city was then laid down on a map and confirmed by law, " to remain, from that time forward, without alteration." Streets were also laid out, some of which were crooked enough. The city then contained by enumeration, " one hundred and twenty houses, with extensive garden lots," and one thousand inhabitants. One of the first acts of the city authorities, after the incorporation of New Amsterdam, was the framing and passage of an order similar to the one promulgated in 1648. From this it is inferred that but little attention was paid to the previous proclamation, and as a consequence several fires had occurred, " and further dangers are apprehended." Then the ordinance decrees that it is incumbent on the fire officials " to perform their duties as fire wardens according to the custom of our Fatherland," and names the following as such fire wardens: Hendrick Hendrickson Kip, Govert Loockerman and Christian Barents, " who are hereby authorized to visit all the houses and chimnies within the city jurisdiction."

In 1657 the progress of the city became so marked that it was thought appropriate to give to its thoroughfares the names of streets, which was accordingly done, and they are enumerated as follows:

T' Marckvelt (the Marketfield), De Heere Straat (the principal street), De Hoogh Straat (the High Street), De Waal (the Wall), T' Water (the Water), De Perel Straat (the Pearl Street), aghter de Perel Straat (behind the Pearl Street), De Brouwer Straat (the Brewer Street), De Winckel Straat (the Shop Street), De Heere Graft (the principal canal), De Prince Graft (the Beaver Canal), T' Marckvelt Steegre (the Marketfield Path), De Smits Valley (the Smith's Valley).

The Dutch burghers did not stop here. They had put their hand to the plow and were not going to turn back. In addition to the foregoing measures for the common safety in case of fire, a rattle-watch of eight men was established. The duties appertaining to this watch were imposed upon each of the citizens by turn. Streets were for the first time paved with stone. There were no sewers, and the pavement extended to the width of only ten feet from the front of the houses, the center of the street being left bare for the more easy absorption of the water.

The inauguration of these reforms must have transformed the budding city, from a condition which Governor Stuyvesant on his arrival had designated as "low," into one of comparative order and shapeliness. The hog-pens, and other offensive structures, must have also disappeared from the public thoroughfares, while, no doubt, a more substantial order of buildings had taken the place of the houses which were "built of wood and covered with reeds and had wooden chimneys," for we find the Director-General in a proclamation enlarging upon "the beauties of a well-regulated city, with good dwelling houses and spacious gardens;" and also glowingly dwelling upon "the blessed augmentation of the population and trade of the city."

Towards the latter part of the year 1657 the need of regular leather fire buckets was much felt. None existed in the colony, and the thought of manufacturing them themselves was too visionary and impracticable to be entertained just then. As the Fatherland was depended upon to furnish nearly all the artificial necessaries of life, it was decided to send to Holland for the buckets, as specified in the following resolution:

Whereas, in all well-regulated cities it is customary that fire buckets, ladders, and hooks are in readiness at the corners of the streets and in public houses, for time of need; which is the more necessary in this city on account of the small number of stone houses and the many wooden houses here; therefore, the Director-General and Councillors do authorize the Burgomasters and Schepens of this city, either personally or through their treasurer, to demand immediately for every house, whether small or great, one beaver or eight guilders in sewant; and to procure from fatherland, out of the sum collected in this manner, two hundred and fifty leathern fire buckets, and also to have made some fire ladders and fire hooks; and to maintain this establishment, they may yearly demand for every chimney one guilder.

This tax was promptly collected by the city authorities, but the much coveted fire buckets were still beyond the reach of the city fathers. The resolution, quoted above, looking to the mother country for their procurement, was reconsidered, as it would take a long time before they could have reached this country. So, after waiting some months, it was decided to invoke the aid of the city shoemakers. But the shoemakers of those primitive days lacked confidence in their ability to perform the task assigned them. Four out of the seven Knights of St. Crispin responded to the call to meet the city fathers in solemn and serious conclave. The date of the meeting was the first of August, 1658. The views of each shoemaker were solicited. The first declined "the arduous undertaking;" the second declared he had no material; the third, more enterprising, proposed to contract to make one hundred buckets for the consideration of six guilders and two stuyvers each (about two dollars and fifty cents), and the fourth, after much persuasion, consented to make the remaining fifty upon the same terms.

These are the terms agreed upon:

Remout Remoutzen agrees to make the said buckets all out of tanned leather, and to do all that is necessary to finish them in the completest manner for the price of six guilders two stuyvers each (about two dollars and fifty cents each), half sewant, half beavers, a fourth part of the half beavers to be "passable," three-fourths whole beavers: on these conditions he is to make one hundred buckets, which he promises to do between this and All-Saints' Day. Adrian Van Lair, on the same terms, to make fifty buckets.

But Rome was not built in a day, and at the end of six months from the date of the above agreement, that is to say, on the twentieth of January, following, the one hundred and fifty leather fire buckets were delivered at the Stadt House, where fifty of the number were deposited. The remainder were divided in lots and placed at the residences of nine of the principal inhabitants, namely:

Numbers 1 to 50, in the City Hall; 51 to 62, in Daniel Litschoe's tavern (present Pearl Street, near Wall); 63 to 74, in the house of Abraham Verplanck, in the Smith's Valley, (Pearl Street, near Fulton); 75 to 86, in the house of Joannes Pietersen Vanbruggh (Hanover Square); 87 to 98, in the house of Burgomaster Paulus Leendenen Vandiegrist, (Broadway, opposite Exchange Place); 99 to 110, at the house of the Sheriff (or Schout) Nicasius de Se'le, (southeast corner Broad Street and Exchange Place); 111 to 122, at the house of Pieter Wolfersen Van Couwenhoven, (northwest corner Whitehall and Pearl Streets); at the house of Jan Jansen, Jr., ten; at the house of Hendrick Hendrickson Kip, Sen., ten, (Bridge, between Whitehall and Broad Streets); at the house of Jacobus Backer, ten, (Broad, between Stone and South William Streets).

The burning of a small loghouse on a bluff overlooking the bay, where Castle Garden now stands, led to the establishment of the first fire company in 1658. This organization, disrespectfully dubbed the "Prowlers," consisted of eight men, furnished with two hundred and fifty buckets, hooks, and small ladders, and each of its members was expected to walk the street from nine o'clock at night until morning drum-beat, watching for fire while the town slumbered.

This company was organized by ambitious young men, and was known also as the "rattle-watch." It was soon increased to fifty members, and did duty from nine P. M. until sunrise, all the citizens who could be roused from their beds assisting in case of fire. One of the first fire buckets is still preserved by James Van Amburgh, of Westchester County, whose ancestor was one of these early firemen. The first serious fire had occurred the year before, in 1657, when Sam Baxter's house caught fire—from a blazing log which rolled out of the fireplace during the night—and was completely consumed. It was regarded as the handsomest dwelling in the settlement of the early Dutch, and its destruction gave the needed impetus for the organization of a fire company.

Even the veteran firemen who still survive would laugh if they would read the manner in which those early fire laddies undertook to provide against conflagrations. One of the rules was that each citizen of New Amsterdam was required to fill three buckets with water after sunset, and place them on his doorstep for the use of the fire patrol in case of need. Another Dutch ordinance directed that ten buckets should be filled with water at the town pump, "wen ye sun do go down," and these were to be left in a rack provided for that purpose, so that the members of the "rattle-watch" could readily lay their hands upon them "if ye fyer does go further yan ye efforts of ye men and call for water."

DUTCH WINDMILL.

When the fire was extinguished, the buckets of the citizens that had been used were thrown in a great heap on the common, and the town-crier, mounting a barrel, shouted lustily for each bucket proprietor to come and claim his own. As the stirring nasal cry,

"Hear ye! O! I pray ye,
  Lord masters claim your buckets,"

penetrated to the suburbs of the town, boys ran from all directions, and fought savagely on the grass at the crier's feet, to see who should carry home the buckets belonging to rich men, knowing that the reward would be a cake or a glass of wine, or a small coin.

The prevention of fire was a subject which caused much anxiety and unremitting attention. To see that the ordinances were carried out, frequent examinations were made of the chimneys and houses. These precautions caused much annoyance to the order-loving Dutch matrons, who, doubtless, regarded such visits as an intrusion. The worthy fire functionaries found their zeal but ill-requited. They were often insulted and abused, but they bore it all with true Dutch fortitude, until their female persecutors called them "chimney sweeps." This was the crowning indignity, and not to be borne. Retaliatory measures were adopted. The goede vrouws were summoned before the magistrates and fined for their discourteous conduct. This, it seems, did not mend matters, for the office of fire warden fell into disuse, and the ordinance became a dead letter.

Public wells at this time were found to be no less a public than a private necessity, equally indispensable in time of peril by fire as in the preservation of the public health. The first public well was dug in front of the fort in 1658. This well afforded an abundant supply of spring water, and "it became the great resort of the inhabitants during the remaining period of the Dutch occupation." The public wells were situated in the middle of the streets, and the water was passed from them in buckets through long rows of citizens to the scene of fire. Water was raised from these wells by the old Egyptian method of a balance pole and bucket, a mode still familiar in country parts. So far as drinking purposes were concerned, the water so obtained was very bad.

Dwellings of a more costly character than had previously been known were soon to be erected. In 1657, Peter Cornelisen Vanderveen built a fine house on the present Pearl Street. The year following, Governor Stuyvesant erected a large house in the vicinity of the present Whitehall Street, the name of which street it is alleged has been derived from the white hall of the Dutch governor. Others followed, and the demand thus occasioned induced the establishment of a brick-yard in the year 1659, by De Graff and Hogeboom, and brick buildings after this period became the fashion with all who could afford the additional expense. Compared with more recent times, those dwellings must be considered as extremely inexpensive. A house and lot of the value of one thousand dollars of our present currency would then have been of the first class; they rarely exceeded eight hundred dollars. Rents varied from twenty-five dollars to one hundred dollars.

About the year 1656 several merchants had erected stone edifices, and schools had been established. The houses put up in the earliest period were usually one story high, with roofs of straw and chimneys of wood. These were succeeded by houses of brick and tile—the gable end usually to the street; apparently by a succession of steps from the line where the roofs commenced, the wall on the street, from each side tapering to the top at the center, in a point where often was a weathercock. And frequently on the street front, in iron figures, was designated the year in which the house was built. The street door was divided crosswise in the middle, the upper half having a large brass or iron knocker on it. A porch or "stoop" was at the front, on which the street door opened; and on each side was a bench, on which, in pleasant weather, some of the family were wont to sit and pass their leisure hours, often in company with a friend or neighbor. An alley on one side made a passageway to the rear part of the building, where was the family kitchen with its huge fireplace. The plan of the town at that period was substantially the same as is now found in the same locality. The water line, however, has been carried out far beyond its original place. The fort was located just below the present Bowling Green. From the fort a broad, straight roadway, led back towards the cultivated boweries farther up the island. This was from the beginning the principal street of the town, though not a favorite one for residences on account of its distance from the water. The Dutch called it "De Heere Straat," or Main Street. The English changed its name to Broadway.

The Dutch, in imitation of what was done in Holland, built dykes in Broad Street, as far up as the City Hall. The city was enclosed with a wall or palisades from Trinity Church across Wall Street to the East River.

Like most other Dutch villages of former times, the town of New Amsterdam was not wanting in its supply of windmills. These machines played an important part in those days, when there was no water power convenient. The windmill adjoining the fort, and standing upon the present State Street, was the first of its kind erected by the Dutch. Another windmill occupied the eminence on Broadway, between the present Liberty and Cortlandt Streets. Farther eastward on the heights along the East River shore was another windmill, opposite the ferry landing from Long Island. Another stood upon the south part of the present City Hall Park. Yet another was erected on the North River shore, below the present St. Paul's Church. "These, and several others," says Valentine, " erected from time to time, on prominent points of the landscape, were distinguishing features of the Dutch city of New Amsterdam." The first windmill in Broadway, near Cortlandt Street having decayed, it was ordered in 1662 that there be another erected on the same ground, " outside of the city land-port (gate) on the Company's farm."

The vicinity of Chatham Street, south of Pearl Street, was, in its natural condition, very high ground, and was called Catimut's Hill. It had also at times the names of Windmill Hill and Fresh Water Hill. In 1662 a windmill was erected in this vicinity—west of the present Chatham Street and a little north of Duane Street. This mill was in existence for over half a century. An old windmill, erected, it is supposed, at a very early date on the Bayard estate, stood on the easterly side of Elizabeth Street, midway between the present Canal and Hester Streets. It was still standing for some years after the revolutionary war, the last relic, it is supposed, of that kind of structure in this city.

The British seized the Dutch possessions of New Netherland in 1664. This marked a transformation in the municipal affairs of the city government. But those Batavian pioneers have bequeathed to the city many of their noblest characteristics, which have descended to the present day.

SECTION OF WALL STREET PALISADE.

CHAPTER II.

PRIMITIVE FIRE APPLIANCES.

1664-1731.—The British take possession of New Netherland.—Establishment of a "Burger Wagt."—Inadequate Supply of Fire Buckets and Hooks and Ladders.—Action of Governor Dongan and his Council. — Adoption of Means for the Extinguishment of Fires. — Pavement of Streets.—Appointment of Fire Wardens.—"Throw out Your Buckets."—The City at the Commencement of the Seventeenth Century.

WHEN Governor Nicolls wrested the province from the Dutch, he, in a letter written in 1665, to the Duke of York, said: "Such is the mean condition of this town (New York) that not one soldier to this day has lain in sheets, or upon any other bed than straw." This, however, did not prejudice him to the extent that he could not appreciate the natural advantages of the place. "The best of all his majesty's towns in America," is what he says upon entering it. This is what he predicts of the city: "Within five years the staple of America will be drawn hither, of which the brethren of Boston are very sensible."

During the military rule of Governor Colve, who held the city for one year, everything partook of a military character. Then the Dutch mayor, at the head of the city militia, held his daily parades before the City Hall (Stadt Huys); and every evening, at sunset, he received from the principal guard of the fort, called the "hoofd wagt," the keys of the city, and thereupon proceeded with a guard of six to lock the city gates; then to place a "burger wagt," a citizen guard, as night watches at assigned places. They also went the rounds at sunrise to open the gates, and to restore the keys to the officer of the fort.

On the thirtieth of January, 1674, there was a meeting of civic officials in regard to fire matters. There were present Captain Knyff, on behalf of the Honorable Governor; Anthony De Mill, schout; Johannes De Peyster, Johannes Van Brough, and Aegidius Luyck, burgomasters; William Beekman, Jeronimus Ebbingh, Jacob Kipp, Lourens Van der Speigill, and Guilame Ver Planck, schepens. At this meeting the fire wardens presented a written report of the number of fire buckets and other implements "found by them to be provided." They made a demand for an additional supply of the implements, "requesting that this court will be pleased to order that such fire hooks and ladders as are necessary may be made."

When the city came permanently under British dominion by the peace of 1674, its former exclusive Knickerbocker character began gradually to wear off. At that time almost all the houses presented their gabled ends to the street, and all the most important public buildings, such as "Stuyvesant Huys" on the water edge, at present Moore and Front Streets, and the Stadt Huys or City Hall, on Pearl Street, at the head of Coenties Slip, were then set on the foreground, to be more readily seen from the river. The chief part of the town lay along the East River (called "Salt River" in early days), and descending from the high ridge of ground along the line of Broadway. A great artificial dock for vessels existed between "Stuyvesant Huys" and the bridge over "the canal," where it debouched on the present Broad Street.

As already intimated, New York was in primitive days the "city of hills." Thus, at the extreme south end of Broadway, where the ancient fort formerly stood, was a mound, quite as elevated as the present general level of the street in front of Trinity Church, and thence regularly declining from along that street to "the beach" on the North River. The hills were sometimes precipitous, as from Beekman's and Peck's Hills, in the neighborhood of Pearl Street and Beekman and Ferry Streets, and from the Middle Dutch Church on Nassau Street down to Maiden Lane. Between many of the hills flowed in

DUTCH COTTAGE IN BEAVER STREET, 1679.

several invasions of water, such as "the canal," so called to gratify Dutch recollections, which was an inroad of water up Broad Street. Up Maiden Lane flowed another inroad through Smith's marsh or valley. A little beyond Peck's Slip existed a low water course, which in high tide ran quite up to the Collect, and thence, joining with Lispenard's swamp on the North River side, produced a union of waters quite across the city, converting it occasionally into an island. This accounts for the lowness of Pearl Street where it traverses Chatham Street. There they had to use boats occasionally to cross foot passengers over from either side of the high rising ground.

The importance of taking precautions against the happening of conflagrations was recognized in many ways, as is evidenced by the ordinances framed and the measures adopted from time to time. On the sixteenth of February, 1676, all persons having any of the city's ladders, buckets or hooks, in their custody, were called upon to immediately deliver them to the mayor. It was also ordered that wells be dug, as follows: "One in the street over against the house of Fowliff Johnson's, the butcher; another in the broadway against **Mr. Vandicke's**; another in the street over against Derrick Smith's; another in the street over against the house of John Cavildore; another in the yard or rear of the Cytie Hall; another in the street over against Cornelius **Van**

CITY HALL, WALL STREET.

Borsum's." On the twenty-eighth of February there was published a list of persons that had "noe chimneys, or not fitt to keepe fire in," and an order was issued by the mayor and aldermen calling upon these delinquents to cause suitable chimneys to be built without delay. In January of the following year John Dooly and John Vorrickson Meyer were appointed to inspect all the

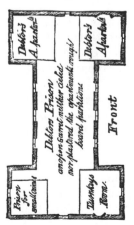 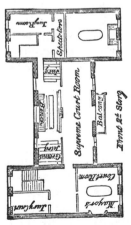 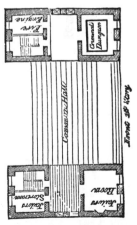

PLAN OF CITY HALL.

chimneys and fire hearths in the city, and on the fifteenth of March, 1683, a law was enacted empowering the appointment of viewers and searchers (fire wardens) of chimneys and fire hearths, to report to the mayor and aldermen, who could impose a fine not exceeding twenty shillings for each default; prohibiting the laying of straw, hay, or other combustible matter in their dwelling houses, or places adjoining the same, "but at a distance from their houses and the streets; and providing for hooks, ladders, and buckets, to be kept in convenient places;" and, further, that "if any person should suffer his chimney to be on fire he should pay the sum of fifteen shillings."

On the ninth of September following, the mayor, aldermen, and commonalty of the city, petitioned the governor to confirm unto them the several ancient customs, privileges, and immunities granted by the former governor of the province, Col. Richard Nicolls, 1665, who incorporated the inhabitants of the city, New Harlem, and all others inhabiting the island of Manhattan, as a body politic and corporate under the government of a Mayor, Aldermen, and Sheriff, etc.

In responding to the petition of the corporation of the ninth of September, Governor Dongan and his council, at a meeting held on December 6, stipulated that the city should "appoint one, or more if necessary, to look after the chimneys for the preventing of fire, and that all houses keep one or more leather buckets."

A public chimney-sweep was appointed for the city (1685), who was to cry his approach through the public streets, and who probably originated the whoop peculiar to his vocation. His rates were fixed by law at a shilling and eighteenpence per chimney, according to the height of the house.

Great damage seems to have been done by fire in January, 1686. The Common Council, at a meeting held on February 28 of that year, referred to the absence of means for the extinguishment of fires, and it was ordered that every inhabitant whose dwelling house had two chimneys should provide one bucket, and for more than two chimneys, two buckets; that all brewers possess five buckets apiece, and all bakers three, said buckets to be provided before September 25th ensuing, under a penalty for neglect of five shillings for each bucket. Five years later, on the twenty-fifth of November, 1691, this order was re-enacted. But there were added the stipulations that the buckets should be provided by the occupants, and the cost thereof allowed them by the landlord out of the rent, and "every man to marke the bucketts with the letters of his landlord's name, upon forfeiture of six shillings, for the use of the citty, to be paid by the tenant on default," etc. The mayor was empowered to acquit "poore people" of the penalty.

At the same time, Derrick Vandenburgh, John Rose, Snert Olphite, and Garrett Rose were appointed to "goe round the towne and view each fireplace and chimney, that they be sufficient and clean swept," with the penalty of three shillings and sixpence to each inhabitant for each defect.

Chief among the substantial indications of progress was the completion in 1693 of the Garden Street Church. It was built in the midst of a beautiful garden, "a great distance up town," fronting a narrow lane called Garden Alley, which afterwards became Garden Street, and is now Exchange Place. This year Wall Street was first paved to the width of ten feet, in front of the houses facing the wall.

A fire occurred in that part of the town called the "Fly" in February, 1692, at which several buckets were lost. Complaints reached the mayor that people of thievish propensities had appropriated them, whereupon His Honor issued an order directing the crier to give notice round the city that the stolen buckets be taken to the mayor immediately so that they might be restored to

VIEW OF NEW YORK FROM THE NORTH, 1679.

Original in possession of W. M. Randell, Office of Board of Fire Underwriters.

their owners. Other appliances besides buckets had been thought of. Two years before the fire in the "Fly," five "brant masters" (fire wardens) had been appointed on January 4, 1690. These fire wardens were: Peter Adolf, Derck van der Brincke, Derck ten Eyk, Jacob Borlen, and Tobeyas Stoutenburgh, and it had been ordered that five ladders be made and provided for service at fires, with sufficient hooks therefor.

In 1693, it was ordered "that every inhabitant in the streets hereinafter mentioned, shall, before the first of August next, cause to be paved, with pebble stones, so much of said street as shall front their respective premises." Thence follows the designation of the streets to be paved, eight in number. The crude condition of the city in respect to its streets may also be inferred from an order made in this year, that "the poisonous and stinking weeds before everyone's door be forthwith plucked up." The above system of paving continued for many years, and it is believed that, up to the time of the Revolution, the "kennel" ran through the centers of the streets, and if sidewalks existed, they were the voluntary work of the adjacent owners. No regulations are to be found in the public ordinances concerning either their construction or repair.

After the revolutionary war, the subject of city improvements was under a commissioner, instead of a committee of the Common Council. Gerard Bancker was the first street commissioner.

Additional precautions were now taken against occurrences of fires. In 1697, the aldermen and assistant-aldermen were authorized to appoint two persons as fire wardens in every ward. The penalty of three shillings was imposed for the neglect to remedy defective flues and hearths—one-half to the city and one-half to the wardens—and if a chimney should take fire after notice had been given to clean it, the occupant was mulcted in the sum of forty shillings. This is the first record of a paid Fire Department in the city of New York. The system had advanced beyond the limits of "viewers" and "overseers," and had reached a point where something like an organization was effected, and arrangements completed for paying, fining, and discharging the men, who were obliged to view the chimneys and hearths once a week. In short, a more prompt and systematic performance of duty was required.

THE WATER-GATE, FOOT OF WALL STREET, 1679.
Original in possession of W. M. Randell, Office of Board of Fire Underwriters.

The practice of having every house supplied with fire buckets now became general, and was continued long after the introduction of fire engines. The manner in which an alarm of fire was given in the night time is graphically told by the Hon. Charles P. Daly: "If a fire broke out at night," he says, "the watchman gave the alarm with his rattle, and knocked at the doors of the houses, with the cry, 'Throw out your buckets!' the alarm being further spread by the ringing of the bell at the fort and by the bells in the steeples of the different churches. When the inmates of a house were aroused, the first act was to throw out the buckets in the street, which were of sole leather, holding about three gallons, and were also hung in the passage close to the street door. They were picked up by those who were hastening to the fire, it being the general custom for nearly every householder to hurry to the fire—whether by day or by night—and render his assistance. As soon as possible two lines were formed from the fire to the nearest well or pump, and when they gave out, the line was carried to the next one or to the river. The one line passed up the full buckets, and the empty ones were passed down the other line.   No one was permitted to break through those lines, and if any one attempted to do so, and would not fall in and lend a helping hand, a bucket of water or several were instantly thrown over him.   Each bucket was marked with the name or number of the owner, and, when the fire was over, they were all collected together and taken in a cart, belonging to the city, to the City Hall.   A bellman then went round to announce that the buckets were ready for delivery, when each householder sent for his bucket, and, when recovered, hung it up in the allotted place, ready for the next emergency."

The first attempt to light the streets was made in November, 1697.   The ordinance reads as follows:

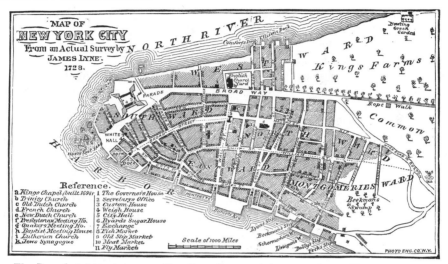

The Board, taking into consideration the great inconveniency that attends this city, being a trading place, for want of having lights in the dark time of the moon in the winter season, it is therefore ordered that all and every of the housekeepers within this city shall put out lights in the windows fronting the respective streets of their city, between this and the twenty-fifth of March next, in the following manner: Every seventh house, in all the streets, shall, in the dark time of the moon, cause a lantern and candle to be hung out on a pole, the charge to be defrayed equally by the inhabitants of said seven houses.

During this period (1697) a night watch was established, composed of "four good and honest inhabitants of the city, whose duty it shall be to watch in the night time, from the hour of nine in the evening till break of day, until the twenty-fifth of March next; and to go round the city, each hour of the night, with a bell, and there to proclaim the season of the weather and the hour of the night."

The erection of the City Hall in Wall Street, at the head of Broad (in 1700), was the great event which established Wall Street as the central point of interest for leading business and professional men.   The City Hall was supported upon brick arches over the sidewalk, under which pedestrians could pass from street to street in all directions.   One of the rooms on the first floor was at a later day appropriated for the reception of the first two fire engines in New York, imported from London.

Four able-bodied men were appointed watch and bellmen for the city in 1702, from November 1 to April 1 following.   They were to go, every hour in the night, through the several streets, publishing the time of the night; to apprehend disturbers of the peace, etc., and to see that no damage be done by fires. A lantern, bell, and hour-glass were provided for them by the city.

The Common Council, on the sixth of November, 1703, ordered that the aldermen of each ward should command the respective constables therein to make a house to house inspection, to ascertain whether the number of fire buckets required by law were kept on hand, and to present the delinquents for prosecution.

New and more stringent regulations were now passed in respect to fires: the fire wardens were directed to keep strict watch of all hearths and chimneys within the city, and to see that the fire buckets were hung up in their right places throughout the wards, and two hooks and eight ladders were purchased at the public expense for the use of the fire department.

This system prevailed, with slight modifications, until the introduction of the hand engines from London.

A law for the better prevention of fire was published at the City Hall on November 18, 1731. After the customary ringing of three bells, and a proclamation had been made for silence, it provided for the appointing of "viewers of chimneys and hearths," to make monthly inspections; the fine of three shillings for neglecting the directions of the fire wardens, re-enacting the fine of forty shillings for chimneys on fire, and establishing a like fine for "viewers" who should refuse to serve, and a fine of six shillings for neglect of duty; providing for the obtainment of hooks, ladders and buckets, and fire engines, to be kept in convenient places; for leather buckets to be kept in every house; a penalty for not possessing the required number of buckets, and a fine for detaining other men's buckets.

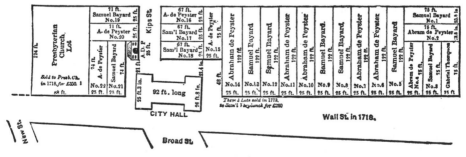

WALL STREET LOTS, DUTCH PERIOD.

CHAPTER III.

THE FIRST HAND ENGINES.

1731-1782.—Introduction of Machines from London.—Newsham's Engine.—Formation of the First Fire Companies.—Who the Original Fire Laddies were.—Location of Stations.—How the Department Force Increased.—Terms of Service.—Privileges and Exemptions.—Act of Incorporation.

THE year 1731 was the beginning of a memorable epoch in the history of New York and its famous Fire Department. Then came into use the new hand fire engines. Then was laid the foundation of that gallant, emulous, and self-sacrificing body of volunteers, the record of whose deeds will read to posterity like an old romance. Just as the chronicles of the doughty Crusaders touch the hearts of the youth of to-day, so will the history of the achievements of the old volunteer companies of the Empire City fire the bosoms of generations to come. This year saw the nucleus of a fine body of athletic men, ever ready to risk life and limb for the public weal. Soon were to be identified with those primitive engines, names that will live forever in our history, such as the Harpers, the Macys, the Townsends, the Goelets, William H. Appleton, Zophar Mills, George T. Hope, Marshall O. Roberts, and James Kelly. It was the beginning of the era of the clattering machine, with its rushing, shouting, bold and dashing attendants, as ready to fight their fellows for the place of honor in the hour of danger as the devouring flames themselves.

On the sixth of May, 1731, the city authorities passed the following resolution:

Resolved, With all convenient speed to procure two complete fire engines, with suctions and materials thereto belonging, for the public service; that the sizes thereof be of the fourth and sixth sizes of Mr. Newsham's fire engines, and that Mr. Mayor, Alderman Cruger, Alderman Rutgers, and Alderman Roosevelt, or any of them, be a committee to agree with some proper merchant or merchants to send to London for the same by the first conveniency, and report upon what terms the said fire engines, etc., will be delivered to this corporation.

The committee named reported at a meeting of the Common Council, held on June 12, 1731, that they had proposed to Messrs. Stephen De Lancey and John Moore, merchants, to send for two fire engines to London, by the ship *Beaver*, of Mr. Newsham's new invention of the fourth and sixth sizes, with suctions, leathern pipes, and caps, and other materials; and that those gentlemen had undertaken to purchase and deliver them to the corporation at an advance of one hundred and twenty per cent. on the foot of the invoice (exclusive of insurance and commissions), and that the money should be paid for the same within nine months after the delivery of the same.

Towards the close of November of 1731 the good ship *Beaver* was sighted off port, and on December 1st workmen commenced to fit up "a convenient room" in the new City Hall for securing the fire engines, and on the fourteenth, the engines being in the meanwhile landed and "secured," a committee was appointed to have them cleaned and the leathers oiled and put into boxes ready for immediate use.

"The importation by the city of these fire engines," says the Hon. Charles P. Daly in his valuable treatise on "The Origin and History of the New York Fire Department," "was an incident of no ordinary importance. There was no subject upon which at that time the inhabitants of the city felt a deeper interest than the most effectual means of extinguishing fires, for the loss of property by conflagration was a calamity to which the city from its first settlement had been particularly exposed."

These engines were designated as No. 1 and No. 2. They were located in separate sheds, in the rear of the City Hall, No. 1 on the east side of the building, and No. 2 on the west side, facing King Street, now Nassau.

The aldermen and the assistant aldermen were in charge of the apparatus

VIEW OF DUTCH COTTAGES.

On the northeast corner of Exchange Place and Broad Street, about the year 1680.

in those days, and they were called overseers. The mayor and aldermen took charge at fires, the public at large being compelled to do fire duty. No one over twenty-one years of age was exempt, and for a refusal to do duty they were liable to a fine of one pound or five dollars.

When the two engines were received by the city from London, they were a great curiosity, the people being fully as much interested as in the days when silver coinages were brought out.

Peter Rutger, a brewer and an assistant alderman of the North Ward, was the first man that ever had charge of a fire engine on Manhattan Island, and John Roosevelt, a merchant, was the second.

In 1677 the city contained three hundred and sixty-eight houses; in 1693 the number was five hundred and ninety-four; in 1696 it was put down at seven hundred and fifty; and when the two fire engines arrived from London, the population of the city was eight thousand six hundred and twenty-eight, and the number of houses was about one thousand two hundred.

Up to this time, as has been shown, the only means of extinguishing fire was the carrying of water in buckets and the use of ladders and fire hooks. These primitive appliances, however, were more effective instruments as fire apparatus than might be inferred in view of the vast and ingenious mechanical appliances and machinery in use at the present day. Architecture had not then, as now, taken the same ambitious flight. The buildings originally were chiefly of one story, and few houses exceeded two stories. The first three story house put up in the city was erected in the year 1696, in Pearl Street, opposite Cedar Street, and was built by a member of the Depeyster family.

Mr. Newsham advertised his engines in the following terms :

Richard Newsham, of Cloth Fair, London, engineer, makes the most substantial and convenient engines for quenching fires, which carries *continual streams* with great force. He hath play'd several of them before his majesty and the nobility at St. James, with so general an approbation that the largest was at the same time ordered for the use of that royal palace.

SCENE AT A FIRE, 1730.
(From an old Fire Certificate.)

The largest engine will go through a passage about three foot wide, in complete working order, without taking off or putting on anything; and may be worked with ten men in the said passage. One man can quickly and with ease move the largest size about in the compass it stands in and is to be played without rocking, upon any uneven ground, with hands and feet or feet only, which cannot be paralleled by any other sort whatsoever. There is conveniency for twenty men to apply their full strength, and yet reserve both ends of the cistern clear from incumbrance, that others, at the same time, may be pouring in the water which drains through large copper strainers. The staves that are fixed through leavers, along the sides of the engine, for the men to work by, though very light, as alternate motions with quick returns require; yet will not spring and lose time the least; but the staves of such engines as are wrought at the ends of the cistern, will spring or break if they be of such length as is necessary for a large engine when considerable power is applied; and cannot be fixed fast, because they must at all times be taken out before the engine can go through a passage. The playing two streams at once, do neither issue a greater quantity of water, nor, is it new, or so useful, there having been of the like sort at the steel-yard, and other places, thirty or forty years, and the water being divided, the distance and force are accordingly lessened thereby. * * * As to the treddles on which men work with their feet, there is no method so powerful, with the like velocity or quickness, and more natural safe for the men. Great attempts have been made to exceed, but none yet could equal this sort; the fifth size of which hath played above the grasshopper upon the Royal Exchange, which is upward of *fifty-five yards high,* and this in the presence of many thousand spectators.

Those with suction feed themselves with water from a canal, pond, well, etc., or out of their own cisterns, by the turn of a cock, without interrupting the stream * * * and play off large quantities of water to a great distance, either from the engine or a leather pipe or pipes of any length required. * * * The five large sizes go upon wheels, well boxed with brass, fitted to strong iron axles, and the other is to be carried like a chair.

It appears, nevertheless, that Newsham had produced nothing new, as all the potent properties of his engine had been for a long time previously known. The superiority of his machine consisted simply in the ingenious mechanical adaptation of familiar principles. In form it resembled the machine in use when engines were worked by hand.

The practical usefulness of the new engines was soon tested, as appears

ROUGH DRAWING OF FIRST HAND-ENGINE.

from the following paragraph in the Boston *Weekly News Letter* of January 6, 1732, under the head of "News from New York:"

Last night, about twelve o'clock, a fire broke out in a joiner's house in this city. It began in the garret, where the people were all asleep, and burnt violently; but by the aid of the two fire engines, which came from London in the ship *Beaver,* the fire was extinguished after having burnt down the house and damaged the next.

Some person, little apprehending, as it may be supposed, that it would descend as a memorial to our day, made the accompanying rough pen and ink sketch of one of these engines, which, though rude and badly drawn, is sufficient to indicate its structure and the manner in which it was worked. This engine, with slight modifications, continued in use down to 1832, and long afterwards, in this city.

The experience of the fire of the seventh of December, referred to above, had doubtless pointed out the necessity of putting the engines in charge of some competent and skillful person, and, accordingly, on the twenty-first of

January following, the mayor and four aldermen were appointed a committee to employ workmen to put them in good order, and to engage persons by the year to keep them in repair and to work them when necessary. Anthony Lamb was accordingly appointed overseer, or, as the office was afterwards called, chief engineer, at a salary of twelve dollars a year, and he and the persons employed by the year under him may be said to have been the first regularly organized Fire Department. The sheds fitted up for these two engines in the rear of the City Hall would not seem to have been sufficiently commodious, and, accordingly, in 1736, the corporation ordered a convenient house to be built "contiguous to the watch house in Broad Street, for their security and well keeping." This building, the first engine house in the city, was in the middle of Broad Street, half way between Wall Street and Exchange Place. The watch house stood at the head of Broad Street, and immediately behind it, in the middle of the street, this engine house was built. Lamb held the office of

ROUGH DRAWING OF HAND-ENGINE.

chief engineer until 1736, when he was succeeded by Jacob Turk, a gunsmith, who appears to have been a man of considerable mechanical skill and ingenuity.

Fire engines were built and for sale in this city six years after their first introduction, as will be seen by the following advertisement from the *New York Gazette*, May 9, 1737:

A Fire-engine, that will deliver two hogsheads of water in a minute, in a continual stream, is to be sold by William Lindsay, the maker thereof. Enquire at Fighting Cocks, next door to the Exchange Coffee-house, New York.

The engines were being constantly changed from one ward to another, to please the aldermen. If an alderman or an assistant could get an engine located in his ward, it was a big thing, and the friends of the alderman would freely build a house to put it in.

Several attempts were made to build engines after those brought over from London, but most all failed who attempted it. One Bartholomew Weldern built two, neither one of which would work.   The price allowed for building an engine in those days was fifty pounds.

Thomas Lote was the first man that ever built an engine in this country that was used. It was known as No. 3, and on its completion was located adjoining "Kalch-Hook Pond." A full description of the company will be found on another page.

In December, 1737, the General Assembly of the colony passed an act enabling the corporation to appoint not more than forty-two able, discreet, sober men, as firemen; an equal number to be appointed out of the six several wards on the south side of Fresh Water. An enumeration of the trades of twenty-eight will be interesting, and is as follows: blacksmiths, 4; blockmaker, 1; cutter, 1; gunsmiths, 2; carpenters, 5; bricklayers, 2; ropemaker, 1; carmen, 2; coopers, 4; bakers, 2; cordwainers, 4.

FIREMEN AT WORK, 1733.

(From an old Fire Certificate.)

The Volunteer Fire Department, so established, lasted for one hundred and twenty-seven years. A high compliment, and one that no doubt was deserved, was paid to the city's firemen in the preamble to this act, in these words: "The inhabitants of the city of New York of all degrees, have very justly acquired the reputation of being singularly and remarkably famous for their dilligence and services in cases of fires," and it was, doubtless, this fact that led to the institution of the voluntary system. This act recites, furthermore, that the firemen "have, at very great charge and expense, supplied themselves, and are provided with two fire engines and various sorts of poles, hooks, iron chains, ropes, ladders and several other tools and instruments, for the extinguishment of fires. They were to manage and care for the fire apparatus," to be "called the firemen of the city of New York," and be ready for service "by night as well as by day." To "compel and oblige them" to be "diligent, industrious and vigilant," the Common Council were empowered to remove any of them and put others in their place, and, as an inducement to fill up the ranks, the firemen so appointed were "freed, exempted and privileged from the several offices of constable and surveyor of the highways, and of and from the being put into or serving upon any juries or inquest, and of and from being compellable to serve in the militia, or any of the independent companies of or in the said city, or any or either of them, except in cases of invasion, or other imminent danger." It was ordained likewise that the firemen enjoy the privileges given by the act of Assembly, on condition of their subjecting themselves to certain cited rules and regulations, of which these are an abstract:

Upon notice of the happening of a fire, they are to take the engines and assist in its extinguishment, and afterwards to wash the engines and preserve them in good order.

If absent from a fire without reasonable cause, to forfeit twelve shillings.

Once in each month to exercise the engines, so as to keep them in good order.

For any neglect of his duty, a fireman might be removed.

Forfeitures were to be recovered before the Mayor, Recorder, or any Alderman.

Thirty-five was the number of firemen chosen. These are their names and occupations: John Tiebout, blockmaker; Hercules Wendover, blacksmith; Jacobus Delamontagne, blockmaker; Thomas Brown, cutler; Abraham Van Gelder, gunsmith; Jacobus Stoutenburgh, gunsmith; William Roome, Jr., carpenter; Walter Hyer, Sr., bricklayer; Johannes Alstein, blacksmith; Everet Pells, Jr., ropemaker; Peter Lott, carman; Peter Brower, bricklayer; Albertus Tiebout, carpenter; John Vredenberg, carpenter; John Dunscombe, cooper; Johannes Roome, carpenter; Peter Marschalck, baker; Petrus Kip, baker; Andrew Myer, Jr., cordwainer; Robert Richardson, cooper; Rymer Brozer, blacksmith; Barnet Bush, cooper; David Van Gelder, blacksmith; Johannes Van Duersen, cordwainer; Martinius Bogert, carman; Johannes Vredenbergh, cordwainer; Johannes Van Sys, carpenter; Adolph Brase, cordwainer; and John Man, cooper; "all strong, able, discreet, honest and sober men."

These firemen served without salary.

The following year (1739) the corporation selected five firemen from each ward, or thirty in all, and passed an ordinance for their regulation or government.

Upon the breaking out of any fire within the city, "all sheriffs, under or deputy sheriffs, high constables, petty constables, and marshals (upon notice thereof), were required to immediately repair to the scene of the conflagration, and with their rods, staves, and other badges of authority, aid and assist in extinguishing the said fires, and cause people to work to extinguish the flames. A part of their duty also was to protect property from the depredations of thieves, and to help the inhabitants to remove and secure their household goods. Thus was formed the first fire company in the city of New York.

Jacob Turk became the head of this new organization, and continued in the office for twenty-five years. Among other things, he introduced the well-known leather cap worn by the firemen to the present day. Turk was succeeded by Jacob Stoutenburgh, a gunsmith, and was one of the thirty firemen originally appointed in 1738. He continued to be the chief engineer down to the Revolution. When he was appointed in 1761, the city had largely increased in population and territory, and, in consequence, the force in the following year was augmented to two assistants and sixty men. After the breaking out of the revolution, it was converted into a military organization

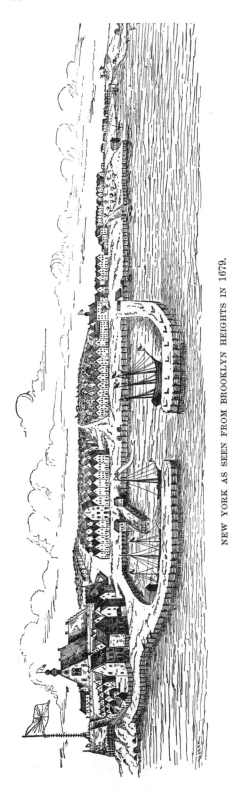

NEW YORK AS SEEN FROM BROOKLYN HEIGHTS IN 1679.

Original in possession of W. M. Randell, Office of Board of Fire Underwriters.

consisting of two battalions, commanded by Stoutenburgh, and was composed of one adjutant, one captain, five lieutenants, and one hundred and thirty-four men. It retired, necessarily, as a part of the military, with the retreat of the American army from the city in 1776, and the extent of the ravages of the dreadful conflagration which followed immediately after the entrance of the British troops was mainly owing to the want of firemen in the city.

The governor's house in the fort, on the eighteenth of March, 1741, was discovered to be on fire, and notwithstanding the efforts of the Fire Department—then but recently organized, and having the benefit of one or two fire engines — that edifice, together with the chapel erected about fifty years previously, and all the other buildings in the fort, were entirely consumed. The conflagration was at this time attributed to the carelessness of a plumber who had left fire in a gutter between the house and the chapel, and it was so reported by the governor to the legislature. A week after, the chimney of Captain Warren's house, near the fort, took fire, but the flames were soon extinguished with little damage. A few days after, a fire broke out in the storehouse of Mr. Van Zandt, which was attributed to the carelessness of a smoker. Three days later, the hay in a cow stable near the house of Mr. Quick was discovered to be on fire. The alarm was given, and the flames were soon suppressed. While returning to their homes, a fifth alarm called the firemen to the house of Mr. Thompson, where it was said fire had been placed in a kitchen loft where a negro usually slept. The next day coals were discovered under the stables of John Murray in Broadway. The following morning, a fire broke out in the house of Sergeant Burns, opposite the fort; and a few hours after, the roof of Mr. Hilton's house, near the Fly Market, was discovered to be on fire. Both were extinguished without much damage, but the rapid recurrence of so many fires alarmed the inhabitants, and a rumor was soon circulated that the negroes had plotted to burn the city. The magistrates met the same afternoon to consult about the matter, and while they were still in session another fire broke out in the roof of Colonel Philipse's storehouse. The alarm became universal; the negroes were seized indiscriminately and thrown into prison. People and magistrates were alike panic-stricken. The Common Council assembled and offered a reward of one hundred pounds and a full pardon to any conspirator who would reveal his knowledge of the plot with the names of the incendiaries. From the eleventh of May to the twenty-ninth of August, one hundred and fifty-four negroes were committed to prison, fourteen of whom were burnt at the stake, eighteen hanged, seventy-one transported, and the rest pardoned or discharged for the want of sufficient evidence. In the same time, twenty-four whites were committed to prison, four of whom were executed.

On December 1, 1741, these additional firemen were appointed: Isaac Van Hook, cordwainer; Abraham Alstyne, Jr., bricklayer; Albertus Tiebout, carpenter; Johannes Alstyne, blacksmith; John Van Zandt, blockmaker; Samuel Bell, blacksmith; John Myer, gunsmith; Peter Hendrickse, carpenter; Ahasuerus Turk, cordwainer; Johannes Powlse, carman; John Apple, carpenter; Benjamin Moore, sailmaker; John Dally, ship carpenter; and Peter Vlierboom, cordwainer.

In this year also a committee of the Common Council was appointed "to inspect the ladders, hooks, etc., and to cause one hundred leather buckets to be made."

The number of houses in the city, in the year 1744, was as hereby particularized:

The west side of Broadway to the river	129
The east side of Broadway, with the west side of Broad Street	232
The east side of Broad Street, with the west side of William Street	324
The east side of William Street, with the west side of Pearl Street	242
The east side of Pearl Street to the East River	214
Total	1,141

Professor Kahn, who visited this city in 1748, thus describes it: "Most of the houses are built of bricks, and are generally strong and neat, and several stories high; some have, according to the old architecture, turned the gable end towards the street but the new houses are altered in this respect. Many of the houses have a balcony on the roof, on which the people sit in the evenings in the summer time; and from thence they have a pleasant view of a great part of the town, and likewise of part of the adjacent water and of the opposite shore. The roofs are commonly covered with tiles or shingles, the latter of which are made of the white fir tree, which grows higher up in the country. The inhabitants are of opinion that a roof made of these shingles is as durable as one made of white cedar. The walls of the houses are whitewashed within, and I did not anywhere see hangings, with which the people in this country seem in general to be little acquainted. The walls are quite covered with all sorts of drawings and pictures in small frames. On each side of the chimney they usually have a sort of alcove, and the wall under the window is wainscotted, with benches near the window. The alcoves, as well as all of the woodwork, are painted with a bluish-gray color."

"The streets do not run so straight," he further adds, " as those of Philadelphia, and have sometimes considerable bendings; however, they are very spacious and well-built, and most of them are paved, excepting in high places, where it has been found useless. In the chief streets there are trees planted, which, in summer, give them a fine appearance, and, during the excessive heat

CITY OF MANHATTAN OR NEW YORK.

A. Shipping Port.	E. The Temple or Church.	J. Lower Town.
B. Bridge for discharging vessels.	F. Parade Ground.	K. City Hall.
C. Fountain or Wells.	G. Meat Market.	L. Custom House and Stores.
D. House of the Governor.	H. Slaughter House.	M. Powder Magazine.

From the collection of charts and plans made by order of the Duke de Choiseul and executed by S. Bellin in 1746.

at that time, afford a cooling shade. I found it extremely pleasant to walk in the town, for it seemed quite like a garden. The trees, which are planted for this purpose, are chiefly of two kinds; the water beech is the most numerous, and gives an agreeable shade in summer by its large and numerous leaves. The locust tree is likewise frequent; its fine leaves, and the odoriferous scent which exhales from its flowers, make it very proper for being planted in the streets, near the houses, and in gardens. There are likewise lime trees and elms in these walks, but they are not, by far, so fragrant as the others. One seldom meets with trees of the same sort adjoining each other, they being in general placed alternately. Besides numbers of birds of all kinds which make these trees their abode, there are likewise a kind of frog, which frequents them in great numbers during the summer. They are very clamorous in the evening, and in the nights (especially when the days have been hot and a rain is expected), and in a manner drown the singing of the birds. They frequently make such a noise that it is difficult for a person to make himself heard."

It was decided, in February, 1749, to build an engine house in Hanover Square, and to procure one hundred new fire buckets. Three years later, in May, the watch prison was designated a house for a fire engine, and six small speaking trumpets were purchased.

On February 23, 1753, a fire broke out in the new Free School House, kept by Mr. Joseph Hildreth, clerk of Trinity Church, which entirely destroyed the building. The steeple of Trinity Church was set on fire several times from the flying coals, but the fire was happily extinguished and the steeple preserved. The whole loss sustained was set down at two thousand pounds.

Peter Clopper was allowed three pounds for building an engine house, "on a vacant lot called Rutgers' Walk, in the east ward of the city." Engine Company No. 26, it is believed, occupied the site of this building in after years in Rutgers Street.

In addition to the law for the better preventing of fire which was ordained on the eighth of November, 1756, an ordinance was passed in November, 1757, decreeing that no person should have, keep or put any hay or straw in barracks or piles in his yard or garden, or in any other place, to the southward of Fresh Water, except in close buildings erected for the purpose; and that no person should have, keep, or put any hay or straw in any house, stable or building within the same limits, that should be within ten feet of any chimney, hearth, or fireplace, or place for keeping ashes, under the penalty of twenty shillings for every offense, one-half of which should be recovered for the church wardens for the use of the poor of the city, and the other half for the person who should prosecute the complaint. The new barracks adjacent to the workhouse being unprotected, a fire engine and fifty buckets were sent there. In order to provide additional and more powerful fire engines, it was decided at a meeting of the Common Council, held on June 20, that the remainder of the money acquired by the sale of the city's fire-arms to General Abercrombie, be sent to England for the purchase there of one large fire engine, one small one, and two hand engines, with some buckets, etc.

In July, Jacobus Stoutenburgh was appointed overseer of the fire engines and appurtenances, agreeing to take care of them and keep them in good order for the sum of thirty pounds per year. The following year Mr. Stoutenburgh was known as the engineer of the department, having as assistants Samuel Bell and Jasper Ten Brook. The working force consisted of twelve men for each of the six wards, of whom the following is the complete roster.

West Ward.—John Kierstadt, Gulian V. Varick, John Van Dolson, Cornelius Heyer, Isaac Stoutenburgh, Jr.; Marselus Garrabrants, George Stanton, George Wells, Abraham Bussing, Robert Harding, Barnardus Swartwout, and Cornelius Cooper.

North Ward.—Peter Hendricks, Aaron Gilbert, John Montania, Francis Barry, Cornelius Turk (cordwainer), Peter Garrabrants, Isaac Stoutenburgh, William Ellsworth, Jr.; Isaac Delamater, John Delamater, Andrew Bell, and Isaac Bogert.

Dock Ward.—Andrew Gotier, John Van Gelder, David pra Provoost,

Josiah Bagley, Daniel Ten Eyck, Charles Phillipse, Andrew Breasted, Peter De Riemer, Henry Deforrest, James Van Varck, and Henry Sickles.

East Ward.—Peter Bogert, John Roomes, John Targier, William Bokee, David Hansen, Samuel Waldrom, Francis Basset, John Van Alstyne, Victor Beecker, David Scott, John Bergen, and William Post.

South Ward.—George Walgrove, Isaac Marschalck, Zachariah Sickles, Aert Houseman, Gerardus Myer, Thomas Lawrence, Jacob Roome, Abraham Labach, Henry Sheaf, Abner Brown, Richard V. Varick, and Daniel Evits, Jr.

Montgomerie Ward.—William Hardenbrook, Anthony Shackerly, Theophilus Hardenbrook, John Elsworth, James Bogart, Jr.; Stephen Crosfield, Tunis Tiebout, John Hardenbrook, Peter Roomer, Peter Ryker, John Dyckman, and Cornelius Van Sise.

No attempt was made to light the streets by public authority until the year

BURNS' COFFEE-HOUSE, BROADWAY (ATLANTIC GARDEN),

In which the first non-importation agreement of the colonies was signed, on the thirty-first of October, 1765, by the merchants of New York.

1762, excepting a temporary ordinance in the latter part of the previous century, requiring the occupants of every tenth house to hang out a lantern upon a pole. An act of Assembly was passed in the above year giving the corporation authority to provide means for lighting the city. In the same year the first posts and lamps were purchased. In 1770 a contract was made with J. Stoutenburgh for supplying oil and lighting the city lamps, for the sum of seven hundred and sixty dollars. In 1774 the city employed sixteen lamplighters. This system of lighting the city remained substantially the same until the contract with the New York Gaslight Company, in 1823, by which certain parts of the city were to be lighted with gas.

Nicholas De Reimer was appointed foreman in the East Ward, on January 4, 1765, in the place of David Hansen, deceased; and Nathan Fish was appointed a foreman in the place of David Scott, who had removed to Albany.

On October 14, John Silvester was appointed a fireman in the place of Andrew Gotier, the then assistant foreman in the Dock Ward.

In 1767 it was directed that all the roofs in the city should be covered with slate or tiles. For some years, however, tiles alone were used, the first building roofed with slate being, it is said, the City Hotel, in Broadway, erected about 1794.

The number of firemen in the city had been increased by February 1, 1769, to one hundred and thirty, among whom the following were foremen: Jacob Roome and Robert Harding, in the West Ward; George Stanton, Gulian Varick, and Andrew Bell, in the North Ward; Peter Bogart and Charles Phillips, in the East Ward; Isaac Marschalck, in the South Ward; and William Hardenbrook, in Montgomerie Ward. Jacob Stoutenburgh was still engineer, with Joseph Ten Brook and Isaac Stoutenburgh, Jr., as assistants.

The law prescribing a penalty for permitting chimneys to take fire through neglect to keep them clean became practically obsolete because of the unwillingness of neighbors to turn informers and help to prosecute for violations of it. It was therefore deemed necessary in November, 1771, to appoint Johannis Myer to perform that disagreeable but necessary service; and the penalties were to be devoted to a firemen's fund for the purchase of material required by them in the prosecution of their duties. The engineer in this year, for "maintaining" ten engines and for his own salary, drew the sum of thirty-three pounds and six shillings. The following year a third assistant engineer was appointed, and three additional engines were purchased.

In May, 1772, John Burns, peruke maker, and Peter G. Waldron, were appointed firemen for the South Ward. In July, Alderman Andrew Gautier was authorized to purchase two fire engines belonging to Thomas Tiller; and in September to purchase one belonging to Davis Hunt. George Stanton and Jacob Roome were recorded as assistants to engineer Stoutenburgh; George Waldegrove was foreman, and John Brower assistant, in the West Ward; John Bell, also foreman, in the West Ward; Jacob Brower and Gulian Varick were in command of two small fire engines; Isaac Meade was foreman of the engine near St. Paul's church; Andrew Bell in command of the engine at the barracks; Theophilus Hardenbrook, foreman in charge of engine in St. George's Square; and John Quackenboss in command of the company located in the "Out Ward," lately organized, which consisted of David Henry Mallo, George January, John Walters, Henry Shute, Garrett Peterson, Isaac Van Duerson, John Simerendyck, Richard Edmonds, Valentine Arnolds, Francis Sawyer, Mathias Feer, John Stout and William Crolius.

Five acres on Broadway were purchased during the year 1773, and buildings erected at a cost of about eighteen thousand dollars, for the New York Hospital. Before their completion their interior was burned out by an accidental fire, and the work thus retarded for a considerable time.

"The Provost House," at the Battery, wherein dwelt Governor Tryon, was consumed by fire at midnight on December 17 of this year. The family escaped with difficulty. The governor's daughter leaped from the second story window, and her maid, Elizabeth Garrett, afraid to follow her, was burned to death. Greater mischief would have been wrought but for the snow on the adjacent buildings.

Christopher Colles, in 1774, had partly constructed a reservoir in Broadway, near Pearl Street, the completion of which was stopped by the Revolutionary war.

Isaac Bangs, a New England trooper of 1776, thus describes the New York of that period: "I spent most of the day in viewing the city, which is more extensive than I imagined. It is nearly as populous as the town of Boston. The public edifices are more numerous, yet not in general so magnificent as those of Boston. * * * On the southwest part of the town, which is a point between the two rivers, is a very strong and costly fort, built by the king's troops. Outside the fort, at the edge of the water, was a battery, erected at a vast expense to the king, of hewn stone, being about ten feet high, and having the inside filled up to form an inclined plane, sloping inwardly down to a wall one and a half feet high. Over this the cannon were to play. But as so low a wall would not be a sufficient cover for the men, our people were busily employed in making a turf wall upon the stone wall, and when we arrived, had almost finished as complete a battery as ever I saw. From the above-mentioned fort, a spacious street, running east-northeast in a straight

VIEW OF NEW YORK FROM THE NORTH, 1679.
From painting in possession of W. M. Randell, Office of Board of Fire Underwriters.

line, reached without the town above a mile. In this, near the fort, is the equestrian statue of George III." Lieutenant Bangs refers to the "new" water works, and says that the well water is very bad and unwholesome, "so that the inhabitants prefer to buy water for making coffee, out of carts employed in carrying it around the city." One Sunday he dropped into a church, but could not understand a word of the service because it was all in Dutch. On another Sunday, this observant soldier says: "In the forenoon I attended public worship at the Congregational meeting; was very much disappointed with the preaching. The parson had invited a chaplain of the army to do his work for him, who performed it miserably. Being tired of such nonsense as I heard in the forenoon, I tried the Church of England in the afternoon. But the satisfaction I received from the substance of an excellent sermon was greatly abated by the pedantic behaviour of the priest, the irreverent conduct of the people, and the foolish parade of ceremonies. I am determined next Sunday (unless I find better entertainment) to attend worship with the Dutch priest, whom I heard last week, choosing rather to worship where I understand nothing than to hear and see such folly."

On the fifteenth of September, 1776 (soon after the disastrous battle on Long Island), the British troops took possession of the city, and in their train were refugees from all sections. Later, traders and speculators came in hordes by every transport fleet from Great Britain, and a large business sprung up in the purchase and sale of army supplies, but the city itself found no profit in this abnormal traffic. The streets and buildings were allowed to go to decay, with the exception of temporary repairs for sanitary reasons, and the glories of the once thriving city were but a story of the past.

Up to 1776 there were but seven engines and two bucket and ladders, or trucks, although there were building at the time one for No. 8. During the early part of this year the whole force of the Fire Department, consisting of a little over one hundred and seventy, formed themselves into a home guard, with Jacob Stoutenburgh as chief, but virtually under command of General Washington.

Two terrible conflagrations added to the measure of distress and ruin. Hardly had the British troops taken possession, ere (on the twenty-first of September, 1776,) a disastrous fire, breaking out in a small wooden house on the wharf near Whitehall, occupied by dissolute characters, spread to the northward, and consumed the entire city westward of Broadway to the very northernmost limit. In this terrible calamity, which owed its extent to the desertion of the city and the terror of the few remaining inhabitants, four hundred and ninety-three houses were destroyed, including old Trinity and the Lutheran Church. Another destructive fire broke out on Cruger's wharf on the third of August, 1778, and burned about fifty-four houses.

The cause of so many houses being burned was attributed to the military taking the directions of the fire from the firemen. The commander-in-chief, to whom complaint was made by the citizens, gave general orders that in future no military man should interfere with any fire that might happen within the city.

The following is a list of the number of houses burned (1778): Col. Wm. Bayard, six houses and stores; Messrs. John and Henry Cruger, six houses; Gerardus Duyckinck, seven houses; Peter Mesier, two dwelling houses; David Provost, four houses and two pulled down; Capt. Thomas Brown, four houses; Mr. Varick, one house; estate of Andrew Meyer, one house.

Several of the inhabitants were restrained from going out to assist at night from a fear that they might be arrested as suspicious persons. In fact, several decent citizens were sent to the provost guard for examination, and some had to stay there two or three days until their "loyalty" could be made out. In one case, even a good loyalist, sometimes inclined "to taste a drop too much," was, by misapprehension of his character and in the excitement of the moment, hung up on a sign-post at the corner of Cherry and Roosevelt Streets.

These fires occurred while the British held possession of the city, and excited a fear at the time that the "American Rebels" had purposed to oust them by their own sacrifices, like another Moscow. It was, however, established that they were the result of accident and not of design.

After the great fire of 1776, Major-General Jas. Robertson issued the following proclamation:

Whereas, There is ground to believe that the Rebels, not satisfied with the Destruction of Part of the City, entertain Designs of burning the Rest. And it is thought that a Watch to inspect all the Parts of the City to apprehend Incendiaries and to stifle Fires before they rise to a dangerous Height might be a necessary and proper means to prevent such a calamity. Many of the principal inhabitants have applied to me to form such a Watch and have all offered to watch in person, etc.

The Revolution caused an abrupt break in the municipal history. The meetings of the Mayor's Court of Quarter Sessions and the Common Council ceased after July 4, 1776. On the occupation of the city by the British they were not resumed; but, the city being placed under martial law, military courts of police took their place. When, after this seven years' blank, the forms of municipal government were restored, it was under the constitution of the State of New York adopted in 1777.

The mayor and superintendent-general, in 1778, made proclamation to the citizens that John Norris, at the corner house, near the Main Guard, and David Henry Mallows, near the Tea Water Pump, had the care of the chimney-sweeps, and that on a note in writing being left at either of their houses, a sweep would be sent to the place designated. A fine of five pounds, previously established, it was declared, would be punctually exacted from every inhabitant whose chimney should take fire through neglect. Each chimney should be swept once in every four weeks. Similarly, notice was given that John Roome was appointed to examine the stoves put up in the city, and the places allotted by the inhabitants to keep their ashes in. The inhabitants were reminded that "the injudicious method of firing stoves, and keeping ashes, having often endangered this city, it is expected that the citizens will punctually attend to such directions as Mr. Roome may judge necessary, in order to prevent the calamity of fire, which is equally to be dreaded by every inhabitant."

On June 14, 1780, by permission of the commandant, a scheme was devised and put in operation for the purpose of procuring an additional number of fire buckets for the use of the city. The prizes offered ranged from one thousand dollars to eight dollars. There were one thousand five hundred and two prizes, four thousand four hundred and ninety-eight blanks, and six thousand tickets at four dollars each, representing twenty-four thousand dollars, subject to a deduction of fifteen per cent. This scheme, when launched, was backed up with this admonition: "Depending on the liberality of those who wish to promote the common good, as well as to secure their own private interest, a large number of buckets are already contracted for and will soon be completed. As the safety of every individual is, in this measure, blended with public utility, it is not doubted but the same laudable spirit which on many former occasions has readily exerted itself, will again step forth for the speedy accomplishment of so necessary a purpose."

A number of citizens formed themselves into companies, in January of 1781, calling themselves by the names of the Friendly Union, Hand-in-Hand, and Heart-in-Hand Fire Companies. Their object was to undertake every service in their power, in case of fire, by removing and securing the effects of such of their fellow citizens whose situation, at such time, should require their attention. In order to be distinguished, they wore round hats with black brims and white crowns. They were exempted from handling buckets, or assisting in working the engines.

The troops in garrison were found to be derelict in the matter of complying with the order for cleaning of chimneys, and it was requested that in future the officers quartered in this city once in every month "will send to this office (barracks office, Maiden Lane) for an order for the sweeping of their chimneys."

The whole increase of the city during the century of English domination did not exceed twenty thousand, an increase which seems at the present day vastly disproportionate to the commercial and agricultural advantages of the city and province. But this surprise will decrease when the jealous and narrow-minded restrictions thrown around the colony are considered. As early as 1705 Governor Cornbury, writing from New York to his official superiors in England, expresses himself in these terms: "I hope I may be pardoned if I declare my opinion to be that all these coloneys, which are but twigs belonging to the main tree (England), ought to be kept entirely dependent upon and subservient to England, and that can never be if they are suffered to go on in the notions they have, that as they are Englishmen, so they may set up the same manufactures here as people may do in England."

The Department (up to 1776) consisted as follows:

Engine Company No. 1—Location, rear of City Hall.

Engine Company No. 2—Rear of City Hall,

Engine Company No. 3—At Kalch-Hook Pond.

Engine Company No. 4—Broadway and a lane leading down to Jansen's windmill, midway between Little Queen and Fair streets.

Engine Company No. 5—On "Smit Valley," now Pearl street.

Engine Company No. 6—Crown street, near King, now Nassau.

Engine Company No. 7—Duke street, leading down to Terry, now Stone.

Engine Company No. 8—At the Tar Pits, foot of now Maiden Lane.

Truck Company No. 2—Fair, near King street.

Truck Company No. 2—S. E. of the Battery, adjoining the Basin.

During the war the Department was completely demoralized, but two engines having survived. Most of the members were killed, and when the British evacuated the city only one of the engines left would work.

VIEW OF NEW YORK HARBOR, FROM NAGER, FORT HAMILTON, 1769.
Original in possession of W. M. Randell, Office of Fire Underwriters.

CHAPTER IV.

BEGINNING OF A NEW ERA.

1783–1797.—The British Evacuate the City.—"Henceforth New York was to move on her Marvelous Career."—Address of the Firemen to Governor Clinton.—Formation of a new Fire Organization.— The Fresh Water Pond.—New Companies Organized.—Fire Buckets and Their Uses.—Location of Engine Houses.

ON the twenty-fourth of March, 1783, Robert R. Livingston, the Secretary of Foreign Affairs, notified General Washington, then at West Point, of the agreeable intelligence of a general peace, and on the ninth of April following, at twelve o'clock, peace was proclaimed from the steps of the City Hall by the town major. On the twenty-fifth day of November the American army, under the command of Major-General Henry Knox, marched from Harlem to the Bowery Lane, where they remained until one o'clock, when, the British posts being withdrawn, the American column marched in

VIEW OF NEW YORK, GOVERNOR'S ISLAND, THE RIVERS, ETC., FROM LONG ISLAND, 1776.

and took possession of the city. The new era began upon this day; henceforth New York was to move on her marvelous career. In a few years she appears, reorganized, rebuilt, with new architecture, new institutions, *facile princeps*, the imperial city of the continent. The compact part of the city extended to Chambers Street on the north and to Catharine Street on the east. Fort George stood on the north end of the Battery, and barracks for soldiers on the south end. The upper barracks were in the park, on Chambers Street. The prison, new prison, and house of correction were in the park, the latter where now stands the City Hall. The fresh water pond on Centre Street was in part surrounded by hills. The hospital building stood near Broadway and Duane Street. A line of fortifications extended from the high grounds on the east part of the city to Bunker Hill, near Grand Street, between the Bowery and Broadway, and westward across Broadway to another eminence; fortifications were also erected farther west of Broadway, near the river, on a line with Fourteenth Street. All beyond was cleared fields.

In the lower parts of the city there was little to be seen but heaps of ruins. By far the greatest part of the buildings were composed of wood and covered with shingles, bricks and stones being very little used. Washington and West Streets were not in existence, and the project of making new grounds by encroachments on the rivers had been scarcely thought of. In a secluded spot, in the present Reade Street, near Broadway, was a burying ground for people of color, in the neighborhood of which there was scarcely to be found a single house; and immediately to the northward stretched fields and meadows, which extended far and wide. Very few streets were paved, and the workmanship of these few was performed in such a manner as would now be deemed very awkward; one gutter running through the center, which was the lowest part of the street, and the elevation on both sides being towards the houses. Of banks and insurances offices there was not one in the city. At the commencement of the revolutionary war there were nineteen places of public worship; but at its close there were only nine. Trinity and the old Lutheran Church were consumed by the great fire, November 21, 1776, and the other churches, as well as the college, were used by the British as barracks, jails, hospitals, and riding schools.

The Bank of New York was the first banking institution established in this city, commencing operations in 1784, although not chartered until 1791, the banking house being located on the corner of Wall and William Streets. It was followed by the Manhattan Company, incorporated in 1799, located at No. 23 Wall Street; by the Merchants' Bank, incorporated in 1805, located at 25 Wall Street; by the United States Bank, located at 38 Wall Street, about 1805; by the Mechanics' Bank, incorporated in 1810, located at 16 Wall Street. These were the pioneer banking institutions, which were soon after rapidly increased in number.

Insurance companies were in existence in this city still earlier than banks. "We believe," says Valentine, "the first institution of the kind after the Revolutionary War was called the Mutual Assurance Company. We find that in 1815 there were already thirteen insurance companies established in Wall Street."

The principal event which settled the character of Wall Street as the center of interest in the city, and which brought about it the leading men of business and professional life, was the erection of the old City Hall, opposite Broad Street, in 1700; which building became afterwards the Capitol of the United States, and the site of which is still used for public purposes, thus perpetuating the influence of the original selection of that site down to the present day. The City Hall remained in use for the objects for which it was erected about a century. After the Revolutionary War this building received additional historic interest as the first place of meeting of the Congress of 1789, and the inauguration of George Washington as president.

Shortly after the British troops had taken their final departure, this manly missive (a *fac-simile* of the original) was penned:

*To His Excellency George Clinton Esq
Governor of the State of New york in Ameri=
-ca &c.ª   May it please your Excellency*

As the Change of Government has now taken place on the Arrival of your Excellency in this City—We the Fire Engineers of the several Fire Engines, and Companies belonging to the same, beg leave to lay before your Excellency, the State and Condition of the Fire Engines &c.ª—as also of the several Companies and Number of Men now belonging to the same.

We further beg leave to represent to your Excellency that the Fire Engines with the other implements belong=-ing, were before the late Fire all in good Condition, and the Companies under good Order and Regulations: And as there are at present a Number of Fire Buckets wanting, and also some Necessary to be done (Occasioned by the late Fire) to the several apparatus belonging to the Engines, which require immediate dispatch. not knowing how soon they may be wanted—We think it Our duty, and therefore take this early Opportunity to represent this matter to your Excellency, as the safety and preservation of this Metropolis at Times depend greatly in keeping the Engines in good Order.

We now beg leave to inform your Excellency, that we held a Commission Jointly and Severally, under the late Governor Robertson, and are happy to say we always gain'd applause from the Citizens for our good Conduct in the Alarming time of Fire in this City — Should it please your Excellency to Continue us in this office under your Administration we will always Act with such Conduct, as we make no Doubt will, when Called upon in Time of Fire gain the applause of your Excellency, as well as in the late Fire we have of the Citizens. — — We

Remain with Great Respect
Your Excellency's Most Obed't
Most Hum.le Serv.ts
John Balthasar Dash.
George Stanton
Francis Dominick
Jeronemus Alstyne

New York 27th November 1783.

A List of the Names of the Foremen and Commons men, belonging to the Several Fire Engines, with the Numbers of the Same, —

Engine —

		Men
N:	Jacob Boelen, Foreman	12
2,	John Burt Syng — Do	12.
3,	John C. Cuntzius — Do	16.
4,	John Post — Do	13.
5.	Daniel Penryck — Do	22.
6	Nicholas Carmer — Do	21
7,	Ahasuerus Turk — Do	24,
8	Henry Riker — Do	23.
9,	Charles Doughty — Do	16.
10	Isaac Meade — Do	22
11	Christopher Henniger — Do	16,
12	John B. Dash Jun. — Do	12,
13.	Richard Deane — Do	12.
14.	Benjamin Birdsall — Do	10,

Men belonging to Ladders and hooks }—

N. 1.	Daniel Cottong Foreman	12.
2.	William Wright — Do	10

253

What was recognized as the upper extremity of Broadway in 1784, and the utmost limit of the city pavement, was the site of St. Paul's Chapel. The fields were open to the north as far as a line ranging eastwardly from Warren Street, where the prospect was bounded by those more useful than agreeable objects, the bridewell, the poorhouse, the goal, and the gallows. Towards the west, however, there was nothing to obstruct the view of the North River but two low houses at the corner of Vesey Street and the college building. The "fields," as the area comprised in the park was then called, were neither enclosed nor planted. The streets leading from Broadway to the river had been laid out as high as Warren Street, yet they were but partially built upon, and, for the most part, with houses of an inferior description. None above Dey Street had been regulated and paved; nor had the ridge, commencing near the Battery and extending the length of the island, been dug through as far

ANCIENT VIEW OF THE PRESENT JUNCTURE OF PEARL AND CHATHAM STREETS, CHATHAM
SQUARE AND BOWERY, 1761.

A. Catimut Hill.	D. Jews' Burying Ground.	G. Road to the Bowery (present
B. Fresh Water.	E. Rutger's Farm House.	Pearl Street.)
C. Fresh Water Bridge.	F. Bowery Road.	H. Road to the City.

even as Cortlandt Street. Great Dock Street, or that part of Pearl between Whitehall and Coenties Slip, with the other streets in the neighborhood in the immediate vicinity of Fort George, within which the Colonial Government House was situate, had long been considered the court end of the town. But, even before the revolution, Wall Street was regarded as a rival seat of fashion, to which it established an exclusive claim, and maintained it until superseded by Park Place (or Robinson Street). Little Dock Street, now merged in Water Street, and that part of the original Water Street which lay adjacent to the Albany pier, were occupied by the river trade; while the remainder of Water Street, and such parts of Front Street as had already been recovered from the river, formed the emporium of foreign commerce. This, indeed, was the case as far up as the Coffee House Slip, and gradually extended to Maiden Lane, at the foot of which was the *Vly* market and the Brooklyn ferry; whilst at the head of it stood the Oswego Market, fronting on Broadway. Above, on the East River, as far as Dover Street, the wharves were chiefly occupied by down-easters with their cargoes of notions, or by Long Islanders with their more substantial freights of oysters, clams, and fine white sand. Beyond Dover Street, the shipyards commenced, extending at first no farther than to the "New," or, as it is now called, "Pike" Slip. Crossing from Dover to Great Queen (since Pearl) Street, and following the latter beyond its intersection with Chatham Street, and along that part of Pearl then called Magazine Street, the "*Kolch*," or "Fresh Water Pond" was reached; whence, through the "Tea Water Pump," in Chatham Street, the city was supplied with water for domestic use, distributed to the inhabitants by means of carts surmounted by casks. Nor was this the only use made of the "Collect," as it was called in English. Its southern and eastern banks were lined with furnaces, potteries, breweries, tanneries, ropewalks, and other manufactories, all drawing their supplies of water from the pond.

Numerous fire buckets had disappeared from time to time—expropriated or irremediably damaged. So great had the deficiency thus created become, by the commencement of 1784, that the Common Council appointed a committee to ascertain the number wanting, and to make contracts for new buckets.

The first regular organization of the Fire Department of the city of New York appears to have been effected on the fifteenth of February, 1786, when it was ordered by the Common Council that the following persons be appointed firemen, during the pleasure of the Board:

William Ellsworth, John Stagg, Francis Bassett, Isaac Mead, and John Quackenboss, engineers.

HOOK AND LADDER MEN.

Company No. 1.—David Contant, Edward Lowvier, John Vernon, Gilliaum Cornell, Jacob Abramse, Edward Patten, Christian Stamler, Thomas Underhill, Anthony Abramse, Abraham Schenck, Thomas Skaats, Rinior Skaats, and Daniel Fagan.

Company No. 2.—William Wright, Timothy Russell, Christopher Halsted, George Deiderich, Thomas Lubbary, John Hacbain, Daniel Lawrence, Samuel Carmen, James Russell, Matthew Bird, Henry Rogers, and David Rosette.

ENGINE MEN.

Engine Company No. 1.—Benjamin Birtsell, Thomas Ash, James Tyler, Peter Demilt, John Buskirk, Richard Davis, Jurden Lawrence, John Van Varick, Theodorus Deforrest, William Carman.

Engine Company No. 2.—Jotham Post, foreman; Jeremiah Ackerly, Frederick Shober, Daniel Kingsland, John Simpson, John Titus, Peter Shop, John DeGroot, William Nicols, Patrick Seamons.

Engine Company No. 3.—Guilliaum Varick, foreman; Bartholomew Skaats, William Covenhoven, Gerard Smith, Jacob Brower, John Kemper, John De Le Montague, William Van Dolsem, John Henry, George Gozman.

Engine Company No. 4.—Sylvester V. Buskirk, John Rarsi, Thomas Bruen, John Philips, Elbert Anderson, Burger Van De Water, William Hunt, John Van Voorhis, Elias Stillwel, John Houseman. (Its engine was removed in February, 1793, from the City Hall to the theater in John Street.)

Engine Company No. 5.—Frederick Eachart, George Peck, Garret Van De Water, William McKinney, Peter Thompson, John Cole, Abraham Eachart, William Remmey, Nicholas Hillman, and Caleb Pell.

Engine Company No. 6.—Abraham F. Martlings, foreman; William Day, Joseph Smith, William Jennings, Conrad Heasner, Thomas Campbell, Valentine Vaughn, Jacob Day, Joseph Smith, Jr.

Engine Company No. 7.—John Post, Jacob Tabley, James Townsend, Thomas Hazard, Elijah Cook, Anthony Ford, John Day, John Smith, William Mooney, William Dean, Stephen Coles, Jacob Smith, Abel Hardenbrook.

Engine Company No. 8.—David Morris, Henry Spingler, Anthony Brown, James Quackenboss, Dowe Talman, David Van Derbeck, Isaac Sherdewine, Abraham Brevoort, Philip Smith, Christopher Fegenhan, Isaac Austin, John Rose, Frederick Mabie, Andrus Cole, Abraham Riker, Charles Hardenburg.

Engine Company No. 9.—Edward Doughty, John Betts, John Clark, Jr., John Doughty, Samuel Doughty, Abraham Bond, Henry Bausher, Charles McLain, John Anderson, Jacob Cushun, Moses Egbert, James Stewart, Andrus Ten Eyck, Richard Ten Eyck, Thomas Burns, Daniel Barbee, Nathan Strong, and John Astin.

Engine Company No. 10.—Gabriel Furman, foreman; Garrit Peterson, Gideon Kastang, Aaron Dow, Josiah Furman, Jacob Tier, Peter Balmer, Garrett Quackenboss, Frederick Gants, John Faulk, John Odel, James Miers, Oliver Hubbs, Leonard Fisher, James Balmer, John Binkes, Richard Furman, Andrus Thompson, James Renolds, William Collister, John Hogelandt, Valentine Tatter, and James Hawkins.

Engine Company No. 11.—Daniel Ten Eyck, Evert Hessells, Jacobus Quirk, Andrew Myers, William Myers, Adam Keyser, Abraham Ten Eyck, James Moore, Henry Sickles, Samuel Wessells, Gerardus Burger, Joseph George, William Brown, Benjamin Shyrkird, John Murray, James M. Cullen, Moses Smith, John Devine, John Young, John Nicolls, Jacob Morris, Joseph Corrie, Augustus Sidell.

Engine Company No. 12.—Henry Riker, John Brevoort, Thomas Franklin, Jr., John Seagar, Robert Johnson, Donald McKay, Henry Titus, Willett Seaman, Jacob Seaman, John Gassner, Joseph Stringham, Jonathan Dickinson, John Walter, Andrew Merrill, John Webb, Abraham Polhemus, Thomas Stagg, Burling Martin, Mathias Warner, John Aurther, Henry Mitchell, John Evans, Enoch Carter, and Daniel Hitchcock.

Engine Company No. 13.—William Borkee, foreman; Victor Baker, Ezekiel Robins, William Post, John Young, Richard Norwood, William Shotwell, Thomas Warner, Cornelius Ricker, James Woodward, Walter Hyer, Richard Pinfold, Adolph Degrove, John Lawrence, Thomas Saunders, George Archeart, John Alstine, William Smith, Jr., James Lent, Nicholas Carmer, James Beekman, William Allen, Henry Ricker, John Smith.

Engine Company No. 14.—Captain Jacobus Bogart, Jacob Resler, Abraham Brower, Bisset Weeks, Isaac Vaardenburg, John Ritter, Burget Shellhouse, Ernest Awick, Marmaduke Earl, Peter Lawrence, Francis Moore, Michael Nistel, Thomas Lincker, John Kiersted, Valentine Shemeal Medrif Eden, John Baldrige, Morris Earle, James Blanchard, Abraham Delamater, Samuel Johnston, George Garland, John Carrow, and Cornelius Van Alen.

Engine Company No. 15.—Ahasurus Turk, George Warner, Alexander Hosack, John Buxton, Charles Bush, Christian Shultz, Abraham Anderson, William Ellison, Jonas Colong, Cornelius Warner, Garret Walgrave, George

Walgrave, John Mowatt, John Mildeberger, Stephen Rose, Peter Garbrance Samuel Walgrave, James Kip, George Smelzel, Josiah Jones, Charles Warner, Robert Carter, Thomas Barrow, and George Webster.

In May, 1785, a fire engine was purchased of Richard Deane for the sum of forty pounds sterling. In July of that year the French church was burnt. In October, as "the season in which fires most frequently happen was approaching," the law for the better preventing of fire was published in the newspapers of the city, so that no one could plead ignorance.

Although no effort appears to have been made by State laws prior to 1787 to organize any force of men specially charged with the extinguishment of fires in this city, it is worthy of note that two previous enactments had been made looking toward the prevention of fires, one in 1785, and the other the following year. The first of these laws was aimed at "the pernicious practice of firing

RESIDENCE OF GOVERNOR LEISLER (IN THE FORT.)
Said to have been the first brick building in New York.

guns, pistols, rockets, squibs, and other fireworks, on the eve of the last day of December, and the first and second days of January," and provided for a fine of forty shillings for the offense of firing off any gun, etc., within a quarter of a mile of any building on the days named. In the event of the fine not being paid, then the offender went to jail, "there to remain without bail or mainprize for the space of one month."

The other, passed in 1786, was directed against "the storing of pitch, tar, turpentine, resin, linseed oil, or shingles," as well as against the firing off of guns, pistols, etc. It prohibited the storing of any of the substances named in any place "south of fresh water in said city," under a penalty of ten pounds. But any ship chandler was allowed to have "near his door in the open street" not to exceed twenty barrels at any one time, "in order the more readily to supply the merchant ships, and others who may have occasion for small quantities of such commodities." Any person discharging any firearms or fireworks "on any lane, street, or ally, garden, or other enclosure, or in any other place where persons usually walk " south of fresh water," was liable to a penalty of twenty shillings, or to be imprisoned for ten days. If the offender were a slave, it was provided that he was to be " publickly whipped on the naked back as many times as the justice shall prescribe, not exceeding thirty-nine."

On March 15, 1787, the first act regulating the keeping and storing of gunpowder was passed. By this law, any gunpowder in greater quantity than twenty-eight pounds, found by any fireman outside of the powder magazine and within one mile of the City Hall, was forfeited to the use of such fireman, without the formality of any legal process whatever

On November 1, 1780, the Hand-in-Hand Fire Company was organized. Certain rules and regulations were at various times agreed on, and adopted at a meeting held at the Coffee House on November 20, 1788. " The utility of associations for the purpose of averting as much as possible the ruinous consequences which may occasionally happen by fire," the preamble recites, " induced a number of individuals to form themselves into select companies, with the laudable view of affording their particular aid to each other, and to the community at large." Under this impression the society was formed. Among the articles of association was one requiring that each member should provide himself with two bags, consisting of three-and-a-half yards raven's duck (with proper strings), marked with the owner's name at length, and " H. H.," the initials of the company; also with a round hat, the crown to be painted white, and thereon the letters " H. H.," painted black, as large as the crown would permit of; which hat should be considered as the badge of distinction of the company in case of fire. Another article provided that there should be a watchword given by the president or vice-president, in order to prevent deception from intruders at the removal of effects in case of fire; and the watchword was to be demanded by one of the members, who should be placed as sentinel at the house or store in danger.

The earliest state law providing for the protection of the city from the ravages of fire, and upon which is founded all subsequent legislation relating to the appointment and equipment of firemen, is that passed on March 19, 1787, entitled "an act for the better extinguishment of fires in the city of New York." By that act, the Common Council was authorized and required to appoint "a sufficient number of strong, able, discreet, honest, and sober men, willing to accept, not exceeding three hundred in number of the inhabitants, being freeholders or freemen of said city, to have the care, management, working and using the fire engines and the other tools and instruments, now provided or hereafter to be provided for extinguishing fires, * * * which persons shall be called The Firemen of the City of New York; and who, with the engineers of the same city are hereby required and enjoined to be ready at all times, as well by night as by day, to manage, work and use all the same fire engines, and other of the tools and instruments aforesaid."

The firemen so appointed were made subject to such rules as the Common Council might prescribe "for the frequent exercising, trying and using of the same fire engines, tools, and other instruments."

It was decided in February, 1788, to remove the engine located in Nassau Street to a house to be erected on the ground belonging to the Reformed Protestant Dutch Congregation adjoining the North Church.

In January, 1789, the following appointments were made: George Titlar and James Ketchum to Engine No. 11, vice Jacobus Quick and Henry Sickels, resigned; Abraham Moore to Engine No. 14, vice Bisset Weeks; Isaac Vervelen to Engine No. 8, vice Dowe Talman; Oliver Mildeberger to engine No. 12, vice Henry Riker; George Seal and Thomas Saunders to Engine No. 13, vice George Arhart and Richard Penfold; John Halsted and Samuel Carman to Hook and Ladder Company No. 2, vice Daniel Lawrence and David Rosette, William Pinckney to Engine No. 5, vice William Rammey; and William Peterson, Jeremiah Wood, and Jacob Free to "Out Ward" Engine, vice James Balmer, John Fasch, and John Binckes.

On the thirteenth of May the following appointments were made: Ebenezer C. Kilburne to Engine No. 15, vice Alexander Hosack, resigned; Thomas

NEW YORK IN 1672.

Stevenson to Hook and Ladder Company No. 1, vice Edward Lowvier, resigned; Samuel Sneeden, Garrett Debow and Robert Roberts to Hook and Ladder Company No. 1, vice Anthony Abramse, Isaac Abramse, and Thomas Underhill, removed from the city; John Simmons to Engine No. 6, vice Thomas Campbell, resigned; David Ackerman to Engine No. 14, vice Thomas Lincoln, displaced; John J. Bogert to Engine No. 14, vice Samuel Johnston, deceased; Cornelius Sebring to Engine No. 14, vice John Kiersted, resigned; and Isaac Cock to Engine No. 12, vice John Segar, resigned.

The meddlesome and often obstructive character of the help given to the firemen by boys and excitable young men, which caused so much trouble and anxiety in later times to the controllers of the Department, seems to have developed itself as early as 1789, for it is recorded as a decree of the august and reverend fathers of the city, that after the twelfth of August of that year no person under the age of thirty years should be appointed to the office of a fireman. But that law proved to be a decided drawback instead of a benefit to the Department, and it was therefore repealed in the following November.

The fire engines of the smallest size were used to approach nearest to the fire, and were, therefore, best adapted for the "leaders" to convey water through windows and narrow passes. When the "leaders" were used, none but firemen were willing to support them, and "it was attended by a general wetting by the water which gushes out of the seams." The foreman of these engines petitioned the Common Council for an assignment of ten men to each company, and their petition was acceded to in March, 1790.

A project was conceived about the year 1789 for converting the Fresh Water Pond, and the grounds adjacent, to the embellishment of the city. A company was formed with that view, and a plan drawn, laying out a park, embracing the great and lesser Collect, and extending from the north side of Reade Street to the present site of Grand Street, so as to include the eminence called "Bunker's Hill." The "Little Collect" commenced at the foot of the hill, on the north side of Reade Street, and was divided from the principal pond by a mound or knoll, through which Pearl Street was carried. On this knoll stood the "Old Powder House," from which the street leading to it from Broadway, now part of Pearl Street, derived its name of Magazine Street.

METHOD OF CARRYING FIRE BUCKETS.

The plan for the conversion of the Collect, as stated, fell through, principally because the supposition of the city's ever extending so far out upon the island was thought by capitalists too visionary to be acted on. Another project, of a more utilitarian character, was subsequently entertained, namely, to connect the Collect with both rivers, thus converting it into a dock, with wharves and warehouses surrounding its margin. But such were the limited views generally prevalent at that day in regard to the probable increase of the city in size, business, wealth, and population, it was believed the dock would never be wanted.

Between 1787 and 1790 the streets leading from Broadway to Hudson River, from Cortlandt Street upward to the hospital, were regulated, and some of them paved. On the west side, Broadway was paved as far out as Warren Street, and large and substantial brick houses were gradually making their appearance. Greenwich Street, in which the most conspicuous object was the Bear Market, now superseded by the more extensive erection dignified with the name of Washington Market, was prolonged, by leveling high grounds extending northward from the foot of Warren Street, where stood Vauxhall House and Garden, once the seat of Sir Peter Warren. In this year the first sidewalks in the city were laid on the west side of Broadway, from Vesey to Murray Streets, and opposite for the same distance along the bridewell fence. These were narrow pavements of brick and stone, scarcely wide enough to permit two persons to walk abreast.

On March 24, 1791, the Legislature passed a law prohibiting the erection of wooden buildings of three or more stories below what is now Canal Street. All buildings to be erected within this space should be constructed of stone or brick, and should be covered, "except the flat roof thereof," with slate or tile. But such flat roof "may be composed of board or shingles, provided it does not exceed two-fifths of the space of the roof, and be surrounded by a substantial balcony or balustrade." An exception is made to the roofing of existing buildings, and also in favor of buildings erected on ground "not capable of sustaining a foundation, upon which a stone or brick structure can be sustained." This latter exception authorizes the erection of wooden buildings on such grounds within the limits named, after the filing of a favorable report of the majority of five disinterested persons appointed by the mayor to examine the condition of the ground in question.

A revised law for preventing and extinguishing fires was passed on November 10, 1791, which, among other provisions, called for the appointment of fire wardens in the respective wards of the city. In accordance therewith the following appointments were made:

First Ward.—John Remsen and Thomas Ludlow.
Second Ward.—Walter Bicker and George Harsen.
Third Ward.—Jeronimus Alstyne and William Hardenbrook.
Fourth Ward.—George Stanton and Anthony Post.
Fifth Ward.—John Franklin and Benjamin Egberts.
Sixth Ward.—William Arnold and Jacob Harsen.
Seventh Ward.—Richard Varian and Charles Wright.

As marks of distinction at fires, and insignia of official position, it was decreed by the same law that the wardens should wear caps and carry certain wands and trumpets. And it was further ordered that all fines recovered as penalties for violations of the fire laws should be paid to the engineer, and by him appropriated as the fire marshal should direct.

In this year belong the earliest extant records of any fire company in the city, namely, those of Engine No. 13, which began in the month of November; also, the first written report known to have been made of the doings of the Fire Department proper, was made on the fourth of this month. The meeting was held in the house of Jacob Brouwer, in Nassau Street. The minutes of this meeting inform us that "engineers, firemen, and representatives" attended, but that the engineers and foremen were the only "representatives" present. The engineers were: Ahasuerus Turk, chairman; William J. Elsworth, John Stagg, Francis Bassett, Isaac Mead, and John Quackenbush. The foremen were: Abraham Franklin, secretary; Abraham Brouwer, James Beekman, Thomas Franklin, Evert Wessels, Gabriel Furman, John Post, Joseph Smith, Frederick Eckert, Sylvester Buskirk, Bartholomew Skaats, Jackamiah Ackerly, Thomas Ash, John B. Dash, Archibald Kerly, William Wright, David Coutant, John Clark, and David Morris. These names represent some of the most respectable residents of the city.

The Fire Department, on the twentieth of December, 1791, held a meeting of representatives of their organization, authorized by their different companies, and framed a constitution, for the purpose of establishing a fund for the relief of unfortunate firemen whose misfortune was occasioned while doing duty as firemen. This constitution reads as follows:

ARTICLE I. A fund, which shall be called The Fire Department Fund, shall be established with the moneys arising from chimney fires, certificates, and donations, and with such other moneys as may hereafter be agreed on by such fire companies as have already agreed or may hereafter agree to fund the same.

ART. II. The Fire Department shall be represented as follows, viz.: The engineers to send one; a company composed of eighteen men or upwards to have two, and under eighteen, one representative; and such company to choose them on or before the first day of June in every year.

ART. III. There shall be annually chosen, by ballot, by the representatives, out of their own body, a President and Vice-President, and out of the whole body of Firemen, at their first meeting, nine Trustees, a Treasurer and Secretary, which Treasurer shall give security to the Trustees for the faithful performance of his trust.

ART. IV. The Trustees shall class themselves in three classes, viz., Nos. 1, 2, and 3. No. 1 shall go out the first year, No. 2 the second, and No. 3 the third year, and the representatives shall choose three new Trustees annually, at a meeting which shall be called by the President, or, in his absence, by the Vice-President, on the first Monday of July in every year, and as much oftener as any five representatives may require it.

ART. V. The Trustees shall have the sole disposal of the moneys in the funds, which shall be for the relief of such disabled Firemen, or their families, as may be interested in this fund, and who may, in the opinion of a majority of the Trustees, be worthy of assistance.

ART. VI. At a meeting of the representatives, they shall have a right to inquire into the application of the funds, and, in case of a misapplication, or malconduct of any member, they shall have a right to call them to account, and, if found guilty of a breach of trust, shall be displaced, and a new Trustee or Treasurer elected.

In the month of December of this year, Nathaniel Hawkhurst, and some others in the vicinity of Burling Slip and Queen Street, proposed to the Corporation to purchase at their own expense a fire engine, and a proper place for its reception, if the Board would appoint them firemen. The proposal was accepted. In the same month, upon the representation of Foreman Kerley and the firemen of the engine located in Cherry Street, that it was too small for the service required of it, steps were taken to procure one of proper size, the Cherry Street engine to be removed to the almshouse. On the eighteenth of April, 1792, a fire engine, lately imported from London, was purchased from John W. Thompson for ninety pounds sterling.

The organization of the Fire Department up to January, 1792, consisted exclusively of engineers and foremen. The firemen, who were excluded, felt that they had a right to be represented, and they succeeded in carrying their point. By this change each company consisting of eighteen men were entitled to send two representatives, and each company consisting of less than this number was entitled to send one representative. Instead of all the engineers being members of the organization, only one of them was admitted to membership. The following were elected officers: John Stagg, president; Ahasuerus Turk, vice-president; William J. Elsworth, treasurer; Abraham Franklin, secretary.

The old Kennedy House (the Washington Hotel of later times) was located at No. 1 Broadway. This building was an object of great historic interest. It was, during the Revolution, occupied successively by Cornwallis, Clinton, Howe, and Washington, and here André commenced his correspondence with Arnold. The house was erected in 1760, by Hon. Captain Kennedy, afterwards Earl of Cassilis. The great fires in 1776 and 1778 occurred while the British held possession of the city. This building was pulled down by Cyrus W. Field, who built a more pretentious structure on its site.

The authorities went into the business of manufacturing their own engines —or, rather, experimenting therein—in 1792, and had the satisfaction of receiving a report in June of that year from Engineer Ellsworth, to the effect that the engine had been successfully finished. It was deposited "in the rear of Mr. Mesier's lot, south of Cortlandt Street," under the direction of the aldermen and assistant aldermen of the Fourth Ward.

About the same time the small engine at the almshouse was removed to the Seventh Ward, to be located as the aldermen of that ward and the assistant aldermen of the Sixth Ward should determine. This was the origination of Engine Company No. 19.

The manner of obtaining water at fires was principally by raising it in hand buckets from the slips, which the inhabitants considered a most disagreeable duty. The experiment of a copper pump for drawing water out of the river was suggested in the Council in July, 1792, and provoked a heated

OLD KENNEDY HOUSE, NO. 1 BROADWAY.
Washington Hotel of later times.

debate on the utility of the measure, etc. It was agreed to, and the engineer was ordered to superintend its construction.

The pump was completed by January, 1793, and deposited in the engine house at the rear of the City Hall, and Richard Kip, and his father, James Kip, were charged with the management of it.

In January, 1793, upon the representation of Engineer Ellsworth, that, on account of the increase in the number of engines and firemen, an additional engineer had become necessary, the Common Council appointed Ahasuerus Turk an engineer.

The fire engine house in Greenwich Street was removed in July, to the Hay Scales, in front of the basin at Thames and Little Queen Streets.

Owing to the heavy fall of snow during the month of December, sleds were built for conveying Engines No. 17, 18, and 19, to fires, and two additional men were added to Engine Company No. 19, who, because of their "remote situation from the body of the city, found it difficult to transport their engine."

In 1793 the Common Council embodied all its rules for the conduct of the Fire Department in a single ordinance. This ordinance is too valuable and too quaint a document not to be given nearly *verbatim:*

"That the inhabitant and owner of every house in this city having less than three fire-places shall provide one Leather Bucket; and having three fireplaces and under six, two; and having six fireplaces and under nine, four; and having nine Fire-Places and upwards, six; and of every Brew-House, Distilling and Sugar House, nine Buckets; and of every Bake House four Buckets, each of which Buckets   *   *   *   shall be sufficient to contain at least two Gallons and an half of Water, and shall be marked with at least the initial letters of the Landlord's Name, and shall be hung in the entry or near the Front Door   *   *   ready to be used for extinguishing fires, when there shall be occasion. The buckets to be got at the expense of the owner of the house, the tenant having the right to deduct the cost of the same from his rent. Penalty, six shillings for each bucket not provided.

So many Firemen shall from time to time be appointed in each of the Wards of this city as the Common Council shall deem proper, and shall be called Fire Wardens, whose Duty it shall be, immediately on the cry of fire, to repair to the place where it shall be, and to direct the inhabitants in forming themselves into Ranks for handing the Buckets to supply the Fire Engines with Water, in such places and in such manner as they may think will best answer the purpose, under the direction of the Mayor, Recorder, and Aldermen, if present.

This ordinance further provides that the mayor, recorder, aldermen and assistants shall carry at fires "a white wand, at least five feet in length, with a gilded flame at the top; and each of the fire wardens shall wear upon those occasions a cap with the city arms painted on the front, and the crown painted white, and carry in his hand   *   *   a speaking trumpet painted white."

This ordinance also provides that when a fire occurs the watchman shall give notice to the fire wardens, whose names and addresses are required to be hung up in the watchhouse. "And it is enjoined on the inhabitants to place a lighted candle at the front window of their respective houses, in order that the people shall pass through the streets with greater safety." The men are also required at least once a month to exercise with their engines, etc., and to wash, clean, and examine them, under a penalty of six shillings; and for every failure to attend at the fire, and for leaving his engine while at a fire, and for failure to do his duty at a fire, a fine of twelve shillings is imposed, and to be removed from office as fireman. The chief engineer is required to see that all buckets are collected after fires, and carried to the City Hall, "and placed upon the pavement there under the Hall, so that the citizens may know where to find them."

The fire wardens are required to examine the houses and buildings in their respective wards, and to see that "they be properly furnished with buckets;" and also to examine fireplaces, chimneys, outhouses, and buildings, stoves and pipes thereof, and give notice of any danger or deficiency to the mayor or recorder, who can impose a fine of ten shillings, if he feels so disposed. Stoves could be erected without the approval of the fire wardens, but subject to fine of twenty shillings.

The need of street numbers had been for some time rendered apparent by the increasing growth of the city, and, in 1793, the corporation appointed a committee to prepare and report a feasible system. This was done, and the proposed method, beginning at the next house in every street terminating at either of the rivers, at the intersection of the main street next the river, and numbering all houses below these intersecting streets, beginning with No. 1, looking upward in all the main streets and downward in all the slips, and so on to the end of the street or slip, was adopted by the corporation.

In 1793 the Fire Department consisted of twenty engines, two hook and ladder companies, twenty-two foremen, thirteen assistants, and three hundred and eighteen men.

About the year 1794 the fire engines were of a very inferior quality; and no water was to be had except from wooden-handle pumps. By a law of the corporation, every owner of a dwelling was obliged to procure a fire-bucket for every fireplace in the house or back kitchen. These buckets held three gallons, and were made of sole leather. They were hung in the passage, near

THE CLERMONT.
Fulton's First Steamboat.

the front door, and when the bell rang for fire the watchmen, firemen, and boys, while running to the fire, sang out, "Throw out your buckets." These were picked up by the first to come along. Two lines were formed, from the fire to the nearest pump; when the pump gave out the lines were carried to the nearest river; one line passed down the empty, the other passed up the full buckets. It was seldom that any person attempted to break through these lines. As we have said elsewhere he would be roughly handled if he tried it. The firemen expected every good citizen to give them aid.

Up to 1795 private citizens had furnished the fire-buckets. This plan did not prove satisfactory. As an improvement, each engine house was furnished with two poles, of sufficient length to carry twelve buckets each. These poles were carried on the shoulders of firemen when going to fires, as may be seen represented in engravings on old firemen's certificates. The general rule that prevailed was, that the first fireman to reach the engine house after an alarm of fire should have a right to the pipe, and take it with him to the fire;

that the next four firemen to arrive should bear away the bucket-poles; and that the rest of the company should run off with the engine, "bawling out and demanding the aid of citizens as they proceeded on."

The small engine and house in Gold Street were removed in May, 1795, to the neighborhood of the hospital; and it was ordered that a new house be erected in Gold Street for an engine about to be purchased. Orders were also given for the erection of an engine house in the vicinity of that existing in Maiden Lane, which had become unfit for use, and had to be removed from Mr. Rutger's lot, on which it stood.

An amendment to the building laws was recommended in February, 1795, that no building, excepting those of stone or brick, and covered with slate or tile, should be of any greater height from the level of the ground to the lower part of the roof than twenty-eight feet, and that the pitch of the roof should not exceed ten inches per foot.

A fire engine was located adjacent to the Methodist Church, in the Seventh Ward, in June of this year. In October, an ordinance was passed compelling the Tea Water men to supply the engines with water in case of fire.

The Fresh Pond, or, as the Dutch designated it, *Kolch*, which name had been corrupted into the "Collect," was the scene of one of the most interesting events that the world ever saw. That was nothing less than the original experiment in steam navigation. Here, in 1795, was exhibited by John Stevens, of Hoboken, a boat with a screw propeller driven by a steam engine. The next year another experiment was made in the same place by John Fitch, the real inventor of steam navigation, with a ship's yawl, into which he had placed a rude steam engine of his own construction, with paddle-wheels at the sides of the boat. These experiments, with Fitch's invention, were made in the presence and under the inspection of Chancellor Livingston, and Stevens, and Roosevelt, and doubtless afforded many of the facts and suggestions through which Fulton made the art available for useful purposes.

Five men were added to each Hook and Ladder Company in November, 1796.

John Bogert, a member of Engine Company No. 14, was appointed a fire warden in December, and on the third of the following month, Abraham Coddington was appointed to take his place in the company.

On December 9, about one o'clock, a destructive fire broke out near the center of Murray's Wharf, Coffee House Slip, which, notwithstanding the exertions of all the engines, and a vast concourse of the citizens, could not be got under until it terminated at the Fly Market, and having consumed nearly fifty buildings, the property of a number of citizens, some of whom, in consequence, were reduced from affluence to indigence.

The location of engine houses in 1796 was as follows:

No. 1 Engine House, opposite Groshan's brewhouse, Barley Street.
No. 2 Engine House, near the new Methodist Church.
No. 3 Engine House, Nassau Street, opposite City Hall.
No. 4 Engine House, fronting the Playhouse, John Street.
No. 5 Engine House.
No. 6 Engine House, at the College Wall, Murray Street.
No. 7 Engine House, Cliff Street, by the Church Wall.
No. 8 Engine House, adjoining the Gaol yard.

No. 9 Engine House, Whitehall Street, near the Government House.

No. 10 Engine House, top of Catharine Street, in Chatham Street.

No. 11 Engine House, Hanover Square.

No. 12 Engine House, at the junction of Pearl and Cherry Streets.

No. 13 Engine House, near Ferry Stairs, Fish Market.

No. 14 Engine House.

No. 15 Engine House, in Nassau Street, opposite the Federal Hall.

No. 16 Engine House, in Liberty Street, near the New Dutch Church.

No. 17 Engine House, near the New Slip.

No. 18 Engine House, on the Hill, John Street near Pearl Street.

No. 19 Engine House, Hester Street, near Bowery Lane.

No. 20 Engine House, Greenwich Street, at the new Albany Pier.

No. 21 Engine House, adjoining the burial ground of the Baptist Church, Gold Street.

No. 22 Engine House, George Street.

A new engine was purchased in January, 1797, for Engine Company No. 1, and the membership raised to twenty. At the same time the petition of Peter Curtenius and others for a fire engine in Greenwich Street, between Reade and Lispenard Streets, was granted.

John Halsey represented to the Common Council in February, 1797, that he would undertake to import from Hamburg two fire engines, with long hose, to convey water from the river into the interior of the city, of superior quality, and on cheaper terms than similar machines could be manufactured in this country. The Council gave Mr. Halsey encouragement, and appointed a committee to communicate with him.

DESIGN ON OLD FIREMAN'S CERTIFICATE.

CHAPTER V.

IMPROVEMENT IN FIRE EXTINGUISHING METHODS.

1798-1811.—Act of Incorporation (1798).—Formation of Fire Insurance Companies.—Additional Fire Engines.—Description of the City about the close of the Eighteenth Century.—Rapid Extension of New York.—Great Fire of 1804.—Fire Plugs.—Another Destructive Conflagration (1811).

THE act of March 19, 1787, limited the number of firemen to three hundred, to be nominated and appointed by the Mayor and Common Council, and they were by its provisions enjoined to be ready at all times, as well by night as by day, to manage, control, and use the fire engines to be provided, and were exempt from service as constables, jurors, and militiamen, and placed generally under the regulation of the city government. In 1792 the number was increased to four hundred and fifty. On the twentieth of March, 1798, however, upon a petition of the firemen praying to be incorporated, the more effectually to enable them to provide adequate funds for the relief of disabled and injured firemen, and for the purpose of extinguishing fires, they were incorporated under the name of the Fire Department of the City of New York.

The members of the Department and their successors were accordingly rendered capable of suing and being sued "in all courts and places whatsoever, in all matters of actions, suits, complaints, causes and matters whatsoever, and that they and their successors may have a common seal, and may change and alter the same at their pleasure."

By this act, the firemen belonging to any of the engines of the city of New York were declared to be and to continue as such until the year 1818 a body politic, by the name of the "Fire Department of the City of New York." They and their successors were declared capable of purchasing, holding, and conveying any estate, real or personal, for the use of the said corporation, not to exceed the sum of twenty thousand dollars. The said representatives, on the second Monday of December in every year, elected by ballot, out of their own body, a president and vice-president, and out of the whole body of firemen, three trustees, a treasurer, secretary, and collector. The first representatives, as named by the act, were Daniel Hitchcock, Thomas Tom, Nicholas Van Antwerp, James Parsons, Jr., William Hardenbrook, Matthias Nack, Samuel Lord, Nicholas Roome, Leonard Rogers, Cornelius Brinckerhoff, Joseph Smith, Israel Haviland, John Pritchett, James Robinson, Robert McCullen, Augustus Wright, William Hunter, Elijah Pinckney, Isaac Hatfield, Garret Debow, Adam Pentz, John Perrin, Adam Hartell, Moses Smith, William Brown, John Lent, John Utt, Uzziah Coddington, Jr., Peter Embury, James Van Dyck, Thomas Timpson, Joseph Newton, William Degrove, William Baker, Thomas Demilt, William A. Hardenbrook, Isaac Tirboss, Henry Rogers, John Dominick, and Joseph Webb. Daniel Hitchcock was named as the first president; Thomas Tom, vice-president; Frederick Devoe, Jacob Sherred, James Stewart, John Striker, James Tylee, Benjamin Strong, Thomas Brown, Stephen Smith, and Christopher Halstead, trustees; Nicholas Van Antwerp, treasurer; James Parsons, Jr., secretary; and Martin Morrison, collector.

The trustees were divided into three classes; the first class to go out of office the first year; the second, the second year; and the third, the third year. These trustees managed the affairs and disposed of the funds of the corporation according to the by-laws, rules, and regulations.

The funds of the corporation were obtained from chimney fines, certificates, donations, etc.

The incorporation of the Fire Department appears to have acted as a signal for the formation of fire insurance corporations. That arm of the commerce of our great city, now grown so powerful and far-reaching, holding within its sweep untold millions of capital, was represented at this period, so far as the

DUTCH COTTAGES, BROAD AND GARDEN STREETS, 1800.

statutes of this state indicate, only by two companies, known as "The United Insurance Company" and "The Mutual Assurance Company."

The latter company was incorporated in 1798, March 23, on the mutual plan, and among its incorporators are to be found names familiar to all insurance men, many of which will be found intimately associated with the history and progress of life, as well as fire insurance in this city. They embrace such names as Thomas Pearsall, Nicholas Gouverneur, Abraham Varick, Wynant Van Zandt, Samuel Franklin, John Thompson, Robert Lenox, Gulian Verplank, Samuel Bowne, and Leonard Bleecker.

The first intimation in the municipal records of the Fire Department, of trouble arising from personal disagreements among members of a company, is given in the proceedings of the Board of Aldermen dated February 12, 1798. Therein it is set forth that the foreman and other members of Engine Company No. 7 complained against Jacob Tablie, one of their number, for rude and improper conduct, for refusing to observe the rules and regulations of the company, and disturbing the harmony thereof. The Board heard Mr. Tablie in his own defense, and concluded that the best interests of the company and the department demanded his removal, which was immediately effected, and John Drake was appointed in his stead.

A new fire engine was "imported" from Philadelphia in February, 1798, and placed in charge of Engine Company No. 15, stationed at the City Hall, and their old engine was packed off to the Seventh Ward.

Two fire engines arrived from Hamburg in the spring of 1799, and measures were taken for the erection of a house for them in the yard of the almshouse. In the month of September the following persons were appointed to take charge of those engines:

Foreman, Abel W. Hardenbrook, tinplate worker; Assistant Foreman, William Janeway, brewer; Richard L. Mott; Benjamin Carpenter, carpenter; Silvenus Pine, merchant; Samuel Hutchins, grocer; Richard Collis, paper manufacturer; Jacob Smith, turner; Enoch Buxton, shoemaker; Abraham Alstine, cabinetmaker; Jacob Shatzel, grocer; Christian Hyle, joiner; Peter Wooley, shoemaker; Harmanus Rutan, porter; John Cromwell, grocer; Levi Weeks; William Miller, carpenter; John McKay, painter; Eli Knapp, shoemaker; David Colon, chairmaker; Henry Seibe, grocer; Ezra Weeks, carpenter; Daniel Tyler, coach painter; William Post, cooper; John McComb, mason; Robert M. Thompson; George Minuse, joiner; Tunis Riker; Joseph Cook; William Hardenbrook, Jr., brassfounder.

The jail bell of the old bridewell possessed a peculiar sound, known from all others. "I remember," writes an old New Yorker, "its sounding for a break-out by the prisoners, about the year 1800. Old Peter Lorillard, the tobacconist, was shot by a prisoner whom he tried to arrest. It was some months before he recovered." The shooting caused quite a sensation at the time.

About the year 1800 New York fairly overleaped the boundaries that seemed for a while to confine it. A line of low grounds and watercourses extended quite across the island, from the great swamp on the East River, through the Fresh Water Pond and Lispenard's meadows, to the Hudson, cutting off the city from the high ground beyond. For a long time the only public highway over this low ground was the Boston road (now called the Bowery), which passed over a bridge near the head of Roosevelt Street. Recently a passage had been made on the shore of the Hudson, pretty nearly answering to the present Greenwich Street. But the growth of the city naturally caused it to expand beyond its former limits, and with the beginning of the nineteenth century the city began its progress " up-town."

About this time St. Paul's steeple was on fire, and was saved by a sailor climbing up the steeple. The great tea-water pump in Chatham Street was, when an emergency arose, utilized to extinguish the flames. Hundreds of water carts supplied housekeepers with this pure water, and as the fire occurred on a Sunday, all these water carts were employed in taking water to St. Paul's and the fire engines.

In January, 1800, the small Engine No. 21 was removed from the engine house in Gold Street, near the Baptist Meeting House, to the house in Greenwich Street, near the Industry Furnace, in the place of the old Engine No. 1, which had been removed to Engine House of No. 23, in Broadway, near the Hospital.

On the thirteenth of this month Uzziah Coddington, attached to Engine Company No. 14, was appointed a fire warden. On the twenty-seventh of the same month, Nicholas Van Antwerp, of Engine Company No. 11, was promoted to the position of an engineer.

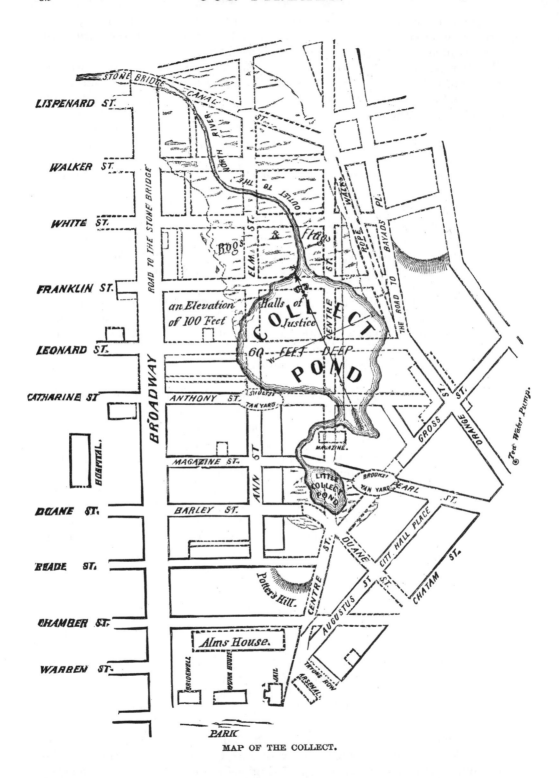

MAP OF THE COLLECT.

Thomas Howell imported two fire engines from London in December, which the Corporation purchased from him for the sum of four thousand dollars. At a conference between the engineer and a committee of the Common Council, held in the same month, the following disposition of the new engines and alteration of some of the old ones was agreed upon:

The large engine (imported) was placed in the corner of the yard of the City Hall, and an engine house built adjoining the house of Mr. Verplank. It was numbered 3, and allowed a complement of twenty-four firemen. The other lately imported engine was placed in the jail-yard in the house where No. 8 lay, receiving that number, and being allowed twenty men. Old No. 8 was removed to the Furnace at the North River, and numbered 1, and its company increased to thirteen men. Engine No. 3 was removed to the Hospital, and numbered 23, to replace the engine sent to Poughkeepsie—No. 1—then at the Hospital, being out of order and useless. Engine No. 21, then at the Furnace, was returned to its original stand in Gold Street, near the Baptist Meeting House. The company of the old Engine No. 3, consisting of ten men, was put in charge of the new engine in the yard of the City Hall, and its strength increased to twenty-four men. The company belonging to Engine No. 8, consisting of thirteen men, was placed in charge of the new engine in the jail-yard, and the force increased to twenty men.

In addition to the foregoing, the Council committee recommended that a new engine house be built at the head of the Common Sewer, at Burling Slip, near Pearl Street, for Engine No. 18, and with respect to the floating engine, that a boat be immediately procured for it, and placed in one of the most central slips on the East River, with a force of thirty able-bodied men. Protests were subsequently presented against this location for the engine house, and it was decided that a more eligible site would be at Beekman's Slip, directly in the rear of a fountain erected by the Manhattan Company for supplying shipping with water. As these changes and assignments called for the employment of an additional number of fifty-one men, which would increase the firemen to a greater number than the law allowed, it was decided to apply to the legislature to increase the number of firemen to six hundred.

The Fire Department consisted of a single engineer, who received his appointment from the Common Council, and who was invested with absolute control over the companies, engines, and all else that pertained to the organization; a number of fire wardens, commissioned by the same authority to inspect buildings, chimneys, etc., and to keep order at fires; and several voluntary companies under the direction of a foreman, assistant, and clerk of their own choosing. A few engine houses had been built; the greater part of the hooks and ladders, buckets, etc., were deposited for safe keeping in the City Hall. Several of these pioneer companies retained their organization up to the time of the disbandment of the Volunteer System.

At this time, the city, though the metropolis of the western world, was a mere village in comparison with the city of to-day. The city proper was bounded on Broadway by Anthony, on the North River by Harrison, and on the East River by Rutger Streets; and even within these limits the houses were scattering, and surrounded by large gardens and vacant lots; Broadway ended at Astor Place, where a pole fence, stretching across the road, formed the southern boundary of the Randall Farm, afterwards the endowment of the Sailors' Snug Harbor.

In November, 1802, the engine house in Hanover Square was removed to the Old Slip. On the twenty-ninth of the month the engine house of No. 4 in Nassau Street, between John and Fair Streets, was removed to the public ground near the office of the Kine-pock Institution.

According to the report of the fire wardens of the Third Ward there were, in March, 1803, one thousand three hundred and thirty-eight fire buckets, and a deficiency of six hundred and fifty-two. The inhabitants of that ward were opposed to throwing out or carrying their buckets to a fire; and so frequent had become the loss of buckets at fires, and on account of the impediments which existed in getting payment for those lost from the corporation, that many of the Third Warders were in a revolt against the system, and declared they would not lend their buckets at all. In May one thousand fire buckets were ordered by the corporation for the use of the firemen. Engine No. 23 was destroyed at a fire which occurred in this month.

FIREMEN AT WORK, 1800.
From an old Fire Certificate.

One of those terrible fires which were wont to ravage the city periodically before the introduction of fire-proof buildings and the existence of an efficient fire department, broke out on the eighteenth of December, 1804, in a grocery in Front Street, and raged with fury for several hours, burning the old Coffee House, on the corner of Pearl and Wall Streets, the scene of so many patriotic gatherings in the days of the Revolution, with many other of the old landmarks of the city. Forty stores and dwellings were destroyed by the fire, which was supposed to have been the work of an incendiary. The loss of property was estimated at two millions of dollars.

Even so early as this year the necessity of settling a regular plan of streets, for a distance of eight miles in length, and the width of the island, was anticipated by the legislature, and a plan was established by law comprehending in its features the cutting down of mountains and the filling up of valleys to a regular and uniform grade over all that extent.

In December the number of fire wardens in each ward was increased to six. Gilbert Aspinwall resigned as warden, and John Ellis was appointed in his stead.   John De Peyster and John Kane were appointed additional fire wardens in the Second Ward; Thomas Taylor, John L. Van Kleeck, and William H. Ireland in the Third Ward; and James Taller in the Fourth Ward.

In 1805 another fire ordinance was passed, which is in many respects similar to that of 1793. It is more comprehensive, however, and the fines imposed are in U. S. currency.

It provides, in addition to the other, substantially as follows: The firemen of the city to consist of one chief, and as many other " engineers, fire wardens, hook and ladder men, and other firemen," as may be appointed by the mayor, etc., as firemen, and be distinguished by the said appellations.

The chief is to have control of the firemen, subject to the Common Council, and the engineers shall take proper measures for having the several engines " placed, filled and worked," at fires. He is also to have charge of the repairs of engines, and to see that they are kept in good working order.

It changes the distinguishing badges, etc., to be worn by fire officials at fires, as follows:

In order that the members of the Common Council, Engineers and Fire Wardens, may be more readily distinguished at Fires, the Mayor, Recorder, Aldermen, and Assistants, shall each have on those occasions a white wand of at least five feet in length, with a gilded flame at the top, and each of the engineers shall have a leather cap painted white, with a gilt front thereto, and an Engine painted thereon, and have a good speaking Trumpet painted black; and each of the Fire Wardens shall wear a like cap with the City arms painted on the front and the Crown painted black, and have also a speaking Trumpet, painted white. And the names and places of abode of the members of the Common Council, Engineers and Fire Wardens, shall from time to time be fixed up in writing in the Watch Houses by the Aldermen respectively in whose Ward the Watch House shall be.   *   *   * And, moreover, it shall be the duty of every Watchman, upon the breaking out of fire at or near his Watch Station, to alarm the citizens by the crying of fire, and mentioning the street where it shall be   on his way to the nearest Watch Station, "so that the citizens and firemen generally be made acquainted where and in what Street to repair."

But if a chimney take fire after the watch is set, the watchman is enjoined to prevent the ringing of any bell, so that the firemen and citizens be not unnecessarily alarmed.

The former provision as to the placing of a lighted candle in the front window, is renewed here, and reappears in all ordinances down to the year 1860.

The hook and ladder men shall be divided into companies, which shall each choose a foreman, assistant, and clerk, out of their own number. They are required, under penalty of one dollar and fifty cents, in case of fire, to bring the necessary hooks and ladders to the scene of the fire, and to use the same, under the direction of the members of the Common Council and engineers, and after the fire is extinguished, to return them to where they are usually deposited.   The capacity of the fire buckets is increased to two-and-a-half gallons.

The firemen (other than engineers, fire wardens, and hook and ladder men), shall be divided into companies, one to be assigned to each of the fire engines belonging, or that may hereafter belong, to the city, and each company shall choose a foreman, assistant, and clerk out of their number.

It became apparent in 1805 that the means employed for the extinguishment of fire required, and were susceptible of, much improvement.   The increasing extent of the city and its population enhanced the possibilities of frequent and dangerous fires, at the same time that it supplied the means and indicated the propriety of putting the Fire Department upon a more effective and systematic footing. The utility of the floating engine had been fully established. But as it could not always be moved in due season to the place where it was wanted, it was proposed to procure another of the same kind. For a similar reason, and also because at some seasons the ice or other causes might wholly prevent the floating engines from being moved, it was recommended that two engines of like power be procured and placed on wheels, for service within the city. These latter were not intended as substitutes for the floating engines, but it was thought that four engines of the power specified were not more than could be usefully and profitably employed on many occasions. Certain of the engines then in use—Nos. 2, 5, 6, and 16—were both too small and greatly out of repair, and it was decided to sell them, and that

VIEW OF OLD DUTCH COTTAGES,

In William Street, looking from corner of Liberty Street towards Maiden Lane, 1800.

in future uniformity in size and power in engines be attended to throughout the department. The screws of the leaders were of different sizes, which led occasionally to trouble at critical moments. Uniformity in that respect, too, was to be observed regarding engines of similar power, and every common engine should have at least four leaders of forty feet each.

In May, 1805, it was decided to build a new engine house in the Seventh Ward on a site offered by Smith Place in Rivington Street, between Third and Fourth Streets, and the chief engineer was ordered to furnish one of the best of the small engines for the company to be established there. On the thirteenth of the month the engine house in the City Hall yard was extended so as to admit of the reception of the engine then stationed in Nassau Street on ground belonging to the Presbyterian Church. The chief engineer was authorized, in September, to station fire engines at Greenwich Street, and form a new company. Divie Bethune, Jeremiah F. Randolph, Hector Scott, Peter H. Wendover, and Samuel L. Page, Jr., were appointed fire wardens of the Eighth

Ward. Engine No. 13, situated at the Fly Market, was given a new location at the head of Burling Slip, in December. In the spring of the following year a new fire engine house was erected on the ground of the New Dutch Church in Liberty Street. About the same time Hugh McCormick, of No. 2 Jacob Street, was appointed a fireman of Company No. 7, instead of John Minuse resigned; Nehemiah Ludlam, Philip Ruckle, and Walter Whitehead were appointed to No. 15, instead of James Bertine, Jeremiah Woods, and Jacob Peterson, resigned; Abraham Dwyer, David Hubbs, John Gillmour, and Benjamin Haight, to Company No. 13, instead of John Heyer, Frederick Miller, Samuel Burtis, and John Cavanagh.

The streets were swept twice a week by the inhabitants, each opposite his own house; and for the collection of garbage a bell-cart came round daily in each street. The city was lit by lamps, with oil. Wood was the principal article of fuel, and hickory was deemed the best. The chimneys were swept by small negro boys, whose street cries in the morning drew forth many a denunciation from those whose slumbers were thus disturbed. With the break of day did the streets ring with their cries of "Sweep, ho! sweep, ho! from the bottom to the top, without a ladder or a rope, sweep, ho!" to a chorus or cry, in which often were added dulcet sounds of real harmony.

In 1807 there was a number of the old Dutch houses still standing, with their gable ends to the street, and the date of their erection in iron figures placed in the wall in front. Several of these stood in Broad, William, Garden, and Pearl Streets; two stood at the head of Coenties Slip, west side, near Pearl. The dates generally were from 1696, 1697, 1701, and 1702, showing that the city was pretty much confined to the near proximity of the old Dutch Church in Garden Street, built in 1693, and below Wall Street. Every one of these buildings has long since disappeared.

The city, at the time in question, contained about sixty thousand inhabitants. A large majority of the residents dwelt below Cortlandt Street and Maiden Lane. A sparse population then occupied that portion of the island which lay above the site of the New York Hospital on Broadway, and the grounds stretching northerly, now covered with magnificent buildings, were then graced with the sycamore, the elm, the oak, the chestnut, the wild cherry, the peach, the pear, and the plum tree, and further ornamented with gardens appropriated to horticultural products, with here and there the artichoke, the tulip, and the sunflower. Where now stand the Astor Library, the Mercantile Library, the Academy of Music, the Cooper Institute, and the Bible House, old Dutch gardens were abundant, cultivated with something of the artistic regularity of the Hollanders, luxuriating in the sweet marjoram, the mint, the thyme, the currant, and the gooseberry. Avenues, squares, and leading roads had not yet been laid out, and the street regulations in paving and sidewalks had reached but little above the City Hall Park, and in the Bowery only within the precincts of Bayard Street. The present City Hall was in a state of erection, and so circumscribed, at that time, was the idea of the city's progress, that the Board of Supervisors, by a slender majority, after a serious discussion, for economy's sake, decided that the postern part of the Hall should be composed of red stone, "inasmuch as it was not likely to attract much notice from the scattered inhabitants who might reside above Chambers Street."

Fire plugs were first introduced in 1807, the first plug being put down at the corner of William and Liberty Streets. The chief engineer approved of it so highly that he recommended that each block in the city be similarly supplied.

In June of this year a petition of residents in the vicinity of Corlears Hook for a fire engine was acceded to, and old No. 1, which had been superseded at the Methodist Meeting House by a larger engine, was sent there.

The full strength of the Fire Department was eight hundred and sixty-nine men, as compared with seven hundred and sixty-one in the previous year (1806). It was made up of seven engineers, forty-eight fire wardens, seven hundred and seventy-eight fire engine men, and thirty-six hook and ladder men. The number of fire engine companies was thirty-four, of which Nos. 28 and 33 were the smallest, having only ten men each, and Nos. 25, 3, and 8 were the largest, having forty, thirty-two, and thirty men respectively. The floating engine was in charge of forty men. There were only two hook and ladder companies. In November the strength of Engine Company No. 25 was raised to fifty. Two years after, in December, the full strength of the department was nine hundred and fifty-five men, of whom seven were engineers, fifty-five fire wardens, eight hundred and forty-seven fire engine men, and forty-six hook and ladder men—an increase of twenty-eight men over the previous year (1808).

An ordinance, passed January 11, 1808, provides that the Fire Department shall consist of " a chief engineer, and as many other engineers, fire wardens, fire engine men, hose men, and ladder men," as may be appointed by the Common Council. It gives absolute control in case of fire to the chief engineer over men and machines. The chief engineer must make examination of all apparatus, etc., at least once in six months, and report the same, with list of force, to the Common Council, to be published. He had charge of repairs, and was required when a fire was over to send all private fire buckets found in the vicinity to the City Hall for identification. The provisions are substantially as in the 1805 ordinance, with the exception of some additions and alterations which it is not necessary to notice.

The following appointments were made in March, 1809: William W. Gallatian, upholsterer, 28 Beaver Street, to Engine Company No. 3, vice Jacob P. Roome, resigned; James Segoine, shoemaker, 53 Water Street, to Engine Company No. 11, instead of Daniel Updike, resigned; Andrew M. Arcularius, grocer, 151 Fly Market, to Engine Company No. 24, vice Alexander Nicoll, resigned; and Lewis Thomas, wheelwright, Greenwich Street, to Engine Company No. 27, in place of Abraham Powles resigned.

A hook and ladder company, consisting of ten men, was established in the village of Greenwich in the summer of 1809. The members of the company were: Henry Blacklidge, James Reeves, Andrew Hegerman, John Jennings, William Lezong, William Welling, John H. Blanck, William P. Gilbert, Thomas Sherwood, and John Brown. This was the origin of Hook and Ladder Company No. 3. Messrs. Sherwood and Hegerman remained only about one month with the company, and were replaced by Isaac De Boise and Andrew Blakeley.

The expenses incurred by the city for supplies to the Fire Department for the eight years ending 1809 amounted to forty-three thousand eight hundred and eighty-eight dollars, and it was suggested that, inasmuch as the fire insurance companies were greatly benefitted by the existing organization of the Fire Department, they should be called upon to defray some proportion of the expense.

The engine house standing on the burial ground of the congregation of the First Presbyterian Church, was donated to the church society by the city in May, 1809.

An attempt was made on the evening of the thirtieth of November, 1809, to set fire to the range of wooden buildings in Front Street, between Crane Wharf and Beekman Slip, by placing a coal of fire in some damp powder, and laying the same in a pile of staves at the rear of the store, No. 203 Front Street. The mayor, DeWitt Clinton, issued a proclamation, offering three hundred dollars reward for information which would lead to the discovery of the incendiaries.

Among the appointments made in March, 1810, we find Philip W. Engs, accountant, 222 William Street, in place of John McGregor, resigned, to Engine Company No. 21; and John Vreeland, merchant, Broadway, vice Andrew Maverick, resigned, to Engine Company No. 16.

The population of the city in 1810 was over ninety-six thousand; having added thirty-six thousand in ten years, and increased nearly threefold in twenty years. The city had extended with unprecedented rapidity, and, at the time mentioned, it covered more than four times the area that it embraced twenty years before. Broadway had been opened through to the Bowery, and on either side streets had been laid out as far up as Amity and Great Jones Streets. To the east of the Bowery, the streets running eastward were laid out as high up as North (Houston) Street, which had been fixed as the permanent boundary of the city; and crossing these, the present streets were laid out as far east as Norfolk Street.

The city was again devastated by a terrible conflagration (May 19, 1811), which broke out about nine o'clock on Sunday morning, near the northwest corner of Duane and Chatham Streets. The steeple of the Brick Church, and the cupola of the jail caught fire.

DRAWING ON FIREMAN'S CERTIFICATE.

CHAPTER VI.

ADOPTION OF A PLAN FOR THE FUTURE CITY.

1811-1822.—Two Sailors and a Prisoner Distinguish Themselves.—Laying of the Corner-stone of the City Hall.—Extension of Fire Limits.—Enactment of Laws for the More Effectual Prevention of Fires.— Duties of Firemen.—The Use of Fire Buckets Superseded by Hose.

ONE of the most important events of this period (1811) was the adoption of a plan for the future city, to which we owe the parallel streets and broad avenues of the upper part of the island, which contrast so strongly with the narrow streets and crooked lanes of the down-town locality. This plan was due to Simeon Dewitt, Gouverneur Morris, John Rutherford, and S. Guel, who had been appointed by the legislature in 1801, as commissioners to lay out and survey the whole island to Kingsbridge into streets and avenues. By the proposed plan, the streets beginning with the first on the east side of the Bowery above Houston Street, numbered upward to the extreme end of the island. These were intersected by twelve avenues, numbering westward from First Avenue—the continuation of Allen Street—to Twelfth Avenue upon the shores of the North River. As avenues were afterwards laid out to the east-ward of the former, they were designated by the names of the letters of the alphabet A, B, C, and D. By this plan, the island was laid out with admirable regularity, while the squares and triangles which were formed by the junction of those time-honored thoroughfares which could not be removed, were con-verted into public parks for the adornment of the city. The despised Potter's Field became the beautiful Washington Square; the Bowery and Broadway met amicably in Union Square; Madison Square was formed from the union of the Old and the Middle Roads; the great salt meadow on the eastern side of the city was drained, and Tompkins Square, with hundreds of city lots, sprung up from its depths; valleys were filled up, hills were leveled, and art seemed destined to surmount the difficulties of nature, and to make every inch of New York island habitable ground.

On the nineteenth of May, of this year, the Brick Presbyterian Church took fire, and two seamen distinguished themselves in an especial manner, and at the imminent hazard of their lives, by ascending the steeple of the church which was on fire, and, by their exertions, arresting the progress of the flames until the leader of one of the engines could be brought to play upon it. The cupola of the jail became ignited from flying embers, and a debtor imprisoned therein proved so exceedingly active in helping to extinguish the flames that the Common Council directed their clerk to procure the issuance of a warrant in his favor for sixty dollars, thus restoring him to liberty and fame.

The corner stone of the City Hall was laid September 26, 1803. It was completed in 1812 at an expense of five hundred and thirty-eight thousand seven hundred and thirty-four dollars.

Fire bugs again made their appearance in January, 1811, when they burnt down the ropewalk of Peter Schermerhorn, on Orchard Street, and the mayor offered one thousand dollars reward for their apprehension.

The principal difficulty in extinguishing fires was to procure a sufficient supply of water. In the central part of the city the pumps and cisterns, which were principally relied on, became soon exhausted, and before a line composed of engines and leaders could be formed to the rivers, the fires too often had gained considerable headway. To remedy this defect, it was suggested in June, 1811, that two reservoirs of stone, sufficient to contain two hundred hogshead of water each, be built and located at or near each wing of the City Hall, to be supplied from the roof thereof, and the water to be used for no other purpose than the extinguishment of fires. It was recommended also that the different religious societies in the city be requested to cause to be built a reservoir adjacent to their respective places of worship, to be supplied with water from such places of worship, the water to be used only at fires.

Thomas Brown, chief engineer, resigned his office on November 11, on account of ill health. On the eighteenth of the month the foremen of thirty-six fire engines petitioned the Common Council to appoint Thomas Franklin as chief engineer, and the

OLD FIRE HAT.

prayer of the petitioners was granted. Among the appointments made on the twenty-seventh of this month were: Peter Simons, silversmith, 275 Pearl Street, to Hook and Ladder No. 3, vice Simeon Fawcett, resigned; Mordecai Homan, merchant, 97 Fair Street, to Engine Company No. 3, vice Charles I. Field; William Pulis, butcher, Mott Street, to Engine Company No. 15, vice Walter Whitehead. A patent for a newly-invented fire engine, more powerful in its operations and less expensive in its construction than the existing engines, was granted to Richard Crosby by the United States in the latter part of this year; and the Common Council authorized him, in January, 1812, to construct such an engine for the use of the city.

The frequent fires occurring in the fall of 1811 from no cause that could be reasonably ascribed, left no room to doubt that incendiaries were at their villainous work, and the mayor of the city again offered a reward of three hundred dollars for the apprehension and conviction of the offenders.

The fire wardens in December communicated to the Common Council that as the use of hose had in a great measure superseded the use of fire buckets, the ordinance requiring owners and occupants of houses to furnish buckets, should, in their opinion, be repealed, and also an application should be made to the legislature for an extension of the limits within which wooden buildings should not be erected.

In the following month the Council committee reported upon that communication that, notwithstanding the advantages arising from the use of leaders, cases might arise in the interior of the city when, by a speedy collection of buckets, the fire might be extinguished ere the line by engines and leaders could be formed, and consequently it would be imprudent to discontinue the ordinance as requested. The number of buckets required to be kept, might, however, be reduced by one-third, to lighten the burden on the citizens.

The condition of affairs in the city during the summer of 1812, whilst the national government was prosecuting the war against Great Britain, had become most critical. There were fears of commotions and riots fomented by evil disposed people, which, if allowed to pass unnoticed, might lead to serious and alarming consequences. At this juncture (July, 1812), the members of Engine Companies Nos. 39, 36, and 8, volunteered their services to the chief magistrate, to assist in quelling any riot or disturbance that might arise, reserving to themselves, however, the privilege of being commanded by their own officers, without the interference of any military officer whatever.

An act for the more effectual prevention of fires was passed April 9, 1813. This act made it obligatory that dwelling houses, storehouses, and other buildings, thereafter to be erected within the following boundaries, should be made and constructed of stone or brick, with party or fire walls, rising at least six inches above the roof, " and shall be covered, except the flat roof thereof, with tile or slate, or other safe materials, against fire, and not with board or shingles," within that part of the city to the northward of the point of the Battery, and a line beginning upon the East River, opposite Montgomery Street, thence through Montgomery Street to Cherry Street, thence down Cherry Steeet to Roosevelt, through Roosevelt to Chatham, down Chatham to Chambers Street, through Chambers Street to Broadway, up Broadway to Canal Street, thence, commencing again at Chambers Street and running to Hudson's river, including also the lots of ground on the northerly and easterly sides of the said streets through which the above-mentioned line runs, and including, also, the lots of ground fronting on both sides of Broadway, between Chambers and Canal Streets.

The above designated portion of the city also constituted " the Watch and Lamp District."

Section 66 declared it to be unlawful to store gunpowder, " except in the public magazine at the Fresh Water," and then only in certain designated quantities. Other sections prohibited the storage of sulphur, hemp, and flax, except in certain specified quantities, " in any one place in the city of New York, to the southward of the Fresh Water, nor to the southward of Rutgers Slip, under the penalty of twenty-five dollars. Pitch, tar, turpentine, rosin, spirits of turpentine, linseed oil, or shingles, were similarly quarantined.

, The mayor, aldermen, and commonalty, were re-invested with the power " to appoint (as often as it shall be necessary) a sufficient number of strong, able, discreet, honest and sober men,   *   *   *   being freeholders of the city, to have the care, management, working, and using of the fire engines, and the other tools and instruments   *   *   *   for extinguishing of fires within the said city," which persons are to be called the firemen of the city of New York. During their continuance in that office, and no longer, they shall be exempted from serving in the office of constable, and from being impaneled or returned upon any juries or inquests, and of and from militia duty, "except in cases of invasion or other imminent danger."

Upon the breaking out of any fire within the city, the law required the sheriffs, deputy sheriffs, constables, and marshals, upon notice thereof, to repair immediately to the scene of the fire, with their rods, staves, and other badges of authority, and aid and assist in the extinguishing of the said fire, and cause the firemen in attendance to work; to prevent any goods or household furniture from being stolen; to seize all persons found stealing or pilfering; and to give their utmost assistance in removing and securing goods and furniture. They were subordinate to the mayor, recorder and aldermen, or any of them.

In case of fire, the mayor, or, in his absence, the recorder, with the consent and concurrence of any two of the aldermen, might order buildings to be pulled down.

CANAL STREET IN 1812.

The Common Council was authorized to pass ordinances for the extinguishment and prevention of fires; and also to regulate the keeping, carting, conveying, or transporting of gunpowder, or any other combustible or other dangerous material, within the bounds of the city; also to regulate the use of lights and candles in livery and other stables; to remove or prevent the construction of any fireplace, hearth, chimney, stove, oven, boiler, kettle, or apparatus, used in any manufactory or business, which might be dangerous in causing or promoting fires.

Jameson Cox, baker, 15 Charlotte Street, was appointed a member of Fire Engine Company No. 21, on June 7, 1813, in place of Joseph Vail, who had enlisted in the regular army. Cornelius W. Lawrence, merchant, of No. 174 Water Street, who, in after years, become mayor of the city, joined Engine Company No. 18 on July 12 following.

From the proceedings of the Common Council (November 29, 1813), it appears that the chief engineer (Thomas Franklin) proposed an amendment to the law, establishing a uniformity in the caps of firemen, which was agreed to, and the law directed to be amended accordingly.

On the tenth of January, 1814, the chief engineer reported that during the preceding year the sum of one thousand and ninety-two dollars and twenty cents had been received and collected from fines, which were applied to the relief of disabled firemen and their families, and for educating about seventy of their children. On the above date it was resolved that the staves of office to be carried at fires by members of the Common Council be similarly constructed with those lately made, (viz., with a gilded flame at the top), "and that the justices of the police and the superintendent of repairs be furnished with staves, to be used on like occasions."

The estimated value of the property belonging to the Fire Department at the close of 1814 was as follows:

15 brick buildings	$5,250.00
32 wood buildings	4,800.00
2 lots of ground	1,600.00
41 engines	26,200.00
Floating engine and boat	1,400.00
4 old engines not in use	750.00
13,085 feet leather hose	8,548.00
1,000 fire buckets	1,500.00
4 trucks, 15 ladders, and 20 fire hooks, etc.	1,200.00
Signal lanterns, torches, axes, etc.	150.00
Drag ropes	70.00
Stoves and pipes	150.00
Hose wagon	175.00
1 copper pump	30.00
20 loads nut wood	90.00
Total	$51,913.00

The extension of the city and the opening of new streets, though greatly checked, was not wholly suspended by the prostration of business consequent upon the unsettled condition of public affairs.

Immediately after the plan of the upper part of the city was definitely arranged, the Third Avenue was ordered to be opened and regulated from Stuyvesant Street to Harlem River, and a few years later a part of First Avenue was also brought into use. Several of the old streets in the lower part of the city were widened, straightened, and extended.

Soon after the return of peace (war of 1812), Broadway, above Canal Street, and Spring and Broome Streets, began to be occupied with buildings, and that portion of the city advanced rapidly in improvements and population.

But the greatest public work of this kind undertaken during this period was the opening of Canal Street. An immense canal was opened from the Collect to the Hudson River, by which a vast extent of low grounds was drained, and the pond itself almost annihilated. Over this canal was thrown an arch of substantial mason work, upon which was built one of the most spacious and elegant thoroughfares in the city, the whole of which cost about one hundred and fifty thousand dollars.

The firemen having determined to apply to the legislature to enact a law granting them certain privileges, and the renewal of their charter, deemed it expedient to place in the hands of the representatives the following calculations, showing the principles on which their petition was founded:

From this record it appears that there were in

1795,	5 fires and	9 alarms.			1805,	13 fires and	6 alarms.		
1796,	6 "	6 "			1806,	23 "	6 "		
1797,	10 "	9 "	Averaging		1807,	21 "	10 "	Averaging	
1798,	6 "	5 "	13⅗ per annum.		1808,	23 "	14 "	31⅖ per annum.	
1799,	6 "	6 "			1809,	16 "	25 "		
1800,	9 "	9 "			1810,	25 "	19 "		
1801,	11 "	6 "			1811,	26 "	27 "		
1802,	10 "	7 "	Averaging		1812,	20 "	23 "	Averaging	
1803,	9 "	8 "	19⅗ per annum.		1813,	37 "	39 "	55⅘ per annum.	
1804,	16 "	13 "			1814,	29 "	32 "		

By this it appears that their duty had increased in a four-fold proportion in the space of twenty years. From actual calculation on the average of the preceding five years, there was an increase of two hundred and seventy-five hours actual duty per annum, or two hundred and seventy-five days in ten years, allowing ten hours for a day.

The amount of the Fire Department Fund, December 1, 1814, was ten thousand six hundred and twenty-two dollars and thirty-eight cents; the amount of moneys paid the previous year for the relief of indigent firemen, their widows, and the schooling of their children, was one thousand five hundred and eighty-six dollars and twenty-five cents.

SCENE AT A FIRE.
From a Fireman's Certificate.

The recommendation of the Common Council to the several religious congregations of the city to build cisterns at their respective churches, heretofore recorded, was entirely ignored, although it was a measure that would redound to the safety of the churches as well as of the adjacent property. The corporation had within the years from 1810 to 1814 displayed great interest in the organization and system of the Fire Department, procuring the best attainable apparatus; but its efforts were still handicapped by the lack of a sufficient supply of water. It was, therefore, decided in February, 1814, to apply to the legislature for an act empowering the corporation to build cisterns when and where it seemed advantageous to do so.

During this year five engines of six and one-half inch caliber and the necessary appurtenances, also a new truck for the Hook and Ladder Company at Greenwich, were purchased. The old Engines Nos. 20 and 23 were sold, the former for four hundred dollars cash, and the latter to the Pleasant Valley Manufacturing Company for six hundred dollars at six months.

On April 11, 1815, there was passed "An act for the more effectual prevention of fires in the city of New York." This extended the fire limits from "a line, beginning at the North River, at a place called Dekleyne's Ferry, a little to the northward of the state prison to the road commonly called the Sandy Hill Road, to the northward of the Potter's Field and the house of William Neilson, to the Bowery, to a street commonly called Stuyvesant Street, to the East River."

The Common Council adopted a resolution (March 25, 1816), on the petition of a number of carpenters and others, suspending the duties of the fire wardens under the ordinance prohibiting the storing and seasoning of lumber on premises within the fire limits, the enforcement of which, it was alleged, would inure to the loss and inconvenience of those tradesmen. But a fire occurred in November in Water Street, which was much intensified and caused much damage by reason of the burning of a quantity of lumber, stored in the immediate vicinity, which caught fire. The Common Council soon after repealed the resolution of the twenty-fifth of March.

OLD FIRE CERTIFICATE.

The Fire Department (Act, April 12, 1816,) was continued as a body corporate and politic, in fact and in name, until the first day of May, 1838, "with all the rights, powers, and privileges, and subject to all the provisions, restrictions, limitations, and conditions mentioned and contained in the act entitled 'An act to incorporate the Firemen of the city of New York.'"

The fire engine companies kept importuning the corporation for an increase in their membership, and it was, in consequence, found necessary in August, 1816, to make a regulation that all companies having engines of six and one-half inch caliber should have twenty-six men, and those that had a greater number be reduced to conform thereto, except the companies in the out wards, as to the strength of which the chief engineer should determine. Among the appointments made in this month are these:

Alexander Wiley, Jr., 98 Greenwich Street, to Hook and Ladder No. 1, vice William Sterling, resigned; John R. Lecount, grocer, to Hook and Ladder No. 2, in place of Samuel Weeks; Rowland Gardner, hatter, 38 Chatham Street, to Fire Engine Company No. 5, vice John Matthews; John Van Houten, carpenter, to Fire Engine No. 29, vice Joseph Simmons, resigned. In September, Ephraim Badeau, hatter, 6 Bowery Lane, and Benjamin Scribner, accountant,

Catharine Street, to Hook and Ladder Company No. 2; John Hitchcock, merchant, Peck Slip, to Engine Company No. 7; and Richard Townley, merchant, to the same company.

At a fire in John and Water Streets in December, Isaac Skaats, George Herrick, and John Talman had their limbs broken, incapacitating them from further duty. In April, 1817, the Common Council ordered that the sum of three hundred dollars be distributed among them.

These fires and a fire in Mott Street at about the same time, were of incendiary origin, and Jacob Hays, one of the city marshals, was mainly instrumental in bringing the miscreants to justice, for which service he was awarded a sum of three hundred dollars.

The number of engineers was increased, on December 23, 1816, from eight to ten.

The first hydrant ever used in New York was located in front of the dwelling house of Mr. George B. Smith, of Engine Company No. 12, in Frankfort Street, in the year 1817. This was the origin of the hydrant system in this city.

Any fireman, while in the performance of his duty as such, who should so maim or injure himself as to render him thereafter unable to perform the duties of a fireman, or who should have so maimed himself since the fifth of the preceding May (Act, February 28, 1817), was entitled to the benefit of the law passed the twelfth of April, 1816, fixing the time of service of firemen at ten years.

The leading features of the ordinance, passed May 5, 1817, are as follows:

The Fire Department to consist of a chief engineer, who shall have an annual salary of eight hundred dollars, payable quarterly, and as many other engineers, fire enginemen, hosemen, and hook and ladder men, as may from time to time be appointed by the Common Council. The chief engineer had the sole and absolute control and command over all the engineers and other persons of the Fire Department. It was his duty to examine—twice in every year—into the condition and number of the fire engines, fire buckets, and other fire apparatus, and fire engine houses belonging to the corporation, and report the same—once a year—to the Common Council, together with the names of all the members of the Fire Department, and the respective associations to which they belong; to cause all the private fire buckets which may remain after any fire is extinguished, to be collected and conveyed as soon as possible to the City Hall, to be there deposited, in order that the citizens may know where to find them; to report in writing all accidents by fire that may happen in the city, with the causes thereof, as well as can be ascertained, and the number and description of the buildings destroyed or injured, together with the names of the owners and occupants, to the city inspector, who shall keep a faithful register of the same. As many of the freeholders, or firemen, of the city, as the Common Council may deem proper, shall, from time to time, be appointed in each of the wards, to be denominated fire wardens; each of whom to be assigned and attached by the mayor to such company of firemen, having charge of a fire engine, as he shall think proper, and shall report himself to the chief, or other engineer, at every fire. The fire wardens of each ward to form a separate company, and each company to choose out of their own number a foreman and clerk, to make rules, regulating the time and manner of conducting their elections, etc. It was the duty of the said fire wardens, immediately on the alarm of fire, to repair to the place where it may be, and aid and assist in procuring supplies of water to the fire engines to which they are respectively assigned; and to such other fire engines as the chief engineer or other engineer may direct them to attend; to prevent the hose from being trodden on; and to keep all idle and suspected persons at a proper distance from the fire, and from the vicinity. Other duties were also imposed on the fire wardens, namely: twice a year, in the months of June and December, and as much oftener as they should think proper, to examine the dwelling houses and other buildings in their respective wards, to see that they are properly furnished with fire buckets; to examine the fireplaces, hearths, chimneys, stoves, and pipes thereto, ovens, boilers, kettles, or apparatus which, in their opinion, may be dangerous in causing or promoting fires, and the places where ashes may be deposited; * * * to enter into and examine all buildings, livery and other stables, hay boats or vessels, and places where any gunpowder, hemp, flax, tow, hay, rushes, fire wood, boards, shingles, shavings, or other combustible materials, may be lodged; * * * to make report whether any, and what cases of violations of the laws of this state, prohibiting the construction of wooden buildings within certain limits, etc.

The duties of firemen are thus defined:

As often as any fire shall break out in the said city, to repair immediately upon the alarm thereof, to their respective engines, hose wagons, hooks and ladders, and convey them to or near the place where such fire shall happen, and there, in conformity with the directions given by the chief engineer or other engineers, shall work and manage said engines, or apparatus and implements, with all their skill and power; and when the fire is extinguished, shall not remove therefrom but by the direction of an engineer; when they shall return their respective hose wagons, hooks and ladders, engines and apparatus, well washed and cleaned, to their several places of deposit." * * * The penalty for neglect of duty was as follows: for neglect to wash and clean the fire engines at stipulated times, for every default, one dollar; for neglect to attend at any fire, or leave his fire engine or other apparatus while at any fire, without permission, or shall neglect to perform his duty on such occasion, without reasonable excuse, for every default, three dollars; "and if any fireman shall neglect to do his duty as such, in attending at fires, or in working, exercising, managing, trying, or using the said fire engine, or other implements, or apparatus for extinguishing fires, every such person shall, besides the fines and penalties aforesaid, be removed and displaced from his station.

The ordinance further recites:

In order that the members of the Common Council, engineers, and fire wardens may be readily distinguished at fires, the mayor, recorder, aldermen, and assistants, shall severally bear, on those occasions, a wand with a gilded flame on the top; and each of the engineers shall wear a leathern cap, painted white, with a gilded front thereto, and a fire engine emblazoned thereon, and shall also carry a speaking trumpet, painted black, with the words 'Chief Engineer,' 'Engineer No. 1,' etc., as the case may be, in white, which shall also be painted on their caps respectively; and each of the fire wardens shall wear a hat, the brim black, the crown painted white, with the city arms blazoned on the front, and shall also carry a speaking trumpet, painted white, with the word 'Warden,' in black painted thereon.

The firemen, when on duty, shall wear leathern caps, in the form heretofore used; and the said caps (except those worn by the Floating Engine Fire Company) shall be painted and distinguished in the manner following, viz.: the foremen of each of the fire engine companies (except the Floating Engine Company) shall wear a cap, painted black, with a white frontis-piece, and the word 'Foreman,' with the initials of his name and the number of his engine painted thereon in black; and the firemen of the said fire engine companies (except as above excepted) shall wear a cap, painted black, with the initials of their names and the number of the engines to which they belong painted in the front thereof, in white. The foreman of each of the hook and ladder companies shall wear a cap, painted black, with a white frontispiece, and the word 'Foreman,' and the initials of his name, and the number of the company to which he belongs, and a hook and ladder painted thereon, in black; and the members of the said hook and ladder companies shall wear a cap, painted black, with the initials of their names, and number of the company to which they belong, with a hook and ladder painted in the front thereof in white. And the foreman of each of the fire hose companies shall wear a cap, painted black, with a white frontispiece, and the word 'Foreman,' and the initials of his name and the number of the company to which he belongs, and a coil of hose painted thereon, in black; and the members of the said fire hose companies shall wear caps, painted black, with the initials of their names and the number of the company to which they belong, with a coil of hose painted thereon, in white. And the assistants to each respective company shall wear caps, painted in the same manner as that of the foreman of the company, with the word 'Assistant' in lieu of the word 'Foreman.'

The ordinance also provided that the names and places of abode of the members of the

Common Council, engineers, fire wardens, and foremen of their respective companies, and bell ringers, annually, in the month of December, should be printed and set up in the several watch houses in the city, by the city inspector; and whenever fire should happen in the night, the watchmen should give notice to each of the members of the Common Council, engineers, fire wardens, foremen, and bell ringers within their respective watch districts. Moreover, it was the duty of every watchman "upon the breaking out of any fire to alarm the citizens by crying 'Fire,' and mentioning the street where it may be, so that the firemen and citizens may thereby be generally directed where to repair. In case, however, that a chimney only should be on fire—either by day or night—the fire bell at the City Hall, and the bells of the several churches shall not be rung; but only on occasions where a building shall be proclaimed to be on fire. And it is enjoined on the occupants to place a lighted candle at the windows of their respective buildings, when fire may happen at night, in order that citizens may pass along the streets with the greater safety.

Constables and marshals were also, on an alarm of fire, to repair to the place of such fire, with their staves of office, and to attend and obey such orders as might be given them by the mayor, recorder, or any of the aldermen or assistant aldermen.

Owners or occupants of every dwelling house, having less than three fire places shall provide one leathern bucket; and having three fireplaces and less than six, two leathern buckets, and having six fireplaces and less than nine, four leathern buckets; and having nine fireplaces and upwards, six leathern buckets, to be marked with at least the initial letters of the owner's name with the number of the house to which it belongs, and the name of the street in which such house is situate. Every brewhouse, distillery, sugarhouse, soap and candle manufactory and ship chandlery store, to provide nine leathern buckets, every bakehouse and air furnace to provide six, over and above the buckets provided for their respective dwelling houses. Each of these buckets to contain two gallons and a half of water, and to be suspended in some convenient place, ready to be delivered and used for extinguishing fires, when any should occur. Such buckets, moreover, to be furnished and provided at the expense of the inhabitant or occupant of said premises.

And if such inhabitant or occupant be a tenant, the price of such leathern bucket shall be allowed and deducted out of the rent, unless there be a special agreement between the parties to the contrary." "It shall nevertheless be optional," the ordinance declares furthermore, "with any owner of a dwelling house, as aforesaid, to surrender and deliver over to the mayor, aldermen and commonalty such number of leathern buckets not exceeding one-half of the whole number such dwelling house is required to have; which buckets, when surrendered and delivered over to whomsoever the Common Council shall direct, shall become public buckets; and shall be deposited in such suitable place or places, in each ward, as they shall direct, and for which the owner of every such dwelling house, thereafter, from so many leathern buckets as shall be so surrendered and delivered over, and the same shall also be registered in a book, to be kept for the purpose, by the city inspector.

With some of the church congregations it was made the express duty for the sextons to ring the bells at an alarm of fire, and with others it was an implied duty. At the fire on December 19, 1818, only a few of the bells were rung, and in consequence a large proportion of the firemen were not alarmed.

This fact was taken cognizance of by the Common Council, who convened a meeting of church officers, whereat it was arranged that no such neglect of duty should occur thereafter, and, to facilitate matters, it was made the duty of the watchmen at the cry of fire immediately to alarm the sextons.

The propriety of taxing the fire insurance companies of the city for the whole or a proportion of the expense annually incurred for the Department was discussed in the Common Council in December, 1818, and the Committee on Applications to the Legislature were directed to inquire into its expediency.

On the twenty-seventh of December, 1819, the Committee on the Fire Department reported that the fire buckets were rapidly being superseded by the use of hose, and, on their recommendation, the use of fire buckets at fires was dispensed with.

Very soon every new engine was furnished with suctions, and the old machines were altered so as to use them. There was also an active and increasing demand for an additional supply of hose and hose carriages. The latter, at this time, consisted of a reel placed on the axle of two cartwheels, and was the invention of foreman David J. Hubbs. It was either attached to the engine by tail hooks, or drawn by two members of the company. "Hubbs' Baby," as the simple contrivance was called, was the origin of the hose companies.

THE FIRST HOUSE LIGHTED WITH GAS,
No. 7 Cherry Street, residence of Samuel Leggett, First President of the New York Gas Company.

According to the Comptroller's report for the year 1819 the amount expended for building engine houses in Fayette and Rose Streets, and at Greenwich, for ground and buildings, and building a house on Beaver Street, was twenty-one thousand and ninety-six dollars, and on account of engines to A. W. Hardenbrook, five thousand and ninety-six dollars and seventeen cents.

The floating engine had practically been in disuse during the year 1818, lying aground most of the time in her slip at the foot of Roosevelt Street. In the summer of 1819 it was taken to the Corporation Yard on Leonard Street, and there set up as a supply engine for extinguishing fires in that part of the city. A company was formed to manage it, called Supply Engine Company No. 1, and consisting of Jacob P. Roome, foreman; Jacob Smith, Jr., assistant; William Roome, Isaac Skaats, William M. Wilson, and John Bowman. This company was stationed over a large well of water in the Public Yard, from which she was never moved, and, consequently, never used only when the fire happened in the immediate neighborhood. The duties of the company, therefore, were much less arduous than those of other firemen, except the fire wardens. The Common Council, in view of these facts, decided in January,

1829, that no person should be eligible for membership in that company who had not borne the burden of the day by doing more active duty a few years previous, and, accordingly, fixed the necessary qualification for membership therein at a five years' service in the Department. But this action was repealed in February, 1830, for various reasons, among which were, that the term of service of firemen had been reduced from ten to seven years, and that during the existence of the restriction there had not been a single application for membership.

In conformity with an act passed in April, 1820, the fire wardens of the city were clothed with authority, in June of that year, to discharge the duties of health wardens, and were placed under the control of the Board of Health.

The value of the estate vested in the Fire Department as public property in 1820 was seventy-two thousand seven hundred and eighty-nine dollars.

The Common Council, on December 26, 1820, reduced the salary of the chief engineer, which had been eight hundred dollars, to five hundred dollars per annum. This ordinance also adopted the main features of the ordinance of May 5, 1817, and ordained that "no person shall be elected a fireman until he shall have attained the age of twenty-one years.'

On the tenth of June, 1822, the Common Council ordained that whenever the office of any of the engineers of the Fire Department shall become vacant, it shall be the duty of the engineers of that Department to nominate five persons from among the foremen as suitable persons to supply such vacancy, and to give notice thereof to the foremen of the fire companies, and to require them to meet at such time and place as the said engineers shall appoint; and that the said engineers and firemen shall then and there, or at such other time and place as they may appoint by joint ballot, designate from the persons so nominated the person whom they may wish to fill such vacancy; and that no person shall be considered as so designated who shall not receive a majority of all the votes which shall be given.

FROM AN OLD PITCHER,
Presented to Chief Gulick.

CHAPTER VII.

GROWTH OF THE CITY AND THE DEPARTMENT.

**1822-1835.—An Epoch in the City of New York.—The Yellow Fever Epidemic.—Enactment of New Build-
ing Laws.—The City Increasing with Unprecedented Rapidity.—The Services of Volunteers Dispensed With.—Location of Engine Houses.—Praise for the Fire Department.—Public Cisterns.—
Insufficient Supply of Water.—Formation of a Hydrant Company.**

THE year 1822 forms an epoch in the municipal history of New York. The
yellow fever, which had so often spread suffering and death among the
inhabitants, made its last eccentric visit to our city in the autumn of
that year. The people of the lower wards fled at its approach; the banker
closed his doors, the merchant packed his goods, and churches no longer
echoed the words of Divine truth. Hundreds of citizens fled the city altogether.
But a few days elapsed from the first alarm, and business had found a refuge
and a resting place. What was then the village of Greenwich, and is now the
Ninth Ward of the city, suddenly became the center of trade and commerce.
At a little distance from the spot where the larger merchants had made
their temporary homes, ran a secluded country lane called Southampton Road.
Trees that were ancient even in the time of the Revolution spread a grateful
shade in the sultry days of summer. A convenient nook by the side of this
quiet lane was chosen by a considerable number of Scotch weavers who had fled
from the pestilence. This new home they called Paisley Place. Seventeenth
Street, from Sixth to Seventh Avenue, is now the site of the spot where the
Scotch weavers once·hummed their native airs and sent the shuttle flying. It
formed part of the great Warren estate. Admiral Warren, who died in
Ireland in 1752, was an adopted citizen of New York, and had exercised considerable influence in the affairs of the colonial government. He had been
knighted for his services in the royal navy while in command of a fleet on this
station. The admiral married a daughter of Stephen De Lancey, an eminent
New York city merchant. In the square now formed by Bleecker, Fourth,
Perry, and Charles Streets, stood the Warren mansion, and through its
illuminated courts flashed far and wide the splendors of its gayety and fashion,
renowned in the city, and on the trim lawns and terraces around the building
often trod the feet of beauty. For forty years previous to 1867 the homestead
was owned by Abraham Van Nest, a prominent merchant. A considerable
portion of the Warren estate, including the little Paisley nook, passed into the
possession of the Astor family.

The strength of the Department in June, 1822, was one thousand two hundred and sixty-nine men, including engineers and fire wardens; forty-six engines,
including two at the new almshouse; four hook and ladder trucks; one hose
wagon, with ten thousand two hundred and forty-five feet of hose in good order

(including six hundred feet at the new almshouse); one thousand two hundred and ten feet of hose ordinary; and eight hundred and eighty feet bad; two hundred and sixty-eight fire buckets, seventeen ladders, twenty-three hooks,

FIRE DEPARTMENT,
CITY OF NEW-YORK.

It is hereby **Certified**, That

Samuel S. Smith

has been a **FIREMAN** of the City of New-York, **Ten Years**, and is therefore, pursuant to the Act of the Legislature of the State of New-York, entitled "An Act granting privileges to the Firemen of the City of New-York; passed the 12th day of April, 1816; exempted from serving as a Juror in any of the Courts of this State, and from all Militia Duty, except in cases where the Militia are ordered into actual Service.

In Witness Whereof, We the Clerk of the Common Council of the said City, and the Chief Engineer, have, pursuant to the said Act, subscribed these presents, this *Tenth* day of *August* 1826

J. Morton   Clerk C. C.

Jameson Cox   **Chief Engineer.**

FAC-SIMILE OF FIREMAN'S CERTIFICATE, 1826.

one machine for throwing down chimneys, and one copper pump. In February, 1821, old Engine No. 3 was sold for six hundred and forty dollars, and a new one purchased for seven hundred and fifty dollars; in June, old No. 25 was sold for three hundred dollars exclusive of hose, and a new one purchased at a cost of eight hundred and eight dollars; in October, old No. 5 was sold to A. W. Hardenbrook for five hundred dollars; in November, old No. 9 was sold for six hundred dollars, During 1822 (up to June) three new engines, Nos. 5, 9, and 28, were built at the corporation yard under the direction of Jacob Roome, superintendent of repairs, at a cost of five hundred and ninety-six dollars each, at least one hundred and fifty-four dollars apiece lower than the corporation had theretofore paid for engines of a similar size, and in point of workmanship and in other respects far superior (it was claimed) to any other belonging to the corporation.

A building law was enacted by the legislature, April 12, 1822, looking to the more substantial construction of new buildings, and the imposition of penalties for any infraction of the same. Yet another act was passed the following year (April 9, 1823) of a similar nature, requiring that certain buildings should be fireproof. Other laws, of like scope and tendency, were passed at various subsequent dates.

So eager were young men to put on the red shirt and the helmet of the fireman and be recognized as such, that it was only by the most rigid supervision and discrimination they were prevented from being enrolled in the companies, and the law was on all occasions strictly enforced. But in the winter of 1822-'23 a great deficiency of firemen was experienced, and a memorial was presented by the Fire Department to the corporation praying for an amendment of the law so as to permit young men between the ages of eighteen and twenty-one to be chosen as firemen. But inasmuch as the law passed April 9, 1813, prescribed that none but freeholders and freemen were eligible, the Council decided that they had not power to do as requested.

Valentine Vandewater, Jameson Cox, Philip W. Engs, and Uzziah Wenman were appointed engineers in December, 1822, in place of Benjamin Strong, James Scott, Hays Pennell, and John Colville, resigned.

For the six years preceding 1823 the cash expenses of the corporation for engines and apparatus, including the ground purchases and the engine houses erected, amounted to seventy-nine thousand nine hundred and ninety-six dollars and ninety-four cents, averaging thirteen thousand three hundred and thirty-two dollars per annum. The value of the estate vested in that species of public property was estimated in 1820 at seventy-two thousand seven hundred and eighty-nine dollars.

The number of engine companies (including hook and ladder companies) in January, 1823, was forty-seven, to which one thousand two hundred and fifteen men, all told, were attached, all of whom, when they should have served ten years from 1816, were to be exempted from serving as jurors, and all military duty thereafter. These facts suggested the question whether the existing number of engines was not more than was needed, and whether some of them could not be dispensed with, in view of the fact that the sum of nine thousand five hundred and sixty-six dollars was asked for in the annual estimate for departmental expenses for 1823 for the Fire Department. At that period no city in the Union incurred fire department expenses in anyway proportioned to the city of New York. In Philadelphia the engines and apparatus were furnished by individuals, and the privilege of exemption from jury and military duty were considered a sufficient remuneration, the City Council only appropriating about two thousand dollars towards the necessary repairs. The same economical system was pursued in the other cities throughout the United States. Mayor Allen, calling the attention of the Common Council to this matter, said that while they were drawing upon the property of the citizens in taxes so large an amount for fire purposes, and at the same time compelling them to perform nearly double duty as jurors in consequence of the exemption granted the firemen, it was no more than reasonable that the benefit to be derived in a public point of view should be commensurate with the sacrifice. Before the establishment of fire insurance companies in New York, the benefits derived from the Fire Department were perhaps equal to the expenditure. But it was very questionable then, when almost every species of property liable to be destroyed or injured by fire was insured against loss, whether any material

COAT OF ARMS, OLD VOLUNTEERS.

public benefit was derived. The subject was of sufficient importance to the Common Council to cause an inquiry to be instituted whether the finances could not be relieved by a reduction of the expenses for the Fire Department. On the thirteenth of January the Common Council decided to apply to the legislature for authority to assess and levy annually a tax on fire insurance companies to be applied towards defraying the expenses of the Fire Department.

In conformity with the presentation of the condition of the finances by Mayor Allen, and his suggestion that retrenchment be introduced, if possible, the chief engineer, in July, 1823, reported that retrenchment was practicable only in the matter of hose, substituting hemp hose for leather, which was only half the price.

The strength of the Fire Department in June, 1823, was one thousand two hundred and eighty-four men, all told; forty-six engines, including two at the new almshouse; four hook and ladder trucks, one hose wagon, and eleven thousand five hundred and seventy-five feet of hose, good, bad, and indifferent; two hundred and eighty-five fire buckets, sixteen ladders, twenty-three hooks, one machine for pulling down chimneys, and one copper pump.

The engine houses were located as follows:

Engine.
1. Duane Street Market.
2. Eldridge, near Division Street.
3. Beaver, near Broad Street.
4. Ann Street, North Dutch Church.
5. Fulton Street, North Dutch Church.
6. College Yard, Murray Street.
7. Rose, near Frankfort Street.
8. Chambers, near Cross Street.
9. Marketfield, near Broad Street.
10. Fifth Street, near Second Avenue.
11. Old Slip.
12. Rose, near Frankfort Street.
13. Fulton Street, Fireman's Hall.
14. Vesey Street, near Church.
15. Christie, near Bayard Street.
16. Corporation Yard, Leonard Street.
17. Roosevelt, near Cherry Street.
18. Fulton Street, Fireman's Hall.
19. Eldridge Street, near Division.
20. Cedar, near Washington Street.
21. Fireman's Hall, Fulton Street.
22. Hester, near Orchard Street.
23. Hospital Yard, Anthony Street.
24. Prince and Wooster Streets, Watch House.
25. Tryon Row.
26. Madison, near Rutgers Street.
27. Watts, near Greenwich Street.
28. Mercer Street, near Prince.
29. Christopher and Hudson Streets.
30. Christie, near Stanton Street.

Engine.
31. Leonard, near Church Street.
32. Hester, near Orchard Street.
33. Cherry Street, near Corlears Hook.
34. Christopher and Hudson Streets.
35. Harlem Village.
36. Spring Street Church, near Varick Street.
37. Christie, near Stanton Street.
38. Bloomingdale Road, House of Refuge.
39. Vesey and Church Streets.
40. Mulberry, near Broome Streets.
41. Delancey and Attorney Street.
42. Foot of Roosevelt Street.
43. Manhattanville.
44. Columbia, near Stanton Street.
45. Yorkville.
46. Rose Hill.
47. Tenth Street, near Avenue D.
48. Fitz Roy Road, near Nineteenth Street.

H. and L.
1. Beaver, near Broad Street.
2. Tryon Row.
3. Christopher and Hudson Streets.
4. Eldridge Street, Watch House
5. Delancey and Attorney Streets.
6. Mercer, near Prince Street.

Hose.
1. Tryon Row.

Besides the regularly appointed firemen, there were attached to each company a number of self-constituted firemen, who were known as "volunteers." Their services, it appears, were not appreciated by the Common Council, and on the twenty-first of June, 1824, a resolution was approved, and directed as a circular to each company, ordering them to dispense with the services of these men, and, in case of their non-compliance, to send the engine, hook and ladder, or hose cart, as the case might be, to the Corporation Yard, and report the company to the Common Council.

In June, 1824, the condition of the Fire Department called forth great praise from a special committee of the Common Council, who made a tour of inspection, and declared that it was not surpassed by any other in the United States. The volunteer boys, who assumed the dress and authority of firemen, attached to companies, were the source of much annoyance, by causing false alarms of fire, whereby the members were constantly harassed and fatigued, and the machines injured to a great degree.

At this time the city was increasing with unprecedented rapidity. From actual enumeration, it appeared that in the year 1824 more than sixteen hundred new houses were erected, nearly all of them brick or stone. The price of real estate was also greatly increased. The erection of churches and other public edifices had become so frequent an occurrence as to forbid notice of each particular case. On the west side of the island the city proper was verging, nearly to Greenwich Village, which was also expanding into a large and well-built suburban ward. Eastward from the Bowery a settlement was springing up quite beyond the compact part of the city. In the middle portion, on both sides of Broadway, were many half rural residences of retired merchants and men of wealth. The old Potter's Field was becoming an obstacle to the city's progress in that vicinity, and it was accordingly determined to level and grade it, to be kept as a public promenade—the present Washington Square.

Jameson Cox was elected chief engineer of the Department at the meeting of the Common Council held on December 6, 1824, and among the appointments made in January of the next year were those of William P. Disosway, merchant, 45 Pearl Street, to Hook and Ladder No. 1, vice Hugh Aikman, who joined the Supply Company; Richard Carman, carpenter, 60 Stone Street, to Engine Company No. 3, vice Joseph Swaine, resigned; Samuel B.

SPECIMEN BOWERY BOYS.

Warner, sailmaker, 8 Garden Street, to Engine Company No. 3, vice Edward Ogden; Edmund Willetts, cartman, 196 Eldridge Street, to Hook and Ladder No. 4, vice John Varick, resigned; George Bijotat, upholsterer, Bowery, to Engine Company No. 19, vice Thomas Asten, term expired.

According to the report of Chief Engineer Jameson Cox, the condition of the Department in June, 1825, was:—Forty engines in good order, four indifferent, and two ordinary; four hook and ladder trucks and one hose wagon, ten thousand five hundred and seventy-four feet of hose, two hundred and twenty-eight fire buckets, eighteen ladders, and twenty-three hooks. With companies complete, the force would number one thousand three hundred and nineteen men, all told, but there were two hundred and thirty-one vacancies. During the year engine houses had been built for Companies Nos. 10, 19, and 33.

The Committee on the Fire Department reported on the twentieth of June on the subject of constructing public cisterns, and recommended a resolution, which was adopted, that the street commissioner be directed to prepare ordinances for the construction of ten public cisterns, the same to be used on the occasion of fire by the Fire Department. Subsequently, on the nineteenth of December, 1825, ordinances were passed for the construction of five additional cisterns. On the twenty-third of the same month, the Committee on the Fire Department were instructed to inquire into the expediency of filling all the public cisterns with water forthwith, and the fire companies were requested to volunteer their services to carry the above into effect.

A resolution was referred to the Committee on the Fire Department, in conjunction with the chief engineer, to mature a report to the Board of some more energetic and efficient plan to protect the firemen when on duty at fires from the encroachments of the surrounding populace. On the thirtieth of January, 1826, the committee reported the following resolution, which was adopted:

Resolved, That his honor, the mayor, be requested to address a circular to each of the foremen of the several companies of fire wardens, calling their attention to that section of the law pointing out their duties at fires, and that each of them would enforce the same on the members of their companies, and that the penalties which may hereafter be incurred by the constables and marshals of the city for not attending fires, be enforced.

On the second of January, 1827, seven additional cisterns were ordered by the Common Council, and eighteen on the twenty-fifth of August, 1828.

The firemen of the city were an incorporated body, under the name and title of the Fire Department of the City of New York, and had certain emoluments allowed them, which they appropriated to charitable purposes, such as giving pensions to widows of deceased firemen, making donations to indigent disabled firemen, and furnishing necessary clothing to children of firemen, so as to enable them to attend the public schools. Each company appointed annually two of their number to represent them in the Fire Department, and such representatives, when assembled, appointed out of the body of firemen in the city a Board of Trustees, who were intrusted with the funds, and at whose discretion widows were put on the pension list, and donations were made. In consequence of severe and heavy losses which the Department had sustained in 1826 by several moneyed institutions in the city, the Board of Trustees had come to the conclusion that they would be under the necessity of suspending the pensions and donations, unless they received assistance from their fellow-citizens. In January, 1827, the Common Council, recognizing the close connection between the interests of the firemen and the Corporation, decided that it was proper and judicious to extend a helping hand, and directed the comptroller to issue his warrant for one thousand dollars in favor of the treasurer of the Fire Department Fund. Two years after another one thousand dollars was donated, because the frequency of fires in the fall of 1829, and the consequent increasing demand on the treasury of the Fire Department Fund from disabled and sick firemen, had left the treasury in December of that year almost exhausted. As many as eighty-eight widows, and a large number of orphan children, had to be provided for in that year.

At a fire at the Vauxhall Garden in August, 1828, one of the engine companies, and several members of other companies, refused to perform service, and a rumor prevailed throughout the city that the firemen as a body had refused to obey orders, which caused general alarm among the inhabitants. Upon investigation, it was found that the demoralization was very limited, and measures were taken to keep up the efficiency of the force.

Jameson Cox, chief engineer, presented his resignation on December 8, 1828, which was accepted. Philip W. Engs, Samuel J. Willis, and Uzziah Wenman were candidates for the position. Mr. Wenman was elected.

"Firemen's Hall," in Fulton Street, had accommodations for four engines. The placing of so many machines in one immediate vicinity had been found to be prejudicial to the services of the Department, and in some instances to be a nuisance to the neighborhood. These facts, superadded to the necessity of providing engines for the upper part of the city by taking from the lower part those that could well be spared and were poorly supplied with men, had gradually caused the reduction of the number of engines there until, in February, 1829, only one was left, and the removal of that, too, had been decided on. The corporation concluded that the ground occupied for Fireman's Hall being no longer needed, they would sell it by auction, which was done on April 1.

In June, 1829, there were in the Department forty-eight engines, five hook and ladder trucks, with twenty-six ladders and twenty-nine hooks, and one thousand four hundred and thirty-two men with full companies, but only eight hundred and sixty-nine in actual service, there being five hundred and sixty-three vacancies.

Engine No. 28 was located on corporation ground on Mercer Street, and the council had directed that Hook and Ladder No. 6 should also be stationed there. It was therefore decided, in August, 1829, to erect a two-story brick building on the lot, in which, besides housing these companies, a ward court could be accommodated and the meetings of the Fire Department be held. Hence the origin of the present Firemen's Hall.

Although the natural advantages of New York in other respects were not excelled, nor perhaps equalled, by any city in the world, yet it had to be admitted that the supply of water for household purposes and for the extinguishment of fires was, in 1829, very meager. Various schemes had been adopted for the purpose of bringing water into the city, but none had as yet complied with the main object of their charters, so far as the public was concerned, and it was found that similar incorporations of private individuals, whether they proposed at their commencement to furnish pure and wholesome water or pure and first quality gas, had an eye only to the profits of their incorporations, and the public suffered under their monopolies.

The water pipes of the Manhattan Company extended to such parts of the city as they deemed advisable to put them in on the score of profit, and the upper part of the city, although not possessed of good water, had it, however, of a quality superior to that supplied by the Manhattan Company, and, therefore, the residents were unwilling generally to take the Manhattan water. The result was that all that part of the city lying above Grand Street, on Broadway, or Pearl Street on the east side of the city, did not have the use of the Manhattan water for the purpose of extinguishing fires. It became necessary, therefore, for the corporation to obtain a supply of water for that purpose to the upper part of the city.

The breadth of the island at Grand Street was then reckoned about two miles, and this did not materially differ as high up as Fourteenth Street. The extreme distance between those points was, consequently, one mile, and to bring water from either river at the extreme distance would require twenty-six engines, and thus the whole engine establishment could not form two lines. The furnishing water by engines from the rivers was not only too limited a mode to be at all relied on for that section of the city, but was also too laborious on the firemen.

Another mode of supply was by cisterns, which was in operation at this period to a limited extent. The corporation had forty public cisterns, at a cost of twenty-four thousand dollars, which usually contained one hundred hogsheads. To provide for the section of the city between Fourteenth and Grand Streets on Broadway, and Fourteenth and Pearl Streets on Chatham, by cisterns, would require the construction of at least sixty additional cisterns, on the scale of a cistern for each one thousand square feet, which, at an expense

BULL'S HEAD IN THE BOWERY.
[Between Bayard and Pump Streets, now Canal Street, 1783.]

of six hundred dollars each, would call for an expenditure of thirty-six thousand dollars.

In March, 1829, the corporation decided to lay down two lines of iron pipes for the security against fire of the section of the city before described, one line of tubes to run from Fourteenth Street through the Bowery, to its termination at Chatham Street, and a line of tubes from Fourteenth Street through Broadway to Canal Street, connecting with a reservoir containing two thousand hogsheads (or as much as twenty cisterns) on Fourteenth Street.

The Committee on the Fire Department reported on the sixteenth of November, 1829, that, although they had excavated only fifty feet in depth at Thirteenth Street, yet the quantity of water would be sufficient to fill the reservoir and pipes, as it was estimated that seventy hogsheads of water were issued in a day; that the cast-iron tank was received from Philadelphia, and that the same should be inclosed with a brick or wooden building—the cost of the former being estimated at three thousand five hundred dollars, and of the latter two thousand dollars. Which report was agreed to.

A fireman should have experienced five years' service before he was eligible for appointment as a warden. In consequence of the reduction of the term of service of firemen from ten to seven years, the wardens encountered no small difficulty in procuring the aid of such competent persons as were willing to do the duty of wardens for the short space of time—two years—during which they were eligible for office. The ordinance affecting this matter was therefore amended in November, 1830, reducing the term of service for eligibility from five to three years.

The legislature, on April 16, 1831, extended the charter of the firemen of the city of New York, passed March 20, 1798, to the year 1860. The corporation was likewise empowered to purchase, hold, and convey any estate, real or personal, for the use and objects for which the said corporation was instituted, "but such real or personal estate shall not exceed the sum of fifty thousand dollars."

This act was amended March 25, 1851, by which the said corporation could hold and convey any estate, real and personal, for the use already mentioned, but not to exceed the sum of one hundred thousand dollars.

An important state law, relative to the prevention of fires in the city of New York, was enacted on the twentieth of April, 1830. This law was quite lengthy, containing forty-two sections. Reference can be made only to its general features. Party walls, the law declared, shall be constructed of stone or brick; outside party walls shall not be less than eight inches thick, except flues of chimneys; party or end walls shall rise and be extended to the roof, and so far through the same as to meet and be joined to the slate, tile, or other covering thereof, by a layer of mortar or cement; beams and other timbers in the party walls shall be separated from each other, at least four inches, by brick or mortar; all hearths shall be supported with arches of stone or brick. No timber shall be used in the front or rear of any building within such fire limits, where stone is now commonly used; every building within the fire limits, which may hereafter be damaged by fire, to an amount equal to the two-thirds of the whole value thereof, after the lapse of at least fifteen years from the time of its first erection, shall be repaired or built according to the provisions of this act; no wooden shed exceeding twelve feet in height at the peak shall be erected within the fire limits.

A large part of the act is devoted to the regulation of the keeping and storage of gunpowder.

A law, forming a hydrant company, was passed by the Common Council on July 16, 1831. This company consisted of a foreman, assistant, a clerk, and twenty men, who were firemen and hydrant men. It was their duty, on an alarm of fire, to proceed to the hydrants, and see to the water being properly let out, that the hydrants were not injured, that they were properly secured and put in order after the fire was extinguished; and also to see that the stop-cocks were kept in order; and generally to attend to the engines being supplied with water from the reservoir; to report all injuries and defects which they might discover in any part of the works, to the chief engineer. The caps of said company were painted black, and had the words "Hydrant Company" on the frontispiece thereof.

A Fire and Building Department was created and organized by a law passed and approved in October, 1831. It was composed of three "discreet and proper persons," known as the Commissioners of the Fire and Building Department, and the commissioners were respectively designated a superintendent of buildings, chief engineer, and commissioner of the Fire Department.

The duty of the superintendent of buildings required him to advertise for estimates for all public buildings which might thereafter be erected under the authority of the Common Council, for all repairs to public buildings then in use, etc.

It was the duty of the chief engineer to report the names of persons who may be designated by the engineers and foremen as suitable persons to be appointed by the Common Council to fill vacancies in fire companies; in all cases of fire to have the sole and absolute command and control over all engines and members of the Fire Department; to direct the other engineers to take proper measures that the fire engines were suitably arranged and duly worked; to examine, once in every month, into the condition and number of the fire engines, and buckets, and other fire apparatus, and fire engine houses; and report the same to the Common Council twice in every year; and whenever any of the engines and apparatus should require to be repaired or new ones built, the chief engineer should personally inspect the building of the same; to report in writing all accidents by fire, with the probable causes thereof, etc.

Further, the commissioners should give their personal attention and supervision to the laying down of all such water pipes as the Common Council may direct, take charge of the reservoir and water establishment in Thirteenth Street, see that the hydrants were in order, etc.

The commissioners were obliged to give bonds in the sum of five thousand dollars, besides being sworn, for the faithful performance of their duties.

Pursuant to the organizing of the new Department, the enlargement of the house of Fire Engine Company No. 10, the erection of a two-story brick house on the lot corner of Delancey and Attorney Streets for the accommodation of a fire engine, hook and ladder company, and hose truck, the building of a hose house in Wooster Street, near Houston Street, the procuring of four thousand feet of hose, and the construction of a new engine for Company No. 11, were undertaken immediately.

In March, 1832, the fire limits were extended so as to include all that part of the city beginning on West Street, one hundred feet northerly from Spring Street, and running thence northerly along West Street to Bank Street, thence easterly through Bank Street to Greenwich Lane, thence southerly through Greenwich Lane to the east side of Sixth Avenue at a point northerly one hundred feet from Eighth Street, thence westerly along Sixth Avenue to a line distant southerly one hundred feet from Amity Lane, thence easterly and parallel with Amity Street to a line distant westerly one hundred feet from Greene Street, thence southerly and parallel with Greene Street to a line distant one hundred feet northerly from Spring Street, and thence westerly and parallel with Spring to West Street, at the place of beginning.

Also beginning at the Bowery, one hundred feet northerly from Rivington Street, and running thence northerly along the Bowery to a line distant southerly one hundred feet from North Street, thence easterly and parallel with North Street to Orchard Street, thence southerly along Orchard Street to a line distant one hundred feet northerly to Rivington Street, and thence westerly and parallel with Rivington Street, to the Bowery at the place of beginning.

The city in 1832 embraced a population of one hundred and eighty thousand souls, a collection of about thirty thousand houses, a tonnage of three hundred thousand four hundred tons, exclusive of ten thousand five hundred tons of steamboats, and an assessed value of property, including thirty-seven millions of personal estate, of one hundred and fourteen millions of dollars. Her lighted and paved streets, lined with houses, extended to Thirteenth Street on the North River, to the dry dock on the East River side, and to Thirteenth Street on "the Broadway and Bowery Streets." All the modern streets were straight and wide, graduated to easy ascents and descents; and where formerly very narrow lanes existed, or crowded edifices occurred, they had either cut off the encroaching fronts of houses, as in William Street and Maiden Lane, or cut through solid masses of houses, as in opening Beekman and Fulton Streets. The bounds of the city had been widened both on the North and East Rivers by building up whole streets of houses at and beyond Greenwich Street on the western side, and at and from Pearl Street on the eastern side.

OLD SUGAR HOUSE AND MIDDLE DUTCH CHURCH.

The proviso in the law forming a hydrant company approved July 16, 1831, was repealed in May, 1832, and thenceforth is was ordained that no individual could be eligible for appointment as hydrant man unless he had served as a fireman for at least three years.

Although *quasi* officers of the municipality, it was charged that certain firemen frequently exhibited as much indifference to the injunctions of the authorities as might be looked for only from the lawless class. Hence, in July, 1832, it became necessary to promulgate a law ordaining that any fireman found guilty of an offense against the ordinances of the Common Council, and having thereby resigned or been expelled, should not be eligible to an appointment to any office of trust, in any company, nor reappointed a firemen in any case.

Also, it was not uncommon for the foreman or engineer of an engine company to hire out the engine, and to lend it, on his own responsibility, which was subversive of all semblance of discipline, and impaired the efficiency of the

particular company.   Consequently, a provision was incorporated in the law
of July, 1832, that no fire engine should be let out for hire, or lent, in any case,
without permission from the alderman or assistant alderman of the ward
wherein it was wanted to be used, and the chief engineer, in default thereof,
and the fireman so offending, would be removed from the Fire Department.

During the prevalence of the epidemic of cholera in 1832 the working
force of the Department was much weakened by reason of sickness and death.
Very often not enough men, nor even supernumeraries, boys and youths who
loved to linger in the shadow of the engine house and be permitted to mingle
with the hardy fire fighters, could be mustered to drag the engine to the scene
of the conflagration.   Horses had to be brought into requisition, as is attested
by the fact that in November, 1832, the comptroller was authorized to pay the
bill of James Gulick for eight hundred and sixty-three dollars and seventy-five
cents, for horses " to drag the engines and hook and ladder trucks to the fires
during the late epidemic."

The custom was in those days, upon the outbreak of fire, to ring the church
bells as well as the fire bells, and when the fire happened during the night, the
watchman in his tower should ring the alarm, and hang out of the window of
the cupola a pole with a lantern on the end pointing in the direction of the
fire, so that the firemen and citizens could readily know the whereabouts of the
fire.   Further, the watchmen (the police) were obliged to call out the street or
between what streets the fire was located.   The laws of the municipality
regarding these observances were inflexible, delinquency on the part of the
bellringers or the watchmen being visited with severe penalties.

The cost of supporting the Fire Department by the city varied considerably.
In 1830 it amounted to twenty-two thousand nine hundred and sixty-two
dollars.   The actual number of fires that happened in that year were one
hundred and nineteen; false alarms, one hundred and twenty-five; and the loss
of property, one hundred and fifty-seven thousand one hundred and thirty-five
dollars.   In 1831 the expenses of the Department amounted to twelve thousand
nine hundred and eighty-four dollars.

Careful calculations showed that although it cost in 1832 only eighteen
thousand dollars to maintain the Fire Department, the individual firemen
were taxed in their services two hundred and eighty-four thousand five
hundred dollars annually.   It is true their labors were rendered voluntarily,
and they had an equivalent, but it did not render it less imperative on the city
authorities, as the common guardians of this great community, to diminish the
labors and personal exposures and risks of that meritorious, skillful and
patriotic class of citizens.

The melancholy tidings of the death of the illustrious La Fayette, the friend
and companion of Washington, the adopted son of America, the brave and
faithful defender of liberty in both hemispheres, reached New York on June
19, 1834, just one month after his demise in Paris.   Suitable honors were of
course to be paid to the memory of this splendid character by the municipal
authorities, and, in these days, no civic parade would be complete without
the participation and presence of the members of the Fire Department in
the usual and formal manner, a meeting was called whereat the following
preamble and resolution were adopted, and programme for the parade
agreed to :—

Whereas, we have learned of the death of General La Fayette, the tried patriot, the firm and devoted friend of America and her free institutions; he, who forsook the blandishments and ease of a luxurious court, who gave his fortune and risked his life for the independence of our happy Republic, therefore,

Resolved, That we, the firemen of the city of New York, will unite with our fellow-citizens on Thursday, the twenty-sixth instant, in paying such tribute of respect as the eminent virtues and patriotic services of one of America's dearest sons demand of a grateful and affectionate people.

The exempt firemen also attended in a body.

The Department assembled at Hospital Green, and the line was formed under the direction of the Grand Marshal, James Gulick, assisted by his aids, in the following order:

First, Fire Department Banner.

Second, Grand Marshal and two Aids.

Third, President, Vice-president, Trustees, Treasurer, Secretary, and Collector of the Fire Department.

Fifth, Exempt Firemen.

Sixth, The banners and implements equally distributed through the line, under the direction of the different marshals. The Brooklyn and Williamsburg firemen in the center.

After the ceremonies, the procession reorganized and proceeded up Greenwich Street to Canal, through Canal to Broadway, up Broadway to Grand Street, through Grand Street to East Broadway, down East Broadway to Chatham Square.

The alleged improper and riotous conduct of the members of several companies of the Department, and the congregating of idle and dissolute persons in the engine houses, had been for several months the subject of complaint from residents in the vicinity of engine houses. Boys and young men, too, obtained very ready access to the engines, and made it a matter of amusement to raise an alarm of fire as an excuse or cover to get the engines out and have a run. Evidently the engine companies could prevent these scenes. But in cases of fire the companies desired some assistance from these boys and young men, which induced them to countenance the assemblages. The Common Council investigated the complaints, and in October, 1834, reported that the members of some of the companies could not be depended upon to prevent the engine houses being entered and frequented by persons other than those belonging to the Fire Department, and suggested the enactment of a law providing a remedy.

That a prompt alarm of fire might be given, a watchman was stationed at all times in the cupola of the City Hall. The law so providing was approved by the mayor, April 1, 1835. The chief engineer, by and with the consent of the mayor, was empowered to appoint a competent number of persons to perform the duty of such watchmen, day and night, subject severally to removal by the chief engineer. These bellringers, nevertheless, were amenable at all times during the night to the rules and regulations of the Watch Department. On the occurrence of any fire, the City Hall bell should be rung by the watchman on duty in the cupola, and the ringing thereof maintained during the continuance of the fire. Notice of the locality of the fire was given by ringing said bell in a manner prescribed by directions given by the committee on fire and water and the chief engineer, and by hanging out a light in the direction of the fire. For neglect of any of the duties required by this law, the penalty imposed was removal from office by the chief engineer or captains of the watch.

Upon the happening of any fire, the several watchhouses and market bells were rung, and also all other alarm bells, and the same was done whenever any one alarm bell should ring, and the ringing thereof continued until the city bell had stopped.

It will be seen from these facts that the Fire Department kept pace with the growth of the city. The people were quick to recognize the importance of keeping up, both in numbers and efficiency, a body of men so necessary to the welfare of the growing metropolis. Year by year, nay, almost month by month, additions to the Department were made, and alterations effected to improve it. The enactment of the new building laws was a great help to the firemen, and its enforcement gave them a great advantage over their natural enemy—an advantage which prior to this they did not possess.

It will also be noted how eager the firemen were to maintain an *esprit de corps*. Before the period we are just concluding efforts had been made to diminish the number of the hangers-on of the Department. As the city grew these parasites increased, and the difficulty was all the greater to keep them off. We have shown how persistently and honorably the firemen endeavored to abate this nuisance. They could not wholly dispense with the services of outsiders, but those whom they did employ they took care should be of the best quality attainable.

It was only natural in the period we have just discussed that the Department should complain of the insufficiency of water. That was not a matter that could be attended to until science had a greater play than she experienced in those days. Indeed up to the present there has been a constant cry that New York has not all the water she needs. In the past as in the present the firemen did the very best they could to utilize what was at their disposal for the benefit of the city.

RESCUE OF A CHILD.

CHAPTER VIII.

FEUDS AND THEIR SUPPRESSION.

1835-1842.—Frequency of Fires.—Element of Rowdyism in the Department.—Bitter Feuds between Companies.—The Importance of the Services of the Fire Department Universally Admitted.—A Proposition to Elect and Appoint Five Fire Commissioners.—Efforts to Suppress " Volunteers."

MAYOR LAWRENCE, in September, 1835, called the attention of the Common Council to the frequency of fires, and particularly the one in Fulton, Ann, and Nassau Streets, and also the fire in Water Street and Maiden Lane, by which a large amount of property was destroyed and lives lost. He expressed the belief that these were the work of incendiaries, and he suggested the propriety of offering a reward for such information as should lead to the detection and conviction of the criminals. The Council empowered him to do so in his discretion, and, accordingly, a proclamation for five hundred dollars was issued.

Not more than a fortnight after the issuance of this proclamation another large fire broke out in Franklin and Chapel (now College Place) Streets, bearing every mark of being of incendiary origin, and another reward of five hundred dollars was offered.

Then followed the terrible conflagration of December 16, which destroyed in one night twenty million dollars' worth of property, and dislodged more than six hundred mercantile firms. By that calamity the extensive resources and irrepressible energies of the citizens were developed, and it forms a proud record for the pages of history that not a single mercantile failure resulted therefrom, and many of the heavy sufferers were among the most active in aiding the widows, orphans, and infirm persons reduced to poverty and dependence.

The element of rowdyism in the Fire Department hitherto referred to as being so pronounced that the citizens begged for the interference of the authorities, again manifested itself at a fire which occurred on the night of January 1, 1836, when Alderman Purdy, representing the Tenth Ward, was set upon and mercilessly beaten by members of Engine Company No. 10, who were also accused of abandoning their engine on that occasion. For the latter offense, nine officers and members were expelled the Department, and ten were suspended for not complying with the requisitions to appear before a committee of the Common Council and testify in reference to the assault on Alderman Purdy.

With the opening of the spring of 1836, the number of fires in the city had increased to an alarming extent, and a proportionate increase in the number of firemen had become necessary. This increase was not attainable, by reason of the citizens being deterred from becoming firemen in consequence of the arduous and toilsome duties which the members of the Fire Department were incessantly called upon to perform. As the increase was absolutely necessary for the safety of the city, it became a duty incumbent on the authorities to encourage citizens to join the Fire Department by lessening, as far as possible, the labors of the firemen, as well as removing such impediments to their exertions as existed.

Among those impediments, that caused by young men—who appeared at fires in the garb of firemen—was especially prominent. The engineers had no control over them, and their insubordination, utter lawlessness, and the confusion they created, proved a continual source of annoyance and serious hindrance both to the engineers and the regular firemen, a great majority of whom would gladly dispense with their precarious assistance if by so doing they could be freed from all suspicion of participating in riots created by these boys,

JUNCTION OF BROADWAY AND THE BOWERY, 1831.
(Union Square.)

and which, instead of being assigned to their true cause, were attributed to the members of the Fire Department.

To accomplish these two purposes, it was determined to appoint four persons to each fire engine and hose company, and two persons to each hook and ladder company, to take care of the apparatus and assist generally, and making it the duty of all members of the Department to prevent persons not belonging to the Department, especially boys, from entering any house or handling any apparatus belonging to the Department, said appointees not to be considered as firemen, and to be paid at the rate of one hundred and fifty dollars per annum.

The Third Ward Hose Company, whose origin was traceable to the conflagration of December, 1835, tendered its services to the corporation in March, 1836, which were accepted, and they were recognized as a volunteer fire company, attached to, but not a part of, the Fire Department.

From the report of the chief engineer, John Ryker, Jr., it appears that the condition of the Fire Department on October 3, 1836, was :

Forty-nine engine companies,

Six hook and ladder companies,

Nine hose companies,

with an active available force of nine hundred and thirty-seven men.

Half a century ago it was an honor to be an alderman or an assistant. They were elected by their fellow-citizens for their integrity and ability, and as a consequence, were entrusted and invested with privileges and functions of a magisterial nature. Hence it came about that, next to the mayor of the city, they were, perhaps, among civic functionaries, the most important. That was their status as concerns fires, for to them (as the law prescribed) the marshals and constables, repairing immediately on the alarm of fire with their staves of office to the scene of the fire, should report and should conform to such orders as might be given them by the mayor, the alderman and assistant of the ward, or by any one of the aldermen, for the preservation of the public peace, and the removal of all idle and suspected persons or others not actually or usefully employed in aiding the extinguishment of such fire, or in the preservation of property in the vicinity thereof, and if any marshal or constable should not attend at such fire or should neglect so to report himself, or to obey any orders that were given him,

PITCHER.
Presented to Chief Gulick.

he should, unless he had a reasonable excuse, to be determined by the mayor, forfeit and pay five dollars for each offense.

Two persons were appointed to each fire engine and hose company (ordinance May 10, 1836), and two persons to each hook and ladder company within the lamp and watch district, their duty consisting of keeping all the apparatus of the companies in complete order and ready for immediate use; upon every alarm of fire they repaired forthwith to the house of the engine, hose, or hook and ladder company to which they were attached, and assisted the members in conveying the engine, carriage, or truck to the fire, and there assisted the company in getting the engine to work, or the hose ready for immediate action, under the direction of the officers of the company to which they belonged; and during the time such engine or hose carriage was employed at a fire, the two persons named in the ordinance took charge of the hose, and prevented any persons from treading on, or otherwise injuring the same. They also assisted the members, when the engine or hose carriage was discharged from duty, after the putting out of a fire, in taking up the hose and other apparatus, and assisted in conveying them, together with the engine or hose carriage, etc., to the house appropriated for it, and there washed and dried the hose, and cleaned and put in complete order all the apparatus, so as to be ready for immediate use, taking care, however, in no case to meddle with the works of an engine.

Those persons, similarly appointed and attached to a hook and ladder company, preserved the truck and apparatus belonging to their company from injury during the fire; assisted the members in raising or moving ladders and hooks, and rendered assistance, after the fire, in getting the apparatus to the house, etc.

"Among the novelties of New York," it was remarked by an observant writer (1837)) "there is nothing perhaps which strikes a stranger with more surprise than the frequency of fires. There is scarcely a day from January to July, and from July to January, when there is not an alarm—a cry of fire—and a ringing of bells. But a single alarm, for each day in the year, would be too low an average. To say the bells are rung and the firemen called out five hundred times in the three hundred and sixty-five days, would not exceed the truth."

"Strangers are very often alarmed," continues the same writer, "as well as surprised, at the frequent cries of fires in this city, and fancy from the hideous outcry of the boys and the rueful jangling of the bells, that the fire is close to, if not within their very lodgings; and that New York is, every day, on the verge of a general conflagration. To this alarm, the bells very much, perhaps needlessly, contribute. As soon as an alarm of fire is given they fall to ringing in all quarters with great zeal and force; and some of them continue their clamor for a considerable time after the danger is past, or after the alarm is ascertained to be a false one. The first in the field, the most vigorous in action, and the last to quit, is the bell of the Middle Dutch Church. Who the ringer of that bell is we do not know; but this we will aver, that he labors with a zeal and perseverance that are quite astounding. We fancy he, now and then, gets up in his sleep to exercise his vocation. At any rate, whether asleep or awake, he seems to have a remarkable fondness for pulling at the end of a rope."

Severe and bitter quarrels were often the result of placing two engine companies under the same roof. This was illustrated by the perpetual and bitter feuds between Companies Nos. 34 and 29 and Hook and Ladder Company No. 3, whose houses, on the corner of Hudson and Christopher Streets, adjoined and were connected. The residents of the Ninth Ward, in the immediate vicinity, were much disturbed by the disorderly conduct of the members of these companies, regular and volunteer, and they memorialized the Common Council for an abatement of the annoyance by the removal of the engine companies. An investigation was made on the part of the Council, and so well established was the fact that gross scenes of outrage and abuse had often been perpetrated that the corporation took possession of the engines and placed them in the public yard until other locations for them should be determined on. The hook and ladder company was completely exonerated by the investigation, being declared to be a well regulated, efficient, and valuable company. The upshot of the matter was that the house corner of Hudson and Christopher Streets was sold, and the bellicose engine companies were located respectively on Morton and Bank Streets.

In May, 1838, the laws and ordinances relating to fires and the Fire Department were amended and modified so that the Department should consist of a chief engineer, nine assistant engineers, a water purveyor, and as many fire wardens, fire engine men, hosemen, and hook and ladder men as might from time to time be appointed by the Common Council. The chief engineer should be nominated by the engineers, foremen, and assistant foremen; and the assistant engineers by the foremen and assistant foremen of the fire companies, respectively, to the Common Council for appointment, and should hold their offices during the pleasure of the Common Council.

The salary of the chief engineer was fixed at twelve hundred dollars per year.

The water purveyor should be appointed by, and hold office during the pleasure of the Common Council, at a salary of one thousand dollars per year, take charge of the public reservoirs and establishments of water for the extinguishment of fires.

The engineers, foremen, and assistant foremen, should meet on the first Tuesday in June annually for the purpose of nominating a suitable person for chief engineer.

So many of the freeholders or freemen as the Common Council deemed proper should from time to time be appointed in each of the wards of the city, denominated fire wardens, assigned and attached by the mayor to such company of firemen as he should think proper, the fire wardens of each ward forming a separate company.

The names and places of abode of the members of the Common Council, engineers, fire wardens, and firemen of the respective companies, and bell ringers, were annually, in the month of June, printed and set up in the several watchhouses by the city inspector, and whenever any fire happened in the night, the watch gave notice to them within their respective watch districts.

PAINTING ON NO. 3 ENGINE, OF WILLIAMSBURG.

Mayor Aaron Clark, in his annual message, referring to the Fire Department, said that their importance was universally admitted. They were to be congratulated, he said, upon their efficiency and usefulness, and the general harmony then prevailing among the companies composing the department, consisting, as it did, of a numerous body of citizens engaged in various pursuits and businesses, and voluntarily associated for the preservation of property and life from the ravages of conflagration, it had become identified with the safety and the happiness of the citizens. For intrepidity, skill, and firmness of purpose "in the summer's heat and the winter's cold," their firemen were unsurpassed by those of any country.

In July, 1838, the insurance companies urged upon the authorities the passage of an ordinance for the appointment of commissioners to investigate the causes of fires.   The Common Council responded with a law to appoint three persons at a salary of one thousand dollars each per annum, who should attend at all fires, and immediately thereafter investigate the cause thereof, and file a report of the evidence taken and the result of their investigation.

The ordinance was to go into effect on the first of August, 1838, provided that the sum of four thousand dollars had been previously paid into the city treasury by one or more of the insurance companies, for the purpose of defraying the expenses incurred by the commission, which latter should continue in force so long as one or more of the companies should on or before June 1 in each year pay a similar amount.

The city in 1838 was divided into five districts, which were pointed out by the bell as follows:

First District—one stroke of the bell.

Second District—two strokes of the bell.

Third District—three strokes of the bell.

Fourth District—four strokes of the bell.

Fifth District—a continual ringing.

The First District was comprehended by a line from the foot of Murray Street to the City Hall, and in a line from the northwest corner of the City Hall parallel with the North River, to Twenty-first Street.

The Second District was bounded by the latter line, and a straight line from the City Hall to Third Avenue at Twenty-first Street.

The Third District was bounded by the latter, and a line from the City Hall to the East River above the dry dock.

The Fourth District was bounded by the latter, and comprehended all the space between that and the East River, as far down as Frankfort Street.

The Fifth District was all that part of the city below Frankfort and Murray Streets.

The encouraging and well-deserved compliment paid the Fire Department by Mayor Clark in 1838 was echoed in 1839 by Mayor Isaac L. Varian, who said, in addressing the municipal legislature, that it deserved their fostering care.   During the past year the amount of property destroyed by fire was small, compared with former years.   The introduction of water for the purpose of extinguishing fires through pipes and hydrants had afforded additional facilities to the firemen, and on the plan the pipes were being laid, a farther extension of them was deemed advisable, and contracts were made for the supply of six thousand five hundred water pipes.

A proposition was submitted to the legislature in June, 1840, without any application on the part of the Common Council, in regard to the Fire Department of this city, which was adopted by one branch of that body, but in the other was not acted on, and did not become a law.   This proposition was to deprive the Common Council of all control over the Department, and place it in the hands of persons who were not in any way responsible to the public authorities, while it left the whole expenses of the Department to be paid from the treasury.   Such a measure was not acceptable to the Common Council; and instead of removing the difficulties which had in former years operated injuriously against the Department, would have added, the Council claimed, new ones of a more serious character.

Since 1836 the introduction of political feelings and views into the general management of the Fire Department had materially affected its usefulness and tended much to produce the evils which the law above referred to was designed to remedy.

It was directed by the Common Council, March 11, 1840, that a cupola and alarm bell be placed on Center Market, and that the expense thereof be paid out of the general appropriation for the Fire Department, and that the superintendent of buildings and repairs, under the direction of the joint committee on fire water, contract for the same.

It was decreed also that a watchman should, at all times, be stationed at the cupola of the City Hall, reservoir, Center, Essex, and Jefferson Markets, for the purpose of giving an alarm whenever a fire occurred. The fire and water committee, by and with the consent of the mayor, appointed a competent number of persons to perform such duty by day and night, who were severally removable by the committee. These men were paid for their services, at the rate of two dollars per day, on their bills being certified by the chairman of the fire and water committee.

In the winter of 1841 it was sought to still further amend and modify the laws respecting the Fire Department. The firemen were to be appointed by and under the control, supervision, etc., of five commissioners, elected and appointed by the representatives of the New York Fire Department, holding office for five years, at one thousand dollars each per annum, to be known as "The Commissioners of the Fire Department of the City of New York," and no person should be appointed as a commissioner who had not served at least five years as a fireman. The commissioners should have power to appoint a chief engineer and seven assistant engineers, subject to removal at any time by said commissioners. They should have power to appoint the firemen, and to purchase all apparatus; to appoint on the recommendation of the alderman and assistant alderman of each ward, five persons to each ward, to be denominated " Fire Policemen ; " to appoint two persons as cleaners ; and to regulate and fix the salaries of chief and assistant engineers, the fire policemen, and the cleaners.

The salary of the chief engineer, it may be observed here, varied considerably. In 1819 it was $800 a year; in 1820, $500; in 1834, $1,000; in 1838, $1,200; in 1839, $500; in 1841, $1,000 ; in 1844, $1,500; in 1848, $2,000; in 1855, $3,000, and from 1857 to 1865, $5,000. Long before 1841 the chief engineer was the appointee of the Common Council, then he became the annual choice of the engineers, foreman and assistant foreman. In 1842 an ordinance was passed by which the chief engineer was nominated by the firemen, appointed by the Common Council and served until a majority of the firemen desired a new election. At various times there were heated arguments as to the best method of appointing or electing a chief engineer. The citizens showed their interest in the Department by joining in these discussions through the press. The opinion of the majority prevailed that that important officer should be the selection of the whole Department, and so we find that in 1853 a law was passed fixing his election by the firemen, who balloted for him every three years.

The regular firemen continued to be much harassed by so-called volunteer associations, their good name tarnished, and their efforts often frustrated. The Common Council again (November 10, 1841) denounced these volunteer associations and the practice of permitting them to assume the garb of firemen, and to mingle in the duties thereof. This, the ordinance declared, was not only in direct and open violation of the ordinances of the Common Council, but was calculated, in its results, to demoralize the character of youth, and bring reproach upon the Department, by the riotous and disorderly conduct in which these young men were so often engaged. Hence, the officers and members of each company were ordered forthwith to disband all associations of volunteers, and upon no occasion to suffer or permit them to have access to the public property; and all magistrates, watchmen, and police officers, were requested to prevent the congregating of all boys around or in the vicinity of the engine, hose, and hook and ladder houses, to the end that members of the Fire Department might be recognized as such, and be held responsible for all deviation from the path of duty, and the requirements of the ordinances of the Common Council.

ORIGINAL PAINTING ON NO. 3 ENGINE, WILLIAMSBURG.

Fire companies were interdicted from removing their apparatus out of the district in which the same was located, below Fourteenth Street, in case of fire, or an alarm of fire, under the penalty of being subject to expulsion or suspension from the Fire Department, unless they should be permitted so to do by the chief or one both assistant engineers.

The fire districts were laid out as follows:

The First Fire District shall embrace all that part of the city lying north of a line from the foot of North Moore Street to the Halls of Justice, and west of a line running from the Halls of Justice, through Lafayette and Irving Places.

The Second Fire District shall embrace all that part of the city lying east of the first district, and north of a line running from the Halls of Justice to the foot of Roosevelt Street.

The Third Fire District shall embrace all that part of the city lying south of the first and second districts.

Engine Companies Nos. 22, 38, 42 (June 22, 1842), consisted of sixty men each, and all other engine companies of thirty men each; hose companies with four-wheeled hose carriages, of twenty-five men each; hose companies with two-wheeled hose carriage, eighteen men each; and hydrant companies, of fifteen men each; and the chief engineer was directed not to allow the above-named companies to exceed the number of men specified.

Engine Company No. 9 thereafter should be known as Hose Company No.

35; Engine Company No. 47 as Hose Company No. 34; Engine Company No. 17 as Hose Company No. 37; Third Ward Hose Company as Hose Company No. 27; Fifth District Hose Company as Hose Company No. 28; Hose Company No. 44 as Hose Company No. 29; Hose Company No. 43 as Hose Company No. 31; Hose Company No. 42 as Hose Company No. 32; making the number and locations of the fire apparatus as follows:

ENGINE COMPANIES.—Their Numbers and Locations.

No. 1, Clinton Square, foot of Duane Street.
No. 2, Eldridge, near Division.
No. 3, Orange, near Prince.
No. 4, North Dutch Church, near Ann Street.
No. 5, North Dutch Church, near Ann Street.
No. 6, Reade Street, near West Broadway.
No. 7, Rose Street, near Frankfort Street.
No. 8, Ludlow, near Broome Street.
No. 9, Disbanded.
No. 10, Third Street, near Bowery.
No. 11, Wooster, near Prince Street.
No. 12, William, near Duane Street.
No. 13, Duane, near William Street.
No. 14, Corner of Vesey and Church Streets.
No. 15, Christie, near Walker Street.
No. 16, Disbanded.
No. 17, Disbanded.
No. 18, Amity, near Sixth Avenue.
No. 19, Elizabeth, near Grand Street.
No. 20, Cedar, near Greenwich Street.
No. 21, Lumber, near Cedar Street.
No. 22, Chambers, near Centre Street.
No. 23, Anthony, near Broadway.
No. 24, Seventeenth Street, near Ninth Avenue.
No. 25, Twenty-third Street, near Fifth Avenue.
No. 26, Madison, near Rutgers Street.

No. 27, Watts, near Greenwich Street.
No. 28, Disbanded.
No. 29, Horatio Street, near Ninth Avenue.
No. 30, Disbanded.
No. 31, West Broadway, near Beach Street.
No. 32, Hester, near Allen Street.
No. 33, Gouverneur, near Henry Street.
No. 34, Christopher, near Hudson Street.
No. 35, Harlem.
No. 36, Varick, near Vandam Street.
No. 37, Delancey, near Allen Street.
No. 38, Nassau, near Ann Street.
No. 39, Doyers, near Chatham Square.
No. 40, Mulberry, near Broome Street.
No. 41, Corner Delancey and Attorney Streets.
No. 42, Beaver, near William Street.
No. 43, Manhattanville.
No. 44, Houston, near Lewis Street.
No. 45, Yorkville, Third Avenue.
No. 46, Twenty-fifth Street, near Bull's Head.
No. 47, Disbanded.
No. 48, Thirteenth Street, near Sixth Avenue.
No. 49, Harlem.
No. 50, Bloomingdale Road, Harsenville.

HOSE COMPANIES.

No. 1, 4-wheeled, Duane, near William Street.
No. 2, 2 " William, near Duane Street.
No. 3, 2 " Centre, near Hester Street.
No. 4, 2 " Attorney, near Delancey Street.
No. 5, 4 " Mercer, near Prince Street.
No. 6, 4 " Gouverneur, near Henry Street.
No. 7, 2 " Christie, near Stanton Street.
No. 8, 4 " Cedar, near Nassau Street.
No. 9, 4 " Mulberry, near Broome Street.
No. 10, 2 " Roosevelt, near Cherry Street.
No. 11, 2 " Jefferson Market, Sixth Avenue.
No. 12, 4 " Seventeenth Street, near Ninth Avenue.
No. 13, 2 " Eldridge, near Division Street.

No. 22, 2-wheeled, Hester, near Allen Street.
No. 23, 2 " Charles, near Hudson Street.
No. 24, 2 " Renwick, near Spring Street.
No. 25, 2 " Leonard Street, near Broadway.
No. 26, 2 " Monroe, near Jefferson Street.
No. 27, 2 " Corner of Vesey and Church Streets.
No. 28, 2 " Chambers, near Centre Street.
No. 29, 2 " Willett, near Rivington Street.
No. 30, 2 " Bowery, near Thirteenth Street.
No. 31, 2 " Willett, near Rivington Street.
No. 32, 2 " Third Street, n'r Bowery.

No. 14, 2-wheeled Elizabeth, n'r Bayard Street.

No. 15, 2 " Essex Market, near Grand Street.

No. 16, 2 " Beaver, near Broad Street.

No. 17, 4 " Fifth Street, near Second Avenue.

No. 18, 2 " Franklin Market, Old Slip.

No. 19, 2 " Cortlandt Alley, near Canal Street.

No. 20, 2 " John, near Dutch Street.

No. 21, 2 " Henry, near Catharine Street

No. 33, 2-wheeled Sullivan, near Prince Street.

No. 34, 2 " Tenth Street, near Avenue D.

No. 35, 2 " Mercer, near Bleecker Street.

No. 36, 2 " Henry, near Catharine Street.

No. 37, 2 " Monroe Market.

No. 38, 2 " Amity Street, near Sixth Avenue.

HYDRANT COMPANIES.

No. 1, John A. Blackledge, Foreman.

No. 2, Allen R. Jollie, Foreman.

No. 3, Daniel Coger, Foreman.

HOOK AND LADDER COMPANIES.

No. 1, Beaver, near Broad Street.

No. 2, Chambers, near Centre Street.

No. 4, Eldridge, near Walker Street.

No. 5, Corner Delancey and Attorney Streets.

No. 6, Mercer, near Prince Street.

No. 7, Harlem.

No. 8, Disbanded.

No. 9, Disbanded.

No. 10, Third Avenue, Yorkville.

Fire wardens to the number of six were stationed in each of the First, Second, Third, Fourth, Fifth, Sixth, Seventh, Eighth, Ninth, Tenth, Eleventh, Twelfth, Thirteenth, Fourteenth, Fifteenth, Sixteenth, and Seventeenth Wards.

The Common Council, on September 7, 1842, by ordinance, established the offices of a chief engineer, a superintendent of the aqueduct works, a water purveyor, and a register of rents, to hold their respective offices during the pleasure of the Common Council, unless sooner removed for cause by the Croton Aqueduct Board, with the concurrence of the Joint Croton Aqueduct Committee. The chief engineer, under the direction of the Croton Aqueduct Board, had the general executive care and superintendence of the Croton Aqueduct Works.

The superintendent and water purveyor had the care of laying down all the distributing pipes, hydrants, and stop-cocks, under the direction of the chief engineer and Croton Aqueduct Board; examined into, and reported to the Croton Aqueduct Board all applications for water, and generally did all such duty assigned to them; they attended all fires, provided against all unnecessary waste of water, and saw that all hydrants were closed at the termination of each conflagration.

The salary of the chief engineer was increased to one thousand five hundred dollars per annum.

FIRE APPARATUS.

CHAPTER IX.

INTRODUCTION OF THE CROTON SERVICE.

1842-1853.—Much Rioting among the Companies.—Condition of the Department.—The City Divided into Three Fire Districts.—The Morse Magnetic Telegraph.—Erection of a Water Tower.—The Hague Street Disaster.—Chief Carson's Charges.

THE introduction of the Croton water into the city called for a thorough reorganization of the Department. That worthy and patriotic class of citizens would no longer be required to perform the laborious duty of dragging their engines for miles ; and the services of the boys who congregated about the engine houses for the purpose of assisting to convey the engines to the fires would no longer be required. The period had now arrived—the summer of 1842—when the city authorities could with perfect ease, and with proper regard for the laborious exertions of the Fire Department, prevent boys and young men, not members of the Department, interfering in any manner with, or performing the duties of, firemen. When these excrescences should be lopped off from the Department, the high character and worth of the members proper would be at once appreciated, and the people would bear witness to their services and usefulness.

Serious and disgraceful fights and riots had occurred in the autumn of 1843 between different fire companies, principally originating with low and violent characters whose respective companies had been disbanded and broken up by the corporation, and who attached themselves to others on occasions of fires, to create fights and disorder, thus degrading the character and impairing the usefulness and discipline of the Fire Department. In order to prevent the repetition of such outrages, and effectually protect the respectable and well-disposed, the chief engineer, C. V. Anderson, solicited the Common Council for the establishment of a fire police, consisting of not less than twenty men, who should assemble at each fire to protect property and to suppress tumult.

The Common Council had no power to create such a body, and, therefore, a memorial to the legislature was prepared for authority to do so.

The condition of the Fire Department in August, 1843, was: thirty-seven engines in good order, two in indifferent order, and two rebuilding; thirty-eight hose carriages in good order, and one rebuilding; eight hook and ladder trucks, with forty-seven ladders and fifty-one hooks, and forty-eight thousand nine hundred feet of hose. There were then in the Department thirty-nine engine companies, forty hose companies, eight hook and ladder companies, and three hydrant companies, and one thousand six hundred and sixty-one men.

In March, 1843, in consequence of certain serious disturbances in the Department, the disbandment of certain companies, and among others of Engine Company No. 34, was recommended. The evidence concerning the fights between Engine Companies No. 34 and 27 substantiated the allegations of frequent and violent attacks, while not a solitary complaint had been made to the competent authorities, both companies having "preferred to fight it out to calling on the Common Council for protection." Engine Company No. 34 was disbanded, their apparatus returned to the public yard, and their house given to Hose Company No. 40. In May of that year No. 34 was reinstated.

In August, 1844, there were in the Department thirty-nine engines in good order, and one in indifferent order; thirty-eight hose carriages in good order, one indifferent, and two building; eight hook and ladder trucks, with forty-six ladders and forty-nine hooks; thirty-one thousand eight hundred and fifty feet of good hose, and six thousand two hundred and fifty feet of hose in ordinary, making in the whole thirty-eight thousand one hundred feet of hose; forty-one

DANCING FOR EELS, CATHARINE MARKET.
Original in rooms of the Veteran's Association, Eighth Street.

engine companies (one of which performed duty with a hose carriage), forty-one hose companies, eight hook and ladder companies, and one hydrant company; one thousand five hundred and eighty-one men.

In May, 1845, there were thirty-nine engines, thirty-eight hose companies, seven hook and ladder companies, and two hydrant companies. Thirty-three of the engines were located below Twenty-eighth Street, and of those thirty were six and one-half inch cylinder engines, one ten inch, and two nine inch cylinder engines.

The introduction of the Croton water, while it had added vastly to the ability of the Department to answer the ends of its organization, had likewise suggested various improvements. Hose carts had been multiplied, and had proved to be in many cases advantageous substitutes for the fire engine. From the lightness of their construction, they could be run with much greater facility to points where they were suddenly required, and being able from the hydrants to throw water to the elevation of ordinary buildings, they were found to equal in efficiency for the extinguishment of fires the class of engines principally used before the introduction of the water, and then constituting in numbers the bulk of the engine force.

During the year ending August 1, 1845, there were three hundred and fifty alarms of fire, two hundred and sixty of which called for the employment of the Department and its apparatus, and ninety arose from trivial causes. The amount of property destroyed during the same period (excluding the fire on July 19 in New and Broad Streets) was four hundred and seventy-four thousand eight hundred and thirty dollars. In the months of May and June alone there were sixty-seven actual fires.

The following is a return of the engine, hose, hook and ladder, and hydrant companies; their apparatus, places of deposit, condition, etc., together with the names of the engineers and foremen, on September 22, 1845:

Cornelius V. Anderson, chief engineer; W. Wells Wilson, George Kerr, Alfred Carson, Charles Forrester, Philip B. White, Owen W. Brennan, James L. Miller, Henry J. Ockershausen, Aaron Hosford, assistant engineers.

ENGINE COMPANIES.

No. of Engine.	When Built.	Condition.	Foremen's Names.	Place of Deposit.
1	1827	Good.	Stephen T. Hoyt.	Clinton Square, foot of Duane Street.
5	1822	Good.	Hiram Arents.	40 Ann Street.
6	1839	Good.	H. C. Flander.	106 Reade Street.
7	1815	Condemned.	Alex. D. Renton.	6 Third Street.
8	1800	Good.	James Tyler.	91 Ludlow Street.
9	1824	Good.	Wm. M. Guest.	Corner 48th Street and 8th Avenue.
10	1824	Good.	John J. Terhune.	27th Street, near 10th Avenue.
11	1833	Good.	Abraham B. Purdy.	118 Wooster Street.
12	1828	Good.	John Gildersleeve.	74 Delancey Street.
13	1829	Good.	Danl. S. Weeks.	5 Duane Street.
14	1832	Good.	Hy. B. Venn.	Corner Church and Vesey.
15	1831	Good.	Nichls. T. Wilson.	49 Christie Street.
16	1825	Good.		152 20th Street.
18	1825	Good.	Peter A. Banta.	132 Amity Street.
19	1824	Condemned.	M. Eichells.	199 Christie.
20	1826	Good.	Horace F. Deen.	126 Cedar.
21	1835	Good.	Charles Daly.	5 Temple.
22	1840	Good.	Garrett B. Lane.	36 Chambers.
23	1833	Good.	Geo. McKinley.	Anthony (Worth), near Broadway.
24	1818	Good.	A. Lanson J. Brown.	255 17th Street.
25	1813	Good.	Arthur Gillender.	Bloomingdale Road and 24th Street.
29	1824	Good.	Thomas Lawrence.	14 Amos Street.
31	1823	Good.	Wm. H. Whitehead.	West Broadway, near Beach Street.
32	1838	Good.	Thos. Cooper.	101 Hester Street.
34	1823	Good.	David Broderick.	Christopher, near Hudson Street.
35	1827	Good.	Robt. Crawford.	121st Street, near 3d Avenue.
36	1836	Good.	John D. Brower.	Varick, near Vandam.
38	1842	Good.	John W. Schenck.	Ann, near Nassau.
41	1829	Good.	Joseph Hyde.	Corner Delancey and Attorney Streets.
42	1842	Good.	Hy. J. Mabbett.	88 Nassau Street.
43	1827	Good.	Danl. F. Tiemann.	Manhattanville.
44	1828	Good.	Isaac Sellick.	2d Street, near Lewis.
45	1837	Good.	Wm. Fulmer.	3d Avenue, Yorkville.
46	1835	Good.	Chas. H. Smith.	349 3d Avenue.
48	1827	Good.	Robt. Sutters.	152 20th Street.
49	1826	Good.	Epenetus Doughty.	126th Street, (Harlem).
50	1840	Good.	Wm. Holmes.	Harsenville (Bloomingdale Road).

HOOK AND LADDER COMPANIES.

No. of Engine.	When Built.	Condition.	Foremen's Names.	Place of Deposit.
1	1843	Good Order.	Wm. H. Geib.	34 Chambers Street.
2	1839	Good Order.	Theodore R. De Forrest.	24 Beaver Street.
3	1840	Good Order.	No Company.	Horatio, near Ninth Avenue.
4	1845	Good Order.	Henry Morris.	Eldridge, near Walker Street.
5	1844	Good Order.	Wm. S. Lacour.	Corner Delancey and Attorney Streets.
6	1838	Good Order.	James M. Murray.	Mercer Street (Firemen's Hall).
7	1837	Good Order.	Johnson Gillen.	126th Street.
10	1839	Good Order.	Wm. Ackerman.	3d Avenue, corner 85th Street.

HOSE COMPANIES.

No. of Engine.	When Built.	Condition.	Foremen's Names.	Place of Deposit.
1	1834	Good.	Wm. H. Heath.	5 Duane Street.
2	1838	Good.	James Hudson.	262 William Street.
3	1838	Good.	James Elkins.	202 Centre Street.
4	1845	Good.	D. M. Smith.	Corner Delancey and Attorney Streets.
5	1835	Good.	Reuben B. Mount.	Mercer Street (Firemen's Hall).
6	1845	Good.	Addison B. Wight.	Gouverneur Street, near East Broadway.
8	1836	Good.	John W. Moore.	74 Cedar.
9	—	Building.	Hy. S. Mansfield.	174 Mulberry Street.
10	1838	Good.	John P. Hopkins.	111 Roosevelt Street.
11	1835	Good.	John W. Stinman.	14 Amos Street.
12	1837	Good.	Lewis Carpenter.	244 17th Street.
13	1844	Good.	John H. Blake.	Mangin, near Delancey Stret.
14	1845	Good.	Hy. A. Burr.	2 Elizabeth Street.
15	1837	Good.	George Baker.	1 Eldridge Street.
16	1838	Rebuilding.	G. Callender.	24 Beaver Street.
17	1836	Good.	James Graydon.	40 5th Street.
18	1838	Good.	Thos. Minniette.	Franklin Market (Old Slip).
19	1838	Good.	Philip Lawrence.	Cortlandt Alley, near Canal Street.
20	1838	Good.	Genest M. Ottignon.	Ann Street, near Nassau Street.
21	1838	Good.	Franklin Waterbury.	Henry, near Catharine Street.
22	1838	Good.	Richd. H. Welch.	101 Hester.
23	1840	Good.	Wm. Cooper.	Horatio, near Ninth Avenue.
24	1839	Good.	Saml. Freer.	Spring Street, near Greenwich Street.
25	1845	Good.	James E. Fountain.	Anthony, near B'way.
26	1840	Good.	Joseph Casilear.	166 Monroe Street.
27	1836	Good.	Peter L. Seely.	Corner Church and Vesey.
28	1844	Good.	Nathan Lane.	32 Chambers Street.
29	1841	Good.	Rodman E. Field.	77 Willett Street.
31	1841	Good.	Theodore Tucker.	5 Walnut Street.
32	1842	Good.	James L. Haight.	6 3d Street.
33	1841	Good.	Hy. Colgrove.	Sullivan, near Prince.
34	1842	Good.	Jerh. Simonson.	10th Street, near Dry Dock.
35	1840	Good.	Wm. M. Cahoone.	199 Mercer Street.
36	1840	Good.	Francis B. O'Connor.	Henry, near Market Street.
38	1843	Good.	John Gillelan.	132 Amity.
39	1838	Good.	Wm. J. Thompson.	349 3d Avenue.
40	1843	Good.	John A. Cregier.	168 Barrow Street.
41	1843	Good.	Robt. Zabriskie.	67 Watts Street.

HYDRANT COMPANIES.

1	—	—	Thos. Nichols.	
2	—	—	Chas. H. Clayton.	

From the foregoing report it will be seen that the Department was possessed of thirty-five engines in good order, and two condemned; thirty-six hose carriages in good order, and two rebuilding; eight hook and ladder trucks, with forty-four ladders and forty-eight hooks; thirty-seven thousand two hundred feet of hose in good order, and two thousand five hundred feet of hose in ordinary, making in the whole thirty-nine thousand seven hundred feet of hose; thirty-seven engine companies, thirty-eight hose companies, seven hook and ladder companies, and two hydrant companies; one thousand five hundred and sixty-seven men.

About 1852 the Common Council adopted an ordinance dividing the city into three fire districts, and confining the apparatus and labors of the firemen to the district in which their apparatus were located. The object of the ordinance was to lessen the duties of the firemen, and to prevent the great destruction of the apparatus which was caused by their being uselessly dragged over the city at every alarm of fire. In consequence, however, of the imperfect alarms of fire, it was considered unsafe to enforce strictly the ordinance.

It was generally conceded that ten thousand dollars per annum was a low estimate of the expense of repairs to the fire apparatus.

During the year ending August 1, 1846, there had been two hundred and fifty-eight fires and one hundred and thirty-nine false alarms of fire. Many of the fires had no doubt been extinguished before the alarm had reached the nearest bell station, yet, in consequence of there being no means afforded of notifying the bell-ringers of the extinguishment of the fire, or that the alarm

FIREMAN'S CERTIFICATE.

was a false one, the bells were rung, and the firemen called unnecessarily from their business or their rest, thereby causing a loss of time and money to them and the apparatus dragged for miles over the city, creating a useless expense to the city. The Common Council, in November, 1846, in view of these facts authorized the introduction of Morse's magnetic telegraph into the Department.

Action was also taken in the matter at a meeting of the engineers and foremen held December 1, 1846, at which Mr. James L. Miller, of the engineers, offered the following:

Resolved, That a committee of five be appointed from this body to urge upon the members of the Common Council the propriety of adopting the plan recommended by the chief engineer, in relation to the magnetic telegraph for the use of the Fire Department.

The resolution was unanimously adopted, and the following committee appointed : James L. Miller, of the engineers, Lawrence Turnure, Hose 36; Abraham B. Purdy, Engine 11; James W. Barker, Hydrant 2; John A. Cregier, Hose 40.

The number of fires was increasing every succeeding year, and occurring, as many of them did, under very suspicious circumstances, it appeared necessary that their origin should be investigated. During the night of the second of May, 1846, within about six hours, ten fires occurred, all of which, except one (the *True Sun* building), commenced in stables, and were no doubt the work of design. Nothing but the extraordinary exertions of the firemen prevented several serious conflagrations.

Successive acts of the legislature had reduced the term of service of firemen until, on November 16, 1847, a law went into effect making the period of servitude five years.

The various engine, hose, and hook and ladder companies, were granted the use of the Croton water, on paying the expenses of the introduction.

During the years 1847-'8, the fire districts were laid out as follows :

First District.—The First Fire District shall embrace all that part of the city lying north of a line from the foot of North Moore Street to the Halls of Justice, and west of a line running from the Halls of Justice through Lafayette and Irving Places.

Second District.—The Second Fire District shall embrace all that part of the city lying east of the First District, and north of a line running from the Halls of Justice to the foot of Roosevelt Street.

Third District.—The Third Fire District shall embrace all that part of the city lying south of the First and Second Districts.

For the purpose of guiding the firemen more correctly to the fire, the districts are subdivided, and the district bells will be rung as follows. First District, first section, one stroke; First District, second section, two strokes; Second District, first section, three strokes; Second District, second section, four strokes; Third District, first section, five strokes; Third District, second section, six strokes.

For assistance, the signal will be the continual ringing of all district bells, except that on the City Hall, which will always ring the section in which the fire is raging.

Permission was granted (December 2, 1847,) to Hugh Downing and Royal E. House to costruct a line of telegraph, by setting posts in the ground, and extending from Fort Washington to the Bloomingdale Road, thence along said road to Sixth Avenue, to the fire station at Jefferson Market, thence to the fire stations at Centre and Essex Markets, thence to the City Hall, to the Merchants' Exchange. This permission was coupled with a proviso that Downing and House should put up the necessary wire and apparatus, and keep the same in order, and give the free and perpetual use of the invention for communicating alarms of fire from the City Hall to the different fire stations, and nstruct the different bellringers in the use of said invention, and commence and continue the communication themselves, until the bellringers were instructed, in consideration of which they received from the city the sum of five hundred dollars.

The salary of the chief engineer was increased to two thousand dollars July 8, 1848.

The resignation of C. V. Anderson, chief engineer of the Fire Department, on November 22, 1848, was accepted, to take effect from the time a successor was appointed.

Alfred Carson was appointed to the vacancy of chief engineer of the Fire Department on December 7, 1848, and Clark Vanderbilt appointed an assistant engineer in place of Alfred Carson, promoted.

The fire limits (Act March 7, 1849,) were extended so as to embrace all of the city situate to the southward of a line drawn one hundred feet north of Thirty-second Street, extending from east to Hudson River. All dwelling

OLD FIRE HATS.

houses, stores, storchouses, and all other buildings, after the passage of this act, to be built or erected within the fire limits, "shall be made and constructed of stone or brick, or other fire-proof materials, and shall be constructed with party or outside walls."

The Act (section 28) further provides:

"The duties and powers that were by law conferred upon the fire wardens   *   *   * prior to the passage of an act entitled 'An Act for the Establishment and Regulation of the Police of the City of New York,' passed May 4, 1844, as well as the duties and powers of fire wardens conferred upon the police by the said act, and by the act to amend the same, passed May 13, 1846, are hereby conferred upon the assistant engineers of the Fire Department, and upon their successors in office."

The duties appertaining to assistant engineers are detailed at length. Their compensation, the act declared, should be fixed by the Common Council, but should not exceed the sum of five hundred dollars per annum.

An office, denominated the Department of "Repairs and Supplies," was created by the legislature April 2, 1849, " which shall have cognizance of all repairs and supplies of and for roads and avenues, public pavements, repairs to public buildings, to fire engines and apparatus of the Fire Department, and the chief officer thereof shall be called the commissioner of repairs and supplies. There shall be four bureaus or branches in this department, and the chief officers shall be respectively denominated the ' superintendent of roads,' ' superinten- dent of repairs to public buildings,' ' superintendent of pavements,' and ' chief engineer of the Fire Department.' "

The salary of the water register in the Croton Aqueduct Department, July 21, 1849, was fixed at one thousand five hundred dollars per annum ; the salary of the deputy water register at one thousand dollars ; and the salary of the water purveyor, in Bureau of Pipes and Sewers, was placed at one thousand five hundred dollars per annum. In October following the assistant engineers of the Fire Department, for the performance of the duties of fire wardens, were paid five hundred dollars per annum each.

In the summer of 1849 the condition of the Fire Department was such as to merit the confidence of the authorities and of the community at large. For efficiency it had never been excelled, and the promptness, zeal and fidelity with which the members discharged their arduous and self-imposed duties drew forth the warmest encomiums from those in authority. The force at that time consisted of about one thousand six hundred men, three first-class engines, six second-class engines, twenty-four small engines, nine hook and ladder trucks, eighteen four-wheeled hose carriages, twenty-five two-wheeled hose carriages, and fifty thousand feet of hose. The city was divided into three districts, the lower one containing the greatest amount of valuable property, covering comparatively a small space of ground, while the limit of the other districts was bounded only by the extent of the island. That imposed upon the firemen in the upper districts an unusual and oppressive amount of labor, and it was consequently proposed, as being in accord with the best interests and the desires of the citizens residing in the upper part of the city, to form a new district, comprising all that part of the city north of Twenty-second Street.

A water tower was erected in this year on the rear of lots on the north side of Twenty-second Street, between First and Second Avenues, and a bell weighing eight thousand pounds placed therein.

A most appalling disaster occurred on the morning of February 4, 1850. A steam boiler exploded in a large building, 5 and 7 Hague Street, completely demolishing it, and burying beneath its ruins one hundred and twenty persons, of whom sixty-four were killed and forty-eight wounded. The Fire Department rendered invaluable service in rescuing the imperilled people and in saving adjoining property from destruction by the fire which ensued, for which services they were the recipients of the sincere thanks of the Common Council. Details of this awful calamity will be found elsewhere in this book.

The Board of Fire Wardens organized, in compliance with the laws for the more effectual prevention of fires, passed March 29, 1850, were sworn in on April 30, 1850. They were divided into three classes by lot, drawn by the president of the Fire Department, Zophar Mills, as follows :

Class One, to serve for the term of one year : John Kettleman, Charles L. Merritt, Samuel Waddell, and John B. Miller.

Class Two, to serve for the term of two years: John Rese, Thomas Boese, Franklin Waterbury, and Wm. Drew.

Class Three, to serve for the term of three years: Benjamin Cartwright, James Gilmore, Francis Hagadorn, and William B. Hays.

Their organization was completed on May 7, 1850.

The whole number of complaints of violations of the laws, made to the Board during the year ending April 1, 1851, amounted to six hundred and fifty-one. The number of old and dangerous buildings examined and reported to the chief engineer of the Fire Department as being exceedingly dangerous in case a fire should occur in either of them, forty-four. The quantity of gunpowder seized and delivered to the trustees of the Fire Department was one hundred and fifty-seven kegs and twenty cases, containing fifty canisters each.

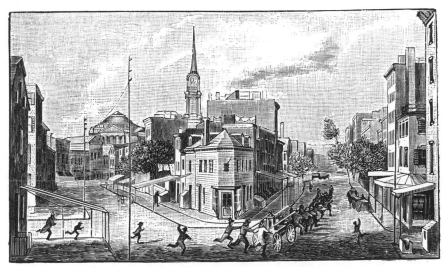

GOING TO A FIRE (CENTRE MARKET).

Although the disreputable element in the Fire Department had been gradually growing less for some years, owing to the judicious and unrelenting weeding-out process in operation, still even at this date (the Fall of 1850), there were disagreeable and emphatic evidences of the existence of a rowdy crowd, upon whom a writ of ejectment should be served. At a fire in Gansevoort Street on the afternoon of August 7, Engine Company No. 34 detached the hose of Hose Company No. 35. At a fire in University Place on August 14, Engine Company No. 4 hindered Hose Company No. 35 from attaching to a hydrant, and William Story, of No 4, made a personal assault on the foreman of the hose company. Hose Company No. 16 assaulted Engine Company No. 19, and injured their apparatus whilst they were going to a fire on the morning of August 16. Hose Company No. 13 was accused of several attacks on Hose Company No. 6; Hose Company No. 14 was reported for attacking Hose Company No. 26, and injuring their apparatus. Of these complaints the charge of Engine Company No. 19, implicating Hose Company No. 16, was the most serious, disclosing circumstances of the most aggravating character, and showing the premeditated nature of one of the most dastardly outrages that had ever disgraced the Fire Department. The apparatus of both companies were nearly new, having been in use only a short time. The carriage of No. 16 had been accidentally run into, upset and much damaged by the engine on August 14. Two evenings thereafter, as Engine Company No. 19 was proceeding up Third Avenue to an alarm of fire—doubtless raised for the express purpose—they were assailed by a large party of rowdies, several of their members seriously injured and driven from their engine, which was then wantonly upset and considerably damaged. Owing to threats made by persons connected with No. 16 there were good reasons for believing that the outrage had been perpetrated by them. Complaints were also made against Engine Company No. 16 by Engine Companies Nos. 24 and 34. An investigation resulted in the disbandment of No. 16, and the Common Council expressed their determination to arrest the spirit of rowdyism which seemed to be spreading in the Department, and which had so great a tendency to impair its character and efficiency.

A new fire district was formed January 5, 1850, and included all that portion of the city north of a line drawn through the center of Twenty-second Street, from the East to the North River. An additional assistant engineer was also elected.

The act of March 29, 1850, restored the office of fire warden, which had been abolished by the act of May 7, 1844, and declared, "that such fire wardens shall be twelve in number, and shall be selected from firemen of the city of New York, exempted by law from duty, at the time of such selection, whether then in active duty or not, and shall be appointed by the Common Council upon the nomination of the representatives of the Fire Department, by a majority of the votes cast by them for that purpose."

The fire wardens were divided into three classes (four in each class), by lot, to be drawn by the president of the Fire Department, or in case of his absence, by the vice-president, or by one of the trustees, at a time and place to be notified to said fire wardens. The classes were respectively numbered One, Two, and Three, according to the term of service of each. Class One served one year, Class Two served two years, Class Three served three years, and until their successors were appointed.

Their duties were defined substantially as follows: they were to inquire and examine into any and every violation of any of the provisions of the acts previously passed for the prevention of fires in the city of New York; to give, or cause to be given, a notice, in writing, signed by at least one of them, to the owner and builder respectively, of any such dwelling house, store, storehouse, building, ashhole, ashhouse, wooden shed, wooden building, or frame building, which should, after the passage of the act, be erected, altered, or enlarged. It was their duty also to report to the chief engineer the location of and particular circumstances attending any building constructed, or in the course of construction, deemed unsafe; also to report all cases where goods were improperly stored in any building, so as to hazard the lives of firemen, or where any building should from any cause have become unsafe. They should attend all fires in the fire districts respectively to which they were allotted, and to wear at such fires the usual fire cap, with the words "Fire Warden," and the number of such district, conspicuously painted thereon, in white, on a black ground. Their compensation, as fixed by the Common Council, was two hundred and fifty dollars per annum each.

This act also abolished the office of assistant engineer.

Chief engineer Alfred Carson, on September 30, 1850, submitted his yearly report to the Common Council, in compliance with the requirements of law. This report was charged with dynamite, and few of the leading city officials escaped unscathed, as its contents were scattered broadcast, hitting right and left, and sparing none. Members of the Common Council, police justices, aldermen, ward politicians, prominent firemen, and police captains, were fiercely and ruthlessly assailed. Chief Carson, to do him justice, seemed at least to have the courage of his convictions, but his discretion and judgment cannot be commended. That there were abuses, and very serious ones, in the Department, which called for remedial measures, none will deny. Many of these abuses struck at the very root of all semblance of authority and discipline in the Department, but they were the inherited development of a long number of

WASHINGTON'S RESIDENCE.

Franklin House, head of Cherry Street, 1790, as it appeared in 1850.

years of misgovernment and mismanagement. No one man or official was responsible, nor could the evils complained of by Chief Carson be remedied by the most enthusiastic reformer or powerful official effort, except by the most revolutionary method. In fact, these abuses had grown up gradually, until they had become firmly rooted in the system and become a part, and a controlling part, of it. Firemen had inherited prejudices and resentments, and had come to regard themselves as possessed of exceptional privileges, and a large portion of the community, by their acquiescence or active support, helped to confirm them in this belief. The times, generally, viewed from the better ordered standpoint of the present day, were sadly out of joint. There seemed to be a less regard for the law, and the administrators of justice often dispensed it with a very partial hand. Ward politics dominated the bench, and moulded all public action. It was a time when mob rule was a power in the city. We had then no police force worthy of the name, and the rougher element had no wholesome terror of the law, for even if arraigned for trial the rough who had committed himself was sure to find sympathy for his misdeeds among the politicians who controlled primary elections, a class from which were recruited the police justices, and even higher judicial dignitaries. These police justices, it may be noted, had had for a long time previously control of the police force, and they held their tenure of office more by protecting the turbulent element than by enforcing the laws and protecting law-abiding citizens. The firemen were a powerful and representative body of men. In pluck and daring we may not look upon their like again. They were both feared and respected. They could extinguish the political ambition of the most popular citizen as readily as they could put out the light of a blazing tar barrel. Their influence was far-reaching, and whenever they saw fit to indulge in a family jar, it was, as a rule, considered the safer course to let them severely alone and settle their difficulties among themselves.

Therefore, Chief Carson proved to be a reformer in a non-reforming age. No one wanted his reforming nostrums, or cared a straw about his charges, recommendations, or complaints. He was whistling against the wind, and was voted a crank. If Mr. Carson, it was argued, didn't like things as he found them, why did he accept office? The Department was no better or worse than it had been under his predecessor, who was a man of sterling integrity and strict official honor; but the intrepid—if bumptious—firemen found nothing to complain of; then why should Chief Carson? The chief's focal point of observation was sadly at variance with that of his colleagues and official superiors. There was a wide divergence in their views on these matters.

Mr. Carson's indictment was voluminous, and contained any number of counts. He found fault, for instance, with the method of appointing the fire-ringers from the police force, complained of their "gross neglect," their "utter irresponsibility," to the chief engineer, and suggested that the appointing power and control of these functionaries be taken out of the hands of the mayor and chief of police. He cited aggravated cases of neglect of duty of those fireringers, "which change and neglect," says the report, "not only shamefully jeopardizes property worth millions of dollars, but cause the firemen much unnecessary labor, through false alarms at the towers, and often lulling a whole district in a false security by striking the bells wrong, and giving no alarm when fire actually exists." The delay in the repair of the engine and hose houses was another source of unhappiness to the troubled soul of the censorious chief. The superintendent of public buildings, who had charge of such matters, came in for his share of the general fault finding, and Mr. Carson, as a remedy, petitioned for a transfer of the repairs and alterations of the different engine, hose, and hook and ladder houses, to the chief engineer.

Another evil against which the official soul of Chief Carson was up in arms, and against which he inveighed in the most emphatic and forcible terms, was "the outrageous spirit of rowdyism of certain clubs of desperate fighting men, called 'Short Boys,' 'Old Maid's Boys,' 'Rock Boys,' etc., organized after the mode of the clubs of London and Paris, whose members were shot down like dogs by the firemen of the latter city, and finally suppressed, as were the clubs in London some years since by the city authorities." Chief Carson was especially vehement in his references to the conduct of these "clubs." "These clubs," he repeats, "make deliberate and bloody attacks on our firemen while going to and returning from fires, destroying the apparatus, and often, by stratagem, putting certain companies in collision with each other, individual members against each other, and creating in every way endless broil and confusion in the Department. * * * I have had many of these villains," the chief goes on to say, "arrested for upsetting our engines, cutting the hose, beating our firemen almost to death, etc., but they were no sooner in prison than the captains of police, the aldermen, and judges of police, would discharge them, to commit fresh attacks on the firemen the following night, and while reeking with a terrible revenge for their arrest and temporary confinement." Some of these "club" men Chief Carson dubs "brutal looking monsters." * * * "The Old Maid's Boys," continues the chief, growing vehement, "a fearful and most deadly club, seized Hose No. 14, ran up alongside of Hose No. 26, attacked the firemen, upset the carriage, etc., doing considerable injury to the carriage." "But why," he asks, desperately, "recount these daily and daring outrages, when these bloodthirsty creatures are thus encouraged and liberated by aldermen, on whose conscientious watch-

fulness and unsullied integrity the people rely for the incarceration and severe punishment of these abandoned and heartless fiends."

The remainder of this bulky report is mainly taken up with the troubles existing among certain inharmonious bodies of fire laddies. From this it appears that William M. Tweed, the one time boss, and then foreman of Engine Company No. 6, was expelled for lead-

OLD LEATHER FIRE BUCKETS.

ing in an attack on Hose Company No. 31, and his company suspended for three months. The Common Council, however, to the deep disgust of Chief Carson, failed to ratify this sentence, and Mr. Tweed was let off with a suspension of three months. These Chief Carson calls "revolting facts."

There were in the Department twenty-five engines in good order, three in ordinary condition, and six building; thirty-two hose carriages in good order, thirteen indifferent, and two building; six hook and ladder trucks in good order, two indifferent, and one building; with forty-five ladders and seventy-four hooks; forty-five thousand three hundred feet of hose in good order, and nine thousand six hundred and fifty feet in ordinary condition, making in all fifty-five thousand nine hundred and fifty feet of hose; also thirty-four engine companies, forty-seven hose companies, nine hook and ladder companies, and one thousand eight hundred and ninety-eight men.

During the year ending August 1, 1850, there had been two hundred and eighty-nine fires, by which the loss or damage to buildings amounted to two hundred and seventy-eight thousand seven hundred and twenty-five dollars, including fourteen thousand dollars by the explosion in Hague Street, and in stock, furniture, etc., to one million sixteen thousand three hundred and sixty-eight dollars, including seventy thousand dollars by the explosion in the Hague Street fire.   There had been one hundred and ninety-two alarms.

By ordinance of November 25, 1850, the city was divided into eight fire districts.   The First District comprised all that part of the city lying north of Twenty-second Street and east of Sixth Avenue; the Second District comprised all that part of the city lying north of Twenty-second Street and west of Sixth Avenue; the Third District comprised all that part of the city bounded and contained as follows: Beginning at the foot of North Moore Street on the North River, and extending easterly in a straight line to the corner of Leonard and Church Streets, thence northerly in a straight line to the corner of Eighth Avenue and Twenty-second Street, thence westerly along Twenty-second Street to the North River, thence southerly along the North River to the place of beginning.   The Fourth District was bounded as follows: Beginning at the corner of Leonard and Church Streets, running thence northerly in a straight line to the corner of Eighth Avenue and Twenty-second Street, thence easterly along Twenty-second Street to Lexington Avenue, thence southerly in a straight line to the corner of Elm and Leonard Streets, and thence westerly in a straight line to the corner of Church and Leonard Streets.   The Fifth District was bounded as follows: Commencing at the corner of Elm and Leonard Streets, and running thence northerly in a straight line to the corner of Lexington Avenue and Twenty-second Street, thence easterly along Twenty-second Street to the East River, thence southerly and along the East River to Fourteenth Street, thence southwesterly in a straight line to the corner of Leonard and Orange Streets, thence westerly in a straight line to the place of beginning.   The Sixth District: Beginning at the corner of Leonard and Orange Streets, and running thence easterly in a straight line to the foot of Market Street, on the East River, thence along the East River to Fourteenth Street, thence southwesterly in a straight line to the place of beginning.   The Seventh District: Beginning at the foot of Market Street on the East River, and running thence westerly in a straight line to the corner of Leonard and Elm Streets, thence southerly along a straight line, intersecting Wall Street at the junction of Nassau, Wall, and Broad Streets, and continuing through the Battery to the North River.   The Eighth District: Beginning at the foot of North Moore Street, on the North River, and running thence easterly in a straight line to the corner of Leonard and Elm Streets, thence southerly along a straight line, intersecting Wall Street at the junction of Nassau, Wall, and Broad Streets, and continuing through the Battery to the North River.

In case of fire in the First District, the signal shall be one stroke from the alarm bells; in the Second District, two strokes; in the Third District, three strokes; in the Fourth District, four strokes; Fifth District, five strokes; Sixth District, six strokes; Seventh District, seven strokes; Eighth District, eight strokes.

On the twenty-fifth of January, 1851, a resolution was approved by the mayor, directing the commissioner of repairs and supplies to contract with Richard H. Bull for the immediate completion of the telegraph wire and apparatus to all the fire alarm stations in the city, and the sum of six hundred dollars was appropriated to pay for the same.

By the act of July 11, 1851, the heads of departments, except the Croton Aqueduct Board, were elected every three years.   The heads of departments nominated, and by and with the consent of the Board of Aldermen, appointed the heads of bureaus in their several departments, except the chamberlain, the receiver of taxes, and the chief engineer of the Fire Department. The chief of the Fire Department "shall be elected in the same manner as is now or may hereafter be prescribed by law."

The strength of the Department on August 1, 1851, was twenty-six engines in good order, three ordinary, four building, and one rebuilding; forty-one hose carriages in good order, two ordinary, and six building; six hook and ladder trucks in good order, and two ordinary; forty ladders, and eighty-five hooks; forty-three thousand three hundred feet of hose in good order, fifteen thousand two hundred feet ordinary; thirty-four engine companies, forty-nine hose companies, eight hook and ladder companies, and three hydrant companies. There were two thousand two hundred and eleven men in the Department; if the companies were full there would have been two thousand eight hundred and eighty-eight men.

During the year ending August 1, 1851, there had been three hundred and nineteen fires, by which the loss on buildings amounted to one hundred and fifty-nine thousand four hundred a n d fifty-five dollars, and on wares five hundred and forty-eight thousand a n d twenty-three dollars, making the loss by fire seven hundred and seven

FIRE HYDRANTS.

thousand four hundred and seventy-eight dollars. There had been two-hundred and thirty-eight alarms. These facts show an increase of thirty fires and forty-six alarms over the preceding year, but, at the same time, a decrease of five hundred and eighty-seven thousand six hundred and twenty-five dollars in the destruction of property.

The fire companies in the northern section of the city had long suffered great inconvenience for the want of a proper alarm. For their relief an iron tower was built on Thirty-third Street. A lot was procured for the erection of an iron tower in Spring Street, near Varick, which was much needed. The tower on Centre Street was much dilapidated and insecure, with a bell weighing only four thousand pounds. During a high wind, or an alarm, the tower would vibrate in a very noticeable manner. Its demolition was recommended, and a new tower to be put up on the lot where Engine No. 9 was located on Marion Street. The Jefferson Market bell tower was destroyed by fire on the twenty-ninth of July, and an iron tower was erected in its stead.

The connection of the bell towers with Fire Headquarters by telegraph was completed in the summer of 1851. Instantly the effectiveness of the connections was recognized, as the firemen were saved much unnecessary labor by the prevention of the numerous false alarms which had theretofore misled them.

The report of Chief Engineer Alfred Carson in this connection is worth recording.

"The entire (telegraphic) apparatus," says Mr. Carson, "is necessarily of very delicate construction, and must be used with great care by the bellringers, or it at once becomes utterly inoperative. And it grieves me to inform you (the Common Council) that the telegraphic apparatus is often seriously injured, either by the bellringers themselves, or by some of the numerous friends who unceasingly visit them, who often use it without occasion, simply to gratify their curiosity, thereby misleading and creating general confusion at the bell towers throughout the city, and, of course, throughout the Department."

The fire limits of the city, in the winter of 1851, were extended from Thirty-second Street to Fifty-second Street.

In January, 1854, Engine Companies Nos. 1,2, 4, 5, 6, 7, 8, 9, 11, 12, 13, 14, 15, 16, 17, 18, 19, 20, 21, 22, 23, 24, 25, 26, 28, 29, 30, 31, 32, 33, 34, 35, 38, 41, 42, 43, 44, 46, 48, and 49, Hose Companies Nos. 1, 2, 3, 4, 5, 6, 7, 8, 9, 10, 11, 12, 13, 14, 15, 16, 17, 18, 19, 20, 21. 22, 23, 24, 25, 26, 27, 28, 29, 31, 33, 34, 35, 36, 37, 38, 39, 40, 41, 42, 43, 44, 45, 46, 47, 48, 49, 50, 51, 52, 53, and 54, Hook and Ladder Companies Nos. 1, 2, 3, 4, 5, 6, 7, 8, 9, and 11, were in possession of houses in good condition. The houses of Engine Companies Nos. 10 and 45, Hose Company No. 30, and of Hook and Ladder Company No. 10 were in a dilapidated condition, but yet occupied by them. The apparatus of all the companies were in good order, except those of Engines Nos. 20 and 36. Engine Companies Nos. 3, 27, 36, 37, and 40 ; Hose Companies Nos. 32, 55, and 56, and Hook and Ladder Companies Nos. 12 and 13 had no locations, except that Engines Nos. 36 and 37, and Hose Companies Nos. 55 and 56 were doing duty from temporary houses. Engine Company No. 39 occupied a temporary house, but a building was in process of erection for them in Thirty-first Street, near Seventh Avenue, and the engine in use by No. 9 was to be appropriated to their use.

It was made the duty of the policemen on duty, whenever an alarm of fire had been raised during the night, to give notice thereof to the several firemen residing within their respective beats, at their places of residence, who, in accordance with the fire regulations, ought to turn out on occasion of such alarm. Each fireman was required to deliver to the captain of police for the district in which he resided a statement of his name and place of residence, and the captains should furnish the several policemen under their charge with the names and residences of firemen residing within the respective beats of such policemen.

All third class engines were allowed in future ten additional men, so as to make their full complement forty.

The chief of police was authorized and required (Act, April 16, 1852) to make an investigation into the origin of every fire occurring in the city, and for that purpose he was invested with the same powers and jurisdiction as were possessed by the police justices.

At any alarm of fire it was the duty of the captains of police (Act. April 13, 1853) nearest the scene of conflagration forthwith to proceed to the same, with the reserve corps of their command, to be diligent in preserving order and in protecting property. The chief of police should also repair to the scene of the fire, and, with the assistance of the police force, use every exertion to save and protect property, and remove or cause to be removed, all idle and suspicious persons from the vicinity of the fire.

The hydrant companies were decreed to be of very little service, and it was believed that they might be dispensed with without detriment to the Department.

During the year 1853 several extremely violent fights took place between fire companies. Pistols and other dangerous weapons had been brought into requisition, and the apparatus upset and nearly destroyed. The worst of these encounters were between Engine Companies Nos. 6, 18, and 44, and Hose Companies Nos. 16 and 17. Yet no punishment had been inflicted, although the facts had been duly reported to the Common Council, who, instead of investigating the circumstances, allowed the matter to lie for several months, and then directed the chief engineer to return the apparatus which he had taken from them. If these acts of insubordination had received proper attention, and the persons who were found guilty of any serious offense were expelled forthwith, disbanding the companies to which they were attached, and transferring the unoffending members to other companies, the number of companies would have been reduced (for which the authorities had been clamoring), and the Department would have got rid of the persons who were bringing reproach upon it.

OLD FIRE HAT AND FRONTS.

In July, 1853, the chief engineer, in compliance with a resolution of the Common Council, reported that he was quite satisfied of the great utility of the fire-alarm telegraph system introduced by Mr. Robinson, and he counseled the purchase of it. He had seen the immense advantages of it in regulating the striking of the several bells, as by means of it the alarms were always correctly transmitted, and at the same moment, from the station first discovering a fire to each and every one of the other stations. The apparatus could therefore be taken with greater dispatch to the vicinity of fires, and the labor of the firemen and the wear of the apparatus were materially lessened.

In the reports of the chief engineer for the years 1851, 1852, and 1853, the official action and integrity of the Common Council were brought into question, and the chief engineer indulged in epithets towards the members couched in language so unbecoming his position and so gross as to induce the belief that designing men were using him as a medium for venting their spleen upon the authorities. That was more than the aldermanic soul could endure, and Mr. Carson's decapitation was contemplated.

Soon petitions began to roll into the aldermanic chambers from various engine and hose companies, asking for the removal of Chief Carson. The Board of Aldermen, therefore, felt called upon to take action, and they passed a resolution at a meeting held on September 15, 1853, designed to ingloriously put an end to the career of the chief. This was referred to the Board of Assistant Aldermen for their concurrence, by whom it was shelved, and it never again saw the light of day.

By an act of the legislature, passed July 18, 1853, the salaries of the fire wardens were fixed at five hundred dollars per annum, instead of two hundred and fifty dollars, which they were in receipt of theretofore.

In December, 1853, the sum of twenty-four thousand eight hundred and eleven dollars was appropriated for a new building for the use of the Fire Department, to be called "Firemen's Hall," located in Mercer Street, between Prince and Houston Streets, of which more is said elsewhere.

The following table shows the population of New York City for a number of years:

Year.	Population.	Year.	Population.	Year.	Population.
1674,	3,000	1746,	11,717	1820,	123,706
1678,	3,430	1756,	13,040	1825,	166,000
1703,	4,436	1771,	21,863	1830,	203,007
1712,	5,840	1786,	23,614	1835,	270,089
1723,	7,243	1790,	33,131	1840,	312,710
1731,	8,622	1800,	60,489	1845,	371,223
1737,	10,664	1810,	95,519	1850,	515,394

ANCIENT METHOD OF FIRE EXTINGUISHING.
[From Fireman's Certificate, 1789.]

CHAPTER X.

ABOLISHMENT OF THE VOLUNTEERS.

1854—1865—Creation of the Board of Fire Department Commissioners.—Peter Cooper's Plan.—How Abuses had crept in.—Charges in the Newspapers.—Investigation held.—Location of Companies. —Burning of the Cupola of the City Hall.—Exit the Old Volunteers.

IN 1854 the Fire Department of New York was composed of nearly four thousand citizens, who devoted their time and exertions to the public service without any reward except the satisfaction derived from the faithful discharge of their duty as citizens. It was conceded that that branch of the civil service possessed the capacity for government in itself at least equal to that of the citizen soldiery who were left in the free and full management and control of their own internal affairs. Besides it was seen that the system of administering the affairs of the Fire Department through the Common Council was burdensome to the latter body, interfering with its more legitimate business, and had operated in experience unfairly and injuriously to the Department, greatly impairing its efficiency. An ordinance was therefore introduced creating a "Board of Fire Department Commissioners," composed of three persons from each of the eight sections of the fire districts, and three from that portion of the city known as the Twelfth Ward, two from each district being exempt firemen, and the third one of the active firemen of the city. The chief engineer should be an *ex officio* member of the board and all its committees.

The venerable Peter Cooper gave some attention to the prevention and extinguishment of fires, and communicated with the Common Council in that respect, February, 1854. The plan and principle which he advocated were designed to make the performance of fire duty a dollar-and-cent interest to some three-quarters of all the officers in the employ of the city government. He recommended the placing a boiler-iron tank, thirty feet in height, on the top of the existing reservoir on Murray Hill. That tank was to be filled, and kept full of water, by a small steam engine. Further, he proposed that the City Hall should be raised an additional story and covered with an iron tank that would hold some ten feet of water, the outside of the tank to be made to represent a cornice around the building. With that greater head and supply of water always at command and ready for connection with the street mains, the moment a signal was given from any police station it was apparent that all the hydrants could be made efficient to raise water over the tops of the highest houses in the city. Also he would cause to be placed in every street, at convenient distances, a small cart containing some three hundred feet of hose. These carts should be so light that one man could draw them to the nearest hydrant to the fire, and bring water on the fire in the shortest possible time. With that arrangement he proposed to make it the interest of every man in the police to watch incendiaries and thieves, and to use every possible effort to extinguish fires as soon as they had occurred.

Mr. Cooper had presented a similar programme twelve years previously.

In the spring of 1854 there were but one first-class engine in the Department, No. 38, nine and one-half inch cylinder; four second-class, Nos. 14, 21, 22, and 42; and three third-class, Nos. 5, 13, and 20. Nos. 14, 21, and 42 were each eight and one-half inch cylinder; No. 22, eight inch; Nos. 13, 7, 5, and 20, each six and one-half inches. The complement of men allowed to each company was as follows:

Engine No. 38 (first-class Philadelphia style), nine and one-half inch cylinder, sixty men; No. 22 (second-class piano), eight inch cylinder, fifty men; No. 42 (second-class piano), eight and one-half inch cylinder, fifty men; No. 14 (second-class Philadelphia), eight and one-half inch cylinder, seventy men; No.' 21 (second-class Philadelphia), eight and one-half inch cylinder, seventy men; No. 5 (third-class New York style), six and one-half inch cylinder, forty men; No. 13 (third-class New York improved), seven inch cylinder, forty men; No. 20 (third-class New York improved), six and one-half inch cylinder, forty men.

The chief engineer was elected, every three years, by the members of the Fire Department, by ballot. The election for this office took place on the first Tuesday after the first Monday in February, 1854, and thereafter every succeeding three years.

The chief engineer was ordered not to receive any annual returns from companies but such as had conformed to section first of the ordinance, passed June 22, 1842, relative to the Fire Department, as fol-

OLD JEFFERSON MARKET FIRE TOWER.

lows: "The Fire Department of the city of New York shall consist of a chief engineer, assistant engineers, fire-enginemen, hose men, hook and ladder and hydrant men, who shall be citizens of the United States, of the age of twenty-one years and upwards;" and in future to receive no return of members to fill the vacancies in companies unless the foreman and secretary had made affidavit that such persons were citizens of the United States, and twenty-one years of age and upwards.

The Common Council instructed the mayor to appoint three persons to act as bellringers at each of the different alarm districts, such persons to be selected from among the exempt firemen. The bellringers, so appointed, received as remuneration for their services the sum of five hundred dollars each per annum, and were subject to removal by the mayor for misdemeanor or negligence of duty.

As foreshadowed by the action of the Board of Aldermen in their attempt to dismiss Carson, Chief Engineer, from office, and notwithstanding that numerous petitions from fire companies had requested such action, seemingly justifying it, there was yet a dormant feeling of dissatisfaction which manifested itself only after the inauguration of the new Council in 1854. In February of that year a committee of representatives of the Fire Department, Carlisle Norwood, D. Milliken, and Henry W. Belcher, presented a petition to the new Board, setting forth that during the preceding three or four years serious and gross abuses had crept into the Department by which not only its morals had been impaired, but its efficiency and discipline had been destroyed. The great majority of the firemen were of every vocation, the merchant, mechanic, artisan, from the professional and laboring classes; and that majority in point of character and respectability would challenge comparison with any other institution in the country. Their aim was to discharge the self-imposed duty with fidelity, and to elevate the character of their body; but to accomplish that they should be sustained by the authorities. That support had not been accorded for the preceding few years; for owing to a personal difficulty between the head of the Department and the municipal government, the latter had by every means in their power set at defiance the authority of the former, disregarded his recommendations, and thus given every encouragement to the riotous and disorderly to carry out their infamous and wicked designs without restraint. The result was that the Department which should have been the pride and the boast of the city had become a by-word and reproach; charges of a heinous nature were freely made against some of its members through the public prints, which want of power on the part of the Department prevented them from investigating.

JEFFERSON ASSEMBLY ROOMS.

In connection with this matter a special meeting of the representatives of the Fire Department was held in Firemen's Hall on February 13, 1854, at which resolutions were adopted, stating that among the causes which had mainly brought about the deplorable condition of the Department had been prominently the flagrant conduct of the city government, which, instead of endeavoring to preserve the discipline and character of the Department, had done all in their power to destroy them by the indiscriminate creation of firemen, the restoration to membership of men expelled for bad conduct, the encouragement and license given to the riotous and disorderly by their neglect to punish them when brought before them; in a word, by the wholesale abuse of their authority to gratify personal ends and political purposes.

On the fourth of May, 1854, it was stated in a daily newspaper in regard to the Broadway catastrophe, that the chief engineer testified that within his knowledge a gang of men, wearing the garb of firemen, attended fires for the purpose of stealing; that he had known members of the Fire Department to be caught thieving; that in one case of a member expelled for stealing at a fire the Common Council had reinstated him; that a member, then foreman of an engine company, had been thus expelled and reinstated; that sometimes persons had attended fires dressed as firemen though not members of the Department; and that, in his judgment, more than one-half the fires that had occurred were the work of incendiaries.

The Common Council requested the chief engineer to inform them whether he had been correctly reported. He replied, on May 15, 1854, that if the evidence had been fully and correctly reported their inquiry would have been unnecessary. His reference to the reinstatement of persons expelled for stealing applied to the Common Council of 1853 and not to that of 1854. Attempts had been made to establish the fact that some of the persons killed were in the building for the purpose of stealing instead of extinguishing the fire, and that clothing recognized by the proprietors of the store as belonging to their stock was found upon some of the bodies. That was published far and wide, and made the occasion of severe comments on the Fire Department. The evidence adduced, however, showed that no clothing whatever from the establishment was found upon any of the bodies, except such as was placed under and upon them by their comrades after rescuing them from the ruins, in order that they might be carried to the hospital as comfortably as possible.

The following complement of men was allowed the different engine, hose, and hook and ladder companies, viz.: First class engines, sixty men; second class engines, fifty men; third class engines, forty men; hose companies, twenty-five men; hook and ladder companies, forty men. Hydrant companies to remain the same as previously.

The strength of the Department in September, 1854, consisted of thirty-three engines in good order, seven ordinary, and eight building; forty-three hose carriages in good order, seven ordinary, and six building; nine hook and ladder trucks in good order, two ordinary, and one building. The trucks were supplied with all necessary implements. There were in use forty thousand six hundred and fifty feet of good hose, and fifteen thousand eight hundred feet ordinary; forty-eight engine companies, fifty-seven hose companies, fourteen hook and ladder companies, and four hydrant companies; two thousand nine hundred and fifty-five men. If all the companies were full, there would have been four thousand four hundred and eighty men.

During the year ending September, 1854, there had been three hundred and eighty-five fires, with a loss on buildings of eight hundred and twenty-seven thousand and twelve dollars, and on wares two million and seventy-three thousand two hundred and seventy-two dollars. There had been two hundred and twenty-one additional alarms, mostly caused by burning chimneys, spirit-gas explosions, etc., while for the residue no real cause could be ascertained. The loss was large compared with former years. Doubtless one-half the fires were the result of incendiarism, and one-quarter of carelessness.

Captain Ditchett, of the Fourth Ward police, proposed for the better prevention of personal injury and loss of life, and of interference with the firemen while on duty at a fire, that policemen be stationed with flags by day and lighted signals at night at proper distances on the streets leading to fires, and all persons passing, or who persisted in remaining within, the lines, should be arrested, unless they had business there. To adopt that plan it would be necessary to procure a badge for the Department, to be worn by members at fires when not in fire dress; and a law should be passed making it a penal offense for any person to wear the badge, or other insignia of the Department, except firemen, which would act as a salutary check on rowdies and thieves prowling about fires, and enable the firemen to discharge their duties more effectively.

Following are the names of officials and the locations of company quarters for the years 1854-'5:

Alfred Carson, chief engineer; office, 21 Elizabeth Street.

Assistant Engineers.—Michael Eichell, John A. Cregier, Moses Jackson,

These are to Certify that William E. Bishop is pursuant to Law nominated and appointed
One of the Firemen of the City of New York

John S. Giles Treasurer Fire Dept.   D. T. Valentine Clerk Common Council
February 1st 1849

FIREMAN'S CERTIFICATE.

Henry H. Howard, Peter N. Cornwell, John Baulch, John Decker, John C. Oliver, William Simpson, John H. Brady, William H. Ackerman.

Fire Wardens.—Thomas Boese, John Reese, William B. Hays, Henry Lewis, John T. Harding, Isaac T. Redfield, John B. Miller, William Wessels, John Crossin, David Theall, Floyd S. Gregg, Charles L. Merritt, John Lynes, clerk. Meet once a month. Office, 21 Elizabeth Street.

LOCATION OF ENGINE COMPANIES, ETC.

Name.	No.	Location.
Hudson,	1,	West Forty-seventh Street, near Eighth Avenue.
Excelsior,	2,	21 Henry Street.
Broderick,	3,	(No location.)
Niagara,	4,	Mercer, near Amity Street.
Protection,	5,	61 Ann Street.
Americus,	6,	Henry, near Gouverneur Street.
Lexington,	7,	East Twenty-fifth Street, near Second Avenue.
Manhattan,	8,	71 Ludlow Street.

Name.	No.	Location.
United States,	9,	47 Marion Street.
Water Witch,	10,	West Twenty-seventh Street, near Tenth Avenue.
Oceanus,	11,	Wooster, near Prince Street.
Knickerbocker,	12,	East Fiftieth Street, near Third Avenue.
Eagle,	13,	5 Duane Street.
Columbian,	14.	Church, near Vesey Street,
Peterson,	15,	49 Christie Street.
Croton,	16,	165 West Twentieth Street.
East River,	17,	Mangin, near Delancey Street.
Atlantic,	18,	Thirteenth Street, near Avenue C.
Lafayette,	19,	199 Christie Street.
Washington,	20,	3 Temple Street.
Fulton,	21,	Anthony Street, near Broadway.
Protector,	22,	Chambers, corner Centre Street.
Waverley,	23,	223 Twelfth Street.
Jackson,	24,	West Seventeenth Street, near Ninth Avenue.
Cataract,	25,	Broadway, near East Twenty-sixth Street.
Jefferson,	26,	6 Third Street.
Fort Washington,	27,	Carmansville.
Pacific,	28,	Fourth Avenue, corner East Twenty-seventh Street
Guardian,	29,	14 Amos Street.
Tompkins,	30,	East Twenty-second Street, near Second Avenue.
Hope,	31,	West Broadway, near Beach Street.
Bunker Hill,	32,	101 Hester Street.
Black Joke,	33,	Fifty-eighth Street, near Broadway.
Howard,	34,	Christopher, near Hudson Street.
Columbus,	35,	Third Ave., near One Hundred and Twenty-first St.
Equitable,	36,	Broadway, corner Sixty-ninth Street.
Tradesmen,	37,	Fifty-ninth Street, near Third Avenue.
Southwark,	38,	28 Ann Street.
Lady Washington,	40,	Crosby, near Broome Street.
Clinton,	41,	Attorney, corner Delancey Street.
Empire,	42,	2 Murray Street.
Manhattan,	43,	Manhattanville.
Live Oak,	44,	Houston, near Cannon Street.
Aurora,	45,	Eighty-fifth Street, corner Third Avenue.
Relief,	46,	Third Avenue, near East Twenty-sixth Street.
	47,	Yorkville.
Mazeppa,	48,	West Twenty-fourth Street, near Seventh Avenue
Pocahontas.	49,	One Hundred and Twenty-sixth Street, Harlem.

HOSE COMPANIES.

Name	No.	Location
Eagle,	1,	Madison, near Pike Street.
Knickerbocker,	2,	5 Duane Street.
Independence,	3,	211 Hester Street.
Marion,	4,	Attorney, near Delancey Street.
New York,	5,	Fireman's Hall, Mercer Street.
Croton,	6,	23½ Gouverneur Street.
Ringgold,	7,	East Thirteenth Street, near Fourth Avenue.
City,	8,	75 Cedar Street.
Columbian,	9,	174 Mulberry Street.
Liberty,	10,	Dover, near Pearl Street.
Gulick,	11,	14 Amos Street.
Washington,	12,	51 Horatio Street.
Jackson,	13,	Mangin, near Delancey Street.
Atlantic,	14,	19 Elizabeth Street.
Fulton,	15,	1½ Eldridge Street.
Tompkins,	16,	Houston, corner First Street.

Name.	No.	Location.
Clinton,	17,	40 Fifth Street.
Franklin,	18,	28 Beaver Street.
American,	19,	52 Greene Street.
Humane,	20,	30 Ann Street.
Hudson,	21,	Foot of Duane Street.
Phenix,	22,	101 Hester Street.
Perry,	23,	51 Horatio Street.
National,	24,	315 Spring Street.
United States,	25,	Anthony Street, near Broadway.
Rutgers,	26,	Norfolk, near Division Street.
Neptune,	27,	106 Reade Street.
Pearl,	28,	Chambers, corner Centre Street.
Continental,	29,	77 Willett Street.
Laurel,	30,	West Twenty-seventh Street, near Tenth Avenue.
Putnam,	31,	5 Jackson Street.
Index,	32,	West Forty-eighth Street, near Eighth Avenue.
Warren,	33,	Sullivan, near Prince Street.
Star,	34,	Tenth Street, near Dry Dock.
Fifteenth Ward,	35,	199 Mercer Street,
Oceana,	36,	205 Madison Street.
Madison,	37,	Broadway, near East Twenty-sixth Street.
Amity,	38,	132 Amity Street.
Metropolitan,	39,	Third Avenue, near East Twenty-sixth Street.
Empire,	40,	142 Barrow Street.
Alert,	41,	67 Watts Street.
Mazeppa,	42,	West Thirty-fourth Street, near Tenth Avenue.
Pioneer,	43,	One Hundred and Twenty-third St., cor. Third Ave.
Washington Irving,	44,	West Thirty-first Street, near Seventh Avenue.
Red Jacket,	45,	East Thirty-third Street, near Third Avenue.
America,	46,	83 Nassau Street.
Howard,	47,	Fourth Street, near Avenue D.
Americus,	48,	Eighty-fifth Street, corner Third Avenue.
Lady Washington,	49,	126 Cedar Street.
Corlies,	50,	10½ Mott Street.
Relief,	51,	East Fiftieth Street, near Third Avenue.
Undine,	52,	Harlem.
Naiad,	53,	179 Church Street.
Eureka,	54,	153 Franklin Street.
	55,	52 Amos Street.
	56,	140 Varick Street.

Hook and Ladder Companies.

Mutual,	1,	Chambers, corner Centre Street.
Chelsea,	2,	West Twenty-fourth Street, near Seventh Avenue.
Phenix,	3,	132 Amity Street.
Eagle,	4,	20½ Eldridge Street.
Union,	5,	91 Ludlow Street.
Lafayette,	6,	Firemen's Hall, Mercer Street.
Mechanics,	7,	Harlem.
Empire,	8,	West Forty-eighth Street, corner Eighth Avenue.
America,	9,	East Twenty-ninth Street, near Second Avenue.
Narragansett,	10,	Eighty-fifth Street, near Third Avenue.
Knickerbocker,	11,	153 Franklin Street.
Friendship,	12,	East Thirteenth Street, near Fourth Avenue.

Hydrant Companies.

No. 1, Seventh and Eighth Districts. No. 3, Third and Fourth Districts.
No. 2, Fifth and Sixth Districts. No. 4, Fifth and Sixth Districts.

Fire Districts.

First District.—All that part of the city lying north of Twenty-second Street, and east of the Sixth Avenue.

Second District.—All that part of the city lying north of Twenty-second Street, and west of the Sixth Avenue.

Third District.—Beginning at the foot of North Moore Street, North River, and extending easterly in a straight line to between Church Street and Broadway in Leonard Street, thence northerly in a straight line to the corner of Eighth Avenue and Twenty-second Street, thence westerly along Twenty-second Street to the North River.

Fourth District.—Beginning in Leonard Street, between Church Street and Broadway, running thence northerly in a straight line to the corner of Eighth Avenue and Twenty-second Street, thence easterly along Twenty-second Street to Lexington Avenue, thence southerly in a straight line to between Broadway and Elm Street, in Leonard Street, and thence westerly in a straight line to Leonard Street, between Church Street and Broadway.

Fifth District.—Commencing in Leonard Street, between Elm Street and Broadway, and running thence northerly in a straight line to the corner of Lexington Avenue and Twenty-second Street, thence easterly along Twenty-second Street to the East River, thence southerly and along the East River to Fourteenth Street, thence southwesterly in a straight line to the corner of Leonard and Orange (Baxter) Streets, thence westerly in a straight line to the place of beginning.

Sixth District.—Beginning at the corner of Leonard and Baxter Streets, and running thence easterly in a straight line to the foot of Market Street, East River, thence along East River to Fourteenth Street, thence southwesterly in a straight line to the place of beginning.

Seventh District.—Beginning at the foot of Market Street, East River, and running thence westerly in a straight line to Leonard Street, between Broadway and Elm Street, thence southerly along a straight line intersecting Wall Street at the junction of Nassau, Wall, and Broad Streets, and continuing through the Battery to North River.

Eighth District.—Beginning at the foot of North Moore Street, North River, and running thence easterly in a straight line to Leonard Street, between Broadway and Elm Street, thence southerly along a straight line intersecting with Wall Street at junction of Nassau, Wall, and Broad Streets, and continue through the Battery to North River.

In case of fire, the signals from the alarm bells were as follows: First District, one stroke; Second District, two strokes; Third District, three strokes; Fourth District, four strokes; Fifth District, five strokes; Sixth District, six strokes; Seventh District, seven strokes; Eighth District, eight strokes.

For assistance, the signal consisted of the continual ringing of the City Hall and all district bells.

The state legislature enacted a law, March 29, 1855, by which five commissioners were elected by the Fire Department, and to be known as "The Commissioners of the New York Fire Department." The commissioners so elected drew for the term of their respective offices, say, one for the term of five years; one for the term of three years; one for the term of two years; and one for the term of one year; "and, annually thereafter, there shall be elected one commissioner to hold his office for the term of five years."

No person was eligible as such commissioner unless, at the time of election, he was an exempt fireman, and had ceased to be a member of the Fire Department, for at least three years prior to said election. Their duty consisted in inquiring into all applications for the organization of volunteer fire companies; no volunteer fire companies could be organized unless approved by said commissioners; unless—in case of disagreement by the commissioners—a three-fourths vote of all the members should overrule the decision of the commissioners.

The Corporation of the Fire Department, by act of the legislature, April 3, 1855, were permitted to hold real and personal estate, but not to exceed the sum of one hundred and fifty thousand dollars.

VIEW OF BROADWAY, 1800.
Trinity Church. City Hotel.

Members of the Fire Department (ordinance June 14, 1855) were required, when on duty as firemen, to wear the leathern cap as previously in use, or a badge. The badge was made of Prince's metal, bearing the words "New York Fire Department," each badge bearing a distinct number, in raised figures thereon, of white metal. The badge worn by exempt firemen was composed of white metal, with the figures thereon of Prince's metal, but in all other respects similar to the badge used by the active members of the Department. Said badges were struck from separate dies and numbered as the commissioners of the Fire Department might direct.

This ordinance made it the duty of the police, when a fire occurred, to form a line, at least two hundred feet distant from the said fire, on either side thereof; and under no circumstances should they permit any person to pass said line, unless said person should wear the uniform or badge of the Fire Department, the uniform of the insurance patrol, or be a member of the Common Council, a member of the Police Department, or an owner or resident of property within the prescribed lines.

The salary of the chief engineer was increased to the sum of three thousand dollars per annum.

The fire limits were extended to a line south of Forty-second Street, from the East to the Hudson River, on the fourteenth of April, 1856. This act required that buildings erected or to be erected within the fire limits should have front and rear walls, and side walls on both sides, whether such side walls be outside or party walls; and these outside and party walls of every such dwelling house, store, storehouse, or other building, should be constructed of stone, brick, or iron, and started and built upon foundations of stone or brick.

In August, 1856, the state of the Department had never been so encouraging or its working more perfect, and that too while laboring under many disadvantages. The Department consisted of fourteen engineers, one thousand six hundred and forty-four engine men, one thousand one hundred and twenty-eight hose men, three hundred and sixty-six hook and ladder men, and thirty-three hydrant men, amounting to a total of three thousand and eighty-five men, an increase of four hundred and fifty-four over the roll of 1855. These were divided into forty-six engine companies, fifty-eight hose companies, fourteen hook and ladder companies, and four hydrant companies. There were thirty-five engines in good condition, five ordinary, five building, and one rebuilding; forty-nine hose carriages in good condition, six ordinary, two building, and one rebuilding; twelve hook and ladder trucks in good condition, and two building. There was a total of sixty-eight thousand seven hundred and fifty feet of hose in use.

The loss by fires during the year ending July 31, 1856, was six hundred and thirty-two thousand and thirty dollars, being a decrease of five hundred and thirty-five thousand and eighty-nine dollars from 1855.

The rowdies had for a long time remained quiet, and it was hoped that the Department would not again be molested by them. But of late three attacks had been made. In one case Engine Company No. 41 were proceeding at great speed to a fire, when they were set upon by these miscreants with clubs, slung-shots, and stones. Several members of the Department were knocked down, one of whom was run over by the engine and was seriously injured. Another, Hose Company No. 15, were attacked while attending to their duty, the men driven away, and the carriage upset in the street. The third was an attack on the engine house of Company No. 32 by a gang of rowdies. It was useless to look to the police justices for redress, for it was well known they dared not grant it, the political influences of the gangs being so great.

An ordinance to reorganize the Fire Department was introduced in July, 1856. It provided among other things for one chief engineer, eighteen assistants, and as many fire engine men, hook and ladder men, and hose men as were then or might thereafter be appointed by the Common Council in accordance with the provisions of "An act for the better regulation of the firemen in the city of New York," passed March 29, 1855. The chief and his assistants should severally be elected by the firemen by ballot. The first election for chief engineer should take place on the first Tuesday after the first Monday in February, 1857, and thereafter every three years; and the first election for assistant engineers on the first Tuesday after the first Monday in June, 1857. The chief engineer should at the time of his election be a fireman who had served the full term prescribed by law; should receive a yearly salary of three thousand dollars. Each of the assistants should be a fireman who had served three years, and should be an actual resident of the district in which he was nominated, and for which he was elected.

No fireman, while under suspension for any violations of the provisions of the ordinance, should be permitted to wear a fire cap bearing the frontispiece of the company to which he was attached nor allowed to vote, nor permitted to frequent the house occupied by his company, or take part in any of the meetings of said company.

At the quarterly meeting of the Board of Engineers and Firemen, held on September 4, 1856, it was decided that the number of men at that time allowed to the different fire companies, namely, first-class engines, sixty men; second class, fifty men; third class, forty men; hose companies, twenty-five men; and hook and ladder companies, forty men, was sufficient to perform the necessary duties of the respective companies, and that any further addition to companies by the Common Council would be prejudicial to the best interests of the Fire Department.

CHIEF DECKER AND BOARD OF ENGINEERS, 1862.

This action was deemed necessary because of a resolution adopted by the Board of Councilmen to increase the force of Hose Company No. 9 five men, on the face of the remonstrance and protest of the chief engineer of the Department. The Board of Aldermen concurred in the action of their legislative brethren, and filed away the communication of the fire chief for future action on the kalends of February.

Harry Howard, of No. 108 Leonard Street, was elected chief engineer on February 3, 1857.

In January, 1858, the Fire Department was composed of fifty-two engine companies, sixty-two hose companies, fifteen hook and ladder companies, and four hydrant companies, with a force of over two thousand men. The estimate for that year for apparatus, and their repairs, etc., was sixty thousand dollars, and fifty thousand dollars for expenditures for buildings and repairs to them, salaries, and lighting the engine and other houses. The real estate and houses on leased ground belonging to the corporation, in use by the Department, were valued at three hundred thousand dollars, and the apparatus at seventy-five thousand dollars, the interest on which, at six per cent., would amount annually to twenty-two thousand five hundred dollars, making the total yearly cost of protecting the city against fires, independent of the use of the water and hydrants, about one hundred and thirty-two thousand five hundred dollars.

The voluntary service of the members of the Department frequently bestowed at the hazard, and often the sacrifice, of their lives, had given them a strong claim to the good will of the Common Council and of the citizens generally.

The introduction of steam fire engines into the Department had been the subject of consideration for the preceding two years, and an appropriation was made in 1857 of nineteen thousand five hundred dollars for the purpose of testing the experiment. But no definite steps had as yet been taken toward purchasing any apparatus of that description.

On the fourteenth of April, 1858, an act was passed by the legislature extending and continuing in force until the first of May, 1880, unless sooner altered, modified, or repealed, the act incorporating the firemen of the city of New York, passed March 20, 1798, and all acts and parts of acts relating to said incorporation.

In February, 1858, one year after the selection of Chief Howard, the Department consisted of fourteen engineers, one thousand eight hundred and fifty members of engine companies, one thousand two hundred and fifty-seven members of hose companies, and four hundred and fifty two members of hook and ladder companies; making a total of three thousand five hundred and fifty-nine men, an increase of four hundred and seventy-four over the number on the rolls one year before. These were divided into forty-eight engine companies, sixty hose companies, and fifteen hook and ladder companies. There were forty-nine engines in good condition, nine ordinary, and two rebuilding; forty-three hose carriages in good condition, sixteen ordinary; eleven hook and ladder trucks in good condition, and four ordinary; twenty-seven hose tenders in good condition, seven ordinary, and fifteen building. There were in use thirty-three thousand four hundred feet of hose in good order, thirty-seven thousand four hundred and fifty feet in ordinary condition, and ten thousand four hundred feet in very bad condition.

There was a large decrease in the amount of losses by fire during 1857 as compared with 1856. Total number of fires for the year ending July 31, 1856, three hundred and fifty-four; alarms, one hundred and nine; total loss by fire, six hundred and thirty-two thousand and thirty dollars. Total number of fires from February 17, 1857, to February 17, 1858, three hundred and twenty-two; alarms, one hundred and ninety-eight; total loss by fire, four hundred and twenty-eight thousand two hundred and sixty-six dollars.

All hook and ladder companies (ordinance January 7, 1857) were allowed ten additional men; all the hose companies, thirty men; all first class engines, seventy men; second class engines, sixty men; and third class, fifty men.

The Street Department superintended the making of, repairing, and lighting the public roads and avenues; constructing, repairing, and lighting the public buildings; repairing wells and pumps; supplying the public rooms and offices of the corporation, the court rooms, the police station houses, the engine, hose, and hook and ladder houses; and the public markets, with fuel, stationery, printing, and all other things necessary therefor; constructing and repairing fire engines, hose carts, hooks and ladders, hose, and other machines and apparatus for the use of the Fire Department. There were two bureaus in the Street Department, namely, a bureau for the building and repairing of wharves and piers, called the Bureau of Wharves; a bureau for constructing and repairing the public buildings, and repairing of wells and pumps; for the supplying of the public rooms and offices of the corporation, the court rooms, the police station houses, the engine, hose, and hook and ladder houses, and public markets, with fuel, stationery, printing, and all other things necessary therefor, called the "Bureau of Repairs and Supplies;" a bureau for repairing fire engines and fire apparatus, under the direction of the chief engineer.

While proceeding to a fire in July, 1857, Chief Engineer Harry Howard

WINTER SCENE, BROADWAY AND PRINCE STREET, 1857.

was attacked with paralysis, the consequence of severe fire duty which he had previously performed.

An ordinance for the better regulation of the Fire Department went into operation on March 29, 1858. It became the duty of firemen to prevent boys or disorderly characters from congregating in or about the place of deposit of the various apparatus, and not to allow the said place of deposit to be used for any other purposes than those directly connected with the performance of their duty as firemen. No persons other than members and exempt members of the company, or of the Fire Department, in good standing, were allowed to sleep in any engine, hose, or hook and ladder house; the street doors should not be kept open, except while persons were passing in and out, or while any necessary repairs or cleaning were being performed. Good order should be preserved in and about the houses occupied by their respective companies. In going to or returning from a fire, the drag-rope was the proper place for the

firemen, except the officers in command. These should prevent all boys and
noisy improper persons from taking hold of the rope. On no account should
a person, other than a member of the company, or a member or exempt member of the Fire Department, known to at least two of the members of the
company present, be allowed to manage or have any control of the tongue
or tiller of any apparatus in going to or returning from a fire. The officers
and members of each and every company, when returning with their apparatus
from a fire, or alarm of fire, were warned against any racing of their company
with any other company, and cautioned to abstain from any conduct that
would be likely to cause a breach of the peace, or reflect discredit on the Fire
Department. Also it should be their duty to use all endeavors to cultivate
good feeling among the members.

On the morning of August 18, 1858, a fire broke out in the City Hall. It was
generally supposed that the fire was caused either from the burning candles,
used in the windows of the City Hall for the illumination on the night preceding, on the occasion of the celebration of the completion of the first Atlantic
telegraph cable, or from the fireworks discharged from the roof, the remains
of which retained fire, and lodged in some unperceived place on the roof, or in
some of the attics of the building, and suddenly burst forth into flames. The
testimony taken at an investigation clearly established the fact that the fire
originated from the remains of the fireworks and the empty boxes and cases
used for them which were left on the roof.

A short time after the discovery of the fire the cupola became enveloped in
flames. The fire then descended through the roof to the attic rooms, and soon
to the governor's room. The valuable paintings, however, in the latter room,
had been previously removed with great care, so that none of them were
destroyed, or even injured, except one slightly damaged in taking it down.
The flames were subdued at two o'clock A. M., after destroying the cupola, the
greater part of the dome, the roof and the attic rooms in the front part of the
hall, and considerably injuring and defacing the governor's room. The bell-
cupola was also damaged, but the heavy frame work remained sufficiently
strong to sustain the bell. The loss was estimated at fifty thousand dollars.
No public written documents or records deposited in the several offices in the
building were destroyed or injured. There were, however, in one of the attic
rooms a large number of printed proceedings of the Common Council of each
Board thereof, together with some other books, which were nearly all
destroyed, or so much damaged as to be almost worthless. Duplicate copies
of all those printed books were, however, in the City Library room, uninjured.
The noble exertions of the Fire Department succeeded in saving both wings of
the Hall from fire, and for the skill and success with which the members
battled the flames, they received the thanks of the Common Council and the
benedictions of the people at large.

The working organization of the Fire Department in February, 1859,
consisted of fourteen engineers; one thousand nine hundred and twenty-two
members of engine companies; one thousand two hundred and sixty-two
members of hose companies; and five hundred and two members of hook and
ladder companies; a total of three thousand seven hundred men, an increase
of one hundred and forty-one over the previous year. The number of men
allowed to each company were to first class engine companies, seventy men;

second class, sixty men; third class, fifty men; hook and ladder, fifty men; and hose, thirty men. The amount of loss by fire showed an increase over 1858.

The Department had been much agitated on the subject of steam fire engines, and the merits of the innovation on hand power had been freely commented upon not only in the Department, but by all classes of citizens. The Common Council had for the use of the city two large steam fire engines from Messrs. Lee & Larned, patentees. Those engines had been completed and experimental exhibitions of their powers had been given at different times. They had also been put in practical operation on two occasions, namely, at the fire in Duane Street on the evening of January 17, 1859, and at the fire in South Street on January 24. But these tests failed to satisfy the members of the Department of the value of the steam fire engines, who stated that the expectations hoped from their introduction had not been in any manner realized.

In the light of present experience the following comment of the chief engineer, in this connection, is strange and interesting reading.

The steam engines then owned by the city, said the Chief, were large in size and powerful in action, and if permitted to discharge water at every fire would entail more damage by that element than the one it was sought to subdue. The propriety of their introduction into general use was questionable in his judgment, though their services might be rendered effective on extraordinary occasions when the Department might be called on to do extra or laborious duty. In that respect they might prove an addition as an auxiliary branch of the Department; but to be relied upon as the effectual weapon of defense against fire, he was disposed to question their capability and quickness in operation. The city of New York was protected by a Volunteer Fire Department unequaled in the world, and on their promptitude in responding to the call of duty the community relied for protection against the ravages of fire.

At a meeting of the representatives of the New York Fire Department held on May 20, 1859, the following persons were elected Commissioners:

Thomas Lawrence for the full term of five years, in place of John W. Schenck, whose term of office had expired. John J. Gorman, to serve four years, in place of Nelson D. Thayer, resigned. Ernest W. Brown, to serve three years, in place of Robert H. Ellis, resigned; and William M. Tweed, to serve two years, in place of William Wright, resigned.

During the summer months of 1859 several fires had occurred in the upper portion of the city evidently the work of evil-disposed persons. The Common Council, therefore, authorized the mayor to offer a reward of one thousand dollars for the detection and conviction of the offenders.

The several fire insurance companies doing business in the city made a proposition to the city government to furnish and present a steam fire engine to the corporation. This proposition was accepted on the eighth of February, 1859.

At an election held by the members of the Fire Department on the third of March, the following nominations for assistant engineers were made, viz.: For the First District, G. Joseph Ruch; for the Second District, John Brice; at large, Daniel Donnovan, John Decker, William Hackett, Peter N. Cornwell, Edward W. Jacobs, Elisha Kingsland, John A. Cregier, Stephen Mitchell,

Timothy L. West, and John Baulch. They were confirmed by the mayor July 12, 1859.

John Decker succeeded Harry Howard as chief engineer of the Department in February, 1860. The working force then consisted of fourteen engineers, two thousand two hundred and thirty-four members of engine companies, one thousand four hundred and eleven members of hose companies, five hundred and eighty-two members of hook and ladder companies, making a total of four thousand two hundred and twenty-seven men, an increase of five hundred and twenty-seven over the force for 1859. These were divided into fifty engine companies, fifty-six hose companies, and seventeen hook and ladder companies.

Chief Decker, as well as his predecessor, took up the controversy on the subject of steam fire engines for the Department, condemning their use. He said that at large fires they were serviceable auxiliaries to the hand engines, but they could never take the place of the hand apparatus, as eight fires out of every ten that occurred were brought under subjection by the quickness of operation of the hand engines, so that there was no necessity for placing the steamers to work.

A resolution was introduced in the Board of Aldermen at the meeting held on January 10, 1861, directing that the legislature be memorialized for the passage of an act transferring the entire government of the Fire Department from the mayor, aldermen, and commonalty of the city of New York to the Board of Fire Commissioners, reserving only to the mayor, etc., the control, supervision, and ownership of the real estate, buildings and apparatus of the Department. The proposition was lost by a vote of six to eleven.

It had been represented to the Board of Aldermen that the Commissioners of the Fire Department had neglected and refused to report to the Common Council for approval their proceedings in the investigation of charges against members of the Department, with their decision thereon, claiming and insisting under authority of the laws creating the Board of Commissioners, passed March 29, 1855, as amended by the act of March 2, 1861, that their decisions were final and conclusive.

The Common Council regarded such claim as being derogatory of their authority and repugnant to the spirit of the laws, which provided an appeal from the decisions of all tribunals of inferior and limited jurisdiction, and decided to take steps to establish its falsity.

There was a force of four thousand and forty men in the Department in June, 1861. The total number of fires for the year ending May 31, 1861, was four hundred and three, and the total loss one million three hundred and forty-seven thousand two hundred and ninety-seven dollars, one-third of which was lost at one fire in Warren Street, in November, 1860. The following companies had been provided and were doing duty with steam fire engines: Nos. 2, 6, 7, 8, 26, 38, 42, 46, 47, and Exempt Engine and Hose Company No. 57. In addition to those, the Common Council had authorized the providing of steam engines for Companies Nos. 5, 21, 33, and Hose Company No. 52, making a total of sixteen steamers, which was considered a sufficient number for any ordinary emergency.

Never since the organization of the Fire Department had that institution been in a more thriving condition, nor had its prospects presented a fairer aspect than in 1862. During the year the general conduct of the members had

been exceptionally good, the causes of complaint being fewer than in any preceding year, and the several companies appearing to vie with each other in
their endeavors to uphold before the whole community the long-established,
generally good reputation of the organization.   The working force consisted of
three thousand eight hundred and fourteen men, a decrease of four hundred
and thirteen from 1861.   The total number of fires for the year was three
hundred and eleven, and the total loss one million four hundred and twenty-
eight thousand five hundred and eighty-four dollars.

A large fire occurred in January, 1862, at the corner of Fulton and Pearl
Streets.   Owing chiefly to the large quantities of oils stored in two of the
buildings, the fire spread with such fearful rapidity that it was only by the
most extraordinary exertions on the part of the firemen that the city was
saved from a conflagration second only to those of 1835 and 1845.

RUSHING TO THE CONFLICT.

On a requisition made upon him by the Secretary of War, Mayor Opdyke
dispatched to Fortress Monroe, in Virginia, on April 17, the two powerful
hand engines built for and used by Engine Companies Nos. 16 and 31. Assistant
Engineer John Baulch, together with two members from each company, proceeded to Fortress Monroe with the apparatus, and were employed to take
charge of them.

The gross expenditure for the Department for the year 1862 amounted to
three hundred and eighty thousand five hundred and twelve dollars and fifty-
six cents; for the year 1861 it amounted to three hundred and thirty-seven
thousand eight hundred and ninety-one dollars and seventy-eight cents, showing an increase for 1862 of forty-two thousand six hundred and twenty dollars
and seventy-eight cents.   Much of this expenditure was incurred for fire
machines and apparatus, including a number of steam engines.

At a meeting of the representatives of the New York Fire Department, held on May 12, 1863, John J. Gorman was elected fire commissioner for the ensuing five years.

During the year 1862-'63 the loss by fire amounted to one million one hundred and ninety-one thousand nine hundred and twenty-two dollars. The number of fires was two hundred and sixty-eight.

The working force of the Department at the close of the year 1863-'64 numbered three thousand nine hundred and sixty men, a decrease of two hundred and sixty-two from the previous year. The total loss amounted to two million nine hundred and thirty-five thousand and fifty-four dollars. The increase in loss was principally due to the numerous fires that occurred during the riots of 1863, the amount for July alone footing up one million one hundred and twenty-five thousand and sixty-eight dollars.

Intimation was given early in the year 1865 of the change that was so soon to take place in the constitution of the Fire Department. Certainly no city in the world possessed a more complete fire organization in the number of engines, the effectiveness of the steam machines, the copious supply of water, or the gallant army of Volunteers directing these means for the preservation of property. The generosity and public spirit of the firemen could not be more highly appreciated, and nothing could efface the glorious records of their previous history, so full of instances of heroic daring and unselfish toil. Many of its friends, however, were of the opinion that the system so admirably adapted to a small city was not suited to a metropolis, and that economy, as well as the new machinery, demanded a change.

On March 30, 1865, the legislature passed an act creating a "Metropolitan Fire Department." On the thirty-first of March Chief Engineer Decker sent a communication to the Common Council requesting instructions in relation thereto. As some time would necessarily elapse before the new system could be properly and efficiently placed in a position to meet all that would be required therefrom in respect to the full protection of the lives and property of the citizens—the substitution of a paid system in place of the Volunteer organization—and as much suffering, and perhaps loss of life, might ensue in case of a disastrous conflagration unless the volunteer organization were continued in service, the Common Council urged upon the officers and members of the Department the public necessity of their still continuing their previous energetic and humane efforts in arresting on all occasions as theretofore the progress of the devouring element, thereby not only preventing thousands of helpless women and children from being rendered homeless and destitute, but wreathing around the memory of the Volunteer organization of the New York Fire Department a record of fame and usefulness of which both themselves and their children in after time might well be proud.

The four commissioners appointed under the act organized on May 2. Immediately the attorney general of the state in his official capacity and on behalf of the people, sued out an injunction, enjoining them from taking possession of the city's property, also a writ of *quo warranto*, compelling them to show by what warrant they held their office as fire commissioners (the attorney general believing that the said "Metropolitan Fire Law" was unconstitutional).

The matter was tried in the Supreme Court, and finally carried to the

Court of Appeals at Albany. That court on the twenty-second of June deciding the law constitutional, the commissioners took possession of the Department immediately.

The commission consisted of Charles C. Pinckney, president; James W. Booth, Philip W. Engs, and Martin B. Brown.

Whatever the abuse that was heaped upon the Volunteer firemen by those who desired to abolish the system from whatever motive, or whatever the danger that threatened them in the performance of their duty, the firemen, it must be said, were at all times ready and willing to assist to the utmost extent of their ability in preserving the lives and property of their fellow-citizens, and were deserving of unqualified praise for their self-sacrificing actions.

The Department was almost unanimously opposed to any change, and so powerful and unanswerable were their arguments before the committee of the assembly that their friends asserted the use of money (said to be fifty thousand dollars) by the insurance companies alone secured the passage of the act.

While the bill was pending before the legislature its advocates abused the members of the Volunteer Department unstintedly; but notwithstanding that shameful course the firemen did not desert the people, although it was freely asserted that the moment the bill would pass the legislature, they would cease to perform their duty. But the firemen disappointed their enemies, and kept on performing their duty as faithfully and cheerfully as they ever had done, until they were honorably discharged.

"The changes that have occurred," says an old resident and intelligent chronicler of the times, writing in 1862, "within my memory in the city at large, almost defy my own belief. The scenes of a moving panorama scarcely pass with greater rapidity before the vision. It is far from an easy task to recall the objects of local interest which have so suddenly disappeared. Time, and the inexorable demands of commerce and population and progress, are sweeping away all the landmarks associated with the traditions and memories of a past generation."

According to the last official report of the chief engineer of the Volunteer Fire Department, June 30, 1865, the working force consisted of three thousand four hundred and twenty-one men; the organization consisted of the following officers:

OFFICERS:

John R. Platt, president, 79 Murray Street; Sylvanus J. Macy, vice-president, 189 Front Street; Samuel Conover, secretary, 27 and 29 Pine Street; John S. Giles, treasurer, 174 Canal Street; and David Theall, collector, 130 East Fifty-first Street.

BOARD OF TRUSTEES.

Jonas N. Phillips, president, 16 Wall Street and 36 West Twelfth Street; Geo. F. Nesbitt, secretary, 79 Lexington Avenue.

BOARD OF FIRE COMMISSIONERS.

John J. Gorman, president, 52 Ninth Avenue; Thos. Lawrence, 182 Waverley Place; Edward Bonnell, 298 Bowery; William M. Tweed, 197 Henry Street; Thomas Flender, 201 West Fiftieth Street.

CHIEF ENGINEER.

John Decker, 334 Broome Street.

ASSISTANT ENGINEERS.

Name.	Occupation.	Residence.
Elisha Kingsland	Melodeon maker	44 First Street.
Timothy L. West	Carpenter	259 West Seventeenth Street.
Wm. Lamb	Carpenter	62 West Twenty-first Street.
Joseph L. Perley	Machinist	110 Cannon Street.
Eli Bates	Mason	4 Patchen Place.
James Long	Blacksmith	3 Harrison Street.
Bernard Kenney	Horseshoer	94 Rivington Street.
Bartley Donohue	Butcher	112 East Thirty-third Street.
Thomas Duffy	Mason	44 East Fifty-third Street.
John Hamill	Mason	47th St., bet. 7th and 8th Aves.
Michael Shaughnessy	Liquor Dealer	390 Eighth Avenue.
Alex. V. Davidson	Clerk	356 West Fourth Street.
Thos. Sullivan	Clerk	102 East Thirteenth Street.
Peter Weir	Bricklayer	116 Leonard Street.
Gilbert J. Orr	Machinist	4 Centre Street.
Thomas Cleary	Varnisher	100 Cedar Street.
Michael Halloran	Clerk	86th St. and 4th Ave.
Abram Horn	Carpenter	Manhattanville.
Geo. H. E. Lynch	Clerk	Sylvan Place, Harlem.

RESPONDING TO AN ALARM.

CHAPTER XI.

LIFE AMONG THE VOLUNTEERS.

Scenes and Incidents, Grave and Gay.—Historic Memories.—Distinguished Firemen.—Refreshments and Amusements.—Morality and Temperance.—At the Theater.—Songs and Singers.—Luxurious Furnishing of an Engine House.—A Temperance Orator's Only Speech.

AS time rolls on the interest in the old Fire Department of New York seems to deepen. There is nothing like the institution in the history of any other city of this continent or in fact in Europe. So, too, does the New Department stand head and shoulders above any fire department in the world. The doings of both make a chronicle more interesting than any romance or novel. Apart from the dry record of fires attended by the old fire laddies, and the details of the establishment of the Volunteers, are incidents and stories worthy of the attention of posterity. Not only to the student of the manners and customs of bygone times, but to the general reading public are these matters full of interest, and which never weary in the retelling. These facts the writer has gathered from the most reliable sources. Men over whose heads the snows of eighty winters and more have passed have contributed their experience. Others whom we would call old, but whom the octogenarians consider youthful, have likewise added their quota of information. In these and the succeeding chapters we propose to place before the reader a picture of the life of the Volunteers, and a graphic sketch of the paid Department. The fights, the songs, the brave deeds, and the social life of the firemen are here set down, we hope, in the plain and simple language of the impartial historian.

For more than half a century the Volunteers embraced the very best classes of the citizens of New York. Subsequently their numbers were augmented by " runners," unofficial firemen, of a different grade, who, though no less zealous in the performance of duty, were full of fun, frolic, and fight, making the history of their times decidedly lively. Among the distinguished names in the Mutual Assistance Bag Company, which was organized in 1803, and was the forerunner of the present fire insurance patrol, were those of the Bleeckers, Beekmans, Cuttings, De Peysters, Irvings, Laights, Roosevelts, Stuyvesants, Swartwouts, and Ten Eycks.

Among other well-known names of citizens, highly respected, who were in the old Fire Department are those of Zophar Mills, George T. Hope, president of the Continental Fire Insurance Company, W. L. Jenkins, president of the Bank of America, Carlisle Norwood, president of the Lorillard Fire Insurance Company, Jordan L. Mott, the well-known merchant; Thomas Monahan, president of the Fulton Bank (of Engine Company No. 4, afterwards of Hose Company No. 1); Frederic E. Gibert, capitalist and philanthropist, foreman of No. 4, founder of the New York Club and for twelve years its president.

In 1841 **Mr. Gibert** acted as a second to Mr. William Heyward, of South
Carolina, when the latter fought a duel with August Belmont.   Peter and
Robert Goelet, the millionaires, belonged to Engine Company No. 9; Morris
Franklin, president of the New York Life Insurance Company, was foreman
of No. 25 (known as the "brass back engine"), and had several narrow escapes
from death; James F. Wenman, ex-park commissioner; William H. Webb,
the shipbuilder, ran with Live Oak No. 44; John R. Steers, who built the yacht
"*America*," was also a member of Engine No. 44; John W. Degrau, who was
born in 1797.   At the time of the Philadelphia Centennial Exhibition it was
proposed to send to that city a delegation of the veteran firemen, but not a
man could be found who was not his junior.   After the fire of 1835 Mr. Degrau
raised two hose companies and one thousand six hundred dollars for the
purpose in one day.   He could remember catching fish the whole length of
what is now known as Canal Street, from Broadway to the North River.
His playmates were the Roosevelts, the Goelets, the Irvings—Washington
Irving's father kept a dry goods store in William Street—General Morris,
Drake, the poet, and Mr. Hackett, the actor.   Then there was Adam W.
Spies, the successful hardware merchant, now eighty-six years old and wealthy.
Mr. Spies was president of the Stuyvesant Insurance Company, had traveled
over Europe, an amateur artist of no inconsiderable talent and full of infor-
mation on a variety of subjects.   He was a member of Engine Company No. 5,
and a fire warden.

Some of the old firemen have found congenial occupation on Jersey Heights,
such as Charles Merrill, formerly secretary of Columbia Hose Company No. 9;
Larry Welsh, foreman of Howard Engine Company No. 34; James R. Tate,
formerly foreman of Marion Engine Company No 9 ("Old Rock").   In
Hoboken, there are David Satters, formerly of Harry Howard Hose Company
No. 55, now foreman of Hoboken Engine Company No. 1; Gus Willis, of old
Empire Engine Company No. 42, now of Hoboken Engine Company No. 1; E.
Gilkyson, formerly of Neptune Hose Company No. 27; Sam Archer and James
Kenny, now chief engineer of the Hoboken Fire Department.

Of the quality of the old firemen, Mr. William Brandon, speaking in 1884,
remarked: "The majority of people have no idea of the number of judges,
aldermen, prominent officials, and millionaires they see and hear of in the city
of New York who were firemen once, lithe, agile, and careless of themselves as
they climbed the ladder in summer to the roofs of tall houses, handled the almost
frozen hose in the depths of winter, when it was like sheet-iron, and encountered
danger and death at all seasons."   Thomas Coman, of Engine Company No.
13, rose to be president of the Board of Aldermen; so did Alderman Kirk of
the same company; of Hose Company No. 60, were John Clancy, editor of the
Leader, subsequently county clerk; Congressman Morgan Jones, Supervisor
Walter Roach, and Police Captain Edward Walsh.

James F. Wenman, the ex-park commissioner, later treasurer of the
Veteran Firemen's Association, whose headquarters are in East Tenth Street,
was one of the most active of the old firemen.   In 1876 he saved the life of a
servant girl.   It was at a fire at the New York Club house.   The girl had
endeavored to escape by going out on the broad ledge of the main cornice.   The
flames were behind her, and a step would have precipitated her to the pavement, seventy feet below.   The firemen had reared an extension ladder, but it

was found to be ten or twelve feet too short. Mr. Wenman made his way to the roof, seized the girl, and half pulling, half dragging her, finally succeeded in getting her to the roof of an adjoining building.

The fireman's pride in his profession was demonstrated in a thousand and one ways, as also was his fond regard for the seemingly sole object of his affection outside of his domestic relations. As one of numerous illustrations that could be given, it is related that Foreman Thomas Conner, of Clinton Engine Company No. 41, being compelled through illness to resign his office, expressed the hope in his letter of resignation, October 9, 1837, that with their new engine soon to arrive, his company would be able "to cope with anything that runs on four wheels." "When you bring her home," he added, "I hope I will be able to help you escort her to the house. I am in hopes when the new machine arrives, at the first alarm of fire at night to see that double rope, that you have been so long talking about, manned inside and out, with young Gulick ranged ahead with the old 'Stagg,' placing the animal in the most conspicuous style. I shall try to take her out the first night."

Benjamin Strong, whose term of service began as far back as 1791 and continued up to 1822, was one of the most enthusiastic volunteers. His heart and soul were engrossed in the pursuit, and his activity was unremitting. At the first stroke of the alarm bell, even at night and even when age was beginning to make its enfeebling influences apparent, he donned his fire cap and joined the hastening throng of his hardy and intrepid comrades. He communicated his enthusiasm to his sons and daughters, who took an honorable pride in their father's devotion to duty. Even after he had resigned from the Department, he was always disappointed not to be called from his bed when there had been a night alarm.

An amusing story is told of how a distinguished member of the Association of Exempt Firemen came to join the Department. It was about seventy years ago that the occurrence took place. An "Old Vamp," then in his prime, was sitting in an old tavern in Nassau Street, when he heard some of the boys talking about joining an association. He then thought he would like to belong to something or other. So, when he went home, he told his mother that he wanted to join a society, he did not much care what it was. There was a great revival going on in those days in the old Duane Street church, and, like all good mothers, she told him to come along with her and join the church. "Well," said he, "I don't particularly care what it is, but I must belong to something." So down to the church he went, but the minister told him he must go on probation for three months before he could join. When the three months had expired, he called on the "Dominie," but was still told that he must wait two months longer. Some three months passed, when the deacon met our friend walking down Hudson Street, in a neat red shirt and a fancy pair of suspenders, bearing a number upon his back, and a coat thrown over his arm. "Ah!" said the deacon, "you are the one I want to see. You have not been to church of late." "No, deacon, that probation was too long for me." "But," said the deacon, "your probation is at an end; you can now join the church." "Too late, deacon, too late. I've joined an engine company down here, and its going to take all my time to look after fires. I'm laying for one now. You see I was bound to join something, and these fellows let me in without any probation; all I had to do was to shake down my little two dollars and I was called a member. Call around and see us, deacon. We have got as bully a little engine as ever stretched into a fire."

Considering the superior class of men composing the Volunteer Department, the morals of the members must necessarily have been of a corresponding kind. This will be readily understood from some peculiar entries made in the minute books of the companies. For instance, in the book of Engine Company No. 21 is found the following: "Wm. A. Baker reports Mr. Crossthwaite as saying, 'Damn the odds.' The secretary reports Mr. W. A. Baker for saying to John E. Norris (during an altercation between the two), 'You be

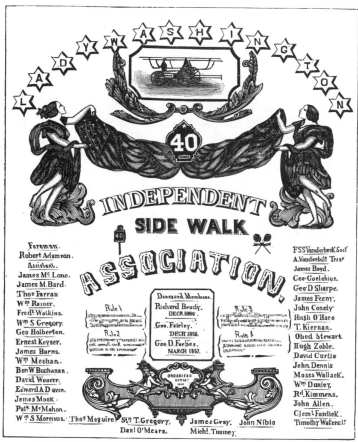

CERTIFICATE OF THE INDEPENDENT SIDEWALK ASSOCIATION.

damned, you damned old Dutch hog.'" As nothing but the very gravest matters are recorded in the minutes, it is clear that the offense of using impolite language is the worst the fire laddies of that period (1810) can be accused of. It would seem that those old Volunteers had quite a profound veneration for their engine houses, from the rules and regulations they made for the maintenance of discipline. Under date of February 10, 1830, we find on the minutes of Engine Company No. 13, that Mr. Tonnele was fined twice for swearing and once for chewing. Chewing! What would our valued firemen of to-day say if the commissioners passed such a resolution as the following, which appears on the book of No. 13, on November 28, 1829:

Resolved, That if any member be found smoking a segar or chewing tobacco in the Engine House at any time, he shall be fined twenty-five cents for every offense.

Such an order would, undoubtedly, cause a conflagration to-day. "What!" said a fireman to the writer, "fire without smoke! Never! It is against the laws of nature." Time after time were the men fined for a breach of this rule, the occurrence always being gravely recorded on the minutes. Poor Tonnele appears to have been a slave to the weed and forfeited many a dollar for the sake of a "quid." Swearing was regarded as heinous as chewing. One of the by-laws of Pearl Hose Company No. 28, in 1854, was: "If any member, while on duty or at meetings, shall persist in improper conduct, or in using profane or improper language, he shall be expelled, provided that two-thirds of the members present vote therefor."

Quite a revenue was derived from the infliction of fines. Here is the schedule of Clinton Engine Company No. 41, in 1823:

Foreman and assistant foreman, for neglecting to impartially enforce all laws that shall be adopted by the company.............	$1.00
For the treasurer neglecting to render a true statement of the funds when requested by the foreman or assistant.......	1.00
For a member neglecting to repair after engine to fire when alarm has sounded and engine gone............................	0.75
For going direct from home without his fire cap....	0.25
For not coming to order when called by the chair..................	0.25
Absence from regular or special meeting...........................	0.50
Not answering to name at roll-call (except he be within sight of engine-house)...	0.12½
Quitting meeting without leave of chairman	0.50
Introducing politics at meeting, improper behavior, using indecent language, profane swearing, or being intoxicated at any meeting of company..	1.00
Shoving at engine, instead of dragging on rope when under way...	0.25
Failing to report chimney on fire within forty-eight hours of knowledge of fact..	1.00

These were the regular fines, but there were others imposed according to the will of the majority of a meeting when special reports were made as to the conduct of members. We take Engine Company No. 13 as an example. In May, 1800, Henry Carmer, a clerk, in the Branch Bank of the United States, tried to be excused for not attending the monthly "washings." After much discussion he was fined two shillings for each absence. At this meeting each man "chipped in" one shilling to pay the tavern bill. At a meeting of this company in November, 1794, at Hunter's Hotel, when twenty-three members were present, the fines collected amounted to £3 1s. The "offenses" of those days make very amusing reading. On May 13, 1818, delinquents of No. 13 were called upon to "show cause," when James Burling was fined twenty-five cents "for not giving an unequivocal answer." In 1821 Richard Ustick was fined fifty cents "for using the trumpet contrary to law," and subsequently fifty cents "for leaving the engine at an alarm of Fire to get his Fire Clothes," but in the latter case the fine was remitted. In the same year John C. Hegeman was declared "finable for appearing at the Engine at a Fire without the initials of his name on his cap." Some of the excuses are no less remarkable than the fines. Here is one from No. 13:

January 15, 1807. (Fire at 1 A. M., in Fair Street.) Harris Sage's excuse (for absence) is received. He says at the time of the above Fire he was locked in some one's Arms and could not hear the Alarm.

Joseph Giraud, in 1807, said he could not attend a "washing" because of a severe pain in his face, and he was "under the necessity of having a Jaw Tooth Extracted." The companies, in all cases, were determined to have their pound of flesh, and never failed to dun a member for his fines. In cases of fractiousness the delinquent was expelled, and finally proceeded against by the corporation attorney. Here is a specimen of a delicate note sent by the considerate secretary of No. 13 to a bold, bad, wicked, and defiant member :

NEW YORK, Nov. 12th, 1835.

SIR,—It is with extreme regret that I find myself obliged to inform you that at the last quarterly meeting of Eagle Fire Engine Company No. 13, held on the 11th inst., you were expelled from that Company for neglect of duty and numerous infractions of the Bye Laws of the Company.

Enclosed I hand the account of the Company against you, which I have been directed to collect, and as authority is vested in me to Commute the same if I think proper, I would advise your calling upon me immediately, or I fear I shall receive instructions to place it in the hands of the Corporation Attorney to be sued for.

I trust, sir, the information, which I am obliged in the discharge of my duty to communicate, may engender no ill-feeling between us. I remain,

Yours, etc.,

J. HUNTER GRAHAM, *Secretary.*

Call at No. 1 Jones Lane.

In addition to the fines mentioned above, there were, of course, others, and heavy ones, for non-attendance at fires. But, as a rule, the attendance was very prompt. Indeed, nothing stopped the boys from turning out at the first alarm. Whether at church, wedding, fair or funeral, off they would start at the sound of the bell. In the chapter of fires of the Old Department a notable instance of the devotion of the men to their duty is given in the case of the ill-fated "Andy" Schenck, who quitted his pleading sweetheart to go to his death. An incident not quite so mournful occurred one night in 1857. Watch night services were being held at the old colored church, corner of Leonard and Church Streets. The congregation had been worked up to the highest pitch of devotional enthusiasm, when the City Hall bell, ringing out its warning note, changed like a flash the aspect of the scene. Many members of Engine Company No. 21 were scattered in different parts of the church, and they at once made a rush for the door. Guarding the portal, however, was a saintly colored giant, a worthy deacon, pious and muscular. His sense of propriety was, so to speak, knocked all of a heap at the seeming irreverence of the fire laddies in their helter-skelter race from the sanctuary. St. Peter himself could not be more determined in keeping the wicked out of heaven than this stalwart deacon was in keeping them in church. He braced himself for a great effort. Lifting his eyes to heaven and his formidable bunch of fives in pugilistic shape, he prayed, "Lord, forgive me for what I am about to do, and may Thy name be ever praised." There was a "dull thud." His ham-like fist had fallen upon poor Jim Weir's left eye, and the foreman was hurled clear across an aisle into a pew, landing in the lap of a prayerful old lady. But the self-sacrificing, dutiful Jim was not to be deterred by a little accident of this kind. With an apology to the devotional dame, and a word of warning to the earthly St. Peter, he picked himself up, gained the street with his companions, and attended the fire. The recording angel duly registered the blow of the deacon, and then wiped it out with a tear, but it was not quite so easy to wipe out Jim Weir's black eye. During two weeks the gallant foreman walked about with his eye in mourning, and his feelings in a state of effervescence, for his friends gave him no peace about his church adventure. But one night it was Jim's turn to give the recording angel something to do. He met the good deacon accidentally, and "sailed right in," and when he got through with him the burly saint thought that he had been having a bad quarter of an hour in purgatory. Weir's eye visibly improved after that.

A notable example of what a fireman will endure in the performance of his duty is found in the annals of the Old Department. On January 8, 1854, when the Lafarge House and Tripler Hall, on Broadway, were destroyed, T. F. Goodwin, foreman of Hose Company No. 35, was so persevering in holding his pipe to the flames that his boots were burned to a crisp on his feet. "Where," asked the *Herald* of the next day, "can man go and find deeds of greater hero-

CANAL STREET AND BROADWAY, 1812.

ism than this in the history of the New York firemen? With no other incentive than merely to save property and roll back the waves of fire, we see this man entering the very jaws of death, and standing there—doing battle until the enemy had burned his weapon from his hands and his garments from his body."

After working for hours at a fire the men would naturally feel hungry. On their way home they would have their choice of supping upon hot corn or baked pears. These dainties were to be had from women who peddled them. Or they might visit places of refreshment, more pretentious than the street stand, such as Holt's cellar on Fulton Street. This place was open all night, so that the fire laddies out late could be sure of hot coffee and hash. Many of its patrons are now owners of brownstone houses. Among the women who used to minister to the comfort of the laddies was the servant of a member of No. 11 Engine, Mr. Benjamin Aymar. She was known as "Molly." Molly considered herself to be permanently attached to No. 11, and stood up for the superiority of the machine under all circumstances. She boasted that she belonged to "ole 'Leven," and used to say, "I allers runs wid dat ole bull-gine." On one occasion, in 1818, a blinding snowstorm prevailed when a fire broke out in William Street. The boys had the utmost difficulty in dragging their engine through the snow-obstructed streets, and had not men enough on the rope. Molly came along, hitched on to the rope and helped to drag the machine to the fire. This deed of Molly's was often recounted in the station houses. By the way, it was at this fire that Daniel F. Tiemann first did active duty as fireman. Twenty years after he was promoted to be foreman of Cataract Engine No. 25, when she lay in "Love Lane," now Twenty-third Street. When he removed from the Sixteenth Ward to Manhattanville, he became foreman of No. 43. He was for years in the Board of Aldermen and at last mayor, and also served in the Senate. While an alderman Mr. Tiemann got a resolution passed in the board, providing that no liquor should be paid for by any company, and ordering the appointment of a steward to furnish coffee and cakes at fires. His company (No. 41) discharged a steward in 1838 because he "had not done the company proper justice," and elected Henry Hemmingway to fill the vacancy. Two years before this company was a little under the weather financially. Landlord Winslow presented a bill for refreshments, and it was ordered, "Having not money sufficient to pay it, motion was made that we pay him all we had in our funds, which was eight dollars, and let him wait a future day for the remainder." No doubt mine host waited till the cloud rolled by. Once a Boniface charged the company "an exorbitant price for refreshments," and the following simple and straightforward way of meeting the bill was adopted:

Resolved, That the treasurer call on him and offer a fair price. If he did not take it, not to (pay) him at all.

When Mr. Tiemann was running for state senator he had for his opponent (whom he beat two to one) the famous Harry Genet—"Prince Harry"—whose connection with the "Tweed Ring" brought him subsequently into trouble.

A well-remembered entertainer of the firemen was Colonel Turnbull, of the One Hundred and Thirty-third Regiment, the police regiment in the brigade that was raised for the war of the Rebellion. Turnbull was captain of the Eighth Precinct in 1854. A fire which destroyed the City Assembly Rooms, Nos. 440 to 450 Broadway, on December 20 of that year, was fatal to James T. Laurie, of Hose Company No. 7. The rear part of the building fell on him and killed him instantly. The body was recovered and taken home. The night was bitterly cold, and the firemen suffered a great deal. When the fire was out Captain Turnbull said: "Come along with me, boys, and get something warm." He took Hose Companies Nos. 7 and 14 to his private residence in Grand Street, and there regaled them with hot coffee and plenty of good things to eat. This timely act of kindness saved many from being stretched on a bed of sickness.

Sometimes the firemen gave entertainments that were of a remarkably *recherche* character. Oceana Hose Company, No. 36, gave such a one on December 8, 1852, at their carriage house in Madison Street. A description of it in the *Herald* will give an idea of the "style" that was put on by Oceana:

On approaching the house we found the street lined on both sides, for about a block, with carriages, and imagined for a moment we had dropped down in the region of Upper-tendom, instead of the house of a fire company. The house is fitted up throughout in a style not surpassed, if equalled, by any other of a similar kind in the city. The walls were tastefully decorated with appropriate engravings, and in the back part of the room was the book-case well filled with a collection of useful and entertaining books. The drawing-room was fitted up in a style truly magnificent, and would vie with those of some of our merchant princes in Fifth Avenue and elsewhere. The carpet upon the floor was of Brussels tapestry, and the windows were hung with damask and lace inside curtains. In fact, everything in and about the house was arranged in a style of splendor and convenience such as we have never seen equaled by any company in the Department, and we understand it has been done entirely at the expense of the members themselves, the whole cost being about one thousand two hundred dollars. We could add much more in regard to this, but for want of space must pass on to the entertainment. During our stay the house was crowded with ladies and gentlemen, all seemingly much pleased with the hospitable and generous manner in which they were received by the members of the Oceana; and we must say we never saw con-

TAMMANY HALL, 1830.
[Site of the *Sun* Building.]

gregated together on any occasion a greater array of beauty than we witnessed on this. An abundance of choice cake, lemonade, wines, creams, jellies, etc., were partaken of with a zest by the many charming ladies present. A band was in attendance during the evening which served to enliven the scene. The whole affair was of such a character as to reflect the highest credit upon the Company and the committee (Messrs. W. D. Wade, W. A. Woodhull, T. L. Parker, junior, and A. Slote), under whose especial supervision it was got up, and for pleasure could not be surpassed. It was a happy evening for all concerned, and its pleasures will not soon be forgotten. But it is unnecessary to say anything further in praise of the entertainment. The members have ever deserved and sustained a good name, not only in the Department, but among the public at large, and we feel a pride in having such a company in our midst, to whom we would point as a proud example for others to imitate.

The temperance societies of 1840 made an effort to win over the firemen,

and in a measure succeeded.   Almost all the members of Engine Company
No. 18 signed the pledge, and became ardent propagandists.   They were
encouraged and rewarded by the Ninth Warders, who presented them with a
silken banner.   The presentation took place in the Methodist Episcopal Church
in Bedford Street, and it was a great day for the boys.   The banner was
presented by Miss Downey, sister of Captain Jack Downey (afterwards of the
Fire Zouaves).   The fire laddies entered the church in their uniform, and were
seated in the front pews.   Among the members were Henry Wilson (subsequently a merchant at No. 311 Bowery), Samuel J. Gillespie, Nelson D. Thayer
(who was given charge of the banner), Charles W. Cornell (who later on went
to live in California), John Boyd, David Milliken (a president of the Fire
Department), John Ayres, John Kettleman, and Leonard De Cline.   The
church was thronged with young ladies, wearing red ribbons with the number
of the company attached—their attachment, by the way, to several members of
the company being a well-known fact.   Mr. Wilson returned thanks on behalf
of the company.   "Why shouldn't we join the temperance movement?" said
Mr. Wilson.   "Are we not of all men the most steadfast believers in the
efficacy of water?   Why, we could not get along without water.   It is our
native element, and may we always have enough of it."

Among the other companies who joined the teetotallers were Hose
Companies Nos. 13 and 5, Engine Companies Nos. 27 and 41.   The Common
Council, as a recognition of this still further sacrifice on the part of the firemen,
presented to each of the companies a brass trumpet.   On one occasion in 1842,
after temperance services in the Forsyth Street Methodist Episcopal Church,
Hose Company No. 2 had a grand teetotal "blow-out" in its house in Eldridge
Street, to which it invited Engine Company No. 18.   The boys were got up in
magnificent style in red shirts and showy suspenders with wonderful needle-
work.   The deacons of the church were also there, and, of course, all the
pretty girls, wearing red roses.   Tea and coffee, hot rolls and cake, and so on,
were dispensed with prodigality.   Speeches were made in public and in private
—the private ones being made to the young ladies—"The Learned Blacksmith,"
"On Old Long Island's Seagirt Shore," and other songs were sung, and
generally a splendid time was had.   The fire laddies got lots of fun out of their
temperance proclivities.   A comical story is still told by John J. Mount, of
Hose Company No. 2.   The Sackett's Hall Temperance Society in Division
Street was one of the great centers of teetotal propagandism.   Young Mount,
now a police captain, and the brother of James R. Mount, was here a constant
attendant, but a remarkably silent member.   It was the custom to have
impromptu speeches made.   At length young John Mount, inspired by what
others did, conceived the idea of making an off-hand speech.   He had another
brother, George, now dead, who had a literary gift, and to him he applied to
write him an "impromptu" speech.   George wrote it, and at great length.
For weeks and weeks the gallant fireman applied himself to its study until he
had every word of it by heart.   Then on a certain night, when the hall was
crowded he modestly took a seat among the audience.   After several orators
had got through brief exordia, other speakers were called for by the chairman.
Now was the supreme moment.   Up jumped Mount to the intense astonishment
of all who knew him, and, with his heart going pit-a-pat, he proceeded
towards the platform.

"Hullo! Jack, what's the matter with you!" cried one. "Come off!" sarcastically said another. "Are you going to sing!" observed a third, while the girls tittered.

But the bold fireman knew the power he had acquired, and, ignoring the quizzical remarks of his friends, mounted the rostrum. He began timorously, but in a few moments caused the audience to open its eyes as well as its ears. Such a flood of rhetoric it had not been accustomed to. Close argument, flights of fancy, stirring appeals, and picturesque descriptions, followed each other in swift order. The meeting was roused to enthusiasm, and when, after an hour of this kind of thing, he took his seat in the middle of the hall, he was cheered again and again, and congratulated on all sides. A great orator had appeared, a genius had been discovered. Managers of other societies gathered around him anxious to secure dates. Young Mount engaged himself to speak at nearly a dozen places. But, alas! for the morrow. He could not deliver the same speech again, and had no other ready. Consequently that was his last as well as his first appearance on the teetotal platform. Rather than "give himself away" he abandoned the temperance movement, and it knew him no more. But he had made himself famous—for the time being.

One of the queer characters of the old days was "Rooster Kelly," who used to run with Engine No. 30. He was remarkable for the tall stories he used to tell, and for the interesting way he had of making them appear truthful. Years after the disbandment of the Volunteer Department, he related the following story about "Old Mose:" "Mose ran with old Forty. He keeps a billiard saloon in Honolulu now. I kin remember the night him and Orange County—he was our foreman—had it nip and tuck. They were both bully boys, but Orange County kinder got the bulge on him after a four hours' tussle. One night, Orange County, Mose and me, Tom Hyer, Captain Tom Reeves, and Alick Hamilton, were down in Bob Wanamaker's saloon, corner of Reade Street and Broadway, when the fire bell rang. The fire was down in Wall Street. Just after he got there, somebody threw a stone out of the third story window of the house next door to the fire. Well, that stone struck Orange County on the shoulder, bounced off, and struck the rooster that was standing next to him handling a bucket, and killed him deader'n a door nail."

Moses Humphrey, or "Old Mose," as he was called, was the typical "Bowery boy," whom Frank Chanfrau, the actor and fireman, caricatured in his famous play. "Mose" belonged to Engine 40 (Lady Washington). Chanfrau's impersonation was not pleasing to the majority of firemen, who regarded it as a libel upon themselves. *America's Own, or the Fireman's Journal,* of which Anthony B. Child was the editor, took the actor severely to task. By the way, it was in this paper that Maggie Mitchell received her first notice at her *debut* in the Bowery Theater. The *Journal* praised Chanfrau as an actor, but added: "It is ridiculous to attempt to make a part out of such a character as Mose is represented to be. His benevolence, and the clap-trap manoeuvres of the stage, are all sham. The effect of this character upon the juveniles who visit the theater is plainly visible, as they take every opportunity to imitate the character. Its effects upon the Fire Department are serious, in the estimation of those who are not acquainted with its members, as they set every fireman down as a 'Mose,' degrading to youth."

One of the arts cultivated by the old firemen was the art of music. As sailors work best when they have some one to sing to them or fiddle to them, so the fire boys worked with a greater will when they heard a song. How vigorously they used to dash down the brakes when a good chorus was being sung around them! One of the singers of the olden time was James Hurley, an old Fifth Street schoolboy, who was known as the " Sweet Singer of the Dry Dock." Hurley belonged to old Forest Engine No. 3, and at every fire he encouraged the boys with his songs. Once, at a fire that broke out at Houston Street and the Bowery, a thousand men stood around and heard one hundred fire laddies of No. 3 take up the burden of Jimmie's song, which was the old pathetic Irish ballad " Shule, shule, shule agra." A few weeks later Hurley joined the Ellsworth Zouaves, and was one of the first to fall by a Southern bullet among the mountains of Virginia.

Live Oak Engine No. 44 was known as " Old Turk," and the " Singing Engine." William H. Webb, the shipbuilder, was a member. The early members were mostly shipyard men, and the greater part of them good vocalists. Chief among them was Frank Walton, a tall sawyer, who was called the " Minstrel Boy of the Sawpit." One evening in April, 1849, a fire broke out near the Eagle Tavern, and a rival engine to " Old Turk " did so badly that the members were hissed. A young lady opposite, standing at her window, heard Walton sing, and after the fire invited him into her parlor, and accompanied him on the piano while he sang her a fireman's ditty. After this he became a constant visitor, and finally married one of the belles of the Eleventh Ward.

But Walton could sing anywhere. Coming home from the old Chatham Theater one night Walton and a companion sat down on a stoop in East Broadway to rest. There were no railroads in that neighborhood then. Walton sang "Napoleon's Dream," and soon every window for blocks around was filled with admiring nightcaps, and even staid old Quakers from Henry Street listened to the song. Walton took the gold fever in '50 and went to California. Being unable to pay his way on board he sang his way to 'Frisco. To the astonishment of the New Yorkers who thought Walton was in New York, he made his appearance in the mines with a slouch hat, coat on his arm, and a red shirt, on which a badge of " 44 " shone resplendent. He sang his way to the hearts of the miners, and in one week was the best known man in the mine. But the tide turned ; reverses met him at every step, and far from home and the scene of his early exploits, Old Turk's Mocking Bird one cold winter night folded his fire coat around him and slept his last sleep. The winter winds of the Nevadas sang to sleep the " Minstrel Boy of the Sawpit."

Opposite the historical Tea-water Pump (of which mention is made elsewhere) stood the Tea-water Tavern, where the boys also quenched their thirst quite as often, but with a more dire effect. It was in this old hostelry when rivalry first grew strong between the engine companies, that No. 3 gathered in solemn conclave over a bowl of steaming punch, to decide the momentous question of painting their new engine. The old Tea-water Pump had been given that day a fresh coat of pea green, and an honest fireman coming to the meeting had noticed the pretty contrast with the white snow piled all about it. So, rising in his seat and speaking with sincerity and profanity, he addressed the chair: " I don't care a d———, fellers, what color yer paint the ole gal, if ye'll only listen to me an' paint her green." This speech got abroad, and when No. 3

COMPANY AND DEPARTMENT FIRE BADGES.

afterwards extinguished a fire it was reported that she had "painted it green." Indeed, so proud did the boys become of the expression that they embodied it in a rude ditty which they never failed to sing, to the frantic rage of their rivals, when returning from a fire:

> We are coming back rejoicing,
> The liveliest boys you've seen;
> We've beat them other fellers
> At the fire we painted green.

But alas, poor No. 3! The day came when three small fires broke out within twenty-four hours, and as ill luck would have it No. 3 was last at all of them. Then was there great rejoicing among the enemy, and a terrible battle fought by the chagrined members of No. 3. Some one wrote a poem of praise over this event, beginning:

There is an engine house
  Not far away,
Where they are last at fires
  Three times a day.

Oh, how the boys all scream,
  When they see Three's put on steam,
For the fires they can't paint green
  Three times a day.

Even the stage was invaded by the old firemen, as the following entertaining facts will show. Engine No. 27 was located east of the Bowery. Its volunteer members were principally mechanics, such as ship-carpenters, calkers, shipsmiths, boatbuilders, riggers, and the like. They would all drop their tools at the screw dock, at the foot of Pike and Market Streets, on the instant a fire alarm was sounded in the daytime, oftentimes to the disgust of the "bosses." They were a hardy lot, who had their headquarters at the Sawdust House in Walker Street, kept then by Yankee Sullivan. The old Chatham Theater was only five minutes' walk from the engine house. One of Twenty-seven's boys was John J. Mount, a boatbuilder, afterwards captain of the Nineteenth Precinct police, already referred to as the temperance orator. Mount had a taste for the stage and became captain of the "supes" at the Chatham Theater. One Saturday night on his return to the engine house from his histrionic labors he imparted a piece of news to the boys. On Saturday nights very few of them went home, having all Sunday to sleep in, provided there were no fires. The supernumerary captain told the lads that on the following Monday "Cherry and Fair Star" was to be brought out at the Chatham in grand style, with Mrs. Harrison, an English importation, as Fair Star. He told them an alluring story of the armor, shields, spears, banners, all of the most gorgeous description, in the play, and said that the management required thirty or forty extra "supes" to don the habiliments of pageantry and war, and give *éclat* to the spectacle. The captain was empowered to enlist the force required, and naturally offered the good thing first to the boys. They jumped at the chance to immortalize themselves on the boards, and nearly every man joined at once. They were required to be at the theater at eleven o'clock the next morning (Sunday) for rehearsal. As their engine and the theater bore the same name the firemen felt they had a sort of affinity with the latter. Their engine was somewhat theatrical. On its back it bore a painting by Quidon, eminent in those days, representing Rolla holding Alonzo's child at arm's length for protection.

On Sunday morning between thirty and forty of the boys entered the back door of the Chatham, some trembling with excitement, some doubtful how they would succeed, and others brave and confident. All was bustle on the stage as they entered for the first time behind the scenes. Jimmy Anderson, an excitable Irishman, was stage manager. Of course, he had been accustomed to bully the "supes," but the new men were made of sterner stuff, and it would have been risky to have bullied them a great deal. Mrs. Harrison, the star, stood talking to some of the actors at the wings. The boys remarked her round cherry face, and thought that she liked her brandy and water. Captain Mount was not a little nervous, for he had undertaken a great responsibility. The firemen were untrained "supes," and would not stand much nonsense in the drilling. Mount marshalled them in line, armed with old sticks and spears. They marched up and down, across, in and out and around the stage, until some of the boys thought it a serious matter, but others thought it great fun, and skylarked occasionally. The skylarking excited the ire of the stage manager, who frowned, and fretted, and swore, and threatened to pull the offenders out of the ranks, which was still greater fun for the boys. One he threatened to throw out of the theater, but it was well for him he did not try it, because the menaced fire laddie was one of the "lightning boys," and the manager, had he tackled him, would have thought a mule had kicked him. However, they did very well, and remained at the theater until dark, there being no alarm of fire that day. Had there been, they would have left pell-mell, for "running wid der masheen" was paramount to business and everything else. Indeed, there were cases where firemen had left the altar, half married, to attend a fire.

After relating their experiences to the few they had left around the engine house, the "supes" went home, more fatigued than if they had worked all day at a fire. The scene on the stage next night was a strange one to them. Scene shifters, stage carpenters, property men, and others, were up to their eyes in business. The firemen were taken to the supernumeraries' dressing room under the stage, and there accoutred. Their jokes at each other's expense were bandied about, such as "Scotty, your gal ought to see you now!" "Nosey" (to one who had a decidedly Roman nose), "take a reef in your bugle, so the audience can see your helmet!" "Jimmy, if your mother knew you were here and dressed up so wouldn't she be proud of you!" Mount was busy showing the men how to put their stage clothes on. They went on in the grand pageantry scene, and the stalwart firemen certainly looked well, and marched well, as the audience warmly applauded them. The sea of faces before them, and the tumultuous cheering, had a novel effect upon the new "actors." After the grand tableau, which concluded the piece, the firemen doffed their gorgeous dresses. While taking off their harness, Captain Mount went to them and said he wanted four of them to go on in civilians' dress in the next piece, "The Hazard of the Die, or the Ruined Gambler," and that the rest might go in front and see the play. He began to select the best dressed in the party. John Rogers was attired in a resplendent blue coat, English cloth, long and square-tailed, with velvet collar and fancy gilt buttons—very fashionable in those days. Rogers would not have gone on in his own dress for any amount of money, and would rather forfeit his week's salary—twenty-five cents. However, he lent his "nobby" coat to one of the boys, taking his in exchange. The scene opened with the gamblers throwing dice. The four firemen took a hand in, and were saluted by their comrades in front with such remarks as these: "Johnny, don't let him cheat you!" "He's fingering the dice!" "Who'd you borrow that coat of?" etc., etc.

When the piece was over they all left the theater. Just as Rogers was exchanging coats again, an alarm of fire was sounded, and away the late "supes" went helter-skelter to the engine house, meeting the engine as she was coming into Chatham Street. It was an all-night fire, and they thought no more of theatricals. Only five of the men went through the "run" of the piece, which lasted two weeks. It was lucky for the management that there was no alarm of fire on the opening night, for assuredly the firemen "supes" would have dashed off in their stage attire to attend to the fire, and leave the play to take care of itself.

On January 27, 1854, Mr. J. Purdy of the National Theater paid a graceful compliment to Clinton Engine Company No. 41, in having his band serenade them. The boys were suddenly attracted by the sweet sounds that greeted their ears, and soon the denizens of the neighborhood turned out to listen and to applaud. The company subsequently passed a resolution of thanks in the following words:

The members of 41 greatly appreciate so tasteful a compliment. Our best wishes accompany the manager of the National Theater and his talented company in the career of eminence and prosperity which they so well deserve.

A party of four, consisting of William M. Tweed, Adolphus Borst ("Bill Post"), William Drew, and John Garsight ("Dandy Gig"), sat in the house of 12 Engine in Rose Street on the evening of the famous 1835 fire. They were all volunteers. The corporation was supposed to furnish the engine houses with coal for heating purposes, but for various reasons they were often without it, and the members had to make shift as best they could, sometimes purchasing fuel out of their own pockets, oftentimes receiving it as a donation from neighbors, and not infrequently "foraging" for it. The quartette above named found that their supply of coal had been exhausted. Tweed suggested that they forage for it, and, accompanied by Borst and Drew, carrying a couple of buckets, paid a visit to the nearest coal yard, at the corner of Dover and Pearl Streets. Tweed, hardly as fleshy then as when he imperiously controlled the politics of the metropolis, scaled the fence, astride of which perched Drew, while Borst kept a lookout for the "leather heads," as the police were then termed. The buckets were passed to Tweed, by him filled with coal, and returned to Borst on the sidewalk. The party managed to get back to the engine house without being detected, and lit a fire in the small sugar-loaf stove, and set about making themselves comfortable for the evening. On the previous night they had been called to a small fire. The engine was of the goose-neck pattern, and the men were in the habit of jumping sidewalks with it. In doing so the king bolt had been broken, and the apparatus had been turned in, tongue first, being unfit for duty until repaired. Tweed and his companions were just beginning to reap the reward of their raid on the coal yard—for, as has been said, the night was bitterly cold—when the alarm for the great fire was given. The party, leaving their damaged engine in the house, hurried to the scene of the conflagration, and were there continuously on duty for the subsequent forty-eight hours.

FIREMAN'S EMBLEMS.

CHAPTER XII.

STORIES OF THE COMPANIES.

Racing Rivals.—A Tragedy in the Tombs.—The Tea-water Pump.—Celebrated Combats and Champions.—
The "Battle of the Boots."—The Big Bowery Fight.—Old "Mose."—Chivalry of the Firemen.—
Foraging for a Supper.—Hard Work at the Fires.

THE way they used to do things in the Forties is told by an old fireman of Hook and Ladder No. 4. "I joined Hook and Ladder No. 5," he said to the writer, "in the spring of 1845. She was called the 'Screamer,' and we were as proud of her as some of the survivors are now (1886) of their certificates on their walls. I was a youngster then, and used to lay awake at nights fearful lest I should miss an alarm. We used to have fine times at the station house. On fine nights we used to sit around the door and sing. I was mighty fond of music, and was so taken with Big McCollum's singing that I joined Truck 4 just to hear him. That was in 1860. She was known officially as Eagle Hook and Ladder No. 4, and lay in Eldridge Street, near Canal. Just above us in Christie Street was Peterson Engine Company No. 31, and we had many a muss with that company. We got up a song on them once like this:

> The silver hook and ladder,
> The pretty, golden Four,
> To make Thirty-one the madder,
> Wash the paint from off her door.

"The youngsters in the street used to take sides, and when one crowd met another and heard this song sung, a fight was sure to result. One night there was a row in front of our house, and our foreman, Jack Halligan, thinking the lads had done each other enough damage took the hose and washed them off the street. At that time there was another big rivalry going on between Americus, nicknamed 'Big Six,' of which Bill Tweed was a member, and Engine Company No. 41, called the 'White Ghost.' They were always looking for each other at a fire, and washing each other. Well, Big Six got an assistant secretary, and a 'White Ghost' boy heard of it. At the next meeting of his company he got up and said:

"'Mr. Chairman, I move we have an assistant sec. I don't know what an assistant sec. is, but No. 41 has got one, an' I'm hanged if we ought to let them pukes lay over us.'

"All the other fellows thought just as he did, so they voted themselves an 'assistant sec.,' without in the world knowing what he was to do. They also got up a song which ran something like this:

Number Six has come on deck
With a new assistant sec.,
        Do ye mind?
He's as dirty as its water,
Tho' he thinks himself a snorter,
But he really hadn't oughter,
        Do ye mind?

"Oh, the races we used to have with the boys of No. 31! Either company first at the brow of Chatham Hill, where Chatham Square is now, would wait for the other, and then there would be a tight race down the hill to the fire. It made a good deal of bad blood. Some time in 1861 a fire broke out one night in the lower part of the old Eighth District. We went down the hill with all the boys hanging on to the ladders, except two at the tongue and one at the tiller. Engine No. 31 was right behind us. She crowded us mighty tight, and when she saw her chance at Mulberry Street, she jumped into us and upset the truck in the gutter. We lay all over the street, as if knocked over in battle, and the others went right on with yells of derision. Our truck was wrecked. But we got our revenge, when they came back, and many of them went home with broken jaws and sore heads. Next Sunday there was an alarm from the Seventh District. We had fixed up the old engine, and we had her to the top of the hill in a jiffy. Thirty-one met us, but we left them behind. When they arrived they turned the hose on us, and we had to sail right in and take it away from them, and washed three or four of them across the street. We fought all the way back, and 'laid out' several men before we got to Eldridge Street. Then the populace took a hand in, and for about four hours there was the biggest riot seen before the war. Bricks and stones were going around without owners, and half-a-dozen shots were fired. One fellow held his revolver in his coat-tail pocket, and fired her off at random. The police arrested five firemen and several runners, but through political influence they were never brought to trial."

In early days, before the introduction of the telegraphic system, notice was given of a fire by the ringing of bells. In 1835 it was ordered that a watchman be stationed constantly in the cupola of the City Hall to give the alarm. The bell was rung during the continuance of the fire, the locality of the blaze being indicated by ringing the bell in a prescribed manner, and by hanging out at night a light in the direction of the fire, and by day a flag. The watchhouses and markets had bells which were utilized for the same purpose, and the churches also rang their bells. Then watchmen were stationed in the cupolas of the Halls of Justice, the Reservoir, and Center, Essex, and Jefferson Markets, and received one dollar and seventy-five cents a day. In 1842 the city was divided into districts, and each district into sections, and a certain number of strokes for each section indicated the location of the fire. Each bell had its peculiar tone which a fireman soon learned, and could tell at once where the conflagration was. In 1844 the watchmen were legislated out of office, and three exempt firemen, appointed by the mayor, acted as ringers in each district. Their salary was six hundred dollars a year, increased in 1864 to one thousand dollars. At various times the regular bell towers were located at the City Hall, Essex Market, Center Market (afterwards Marion Street), Washington Market, Macdougal Street, Jefferson Market, Union Market, Twenty-second Street and First Avenue,

Thirty-third Street, Fifty-first Street, Mount Morris, Yorkville, the Post-office, and the Tombs.

Connected with the last-named cupola is a dramatic story, which we have referred to in a chapter on fires of the old Department. Alderman Clarkson Crolius, of the Sixth Ward had long urged the desirability of a bell-tower on the Tombs prison for fire alarm purposes. At last, in 1842, he succeeded, and in November of that year it was completed save for a few finishing touches. The finishing touches, however, were not given, for on the eighteenth the cupola and a part of the roof were destroyed by fire, and the building threatened. The rumor that the fire was started for the purpose of rescuing John C. Colt, who was to have been executed on that day, was unfounded. Mr. Crolius made a thorough investigation and wrote a long report to the Common Council. On the previous day the alderman had inspected the tower. The watchman's room was built of pitch pine, and

BURNING OF THE TOMBS' CUPOLA.

was to have been lined with tin. Alderman Crolius warned the watchman not to light a fire till the tin had been put in. But his warning was disregarded. The man made a roaring fire which, in the early hours of the morning of the eighteenth, ignited the woodwork and destroyed the structure. While the fire was blazing and the engines rattling outside, Colt, within his cell, took his own life and cheated the gallows.

Colt was a bright young man, well-connected and with numerous friends. By profession he was a teacher of bookkeeping. He was born at Hartford, Connecticut, where his father possessed a manufactory of silks and woollens. His brother was the renowned Samuel Colt, the inventor of the revolver, who had a checkered career. John got into financial difficulties in this city and had to borrow money. One of his creditors was Samuel Adams, who dunned his debtor. Colt was then living at No. 11 Elizabeth Street, a house owned by James R. Mount's father-in-law. One day Adams went to John Colt's office and annoyed him. They quarrelled, blows were struck, and the hot-headed Colt struck his adversary on the temple with a stone pitcher. The blow was instantly fatal, and Adams fell dead. Colt rushed out, thoroughly alarmed by his rash act, and walked about in a terrible state of excitement. No one had seen the deed. The thought struck him that he could quietly get rid of the body and save his reputation. He packed the body in a barrel and had it conveyed at night to the ship Kalamazoo, lying at the foot of Market Street, but the contents of the barrel were discovered, and this secret means of getting rid of the corpse told against him and helped to convict him of wilful murder. On the night previous to the day set for his execution he was visited by Alderman Crolius and Sheriff Monmouth B. Hart, who was a friend of his. Colt had had a love intrigue, and the woman with whom he had been living was young, handsome, and of respectable family. He asked that he be allowed to be united in marriage with her. She was then in the warden's room, for she had been a constant visitor during the young man's imprisonment. Colt's request was granted. At twelve, midnight, the Rev. Dr. Lampson arrived, and the ceremony was performed. Upon its conclusion the convict prayed that he might be left alone for a few minutes with his wife. It was done, and then, so it was supposed, the devoted but unfortunate girl passed him a dirk knife which was to save him from the disgrace of a hangman's halter. Colt concealed the weapon in the waste pipe of the closet. The parting with his wife was an agonizing one. Each knew that by the act of the other they would never meet again alive in this world. Next morning, when the excitement of the fire had subsided, and his cell door was opened, young Colt was found dead, reclining on a settee, with the dirk knife in his bosom. About an inch of the blade had penetrated his heart. A few days before he had asked for and been given a work on anatomy, presumably to learn how most easily and effectively he could compass his own death. The knife was given by Mr. Crolius to Chief of Police Matsell. Two or three days previously his brother Samuel had exploded an invention of his, a torpedo, in the North River, and this circumstance gave rise to the rumor that he had been concerned in the conflagration to effect John's rescue. But it was untrue.

Chowder parties were often given by the companies, and these were notable events for the district. A large number of guests would be invited, and, of course, the big wigs. Lots of fun was to be had at these gatherings. After the eating and drinking dancing was indulged in, not the modern waltz, with its ungainly and vulgar variations, nor even the regulation square dance, but the good old-fashioned gymnastic exercise known as the step-dance. The accompaniment was often a banjo, sometimes a fiddle, and sometimes a flute, but whatever the music the enthusiasm of the dancers and the enjoyment of the spectators were always the same—superlative. Then, again, songs were sung and amusing stories told—stories about fires and firemen—but speeches were tabooed. Even in those slow-going days (slow in comparison with our own) people thought life was too short to indulge in or listen to the "long talk." Nearly ten years ago an old fire laddie, John Rogers, of Hose Company No. 39, gave his reminiscences in a pamphlet, and in reference to these parties said:

"About once a week we would procure a chowder pot, and with a halibut's head and 'fixin's' get up a chowder as was a chowder, the wherewith to pay for the same being collected by one of the boys going round with the hat. We did not eat the chowder in the dark, but had the engine house lighted on chowder nights with candles purchased at a neighboring grocery. Many of the boys lived near by, and these furnished from their homes plates and spoons sufficient to go round, and I venture to assert that no game supper with brilliantly lighted halls and music was ever enjoyed more than our chowder."

The engine house was their sanctuary—their loved sanctuary—and no priest could have a greater regard for his than the firemen for theirs. The inducement must have been exceedingly strong to get the boys away from it. All the amusement they wanted they could get there. Indeed, in those times their wants were few and their indulgences moderate. They did not even aspire to three cent cigars, one or two cents furnishing a weed satisfactory to their tastes. "One of the boys," says an old timer, "induced us one night to go a short distance from the engine house to a raffle for a stove with dance accompaniment, but we did not feel at home. I remember if there were some good looking girls present we could enjoy ourselves better in the old engine house in the dark a good deal. 'Our house' was not quite so large or so well appointed as the engine houses of the present day, being, I should say, about 30 by 14 feet, our engine, 10 by 4, standing in the center. We had no gas in the house, and, in fact, no lights whatever at our gatherings, being allowed so much oil a month from the Corporation yard, bare-

THE COLLECT ONE HUNDRED YEARS AGO.
[Present site of the Tombs, etc.]

ly sufficient to supply our torches and signal lanterns while going to and at a fire, consequently we could use none in the engine house, except in setting things to rights after a fire, and at our monthly meetings. When gathered o' nights in the dark knowing each other by the voice we would talk on the passing topics of the day until we had talked out, when some of the boys would call for a song. Dick Flannigan, a fine singer, and still living, was generally called upon first, and would respond to the call with 'Red Robin,' 'The Angel's Whisper,' or some other popular ballad of the day, when it would be his ' call,' with a response immediately from the member called upon, and so, in free-and-easy fashion, without light and without beer, so much in vogue to-day, we passed away the evenings when no loud alarm rang out to call us forth to stay the flames. What with our score of singers and yarn spinners (many of the latter had learned to spin yarns on shipboard), the hours passed pleasantly and innocently, albeit rough (and ready) mechanics, with little worldly polish. Not infrequently were these sittings interrupted by shaking at the door and the cry of ' Turn out, here ! fire ! fire !' when all would start to their feet on the instant, the doors be flung open, the rope paid out, and forth we would dash in the direction of the fire, our 'souls in arms and eager for the fray.'"

But these routine amusements were broken in upon by the grand chowder parties, as we have said. Among the companies who were famous, in those later days of the Volunteers, for these suppers, were Hose Companies Nos. 33, 36, and 38, and Engine Companies Nos. 42 and 44. Even under the new régime the old boys kept up the old practice of giving Saturday night "chowders," especially the Warren Hose Company No. 33, which had merged into the Warren Association. There were times, however, when the firemen yearned for something a trifle more toothsome than chowder, and would go a little way out of the straight moral path to obtain it. A story is told of Hose Company No. 60 (M. T. Brennan). The editor of the old *Leader*, John Clancy, was for many years its foreman; he was the only journalist in the old department who ever held that rank. On one occasion No. 60 decided to treat themselves to a banquet. They went to the tremendous expense of buying a bushel of oysters, and clapped them in the kettle on the stove in the engine house, then in Elm Street. Martin J. Keese, who was once foreman of the company and later custodian of the City Hall, happened to drop in, viewed the preparations for the feast, and then thoughtfully informed the boys he had seen two magnificent chickens hanging out of the window of one of the members.

"What!" cried Clancy, "one of our boys with chickens, and we not invited! Let us have them here and then invite the churlish fellow."

At once a delegation was sent out to bring in the fowl. Keese tenderly unhooked the chickens while his companions saw that he was not interfered with in the transfer, and the triumphant party returned, and put in the chickens with the oysters. The delicious odor that floated out on a gentle breeze brought heads to many a window and water to many a mouth. Right opposite the engine house lived a Mrs. Hogan, who was attracted by the aroma.

"Arrah, boys," said the old lady, "what in the name of goodness have yez there? It's like a hevenly drame."

"It's a pot of elegant soup," said the genial John, and filling a bowl with the mixture he took it over to the good dame.

When he returned he heard a yell from Mrs. Hogan. "Oh! bad 'cess to yez, ye bastes, yez have cooked the chickens widout takin' out the enthrails. Och! I'm poizened."

A shout of laughter from the engine house caused Mrs. Hogan to use more rhetoric than she had intended.

But supper-parties and dancing-parties were not the only amusements indulged in by the fire-laddies. Some of them were addicted to that form of amusement which modern slang calls "mashing." To be sure, there is no reason why a fireman should not have an innocent flirtation as well as other citizens. Among the unfortunate flirtations was this one: A well-known actress, remarkable for her pretty face, was staying with a married friend in a cross-town street. She was in the habit of writing in one of the back rooms, and right opposite the window at which she sat was the abode of a young fireman. He had straw-colored whiskers, a sad-looking eye, and a flat face, but he thought himself handsome. Day after day he used to stare out of window at the handsome actress, till she came to regard him as a curiosity. Mistaking her glances, he felt emboldened to waft her kisses, and blushed while he did it. Then he made inquiries among the servants, and learned that the front room was occupied by Mrs. Smith. Upon this he squared his elbow and wrote a missive full of respectful love and devotion to Mrs. Smith. Unfortunately, Mr. Smith, who was a man of an extremely jealous disposition, found the letter on the hall-stand, opened it, and turned pale with rage when he read the allusion to the supposed flirtation. He caused one of his work-girls to write an answer. The young fireman responded, more love-missives passed to and fro, and at last an appointment was made. Mr. Smith was convinced his wife was false, and determined to destroy her lover before her face. The interview was held, and its uproarious character attracted the attention of the actress. She rushed in, found the wife dissolving in tears, her husband accusing her while flourishing a revolver, and the young man in a corner stupefied by the reception he met with. An explanation followed, laughter took the place of tears, and the machine runner raced off quicker than ever he did to a fire.

The engine was, so to speak, the apple of the eye of the old fireman. Once a fireman was seen to publicly hug and kiss his engine, after she had got the best of a rival company's engine. Again, a fire laddie, who would not have shed a tear for any trouble of his own, cried like a child when his machine was "washed." The public took an amazing interest in Fire Department matters. The "mysterious disappearance" of the picture on the back of Engine No. 14, about 1850, kept the whole city talking for days. She was a "crack" little engine and a great favorite. Harry Venn and Peter Ottignon

HARRY VENN,
Foreman Engine Company No. 14.

(the Jolly Butcher), two of the most popular firemen of the city, had been foremen of her. When Ottignon was foreman the boys had the engine painted regardless of expense. The "engine artist" of the time was Quidor, who put what was regarded as a fine painting on her back, representing a handsome Indian and his squaw. One day, however, they got into a fight with another company, and as a punishment their engine was sent to the corporation yard—the greatest disgrace that could befall a company. The boys were naturally very downcast, but before the corporation truck had arrived to take away the "beauty," the painting was removed from her back, and hidden in a cellar. The lads were resolved to have some memento of her. When the Fire and Water Committee, however, found out what was done, they were indignant, and set detectives to work to look for that Indian and his squaw, and the daily newspapers were full of the accounts of the search. Only a few of the men were in the secret. In time No. 14 was reinstated in her old house, and then suddenly and mysteriously one bright morning the missing back was found attached to the engine. In the meantime the Indian and his squaw had traveled six thousand miles. This is how it happened: One of the old members of the company was Jim Lyons, who afterwards became a mate on board of one of the Havre Line of packets. The back was taken to his boarding house one night, and next day Lyons sailed for France, and, when he returned, brought back the engine plate with him

This pretty little engine once had a terrific struggle at a fire with No. 34 (Old Howard). It was one of the most exciting contests known in the old Department, and is thus graphically described by an eyewitness, John D. Brower, one of the "vets," who subsequently went to San Francisco: "A fire had occurred in 'Mackerelville.' No. 34 had come from Christopher and Hudson Streets, and had secured a good position for drawing water from a pond in the vicinity, her suctions running out about level with the box of the engine. There were several other short liners at work, passing the water from a pond nearer the fire, but as it threatened to be a big fire before it got through, and the 'Rovers' knew they had a good thing, Thirty-four remained at its original place. Pretty soon the engines from away down-town arrived, and among them No. 14 from Vesey Street. When hailed by No. 34 to take their water, the boys cried 'Yes, yes,' for it was considered as showing a mean spirit or the white feather to refuse an offer of that kind. So after dragging her over several little hills and valleys, 14's boys turned her round to 34's butt, and made ready to take her water. No. 34 had already been working slowly, 'charging the hose,' as they called it, and when No. 14 gave the word in went the butt, and to work they went in good earnest, and the drumming of the engines in that line was music to the ear of the fireman, and tended to hurry him on to the scene of the fight, or the fun, when blocks away. It was a damp, drizzly night, with a cold wind from the east, but there were men surrounding those two engines, the pride of the Department, stripped to the buff, and working as they never could or never would work at anything else. There were around No. 14 Pete Ottignon, foreman at that time; Harry B. Venn, who had just resigned the position; Phil Jonas, Johnny Baum, Jim Johnston, Alf Chancellor, Boss Talliant, Dick Logan, Sam Baisley, Alex. Dunscombe, John Decker (a Volunteer at that time), and others, cheering, working, and striving, as though their lives were at stake to prevent one drop of water from running over 14's box. The first encounter lasted nearly ten minutes—a long time if a watch was held over men working as they were, when the order ' 'vast playing' came down the line, an order which was quite welcome to No. 14, but not quite so welcome to No. 34; for when the butt was taken out the water was found to be up to the bend. Then the friends of 34 became deeply concerned as to the duration of the fire; 14 was also by no means a disinterested party as to its continuance; in fact 14 would have hailed with joy about that time the order to 'to take up,' and those of 34 would prefer seeing another cowshed or an old stable go rather than miss this glorious opportunity at one of the most energetic and efficient companies in the old Department. Then came a lot of 'chin,' criticisms, and opinions, as to whether 14 could or could not take the water, and in justice to her brave fellows it must be stated that it was thought at the time that the soft ground she stood on, made worse by the water from 34's butt every time it was taken out, helped in a great measure to bring on the misfortune that at last befell her; for while she stood fairly up so that the men could get at their work, she rattled the water out after it got to the bend as fast as it came in, making it rather lively for the engine ahead. But no quarter was given or taken in such matters; 'Up to the bend' did not frighten anybody. Those little engines could not get a good hold of the water until it was about there, but when it rose above that particular place, then look out for squalls. And in justice, too, to 'Old Howard' and her heroes, it was acknowledged that her butt on this occasion was not one to be trifled with. Drawing the water as she did with a level suction, it came from her butt almost as solid as a board, and to those not acquainted with the qualities of those little engines, it would seem almost impossible for one of them to throw the stream 34 showed that night, or for one of them to take it as long as 14 did.

UP TO THE BEND.
[Old 14 washed by 36.]

By this time the position of the engines was breezed around, and the friends of both came hastening to their aid, until quite a crowd had assembled around both the contestants.

"At length the word came again for water, and all went to work with a will. They stood in rows three or four deep, and as fast as a man would drop off the brakes he would pass to the rear, and another would instantly take his place. When next the order ''vast playing' came down the line, the water was a trifle lower, and it was barely perceptible, but it gave encouragement to 14's crowd for the time, and delayed the hopes of those at the engine behind her, who were inwardly wishing for the fire to last a while longer. By this time 14 had settled in the soft ground almost up to her hubs, and therefore made much harder work of it. However, 34 was in pretty much the same condition, so it was also as fair for one as the other. The word again came, and never did the fire laddies work with better spirit and energy than they did that night. They worked with a will known only to those who have been placed in the like 'hole.' The water began to rise—slowly, to be sure, but it was rising. Then it was a sight to see the brave fellows of 14 and her 'crowd' exert themselves in order to keep her free. Harry Venn, towering like a chief among heroes, stood on the rope-reel waving his trumpet over those at work on the brakes, and cheering them on by all sorts of endearing appeals. It soon became evident, however, from the dull heavy sound of the brakes, that it was as Johnston said, 'beginning to look dusty;' the water was rising, she was nearly full. Then a cheer around 34 told of confidence restored on her side. And then both sides stopped again, when the word was passed up the line, 'three-quarters full.' The hair on Logan's head stood straight out now, and Baum, Dozey, Baisley, Johnston, and Jones were all more or less grouty. Anything but a 'wash' for them. Venn looked distrustingly at the settled condition of the engine in the ground, examined the chains, and surveyed the scene like a man who felt that at any rate he was doing his best. All this time 34 had kept on working moderately, to keep the hose well charged, and when the word again came, at the first stroke of 14 in went the butt. This 'round' was of long duration, and, despite the heroic efforts of those willing hands to save her, the water gradually rose. One would have expected to see the brakes fly, as they did, that they would tear the little engine to pieces. Just so with 34. They were hammering the wood with a will, while a long drawn cheer from the crowd around her told those at the brakes they were not striving in vain, and made the cold, damp night air ring with life and animation. And when the word was passed down 'She's up to the rabbits,' followed soon after by the two single words, to delight or dismay, as the case might be, the firemen of long ago, 'She's over!' one would have thought that a Malakoff or a Gibraltar had been successfully stormed that night at Mackerelville.

"But there she stood, plucky little 14, when the order came to 'take up' full and dripping over. Her 'boys' had done their best, and there was no fault to find with the engine, yet she had received a stain upon her fair fame that would follow her for years, or until such time as the doubtful favor might be returned, if ever there was a possibility.

"Yes, there stood 14, pretty as a picture, even in her defeat, just out from the painter's, with a finely polished surface of black, ornamented and striped in gold, her silver-plated work shining with care, her burnished levers glistening in the torchlight, while her members and volunteers, and in fact the whole crowd around her appeared like men who had not been invited to take anything for a week. All old firemen know how galling it was in such cases to let water out by the way of the tail screw that they failed to pass over the leader bow. All the vets have been there. But so particularly hard did the result of this encounter at Mackerelville grate on the feelings of the members of 14 that the very next afternoon they sent a delegation to 14's house, with a request to measure her cylinders. Of course it was granted, and they were found to be like all others, except 38 and 42, in the department, just six and a half. It had been a fair and square tussle, engine to engine, fireman to fireman, pluck had been the same on both sides, but the luck was this time all on 34's."

The John Rogers already referred to has given reminiscences of rivalry in the old days. "The machine I 'run' with and thought the world of," said Rogers, "'laid' east of the Bowery, near Division Street, and was of the.

little 'goose-neck' pattern, with six-inch chambers, and capable, with our crew at the brakes, of 'taking the water' of any neighboring engine and no favors asked. The sounding and inspiriting calls consequent upon forming a line in those days many yet remember. To me the grandest and most exciting affair that could be improvised was the various engines working in line at a fire when the flames were aggressive. I can see the line now, hear the stentorian shouts of the foreman, the uproar of voices generally, the pounding of the rapidly-moving brakes, and other noises incident to a fire. A fire breaks out in Beekman Street, above Cliff. The bells sound the alarm ; out rolls the engine, and down they go, the first making for the dock, where they are wheeled about, the wheels against the string-piece of the dock. Two men jump to each side of the engine, unbuckle the suctions (of sole leather, the baskets of brass) and screw them them to the tail of the engine. By the time

CONFLICT BETWEEN COMPANIES.

this is done, the 'butt' is unbuckled and the hose reeled off by two or three members, who start with it up street, dragging its length (two hundred feet) not slowly along by any means, the man first at the engine house and the first man at the tongue being entitled to hold the butt into the engine which is to take the water from the one on the dock, a rule with all companies.

"By the time these movements were effected another engine would come thundering down street, the foreman in charge of the first shouting at the top of his voice, 'Take our water, boys?' 'Yes,' would be the reply in most cases, when round would go that engine in position to 'take our water,' its hose reeled off and carried farther up the street to connect with the next engine coming along, and so on until the line was formed from the dock to the fire. The line formed and all being in readiness for the work in hand, the foreman of the engine on the fire (the one nearest the latter) would give the command to his company : 'Play away !' which was repeated all down the line to the engine 'at suction' on the dock, when the most enlivening and exciting scenes would be witnessed. Necessarily the suction engine had the longest stroke, from the fact that she had to draw the water before forcing it through her four lengths of hose, the two operations requiring great pressure upon the brakes. With the order to 'Play away !' the man holding the butt of the suction engine, assisted by two others who 'lightened up the hose,' would begin to brace his muscles and make ready for the coming of the rushing water. The force of water was immense as the stream poured into the receiving engine shortly after the commands of the foreman, 'Stand by your brakes, men !' 'Put in the butt' (to the holder of the latter), and play away, men !'

"The old-timer recollects well the music (enlivening to his ears) that followed these commands, and the young men of the present day can imagine how exciting it was to see twenty partially stripped men (ten on a side) manning the brakes of a short-stroke engine and dashing her down at the rate of sixty or seventy strokes a minute, some with their hair floating about their faces at every stroke, while that of others was confined by closely-fitting skull-caps of red or striped flannel. Then upon the front of the engine the foreman would jump, and through his trumpet, or without the mouthpiece, shout to his men such stimulating cries as these : 'Every one of you, now, will you work ?' 'Work her lively, lads !' 'You don't half work !' 'Now you've got her !' 'Stave her sides in !' 'Say you will, now !' and so on, his body swaying to the motion of the brakes, and he giving up only when his voice was gone, when some strong-bodied and loud-voiced member would relieve him. The men who worked at the brakes were now tired out, and were in turn relieved in a minute or minute and a half, that being as long as a man could work on the brakes in that position, the labor being so violent and exhausting. But there were plenty on each side the engine ready to fall in when the exhausted ones fell out, and an expert thing it was to fall in and catch the arm of the brake, between which and the box of the engine many a finger has been crushed, maiming many a fire-laddie for life. I could go on talking about 'playing in line' for hours—how one engine would 'nigger' another by getting eight or ten strokes ahead before the water from the butt could be discharged, how the man holding the butt would get knocked down for not taking it out of the engine he was supplying soon enough to please other parties. I could dwell on the 'boiling,' 'slopping,' and final 'washing,' and how the discomfited company of the washed engine would, in many cases, go in for a free fight in order to vent their mortification in not being able to play the water out as fast as the rear engine had played it in, resulting in a 'wash.'"

There were many fights, and hot ones, too, in the old department, but they grew out of a natural emulation and were not lacking in a certain rugged element of chivalry which promoted manhood, though somewhat at the expense of public order. The murderous revolver and assassin-like disposition which now mark its use were unknown in those days. The combats were fair hand-to-hand fights between man and man, and he who resorted to any other weapon than those which nature supplied was accounted a ruffian or a coward.

But when big fires happened all individual bickerings were sunk in a unanimous resolve to do their duty. This was notable in the great fire of 1811, which began on a Sunday, when all the firemen fraternized. Some unknown writer contributed to the papers across the ocean an original poem on what he called "The Clasped Hands of the Fire Brigade." The first stanza read:

> They came from the altar to face the flame,
> From prayer to fight with fire;
> And the flame which burns but never binds
> Was a bond to draw them nigher.

On Sunday morning, July 26, 1846, a big fight occurred in Broadway between the runners of several fire companies. The companies involved were Engine Companies Nos. 1, 6, 23, 31, and 36. The fight lasted a considerable time, and many of the combatants received more than they bargained for in their desire to have some fun. Subsequently, Andrew McCarty and Jeremiah Haley, of No. 1, and Alexander McDonald and Daniel Davenport, of No. 5, were expelled. On August 5, all the companies concerned were disbanded by order of the Common Council. In view of the magnitude of the combat, the Aldermen considered they could not overlook the affair. The battle had raged all the way to Canal and Hudson Streets, and attracted an immense crowd of citizens. After the disbandment, there was not a single fire company left in the Fifth Ward. Benjamin J. Evans, who first began to run with No. 31 in 1843, became its assistant foreman, and subsequently joined Hose Company No. 5, on November 16, 1850, has given the writer the following particulars of this big fight:

GOVERNOR'S HOUSE AND CHURCH IN THE FORT.
[Dutch Period.]

"We were called out from our quarters in West Broadway on a still alarm, our foreman singing out, 'Come, pull away, boys, for West Broadway's alive!' As we were returning home, opposite the Park, we met Engine No. 6, and she commenced to bark. Then along came Equitable, and she thought she would help No. 6, but found that she was in a mighty pretty fix herself. No. 5, just then turned up near Ann Street, and the 'Short Boys" cry greeting their ears, they said, 'Let us go and help old 31, and make the Short Boys feel sick.' Chief Engineer Anderson was standing at the time on the Astor House steps. No. 6, which then lay in Reade Street, began to 'bear' at us, and a fight resulted. In the midst of it, No. 1 Engine, which lay at the foot of Duane Street, appeared and sided with No. 6. Then Engine 23, of Leonard Street, turned up and sailed in with us. No. 36 followed quickly, taking Six's side. Pipes, axes, and any weapon handy, were used in the fight. It was a terrific fight, and lasted a long while. At last, Anderson succeeded in putting a stop to it, and made us go down Canal Street instead of through Chambers, so as to avoid our foes. Foreman Jack Whitehead and Assistant Foreman Bill Whitehead were tremendous big men, whom nobody cared to tackle single handed. Before the fight No. 5 sent their engine home in charge of a few men, and this precaution saved them from being disbanded."

Evans, one afternoon, while assistant foreman of No. 31, was with Engine No. 5, and got into a "muss" with No. 11 in Eighth Avenue. No. 11 "wiped the street" with him and his chums, and at last the men of No. 5 made off and Evans was left with only Uzziah Wenman to stand by him. After 31 was disbanded he joined 14 Hose, and subsequently he organized new 31. Evans went to the war with the Twelfth Regiment, N. Y., in April, 1861, and was taken prisoner at Harper's Ferry. His was the first regiment in Washington on May 24, 1861. Evans crossed the Long Bridge at Washington, and saw the rebel flag flying on the Marshal House about four in the morning. About five o'clock word was brought that Ellsworth was shot at Alexandria. After the war he went back to No. 31. Mr. Evans is now fifty-six years old, and connected with the Fire Department in Jersey City.

A single combat was the result of the rivalry between Engine Companies Nos. 30 and 44 ("Old Turk"). No. 30 lay in Christie Street, and Jack Teal was the foreman. Jim Jerolomon was the giant of No. 44, standing six feet four in height. In Chief Gulick's time No. 44 lay in Houston Street, near Lewis, and Bob Penny was foreman. On a Saturday afternoon a fire broke out in Milton Smith's stables, at Avenue D and Sixth Street. No. 44 was the first to reach the fire, and took suction from the foot of Sixth Street. No. 37 engine, which lay in Delancey Street, was friendly to No. 44, and was on her way to the fire, when Penny ran down to Union Market and told No. 37 to go to Fifth Street, the object of this being to make No. 30 take No. 44's water and get washed. Soon No. 30 came in, and Penny asked Teal, who commanded No. 30, to take Forty-four's water. Teal replied, in a sarcastic manner: "Take yer water? Ye-e-s; why wouldn't we take it?" No. 30 got into line, and 44 butted into her. The butcher boys of Christie Street were good men, and held their own for a time, but when Penny got the stout lads from the shipyards on the brake of Old Turk nothing could equal them, and in fifteen minutes No. 30 was boiling over. Penny asked Gulick to send an engine to take Forty-four's water. "Can't 30 take it?" asked the chief. Penny replied that a dozen Thirties couldn't take it. Gulick then ordered No. 30 away, and as Jerolomon took the butt out of 30 he squirted the water over "Thirty's fellers." Teal, who was a much smaller man, then struck Jerolomon, and a fight was the result. The next day Teal and Jerolomon met in Yorkville and fought. On the third round Teal claimed that Jerolomon was biting him, and on removing his shirt the print of teeth was found on his shoulder. The combat was then broken up. Teal was a joiner, and considered one of the best fighters of the time. Jerolomon was at another time a member of No. 17 engine, when she lay in Jackson Street, then Walnut.

In the year 1824 James P. Allaire, of the old firm of Allaire Bros., was foreman of "Black Joke" Engine Company No. 33. The name was given her in honor of an Albany sloop which distinguished herself in the war of 1812. She was painted a "nigger" black on the body, and had a gold stripe running all the way around. In 1832 her headquarters were in Gouverneur, between Henry and Madison Streets, and Malachi Fallon was her foreman. She had on her ropes about forty men, nearly all of them being fighters. The company was known as a fighting one and "a pretty hard crowd." Fallon, after leaving No. 33, became chief of police of San Francisco, California. In 1842 James Burbridge was her foreman, and among the runners were two gigantic negroes, one named John Arno alias "Black Jack," and the other was called "Black Joe." Those darkeys made themselves very serviceable around the engine house, and felt themselves highly honored in being asked to do anything. They were not, however, allowed to bunk in the engine house. In the summer of 1842 No. 33 had a severe fight with No. 5 Truck and Hose Company No. 4. There had been a fire in Monroe, near Gouverneur Street, and these two companies combined to "lick" No. 33. And a terrible thrashing they gave 33, the fight lasting almost an hour; bloody heads, broken noses, black eyes, and torn clothes being plentiful. The fight originated in a supposition that while at work at the fire the men of No. 33 "splashed" water over the men of Nos. 4 and 5 while they were playing on the ruins. No. 33 denied that they had done so, but insisted upon having a fight, and they got it. In 1843 No. 33 was disbanded, but was reorganized in 1844, with ex-Alderman Peter Masterson as its foreman.

In 1832 No. 33 got into a difficulty with Engine Company No. 11. A fire occurred in Pearl Street, near Maiden Lane. No. 11 was taking water from the dock and supplied No. 33. Both companies were noted for their strength. No. 11 tried to "wash" No. 33, and failed after working all night. When daylight broke, the boys, tired out, went to breakfast, and then the runners or hangers-on of the engines took their places to keep up the supply of water. These "irregulars" were animated with the same sentiments that characterized the great men they were

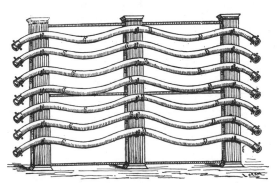

RACK FOR DRYING LEATHER HOSE, 1840.

permitted to follow, and again it was sought to get No. 33 over, but in vain. Then No. 11 charged No. 33 with "niggering." This meant only working at intervals and compelling the supply engine to take out its butt. Hot words followed, and it was decided to settle the matter by a fight. As a rule champions were selected for the companies, and the rule was observed on this occasion. The engines were deserted, a ring was formed, and at it the gladiators went. In the midst of the fun the gigantic Gulick appeared upon the scene. He was the Chief Engineer. He settled the contest immediately. A blow from his fist was like a kick from a horse. He sailed right in and scattered the ring and the fighters in a minute.

No chief had ever so great a hold upon the firemen as James Gulick had. We refer in the chapter upon fires to the refusal of the men to work after the great fire of December, 1835, when the Common Council deposed him from office. Here is another instance of the affection the boys had for him. It was in the beginning of the same year, January 4, that a fire broke out in Centre Street, adjoining the works of the New York Gas Company, which destroyed two houses. Against the gable end of one of the burning buildings a large number of barrels of resin were piled. The firemen worked diligently to save these by rolling them into the street, and the night being intensely cold, some one kindled a small fire in the street with a part of the contents of a broken barrel, which the workmen employed by the gas company attempted to extinguish. They were warned by the firemen to desist, and a big, heavy fellow, who insisted upon putting out the fire, was shoved away. Thereupon a large number of his friends attacked the few firemen around the fire. Other firemen flew to the assistance of their comrades, and a regular fight ensued. The laddies conquered. Gulick heard of the affair, and, hastening to the scene, exclaimed: "What does all this shameful conduct mean at this moment?" One of the workmen flew at him and struck him from behind over the head with an iron bar. His fire-cap, however, protected him from serious injury. Turning upon his assailant the powerful Chief pursued him across the ruins of the fallen wall, and threw him down upon the bricks. Immediately some thirty or forty workmen surrounded Gulick. Then the cry was raised, "Men, stand by your Chief!" and in a twinkling the assailants were quickly routed and took refuge in the gas-house at the corner of Centre and Hester Streets. Gulick, by almost superhuman efforts, got into the gas-house first to prevent the excited firemen from entering. Amid volleys of coal-buckets he called upon the rioters inside to behave themselves and they should be protected. He was replied to by being rushed at with a red-hot poker; but, fortunately, his trumpet was under his arm, with its large bowl in front of him, through which the hot poker passed. He jumped from the stoop crying in stentorian tones: "Now, men, surround the house; don't let one of them escape!" They were all, or nearly all, arrested and locked up after receiving a sound drubbing. The firemen got very excited, and it seemed that a big riot would ensue. They rushed into the gas-house and attempted to destroy the machinery, and a dreadful explosion was imminent. But the Chief's firmness prevailed, and in a short time he quieted the men and restored peace.

One of the most famous fights of the old fire laddies goes by the name of "The Battle of the Boots." It is not a dignified name for a battle, still the conflict was a very heroic and very bloody one. There are several still living who participated in the affair. It took place in the summer of 1842, and was the result of an old feud between engine companies Nos. 27 and 34, and came off after extinguishing the fire in the New House furniture store, the shop attached to which is in Van Renwyck Street, which runs from Spring to Canal Street. That street is now called Renwick Street. Both companies were composed of smart men, both had made good records, and their rivalry was warm. The brave and unfortunate Dave Broderick was then foreman of No. 34. John J. Mount, as already stated above, was one of the Volunteers of No. 27. Mount was one of the gay and festive Butt Enders, an association around Clinton Market, at the foot of Spring Street, who used to run with No. 27. Previous to this fire in Van Renwyck Street No. 27 was caught shorthanded and at a disadvantage by their opponents, and sustained a defeat. Although they laughed at it, and indeed seemed to regard it as a good joke, this severe check was brooded over by No. 27, and they determined soon to get even with their opponents. All the Volunteers went up and joined the roll of No. 27 and then looked out for the "enemy." No. 27 ran to several fires without coming in contact with No. 34 until this fire in Van Renwyck Street occurred. No. 27 was early on hand, took the dock, gave water to their hated rivals, who in turn gave their water to some other engine. All the boys worked magnificently. Their first duty was to the public—to put out the fire—and no private interests were supposed to interfere with this.

About ten o'clock at night the fire was got under, and all the engines took up their hose. For some time No. 27's plan of battle had been arranged by Ely Hazelton, their "boss" warrior, the Napoleon and Achilles of the company. The signal for the fight was to be the word "boots," and when that was given every man was to "sail right in." Well, the ropes were lined inside and out, and No. 27 had all their friends around. When they got near Hudson Street they were almost abreast of No. 34. No. 34 was about to turn the corner, but three parts of No. 27's rope stretched across the way. Now was the moment; now had the hour of revenge arrived.

"Boots!" thundered the muscular and stentorian Hazelton.

Down went the ropes, up went the avenging hands of the lads of No. 27, and in a twinkling they were pummeling their opponents. Blows were rained with stunning force and bewildering rapidity, while the exchanges were few and far between. But the rush of No. 27 was like the fall of a mountain torrent reinforced by the 'whelming flood of a winter's storm, and the unfortunate boys of No. 34 were overpowered and swept away. The foreman and assistants in those days used to walk in rear of the engine. Foreman Broderick was far in the rear when the battle began, and, scarcely realizing what had happened, was marching up Hudson Street, near Spring, when he received a gentle hint of what was going on. One of the young fellows of No. 27 noticed the redoubtable Dave coming along. The temptation was too great, and he let fly at Broderick, who, as the old chroniclers of the tournaments say, "bit the dust." Dave's hat fell off and was lost to him. It became the trophy of No. 27. The boys of No. 34 rallied, but their opponents were this time determined to conquer or die, and full of enthusiasm charged *en masse* on No. 27 and drove them up the street. In the struggle Mount was struck in the stomach by the stave of a barrel and badly gashed. No. 34 was already whipped when its foreman and assistants put a stop to the further progress of the fight.

Broderick's fire cap was picked up, and carried in triumph by No. 27 to their engine house in Desbrosses Street, where it was placed on the flagstaff, and remained on exhibition all next day. The headquarters of this company was at Joe Orr's saloon, at the corner of Desbrosses and Greenwich Streets. Broderick called there on the afternoon following the fight, accompanied by Mike Walsh, Johnny Ketcham, and several other members of his company to negotiate for the return of his official headgear. Hazelton and some of his chums were there. The peace propositions did not proceed satisfactorily; indeed they resulted in a row. Walsh had his fingers broken, Broderick was run out of the place, and his aid-de-camps scattered. Dave was pursued into Washington Street, and he ran for safety into the restaurant kept by Budd. Mount saw his flight, and noticed the infuriated crowd that chased him. He at once stepped in between the pursued and pursuers, and arrested further hostilities. "You ought to be ashamed of yourselves," said he, "so many of you to attack one man. Let him have fair play." The temper of the crowd cooled, they acknowledged the justness of the rebuke, and allowed the young fireman to have his way. Mount then escorted Broderick to the latter's place.

at the corner of Commerce and Hudson Streets, and was warmly thanked for his generous interposition.

Hazelton, the fighter, subsequently came to an untimely end. He gave himself up to drink, and all efforts to reform him were in vain. In 1850 he went on a spree, and one night he took an awl, put the point to his head, and drove it into his brain with a mallet. He died almost instantly.

Nearly the entire time of the Common Council was taken up in settling the disputes between Broderick's company (No. 34) and No. 27. They were always bitter enemies, and never lost an occasion to quarrel. Generally the battle ground was near Sweeney's Hotel, and not a meeting of the Council passed without the friends of both companies being present in force, carrying bludgeons, sticks, hooks, and every kind of fighting implements, as evidence for and against one another—trying to prove which was the aggressive party.

RESIDENCE OF JACOB STOUTENBUGH, FAIR ST.
First Chief Engineer of Fire Department, 1735.

No. 40 ("Lady Washington") housed in Mulberry Street, near Grand. Her foreman and assistant foreman were Joseph Primrose and John Carlin, brother of William Carlin, who subsequently owned and kept the hotel on Fourteenth Street, opposite Macy's. Among the most conspicuous of her fighting men were: Mose Humphreys, a type setter (afterwards the prototype already referred to of Chanfrau's Mose in a "Glance at New York"), who died in the Sandwich Islands, where he had married a native woman, and reared a large family of young natives; and Jim Jeroloman, a shipbuilder, six feet four inches tall, who wore earrings, and who challenged "Yankee" Sullivan to a prize fight, but was easily beaten.

There were several other popular fire companies more or less in sympathy and in aggressive alliance with one or other of the above companies. Among these were No. 44 ("Live Oak") at the foot of Houston Street; No. 30 ("The Tompkins"), of which Tom Hyer was a member; No. 34, at Christopher Street and Hudson, of which Dave Broderick was foreman, and Bill Poole—the only man who ever beat John Morrissey—was a member; and No. 33, afterwards "Big Six," of which William M. Tweed and Malachi Fallon were then only modest privates. Its foreman was Sam Purdy, who afterwards became the first lieutenant-governor of California. Purdy's father was the rider of Eclipse in his junior race on the Long Island course with Henry.

Between Nos. 15 and 40 an ill-feeling had been for a long while brewing. Both companies when running to down town fires used frequently to meet in Chatham Street, and fright the town from its propriety with angry wranglings, or with excited shouts as they would "buck" the pavements, one on either side of the street, and engage in a furious contest of speed in their rival efforts to be first at the fire. On this remarkable occasion, however—it was a bright.

summer Sunday—the two companies, after several hours of arduous duty at a fire in South Street, near Wall, turned homeward about the same time, and passed up Pearl Street together, in dangerous proximity to each other. The ropes of both sides were—as usual on Sundays—fully manned. Probably five hundred men confronted each other on either side. It had been rumored early in the day that No. 40 intended to attack No. 15, and destroy its boasted invincibility. The presence in the ranks of the former, of several noted fighters

FRONT AND TRUMPET OF WM. M. TWEED.

from 34 and 44, lent color to this report, and the hostile companies were followed by an army of expectant lookers-on and partisans.

The two wheeled into Chatham Street together, No. 15 leading. No. 15 turned eastward on its usual way homeward, via the Bowery. No. 40 should have taken the westward course down Chatham Street to its house on Mulberry Street, but instead of doing so, followed its rival until the broad space of Chatham Square was reached. Here the two companies came abreast, and the satirical chaffing which up to this had marked their antagonism swelled into a chorus of mutual taunts and menaces. So they continued, until the Bowery was reached. At the head of 15's rope was "Country" McCluskey, confronted by the formidable Jim Jeroloman at the head of 40. At the rear of the line Hen Chanfrau was opposed by Mose Humphreys. Both sides were by this time ripe for conflict.

The two foremen, Colladay, on the part of No. 15, and Carlin, on the part of No. 40, passed rapidly up and down their respective lines, ostensibly endeavoring to preserve the peace, but in reality stimulating the courage and exciting the pride of their partisans. "Now, boys, no fighting," said Colladay, audibly, adding in an undertone, "but if they will have it, give it 'em good!" "Be quiet, men," said Carlin, loudly ; then in a lower tone, "till they begin, then go in!" The vociferations of the opposing companies grew meanwhile louder and more threatening, until at last words being exhausted, both sides began to "peel" for the conflict which was felt to be inevitable. Jeroloman took out his earrings and put them in his pocket.

Passing from Chatham Square into the Bowery, the opposing companies, which up to that point had moved side by side, surrounded by a dense crowd, were, by the narrowing limits of the latter street, forced into collision. That proved the signal for the fray. The lines of each were extended nearly an entire block. The instant McCluskey and Jeroloman came within striking distance of each other, they dropped their respective ropes and became fiercely engaged. The shock of battle rolled down the line, and quicker than it takes to write the words, one thousand sturdy, stalwart fellows were fiercely grappling each other in a hand-to-hand fight. The din was frightful ; louder than the furious exclamations that filled the air could be heard the resounding blows. The fighters were so thick that there was scarcely room for one to fall. Combatants who, so to say, felt themselves knocked down, were upheld by the pressure of the surrounding throng, and those who were unlucky enough to find mother earth were nearly trampled to death by the feet of friend and foe before they could escape. The leaders on both sides did their very best to maintain their reputation for courage and personal prowess. McCluskey, after a hot and desperate struggle, thrashed Jeroloman, Freeland triumphed over a noted fighter of No. 40, known as "Orange County," and other champions of No. 15 were making it all right.

The most conspicuous opponents at the other end of the line were Hen Chanfrau and Mose Humphreys. Both were pure-blooded Americans and men of noted bravery. At the crisis of their little difficulty, when victory appeared somewhat uncertain on whose gladiatorial arm to perch, a handsome bright-eyed lad of twelve years ran quickly out of Alvord's hat store, in which he had acted as clerk, and nimbly mounting an awning-post, shouted down to one of the combatants, who had just then pressed his antagonist backward over the tongue of 40 engine, and was pounding him very industriously, "Give it to him, Hen ; Julia is looking at you from the window! Don't choke him ; give him a chance to holler enough!" This nimble and encouraging youngster was Frank Chanfrau ; and Mose Humphreys, who presently chorussed Frank's advice with a hearty acknowledgment of defeat, was to suggest to the then comedian in embryo a type of character which won him a double fortune and an enduring fame.

The fight lasted about thirty minutes. It resulted in the total defeat of No. 40, who abandoned their apparatus and fled precipitately. The victorious 15, determined to humiliate their antagonists in the most bitter manner known to the Volunteer firemen of that day, seized the captured engine—which was beautifully painted in white and gold—dragged it to a pump, and deluged it with water. They held possession of it for hours, but finally released it to John Carlin. They, however, refused to permit any of "40's fellows" to enter their bailiwick, and the latter were made to suffer the additional mortification of seeing their beloved "Lady Washington" drawn home from the scene of their defeat at the tail of a cart. This notable battle terminated hostilities between 15 and 40.

William H. Philp, a well-known artist and a whilom fireman, has many pleasant reminiscences to recall. One is the serenade and the torchlight procession in honor of Jenny Lind. During her first visit to this country she had given the proceeds of one of her concerts to the Firemen's Widow and Orphans Fund. In recognition of her generosity the firemen subscribed for the purchase of a copy of Audubon's Book on Birds, a very rare and costly work, and this was presented to her by a committee of firemen at the Irving House, corner of Broadway and Chambers street. It was a beautiful night, and the whole department turned out with bands of music and torches. Broadway was crowded. Halting in front of the hotel the committee entered and made the presentation. Then Jenny Lind appeared on the balcony and bowed her acknowledgments many times, deafening cheers following each bow, torchlights waving and bands playing.

Mr. Philp went on the famous excursion to Philadelphia in 1852, where the Department were received by the municipal authorities, and the firemen shown about the city and most hospitably entertained. Mr. Philp thinks that it was about this period that the New York Fire Department reached the greatest epoch of its glory; there was an *esprit du corps* in the department and a manly zeal in the discharge of duty not surpassed at any later period. It was witnessing the feats of the firemen at the Hague street explosion that inspired Mr. Philp with a desire to become a fireman, and he always took an active part with his company during the three years that he served. He was present at the Pearl street fire in 1850; at the fire in the drug store of McKesson & Robbins, where a number of the firemen were injured by the spattering of vitriol from broken carboys; at the Jennings clothing store fire, opposite City Hall Park, and at the burning of the Great Republic, the largest sailing vessel then afloat.

The most trying fire ever attended by Mr. Philp was that in Broadway, between Grand and Howard streets, in the winter of 1853. It was a bitter cold night; the water froze in sheets on the firemen's backs while their faces were exposed to the heat of the fire. Many were totally benumbed, and one or two firemen were killed by falling walls. Mr. Philp declares that he endured nothing throughout the war of the Rebellion equal to his suffering on that memorable night. He is a member of the Volunteer Firemen's Association.

CHAPTER XIII.

MEMORABLE INCIDENTS.

Running on the Sidewalks.—Attacked by Rowdies.—Concealing a Hydrant.—The Bunking Rooms.—
Heroism of an Old Fire Laddie.—A Gallant Rescue.—Target Companies.—Knights of the Round
Table.—Frank Clark, of "Old Turk."—A Fireman becomes a Monk.

THE weekly papers had published in 1854 articles reflecting upon the Department, and particularly referring to the rowdies who were permitted to run with the engines. On the twenth-fourth of January a special meeting was held at Fireman's Hall by the Board of Engineers and Foremen, and a committee was appointed to investigate the charges. The committee consisted of John Lynes, Hose Company No. 9; Noah L. Farnham, Hook and Ladder Company No. 1; John D. Dixon, Hose Company No. 54; Julian Botts, Engine Company No. 38; and William Tappan, Engine Company No. 7. The alleged rowdyism was shown to be due to the irresponsible runners who tacked themselves on to the companies.

The firemen at all times naturally took the shortest cut to a fire and the easiest road. The easiest was the sidewalk, which they used to clear like a flash of lightning. It was alleged that there was danger in this, and that it interfered with the liberty of the citizen. Nevertheless the boys thought it much better to run smoothly over the sidewalk than to bump along over the cobble stones. On May 20, 1853, the Common Council took the matter in hand. Alderman Smith proposed a resolution, notifying the engine companies that they would be dissolved if known to run on the sidewalk. In reference to this the *Fireman's Journal*, edited by Mr. Anthony B. Child, said on the following day:

"If Alderman Smith's resolution becomes a law we hope more attention will be paid by the authorities to the condition of the streets. In some of our principal thoroughfares it is almost impossible to drag an apparatus in the street. Not only is there severe labor requisite for such an act, but there is also the risk of the apparatus breaking down and danger to the men. If our streets were kept in a passable condition the firemen would not be obliged to take the walk. The firemen have to complain, not only of the deep ruts in the streets, but the manner in which they are lumbered up for building and railway purposes, thus giving the firemen but one resource—either to take the walk, or turn back and go six or seven blocks out of their way."

Through the death of a man the Grand Jury took notice of the infraction of the ordinance.

Sometimes the firemen were exceedingly annoyed by gangs of ruffians. About twelve o'clock on Thursday night, October 15, 1860, the Twenty-second Street bell started an alarm in the Third District. Engine Company No. 19 rolled out their machine and took the usual route, through Christie Street to Second Avenue, and then started up-town. Most of its members lay in the direction of Grand, Hester, and Walker Streets at that time. Those who rolled out the engine generally had to take her all the way up to the fire alone, with the exception of such slight help as they picked up on the way. On this occasion there were only six persons in the house when the alarm was given, but they were augmented by three or four strangers. As they neared the corner of Nineteenth Street a hundred ruffians or more saluted them with a volley of heavy stones, brickbats, etc., knocking down and injuring severely two of the members and one of the strangers. The rest were assaulted with clubs, sticks, etc., and were forced to leave their engine. The blackguards upset the engine, broke her tongue, smashed the large silver eagle on the top of the machine, and left her. One of the firemen had his nose broken.

No. 19 was always friendly with other companies, and her friends determined to stand by her in this emergency. One night the fire bell as set going, and several companies lay in wait in the vicinity in which No. 19 had encountered the ruffians, and through which she would come now. The gang, however, seemed to be apprehensive, and was afraid to come out. A gentleman who wrote about the outrage said:

"Now if these gentlemen (the gang) wish to have a pleasant evening's sport let them try the same game when she (No. 19) is coming from a Fourth or Fifth District fire. The companies are determined to take the law into their own hands. If they find these gentlemen they will give them the punishment they deserve."

Foreman J. J. Tindale, in reference to this letter, wrote that his company had no fighters in it, deprecated retaliation, but hinted pretty strongly that his men were able to take care of themselves.

At the great fire in New Street in 1845 the "innocence" of a fireman, or else the churlishness of a tradesman nearly caused loss of life. A fireman, named Sullivan, went into a grocery, kept by a German on the corner of Beaver and Pearl Streets, and had some refreshment

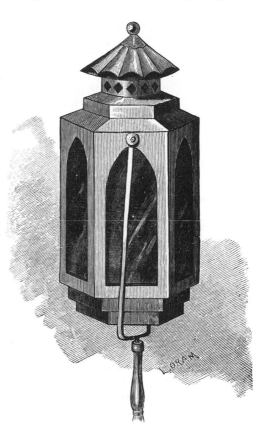

CHIEF ENGINEER ANDERSON'S SIGNAL LIGHT.

He told the storekeeper to charge the refreshments to his company, but the German, not relishing the idea, seized a large cheese knife, and striking Sullivan with it, laid open all one side of the fireman's head, inflicting almost a mortal wound. His comrades heard of the affair, and about forty of them hastened full of indignation to the spot. They utterly demolished the store, and were nearly killing the German, when the police arrived and rescued the tradesman.

One of the companies that felt extremely proud of itself and its engine was Hose No. 9. It could fairly lay claim to the title of a "crack" company. No. 9 was known as the "Silver Nine," because of the silver mountings of its carriage. Among her best known foremen were Harry Mansfield. Silver Nine lay in Mulberry Street near Broome. It was customary with all the companies, upon getting their machines back after repairs or redecorating, to give a grand feast. On one occasion the Silver Nine came back resplendent from the repair shop, and the boys did the honors in grander style than ever. Towards the close of the feast they became somewhat boastful, and declared that no company in the world could pass them. Some of its rivals—for no good company was ever without a rival—heard the boast, and resolved to "take the shine" out of Silver Nine. This company was the first to introduce bells on its hose carriage, and was, in consequence, looked upon as foppish.

A compact was entered into between No. 19 Hose (of which Uzziah Wenman was a member), Nos. 38, 15, and 3 Hose, to play a trick upon the boastful Silver Nine. It was determined that they should pass her four times in one night, and so forever dethrone her from her proud pre-eminence. A sham fire was to be started up-town about two o'clock on a Sunday morning. No. 9 would start out, the four companies in the conspiracy would lie in wait for her at certain points of the route, and each pass her in succession as she came along.

Hose 38 was to set fire to a lot of tar barrels about the corner of Seventeenth Street and Sixth Avenue, and then the hose companies were to be with their men all ready and waiting for Hose No. 9 to come along. As each company would keep its men fresh for the race, while, of course, the members of No. 9 Hose would be running all the time, it was calculated that each one of the four companies, fresh, would be able to pass No. 9, exhausted.

In the earlier part of Saturday evening the rope of No. 9 was laid out on the sidewalk ready for instant use, when a real fire broke out about nine o'clock at the foot of Market Street. This fire was no sooner put out than another occurred about eleven o'clock in Elm Street. It happened that at each of these fires Silver Nine was passed by other companies. The boys were more put out than the fire, and they were chafing at their defeat, when the sham fire was started up-town. Silver Nine dashed out, hoping to be the first this time, but, alas, the plot was too well laid, and she was passed by each of the companies in the conspiracy according to arrangement. This was six times in one night she was passed, and such a series of defeats was almost unprecedented in the Department. The glory of Silver Nine was gone forever, and she never boasted more.

It must be said for No. 9 that she did not resort that night to any of the customary tricks to avoid being passed. Sometimes when a company saw itself on the eve of being outrun its foreman would shout, "Round to, and go back for more men!" or, "Stop, and fix that wheel!" and in these cases there was no race. Occasionally, in trying to pass each other, engine or hose companies would be driven into piles of bricks, or holes, and men and machines would be injured. Companies used to hide behind walls, or piles of bricks, until rival companies came along, and would then rush out. This was a direct violation of the law, and was a common occurrence.

Once an engine company saw itself in danger of being passed in Dominick Street by a hose company, and it ran the latter upon a pile of bricks. The hose company, however, again came gamely up to the scratch, and in Varick Street was nearly passing its rival, but the men of the latter cut the straps that held up its arms, which fell among the men on the rope of the hose company, endangering their lives.   Conduct like this every one condemned as cowardly and unworthy.

Many a fight has occurred for the possession of a hydrant.   If a hose company arrived early at a fire it might possibly get a stream on from its own hose.   But the engineers did not care for this, as they considered it ineffective; they desired the more solid and telling stream from an engine, and not infrequently would order its hose company to back out of the line and give its water to an engine.   On one occasion a very funny, but, withal, fierce, fight took place for the possession of a hydrant.   The survivors often laughed over it.   Hose No. 14 was a popular company, and Henry A. Burr was foreman of it, and W. W. Corlies assistant foreman.   One dark night there was a fire up-town, where the streets were then poorly paved and worse lighted—in fact, not lighted at all in some places.   In one of these dark spots, not far from the fire, Burr, as the company dashed along, saw the outline looming up of a big hydrant.   He instantly made for the hydrant, but found another man clutching at it also, a member of a rival company that had come along.   Burr and the other fellow contended for that hydrant in the darkness; then, finding the fight going against him, Burr called for his men, who came.   Then the other chap called out for his men, who came, and a fierce struggle took place in the dark for the supremacy and the hydrant.   The fight was terminated in a curious way.   One of the men, who was smoking while the rest were squabbling, lit a match at the end of his cigar and looked at the object for whose possession they were fighting all around him.   Then he burst into a loud laugh, and no wonder; for what they thought was a hydrant wasn't a hydrant at all.   It was only a buried cannon, with half of it sticking out of the ground.   This discovery ended the fight.

A volunteer, belonging to No. 14 Engine, conceived what he thought a magnificent idea to become solid with the company.   A new district had been opened up, and the firemen were not very well acquainted with it.   But the volunteer, in rambling through the locality, noted a fire plug, and impressed its position on his memory.   One night a fire occurred in this section, and the volunteer made a dash for the plug.   He saw an old barrel near, clapped it over the plug, and sat on it.   He began to smoke and assumed as graceful and careless an attitude as though he were an accomplished actor.   An opposition company, dashing up and finding no hydrant, caused the volunteer to smile and chuckle.   He was thinking of how proud Fourteen would be of him when they came along.   He would then off with the barrel and reveal his treasure.   But he didn't get the chance.   Another company coming along saw the man on the barrel, and something about him made them suspicious.   Perhaps he seemed too lazy and indifferent on the barrel.   They rolled him off his seat, lifted up the barrel, and discovered the hidden hydrant. Alas, for that zealous runner and genius!   He did not consort with No. 14 for a long time after.   It was weeks before he was able to run, and more weeks before he could sit even on a chair.   As for hydrants he never again sat on one.

The rivalry of the companies to get first to a fire originated the bunking system.   The first companies to adopt its practice were the old rivals, Engines Nos. 5 and 14.   The late Mayor Tiemann fought against the system because, he said, it would cause the ruin of many a young man. The Engine Companies Nos. 12 and 21 began bunking. Ex-Mayor Wickham, Charles E. Gildersleeve, and Andrew C. Schenck, of Hook and Ladder Company No. 1, organized a bunk room in order that the company when going to fires might not be outstripped by Hook and Ladder Company No. 4. "Andy" Schenck, to be near the tiller of the truck—which was the post of honor—threw the floor carpet upon the ladders, and slept on it. The instant an alarm was sounded, he slid down and seized the tiller. Mr. Wickham took for his pillow the lowest of the steps leading to the room above. When the company moved into its new house, each member contributed twenty-five dollars towards furnishing it. Engine Company No. 33 made friends with the sexton of All Saints' Episcopal Church (afterwards turned into a machine shop) in Grand Street, near Pitt, the members lying in the pews, and using the ends of the cushions for bolsters. This was very nice and very comfortable, but 'ere long they were turned out and then hired the second story of a house in Scammel Street, one hundred and fifty feet from their engine house, and paid for it themselves. Some of the bunk rooms were remarkably orderly : no talking, for instance, was allowed in No. 38's after ten P. M. No. 36 would not permit card playing under penalty of fine or expulsion, or allow any drunken person to be brought to the house under the same penalties. When the city built engine houses the men were furnished with comfortable quarters.

When the new Department came into existence they used the old houses, but as improvements were made in the machines, and steamers became general, the houses were altered to suit the new order of things, or more suitable ones were built.

One of the most remarkable acts of heroism known to the annals of the old Fire Department, says Mr. John A. Cregier, was done by James R. Mount. On March 17, 1852, a fire broke out in a paint and paper hanging store at 89½ Bowery, cutting off the retreat of men, women, and children, who lodged in the third story. When Mount's company, No. 14 Hose, of which he was foreman, arrived, they found the inmates in a perilous position. Heartrending cries for help came from the windows. At one window a woman held a child, and was about to throw it into the street, when Foreman Mount cried out to her not to do it, and that he would go up to her. The gallant fireman started, but found his task no easy one. Under the stairs had been stored cans of paint, varnish, and oil. The stairs were partly burned through, and the flames and smoke were almost impassable. Fireman Joseph Skillman, who was afterwards killed at the Coffee Mills fire in Fulton Street, endeavored to dissuade his foreman from going up the stairs. "You will never come out alive," said Skillman. But Mount felt it to be his duty, and could not be deterred. Wrapping his coat around his head he dashed through flame and smoke up the stairs. At the top of the first flight he met a girl. She was too dazed and frightened to let Mount assist her, and she fainted. The foreman picked her up and cried out to Skillman that he would throw her down. He did so, and Skillman caught the insensible girl at the foot of the stairs. The devoted fireman then mounted to the next flight of stairs, at the head of which he found a man lying in what Mount first thought was a state of insensibility. The fireman put his hand down and felt him. The man was dead. There was no time to waste, so the gallant man started up the third flight. At the top he found another dead man in his night clothes. This man had, on the first alarm, got out, but had returned to secure forty-nine dollars in gold that he had left in his room. Next day the money was found clutched in his hand. His treasure was dearer to him than his life, and in foolishly striving to regain the former he sacrificed the latter.

Mount passed towards the front room through smoke so dense that he could almost shove it away with his hand. He opened the door, went in, closing the door after him, and found two women, two children, and two men, in a terrible state of excitement. Mrs. Muller was the woman who wanted to throw her child into the street. Mount calmed the frantic mother, and told them all to remain quiet for a few minutes, when he would return. Tying his coat about his head, he went back by the stairs, which were now almost burned away, passing on the landings the bodies of the dead men. He reached the street more dead than alive, but the fresh air revived him. In the meantime Skillman and his comrades had procured a ladder, thinking that Mount could not possibly get back by the flaming staircase. The ladder was reared against the side of the house, but unfortunately it reached only to the second story. Then they got a hogshead, and on this placed the ladder, which now reached within four feet of the

A GALLANT RESCUE.
Fireman Mount saves the lives of two women.

windows of the third story. At this time the flames from the cans of varnish, oil, etc., burst into the street, and the sidewalk appeared to be on fire. When the ladder was reared on the hogshead no one appeared anxious to ascend. Mount said, " I will go," and directed them how to hold the ladder. The flames were now licking the rungs of the ladder, but up the brave fireman went.

The first to make their escape were the two men, who lowered themselves from the window to the top of the ladder. Coward-like, they left the women and children to die. One was the husband of Mrs. Muller. The first time Mount went up, Mrs. Muller handed him one of her children. On his next ascent he received another child. The third time he rescued Mrs. Muller and had great difficulty in doing so. He'had to stand on the top rung of the ladder, holding on to the sill with his left hand. The woman clung around his neck. Then he felt for the top rung in making his way down, and slowly descended while the ladder shook as if it would fall. One misstep and death awaited them on the sidewalk. His comrades below held on for dear life. The last woman, Mary Koephe, weighed two hundred and twenty-five pounds. She was in her night dress, and sat on the window sill with her legs out, thoroughly frightened. Mount told her to hold on firmly to him, and she did so. When the gallant man had got down about two-thirds of the ladder, he fainted from over-exertion. His comrades instantly understood the situation, and ran to him; his burden fell into the firemen's arms. Th enthusiasm of the spectators found vent in repeated cheers. Mount was taken to Harry Raveno's store, ard the doctor found that he was suffering from the inhalation of smoke. When he revived, he vomited, felt better, and went home. His hands were burned, and his clothing, of course, was ruined.

Mr. Mount was also presented with a testimonial by the members of his company. The testimonial was a magnificent gold chronometer watch and chain, valued at two hundred and sixty dollars. The presentation took place at Moss's Hotel, corner of Bowery and Bayard Streets, to which a number of prominent citizens and members of the Fire Department were invited. Mr. W. J. Williams presented the watch in a neat speech. Mr. Mount replied in feeling language. "Words," he said, "are but the sparkling bubbles upon the ocean of feeling; but if you could look down in the lower depth of my inner heart, you would see the pearls and diamonds of a gratitude which I am unable to express." In addition to Mr. Williams the donors were Messrs. Herman Krall, P. H. Cooley, Levy L. Lyons, William Mash, and James L. Clute.

This brave deed of Mount was subsequently the occasion of a fight in the Common Council, the humors of which were given in the daily papers of the period. A committee of the Board of Aldermen reported in favor of appropriating three hundred dollars "to the purchase of some suitable testimonial, to be presented to Mount in recognition of his gallant services." On January 3, 1853, Alderman Wesley Smith (of the Eleventh Ward), who was foreman of Hose Company No. 34, called up the report, moved its adoption, and was seconded by Alderman Bard (of the Fourteenth Ward). Smith was remarkable for his great height. Alderman Sturtevant (of the Third Ward), one of the most pugnacious men in the Board, desired to know "whether Mr. Mount had done anything more than any other man would have done—any one sitting around that Board." "Yes," said Bard, promptly. "Anything more than the gentleman of the Fourteenth himself would have done?" superciliously inquired Sturtevant. Mr. Bard said he was not there. "Then more shame for you. Mr. Mount was there and had the opportunity ——" Alderman Sturtevant was going on to say, when he was interrupted by Mr. Smith, who inquired whether the gentleman was speaking for or against the resolution.

Alderman STURTEVANT:—"If the gentleman will have a little patience. or exercise what he is not distinguished for, a little civility and politeness, he'll find out what I am talking about. Here is a report before us in favor of awarding three hundred dollars, or three hundred dollars' worth, to Mr. Mount for doing what any true-hearted fireman would be glad to have the opportunity of doing. And I am sure my friend of the Fourteenth, with his fat, cheerful countenance, wishes he had been there and the tall Son of York——"

Here Alderman Smith jumped up to make a point of order. Alderman Sturtevant, he said, was personal, contrary to the rules of the Board. The president ruled against Sturtevant, but that irrepressible alderman continued his remarks in the same strain. Again he was interrupted, other aldermen joined in, and there was quite a hubbub. But Sturtevant managed once more to get the floor, and repeated "the Tall Son of York."

"Mr. President," cried Mr. Smith, excitedly, "if this is to be permitted I must ask your leave to throw an inkstand at his head, which I will do, so sure as I sit here, if he repeats those words."

The president interposed. The disorderly city father said: "I mean to do so. But neither the president nor any one else is to tell me what language I am to use, and when I say, without intending any offense, the tall Son of York ——" splash went the inkstand, but the other aldermen promptly interfered to prevent hostilities, and the debate was resumed, Sturtevant arguing that they had no right to put their hands in the city treasury for such a purpose. Finally the testimonial was voted. This incident in the Common Council was long remembered. A year or so afterwards, when Brougham produced his burlesque of "Pocahontas" at Wallack's Theater, he referred to it in the following lines which "caught" the house:

> "Shut up, dry up, or go to bed,
> Or I'll throw an inkstand at your honorable head."

The old Volunteer firemen of the city of New York have the honor of being the first to extend the right hand of fellowship to their Southern brethren. In the early part of 1867 the members of "Independence" Hose Company No. 1, of Columbia, S. C., having had all their equipments destroyed during the war, appealed to the Northern firemen for old hose, and such apparatus as they had cast aside, in order to re-establish their old department. Mr. Henry Wilson, who was president of the New York Firemen's Association, immediately called together the members, and steps were at once taken to see what relief could be afforded them. A committee was appointed to raise funds, and in less than one week they realized over five thousand dollars. A new silver-mounted hose carriage, with ten lengths of new hose, was procured, one hundred fire hats, red shirts, belts, trumpets, and white hats for the chief engineer and assistants, were purchased, and shipped early in March of the same year on the steamer "Andalusia." A committee of fourteen was appointed to proceed to Columbia and make the presentation. This committee consisted of Henry Wilson, president; Alderman William Lamb, Trustee, Frederick A. Ridabock, Robert Wright, Lewis J. Parker, Thomas C. Burns, Peter Y. Everett, John Underhill, Joseph W. Lamb, Frank Burns, Abraham Clearman, Jones L. Coe, and J. W. Downing. At the earnest solicitation of Mr. Ridabock, the committee went by rail, which was no doubt the means of saving some of the lives of the committee, as the steamer "Andalusia" took fire when twenty-four hours out, and with all its valuable cargo was totally destroyed, and twelve lives lost. The committee went by the way of Philadelphia, Baltimore, Fortress Monroe, Norfolk, Wilmington, and Charleston, being received at all these places by the firemen of each city. While at Charleston the mayor, Common Council, Chief Engineer M. A. Nathans, and the whole fire department, as well as the citizens, turned out to greet them. The following morning after their arrival in Charleston, the steamer " *Manhattan* " came into port with the sad news of the loss of the steamer " *Andalusia*," and bringing the rescued passengers. The association had only one thousand dollars insurance on the carriage, the whole having cost over five thousand dollars. The committee were greatly dejected over their loss, and wanted to return home immediately, but the Columbia firemen insisted on their visiting their city, which they did, receiving a most cordial welcome. The committee resolved to duplicate their loss as soon as they got back to New York. On their return home they were the guests of the firemen at Richmond, Washington, Baltimore, and Philadelphia. As soon as they got back to New York they ordered another carriage built, duplicated everything lost on the ill-fated steamer, and in June of the same year shipped it on the steamer " *Manhattan*." Messrs. Henry Wilson, William Lamb, Thomas C. Burns, Abraham Clearman, and Lewis J. Parker, being sent to present the same. They reached Columbia in safety, the people turning out in mass to greet them. President Henry Wilson made the presentation in a most impressive speech. Governor Orr, General Barton, Mayor Starke, Hon. S. W. Malton, Chief Engineer McKenzie, and the whole Fire Department being present. Captain Macky, of Hose No. 1 received the gift.

The two carraiges with all the equipments cost over ten thousand dollars, and the carriage still stands as a monument to the noble generosity of the old Volunteer firemen of New York City.

Between 1855 and 1861 target excursions were a great feature throughout the city of New York. It was not an uncommon thing to see from ten to fifteen pass the *Herald* office every day, while on Thanksgiving and Christmas Day they would exceed one hundred in number. Most all emanated from some one engine, hose, or hook and ladder company. They were well drilled and would put to blush some of the militia companies of the state. Among those that had their origin from the fire department were the Gulick Guards, named after Chief Engineer James Gulick. Oceanus Guards from Engine 11, Peterson Light Guards from Engine 15, Marsh Light Guards from Hose 33 and 40, Baxter Light Guards Hook and Ladder 15, Wildey Guards Engine 11, Washington Guards Engine 20, Union Guards Hook and Ladder 5, Atlantic Light Guards Hose 14, Live Oak Guards Engine 44, Americus Guards Engine 6, Columbia Guards Engine 14, Poole Guards Engine 34. Ringgold Guards Hose 7, Center Market Guards Engine 40, and many others that might be named. The Knickerbocker Guards from the Bowery and Lindsey Blues were also started by firemen.

In 1857 a general parade of all the target companies in the City took place, Fire Commissioner Henry Wilson, being commander-in-chief. One hundred and twenty-seven companies turned out, which were divided into two divisions, the first being under command of William Wilson, at one time alderman of the first ward, and, during the war, colonel of the Sixth New York Volunteer Regiment, stationed so long at Santa Rosa Island, and the second under command of John Creighton. Fernando Wood was at that time mayor of the city, and he furnished all the muskets which were delivered to the several companies from the police-station houses by the captains of each ward.

It was on the twenty-third of April, 1857, that the parade took place, over twelve thousand men being under arms. On the staff of Commander-in chief Henry Wilson rode Lloyd Aspinwall, Wm. H. Disbrow, G. Mansfield Davis, Dudley S. Gregory, Jr., and Samuel C. Thompson. On Colonel Wm. Wilson's staff were Alexander C. Lawrence, William Mulligan, Alexander Mason, James E. Kerrigan, Captain James Turner, and Charles A. Waters. On the staff of General Creighton were Wilds P. Walker, Ald. Thomas

BALL TICKET, GULICK GUARDS.

McSpedon, Peter Y. Everett, Sam Suydam, Councilman Horatio N. Wild, and Alexander Ward. The several companies were neatly equipped. In fact it was one of the most extensive parades ever witnessed in the city prior to the war. Business was suspended, stands erected all along the route or line of march, and the streets were crowded with thousands of people. Many of the companies wore red shirts, some blue overcoats, while others wore uniforms— not the state militia uniform.

The Knights of the Round Table were among the most noted organizations of the old Department. It originated among the members of Lafayette Hook and Ladder Company No. 6, located under Fireman's Hall, Mercer Street. It was organized in the fall of 1848, James P. Decker, Jr., being chosen the first president. The "Knights" convened but once a year—Christmas Eve— and the occasion was one of great enjoyment. Among its members was a large number of the theatrical profession, as well as members of the Fire Department. A grand supper was the principle feature of the gathering.

The supper took place at eleven o'clock at night, and was continued until the wee hours of Christmas morning. "Tom and Jerry" was the opening drink for the night's festivities. The tables were loaded down with all the viands of the season. Among its members were several firemen of Hook and Ladder No. 6. Among those who were at various times elected president were: John K. Evans, S. F. E. Kirby, Washington Barton, George W. Williams, James Kellock, Augustus Hamilton, and Peter Y. Everett. At the head of the table could always be seen Daniel Carpenter, superintendent of the Police Department, Lester Wallack, Dolly Davenport, E. P. and George Christy, old Blake, the actor, the Buckley Brothers of Buckley Minstrels, John Underhill, Charley Dobbs, and Joseph R. Wheeler, of Hook and Ladder 6; Richard P. H. Able, of Engine 28; Charles Ryerson, assistant foreman of Hook and Ladder 6; Col. W. R. W. Chambers, of Hose 22; Captain Turnbull, of the Eighth Ward police; James Moffatt, John H. O'Neil, and John K. Costigan, of Hook and Ladder 6. The feasts were always held in the basement of Fireman's Hall, the tables extending seventy-four feet in length, and

FOREMAN GRATACAP'S HAT.
(Saved from Crystal Palace Fire.)

on either side could always be found old Eph. Horn, Jerry and Dan Bryant, Tom Pendergast, Bob Hart, George Sherwood, Campbell N. Gole, Assistant Fire Marshal Henry O. Baker, John McCool, city register, and of Hose 24; Frank Raymond, Hose 5; James Timothy, property man of Wallack's Theater, and assistant foreman Hook and Ladder 6; Ed. F. Gillett, George Blanchard, Harry Peck, Charles Parsloe, of "My Partner" fame; Nelse Seymour, Brown Atkins, Sandy Spencer, Judge A. A. Phillips, of Engine 40; Ex-chief Engineer Elisha Kingsland, Assistant Engineers Timothy West and Charley Miller, of Engine 34. Wit and humor abounded, intermingled with anecdotes, songs, ballads, and jokes, which kept the whole party in one continual uproar, the Knights of the Cork always endeavoring to outdo one another with all sorts of gags and puns. Among others who never failed to be present were Robert Wheeler, Frederick Melville, Fernando Wood, Jr., Charles Nesbitt, Harry and Joe Smith, James Turner, Oliver Lakeman, Jack Coburn, and a host of others that might be named. The last feast was held on Christmas Eve, 1880, Harry Wines, ex-captain of police, being the last president.

Of the many "Liberty Poles" erected in the city the best known was, perhaps, "Tom" Riley's. It stood at the southwest corner of Franklin Street and West Broadway. It was the scene of many a gathering on holidays. These contests took place between rival engines, and these exciting trials attracted numerous spectators, beside members and friends of the Department. Each company was jealous of the reputation of the pumping power of its engine, often challenges were issued to decide the question, and Riley's Liberty Pole was most often selected at which to make the trial. The pole was marked in various places with figures indicating the number of feet high that the several companies had played. Its height has been given as

RILEY'S HOTEL AND LIBERTY POLE.

one hundred and thirty-seven feet. Especially on Thanksgiving Day would crowds of enthusiasts gather to see the machines work. The judges sat on the roof of Mr. Riley's hotel and reported the respective heights. Among the trials at Riley's Liberty Pole was a notable one in 1855. The Exempt Engine Company had been organized on November 14 of the preceding year at the house of Mr. H. B. Venn, No. 298 Bowery. The company had procured the abandoned engine of No. 42, which, on account of its great weight, was called the "man killer." On the twenty-fourth of January, while the snow was falling heavily, one hundred and ten exempts marched with the engine to Riley's, and were watched by a big crowd. The trial was a great success, and the company celebrated the event the same evening by a cold collation at Brooks's Rooms in Broome Street.

Riley's pole was first put up in 1834, on Washington's birthday. It was a great day for the Democrats who erected it. There was a feast, there were speeches, and other appropriate exercises. Unfortunately it did not long remain standing. It was struck by lightning in the following year, and so injured that it had to be taken down. Another pole was erected at the expense of the Democrats. It was removed in 1858, and long after "old timers" used to visit the spot where it had stood to talk over the memories of bygone days. Riley's hotel has since been torn down, and a six-story structure for business purposes was built on the site. The old hydrant near it was left standing.

As we have intimated elsewhere, "Old Turk," No. 44, was a famous engine. The most prominent of the old "Forty Fourers," and one whose name even

FRANK CLARK.

to-day is a household word among all old firemen, was Frank Clark, one of the most remarkable men who ever ran with the "masheen." Clark was born in Paterson, N. J., in 1824, the same year that 44 was organized. He came to New York, and of his school days in Fifth Street he says : "The first day we went to the school the gang tried to pitch the teacher out of the window, but instead got pitched out themselves." Clark was indentified with 44 from boyhood. According to himself he "jined" at eleven years of age.

In the early days of 44 the firemen were divided into two clases—regulars and volunteers or runners. While Sam Allen was foreman the volunteers bunked in a house directly opposite the engine house, in Houston Street, between Cannon and Lewis Streets. One night Allen locked the engine house, and going to the bunkers' quarters made an offer of a brand new suit of clothes to the first volunteer who would roll the engine in case of a fire during the night. The volunteers turned into their bunks with their trousers stuck into their boots beside their beds and ready to be jumped into as soon as the alarm sounded. At midnight the Union Market bell " came in " for a fire in the Sixth District. The volunteers jumped into their trousers and rushed across the street only to find the engine already in the street, and Clark on the tongue with neither boots nor trousers on. From that night until his death 45 and Frank Clark were synonymous terms among firemen, not only in New York but in almost every city in the Union. He became a member of 44, and afterwards foreman, a position of honor and power in those days. He led " Old Turk " to Washington to see Pierce inaugurated, and to Philadelphia, where they were received by Bill McMullen's Moyamensing Hose and created a sensation. While foreman of Old Turk Clark married, and on the night of the wedding escorted his bride home from the church. When within a few yards of the bride's house the bell struck six, and Clark left his bride at her door while he rushed to the house, seized his trumpet, and led 44 to the fire in his wedding suit, and for three days never saw his bride. This was at the great Sugar House fire, which lasted three days. When called to account for his conduct he replied :

"What wus a feller goin' to do? Let the injin get passed?"

Volumes might be written about Clark and his exploits. He became prominent in politics, but was not suited for a leader. He was an "Old Line Democrat" of the most pronounced type, and this lost him place time and again. He was not a selfish man, and for forty years he was known to almost every man, woman and child in the Eleventh Ward, and was as much of a boy in his ideas at sixty as he was at twenty. He was "Frank Clark of old 44," and he gloried in his title. The proudest day of his life was when he led 44 on Evacuation Day parade in 1883. Old Turk turned out two hundred strong, and thousands flocked to see her. From far and near the old eastsiders who had moved away years before came back to their old stamping ground. Clark with his red shirt and fire cap, and a silver trumpet covered with flowers, was a prouder man that day than any monarch on earth.

The affection entertained by the people for the men of Old Turk may be gleaned from a letter written to the *Sun* by Mrs. Edward Moynihan, of No. 298 Seventh Street, a few days before the parade. Mrs. Moynihan spoke in glowing terms of old 44 and said :

"They tell me that the old firemen may be short of funds for a band. If that is so, I will freely contribute whatever may be lacking. All I ask is that they march past my window so that I may once more see about all there is left in the Eleventh Ward to remind me of the past." The old lady's wish was gratified. Old 44 marched past her window. As Mrs. Moynihan, bent with age and resting on the arm of her son, appeared at the window, Clark lifted his hat and raised his trumpet, when two hundred of the flower of the old Fire Department raised their helmets and remained uncovered until they passed the old lady's window. It was a memorable day in the Eleventh Ward, and there were few dry eyes among the men of Old Turk. The aged lady had seen old 44 for the last time.

At all demonstrations and at their funerals Clark was a prominent character. Attending a funeral of one of his old comrades he requested that, if he himself should die on Monday, he be kept in until the following Sunday, so that all the old boys might have a chance to go to his funeral. Two weeks from that day his wish was gratified. He died on Monday, May 4, 1884, and his funeral took place on Sunday, May 10. It was the largest demonstration ever witnessed at the funeral of a Volunteer fireman not killed in the discharge of his duty, and among the floral tributes was the motto of old 44 :

Extinguish one flame and cherish another.

Old 44 was also remarkable for her six stalwart Pennys, who were known all over the city as "Old Turk's Big Pennys." Once a foreman of a rival company had a dispute with 44's foreman as to the relative merits of their respective companies, and offered to back his opinion by betting drinks for the two. In those "good old days" good old whiskey could be had for three cents a glass, and the rival foreman banged down six cents on his engine. He had a well-founded conviction that 44's foreman was penniless. Rueful 44 thrust his hands into his empty pockets and looked along the line. His sad eye lighted on one of the Pennys, and a ray of hope entered his thirsty soul. He whispered to this particular stalwart Penny, who whispered to his brothers, and at once each of the six namesakes slapped a penny upon the engine amid a roar of laughter from the spectators. The challenger laughed too and took the whole crowd over to "Johnny" Muldoon's, at Third and Lewis Streets, where they fraternized. As they drank each other's healths Nigger Shee sang the following refrain of the old song:

> I went down town to see my posey,
> Who did I meet but Jim Along Josey.
> Hey, Jim Along, Jim Along Josey,
>   Hey, Jim Along,
>   Jim Along Joe.

John McDermott ("Old Time Enough"), of Excelsior Engine Company No. 2, derived his "nickname" from a peculiarity, the cause of which he tells in this way: "Of course you know that in those days every other man in the Department had a nickname, and if he was at all prominent as a fireman, he was known all over the city by it every bit as well as by his proper name. Indeed many knew him by his nickname who would have been puzzled if asked his right name. As secretary, foreman and in other positions, I always tried to smooth over the little quarrels which were sure to come up. One would present charges against the other for this or that offense, and insist that they be forwarded to headquarters. I knew that a little delay would in every case cause the parties concerned to forget all about them, so my customary reply—indeed it became stereotyped—was, 'Oh, time enough.' Perhaps I may have carried this thing a little too far, but it got me the nickname as my reward, and I suppose I'll bear it to the day of my death.

"Excelsior was known as the Quaker Company, because when I joined it a great many of the boys' fathers were old Broadbrims. Most of the members—among whom I recall Mayor Westervelt's son; Ed. Knight, Librarian of the Supreme Court; ex-Coroner Pat Keenan, ex-Alderman Bryan Reilly, Zophar Mills, and others—belonged to good families, so that we had none of the fighting element with us. It wasn't at all unusual for us to have a forty or fifty-dollar supper after a fire, and in those days forty dollars would buy a great deal of good grub. Some of the wealthier fellows belonged to it, as they did to other companies, to enable them to escape jury duty, and not a few of them would regularly pay as fines every month ten or fifteen dollars. When I joined No. 2 the house was at 21 Henry Street—I believe it is a butcher shop now—but in 1865 we moved to East Broadway, between Catharine and Market Streets.

"In the autumn of '52 a grain-elevator at the foot of Roosevelt Street caught fire on Sunday morning. It was only a few blocks from the house, and we happened to be on hand before the alarm was given. Jack Sloper—he was a sort of left-handed Mascot to me always—and I had the pipe down in the hold of the elevator. We heard a noise and happened to back out just in the nick of time, for the machinery had given way. When the ships Great Republic, White Squall and others were burned at the foot of Dover street, the same Sloper and I were on one of the vessels. We had the pipe and were lying on our stomachs between decks, with half hatch on. The gas generating in the hold of the vessel exploded, driving the other half of the hatch up and knocking us heels over head."

Mechanics' Hose No. 47 had a member whose history, though brief, is noteworthy. Daniel Kelly was born in the Eleventh Ward, hailing from the famous old Dry Dock, which has but recently become a thing of the past. Kelly joined No. 47 in 1859. He was a man of great strength, brave as a lion, but very quiet. He became foreman of Mechanics' Hose. About twenty-five years ago, on the Fourth of July, at a fire in Columbia Street, the foreman of a rival of No. 47 attempted to strike Kelly with his trumpet. Kelly simply grabbed the man, threw him across his knee, and spanked him like a schoolboy amid the roars of the crowd. When Kelly had served his time he resigned, and dropped out of sight.

BROTHER BONAVENTURE RECOGNIZES AN OLD FRIEND.

[Mechanics' Old-time Foreman.]

Some years ago a visitor desired to see the monastery at Hoboken, and was referred to Brother Bonaventure. The brother and the visitor were passing through the house when the former suddenly turned and pressed the hand of the visitor, exclaiming "How do you do, Joe? Don't you remember me?" Brother Bonaventure was Daniel Kelly, Mechanics' old-time foreman, and "Joe" was one of his former comrades. The monk told his friend that was the only way he could save his soul. Kelly was brought up within the sound of the old Mechanics' bell. Within the monastery was a bell which rang for prayers at midnight. The recluse explained that a special indulgence was granted to the monk who first responded to its peal. Brother Bonaventure's experience and practice in invariably being the first to answer the old fire bell stood him in good stead now, and he gained all the indulgences.

CHAPTER XIV.

FIRES OF THE OLDEN TIME.

History of Some of the Great Conflagrations that have Devastated New York.—The Alleged Incendiary
Slave Plots of 1741 and 1796.—The Revolutionary Struggle and the Attempts to Burn down the
City.—Disastrous Fire of 1811.—A Sailor's Gallant Deed.—The Old Jail Bell and its History.

THE greatest calamities that have befallen New York have been its
destructive fires. Within the comparatively brief space of one hundred
years she had suffered more from the "devouring element" than any
city in the world. The rapidity with which these striking events succeeded
each other is remarkable. The years 1741, 1776, 1778, 1804, 1811, 1835, 1839,
and 1845 are in the history of the city memorable for the ruin and misery
occasioned by mighty conflagrations. In the intervals innumerable other fires
had occurred, some of them resulting in loss of life and great destruction of
property, but those of the years just mentioned surpass all others in their
extent, intensity, and far-reaching effects. But the frequent recurrence and
remarkable destructiveness of these fires are no reflection upon the zeal and
courage of the noble men who had volunteered to fight the flames. That
gallant body had only meager means and unscientific appliances to help them
in their arduous labors. All that brave and watchful men could do they did,
and mortal men could do no more.

With the exception of Constantinople New York has, perhaps, suffered
more frequently from conflagrations than any city in the two worlds.
Hamilton said in his time that one could not be twenty-four hours in New
York without hearing an alarm of fire. This observation was repeated by a
writer who published a small work in 1837, called "A Glance at New York,"
who added that one alarm a day would be a small average, and that it would
be nearer the truth to say that the firemen of New York were called out five
hundred times a year—a statement which all familiar with New York at that
time have corroborated. Many of these were undoubtedly false alarms,
raised by boys for the pleasure of running after the engines. The fire of
London in 1666 was bigger than anything this city has seen. Four hundred and
thirty-six acres were laid waste, eighty-nine churches destroyed, with thirteen
thousand two hundred houses, leaving two hundred thousand people temporarily without homes. The fire of Hamburg in 1842 burned sixty-one streets,
containing one thousand seven hundred and forty-seven houses. The Chicago
fire laid waste over five acres, and left one hundred thousand of her citizens
homeless. But if the frequency of fires in the city, the magnitude of some of
them, and the amount of property destroyed, be collectively considered, it will
be seen that New York, perhaps, has suffered more heavily from this kind of
calamity than any other city of modern times. Still these conflagrations have

in the end proved of great benefit by causing more spacious and elegant edifices to arise, phœnix-like, out of their ashes.

The first great fire, or rather series of fires, in 1741 was said to be the work of negro slaves. Dr. John Gilmary Shea in 1862 published a paper on the subject, carefully analyzing the evidence for and against the alleged plot. Slavery was almost coeval with the settlement of this city, says Dr. Shea. When the fort was begun in 1625, and colonization properly commenced, the Dutch West India Company immediately promised to each patroon " twelve black men and women out of the prizes in which negroes shall be found." The negroes taken on an enemy's ship were thus sold here as slaves, irrespective of their former condition. Indians were similarly treated. Slaves were also brought in directly from Angola and other parts of Africa, and indirectly through the Dutch West India Islands. Thus the element of negro slavery was introduced and extended during the Dutch rule. Fort Amsterdam itself, that cradle of New York, was finally completed by the labor of negro slaves, whose moral condition was utterly ignored. When the English came they accepted slavery, and gave it the sanction of municipal law.

As time rolled on the laws bore heavily upon the poor negro, and too often the slaves were goaded to commit deeds of violence. Fearful was the retribution. Two slaves of William Hallett—an Indian man and negro woman—of Newtown, Long Island, in 1707 murdered their master, his wife, and their five children, in revenge for being deprived of certain privileges. The woman was burned, the man was suspended in gibbets and placed astride a sharp iron, in which condition he lived some time, and in a state of delirium which ensued, believing himself to be on horseback, would urge forward his supposed animal with the frightful impetuosity of a maniac, while the blood oozing from his lacerated flesh streamed from his feet to the ground.

A conspiracy followed, terrible scenes of bloodshed ensued, and severer laws were enacted. In 1741 the city was in a state of panic. The midnight sky was reddened with the flames of the incendiary, and no man's property seemed safe from the torch of the conspirator. The city contained about eleven thousand inhabitants, and of these about one-fourth were negroes. In those days the governor (Lieutenant-Governor Clarke, an Englishman) resided in Fort George, which stood on an eminence south of Bowling Green. In this fort stood a church, built by Governor Kieft, the king's house, barracks, etc. The church was of stone, but covered with a shingle roof. On the eighteenth of March, about one o'clock in the day, a fire broke out in this roof, and as the wind was high the flames spread rapidly. The fire bell rang out, and thousands flocked to the scene. Just ten years before the new fire engines had been introduced and something like a fire department organized. These slow and unwieldy machines came lumbering to the spot, manned by firemen in civilian costumes as clumsy and uncouth as well could be devised to prevent freedom of limb and muscle. The bucket lines were formed, but not too rapidly, and the contents of the buckets half spilled before reaching the engine. And still the flames mounted high. The ships in the harbor thought the whole city was afire. Soon the church, the king's house, and other buildings in the fort were reduced to ashes. The flames spread beyond the fort, and the rest of the town was menaced, but the further progress of the fire was arrested. A few weeks after four or five other fires occurred in different parts of the city, and then was heard the cry "The negroes are rising!" Everywhere the slaves were hurried to jail, and a wild search was made for suspicious persons. Trials, executions, and bloody laws followed fast till the panic was allayed, and the city became sane and safe again. Four white people were hanged,

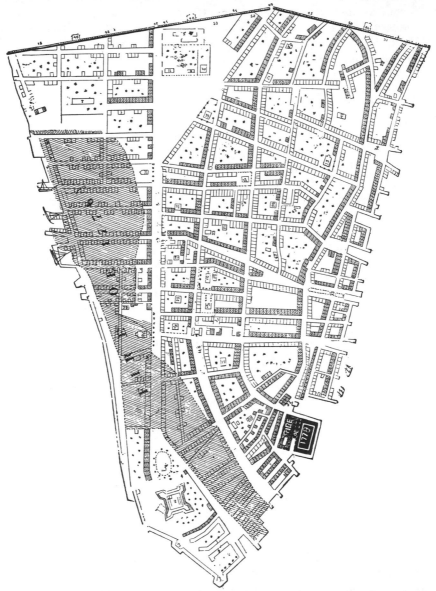

MAP SHOWING PORTIONS OF CITY DESTROYED BY GREAT FIRES OF 1776 AND 1778.

fourteen negroes burned, eighteen executed, and seventy-one transported to the West Indies and sold.

The next great fire occurred in the stirring times of 1776, and is connected with the battle of Long Island. New York appears to have been a coveted prize for the British, and early in 1776 Howe dispatched General Clinton secretly to attack it.   Dr. Benson J. Lossing, in his History of New York City, says that General Washington, suspecting New York to be Clinton's destination, sent General Charles Lee thither, and on the evacuation of Boston in March the commander-in-chief marched with nearly the whole of his army to New York, arriving here in the middle of April.   He pushed forward the defenses of the city begun by General Lord Stirling.   Fort George, on the site of Fort Amsterdam, was strengthened, numerous batteries were constructed on the shores of the Hudson and East Rivers, and lines of fortifications were built across the island from river to river not far from the city.   Strong Fort Washington was finally built on the highest land on the island (now Washington Heights) and intrenchments were thrown up on Harlem Heights.   In the summer Washington made his headquarters at Richmond Hill, then a country retreat at the (present) junction of Charlton and Varick Streets.

On the 10th of July copies of the Declaration of Independence were received in New York.   The army was drawn up in hollow squares by brigades, and in that position the important document was read to each brigade.   That night soldiers and citizens joined in pulling down the equestrian statue of King George, which certain tories had caused to be set up in the Bowling Green only six years before.   They dragged the leaden image through the streets and broke it in pieces.   Some of it was taken to Connecticut and moulded into bullets.

At the close of June, 1776, a British fleet arrived at Sandy Hook with General Howe's army, which was landed on Staten Island.   After the landing they were joined by forces under Sir Henry Clinton, who had been repulsed in an attack upon Charleston, S. C.   Hessians (foreign mercenaries hired by the British Government) also came, and late in August the British force on Staten Island and on the ships was more than twenty-five thousand in number. On the twenty-fifth of August over ten thousand of these had landed on the western end of Long Island, prepared to attempt the capture of New York. Washington, whose army was then about seventeen thousand strong, had caused fortifications to be constructed at Brooklyn, and he sent over a greater part of his forces to confront the invaders.   The battle of Long Island ensued and was disastrous to the Americans.   Washington skillfully conducted the remainder (not killed or captured) in a retreat across the East River, under cover of a fog, to New York, and thence to Harlem Heights at the northern end of the island.   The British troops followed tardily, crossed the East River at Kip's Bay, and after a sharp battle on Harlem Plains took possession of the city of New York, or what was left of it.

The British had pitched their tents near the city, intending to enter the next morning and were in repose.   The whole camp was sunk in sleep, and only the sentinels were awake, pacing their weary rounds.   Suddenly, at midnight, arrows of lurid flame shot heavenward from the lower part of the town.   The city seemed to be on fire.   Afterwards it was asserted that the Americans had formed a scheme to burn down New York rather than let it fall into the hands of the English enemy.   At any rate, a conflagration was started, accidently or designedly, at the foot of Broad Street.   There were few citizens able or disposed to fight the flames, for most of the inhabitants had fled the town.   In the space of a few hours five hundred buildings were destroyed. The soldiers and sailors from the vessels in the river were ordered ashore, and they succeeded in staying the flames before they reached Wall Street. It was General Greene who had simply urged the destruction of the city by fire —a measure afterward so effectively adopted by Count Rostopchin, Governor of Moscow, to arrest the career of Napoleon. General Greene's idea was to deprive the British of the advantage of having their winter quarters established in New York. His reasons for this measure were sound, says W. L. Stone in his History of New York, and ought, doubtless, to have been adopted. Washington also was believed to have been of the same opinion, especially as two thirds of the property which it was proposed to destroy belonged to undisguised loyalists. But Congress would not allow the sacrifice, and on the fifteenth of September the city was in full possession of the English.

At this time, according to Hugh Gaine, in his *Universal Register* for 1787, New York contained about four thousand two hundred houses and thirty thousand inhabitants. It would seem as if the idea of firing the city—though given up by Washington and Greene—was still cherished by some of the residents of the city. Scarcely had the British fairly taken possession, when, on the night of the twentieth of September (only six days after they had marched in) a terrific fire broke out which was not subdued until one thousand houses, or about one fourth of the city, were reduced to ashes. Although the value of the property destroyed does not discount that lost sixty years after in the Great Fire of 1835, yet it will be seen that its ravages were of far greater extent. The fire was first discovered in a low dram-shop in Whitehall Slip, called the "Fighting Cocks," tenanted by abandoned men and women. In a few minutes afterward flames were seen to break forth from several other buildings, lying in different directions, at the same instant. For some time previous the weather had been dry, and at the moment a brisk southerly wind prevailing, and the buildings being of wood and covered with shingles, the flames soon caught the neighboring houses and spread with inconceivable rapidity. The fire swept up Broad and Beaver Streets to Broadway and thence onward, consuming all that portion of the town lying on the North River, until the flames were stopped by the grounds of King's (Columbia) College at Mortkill Street, now Barclay. St. Paul's Church was, at one time, in great danger. Fortunately, however, the roof was flat with a balustrade on the eaves. Taking advantage of this circumstance, a number of citizens ascended to the balustrade and extinguished the flakes of fire as they fell on the roof. Trinity Church, with the Lutheran chapel, on the opposite corner of Rector Street, was also destroyed. The Rev. Dr. Inglis was then rector of Trinity, and this sacred edifice, his parsonage and the Charity School (two large buildings) were consumed, entailing a loss of church property to the value of twenty-five thousand pounds. The organ of Trinity alone cost eight hundred and fifty pounds. "The ruins," says Dunlop (who wandered over the scene at the close of the war), "on the southeast side of the town were converted into dwelling places by using the chimneys and parts of walls which were firm, and adding pieces of spars with old canvas from the ships, forming hovels—part hut and part tent." This was called Canvas Town, and there the vilest of the army and Tory refugees congregated.

Captain Joseph Henry, afterward a judge in Pennsylvania, has given, in his "Campaign against Quebec," a vivid description of "the great fire of 1776." He had just returned from Quebec, and was standing on the deck of the ship in the bay when the fire broke out. Captain Henry writes : "A most luminous and beautiful, but baleful, sight, occurred to us—that is, the city of New York on fire. One night (September 21) the watch on deck gave a loud notice of this disaster. Running upon the deck we could perceive a light, which at the distance we were from it (four miles) was apparently of the size of the flame of a candle. This light to me appeared to be the burning of an old and noted tavern called the 'Fighting Cocks' (where ere this I had lodged), to the east of the Battery, and near the wharf. The wind was southerly and blew a fresh gale, the flames at this place, because of the wind, increasing rapidly. In a moment we saw another light at a great distance from the first up the North River. The latter seemed to be an original, distinct, and new formed fire, near a celebrated tavern in the Broadway called 'Whitehall.' When the fire reached the spire

TRINITY CHURCH, DESTROYED BY FIRE, 1776.

of a large steeple, south of the tavern, which was attached to a large church (Trinity Church), the effect upon the eye was astonishingly grand. If we could have divested ourselves of the knowledge that it was the property of our fellow-citizens which was consuming, the view might have been esteemed sublime, if not pleasing. The deck of our ship, for many hours, was lighted as if at noonday. On the commencement of the conflagration we observed many boats putting off from the float, rowing rapidly toward the city. Our boat was of the number. This circumstance repelled the idea that our enemies were the incendiaries, for indeed they professedly went in aid of the inhabitants. The boat returned about daylight, and from the relation of the officer and the crew we clearly discerned that the burning of New York was the act of some madcap Americans. The sailors told us in their blunt manner that they had seen one American hanging by the heels dead, having a bayonet wound through his breast. They named him by his Christian and surname, which they saw on his arm. They averred he was caught in the act of firing the houses. They told us also that they had seen one person who was taken in the act tossed into the fire, and that several who were stealing and suspected as incendiaries were bayonetted. Summary justice is at no time laudable, but in this instance it may have been correct. If the Greeks could have been resisted at Persepolis, every soul of them ought to have been massacred. The testimony we received from the sailors, my own view of the distant beginnings of the fire in various spots, remote from each other, and the manner of its spreading, impressed my mind with the belief that the burning of the city was the doing of the most low and vile persons, for the purposes not only of thieving, but of devastation. This seemed, too, the general sense, not only of the British, but that of the prisoners then aboard the transports. Lying directly south of the city and in a range with the Broadway, we had a fair and full view of the whole process. The persons in the ships nearer to the town than we were uniformly held the same opinion. It was not until some years afterward that a doubt was created, but for the honor of our country and its good name an ascription was made of the firing of the city to accidental circumstances. It may be well that a nation in the heat and turbulence of war should endeavor to promote its interests by propagating reports of its own innocency and prowess, and accusing its enemy of flagrant enormity and dastardliness (as was done in this particular case), but when peace comes let us, in God's name, do justice to them and ourselves."

At this distance of time it is difficult to say whether the fire was or was not the result of incendiarism on the part of the disaffected Americans. Even reliable contemporaneous writers differ widely in their opinion on the subject, some affirming positively that the city was set on fire, and others, again, quite as positively affirming the contrary. Later writers, with all the facts before them and after an impartial survey, are inclined to believe that the fire was the result of a deliberate design ; nor, if the newspapers and correspondence of the day can be believed, is there much room left for doubt. According to these authorities one man was seized in the act of setting fire to the College, and he acknowledged to his captors that he had been employed for the purpose. A New England captain, who was seized at the same time with matches in his pocket, also confessed the same. A carpenter, named White, was observed to cut the leather buckets which conveyed the water. "The next day, Saturday," says Steadman, in his History of the American War, "a great many cartloads of bundles of pine sticks, dipped in brimstone, were found concealed in cellars of houses to which the incendiaries had not had time to set fire." "The rebels," says the Rev. Charles Inglis, in writing on the same subject a few days after to the Venerable Society for the Propagation of the Gospel in Foreign Parts, "carried off all the bells in the city, partly to convert them into cannon and partly to prevent notice being given speedily of the destruction they meditated against the city by fire when it began. . . . . . Several rebels secreted themselves in the houses to execute the diabolical purpose of destroying the city." Notwithstanding, however, this seeming mass of testimony, it was found impossible to obtain legal proof sufficient to fasten the act upon any particular individual—for all who had been caught at the time with matches, etc., had been killed on the spot by the soldiery—and the result was that several of the citizens, who had been arrested and imprisoned on the charge of being the incendiaries, were acquitted.

Two years after this event, on August 3, an hour after midnight, a fire broke out in the store of Mr. Jones, ship-chandler, on Cruger's Wharf. Sixty-four dwelling-houses, besides stores, were consumed, and two small vessels were burned. On this occasion the firemen were assisted by the military, with Colonel Coburn and the other officers of the Thirty-fifth Regiment.

On December 9, 1796, a great conflagration, known as the "Coffee House Slip Fire," took place. It began between one and two A. M., in Robinson & Hartshorne's store on Murray Wharf (now the eastern end of Wall Street), and extended to Maiden Lane, consuming a part of the old Fly Market and rendering necessary the pulling down of another part of it. So rapid was the spread of the flames that all the buildings below Front Street, from Murray Wharf to the Fly Market, over fifty in number—many of them large and well-stocked stores—were in ashes in about four hours, and one of the engines (believed to be No. 18) was thrown into the river to save it from being burned. In this year, as in 1741, the negroes were accused of forming plots to burn down the city. In the previous year seven hundred and thirty-two persons had died from yellow fever, and the people were still nervous and excitable after that dreadful scourge. In the month of December, 1796, the Fish Market was torn down for the purpose of arresting a very destructive fire. The *Minerva* of December 9, then edited by Noah Webster, and a few years afterwards by Zachariah Lewis, when its name was changed to the *New York Commercial Advertiser*, thus notices this conflagration: "About one o'clock this morning a fire broke out in one of the stores on Murray's Wharf, Coffee House Slip. The number of buildings consumed may be from fifty to seventy—a whole block

VIEW OF BROADWAY, NEW YORK, BETWEEN HOWARD AND GRAND STREETS, 1840.

between the above slip, Front Street, and the Fish Market. The progress of the fire was finally arrested by cutting down the Fish Market."

So many fires occurring about the same time led many of the citizens to believe that the slaves were again conspiring to destroy the city. Great excitement was caused and much preparation made to guard against such a calamity. The same paper of the fourteenth instant following says: "*Serious Cause of Alarm.*—Citizens of New York, you are once more called upon to attend to your duty. It is no longer a doubt, it is a fact, that there is a combination of incendiaries in this city aiming to wrap the whole of it in flames! The house of Mr. Lewis Ogden, in Pearl Street, has been twice set on fire—the evidence of malicious intent is indubitable—and he has sent his *black man,* suspected, to prison. Last night an attempt was made to set fire to Mr. Lindsay's house in Greenwich Street. The combustibles left for the purpose are preserved as evidence of the fact. Another attempt, we learn, was made last night in Beekman Street. A bed was set on fire under a child, and his cries alarmed his family. Rouse, fellow-citizens and magistrates! Your lives and property are at stake. Double your night-watch and confine your servants."

The Common Council on the fifteenth of December, 1796, passed resolutions, offering five hundred dollars reward for the conviction of offenders, and recommended that good citizens in the several wards should arrange themselves into companies or classes, "to consist of such numbers as shall be necessary for the purpose of keeping such watch for the safety of the city." A citizen of that day, in writing to a friend, also says: "The yellow fever produced not such extraordinary commotion. The present alarm—as it is contagious—may be called the *fire fever.*" The "fever," however, soon died out, as the precautions taken had the desired effect, even if there had not been any actual design or conspiracy.

In connection with the Coffee House Slip fire is an interesting story told by Mr. Philip W. Engs, who was president of the Association of Exempt Firemen in 1857: "On this occasion one of the stores was found to contain several kegs of powder, when an individual by the name of Richardson Underhill entered the store, took the powder from thence, and, placing it in an open boat, rowed off into the stream, and remained there with it until the fire was extinguished. This same person, when in the year 1798 New York was so terribly visited with yellow fever, at the hazard of his life nursed the sick and cared for the dead, and yet to the disgrace of human nature, and because in his business matters he had been guilty of improprieties, was suffered to die and be buried from our then miserably-kept almshouse (in Chambers Street). 'Ingratitude, thou marble-hearted fiend!'"

On January 17, 1800, the city was again alarmed in consequence of the occurrence of several fires. One was P. Dunstan's house in the neighborhood of the New Banks, in the northern part of the city. The second was on board the ship "*Admiral Duncan*" at Salter, Son & Co.'s wharf, near Old Slip. It was impossible to save the vessel, which was cut loose from the wharf. The "*Admiral Duncan*" drifted among the shipping, setting fire to some, bobbed about among the wharves, and was finally consumed off the Battery.

Mr. Engs again writes of a fire on May 22, 1803, at No. 37 Vesey Street, known as the New York Bread Company's Bakery. "This building," he says, "was remarkable for its thickness of walls and general strength, and had been erected by a stock company for the purpose of putting down the price of bread, in which the people were at that time much imposed upon, as well as in the quality. The general interest felt in the success of this enterprise caused great excitement when it was known the building was on fire, and strenuous exertions were made to save it. A very remarkable incident occurred at this fire. A ladder being raised to the cornice in the rear was, from the necessity of getting all the elevation possible, placed too nearly erect. Two firemen had reached its top, when the cry below was, 'The wall is falling!' One of the men slipped down by the rungs. The other, being higher up, and the cornice above him on fire, gave a sudden jerk to the ladder which threw it with great force across the yard, precipitating him through a glass window in the second story of a house, and landing him on the floor without any very serious bruises. It was supposed that the preservation of his life was owing in a great degree to his having on a fire cap, without which he could not have passed through a glass window without dangerous gashes in the head. As it was he was tolerably well scratched, but yet able to get up and go home. There is so much romance connected with this leap that it might be set down among the doubtful, were it not for the statement being confirmed by our former chief engineer, Mr. Uzziah Wenman, who, at that time a young lad, lived with his father in a house fronting on Partition (now Fulton) Street, in the rear of this fire." Here Mr. Engs makes an "odious comparison" in the following manner: "The walls of this building did not fall, and the premises were repaired, and subsequently occupied as a warehouse. I occupied it in later years, and considered it a model as to thickness of wall, by which our laws in relation to building might have been properly guided. Within two or three years that building was taken down to give place to one of those elegant warehouses which are now ornamenting that part of our city, but not one among which would bear such a heat as the Old Bakery walls endured without tumbling to the ground."

This interesting old fireman continues: "It was during this year (1803) that the Lumber Yard Fire, on the premises of Mr. Bonsel, took place, the flakes from which, when in a blaze, were blown on to St. Paul's Church steeple, at a great height from the ground, causing it to take fire, and threatening the destruction of that part of the city, the wind being very high. Despair was in every countenance, but a gallant sailor volunteered his services to climb the lightning rod, taking with him a cord, which he made fast at one end, and then let it down to the ground. A bucket was then tied to it, and, being filled with water and a tin cup placed in it, was hoisted up to the noble fellow, who, holding on to a column with one hand, used the tin pot with the other to cast on water, and extinguished the fire kindling on another column in the highest part of the steeple, thus preventing immense destruction, and doing the city a great service, which, it is gratifying to say, was not forgotten, but met with proper notice and reward." The hero's name, however, seemed of no consequence.

On the eighteenth of December, 1804, the progress of the city was again impeded for a short time by a disastrous fire, which began at two o'clock in the morning in a grocery on Front Street. The air was cold, and a high wind blowing, and the engines late in their appearance. The buildings from the west side of Coffee House Slip, on Water Street, to Gouverneur's Lane, and thence down to the East River, were swept away, and crossing Wall Street, the houses upon the east side of the slip were burned. Among them was the old Tontine Coffee House, so celebrated in its day, and which had a narrow escape in the great fire of 1835. Most of the buildings being of wood, their destruction caused new and fire-proof brick edifices to be built in their places. About forty stores and dwellings were consumed—fifteen on Wall Street, seventeen on Front, and eight on Water Street—the value of the property destroyed amounting to two million dollars. The fire was supposed to have been the work of eleven incendiaries, from anonymous letters sent to a merchant previous to the event. A reward of five hundred dollars was accordingly offered by the mayor for the apprehension of the guilty parties, but no one was arrested.

On August 25, 1808, a general alarm of fire was given at 1 A. M. It began at the soap and candle factory of Edward Watkeys, in Nassau Street. The factory was surrounded by several large wooden buildings, which soon were all in flames. The Department struggled for at least two hours, and the fire was not subdued till six buildings were destroyed. The loss of life, however, was great, for four persons perished in the flames.

The War of 1812 was a period of darkness and depression for New York, but the city's resources were additionally crippled by the terrible conflagration of May 19, of the preceding year (1811.) The fire broke out on Sunday morning in Lawrence's coach factory in Chatham Street, near Duane, and raged furiously for several hours. Mr. John W. Degrauw was then a small boy in a store in the Bowery with his uncle. Passing by at the outbreak of the disaster he ran down Chatham Street crying "Fire!" and soon got the old jail bell near the City Hall ringing. A brisk northeast wind was blowing at the moment, and the flames, spreading with great rapidity, for some time baffled all the exertions of the firemen and citizens. Between eighty and one hundred buildings on both sides of Chatham Street were consumed in a few hours. Mr. G. P. Disosway was then a Sabbath-school boy and a teacher in a public school room near by, at the corner of Tryon Row. The school was dismissed, and, as usual, proceeded to old John Street Church, while thick showers of light, burning shingles and cinders were falling all over the streets. That was the day of shingle roofs. When the teachers and scholars, their number very large, reached the church the venerable Bishop McKendall occupied the pulpit, and seeing the immense clouds of dark smoke and burning embers enveloping that section of the city, he advised the men "to go to the fire and help in its extinguishment and he would preach to the women and children." This advice was followed.

By this time the scene had become very exciting, impressive, even fearful. The wind had increased to a gale, and far and wide and high flew the flakes in whirling eddies, throwing burning destruction wherever they lit or fell. The lofty spires near by of the Brick Meeting Church, St. Paul's, and St. George's Chapel, enveloped in the flying embers, soon became the special objects of watchfulness and anxiety. Thousands of uplifted eyes were directed to these holy places, threatened with destruction. But there was no cause for fear. Near the ball at the top of the Brick Church a blazing spot was seen outside, and apparently not larger than a man's hand. Instantly a thrill of fear evidently ran through the bosoms of the thousands crowding the park and the wide area of Chatham Street. "They feared the safety of an old and loved temple of the Lord," says an old chronicler, "and they feared also, if the spire was once in flames, with the increasing gale, what would be the terrible consequences in the lower part of the city."

"What can we do?" was the universal question. "What in the world can be done?" was the query in everybody's mouth. The kindling spot could not be reached from the inside of the tall steeple, nor by ladders outside, neither could the most powerful fire-engine of the day force the water to that lofty height. With the deepest anxiety, fear and trembling all faces were turned in that direction. At this moment of alarm and dread a sailor appeared on the roof of the church, and very soon he was seen climbing up the steeple, hand over hand, by the lightning rod, a rusty, slender piece of iron. The excitement became intense, and the perilous undertaking of the daring man was watched every moment, as he slowly, grasp by grasp, foot by foot, literally crawled

Barnum's Museum. St. Paul's Church. Astor House.
PARADE OF THE PURDY GUARDS, 1843.

upwards by means of this slim conductor. Many fears were expressed among the immense crowd, watching every inch of his ascent, for there was no resting place for hands or feet and he must hold on or fall and perish. Should he succeed in reaching the burning spot how could he possibly extinguish it, as no water, neither by hose nor bucket, could be sent to his assistance? At last he reached the kindling spot, and, firmly grasping the lightning rod with one hand, with the other he removed his tarpaulin hat from his head and by blow after blow beat out the fire. Shouts of joy and thanks greeted the noble fellow as he slowly and safely descended to the earth again. Who was the hero? He was the father of the Rev. Dr. Hague, pastor of the Baptist Church at the corner of Thirty-first Street and Madison Avenue, who died about 1871. The "Old Brick" was thus preserved from the great conflagration of that Sunday morning. The gallant sailor quickly disappeared in the crowd, and, it was said, immediately sailed abroad, with the favorable wind then blowing. A reward was offered for the generous act, but it was said an impostor succeeded in obtaining it.

The cupola of the Old Jail which stood on the spot now occupied by the Hall of Records also took fire. This was extinguished through the exertions of a prisoner " on the limits." This was the famous institution where unfortunate debtors were confined and deprived of liberty, and without tools, book, paper, or pen were expected to pay their debts. It was a kind of Calcutta Black Hole, and the inmates, having no yard, had to use the top of the building to take exercise. Here they might be seen every hour of the day. Generally discovering fires in the city, they gave the first alarm by ringing the Jail bell. This became a sure signal of a conflagration, and on this occasion they saved the legal pest-house from quick destruction. The Corporation rewarded the debtor who had extinguished the blaze in the cupola. If the building had been destroyed, and its inmates saved, there would not have been much public regret at the loss, for it had been a veritable dungeon to American prisoners of war during the Revolution. After General Washington's success, in the year 1777, in New Jersey, a portion of these poor prisoners were exchanged, but many of them, exhausted by their confinement, before reaching the vessels for their embarkation home, fell dead in the streets. These are some of the historical reminiscences of the " Old Debtors'-Prison " which so narrowly escaped burning in the fire of May, 1811.

" The dependence for water at this fire," says Mr. Engs, " was entirely upon street pumps, private cisterns, and the Manhattan Works. These were plied with all the then existing means, and even the assistance of numerous females was volunteered to pass the buckets. The short supply of water and the strong wind baffled all exertions, and resort was had to pulling down some houses before the progress of the flames could be arrested. In two hours and a half 102 houses were destroyed. Scudder's Museum, situated in Chatham Street, opposite Tryon Row, prevented it spreading farther in that direction, and the open space in Tryon Row arrested its progress there. . . . . . The flakes had caught in forty-three places quite away from the great scene of the conflagration, and this may be accounted for, to a great extent, from the fact that the buildings were nearly all of wood, filling the air with sparks and cinders, which the heavy wind sped on to mischief. In the opinion of the engineers a stop could not be put to this conflagration without applying the hooks and razing the houses in Tryon Row and elsewhere to the ground. The Recorder, Mr. Van Wyck, had the power by law and forbade it, threatening the commanding engineer with expulsion if he gave such orders. It was no time to hesitate, and Engineer Roome, indignant at the interference, cried out, ' Come on, Hook and Ladder ! and you, Pierre Van Wyck, stand on one side, or we will bury you in the ruins !' "

This fire was long remembered in the Department on account of a fatal accident. William Peterson, foreman of Engine Company No. 15, was one of the bravest and most devoted of firemen, and had often signalized himself by his exhibition of courage and zeal. While the Chatham Street fire was at its height Foreman Peterson was suddenly stricken down, overcome by his too great exertion and by exposure to the heat. He was carried home in an almost lifeless condition, and within a few hours he died. The last solemn rites were attended by the whole Department, and the chiselled marble at Greenwood tells to posterity the story of his worth. There was another accident also at this fire. Chief Engineer Thomas Franklin while attempting to pass from one street to another, both sides of which were swept by flames, was overcome by the heat, and his clothes took fire. At once he was drenched with water from the engines, and in an exhausted state was taken home. He soon recovered from his injuries.

On August 3, 1813, an accident occurred at a fire in Ross's buildings in Fulton Street (then called Fair Street), near Broadway, which for long after gave work for the lawyers. Jeremiah B. Taylor, who had no connection with the Department, and, it is said, was not a citizen, was looking on at the burning building, standing near the pipe of Engine Company No. 21. Suddenly a wall fell upon him, burying him and killing him, and cutting off a length of hose. The pipe man escaped without injury, but Foreman Howe suffered from a severe blow on the head from a falling brick. The generous-hearted firemen

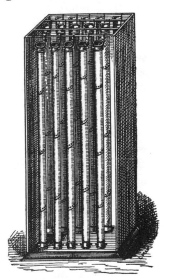

HOSE RACK.

at once set on foot a subscription to relieve Taylor's family, and raised between seven and eight hundred dollars. His funeral was attended by the whole Department, and the expenses paid by the men. Subsequent discoveries, however, showed that the firemen's charity was misplaced, and the fund was then held for their own benevolent purposes. Taylor's heirs, however, began suit, and for years the litigation dragged its slow length along, and finally became a dead letter.

The next few years have a record of accidents. On August 31, 1815, William Meekleworth, our old chronicler P. W. Engs and A. Lent were knocked down by the fall of the cornice of Zion Church in Mott Street, and Meekleworth was very much hurt. On December 3, 1816, George Herrick fell from the loft of Mr. Allen's store in Water Street, while on duty at a fire, was buried under some fallen bricks, and had his leg broken. On June 22, 1820, Charles W. Abrams, of Engine Company No. 18, died in consequence of injuries sustained at a fire in Broadway, and was buried in Trinity Church yard. The fatal fire in Broadway began at Cram's distillery, and thirty-six houses were burned. Early in the present century turpentine distilleries were allowed to be erected on and about the old Collect, between Orange and Rynders Streets, considered in 1820 to be the upper part of the city. These distilleries would burn out two or three times a year, calling for machines to be drawn to them from the distant parts of the city without being able to do any good, as it was impossible to arrest the flames by water, and there were no houses so near as to be much in danger. The nuisance became so great that firemen and other citizens applied to the authorities to forbid their location within the "lamp and watch district," and the distilleries were finally driven out. On January 24, 1821, at three A. M., an alarming fire broke out in a house in Front Street, near Crane's Wharf, which destroyed twenty-four buildings and did much injury to seven others. A number of vessels at the wharf were also injured. The weather was so cold that the hose was with difficulty kept from freezing.

The Department suffered a loss at a fire at a ship-yard on March 24, 1824. It occurred in the yard of Adam & Noah Brown, bounded by Stanton Street, Houston Street, Goerck Street, and the East River. There were two steamboats and two ships on the stocks, under cover of the ship-house. Early as was the hour, half the city seemed aroused and hastened to the scene of the conflagration. The firemen rapidly put their engines to work, but their enemy had got a good way ahead of them. The steamboats on the stocks were nearly finished, and Mr. Adam Brown, who was present, determined to make an attempt to launch them. A strong force of workmen and citizens was got together, and the effort was made. They were aided by the firemen, especially by Engine No. 33, under Foreman James P. Allaire and Assistant Foreman Ebenezer Worship, who endeavored to check the flames at that point. But in vain; the conflagration spread so rapidly that the workmen were driven from the vicinity of the stocks, and the attempt had to be abandoned. Engine No. 33 stood her ground bravely; but, unfortunately, was in a moment almost surrounded by fire. "Jump for your lives!" cried hundreds of spectators who saw the peril of the men. Some of the firemen were able to get away, but Charles Forrester, Philander Webb, Jeremiah Bruce and Harry Esler had to jump into the river to escape the flames. They were quickly rescued, but their engine was destroyed, nothing remaining of it but a blackened scrap-heap. The fire now raged furiously and unchecked, and in the space of an hour every vessel and all the property in the yard were burned.

A still sadder event occurred on March 8, 1827, when two firemen were killed. It was during a fire at Bowen & Co.'s store in Maiden Lane. A ladder had been placed against the building to enable the firemen to get their hose to play into the interior. David W. Raymer, of No. 40 Engine, stood at the top, Assistant Foreman Francis Joseph, of No. 1 Engine, under him, and just below a third man. The smoke and flame that poured out of the windows obscured the top of the building so that no one perceived the wooden cornice was tottering. Without the slightest warning down it crushingly came, smashing the ladder and burying three men. There was a simultaneous rush of firemen to the spot to extricate their unfortunate comrades. Quicker than it takes to write the words, the blazing cornice was removed, flung aside, and the wounded men lifted tenderly out. It was found that Raymer and Joseph were very severely injured, but that the third man had escaped with trifling hurts. Raymer and Joseph were conveyed to hospital, but the former survived only an hour, and the latter died before morning. There was universal mourning for those brave men, for they were well known and liked for many estimable qualities. The two were buried on the same day, the Fire Department attending the joint funeral in a body. The Department collected a handsome sum of money for Raymer's destitute widow and orphans. Fifty years afterwards Mr. Charles Forrester, of No. 33 Engine, which was destroyed in 1824, was giving reminiscences of the old days, and remarked that firemen were more reckless in those times than in later years. "They didn't care so much for their lives," said Mr. Forrester, "they ran up slate roofs, for instance, in a most careless fashion."

In reference to the deaths of Raymer and Joseph the *Commercial Advertiser* of that date had the following pertinent remarks: "Thus we have lost two valuable members of the Society by the careless manner in which buildings are suffered to be erected in this city, and until we have a law clearly defining the manner in which houses should be constructed the lives of our firemen will be endangered not only by overhanging wooden gutters and cornices, but in many other respects. One of the morning papers speaking of the melancholy accident of yesterday suggests the propriety of the more general use of copper gutters which are secured in such a manner to the building as to prevent their falling in case of fire."

In May, 1828, many fires had occurred in the upper part of the town, and it was supposed they were the work of incendiaries. The greatest of them occurred on the twenty-sixth, when the Bowery Theater was destroyed. A colored man was apprehended on suspicion, and he confessed to having been hired to set fire to the building. The fire originally broke out in Chambers & Underhill's livery stable in Bayard Street, about a quarter before six o'clock in the evening. The wind blew freshly from the southwest, and in a few minutes six or seven wooden buildings in the vicinity were enveloped in flames. The firemen could not prevent their progress, the buildings being full of combustible materials. The fire soon communicated to the Bowery Theater, both in front and in the rear in Elizabeth Street. The flames were driven by the wind full upon the play-house, whose side wall was fire proof, with iron shutters to the windows. At length the wooden cornice took fire. The flames singing the ends of the rafters were driven violently into the interior of the building. A pyramid of flame rose from the burning roof to an immense height with a dazzling intensity of brightness and heat that drove back the bystanders, and shed over the city a light like that of day. The roof, chimneys, and the west wall

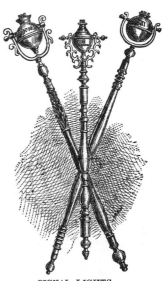

SIGNAL LIGHTS.

shortly after fell, and the fire raged inside about three hours. But when the cornice fell it brought down death with it. John Bradshaw, of Engine Company No. 21, was at work beneath it and was crushed to death. It was impossible to rescue the body, and it was not until weeks after that the mangled remains could be dug out. A young man, Benjamin Gifford, Jr., who lived at No. 139 Madison Street, and who used to run with the engines, was also supposed to have perished in the ruins. Bradshaw's funeral, at No. 2 Liberty Street, was attended by his company. The Rev. Mr. Feltus officiated and delivered a very appropriate and feeling address to the firemen.

The buildings beyond the theater were also consumed with much rapidity, being full of ardent spirits and other inflammable articles. At one period of the conflagration the gas in the pipes which supplied the theater became ignited, and the effect which its instantaneous combustion produced on the distant spectators was like that of lightning. Others supposed it was the explosion of gunpowder. An individual was on the roof of the theater when the flames began to envelop it. He escaped with great hazard from his peril by letting himself drop from the eaves about twenty feet to the roof of an adjacent building. Part of the rear wall fell during the night and the remainder fell in the morning.

When the fire first broke out, there was great difficulty experienced in getting a supply of water, and it was not until a line of engines was formed, extending from the scene of the conflagration to the East River at Catharine Slip, and another line from the corporation supply engine at the corner of Leonard and Elm Streets, that the fury of the flames could be arrested. The engine from Yorkville was brought down by three horses, and the firemen of Brooklyn assisted with promptness and activity. It was not until eleven o'clock that the fire was subdued. All the properties of the Bowery Theater

OLD NORTH BATTERY, FOOT OF HUBERT STREET.

were destroyed, and some persons escaped from it with difficulty. Mrs. Gilfert, the wife of the manager, was to have had a benefit, and as a full house was expected, it was a fortunate circumstance that the fire broke out before the hour of admission. The roof of the building was sheeted with lead, which soon melted from the intensity of the heat. Sixty thousand dollars insurance had been effected which did not cover the whole loss. Five horses and several carriages and gigs were destroyed in the livery stable. The Shakespeare Tavern, kept by D. Scribner in the Bowery, was burned.

The *Commercial Advertiser* of May 28 (ten days after the fire) said:

It is very much to be regretted that the police, with the mayor at the head of it, should not be prompt and efficient on such occasions. The watch was not seen on Monday when the first fire broke out, and very few constables made their appearance on the ground. The consequence was that an idle crowd, with a whole gang of thieves and pickpockets, interrupted the operations of the firemen, and prevented property from being saved if they did not actually assist in its destruction. When the mayor was compelled to preside as a judge in the sessions, half the year round, we well recollect that the duties of the office, as related to the Police Department, were faithfully attended to by Messrs. Clinton and Colden, and that all the officers were required to attend on occasions of fire. Such was also the case with Mr. Hone after the judicial functions of the office were removed. He was indefatigable as a police officer, and generally among the first on the ground at a fire. The presence of the mayor is not only necessary to control the spectators, who can do no good, but to inspirit the firemen, to whose laudable exertions he should be a witness.

The *Morning Courier* of the day of the fire had the following notice:

BOWERY THEATER.—A CARD.—Mrs. Gilfert's Benefit. Mrs. Gilfert respectfully announces to her friends and the public that, having recovered from her recent severe indisposition, her benefit, which in consequence of that event was postponed, will take place this evening, the 26th inst. Upon this occasion will be performed the TRAGEDY OF THIRTY YEARS; or, the Life of a Gambler—heretofore received with the most distinguished approbation. The part of Georgette, for this night only, will be personated by Miss Sophia Gilfert, being her first appearance. THE HUNDRED POUND NOTE will also be presented, the part of Billy Black by Messrs. Roberts and Chapman. Mdme. Labassee will dance her favorite *pas seul*, "I've been roaming." Mons. Barbere and Mad'slle Celeste will appear in a grand *pas de deux*. Seiltanzer Herr Cline will perform on the elastic cord, displaying many novel and highly effective evolutions. ☞ Seats may be secured at the box office.

The large number of fires previous and subsequent to the burning of the Bowery Theater caused the various insurance companies to offer a reward of one thousand dollars for the apprehension and conviction of any incendiary. The following presidents signed the advertisement:

E. Lord (Manhattan), T. R. Mercen (Equitable), John Slidell (Traders'), A. M. Muir (Etna), Jacob Drake (Fireman's), J. T. Champlin (Farmers'), James Swords (Washington), R. Whiley (North River), Thomas Hertell (Phenix), A. Bloodgood (Contributorship), Henry Rankin (Globe), Gabriel Furman (Mutual), E. H. Laight (Eagle), R. Havens (Howard), J. Lawrence (Merchants'), Noah Jarvis (Mechanics'), John McComb (Lafayette), Allen Clapp (Jefferson), E. Tibbetts (Franklin), and J. C. Hart, secretary of the Chatham.

The year 1829 was prolific of misfortunes to the Department. There were many fires, but though not serious in themselves they proved disastrous to the firemen. At a fire in a dwelling house in Broome Street, near Sheriff, on April 23, a ladder had been raised to facilitate the efforts of the hosemen. On the ladder were Messrs. Conklin, Titus and Chappell, of No. 14 Engine, and William Stoutenburgh, of No. 5 Engine. Without any sign of warning the front of the building suddenly fell outwards, breaking the ladder in two and burying the men in the ruins. Their escape from death was miraculous. In a few seconds the firemen were extricated, and, strange to say, only one was found to have sustained any serious injury. This was Titus, who soon recovered. Much the same kind of accident happened on July 9 to members of Hook and Ladder Company No. 1. At a fire in a four-story store, No. 28 South Street, some of the men were injured by the falling of a ladder, and several other firemen were buried in the ruins of the fallen gable end of the building. They were all saved from death, but some of them were so severely injured that at first it was thought they would die. Happily they recovered. A tremendous storm struck the city some few weeks after, on August 15, and at half-past three in the morning the lightning set fire to a house at the corner of Mulberry and Hester Streets. The Secretary of No. 21 Engine makes a satirical remark at the end of his report of this occurrence: "The engine was dragged to the fire," he says, "through one of the most severe storms of thunder and rain experienced for many years, the flashes of lightning following each other almost instantaneously, and the rain pouring down in torrents. It was also slyly reported (how true I know not) that some of the members—rather short, to be sure—had to put their swimming powers in operation to reach the fire."

Three fatal accidents occurred in 1832. On July 5, Cornelius Garrison, a member of Engine Company No. 32, was killed at a fire, and on September 25, Nathaniel Brown and James Hedges, members of Engine Company No. 42, met the same fate.

The City Hotel was burned on April 24, 1833. This vast structure occupied the whole block west of Broadway, between Cedar and Thames Streets. It was about one hundred feet in length by sixty feet in breadth. It was owned by John Jacob Astor, who purchased it about 1830 at a cost, including the land, of more than one hundred and twenty thousand dollars. It was one of the most exciting fires of the period, from the narrow escapes attending it and for the gallantry of ex-Chief Engineer U. Wenman. About ten in the morning smoke was seen issuing from the roof of the hotel, south end, rear side. At first a barrel of water would have extinguished it, but the great height of the building rendered it inaccessible to the firemen, and the consequence was that in a short time the southern half of the roof was in a blaze, sending its immense volumes to the skies, and in half an hour the northern part of the roof had shared the fate of the rest. As soon as the fire had descended within reach of the firemen's powers, they poured in upon it a flood of water from every direction, and finally subdued the flames, leaving the three lower stories uninjured, except by water. The upper story, as well as the attics of the roof, was destroyed, except the walls. In the attempt to check the progress of the fire, eleven persons ascended the upper story, immediately under the roof. Among them Mr. Jennings, the keeper of the hotel, Mr. Uzziah Wenman, who the year before was chief engineer, Mr. Charles Baldwin, lawyer, Mr. Thomas Austin, a city auctioneer, Mr. A. S. Fraser, a clerk of Mr. Aaron Clark, and Mr. James Thompson. Absorbed in their work of trying to save the building, they did not notice the progress of the flames. The greater part of the ceiling of the upper story fell, and the fire then rushed up the scuttle and cut off their retreat by the staircase. The structure was so high that no ladder could be raised to relieve them, nor even near enough to throw a rope by which they might descend. In this perilous situation, on the verge of the roof, and the raging element making frightful advances toward them, they had for some time a melancholy prospect of being crushed by the fall of the burning timbers around them. One or two exclaimed, "We are lost!" Long ladders were spliced, but for some moments all efforts to reach them were in vain. Calmness was recommended in this dreadful emergency. The ex-chief with an axe which he had brought with him cut away the skylight. Samuel Maverick, an exempt fireman, was in the story beneath, and, by extraordinary effort, with the assistance of a flag-staff, sent up the end of a drag rope. Providentially it stuck fast. Assistant Alderman Day, of the Eighth Ward, took this drag rope, which was very heavy, and about one hundred and fifty feet in length. Nevertheless, he made several coils, and ran with it along the gutter, where a slight inclination or false step would have dashed him to the ground. Mr. Wenman seized the rope and fastened it to the dormer casement. He then began lowering his companions, beginning with Charley Baldwin, who was much larger than himself. The situation was watched with great anxiety. Broadway was lined with people from Rector Street to the Park, and the adjoining roofs, windows and balconies were filled with spectators. The work of destruction proceeded rapidly, and the flames burst through the roofing with such violence as to throw the tiles off in masses, which tumbled down upon the pavement below, to the imminent danger of the firemen and others beneath.

When all his companions had been relieved, a ladder was brought to the interior of the fourth story, which reached to the attic, and on that Mr. Wenman was enabled to descend. His hands had been much cut by holding to the rope while he was letting down the other men. One of these imperilled persons had given up all hope, but he manifested a great degree of coolness. He waved his hands to his friends below, bidding them, as he believed, a last farewell. For a long time the rumbling of scarcely a cart or carriage was to be heard in that part of the city. Business seemed to pause while the work of destruction was going on.

There were some casualties, but not of any moment. One of the hook and ladder men of No. 2 was somewhat severely cut in the face by the falling of a tile from the roof. He had his wound dressed, and then manfully returned to his duty. Another man was badly scalded by the molten lead falling on him. Although the destruction of property was immense, yet it was calculated that, by the excellent supply of water from the hydrants, one hundred and fifty thousand dollars' worth of property was saved. The damage to the building was about ten thousand dollars; insured. The occupant, Chester Jennings, was also insured to a much greater amount than his loss. The hotel was crowded with guests, and for days before applicants had been refused.

The first trouble of any account between the firemen of the city of New York and the authorities was the "Bailey trouble," which occurred in 1828. John P. Bailey, who was the foreman of United States Engine Company before John Ryker, Jr., and who was a manager in the old Sugar House at the corner of Church and Leonard streets, was in command of his company at a fire, and refused to allow Thomas Shephard, the Assistant Alderman of the Fifth Ward, to go through the fire lines. Shephard left threatening vengeance, and on August 11, 1828, had Bailey dismissed. The firemen thought this unjust, and at the next fire, which proved to be at the Vauxhall Garden, which then ran through from the Bowery to Broadway, after they had done their duty and put out the fire, they turned their caps and dragged the engines home by the tail ropes, and gave other evidences of their feeling in the matter. The affair created great excitement at the time, and Bailey was finally reinstated in his command.

RESCUE OF A WOMAN.

CHAPTER XV.

OTHER DESTRUCTIVE CONFLAGRATIONS.

Accidents to Firemen.—Two Hundred Families Rendered Homeless.—The Calamity at Niblo's Old Theater and Burning of the New.—The Bowery Theater in Flames Three Times.—An Old Play Bill.— Revolt of the Firemen on Account of Chief Gulick.—Introduction of Politics.—Destruction of the Old National Theater.—A Scene of Magnificence and Splendor.—A Million Dollar Conflagration in Water Street.

ON April 30, 1833, at eleven o'clock at night, a destructive fire began in the large stable of Kipp & Brown, corner of Hudson and Bank Streets, in that part of the city then called Greenwich Village, and which old newspapers describe as being two miles from Wall Street. The contents of the stables were very combustible, and large flakes of fire and burning shingles fell upon the buildings adjoining which caught almost immediately. The wind was from the eastward, and its strength helped to spread the flames. In the stables were forty-seven horses, and their agonizing cries were dreadful to hear. It was impossible to save them, they were all burned, and next morning they were found lying in rows, side by side, just as they had stood in their stalls. The population in that part of the city was very dense, very many were foreigners, and few were above comfortable circumstances. The houses were generally two stories, many of them with brick fronts. In less than twenty minutes the block bounded by Hudson, Bank, Greenwich, and Hammond Streets, and containing sixty or seventy dwellings, was destroyed. One hundred and fifty or two hundred families were rendered homeless. The scene of confusion and consternation was almost indescribable. A hundred or more families who had removed their furniture to places supposed by them to be secure were seen flying in every direction before the fury of the all-devouring element. In many instances furniture, after being removed, was destroyed by fire. Through the dense cloud of smoke and burning cinders children half naked were to be seen running to and fro, crying for their parents, and parents in despair shrieking the names of their children. Among those who exerted themselves to arrest the progress of the flames were Aldermen Murray, Whiting, Robinson, and Peters, who remained on the ground till morning. The fire was said to have been caused by a woman to revenge herself on a man who had slighted her. The loss was about one hundred and fifty thousand dollars.

On September 5, 1833, on the way to a fire, Engine No. 41 and Engine No. 3⁷ were running a race with the characteristic emulation of the day. It was almost a neck-and-neck affair, and along the route hundreds of persons ran cheering the contestants. No. 41 was just about passing its rival, when a horse and wagon ran into the head of the rope. It was at a corner around which the wagon was coming. The men, taken unaware, let go their hold of the rope, and several were thrown down, and among them Mr. Sutton. Mr. Sutton was struck by the king-bolt of the engine and dragged some distance. This put a stop to the race, and that gentleman was picked up much injured. A more serious event happened on March 7, 1834. A fire broke out in the store of Maitland, Kennedy & Co., at Front and Depeyster Streets, at which Mr. John Knapp, of Engine No. 32, was killed. The firemen were doing good work, and though it was seen that the building would be gutted, the men had the satisfaction of knowing that they were confining the fire to that

MONUMENT TO FIREMEN WARD AND UNDERHILL (CLARKSON STREET).

building. Mr. Knapp was standing in the doorway playing on the flames with the pipe which he held. His comrades suddenly noticed the front wall bulging and gave the alarm. Knapp dropped the pipe to effect his escape, but before he had got a few steps from the building he was overwhelmed by the falling torrent of bricks. Bruised, mutilated, disfigured, Mr. Knapp was taken from under the mass, but life was extinct. The dismay among the men of No. 32 was inexpressible. Placing their dead comrade upon their engine, they detached their hose and sorrowfully bore the body home.

A few months subsequent to this, on July 1, another calamity occurred. We quote the details from the minutes of Engine Company No. 13: "This morning, about a quarter before three A. M., a fire was discovered in the store of Haydock, Clay & Co., 273 Pearl Street. The entire stock of goods was destroyed and also the building. Toward the latter part of the fire an accident happened which cast a gloom over the happiness of a large and highly respectable body of young men belonging to the Fire Department—the death of Messrs. Eugene Underhill and F. A. Ward, both members of this company. They died in the honorable and fearless discharge of their duty. What made their sudden death more deeply felt was that there seemed an unusual flow of spirits among the company who were almost to a man witnesses of the scene and standing near the building when the wall fell, and many of them had been in the building during the fire and almost by a miracle escaped. On Wednesday, second instant, they were followed to the grave by a large concourse of citizens. The procession started from Broadway (Hospital   ) down Beekman Street to Pearl Street, when the procession halted to receive the remains of Mr. Ward, then moved up Madison to Market, up Market to Henry Street, where the procession then halted again to receive the remains of Mr. Underhill.

ORDER OF PROCESSION.

FIRST,

THE HEAD OF FIRE DEPARTMENT.

With the Fire Department Banner, then Members of the New York and Brooklyn Fire Departments with Banners placed at Equal Distance in the procession. Then the Hearse containing the Body of Mr. Ward.

Supported by Eight Pall Bearers in the following order :

KNAPP,		FITZGERALD,
MILLER,		FRANKLIN,
GLARHAM,	WARD.	C. MILLER,
SHARP,		MITCHELL.

The Friends and Relations of the Deceased.

J. T. MOORE,		TOMPKINS,
MICHALETTI,		MACY,
SILLECK,	E. UNDERHILL.	VARIAN,
GRAHAM,		PHILLIPS.

The Friends and Relatives of Mr. Underhill, then the Members and Volunteers of our Company Followed by the Members of No. 10.

"The procession moved up Henry Street to Gouverneur Street, through Gouverneur Street to Grand, down Grand to Broadway, up Broadway to Houston Street, through Houston to Varick Street to the burying-ground. The procession then opened from the front so as to let the left of the line countermarch into the yard.

"They were buried as they were found, *Side by Side.* One Monument will Cover the Remains of those two Young Men who were Cut off in the prime of life—the Dawn of Manhood. Peace to their ashes."

And now we come to one of the most memorable years in the fire history of New York—1835. To that great conflagration, so sweeping and so dire in its results, we feel it necessary to devote special chapters which follow this one. It was a year in which a fire fiend seemed to have taken possession of the city. We will mention here only one or two fires which, though large, were yet dwarfed by the terrible calamity of December 16. On June 8 no less than two hundred families (as in 1833) were rendered homeless by a fire that broke out in the rear of 209 Elizabeth Street. It was a fearful night for that thickly populated district. Every building on the block bounded by Prince, Mott, Elizabeth, and Houston Streets was swept away by the flames. Women and children fled screaming from the roaring element, and considering the little army that had been housed in the burning buildings, it was marvelous how any escaped with their lives. The firemen behaved splendidly in getting these people safely away.

On September 17 Niblo's Garden had a narrow escape. For a neighbor it had a fireworks manufactory. About one o'clock in the afternoon the spontaneous combustion of some articles took place. Three or four explosions in rapid succession alarmed every one in the locality, and the firemen were called. Before they reached the scene, however, the fire had spread to Niblo's Garden, damaging it to the extent of fifteen thousand dollars. But a fatality was a still sadder result of the conflagration. The persons employed in the theater, and who were preparing for the evening performance, had barely time to escape before the building was enveloped in flames. A colored boy named Isaac Freeman was slow in getting out. In the upper part of the building two firemen were fighting the conflagration. One was Fire Warden Purdy, Jr., of the Tenth Ward (a son of Alderman Purdy), and the other W. Harris, of No. 2 Company. Volumes of thick black smoke accompanied by tongues of fire suddenly rolled around them. The firemen called to Freeman to get on his knees and crawl along with them. But Freeman was almost instantly suffocated, and Purdy and Harris then made a dash through the flames and with difficulty got through a window. They crawled along the gutters, and at last, amid the congratulatory shouts of the crowd, succeeded in reaching a ladder. Purdy's left hand was badly burned and his hair and face scorched. Harris escaped without injury. The fire did not prevent a concert taking place next night as announced. It was Mons. Gillaud's Benefit Concert, at which Signorina Albina Stella, Mrs. Franklin, Signor Montressor, and other well-known artists of the day assisted. The loss was about fifteen thousand dollars.

In early years a circus called the "Stadium" was established on the northeasterly corner of Broadway and Prince Street. These premises were purchased when Bayard's farm was sold off in lots by Mr. Van Rensselaer, and occupied the site of the Metropolitan Hotel and Niblo's Garden. Shortly after the War of 1812 the inclosure was used as a place for drilling militia officers who were cited to appear at the "Stadium" for drill. The circus edifice was surrounded by a high fence, the entrance being on Prince Street. Afterwards two brick buildings were erected on Broadway, one of which was for some time occupied by James Fenimore Cooper, the novelist. William Niblo, previously proprietor of the Bank Coffee House in Pine Street, removed to this locality in the year 1828, and established a restaurant and public garden. In the center of the garden was still remaining the old circus building, which was devoted by Mr. Niblo to exhibitions of theatrical performances of a gay and attractive character, which soon attained such popularity as to induce him to erect a building of more pretensions as a theater. This edifice was constructed even with a line of Broadway, but having a blank face on that street, the entrance being from within the garden. The latter was approached from Broadway. The interior of the garden was spacious and

adorned with shrubbery, and walks lighted up with festoons of lamps. This
view shows the condition of Niblo's Garden before the erection of the theater
on Broadway at present.

Five days afterward the famous Bowery Theater was burned. This unfortunate playhouse has had many such experiences. One of the first was on
November 20, 1826, and was in consequence of a flaw in a gas pipe. The 1828
fire is already described. The accident of 1826 occurred about 5 P. M. The gas
must have been escaping some time, as the moment a lamp was lighted the
flames ran up to the gallery. They burned through the gallery in the saloon,
but fortunately no great damage was done. The fire was extinguished by
buckets only, without the aid of the engines. On September 22, 1835, how-

NEW YORK THEATER, AFTERWARD BOWERY THEATER.
(Erected 1826.)

ever, it was entirely destroyed. The fire began, singularly enough, about the.
same hour, 5 P. M. In a short time, notwithstanding the efforts of the Fire
Department, the edifice was a total loss. Engine Company No. 26 was indefatigable amid the falling timbers. One of its members, George Mills, had his
leg crushed by a falling beam, and it was feared that he would lose the limb.
Mr. T. J. Parsons, in the employ of Messrs. Benedict & Benedict, of Wall Street,
was also injured by a beam which fell on his head. An inventive genius of
the time, Matthew Carey (at that date a very old man), had suggested the
plan of covering adjacent buildings, while a fire was in progress, with wet carpets, blankets, etc., a plan which was the forerunner of the present method of
the Fire Insurance Patrol. His scheme was tested at this fire, and, it was said,
proved eminently successful in saving property. Forty-five minutes after the
outbreak the roof and part of the rear wall fell in. Half an hour afterward
the front wall came down, injuring the persons named above and several

others. One hundred and fifty thousand dollars were swallowed up. The building and lot were owned by Hamblin, Hamilton & Gouverneur. Hamblin was the sole owner of the scenery, properties, wardrobe, etc. Miss Medinas, one of the actresses, lost twenty thousand dollars, which included manuscript copies of "Norman Leslie," "Rienzi," "Pompeii" and "Lafitte." Mr. Gates, an actor, lost five hundred dollars. On the previous evening, Miss Waring, an actress, had met with a very serious accident. During the performance one of her legs was fractured. Nevertheless, it was declared that this fire was a fortunate occurrence for the city. The theater had stood in the way of opening Canal Street, and it was thought that the destruction of the large and expensive edifice would permit the proposed plan to go into execution. The theater was rebuilt on an enlarged scale—indeed, made the largest edifice in the city, but it met the same fate in the following year, and the occurrence is described further on.

The city had only a brief respite before it experienced another series of memorable fires. A notable circumstance occurred on February 18, 1836. The extensive printing and book manufacturing establishment in Mulberry Street, widely known as the Methodist Book Concern, was burned. Nothing of value could be rescued ex-

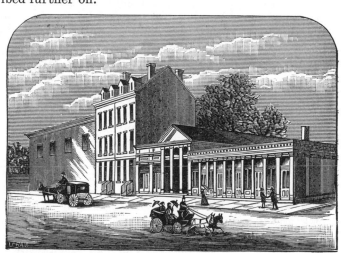

NIBLO'S GARDEN, 1828.

cept the account books of the *Christian Advocate and Journal.* In the morning fragments of burnt books were found on Long Island. As in 1835, the night was intensely cold, and the hydrants frozen, so that it was impossible to procure water. The singular circumstance was that one of the fragments found on Long Island was a charred leaf of the Bible, containing the sixty-fourth chapter of Isaiah. Very little of the leaf was legible, except the eleventh verse of that chapter, which reads: "Our holy and our beautiful house, where our fathers praised thee, is *burned up with fire,* and all our pleasant things are laid waste." This discovery occasioned much comment at the time. More than two hundred persons were thrown out of employment. The loss of this establishment and its valuable presses and stereotype plates was severely felt by the Methodist Episcopal denomination, the accumulation being the result of forty years of persevering industry, and the calamity occurring at a most unfavorable time, the Great Fire of '35 having rendered bankrupt many of the insurance offices.

In this year (1836) we strike upon a portion of the history of the Old Fire Department, where its members allowed their personal predilections to overcome their sense of public duty. The trouble originated in the famous fire of the preceding year. The citizens, as well as the press, on the day after the December conflagration of 1835, laid great stress on Chief Engineer Gulick's ability as a fireman, many claiming that it was his fault that the fire had gained such headway and that so much property was destroyed. They never gave it a thought that the firemen had been up two nights before, or the lack of water. Gulick was a very determined, independent, outspoken man, and when his pride was piqued, especially as to his qualifications as a fireman, he was up in a jiffy. He stood six feet two inches, was stout, and said to have been the finest looking man in the Department. The result of the many rumors caused the Common Council, who in those days had control of the Department, to order an investigation to be made. The discussion continued until May, 1836, when the Fire and Water Committee held a special meeting, at which Alderman Paul, of the Fourth Ward, made a long speech in denunciation of Gulick, charging him with having done certain things at the fire that was the means of aiding its extension in place of arresting its progress. Gulick was standing in the lobby at the time, while the room was crowded with citizens and firemen, all deeply interested in the proceedings. Gulick became quite excited over what old Paul stated, and he gave the alderman the lie, and left the room. At the conclusion of the meeting the committee went into secret session, and unanimously agreed to report in favor of removing Gulick at the next meeting of the Board, which was to be held on the following day.

About the time they were to convene (May 4, 1836) a fire broke out in Union Market, at the junction of Houston and Second Streets. Gulick was not aware at that hour what decision the Fire and Water Committee, had arrived at, but while at work at the above fire, which consisted of two small brick buildings, Charles G. Hubbs, of Engine Company No. 13, whom it seemed had learned the secret intention of the Fire and Water Committee, came up to Gulick and told him what he had heard. Gulick would not believe it at first, but when assured by Hubbs that it was so, Gulick went away from the fire, turning his cap as he did so. The men saw at a glance that something was wrong. Several ran after him, and soon learned that he was to be their chief no longer. The fire had been nearly subdued, when the firemen started for home. About an hour afterward it broke out anew, when all the firemen came on the ground with their apparatus, and their hats turned. They refused to go to work, when Charles H. Haswell, foreman of Engine Company No. 10, mounted the box of his engine and made a long speech to the men, contending that the removal of Gulick was an insult to the Department, and that his command should not go to work, let the consequences be what they might. So the firemen all agreed to side with Haswell. At this stage of the proceedings Carlisle Norwood, President of the Lorillard Insurance Company in 1875, came on the ground, and, seeing the state of affairs (the fire still raging at the time), went to Haswell and appealed to him not to create discord among the men. Haswell was unrelenting, and while Norwood stood conversing with him, John Coger, foreman of Engine No. 8, afterward assistant engineer, came up. Norwood appealed to Coger to get his company to work, as there was no knowing where the fire would terminate unless some efforts were made to arrest its progress. Coger consented to put his men on the brakes, but had no sooner brought a stream to bear on the fire than his hose was cut in several places. Several of the leading firemen, with Mr. Norwood, now consulted together as to what was best to be done; when it was finally decided that the only hope lay in getting Gulick to return to the fire, and for him to get the men to go to work. Thereupon Benj. H. Guion, one of the Fire Wardens, went in search of Gulick, and succeeded, after repeated entreaties, in getting him to resume command of the Department until the fire was extinguished. As Gulick hove in sight cheer after cheer rent the air from the members of the Department. He marched down among the men, with Carlisle Norwood on the one side, and Mr. Guion on the other, and exclaimed to the members of the Department: "Now, boys, let's all go to work and put out this fire, and we will attend to the Fire and Water Committee afterward." And so they did with a will, and the fire was soon after extinguished.

Just previous, however, to Gulick's reaching the fire the last time, word had been sent down to Mayor Lawrence of the demoralized condition of the firemen, and the great destruction of property that was sure to follow. The mayor started post haste to the scene, and undertook to direct the firemen, but they paid no attention to his orders. They hooted at him, and cheered incessantly for Gulick. The result was that the mayor was finally compelled to leave, and started for his office swearing vengeance on Gulick for

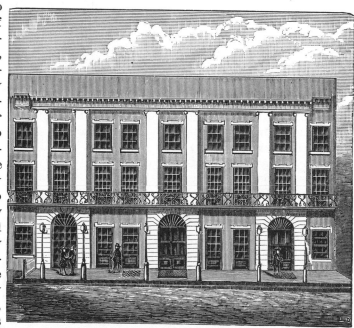

BURTON'S THEATER, CHAMBERS STREET.

the insults offered him by the firemen. On reaching the City Hall he found the Common Council in session; he at once made known to them the state of affairs at the fire, and urged the removal of Gulick at once. The result was that his wishes were complied with. The news spread like wildfire throughout the city—the Common Council having appointed, as Chief, John Riker. When the firemen learned that Gulick had been decapitated, they called special meetings and passed resolutions that Gulick must be reinstated, or they would abandon their engines. Efforts were made to induce Riker to resign, but without avail. The several companies kept on doing duty, but all the while urging the reinstating of Gulick. When they found that the Common Council would not accede to their requests, they marched up to the City Hall in a body and tendered their resignations. The course thus pursued by the men was in no way aided by Gulick, as he remonstrated against their withdrawing from the Department on his account.

Many of the old exempt firemen and citizens seeing that the city was now without a department, tendered their services, and took command of the several companies. The old members then organized themselves into what was known as the "Resigned Firemen's Association." Wm. Corp, foreman of Engine Company No. 4, and in after years paying teller of the Bank of New York, was chosen president. So matters jogged along until autumn, Riker remaining Chief, when the firemen got together and nominated Gulick for Register. They then appointed a committee to wait on the Tammany Hall Convention, to request them to indorse Gulick, nearly all the firemen being Democrats in those days. As Tammany would not agree to their demands, they waited on the Whig party, the latter having always been in the minority, and they were very willing to take up Gulick. The result was that he was elected by over seven thousand majority.

The following spring the firemen dovetailed with the Whigs again, and for the first time the Whigs got the control of the Common Council, each candidate, however, on the Whig ticket being pledged to remove Riker, if elected. As soon as they got in power they gave the chief engineership to Mr. Corp, President of the "Resigned Firemen's Association," but he declined the honor, so they made Cornelius V. Anderson chief. Then all the old members went back into the Department. During 1836 the Common Council passed an ordinance that the Board of Foremen and Assistants should elect the chief, this being the first concession made to the firemen.

To bring this subject to a close we must skip three years and come to 1839, when the Democrats again got control of the city ; they at once determined to remove Anderson. In order, therefore, to obtain a majority in the Board of Foremen and Assistants they got together twenty prominent men of their party, among whom were Oliver Charlick and Superintendent of Police John A. Kennedy. Each of the twenty got ten men and formed twenty hose companies, which the Common Council agreed to confirm as firemen, thus sending forty new votes into the Board of Foremen. The meeting at which these twenty companies were legalized was not held until near midnight, the object being to get certain members to go home before the "job" was rushed through. David Graham, a well-known lawyer, then Assistant Alderman of the Fifteenth Ward, smelt a mouse, tarried and soon learned what was going on. As the members of the Council took their seats, just fifteen minutes before twelve, Graham arose from his chair, and, in his loud, stentorian voice, exclaimed : "At this dead hour of the night you are going to do the darkest deed ever perpetrated by human being." He then took his hat and left the Chamber. The "job" was, however, put through, and Edward Hoffmire, the Ring candidate for chief, was, by the addition of these forty votes, elected over Anderson by nine majority. None of these new companies had ever any location or apparatus. When Charlick used to be asked what company he belonged to he would reply : "I belong to one of these things that spins around in the middle (meaning a reel), but I have never been able to find out where she lays."

The day following Hoffmire's election the papers came out with long articles denouncing the action of the Common Council, while many of the leaders of the Democratic party saw that the successful scheme would eventually be a detriment to them politically, and, moreover, they found they were doing themselves no good by fighting the firemen ; the result was that Hoffmire was never confirmed as chief engineer. Soon after the firemen passed a resolution at Fireman's Hall that no member could vote who had not been an active fireman three months, and thus killed the new Hose cart members—the "June Buggs," as they were called—not over half a dozen companies ever becoming permanently organized. Anderson remained chief until relieved by Alfred Carson. Gulick was for many years in the crockery business. After serving three years as Register, he ran for a second term, but was defeated. His salary was from eighteen to twenty thousand per annum, but he lent and spent to such an extent that all he had soon vanished. He finally got down in the world, losing all ambition; in fact, he seemed humiliated at his defeat, and thought every friend had failed him, and he finally sank so low in life that he died in the most extreme poverty, and without a friend near at hand to administer to his wants.

Very many unimportant fires happened while the firemen were in this state of "passive resistance." Everybody took a hand in the discussion. In the daily papers of the period the fire engine companies published "cards" almost every morning, invariably beginning satirically thus : "Whereas the Common Council, *in their wisdom,*" and ending by telling the public they, the firemen, had resigned because of the bad treatment by the aldermen of Chief Engineer Gulick. The *Morning Courier and New York Enquirer* of September 24, 1836, had the following paragraph :

This morning, at about three o'clock, a fire was discovered in the small wooden Church of the Nativity in Avenue D, one door from Fourth Street, which was entirely destroyed, and a brick building adjoining. The flames also extended to a number of small tenements in Fourth street, which were burning when we went to press. We are sorry to add that a great number of the Fire Department were inactive lookers-on at the conflagration.

In reference to this celebrated fight the *Morning Courier and New York Enquirer* of September 26, 1836, has a long leading article, which we here reproduce in a condensed form :

A difference has arisen between most of the fire companies of this city and the Corporation, in consequence of which many of the former at the fire which took place on Saturday morning early remained inactive spectators of the conflagration and have resigned . . . . Our intention is to avail ourselves of this opportunity to point out the necessity that exists for the introduction here of a totally new system for the extinguishment of fires. In this respect, too, it is very evident that we have not kept pace with the vast increase of the population and extent of the city . . . . When fire companies were formed, the members composing them were known to the whole community . . . . But the case is now materially altered. The firemen are still generally, it is true, held to be a very meritorious body of men, but the individuals composing it are little known or cared for. How, under this state of things, they have remained efficient so long as they have is a matter of astonishment. . . . . Of late years, however, a system of pecuniary rewards to a small extent has grown up; the Chief Engineer and six assistants have had salaries allotted to them, and now the firemen generally work for nothing, though as there were loaves and fishes to be distributed they ought to have something to say in the distribution . . . . . .

We are evidently at present arrived at that state of things that the best interests of the city imperiously require that a system for the extinguishment of fires should be introduced here commensurate with its increased extent . . . . In casting about as to what that system ought to be, the cities of the continent of Europe will afford us no guide. There fires are so very rare, and fire insurance so little resorted to, that the cases are not at all similar. In London it is different. There fires are frequent—though not as frequent as here—and insurance against fires is generally resorted to. Now we find in London that the measures adopted for the extinguishment of fires are under the control of the Fire Insurance Companies, and indeed that they cheerfully defray the greatest part of the expense . . , . It is their duty and interest to investigate the causes of fire . . . . The fire engines in London are chiefly built at the expense of the fire companies—they too pay the firemen. These firemen are ticket-porters, watermen, mechanics, etc., who can readily quit their occupations when a fire occurs.

After describing the emulation of the London firemen and their rewards, the *Courier* continues :

We are not prepared to say that it would be desirable to introduce a system of pay here at once, but that it will eventually be necessary we have no doubt. A gradual adoption of it would probably work best. Pay to the head engineer and to one or two men employed in taking care of the engine—by which the crowds of boys we now see about our engine houses would be avoided—is perhaps now all required. Horses should assuredly be immediately used for conveying the engines to a fire. We learn that in London the fire engine is placed ready for use in a vehicle, to which horses standing in a stable close by are immediately attached on an alarm of fire, and it is strange that so obvious an advantage should not have been introduced here. The necessity for it becomes daily more apparent as the city increases.

On May 26, 1836, Richard S. Ritchie, a member of Engine Company No. 6, was killed at a fire.

About four o'clock on the morning of July 19, 1836, a fire was discovered in the large four-story brick building, 117 Nassau Street, belonging to the American Bible Society, and used as their printing establishment by Daniel Fanshaw. There were nineteen power presses in the building, together with type, which were destroyed with the building. Loss, one hundred and forty thousand dollars.

Once more, in 1836, was the Old Bowery Theater burned down. On September 22 at 4 A. M. smoke was seen to issue from the center of the roof, and in a very few minutes the whole building was completely enveloped in flames. So sudden and so rapid was the conflagration that it was impossible to save the building when the firemen arrived at the spot. The wardrobes, the valuable properties, in fact everything was swept away, except the clock, a piano, and the large mirror of the greenroom. A man, named Frederick, who was employed as a sort of janitor, slept in the building, and had a narrow escape of his life. He managed to get, but in his night clothes, safely out into the street. The upper portion of the side walls fell on Nos. 40 and 44 Bowery, and crushed in the roofs. Mr. Hamblin, the lessee, estimated his loss at from seventy-five thousand to one hundred thousand dollars, not a cent of which was insured, the policy having expired three days before, and the negotiations for the new one had not been completed. The loss to the members of the company was very great.

At ten o'clock in the morning several people were standing in the portico of the ruins when one of the burned beams fell from aloft, striking Frederick Parsons, of No. 26 Reade Street, on the head, and injuring him severely. A boy, named Thomas Butler, living at the Bull's Head, was also struck on the shoulder, which was dislocated.

The following was the advertised programme for the performance at the Bowery Theater:

Fourth night of the New Drama entitled "Lafitte, the Pirate of the Gulf," by Miss Louisa H. Medina, authoress of "Last Days of Pompeii," "Norman Leslie," Rienzi," and a number of other pieces.

THIS EVENING, September 22, will be presented the Drama of LAFITTE, THE PIRATE OF THE GULF.

Lafitte	Mr. Hamblin.	Theodore	Miss Waring
Alphonso	Harrison.	Constanza	Mrs. Harrison.
Gen. Jackson	Woodhull.	Oula	Mrs. Herring.

Seven days after this event fire was discovered in a brick building in the rear of Guppy's large sugar house on Duane Street, at about three o'clock in the morning. The flames communicated to the sugar house, which, with its contents, was entirely destroyed. Loss, one hundred and fifty thousand dollars.

The adjoining buildings were touched by the flames, but the firemen saved them. At this fire several old citizens, who for years had been on the exempt list, manned the engines, and among them was the venerable ex-alderman of the Second Ward. Soon after the fire began one or two interlopers, when they saw ex-Chief Engineer Gulick come along, attempted to raise a groan. They were immediately ordered into custody.

In the following year there was another melancholy occurrence. Fire was discovered about 4 A. M. at No. 109 Washington Street, and before the engines got to the spot the building was doomed. Hose Company No. 13 was nearest to the burning building, and the alarm was given that the walls were tottering. Thomas Horton, of No. 13, was the last to run, and was caught in the fall of the north gable end of the wall and instantly killed. He had been only a week a member of the company, and in the minute book the entry of his election was next to the record of his death. His funeral took place from No. 34 First Street, and a large number of firemen, including Chief Engineer Anderson, attended. Most of the companies carried banners draped in mourning, and on the banner borne by his own company was the inscription, "His death was occasioned in the discharge of his duty." Again, on February 6, 1838, a gallant fireman fell. At a fire in a row of buildings in Laurens Street (now South Fifth Avenue), between Broome and Spring Streets, occupied by Peter Lorillard, tobacconist, the rear wall of one of the buildings fell. John Buckloh, of Engine Company No. 19, who at the time was standing on a short ladder against the wall holding the pipe, was buried beneath the rubbish. He had a grand funeral, the mayor, the Common Council and a large body of citizens attending the obsequies.

It was at the fire in the stable in Laurens Street that a most thrilling incident occurred. The men were working away bravely and were standing on some well-filled bags. "Give them another wetting, boys," said Chief Anderson, as he was about leaving the scene. The men subsequently discovered that they had been standing over what might have been their graves—the innocent looking bags contained powder. They had been left there by a cartman, who had brought them from a packet ship late one afternoon, and, knowing that the store where they were to be deposited was closed, had taken them to his stable, intending to leave them there until morning. For some time after the firemen looked out for bags when they were called to a conflagration.

February 18, 1838, saw the ill-fated Bowery Theater destroyed for the third time. As on other occasions it occurred, fortunately, at a time when there was no performance. It began about two o'clock on Sunday morning in a carpenter shop on the third story, and in a little while the large and handsome edifice fell. The iron safe, containing money and all the books and papers of the establishment, was saved. The wardrobes, valued at seven or eight thousand dollars, were lost, and the scenery, machinery, and stage property, estimated at fifty-two thousand dollars, were also destroyed. There was no insurance on the wardrobes, scenery and other properties. Insurance to the amount of thirty-five thousand dollars had been effected upon the building, which, it was supposed, would not cover one-half of the whole actual loss. Very few of the actors had any property in the theater. Of the origin of the fire there was but one opinion—it was the work of an incendiary.

Fire broke out in the soap factory of Baurmeister & Scheplin, situated in the rear of No. 160 Hammond Street, on August 1, 1838. Before the progress of the flames could be checked large portions of the block of buildings bounded by Hammond, Washington, Perry, and West Streets were destroyed. A very large number of families were by the calamity deprived of their homes and turned out upon the world with but little more property in their possession than they carried upon their backs. By this fire fifty buildings were destroyed, the loss aggregating many thousands of dollars. On July 25, 1839, a fire broke out in the paint shop attached to a wheelwright's shop on Sixteenth Street, between Ninth and Tenth Avenues, owned and occupied by Mr. Martin, which with the contents was entirely destroyed. The fire communicated to the next building on Sixteenth Street, and to the rear of a range of buildings on Tenth Avenue between Sixteenth and Seventeenth Streets, all of which were burned. The loss was thirty thousand dollars.

ITALIAN OPERA-HOUSE, AFTERWARD NATIONAL THEATER.

One of the most destructive fires since that of 1835 broke out on Monday afternoon, September 23, 1839. The volumes of smoke rolling over the city and the general alarm created soon spread the news of its locality—the National Theater, corner of Leonard and Church Streets. The great combustibility of the material in the building explains the rapidity with which the fire marched in its destructive course. Three fine churches shared the fate of the theater. Some of the persons employed in the latter discovered fire in the vicinity of the gas-room, which they endeavored to extinguish with a small force-pump, but in a few minutes they were compelled to beat a hasty retreat. Before six o'clock, or a little after the outburst of the flames from the roof of the theater, the fire had communicated to the French Episcopal Church, corner of Franklin and Church Streets, and to the African Church opposite, on the corner of Leonard and Church Streets. The rear gable end and a part of one of the side walls of the playhouse fell, burning the rear part of the two story brick front dwelling No. 14 Leonard Street. The Dutch Reformed Church in Franklin

Street, between Chapel and Church Streets, the inside of which, together with the roof of the two story schoolhouse next adjoining, and belonging to the church, was also destroyed. It was a scene of great magnificence and splendor, and also a peculiar one. In the neighborhood of the churches were houses of ill-repute, and the unfortunate inmates of these dwellings rushed frantically out in the attire in which the alarm found them, to add to the terrific grotesqueness of the picture. Thousands of persons congregated in the vicinity, pushing and struggling from one point to another, shouting and cursing and swearing. Odd-looking stage properties were thrown from the theater, sacred vestments and furniture hurled from the churches, and flaunting finery dragged from the temporary homes of the unfortunate. Carts and wagons were pushed here and there, the excited owners of property striving to save all they could. It was a scene worthy of a painter's pencil. The clamor of trumpets and voices, the steady working of the engines, the moving masses, the screaming of women, and the helter-skelter passage of every sort of furniture borne off or heaped upon the streets; bibles, prayer books, altar ornaments, and the sacred chalice, mixed up with gorgeous theatric costumes and tomes of Shakespeare, and librettos and scores of Rossini, Bellini, and Auber, and wardrobes and gewgaws of a more ambiguous character, thrown from houses of ill-fame on fire or threatened in the vicinity; the troops of actors, orchestral performers, the retinue of supernumeraries and scene shifters running to and fro, mingled with the cries of the colored people, of French citizens, looking unutterable despair on the combined havoc of all that was dear to them as the source of their livelihood, or upon the temple where they worshipped—all these scenes—fearful realities—defy description. The whole spectacle, in fact, the blending of things sacred and profane below, heightened by the sea of flame and smoke above, presented a lively tableau—a serio-grotesque picture. Through it all the firemen worked calmly, persistently, and successfully. But notwithstanding their efforts four hundred thousand dollars were swallowed up that evening.

In connection with this fire we meet with the name of Mr. James Wallack, the father of the famous actor, Mr. Lester Wallack. His loss was estimated at twenty-five thousand dollars—no insurance. The theater was owned by Messrs. Ayman & Co. and O. Mauran, and was leased to Mr. Wallack. The building was valued at sixty thousand dollars and insured for thirty thousand dollars. The French church was a splendid edifice of white marble, the portico in front supported by very large granite pillars. It was erected in 1822, and cost about eighty thousand dollars. The fine organ and most of the furniture were saved, but very much damaged. There was an insurance of twenty-four thousand dollars. Of the Dutch Reformed Church, the Rev. J. Harkness, pastor, only the walls remained. It was insured for ten thousand dollars. The Zion African Methodist Episcopal Church was built in 1820, and cost eighteen thousand dollars. It was insured to the full amount of its value. Numerous other buildings, dwelling houses, etc., were more or less injured—some nearly destroyed.

The above fire was destructive enough, but the next one in the month of October was a million dollar calamity. On October 5, at 11.45 P. M., the secretary of an engine company writes: "Fire corner of Eldridge and Broome; engine did not roll owing to her being out of order." An hour and a quarter

after, a fire that assumed alarming proportions broke out in the fur store of
Halsey & Co., in Water Street, near Fulton.   The wind was blowing fresh at
the time, and the flames swept through Water Street and Burling Slip, Pearl and
Fletcher Streets.   The United States Hotel (which previous to that time had been
called Holt's) was in imminent danger.   It was saved by placing wet blankets
in each window fronting the fire.   It was a terrible night for the Department,
whose energies were taxed to the utmost.   Whole blocks were swept away,
and the destruction of property was enormous.   For eight hours the fire lasted,
illuminating the whole city.   This great conflagration was considered to be
second only to that of 1835.   Two-thirds of the block bounded by Water Street,
Burling Slip and Front Street, together with several new stores in Water Street,
between Burling Slip and Fletcher Street, and two or three buildings in Fletcher
Street, one of which was occupied by John T. Hall, a member of a fire company, were consumed.

The night of January 30, 1840, was an extremely busy one for the firemen.
From seven o'clock in the evening until the dawn of the following morning they
had scarcely any respite from their labors, one alarm succeeding another with
remarkable rapidity.   For the few months preceding fires had been singularly
numerous, and the sound of the fire bell had fallen with regular and mournful
cadence upon the tired ears of the firemen.   It seemed as though the destroying angel had been sent abroad.   On this night the first conflagration broke
out at 7.15 P. M. in Front Street, near Broad Street, destroying a grocery.
Then a fire half consumed Forker & Co.'s ship-chandlery store in South, near
Dover Street.   There were other alarms besides.   The South Street fire had
not been entirely subdued, and at three o'clock in the morning it broke out
afresh.   The flames communicated to the immense tea-store of Thomas H.
Smith and to five other stores.   Smith's was occupied as a public store.   One
of the five stores was the extensive one of J. J. Hix.   They were all destroyed.
The public store covered an area fifty by two hundred feet.   The total loss was
estimated at over one million dollars.

The tenderest expressions of sympathy from firemen were called forth by
the death of two of their comrades on April 15, 1840.   Assistant Engineer
James S. Wells and James Glasgow, a member of Hose Company No. 15, were
killed by the falling of a wall at a fire in Eldridge Street.   A meeting of engineers, foremen and assistants was held at Firemen's Hall on the sixteenth, upon
the call of Chief Engineer Anderson.   Mr. Anderson proposed a funeral programme, which was approved, and on the motion of Mr. Kane, Colonel Thomas
F. Peers was appointed marshal for the occasion, with the following aids:
Owen W. Brennan, John Carland, John T. Rollins, George F. Ramppen, and
Joseph W. Long.   On motion of Mr. Suydam, Daniel R. Suydam, Carlisle
Norwood and Edward Brown were appointed a committee to draft resolutions
of sympathy, and reported the following:

Resolved : That in the dispensation of an all-ruling Providence by which Messrs. James S.
Wells and James Glasgow have met with a sudden death, we have to deplore the loss of two
valuable members of the Department—men whose private virtues and strict integrity had
endeared them to all, and whose decease has left a blank in their families which cannot be
filled.

Resolved : That this Department do sympathize deeply with the relatives of the deceased
on this mournful event, and that they will testify the regret which they feel by attending in

a body the funeral to-morrow (Thursday) afternoon, and by wearing crape on the left arm for thirty days.

Resolved : That a copy of the foregoing resolutions be forwarded to the familes of the deceased, signed by the officers of the meeting and published.

May the same all-wise and beneficent Providence sustain the widow and fatherless in their affliction.

The Fire Departments of Brooklyn and Williamsburg were invited to attend the funeral. The pall-bearers were James Gulick, John Ryker, Junior, Michael O'Connor, Halsey R. Mead, Allen R. Jollie, Daniel C. Selleck, William P. Wallace, and Elijah T. Lewis. On the following day the various companies met in Canal Street. The line was formed on the north side of the street, the right resting on Hudson Street. Engine, Hook and Ladder, Hose, and Hydrant Companies No. 1 together constituted the base or right of the line ; Engine, Hook and Ladder, Hose, and Hydrant Companies No. 2 were next, and in the same order to the left ; Engine Company No. 49 was on the extreme left.

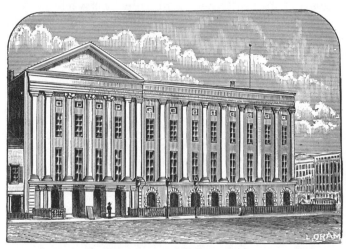

ASTOR PLACE OPERA HOUSE.

In May, 1841, there were several extensive fires. On the seventh five five-story warehouses were destroyed in Pearl and Water Streets. On the nineteenth four hundred thousand dollars' worth of property was destroyed in buildings whose site had been swept by the fire of 1835.

But on the twenty-ninth a still more notable fire occurred. The new National Theater had been in existence only two years since its first destruction in 1839, when it again went down before the devouring element—its destruction this time being the work of incendiaries. The manager was Mr. Burton, his stage manager Mr. Wemyss. When these gentlemen entered the house about five o'clock (it was Saturday), they were met by one of the company, Mr. Okie, who said that he thought he smelt fire. Investigation proved the accuracy of his surmise. In the prompter's box fire was found in three places, and in the pit ticket office a quantity of spirits of turpentine was discovered to have been thrown into a box of loose rubbish, and the office on fire in two places. The bottom of the rear door of the office was also found burning. These were scarcely extinguished when Mr. Russell, the treasurer, and his assistant, Mr. Glessig, found that a fire had been started under the staircase leading from the rear of the box-office to the suite of apartments above, occupied by Mr. Russell and his family. It was only with the greatest difficulty that this conflagration was extinguished. But this was not all. In a room in the second story adjacent to Mr. Russell's rooms two other fires were found burning; spirits of turpentine had been strewn over a pile of theater tickets, and in another part of the room manuscript music and other papers were on fire. These fires having been extinguished a roll of paper thrown from an upper story window into Leonard Street was found to contain a quantity of friction matches. Below was the Turkish Saloon, where a box of matches of a like kind was found. It was clear that an attempt had been made to fire the saloon also, and that there was more than one incendiary. Notwithstanding his alarming discovery Mr. Burton decided to let the performance go on.

At the close a thorough search was made of the premises, and nothing suspicious was found. At 3:30 A. M. Mr. Russell went to bed. He could not sleep, however, and at six o'clock arose, went to the stage door in the rear, and stood talking to the private watchman. In a few minutes, to the treasurer's astonishment, flames burst from different parts of the building, and with amazing rapidity they spread. Indeed Mrs. Russell had a narrow escape of her life. Her husband dashed to her room, rolled her up in the bed clothes, and with difficulty got her out of the burning building. The walls of the theater proved to be of the flimsiest, and in a short time the rear wall and the side wall on Franklin Street both gave way. It was a miracle that numbers were not crushed to death in the adjoining houses. Engineer John T. Rollins, who lived close by the theater, was on the spot in a few moments. He went inside, and found the stage blazing, and it was his opinion that the fire had been started half an hour before. Chief Engineer Cornelius V. Anderson said that within fifteen minutes of its discovery he saw the fire bursting through, at the back of the theater. He warned all the people living in the rear to clear out, for he noticed the miserable walls, unable to bear the weight of the roof, bulging and cracking everywhere. But the chief engineer's warning was too late in one instance. In Franklin Street was a notorious house, kept by Julia Brown, a woman remarkable for her good looks. She escaped, but one of her unfortunate boarders, a woman, was killed by the falling wall. Next day her body was discovered by Zophar Mills. Mr. Burton had, but a few days before, brought his valuable wardrobe from Philadelphia, and it was lost. Miss Cushman, the celebrated tragedienne, who was playing here, and Messrs. Shaw and Howard also lost heavily. Among the adjoining edifices injured or partly burned were the French Protestant Episcopal Church, the Dutch Reformed Church in Franklin Street, and the African Church on the corner of Leonard and Church Streets, opposite the playhouse. The work of destruction lasted only one hour.

On March 31, 1842, there were three fires—one of great magnitude. The whole of two large blocks of dwellings, including at least one hundred houses, was laid in ruins. At least two hundred and fifty families were rendered homeless. The fire originated in a two-story house, occupied as a grocery and dwelling. At least forty or fifty of the houses were worth from three thousand to four thousand dollars each, the aggregate being about three hundred thousand dollars, and the furniture destroyed being worth twenty or thirty thousand dollars. On May 31 J. Harker & Bros., Nos. 80 and 82 Cliff Street, publishers, lost one hundred thousand dollars in a fire.

CHAPTER XVI.

OLD VOLUNTEERS FIGHTING FIRE.

More Fires of the Olden Time.—A Terrible Snow Storm and Burning of the Tribune Building.—The Bowery Theater Destroyed for the Fourth Time.—The Awful Fire of 1845.—Thrilling Incidents.— Niblo's Garden in Flames —The Fearful Hague Street Disaster.—The Harper's Fire.—The Park Street Theater,

A TERRIBLE snow storm swept over New York on February 4, 1845, and the cold was intense. At four o'clock on the morning of February 5 the office of the *New York Tribune*, occupying the corner lots Nos. 158 and 160 Nassau Street, was destroyed by fire. A boy had lighted a stove, and in half an hour the apartment was in a blaze. The fire engines were at a disadvantage in this great storm. The streets were almost impassable; some of the machines could not get out of their stations at all, and those that did could scarcely be dragged through the streets. Some of the engines were pulled a few rods, and then the task had to be given up. The hydrants were found to be frozen and had to be broken open with axes. Hence it was no wonder the *Tribune* building and the adjoining structure on the corner of Spruce and Nassau were entirely destroyed in a short time. There were some narrow escapes. One of the proprietors, Mr. Graham, and a clerk were asleep in the second story, and when aroused found the door and stairway afire and egress that way cut off. They saved themselves only by jumping from the window. The compositors in the fifth story and the pressmen in the basement got out with great difficulty. Tammany Hall was at one time in imminent danger. The rear part, connecting with the *Tribune* building, caught fire, but the firemen succeeded, by hard work, in extinguishing the flames. The publishers, Greeley & McElrath, publicly thanked the fire laddies for their labors. The office was temporarily located at No. 30 Ann Street (formerly the *New World*).

A few months after the *Tribune* fire came a greater conflagration—the total destruction, for the fourth time, of the ill-fated Bowery Theater. Indeed, this year (1845) is very remarkable for the number of disastrous fires which occurred in the city. The "new historical drama" of "Robin Hood, the Outlaw," was to have been played that evening (Friday, April 25), and Mr. Davenport, a popular actor of the period, was to have taken his benefit. As on previous occasions, the calamity was the work of a diabolical incendiary. The supposition is proved by the fact that the flames first proceeded from a vault filled with shavings under the carpenter's shop, to which there was access by a trap door. The carpenter's shop was on the south side of the theater, from which it was separated by an iron fire-proof door. It was about

six o'clock when the flames were discovered, and before the fire-proof door
could be closed they caught the scenery, and, like a flash, the whole house
was ablaze.   When the engines arrived the theater was already doomed.
The carpenters and actors had manfully struggled, but in vain, to save the
wardrobes.   Dense volumes of smoke drove them back.   The firemen mainly
directed their efforts to saving the block of three-story houses opposite, and
succeeded after great exertions.   At first, however, there was great danger of
a wide-spreading conflagration.   One of the greatest calamities feared was lest
the gas-house next the theater should take fire and explode.   Happily, however, the flames did not touch it.   When the fire burst through the roof and
windows of the playhouse the scene became one of mingled grandeur and

BURNING OF THE OLD TRIBUNE BUILDING.

terror.   The roaring of the flames, the breaking of glass, the cracking of the
burning rafters, the continuous thud, thud, of the well-manned engines, and
the hoarse voices of the foremen as they gave the necessary directions, all
combined to increase the excitement.   In about half an hour the fire was at its
height, blazing with fearful intensity.   The glowing heat was almost unbeara-
ble, affecting the houses opposite; it was so intense, indeed, that those buildings
were often concealed under a dense cloud of steam from the constant streams
of water thrown on them by three engines.   Soon the roof fell in and the fiery
furnace sent forth a cloud of ignited particles, which spread to a great distance,
and endangered the surrounding property.   About a quarter before seven the
peak of the rear wall on Elizabeth Street fell outward with a fearful crash, and
several persons narrowly escaped death.   About ten minutes later the north
half of the end wall also fell, and five minutes later the remaining half.   The

wind being from the northeast the heat and main body of the flame were felt most on Elizabeth Street. As the flames burst forth from the front windows and caught the heavy cornice the whole interior was revealed to those on the roofs of the opposite houses, and the furniture of the saloon, the pictures, glasses, sofas, etc., could be distinctly seen as each became a prey to the spreading flames. When the heavy cornice in front fell many persons were standing on the steps and narrowly escaped death, but some were slightly bruised. The houses on either side several times caught fire, and the roofs of some of them were destroyed. The inmates threw their furniture out of the windows, and the scene became one of disaster and confusion. The house of Mr. Cox, on the north side of the theater in Elizabeth Street, was much injured. Several small tenements in this street were nearly a total wreck, and some of the inmates escaped with difficulty. One poor woman had barely time to snatch up her two children before her room was in a blaze. She forced her way through the flames and smoke into the street. The children were uninjured, but the mother was burned in several places.

Among the buildings very considerably damaged were the Bowery Hotel (Nos. 50 and 52), Shaw's Hotel, south of the theater in the Bowery, and the store of Mr. Cort, plumber. The loss of T. S. Hamblin and James R. Whiting was very heavy. Mr. Hamblin's loss in stock, stage appointments and wardrobe was about one hundred thousand dollars, and no insurance. The veteran manager was at his home in Franklin Street when his acting manager, Mr. Davenport, rushed into the house with the news of the conflagration.

"There go the labors of seven years!" said Mr. Hamblin, sadly, as he reflected upon the previous misfortunes that had befallen him. Then he brightened up in his characteristic, enterprising way, and exclaimed: "But we are not dead yet, boys!"

In the next month the city was again startled by a destructive conflagration. Fire was discovered on May 31 in the stables of Peters & Palmer in Eighteenth Street, which were entirely consumed, with twenty horses. From thence the fire spread to a range of twelve two-story houses on Eighteenth Street to Sixth Avenue, and with the exception of two or three two-story brick houses on the corner of Sixth Avenue, crossing into Nineteenth Street, destroyed about a dozen dwellings on the south side and five or six on the north side, besides the roofs of six or eight brick dwellings; thence through to Twentieth Street the flames destroyed a large number of dwellings, nearly the whole of which were occupied by poor families, and some of whom had lost their all. The number of persons who were burned out was not less than four hundred. One hundred buildings in all were destroyed, and the loss was one hundred thousand dollars.

Not since 1835 had there been so calamitous a fire in the city as in the month of July of this year (1845). Perhaps it would be more accurate to say that it was the most fearfully destructive fire in the annals of the Department, for thirty lives were sacrificed on that terrible morning of July 19, and many persons were injured. Over three hundred buildings were burned down, and more than ten million dollars' worth of property laid waste. The event is still fresh in the memory of many of our old citizens and firemen, and they still recollect the mourning that long characterized the city over the loss of so many estimable men and the injury to so many others. The fire broke out about 3 A. M. in the sperm oil establishment of J. L. Van Doren, No. 34 New Street, and soon spread to a chair factory adjoining. Chief Engineer Anderson and the Department were quickly at work, but in spite of their efforts the fire traveled with great rapidity, extending to Exchange Place, Broad Street, and finally to the large storage house of Crooker & Warren, on the latter street. This building, it seems, was stored with saltpetre; it had hardly been on fire ten minutes when it blew up, the shock breaking over a million panes of glass throughout the whole city, even up as high as Canal Street. Not a vestige of the edifice was left except the bricks, while six or seven of the adjoining buildings were partly demolished.

The explosion shook the city like an earthquake. It was felt in Jersey City and Brooklyn, while the report was plainly heard away out to Sandy Hook. Engine Company No. 22 was stationed directly in front of the ill-fated building, and had one stream on the fourth story. Garret B. Lane was then foreman. Soon after he had got his engine to work he discovered a heavy black smoke rolling up the stairway, which at once struck him that the lower portion of the building was on fire. He ordered his men to back out, which they did with much difficulty, as the smoke was so dense that they were nearly suffocated. All got out in safety except Francis Hart, Jr. Hart remained to let down the hose, and when he tried to descend the flames and smoke were so great as to prevent him, and he went on the roof of the chair factory. He clambered from that building to the corner of Broad and Exchange Streets, breaking each skylight as he proceeded over the roofs, but found no stairs leading from any. Finding himself thus on the third building from the chair factory, without any means of getting down, Hart sat in the scuttle. "I did not then consider myself in any danger," he subsequently reported to an investigating committee. "I had been there about five minutes when I heard the first explosion—a species of rumbling sound—followed by a succession of others of the same kind. The gable of the house next to this corner shook with the first and successive explosions, so that I had prepared myself, if it threatened to fall, to jump through the scuttle of the corner house. After the small explosion the great explosion took place, the noise of which seemed to be principally below me. I perceived the flames shooting across the street. I felt the building falling under me, and the roof moved around so that a corner of it caught on the opposite side of Exchange Street and was thrown off into that street. As far as I could judge the whole roof that I was on moved in one piece, and the walls under it crumbled down beneath it. I think there were some fifteen or eighteen small explosions. I could see one engine from the roof I was on."

How Hart finally escaped death reads like a page in a romance, such as Jules Verne might imagine. Just as the members of No. 22, of which Mr. Waters was foreman, had got about twenty feet away from the building, it blew up. The engine of No. 22 was blown clear across the street, and buried beneath the ruins, where it was finally consumed by fire. Hart, who had managed to reach the roof, had passed to the roof of the adjoining building when the explosion took place. He was carried on the top of the roof upon which he was standing, clear up into the air, and landed in safety on a building on the opposite side of the way, the only injury that he received being the dislocation of one of his ankles.

Augustus L. Cowdrey, a young and promising lawyer, a member of No. 42, was in company with Dave Van Winkle, of Engine No. 5, holding a pipe in another building, when another explosion took place, and that was the last ever seen of young Cowdrey. Van Winkle was blown clear out into the street, and escaped with slight injuries.

Some of the fire engines near the building were shivered to atoms. The explosions were accompanied by shocks resembling earthquakes, and so powerful as to shatter windows within the circuit of a mile. The doors of the American Exchange Bank, in Wall Street, were burst open with a loud crash. The City Bank doors were also burst through. Massive iron doors and window shutters were bent and twisted in every direction. The explosion not only carried away three buildings and shattered doors and windows, but it hurled flames and burning timbers into adjoining warehouses. The buildings which stood on New Street, from Wall to Exchange Place and thence to Beaver Street, were laid in ashes. A famous place of resort on Beaver Street known as the Adelphi Hotel was destroyed. Thirty or forty valuable stores with their contents were consumed. The splendid hotel known as the Waverly House on Broadway, with twelve warehouses on Broad Street, on both sides from Wall Street to Exchange Place, and thence to Beaver Street; Exchange Place, from Broadway to Broad Street, and from Broad to William Street, and silk warehouses and dry goods stores were de-

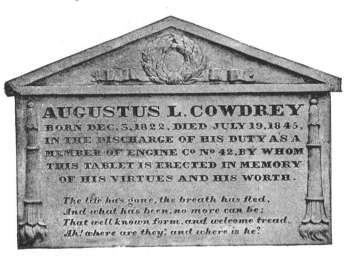

MONUMENT OF A. L. COWDREY.

stroyed—forty buildings in all. The loss by this fire was greater than all the fires since 1835.

The extent of the conflagration was quickly known on the other side of the East River, and among the companies that came from Brooklyn was Jackson Engine Company No. 11, who performed such efficient duty that they were tendered a fine collation by the citizens at Brown & Hall's on Bridge Street. No. 7 of Williamsburg and Nos. 3, 4, and 5 of Newark did noble duty. The Croton Hotel, the Philadelphia Hotel, the Pearl Street House, the City Hotel, and the Broad Street Hotel were open for three days free to all the poor people that were burnt out.

During the fire Engine Company No. 38 was stationed on Bridge Street, No. 25 at the Bowling Green, and No. 13 at the corner of Morris and Greenwich Streets. Among the prominent persons encouraging the firemen were Mayor W. F. Havemeyer, George W. Matsell, then a justice of the peace, afterwards president of the Police Board; ex-Chief Engineers Gulick, Wenman, and Riker, the three last rendering valuable service. Lafayette Hook and Ladder Company No. 6 were the hardest-working truck company at the fire.

They, with Hose Company No. 22, were feasted at the Astor House, by invitation of Coleman & Stetson. James M. Murray was then foreman of Hook and Ladder Company No. 6, and Richard H. Welch foreman of Hose Company No. 22. The Delmonico brothers had a very narrow escape. They kept the bon-ton restaurant in those days, but their property was saved through the efforts of Engine Companies Nos. 30 and 40 of this city, and No. 7 of Williamsburg. The Delmonicos gave them a splendid repast before they started for home, and one of the brothers afterwards joined the Department.

The calamities at this fire were so unprecedented that a special committee of the Common Council was appointed to investigate the cause of the occurrence, and report upon the proceedings at that conflagration. The committee consisted of Messrs. Emanuel B. Hart, B. J. Meserole, James C. Stoneall, Geo. H. Purser, Archibald Macclay, Jr., and Joseph C. Albertson. In the course of their report the committee say: "If the person who had charge of the public bell on the City Hall had struck it, as was his duty, the fire would have done very little damage, not extending beyond the building in which it originated. But Mr. Henry J. Ockerhausen, one of the engineers, who resided in Rose Street, states that a fireman, attached to No. 5, came from Fulton Street to his (Mr. Ockerhausen's) house, to inform him of the alarm. Mr. Ockerhausen dressed himself, and had only run as far as Nassau Street, when he distinctly saw the smoke issue from the fire. He heard no bell sounded until he had reached Fulton Street. There he perceived the blaze of the fire, and heard an alarm from the bell on the Post-office Building; but, although he listened attentively for the sound of the City Hall bell, he swears that it was not struck before he reached the fire."

Among the incidents of the fire was the destruction of an old bell which hung in the cupola of the old jail during the Revolution. When the jail was remodeled into the present Hall of Records the bell was taken down, and placed on the Bridewell as a fire alarm bell. Among the old firemen it was cherished as a dear friend of bygone years, and during the chieftainship of John Lamb and "Tommy" (who was dubbed "Pleasant-faced Tommy") it was the principal means of giving notice of a fire. On the destruction of the Bridewell the old bell was placed in a cupola on the house of Naiad Hose Company, in Beaver Street, a house longer devoted to its ancient uses than any other. But this disastrous fire silenced forever the brazen tongue that had for a century given forth its warning notes. Its old enemy at last prevailed, and one decisive victory compensated the fire fiend for many a defeat of yore.

On September 18, 1846, Niblo's Garden was burned again at four o'clock on a Friday morning, the whole building being consumed in two hours. The next evening Gabriel Ravel, of the famous Ravel family of tightrope dancers, was to have had a benefit. The fire originated in the greenroom. One of the firemen, Thomas Boesé, while holding a pipe went so near the flames that his clothing caught fire. Another pipeman, thinking he was doing well, turned a stream of water on him, but the suddenness of the transition from heat to cold paralyzed Boesé. Mr. Boesé afterwards became clerk in the Register's Office. The old passion, however, was strong within him, and whenever the City Bell sounded an alarm, he would drop his pen, blotting his book, and rush in the direction of the fire. In 1872 he was appointed clerk of the Superior Court.

The theater was rebuilt, and opened July 3, 1849, under the management of Chippendale & Sefton, with the Ravels, and with a dramatic company that included Mr. Charles Burke. This famous playhouse was originally established by Mr. William Niblo (from whom it took its name) when Jackson was President. It was a house and garden of entertainment, and quickly sprang into popularity, becoming at last the house of the most distinguished artists. In 1837 Mrs. Watson, Mrs. Bailey, Mrs. Knight, Mr. Plumer, and Mr. T. Bishop appeared there in concert. Joseph Jefferson—father of the present renowned comedian of "Rip Van Winkle" fame—produced musical farces there. Other noted players were Mrs. Maeder and Clara Fisher. Burton was the reigning star at Niblo's in 1839, and that year witnessed the first production of the Ravel pantomime "The Green Monster," which kept the stage for many years. In the fall of that year Mr. Wallack leased the house—his National Theater having been burned—and brought forward the renowned Miss Vandenhoff. In 1842 Tom Placide acted there. Next year saw the

NIBLO'S GARDEN, 1845.

debut of E. L. Davenport, who on August 9 played Frederick Fitzallen in "He's not Amiss." On the fifteenth of September the opera of "Lucia" was first given there, and in the company were Signoras Majocchi, Thamesi, and Miss Coad, and Signori Valtelina, Antognini, Albertazzi, and Maggiori. Mr. W. Corbyn brought out John Brougham in the autumn of 1844.

The features of the season of 1846 (the year of its destruction) were H. Placide's Haversack in the "Old Guard," Hackett's Falstaff, George Holland's Mr. Golightly, and a series of impersonations by Burton.

A fire that broke out in the Duane Street sugar house on the night of April 2, 1848, caused the death of three gallant firemen and severe injuries to two others. The front wall of the building suddenly fell into the street, burying George Kerr, assistant engineer, and Henry Fargis, assistant foreman of Engine Company No. 38. Mr. Jennings, of Hose Company No. 28, Mr. Robert Roulston, of Hose Company No. 38, and Mr. Charles J. Durant, of Hose Company No. 35, were severely injured by the falling bricks and timber. Mr. Durant was so severely hurt that he died a few days after. Mr. Kerr had charge of the Department on that occasion, and the owners of the structure, in defending the stability of their building afterward, claimed that Kerr and Fargis had rashly exposed their lives and those of their men. But it was proved that the edifice was of the flimsiest description. Chief Engineer Anderson, in a letter to the Common Council on this event, says : " As an evidence of the insecurity of the wall, I would call attention to the fact that when it fell outward there was not the least appearance of fire in that story.   *   *   *   Mr. Kerr, so far from being rash or imprudent, was one of the coolest, most experienced, and judicious engineers that the Department has ever had.   *   *   *   Mr. Fargis was a young man of high promise in and out of the Department, and had won the confidence and esteem of all who knew him.   *   *   *   The death of two such men is a public calamity, and if by care and proper precaution such melancholy accidents can be prevented hereafter, I have the fullest confidence that your honorable body will take every step to insure the consummation of an end so desirable."

The joint funeral of these unfortunate firemen was the greatest public demonstration the city had ever seen. Fully fifty thousand persons witnessed the obsequies. The funeral service was held on April 4 in Dr. Ferris's Church, in Market Street. Mr. Zophar Mills was marshal of the immense procession, the order of which was as follows : Exempt Firemen ; the Fire Department in the order of companies ; body of George Kerr ; assistant engineers as pall bearers ; relatives and friends ; chief engineer ; body of Henry Fargis ; members of Engine Company No. 38 as pall bearers ; officers of Fire Department ; Common Council ; chief of police and aids ; jewelers and silversmiths ; citizens.

The engine house of Engine Company No. 11 was injured by fire on April 18, 1848, which broke out in Wooster Street, near Spring, and destroyed twelve buildings, causing a loss of one hundred and seventy-five thousand dollars. A few weeks afterward, on May 26, a dreadful event happened. The large stables of Kipp & Brown, on the corner of Ninth Avenue and Twenty-sixth Street, were burned, when twenty-seven stages, one hundred and thirty horses, a large number of swine, three thousand four hundred bushels of grain, and forty tons of hay, were destroyed. Messrs. Kipp & Brown were old members of Engine Company No. 10, their names were household words in the city, and consequently much sympathy was expressed for them.

As great a calamity occurred on November 18 of the same year, when another stable, that of Messrs. Murphy, at the corner of Third Avenue and Twenty-seventh Street, was burned down. Indeed, a continuous series of fires spread dismay everywhere. All night, and till the dawn of morning, the warning bells rang incessantly. From the reflection of the fires every street in New York was filled with lurid light. The hearts of the citizens sickened at the sight of the whole city wrapped in the light of conflagration and with a high wind blowing. In Messrs. Murphy's stables were one hundred and seventy-five horses. They stood to their halters while the flames gathered around them. Firemen and citizens had rescued about twenty-five of the poor brutes, when portions of the roof began to fall, and then no one dared venture again into the stables. It was an awful picture to look upon. The horses, held by their halters, reared and sent forth terrific shrieks and groans, but one by one they fell and perished in the flames. One animal broke loose and rushed out of the burning building, but before it could be secured it neighed in a frenzied sort of way and then rushed back into the flames. The fearful sounds emitted from the stables would have melted a heart of stone. But not alone was there solicitude for these poor brutes. The flames had communicated to several small wooden buildings in the rear of Twenty-eighth Street, occupied by needy families. Women were running in every direction, seeking their children, and children seeking their parents. One of the most gallant rescues on record happened on this awful night. One woman, supposing that her child was still in her burning dwelling, with the frenzy of despair rushed into the house and ascended the stairs to the second story, but the heat was so great she was forced to return. But a noble fireman had been before her, and he soon appeared, bearing in his arms the object of the distracted mother's love. In a moment more the baby was in her arms, and, shrieking with joy and in an ecstasy of delight, she fell upon her knees and called down the blessings of heaven on the deliverer of her infant. It is such acts as these that endear the firemen to the citizens. Even amid that scene of confusion stern men were deeply affected by the sight they witnessed.

PARK THEATER, 1831.

In the center aisle of the stable thirty-three stages were arranged and only seven were saved. In the rear of the building thirty very beautiful sleighs were destroyed. Behind the building the St. Barnabas Protestant Episcopal Church caught fire some time after and went down before the flames. Then the Rose Hill Methodist Church with its parsonage ignited and was barely saved. Next the Public Schoolhouse No. 15 adjoining was enveloped and was soon a pile of ashes.

Ding, dong, ding, dong, tolled the bells. Another fire at the corner of the Bowery and Broome Street. Here several buildings were laid in ashes, and the Baptist Church, No. 350 Broome Street, was much damaged. In this locality, Mr. Thomas Cochran, of Hose Company No. 9, was seriously hurt by falling from the roof of a back building. While these fires were raging, still another large stable at the corner of Thirty-fifth Street and Eighth Avenue, with two wooden buildings, were razed through a conflagration. And as the gray dawn was breaking, still one more stable was ablaze in the rear of No. 103 West Seventeenth Street, and here four valuable horses were burned to death.

Mme. Adele Montplaisir, the celebrated ballet dancer, was to have taken a benefit on December 16, 1848, at the Park Theater—then the most fashionable resort in the city. At 6.15 P. M., one hour before the doors were to have been opened, while some members of the ballet were in the dressing room, smoke was seen issuing from the rear window in Theater Alley. One of the young ladies had carelessly pushed a gas jet near some playbills. The result was that, for the second time, the theater was burned down. The building was owned by Messrs. Astor & Beekman, and was valued at thirty thousand dollars. It was the first fire at which Mr. Alfred Carson officiated as chief engineer.

The Park Theater was commenced in 1795 by Lewis Hallam and John Hodgkinson and others, all professional actors. The theater was situated in the center of the block, the entrance being on the north side of John Street, midway between Nassau Street and Broadway. The new theater was finished about the year 1798, at a cost of one hundred and seventy-nine thousand dollars. The exterior of the building was plain, but the interior was fitted up with much elegance. On the night of May 24, 1820, it was consumed by fire. The theater was rebuilt in April, 1821. It was not again rebuilt after the 1848 fire.

Abraham Brown, a fireman, effected a gallant rescue at a fire in the house of Mr. Ward, in Catharine Street on April 11, 1849. In the confusion Mrs. Ward had left behind one of her children, a two year old girl. Brown heard the distracted mother bemoaning the loss of her child, ascended a ladder, and effected an entrance through the front window. He found the baby in a back room lying on a bed. He picked her up, and though flames and smoke barred his way he dashed through them and brought the child into the street at the risk of his life. Unhappily, the babe was dead.

On a bright, pleasant, wintry morning, the fourth of February, 1850, at twenty minutes after eight o'clock, the citizens of the Fourth Ward and vicinity were startled by a loud explosion which rent the air, and caused many buildings in Pearl and Frankfort Streets to shake from their very foundations, and shattered many hundreds of panes of glass, the fragments of which were hurled in every direction on the pedestrians who were wending their way to their places of business. A few moments, and the sad news spread like wild-fire that a fearful explosion had taken place at Nos. 5 and 7 Hague Street, that both buildings had been blown into atoms, and that one hundred human beings were buried beneath the ruins. The report proved too true, for it was soon discovered that the two hundred horse-power boiler in the extensive press room and machine shop of A. B. Taylor & Co. had exploded; that at the time over one hundred people employed by Taylor & Co. and St. John, Burr & Co., hatters, were at work on the premises. It was claimed by those that witnessed the terrible explosion that the building was lifted full six feet from its foundation, and then fell a mass of ruins. Instantly flames burst out in every direction, and here and there could have been seen legs and arms sticking out from the ruins, while the most piercing shrieks could be heard from those buried in their living tomb.

The firemen were not long in reaching the scene of disaster, with Chief

Engineer Alfred Carson at their head. A general alarm having been sounded, nobly did the members of the Department turn their untiring efforts toward rescuing those still alive. They soon controlled the flames, and then body after body was carried out, some mangled and bruised beyond recognition. Among those early on the spot were Zophar Mills, Harry Howard, Recorder F. A. Tallmadge, Chief Matsell, J. Murray Ditchett, Joe Keefe of Engine 21;

HAGUE STREET EXPLOSION.

while among the companies who mounted the hot bricks were Engines 4, 5, 13, 14, 22, and Hook and Ladder 1 and 4. All the down-town companies lent a helping hand. Wm. Story, of No. 4, at the risk of his own life, rescued many, among them a little boy named Freddie Tieman. Story had to crawl down into a hole seven feet before he could get to where the little fellow lay. He was alive, and the first word he said was, "Mr. Fireman, that fire is close to my feet." Story gave him his fire cap and told him to put it over his face to keep the steam off, and he would put a stream on the fire. The lad did as he was told, and waited for the hour of deliverance. While he lay thus wedged in between two heavy beams he heard others beneath him giving way to the agony of despair. His words to those were: "What's the use of giving up? The firemen are hard at work; they will get us out if anybody can."

They finally sawed away a large timber, Zophar Mills superintending the whole affair, and the little hero was saved. Away down near the bottom lay another brave little fellow, whose name is still stamped upon the heart of many an old fireman, one Samuel Tindale, fifteen years old, and by him one of his comrades, Thomas Vanderbilt, nineteen years old. Around them were burning timbers and hissing bricks. Tindale soon made known his whereabouts, and the firemen worked like beavers to rescue him. His brother was quickly by his side, and when the boy heard him he said: "Go tell mother I am still living;

EXTRICATING BODY OF S. J. TINDALE FROM THE RUINS.

not to worry; that I hope soon to get out." At the same time he told the firemen he was up to his neck in water, and said: "You must stop that water or I shall drown; there is a stick across my leg, and I cannot move."

The firemen kept carting away basket after basket of rubbish, and finally worked their way down to an old side door, where they made considerable headway, when young Tindale hallooed to them that he was scorching. Finally they got near enough to hand him a blanket. As he took it he said there was a dead man lying alongside of him. All day long he remained in the same position. It seemed a miracle how he ever survived; but his brother remained by him, encouraging him and furnishing him with stimulants. About nine o'clock at night it was found that a heavy iron bar held him fast. About eleven

o'clock he said he thought they could not save him, and exclaimed: "I shall be the third one who has been killed by this affair." He had no idea how many had fallen victims in this deplorable disaster. At one o'clock the iron bar was lifted, when it was discovered that another bar still held him a prisoner. As soon as the poor boy heard this he exclaimed: "Pull me out, whether you draw my legs off or not!" On worked the firemen, never faltering for a moment, and at four o'clock in the morning, amid the shouts of all, the noble youth was lifted out and borne to Dr. Traphagen's drug store, No. 308 Pearl Street, where he died shortly after. He had been twenty hours in the ruins.

Sixty-four persons were killed, the greater portion of whom were young men and boys, while about seventy were injured. Among the latter was John Vanderpool of Engine 15. He succeeded in rescuing a young lad named

George West, William Merritt of Hose 13, and Henry A. Burr. The Common Council, headed by Mayor Westervelt, did all they could to aid the sufferings of the wounded and the families of the dead. No fire ever occurred in this city that was attended with a greater loss of life.

Names of killed and wounded in the Hague Street explosion:

LIST OF KILLED.

1. Peter Hyde, 18 years, born in Brooklyn.
2. George Hyde, 28 years, born in Brooklyn.
3. Levi Hall. 28 years, born in Connecticut.
4. Adam Nealty, 33 years, born in Ireland; residence, Sixth Avenue and Thirty-second Street.
5. Isaiah Marks, (colored) boy.
6. Leonard Brooks, 30 years, born in Rockland County; residence, 54 Oliver Street.
7. Alexander Dixon, 23 years, born in Canada; residence, 29 Front Street, Brooklyn.
8. Henry N. Reed, 29 years, born in New York; residence, 128 Ninth Street.
9. Richard E. Egbert, 30 years, born on Staten Island.
10. Samuel J. Tindale, 15 years, born in New York; residence, 72 Beekman Street.
11. Rufus Whitney, 35 years, born in Boston; residence, Williamsburg.
12. John Dougherty, 19 years, born in Scotland; residence, Brooklyn.
13. James Brooks, 23 years, born in New York; residence, 54 Oliver Street.
14. Abraham O. Kelsey, 31 years, born in New Jersey; residence, Rivington Street.
15. Robert Hyslop, 27 years, born in Scotland; residence, 412 Pearl Street.
16. Patrick Burns, 29 years, born in Ireland; residence, Division Street, Brooklyn.
17, John Rogers, 34 years, born in New York; residence, 38 Mott Street.
18. Daniel Dougherty, 16 years, born in Ireland; residence, Brooklyn.
19. George T. Worrell, 17 years, born in New York; residence, 636 Fourth Street.
20. Lemual B. Whitney, 27 years, born in Brooklyn; residence, Church Street.
21. Loren King, 22 years, born in New York; residence, 61 Oliver Street.
22. Jesse Huestis, 14 years, born in New York; residence, 87 Beekman Street,
23. Frank Bartlett, 14 years, born in Hudson; residence, 74 Frankfort Street.
24. Owen Brady, 14 years, born in New York; residence, 115 Willett Street.
25. James Taill, 33 years, born in England; residence, 84 Frankfort Street.
26. Joseph Lockwood, 45 years, born in Connecticut; residence, Beekman Street.
27. George Harwood, 25 years, born in England; residence, 227 Eighth Street.
28. Joseph P. Hurd, 27 years, born in Connecticut; residence in Brooklyn.
29. Joseph Harvest, 29 years, born in England; residence, 323 Delancey Street.
30. Alexander Herglas, 33 years, born in Ireland; residence, 63 Third Avenue.
31. William Elliot Townsend, 13 years, born in New York; residence, 328 Ninth Street,
32. Seneca Lake, 36 years, born in New York; residence, 137 Seventh Street.
33. William Baudoine, 22 years, born in New York; residence in Cannon Street.
34. Thomas Vanderbilt, 26 years, born in New York; residence, 106 Cherry Street.
35. James Kearney, 35 years, born in Ireland; residence not known. Buried by the city.
36. Joseph Eisinger, 19 years, born in France; residence, 16 Pike Street.
37. Matthew McLaughlin, 22 years, born in New York; residence in Broome Street.
38.
39.
40. All these bodies remained without identification. Some of them were never
41. identified, even by the most careful scrutiny which could be made by anxious
42. friends.
43.
44. William Collins, aged 24, born in Ireland; resided at 337 Pearl Street.
45. Lawrence Christal, aged 23, born in New Jersey; resided at 272 William Street.
46. Robert Ross, aged 40, resided in Brooklyn.
47. James Guillifer, aged 40, born on Long Island; resided at 74 Middagh Street, Brooklyn.
48. Gearge Neal, aged 15, born in New York; resided in Brooklyn.

49. Isaac H. D. Osborn, aged 32, born in New York; resided at 61 Avenue D.
50. George Ford, foreman for Taylor & Co., aged 35, resided in South First Street, Williamsburg.
51. Wm. K. Bartlett, aged 17, born in New York; resided at 74 Frankfort Street.
52. Stephen Coburn. aged —, birthplace and residence not ascertained.
53. James Granger, aged 23, born in London; resided in Brooklyn.
54. George H. Davis, aged 37, born in Massachusetts; resided at 291 Pearl Street,
55. John Thurston, aged 15, born in Brooklyn; resided in Brooklyn.
56. Robert H. Stremmel, aged 13, born in New York; resided at 174 Newfolk Street, Brooklyn.
57. Cornelius Dougherty, aged 15, born in Scotland; residence not stated.
58. Charles Knowlton, aged 35, born in England; resided at 632 Fourth Street.
59. Thomas Farrell, aged 24, born in Ireland; resided at 269 Madison Street.
60. Peter Donahue, aged 32, born in Ireland; resided at 3 Oak Street.
61. One body not identified,
62. One body not identified.
63. James S. Crincy, aged 39, residence not known.
64. William E. Merritt, aged 26, residence in Beekman Street. His body was covered with contusions and burns, and presented a most pitiable appearance. Though attended with the greatest care, he survived his injuries only one week. He was a cousin of John J. Tindale, ex-president of the Fire Department.

LIST OF THE WOUNDED.

James Flood, badly injured in the face and thigh; his cheek required to be stitched together.
Patrick McPhillips (boy), knee badly fractured.
Thomas Weed, leg broken, and otherwise bruised.
H. D. Smith, shoulder blade broken.
S. H. Smith (boy), leg broken.
John Rogers, arm badly injured.
Francis Hyde, burned and injured in the face and arm.
W. Quinn, bruised very severely.
Henry Geefider, badly bruised and leg injured.
James Odell, leg broken, taken to Brooklyn.
Norvin N. Canfield, shoulder injured.
George Lewis, severely bruised.
James Hyatt, badly cut on the head.
Mr. Gregg, spine fractured, probably a mortal wound.
James Thompson, leg and knee bruised.
Henry Gerarder, badly scalded and bruised.
John Brown, severely burned.
Francis Lynch, arm broken; fell from third floor to cellar.
Lewis Daly, watch-case maker, head, legs, and arms badly bruised.
Charles Dougherty, blacksmith, severely burned and bruised.
Thomas Brooks, leg broken.
John J. Thompson, compound fracture of the leg and arm.
George H. Rowland, leg very badly bruised.
John C. King, arm and back severely injured.
C. O. Jessup, head and face bruised and cut.
Maurice L. Canfield, injured in the chest.
A. Aldridge, leg and arm much bruised.
James Taill, slightly bruised.
William Taill, slightly bruised.
John Mills, slightly bruised.
A. B. Martindale, slightly bruised.
Joseph Amble, slightly bruised.
J. Deberry (boy), slightly bruised.
Wesley S. Rowland, leg somewhat bruised.

Ellis C. Craig, slightly bruised.

Robert King, slightly bruised.

William Procter, slightly bruised.

Samuel Ding, slightly bruised.

William Gowanloch, slightly bruised.

Robert Stimel, slightly injured in the head.

George West, slightly injured in the head.

John Fagan, slightly injured in the head.

William Quigg, internally injured.

J. Tindell, considerably hurt.

Abram Mills, considerably hurt.

Frederic Stimmel (boy), not much injured.

Henry C. Burr, one of the firm of St. John, Burr & Co., slightly injured.

William Delander, badly scalded in the hands, his face badly bruised, and his shoulder-blade severely injured. He extricated himself from the ruins, and sustained most of his injuries in doing so. They did not prove fatal.

John L. Guyre, a member of Engine Company No. 14, at a fire in Front Street, on April 24, 1850, fell through a hatchway and was killed. A large concourse of firemen attended his funeral, and the members of his company raised a handsome monument over his tomb in Greenwood Cemetery. On June 6 a woman, with an infant in her arms, appeared at a window of a burning dwelling in Twenty-ninth street, near Lexington Avenue, and piteously cried for help. Reckless of danger, Foreman Joseph Davison, Assistant Foreman John Rogers, and William Minor and William Seaman, of No. 39 Hose Company, rushed into the flames. For some minutes they were hidden from view, and the suspense of the onlookers was intense. Then Rogers and Minor were seen descending the stairs bearing both mother and child and all considerably burned. When they emerged into the street with their precious burdens, the enthusiastic shouts of firemen and spectators were almost deafening.

In 1853 several firemen were killed in the performance of their duty. In the previous year, on September 25, Arthur J. Evans, one of the brave Mount's comrades, of Hose Company No. 14, lost his life at a fire in Palmer's chocolate factory in Duane street. On May 31, 1853, George W. Trenchard, foreman of Hose Company No. 16, was killed at a fire in Essex Street. On October 30, Michael O'Brien, of Hook and Ladder Company No. 11, and John S. Carman, of Engine Company No. 5, were killed at a fire in the Fowler Buildings, corner of Fulton and Nassau Streets.

On December 10, 1853, Franklin Square was the scene of one of the most disastrous of conflagrations. Several buildings were within a few hours transformed from gigantic warehouses, into smouldering ruins, and hundreds of artisans and workmen engaged in comfortable occupations were within the same time robbed of employment and thrown destitute upon the world. The fire began a little after one o'clock in the afternoon in the extensive publication establishment of Harper Brothers just after the employees had returned from dinner. It was said that a boy had dropped a lamp into the camphene in the engine room, which would account for the rapid spread of the flames. The building being filled with paper and matter of a light and combustible nature, the ignition from roof to basement was almost like the flashing of powder. By two o'clock nothing was standing of the immense warehouse except the outside walls, and within those the angry flames were sporting like infant demons. At this hour the apprehension was very great. There was no reason to doubt the destruction of many blocks in the vicinity. The wind was very high, and huge coals of fire were carried off to the distance of Beekman Street, and even there fell thick and fast upon the roofs of buildings and the heads of spectators. From Harper's buildings the flames ignited the opposite side of Pearl Street, although very wide at this spot, and for a time there was every appearance that this block would be licked by the increasing fire. Soon after the fire a heavy cloud of smoke hung over the city, filling many of the down-town streets to a burdensome degree. There were many narrow escapes. One young woman jumped out of a window and fortunately escaped injury. Another young woman had her dress take fire and saved herself by stripping it off. Policeman Masterson took her to the Chief's office.

As soon as the fire had extended across Pearl Street the efforts of the firemen were divided. The first building which caught on this side of the street was the Walton House, of Revolutionary memory. This was No. 326 Pearl Street, and every effort of the hard-worked firemen to preserve it on account of its historical associations was of no avail. In a few moments it was completely gutted. The Walton House was a large three-story edifice

BURNING OF HARPER BROTHERS' BUILDING.

built in the English baronial style of the last century. It was erected about 1754 by an aristocratic gentleman from whom it took its name. Finally it was turned into a boarding house. Adjoining the Walton House was the Franklin Square Hotel, which shared the fate of its neighbor. Next to this hotel was the extensive bakery of ex-Alderman James Kelly, No. 330 Pearl Street. For a long time it was feared this would go with the rest, but Mr. Kelly being an old favorite of the Fire Department, and an ex-member himself, every nerve was strained to save his dwelling. Wet blankets were hung out of the windows, and his roof was kept well-flooded. A hole was burned through his roof, but the house sustained very little other injury. As evening advanced the fire had a terrific beauty of its own. Harper's was one mass of rubbish, comprising six houses on Cliff Street, running through to Pearl and taking in the same number of houses on that street. On the opposite side of Cliff Street the buildings Nos. 81 and 83, also occupied by Harpers, were much scorched. Adjoining Harper's buildings, next to

Ferry Street, was the large publishing house of George F. Coolidge & Brother, which also fell before the fiery blast. The fire was stopped on the side toward Ferry Street at No. 319, the drug store of W. W. Thayer, which was somewhat damaged by water. On the other side the fire was arrested at a new building which the Harpers were erecting, in addition to three other buildings. There the flames met with nothing but a shell of a house of stone, and had it not been for this the work of destruction would probably have extended much farther. In all sixteen buildings were burned, and four or five more or less injured.

The energy of the firemen on this occasion was said to be very noticeable. For a long time before there had not been so large a turnout of the Department. Almost every engine in the city was on the ground, and even the Harlem engine was on hand. The bells rang a general alarm, which had not been done for months before. There were present four of the Brooklyn companies, Nos. 1, 4, 5, and 7. The Brooklynites formed a line through Peck Slip and took their suction from the dock. Of our firemen the *New York Herald* of that date said:

We cannot again refrain from speaking of the noble conduct of our firemen. At the time the fire broke out there were some six hundred human beings in the establishment of Messrs. Harper, men, women, and children, and immediately upon giving the report of the fire the greatest consternation prevailed—every window was filled with frantic souls crying for help. We are told there was abundance of time for every one to come down safely, but in the terror of the moment all rushed for the windows. The firemen immediately mounted their ladders, and brought all down in safety to the ground, perilling their own lives in doing so. * * * Amid crackling timber and hissing flames they forced their way, regardless of every peril in their efforts to roll back the billows of fire. Some idea can be formed of the degree of heat, considering the fact that it was difficult at times to bear it even in the upper part of Franklin Square. Yet amid all this for three long hours the heroic firemen worked at their engines, and yielded not till they were masters of the angry element.

Hook and Ladder Company No. 1 (Mutual) was the second apparatus on the ground, and by means of their ladders several girls made their escape. Some of the members of the company directed their efforts to rescue the safes. They got out the larger seven feet high one, and Mr. James Harper requested them to rescue the smaller, but it was impossible. Hook and Ladder Company No. 6 had the task of throwing down the walls on the Pearl Street side; on the Cliff Street side No. 11 did the same work; Nos. 2, 3, 4, 5, and 8 were at work in different parts. All the ladders of No. 1 were broken by the fall of a portion of the Cliff Street wall.

The loss to the Harpers was eight hundred thousand dollars; Coolidge & Bros., two hundred thousand dollars; and taking the other firms and houses altogether nearly one million five hundred thousand dollars. Ten years before on June 1, 1842, the firm lost one hundred thousand dollars through a fire.

In the newspapers of December 12, 1853, under the heading "The Firemen," we find the following advertisements:

A CARD.—Oceanus Fire Engine No. 11 return their sincere thanks to Mr. Joseph Carlisle, of Centre and Leonard Streets, for the bountiful supply of refreshments furnished them after their return from the fire in Pearl Street.

By order.   DAVID BAKER, *Foreman.*
WM. J. LEWIS, *Secretary.*

A CARD.—At a special meeting of Hook and Ladder Company No. 4, held at the truck house after the return from the fire in Pearl Street, it was unanimously

Resolved, That the thanks of the company be tendered to Mr. and Mrs. John Baulch for the bountiful supply of refreshments furnished us after the above fire.

JOHN CORNWELL, *Chairman.*

JOHN SLOWY, *Secretary.*

On December 14 Foreman Chas. F. Meyons and Secretary Martin Wise published a similar card in reference to Mr. James Kelly.

A fire that broke out on December 26, 1853, in a store in Front Street, spread to the shipping in the docks. Among the vessels burned was the big ship Great Republic (three hundred and twenty-five feet long and four thousand five hundred and fifty-five tons burden). The total loss was six hundred thousand dollars.

The gallantry of the firemen was conspicuous at the burning of Tripler Hall and the Lafarge House on Broadway, nearly opposite Bond Street, on

TRIPLER HALL OR METROPOLITAN HALL, 1854.

June 8, 1854. T. F. Goodwin, foreman, and Hugh Curry, both of Hose Company No. 35, particularly distinguished themselves by their courage. The fire caught from one of the hotel furnaces under the orchestra box of the concert room, and in one hour the buildings were in ruins. Tripler Hall was built by Mr. Tripler, and first opened to the public on the fourteenth of October, 1850, and could seat four thousand persons. It was a concert room in the Lafarge House. The Lafarge House cost three hundred thousand dollars, and was leased to Wright, Laniers & Co., for fifty-four thousand dollars a year. It was elegantly furnished.

Among the first of the brilliant stars who occupied the boards of the Lafarge House was Jenny Lind, who was hailed as the "Gifted Swede," and welcomed as "Sweet Warbler," in a motto at Castle Garden. Indeed, Tripler Hall was built especially to accommodate the large audiences which evening after evening flocked to hear the Swedish Nightingale. It was costly and magnificent beyond anything at that time in the city, and cost one hundred thousand dollars. It was the largest music hall in the world, except the opera houses of London, Milan, and Havana. But the first voice heard within its walls was that of the sweet singer Madam Anna Bishop. Then followed Jenny Lind. Here also Miss Catherine Hayes entertained crowded and distinguished audiences; here Alboni and Madame Sontag sang; and here the monster Jullien Concerts drew immense houses night after night. The name of the concert room had been changed to Metropolitan Hall, and the last announcement previous to its destruction in 1854 was for Wednesday evening, January 18, when the ballroom of the Lafarge House, communicating with the concert room, was to have been thrown open for ladies and gentlemen patronizing Jullien's Grand Ball Paré, to obtain admission to which full evening dress was indispensable. The hall was also used for political and other meetings. There were heard the ringing tones of Thomas D'Arcy McGee, the Irish patriot of 1848, who had to fly from his country. Other well-known names in its history are those of Lucy Stone, Lloyd Garrison, and Wendell Phillips.

The work of rebuilding the hotel and theater was at once begun, and on the eighteenth of September the "Great Metropolitan Theater and New York Opera House" was opened with a poem spoken by Harry Eytinge, the song of "The Star Spangled Banner," and Bulwer's play of "The Lady of Lyons." Brief, however, was the second period of the brilliant career of the Metropolitan. Toward the close of 1854 the famous Italian priest Gavazzi, who had abandoned the Catholic Church, made his appearance in this country on a crusade against his ancient faith. He was a man of keen intellect, and his eloquence was forceful and earnest. Everywhere he went the Catholic part of the population, especially the foreign element, opposed him most strenuously. His life was threatened, and vengeance was vowed against him if he persisted in his attacks. Saturday night, November 8, Gavazzi lectured at the Metropolitan. Although threats had been made to tear down the building should the apostate priest speak there, it was not thought that any serious results would follow. He had spoken there before and had not been interfered with. On this occasion Father Gavazzi lectured to five thousand persons, and the meeting passed over tranquilly. A few hours after its close, however, the building was in flames, and the efforts of the firemen could not save it from destruction.

OLD FORT GEORGE.

CHAPTER XVII.

FINAL FIRES OF THE OLD DEPARTMENT.

Great Loss of Life at the Jennings Fire —Charity's Compassionate Hand.—" Andy " Schenck's Marriage and Untimely Death.—The Crystal Palace Conflagration and Destruction of Engines.—Joseph Skillman's Death.—Fires Through the Draft Riots, and Heroism of the Firemen.—Exciting and Perilous Times.—Alleged Southern Plot to Burn Hotels in 1864.

ABOUT 3 A. M. on September 3, 1849, the noble packet ship Henry Clay, lying at the foot of Fletcher Street, was discovered to be on fire amidships. The alarm was given by the Fulton Market bell, which struck as the first glare of light shone up, and although the firemen were promptly on the spot some delay occurred in starting the various hydrant streams. Hose Companies 1, 2, 3, 8, 10, 15, 18, 21, 25 and 28 were on hand and furnished water to Engines Nos. 5 (which was first to work), 20, 38, 14, 2, 13 and 21. No. 13 was obliged at first to use suction in consequence of the small number of hydrant lines.

A fearful loss of life in the Fire Department occurred on Tuesday night, April 25, 1854. It broke out at eight o'clock in the clothing store of William T. Jennings & Co., No. 231 Broadway, and defied all the efforts of the firemen. On the south of the building stood the American Hotel, and on the north the establishments of Meade Bros., photographers, and of Mr. Batchelor, hairdresser. John A. Cregier was standing on the roof of Meade's building in company with another engineer, Noah L. Farnham. They let down to the street the halyards of the flagstaff, and with great difficulty succeeded in drawing up one end of a length of hose. Scarcely had they begun to play on the fire when the rear wall of Jennings's buildings suddenly toppled over backward upon the extension, letting the upper floors fall upon thirteen or fourteen firemen who were in the second story of the burning store. There was, it seems, a huge iron safe in the upper story, and this dashed through the several floors to the basement, instantly killing two firemen. The scene around that fire, when it was known that over twenty firemen were buried beneath the ruins, beggars description. It required but a moment's thought, and then the members of the Department rushed into the building, regardless of their own lives, to rescue those of their comrades. Cregier directed the pipe of his hose toward a part of the burning roof that hung over the spot where the men were buried, and which seemed about to cave in.

" Stop that water !" called a voice from below, " it is scalding the men "— not the buried men only, but the gallant fellows who were trying to extricate them.

More perilous, however, than the scalding water were the heavy rafters on the eve of falling, and Cregier cried out in stentorian tones, while still flooding the place with water :

"It can't be done; the roof will go;" and by his decision he saved many lives.

All night long they worked, braving danger at every turn, and not until they had taken out the lifeless remains of eleven of their comrades, with some twenty bodily injured, did they retreat from the ruins. Of those who fell in the discharge of their duty were John O'Donnell, of Engine 42, a son of Coroner O'Donnell. He was in the ruins over eight hours, and conversed with his friends until rescued. He died in the New York Hospital the same night. James McNulty, of Engine 20, Andrew C. Schenck, of Hook and Ladder 1, John A. Keyser, of Hose 8, two brothers, Daniel and Alexander McKay, of Engine 21, a boy named Michael Flynn, a runner of Hose 53, James E. Deegan, of Hose 18, an old man named Wilson, a runner of 21 Engine, and one John Reinhardt. Some of the ruins having been reached by cutting holes through the basement walls of Meade's building, "Andy" Schenck was seen to be dead, and young O'Donnell so bruised that the top of his head, as an old fireman expressed it, was "as big as a stove and just about as black." Dr. O'Donnell had been anxiously pacing in front of the ruins waiting for his son to be brought out. Hugh Gallagher, of Engine Company No.

JENNINGS' FIRE.

23, was found pinned against a wall by a heavy safe, which had fallen from the floor above.

Of poor Andy Schenck it is related that when the alarm for the fire sounded that night he was calling at the house of the young lady to whom he was engaged to be married, and who earnestly urged him to stay. "No," said he, after some hesitation, "I'll go to this fire, and this is the last fire I will go to." It was indeed his last, for there he found his grave. Among those who miraculously escaped being killed were Zophar Mills, Jacob Larrick, of Hook and Ladder No. 6, ex-Comptroller Brennan, then captain of the Sixth Ward police; Chief Engineer Harry Howard, and Timothy L. West.

The following are the names of the wounded: Matthew Gilligan, Engine 21; Hugh Hart, Engine 21; E. Gillespie, Engine 21; Patrick Feeney, Engine 21; Patrick Waters, Engine 21; John Newman, Engine 21; Joseph R. Wheeler,

Hose 5; Charles Kratz, Hook and Ladder 11; Robert Brewster, Engine 6; Philip McHugh, Engine 15; Charles Parks, Hose 25; Charles Daly, Engine 20; Patrick Gorman, Engine 15; John J. Shaw, Hose 8; Hugh Gallagher, Hose 25; Timothy Shinley, Engine 15; Peter Curran, Engine 10; Charles Wheeler, Hose 25; Augustus Hoyt, Hose 10; William Basset, Hose 54; Thomas Flennan, Engine 15; John Lewis, Hose 21; John Atkinson, Hose 49; William Moran, Engine 21.

When the sad news was announced in the journals of the following day, thousands upon thousands congregated around the ruins and at the dead-house in the hospital yard to view the mangled remains of those brave but unfortunate men. The firemen of Brooklyn, Jersey City and Newark held meetings of sympathy, while in the Common Council Alderman Blunt presented a series of resolutions upon the death of the firemen, and one thousand five hundred dollars was appropriated to defray their funeral expenses. The Board of Foremen and Engineers met and passed resolutions, presented by Timothy L. West, and it was agreed that the Department turn out in a body to pay the last tribute of respect to their deceased brethren.

The citizens also came forward with donations to the families of the deceased, among whom were Barney Williams, Drumgold . & Proch, and Coleman & Stetson, of the Astor House. The remains of the brothers McKay, James McNulty, John A. Keyser, A. C. Schenck, John R. O'Donnell and James E. Deegan were buried from the City Hall, the procession being one of the most solemn ever witnessed in this city. Engine Company No. 40 carried the department banner, and the whole Fire Department, and the City Council, headed by Mayor Westervelt, turned out. The line of march was up Chatham to the Bowery, then through Astor Place to Broadway, and down Broadway to the South Ferry. Alexander McKay was killed while endeavoring to rescue his brother Daniel, and McNulty died soon after being conveyed into Rushton's drug store, under the Astor House. It seems that there was an iron arch in the rear of the building extending from one side of the edifice to the other which supported the rear wall; this became red hot, and the effect of the water from the pipe of Engine Company No. 22 cracked it, thus letting down the whole rear wall. A coroner's jury was impaneled, with John N. Genin, the well-known hatter, as foreman, and it was decided that the place was set on fire by thieves, three of whom were afterward sent to State Prison. The loss at this fire was estimated at seventy-five thousand dollars, and to this day the old "vets" talk of that lamentable event.

Harry Howard, then Assistant Engineer, testified as follows before the coroner's jury: "At half-past eight o'clock the two upper stories were on fire. I think there were then about fifty persons in the store, firemen and others. Engine Company No. 21's pipe was throwing a good stream of water towards the staircase into the third story. I then discovered a skylight, and ordered the men to get out on the roof of the extension [in the rear of the building] and play water into the front building, * * * but I had no conception of the building falling at this time. If the men had reached the point where I ordered them they would have been saved. Some of them did as I ordered them, and they were not killed; others had not time." The jury censured the builders for the flimsy character of a portion of the structure.

At noon on July 1, 1854, a fire broke out in a furniture store No. 371 Grand Street, at which Mr. John W. Garside, a member of Columbia Hose Company No. 9, rescued three persons—two women and a boy fourteen years old. Mr. Garside climbed up the gutter, being helped up by one of his associates, and, hanging on to the window, succeeded in passing them in safety to the adjoining building. As the last one was being taken out, the window sash, which was held by a button, fell on his arm, and the glass cut his hand severely, and while he was having it dressed at a drug store opposite, the building from which the people were rescued fell in with a crash, not standing five minutes after they had been taken out. Mr. Garside carries an elegant extra jewelled Liverpool gold watch and chain which was presented to him with a box containing two hundred and fifty dollars in gold at a dinner which was given to him at Odd Fellows Hall shortly afterwards. Soon thereafter the Common Council adopted a resolution appropriating one hundred and fifty dollars for a gold medal to be presented to Mr. Garside as a token of reward for his heroic conduct. Mayor Fernando Wood in March, 1855, was deputed to present Mr. Garside with the gold medal. A number of Mr. Garside's friends were present to witness the presentation. His honor the mayor, in his address, highly complimented the gallant fellow on being the recipient of such a well deserved tribute.

The Latting Observatory on Forty-third Street, between Fifth and Sixth Avenues, two hundred and eighty feet high, was destroyed on August 30, 1856. A few months afterwards at a fire in Sixth Street, between Avenues B and C, Engine Company No. 44 and Hook and Ladder Company No. 13 rescued twelve persons, and among the bravest of the rescuers was Joseph L. Perley, who subsequently became President of the Board of Fire Commissioners. The laying of the Atlantic cable was commemorated on August 17, 1858, by an exhibition of fireworks at the City Hall. At midnight the roof was found to be on fire, and the cupola, with its clock, was finally destroyed.

The Crystal Palace in Reservoir Square was burned on the fifth of October, 1858. It was opened on July 14, 1853, for the exhibition of the industry of all nations, and was located in the vicinity of the aqueduct at Forty-second Street. "The fairy-like Greek cross of glass, bound together with withes of iron," says a writer of the period, "with its graceful dome, its arched naves, and its broad aisles and galleries, filled with choice productions of art and manufactures, gathered from the most distant parts of the earth, quaint old armor from the Tower of London, gossamer fabrics from the looms of Cashmere, Sevres china, Gobelin tapestry, Indian curiosities, stuffs, jewelry, musical instruments, carriages, and machinery of home and foreign manufacture, Marochetti's colossal statue of Washington, Kiss's Amazon, Thorwaldsen's Christ and the Apostles, Powers's Greek Slave, and a host of other works of art beside, will long be remembered as the most tasteful ornament that ever graced the metropolis." Beautiful, however, as was this fairy-like palace it vanished in smoke in the short space of half an hour, and fell, burying the rich collection of the American Institute, then on exhibition within its walls, in a molten mass of ruins. The Crystal Palace contained one thousand two hundred and fifty tons of iron, and thirty-nine thousand square feet of glass. A grand concert, which fully ten thousand persons were

expected to attend, had been arranged for the evening.   The total loss was
estimated at two million dollars.

About five o'clock smoke was seen issuing from a large room in the north
nave, and in front of the entrance on Forty-second Street.   The flames spread
with incredible rapidity in every direction.   There were about two thousand
persons scattered about the edifice at the time, all of whom, the moment the
alarm of "fire!" was raised, made a rush for the Sixth Avenue entrance, the
doors of which were thrown open.   The entrance on Fortieth Street was
closed.   Under the direction of ex-Captain Maynard, of the police, and several
of the directors the crowd was conducted safely to the street.   Mr. Smith, an
employee in charge of the jewelry deparment, saw the fire and ran back to his
case of jewelry.   He dragged the case from its fastenings along the gallery,

DESTRUCTION OF THE CRYSTAL PALACE.

down a flight of stairs, and into the street.   He was almost the last person
out, and had a narrow escape of his life.   The view from the street and
neighborhood was very grand, and thousands of persons flocked to the
conflagration.   The firemen of the district were soon on the spot, and twenty
or thirty streams were thrown into the building, but without having any visible
effect.   Many firemen rushed into the edifice, hoping to save the apparatus
that were on exhibition, but they were compelled to retreat on account of the
smoke.   Again and again they gallantly rushed into the palace, and eventually succeeded in saving the carriage belonging to No. 40 Hose Company
(Empire), and the carriage of No. 36 Hose Company (Oceanic).   However, the
carriages of No. 1 Hose Company (Eagle), and No. 6 Hose Company (Croton)
engine of No. 16 (Gotham), Hook and Ladder No. 1 (Mutual), and Engine
No. 28 (Pacific) were destroyed.

Mr. Frederick W. Geissennainer, chairman of the Board of Managers of the American Institute, was standing in the south nave when the fire broke out. He ran to the Forty-second Street entrance, where he discovered a quantity of wooden patterns of the ironwork used in the construction of the palace enveloped in flames. The pitch-pine floors only invited the flames, which licked over the planking, rolling up dense clouds of smoke, nearly suffocating those in the north nave. After despatching a man to turn off the gas, Mr. Geissenhainer ran to a hydrant with hose attached, near the north nave, and caused the water to be turned on. Owing, however, to the lowness of the water in the reservoir it was of no avail. There was no hope of saving the building, and the employees and officers turned their attention to all the nooks and retired spots they could get at in order to drive out any lingering persons.

The flames ascended to the second floor and seemingly rolled along the surface of the woodwork like molten iron, at a speed as rapid as the ordinary pace of a pedestrian in the street. After going through two of the galleries Mr. Geissenhainer proceeded to the picture gallery. He went behind the panorama, thinking that the men who were engaged in winding it for the evening exhibition might still be there. When he returned he found both stairways in a blaze. He ran to one of the towers, and finding one board displaced in the floor he easily removed another and slid down the iron pipe leading from the water tank to the floor below, and a moment after escaped from the building. The last person had scarcely left when the dome fell in with a terrible crash, just twelve minutes after the fire was discovered. One old gentleman was found senseless at the foot of one of the stairways, having failed to escape. He was rescued just before the dome fell.

It was said that the fire was the work of incendiaries who ignited papers in the lumber room. The amount of property destroyed was over five hundred thousand dollars. Among the property destroyed were several valuable steam engines, and some fine pictures belonging to Mr. Furis, of the "Root Gallery," corner of Broadway and Franklin Street.

Next day thousands visited the ruins. Eight of the turrets and a portion of the iron framework of one of the galleries were left standing. The whole area to the depth of three or four feet was covered with broken pillars and columns, melted glass, and disordered machinery. Wandering among the rubbish were many exhibitors searching for any of their property that might be worth saving. A large heap of coal, about fifty tons, continued to burn all day, and all attempts to extinguish it were unavailing. Comptroller Flagg, when the palace fell into the hands of the city, had the concern insured for fifty thousand dollars in ten companies—five thousand dollars in each.

On October 8, three days after the fire, the chief engineer issued a call for a mass meeting of the Department at Firemen's Hall, to consider the best means of replacing the apparatus destroyed. Mr. Howard occupied the chair, and James F. Wenman officiated as secretary. The chief engineer stated that it was useless to petition the Common Council to replace the engines and hose carriages burned, as there was no appropriation for the purpose, and it might require years to get them to act on the matter. A resolution was offered to appoint a committee of thirty to solicit subscriptions toward rebuilding the machines. This was strenuously objected to on the part of many of the foremen, who held that it was the duty of the Common Council to make good the loss of corporation property, and at all events they contended that only officers of the Department were entitled to meet in that hall. But the resolution prevailed, and the following committee was appointed:

David Milliken, Wm. H. Wickham, Matt. T. Brennan, John S. Belder, Noah L. Farnham, John A. Cregier, Henry B. Venn, Henry H. Graham, Philip W. Engs, John Lynes, Wm. A. Woodhull, James Smith, Carlisle Norwood, Charles McDougall, William Williams, James A. Carolin, Albert J. Delatour, John Clancy, Alonzo Slote, Zophar Mills, Henry A. Burr, Andrew J. Garvey, William Thompson, John Fox, David Budd, George R. Connor, Walter Smith, William Raines, Cora Osborne, and James Y. Watkins.

ELM STREET FIRE.

For several years from 1858 there was an absence of great fires, but still there were many lively and many sad nights of conflagration for the Department. No. 5 Engine was buried by the fall of a wall, and some of the men injured, on December 29, 1859. Daniel Scully, of Engine Company No. 40, with members of his company, rescued six persons at a fire in Elm Street on February 2, 1860. He climbed to the third story by means of the leader, and handed the tenants down to men at the windows, one after the other. The Common Council presented him with a gold medal. James R. Mount, at that time foreman of Hose Company No. 15, distinguished himself on this occasion by saving two persons. About twenty persons were suffocated or burned to death. This calamitous fire led to the Common Council passing an ordinance compelling the placing of fire escapes on all tenements. For the first time their attention was turned to this necessary adjunct of such buildings. Hook and Ladder Company No. 4 saved several persons at another fire in Doyers Street. July 26, the same year, Thomas Cox, of Hose Company No. 50, was killed at a fire in Broad Street. On December 3 several persons were saved by firemen in No. 203 Division Street. Fifteen days later the new steamship "*John P. King*" was burned at Pier No. 4, North River. Several members of No. 38 Engine were playing on the flames in the engine room. The vessel was cut loose and towed out into the stream, to the astonishment of the firemen. Two or three jumped from the blazing steamer and were picked up by boats. Thomas R. Smith, who was rescued by the police boat, was much less concerned at the danger to which he had been exposed than at the loss of a new length of rubber hose and a brass pipe belonging to his engine. He almost wept over the loss.

Very disastrous was the fire that broke out in the lower part of the city on December 29, 1859. About five o'clock in the morning the Second Ward police were alarmed by observing smoke issuing from Black, Gramm & Co.'s store, No. 53 Beekman Street. In the meantime the flames spread rapidly, and in the course of half an hour extended to No. 61, only one door from the police station, and occupied by several parties. The large paper warehouses of Bulkley & Co. and Cyrus W. Field were adjoining, and caught fire. Admirable efforts were made to

FIRE—WILSON'S CRACKER BAKERY.

stay the fire, but in vain, and it reached the other side of Ann Street, catching Nos. 90 and 92, and sweeping onward until it reached Nos. 83 and 85 Fulton Street. A wall unexpectedly fell into the street, burying No. 5 engine, and some of its members were injured, but not seriously.

Joseph Skillman, of Hook and Ladder Company No. 15, was killed at a fire in Fulton Street on February 8, 1861. The cold was intense. The members of No. 38 protected their engine from the cold wind by building around it a thick wall formed of bundles of wrapping paper. A number of small fires occurred in 1861 and 1862.

A very destructive fire occurred on January 1, 1863, in Fulton, Gold and Beekman Streets. The cracker bakery of John T. Wilson & Co., and other business and manufacturing establishments at Nos. 66 to 79 Fulton Street, Nos. 56 to 60 Gold Street, and Nos. 69 to 79 Beekman Street, were damaged or destroyed. The firemen had not experienced such a fearful conflagration for some time previously. In a building adjoining the bakery there lay the body of a man who had died the day before. Some of the members of Pearl Hose Company No. 28 went in and found the body laid out on a board, near a window in the second story. Strange to say, above the chamber of death there were signs of jollity—a table was set for New Year's callers.

At another cracker bakery fire (Goodwin's, No. 209 Cherry Street) on February 3, 1863, loss of life occurred. Three firemen—John Slowey and George W. Badger, of Engine Company No. 19, and Thomas Sweeney, of Engine Company No. 6, were buried by a falling wall. Slowey and Badger died of their injuries. Every company passed resolutions of sympathy and sorrow. Hose Company No. 36 eulogized Mr. Badger for his "correct, manly deportment and many sterling qualities which have endeared him to all." His funeral took place from the Stanton Street Baptist Church, the services being conducted by the Rev. Dr. Hiscox and the Rev. Dr. Armitage. The Fire Department, with its banner (carried by Phenix Hose Company No. 22),

BEEKMAN STREET FIRE.

escorted the hearse to Fulton Ferry on its way to Greenwood. The Board of Foremen acted as a guard of honor. Mr. Slowey entered the Department in 1849 as a member of Engine Company No. 15. He afterwards joined Engine Company No. 19, when it had but seven members, and became its foreman. His friends raised six thousand dollars for the benefit of his widow and three orphans. At the firing of the Colored Orphan Asylum, at Forty-third Street and Fifth Avenue, during the Draft Riots, July, 1861, the chief engineer, with his own hands extinguished the burning brands. The desperate ruffians threatened to kill him if he persisted in thwarting their diabolical purpose. Standing upon the steps of the building the bold fire chief appealed to the infuriated crowd of two thousand half drunken wretches. The mob again set fire to the building, and Decker and his gallant little band extinguished the flames. This thoroughly exasperated the shameless crew, and the scoundrels advanced upon the chief engineer. His men determinedly closed around him, and the cowards were afraid to carry out their intent to injure the chief. But they eventually succeeded in burning down the Asylum. Some twenty of the poor little orphans were seized by the mob. A young Irishman, Paddy McCaffrey, with four stage drivers of the Forty-second Street line and Engine Company No. 18, dashed in upon the fiends and rescued the children from their grasp. They struck right and left, and in triumph bore the little ones off to the Thirty-fifth Precinct Station House.

The heroism of the New York firemen in these days of danger was the theme of the public press and of all well-disposed citizens. While some buildings were burning at Fourteenth Street and Avenue C, Assistant Engineer Elisha Kingsland tried to remove a wagon in the street to make room for the approach of a carriage.

"If you touch that wagon I'll blow your brains out," cried a ruffian, who was backed by hundreds of his kind.

COLORED ORPHAN ASYLUM.
[Burned down by Rioters, July, 1861.]

The engineer got upon the wagon and shouted, "If this fire continues, it will cross the street and burn the houses of your friends."

"Get down from there! Shoot him! Mangle them!" were the responses.

Nevertheless, Mr. Kingsland gained his point. Again, at the corner of Twenty-ninth Street and Broadway, Chief Engineer Decker, Assistant Engineers William Lamb and Elisha Kingsland had a hand-to-hand fight with a big crowd. Lamb was knocked down, but his comrades set him on his feet, and they finally succeeded in arresting three of the ringleaders who were stealing bales of silk.

The *New York Tribune*, of July 20, 1863, says: "During the progress of the fire on the corner of Second Avenue and Twenty-first Street, on Monday afternoon [July 13] Lafayette Engine Company No. 19 were threatened by the mob that if they attempted to extinguish the fire, or in any way endeavored to save the building, they would be instantly stoned. Nothing daunted, the brave and energetic foreman, Mr. James G. W. Brinkman, urged his men to instantly stretch their hose and make preparations to save the building. Thereupon the mob cut the hose and endeavored to break the engine; but being assailed and driven off by the company with the assistance of the police, they carried out their destructive propensities in other directions. At the burning of the lumber yard, corner of Avenue C and Fourteenth Street, on Wednesday morning, pretty much the same scenes above described were enacted. The company worked at the fire for six hours and succeeded in saving a considerable amount of property. The police of the Seventeenth Precinct speak in great praise of the members of this company, who, led by their foreman and Assistant Engineer Kingsland, assisted, in conjunction with the members of the precinct, in dispersing mobs and saving the dwellings and property of the residents of the ward. . . . In the absence of the police of this precinct (they being stationed in the more riotous parts of the city), these firemen actually patrolled the ward day and night, and thus rendered a service which will not be soon forgotten."

In some portions of the city the firemen organized themselves into patrols for the protection of their respective neighborhoods. The firemen in the Seventh Ward placed themselves under the command of Captain Rynders and John McDermott, foreman of Engine Company No. 2. The members of Engine Company No. 20 and Hose Companies Nos. 8, 18 and 49, organized a First Ward patrol. Hose Companies Nos. 26 and 31, Engine Companies Nos. 7 and 12 and Hook and Ladder Company No. 10 are mentioned as conspicuous in this service. Escaping and terrified negroes found protection in the engine houses of Engine Company No. 13, in Duane Street, and Engine Company No. 2, in Henry Street.

Some idea of what the firemen had to contend with may be gathered from the following estimate, made by Fire Marshal Baker:

Monday, July 13, 1863.

11:05 A. M.—No. 677 Third Avenue, brick building, Provost Marshal Jenkins's enrolling office; three buildings destroyed. Total value about twenty-five thousand dollars.

3:05 P. M.—Lexington Avenue, between Forty-fourth and Forty-fifth Streets, two brown-stone dwelling houses and their contents, valued at seventy-eight thousand dollars, totally destroyed.

4:35 P. M.—Forty-fourth Street, between Fourth and Fifth Avenues, Bull's Head Hotel, brick building, owned by Mr. Allerton, destroyed with its contents. Loss about seventy thousand dollars.

4:50 P. M.—A five-story brick building, northeast corner of Twenty-first Street and Second Avenue, used for manufacturing firearms by Marston & Co., completely destoyed, together with contents. Loss about seventy-five thousand dollars.

5:15 P. M.—No. 1140 Broadway, Provost Marshal B. F. Manierre's enrolling office, twelve brick buildings destroyed, the whole block on Broadway, from Twenty-eighth to Twenty-ninth Street, and buildings on Twenty-eighth and Twenty-ninth Streets. Total value, including their contents, one hundred and twenty-five thousand dollars.

6:50 P. M.—Fifth Avenue, between Forty-third and Forty-fourth Streets, Colored Orphan Asylum, brick building, totally destroyed. Loss about thirty-five thousand dollars.

8:18 P.M.—No. 429 Grand Street, enrolling office and dwelling of Provost Marshal Captain John Duffy, brick building, sacked and burned. Loss, including contents, about ten thousand dollars.

9:20 P. M.—No. 62 Roosevelt Street, frame dwelling, occupied by colored people. Damage about one hundred dollars.

9:27 P. M.—Eighty-seventh Street, residence of Postmaster Abram Wakeman, totally destroyed. Loss twenty-five thousand dollars. The Twenty-third Precinct Police Station, directly in the rear, on Eighty-sixth Street, caught fire from sparks and was also destroyed. Loss about fifteen thousand dollars.

Tuesday, July 14.

3:30 A. M.—One Hundred and Twenty-ninth Street, corner of Third Avenue, six frame buildings were burned. Total value about twenty-two thousand dollars.

12:22 P. M.—Eleventh Avenue and Forty-first Street, hotel owned by Mr. Allerton, brick building destroyed. Loss about fifteen thousand dollars.

3:04 P. M.—Weehawken Ferry-house, frame, foot of Forty-second Street, North River. Loss six thousand dollars.

THE MOB'S DESTRUCTIVE WORK.

[Thirty-second Street, between Sixth and Seventh Avenues.]

5:03 P. M.—Nos. 73 and 75 Roosevelt Street, brick front, two dwelling houses, occupied by colored families, totally destroyed. Loss three thousand dollars.

11 P. M.—No. 163 East Twenty-second Street, Eighteenth Precinct Station House, brick building; also the fire alarm bell tower, and No. 51 Engine House, all destroyed. Loss about twenty thousand dollars.

11:45 P. M.—No. 24 East Thirty-third Street, dwelling house of Mr. Jared W. Peck, port warden, brick building; a library, valued at five thousand dollars, destroyed; the building fired. Loss by the fire about one thousand dollars.

Wednesday, July 15.

2:40 A. M.—Avenue C, corner of Fourteenth Street, lumber yard of Ogden & Co. Damage about two thousand dollars.

10:50 A. M.—No. 91 West Thirty-second Street, three brick tenement houses, occupied by colored people, all destroyed. Loss about fifteen thousand dollars.

The total amount is estimated at three hundred and sixty thousand one hundred dollars.

At a fire in Twenty-ninth Street, on December 2, 1863, John Brown, Assistant foreman of Hose Company No. 30, rescued some persons from the flames, and for his gallantry received a silver trumpet from the Common Council. Eight hundred and sixty-seven thousand three hundred and thirty-four dollars was lost in the destruction of Auffmordt & Hessenburg's extensive establishment in Duane Street on January 16, 1864. John Fitzpatrick, of No. 34 Engine, had just emerged from the building with two children, when the wall fell and he narrowly escaped. Not so, however, George W. Burridge, an honorary member of No. 42 Engine, who was caught under the wall and instantly killed.

Between one and two o'clock on Sunday morning, May 29, 1864, a fire broke out in the second-hand furniture store No. 75 Division Street, owned by Bernard Heller, who also occupied the upper part of the building as a dwelling. When the doors were broken open the fire was seen burning in the center of the store. The flames immediately rushed out at the door, and extended up the front of the building, which was of wood, and two stories and an attic in height. The occupants of the premises were aroused, but too late to escape by the stairs, which were at the rear part of the store. Engine No. 31 and Hook and Ladder Company No. 11 were quickly on the spot, and it was through their exertions that Mr. Heller and his wife and four children were taken from the second floor, through the windows. Mr. Heller had fallen on the floor, where he was found by the firemen nearly exhausted. He was very badly burned about the face and hands, and his wife was also much injured about the breast, face, hands, and arms. The youngest child, a boy ten months old, was severely burned. Three girls, five, seven. and eight years old respectively, were rescued uninjured. The firemen carried the baby and one of the girls to the hospital. Frank Mahedy, foreman of No. 31, whose untimely end while chief of battalion in the new Department is recorded in another chapter, distinguished himself in rescuing the family. So, too, did Thomas McGrath, of the same company. In a short time the entire building was enveloped in flames, when the front wall bulged. Assistant Engineer Perley ordered the firemen out of the building, but the order being misunderstood was not obeyed. Shortly afterwards the chimney fell, which carried down the floors, and several firemen were buried beneath the timbers. They were soon extricated, however, from their perilous position. Mahedy was very badly bruised, but had no bones broken. He was taken to the engine house and his hurts attended to by a surgeon. Messrs. John Armstrong and Eberhardt, of the same company, were also much bruised, as were also Roundsman Witcomb, of the Seventh Precinct, and several others. Jacob Deitschburger, a cigarmaker, who occupied a room in the attic, jumped from the roof to the awning, escaping with only a few bruises. A child named Batti, three years old, was burned to death in the building, without the knowledge of the firemen.

July 11, 1864, at 1 o'clock A. M., the steamboat "*John Potter*" was destroyed by Fire at Pier No. 1, North River. Several companies were on the dock with their apparatus and while busy at work were surrounded by the fire. Southwark Engine Company No. 38 had to abandon the big old white hand engine belonging to Fulton Engine Company No. 21, temporarily placed in their charge. The small jumper of City Hose Company No. 8 was also abandoned. The truck of Mutual Hook and Ladder Company No. 1 was dragged off the dock in time to save it from destruction. A large number of firemen had to jump overboard and were picked up by small boats, or had to climb out as best they could. No lives were lost.

The Lafayette Theater, in Laurens Street, with several adjacent buildings, was entirely destroyed by fire on Thursday, April 10, 1829. The loss was two hundred thousand dollars. Henry Yates owned the theater, and had not a cent insured.

FIRE IN DIVISION STREET, MAY 31, 1864.

On July 13 a famous place of amusement was destroyed—Barnum's Museum, which then stood at the corner of Ann Street and Broadway. It was about noon when the fire broke out, and at that hour there were few persons in the building, so that no human lives were lost, but half a million dollars' worth of property was destroyed. It was a unique scene, and afforded opportunity for a great deal of graphic and humorous writing in the press. The firemen had much fun with the monkeys, the whale, the bear, and the "Happy Family." The Fat Lady and the Giantess were handed out in safety with the tenderest solicitude for their welfare. Several of the laddies said they were completely smitten with the woolly-headed Albino woman. The enterprising Barnum soon erected another and a more splendid edifice, the burning of which gave occasion for similar gallantry on the part of the New Department in 1868.

But a serious and almost tragic affair took place about the same time in Forty-fourth Street, west of Eighth Avenue. This was the site of the old village of Bloomingdale, where vegetable markets abounded. Several houses were on fire, and at an upper window of one of them a woman appeared with a child in her arms. The fire at Barnum's left this locality short of its complement of engines, and no hook and ladder company was at hand. But

BURNING OF BARNUM'S MUSEUM.
[July 13, 1865.]

the members of Equitable Engine Company No. 36 were equal to the occasion, and adopted an ingenious mode of saving life. One of the men climbed up the front of the building by the windows until he reached the room in which the woman stood. A comrade stood in the window below. Two others stationed themselves in the window on the lower floor. Others held a bed beneath, and then, first the child and afterwards the woman were lowered from story to story, and dropped on the bed. The spectators hailed this daring act with cheer upon cheer.

In Trinity Church yard, facing Broadway, is a memorial shaft and tablet, commemorative of the death and burial of a number of firemen.   On the front of the tablet is this inscription:

ERECTED BY THE
ACTIVE AND HONORARY MEMBERS OF EMPIRE ENGINE COMPANY, No. 42.

COMMITTEE: H. METZGER, G. J. ORR, J. LETSON, J. D. COSTA, J. Y. WATKINS, JR.

The left hand side of the tablet bears the following:

AUG. L. COWDREY

Born Dec. 3rd, 1822. Killed July 19th, 1845, while in the discharge of his duty as a Fireman at the Great Fire.

JNO. B. O'DONNELL

Born August 16th, 1832. Killed April 26th, 1854, while endeavoring to rescue his brother Firemen from the ruins of the burning building, No. 231 Broadway.

GEO. W. BURRIDGE

Born March 12th, 1833. Killed Jan. 16th, 1864, while in the discharge of his duty as a Fireman at the fire at No. 146 Duane Street.

The right hand side of the tablet bears the following:

Col.
NOAH L. FARNHAM

Born March 1st, 1829. Died Aug. 14th, 1861, from wounds received at the Battle of Bull Run, Va.

Lt. TIMOTHY KING

Born Sept. 27th, 1833. Killed May 31st, 1862, at the Battle of Fair Oaks, Va.

Sgt. WM. R. FINCH

Born Feb. 18th, 1831. Died July 7th, 1863, while in the U. S. service at Baton Rouge, La.

FIREMEN'S MONUMENT, TRINITY CHURCHYARD.

The last hour of the gallant old Volunteers was at hand, and their last duty was marked by disaster to themselves.   On August 21, 1865, several of these brave and devoted citizens were injured by the falling of a wall at Nos. 203 and 205 South Street.   A fire extended from No. 204 South Street to the bonded warehouse of J. J. Hicks at No. 401 Water Street, and the loss amounted to three hundred thousand dollars.   The beloved engines had thrown their last streams, the noble men who had risked their lives for their fellow citizens stood silent and mournful in the station houses.   The ties that had bound them together were broken, and they made way for the New Organization, which is perpetuating their glory, their daring, and their historic self-sacrifice.   The deeds of the Old Volunteers have gone into history and will live forever.

CHAPTER XVIII.

THE GREAT CONFLAGRATION OF 1835.

A Night of Destruction and Terror.—Seventeen Degrees below Zero.—Frozen Rivers and Frozen Engines.—Twenty Million Dollars' Worth of Property Swept Away.—A Mountain of Flame Lighting up the Bay.—Despair of the Citizens.—Gallant Struggles of the Firemen.—Alexander Hamilton's Views.

THE most destructive fire that has visited New York, the third greatest on this continent, needs at least a chapter to itself. The great conflagration of 1835, though of world-wide fame, has never been fully told with all its incidents and all its consequences. It was a terrible day for the first city of the land. The destruction was fearful, and so were the results. In a few months the United States banks suspended payment; then followed the commercial distress of 1837, and for a time business seemed paralyzed. Next came bankruptcy after bankruptcy in quick succession, and soon the banks of the State stopped payment for one year. The legislature legalized this necessary public act. The gloomiest forebodings prevailed, and well they might, considering the terrible reverses which the Empire City experienced from this memorable fire. But if the destruction was so great, the rebuilding and the recovery were no less marvelous. New York quickly arose from her ashes, and acres of splendid granite, marble, brown stone, and brick stores filled the entire space that had been swept by the flames.

Three years before the terrible conflagration of December, 1835, there was a visitation of Asiatic cholera, which had recurred season after season, carrying off numbers of the population, and spreading consternation throughout the city. In the summer of 1835 the epidemic seemed to have exhausted itself, and the harassed people were congratulating themselves upon a bright and happy future when another cloud spread over them to dash their spirits, and misfortune once more drove them almost to despair. The fearfulness of the night was intensified by the depth of the snow, the tempestuousness of the weather, and the extreme bitterness of the cold, for the thermometer was far below zero. And yet our bold, self-sacrificing firemen did their whole duty— did it, too, under the most adverse circumstances. Two nights previous to this disastrous event the men had been on duty at two heavy fires, one at Christie and Delancey Streets, at which some half a dozen buildings were consumed, and the other on Water Street. The latter broke out in a spike and nail establishment belonging to Fullerton & Peckerings, No. 173, which was totally destroyed. When the fire was at its height the side walls fell out, crushing in No. 171, the latter taking fire almost instantly, and was the means of communicating to several others. Seven buildings and two carpenter shops were destroyed. Consequently the firemen came to this biggest of fires almost fagged out.

The flames raged from sixteen to twenty-four hours, swept away six hundred and seventy-four buildings, covering seventeen blocks, and fifty acres of ground, in the very heart of the city. It destroyed the section which contained the banks, the Stock Exchange, the Post Office, two churches, the dry goods warehouses, and some of the finest buildings in the city. The losses were

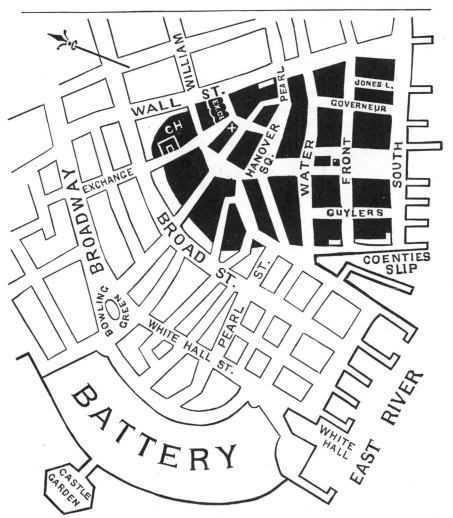

The black blocks are those destroyed by fire. X shows where the fire commenced.

MAP SHOWING BURNED DISTRICT.
[Great Fire of 1835.]

estimated at twenty million dollars, which, in proportion to the size and wealth of the New York of to-day, is equivalent to what two hundred million dollars would represent now. The great fire of 1835 had never had an equal in any English speaking country since the destructive fire of London in 1666.

On Wednesday night, the sixteenth of December, the brazen tongue of the old jail bell, near the City Hall, and other fire bells, rang out their dreadful alarm upon the frosty air. The gusty wind blew the warning sounds east, west, north, and south. Out tumbled the gallant fire laddies, and through the snow-covered streets, assisted by the excited citizens, dragged their engines. A private watchman, Peter A. Holmes, while patrolling his beat, had discovered smoke issuing from the five-story building, No. 25 Merchant Street, which extended through to Pearl Street, and was occupied on the first floor by Comstock & Andrews, fancy dry goods merchants, and the upper part by Henry Barbaud, a French importer. In twenty minutes the flames spread to Exchange Place, then to Water Street, taking both sides of Old Slip and Coenties Slip, then to Beaver, to Jones' Place, to Front and South Streets. The breeze from the N. N. W. amounted almost to a gale. The rivers were frozen solid ; so thick indeed was the ice that the firemen had to cut through it to clear the ends of the pier before they could strike water. Several of the engines were lowered down on the ice and there worked by the men. Every cistern and well was frozen in like manner. As the water from the rivers was pumped into the hose it froze in part and choked the flow. The firemen worked hard, stamping upon the hose to break the ice, and laboring at the pumps. The streams that were thrown by hydrants and engines were blown back in the faces of the toilers, falling congealed at the feet of the firemen. These efforts seemed to add only to the fury of the elements.

Many of the buildings were new storehouses with iron shutters and copper roofs, and so intense was the heat that the metal was melted and ran off the roof in streams. The harbor was lighted up brilliantly, the water looking like a sea of blood. Every spar and every rope in the ships was distinctly visible. Clouds of smoke, like dark mountains suddenly rising into the air, were succeeded by long banners of flame, reaching to the zenith and roaring for their prey. Street after street caught the terrible torrent, until acre after acre was booming an ocean of flame. The Tontine Building (Hudson's News Room), which had a shingle roof, caught fire, and dark smoke in huge masses tinged with flickering flashes of bright flame, burst from all the upper windows. The Tontine was on the north side of Wall Street, and had the flames consumed this building, nothing would have saved the upper part of the city. The old Tontine Coffee House was the exchange of the city, and Buyden, its keeper, is described as a rough but pleasant old fellow. It is related of him that when the first anthracite coal was offered for sale in New York, he tried it in the hall of the Tontine. He pronounced the new article worse than nothing, for he had put one scuttle into the grate and then another, and after they were consumed he took up two scuttlefuls of stones. Two solitary engines, with what little water they managed to obtain, were throwing their feeble and useless streams upon the flaming stores opposite, when Mr. Oliver Hull, calling their attention to the burning cornice of the Tontine, promised to donate one hundred dollars to the Firemen's Fund "if they would extinguish that blaze." In the vicinity was No. 13 Engine, of which Mr. Zophar Mills (who is still living) was foreman. Seeing the danger and knowing that in the ordinary way the hose would not convey the water to the top of the Tontine, Foreman Mills directed his men to get a counter which had been taken out of one of the stores, and to place on the top a gin or brandy puncheon and hold the nozzle so that the water could be thrown on the shingles of the building. By this means the fire was kept under at this point, and the upper part of the city was saved. This was at about four o'clock in the morning, and the cold was so penetrating that it was almost next to impossible to hold the nozzle of the hose in position. Thousands of citizens had flocked to the scene, and their aid was welcome to the tired firemen.

Subsequently there was a controversy as to what company was entitled to the reward for, and honor of, extinguishing the blazing cornice. The dispute was referred to Mr. Hull, the gentleman who offered the reward, who wrote a letter to Mr. Zophar Mills in which he says:

"Other firemen came in to assist from various directions; but the company to whom I spoke, and who piled up the packages on the counter, are, in my estimation, mostly, if not entirely, entitled to the honor of extinguishing the fire. I stood at the corner of Water Street, and observed the whole transaction. Several firemen afterwards called at my store, and stated that they had assisted in preventing the fire from crossing Wall Street at various places, and all of them appeared very much to rejoice in their success in arresting the fire, and seemed desirous to share in the honors. I do not remember which company I paid the money to, but remember that there was some controversy between 8 and 13 as to which was entitled to receive it. But, as it went into the Charitable Fund of the Fire Department, that was not deemed of much consequence. I make this statement with much pleasure, as I consider that we were indebted to the great exertions of our brave fellow citizens the firemen, on that disastrous night, in preventing the fire from crossing Wall Street, thus saving millions of property, and our beautiful city from probably entire ruin."

It was clearly proven at the time that the counter referred to was placed by Engine Company No. 13 upon the sidewalk and an empty liquor cask placed thereon. On the erection thus made Wm. Fitz Randolph held the pipe of Engine No. 13, while Alfred Willis was engaged in raising the hose. The pipe was held at as great an elevation as possible, and by the united force of the company applied to the engine, an unusually strong stream was forced upon the burning cornice. The following certificate was drawn up and signed by witnesses of the action:

We, the undersigned, do hereby certify and declare that we were present at the great fire on the night of the sixteenth of December, 1835, and that we saw the stream of water from the pipe of Fire Engine No. 13 reach and extinguish the fire on the cornice of the Tontine Building which was then in a blaze and burning rapidly.

James S. Leggett, 183 Allen Street; William Fitz Randolph, 36 Cortlandt Street; William H. Patten, 266 Washington Street; Cornelius T. Nostrand, 179 West Street; Isaac Tice, 201 Grand Street; Isaac D. Brown, 10 Peck Slip; Alfred Willis, 36 Cortlandt Street; George D. Jamison, 36 Cortlandt Street; John S. Williams, 169 South Street; Robert S. Barnes, 201 Pearl Street; William S. Moore, 81 Maiden Lane; John Barry, 79 Catharine Street; George Ferguson, Jr., 28 Oak Street; D. Berrien, Jr., 240 Pearl Street; Henry Fourat, 24 Rose Street; John Sutphen, 76 Wall Street; James Whitlock, 24 Eldridge Street; Thomas D. Howe (engineer having the company in charge), 90 Orchard Street.

Onward, still onward, swept the fiery besom of destruction. The hydrants were exhausted—the engines had long been frozen up with their hose. Westward, the South Dutch Church, which had been made the hasty depository of stores of precious goods, was in flames, which threatened to extend to Broad Street throughout. At this supreme moment a man was caught setting fire to the house at the corner of Stone and Broad Streets. Was he a maniac or maddened by liquor? The excited citizens paused not to inquire, but seizing this fiend in human shape lynched him on the spot. On the south a desperate struggle was made at Hanover Square. The firemen had turned their energies to saving property. In that large space was piled an immense amount of goods, thought to be perfectly safe in that spot. There was accumulated the stock of all the French stores, a mass of silks, satins, laces, cartons of dresses, capes, cashmere shawls, and the richest kind of fancy articles, forming a little mountain sixty feet wide by twenty-five feet in height, or nearly one hundred feet square. The large East India warehouse of Peter Remsen & Co., situated on the northeast corner of Hanover Square, was at this moment an object of absorbing interest. It was filled with a full stock of valuable goods. Before the fire reached it goods were cast out of the windows in the upper stories into the street, and with merchandise from the lower floors were piled up with the rest of the large mass in the square. But the warring flames came swiftly on. Just as the goods were stacked a gust of flame, like a streak of lightning, came from the Remsen building, and shooting across the square, blown by the strong wind, set fire to the entire mass. In a few minutes the costly pile was reduced to cinders, it disappeared like figures in a dissolving view, and then the fire was communicated to the houses opposite. Notwithstanding the presence of this mighty furnace, the cold was so intense that the firemen were compelled to take the fine blankets saved, and, cutting a hole through them, convert them into temporary cloaks. In this attire they were seen at daylight dragging home their engines, many of the men so exhausted by fatigue that they were asleep as they walked. One entire company, thus accoutred, had artificial wreaths and bunches of artificial flowers of the richest kind in their caps, taken from the wreck of matter, and presenting a very singular contrast with their begrimed faces and jaded appearance.

It is said the illumination was so great that it was observed at places a hundred miles distant. At one time turpentine which took fire on the wharf ran down into the water and floated off, making a blazing sea many hundred yards square. The shipping in the docks of the East River was endangered, and saved only by strenuous exertions and its removal into the stream. The brig "*Powhattan,*" lying between Murray's Wharf and Coenties Slip, caught fire, but the flames were soon extinguished. No. 33 Engine was run upon the deck of a brig, in order to take the water with her suction, and played into No. 2, which gave her water to No. 13. This last engine (Mr. Zophar Mills's), as already stated, played in the fire at Wall Street. The members of No. 33 Engine, according to Mr. Charles Forrester, "had their own fun on the deck of the brig. The cook on the vessel made a fire in the galley, and six men would get in there and shut the doors, and when they got thawed out a member outside would place his fire cap over the pipe and smoke them out; then a new set would go in, and so it was kept up through the night. The engine did not cease working until daylight, when she stopped for a few seconds, and upon the orders to start again she was found so frozen that they could get no water through her. The company was then ordered home to thaw out."

To depict the scenes of that awful night would require a volume in itself. The surging crowds, the struggle of the police to restrain them, the thousand and one pieces of property rescued from the burning or endangered buildings, and carried hither and thither, the innumerable thefts, the shouts of the assembled thousands, the fights ending in bloodshed, the roar of the flames, and the hoarse creaking of the laboring engines no pen can do adequate justice to. It was a saturnalia for the lawless of the populace. Men, and women too, seized on the cases of wine and barrels of liquor that were thrown about anywhere and everywhere. It is supposed that a thousand baskets of champagne were broken and destroyed, the tops being unceremoniously knocked off, and the contents drunk by the maddened throngs surrounding the fire. An immense quantity of baskets of champagne were seen floating in the docks, and cheese and provisions were scattered there and about the slips. It was soon seen that to save the rest of the city several buildings must be blown up to check the progress of the fire. James Gulick, the hero of the "June Bugs," who was then chief engineer, decided to blow up the houses that were immediately threatened. Chief Engineer Gulick sent for some kegs of gun-

BURNING OF THE MERCHANTS' EXCHANGE.

powder, but a sufficiency could not be obtained in the city—not being allowed as an article of merchandise. Other messengers were sent in hot haste to the fort on Governor's Island, but in vain. Though a most bitter night, a navy barge was despatched, against a head tide, to the magazine at Red Hook, a distance probably of four or five miles from the Yard for a supply of powder.

Then when the first faint streaks of dawn were struggling with the unnatural redness in the sky, a corps of marines arrived with some powder, and the demolition of the buildings began, but it was not till noon of Thursday that the necessary break was made at Coenties Slip. It was truly remarkable, the characteristic *sangfroid* with which the sailors of Captain Mix's party carried about, wrapped up in a blanket or a pea-jacket, as it might happen, kegs and barrels of gunpowder, amid a constant shower of fire, as they followed their officers to the various buildings indicated for destruction. On the north side the extraordinary strength of the Wall Street buildings—many of them resisting firmly the assaults of the destroyer, and none of the walls crumbling and falling into the street, as is too generally the case—did more for the safety of that part of the city than anything within the power of human effort. For hours it was doubtful whether the flames could be resisted here, and, if not, there was little hope that they could be before reaching Maiden Lane.

The advent of the marines and sailors from the Navy Yard had a beneficial effect upon the crowds. The marines, eighty in number, under command of Captain Walker, formed a complete chain of sentinels along South Street, from the Fulton Ferry to Wall Street, and up Wall to the Exchange. They kept their posts all night, and thus afforded great protection to the property exposed. Great prices were offered and given for help in removing goods. One merchant is said to have purchased a horse and cart on the spot for five hundred dollars with which he succeeded in saving his stock. Leary, the hatter, in the midst of the fire gave away hats to any fellow who would help him remove a bundle. To one fellow he gave a hat who handed it back. "What's the matter?" "It doesn't fit," was the saucy reply. "Give me one to fit, if you are giving away hats." Many of the merchants, in the excitement of removing their goods, gave away blankets or anything to poor people who aided them. One poor man had removed several valuable packages to a place of safety. "Here's a coat, a pair of pantaloons, and a blanket for you," said the merchant, handing over the articles.

The violence of the gale continued all night. Burning embers were carried across the East River to Brooklyn, and set fire to the roof of a house, which, however, was speedily extinguished. Mr. John A. Meyers, of One Hundred and Fourth Street, near Ninth Avenue, who celebrated his golden wedding with four generations on February 8, 1886, was then living in a farmhouse on the site of the present Joralemon Street, Brooklyn, said that on the following morning he found the space around his dwelling black with embers flown over from the great fire. The grandest and most inspiring views were from Brooklyn, Weehawken, and Staten Island. Thence the whole city seemed in one awful sheet of flame. The merchants, aided by the firemen and the well-disposed citizens, devoted themselves to removing to places of supposed safety such property as could in their haste be got together. With this intent an immense quantity of goods was placed in the Merchants' Exchange in Wall Street and in the Reformed Dutch Church in Garden Street, where it was presumed they would be secure. But in a short time these buildings with their contents were reduced to ashes. The Exchange was one of the largest edifices in the city, situated on the south side of Wall Street, and embracing one hundred and fifteen feet of the front between William and Hanover Streets. It was three stories high, exclusive of the basement, which was considerably elevated. Its southwest front was one hundred and fourteen feet on Exchange Street. The front on Wall Street was of Westchester marble. The first and second stories of the Ionic order, from the Temple of Minerva Pallas, at Prigue, in Iona; a recessed elliptical portico of forty feet wide introduced in front. A screen of four columns and two antæ, each thirty feet and three feet four inches in diameter above the base, composed of a single block of marble, extended across the foot of the portico, supporting an entablature of six feet in height, on which rested the third story, making a height of sixty feet from the ground. The principal entrance to the rotunda and exchange room was by a flight of ten marble steps, with a pedestal at each end. On ascending to the portico three doors opened to offices. The vestibule was of the Ionic order, from the little Ionic Temple of Illysus. The exchange room, which was the rotunda, was seventy-five feet long, fifty-five feet wide, and forty-five feet high, to which were attached four principal rooms, and in the rear of the rotunda another, used for the auction sales of real estate, shipping, and stocks. The building was begun on the first of April, 1825, and occupied twenty-seven months in its erection, having first been occupied in July, 1827. The plan was that of the architect, Mr. E. Thompson.

This structure long resisted the flames. It did not catch until 2 o'clock on Thursday morning. The end in which the spire pointed to heaven, in the background, was the spot where it was fired. It extended from that point to the cupola and dome. In the centre of the rotunda was erected, by the liberality

RUINS OF MERCHANTS' EXCHANGE AFTER GREAT FIRE OF 1835.
[Rear View.]

of the merchants of the city, a statue of General Alexander Hamilton, sculptured by Ball Hughes. The statue was about 15 feet high, including the base on which it was elevated, and chiselled from the whitest marble. The figure represented him holding a scroll in the left hand, resting on the thigh, and a scarf partly covering the body. For a long time this splendid statue was seen towering brightly amidst the sea of flames that dashed against its crackling base, seeming to cast a mournful glance on the terrific scene. About four o'clock the magnificent dome caved in with an awful crash, one lurid glare ascended to heaven, and then the marble effigy of Hamilton fell nobly, perishing under the crush of the edifice of which it had been, as it were, the tutelary genius. But one gallant effort had been made to save it by a young officer from the Navy Yard with a party of four or five blue jackets. They had actually succeeded in partly removing it from the pedestal when the warning cry was uttered that the roof was about to fall, and they had to seek safety in flight.

Another fine sight was the handsome church of the Rev. Dr. Matthews, in Garden Street. For a long while it withstood the mass of flames in their course towards Broad Street. The church possessed a famous organ. Many and many a solemn dirge had been played upon it at the burial of the dead, and now, the holy temple being on fire, some one commenced performing upon that organ its own funeral dirge and continued it till the lofty ceiling was in a blaze. The music ceased, and in a short time the beautiful edifice, with its noble instrument and immense quantities of goods stored inside and out, were all irrecoverably gone, nothing escaping save the long-sleeping dust and bones of the buried dead. Above the church the bright gold ball and star on the highest point of the spire gleamed brilliantly, and still, while they were both shining on the deep blue concave with an intensity of splendor which attracted general remark, gave one surge and fell in all their glory into the heap of chaos beneath them.

On the following day the heart of the city seemed to have ceased to beat. Of business there was none ; New York was stricken as with paralysis. From five to ten thousand persons had been thrown out of employment, and universal sorrow prevailed. The people gathered in their thousands around the smoking ruins and sadly thought of the many families whose daily bread was gone. Swiftly flew the news to other cities, and sympathy of a practical kind was the response. The same locomotive that early on Thursday morning carried the tidings of the fire to Newark brought to the city within an hour afterwards the New Jersey engines, which at once went to work. The conduct of the Philadelphia firemen was noble. Immediately on the receipt of the intelligence from New York 400 of them organized themselves and started to come on. Unfortunately, by the breaking down of one of the cars on the railroad, a large number of them were obliged to go back, but some arrived early on Saturday morning, and the remainder followed with as little delay as possible. Stations were assigned them amid the ruins, and they went to work with great spirit and excellent results. On the succeeding nights, patrol duty was done by the Third and Ninth Regiments and the light infantry companies. Civic patrols were also formed in several wards, and thus property to a great amount was saved from depredation. Large quantities of merchandise, carried off in boats on Wednesday night were secreted on the Long Island and Jersey shores and in the upper wards of the city.

The scene at Police Headquarters was indeed heartrending. The squalid misery of a greater part of those taken with the goods in their possession, the lies and prevarications to which they resorted to induce the magistrates not to commit them to prison, their screeching and wailing when they found they must relinquish the splendid prizes they had made during the raging of the fire, and the numbers in which they were brought by the police and military, exceeded any scene of a similiar kind on record. For the previous three days and nights every place capable of detention was crammed with these miserable objects—sometimes as many as one hundred being in confinement at the same moment. Hundreds were discharged without detention or other punishment than merely taking from them their plunder ; and but very few of the whole number, even those who had stolen hundreds of dollars' worth, could be convicted, in consequence of the impossibility of the identification of the property stolen.

Mr. James Gordon Bennett, the elder, was then, by his characteristic enterprise and liberality, building up his paper, the *Herald*. In his issue of December 18 he gives the following graphic description of his visit to the ruins on the morning following the fire:

"At nine o'clock yesterday morning I went to see the awful scene. It was heartrending in the extreme. I walked down William Street. Crowds of people of both sexes were wandering in the same direction. It was piercing cold, and every other person had a woollen comforter wrapped around his neck. On approaching the corner of Wall and William Streets the smoking ruins were awful. The whole of the southern side of Wall Street was nearly down. The front walls of the Exchange were in part remaining, covered with smoke and exhibiting the effects of the fire. The splendid marble columns were cracked in several parts. The street was full of people, the sidewalks encumbered with boxes, bales, bundles, desks, safes and loose articles. There was no possibility of then proceeding further down William Street. Both sides were burned down and the streets were filled up with hot bricks, burning goods and heaps of rubbish. United States soldiers were stationed here and there to protect the goods, yet the boys, men and women, of all colors, were stealing and pilfering as fast as they could. From this spot I proceeded down Wall Street in the center. I saw the *Journal of Commerce* sign—all the rest gone. The various brokers' offices to the right were a heap of ruins. The Josephs, the Allens, the Livingstons and various others, all in ruins. From the Exchange down to the river, one side of Wall Street is a heap of ruins.

"On going down Wall Street I found it difficult to get through the crowd. The hose of the fire engines was run along the street and frozen. The front blocks of houses between Exchange Place and Pearl Street, on Wall, were standing, behind which were all ruin and desolation. At the corner of Wall and Pearl, on looking southwardly, I saw a single ruin standing about half way to Hanover Square. I proceeded, climbing over the hot bricks, on the site, as I thought, of Pearl Street—but of that I am not sure—till I got to the single, solitary wall that reared its head as if it was in mockery of the elemental war. On approaching I read on the mutilated granite wall, "Arth— Tap —n, 122 Pe—l Street." These were all the characters I could distinguish on the column. Two stories of this great wall were standing—the rest entirely in ruins. It was the only portion of a wall standing from the corner of Wall Street to Hanover Square; for beyond that there are nothing but smoke and fire and dust.

"Proceeding along on the ruins, sometimes on Pearl Street, sometimes out of it, I found several groups of boys and men digging among the hot dust and bricks. 'What are they doing?' 'Damn them,' said he, 'they are looking for money. Some of them have found gold pieces and others franc pieces.' 'Hillo?' cried a dirty looking little fellow, 'I have got something.' In several other places there were small groups of pilferers and thieves. In the center of Hanover Square I found a variety of goods and merchandise burning. Several men and boys were warming themselves at a fire made of fine French calicoes and Irish linens. Here the smoke was intense. From Hanover Square I could neither proceed south, east nor west. William Street, Pearl and down to the wharf were all impassable. The smoke was suffocating. The whole of the space between the corner of William and Pearl up to the Exchange, with all the streets, stores, etc., I saw to be a sad heap of utter ruins. ' Good God !' said a man to me, ' what a sight !' ' What a sight, truly !' said I. From this spot, near the *Gazette* office which was entirely burned down, I returned the way I came, climbing over burning bricks, knocking against boys, encountering bales and boxes, till I again reached a firm footing in Wall Street. I then proceeded down the nothern side of Wall Street to the wharf below. The crowd of spectators was greater here than ever. The street was full of boxes and goods. I felt quite cold. I saw a large group of men stirring up a fire in the center of Wall Street, between Water and Front, which is here wide. On going near to warm myself I found the fire was made out of the richest merchandise and fine furniture from some of the elegant counting rooms.

" I proceeded to Hudson's News Room, which escaped, having been on the windward side of Wall Street. I could not find an entrance. It was full of goods and bales of merchandise. I proceeded to the corner of Wall and Front Streets. Here I saw a horrible scene of desolation. Looking down South Street toward the south nothing could be seen but awful ruins. People were standing shaking their heads and stamping their feet—still quite cold—and uttering melancholy exclamations. A small boy at the corner was caught by an honest black porter stealing some goods. ' What are you going to do with that ?' asked the porter. ' Nothing,' said the boy. ' Then lay it where you found it and go to the watch house with me.' The rascal attempted to escape. He cried out. ' Let the scoundrel go !' said a gentlemen, and straightway the honest black man gave him a kick and let him run.

" From the corner of Wall Street I proceeded southwardly, for I cannot now talk of streets ; all their sites are buried in ruins and smoking bricks. No vessels lay here at the wharves ; all were gone. I went down the wharf ; the basin was floating with calicoes, silks, teas, packing cases, and other valuable merchandise. Piles of coarse linen and sacking encumbered the street. The carts were busy driving the mutilated goods away. Going a little further south, on what was formerly Front Street, I encountered a cloud of smoke that burst from a smoking pile of stores. I was almost suffocated. Emerging from this sirocco I found myself near a group of boys and ragged men huddling round a fire made of some curious species of fuel. All around appeared to be large heaps of small dust. The fragrance was fine. I asked one of the boys, ' What is that ?' ' Tea, sir,' said he, with perfect nonchalance ; ' fine Hyson tea ; doesn't it make a fine fire ? Come, Jack, throw in a little more of that fuel,' and sure enough he did. A fire was hissing away, made out of tea boxes and fine Hyson tea itself. Several little dirty girls were here gathering up Hyson tea and putting it away in baskets. Proceeding further, I encountered hogsheads of raw sugar, half emptied, and their contents strewed, like the Hyson tea, over the pavements and bricks. Boys and girls were eating it as fast as they could.

" I could not get further than a short distance down Front from the corner of Wall. The smoke, ruin, hot bricks, and all were too horrible to get over or through. Retracing my steps, I returned up Wall Street. The same scenes presented themselves to me. The crowds were immense. Carts, porters, merchants, brokers, bankers, women, children crowded from Front to the bottom of Wall Street. I passed the solitary columns of the Exchange, I

under the corner of Broad Street, and attempted in that direction to reach
the southwest part of the scene of conflagration. All Broad Street was
crowded with goods, merchandise, carts, porters, and crowds. I attempted
several times to thread my way down to the wharf at the foot of Broad Street.
I could not do it. From the center of this street, looking to the left over the
buildings in the direction of William, I saw nothing but flames ascending to
heaven, and prodigious clouds of smoke curling after it as if from a volcano.
Emerging from Broad Street I went up by a narrow street to the Bowling
Green. Here was deposited on the sidewalks half a million of fine goods.
The whole street was lined. Clerks were standing around the several piles
watching them. I went down Whitehall Slip. It was equally crowded with
rich merchandise. One whole end of the Battery was covered with the richest
silks, sarsnets, brocades, and woollen cloths. The plunderers were here quiet.

RUINS OF MERCHANTS' EXCHANGE AFTER FIRE OF 1835.
[Front View.]

busy. Several were caught, and sent to the watchhouse. I turned the corner
at the southern end of South Street, and wended my way along the wharves
in the direction of Coenties Slip. I found all the merchants in Front Street
busy removing their goods.

"On reaching the corner of Front Street and Coenties Slip the most awful
scenes burst upon my eyes. I beheld the several blocks of seven story stores,
full of rich merchandise, on the northern side of the slip, in one bright, burning, horrible flame. About forty buildings were on fire at one moment. The
front on the slip was piled up with goods. 'What nonsense!' said the people,
'the goods will burn up also.' Here the crowd was immense. All the upper
part of the slip on the northern and eastern side was burning or burned up. At
the southern corner of Pearl and Coenties Slip it was just passable. All to the

the right was on fire, and every store back to Broad Street it was feared would go. Pushing through the crowd, I attempted to get back to Broad Street through Pearl. It was hardly possible, so much was the street encumbered with goods, crowds, and carts.

"From this point I retreated up Broad Street through an immense crowd to the Custom House, to which the Post-office had retreated. Here I found a few of the Post-office clerks in an apartment leading from Pine Street, all in an awful state of confusion. They scarcely knew what they had lost or saved, and could not tell when the mails would be ready. On falling in with several of our most respectable citizens, I said, 'Awful! horrible!' 'Truly, truly,' said they, 'we are all ruined; I have two sons gone; each of their stores is burned down. The insurance companies will not be able to pay five shillings in the pound. New York is bankrupt. New York is put twenty years back. Philadelphia and Boston will now start ahead of us.' 'What shall be done?' asked I. 'Shall we not go to war with France?' 'Tush! tush!' said he. 'The surplus revenue ought to pay for this night's work. We paid it to the government—let them give it back to us; we are ruined and bankrupt.'

"There were five hundred stores destroyed. Many of them were worth three hundred thousand dollars. Put them at forty thousand dollars each average, and we have a loss of twenty million dollars—the probable truth. To cover this loss there are twenty-six insurance companies in operation with a capital of nine million four hundred and fifty thousand dollars. Probably two-thirds of this is good for the losses—say six millions. Add two millions insured in Boston and elsewhere, makes eight millions of insurance, which, all paid, leaves a dead loss of twelve millions of dollars to individual merchants and owners of real estate. Some of the oldest families in the city are ruined."

Of the six large morning newspapers only two escaped the general wreck— the *Mercantile* and the *Courier and Enquirer*. The *Daily Advertiser*, *Journal of Commerce*, and *Gazette* were burned out of both printing and publication offices; the *Times* of printing office only. The *American* among the evening papers was entirely destroyed. All Mr. Minor's periodicals, *Railroad Journal*, *Mechanics' Magazine*, etc. etc., were included in the wreck. The printers of the *Knickerbocker* also. The following were the number of buildings destroyed on each street:

Water	41	Old Slip	33
South	37	Jones' Lane	10
Front	80	Gouverneur Lane	20
William	44	Exchange Place	62
Beaver	23	Exchange Street	31
Stone	60	Guyless Alley	20
Mill	38	Hanover Square	3
Pearl	70	Merchant Street	25
Hanover	10		
Coenties Slip	10	Total	674

Arthur Tappan & Co. escaped the absolute ruin in which so many were involved. Their store being of stone, and having window shutters of thick boiler iron (put on after the mobs of 1834), withstood the flames for nearly an hour, while all was in a blaze around it, so that the books and papers, and a very large amount of goods, probably one hundred thousand dollars' worth, were carried out, and after two removes placed beyond the spread of fire. The energy and daring with which the colored people pressed to save these goods greatly impressed the bystanders. It was with difficulty they were restrained from rushing in after the flames had burst out at the door.

Arthur Tappan had an insurance effected on his store and goods to the amount of three hundred thousand dollars at one of the Boston offices. No office in New York City would insure him because he was an abolitionist.

On the second night after the conflagration a couple of gentlemen observed a stout woman making up Pearl street, near the corner of Wall street, with a large bundle under her cloak. When she saw the gentlemen looking at her, she immediately commenced singing "Hush-a-by, baby," etc. The gentlemen, thinking that the poor baby was quite worrisome, offered their aid to quiet its infant restlessness. "Oh, bless your honors, she's asleep now." The gentlemen still persisted in having a peep at the blooming little cherub. She resisted, but in vain. On opening the cloak, they found that the dear little creature, in the terror of the moment, had actually changed into an armful of the richest silk and satin goods, slightly burnt at the ends. The affectionate mother was immediately secured.

During the fire a store was burnt in which was contained eight hundred thousand pounds of lead, belonging to a merchant in Philadelphia. After the fire was over, and the rubbish removed, it was found that the lead had melted into large masses, so that the owner was obliged to *quarry* it out.

The quantity of French goods destroyed was very great. Out of twenty-seven French importing merchants, twenty-three had been completely burned out. There were only four left in the city, and of these, but one of any magnitude—H. Boerdam & Co. French goods advanced twelve per cent. About twelve hundred packages of Manchester print goods were alone destroyed in Exchange Place, commonly called Calico Row. Of linens, also, a large quantity had been destroyed. Stephen Whitney lost $500,000 in houses and real estate; John Suydam, probably $200,000 in stores and insurance stocks. Out of $200,000 in insurance stocks, Dr. Hasack, who died four days after, only saved $20,000. About ten crockery stores were completely destroyed, and also nine or ten hardware. The McNeals, of Salem, were the losers of the great cargo of tea in the store of Osborne & Young. On Tuesday, the day before the fire, they were offered $60,000 profit on the whole cargo. They said to their supercargo, "Shall we take it?" "I would advise you not," said he. "You can, by keeping it a month, make $200,000." They did so, and lost the whole. After the fire the supercargo recalled the conversation and regretted it. "No," said they, "it is all for the best. Providence knows better than you do. It might have been bought by some one that could not bear the loss so well as we can." Noble fellows! Probably about four thousand boxes of sugar of all kinds had been destroyed, and at least forty thousand bags of coffee. On Old Slip there were piled up at least five thousand bags.

Gabriel P. Disosway, of the firm of Disosway & Brothers, 180 Pearl Street, near Maiden Lane, writing some years after the occurence, has given one of the best accounts of the fire. "I then resided in that pleasant Quaker neighborhood, Vandewater Street," said he, "and, hearing an alarm of fire, hastened to the front door. I put on an old warm overcoat and an old hat for active service on my own hook. Years afterwards these articles, preserved as curiosities, bore marks of the heat, sparks and exposure of that fearful time. . .

My own course that night was to obtain voluntary aid, and, entering the stores of personal friends, remove, if possible, books and papers. . . It is impossible to imagine the fervent heat created by the increasing flames. Many of the stores were new, with iron shutters, doors and copper roofs and gutters, 'fireproof' of first-class, and I carefully watched the beginning and the progress of their destruction. The heat alone at times melted the copper roofing, and the burning liquid ran off in great drops. At one store, near Arthur Tappan & Co.'s, I warned some firemen of their danger from this unexpected source. Along here, the buildings were of the first-class, and one after another ignited under the roof, from the next edifice. Downward from floor to floor went the devouring element. As the different stories caught, the iron closed shutters shone with glowing redness, until at last forced open by the uncontrollable enemy. Within, they presented the appearance of immense iron furnaces in full blast. The tin and copper bound roofs often seemed struggling to maintain their fast hold, gently rising and falling and moving until, their rafters giving way, they mingled in the blazing crater below of goods, beams, floors and walls.

"On the north side of Hanover Square stood the fine storehouse of Peter Remsen & Co., one of the largest East India firms, with a valuable stock. Here we assisted, and many light bales of goods were thrown from the upper windows, together with a large amount of other merchandise, all heaped in the midst of the square, then thought to be a perfectly secure place. . . . Water Street, too, was on fire, and we hastened to the old firm of S. B. Harper & Sons, grocers in Front Street, opposite Gouverneur Lane, where there appeared to be no immediate danger. The father and sons had arrived, and we succeeded in removing their valuables. As we left the store after the last load a terrible explosion occured near by with the noise of a cannon. The earth shook. We ran for safety, not knowing what might follow, and took refuge on the corner of Gouverneur Lane, nearly opposite. Waiting for a few minutes a second explosion took place, then another and another. During the space perhaps of half an hour shock after shock followed in rapid succession, accompanied with the darkest, thickest clouds of smoke imaginable. The explosions came from a store on Front Street, near Old Slip, where large quantities of saltpeter in bags had been stored. Suddenly the whole ignited, and out leaped the flaming streams of these neutral salts, in their own peculiar colors, from every door and window. Some might have called them fireworks. . . . One of the most grand and frightful scenes of the whole night was the burning of a large oil store at the corner of Old Slip and South Street. It was four or more stories high, and filled with windows on both sides without any shutters. This was before the days of petroleum and kerosene, and the building was full of sperm and other oils. These fired hogshead after hogshead, and over the spacious edifice resembled a vast bonfire or giant beacon, casting its bright beams far and wide on the river and surrounding region, but finally the confined inflammable mass from eaves to cellar shot out with tremendous force through every window and opening, and soon all disappeared except the cracked, tottering, and falling walls. . . . I sought the premises of Burns, Halliburton & Co., one of the most popular firms of that day. They were the agents of the Merrimac and other works, and had an immense valuable stock of calicoes, muslins, and flannels. In one of the upper lofts I met a member of the firm, Mr. Burns, one of nature's noblemen, since dead, with his other partners, and he was weeping. 'Too hard,' said he, 'after all the toil of years, to see property thus suddenly destroyed!' 'Cheer up,' we replied, 'the world is still wide enough for success and fortune,' and so it proved to him and many other sufferers.

"From Maiden Lane to Coenties Slip, and from William street to the East River, the whole immense area, embracing some 13 acres, all in a raging uncontrollable blaze! To what can we compare it? An ocean of fire, as it were, with roaring, rolling, burning waves, surging onward and upward, and spreading certain universal destruction; tottering walls and falling chimneys, with black smoke, hissing, clashing sounds on every side. Something like this, for we cannot describe it, was the fearful prospect, and soon satisfied with the alarming, fearful view, we retreated from our high lookout.

"Not long after we left our high standpoint it was enveloped in the universal blaze, and soon the Garden Street Church, with its spire, organ, and heaps of goods stored within and out side, was consumed. There, too, was lost the venerable bell which had been removed at an early period in New York history from the old St. Nicholas Church within the present Battery. 'What more can be done to stop the progress of the flames?' became the anxious and general inquiry. Mr. Cornelius W. Lawrence, the Mayor, appeared with his officers, and, after consultation, it was determined to blow up some buildings, and the east corner of Coenties Slip and Coenties Lane (a narrow street) was selected as the proper place to begin the necessary work. On the opposite was the store of William Van Antwerp & Co., hardware dealers and relatives of the writer, who, engaged at this point in saving goods, could see the necessary

OLD POST-OFFICE BELL TOWER.

preparations for the blast. The building to be blown up, I think, was occupied by Wyncoop & Co., grocers. It was large and of brick. Colonel Smith soon arrived with the powder, and a gang of officers and sailors from the Navy Yard, and none else were permitted to interfere. They commenced mining in the cellar, and, placing heavy timbers upon the powder kegs and against beams of the floors, everything was soon ready for the explosion. A friend near by said to an old tar, 'Be careful or you will be blown up!' 'Blow and be ——!' was the careless and characteristic reply to the warning; but, all having been admirably and safely arranged, the crowd retreated. The torch was applied, and in an instant the report followed; then the immense mass heaved up as if by magic, and losing its fastenings, from the cellar to the roof, tottered, shook and fell. A shout went up from the gazing spectators, and at this point the common danger was evidently arrested, thanks to Colonel Swift, Lieutenant Reynolds, and Captain Mix of the Navy and their noble, brave sailors. Heroism can be as much displayed at a terrible catastrophe of this kind as on the bloody field of battle, and it was to-night. This party of miners arrived about 2 o'clock in the morning, when their important work commenced. They continued it successfully in another direction; indeed, it was believed that the conflagration was at last checked by this blowing up of the buildings.

"Wearied with watching, labor and anxiety, thousands wished for the return of day, and at length a dim, increasing light in the east, but enshrouded with dull, heavy clouds of smoke, foretold the coming morning. And what an unexpected, melancholy spectacle to thousands did New York present! The generous firemen from Philadelphia soon after made their appearance, but the fire had been checked. The immense remains continued to blaze and burn for many days. We could now travel around the bounds of the night's destruction, but no living being could venture through them.   Many a merchant living in the upper section of the city went quietly to bed that night, and strange as it may seem, when he came down town the next morning, literally could not find his store, not enough of his stock remaining to cover his head—every yard, ell, pound, gone! There were official statements of several stores, in each of which a quarter of a million dollars in goods was consumed, with books, notes, and accounts. New York the next day sat, as it were, in sackcloth and ashes, and real sorrow began to appear on men's faces as the losses and ruin were discovered by the light of day.

"During the conflagration, then under full headway toward Broad Street, the presence of mind of one man saved much property. This was Downing, the oyster king, of Broad Street fame. Water was out of the question, and at this emergency he thought of his supplies of vinegar, which were large, and with careful application by pailful after pailful a large amount of property was saved in that direction from the general destruction.

"In the estimated thirteen acres of the burned district only one store escaped entire. This was occupied by the well-known John A. Moore of this day in the iron trade on Water Street, near Old Slip. Watched inside, and fire proof, in their wildest career the rapid flames seemed, as it were, to overleap the building, destroying all others. There it stood solitary and alone amidst surrounding entire destruction, as a sad monument stands alone amid the general ruin."

Among those who were deeply affected by this calamitous fire was the celebrated Colonel Alexander Hamilton. Colonel Hamilton wrote the following letter in reference to the fire to the *Mercantile Advertiser and New York Advocate:*

In the anxious state of the public mind will you permit me to suggest a few reflections, which appear to me not unworthy the attention of those who hold important stations controlling the destinies of the community. In the first place, it is not necessary to magnify the distressful consequences of the disastrous conflagration, in which we have all, rich and poor, a most painful subject of contemplation. The evil is not without its remedy, and in such a community as ours it cannot be of long endurance. The common inquiries are everywhere heard, "What is to be done?" "Where is the mischief to end?" "From what quarter are we to look for assistance?" To all which interrogations the answer is readily suggested, by a recurrence to the immense pecuniary ability of the country, which, if wisely administered, cannot fail to afford immediate relief. In the onset, it is important that our insurance companies and our banking institutions should, in their respective capacities, create conservative committees to ascertain the losses which they have actually sustained, and their means of meeting them. These are certainly necessary preliminary steps, and essentially important. This being determined on, it will then be advisable that application should be made to Congress to place at the disposal of our State government whatever amount of money it may judge proper to employ in order to administer to the urgent wants of this crisis. The necessity of some legislative interference cannot be questioned, and if promptly given when the legislature meets in January, the benignant influence of confi-

FIRE OF 1835.
[From Coenties Slip.]

dence will be generally felt. In order to extend assistance the State Treasury should be authorized to loan on all the good securities, bonds and mortgages, etc., in the possession of the insurance companies, to afford them an immediate opportunity to pay the amount of their indebtedness on their policies of insurance, without which they will have to depend on the dilatory course of law, and, in the operation, necessarily increase the distress by extending the embarrassment to others, and thus, independent of the procrastination, defeat the very object in contemplation. In the panic of 1832 the Bank of England advanced on title deeds, bonds and mortgages, etc., with a promptness and vigor at once honorable to that noble institution and to the government which sanctioned the assumption of such a responsibility. These negotiations were made on the character of the applicants, free from all petty cavilling, which saved Great Britain from bankruptcy. It was a measure full of patriotism, intelligence, and worthy the occasion. If, then, the Governor of the State of New York will promptly enter into a correspondence with the United States Treasury to produce an immediate action on the part of Congress, suggesting that in his annual message he will recommend to the Legislature to interpose its credit for the general relief of the public, there can be no doubt that an appropriation will be immediately made. The commercial community will instantly recommence business, the fiscal operations of the country will assume their wonted activity, and the whole community will soon feel the invigorating influence of restoring order and system in place of alarm and chaos.

Is it to be credited that a country which has realized hundreds of millions within the last three years, with its public credit undoubted, should relapse from its high state of prosperity by the deduction of less than twenty million dollars' worth of property? That this will be found the maximum of the loss, I entertain no doubt. The stock of goods in store at this season of the year is well known to be small, and it is equally a fact that a very limited amount of the spring orders have as yet been executed. The open policies of insurance on goods will be found on investigation to attach to valid claims disproportioned to the general apprehension. To make this investigation the more complete, a general insurance committee should be organized, of active, intelligent merchants, of sufficient numbers to appoint adequate sub-committees to make strict inquiries to enable them to compare evidences.

It is necessary that promptness of action should be pursued; every delay but increases the embarrassment, and renders the palliative more difficult of application.

At the public meeting which takes place this evening let the Mayor be requested to address the executive of this State, asking him immediately to enter into a correspondence with our representatives, desiring them to bring this interesting subject, important to the United States, instantly before the National Government, and to solicit him to recommend to the legislature to interpose its credit to procure the only prompt relief which the nature of the case will admit. In the meantime, there can be no doubt as to the course proper for our banks to pursue, which the intelligent gentlemen comprising their direction well know how to apply. In short, a discreet forbearance on the part of the banks, and the prompt action of the Government, will save many of the individuals implicated, relieve the community from further distress, and eventually give new vigor to our commercial enterprise, the vital spirit of our national prosperity.

ALEXANDER HAMILTON.

CHAPTER XIX.

GUNPOWDER CHECKS THE FLAMES.

Ravages of the Great Fire.—Graphic Description by Eye-Witnesses.—Insurance Companies Bankrupted.—
Terror and Dismay.—The Fairest Portion of the City in Ruins.—Action of the Authorities.—
Arrival of Philadel hia Firemen.

A PUBLIC meeting, to express sympathy, took place in the City Hall at noon on December 19. The assemblage was called to order by Judge Irving, upon whose motion the mayor took the chair. The following gentlemen were then appointed vice-presidents on the motion of General Prosper M. Wetmore: Albert Gallatin, Preserved Fish, Louis McLane, George Newbould, Isaac Bronson, Enos T. Throop, Campbell P. White, John T. Irving, Samuel Hicks, George Griswold, James G. King, Benjamin L. Swan, Jacob Lorillard, and Stephen Allen. On motion of General Jacob Morton, the following secretaries were also appointed: Jonathan Goodhue, Prosper M. Wetmore, John S. Crary, John A. Stephens, Jacob Harvey, Reuben Withers, Dudley Selden, Samuel B. Ruggles, George Wilson, Samuel Cowdrey, James Lee, and John L. Graham. The meeting was addressed by Samuel L. Stone, Prosper M. Wetmore and several other prominent citizens, after which the following resolutions were, on motion of James G. King, unanimously adopted:

Resolved, That while the citizens of New York lament over the ruin which has left desolate the most valuable part of this city, and deeply sympathize with the numerous sufferers, it becomes them not to repine, but to unite in a vigorous exertion to repair the loss, that the extent of her commerce, wealth, and enterprise of her citizens justify, under the blessing of Divine Providence, a primary reliance upon her own resources.

Resolved, That we consider it the duty of our citizens and moneyed institutions, who stand in the relation of creditors to those who have directly or indirectly suffered by the late fire, to extend to them the utmost forbearance and lenity.

On motion of Dudley Selden, it was further

Resolved, That a committee of the Mayor and one hundred and fifty citizens be appointed to ascertain the extent and probable value of the property destroyed, and how far the sufferers are protected by insurance. Also with power to make application to Congress for relief by an extension of credit for debts due to the United States, and a return of remission of duties on goods destroyed, and also to ask such other aid from the general state and city governments as may be deemed expedient. Also to ascertain the origin and cause of the fire, and what change, if any, should be made either in the regulating of streets, the erection of buildings, or the arrangements of the Fire Department, to prevent a recurrence of similar calamities, and take such other measures as the emergency may demand.

Resolved, That the committee to be appointed take the earliest and most effectual measures to ascertain and relieve the necessities of those who have been reduced to want by the recent unfortunate event.

On motion of Colonel Murray, it was also

Resolved, That the thanks of this meeting be and they are hereby tendered to the citizens of Philadelphia and Newark for the spontaneous expression of their sympathy in our misfortunes, and that they be especially tendered to the firemen of those cities who, with a promptitude and kindness unexampled, have left their homes at this inclement season to offer their services, and which they are now tendering at the scene of the calamity.

On motion of Prosper M. Wetmore it was finally resolved that the member, of the two Boards of the Common Council be *ex officio* members of the committee to be appointed. The committee, the names of whose members are well-known to-day, was then announced as follows:

Cornelius W. Lawrence, Albert Gallatin, Preserved Fish, Samuel Hicks, Benjamin L. Swan, Dudley Selden, Jonathan Goodhue, Saul Alley, Prosper M. Wetmore, John T. Irving, John Pintard, George Newbould, Samuel B. Ruggles, Jas. G. King, William B. Astor, George Griswold, Enos T. Throop, Samuel Cowdrey, Thomas J. Oakley, George Wilson, Wm. T. McCown, John G. Coster, Walter Bowne, James F. Boorman, Louis McLane, Jacob Lorillard, John S. Crary, Jacob Harvey, Reuben Withers, Ogden Hoffman, Charles King, Edward Sanford, John W. Leavitt, Adam Treadwell, John Leonad,, Geo. G. Robbins, Wm. Neilson, Stephen Whitney, Joseph Bouchand, Jacob Morton, John Wilson, Mordecai M. Noah, Philip Hone, Wm. L. Stone, Rensselaer Havens, Charles W. Sanford, W. Van Wyck, D. F. Manice, John Kelly, H. C. De Rham, Isaac Bronson, Campbell B. White, John A. Stevens, James Lee, Geo. Douglas, Stephen Allen, John Fleming, John B. Lawrence, Wm. B. Townsend, Charles H. Russell, James Heard, Charles Graham, Geo. Ireland, John Y. Cobra, Samuel Jones, Charles Augustus Davis, Robert C. Wetmore, James D. P. Ogden, Andrew Warner, David Hall, James Conner, Robert White, Richard Parnell, Joseph Blunt, Samuel Ward, F. B. Cutting, John H. Howland, John Lang, Daniel Jackson, J. Palmer, Richard Riker, James Roosevelt, Jr., Jas. Munroe, Richard McCarthy, Isaac S. Hone, Peter A. Jay, Amos Butler, Joseph D. Beers, David Bryson, Samuel Swartwout, Walter R. Jones, Philo L. Mills, Morris Robinson, Benjamin McVickar, John Haggerty, Charles Dennison, Geo. W. Lee, Wm. Churchill, Geo. Lovett, G. A. Worth, Edwin Lord, B. L. Woolley, Wm. Mitchell, Burr Wakeman, Wm. Leggett, James B. Murray, Peter A. Cowdrey, John L. Graham, Geo. D. Strong, Jonathan Lawrence, Cornelius Heyer, James Lawson, Samuel S. Howland, James Watson Webb, Wm. M. Price, John Delafield, Jas. McCride, M. M. Quackenboss, B. M. Brown, Wm. B. Crosby, G. C. Verplanck, Wm. Beach Lawrence, Joseph L. Josephs, S. H. Foster, T. T. Kissam, Robert Bogardus, Wm. Howard, Luman Reed, Robert Smith, M. Ulshoeffer, Samuel Thompson, Robert C. Cornell, P. G. Stuyvesant, David Hadden, Benjamin Strong, Wm. P. Hall, Isaac Townsend, Charles P. Clinch, Rufus L. Lord, J. R. Satterlee, David S. Jones, David Austin, Seth Geer, Robert Lenox, Perez Jones, Wm. Turner.

Scarcely had this committee been appointed, when a communication was received from the president of the Board of Trade announcing the names of a committee from that body to co-operate in the objects of the meeting. On motion of Mr. P. M. Wetmore it was resolved that the following gentlemen, deputed from the Board of Trade, be added to the above committee: Gabriel P. Disosway, Robert Gaffrey, Silas Brown, N. H. Weed, George Underhill, D. A. Cushman, Meigs D. Benjamin, Marcus Wilbur, and Thomas Denny.

An investigation was commenced on December 23 (Wednesday) and carried on in the grand jury room on Monday, before Col. Murray, the Chairman of the Committee of Citizens, aided by Justice Lownds, and Messrs. Ward and Jordan, of the Fire Committee of the Board of Assistant Aldermen, relative to the origin and cause of the fire. From a mass of testimony received from numerous merchants, clerks and others, under oath, it appeared to be incontrovertibly established that the fire originated in the store No. 25 Merchant street, and that it was seen simultaneously in the first and fourth stories of that building, occupied by Messrs. Comstock & Andrews, the two intermediate stories occupied on the Pearl street side by Mr. Henry Barbaud, that a report like an explosion of a gas pipe was heard in No. 25 to proceed from No. 28, and soon after the flames seemed to have been enkindled on the first floor, and

ST. PAUL'S CHURCH, 1775.

shot up with the rapidity of lightning through the scuttles in the several floors to the upper story and through the roof. It was the opinion of the committee that it must have been produced by the bursting of a gas pipe, and the distribution of the gas, until it came in contact with the coal in the stove or grate, by which it was ignited. The store No. 25 had been closed a little after five o'clock, and the fires well secured to guard against any accident or injury therefrom. This was the result of a long and critical investigation, and proved that no blame attached to any one.

The Board of Assistant Aldermen held a meeting on the seventeenth of December, 1835. There were present Messrs. Clark, Cleavland, Townsend, Curtis, Brady, Paulding, Greenfield, Jordan, Ingraham, Whitney, Clinch, Stewart, Power and Ward.

The President, James R. Whitney, being absent, on motion of Mr. Townsend, Mr. Ingraham was called to the chair. The following message was received from his honor the mayor:

Mayor's Office, New York, December 17, 1835. Gentlemen of the Common Council: I have requested your meeting this afternoon for the purpose of taking such measures as you may deem necessary for the protection of the immense amount of property exposed to the dreadful conflagration of last night. I propose that the watch be doubled, which will give about three hundred additional guard, and that the mayor accept the volunteer aid of one thousand citizens, together amounting to thirteen hundred. I deem it essential that the property now exposed should be protected as far as practicable. So large a number of citizens in the streets would be likely to notice any appearance of fire, and would doubtless' in case of need, be prepared to aid the firemen in the discharge of their arduous duties.

I need not refer to the occurrences of last night, and to the valuable services rendered by our citizens, but I feel it my duty to acknowledge the aid furnished by Commodore Ridgely and the active personal services of Captain Mix, Lieutenant Nicholas, and the officers, seamen

and marines under their command.   Our acknowledgments are also due to Lieutenant
Temple, of the United States Artillery, and to Geo. Swift.

In conclusion I would suggest to your consideration the propriety of inviting a meeting
of the citizens to consider the emergency in which our business community is placed, and
to devise such measures as may be proper for remedying, as far as possible, the effects of the
serious calamity by which our city has been visited.   If it be the desire of the Common
Council, I will, under your authority, invite the citizens to meet at such time and place as
may appear to be expedient.   C. W. LAWRENCE.

After reading the above message, the chairman offered the following resolutions, which were unanimously adopted, and sent to the Board of Aldermen for
concurrence :

By Mr. Ingraham—*Resolved*, That during the present emergency his honor the Mayor
be invested with full power to employ such additional aid, either to the police watch,
or firemen, as in his judgment shall be necessary, and that this Common Council will
recognize all engagements which he may think proper to make for the protection of the
city from fires, and guarding the property of the citizens, and that the Comptroller pay the
necessary expenses that may be incurred thereby.

Resolved, That his honor the Mayor be requested to call a meeting of the citizens at
such time and place as to him may appear expedient, to devise such measures as may be
proper for remedying the effects of the serious calamity with which this city has been visited,
and from preventing any further extension of the same.

Mr. Cleaveland offered the following resolution :

Resolved, (If the Board of Aldermen concur) that a special committee of five members
from each board be appointed to institute an inquiry into the cause or causes originating the destructive conflagration in the First Ward, on the night of the sixteenth instant,
with power to conduct such inquiry in any manner which to said committee shall seem
judicious, and to report the result of their investigations to the Common Council Committee
on the part of the Board of Assistants, and that Assistant Aldermen Cleaveland, Jordan,
Clark, Stewart, and Townsend, be the committee on the part of this board.   The resolution
was sent to the Board of Aldermen for concurrence.

Mr. Brady offered the following resolution :

Resolved, (If the Board of Aldermen concur) That suitable apartments in the City Hall,
or other public buildings, be offered to the postmaster of this city, for the accommodation of
the post-office, until the general government shall make arrangements therefor.   Adopted
unanimously and sent to the other Board for concurrence.

Mr. Clark offered the following resolution :

Resolved, (If the Board of Aldermen concur herein) That the Mayor of this city be
requested to apply forthwith to the proper department of the Government of the United
States, and respectfully request said government to extend every possible facility to all the
banks in this city, and especially by loaning to said banks a large portion of the surplus
revenue of the United States, and affording relief to the citizens who have sustained loss
by the late fire in this city.

At the suggestion of the chairman, the above resolution was amended by
adding, after the word "requested," the words "in connection with the
presidents of the Board of Trade and Chamber of Commerce."   The resolution thus amended was adopted unanimously, and sent to the Board of
Aldermen for concurrence.

The resolutions of Mr. Ingraham were sent back from the Board of Aldermen with an amendment, by adding the word "military" to the other classes
of citizens whom it was proposed to invest his honor the mayor with
authority to employ, and the amendment was concurred in.

The resolution of Mr. Brady was received from the Board of Aldermen with the following additional resolution, which was concurred in:

Resolved, That a committee of three be appointed on the part of this Board with power to carry the above resolution into effect.

Aldermen Delamater, Banks, and Stilwell were appointed the committee. The resolution of Mr. Cleaveland was received from the Board of Aldermen, that Board having concurred in said resolution, and appointed Aldermen Benson, Taylor, Nixon, and Lovett as their part of the committee.

Mr. Curtis offered the following resolution, which was adopted unanimously:

Resolved, That the northwestern chamber of the City Hall, known as the Superior Court

SCENE OF CONFLAGRATION AS WITNESSED FROM EXCHANGE PLACE.
[From painting in possession of James M. Rankin.]

Room, be placed at the disposal of the merchants of the city for their use as a Merchants' Exchange Room.

Laid on the table.

Mr. Whiting offered the following resolution:

Resolved, That a committee of two from each Board be appointed to act conjointly with the chief engineer, and that they give him all the aid in their power, and that they have power to destroy any buildings they may think proper to prevent any farther extension of the fire.

Adopted; and Messrs. Whiting and Jordan were appointed to wait on the Board of Aldermen with a copy of the resolution.

Mr. Whiting, on behalf of the committee, reported that they had presented the resolution with which they were intrusted to the Board of Aldermen, and that said Board had laid the resolution on the table.

The Board of Assistants met on the eighteenth of December. There were present: James R. Whiting, Esq., President; Messrs. Townsend, Brady,

Paulding, Greenfield, Ingraham, Stewart, Power and Ward. Mr. Ingraham offered the following resolution, which was adopted :

Whereas, The Franklin Market, at the Old Slip, has been destroyed at the late fire, and the butchers having stands therein have been deprived of the same, therefore, *Resolved,* that the Superintendent of Buildings, under the direction of the Market Committee, cause a temporary shed to be erected in Old Slip or Broad Street, for the accommodation of the butchers and others having stalls in the late Franklin Market, until other provision shall be made therefor.

The president offered the following resolution, which was adopted :

Whereas, The late conflagration should admonish us of the absolute necessity of establishing a more perfect and proper organization of the Fire Department, and of the necessity and propriety of being better prepared to resist the ravages of fire; therefore,
Resolved, If the Board of Aldermen concur, that a committee of three from each Board be appointed to devise, with his honor the mayor and chief engineer, some plan and system of operations to be pursued in case this city should again be visited with a fire threatening to be calamitous. Adopted, and the Fire and Water Committee, with the President of this Board, appointed.

Mr. Ingraham offered the following resolution :

Whereas, The late extensive conflagration on the night of the sixteenth of December, instant, was increased to a very great extent by the narrow streets and high stores on each side thereof, and the total destruction of all the buildings in that section of the city, renders it expedient and advisable to alter the route and width of the streets through the same; therefore,
Resolved, That the Common Council recommend to the owners of the lots in that section of the city to meet together on Wednesday next at twelve o'clock, in the Superior Court Room of the City Hall, and take the necessary measures for the adoption of a suitable plan for altering the same before commencing any building thereon. Adopted unanimously.

There are many well-known citizens still living who worked at or witnessed the Great Fire, and among them are Mr. Zophar Mills, Harry Howard, ex-Chief of the Volunteer Fire Department; ex-Chief Justice Charles P. Daly, Mr. William Callender, Mr. George Wilson, of the Chamber of Commerce, and Mr. George W. Wheeler, the only surviving member of Clinton Engine Company No. 41. The reminiscences of these veterans we here reproduce :

"The thermometer was seventeen degrees below zero," said Mr. Mills not long ago, who, with Mr. Wheeler, was discussing this memorable night, "and the fire broke out at about nine o'clock in the evening. The wind was northwest and blowing a gale. The hydrants would not furnish half enough water for one engine, and as the wind made the tide very low there was a great scarcity of water, eh, George?"

"Yes, yes; oh, yes," responded Mr. Wheeler, rubbing his silk hat the wrong way.

"Hence the suctions of the engines could not reach the water in the river, and they had to be lowered in the dark and cold down on to the boats and the decks of vessels. Everything seemed to conspire to cause the greatest conflagration that ever afflicted this city, and cause terror and despair in the hearts of those who witnessed it—what, George?"

"Oh, yes; yes, yes," said Mr. Wheeler, arousing himself from a reclining position for just a moment.

"Hundreds of buildings were burned that did not have a drop of water thrown upon them. I was foreman of Eagle Fire Engine Company No. 13, which was located in Dover street, near Pearl. When the City Hall bell struck the alarm we rolled out——"

"There wasn't any City Hall bell then," interrupted Mr. Wheeler, as he adjusted his stock and high turn over collar.

"You're right, George" (with a brotherly lingering upon the name of George). "It was the bell on the old jail that used to be between the City Hall and Broadway. Well, with a fast run, we were the first company at the fire, which was in Merchant Street, near Wall, a very narrow street. Hanover Street is where Merchant Street was, and it's twice as wide. Two four story stores were blazing from bottom to top, like a carpenter's shop on fire. The fire had already crossed Merchant Street toward Pearl. An engineer ordered me to take my hose into Pearl Street, and, if possible, stop the fire from crossing that street. Five or six stores were then blazing in Pearl

VIEW OF BANK OF AMERICA, CORNER OF WALL AND WILLIAM STREETS.
[From painting in possession of James M. Rankin.]

Street. Our one stream of water seemed almost useless to contend with such a conflagration. There were no iron shutters there then, and in a few minutes twenty windows of the upper stories of the high buildings on the east side of Pearl Street were in a blaze. Although Chief Gulick and every man under him did everything possible to stop the fire, my heart sank within me to notice the awful destruction of property. After the fire crossed Pearl Street it rushed to the river and south to Coenties Slip with little opposition. Over six hundred buildings and property worth twenty million dollars were destroyed. The Merchants' Exchange stood where the Custom House now stands, corner of Wall and Hanover Streets. It was a large white marble building. Chief Gulick ordered me to take my engine to the front. The building was high, and I was ordered away to keep the fire from crossing Hanover Street, and we stopped the fire then and there, to our great joy. We thus saved all of the

buildings on that side of Wall Street, from Hanover to Pearl, the only buildings saved on that side of Wall Street from William Street to the East River.
Am I right, George?"

"Yes, yes," echoed Mr. Wheeler, and, taking a musty book from his pocket,
he straightened up, and said: "Don't you want to know the enjines that
formed our line? No. 33 was at the river. She gave water to 26, and 26 gave
water to 41. Do you remember the pipe of brandy we had to put in the
engine to keep it from freezing?"

"Oh, of course," said Mr. Mills, "I had to put some of the brandy in my
boots to thaw my stockings loose. By the way I made an inquiry some time
ago about the members of my company. I found that eighteen are dead, five
are living, and three I could find out nothing about. In those days each fire
engine was allowed twenty-six men only. The living members are John T.
Hall, of Brooklyn; Cornelius T. Nostrand, of Connecticut; Josiah G. Macy,
of Nantucket; and Zophar Mills, of New York. Chief Gulick is dead. Do
you remember, George, that the Common Council blamed him for not stopping
the fire, and how we turned that Common Council out of office, and elected
Gulick register?"

Chief Justice Charles P. Daly has still a vivid recollection of that night.
Speaking about it on its anniversary in 1885, Chief Justice Daly observed: "I
was nineteen years of age at that time, and I remember on the night of the
fire I was attending a lecture at Clinton Hall. When the alarm came I went
down-town to see what the fire was. When I got there of course, like other
young gentlemen who had been attracted to the scene in the same way that I
had, I set to work to save property. We did secure a great deal, although it
was not saved. We piled it up in Hanover Square, thinking, of course, that
the fire would never reach that locality. But it did, and all the goods that we
had been so zealous about were destroyed.

"On the call of the mayor a meeting was held at the Shakespeare Hotel,
then the principal hotel of the city, which was situated at the corner of Fulton
and Nassau Streets, to take measures for the protection of property, for, of
course, the police were utterly insufficient for such an emergency, and I, with
others, formed an insurance patrol. I captured, I remember, a negro who was
stealing some silks. I was a very active and athletic young man, and I know
I had about as much as I could do to secure him, but I did, and he was locked
up. I think the fact that it was a remarkably cold night is what impresses
itself the most upon my memory. The patrol I spoke of was continued for
several days. There was a public meeting to take measures for assisting those
who had been made destitute by the fire, and for the organization of plans by
which the business firms who were sufferers could continue their business.
Many, of course, were ruined, but some went on again. I attended that
meeting, and if the records say that I spoke and moved a resolution, I probably
did, but I had no impression that I was in public life so early. I was not then
studying for the law, but was engaged in some mechanical occupation."

The eagle-like eye of Harry Howard, ex-chief of the Volunteer Fire Department, sparkles yet, and when spoken to about the great conflagration, he
sighed, and wondered how old the people imagined him to be. "I was only a
'chippy' then," said he. "I was about thirteen years old, and not being of
sufficient age to join the Department, was one of the lads known as runners.

The runners used to do lots of good work, such as pulling on the ropes and working on the brakes. I used to run with Peterson Engine No. 15, of Christie and Bayard Streets. I recollect it was in the evening, and that it was a big fire, and that I couldn't stay at it as long as I wanted to because my boss always made me come home at ten o'clock. I was an indentured boy for eleven years—apprenticed to Abijah Matthews, a cabinetmaker, in Catharine Street. He's dead now. He used to live in *bon ton* style over on East Broadway. All the big bugs lived over there then, especially the Quakers, who were also scattered through Madison, Rutgers and Henry Streets. I was disappointed at having to leave the fire, because I gloried in a big blaze, and the greater the havoc the better I was pleased. I recollect that when the fire broke out the old bell on the Dutch Church, corner of Fulton and William Streets, rang as I had never heard it ring. The engine I used to run with was out of service, laid up for repairs, and I ran to the fire with Phenix Engine No. 22, of Hester Street, between Eldridge and Allen Streets. The fire was around Wall Street and Exchange Place, and spreading fast. There was great excitement. Yes, there were lots of stories about the fire, such as a house being saved in the middle of the burned district, and of a man being thrown over five or six blocks and coming down safe. To be respectful you have to listen to these yarns, but you ain't obliged to believe 'em."

" There can be no topic more interesting than this to an old New Yorker," said Mr. George Wilson, of the Chamber of Commerce, " and I have gleaned many interesting particulars relative to it from the survivors of that day. The Chamber lost its charter in that fire. It was an immense document, with seals and ribbons, and had been given to us by George III a few years before the Revolutionary War. It has not yet been found, but I am confident that it exists. These two portraits," he continued, pointing to the full lengths which graced either end of the room, " are of Cadwallader Colden and Alexander Hamilton, painted for us, and are almost all that we saved from the wreck, except the books. They were carried out of the Merchants' Exchange by patriotic citizens at the risk of their lives. This building—the Merchants' Exchange—which was the finest one destroyed, was one of the largest in the city. The loss of this edifice was a most serious inconvenience to the mercantile community, particularly at such a time of disorder. In it were included not only the rooms I have mentioned, but also those used by the Chamber of Commerce and Board of Brokers ; the Post-office ; the Ship Letter Office and News Room ; the Ship Telegraph Office, several newspaper offices and extensive refreshment rooms.

" The Garden Street or Exchange Place Church, another prominent building destroyed, was erected in 1807. It was a plain, substantial house, of stone, thirty-six by sixty-six feet, with a gallery. The pastor was the Rev. James M. Matthews. It had in it the bell which was originally brought from Holland, but which was destroyed by the fire. A schoolroom adjoined, and there were in the yard a number of ancient tombstones. This building and its grounds were used as a place of refuge, but without avail. The whole was destroyed. In digging the foundation for the extension to the Mills Building some of the bones of those buried here were found. The Post-office, which was among the places burned, was then very small in comparison with its later proportions. Only one of the clerks of that day still lives, and he has been in bad health for some time. Immediately after the fire the Postmaster, Samuel L. Gouverneur, removed it to the Rotunda in the City Hall Park, but not without receiving many indications of dissatisfaction from business men, who complained that it was too far up town !

"Among the well-known business houses which have continued down town to the present time, but were then burned out, were Halsted, Haines, & Co., Howland & Aspinwall, James Bleecker & Son, and Delmonico's. There are many others, but the firm names have so much changed that they cannot be recognized readily. Howland & Aspinwall, B. Aymar & Co., and S. V. S. Wilder, three of the largest mercantile houses, gave notice promptly after the fire that they would cash all paper of theirs which was out in the hands of the sufferers, and their example was followed by many others. Three thousand clerks, porters, and carmen, were thrown out of employment, many of them having families to support. Very heavy losses were inflicted upon French commerce. Only three French importers escaped. One cargo alone, which had arrived and was destroyed before distribution, was estimated to be worth

GALLANT FIREMEN TO THE RESCUE.
[From lithograph by Currier & Ives.]

two hundred thousand dollars. There was little English insurance capital here, owing to restrictive laws against foreign companies, and the loss fell almost entirely upon American companies, many of which were ruined.

"The naval storehouses in Brooklyn, lying directly across the river, caught fire several times, but the flames were promptly subdued. The sails of the schooner 'Alonzo,' lying at the wharf at Brooklyn, were burned. The passengers on the Hudson River boats saw the flames from the Highlands forty-five miles distant, and the light, so says an old chronicler, was also distinctly seen in New Jersey as far as Cranberry. Assistant Postmaster Gaylor, then a boy, recollects seeing it from the court house at White Plains, and others saw it from Morristown, N. J.

"Shanties or sheds were erected near the ruins in South Street, into which the damaged merchandise was removed, and Castle Garden was taken as a depot for the reception of goods which were unclaimed and of which the owners were unknown.

"The *Journal of Commerce* building, which was in the rear of Dr. Matthews's church, was saved by the application of vinegar. Several hogsheads were in the rear of the lot and were unheaded, parts of the fluid being thrown on the roof and other exposed places. Downing saved his restaurant in the same manner.

"The losses of Stephen Whitney, the merchant, and next to John Jacob

Astor the richest man in New York, were reported to be immense—in the neighborhood of half a million dollars. Great complaints were made of the defective architecture of the buildings which were burned. Most of the bricks which were lying in heaps through the streets looked as clean as if mortar had never touched them. In the old buildings, the newspapers of the day said, the mortar was harder than the bricks themselves. The great extent of the fire was ascribed to pernicious inventions to save money. Wooden gutters, cornices and window frames were common. Copper gutters and iron window frames and shutters would have saved the Exchange. The new and lofty building at the corner of Wall and William Streets was on fire at the cornice several times, and with difficulty saved.

"One building was saved in the burned district in Water Street. It was built by Carman for Herman Thorne. He was told that the structure must be fireproof, and declared that it should be so. Although the building stood surrounded by a sea of flames it redeemed his promise and remained uninjured with its goods safe within it.

"While the fire was going on, Louis F. Wilkins, a midshipman, then recently returned from a voyage to the Pacific, heard the agonizing cries of a woman, whose child was left in a building already in flames. He immediately forced his way up stairs, in spite of the warnings of the firemen that he would certainly perish, and rescued the child, which was not in the least frightened, but was, on the contrary, pleased with the brilliancy of the light. He restored it to its distracted mother, who with frantic joy threw her arms about him and exclaimed, 'My God! my God! Thou hast not forsaken me.' Persons were reported to be killed by the fire, but the rumors did not seem to be authenticated. John Lang, of the New York *Gazette*, died shortly after from the excitement and worry the fire occasioned. Among other things noted was that there was danger from melted lead, and that the saltpeter in warehouses in Front Street, near Old Slip, exploded, with a loud noise."

Mr. William Callender, who is now in his seventy-ninth year, and yet looks and feels as hale and active as a man of fifty, has a vivid recollection of old New York. He was not connected with the Fire Department, but, like all New Yorkers in the olden time, he took a lively interest in all that concerned it, and as often as circumstances permitted personally attended most of the conflagrations with which the city was visited from time to time. His remembrance of events which occurred more than fifty years ago is most reliable. Of the Great Fire of 1835 he says:

"The destruction of that night and the suffering that followed were terrible. If you will suppose that to-night all that portion of the city below Canal Street was absolutely and completely swept away, you can form some idea of the extent of that fire. I was chief clerk of the Police Department from 1834 to 1836, and I had to take statements of the losses sustained in that fire. As well as I can remember they footed up over twenty-two million dollars. Insurance companies were wiped out, and millions of the losses were never made good. The night was bitterly cold—seventeen degrees below zero—and the wind blew a hurricane. I stood at the corner of Wall and Pearl Streets, where there is an open space like a funnel. The fire in great sheets of flame leaped across that space, cavorting around in maddening fury. Bales of goods and merchandise that were thrown from the windows were caught up by the wind and whirled about as though they were but flecks of chaff. Rolls of light goods that became untied in their descent from the windows were swept up by the wind and carried off to long distances, and fragments of goods, books, and papers were actually found the next morning on the Jersey meadows. The water supply was had from the reservoir at Thirteenth Street, and from the river, because the hydrants were frozen solid. The tide on the river was so low that it required six engines on a line to bring one stream to play on the fire. Remember these were only hand engines. Of course such means were utterly inadequate to stem the course of the fire.

"The fire broke out in Hanover Street (then called Merchant Street) in the dry goods store of Comstock & Andrews. It spread with great rapidity, the illuminating gas not long before introduced in the city and then in general use in the stores serving to help the conflagration and increase the danger. The Dutch Reformed Church in Garden Street, about two blocks away from the outbreak of the fire, was opened, and valuable goods were taken there and stored, in the belief that they would be safe. The sacred edifice looked in a brief time like a warehouse. The open space at Hanover Square was also piled up with goods from the threatened and burning buildings. Along the slips on South Street were other heaps of valuable merchandise. But the flames continued to increase in fury and these supposed houses of safety with their contents were one after another consumed. The old church building was completely obliterated, and so was the synagogue on Mill Street near South William Street. The Fire Department was powerless to stem the current of destruction."

The action of the gallant Philadelphia firemen on the occasion of this great conflagration needs to be told in detail, and is best related in the words of Mr. J. B. Harrison, of Summitville, Tenn., who, in 1835, was a member of the Franklin Fire Company of Philadelphia. Mr. Harrison, who is a well-preserved gentleman of sixty-nine years, says:

"In the year 1835, December 16, the great fire in New York City broke out. Friday, the eighteenth, the mayor of New York sent for the firemen of Philadelphia to come and help put it out. As quick as the boys of the Ben Franklin heard it twenty-three of us manned the rope and started for the Walnut Street wharf to get on the boat to cross to Camden and take the railroad. The river was so full of heavy floating ice the boat could not cross. There were other firemen there who, when they found they could not cross the river, returned home. We concluded to go to Kensington Road and get on there. When we got to the road we found the ice so thick on the rails that the cars could not run; it was raining and freezing as fast as it fell. We then concluded to go afoot. It was then four o'clock. The word was given. 'Man the rope, boys, we will go to the Trenton bridge and cross the Delaware.' We got to Trenton at twelve o'clock that night, and went to the tavern. When we entered the room we found a large stove red hot. The ice was about an inch thick on our coats and hats. In a short time the ice melted, and the floor was full of water. After we warmed a little, we got up on the seats the best we could to get out of the water and to rest. It was not long, however, till we got cold, and concluded that we had better start on our journey. The word was given, and away we went for the Sand Hills. It was then Saturday morning about four o'clock, and some of our boys were getting weak. On the way we hired a man with a horse to help us along to Sand Hills.

"About five miles from Sand Hills there was a large house, and some of our boys proposed to stop and get some supper, it being nearly night. We halted and asked them for supper ; they would not let us have any, although we offered to pay them well for it. We were forty miles from home, and had not stopped to eat a meal. Some of the boys had given out, and some said they could not go much further. While we were talking to the man of the house, one of our boys stepped to the back part of the house to get a drink of water, and, seeing through the window a large table filled, he called all the boys to come and look. A large table loaded with everything good to eat that a man could wish for was more than our hungry boys could resist, and so we filed in at one door as a large company of guests entered at another. We sat down and ate a hearty supper. The other crowd had to take a stand against the wall until we got through. No one helped us, but we helped ourselves, as it was all before us. When we got through we were polite enough to thank them for supper, and then rolled on to Sand Hills.

BURNING OF THE MERCHANTS' EXCHANGE.
[Dec. 16, 1835.]

"The next day, Tuesday, Fire Company No. 1 came to visit us and offering their services as our escort. We went to see the ruins of the fire, which had been checked by blowing up buildings in advance of it with powder. While we were there we got an invitation to go to a theatre, which we accepted, taking Company No. 1 with us. When we got to the theatre we told them No. 1 was our escort, and we wanted them to go in with us. They refused, and we told them we would go back to our hotel and spend the evening. We had not gone far until we were halted by a messenger from another theatre : 'Franklin boys, come with me ; I will take you to a theatre where you can go in and take whom you wish.'

"On Wednesday I thought I would go and see an uncle in the upper part of the city. Walking along on the sidewalk I was stopped by a cabman, who asked : 'Fireman, where are you going?' I told him. He said that it was too far for me to walk, and took me in his cab. We could not step out anywhere but we were halted by some one wanting to do a kind act for us. We could not spend any money in New York. I bought a few things and laid down the money to pay for them, which was refused. The merchants said : 'You are welcome to anything you want, your money I will not take.'

"When we got ready to go home the New York firemen pulled our engine to the wharf, the mayor appointed a committee to escort us home, and after that the firemen got to visiting from one city to the other."

The following are personal recollections of the great fire by Mrs. Mary LeRoy Satterlee :

"The evening of the great fire in New York City was intensely cold. The bells began to ring an alarm about eight o'clock P. M., and my husband started at the sound which told him of danger to the large warehouses in Pearl Street, one of which his firm occupied. It seemed as if all the bells were ringing their loudest. Mr. Satterlee left our house in Chambers Street, accompanied by his cousin, who was a clerk in the establishment. As the alarm continued, his nephew, a boy of fourteen years, could no longer be restrained, and followed, leaving me very anxious and alone. About ten o'clock the boy returned, saying that the cold was intense, and it was almost impossible to work the engines, and the fire was still raging. He had narrowly escaped being struck by a falling wall. 'Is the store in danger?' I asked. 'No; the wind is driving the flames in an opposite direction, but all hands are helping those whose property is in danger.'

"Eleven o'clock came, then midnight, to find us sitting shivering, dreading to hear, yet most anxious to see, those who had gone to the scene of the calamity. Suddenly our cousin entered, his arms full of books. Icicles clung to his clothing and stiffened his hair. Entirely exhausted by emotion and fatigue, it was some moments before he could relate how the wind suddenly changed and blew as strongly in the other direction and delivering whole blocks to the seemingly uncontrollable flames. I asked for my husband. He had sent up his books and was working with others to get the most valuable part of their stock of silk goods under the roof of the South Dutch Church, never thinking that it could be destroyed before the fire was under control. At three o'clock in the morning—such a very long night—I heard wheels, and my husband returned safe in a carriage piled up with goods. After paying the driver a fabulous sum—for every vehicle was in demand—the goods were tumbled, the wet with the dry, into the hall.

"Next day the fire demon was subdued, but the ruins smoldered sullenly in the best business part of our fair city. The insurance offices were closed, and ruin to some and great loss to many made every heart sad. While the fire was at its height, my sister, who lived in the lower part of the city and was watching the lurid sky and the burning buildings, was told by one of the firemen that she had better pack up all valuables, as, if the fire was not mastered before it reached a certain corner near by, several buildings would be blown up, her house among the rest. She was always calm, but energetic, and seeing that the firemen were terribly exhausted, she summoned her servants, and putting all the tea and coffee they had into large boilers, they got tog ther all the provisions in the house, baked the buckwheat meal into griddle cakes, hailed an early milk cart, and were enabled to feed and refresh every fireman around by calling them into the kitchen ten or twelve at a time. They were almost perished with cold and prostrated by their severe labor.

CHAPTER XX.

NEW YORK'S WATER SUPPLY.

Primitive New York Dependent on Wells and Cisterns.—The Famous and Fashionable Tea-Water Pump.—Love Stories and Tragedy.—Establishment of the Manhattan Company.—The Scheme of Christopher Colles.—Plan to Utilize the Bronx River.—Passage of the Bill for the Croton.—The Celebration in 1842.—The New Aqueduct.

HAVING in the preceding chapters placed before the reader a very full history of the fires under the Old Department, and the consequent heavy losses to the city, it is proper that we should now devote a chapter to the means by which the fire fiend is to be fought. Without a good supply of water the finest engines and the highest state of discipline are almost useless to stay the progress of a fire. The water supply of a city is as great an essential as its drainage and more so than its arrangement of streets or its lighting. To this subject the ancients have devoted their best energies, and the remains of the gigantic waterworks of old Rome attest the truth of the assertion. Hence, we propose to treat, as fully as the scope of this work will allow, the water supply of New York. It is a natural sequence of the history of fires and will properly precede a sketch of the Volunteer Fire Companies.

At a very early day the want of a sufficient supply and a convenient distribution of good water was felt by the citizens of New York. Before the Declaration of Independence considerable expenditures had been made in order to satisfy this want. At first wells were the only sources of supply. There were no public wells before the year 1658, the inhabitants previous to that time having been supplied by private wells within their own inclosures. The first public well constructed (1658) was in front of the Fort. It does not appear that any other wells were sunk in the streets until 1677, at which time an order was promulgated that "wells be made in the following places, by the inhabitants of the streets where they are severally made," viz.:

One opposite Roelof Jansen, the butcher.

One in Broadway, opposite Van Dyck's.

One in the street, opposite Derick Smith's.

One in the street, opposite John Cavalier's.

One in the yard of the City Hall.

One in the street, opposite Cornelis Van Boroum's.

In 1687 seven other public wells were ordered in different streets, for the purpose of defraying the expenses of which the respective premises were assessed; and in the same year the city government undertook to pay one-half the expense, and the neighbors the other half. Public wells, during the earlier part of the last century, were constructed by a contribution of £8 by the city government, and the remaining portion was defrayed by the inhabitants residing in the neighborhood. No person was allowed the use of a well until he had contributed a fair proportion of the cost. About the year 1750 pumps came into use, and a general act was afterwards passed to enable the city to raise a tax for the construction and keeping in repair of the public wells and pumps.

About the year 1690 there were, say, a dozen public wells in the city, standing all of them in the middle of the streets. In 1748 there were many wells, but a portion of the inhabitants preferred to send "out of town" to the Fresh-water Spring—then, and for a long period afterwards, known as the Tea-water Spring. This spring was situated near the present junction of Chatham and Roosevelt Streets. Shortly before the Revolution the neighborhood of the spring was made into a fashionable place of resort at which to procure beverages mixed with pure water. A pump was erected over the famous spring, ornamented grounds were laid out around it, and the "Tea-water Pump Garden"

TEA-WATER PUMP.

held forth its attractions under the most seductive influences. The water of all the other wells and pumps (and there were many scattered over the city) was almost unfit for use.

Before the introduction of the Croton, water was one of the chief commodities for barter in the city. It was delivered by contract as ice now is, or hawked through the streets at a cent or a cent and a half a pail. In some houses this was an important item of expense. Sixty years ago Mr. Davis, of the "Grapevine," in Greenwich Avenue, had an establishment at Beekman and South Streets. He was furnished with forty gallons of water a day from the old spring in Franklin Square, and his bill was thirty shillings a week, or one hundred and ninety-five dollars a year. But Knapp's tea-water, drawn from a spring close by the old White Fort, was the most popular in the olden time, and gave employment to a great many men who made a good living by it. Among these was Mr. Sweeny, the founder of Sweeny's Hotel, who was in former times a waterman. Knapp's famous spring was probably not over six hundred feet from high water mark, and was located on Tenth Avenue near Fourteenth Street. The Ninth Ward was favored with a number of good springs. Going through Thirteenth Street, there was a well where Tracy & Russell's brewery afterward stood. A little further up, at Christopher Street and Sixth Avenue, there was another tea-well which was largely patronized. There were large numbers of wells sunk by the city which were public, but Knapp's spring and the spring in Christopher Street, having obtained a name, had a large patronage from those who could afford to pay for the water.

In 1790 the tea-water pumps became an important aid in extinguishing fires in the vicinity. The other wells in the lower part of the city furnished only a miserable and brackish substitute for water. But here night or day there bubbled up continuously a strong stream of pure cold water, alike the

KNAPP'S TEA-WATER PUMP.

joy of the fireman and the traveler. Some struggling poet of that period, unknown to fortune or fame, wrote a song on the old pump, which the fire laddies of that day were wont to troll as they lounged in their engine house across the street. Two stanzas ran as follows:

In the cool of the day when the breezes are lightest,
    I rest for awhile on the old oaken stump,
Whose roots nestle down in the weeds and the grasses
    That reach to the curb of the Tea-water Pump.

When the fire is put out and the firemen returning,
    How cheerily down the hillside they jump,
Forgetting the smoke, and the heat, and the burning,
    To quench their hot thirst at the Tea-water Pump.

A Mr. Thompson was the occupant of a house in Chatham Street opposite the "Old Tea-water Pump." It appears that the construction of the pump occasioned some inconvenience to the neighbors, as a petition was presented to the Common Council asking that "the inconvenience arising from the spout of the Tea-water Pump projecting over the street" should be removed. The committee appointed to consider the matter decided that the petitioners had just cause of complaint, and the water spout was voted a nuisance. The committee sagely concluded that "if the water carts were ordered to draw up abreast of the spout, near the gutter, and receive the water in rotation, it would remove the obstruction in the street."

This, however, is not the origin of the story of a tempest in a teapot; it is only suggestive of it.

In 1799 a company was incorporated, styled the "New York Manhattan Water Works," with a view to supply the city with pure and wholesome water. The capital of the company was over two million dollars; the charter perpetual, granting the company control over streams and springs on the island of New York and the county of Westchester. When the charter was granted the population of the city was a little over sixty thousand souls; and the previous year the yellow fever had visited the city with all its horrors and virulence, and the minds of all were filled under their calamities with great dread.

The corporation of the city evidenced no disposition to embark in the work. It seems that the Manhattan Company were more intent in making money by their banking operations than accomplishing the avowed objects of their charter, and left the city totally unsupplied with water which could be called pure and wholesome, and over four-fifths of the paved parts of the city without any supply whatever. The works of the Manhattan Company consisted of a well in Cross Street, twenty-five feet in diameter, and two steam engines of eighteen horse-power each; a reservoir on Chambers Street, and one or two small wooden reservoirs.

In 1806 an order was issued removing the old wells and pumps, several of which stood in the middle of Broadway, and establishing others in the sidewalks. These wells had been in existence for one hundred and thirty years.

For the better care of the wells and pumps, laws were passed at the beginning of the present century. The following is a specimen:

On the first Tuesday of May, annually, the Mayor, Recorder and Aldermen, or any five of them, of whom the Mayor or Recorder shall always be one, are authorized to appoint one or more fit inhabitants for each ward of the city to be overseers of the wells and pumps in their respective wards for the ensuing year. Their duty is to cause the wells and pumps to be viewed, examined, cleansed, and put in good order and repair, and to maintain them so; and to keep regular accounts of the money expenses for the same. In case of neglect of duty, the overseers may be each fined five pounds, for the use of the city. They are to account with the Common Council once in three months. Persons willfully injuring the wells or pumps are, on conviction, to be fined forty shillings, or, on refusal or inability to pay the same, they are to be committed to Bridewell for one month, or until the forfeiture and costs are paid. When servants or apprentices do damage to the pumps or wells, the fine shall be paid by the master or owner; and in default thereof the offender shall be sent to Bridewell.

The largest cisterns were built in the vicinity of churches, as for instance, as follows; At St. Stephen's Church, Broome and Christie Streets; St. Thomas's Church, on Broadway; the Bowery Church, between Hester and Walker Streets, and at the Mott Street Church.

Both romance and tragedy are associated with those old city wells. They were the rendezvous of many a tender assignation, and many a love match was arranged while the family pail or kettle was being replenished from the spring. A tragedy which for a long time filled old New Yorkers with sorrow, not unmixed with horror, was enacted at one of those wells, the remembrance of which still lingers in many an old New York family. Juliana Elmore Sands, a beautiful and accomplished young girl, lived with her uncle on the southwest corner of Greenwich and old Provost (now Franklin) Streets. Her youth and beauty, and the mysterious nature of her disappearance, had combined to give to her fate a thrilling, romantic interest. She was described by a "neighbor" in a letter to the papers at the time of the sad occurrence as "uniformly cheerful and serene, and on the day previous to the murder was remarkably so. Her expectation of becoming a bride on the morrow was the natural cause of her liveliness. Her temper was mild and tranquil; her manners artless and

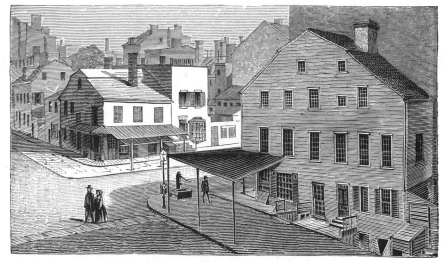

RESIDENCE OF MISS SANDS.
[Southwest corner of Greenwich and Franklin Streets.]

tender; her conversation ever chaste and innocent. She was one of those virtuous characters against whom the tongue of slander never moves."

Miss Sands left the house of her uncle on the evening of Sunday, December 29, 1799, to go sleigh-riding. Nothing more was heard of her until the afternoon of Thursday, the second of January, 1800, when her body was found in a well dug by the Manhattan Company. The well was located in Spring Street near Greene. A coroner's jury rendered a verdict of wilful murder " by some person or persons as yet unknown." On the evening of her disappearance she, as her relatives had supposed, left the house with a young man named Levi Weeks, to whom Miss Sands was engaged to be married. Suspicion at once rested on him. He was arrested and brought to trial. His trial came on before the Court of Oyer and Terminer, Chief Justice Lansing presiding, March 31, 1800. The prosecution was conducted by Assistant Attorney General Colden, and the prisoner was defended by Messrs. Alexander Hamilton, Brockholst Livingston, Aaron Burr, Abram Skinner, James Woods, Charles Baldwin and George Lynch. During the trial the chambers of justice, the avenues of the

City Hall and the streets adjacent were thronged with an eager multitude, anxious to witness the trial. The court room was so crowded that it became necessary to direct the officers "to clear it of all superfluous spectators" before the court could proceed to business. The prisoner pleaded not guilty. The Attorney General opened the prosecution and introduced the witnesses for the people, some fifty in number, the tenor of whose testimony was to connect circumstances of a presumptive nature which might establish proof of the prisoner's guilt. Two witnesses, a man and his wife, who resided in the vicinity of the Manhattan well, declared that at about the time of the alleged murder they heard exclamations of a female in distress, and distinguished the words, "O, Lord! have mercy, do help me!" Witnesses deposed to having seen the tracks of a one-horse sleigh on the morning following the murder.

The evidence for the defence went to prove that the prisoner left Miss Sands's house shortly after eight in the evening, leaving Miss Sands behind in the house; and that he proceeded in his sleigh alone to his own dwelling. The verdict of the jury declared the prisoner not guilty of the crime charged in the indictment, and he was accordingly acquitted.

The Manhattan well, where the remains of Miss Sands were found, was for a long time an object of morbid curiosity. It was also invested with a supernatural degree of interest. Screams, fireballs, and a figure in white were nightly reported to have been heard and seen there. No clue has ever been discovered to clear away the mystery which forever enshrouds the tragic fate of the beautiful, but unfortunate, Juliana Elmore Sands.

Another, but a more pleasing, incident may be recalled in connection with those wells. A story, which for some years was received as correct, was to the effect that the celebrated poem, "The Old Oaken Bucket," had its origin in the author's love of liquor, and was first suggested to him in a remorseful moment in a Bowery tavern. The truth seems to be that on returning one sultry day to his home on Duane Street from his office in the region of Lower Wall Street, the author, Samuel Woodworth, drank a glass of water from one of the old-time pumps of the neighborhood and remarked: "That is very refreshing, but how much more refreshing would it be to take a good long draught from the old oaken bucket I left hanging in my father's well at home." The poet's wife thereupon remarked: "Why wouldn't that be a good subject for a poem?" The poet, taking the hint, sat down and from the depths of his heart poured out the lines which millions have since read with varied emotions.

In July, 1774, the proposal of Christopher Colles to erect a reservoir and to convey water through the several streets of the city was accepted by the Common Council. Mr. Colles's scheme was simply that of the Manhattan Company—to dig large wells, and from them to pump water into reservoirs.

To no single individual is the system of American improvements more indebted than to Christopher Colles. Born in Ireland in the year 1738, he first appears in this country in 1772, as a lecturer upon pneumatics, illustrated by experiments in an air-pump of his own invention. He is also said to have been the first in this country to undertake the building of a steam engine. In 1773 he lectured in this city on the advantages of lock navigation, and one year later he proposed the erection of a reservoir, and the laying down of a system of conduit pipes. With the aid of the corporation a steam pumping engine was erected near the Collect Pond. The engine carried a pump eleven inches in diameter and six feet stroke, which lifted four hundred and seventeen thousand six hundred gallons daily. The war of the Revolution caused an abandonment of this plan.

All the authorities concur in giving to Colles the credit of having been not only the first to propose, but the first to bring before the public, in a practical form, the feasibility and vast national advantage of a system of water communication which should unite the great lakes and their boundless tributory territory with the Atlantic Ocean. This distinguished citizen was also the first (in 1812) to make "formal public proposal for telegraphic intercourse along the whole American coast, from Passamaquoddy to New Orleans."

A semaphoric telegraph was established to signalize intelligence between New York and Sandy Hook, which for many years was under his personal direction. He died in this city on the fourth day of October, 1816, in the seventy-ninth year of his age, and was buried in St. Paul's cemetery.

The ground selected to carry out Mr. Colles's scheme was on the east line of Broadway, between Pearl and White Streets, where a spacious reservoir was constructed. On August 8, 1774, the Aldermen passed the following resolution:

CHRISTOPHER COLLES.

Ordered, That the notherly part of the property of Augustus Van Cortlandt and Frederick Van Cortlandt, fronting on Great George Street, be purchased at six hundred pounds per acre for a reservoir, provided that upon sinking a well there good water be found. If not, the well to be filled up by the corporation.

The water proved satisfactory, and treasury notes to the amount of two thousand five hundred pounds were ordered to be issued to meet the expenses. Subsequently other proposals were made, and in 1798 it was found necessary to look outside the city for a sufficient supply of water, and the Bronx River was mentioned. The yellow fever, which had made great ravages, was said to have been aggravated by the scarcity of good water. Dr. Brown, in his report to the Common Council, underrated the quantity needed. He considered three hundred and sixty-two thousand eight hundred gallons as an ample daily supply, and two hundred thousand dollars as the utmost expenditure required for bringing the Bronx to the city, for laying down twenty miles of pipes in the streets, and erecting two public fountains. The water was to be elevated eighty feet above the level of Harlem River; the machinery for the purpose was to be propelled by the surplus waters from the Bronx, which was estimated to discharge one thousand two hundred cubic feet, or seven thousand four hundred ale gallons per minute. A Mr. Weston, however, estimated that the city would require three million gallons per day.

Up to the year 1816 no serious effort was made to supply the city with a sufficiency of good water. Then the matter was thoroughly discussed, and in August of 1819 Robert Macomb asked permission of the corporation to furnish the city with water. After many inquiries and experiments the first positive step towards something like action on the part of the corporation was taken on the recomendation of the Fire Department in 1829. A report made by Alderman Samuel Stevens in favor of the establishment of a well and reservoir in Fourteenth Street, where water might be distributed, was accepted and favorably acted upon. It was the beginning of the noble Croton Aqueduct.

The Manhattan Reservoir on Chambers Street did not contain a quantity equal to the daily consumption, for it was five times filled and emptied in every twenty-four hours, and the water when distributed for use was in the same state as the water in the pumps and well. The company had on an average laid one mile of pipe, mostly of wood, every year since its incorporation to 1823, and the best pump water on the island, by having a dense population collected around its sources, had lost its purity, and then contained foreign matter destructive to health.

CHAMBERS STREET RESERVOIR.

The Manhattan Company had, however, the ability from their charter, if not to defeat, at least to procrastinate the introduction of water by the city for many years.

In 1823 the legislature of New York incorporated the Sharon Canal Company, with the power to make a canal from the Western boundary of the State of Connecticut to the City of New York. The grant secured the Canal Company all the water on its route for the use of their works and to supply the city with pure and wholesome water.

In 1825 a new company was incorporated, styled the City of New York Water Works, to bring water from Westchester County. But owing to the difficulties in which the company was placed by the opposition of the Sharon Canal and the Manhattan Company, nothing was done and the company voluntarily gave up their grant.

The New York & Harlaem Spring Water Company was incorporated on the 18th of April, 1826, for supplying water from springs supposed to exist in the high lands near Harlaem and Manhattanville. Experiments were made by sinking shafts, etc., but no water was found in sufficient quantity to warrant any further expense, and the company ceased to exist by non-user.

A fifth company was incorporated in 1827, styled the New York Well Company. The water was to be procured on the island by sinking wells on the most elevated grounds. The company made several attempts to procure water, but being satisfied by their experiments of the impracticability of the undertaking, the concern fell through."

In 1825 five additional cisterns were ordered to be constructed. In consequence of a serious fire in the Eighth Ward, the fire companies were ordered to fill all the public cisterns with water. Two years later (1827) seven additional cisterns were ordered; eighteen more in 1828, and sixteen additional ones in 1829. The city then possessed forty public cisterns, at an estimated cost of twenty-four thousand dollars. Each cistern contained usually about one hundred hogsheads of water. But the supply of water was nevertheless insufficient. At least sixty additional cisterns were required for that portion of the city between Fourteenth and Grand Streets on Broadway, and Fourteenth and Pearl Streets on Chatham Street, and on the east side. It was

THIRTEENTH STREET RESERVOIR AND WASHINGTON INSTITUTE.
[Thirteenth Street and Fourth Avenue.]

therefore recommended that the city lay down two lines of iron pipe, for the security of the city in the section mentioned

The firemen built a cistern under the entrance-way to the Old Firemen's Hall in Fulton Street. This was the first cistern ever built in the city, and contained a hundred hogsheads of water. Engine Companies Nos. 13, 18, 21, and 24 share the credit of this work.

Much disagreement and dissension appear to have prevailed among citizens and officials as to the propriety of making the cost of constructing cisterns a public charge. Fully a year had been occupied with such dissensions, when, finally, on March 29, 1827, the Committee on Assessments of the Common Council reported favorably for making the cost of cisterns a public charge. This report was negatived. Public cisterns were, however, established for the use of the Department, some twenty-five additional having been erected up to August, 1828, for which assessments were levied.

In the following year the city authorities set themselves seriously to the task of making a radical change in the whole system. The Committee of the

Board having the subject under consideration made a report in March of this year, and its report was adopted. It declared that, owing to the inferiority of the supply of water provided by the Manhattan Company, the inhabitants above Grand Street would not patronize that corporation, and hence there were no water pipes established in that quarter of the city. The report shows that there were in existence forty public cisterns, which cost about twenty-four thousand dollars, which usually contain one hundred gallons each ; that to supply that portion of the city between Fourteenth Street and Grand Street would require at least sixty additional cisterns, at a cost of about thirty-six thousand dollars, which cisterns would not last longer than twenty to twenty-one years, besides the cost of repairs, etc. The report declared in favor of laying " one line of tubes " along Third Avenue and the Bowery to Chatham Street from Fourteenth Street, and another along Broadway, from Fourteenth Street to Canal Street ; the " tubes " to be twelve inches in diameter. The total expense was estimated (including " five hundred dollars for plugs or hydrants ") to amount to twenty-four thousand five hundred dollars.

The Committee declared that sufficient water for the purpose of extinguishing fires could be obtained "anywhere about the part of the city referred to," and that although such lines of pipes were a considerable distance from the North and East Rivers, they would be sufficient "from the fact of the gradual descent of the ground toward each river." As an additional security it was suggested that, if necessary, "small tubes of six inches diameter may be laid down to subdivide the sections referred to."

On the sixteenth of the following November the Committee on Fire Department reported "that although they excavated only fifty feet in depth in Thirteenth Street, yet the supply of water was found to be sufficient to fill the reservoir, as it was estimated that seventy hogsheads were issued therefrom in a day. A cast iron tank was received from Philadelphia, and the same inclosed in a brick building."

On April 19 following (1830) the same Committee reported that they had erected "on the public ground" on the corner of Bowery and Thirteenth Street a stone tower forty-four feet in diameter and twenty-seven feet high, while there was in course of construction an iron tank of forty-three feet diameter and twenty feet high, and to contain three hundred and five thousand four hundred and twenty-two gallons of water. The pipe was laid on Broadway and nearly completed on Third Avenue and the Bowery.

The memorial of Francis B. Phelps, on the 17th of May, 1830, was the first definite proposal for the introduction of Croton water into the city. New York at that period, as she is to-day, was the commercial metropolis of the Union, furnishing nearly two-thirds of the general revenue. In the year 1800 the population of Philadelphia exceeded that of New York by fifteen thousand. But so steadily did New York begin to "increase and multiply" that before the subsequent decade had elapsed she had overtaken her rival, and by the year 1820 had outstripped her in the race for supremacy. To illustrate the remarkable prosperity that had come upon this city the value of property increased in the year 1831-32 over twenty millions of dollars and the assessed valuation was set down at one hundred and forty-five millions of dollars. But at the same time it was a matter of surprise and regret that the city was almost completely destitute of a supply of good wholesome water, and that there existed any hesitation in securing an abundance of that necessary element. Why was this important measure delayed so long? Because of a powerful, extraneous influence which not only exerted itself in the community, but in the halls of legislation; and because of the powers and immunities granted to the Manhattan Company. In modern parlance, the delay was ascribed to "lobbying" and "lobbyists."

But Mayor Walter Bowne, in his first message to the Common Council, under the new organization of the City Government in 1831, did not lose sight of that most important matter. He said: "Permit me to press on your consideration, with the earnestness which the importance of the subject demands, the expediency of adopting prompt and energetic measures for procuring a copious supply of pure water. Of the practicability of the project no doubt rests on my mind. The ponds and lakes in the mountains of Westchester and Putman offer an inexhaustible supply. The noble aqueducts which were the glory of ancient Rome are now the monuments of her greatness; and one of our sister cities points with pride and exultation to a work of this character which she has years since accomplished."

This question was referred to a committee on the supply of water and extinguishment of fire, and the Board of Assistant Aldermen

MOUTH OF THE CROTON RIVER.

presented an ordinance appropriating five thousand dollars for the laying down of pipes and the further excavation of the well at Thirteenth Street. The diameter of the well was sixteen feet; its depth one hundred and twelve feet, ninety-seven of which had been excavated in solid rock; its bottom sixty-two feet below common high tide. Its capacity was one hundred and seventy-five thousand one hundred and fifty gallons. From the well the water was raised by a steam engine of twelve horse power into an iron tank in a building of octagonal form. The tank was forty-four feet in diameter, twenty and one-half feet high, and contained two hundred and thirty-three thousand one hundred and sixty-nine gallons.

The advantages of the city reservoir in the extinguishment of fires are well demonstrated by the following facts. The destruction of property occurring by fires in New York City from 1825 to 1829 amounted to one million seven hundred and fifty-three thousand six hundred and thirty-three dollars, and the average for the five years was over three hundred and fifty thousand dollars a year. The expense of supporting the Fire Department by the city for the same period amounted to seventy-three thousand six hundred and twenty-seven dollars, or over an average of fourteen thousand seven hundred dollars per annum. During that period there had been four hundred and forty-three fires.

A report, signed by Messrs. Isaac Brown, Stevens, Benjamin M. Brown, Palmer, and Engs, Committee on the Fire Department, adopted on the sixteenth of March, 1829, in relation to the supply of water for the purpose of extinguishing fires, etc., states that, owing to the supply of water for culinary purposes being of a quality much superior to that supplied by the Manhattan Company, citizens residing in the upper part of the city were unwilling to take the Manhattan water, hence no water pipes were laid in all that part of the city lying above Grand Street, or Pearl Street on the east side of the city, and therefore no protection was afforded for the purpose of extinguishing fires.

The following resolution was presented and referred on the fourteenth of July, 1829 :

Resolved, That it be referred to the Committee on Supplying the City with Water to report upon the expediency of offering a premium of five hundred dollars for the best plan for supplying the city with pure and wholesome water, to be approved of by said committee.

In relation to procuring water for the extinguishment of fires, the following resolution was presented and referred on the sixteenth of November :

Resolved, That a competent practical man be appointed and employed to act as a commissioner or agent for the Common Council, to procure information, and to make plans and estimates for supplying the city (abundantly) with pure and wholesome water, said commissioner, or his successor, to be continued as superintendent of this highly-important public business.

The Water Committee was also directed to explore the Croton and other rivers for procuring a supply of water. Nevertheless, assessments for sixteen more public cisterns were presented for confirmation to the Common Council on the seventh of December, 1829.

The following are the locations of cisterns for the year 1830 :

4 at City Hall.
1 at Firemen's Hall, Fulton Street.
2 at Friends' Meeting House, Rose Street.
1 at St. Stephen's Church.
2 at Patten's Church, Broome Street.
1 at Mulberry Street Schoolhouse.
2 at Zion's Church, Leonard and Church Streets.
1 at Gas House, Hester Street.
1 at Watch House, Eldridge Street.
1 at Schoolhouse, Mott Street.
2 at Church, corner of Grand and Mercer Streets.
2 at Methodist Church, Allen Street.
2 at St. Thomas's Church, Broadway and Houston Street.

2 at Bowery, near Pump Street.
2 at Essex Market.
2 at Duane Street Schoolhouse.
2 at King Street, near McDougall Church.
2 at Herring and Amos Streets—Church.
1 at Methodist Church, corner Bedford and Arden Street (now Morton).
2 at Bleecker Street and Broadway.
2 at St. Mark's Church, near Stuyvesant Street.
2 at Baldwin's Church, corner Broome and Ridge Streets.
2 at Baptist Church, corner Delancey and Christie Streets.
2 at Friends' Meeting House, Hester and Elizabeth Streets.

These cisterns were kept filled by details of prisoners, chain gangs from the Penitentiary, which then stood where Bellevue Hospital is now located, who would take the unemployed engines from the corporation yard and fill the cisterns from the pumps and wells around the city.

In December, 1832, Colonel De Witt Clinton finally decided that the city would have to rely on the Croton River. Colonel Clinton had strong confidence in the practicability of delivering the water at one hundred and thirty-seven feet above tide. It actually now stands in the distributing reservoir at one hundred and fifteen feet. He preferred the open canal to the closed tunnel, both on account of the expense of constructing the tunnel and the danger of leakage and breakage. About this time an analysis of the Bronx was made by different chemists, Messrs. Chilton, Ackerly and Griscom, which showed it to be of remarkable purity, not containing more than two grains of foreign matter in a gallon.

On the twenty-sixth of February, 1833, the legislature took steps in the matter. Engineers set to work, and the route was calculated to be nearly forty-seven miles, and the expense four million seven hundred and sixty-eight thousand one hundred and ninety-seven dollars. On February 6, 1834, the Common Council applied to the legislature for a law authorizing a loan of two and a half millions of dollars, to create a stock called the "Water Stock of the City of New York," at five per

FORTY-SECOND STREET RESERVOIR.

cent. interest. The application was granted. The water commissioners appointed D. B. Douglas their chief engineer, and he organized a corps of seventeen engineers, who immediately took the field. I was in the Spring of 1837 that the work was fairly begun, and thirteen sections of the work were let. Three years were allowed for the fulfilment of the contracts. The line was divided into four districts, under Engineers Edmund French, Henry T. Anthony and Peter Hostie.

It was planned that one hundred and fifty-two miles of pipe in the streets would be wanted, and that the expense would be one million two hundred and sixty-one thousand six hundred and twenty-seven dollars.

As the work progressed it was seen that more millions would be required to complete it than the original estimate showed. Grog shops in the vicinity of the laborers were built, and these gave rise to scenes of riot and murder.

In the summer of 1838 (July 10) the comptroller was authorized to sell and dispose of five hundred thousand dollars of the "water stock of the city of New York;" and in the fall of that year (November 2) he was authorized to sell and dispose of a further amount of two hundred and fifty thousand dollars, redeemable in twenty years.

In 1838, during a drought, the Croton stream was gauged and found to be able to supply three times more water than the population required at that time. On May 3, 1839, the legislature passed an act authorizing the construction of High Bridge for the conveyance of the Croton. The total estimated cost of the structure was eight hundred and thirty-six thousand six hundred and thirteen dollars. The High Bridge was contracted for in August, 1839, at seven hundred and thirty-seven thousand seven hundred and fifty-five dollars, and on conditions that it should be completed in August, 1843. The cost of the Aqueduct, including the Bridge, was then estimated to be nine million dollars, over and above the loss of interest on the capital, until the work was finished and productive. In 1840 the original water commissioners, Messrs. Stephen Allen, William W. Fox, Charles Dusenberry and Thomas T. Woodruff, were superseded by Messrs. Samuel Stevens, Benjamin Birdsall, John D. Ward and Samuel B. Childs.

The early part of the working season of 1842 was rainy and occasioned some solicitude, lest the contractors, especially those for the dam, should not be able sufficiently to advance their work to realize the expectations of the citizens to behold the Croton flowing in their streets on the Fourth of July; but after the state of the weather permitted operations to be resumed, the work on the dam was carried on with such diligence and energy that the water in the Croton Lake was raised sufficiently high to flow into the aqueduct with a depth of eighteen inches on the morning of the twenty-second of June. In the following month a jet which threw the water from forty to fifty feet high had been prepared at Forty-seventh Street, and was playing at an early hour on the morning of the second, and was the greatest attraction in the city. The total cost of the Aqueduct was found to be eleven million four hundred and fifty-two thousand six hundred and nineteen dollars and sixty-one cents.

The completion of this great work was celebrated in a fitting manner by the city. A committee of the Common Council stated that the Fire Department had made extensive preparations for the occasion, and hoped the Corporation would do the same. Accordingly the sum of two thousand dollars was appropriated for the purpose—a sum that would have been considered ridiculously small in later days of reckless city expenditure. The president of the Common Council then appointed Aldermen Clarkson Crolius, Jr., Henry E. Davies, Edward D. West, Charles W. Smith, and Frederick R. Lee a committee to take steps to carry out the celebration. The Board of Assistant Aldermen concurred and appointed Messrs. Geo. F. Nesbitt, William Dodge, Daniel Ward, H. C. Atwell, and C. F. Dodge members of the joint committee. Alderman Clarkson Crolius was appointed chairman. Invitations were sent to the corporations of all the cities and towns near at hand. General George P. Morris composed an ode, and the New York Sacred Music Society, through their President Luther B. Wyman, volunteered to sing it on a stage in front of the City Hall. It was arranged that the splendid banner, painted by Mr Allan Smith, Jr., and intended as a present to the Fire Department by the city authorities, should be presented by His Honor Mayor Morris to the Board of Trustees of the Fire Department Fund, who were delegated by the department to receive it at nine A. M. in front of the City Hall.

L. Maria Child, in her "Letters from New York" (1845), thus poetically and glowingly refers to the introduction of Croton into the city:

"But nature is filled with spirits, as it was in the old Grecian time. One of them dwells in our midst, and scatters blessings like a goddess. This lovely nymph, for years uncourted, reclined in the verdant fields, exchanging glances with the stars, which saw themselves in her deep blue eyes. In true transcendental style she reposed quietly in the sunshine, watching the heavens reflect themselves in her full urn. Sometimes the little birds drank therefrom and looked upward, or the Indian disturbed her placid mirror for a moment with his birchen cup. Thus ages passed, and the beautiful nymph gazed ever upward, and held her mirror to the heavens. But the spirit which pervades all forms was changing—changing; and it whispered to the nymph: 'Why liest thou here all the day idle? The birds only sip from thy full urn, while thousands

CITY HALL FOUNTAIN.

of human beings suffer for what thou hast to spare.' Then the nymph held communion with the sun, and he answered: 'I give unto all without stint or measure, and yet my storehouse is full, as at the beginning.' She looked at heaven, and saw written among the stars, 'Lo, I embrace all, and thy urn is but a fragment of the great mirror, in which I reveal myself to all.'

"Then the nymph felt heaving aspirations at her heart, and she said, 'I too would be like the sunshine and the bright blue heavens.' A voice from the infinite replied, 'He that giveth receiveth. Let thine urn pour forth forever, and it shall be forever full.'

"Then the water leaped joyfully and went on its mission of love. Concealed, like good deeds, it went all over the city, and baptized it in the name of Purity, Temperance and Health. It flowed in the midst of pollution and filth, but kept itself unmixed and undefiled, like Arethusa in her pathway through the sea—like a pure and loving heart visiting the abodes of wretchedness and sin.   The children sport with its thousand rills; the poor invoke blessings on the urn whence such treasures flow; and when the old enemy— Fire—puts forth his forked tongue, the nymph throws her veil over him, and hissing he goes out from her presence.   Yet the urn fails not, but overflows evermore.   And since the nymph has changed repose for action, and self-contemplation for bounteous outgiving, she has received

> " 'A very shower of beauty for her earthly dower.'

"She stands before us a perpetual fountain of beauty and joy, wearing the sunlight for diamonds and the rainbow for her mantle.   This magnificent vision of herself, as a veiled Water Spirit, is her princely gift to the *soul* of man; and who can tell what changes may be wrought therewith?"

"To me," says the same writer, "there is something extremely beautiful in the idea of that little river lying so many years unnoticed among the hills; her great powers as little appreciated as Shakespeare's were by his contemporaries, and, like him, all unconscious of her future fame; and now, like his genius, brought to all the people a perpetual fountain of refreshment.   *   * Her name, Crotona, hath the old Grecian sound, but greater is her glory than Callirhoe, or Arethusa, or Agle, the fairest of the Naiads, for Crotona manifests the idea of an age on which rests the golden shadow of an approaching millennium—that equal diffusion is the only wealth, and working for others is the only joy.

"Are you curious to know what conjured up this fair vision to my mind? On New Year's night a fire broke out in narrow and crowded Gold Street. It was soon extinguished, and on that occasion alone the insurance companies estimate that at least a million of dollars' worth of property was probably saved by Croton water.   Fires, once so terrific in this city, are now mere trifles.   The alarms are not more than one to six compared with former years. This indicates that a large proportion was the work of incendiaries, who have small motives to pursue their vocation, now that the flames can be so easily extinguished.   Reflecting on these blessings, I thought how the old Greeks would have worshipped Crotona, and what a fair statue they would have chiseled from their Pentelic marble.   But, after all, what had they so beautiful as our ' Maid of the Mist'?"

High Bridge was completed in 1848.   With the completion of High Bridge the water commissioners appointed by the governor finished their labors, and the whole system came under the charge of the Croton Aqueduct Board.   In 1853–4 an additional pipe of four feet diameter was laid across Manhattan Valley.   In 1858 the construction of the new large reservoir in Central Park was begun, and it was completed in 1862.

In 1860-61 the large iron pipe of seven feet six and five-eighths inches diameter, and equal to the full capacity of the aqueduct, was laid on High Bridge, over which the water had theretofore been passed through two thirty-six inch pipes.   In 1861 another pipe of five feet diameter was laid across Manhattan Valley.   In 1865–6 in pursuance of an Act of the legislature, the masonry aqueduct below Ninety-second Street was discontinued and replaced by two lines of six-foot pipes laid through Ninetieth Street and Eighth Avenue to the reservoir in Central Park.

In 1866 the present high service works at High Bridge were commenced and completed so as to be brought into use in 1870, since which time their capacity has been enlarged by the construction of another pumping engine and the laying of additional pipes. In the same year the construction of the storage reservoir at Boyd's Corners, on the west branch of the Croton River, was begun. It was not completed to be available for use until March, 1873. By an Act of the legislature of 1870, the remaining portion of the masonry aqueduct on Manhattan Island, above the surface of the ground, viz., between Ninety second and One Hundred and Thirteenth Streets, was ordered to be replaced by underground conduits. The conduits decided upon were four lines of four-feet pipes, laid under the surface of Tenth Avenue. They were completed in 1875.

In 1872 the then commissioner of public works purchased the land for the new storage reservoir on the middle branch of the Croton River, near Carmel ;

HIGH BRIDGE.

but for some reason it was not put under contract until October, 1874. It was completed and water let into it in April, 1878.

The total amount expended for works, structures, aqueducts, pipes, etc., etc., connected with the water supply of the city of New York, including maintenance and repairs, from the period of its inception to the first day of January, 1879, was thirty-five million eight hundred and twenty thousand and eighty-one dollars and forty-six cents, of which sum twenty million thirty thousand two hundred and twenty-one dollars and ninety-three cents had been spent to January 1, 1865. The revenue derived from Croton water from its introduction into the city in 1842 to January 1, 1879, amounted to thirty-two million one thousand five hundred and thirty-five dollars and seventy-three cents.

But as the city continued to grow the old aqueduct became inadequate to supply the increasing population with water. For years complaints were made of the scarcity of water, just as in the olden time, and at last the legislature sanctioned the building of a new aqueduct. A charter was obtained in

June, 1883, known as " An Act to provide new reservoirs, dams, and a new Aqueduct, with the appurtenances thereto, for the purpose of supplying the city of New York with an increased supply of pure and wholesome water." Long before 1883, however, the municipal authorities had looked over the ground and mapped out plans. It was deemed wisest to construct the new aqueduct wholly in a tunnel, instead of following the natural contour of the surface of the ground, and thus insure safety and economy. It was found that the Croton was a most unreliable stream. In 1880 there were two hundred and six days in which no water ran over the dam, and other days when millions of gallons ran to waste, there being no means for storing it for drier months. It was resolved to excavate the conduit, except at a few points, by tunnel in the solid rock. It was proposed to construct a dam to impound water to a level of two hundred feet above tide, in order to utilize the utmost flow possible from the watershed of the Croton River. This water area would cover three thousand acres, giving a storage capacity, when filled, of thirty-two thousand million gallons, the top water line of this reservoir being thirty-four feet above the lip of the present Croton Dam.

The new Aqueduct Commission, in their effort to utilize as great a flow from the basin as possible, fixed the dimensions of the new Aqueduct as equivalent to a circle of fourteen feet in diameter, or a discharge of three hundred and twenty-four million gallons daily. This, together with the old Aqueduct, will give a supply of four hundred million gallons daily, to feed which, in a dry year, such as 1880, will require nearly seventy thousand million gallons of stored water in the Croton Basin.

The new Aqueduct begins near the present Croton Dam, in a tunnel of a horseshoe section, within a brick lining, which will extend throughout from end to end. The excavation is at times necessarily in excess of the required dimensions, and slips may extend high into the roof, and at other places heavy timbering is required. The normal section taken out per running foot is two hundred and four cubic feet. The capacity of the finished tunnel is preserved from the starting point until the New York City boundary is reached. It was expected at this point that for the annexed district a distributing reservoir would be built, which would divert a portion of the flow, and hence the flow below this point towards New York would be but two hundred and fifty million gallons daily; the finished diameter of the tunnel thence was reduced to a circle of twelve feet three inches in diameter.

This portion of the tunnel for a length of six and one-half miles, owing to a falling away of the surface, is depressed, and, being under pressure, will be reduced in size and more heavily lined with masonry. It includes the section under the Harlem River, which, owing to the character of the rock, is carried one hundred and sixty feet below the tide level; and the tunnel here, in addition to the heavy brick lining, will also be secured by an interior lining of cast iron two inches in thickness, the section of the tunnel below the river being ten and one-half feet in diameter. On the south side of the Harlem River the tunnel will resume its dimensions of twelve feet three inches, and terminate in a gate house at One Hundred and Thirty-fifth Street. Thence iron pipes will convey the water to Central Park reservoir.

The entire length of the tunnel to One Hundred and Thirty-fifth Street will be thirty and three-quarter miles, being over five miles less than the old aqueduct between tne same points. It will be worked through thirty-four snafts and ten open portals, and the progress may be estimated as thirty-two feet for-

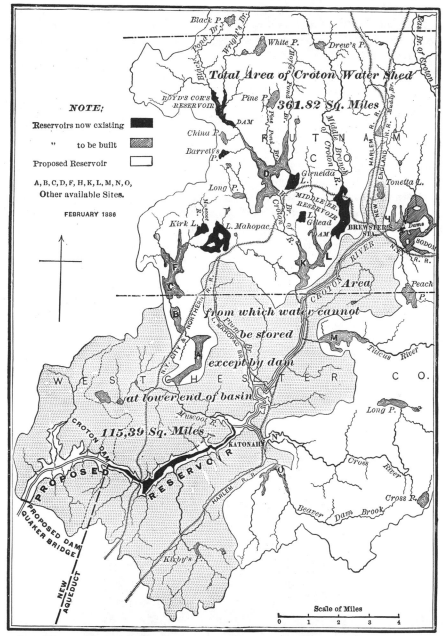

From HARPER'S WEEKLY.

WATER SHED OF CROTON RIVER.

ward per week at each heading. There are about twenty miles of tunnel at present excavated, and about three miles of brick lining completed.

The construction of this Aqueduct will cost from fifteen to twenty million dollars. The contract for excavation amounted to over twelve million dollars.

Not less than six extensive gate chambers will be required for the purpose of emptying portions of the Aqueduct, if it should be found necessary, and for regulating the flow of water from the Storage Reservoir into the city; one of these, near the Croton Dam, is a most intricate structure, calculated to meet the wants of a most unprecedented water service, and will alone cost some five hundred thousand dollars.

Surveys had been made for shallow receptacles, but no sites for dams for over one hundred square miles of the basin could be found, except by means of the Quaker Bridge Dam. To take advantage of the entire drainage of the basin, many declared it absolutely necessary that the dam should be built. The Quaker Dam is located in a deep rocky gorge of the Croton River, about four miles below the present dam. Extensive borings indicate solid rock for the foundation about ninety feet below the bed of the river. The dam proper being one hundred and seventy-eight feet high above this level, makes the total height from the rock about two hundred and seventy feet. The width of the gorge at the bottom is four hundred feet, and the top of the dam is one thousand four hundred feet in length, to be occupied by a river. No water will flow over the dam itself; all freshets and waste will pass by an ample spill-way cut in the rock to the south and west of the dam. There will be about five hundred thousand cubic yards of stone masonry laid in hydraulic cement, and it is estimated to cost between four and five million, and require a little less than five years to build.

So far the work has progressed with great loss of life and injury to limb. Three shifts of workmen occur in twenty-four hours, and the work is continued night and day. The shafts range in depth from over sixty to three hundred and fifty feet. The energy of those in charge has been wonderful, and the labor-saving expedients admirable. As a whole the undertaking has been managed with consummate skill.

GROUP OVER GATE OF GREAT RESERVOIR.

CHAPTER XXI.

IMPROVEMENT AND GROWTH OF THE CITY.

Creation of a Street Commissioners' Department.—Active Measures of Improvement Inaugurated.—
Construction of Wells and Pumps.—The City South of Grand Street Lighted with Gas.—Ancient
Burial Grounds Obliterated.—Public Schools.—Wharves, Slips and Piers.—New Buildings Created.—
The Croton Aqueduct.—Public Cisterns.—City Debt.—Water Pipes.

OPPORTUNITY has been taken at various parts of preceding chapters to
point out many of the leading improvements of former years. It will
now suit our purpose best to take up these improvements at the year
1830, when the records are more definite on the subject, and within the compass of a couple of chapters to mark thenceforth to the present time the rapid

VIEW OF NEW YORK, 1679

progress made, and to record the material growth and prosperity of the city.

A new street was opened in 1830 from Sixth Avenue to Christopher Street,
where it united with Asylum Street, coming in from Eighth Avenue on the
north, and at Sixth Avenue its opening was immediately opposite Fourth
Street, of which, in fact, it was a continuation. The new street received the
name of Asylum Street, and was so known up to December 9, 1833, at which
date it was determined to change the name to Fourth Street. The change was
made in January, 1834.

A Street Commissioner's Department was created by a law passed and
approved October 5, 1831. The duty of the street commissioner required him
to advertise for estimates and to contract for wells and pumps, canals and
sewers, paving or repairing streets, constructing roads, building wharves and
piers; to report such estimates to the Common Council previous to furnishing
contracts; to inquire into the subject matter of all applications to the Common
Council for regulating, paving, or otherwise improving the streets, roads, or
wharves, and report the particular state of the circumstances of each case,
and if necessary a survey or plan of the improvements thereby intended; to

attend to the due execution of all ordinances of the Common Council for regulating, digging, filling, paving, or repairing streets, roads, wharves, and common sewers; to report to the attorney of the Common Council all offenders against the provisions of the ordinance, and particularly of persons guilty of intrusion or encroachment on the public streets or roads; to take the general charge of viewing or determining from time to time whether any and what improvements and repairs are necessary and can be made to any of the streets, roads, etc., and to report to the Common Council the best mode of doing the same, etc.

A deputy street commissioner was appointed to assist the commissioner, etc. Both were sworn to the faithful performance of their duties, and gave bonds respectively in the sums of ten thousand dollars and five thousand dollars for the same.

Active measures were at once begun to forward the work of improvement, and the citizens were not slow to avail themselves of the advantages presented by the official guidance and assistance of the newly organized Department. Steps were taken to fill in the sunken lot on the south side of Fifth Street, between Avenue D and Lewis Street. It was decided to regulate and pave Market Street between Division Street and East Broadway. The street had been widened, but the pavement at this time (the fall of 1831) had become so bad that the thoroughfare was impassable for vehicles. Suitable places for bathing were spoken of, located on the North and East Rivers, to prevent the unsightly exhibitions of naked humanity which had become so frequent along the river front. Wells and pumps were favorably reported for the northeast corner of Suffolk and Rivington Streets, Avenue D and Seventh Street, Third Street between Avenues C and D, Twentieth and Sixteenth Streets, Seventeenth Street near Seventh Avenue, Eighteenth Street, Eighth Avenue near Seventeenth Street, Second Street and Avenue D, Second Street and Avenue B, King Street between Varick and Smith Streets, and the junction of Weehawken and Christopher Streets. The low grounds in the vicinity of Third Avenue and Second Avenue were filled up; the water drained off the grounds at Nineteenth Street and Seventh Avenue. Horatio Street was opened and regulated from Greenwich to West Streets; Washington and West Streets were continued in survey to Tenth Avenue; and Canal Street was lighted with gas from Centre Street to the North River. Permission was given to pave the sidewalks of Sixth Avenue from Fourth Street to Barrow Street.

Increased activity was displayed by the Street Commissioner's Department in 1832. The citizens also evinced their appreciation of the growing necessities of the metropolis, and pushed forward improvements as far as the means of executing them permitted. A well and pump were constructed in Eighth Street, near Third Avenue; and a boring was made for water successfully in Watts Street, between Sullivan and Varick Streets, where a well and pump were built.

In September of this year the rector, churchwardens, and vestrymen of St. Mark's Church petitioned that Stuyvesant and Tenth Streets should be regulated and paved between Second and Third Avenues. Stuyvesant Street was built upon to a considerable extent, and there were a few buildings on Tenth Street. In fact, considering the number and cost of the houses recently erected and being commenced, that part of the city was improving in an unexampled degree. The Common Council did not hesitate to grant the prayer of the petitioners, and the work was immediately begun.

The regulating and paving of Third Avenue between Twenty-third and Twenty-fourth Streets was begun in October, 1832, in conformity with the plan of improving cross sections of the island.

Samuel B. Ruggles, in 1831 and 1832, acquired the tract of land between Third and Fourth Avenues, which he laid out in building lots, forty-two of which he set aside for an ornamental square (now Gramercy Park). He caused a street to be laid out extending from Fourteenth Street to Thirty-first

WASHINGTON MARKET, 1850.
[Showing Old Bell Tower.]

Street, and in testimony of the respect and gratitude justly due the distinguished Washington Irving, he petitioned the Common Council to be permitted to name the Street " Irving Place." His prayer was granted, and the thorough-fare was so named in January, 1833.

Among the numerous improvements which marked the close of the year 1833 were the building of towers and buttresses on the University; wells and pumps at Minetta Street near Macdougal Street, Eighteenth Street near Tenth Avenue; at the intersection of Sixth Avenue and Macdougal Street; in Christie Street between North (now Houston) and Stanton Streets.

Measures were taken to open Twenty-eighth Street from Third to Fourth Avenue. Twenty-eighth Street leads from Third Avenue to a point where

Fourth Avenue, the Middle Road, and the road coming on from the House of Refuge, commonly called the Eastern Post Road, all united, and had become a very considerable channel of communication between the eastern and western parts of the city—and was, in fact, indispensable to maintain the means of passing across.

The name of North Street was changed to Houston Street. Sidewalks were made on West Street from Canal to Harrison Street; on Avenue C, from North Street to Third Street; on Third Street, between Avenues C and D; on Factory Street, between Charles and Hammond Streets; on Fourth Street, between Bowery and Second Avenue.

Twenty-fifth Street, from Second Avenue to the Old Post Road; Nineteenth Street, from Third Avenue to the Bloomingdale Road, and Twenty-fourth Street from Third Avenue to the Old Post Road, were opened. Also, Seventeenth Street, from Sixth to Third Avenue.

Old Slip was filled up to a line with South Street, and Coffee House and Burling Slips similarly filled up, and piers built across them.

Eleventh Street, between First and Second Avenues, and South Street, between Pike and Rutgers Streets, were filled up and regulated, and Sixteenth and Seventeenth Streets, between Third Avenue and Union Place, were regulated.

That open squares in the dense and crowded parts of the city contribute largely to the preservation of the public health, and become enduring ornaments of large cities, seems to have been clearly appreciated in those days. Many inhabitants of the Tenth and Eleventh Wards of the city petitioned the Common Council in January, 1834, to take the property bounded by Allen, Rivington, Orchard and Stanton Streets for the purpose of a public square. Other owners of property in these wards protested against such a course, deeming a public square wholly unnecessary, and because they did not wish to part with their property at that time for any purpose. The remonstrants prevailed.

In this year Third Street, between Lewis and Mangin, was regulated and paved; Gold Street, between Frankfort and Fulton Streets, was widened from twenty-five to fifty feet; Avenue B, from Fifth to Tenth Street, was filled up and regulated; Beaver Street, from William to Broad Street, was widened; Twenty-seventh Street, from Second Avenue to the Old Post Road; Tompkins Square; Eighth Street, from Avenue B to the East River; Gay Street, from Christopher to Sixth Street; Eighteenth Street, from Bloomingdale Road to the land ceded by Peter Stuyvesant; Eighteenth Street, from Third Avenue to First Avenue, and First Avenue, from Eighty-fourth Street to Eighty-sixth Street, were opened. The Hurl Gate Road, north of Eighty-sixth Street, was closed. Whitehall Street, between Marketfield and Front Streets, was lighted with gas. The name of Augustus Street was changed to City Hall Place. Sidewalks were laid on Wooster Street from Amity to Fourth Street, and on Fourteenth Street from Sixth to Ninth Avenues.

The construction of wells and pumps was continued with unabated energy, and as the neccessities of the inhabitants demanded. On Sixteenth Street, between Eighth and Ninth Avenues; on Eighteenth Street, near Ninth Avenue; Twentieth Street, between Seventh and Eighth Avenues; at junction of Ninth Avenue and Seventeenth Street: and on Twentieth Street, near Sixth

Avenue, wells and pumps were built. These works were originally constructed at the expense of the residents. When made conformable to the city regulations, being of proper size, having a sufficient depth of water and properly made, it was customary for the public authorities to take charge of them.

The public improvements which had been commenced during the year 1834 were generally of a character to produce permanent advantages both of safety and convenience to the inhabitants. The question of securing an ample supply of pure and wholesome water had been submitted directly to the people, and their decision in favor of the measure had been made in the manner prescribed by law. In looking to future events connected with their commercial and domestic prospects the fact was not lost sight of that sister cities of other States were entering into competition with a zeal and enterprise which rendered them formidable but not unworthy rivals. Philadelphia and Baltimore, by the completion of their various works of internal communication, were already attracting a considerable portion of the valuable trade of the West, and it became necessary for the people of New York to consider what steps were required to secure their position upon an equality with those enterprising cities.

Arrangements were completed, during 1834, for the erection of buildings on the site of the public yards fronting on Elm and Centre Streets, for a House of Detention for persons accused of crime and for other purposes connected with the Criminal and Police Departments. The foundation for the "Asylum for Lunatics" was laid on Blackwell's Island, and the erection of an Almshouse was in contemplation for the accommodation of the poor and such

OLD MECHANICS' BELL TOWER.

other dependents on the public bounty as had not already been provided for in the public institutions.

Sixth Avenue was opened on June 22, 1835, from Thirty-fourth Street, where it intersected the Bloomingdale Road, to One Hundred and Twenty-ninth Street. Tenth Avenue from Thirteenth to Sixteenth Street was made in the fall of that year; and all the streets and avenues, as laid down on the then map of the city, were opened, up to and including Forty-Second Street, except that part of Forty-first Street between Fifth and Sixth Avenues, it being understood that that land would be required for uses connected with the Aqueduct. Mount Morris Park in Harlaem was mapped out; and plans were prepared for regulating the Avenues and Streets of Harlaem from One Hundred and Ninth to One Hundred and Thirty-fifth Street and from Ninth Avenue to the Harlaem River.

A law was passed by the legislature in the spring of 1836, on the application of the Common Council, authorizing a loan of five hundred thousand dollars for the purpose of raising the means necessary for the erection of public buildings. That measure was resorted to upon the ground that, while a large amount of public property was held for the future advantage of the city, and was increasing rapidly and continually in value, it was obviously unjust to the taxpaying citizens to assess them for all the improvements in progress for the public service. The policy which appropriates the property and the resources of the city to the creation of necessary and permanent improvements for the public service was regarded as sound and judicious; and it was therefore held to be but just to themselves and to posterity, while the public property was held for future accumulation, to transmit the improvements and the obligations by which they were created to those who should come after them.

On the twelfth of May, 1823, the corporation entered into a contract with the New York Gas Company to furnish a sufficient supply of the best quality of gas for all the public lamps south of a line running parallel with Grand Street, and in return for the advantages contemplated to be derived from having that part of the city well lighted, the corporation granted to the New York Gas Company the exclusive privilege of laying their pipes and vending gas in all the streets south of said line. The whole number of public lamps furnished with gas up to September, 1835, was four hundred and forty-four. In January, 1836, there were six hundred and eighty-eight lamps in the city lighted with gas, four hundred and forty-six by the lighters of the New York Gas Company, and two hundred and twenty-two lighted by the lighters of the municipal corporation.

In 1792, when Chambers Street was opened, it passed through the burial ground of the Africans. In 1800 Bancker (now Madison) Street cut through the burial places of the Jews. In 1815 Second Avenue ran through the burial ground of the Methodist Congregation. In 1817 First Street passed through the cemeteries of St. Stephen's Church and of the Methodists. In 1826 First Street travelled over a portion of Potter's Field, and passed directly through the cemetery of the Cedar Street Presbyterian Church. In 1827, in widening Nassau and Liberty Streets, the church vaults of the Middle Dutch Church were cut through and their silent inhabitants removed. In 1830 Elizabeth Street cut off portions of the cemeteries of the Jews and of the Presbyterian Church at the corner of Grand and Mercer Streets. In view of these frequent violations of the sanctity of the grave, the Common Council, in 1823, set apart a portion of the common lands of the city lying between Fifth and Sixth Avenues, and between Fortieth and Forty-fifth Streets, for a public burial ground. The plot contained about twenty-six acres, and the design was to sell or otherwise dispose of portions of it to the different churches, and so to ornament the grounds as to make this Public Cemetery a place of resort for strangers as well as for the citizens; and it was thought that the distance of three miles from the City Hall would effectually protect the spot thus appropriated from any intrusion. But time disclosed the fact that the growth of the city outran even the wildest calculations. The city was even then upon the boundary line of the then proposed Public Cemetery.

In 1825 the grounds occupied as a Potter's Field were filled up and regulated, and the name of the place subsequently became the "Washington Parade Ground." A portion of the common lands lying between Third and Fourth Avenues and Forty-eighth and Fiftieth Streets was afterwards occupied as a Potter's Field, which in 1836 was removed to the "Long Island Farms."

The Public School Society of New York was declared to have been "established for the promotion of the literary, moral, and religious welfare of the rising generation." In 1827 that society consisted of nine schools, containing four thousand five hundred and fifty-eight boys and girls; in May, 1836, there were fifteen schools, containing nine thousand one hundred and eighty-two scholars of both sexes; twenty-six primary schools, containing two thousand nine hundred and forty-six children, and public primary schools for one thousand one hundred and seventy-one colored children. The whole amount expended for that object by the School Society in 1836 was one hundred and thirty-two thousand five hundred and twenty-three dollars and thirty-eight cents, of which eighty-seven thousand three hundred and sixty-four dollars and thirty-one cents was paid by this city.

The enlargement and extension of wharves, slips and piers received a good deal of deserved attention in the summer of 1837. This being emphatically a commercial city, all judicious efforts to invite hither and give security and protection to the vessels of every nation were universally commended.

KISSING BRIDGE ON THE OLD BOSTON ROAD, 1860.
[Fiftieth Street and Second Avenue.]

The formation of public squares at suitable intervals was also actively agitated. It had been the policy of the Common Council, while land was comparatively cheap, to locate such squares as in their opinion would ultimately be wanted. An adherence to that policy allowed of a gradual, cheap and permanent regulation of them.

The system of paving was defective and unnecessarily expensive. A method was suggested which proposed that the spaces in the pavements laid in the usual manner should be filled with a substance which would at once form a solid mass, furnish a smooth and agreeable surface, be impervious to water and not affected by the frost, and yet be favorable to health and economy.

In December, 1837, that portion of Mill Street in a direct line between William and Broad Streets was changed to that of South William Street. It was originally a mere alley connecting with Stone and Broad Streets. William Street was widened and extended from Maiden Lane to Chatham Street in March, 1838.

From the year of its discovery up to the year 1838, this city, at first known as the city of "Niew Nederlands," was considered a commercial city. Those who at so early a period became acquainted with the position of the "Island of Manhattoes" foresaw that nature had prepared a splendid banquet for those who should possess it. They beheld the great rivers of the East and West, and of the far West, the beautiful lakes of the continent, and learned the unsurpassed fertility of the soil which borders them; they felt that at no very distant day New York must become and remain the queen of cities. In such a commercial mart suitable and plenteous accommodations for the craft in which wealth, business and traffic should come were of immense interest. That was verified by the experience of past ages. It was as true of ancient as it was of modern times. The piers and moles of Tyre, Syracuse, Carthage, Alexandria, Athens and other cities formed one of the mightiest of the causes of their superior prosperity. And it was everywhere declared that the perfect safety and convenience for all descriptions of shipping so extensively provided at London, Liverpool, Havre, Naples, Palermo and Boston had attracted and perpetuated much of the business which gave them wealth and power, and would continue in their possession. There was a time when the wharves, slips and piers constructed by this city were "well enough" and perhaps were as ample and extensive as the demand for them justified. But the times were changed, and those important works should change with them. Ships were now constructed of huge dimensions, drawing great depth of water; and the kinds of conveyance by water too had been wonderfully altered and multiplied. The addition and general use of steamboats and towboats in various forms had created a demand for a species of dock room and a sort of exclusive use thereof that had not been dreamt of by any one a few years before. The unconquerable industry and enterprise of the State of New York, as well as of New England and of the "Great West," like the power of a slumbering lion, were only at rest, and would, it was hoped, again spring forth to new achievements and high objects. The natural advantages, and those derived from the various canals and railroads, to be continued and enlarged by the energies of the aspiring, ingenious and indomitable owners of an immense territory, were again to pour their treasures into this city and give it new life, vigor, animation and advancement.

The amount of real estate owned by the corporation in 1839 was fifteen million five hundred and sixty-three thousand nine hundred and twelve dollars and twenty cents, having an income of one hundred and sixty-six thousand one hundred and ninety-two dollars and thirty-two cents. This amount of property, though not producing a sum at all equal even to a lower rate of interest on its value, was still looked upon as a security pledged to the public creditors and as a source from which funds might be obtained, when necessary, to discharge those debts, and no doubt added to the confidence of capitalists who made investments in public stocks.

A large amount of that property was, however, unproductive, and from the rapid growth of the city some part of it was so situated that it might be made to produce a revenue at this time, and by being brought into use be increased in value. The propriety of adopting some plan of leasing the public lands therefore became a subject of serious consideration.

The Water Commissioners were proceeding as rapidly with the Croton Aqueduct as the character of the work and necessary prudence in its erection would admit of. The report made to the Common Council in January, 1839, showed that there had been then expended one million nine hundred and fifty-eight thousand six hundred and seventy dollars and seventy-eight cents, and that the whole line of the aqueduct was then under contract. There had been completed eleven and one-fifth miles, equal to one-fourth of the whole line, and the total amount expended up to May, 1839, amounted to two million three hundred and twenty-six thousand nine hundred and seventy-five dollars and ninety-four cents. The contracts for the work would expire in 1841, and it was conjectural whether the work could be completed by that time. There had been various causes which tended to delay the completion of the work beyond the time originally contemplated, and it would be only under the most favorable circumstances, with the fulfillment of the contracts by all the contractors, and the removal of the difficulties existing as to the mode of crossing the Harlaem River, that such a result could be looked for. The legislature, in the spring of 1839, passed an act prescribing that mode.

The number of new buildings erected within the year 1839 was less than during any similiar period for the previous six years. The whole number so erected was six hundred and seventy-four; in the preceding year the number was seven hundred and eighty-one, and in the year 1837 it was eight hundred and forty. The heavy pecuñiary embarrassments under which the country had been placed produced that result.

About twenty-seven miles of the Croton Aqueduct was completed by May, 1840, and the whole amount expended up to this period was five million four hundred and sixty-five thousand and thirty-six dollars and seventy-one cents.

The number of new buildings erected in the city during 1841 was nine hundred and seventy-one, being an increase over 1840 of one hundred and twenty-one.

The sewer in Canal Street was in such a bad condition in the summer of 1842 that the attention of the authorities was called to it. The refuse from the gas works and distilleries was discharged through it. That, with the accumulation of filth from the city prison, and from the surface of the streets, was not only very offensive to the inhabitants living in Canal Street and the adjoining streets, but the discharge from its mouth at the North River was destructive of the proper uses of the slips into which it emptied, and detrimental to the fish market in Canal Street, the fish there sold having in consequence to be kept in "cars" in the slips adjacent.

The whole amount of expenditure in connection with the building of the Croton Aqueduct from the commencement of the work, say from July, 1835, to August 1, 1842, was seven million six hundred and six thousand two hundred and thirteen dollars and eighty-four cents. On the eighth of June of the latter year the commissioners, accompanied by the engineers, commenced a journey on foot through the Aqueduct, which was completed to the Harlaem River, a distance of thirty-three miles, in the two succeeding days. The whole line having been found in good condition, orders were given to close the openings; which being done, and the dam raised sufficiently to cause the water to flow into the Aqueduct, it was admitted to a depth of eighteen inches at five o'clock in the morning of June 22. A boat capable of carrying four persons, called the "*Croton Maid*," was then placed in the Aqueduct to be carried down by the current, and she completed her singular voyage to the Harlaem River almost simultaneously with the first arrival of the water.

On the arrival of the water at Harlaem on Thursday, June 23, formal notice of the event was given by the commissioners to the mayor and Common Council, who were also informed of the intention to admit it into the Receiving Reservoir at Yorkville on the following Monday.

This intention was completely carried out, the water having been admitted into the reservoir on that day at half past four o'clock P. M. in the presence of a large assemblage, which included the mayor and several members of the Common Council, the governor of the State, the lieutenant governor, and other members of the Court for the Correction of Errors, and many other distinguished persons. A salute of thirty-eight guns was fired. The "*Croton Maid*," which arrived soon afterwards at the reservoir, was hailed with much enthusiasm, and was presented to the Fire Department. The water was retained in that reservoir until July 2, when it was allowed to flow into the iron pipes, which conducted it to the distributing reservoir. At five o'clock on the morning of the Fourth of July the Croton River was in full flow into the reservoir. A jet, which threw the water from forty to fifty feet high, had been prepared at Forty-seventh Street, and was playing at an early hour. At the particular request of the mayor, who stated that the tanks at Thirteenth Street were dry, and the city much exposed if a fire should occur, the water was allowed to flow into the distributing pipes, which had been laid down under the direction of the Common Council.

The citizens and the Council were certainly to be congratulated on the successful introduction of the Croton water. The Aqueduct could furnish daily fifty millions of gallons. No population of three hundred thousand had ever before voluntarily decreed that they would execute such a work. No population but one of freemen would have conceived the idea, for it was undertaken not to commemorate the birth or decease of any monarch, nor to mark a battle-field, or the death or victory of any military chieftain. The stately marble monuments, and the colossal mounds of maimed cannon, only record battles fought. The Croton work was not made for the purpose that the ancient walls of China, Rome, and London, or the more modern walls of Paris, were designed. The great Croton work, voted for by the people, did not contemplate protection from external foes, but it looked to making the population happier, more temperate, and more healthy; and that the countless millions thereafter might enjoy the benefits of the water service.

On the sixteenth of March, 1829, the question of abolishing the system of public cisterns and laying down two lines of twelve-inch iron pipes, one through Broadway and one through the Bowery, and placing a tank or reservoir in Thirteenth Street, on the pinnacle of a rock there situated, was discussed. The plan was pronounced by some to be visionary, and it was declared that water enough could not be procured to fill a tea-kettle, much less the tanks and pipes. The reply to that argument was, "Give us the tank and pipes and we engage to fill them, if we have to carry the water in quart bottles.'' The tank was constructed, the pipes laid down, the hydrants erected. No public cisterns were afterwards made. Every subsequent year added length to the line of pipes, until in August, 1842, they had one hundred and thirty miles, and the Croton River was flowing into that tank and through those pipes and hydrants.

The reception of the Croton water into the city was a matter for universal congratulation. It was an achievement constituting another evidence of the patriotism, scientific and mechanical talent and energy of the citizens ; a work in its conception and execution second only to the Erie Canal. Arrangements were immediately set on foot to conduct it to the market places, to be used in cleansing them, and by which each hydrant in the city might be used in cleaning the streets.

Eighth Avenue in March, 1843, had been paved from Hudson Street to Twenty-fourth Street, and macadamized thence to Fifty-ninth Street, and gravelled from One Hundred and Twenty-fifth Street to McComb's Dam, leaving two and one-half miles to be graded and macadamized, which the inhabitants and owners of property in Manhattanville, Bloomingdale and Chelsea petitioned the Common Council to do.

The whole absolute debt of the city on the twentieth of May, 1843, was twelve million seven hundred and thirty-one thousand five hundred and eighteen dollars and thirty-three cents.

The number of new build-

OLD BOWERY THEATRE, 1863.

ings erected in 1842 was nine hundred and twelve, a decrease of fifty-nine from 1841 ; in 1843 one thousand two hundred and seventy-three, an increase over 1842 of three hundred and sixty-one.

The absolute city debt, both permanent and temporary, in May, 1843, as measured by its stocks, bonds and checks outstanding, was thirteen million six hundred and ninety-seven thousand three hundred and twenty-three dollars and thirty-three cents. This sum, however, included a nominal debt to the commissioners of the sinking fund, as holders of its stocks, to the amount of nine hundred and sixty-five thousand eight hundred and five dollars. With this proper deduction the whole absolute debt may be stated at twelve million seven hundred and thirty-one thousand five hundred and eighteen dollars and thirty-three cents. In addition to the above other certificates of stocks and bonds had been issued under the authority of the corporation to the amount of seven hundred and ten thousand one hundred and sixty-two dollars and sixty-four cents, which was properly regarded a contingent liability, and for which the city was indemnified by absolute liens on real estate situate in the county.

The permanent debt subjected the taxable inhabitants to an annual assessment for interest of seven hundred and thirty-two thousand dollars, or three-tenth mills on each dollar of their assessable property. That tax with the State mill tax constituted a severe burden from the weight of which no speedy relief could be expected. To that was to be annually added a large tax for the support of the municipal government.

The actual amount of the city debt in May, 1845, was twelve million four hundred and fifty-four thousand four hundred and ninety-seven dollars and sixty cents. The condition of the streets had long been the subject of complaint, which, instead of diminishing within the year preceding, had greatly increased. The system of cleaning them by men employed at day's work by the corporation had been condemned as too expensive; while the system of cleaning them by contract had proved inefficient. Mayor Havemeyer brought this subject prominently before the Common Council, and urged them to adopt measures looking to a reformation in that respect.

A system which had been attended with flagrant abuses and had wrought most serious injury to many citizens was that of city improvements, including the opening and regulation of streets, etc., and the imposition of assessments. In times past, it was well known, owners of property had been ruined by measures taken professedly for their benefit as well as that of the city; and it was equally notorious that heavy assessments had been laid and collected, years before, for the opening of streets and avenues, which up to the present time had remained unopened. A recent alleged discovery of want of power in the Supreme Court in regard to the confirmation of assessments rendered action by the State legislature necessary, and, this obtained, a revision of the whole system and its re-establishment on juster principles would, it was hoped, be undertaken.

The total permanent debt of the city in May, 1846, amounted to fourteen million seven hundred and eighty-seven thousand and eighty-eight dollars. One of the obvious means for liquidating the debt and meeting the amount annually required to be provided was the sale of such portion of the city property as was not strictly necessary for city purposes; contemplating, however, the reservation of such lands as public health should require when the densely populated bounds of the city should be limited alone by Manhattan Island.

The estimated value of the real estate possessed by the city in 1846, exclusive of wharves and piers, was fifteen million nine hundred and three thousand dollars. The value of that required under the reservations to be permanently held was fourteen million six hundred thousand dollars, leaving available for such other disposition as the city government might order one million three hundred and three thousand dollars, which produced an annual income of forty-six thousand three hundred and fifty dollars.

In this connection the important question was presented, whether the wharves and piers, estimated as being worth from one and a half to two millions of dollars, and netting an income of scarcely two and a half per centum upon their value, might not, under salutary reservations and restrictions, be sold and an income thence secured more commensurate with their true value. No disposition consistent with the pledges given in creating the debt could be made of the proceeds of such sales except to increase the "sinking fund" provided for the extinguishment of the city debt.

The experiment of using roughly dressed stones for pavements was spoken of in this year (1846), and the utilization of the pauper and penitentiary labor in quarrying and preparing the stones was suggested. The great saving in repairs that such a change in the surface of the streets would effect to the owners of vehicles passing over them, and the increased burdens the same teams would propel, would, it was believed, commend a specific tax upon public conveyances owned in the city, the income of which would go far towards liquidating the expense of the change, while the exemption from the almost intolerable noise and jar, of which the residents of the great thoroughfares were unceasingly complaining, would, with the consent of the owners of property thus benefited, justify a portion of the expense being levied upon them. Another commendable feature of the scheme was that the improvement could be gradually undertaken without the increase of a dollar upon the existing heavy indebtedness, and the change would greatly facilitate and consequently lighten the labor and expense of cleaning the streets.

The expense of lighting the streets and public buildings had reached an amount of considerable magnitude in 1846, the levy for that purpose in that year amounting to one hundred and seventy-four thousand dollars.

ESSEX MARKET BELL TOWER.

The actual amount of the city debt for 1847 was eleven million seven hundred and forty-eight thousand three hundred and seventy-nine dollars and thirty-nine cents. The enormous and increasing expenditures under the head of "Cleaning Streets" called loudly for a thorough change and reform. The net expense for that object during the year was one hundred and seventeen thousand one hundred and ninety-seven dollars and thirty cents. While there was no ground to doubt the fact of the expenditure, there was equally none for supposing that it was for "cleaning" streets, for it was a source of just and general complaint that the streets had never been more neglected, and that very little or no effort had been made to render them comfortable to the citizens.

Water pipes, connecting with the Croton Aqueduct, were laid down through nearly all the streets of the city south of Twenty-third Street, including Eighth Avenue to Twenty-fifth Street, and Third Avenue to Thirty-third Street, and several of the cross streets between Third and Fourth Avenues as far north as Twenty-eighth Street, by May, 1844. In all a total of one hundred and fifty-five and three-quarter miles of pipes had been put down, sufficient to accommodate the existing population south of Twenty-third Street, three hundred and ten thousand. The number of fire hydrants was about one thousand five hundred, and of free hydrants about six hundred.

The number of new buildings erected for the year ending December 31, 1844, was one thousand two hundred and ten.

The actual debt of the city in May, 1845, was twelve million four hundred and fifty-four thousand four hundred and ninety-seven dollars and sixty cents.

In that year Avenue A was regulated between Thirteenth and Twenty-third Streets; Fifth Avenue was paved between Twenty-first and Twenty-third Streets; First Avenue was regulated and graded between Thirteenth and Twenty-fifth Streets, and regulated between Twenty-fifth and Twenty-sixth Streets; Fourth Avenue was numbered from Seventeenth to Twenty-sixth Streets, and opened from Twenty-eighth to Thirty-eighth Streets; and Second Avenue was regulated between Eighteenth and Twenty-sixth Streets, and the road worked through the middle of the avenue twenty-five feet in width between Twenty-ninth and Forty-second Streets. The number of buildings erected in this city during the year 1845 was one thousand nine hundred and eighty, being an increase of seven hundred and seventy over the number for 1844, which shows that the year 1845 had been one of increased activity and prosperity.

Measures were taken to open Madison Square in December, 1845. The corporation, in 1837, applied to the legislature for an act to alter the plan of this city and to erect a square. Such an act was passed in April of that year, and were it not for that act no square could have been erected, inasmuch as it changed the plan of the city laid out by the commissioners under the act of 1807. The application of the corporation for that act may be considered as the first dedication of the ground for a square. The corporation inclosed nearly the whole of the ground with a fence, which may be considered the second dedication, and, as a third act of dedication, purchased from a Mr. Ward a piece of ground lying within the inclosure. The ground within the inclosure belonging to the corporation was the old Potter's Field, which, after it ceased to be a burying ground, was occupied as an arsenal, and subsequently by the House of Refuge and as a burying ground for the House of Refuge. It was the only piece of ground, with the exception of a small gore, that the corporation owned south of the reservoir.

In May, 1846, the total permanent debt of the city amounted to fourteen million two hundred and sixty-three thousand six hundred and nine dollars. The amount appropriated for the support of the city government for that year, including the estimated revenue not assigned to the sinking fund and the amount to be raised by tax, was one million six hundred and seventeen thousand four hundred and eighty dollars.

The net total debt of the city on the thirtieth of April, 1847, was twelve million six hundred and eighty-seven thousand eight hundred and thirty-three dollars and ninety-nine cents. The expenses for lighting the streets, markets, station houses, etc., for 1846, amounted to one hundred and sixty-two thousand eight hundred and thirty dollars and eighty-one cents. There were about two thousand six hundred lamps supplied with gas, and seven thousand six hundred with oil. As the gas afforded more light, and it was believed that the city could be more economically lighted with it than with oil, the gradual discontinuance of oil lamps was begun.

That noble work, the Croton Aqueduct, the enduring monument to the enterprise of New York, of which all were so justly proud, and whose value was each day more and more forcibly illustrated and properly appreciated, fulfilled all the expectations that had been formed of it at its conception, and was rapidly approaching completion. The work at the High Bridge was nearly finished.

The value of the property in docks and slips belonging to the city was estimated at from one and a half millions to two millions of dollars, the net amount of revenue therefrom amounting to about forty thousand dollars annually. That property in the hands of private individuals would, it was believed, produce a revenue bearing some proportion to its value, while under the management of the city it was almost unproductive. The then mayor, Wm. V. Brady, suggested that the wisest course to pursue would be to dispose of a portion at least of that property, and apply the proceeds to the extinguishment of the city debt.

The number of buildings erected in the city of New York during the year 1846 was one thousand nine hundred and ten, a decrease of seventy from the year 1845, which was mainly attributed to the falling off in the First Ward, which was vastly increased in 1845 on account of building on the "Burnt District."

By the tenor of the existing contract (October, 1847) with the Manhattan Gas Light Company, the city had no right to require the company to furnish any of the public lamps with gas north of the line of Sixth Street. The city had long previously outgrown that provision, the line of Sixth Street being then rather a central than an extreme one; and when it was considered that the existing contract would not expire by its own limitation until 1853, it was plain to the dullest perception that it was wholly inadequate to meet the wants of the rapidly-extending city. By mutual agreement the line of Forty-second Street was substituted for Sixth Street.

BROADWAY THEATER, 1850.
[Between Pearl and Anthony Streets.]

The introduction of the Croton water had attracted much attention to the construction of sewers both from the increased necessity which it exacted for drainage and the increased facility which it gave for adapting them to the health and comfort of the citizens. In May, 1848, there were forty miles of sewers in use, ten of which had been built during the preceding year.

The total number of new buildings put up in the city during the year 1848 amounted to one thousand one hundred and ninety-one, a decrease of six hundred and fifty-five from 1847.

The total aggregate of city debt from stocks issued and redeemable from the sinking fund was on the thirty-first of December, 1849, fifteen million three hundred and fifty-six thousand seven hundred and eighty-three dollars. Of that amount three million one hundred and ninety-nine thousand one hundred and five dollars were held by the Commissioners of the Sinking Fund, leaving the net debt of the city redeemable from the sinking fund twelve million one hundred and fifty-seven thousand seven hundred and sixty-eight dollars. The whole amount of stocks issued for the construction of the Croton Water Works was thirteen million eight hundred and thirty-seven thousand dollars. It thus appears that the entire debt of the city had been in reality incurred for the construction of that stupendous work; and of the total amount of debt created for that purpose one million six hundred and seventy-nine thousand two hundred and thirty-two dollars had in fact been already paid, and it was asserted that the revenues of the city then pledged to the redemption of the principal and interest of the city debt would extinguish the whole amount in less than thirty-five years.

The taxing of the personal property of non-residents was a subject that engaged the earnest attention of the city government. A large amount of property, estimated at several millions, annually escaped taxation because the owners resided outside the city. It seemed singularly unjust toward residents that their personal property should be taxed while that of non-residents was exempt, though equally protected and benefited by the laws of the municipal and State governments. The existing law operated as a reward to encourage business men to reside without the limits of the county, and it was therefore suggested that immediate measures should be taken to procure the passage of a law authorizing the taxation of the personal property of non-residents.

The extension of wharves and piers was agitated in 1850. The growing commerce of the city demanded an increased amount of wharf accomodations, the want of which had compelled a portion of shipping to seek a harbor on the Brooklyn and Jersey shores, while the New York wharves could have afforded a more convenient, safer, and better harbor if they had been extended at an earlier period. The existing rates of wharfage had been fixed by the legislature as far back as 1813, when the expense of building wharves bore a very inconsiderable proportion to that of this date. They were then seldom required to be more than two hundred to three hundred feet long by thirty feet wide, and rarely had to be extended into a depth of water of more than from ten to twenty feet; whereas at this date (January, 1850) the length of piers was required to be from four to six hundred feet long by forty feet wide, and to be built in water from twenty to forty feet in depth. Thus while the corporation and owners of water fronts were necessarily subjected to that great additional expense, the rates of wharfage remained as in early days. An application was therefore contemplated to the legislature for the passage of a law authorizing such an increase of the existing rates of wharfage as would correspond with the increase of expense, and pay a reasonable percentage on the investment. Such a law, it was hoped, would serve as a strong incentive to continue the further extension of wharves, thereby affording the additional accomodations so much needed and so long neglected, and would also afford a strong inducement to the proprietors of adjacent property to put up and line the wharves with valuable stores and warehouses, and in that way give life and encouragement to the trading interests and at the same time enlarge the basis of taxable property in the city.

The avenues and roads had not, in the opinion of reliable authorities, received from the Common Council the attention which the necessities of the rapidly growing population demanded. Many years had elapsed since the avenues were opened *in law*. The owners through whose land the avenues were laid had been assessed for such opening and the assessments long paid, and in some instances enforced with oppressive severity. But notwithstanding the great lapse of time since the opening *in law* and the payment of the assessments, yet even at this time some of these avenues had not *really* been opened, but remained in precisely the same condition as if such opening had not taken place and such assessments had never been paid. Some of them, it was true, or rather some portions of them, had been thrown open and the fences removed, but they had never been put, and were not at this time, in a condition to be travelled or used. It was pertinently asked, with what justice or with what good faith the avenues were ordered to be opened, and the payment of the assessment immediately enforced, unless they were required for immediate use? Why did the corporation order them to be opened and enforce the payment therefor, unless it was intended in good faith, immediately afterward, to put them in a suitable condition for public travel and public use? And why had they not been thus improved?

To the inattention to those improvements and to the wants of the overflowing population in the lower wards, and in the long neglect to provide the ordinary facilities for the public to become acquainted even with the geography of the upper wards of the city, was to be traced one of the principal reasons why thousands of citizens had sought residences out of the city, instead of remaining, and locating on this island.

The legislature in 1821, upon the application of the corporation, passed an act to extend the Battery into the North and East Rivers to a distance of six hundred feet, and for that purpose vested the title to the land under the water in the mayor, aldermen, and commonalty of the city and their successors forever, providing that it should not be appropriated to any other use than that of a public ground. By that act the legislature not only authorized that public improvement, but had thrown around it the shield of its high authority as a guarantee against its use except as a public ground, and against any encroachment or invasion of its borders. The area of the Battery at that time was ten and a half acres, and if extended to the distance authorized by the legislature, would cover about twenty-four acres. The prosecution and completion of the work were warmly urged by the then mayor, Caleb S. Woodhull.

The appropriation for lamps and gas in 1849 was two hundred and ten thousand dollars. For the year 1850 it was one hundred and eighty-five thousand dollars.

The great amount of building, paving, and sewering going on tended greatly to obstruct the streets, and left them encumbered with sand and rubbish. Ordinances were suggested providing a remedy.

In 1847 thirty-three suits were instituted in the State of New Jersey against Cornelius W. Lawrence, formerly mayor, to recover the value of a large amount of personal property destroyed by his order at the great fire of 1835. The defense of those suits had been undertaken by the city. Thirty-one of them had been decided in favor of Mr. Lawrence, and the other two were still pending.

EMBLEMS OF THE OLD DEPARTMENT.

CHAPTER XXII.

THE CITY'S UNPRECEDENTED PROGRESS.

Markets and their Ancient Mode of Doing Business.—New York takes Rank as the Third City in Christendom, and Exceeds in Expenditure any other Municipality in the World.—Its Growth and Prosperity Unparalleled.—Ancient Nomenclature of Streets.—Reduction in the Rate of Taxation.—Sales of Real Estate.—Public Works and Construction of Drives and Parks.—The Croton and the Aqueduct.

IN 1851 New York City was, and had been for some years previously, the great emporium of the western world, the very heart of commerce, whose pulsations were felt and responded to in every section of the Union. But it was not wise to rely upon its natural advantages, which made the city pre-eminent in the inducements it offered to commercial enterprise. It was not enough that wharves and piers should be provided for the accommodation of the fleets of sailing vessels. Accommodation should also be provided for ocean steamers, the number of which had increased with a rapidity unparalleled in the history of the world. The immense increase of our maritime intercourse with foreign countries is well illustrated by the following comparative figures of the tonnage employed in the foreign trade:

1840.

Number of vessels	2,048
Tons	570,425
Men employed	23,008

1850.

Number of vessels	3,233
Tons	1,178,598
Men employed	45,359

The coasting trade employed three hundred times as many vessels as the foreign, with a proportionate increase in tonnage.

The amount appropriated and expended during the year 1851 for building and extending piers and wharves and for repairs, alterations and additions, was three hundred thousand dollars, of which sum one hundred and ten thousand dollars was appropriated for building the bulkhead at the foot of Gansevoort Street.

The extension of Second Avenue was being rapidly pushed forward. Eighth Avenue was nearly completed to the width of forty feet as far as One Hundred and Twentieth Street by January, 1852. Broadway was being regulated, and soon after was opened for travel to its junction with Tenth Avenue at Seventy-first Street, and Sixth Avenue was completed to Fifty-seventh Street.

The additional number of gas lamps erected and lighted during the year 1851 was one thousand one hundred and twenty-six, which made a total of gas lamps in the city of six thousand six hundred and ninety-six. The whole number of oil lamps then lighted was five thousand six hundred and two. The wharves and piers were as yet unlighted with gas, and as numerous accidents, some terminating fatally, had been reported, due in great part to the darkness which pervaded these localities, and which also invited depredations upon the shipping as well as upon the various goods which were of necessity sometimes left upon the wharves at night, provisions were made for lighting them with gas.

Nearly eleven miles of public sewers had been laid during 1851, and three thousand two hundred and fifty feet of culverts constructed, together with one hundred and fifty-nine receiving basins.

In May, 1851, Mayor Kingsland suggested the expediency of setting apart some portion of the island as a public park, to be laid out on a scale commensurate with the rapidly increasing population, and one which would afford the citizens more ample accommodations for relaxation and exercise than they then enjoyed. In accordance with that suggestion application was made to the legislature, and an act was passed at the special session held in July, authorizing the Common Council to take for the purpose of a public park the grounds lying between Sixty-sixth and Seventy-fifth Streets, and Third Avenue and the East River. Application was made to the Supreme Court for the appointment of commissioners, to estimate and award the amounts to be paid to the several owners of the property thus to be applied. The right of the Common Council to proceed under that law

VARIOUS STYLES OF OLD FIREMEN'S HATS.

was contested in the Supreme Court by some of the owners of the property interested, and a decision was handed down adverse to the appointment of commissioners under the then existing law. It was therefore determined that renewed application be made to the legislature for the enactment of a law which would meet the exigencies of the case. It was regarded as a matter of deep regret to all interested in the improvement that the contractor for extending the Second Avenue to Harlem had deemed it necessary to open that avenue through the site which a great majority of the people as well as the deliberate judgment of their immediate representatives had fixed upon as the most suitable on the island for the new park, thus marring many of the natural beauties of the location.

In 1853 numerous petitions were sent to the Common Council, setting forth that there existed a necessity for the lighting of the streets all night. When the moon gave light the lamps were kept burning only a portion of the night, and the time of lighting and extinguishing them was determined by the rising and setting of the moon. During stormy and cloudy weather the moon was not visible, could not give any light whatever, and thus the city was left in darkness. Arrangements were accordingly made with the companies to have the streets lighted from dark until daylight throughout the year.

Railroads for city travel were in operation in January, 1854, on Second, Third, Fourth, Sixth and Eighth Avenues.

In February, 1766, the corporation of this city leased to Rev. Mr. Rogers and his associates forever the triangular piece of ground bounded by Beekman and Nassau Streets and Park Row, and occupied in 1854 by the Brick Presbyterian Church, on the express condition that the premises should never, "at any time forever after," be appropriated to private secular uses, at an annual rent of forty pounds, which was paid until September 3, 1785, when the corporation reduced the rent to twenty-one pounds, three shillings. In 1822 the trustees of the Brick Church, at considerable expense, erected a large number of vaults on the church grounds for the interment of the dead, which promised to yield a handsome revenue. The Common Council prohibited interments in the same year south of Grand Street. The board of trustees were desirous of selling their property in 1854, and, petitioning for the removal of the restriction in the grant, offered the city one-quarter of the amount for which the property could be sold, fixing the minimum at $225,000. The Common Council accepted the proposition.

Indifference to commercial progress was evinced in nothing more than in the neglect to provide proper dockage, thus presenting a singular contrast to every other seaport of any magnitude known to ancient or modern commerce. The quays and docks of London, Liverpool, Cardiff, and indeed nearly all English ports were first-class. At St. Petersburg, in Russia, there was (in 1856) one granite pier four miles in extent. At Havre, France, the docks were the principal structures of importance, having cost immense sums, and were justly the pride of its citizens. In fact there was not a city of Europe possessing navigation which did not surpass New York in the necessary provision for the proper convenience and protection of its shipping. Fernando Wood, mayor in 1856, earnestly presented these facts to the Common Council, and urged that measures be taken at once to place New York on an equal footing with the great seaports of Europe.

The system under which the work of street opening was carried on in 1856 originated in 1807, though the operation of the system had become very different from what it then was. The gradual increase of the expensiveness of street openings had become alarmingly perceptible. From 1814 to 1837 the average amount per mile for fees of counsel, commissioners and others employed by them was eight hundred and fifty dollars. From 1837 to 1844 it increased to two thousand three hundred dollars per mile, and in 1855, taking the Bowery opening from Chatham to Franklin Square, as a guide, a distance of about one thousand four hundred and fifty feet, for which upward of twenty thousand dollars had been charged, which was at the astounding rate of over seventy thousand dollars per mile for the same services. In that case the surveyor's fees alone were taxed at five thousand three hundred dollars.

New York inherited from its two old-fashioned ancestors, the Hollander and the Britisher, its present system of public markets. So far as the system was concerned, she stood in 1856 precisely where she did in 1664, when Governor Nichols took New Netherlands from the Dutch; or in 1673, when the Dutch took it as New York back again; or in 1674, when the

British reoccupied it ; or in 1776, when Uncle Sam was born; or in 1815, when he became a man and realized his strength and independence by the treaty of peace with Great Britain.

Mayor Wood considered that ancient mode as wrong and obnoxious to the great republican principle that government should not interfere with private enterprise; that that is the best government which governs the least; that government should avoid becoming a proprietor or restricting the free exercise of individual rights so long as no encroachment was made upon the rights of others or of the community. He therefore recommended the abolition of the system of the sale of the market property and the adoption of the free-trade principle, permitting any individual to open a shop for the sale of meats, etc., the same as for other articles of trade. In 1836 the class known as shop butchers first established themselves in this city in defiance of law at that time,

CITY HALL.

and a strong effort was made to break them up, but it failed. Relief to Broadway, immediate and effective relief from the glut of traffic to the great thoroughfare, gave employment to the thoughts of the City Fathers in 1857, and efforts were contemplated for the accomplishment of so desirable an object. The suggestion of making a parallel avenue contiguous to and in the immediate vicinity of Broadway, by which to draw off some of the travel, received a good deal of consideration, as it would decrease, it was thought, the obstructions to a considerable extent. But the most practical suggestion was that of widening the carriage-way by withdrawing the permission granted to owners of property to occupy a portion of the highway with areas, steps, porticos, etc. An average width of six feet on either side of the street would thus be gained—twelve feet added to the roadway.

In 1854 the subject of erecting a new City Hall was agitated. The old

Alms-house buildings on Chambers Street, which had been for several years used for public purposes, were destroyed by fire about that time, and the necessity for more room, not only for court, but for municipal uses, became so apparent that it was resolved to build a new City Hall. The only steps taken for this purpose appear to have been confined to the adoption of the plans.

No little embarrassment was caused in the discussion of that project by the expressed belief that the old park where the present City Hall stands was too far "down town," and Madison Park (Madison Square) was spoken of as the fittest place for the proposed new Hall, and even Mayor Fernando Wood recommended that site.

In 1861 New York had grown to be the third city in Christendom, and if all who lived within a radius of five miles from its center were included, the population would have been second only to that of London. At that time the union of New York and Brooklyn under one municipal government was much talked of, and was favored by some of the most responsible citizens.

The net amount of the city debt on December 31, 1862, was fifteen million three hundred and five thousand six hundred and sixty-three dollars and fifty-five cents, as against fifteen million five hundred and twenty-one thousand two hundred and ninety-one dollars and seventy-seven cents on December 31, 1861.

Perhaps no city in the world is more favorably located than New York for a well-devised system of drainage. The natural formation of the soil and the close proximity of the rivers surrounding the island greatly facilitate the construction of sewers. To these natural advantages could in a great degree be attributed the absence of a regular system which characterized the sewerage of the lower and more compact parts of the city in 1863, and these advantages had enabled even badly designed sewers in those localities to do their work with tolerable efficiency. The evils arising from a want of system were, however, becoming very apparent, and were constantly increasing. The neglect of a proper system of sewerage had forced the rebuilding of many of the London sewers at an enormous cost to the city, and it was urged as the part of sound policy to anticipate such a contingency by inaugurating as complete a system as human foresight and skill could devise.

It was officially stated in 1864 that the expenditures of the city exceeded in proportion those of any other municipality in the world. This fact was and had been for years the source of continual and well-grounded complaint. The ratio of increase was certainly greatly beyond what might have been reasonably expected from the growth of the city in wealth and population. The following table shows the relative advance for a number of years :

	Population according to Census.	Value Real and Personal Estate.	Tax Levied.
1840	312,852	$252,233,515	$1,354,835.29
1850	515,394	286,061,816	3,230,085.02
1860	814,254	577,230,956	9,758,507.86
1863	1,000,000	594,196,813	11,565,672.18

In the spring of 1864 the lower section of the Central Park was so far completed as to conduce greatly to the pleasant enjoyment of the citizens. The part of the park then in course of improvement was between One Hundred and Sixth and One Hundred and Tenth Streets. Eight miles of carriage roads, five miles of bridle-paths, and twenty miles of foot-walks were then open to the public. The taxable valuations of the three wards adjacent had increased from 1856 to 1862 twenty-seven millions of dollars, due in a considerable extent to the opening of the park. The cost of that improvement, including land, up to the first of January, 1863, was seven million three hundred and seventy-two thousand four hundred and twenty-six dollars.

The growth and prosperity of New York by the advent of the year 1866 were declared to be beyond parallel. Its resources were immense. Population and wealth were pouring into it from all parts of the world. The rich country which surrounded it contributed incessantly to its progress and advancement, and it needed not the gift of prophecy to recognize the fact that before many years the whole island would be crowded with an active and energetic people.

The funded debt of the city on December 22, 1865, was twenty-nine million nine hundred and thirty-two thousand five hundred and seventy-six dollars and fifty cents; and of the county, eleven million three hundred and thirty-three thousand four hundred dollars, together making forty-one million two hundred and sixty-five thousand, nine hundred and seventy-six dollars and fifty cents, of which amount the Commissioners of Sinking Fund held nine million five hundred and eight thousand one hundred and one dollars, leaving a net indebtedness of thirty-one million seven hundred and fifty-seven thousand eight hundred and seventy-five dollars and fifty cents. The whole debt was secured by the entire property of the city, public and private; and the world offered no better security, in 1866, than the public stocks of the City and County of New York.

The city could point with pride to its Croton Aqueduct and reservoirs, its Central Park and its public buildings, connected with and under the charge of the Commissioners of Charities and Correction, as well as those under the charge of the Board of Education. The aqueduct was not only a source of pride, of comfort, and of health, but the revenues derived from it more than paid the interest on the cost of its construction. The Central Park was one of those great public improvements demanded by the spirit of the age, and contributed greatly to the comfort and happiness of all the citizens. It yielded no revenue, but like all other great public improvements, it contributed to the power and prosperity of the city of which it was destined to become so great an ornament.

But the wharves, piers and markets of New York presented a striking contrast to the objects just mentioned. Thus, the great commercial city of the continent had not a single wharf or pier which was not a digrace to it.

Many of the streets of the city had in the course of time changed their names, and these changes doubtless have led to confusion of ideas on the part of readers not conversant with this fact. Following are some of the changes referred to:

Whitehall Street was originally the Winckel or Shop Street. The name was changed from an edifice erected by Governor Stuyvesant called "The Whitehall."

Water Street was so called from being the first street laid out in the bed of the East River.

South Street, the southerly line of the East River shore as finally established.

State Street—originally the ramparts of the Battery. Built upon after the destruction of the fort and the erection of the State House opposite the Bowling Green.

Moore Street—originally the line of the first wharf erected in the city. Colonel Moore, a merchant was a large owner of the lots when first built upon.

Bridge Street in Dutch times led to the bridge across the canal in Broad Street. Name retained from the earliest times.

Stone Street—originally "The Brewers" or Brewer Street. It was the first street paved with stone.

Beaver Street—originally Beaver Ditch.

South William Street—formerly called Mill Street, from the first mill (which was also used as a church) being erected there.

Broad Street—laid out through Blommeart's Valley. A ditch in the centre occasioned the unusual width.

Exchange Place—the old Garden Street. Name changed after the erection of the edifice formerly called the Merchants' Exchange.

William Street—Known at different periods as the Glassmakers' Street, Borgis Joris Path and Smith Street. The northerly part of William Street in compliment to William of Nassau.

Nassau Street was formerly kown as Piewoman's Street.

New Street—One of the thoroughfares of New Amsterdam, was once a novelty and has preserved its cognomen.

Bowling Green—The open place in front of the old fort. Was appropriated for the purpose indicated during the last century.

Greenwich Street—A continuation of the Shore Road leading to Greenwich Village.

Washington Street—Laid out while our hero was in the highest office of the nation.

Wall Street—The line of the city wall or palisade.

Broadway has had various names—the Heere Straat, Great George Street and Bloomingdale Road, all finally merged into the present name.

Maiden Lane—The original "Maid's Path," a rural valley road. Has retained its name from the earliest period.

John Street—After John Harpending, who resided on Broadway. This street, when laid out, passed through his garden.

Cortlandt Street—Laid out through the Cortlandt estate.

Dey Street—Laid out through the Dey estate.

Fulton Street, east of Broadway, was originally Partition Street; west of Broadway it was Broadway Fair Street. A common designation being desirable, it was called after the great engineer.

Gold Street was originally Golden Hill.

Beekman Street was named after the family of that name.

Ann Street was called so after one of the Beekman family.

Vesey Street after the Rev. William Vesey.

Barclay Street after the Rev. Mr. Barclay, of Trinity Church.

Murray, Warren, Chambers and Reade Streets were named under similar circumstances.

Church Street bounded the west side of St. Paul's churchyard.

College Place was laid out along the college grounds.

Ferry Street led to the old Long Island ferry.

Chatham Street was the original road to Boston. Named in compliment to the English statesman.

Cherry Street was run through the road by the cherry trees.

Vandewater and Roosevelt Streets were named after the proprietors of the lands.

Market Street was George Street until a market was built at its foot.

Pike Street was originally Crab Apple Street.

Division Street was so called because it was the division line between the Delancey and Rutgers farms.

Henry Street was called after one of the Rutgers family.

Madison Street was so called to honor President Madison. It was originally Bedlow Street.

Monroe was first Lombard Street, Corlears Street, after Corlear's Hook.

Duane Street—First called Bailey Street. The then mayor was the gentleman honored by the change.

North Moore Street—After one of the officers of Trinity Church. "North" was to distinguish it from another Moore Street.

Desbrosses Street—After a church officer.

Worth Street — Laid out through the Lispenard estate by one of the family, named Anthony. The street became of bad reputation and required obliteration.

POOR HOUSE.
[City Hall Park.]

Canal Street—After a canal that flowed through it from the Collect Pond, where the Tombs now is.

Franklin Street was once Sugar loaf Street.

Varick Street—After the mayor.

Center Street became disreputable as Collect Street; so the name was changed.

City Hall Place was Augustus Street.

Hester Street—After Hester Bayard.

Broome Street—Originally it was Bullock Street.

Spring Street—An old well was situated on the line of this street. It became famous in connection with the murder of Miss Sands.

Bleecker Street—It ran through the country seat of the Bleecker family.

Orchard Street—It ran through the orchard of the Delancey farm.

Mangin, Goerck, Willett, Mercer, Greene, Wooster, Sullivan, Macdougal and Hancock Streets were all named after distinguished families and individuals.

The net amount of the city and county funded debt on December 31, 1866, was thirty million nine hundred and one thousand eight hundred and seventy-eight dollars and thirty-nine cents. Of that amount the sum of ten million seven hundred and eighty-two thousand eight hundred dollars was for Croton Water-works, nine million nine hundred and twenty-three thousand five hundred and seventy-one dollars for Central Park, and fourteen million four hundred and forty-five thousand six hundred dollars for expenses growing out of and connected with the war of the rebellion. The whole debt was well secured, for it was a lien upon the whole property of the city, both public and private.

The tax levy for 1866 was sixteen million nine hundred and fifty thousand seven hundred and sixty-seven dollars and eighty cents, being one million two hundred and fifty-three thousand one hundred and eighty-four dollars and eight cents less than that of 1865. The rate of taxation in 1865 was two dollars ninety-nine cents on every hundred dollars. In 1866 it was only two dollars and thirty cents. The rate for 1866 was based upon an assessed valuation of real estate of four hundred and seventy-eight million nine hundred and ninety-four thousand nine hundred and thirty-four dollars, and of personal estate two hundred and fifty-seven million nine hundred and ninety-four thousand nine hundred and seventy-four dollars, making a total of seven hundred and thirty-seven million nine hundred and eighty nine thousand nine hundred and eight dollars. It was well known that the real estate was assessed only (as a general rule) at but little more than half its market value, and that an immense amount of the personal property of the people escaped taxation entirely. A full assessment would no doubt have reduced the rate of taxation at least one-half.

It was gratifying to the taxpayers to know that fact, and to have learned in addition that, unnecessarily high as the rate of taxation was in New York, it compared most favorably with that of other cities in and out of the State. In Boston, where real estate was assessed at its full market value, and where verified detailed statements of personal property were made by the taxpayers to the assessors, the rate of tax was one dollar and thirty cents; so that, taking into consideration the assessed valuation of property, the rate was as high if not higher than in New York. In Philadelphia where assessed valuations were lower than in this city, the rate was four dollars per hundred on real estate, and thirty cents on personal estate.

In Brooklyn, it was three dollars and forty-one cents; in Rochester, five dollars and sixty-two cents; in Utica, five dollars and sixty-one cents; in Albany three dollars and seventy-six cents; in Syracuse, three dollars and seventy-two cents. In Troy, for municipal purposes only, in addition to the State and county tax, two dollars and fifty cents.

These comparisons were suggestive, inasmuch as a portion of the press had been making continual assaults upon the municipality and its administrators, which had a tendency to create the impression abroad that this city was the "plague spot" of the country. That the standard of many men in public life was low enough, and that the whole system of local government was bad enough, and that the taxes were more than they should be, were freely admitted; but as long as the securities sold at a premium, and that New York possessed the most costly parks, the greatest waterworks, the most extended system of free schools in the country, and a rate of taxation lower than that of her neighbors, the people, amid all their complaints and causes of complaint should have, and doubtless did find, in these facts some ground for congratulation.

In 1867 the new reservoir in process of construction near High Bridge was in rapid progress. The completion of that work was considered necessary for obtaining a supply of Croton water for the whole of the upper part of the island. The sale of a portion of the City Hall Park to the United States Government for a site for the Post Office was being negotiated, and found much public favor. The same could be said of the proposed release to the Government of a portion of the Battery extension for a site for a Revenue Barge Office. The propriety of extending Fifth Avenue through Washington Square and then widening Laurens Street to West Broadway was under consideration. Also the extension of Centre Street through the blocks to Lafayette Place.

The subject of widening Ann Street, which had for some years excited a great deal of attention, was put at rest by the adoption of a resolution by the Common Council rescinding the original resolution, which directed the widening. The action of interested parties in securing at Albany the passage of a law charging the expense of the work upon the city at large instead of making their own property, which would be greatly increased in value, bear its fair and equitable share of such expense, resulted in the defeat of the whole measure, very much to the satisfaction of the public.

The net amount of the city and county funded debt on December 31, 1867, was twenty-nine million six hundred thousand four hundred and sixty-three dollars and thirty-eight cents. Of that sum, eleven million thirty thousand eight hundred dollars was for Croton Water Works; nine million nine hundred and twenty-three thousand five hundred and seventy-one dollars for Central Park; and thirteen million nine hundred and seventy thousand six hundred dollars for expenses growing out of and connected with the war.

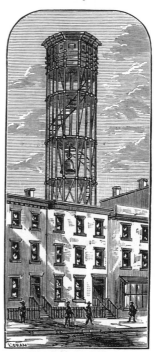

MACDOUGAL STREET BELL TOWER.

In the sales of real estate owned by the city in the year 1867 there was received from the government of the United States for a portion of the City Hall Park as a site for a Post-office five hundred thousand dollars and for a site for Barge Office at the Battery ten thousand dollars.

In 1873 the condition of the financial affairs of the city government was without parallel in the annals of municipal history. It was the commencement of a transition period from an epoch characterized by social demoralization, disregard of the obligations of public duty, official neglect, fraud and crime, towards an era demanding a higher morality and a purer and better standard of public administration.

During this period there had been required the vigor necessary to oppose the methods of malevolent and corrupt officials of the past and forbearance and patience with the inexperience of new incumbents. The task of the restoration of the credit of the city and of protecting the treasury had involved one continued, persistent and unremitting contest with the claimants of the most desperate and corrupt character.

The following statement shows the increase in the city and county debt from 1869 to 1874:

	Gross Debt.	Sinking Fund.	Net Debt.
January 1, 1869	$52,205,430.80	$15,911,501.21	$36,293,929.59
January 1, 1870	66,040.052.22	18,006,310.63	48,033,741.59
January 1, 1871	91,489,466.51	18,115,894.49	73,373,552.02
September 16, 1871, the date on which Comptroller Green took office	116,709,858.51	19,422,333.48	97,287,525.03
January 1, 1873	118,815,229.82	23,348,074.89	95,467,154.93
January 1, 1874	131,204,571.22	24,832,617.50	106,371,953.72

CITY AND COUNTY DEBT.

	Sept. 16, 1871.	Dec. 31, 1873.
Assessment Bonds	$11,824,500.00	$21,927,372.30
Revenue Bonds, anticipating taxes of 1871 and 1873, respectively	22,766,200.00	1,472,547.12
Revenue Bonds, special, payable from building lien		2,034.53
Funded Debt	82,119,158.51	107,802,617.27
	$116,709,858.51	$131,204,571.22

From which it appears that of this increase ten million one hundred and two thousand eight hundred and seventy-one dollars and thirty cents was in assessment bonds alone, for which the city held a direct lien upon the property benefited by the improvements.

Thus the total increase in the debt from September 16, 1871, to January 1, 1874, was fourteen million four hundred and ninety-four thousand seven hundred and twelve dollars and seventy-one cents. The greater portion of the bonds representing that increase was issued for purposes belonging to a former era, and not belonging to the year 1872 and 1873.

The misgovernment of the city in the period heretofore referred to was largely due to a delusion fostered for the worst purposes by designing officials that efficient and honest administration was to be secured rather by certain legislative forms than by the careful choice of good, upright and intelligent instruments. The speedy triumph of public justice over men who had so long plundered the city with impunity, and whose escape from the legal consequences of their crimes had come to be a public scandal, doubtless served to lend emphasis to the fact that no system of law could secure the city against spoliation unless honest and capable hands were supplied to administer it, and unless the judicious selection of public servants was accompanied by methods of strict accountability and by a sustained habit of vigilance in the public mind itself.

The Board of Aldermen on May 16, 1873, condemned the city prison as unfit and unhealthy. They addressed a memorial to the State legislature asking for the enactment of a law to build a new prison. After the law had been passed they came to the conclusion that, in view of the large expense it would entail, it was better to postpone the project, and the Board on September 17, of the same year, passed a resolution to prevent the carrying out of the law authorizing its construction.

For the first time in the history of the government of New York city, the

Common Council, in 1875, consisted of only one board of representatives of the people. Since 1857 there had existed in the administration of local affairs various legislative bodies, the most prominent of which had been a Board of Supervisors, a Board of Aldermen, and a Board of Councilmen, subsequently known as Assistant Aldermen. In addition to these Boards several commissions were from time to time created by law, in each of which was vested combined legislative and executive powers. The results of this divided authority were not satisfactory, and the legislative powers and duties of the several Boards above enumerated had been concentrated in the Board of Aldermen, which was then alone constituted the Common Council.

The liabilities of the city in January, 1875, amounted to, as nearly as they could be computed (for the exact status was not officially known), one hundred and fifteen million one hundred and eighty-seven thousand nine hundred and eighty dollars. In addition to this there was a floating debt, which had been variously estimated at from ten to twenty millions of dollars. Many of the claims constituting that indebtedness were in litigation.

The condition of the public works of the city had attracted of late universal attention. They had been carried on with borrowed money, partly on the security of the credit of the city, and partly on the special security of assessments to be imposed upon the property more immediately benefited. That the works which had been completed on the northern part of the island were and would become of vast public benefit was admitted by all. The only question then remaining was how far some of these works, and others which had been prospected, might not be beyond the existing requirements.

The construction of the Riverside Park drive and the Morningside Avenue had been proceeded with to a considerable extent by the opening of 1875, and the completion of them was strongly urged.

Many of the pavements south of Forty-second Street, and those of some of the avenues were regarded as impediments to travel. Experience had developed the fact that wooden pavements could not be maintained in such a condition as to make them useful or safe. It was therefore recommended that all the streets and avenues in which wooden pavements had been laid, and those in which other pavements were in a condition to impede travel, should be repaved with trap or granite blocks, the only classes of pavements which had met the requirements of commerce and traffic, and the best from a sanitary point of view.

The accommodation provided for crossing the Harlaem River was deemed insufficient. The bridges at Third Avenue and McComb's Dam did not adequately provide for the increasing travel and traffic. Legislative authority had been obtained for tunneling the river, but that work could not be undertaken immediately, and the demand for increased accommodation should be met in some other way. An additional bridge of a temporary character was urgently required, and its erection recommended.

The Central Park was a property of which the citizens were justly proud. The expense incurred in constructing and ornamenting it had been returned to the city in the enhanced value of the property surrounding it and the consequent increase of the taxable fund of the city.

The question of speedy communication between the extremes of the city was forcing itself upon public attention in 1875. The schemes were many which had been suggested to accomplish that purpose, but the results had not been satisfactory. Charters had been granted by the legislature conferring valuable franchises, but from them no advantage to the citizens generally had resulted. So earnest was the desire manifested for securing rapid transit in the city that a board of civil engineers, self constituted, but including gentlemen most eminent in their profession, had undertaken to prepare plans to overcome, if possible, the obstacles hitherto encountered. To some extent a remedy had been provided by tunneling Fourth Avenue above Forty-second Street. That work when completed would give an unobstructed course to passenger trains into and out of the city. The extension of that work southerly to the City Hall over a route which should be nearly the axial line of the city, would go far towards solving the problem of rapid transit.

The city's proportion of the expense for the improvement of Fourth Avenue was three million two hundred thousand dollars.

The tower on the Brooklyn side of the suspension bridge between New York and Brooklyn was nearly finished by the opening of 1875. On the New York side the tower had been carried a few feet above the springing of the arches and would be completed within the ensuing season. The Brooklyn anchorage was within twenty feet of completion and would require about three months to finish it. The castings required to support the cables of both towers had been made. A consolidation of the cities of New York and Brooklyn into one municipality appeared to be only a question of time, and when the bridge should have been completed that union was regarded as a prospective surety.

The extent of the operations of the Department of Public Works, in 1875, may be perceived from the fact that the attention of its officers was constantly required, by not only the works of construction in progress, but by two hundred and seventy miles of street pavements, twelve and a half miles of boulevards and about fifty miles of streets regulated and graded but not then paved; by three hundred and fifty-two miles of sewers with four thousand three hundred and nine receiving basins, and by twenty thousand one hundred and thirty-nine street lamps. There were also distributed through four hundred and ten miles of mains one hundred and five million gallons of Croton water daily, being about one hundred gallons to each of the inhabitants every day. The revenues received by the city from the use of Croton water were about one million two hundred and fifty thousand dollars per annum. During 1875 the Department, among other works of public improvement, constructed thirteen miles of sewers, culverts, and drains with one hundred and twenty-nine receiving basins.

The question of accommodation for travel across the Harlem River again forced itself upon public attention by reason of the frequent interruption at the Third Avenue bridge for repairs, and because of the age and weakness of the structure at McComb's Dam. The rebuilding of the Central Bridge was therefore suggested, and the providing of a steam engine to work the draw of the Third Avenue bridge; and preparations were set a foot for two additional bridges—a suspension bridge half a mile north of High Bridge and a bridge at Madison Avenue.

On the 31st of December, 1876, the net debt of the city amounted to one hundred and thirteen million eight hundred and thirty thousand six hundred and eleven dollars.

A deficient supply of Croton water during 1876 had occasioned much inconvenience, and many remedies had been suggested. The financial condition of the city precluded all thought of undertaking the construction of a new Aqueduct, as the existing one had cost ten millions of dollars when laborers received only fifty cents a day and an additional aqueduct would probably cost double that sum.

The aqueduct conveyed to New York one hundred and ten millions of gallons per day, an amount much beyond the existing necessities, and on the completion of the new reservoirs in Westchester county, that quantity could be furnished regularly during the whole year. These reservoirs would be completed within a year, and then a supply of water, it was believed, would be at hand, sufficient to meet the requirements of the city. Besides, the new high-service water-works for the purpose of supplying water to the elevated localities of the city would soon be finished, when it was hoped water could be furnished in the upper stories of most of the buildings. It was a fact worthy of consideration that during 1876 when there had been an exceptional scarcity of water, there was a sufficient supply for all necessary and legitimate purposes and that as soon as the authorities took steps to stop the waste of water all danger of a failure of supply was at once averted.

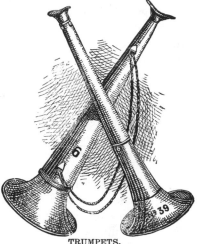

TRUMPETS.

For twenty years (from 1857) the city debt kept steadily increasing. From an indebtedness of about eighteen million dollars at that time, at the expiration of ten years, namely, December 31, 1867, the amount had increased to thirty-two million nine hundred and fourteen thousand four hundred and twenty-one dollars and twenty-six cents. This covered the period of the war, during two years of which, 1863 and 1864, more than twelve million dollars was added to the debt.

From 1867-8 may be dated the accession of the corrupt administration known as "the Ring" to full control. That dynasty continued in power for nearly five years, until 1872. During that period the aggregate debt of the city increased as follows:

December 31, 1868...............................$35,983,647.91
          1869..................................... 47,791,840.28
          1870..................................... 73,373,552.02
          1871..................................... 88,369,3896.0
          1872..................................... 95,582,153.09

Then followed an almost entire change of administration and many sincere efforts to economize expenditures and diminish the increase of the public debt. But these efforts could hardly be said to be successful as the debt continued to increase until on December 31, 1876, the bonded debt amounted to one hundred and nineteen million eight hundred and eleven thousand three hundred and ten dollars and thirty-nine cents. During 1877 a decrease of more than two millions was effected, attributable mainly to the careful and economical management of the finances.

A large amount of block-pavement was laid in 1877. Murray, John, Maiden Lane, Dey, Cortlandt, Rector, Nassau, Ferry, Warren, and Spruce Streets were paved with granite blocks and trap-rock.

The deficient supply of Croton water during 1877 attracted much attention. The supply during the drought in the fall was so diminished as to cause much serious inconvenience. It was expected that the new reservoir, near Brewster's Station, would be completed in the spring of 1878, which would hold three to four millions of gallons. That, with the existing resources, would furnish at all seasons of the year the ninety million of gallons daily which was all that could safely be brought to the city by the existing aqueduct.

The necessity for a larger water supply was again keenly experienced in 1881. It was seen that the single conduit in use for bringing water from the Croton valley and its vicinity would at no distant day prove inadequate for that service. In 1842, when the Croton Aqueduct was completed, New York contained about three hundred and thirty thousand inhabitants, and the daily supply was forty million gallons. The population had increased to one million two hundred and eight thousand, according to the census of 1880, and the average daily consumption of water was ninety-three million five hundred thousand gallons. The subject of an additional source of supply both as an auxiliary to the Croton Aqueduct for general service, and as its temporary substitute in emergency, was, therefore, receiving careful and earnest consideration.

The net funded debt of New York on December 30, 1881, was ninety-eight million three hundred and two thousand eight hundred and fifty-four dollars and eighteen cents. Since 1876 the decrease had been sixteen million six-hundred and forty-five thousand seven hundred and fifty-seven dollars and fifty-eight cents. For 1881 the decrease was three million two hundred and seven thousand and thirty-seven dollars and thirty-eight cents, as against two million nine hundred and twelve thousand one hundred and seventy dollars and ninety-eight cents for the year 1880, which figures were a gratifying comment upon the administration of the municipal finances. The tax rate for 1882, namely, two dollars and twenty-five cents, was materially less than during any year for the previous ten years.

The year 1883 was made memorable in the history of New York and Brooklyn by the completion and dedication to public use of the Bridge which connects them, thus uniting two great cities whose interests are almost identical by a structure great in itself, but greater still in its promised benefits to the best interests of the people of both.

Abundant evidences were to be found in 1884, on every hand, of the continued prosperity and vigorous growth of the city. New avenues of transportation had been opened to and from the interior of the country, great warehouses had been constructed, new exchanges organized, great office buildings had been completed and occupied, and others were in course of construction, manufactories, modest dwellings and palatial residences had been built in great numbers, and the wharves and piers had proven far too limited in number and space to accommodate the foreign and domestic commerce which sought this port.

The net bonded debt of the city on December 31, 1883, was ninety-two million five hundred and forty-six thousand and twenty-five dollars and eighty-eight cents, a decrease during that year of three million five hundred and ninety-five thousand nine hundred and twenty-two dollars and seventy cents.

On the ninth of January, 1883, the State Senate, by resolution, requested the mayor of New York to select and appoint five citizens who in conjunction with himself should, without delay, examine, etc., a plan for a new aqueduct submitted to the mayor by the Commissioner of Public Works, in February, 1882. Pursuant to that resolution the mayor appointed Orlando B. Potter, John T. Agnew, Wm. Dowd, Amos F. Eno, and Hugh N. Camp. Those gentlemen reported to the Senate on March 7.

The legislature subsequently passed an act entitled "An act to provide new reservoirs, dams, and a new aqueduct with the appurtenances thereto for the purpose of supplying the city of New York with an increased supply of pure and wholesome water." That act created a commission consisting of the mayor, the comptroller, the Commissioner of Public Works, James C. Spencer, George W. Lane, and William Dowd, who were empowered and directed to carry out the provisions of the act. At the time of the approval of the act by the governor on the first of June, 1883, one of the gentlemen composing the commission was absent in Europe, and therefore no legal organization could be effected until his return, which occurred late in the month of July. Early in August the commission duly organized, and entered upon the active discharge of its duties.

At the first regular meeting in August, 1883, the Commissioner of Public Works submitted plans for the construction of a dam now known as the "Quaker Bridge Dam," and for an aqueduct from the site of said dam to the Harlem River near High Bridge upon the line commonly known as the "Hudson River Route." That route met with serious opposition from property owners throughout almost its entire length, passing as it did in many places near the existing Croton Aqueduct and through much highly improved and very valuable property. After a good deal of earnest examination of all the schemes proposed the Commission finally decided upon a modification of the "Hudson River Route." A more detailed statement of this subject will be found in a preceding chapter.

FIRST SEAL OF NEW YORK CITY.

CHAPTER XXIII.

VOLUNTEER PARADES AND PROCESSIONS.

Some of the Grand Displays in which the Old Department has Participated.—Celebrating the Opening of the Erie Canal and the Introduction of the Croton.—Commemorating the French Revolution of 1830.—The First Annual and the Triennial Parades.—Torchlight Processions.—Great Parade of 1883.—The Bartholdi Statue Fete.

IN the history of the Volunteer Fire Department its parades are a prominent feature. Even the citizens of Paris are not greater lovers of a street show than are the citizens of New York. A military and civic pageant of this city is never complete without the appearance therein of the firemen, and no body of men comes in for a greater share of applause than the citizens whose business is fighting fire. The Volunteers have graced many and many a parade, and not a few have been entirely their own. To give a detailed description of them all would require many chapters. In this book we can describe only the most important, and briefly refer to the lesser ones.

Independence Day was always considered a proper occasion for a Firemen's Parade. One of the first took place in 1824. The procession was formed in Hospital Green, and proceeded through several of the principal streets to the Bowery Church. Thousands of people cheered the firemen on their way.

When Lafayette arrived in this country the firemen got up a display in his honor. A novel exhibition was given in City Hall Park on September 9, 1824. In the afternoon forty-four engines, the hook and ladder companies, together with two engines from Brooklyn, assembled. General Lafayette, accompanied by Chief Engineer Franklin, reviewed the men and their apparatus, and warmly expressed his admiration of what he saw. The hook and ladder companies, placed in the centre, formed a pyramid of their apparatus, upon the top of which was a miniature house filled with combustibles. Upon a given signal this house was fired, and simultaneously the engines turned their streams upon the burning object, and to the delight of the spectators each hit the object with wonderful accuracy. The spray from the water was remarkably pretty, and as the sunlight shone through the white cloud the brilliancy of the prismatic colors drew forth repeated exclamations of admiration from thirty thousand spectators. Subsequently several companies assumed the name of Lafayette. Engine Companies Nos. 7 and 9 each claimed the honor of first assuming the designation, but No. 19 finally retained it. Hose Company No. 34, Hook and Ladder Company No. 6 and Hose Company No. 4, also at times bore the coveted name.

The opening day of the celebration of the completion of the Erie Canal, November 4, 1825, was one of the finest parades New York had seen. The procession through the city was composed of nearly seven thousand citizens, of different societies, with many cars bearing their respective standards and the implements of their respective arts. It passed through columns of people whose numbers exceeded one hundred thousand. The procession was entirely civic. The aquatic display was exceedingly fine. Twenty-nine steamboats gorgeously dressed, with barges, ships, pilot boats, canal boats and the boats of the Whitehall watermen, conveying thousands of ladies and gentlemen, presented a memorable spectacle. The whole fleet passed down the bay to receive Foreman Clinton and his staff and the committees from the different parts of the country.

The several companies of artillery throughout the State assembled on the auspicious morning and fired salutes in honor of the event. Cannon were placed along the Hudson from Albany to New York at twenty-one places, and beginning at 11 A.M. were fired in succession with one minute interval, beginning at Albany. Then a return fire was made from this city. The report of the cannon from the north and west was received at New York in one hour and forty minutes, and was returned to Buffalo in nearly the same space of time, making a communication on a line of eleven hundred miles in less than three hours.

In the procession the New York firemen presented a magnificent appearance. They headed the Fourth Division one thousand two hundred and fifty-two strong, and were loudly cheered along the whole route. The column proceeded to the Battery and returned by the easterly side of Greenwich Street up Canal Street. The procession occupied one hour and fifteen minutes in passing a given point. The following is the order of the firemen's procession:

JAMIESON COX, *Marshal.*

Assistants.

Nathaniel M. Brown.	Wm. P. Disosway.
Otis Harrington.	Edward Dayton.
Wm. Lockwood.	John P. Bailey.
Neil Gray.	Peter D. Vroom.
Thomas Kennedy.	William Burger.
John W. Degrauw.	Moses Bedell.
Dan. M. Winants.	John G. C. Lord.
E. H. Lacy.	Wm. P. Shipman.
Fred. R. Lee.	Jesse Forshay.
Drake B. Palmer.	George Greig.

Fire Department standard, inscribed "New York Fire Department," borne and supported by members of Company No. 37.

Company No. 6, preceded by their banner. A small car followed, containing two platforms handsomely carpeted and decorated; on the upper platform was a small engine, complete in every respect, with three-eighth inch chambers, from which issued at intervals a stream of water to the distance of fifty feet, being the workmanship of Wm. Corp, a youth who was not a mechanic.

Washington Company No. 20, bearing a small banner. Their engine was mounted on a car drawn by four beautiful black horses; on the platform were two firemen appropriately attired; their grand standard—a portrait of Washington—followed.

Company No. with banner.

Tradesman's Company No. 7, bearing a blue silk banner. In the center of this company was borne a banner of blue silk, six feet by five—a female figure with her right hand upon a spinning wheel, at her feet fruit, etc.; signifying that, notwithstanding calamities by fire, she, by her industry, can obtain a livelihood.

East River Company No. 42 displayed their engine mounted upon a stage, drawn by four beautiful black horses, the two postilions mounted. On the stage in front of the engine were two firemen. Behind were the standard bearers with the company's banner.

Franklin Company No. 39, displaying a handsome banner.

Company No. 15 exhibited their engine mounted on a car drawn by four elegant bay horses.

Equitable Company No. 36, bearing an elegant banner, superbly painted.

Eagle Company No. 13. The engine of this company was mounted on a stage drawn by four milk-white steeds, handsomely caparisoned, and led by four Africans dressed in rich Moorish costume. The engine, with varnish, polishing, etc., was in splendid condition. The four lengths of hose (two hundred feet) were neatly wound on the reel, and covered with a black leather apron, varnished. All the fittings and draperies were extremely handsome, and the banner very fine. On the stage in front of the engine was stationed Edward D. Degrove, a member of the company, in the dress of a fireman, with an American Eagle painted on the frontispiece of his cap. He was supported by Master James A. Gray and Master Alfred Lowber. Committee of Arrangements—Charles I. Hubbs, Gideon D. Angelis, Neil Gray, Richard C. McCormick, Edward W. Degrove.

Scott Company No. 7 appeared with a banner—a view of the fire that occurred at Brooklyn, L. I., on the night of August 1, 1822, the same surrounded by an oak wreath.

United States Company No. 23 exhibited their banner. Four members of the company carried, on a stage handsomely ornamented, an engine of one inch chamber, two feet long, eighteen inches high, capable of throwing water to the distance of sixty feet—being then the best model, and the most effective and complete miniature engine ever exhibited in this country.

DE WITT CLINTON.

Mechanical Engine Company No. 28, with a banner of blue silk suspended from a bronzed pipe and surmounted by a gilt fire-cap.

Hook and Ladder Companies Nos. 1, 2, 3, and 4. Midway from front to rear, in this section of the procession, the four hook and ladder companies were stationed, marshalled by Benjamin J. Scribner. They were preceded by a splendid banner on which was delineated a vivid representation of a fire. One of their trucks followed, drawn by four horses richly caparisoned, the postilions mounted. On each side of the pyramid of ladders, etc., were two firemen in full equipment, bearing axes, etc., and above them waved the "Star Spangled Banner"—the whole representing a correct and beautiful display of this branch of the Fire Department.

Ætna Company No. 16 displayed two very handsome banners.

Manhattan Company No. 8 appeared under a blue banner of very fine workmanship.

Clinton Company No. 41. Their engine, richly painted in orange and highly gilded, was exhibited on a stage surrounded by a balustrade, and drawn by four beautiful blood bays, mounted by postilions. The car was richly ornamented. On the condenser case, the most conspicuous part of the machine, was a beautiful and correct representation (executed by Thomas Grenell) of the arduous and imposing work at that "great pass" through a branch of the Alleghany Mountains known as the "Little Falls of the Mohawk." Next, supported by four members, followed a beautiful and perfect engine in miniature, placed on a stage and decorated with silk drapery, tastefully festooned, displaying appropriate devices. The grand standard of the company, of blue silk, followed, borne by three distinguished members, wearing blue sashes.

North River Company No. 27. The banner of this company, borne and supported by members, represented Amphitrite in her car drawn and attended by Nereids.

Phœnix Company No. 22. Their engine was splendidly burnished, elevated in a tastefully decorated car, drawn by four beautiful bay horses, richly caparisoned.

Company No. 33. Banner of blue silk, five feet square, bordered wth yellow silk fringe.

New York Company No. 31, with an elegant banner, painted by Browerre & Quidor, young artists, natives of the city.

Lafayette Company No. 7, exhibited their handsomely burnished engine, elevated upon a stage, drawn by four bay horses.

Niagara Company No. 10, preceded by their banner of blue silk, with a painting of the Falls of Niagara, by T. Grenell.

American Company No. 4. Their engine was mounted upon a stage, drawn by four fine bay horses.

Chatham Company No. 2, followed by a banner, with an engine painted thereon.

Protection Company No. 5, with a large globular brazen signal lantern burnished.

Company No. 24, with a beautiful miniature engine on the top of a brass pipe, ornamented with ribbons.

Jefferson Company No. 26, Hose Company No. 1, and other companies with a variety of appropriate emblems.

The fire wardens followed with the city arms blazoned on their hats. Their handsome banner was borne by George Jacobs, assisted by Henry H. Gillett, and Augustus Cregier, wardens of the Tenth Ward.

Then came the secretary, treasurer, and collector of the Fire Department, trustees of the Fire Department Fund, president and vice-president of the Fire Department, and engineers of the Department.

One thousand two hundred and fifty-two persons—members of the several fire companies —assembled at St. John's Park, and were marshaled in the procession by Jamieson Cox, chief engineer of the Fire Department, and his assistants. They wore uniform badges, emblematical of their calling. The marshal, his assistants, the engineers, and delegates were distinguished by the magnificence of their decorations.

The following were appointed by the different engine companies delegates to form a Committee of Arrangements:

From the Engineers : Samuel J. Willis.

From No. 1, Charles R. Hatfield.	From No. 22, John Murphy.
From No. 2, John G. C. Lord.	From No. 23, John P. Bailey.
From No. 3, Wm. Lockwood.	From No. 24, Wm. P. Shipman.
From No. 4, Cornelius Romaine.	From No. 25, Morris Franklin.
From No. 5, Peter D. Vroom.	From No. 26, George Greig.
From No. 6, William Civill.	From No. 27, John H. Smith.
From No. 7, Daniel Berrian.	From No. 28, Nathaniel M. Brown.
From No. 8, Otis Harrington.	From No. 29, Samuel Gunton.
From No. 9, Thomas Williams.	From No. 30, E. B. Messeroe.
From No. 10, Henry Palmer.	From No. 31, Daniel M. Winant.
From No. 11, Abraham V. Vandenberg.	From No. 32, James G. Reynolds.
From No. 12, John Teller.	From No. 33, Obadiah Newcomb.
From No. 13, Neil Gray.	From No. 34, E. H. Lacy.
From No. 14, James H. McKenzie.	From No. 36, Moses Bedell.
From No. 15, Thomas Kennedy.	From No. 37, Fred. R. Lee.
From No. 16, John W. Degrauw.	From No. 38, James W. Anderson.
From No. 17, Wm. A. Cox.	From No. 39, Jesse Forshay.
From No. 18, Oliver T. Hewlett.	From No. 40, Richard Cornell.
From No. 19, Wm. B. Odell.	From No. 41, Drake B. Palmer.
From No. 20. Thomas Hopper.	From No. 42, Samuel Brown.
From No. 21, John A. Mitchell.	

Supply Engine :
No. 1, John Groshon.

Hose Company :
Thomas Schieffelin, Jr.

Hook and Ladder Companies :

No. 1, Wm. P. Disosway.	No. 3, Daniel I. Hide.
No. 2, James B. Bird.	No. 4, Thomas Clark.

First Ward, Wm. A. F. Pentz.   Fifth Ward, R. Lowerre.

Third Ward, Wm. Burger.   Sixth Ward, Enoch Dean.

Fourth Ward, John Targee.   Seventh Ward, Ed. Dayton.

Tenth Ward, Augustus Cregier.

Samuel J. Willis, chairman : Neil Gray, secretary.

Delegates to confer with the Corporation : Samuel Jones Willis, Ed. Dayton.

The next parade was on October 15, 1827. It was on the occasion of the celebration of the incorporation of the Department. The firemen turned out very strong, forty-two companies in number. The line of march was up Chatham to Chambers Street; down Chambers to Greenwich Street; thence to the Battery. At the Battery the companies formed in line, and, taking suction from the river, played in rotation.

The Revolution in France in 1830 (the overthrow of the government of Louis Philippe) was duly honored in this city by a parade of the firemen. At a special meeting of the Board of Engineers and Foremen, held at Fireman's Hall, it was unanimously

Resolved, That the members of this Department will unite with their fellow citizens in

WASHINGTON ENGINE COMPANY, NO. 20, CANAL CELEBRATION.

celebrating the late triumphant and glorious contest for liberty and the overthrow of tyranny in France.

Resolved, That the following persons constitute the several committees to make the necessary arrangements :

BADGE COMMITTEE.

F. R. Lee, G. De Angelos, J. Murphy, D. B. Palmer, G. Hamilton.

MUSIC COMMITTEE.

James Gulick, J. S. Huggitt, D. Weeden, E. Winship, P. Baxter.

MARSHAL'S COMMITTEE.

Morris Franklin, A. B. Rich, W. B. Townsend, E. T. Lewis, J. A. Roome.

Resolved, That Uzziah Wenman, W. P. Disosway and D. B. Palmer be a committee to inform the grand marshal of the day of the proceedings of this meeting.

Resolved, That James Gulick be appointed grand marshal, and John Ryker, Jr., and Thomas Howe, deputy marshals for the Fire Department.

W. P. DISOSWAY,   UZZIAH WENMAN,
        Secretary.   *Chairman.*

To the Exempt Firemen :

At a meeting of the Board of Engineers and Foremen held at Fireman's Hall November 18, 1830, it was unanimously

Resolved, That the exempt members of the Fire Department be respectfully invited to join with the firemen in celebrating the late revolution in France.

W. P. Disosway,
Secretary.

Uzziah Wenman,
Chairman.

At a meeting of the fire wardens held at Fireman's Hall, on November 22, 1830, it was, on motion, unanimously

Resolved, That participating in the feelings of our brother firemen, in celebrating the recent success of the liberties of the French people, that we, as a body, join in the procession with our brother firemen.

Resolved, That we assemble at the Hospital Green (in Broadway), at eight o'clock, on the twenty-fifth instant, and that the exempt wardens are respectfully invited to join with us on the occasion.

Cornelius Agnew,
Secretary.

John W. Degrauw,
Chairman.

TWELFTH DIVISION.

Band of Music.

John R. Livingston, Jr., aid, delegated by the marshal-in-chief.

Firemen, and Fire Department.

[That portion of the procession composed of this department contributed greatly to the display, and was under the direction of James Gulick, one of the engineers. In numbers, including those from Brooklyn, they amounted to upwards of one thousand men, and occupied more than a mile of the route, marching in the following order :]

Engine Company No. 4, from the village of Brooklyn, mounted on a car erected on four wheels, which were nearly concealed by elegant festoons of tri-colored cloths, suspended from the stage and supported by gilded pins. The platform on which the engine was placed was covered with handsome carpet, and a grand triumphal arch composed of laurel and other evergreens was erected over the heads of three men, who were on the stage to represent the company in their working costume. In the centre was the motto :

"1776 : LIBERTY : 1830,"

and many appropriate devices, the whole drawn by four horses, followed by the Brooklyn firemen.

Next in order was Engine No. 23 of the New York Department, drawn by two horses, and decorated with American and tri-colored flags and ribbons ; No. 12 placed on a car similar to the first in line, covered with costly Brussels carpet and decorated with luxurious festoons of drapery, composed of the three colors. The horses were led by negroes in Moorish attire ; the hose covered with a patent leather case ; the pipes, levers, etc., elegantly entwined with appropriate ribbons, followed by brass signal lanterns, torches and other implements, beautifully polished and decorated. On either side of the stage was a large American and tri-colored standard. The members followed.

Next came Hook and Ladder Truck No. 1, drawn by members—the drag rope covered with tri-colored ribbons, carriage, ladders, hooks, etc., painted tri-colored, the bottom ladder being blue, the center white, and upper one red. Two small ladders and a hook were erected from the center, from the summit of which were displayed tri-colored and American flags.

Engine No. 1 followed on a car drawn by four superb horses, each nearly thirteen hands high, and said to be the finest team in point of size and power in the State ; the car and engine handsomely decorated.

No. 37, without a car, drawn by six black ponies.

No. 23 had four bay horses, driven by a member seated on a box of the engine. The company followed, bearing the signal lantern (in which was a lighted lamp) and torches, a beautiful miniature engine and other emblems.

Engine No. 2 on a stage drawn by four horses, and handsomely ornamented, displaying at each end an American standard and tri-colored banner.

Hook and Ladder Truck No. 3, drawn by members, flags waving from either extremity.

Engine No. 32, drawn by four brown horses.

No. 5, drawn by members bearing tri-colored and American standards, together with appropriate emblems; the machine beautifully decorated with ribbons, flowers, etc.

No. 40, mounted on a car drawn by four horses, and decorated with the American standard and tri-colored banner, and a superb gilded eagle suspended over the engine.

WEST POINT BAND.

Then Engine No. 46 drawn by four horses without a car.

Miniature No. 33, drawn by one small pony.

No. 33, on a stage drawn by four horses, decorated with tri-colors.

No. 26, without a car, drawn by six horses, followed by members bearing miniature engine and other emblems.

No. 27, drawn by members and ornamented with American and tri-colored flags.

Lafayette Company No. 19, on a car superbly ornamented and drawn by four horses; members following bearing a banner on which was a well executed, full-length portrait of General Lafayette.

EAST RIVER ENGINE COMPANY NO. 42, CANAL CELEBRATION.

No. 14, decorated with flags and drawn by four white horses led by negroes in Turkish costume and followed by members.

Lafayette Company No. 7, drawn by two horses, the company displaying a banner on which was an excellent figure of General Lafayette, as in his youth, on horseback.

Hook and Ladder Truck No. 5, drawn by four horses.

Engine No. 13, ornamented with flags, etc., and drawn by four gray horses led by negroes in Arabian style.

No. 20, drawn by members.

No. 29, also drawn by members, the hose covered with a tri-colored case.

Nos. 41 and 44, on separate cars, ornamented as others previously described, and each drawn by four horses which were driven by members in a masterly style.

No. 11, drawn by members in full working dress, exhibiting a striking contrast with their precursors in the line which elicited the most enthusiastic plaudits from the multitude.

The celebration of the completion of the Croton Aqueduct on October 14, 1842, is a memorable page in the history of New York. Nothing contributed so much to help the gallant firemen in their fights with the flames, and none could better appreciate the benefits derivable from this great work than the fire laddies. They felt that the odds against them in their battle with the old enemy were very considerably reduced. The weather on the day of the celebration was magnificent. A brilliant sun, a sky veiled but not clouded, and a breezy atmosphere were in harmony with the occasion and with the joyousness of the multitudinous population crowded into the city from all surrounding regions to witness and share in the grand jubilee. At sunrise one hundred guns were fired, the bells of all the churches and public places were rung, and in less than an hour the streets were alive with moving masses. The first ceremony of the morning was the presentation of the banner to the Fire Department. C. B. Timpson, Chairman of the Joint Committee on Fire and Water, addressing the Mayor on the occasion, said:

The front [of the banner] represents the Fire Department as having achieved a victory over the devouring element, receiving the blessings and thanks of the widow and her orphans for the protection and benefits derived from it — beautiful emblems of power and beneficence, helplessness and gratitude. They are attended by a hero of the flames. Erect above all stands old Father Neptune, evidently delighted with the victory he has accomplished over his ancient enemy, the demon of fire, by the aid of his skillful and intrepid allies, the firemen of New York. On the other side of the banner the Queen of Cities, represented by a female wearing a crown — the origin of the aqueduct. On the lower part of the border surrounding the picture are emblazoned the arms of the City of New York in basso relievo. The silk on which the design is portrayed measures nine and one-half by seven and one-half feet. Its color is a rich mazarine blue; the fringe, tassels, and cord are amber and crimson. The banner is surmounted and greatly adorned by three separate groups of carving — the centre consisting of a fireman's cap as a base, with a trumpet affixed to the top, on which stands a large eagle with extended wings, measuring three and a-half feet from tip to tip. At each end are trophies, composed of hook and ladder, torch, trumpet, pipe, and axes.

In the course of the speech which the mayor made in reply, his honor said that the banner he was deputed to present was a testimonial from the Common Council of the high appreciation in which they held the services rendered by the Fire Department. He continued:

The Fire Department was organized on the twentieth of March, 1798, from which period to the present time, by its constant vigilance and unceasing and disinterested efforts, the property of our citizens has been protected. Blended with the important services you have thus rendered, you have also performed the important functions of a charitable institution, having for its object the relief of the widows and orphans of your deceased associates; the benefits thus conferred by the Department have been as extensive as their intentions were praiseworthy. This occasion, the celebration of the arrival of the Croton water in our city, is happily selected for the presentation of this banner, as it is to be hoped that among the important benefits to result from that work, not the least will be to relieve your Department of a great proportion of its dangerous and arduous duties. The emblems upon this standard are indicative of the foresight and energy of our citizens, and of the services and humanity of the Fire Department.

Mr. Adam Pentz, President of the Fire Department, made a suitable reply, and among other things, he said:

While some have looked merely to the introduction of pure and wholesome water into this city as being an indispensable requisite of public health and others regarding the distance from which it has been brought and the obstacles overcome as constituting an enduring monument of the enterprise and public spirit of our citizens, the firemen of the city, while participating in the feeling of both these classes, yet with that devotion to their duties by which they have ever been distinguished, rejoice chiefly because that great work, in giving increased efficacy to their exertions, affords additional security to the property of their fellow citizens. It is not, perhaps, too much to say that nearly all the great fires by which large portions of our city have been devastated might have been easily arrested, had the

Department possessed the same facilities for obtaining an abundant supply of water, as that which we now enjoy from the introduction of the Croton.

The magnificent procession was composed of ten divisions. The Fire Department composed the Fourth Division under the direction of Brigadier-General Pentz, assisted by Mr. John T. Dodge and Mr. George C. Ring, aids to the Grand Marshal (General Gilbert Hopkins). Never had the Department made a finer appearance and never did it receive so great an ovation from the people as on this glorious day. The procession was two hours and ten minutes passing a given point. The following was the order of the Fire Department :

At the head of the procession was a band of music brought from Philadelphia by the Neptune Hose Company of that city.

Fairmount Engine Company, of Philadelphia, numbering thirty-seven men, dressed in the uniform of the Philadelphia firemen, viz., glazed hats, drab firecoats and pants, and oil-cloth capes over the shoulders.

Neptune Hose Company, of Philadelphia, fifty-six men, in black fire dress, drawing a splendid four-wheeled hose carriage, silver-mounted.

Engine Company No 3, of Hudson, with their engine, drawn by thirty-two men, and also some members of Engine Company No. 8, of Albany.

Engine Company No. 1, of Poughkeepsie, engine drawn by thirty-five men.

The Fire Department of Newark and New Jersey, consisting of engineers, firemen, and assistants, bearing the banner of the Newark Fire Department. Representatives from the Hook and Ladder and Engine Companies in full uniform, but without apparatus. The men from Newark numbered one hundred and fifty. The New Jersey contingent consisted of Fire Engines, Nos. 1 and 2, each drawn by about forty men in uniform.

The Fire Department of Williamsburgh, about one hundred and fifty men.

The Fire Department of Brooklyn, as follows :

Washington Engine Company No. 1, engine drawn by eighty men, dressed in dark trousers, red shirts, and fatigue caps. Neptune Engine Company No. 2, seventy-four men. Eagle Company No. 4, sixty men. Constitution Engine Company No. 7, one hundred and twenty-five men. American Engine Company No. 9, thirty-nine men. Atlantic Hose and Relief Company, with four-wheeled hose carriage, bearing one thousand feet of hose and twenty-five buckets, thirty men in citizens' dress. Clinton Hook and Ladder Company No. 2, fifty-six men in citizens' dress.

NEW YORK FIRE DEPARTMENT.

Cornelius V. Anderson, *Grand Marshal.*

Assistant Marshals :

W. Wells Wilson,	Dewitt C. Mott,
John B. Miller,	Samuel L. Liscomb,
George Kerr,	Samuel Waddell,
Alfred Carson,	George H. Ramppen,
Charles Forrester,	Zophar Mills,
Philip B. White,	Joseph W. Long,
Owen W. Brennan,	John T. Rollins,

John Rese.

The Grand and Assistant Marshals were dressed in the uniform of the Engineers of the Fire Department, viz., white fire caps, blue coat and trousers. The line was formed in Hudson Street and extended from Christopher to Reade Street. The procession moved at nine A. M. down Hudson to Charles Street, to Broadway, and to the Battery in the following order :

BAND OF MUSIC.

Banner of the New York Fire Department borne on a stage, richly carpeted and festooned and drawn by four white horses, elegantly caparisoned, and each horse led by a black groom in Turkish dress. The banner was supported by the Trustees of the Department. It was designed and executed by Allan Smith, Jr., of New York. The silk on which the fine design was portrayed measured nine and a-half by seven and a-half feet. Its color was a rich mazarine blue. The fringe, tassels, and cord were of crimson and amber. The banner was presented to the Fire Department on the morning of the procession by Mayor Robert H. Morris, and was received by the President, Adam P. Pentz.

The Grand Marshal and two aids and officers of the Fire Department Fund. The Exempt Firemen.

Hudson Fire Engine Company No. 1, drawn by one hundred and twenty-nine members. A small engine was drawn by four boys.

Eagle Hose Company No. 1, drawn by one hundred and forty men. Four wheeled hose carriage painted black and gold.

Mutual Hook and Ladder Company No. 1. Truck drawn by forty men in citizens' dress, dark throughout. A handsome banner.

Chatham Fire Engine Company No. 2. On the back of the engine a portrait of James Wallack as Rolla. Engine drawn by thirty-eight men in uniform. Banner representing the burning of the Bowery Theater.

Niagara Hose Company No. 2. Two-wheeled Hose Carriage, drawn by ten men in uniform.

Forest Engine Company No. 3. Engine drawn by thirty-two men in uniform. Banner borne by six lads in uniform.

Independence Hose Company No. 3. Two-wheeled hose carriage, drawn by forty uniformed men.

ENGINE COMPANY NO. 15, CROTON CELEBRATION.

Lafayette Hose Company No. 4. Two-wheeled hose carriage drawn by fifteen men in uniform.

Protection Fire Engine Company No. 5. Engine handsomely ornamented, and drawn by forty-six men in uniform. A miniature engine preceded, a fac-simile of the large, borne by eight boys.

New York Hose Company No. 5. Four-wheeled hose carriage, drawn by forty men in uniform. A gilded arch spray from the top of the reel surmounted by an eagle. A banner borne by a member and supported by two boys in fire dress.

Neptune Fire Engine Company No. 6. Engine drawn by forty men in uniform. A banner.

Croton Hose Company No. 6. Four-wheeled hose carriage, drawn by twenty-five men in uniform. Large banner representing the Croton Aqueduct. Small banner with the name and number of the company.

Wave Hose Company No. 7. Two-wheeled hose carriage, drawn by twenty men in uniform.

Manhattan Engine Company No. 8. Engine drawn by fifty-eight men.

BAND OF MUSIC.

First Ward Hose Company No. 8. Four-wheeled hose carriage, with panels of handsome pictures. Blue silk banner representing the burning of Dr. Eastburn's church in Canal Street.

Columbian Hose Company No. 9. Four-wheeled hose carriage, drawn by forty men.

Water Witch Engine Company No. 10. Engine drawn by fifty men. Banner representing a fire in Elizabeth Street.

East River Hose Company No. 10. Two-wheeled hose carriage, drawn by twenty-five men.

Oceanus Engine Company No. 11. Engine drawn by thirty-seven men.

Gulick Hose Company No. 11. Two-wheeled hose carriage, drawn by eighteen men.

Knickerbocker Engine Company No. 12. Engine drawn by twenty-six men in uniform.

BAND OF MUSIC.

Washington Hose Company No. 12. Four-wheeled hose carriage, painted cream color and gilt, drawn by fifty men.

Eagle Fire Engine Company No. 13. Engine handsomely painted, drawn by forty men.

Express Hose Company No. 13. Two-wheeled hose carriage, drawn by twenty men in uniform; banner borne by three men, representing the Park, City Hall, and Park Row, the company stretching their hose.

Columbian Engine Company No. 14. Engine drawn by fifty-three men.

CROTON CELEBRATION.

Atlantic Hose Company No. 14. Twelve men in citizens' dress, with badges and without their carriage.

Eagle Hook and Ladder Company No. 4. Truck drawn by fifty-five men; a center-pole with a model of the apparatus; banner.

Victory Hose Company No. 15. Two-wheeled hose carriage, drawn by twenty-nine men banner and two boys bearing brass torches.

Chelsea Fire Engine Company No. 16. Engine red and gold, drawn by fifty-five men with velvet caps, red shirts and dark pants.

Naiad Hose Company No. 16. Two-wheeled hose carriage drawn by twenty-five men.

Clinton Hose Company No. 17. Two-wheeled hose carriage, drawn by twenty-two men.

Union Fire Engine Company No. 18. Engine and banner; sixty-two men in uniform.

Franklin Hose Company No. 18. Two-wheeled hose carriage, drawn by twenty men.

Lafayette Engine Company No. 19. Engine drawn by twenty-six men.

American Hose Company No. 19. Two-wheeled hose carriage, drawn by thirty-two men; banner.

Washington Fire Engine Company No. 20. Engine drawn by forty-three men; banner with figure of Washington, and on the reverse of Lafayette.

Fulton Fire Engine Company No. 21. Engine drawn by thirty-seven men.

Protection Hose Company No. 21. Two-wheeled hose carriage, drawn by thirty-five men; banner.

Protector Fire Engine Hose Company No. 22. Engine drawn by fifty men; brass torches and guide flags.

United States Fire Engine Company No. 23. Engine trimmed with flowers; drawn by forty-two men.

Triton Hose Company No. 23. Two-wheeled hose carriage, drawn by sixteen men.

Jackson Fire Engine Company No. 24. Engine, drawn by thirty-two men.

Eighth Ward Hose Company No. 24. Two-wheeled hose carriage, drawn by eighteen men; two boys bearing torches.

Cataract Engine Company No. 25. Engine, drawn by fifty-three men.

Jefferson Engine Company No. 26. Engine, drawn by thirty-five men; two boys bearing torches.

Van Buren Hose Company No. 26. Two-wheeled hose carriage, drawn by twenty-six men.

North River Engine Company No. 27. Engine, drawn by sixty men.

Third Ward Hose Company No. 27. Two-wheeled hose carriage, drawn by twenty-three men.

Union Hook and Ladder Company No. 5. Boy standing on truck, bearing the motto, "We are pledged to abstain from all intoxicating drinks;" drawn by twenty-eight men.

Guardian Engine Company No. 29. Engine, drawn by forty-four men.

Eleventh Ward Hose Company No. 29. Two-wheeled hose carriage, handsomely decorated, drawn by sixteen men.

Hope Engine Company No. 31. Engine, drawn by fifty-two men; a magnificent banner; boys bearing torches, and a wreath of dahlias.

Putnam Hose Company No. 31. Two-wheeled hose carriage, drawn by twenty men.

Bunker Hill Engine Company No. 32. Engine drawn by fifty men; handsomely painted banner; boys bearing torches and guide flags.

Richard M. Johnson Hose Company No. 32. Two-wheeled hose carriage, drawn by twenty-one men.

Black Joke Company No. 33. Engine, surrounded by men in full dress, drawn by four horses; fifty-eight men in uniform preceding.

City Hose Company No. 33. Two-wheeled hose carriage, drawn by twenty-five men, attended by a delegation of thirteen members of the Liberty Fire Company of Baltimore in appropriate uniform.

Howard Engine Company No. 34. Engine, drawn by eighty-five men, banner of blue silk.

Fifteenth Ward Hose Company No. 35. Two-wheeled hose carriage, drawn by nineteen men.

Equitable Engine Company No. 36. Engine, drawn by fifty-four men; boys bearing guide flags and torches.

Glendower Hose Company No. 36. Two-wheeled hose carriage, drawn by sixteen men.

Tradesmen's Engine Company No. 37. Painted Engine, drawn by fifty-three men.

Southwark Engine Company No. 38. Large, handsomely painted engine, built in Philadelphia, drawn by ninety-four men—four abreast—banner borne on engine, tassels supported by two boys.

Lady Washington Engine Company No. 40. Handsomely painted engine, drawn by sixty men, boys bearing brass signal lanterns and torches.

Clinton Engine Company No. 41. Engine beautifully painted, drawn by fifty-five men, boys bearing brass torches.

Northern Liberty Engine Company No. 42. Large Engine on the same plan as No. 38, drawn by six white horses, preceded by thirty-seven men in uniform; banner; engine followed by hose tender, and also by Engine Company No. 3, of New Haven, as invited guests, attended by band of music; New Haven engine, drawn by thirty-eight men.

Mechanic Hook and Ladder Company No. 7. Truck, elegantly decorated, drawn by thirty-five men; banner.

Engine Company No. 43.

Live Oak Engine Company No. 44. Engine, finely painted and decorated, drawn by ninety men; boys bearing torches and guide flags.

Yorkville Engine Company No. 45.   Engine, drawn by thirty-one men.
Relief Engine Company No. 46.   Engine, drawn by forty-one men.
Mazeppa Engine Company No. 48.   Engine, drawn by thirty men.
Mohican Company No. 50.   Engine, drawn by forty men.

The Committee of Arrangements consisted of the following :

Henry B. Hinsdale, Foreman of Hose Company No. 8, Chairman ; Cornelius V. Anderson, Chief Engineer ; Elijah C. King, Foreman of Engine Company No. 26 ; William Williamson, Foreman of Engine Company No. 13 ; Stephen Kane, Foreman of Hose Company No. 12 ; Henry Snyder, Foreman of Engine Company No. 42 ; William Tupper, Foreman of Engine Company No. 46.

Delegates to confer with Common Council : H. B. Hinsdale, C. V. Anderson.

Number of firemen from neighboring cities..1072
Number in New York Fire Department...3003

    Total...4075

The procession was so long that it was impossible for all to meet at the Battery, or even within two miles of it.   While one branch, therefore, was moving into the line on Broadway by marching toward the Battery, another in the procession was marching up.   In this double line the different fire companies passed and repassed for three quarters of an hour.   The citizen firemen paid marked respect to their guests and one another as they passed, either by moving on with their heads uncovered or by raising their hats.

On the occasion of the opening of the Croton Aqueduct George P. Morris read a poem which was afterwards set to music and sung in every engine house in New York.   Here are the opening verses :

> Water leaps as if delighted
>   While her conquered foes retire ;
> Pale Contagion flies affrighted
>   With the baffled demon Fire.
>
> Round the aqueducts of glory,
>   As the mists of Lethe throng,
> Croton's waves in all their glory
>   Troop in melody along.

It will be observed that all the firemen wore their fire caps with the exception of No. 16 Company, who wore velvet caps, but 16's foreman and assistant had their regulation hats.

On the 24th of June, 1845, the firemen participated in a grand parade on the occasion of the funeral ceremonies in honor of General Andrew Jackson.   All the men were dressed in black and the banners and trumpets were draped in the same somber hue.

Sixty-five companies took part in the big procession when the corner stone of a monument to the memory of George Washington, in Hamilton Square, Yorkville, was laid on October 19, 1847, the anniversary of the surrender of Lord Cornwallis.

On March 8, 1848, the body of John Quincy Adams was received at Whitehall.   A portion of the Fire Department assisted at the ceremonies.   The military and civic procession marched up Broadway, through Grand Street, down the Bowery and Chatham Street to the City Hall.   The Volunteers were represented by the Society of Exempt Firemen, Eagle Hose Company No. 1, Mutual Hook and Ladder Company No. 1, Niagara Hose Company No. 2,

New York Hose Company No. 5, Eagle Engine Company No. 13, Jackson Hose Company, No. 13, Pearl Hose Company No. 28 and Howard Engine Company No. 34.

On the 23rd of July, 1850, the Department was conspicuous in the parade in honor of the memory of President Zachary Taylor.

In 1851 it was determined to inaugurate the first of the annual parades. On the 9th of June a very fine turnout was made with eighteen hundred men, forty engines, forty hose carriages and ten hook and ladder trucks. Companies from neighboring cities took part in the display. The members of the Department contributed to the expenses. The following is the detail of the procession, which occupied three-quarters of an hour in passing a given point :

The line formed four abreast on the west side of Hudson Street, the right resting on Abingdon Square, countermarched down Hudson Street and College Place to Murray Street, up Murray Street and through the Park. Here the procession was reviewed by the Mayor, Common Council, heads of Departments of the City Government, ex-chiefs and assistant engineers ; and then it passed out of the east gate of the Park up Chatham Street and East Broadway to Grand Street. The procession passed down Grand Street to the Bowery and down Broadway to the Park, where it was dismissed. Each company was allowed to parade only the number of men specified by law.

ASSOCIATION OF EXEMPT FIREMEN.

BAND.

Fire Department Banner, borne by Engine Company No. 2.
Officers and Trustees of the Fire Department.
CHIEF ENGINEER as GRAND MARSHAL with Assistants, M. EICHELL and J. P. LACOUR as Special Aids.
Engine Company No. 1, Hose Company No. 1, Hose Company No. 2, Engine Company No. 3, Hose Company No. 3.

BAND.

Engine Company No. 4, Hose Company No. 4.
ROBERT McGINNIS, *Marshal.*
Engine Company No. 5, Engine Company No. 6, Hose Company No. 6, Hook and Ladder Company No. 1.

BAND.

Engine Company No. 7, Hose Company No. 7, Engine Company No. 8, Hose Company No. 8.
T. MONROE, *Marshal.*
Engine Company No. 9, Hose Company No. 9.

BAND.

Engine Company No. 10, Hose Company No. 10, Engine Company No. 11, Hose Company No. 11, Engine Company No. 12.
C. VANDERBILT, *Marshal.*
Hook and Ladder Company No. 3.

BAND.

Hose Company No. 12, Engine Company No. 13, Hose Company No. 13, Hose Company No. 14, Engine Company No. 16, Hose Company No. 16.

BAND.

Hose Company No. 17.
J. A. CREGIER, *Marshal.*
Hose Company No. 18, Engine Company No. 19, Hose Company No. 19, Engine Company No. 20, Hook and Ladder Company No. 4.

BAND.

Hose Company No. 20, Engine Company No. 21.

G. W. VARIAN, *Marshal.*

Hose Company No. 21, Engine Company No. 22, Hose Company No. 22, Hose Company No. 23.

BAND.

Engine Company No. 24, Hose Company No. 24, Hose Company No. 25, Hose Company No. 26.

S. HOYT, *Marshal.*

Hose Company No. 27, Hook and Ladder Company No. 5.

BAND.

Engine Company No. 25, Engine Company No. 29, Hose Company No. 29, Engine Company No. 30, Hose Company No. 30, Hose Company No. 31.

S. M. PHILLIPS, *Marshal.*

PHENIX ENGINE COMPANY NO. 22, CROTON CELEBRATION.

BAND.

Engine Company No. 32, Hose Company No. 32, Hose Company No. 33, Engine Company No. 34, Hose Company No. 34, Engine Company No. 35, Hook and Ladder Company No. 6.

BAND.

Hose Company No. 36.

J. GILLELAN, *Marshal.*

Hose Company No. 37, Hose Company No. 38, Hose Company No. 39, Hose Company No. 40, Hose Company No. 41.

BAND.

Engine Company No. 42, Hose Company No. 42, Engine Company No. 44.

M. JACKSON, *Marshal.*

Hose Company No. 44, Engine Company No. 45, Hook and Ladder Company No. 8.

BAND.

Hose Company No. 45, Hose Company No. 47, Engine Company No. 48, Hose Company No. 48, Engine Company No. 49.

The second annual parade was on June 14, 1852, the third in 1853, and after this there were intervals of three years. The parade of October 13, 1856, was a very imposing affair. The following gives the formation:

ALFRED CARSON, Chief Engineer, *Grand Marshal.*

Assistant Engineers.

JOHN A. CREGIER and HENRY H. HOWARD, *Special Aids.*

FIRST DIVISION.

Assistant Engineers John Baulch and John Decker, *Marshals.*

Visiting Companies:

Association of Exempt Firemen.

Exempt Engine Company.

SECOND DIVISION.

Assistant Engineer Peter N. Cornwell, *Marshal.*

Fort Hamilton Band.

Fire Department Banner, in charge of Engine Company No. 18.

Grand Marshal and Special Aids.

Officers and Trustees of the New York Fire Department Fund.

Engine Company..No. 1.
Hose Company..No. 1.
Engine Company..No. 2.
Hose Company..No. 2.

TURL'S BAND.

Engine Company..No. 3.
Hook and Ladder Company...No. 1.
Hose Company..No. 3.
Engine Company..No. 4.
Hose Company..No. 4.

NORTH CAROLINA BAND.

Engine Company..No. 5.
Hose Company..No. 5.
Engine Company..No. 6.
Hose Company..No. 6.

THIRD DIVISION.

Assistant Engineer Elisha Kingsland, *Marshal.*

WALLACE'S BAND.

Engine Company..No. 7.
Hook and Ladder Company...No. 2.
Hose Company..No. 7.
Engine Company..No. 8.
Hose Company..No. 8.

HELLER'S BAND.

Engine Company..No. 9.
Hose Company..No. 9.
Engine Company..No. 10.
Hose Company..No. 10.

ROBERTSON'S FIRST BAND.

Engine Company..No. 11.
Hose Company..No. 11.
Engine Company..No. 12.
Hose Company..No. 12.
Hook and Ladder Company...No. 3.

FOURTH DIVISION.

Assistant Engineer Wm. T. Mawbey, *Marshal.*

TURNER'S BAND.

Engine Company..No. 13.
Hose Company..No. 13.
Hose Company..No. 14.
Engine Company..No. 15.

DODWORTH'S BAND.

Engine Company..No. 14.
Hose Company..No. 15.
Hose Company..No. 16.
Engine Company..No. 17.

ALBANY BAND.

Engine Company..No. 16.
Hose Company..No. 17.
Hook and Ladder Company...No. 4.
Hose Company..No. 18.

FIFTH DIVISION.

Assistant Engineer Noah L. Farnham, *Marshal.*

ROBERTSON'S BAND.

Engine Company..No. 19.
Hose Company..No. 19.
Engine Company..No. 20.
Hose Company..No. 20.

WASHINGTON BRASS BAND.

Engine Company..No. 21.
Hose Company..No. 21.
Engine Company..No. 22.
Hose Company..No. 22.

NEWARK BRASS BAND.

Engine Company..No. 24.
Hook and Ladder Company...No. 5.
Hose Company..No. 23.
Engine Company..No. 23.
Hose Company..No. 24.

SIXTH DIVISION.

Assistant Engineer Timothy L. West, *Marshal.*

ADKIN'S BAND.

Engine Company..No. 25.
Hose Company..No. 25.
Engine Company..No. 26.
Hose Company..No. 26.

FLOCKTON'S BAND.

Engine Company..No. 27.
Hose Company..No. 27.
Engine Company..No. 28.
Hose Company..No. 28.

HACKENSACK BAND.

Engine Company..No. 29.
Hose Company..No. 29.
Hook and Ladder Company...No. 6.
Hose Company..No. 30.

SEVENTH DIVISION.

Assistant Engineer, James F. Wenman, *Marshal.*

MANAHAN'S BAND.

Engine Company...................................... ....No. 33.
Hose Company.. ....No. 31.
Engine Company.... ....No. 32.
Hose Company..No. 32.

HENWICK'S CORNET BAND.

Engine Company.. ....No. 34.
Hose Company..No. 33.
Hook and Ladder Company.. ....No. 7.
Hose Company..No. 34.

BLOOMINGDALE BAND.

Engine Company..No. 36.
Engine Company..No. 35.
Hose Company.. .. ..No. 35.

STEWART'S BROOKLYN BAND.

Hose Company..No. 36.
Hook and Ladder Company..No. 8.
Engine Company............................. ....No. 37.

EIGHTH DIVISION.

Assistant Engineer Edward W. Jacobs, *Marshal.*

MIDDLETON BRASS BAND.

Engine Company.. ....No. 38.
Hose Company.................................... ....No. 37.
Hook and Ladder Company................................. .. ..No. 10.

NATIONAL GUARD BAND.

Hose Company..No. 38.
Engine Company...No. 39.
Hose Company ....No. 39.
Engine Company..No. 40.

PATERSON BAND.

Hose Company..No. 40.
Engine Company..No. 41.
Hose Company..No. 41.
Hose Company..No. 42.

NINTH DIVISION.

Assistant Engineer G. Joseph Ruch, *Marshal.*

SHELTON'S FIRST BAND.

Engine Company..No. 42.
Hook and Ladder Company..No. 12.
Engine Company..No. 43.
Hose Company.................................... ....No. 43.

WANNAMACKER'S BAND.

Engine Company..No. 44.
Hose Company..No. 44.
Hose Company ....No. 45.
Engine Company..No. 48.

YORKVILLE BAND.

Engine Company..No. 45.
Hose Company..No. 46.
Hook and Ladder Company..No. 13.
Hose Company..No. 48.
Engine Company ....No. 49.

TENTH DIVISION.

Assistant Engineer John Brice, *Marshal.*

WHITWORTH'S BAND.

Hose Company...No. 49.
Engine Company ....No. 50.
Hose Company...No. 50.
Engine Company...No. 51.

SHELTON'S SECOND BAND.

Hose Company ....No. 50.
Hook and Ladder Company...No. 14.
Hose Company...No. 52.
Hose Company...No. 54.

DODWORTH'S SECOND BAND.

Hook and Ladder Company...No. 15.
Hose Company...No. 57.
Hose Company...No. 58.

JEFFERSON BRASS BAND.

Hose Company...No. 60.
Hose Company...No. 61.

The several divisions met as follows, at 10 A. M.:

First Division in Monroe Street, right on Market Street.
Second Division in Monroe Street, right on Jefferson Street.
Third Division in Madison Street, right on Gouverneur Street.
Fourth Division in Madison Street, right on Clinton Street.
Fifth Division in Madison Street, right on Rutgers Street.
Sixth Division in Henry Street, right on Market Street.
Seventh Division in Henry Street, right on Rutgers Street.
Eighth Division in Henry Street, right on Clinton Street.
Ninth Division in East Broadway, right on Gouverneur Street.
Tenth Division in East Broadway, right on Jefferson Street.

The line, four abreast, countermarched up Monroe Street, through Gouverneur, down Madison, through Market, up Henry, through Gouverneur to East Broadway, thence to Grand Street, down Grand Street to the Bowery, up the Bowery and Third Avenue to Twenty-third Street, through Twenty-third Street to the Eighth Avenue, down Eighth Avenue and through Bleecker Street to Broadway, down Broadway through the Park, where the procession was reviewed by the Mayor, Common Council, heads of Departments of the City Government, Board of Fire Commissioners, ex-Chief Engineers, and ex-Assistant Engineers. The line then passed out the east gate and was dismissed.

An exceedingly fine sight was the firemen's torchlight procession on September 1, 1858, on the occasion of the completion of the first Atlantic Cable and the reception tendered Mr. Cyrus W. Field and the officers of the steamships Niagara, Gorgon, and Indus. Seven o'clock was the hour set for the assembling of the Department. The whole city was brilliantly illuminated. The firemen appeared in their characteristic uniform—fire caps, red shirts and black trousers. They met in the neighborhood of Fifth Avenue and Fortieth Street. Marching four abreast, bearing Drummond lights, camphene lamps, Roman candles, Bengal lights, and quite a forest of torches, the procession moved down to Union Square and around the statue of Washington. Thousands of people lined the sidewalks and filled the windows of the route, and the firemen, as they passed, were lustily cheered.

The line did not light up till it reached the statue of Washington, and then the effect was magical. No boys were allowed to carry torches or take any part whatever in the parade. Chief Harry Howard ordered the companies to take their spare hose from their hose racks, reel them on tenders and keep them in the house on the night of the procession, and those who had no tenders to coil the hose and place it near the front doors in order that police and citizens might have free access to the houses in case of fire. Various other precautions were taken to provide for an emergency of fire. The following is the detail of the procession:

FIRST DIVISION.

Assistant Engineer JOHN DECKER, *Marshal.*
The Veteran Association of Exempt Firemen.
Exempt Engine Company.
Ex-Chief and Ex-Assistant Engineers.
Board of Fire Commissioners.
Officers and Trustees of New York Fire Department Fund.
Dodworth's renowned Cornet Band of 40 pieces.

———

Chief HARRY HOWARD, *Grand Marshal.*
Assistant Engineers
JOHN A. CREGIER and JOHN BAULCH,
Special Aids.

———

Fire Department Banner in charge of Marion
Engine Company No. 9.
Friendship Hook and Ladder Company No. 12.
Hudson Engine Company No. 1.
Knickerbocker Hose Company No. 2.
Independence Hose Company No. 3.
Whitworth's Band.
Eagle Hose Company No. 1.
Excelsior Engine Company No. 2.
Marion Hose Company No. 4.
Telegraph Brass Band.
Niagara Engine Company No. 4.
Protection Engine Company No. 5.
Mutual Hook and Ladder Company No. 1.

SECOND DIVISION.

Assistant Engineer PETER N. CORNWELL, *Marshal.*
Robertson's Band.
Americus Engine Company No. 6.
Croton Hose Company No. 6.
Lexington Engine Company No. 7.
City Hose Company No. 8.
Columbian Hose Company No. 9.
Paterson Band.
Ringgold Hose Company No. 7.
Water Witch Engine Company No. 10.
Liberty Hose Company No. 10.
Chelsea Hook and Ladder Company No. 2.
Seventy-first Regiment Drum Corps.
New York Hose Company No. 5.

THIRD DIVISION.

Assistant Engineer ELISHA KINGSLAND, *Marshal.*

Fort Schuyler Band.
Manhattan Engine Company No. 8.
Gulick Hose Company No. 11.
East River Engine Company No. 17.
Jackson Hose Company No. 13.
Excelsior Hose Company No. 14.
Eleventh Regiment Band.
Lafayette Engine Company No. 19.
Tompkins Hose Company No. 16.
Union Engine Company No. 18.
Phenix Hook and Ladder Company No. 3.
Clinton Hose Company No. 17.

FIREMEN'S TORCHLIGHT PROCESSION PASSING WASHINGTON STATUE, SEPTEMBER 1, 1858.

FOURTH DIVISION.

Assistant Engineer W. T. MAWBEY, *Marshal.*

Shelton's Band.
Oceanus Engine Company, No. 11.
Franklin Hose Company, No. 18.
American Hose Company, No. 19.
Turl's Brass Band.
Harry Howard Hook and Ladder Company No. 11
Phenix Hose Company, No. 22.
Protector Engine Company No. 22.
Thos. Manahan's Brass Band.
Eagle Engine Company No. 13.
Humane Hose Company No. 20.
Eagle Hook and Ladder Company No. 4.
Band.
Washington Engine Company No. 20.
Hudson Hose Company No. 21.
United States Engine Company No. 23.

FIFTH DIVISION.

Assistant Engineer TIMOTHY L. WEST, *Marshal.*

Stewart's Band.
Columbian Engine Company No. 14.
Perry Hose Company No. 23.
National Hose Company No. 24.
Union Hook and Ladder Company No. 5.
Jackson Engine Company No. 24.
Edw'd Manahan's Brass Band.
Fulton Engine Company No. 21.
United States Hose Company No. 25.
Williamsburg Brass Band.
Cataract Engine Company No. 25.
Fourth Regiment Brass Band.
Howard Engine Company No. 34.
Rutgers Hose Company No. 26.
Jefferson Engine Company No. 26.

SIXTH DIVISION.

Assistant Engineer JAMES F. WENMAN, *Marshal.*

Governor's Guard Band.
Amity Hose Company No. 38.
Neptune Hose Company No. 27.
Metamora Hose Company No. 29.
Lafayette Hook and Ladder Company No. 6.
Guardian Engine Company No. 29.
Knickerbocker Band.
Knickerbocker Engine Company No. 12.
Laurel Hose Company No. 30.
Mechanics' Hook and Ladder Company No. 7.
Index Hose Company No. 32.

SEVENTH DIVISION.

Assistant Engineer EDWARD W. JACOBS, *Marshal.*

Connell's Brass Band.
Black Joke Engine Company No. 33.
Warren Hose Company No. 33.
Lafayette Hose Company No. 34.
Castle's Band.
Chatham Engine Company No. 15.
Columbus Engine Company No. 35.
Baltic Hose Company No. 35.
Empire Band.
Empire Hook and Ladder Company No. 8.
Equitable Engine Company No. 36.
Empire Hose Company No. 40.

EIGHTH DIVISION.

Assistant Engineer G. JOSEPH RUCH, *Marshal.*

Wallace's Band.
Southwark Engine Company No. 38.
Naiad Hose Company No. 53.
Tradesmen Engine Company No. 37.
Madison Hose Company No. 37.
Lady Washington Engine Company No. 40.
Band.
Washington Hook and Ladder Company No. 9

Pacific Engine Company No. 28.
Metropolitan Hose Company No. 39.
Manhatta Engine Company No. 43.
Pioneer Hose Company No. 34.

NINTH DIVISION.

Assistant Engineer JOHN BRICE, *Marshal.*

Fifty-fifth Regiment Band.
Empire Engine Company No. 42.
Mazeppa Hose Company No. 42.
Narragansett Hook and Ladder Company No. 10.
Franklin Engine Company No. 39.
Adkin's Washington Brass Band.
Clinton Engine Company No. 41.
Washington Irving Hose Company No. 44.
Live Oak Engine Company No. 44.
Excelsior Band.
Valley Forge Hose Company No. 46.
Mechanics' Hose Company No. 47.
Mazeppa Engine Company No. 48.

TENTH DIVISION.

Assistant Engineer DANIEL DONNOVAN, *Marshal.*

Rhonck's Band.
Marion Hook and Ladder Company No. 13.
Americus Hose Company No. 48.
Pocahontas Engine Company No. 49.
Relief Hose Company No. 51.
Sixty-ninth Regiment Drum Corps.
Hope Hose Company No. 50.
Yorkville Band.
Aurora Engine Company No. 45.
Eureka Hose Company No. 54.
Lone Star Engine Company No. 50.
Undine Hose Company No. 52.
Columbian Hook and Ladder Company No. 14.

ELEVENTH DIVISION.

Assistant Engineer WILLIAM HACKETT, *Marshal.*

Dodworth's Second Band.
Baxter Hook and Ladder Company No. 15.
Harry Howard Hose Company No. 55.
Mutual Engine Company No. 51.
Nassau Hose Company No. 56.
Paulding Hose Company No. 57.
New Jersey Brass Band.
M. T. Brennan Hose Company No. 60.
Forrest Hose Company No. 58.
Ion Hose Company No. 59.
Zephyr Hose Company No. 61.
Minute Hose Company No. 62.
North Carolina Band.
Firemen from UNITED STATES STEAM FRIGATE "NIAGARA."
The City Authorities and their Guests.

On the twenty-first of November, 1858, Hibernia Steam Engine Company No. 1, of Philadelphia, visited the city and were the guests of Americus Engine Company No. 6. The Exempt Firemen, called the "Old Guard," of which Mr. James L. Miller was president, gave the visitors a banquet at the St. Nicholas Hotel, at which Mayor Tiemann, Mr. W. T. Milliken, Mr. Morris Franklin, and Mr. R. H. Ellis spoke.

On Monday, October 17, 1859, the Third Grand Triennial Parade of the Department took place. The engines had been brightened up, repainted, regilded and decorated. A profusion of flowers adorned the engines and trucks and carriages. Early in the day a splendid banner was presented by the Common Council to the Department. Mayor Tiemann made the presentation speech, and Mr. Daniel Milliken responded.

By resolution the Board of Engineers recognized on parade " such companies disbanded by the Fire Commissioners as have been placed in service by

"BIG SIX" IN THE VOLUNTEER FIREMEN'S ANNUAL PARADE, OCTOBER 17, 1859.
[Original painting the property of John J. Blair. Painted by Joseph H. Johnson.]

the Common Council, unless previous to the parade the courts declare them legally disbanded, in which case they cannot parade." The uniform was as usual: fire caps, black pants, and firemen's red shirt. It was desired "that no invitation be extended to out-of-town companies for that day; but should any visiting companies appear, a place will be provided for them in the first division of the line."

Line of March.—The Department formed at ten o'clock A. M., on Fifth Avenue, right resting on Thirty-fifth Street, countermarched down Fifth Avenue to Fourteenth Street, to Eighth Avenue, to Bleecker Street, to Broadway; down Broadway, through the Park, to Chatham Street, to East Broadway, to Grand Street, to Bowery, to Fourth Avenue, to the Washington Statue (Union Park), marched around the statue and dismissed.

Invitations were issued to ex-chief engineers, ex-assistant engineers, Exempt Firemen's Association, Board of Fire Commissioners and ex-Fire Commissioners, Exempt Engine Company, Board of Trustees of Fire Department, Board of Fire Wardens, President, Vice-President, Secretary and Treasurer of the Fire Department, and all other officers and ex-officers of the Fire Department.

The Grand Marshal's special directions were:

Smoking in the line will be strictly prohibited. Any violation of this rule will cause the expulsion from the line of the person or persons so offending. In case of fire, the marshals of the several divisions will designate the companies to leave the line, and companies are directed to retain their positions until so ordered. Companies will be prohibited from taking their place in the line with more men than they are entitled to by law. Companies parading with steam engines are directed to take their place in the line without steam. No companies will be permitted to parade with more than one apparatus, except steamers who have tenders used in connection with their engines. * * * * The marshals will appear in dark clothes, red shirts, white comforters, brass trumpets, and their badges of office.

The line moved at noon in the following order, was three and one-half miles in length, and occupied more than one and one-half hours in passing a given point:

FIRST DIVISION.

Assistant Engineer JOHN DECKER, *Marshal.*

Visiting Firemen of Volunteer Fire Departments from other cities.

SECOND DIVISION.

Assistant Engineer PETER N. CORNWELL, *Marshal.*

Colt's Hartford Band.

Open barouche with ex-Chiefs Uzziah Wenman, James Gulick, and Alfred Carson.

Ex-Assistant Engineers.

Association of Exempt Firemen.

Board of Fire Commissioners and Ex-Fire Commissioners.

Exempt Engine Company.

Officers and Trustees of the New York Fire Department.

New York Fire Department Banner, in charge of Harry Howard Hook and Ladder Company No. 11.

Grand Marshal and Special Aids.

Whitworth's Band.

Eagle Hose Company No. 1.

Hudson Engine Company No. 1.

Mutual Hook and Ladder Company No. 1.

Shelton's Drum Corps.

Excelsior Engine Company No. 2.

Niagara Hose Company No. 2.

Independence Hose Company No. 3.

Troy Cornet Band.

Niagara Engine Company No. 4.

Marion Hose Company No. 4.

Protection Engine Company No. 5.

THIRD DIVISION.

Assistant Engineer ELISHA KINGSLAND, *Marshal.*

Turner's Band.

Americus Engine Company No. 6.

New York Hose Company No. 5.

Croton Hose Company No. 6.

Yonkers Band.
Lexington Engine Company No. 7.
City Hose Company No. 8.
Chelsea Hook and Ladder Company No. 2.
Ringgold Band.
Ringgold Hose Company No. 7.
Columbian Hose Company No. 9.
Sing Sing Band.
Manhattan Engine Company, with Tender, No. 8.
Liberty Hose Company No. 10.
Water Witch Engine Company No. 10.

FOURTH DIVISION.

Assistant Engineer WILLIAM T. MAWBEY, *Marshal.*

Sixth Regiment Band.
Marion Engine Company No. 9.
Phœnix Hook and Ladder Company No. 3.
Tompkins Band.
Oceanus Engine Company No. 11.
Minute Hose Company No. 12.
Gulick Band.
Gulick Hose Company No. 11.
Knickerbocker Engine Company No. 12.
Eagle Hook and Ladder Company No. 4.
Middleton Band.
Eagle Engine Company No. 13.
Jackson Hose Company No. 13.
Governor's Island Band.
Columbian Engine Company No. 14.
Tompkins Hose Company No. 16.
Eighth Regiment Drum Corps.
Atlantic Hose Company No. 15.
Chatham Engine Company No. 15.

FIFTH DIVISION.

Assistant Engineer TIMOTHY L. WEST, *Marshal.*

National Guard Band.
Excelsior Hose Company No. 14.
Clinton Hose Company No. 17.
Wannamaker's Band.
Mohawk Engine Company No. 16.
Franklin Hose Company No. 18.
Union Band.
Union Engine Company No. 18.
Lafayette Engine Company No. 19.
Liberty Band.
East River Engine Company No. 17.
Lafayette Hook and Ladder Company No. 6.
North Carolina Band.
American Hose Company No. 19.
Humane Hose Company No. 20.
Washington Band, Newark.
Washington Engine Company No. 20.
Hudson Hose Company No. 21.

SIXTH DIVISION.

Assistant Engineer EDWARD W. JACOBS, *Marshal.*

Union Band.
Union Hook and Ladder Company No. 5.

Protector Engine Company No. 22
Perry Hose Company No. 23.
Hartford Band.
Fulton Engine Company No. 21.
United States Engine Company No. 23.
Mechanics' Hook and Ladder Company No. 7.
Ruble's Band.
Phœnix Hose Company No. 22.
United States Hose Company No. 25.
Fort Washington Engine Company No. 27.
Turl's Band.
Jackson Engine Company No. 24.
Rutgers Hose Company No. 26.

SEVENTH DIVISION.

Assistant Engineer G. JOSEPH RUCH, *Marshal.*

Robertson's Band.
National Hose Company No. 24.
Neptune Hose Company No. 27.
Cataract Drum Corps.
Cataract Engine Company No. 25.
Pearl Hose Company No. 28.
Waterbury Band.
Pacific Engine Company No. 28.
Laurel Hose Company No. 30.
Band.
Metamora Hose Company No. 29.
Empire Hook and Ladder Company No. 8.
Jefferson Band.
Jefferson Engine Company No. 26.
Putnam Hose Company No. 31.
Robinson's Band.
Guardian Engine Company No. 29.
Index Hose Company No. 32.
Drum Corps.
North River Engine Company No. 30.
Narragansett Hook and Ladder Company No. 10.

EIGHTH DIVISION.

Assistant Engineer JOHN BRICE, *Marshal.*

Rohn's Band.
Black Joke Engine Company No. 33.
Peterson Engine Company No. 31.
Hackensack Band.
Warren Hose Company No. 33.
Shelton's Band.
Howard Engine Company No. 34.
Lafayette Hose Company No. 34.
Manahan's Band.
Columbus Engine Company No. 35.
Albany Cornet Band.
Washington Hook and Ladder Company No. 9.
Tradesmen Engine Company No. 37.
Schottio's Band.
Harry Howard Engine Company No. 36.
Mohawk Hose Company No. 39.
Shelton's Band.

Oceana Hose Company No. 36.
Franklin Engine Company No. 39.

NINTH DIVISION.

Assistant Engineer DANIEL DONNOVAN, *Marshal.*

Meyer's Band.
Madison Hose Company No. 37.
Lady Washington Engine Company No. 40.
Wallace's Band.
Southwark Engine Company No. 38.
Alert Hose Company No. 41.
Fifty-fifth Regiment Band.
Amity Hose Company No. 38.
Manhatta Engine Company No. 43.
Stewart's Band.
Friendship Hook and Ladder Company No. 12.
Mazeppa Hose Company No. 42.
Adkin's Band.
Empire Hose Company No. 40.
Pocahontas Engine Company No. 49.
Clinton Band.
Clinton Engine Company No. 41.
Pioneer Hose Company No. 43.
Clinton Band.
Clinton Engine Company No. 41.
Pioneer Hose Company No. 43.

TENTH DIVISION.

Assistant Engineer WILLIAM HACKETT, *Marshal.*

Dodworth's Full Band.
Empire Engine Company No. 42.
Washington Irving Hose Company No. 44.
Ryer's Band.
Live Oak Engine Company No. 44.
Mechanics' Hose Company No. 47.
College Point Band.
Aurora Engine Company No. 45.
Americus Hose Company No. 48.
Castle's Band.
Valley Forge Hose Company No. 46.
Relief Hose Company No. 51.
Rahn's Band.
Marion Hook and Ladder Company No. 13.
Undine Hose Company No. 52.
Drum Corps.
Mazeppa Engine Company No. 48.
Naiad Hose Company No. 53.
Meyer's Band.
Hope Hose Company No. 50.
Harry Howard Hose Company No. 55.

ELEVENTH DIVISION.

Assistant Engineer STEPHEN MITCHELL, *Marshal.*

Palace Garden Band.
Columbian Hook and Ladder Company No. 14.
Nassau Hose Company No. 56.
Empire Band.
Liberty Engine Company No. 50.

Forrest Hose Company No. 58.
Nier's Band.
Paulding Hose Company No. 57.
Mutual Engine Company No. 51.
Band.
M. T. Brennan Hose Company No. 60.
Manhattan Hook and Ladder Company No. 16.
Adkin's Band.
Zephyr Hose Company No. 61.
Ion Hose Company No. 59.
Dodworth's Band.
Baxter Hook and Ladder Company No. 15.

When the Prince of Wales visited New York in 1860 the firemen gave a torchlight procession in his honor on the night of October 13. There were six thousand men in line, who occupied one and a half hours in passing the Fifth Avenue Hotel, from the balcony of which they were received by the Prince. One of the novelties at that time was the appearance of Hook and Ladder Company No. 12, with a calcium light, lent by Professor R. Ogden Doremus. The old "Hay Wagon," decorated with flags, was drawn by Exempt Engine Company, under Mr. Zophar Mills. The enthusiasm everywhere was great, and it was said this was one of the finest displays made by the Department.

The Fire Department made a notable display on Evacuation Day, November 26, 1883. The glittering engines, beautiful horses and stalwart men were as striking as any feature of the parade. Six's big dog barked back at those who cheered him. The Philadelphia disbanded Volunteers were only a shade different from the old New Yorkers, though their long pearl-colored coats distinguished them from the long line that followed ex-Chief John Decker and ex-Chief Harry Howard. The New York Volunteer Firemen made Fifth Avenue look from a distance as if a broad stream of blood was flowing down its roadway. John Decker, stalwart and erect, with his silver trumpet's mouth filled with flowers, conspicuously a favorite with the spectators, Chief Howard, in plain black, limped bravely along the whole route. Howard, Decker and Frank Clark, the foreman of old Live Oak 44, brought out volumes of cheering from the men on the sidewalks. Big Six proved a great curiosity, and the tiger fastened to its brakes beautified the old machine. The engine had been sold to the Government at the general sale of the old apparatus in 1865. The surviving members had made diligent search for it and finally discovered it at Willett's Point. General Henry L. Abbott, commanding the post, gave her up. Mr. William B. Dunley, one of her ex-foremen, and Mr. William Burns, a member, brought the "Old Gal" from Willett's Point to the city. Through the kindness of Commissioner Brennan they were allowed to bring her down on a Department steamboat. When she arrived in New York, ex-Fire Commissioner Blair and Nicholas Martin, an ex-member, with his gray horse, Tiger, were waiting on the pier to receive her. The horse was hitched to the engine, and with Blair and Martin on the tongue she was taken to Blake's livery stable, where ex-Foreman Anthony Burke and other ex-members were waiting to receive her. There was some wrangling among the boys as to who should "back her in," which was observed as an old-time honor, and fell to the lot of Tony Burke. The news soon spread in the neighborhood, and there was great excitement. Men, women and children rushed to see the old engine. After many congratulations the boys retired to a neighboring saloon and drank the health of the members of " Big Six."

Twelve hose was also there, carrying a stuffed dog. The oldest machine of all, Lafayette 19, was a valuable contribution to the show. The red shirts of the men themselves called back the New York of twenty years ago, and whether it was unconsciously or purposely reproduced, even the swagger, the instinctive curl of the upper lips, or the set of the hats were not omitted from the picture they presented. The suburban companies were, some of them, very like the old New Yorkers.

The old Volunteer Fire Company No. 6 was given a reception after the parade by the city club at its rooms in the Bowery. Harry Howard, Assistant Engineer Baulch, George Brown, Major H. Hamilton, Samuel Guthrie, and others were present, and for two hours the stories of the "old days" were re-told. No. 44 held forth in the afternoon at its hall in Avenue D. The Philadelphia Volunteers were to have been received at the military hall. The rain fell in a drizzle, and, finally, steadily and heavily. But the unfavorable circumstances in which the march of the day was made wore the boys out, and they returned home during the evening. A more miserable day could scarcely have fallen to their lot for processional purposes. The firemen were in the fifth division of the parade, and the greeting given them was the heartiest of the day. Unlike the other divisions, every organization was applauded; individuals in the ranks were shouted at, and there were frequent cries to "work her up" as the old machines came into view.

There was a great turn-out of the old Volunteer Firemen in red shirts, black trousers, and leather caps, nearly everybody dragging an antiquated hand engine, hose cart, or "truck," which made a miserable contrast with the splendid steam engines and efficiently fitted hook and ladder machines displayed by the present Department. The "machines" were for the most part handsomely ornamented in the style once familiar to, but until then almost forgotten by, the older citizens of New York. Among the "machines" in line were an engine used in the city in 1825, and a hook and ladder truck and jumper dating back to 1830.

The Fifth Division formed along Fifth Avenue as follows :

On West Thirty-eighth Street.—General LLOYD ASPINWALL, Assistant Marshal, Commanding Staff.

Mounted Police, Captain McCullough.

Battalion of Police.

Superintendent Geo. W. Walling.

Brigade New York Fire Department.

On West Thirty-seventh Street. Assistant Chief Engineer CHARLES O. SHAY. Detachment New York Insurance Fire Patrol.

On East Thirty-seventh Street. Superintendent M. B. WILSON. Detachment Hoboken Fire Department.

On West Thirty-sixth Street. Chief GORMAN. Representatives of Old Volunteer Fire Department, New York City.

On East Thirty-sixth Street. Ex-Chief JOHN W. DECKER. Volunteer Firemen's Association of Philadelphia. Foreman Mortimer L. Johnson. Bellringers of Old Fire Department.

On East Thirty-fifth Street. Protection Engine No. 1, Mount Vernon; Foreman E. J. VOLMAR. Tiger Light Hose, Long Island City; Foreman C. A. LEWIS. Jackson Hose No.

5, Long Island City; Foreman JAMES McKEON. Astoria Hook and Ladder Company No. 1. Volunteer Hook and Ladder Company No. 2, Staten Island; Foreman G. W. DECKER. Wandewenock Hook and Ladder Company No. 1, Newton; Foreman D. P. TREADWELL. Hope Hook and Ladder Company No. 1, Yonkers; Foreman W. H. GURNSEY.

Twenty-one years have rolled by since the disbandment of the Volunteers, and not a few have gone to their last account. But the vigor and the longevity of those gallant men are remarkable, and hundreds of them, happily, still survive. They came to the front once more on the occasion of the unveiling of the Bartholdi Statue on Bedloe's Island, on October 28, 1886. New York saw a magnificent parade that day, and one of its most prominent features was the turnout of the Volunteers in large numbers, and with a portion of their old apparatus. It is no exaggeration to say that of the many attractive sights in that long procession none received greater applause than the Volunteer display. It was one continuous ovation from Fifth Avenue and Fiftieth

THE HURON (BUILT 1760).
[In the Bartholdi Parade.]

Street to the Battery. It was plain that the old firemen were the favorites of New York, and that their memory would never die. There was a perfect exhibition of the gradual improvement of fire apparatus from the earliest times. Two old engines of the period of 1760 and 1784 were mounted on trucks and were regarded as most interesting curiosities. A floral fireman was a noticeable feature, and also a beautiful bronze statuette of the Goddess of Liberty drawn on a carriage. The old-time fire engines of Hoboken, Bloomfield, Flatbush, Staten Island and other suburbs were in line. The Brooklyn Veterans were in the parade with their engines, and a famous hand pump from Hoboken was pulled reverently along. The New York *Herald* of the following day contained the following reference to the fire companies:

But now a ripple of cheering running along the whole extent of the avenue announces what was really the favorite pageant of the day—the fire parade. On came the procession, Marshal Decker leading. Areas of flaming shirts, lines of heavy, crimson lined overcoats, squares of heavy yellow overcoats, garments of gray and blue and black! How gayly they swept by to the refrain of the band and the plaudits of the multitude! To the latter the scene was a revival of the memories of long ago. It was the old Volunteers, with the beloved "machine," that were passing, with heads now grizzled, faces wrinkled, but not a whit less brave, less manly or less gritty than when they fought the flames with their primitive apparatus and fought the faction fights of years ago. Thirty-three "Black Joke," Forty-four "Live Oak," they went by covered with flowers and gay with ribbons. But the applause that hailed them was lost to hearing in the hubbub of cheering that greeted a single stalwart figure limping painfully along with the buff fire coat of old days upon his back and the trumpet of his old command under his arm. And so with "Big Six" engine, refurbished and furnished with a new statue of liberty for the occasion, the old chief Harry Howard went by. Then came fire company after fire company, with decorated engines or hose carriages, and at last gave way to some veteran organizations and kindred associations.

When fifty of the boys in red shirts, black trousers turned up above the mud, and big fire hats came trudging along, hauling an antiquated hand engine, the crowd cheered wildly, and the fire laddies took up the cry of "Hi, hi, hi!" as they passed the President. The leaders of the line waved their big speaking trumpets, and the whole scene for the time was one of unrestrained joy on the part of the firemen and the crowd. The French visitors' contemplated this demonstration with open-mouthed wonder. The faces of the old boys were a

THE UNION (BUILT 1811.)
[In the Bartholdi Parade.]

study. Most of them wore their hair cropped close, and all of them looked robust. There were other old engines, and hose reels and hook and ladder trucks drawn by hand, useful here nowadays only as relics. Among the old "masheens" in the line was the "Union," built in 1811, while a mouldy wreck of a hand pump, worked with cranks, and carried on a four-wheeled truck. was built in 1760, and looked every day of its age.

The following is a list of the firemen in the parade :

VOLUNTEER FIREMEN'S ASSOCIATION.

WILLIAM E. BISHOP, Financial Secretary.   JOSEPH S. BEER, Recording Secretary.

Andrew I. Brush, Merchant, George F. Loftus, Hatter, John J. Blair, John K. Costigan, John Quigg, Martin Senger, William F. Searing, Directors.

Isaac Mills, Sergeant-at-Arms.

Andrew Elliott,	David Simpson,	Edward Murray,	John H. Noakes,
Dennis Moroney,	Frederick Driscoll,	Michael Kane,	J. M. Smith,
J. H. Sleight,	Thomas Higgins,	James Craig,	Stephen D. Hall,

William Smith,
John J. Nagle,
George W. Hall,
F. A. Wood,
Jacob Miller,
Thomas Cowan,
Charles Barry,
Michael Farrell,
Patrick Kelly,
A. I. Brush,
Thos. H. Thomas,
W. T. McLean,
Jacob H. Ackerly,
Fred Haffler,
Peter Boyce,
Ed. Reilly,
Anthony Angels,
Benedic Keland,
Peter Murphy,
W. F. Brower,
Lorenzo Cuddy,
Matt Carren,
Jacob Couterie,
Andrew Jackson,
W. G. Gilchrist,
Adam Feitner,
Michael Kelly,
John Curran,
George Bouscier,
S. J. Harris,
T. F. Devlin,
Gerald Tyrrell,
Wm. Clere,
John Touhey,
J. McDermott,
P. Loftus,
P. Wall,
Henry Ehret,
A. A. Waite,
Henry Clark,
David Brothers,
James Hand,
P. Lynch,
G. B. Alvord,

John K. Costigan,
Charles Holder,
Mortimer Marsh,
Jos. Nobles,
Alfred Robert,
John Hampson,
Dominick Young.
James Leary,
Peter Ward,
J. B. Webster,
John Murray,
John Riley,
Matthew Degan.
James Crawford,
John Hamilton,
James Deane,
Michael Kehoe,
Michael Pettit,
C. J. Smith,
J. W. Sanford,
Philip McGuire,
Wm. Sheehan,
O. E. Scofield,
Francis Clark,
Patrick Connolly,
John D. Barry,
Robert Kennedy,
Timothy O'Keefe,
Michael O'Byrne,
Christian Flannagan,
Isaac Mills,
Benjamin Smith,
Joseph Hunter,
John Dolan,
John Walker,
James Whelan,
Nicholas Miller,
Wm. A. Spring,
Andrew J. Reeves,
F. W. Adam,
John Quigg,
Jacob Woll,
Henry Welch,
Jacob Stroub,
D. Turgg,

James Bisland,
Wm. Gross,
Jacob Bliven.
John M. Lein,
James Bogan,
John Larkin,
Moses O'Brien,
Robert Stevenson,
E. F. Carr,
P. Riley,
M. Kraus,
C. Iles,
T. Leary,
D. W. Gregory,
J. A. Croker,
E. T. Lakeman,
J. Gilmartin,
A. Grimner,
P. J. McPartland,
D. H. Coles,
S. Nash,
H. Kittson,
A. Beattie,
P. Brady,
C. J. Winn,
A. Burke,
T. Lahey,
John E. Drew,
W. J. Wynn,
R. L. Godly,
John Mum,
John T. Muller,
John Geagan,
James Boylan,
John Carroll,
S. B. Williamson,
Geo. Macomb,
D. W. Quinby,
George Chase,
A. G. Smith,
Benjamin Chase,
P. McKeever,
B. Wormley,
Wm. S. Norman,
M. Welton.

Guy Kennedy,
Thomas Bell,
John Kearns,
Thomas Barry,
Thomas H. Crane,
Chas. H. Rowland,
Henry Miller,
Wm. F. Gates,
Peter Seymour,
B. McLaughlin,
Eugene Matthews,
Pat Cook,
Peter Snatch,
Andrew Sanches,
Joseph Stumpf,
Thomas Robinson,
Jacob Guthrie,
Bernard Cregan,
John Metzer,
John Zimmerman,
Thomas Allen,
J. A. Carpenter,
P. O'Connor,
J. J. Blair,
G. W. Hammond,
M. Quinn,
G. A. Sevess,
John G. Magee,
A. J. Thompson,
J. Kenny,
T. Sweeney,
P. Dennis,
J. McKenzie,
P. McCabe,
R. Evans,
J. McNamara,
J. A. Seward,
W. H. Hammond,
H. Close,
E. Brennan,
J. Corrigan,
R. Floyd,
M. Gayte,
J. G. Reilly,

VETERAN FIREMEN'S ASSOCIATION.

George W. Anderson, President; John Moller, Vice-President;

James F. Wenman, Marshal.

O. B. Comings,
N. Hepburn,
J. McCurdy,
B. M. Sweeney,
T. E. Howe,
E. N. Smith,
J. J. Robson,
J. H. Foreman,

W. Murray,
C. Van Blarcom,
J. M. Pierson,
R. Evans,
M. V. B. Smith,
R. Pollock,
T. Cleary,
J. T. Smith,

John McCauley,
C. J. Simmons,
R. McWhinney,
Jno. E. McCaddin,
J. Dawson,
W. Kaess,
R. Cottrell,
D. Bradley,

P. S. De Vries,
D. H. Anderson,
Thomas Barrett,
Thomas Hines,
M. Giblin,
J. Kellaher,
J. Douglass,
J. H. Forshay,

J. H. Bartley,
G. O. Willis,
F. A. Ridabock,
C. Cunneen,
J. H. Johnson,
L. R. Kerr,
Leonard R. Kerr,
Wm. Cahill,
L. Brandner,
H. Webb,
E. G. Snow, Jr.,
J. H. Washburn,
Wm. Brandon,
James O'Brien,
M. Moloney,
W. H. Hayward,
Steve O'Brien,
John M. Lein,
Joseph Hanna,
A. J. Walsh,
J. S. Davidson,
John Earle,
N. D. Thayer,
Thos. McCarthy,
John T. Girvin,
Wm. McAllister,
Colin Gourley,
C. L. Robinson,
Lewis F. Hallen,
Joseph Leary,
Daniel Robinson
M. McAvoy,
L. Loutrel,
J. McCollough,
P. Walsh,
J. H. English,
H. McDonough,
J. I. Slevin,
T. W. Valentine,
Matthew Ellis,
Wm. De Noille,
J. Cunningham,
John Monroe,
P. Ward,
A. T. Anderson,
Thomas Judge,
R. W. R. Chambers
J. B. Prote,
E. T. Bogin,
John Smart,
J. F. Gillen,
Thos. Barrington,
W. H. Caulfield,
Edward E. Wilhelm,
Robt. Canfield,
P. J. Chappell,
J. M. Harnerd,
J. J. McCauley,

P. Singleton,
B. F. Parker,
E. Coe,
T. J. Creeden,
J. Meehan,
T. W. Scott,
W. H. Ryer,
J. A. Linten,
G. T. Patterson, Jr.,
G. I. Hardy,
J. Mateson,
E. A. Bertine,
E. Bland,
G. T. Patterson,
T. Donovan,
Louis J. Parker,
W. H. Boyd,
H. Guenther,
C. A. Childs,
S. Ling,
P. A. Fitzpatrick,
John Monks,
Peter Doelger, Jr.,
G. O. Freeman,
A. C. Hull,
W. M. Tooker,
M. Thompson,
S. F. Cummings,
W. Churchill,
P. Dunleavy,
James Spencer,
Wm. McMahon,
S. L. D. Westbrook,
P. Keenan,
Elward Smith,
P. Miller, Jr.,
John McMahon,
Philip Jordan,
James Flack,
Thomas Tripler,
N. Murray,
A. Monnell,
W. S. Hick,
Nicholas Kent,
Theodore Birdsall,
P. Wannamacher,
John O. Roberts,
W. F. Hayes.
M. W. Wilson
John Vock.
D. D. Naugle,
Nicholas Healy,
P. P. Pullis,
W. B. Dunley,
John Sherman,
John Waydell,
T. J. McCartie,

T. F. West,
John B. Miller,
J. G. Prague,
E. Kingsland,
W. H. Weaber,
B. Owens,
A. J. Fisher,
G. Lambrecht,
C. E. Kemp,
Henry Sturke,
P. Dailey,
P. H. Melly,
E. W. Jacobs,
E. E. Nagle,
J. T. Moller,
D. McLeod,
E. L. Meader,
J. Y. Watkins,
H. Jones
Jas. B. Miller,
J. T. Davis,
John J. Brogan,
W. H. Roberts,
Robert Turley,
J. T. Travis,
John Buckley,
Charles Otto,
Jonas L. Coe,
T. P. Brennan,
W. Dunn,
J. Hampson,
W. Orford,
E. Ward,
G. Borstman,
A. Chancellor,
P. Connery,
A. J. Allaire,
G. Bell,
James McCauley,
James Leary,
C. Von Hagendorf,
J. E. Miller,
J. Crawford,
H. Winkle,
E. Drevet,
D. Garvey,
R. H. Nugent,
A. Sleight,
A. Campbell,
F. Clark,
M. Rouse,
M. Ryan,
F. S. Gwyer,
J. Williamson, Jr.,
J. Binns,
James Higgins,
S. Townsend,

J. R. Platt,
R. C. Mills,
D. Leary,
D. D. Conover,
G. A. Knott,
Wm. Scott,
John H. Stone,
S. M. Robbins,
Chas. W. Caffrey.
Jos. J. McGill,
Benj. Williams,
Charles Stagg,
John D. Minor,
John Byrn,
A. G. Smith,
John Hern,
D. Patterson,
H. K. Woodruff,
G. Isaacs,
Wm. Ranier,
Allen Gallagher,
Isaac H. Tyrrell,
James H. Flood,
Patrick Brady,
W. R. Ricard,
W. H. Richardson,
C, W. Morgan,
Harry Howard,
C. F. Marley,
L. McGee,
J. W. Jacobus,
A. B. Burnett,
T. J. Bishop,
Thomas Scully,
A. McDonald,
M. W. Roberts,
J. J. Gorman,
W. H. Talmadge,
Edward Smith,
D. L. Ormsby,
Peter Dennis,
John Geary,
G. D. F. Closs,
C. W. Harrenberg,
J. F. Daley,
J. J. Cashman,
C. Johnson,
John D. Lobb,
John Hughes,
A. J. Williams,
A. Prothers,
W. H. Perego,
George Wright,
W. M. Randell,
Daniel Day,
Charles Hagan,
A. Yeomans.

LIVE OAK ASSOCIATION.

Peter Maloney, President;   Wm. Landers, Vice-President;

George Moore, Secretary ;   Joseph Nelson, Treasurer ;

Geo. Y. Hughes, J. A. Robson, John Baulch, Honorary Members.

P. Smith,	L. Rhodes,	F. Martin,	W. H. Roberts,
J. Nelson,	H. Fraser,	P. McManus,	J. Weber,
G. A. Moore,	W. Sophers,	H. Centmore,	S. Bailey,
W. H. Landers,	M. Myers,	G. W. Bush,	C. L. Miller,
W. Brennan,	P. Platt,	G. C. Reener,	J. F. Mulholant,
E. Allen,	J. H. Fisher,	J. Quin,	J. Stringer,
J. Fair,	T. J. Carleton,	H. C. Hoffman,	E. T. Simpson,
J. Bowen,	E. McArdle,	W. J. O'Neil,	W. Kelley,
W. H. Vance,	W. McLarty,	J. Peffers,	J. Daly,
J. Cooper,	M. Dowd,	W. J. Nicholson,	G. Mesmer,
P. Miller,	J. Hartshorn,	J. H. Bond,	T. L. Warren,
J. B. Forster,	W. P. Marvell,	T. Angliss,	J. Riely,
J. Hart,	P. Conway,	T. J. Smith,	J. Shields,
E. Looney,	H. Close,	W. Elliott,	A. J. Reeder,
P. Kline,	J. Keating,	C. W. Roberts,	A. Bowe,
H. Metz,	T. W. Cleaver,	M. Bindy,	S. Haysman,
C. Freck,	J. McLarty,	W. Donnelly,	J. Hartman,
J. Donohue,	T. Caldwell,	R. Williams,	John Nelson,
J. Dixon,	J. Riley,	M. Knapp,	Geo. Fisher,
J. Schriner,	H. Young,	H. B. Vitty,	James Smith,
A. Evans,	J. Furlong,	C. McMurray,	John Miller,
M. Dunn,	W. Condit,	W. Barrett,	B. H. Curran,
C. H. Bowland,	W. Dalton,	A. Smith,	Wm. Kelly,
H. Voght,	J. Gordon,	J. Svigs,	Wm. S. Hanno,
S. Bayly,	A. Wilbers,	J. Messmer,	Wm. Donley.

VETERAN ZOUAVE ASSOCIATION, NEW YORK.

Lieutenant-Colonel, T. F. Sheehan ;   Major, J. Van Duersen ;

Quartermaster, F. W. Ritschey ;   Adjutant, P. Schaller ;

Surgeon, E. R. Duffy ;   Senior Captain, F L. Schaefer ;

Junior Captain, John Miller.

G. W. Martin,	J. Hawk,	A. F. Caswell,	J. M. Platt,
Josh Hatch,	W. Dowling,	D. De Voe,	A. Wetherbee,
L. Meek,	W. Miller,	C. Dow,	J. Tierney,
G. Hack,	M. McLaughlin,	G. Schmidt,	J. Miller,
F. Kane,	H. Collyer,	G. W. Lent,	S. Lippencott,
R. Conklin,	W. H. Clarkson,	J. Whalen,	J. Hempstead,
T. Gore,	J. Crimmins,	J. Roundtree,	J. Smith,
M. McCormack,	Chas. Ferris,	W. Carroll,	C. Burnham,
G. Reynolds,	J. Barber,	J. Ewing,	J. Jacques,
C. Walters,	W. Pfeffer,	P. Madara,	J. C. Craft,
C. Earl,	G. Harvey,	N. Hollenbeck,	J. Morton,
S. J. Lowell,	C. McCahill,	Jas. Burns,	A. Kleiner,
M. Clements,	P. Lennon,	W. Fox,	H. Boyd,
D. R. Wood,	T. Demerest,	J. Sharkey,	J. Eder,
J. Bevier,	J. Scheidt,	J. Mosher,	J. Ryan,
J. Festger,	M. Kane,	L. Dyer,	J. Bock,
J. O'Dwyer,	J. Walters,	T. McGiff,	F. H. Vedder,
W. Ferguson,	J. F. Quinn,	H. Duinin,	M. Daly,

VOLUNTEER FIREMEN'S SONS' ASSOCIATION.

C. H. Throckmorton, President.
M'Carthy Drum Corps.

W. Pardee,	James Smith,	H. B. McCarram,	Frank Hoffman,
A. Wilson,	S. R. Williams,	Charles Fellman,	G. H. Walters,
Jacob Schnatz,	C. F. Canfield,	E. J. Smith,	W. L. Flack,
Jacob Roberson,	P. Wannamacher.	C. F. Smith,	John Duafin,
P. E. Ward,	W. Wilmot,	R. Wilson,	J. Woods,
J. E. Purdy,	D. Claffy,	D. Ryer,	W. B. Brown,
W. F. McCoy,	P. Hickey,	W. H. Eaton,	William Harding,
W. Gager,	J. D. Burns, Jr.,	F. E. Bloom,	John Dailey,
Charles McGrath,	E. J. Blair,	W. W. Williams,	J. O. Roberson,
J. Kadley, Jr.,	George Cavanagh,	W. H. Jones,	G. W. Overton,
E. W. Fenton,	Peter M. Bevins,	D. B. Sullivan,	J. J. Ford,
S. Van Wart,	W. P. Evans,	C. H. Kaighin,	R. H. Nelson,
J. S. Hickey,	W. F. Ewing,	D. Higgins,	W. H. Coutrie,
E. A. Johnson,	H. McCaffery,	C. Ryan,	B. J. Loonan,
A. Heffert,	Charles Eaton,	J. J. Pardee,	William Smith,
G. J. Carlton, Jr.,	J. H. Strauss,	William Forster,	G. Ryer,
E. Kline,	A. F. Gugel,	Parry Payne,	J. B. Lawrence,
J. Dolan,	J. Berry,	L. J. Daly,	S. F. Deacon,
J. G. Bryant,	W. Van Wart,	A. Prentiss, Jr.,	C. C. Parish,
P. Schnatz,	P. Hickey,	J. B. Ewing,	J. H. Cornwall.
J. Willse,	S. D. Ward,	John Nichols,	

The remarkable rapidity with which horses are hitched to engines now-a-days astonishes the multitude, and especially foreign visitors who are familiar with the workings of the Fire Departments in European cities. Quick time is made by the New York Fire Department of 1886, but does it make better time than that made by Protection Engine Company 5.

The *Firemen's Journal* of February 10, 1855, says:

"At half past one o'clock on Monday morning a fire broke out in the third story of building No. 140 Fulton Street. The alarm was quickly given, and in five minutes from the discovery of the fire Engine Company No. 5, supplied with water by Hose Company 20, who was first on the ground, had a stream on the fire."

This was rather quick work, considering the Honey Bees and the Humane boys did not have the aid of electricity and horses, but they got to the fire quick all the same.

OLD FULTON MARKET.

CHAPTER XXIV.

THE CHIEF ENGINEERS AND ASSISTANTS.

**All Men of "Character and Undoubted Respectability."—Chiefs whose Names are Household Words.—
The Pride and Boast of the Old Fire Department.—Their Term of Services and Deeds of Heroism.
—An unbroken Succession of Leaders of the Old Volunteers.**

There have been fourteen Chief Engineers of the Old Department, but, owing to the meager records kept at the close of the last century, but little is known of the four first who were technically known as "Overseers." These men, without exception, had the very highest reputation for integrity and fitness. The remark of Mr. Carlisle Norwood is well worth quoting. Here it is :

"Every chief engineer was a man of character and of undoubted respectability."

The following is a tabulated list of those officers :

Anthony Lamb................1732 to 1736	Uzziah Wenman..............1828 to 1831
Jacob Turk....................1736 to 1761	James Gulick................1831 to 1836
Jacobus Stoutenburgh........1761 to 1776	John Ryker, Jr..............1836 to 1837
William J. Ellsworth.......⎱ Combined term	Cornelius V. Anderson........1837 to 1848
Thomas Brown............⎰ of service, 1791 to 1811.	Alfred Carson................1848 to 1857
Thomas Franklin.............1811 to 1824	Henry H. Howard............1857 to 1860
Jamieson Cox..............1824 to 1828	John Decker..................1860 to 1865

ASSISTANT ENGINEERS.

Samuel Bell.............⎱
Jasper Ten Brook........⎰ Assistant Engineers in 1762.

John Balthasar Dash.....⎱
George Stanton..........⎟
Francis Dominick........⎬ Assistant Engineers in 1783.
Jeronimus Alstyne.......⎟
George Waldegrove......⎰

Isaac Mead.............⎱
John Stagg.............⎟
John Quackenboss.......⎬ Assistant Engineers in 1793.
Thomas Hazard.........⎟
Francis Bassett.........⎟
Ahasuerus Turk.........⎰

John Stagg.............⎱
Isaac Mead.............⎟
Ahasuerus Turk.........⎬ Assistant Engineers in 1796.
Thomas Hazard.........⎟
John Post..............⎟
George Warner.........⎰

Name.	Company.	Time of Service.
Thomas Franklin,	Engine 12	1799–1811
Nicholas Van Antwerp	Engine 11	1800–1818
Jacob Smith	Engine 7	1803–1808

Name.	Company.	Time of Service.
John B. Dash	Engine 16	1803–1815
James Stuart	Engine 9	1803–1818
John P. Roome	Engine 14	1808–1824
Hayes Pennell	Engine 15	1811–1822
John Colvill	Engine 4	1811–1822
Benjamin Strong	Engine 13	1812–1821
David J. Hubbs	Engine 13	1815–1824
James Scott	Engine 22	1817–1822
James W. Dominick	Engine 2	1817–1825
Valentine Vandewater	Engine 13	1822–1824
Jamieson Cox	Engine 26	1822–1824
Philip W. Engs	Engine 21	1822–1833
Uzziah Wenman	Engine 39	1822–1828
Samuel J. Willis	Engine 5	1824–1829
James Gulick	Engine 11	1824–1831
Adam W. Turnbull	Engine 40	1824–1829
George Vaugn	Engine 39	1825–1828
Edward Arrowsmith	Engine 7	1825–1830
Jacob Anthony	Engine 14	1828–1834
Thomas D. Howe	Engine 37	1828–1837
Drake B. Palmer	Engine 41	1829–1834
John Ryker, Jr	Engine 23	1829–1836
Jacob A. Roome	Engine 34	1830–1837
Edward M. Hoffmire	Engine 6	1831–1837
David T. Williams	Engine 13	1832–1835
John M. Sands	Engine 40	1833–1835
Edward Blanchard	Hook and Ladder 2	1835–1837
Allen R. Jollie	Engine 29	1835–1837
Daniel Coger	Engine 8	1835–1837
Elijah T. Lewis	Engine 4	1837–1837
Abraham B. Purdy	Engine 11	1837–1838
Wilson Small	Engine 5	1837–1837
John Ely	Engine 37	1837–1838
John Rese	Engine 12	1837–1840
James S. Wells	Engine 36	1837–1840
Daniel C. Silleck	Engine 14	1837–1839
Edward Penny, Jr	Engine 44	1837–1838
Michael O'Connor	Engine 40	1837–1838
Halsey R. Mead	Hose 1	1838–1839
Frederick D. Kohler	Engine 5	1838–1841
Zophar Mills	Engine 13	1838–1842
John L. Berrien	Engine 15	1838–1840
John Coger, Jr	Engine 8	1838–1841
William P. Wallace	Hose 12	1838–1839
William A. Freeborn	Hook and Ladder 4	1839–1842
Josiah W. Long	Engine 21	1840–1840
John S. Kenyon	Engine 49	1840–1842
John T. Rollins	Hose 8	1840–1842
William C. Bradley	Hose 6	1840–1841
Jesse Brush	Engine 31	1840–1841
George H. Ramppen	Engine 19	1841–1842
W. Wells Wilson	Engine 14	1841–1846
John B. Miller	Engine 32	1841–1845
George Kerr	Hose 10	1841–1848
Alfred Carson	Engine 12	1841–1848
Samuel Waddell	Engine 22	1842–1842
Charles Forrester	Engine 33	1842–1847

Name.	Company.	Time of Service.
Sidney B. Alley	Hook and Ladder 4	1842–1842
Philip B. White	Engine 41	1842–1848
Owen W. Brennan	Engine 14	1842–1846
DeWitt C. Mott	Engine 8	1842–1844
Samuel L. Liscomb	Engine 35	1842–1845
James L. Miller	Hose 40	1844–1851
Henry J. Ockershausen	Hose 1	1845–1850
Aaron Hosford	Hook and Ladder 7	1845–1850
Nicholas F. Wilson	Engine 15	1846–1847
John P. Lacour	Hook and Ladder 5	1846–1853
John Barry	Engine 2	1847–1850
Hiram Arents	Engine 5	1847–1847
John A. Cregier	Hose 40	1847–1860
DeLancey Barclay	Hose 16	1848–1849
William W. Corlies	Hose 14	1848–1850
Clark Vanderbilt	Hose 32	1848–1853
Michael Eichell	Engine 19	1849–1855
Thomas Monroe	Engine 14	1850–1853
Robert McGinnis	Engine 38	1850–1851
George W. Varian	Engine 25	1850–1851
Stephen T. Hoyt	Hose 21	1850–1852
Samuel M. Phillips	Engine 34	1850–1853
John Gillelan	Engine 35	1850–1853
Moses Jackson	Engine 16	1851–1856
Richard Kelly	Engine 7	1851–1853
Henry H. Howard	Hose 14	1851–1857
Peter N. Cornwell	Hook and Ladder 4	1853–1862
John Baulch	Engine 13	1853–1864
John Decker	Engine 14	1853–1860
Charles A. Brown	Engine 5	1853–1853
John H. Forman	Hook and Ladder 9	1853–1853
John P. Oliver	Hose 41	1853–1854
William Simpson	Hose 44	1853–1856
John H. Brady	Hook and Ladder 3	1853–1856
Wm. H. Ackerman	Hose 12	1853–1855
Elisha Kingsland	Engine 26	1854–1865
Noah L. Farnham	Hook and Ladder 1	1855–1858
Wm. T. Mawbey	Engine 49	1855–1859
Edward W. Jacobs	Engine 6	1856–1862
Timothy L. West	Engine 24	1856–1865
James F. Wenman	Hose 5	1856–1859
George J. Ruch	Engine 7	1856–1862
John Brice	Hose 42	1856–1865
Daniel Donnovan	Engine 13	1857–1863
William Hackett	Engine 20	1859–1865
Stephen Mitchell	Hook and Ladder 2	1860–1862
John A. McCosker	Hose 52	1860–1863
Thomas Roe	Engine 16	1860–1862
George T. Alker	Engine 38	1859–1865
William Lamb	Engine 25	1862–1865
Joseph L. Perley	Engine 44	1862–1865
Henry Lewis	Engine 41	1862–1865
George McGrath	Engine 51	1862–1865
Eli Bates	Engine 29	1862–1865
James Long	Hose 21	1862–1865
C. W. Ridley	Engine 49	1863–1865
Bernard Kenny	Hose 16	1864–1865

Name.	Company.	Time of Service.
Bartley Donahue	Engine 12	1865–1865
Thomas Duffy	Hook and Ladder 16	1865–1865
John Hamill	Engine 1	1865–1865
Michael Shaugnessy	Engine 39	1865–1865
Alex. V. Davidson	Hose 23	1865–1865
Thomas Sullivan	Hook and Ladder 12	1865–1865
Peter Weir	Engine 21	1865–1865
Gilbert J. Orr	Engine 42	1865–1865
Thomas Cleary	Engine 20	1865–1865
Michael Halloran	Hose 48	1865–1865
Abram Horn	Engine 43	1865–1865
George H. E. Lynch	Engine 52	1865–1865

ANTHONY LAMB was appointed Overseer (Chief Engineer) at a salary of twelve pounds a year. He was an Englishman who had come to the city and established himself as a mathematical instrument maker. He kept for many years a well-known establishment at the sign of the Quadrant and Surveying Compass in the vicinity of Old Slip. He was the father of General Lamb, of Revolutionary memory. Lamb held the office of Chief Engineer, or Overseer, until 1736, when he was succeeded by Jacob Turk.

JACOB TURK was a gunsmith. He held the office of Overseer for twenty-five years. Among other things he introduced the well-known leather cap worn by the firemen to the present day.

JACOBUS STOUTENBURGH, who was, like Turk, a gunsmith, held the office of Overseer from 1762 to 1776. He was one of the thirty firemen originally appointed in 1738. In 1762 he received the title of Chief Engineer. His salary was thirty pounds a year. He continued to be Chief Engineer down to the time of the Revolution. When he was appointed in 1761 the city had largely in-

THOMAS FRANKLIN.

creased in area and population, and in consequence the force in the following year (1762) was augmented to two assistants and sixty men.

WILLIAM J. ELSWORTH was one of the first firemen. In 1791 he was Chief Engineer, and in 1792, when the constitution of the Department was drafted, we find him elected treasurer.

THOMAS BROWN was a fireman in 1738, having been appointed from the Frst Ward. In 1798 Mr. Brown was chosen one of the Trustees of the newly incorporated Department.

THOMAS FRANKLIN, "Uncle Tommy," as he was affectionately styled by the boys, was the first of the old-time chiefs to attain high distinction. His first service was performed with Engine No. 12, which he joined in 1783, and of which he became foreman in 1791. In the year 1799 he was made assistant engineer, and in 1811 Chief Engineer of the Department. He had scarcely been appointed to the latter post when, in attempting to run the gauntlet of blazing buildings on both sides of Chatham Street, he was overcome by the heat, and narrowly escaped being roasted to death in the middle of the street. He was rescued with his clothing in flames, and was carried home in an exhausted condition.

At a great fire in a rope-walk in Orchard Street in July, 1824, the thermometer at the time registering one hundred degrees, Chief Franklin was again overcome, and narrowly escaped with his life. He was elected register, and during the war of 1812 affixed his signature to fractional currency issued by the city to the amount of many millions of dollars. On the occasion of Lafayette's visit to New York Chief Franklin led the parade of the Fire Department.

Mr. Franklin held the post of Chief Engineer from 1811 to 1824, and was an active member of the Fire Department for forty-one years. In 1824 he resigned from active service, to the great regret of the boys, in whose affections "Uncle Tommy Franklin" held a foremost place. It is related of him that he never failed to treat the boys with an almost exaggerated consideration. Even at moments of the wildest excitement, in the thickest danger, he would cheerily shout, "Now, my dear boys, do this, or do that, my dear boys."

·UZZIAH WENMAN.

On the occasion of each firemen's parade after his retirement the old gentleman would stand on the stoop of his house in Broome Street, between Broadway and the Bowery, in full uniform, hat on head and trumpet in hand, and review the procession, receiving the plaudits of his "dear boys" as company after company went by. He passed away in 1830, and was accorded one of the largest funerals ever seen in New York up to that time.

JAMIESON COX was a baker, of Pike Street. He joined Engine Company No. 26 in 1813. In 1822 he was appointed assistant engineer, and chief in 1824. He was an alderman of the Seventh Ward and urged the formation of an alarm company, as the sextons could not be depended upon to give notice of a fire.

UZZIAH WENMAN was born January 22, 1791, in Fulton Street, and died in 1866, having lived just long enough to see the introduction of a new system. He belonged to Engine Company No. 39, and in 1815 was elected its foreman. In 1822 he was appointed assistant engineer and in 1828 Chief Engineer. He was elected to the Legislature, and while there had the firemen's term of service reduced from seven to five years. He was a member of the Croton Aqueduct Commission. He was a brave man, honest in the performance of his duties, and was removed from office (to his credit) because he would not lend himself to the plots of the politicians. One of his most notable acts of coolness and daring was at the burning of the City Hotel on Broadway near Wall Street, in 1829. The chief was left alone on the roof, which was half burnt through and was ready to go down at any moment. His escape was entirely cut off, and there seemed to be not the slightest hope of saving him. The firemen, it was said, lost their heads completely, all sorts of contradictory orders were being shouted, and all was in confusion. Suddenly Wenman stepped to the edge of the roof, and raising his trumpet shouted, "Silence below there!" and in an instant you could have heard a pin drop. Then, through the trumpet, he calmly gave orders to raise a ladder, which only reached half way to the roof, and then lash some poles together and pass him up a light line. It was done, and he tied it round a chimney and came down hand over hand. He had barely touched the street when the roof went in.

JAMES GULICK, one of the most intrepid chiefs who ever directed the destiny of the old Department, served with Engine Company No. 11 until he was appointed assistant engineer in 1824. Standing six feet two in his socks and of superb physique, Gulick was one of the handsomest as well as the most popular firemen of his day. In 1831 he was made Chief Engineer of the Department. At a meeting of active and exempt firemen, held at the Shakespeare Hotel, at the corner of Nassau and Fulton Streets, on the night of September 10, 1831, shortly after he assumed command it was resolved: "That in consideration of the respect we entertain for the character of James Gulick, our newly appointed chief engineer, as well as for the high estimation in which we hold his official capacities as a fireman, a committee be appointed to procure a silver trumpet, to be presented to him in behalf of the firemen of New York." In the following year another testimonial of his worth in the shape of a magnificent silver urn, suitably inscribed, was presented by the representatives of the Department. At a fire in Park Place Chief Gulick bravely rescued, at the risk of his own life, Mr. Morris Franklin, who, while holding the pipe in the attic of the burning building, had been pinned down by the falling timbers of the roof. In 1835 the Common Council, in which a strong opposition to Gulick had been gradually organized, determined to supersede him. The story of his dismissal is told elsewhere, and it will illustrate the popularity of the chief among his men. The self-denial, the suppression of private feeling, and the patriotism of Gulick were conspicuous on this occasion, when, after the firemen had rebelled at his treatment, he flung himself into the breach and restored order and discipline. Immediately after his supersession became generally known eight hundred firemen marched in a body to the City Hall and passed in their

JAMES GULICK.

resignations.   Out of fifteen hundred men scarce seven hundred remained
on duty.   The safety of the city was seriously imperilled.   Engines were
stripped of their ornaments, engine houses were cleared of furniture and
decorations, and whole companies disbanded rather than serve under the new
chief.   Gulick was the idol of the boys, and they would obey none but him.
Tremendous efforts were in vain made to secure Gulick's restoration.   Finding
that nothing could be done with the existing Common Council, the firemen
nominated their darling for Register at the election in that year, and all parties
carried him to victory.   Among other devices displayed on placards during
the campaign was—

Who saved the Cathedral?

JAMES GULICK.

Vote for him for Register.

In honor of their victory the firemen held a grand torchlight procession, over
a mile long, on the night of November 17.   The vote on the thirteenth

ILLUSTRATIVE OF CHIEF GULICK'S CANVASS FOR REGISTER.

assemblyman being a tie, another election was held, and the Whigs nominated
another brave fireman, Morris Franklin, who was elected by a handsome
majority by the votes of his comrades.

From 1842 to 1847 Mr. Gulick was vice-president of the Association of
Exempt Firemen.   He died in 1861, aged sixty-three years.   At the time he
held an office in the Corporation Pipe Yard, at the foot of East Twenty-third
Street.   His generous disposition caused him to neglect making any provision
for his declining years, and he died in comparative poverty.   His funeral took
place at Cranberry, N. J., and was attended by Chief Decker, ex-Chief Wenman, George W. Wheeler, John S. Giles, W. W. Wilson, and a host of other
sorrowing comrades.   No more eloquent tribute to the worth of the departed
chief could have been rendered than the following resolutions passed on the
announcement of his death by the Board of Engineers :

Whereas, The melancholy announcement being made to this Board that another honored, valuable and tried public servant, and for years distinguished as the pride and ornament of the New York Fire Department, has fallen asleep in death, therefore be it

Resolved, That, in our official capacity as Engineers of the New York Fire Department, we learn with sincere sorrow of the decease of James Gulick, ex-Chief Engineer, who departed this life on the evening of Monday, Sept. 16, 1861 ; and that we unite in honoring his remains in such a manner as may best accord with the virtues and character of that great leader in the cause of voluntary aid.

Resolved, That in the death of ex-Chief Engineer James Gulick the New York Fire Department has lost one of its most honorable, fearless, and devoted exemplars, the community at large one of its most spirited and respected citizens, and his relatives and friends one ever found faithful in all the duties and obligations of social life.

Resolved, That no eulogium we can pass in memory of James Gulick can enhance his claims, either as a citizen or fireman—for he was, in the full stature of manhood, "often tried, but never found wanting." The record of his fame can never pass away, nor the brightness of his example be obscured by Time's hand. Hedied full of years and honors, and is now gathered to a glorious reward.

JOHN RYKER, JR., was born in Vesey Street November 25, 1802, and died April 11, 1851. He joined United States Engine Company No. 23, and was appointed assistant engineer in 1829 and Chief in 1836, when Gulick was removed. After his term of Chief Engineer he joined United States Hose Company No. 25. John Ryker was a man of handsome appearance; in character he was generous almost to a fault. It was his misfortune to have been appointed to the most prominent office in the Department in troublous times when dissension reigned. In calmer days his services would have been better appreciated.

JOHN RYKER, JR.

CORNELIUS V. ANDERSON was born April 10, 1818, and died November 22, 1858. In 1830 he joined Hudson Company No. 1. He was a mason and bricklayer by trade, and when he heard that he had been appointed Chief Engineer he was at work laying bricks on a building on the corner of Leonard Street and Broadway. He was a most economical officer, and in consequence antagonized the reckless Board of Aldermen who, at a meeting in 1839, created twenty-four hose companies to bring about his removal. But Anderson was strong in the affection of his men. He was only twenty-eight years old when he became Chief Engineer of the New York Fire Department, a time at when everything was in disorder, consequent upon the appointment of Mr. Hoffmire and the sudden retirement of James Gulick. During the twelve years he occupied this honorable position he gradually won his way into the favor of the firemen, who re-elected him again and again. In the fall of 1848 he was elected Register. While occupying this position (as while chief engineer he doubled the force of the Department, and yet reduced its expenses from seventy-two thousand dollars to thirty thousand dollars) he gave renewed evidence of his sterling honesty by paying into the city treasury forty thousand dollars of surplus fees, while his predecessors had never paid in more than fifteen thousand dollars during a like period of time. In 1851 Mr. Anderson took an active interest in creating the Lorillard Fire Insurance Company, and he was chosen as its president, and continued to act as such until the day of his death. He was also chairman of the Fire Insurance Patrol. In 1856 he was appointed one of the Ten Governors of the Almshouse, in place of William

CORNELIUS V. ANDERSON.

S. Duke, who resigned. For this office he had again been nominated by the Republican party, but declined in consequence of his health. He was mourned everywhere by all. Not alone the firemen who looked up to him with a veneration inspired by time-hallowed associations, but citizens of all classes and conditions joined in sorrowful regrets at the loss of one so useful and so just. The civil authorities, his associates of the Board of Governors of the Almshouse, the Lorillard Fire Insurance Company, the Board of Trustees of the Fire Department, the Board of Fire Commissioners, the Board of Engineers and Foremen, the Board of Representatives, Fire Insurance Patrol, Exempt Engine Company, Hudson Hose Company, and others, all testified, through the public press, their deep sorrow in the loss of Cornelius V. Anderson.

There is a memorable incident in the life of Anderson. It was about the fall of 1843 when an extensive fire broke out in the neighborhood of Hanover Square. Among other merchandise endangered was a quantity of cigars, which, being exposed, were soon carried off by some thoughtless members of the Department. One who had an extra share approached the Chief, and, in a jovial way, offered him a bundle of prime Havanas. Anderson looked him coolly in the face, and said, in his pleasant, quiet manner: "It is easy to steal cigars, but they smoke better when you buy them!" Such was the character of the man. His unimpeachable integrity, his decision, his intrepid courage, his unassuming manners, his mildness, his blunt, outspoken feelings, are traced upon the city's history.

ALFRED CARSON joined Engine Company No. 12 in 1837. In 1841 he was assistant engineer. He became Chief in 1848, served for eight years and then in a close contest with Harry Howard was defeated. After this he rejoined his old company. He died in March, 1880, at his residence, No. 28 Stone Avenue, Jersey City. He left behind him four sisters—Mrs. Haynes, of Brooklyn, one living in Williamsburg, one at Red Bank, N. J., and one in the West. When he retired from the Department he became an insurance surveyor.

One of Alfred Carson's characteristics was his bluntness and disregard of official or political influence when it became necessary to tell the truth. In his report for 1855, speaking of an influence that did much to break up the Volunteer Fire Department, he said :

ALFRED CARSON.

" The law adopted last winter, placing the Department under the supervision of Fire Commissioners, elected by the representatives of the several companies, far exceeds in its usefulness the most sanguine expectations of its friends. The Board has been in existence scarcely three months, yet has rid the Department of a large proportion of the disreputable characters attached thereto ; and ere long those that remain will be reached, unless they conduct themselves in a becoming manner. When misconduct is reported to the Commissioners, they—with the sanction of your honorable body—can remove the guilty parties, and prevent them from again becoming members of the Department. But here their power ends. The miscreants who have been removed can, and many of them do, unite with the runners, and create disturbances between companies. A case of this kind occurred recently ; a company complained of being attacked by a member of another ; on investigation, it was ascertained that the person committing the assault had been previously expelled for offences of a similar nature, and is now but a runner. The aggrieved parties, therefore, had him arrested, but, by giving security in a mere nominal sum to keep the peace for a short time, he was liberated by the judge. As it generally occurs that these rowdies have too much political influence to receive their just deserts from our courts, I would suggest—if constitutional—that application be made to the legislature to clothe the Fire Commissioners with full judicial power, to be used by them only in case of attack, or otherwise interfering with firemen, while in discharge of their duty."

Alfred Carson, chief engineer, was well known for his temperate habits, his favorite beverage being sarsaparilla. Some of his jovial opponents used to say, when he came into a place for refreshments after a fire, "Here comes Old Saxaparill!" One night at a fire on the east side a remarkably zealous foreman, who loved his company like the apple of his eye, and to be her commander was honor enough for him, gave orders to his men after the fire to man the ropes. He did this because he saw a rival company about to start for home. The chief engineer well knew the feeling that existed between the companies, and at once said, "Stand fast!" The foreman of the company, in an excited manner, shouted, "Man your ropes!" In his state of mind he could not see or hear the chief, only the rival company, and the orders of her foreman. Carson, in a louder tone, said, "Stand fast!" The excitable foreman again cried, "Man your ropes!" The assistant foreman called his attention to the orders of the chief, and he replied, "I am foreman of this company." After roll-call, when he had cooled down, an ex-foreman told him he had done wrong, and should have known better, that he would get the company into trouble. He now for the first time began to realize the true condition of affairs, and he asked what he was to do. The ex-foreman told him he had better go over and see the chief and apologize for his conduct. "All right. You know Carson; will you go over with me?" Receiving an affirmative answer, they called on Mr. Carson at his residence. The ex-foreman introduced his companion, who had a slight impediment in his speech, and he instantly blurted out: "Chief at at the fire, I made a ——— fool of myself, and I have come over to apologize and ask your forgiveness for what I have done, as I did not intend any disrespect to you. And now, come, chief, let us go and have a drink."

HARRY HOWARD was born in Manhattanville, now a part of the Twelfth Ward of this city, August 20, 1822, was adopted by a generous Christian lady, Mrs. Sarah Charlesworth Howard, whose name he has always borne and which was afterwards legalized by an act of the Legislature, who brought him up and educated him as if he had been her own son. On Orchard Avenue in Greenwood Cemetery, a monument over Mrs. Howard remains, suitably inscribed, with a life-size marble statue of the lady, to-day attests the gratitude of her adopted son.

Harry was indentured to learn the trade of cabinetmaker with Abijah Matthews & Son, corner of Henry and Catharine Streets, with whom he remained, applying himself with characteristic earnestness, steadiness and perseverance until he became of age. His career as a fireman began April 11, 1840, as a member of Peterson Engine Company No. 15, so-called after their foreman, who was killed at a large fire on Chatham Street, in 1811, located in Christie Street, between Bayard and Canal Streets. But he was no novice, for he, like most strong and active young men in those days, commenced as a runner with that company in 1835. The prominent members of the company were: Nathaniel Bradford, foreman; Matthew D. Green, assistant foreman; John L. Berrian, William J. Vanduzer, Samuel B. Skinner, Nicholas F. Wilson, Henry Chanfrau, Moses F. Odell, who in after years became a member of Congress, and Charles L. Merritt. No. 15 was called the "Old Maid" because she had never been overflowed or washed by any rival engine.

In 1850 Harry Howard was elected foreman of Atlantic Hose Company No. 14, situated on Elizabeth Street directly in the rear of the old Bowery Theater. From that position he was elected in the same year assistant engineer to Chief Carson, in which capacity he rendered such frequent and brilliant services to the Department that he received the warmest thanks from all quarters. The Sixth Ward station house, then located on the Franklin Street entrance to the New York Tombs, was his headquarters, selecting that place because a fire telegraph connected the Tombs prison with the office of the Chief of Police in the basement of the old City Hall. This gave Harry Howard the advantage of learning of outbreaks of fire in distant quarters before he could have been notified by the customary bell-ringing; and enabled him to attend every fire in every district as acting chief until the chief engineer reached the scene. It was the over-exertion thus undertaken that subsequently undermined his health. During the seven years Mr. Howard served as assistant engineer his promptness and dispatch won universal praise. In recognition of his great services, he was elected chief engineer in 1857.

The first act of Mr. Howard, after assuming the office of Chief, was to establish and fit up sleeping apartments, or bunk rooms, for the firemen in all the depositories of fire apparatus

HARRY HOWARD.

throughout the city. This at first was regarded with disfavor by some. But its wisdom was afterwards substantially recognized by the fact that it has been continued to the present day.

He kept the firemen constantly on the alert, and by attacking and subduing fires in their incipiency he was instrumental in saving many millions of dollars of property. The supply of improved fire extinguishing apparatus at that time in use was very limited. There was no steam or horse power to rely upon; everything was done by hand; and it is remarkable how well fires were kept under control with such feeble resources to combat the flames. The losses by fire under Howard's administration as Chief were reduced to such a degree that the rates of insurance were considerably diminished.

He served as Chief Engineer until 1860, when on account of his disabled condition he was obliged to retire from the Department, after completing twenty-five years of active volunteer fire duty. In spite of his remarkable strength and vigor, his great exposures and labor brought on a heavy stroke of paralysis. Being overcome on Grand Street, he fell while running to a fire on East Houston Street, July, 1858. He has never entirely recovered from that affliction, although in other respects he enjoys the best of health—thanks to his life-long abstention from the use of liquors and tobacco. A consultation of the most eminent medical men resulted in the conclusion that the cause of his illness was "exposure, great energy and over-exertion at fires, in performance of the duties of Chief Engineer."

During his active career of twenty-five years Mr. Howard saved the lives of many persons. His rescue of Samuel, the son of A. S. Von Praag, of No. 448 Broome Street, at the fire in No. 231 Broadway, Jennings's clothing house, April 24, 1854, where a number of gallant firemen lost their lives, was a notable instance of his bravery and coolness in time of danger. In the case of the burning of the ship "*Great Republic*," on the twenty-sixth and twenty-seventh of December, 1853, he distinguished himself by such unremitting zeal and perseverance in preventing the entire destruction of that vessel, and so resolutely declined in that instance, as in every other, remuneration for his services, that he received the special thanks of the Board of Fire Underwriters in a letter dated July 22, 1854.

Mr. Howard, while a fireman, represented the Second Assembly District in the Legislature of 1853, was elected alderman of the Sixth Ward in 1854-5, was Receiver of Taxes in 1856. At the close of his connection with the Finance Department as Receiver of Taxes, which he resigned to accept the position of Chief of the Fire Department, he demanded an investigation of his accounts, as millions of the public funds had passed through his hands. A committee of his political opponents pronounced the accounts correct. This is the only instance of a financial officer in this city having his accounts examined at his own request.

Mr. Howard visited the Legislature at the session of 1866, and made an address before the Committee on Cities, for an increase of the firemen's salaries, which resulted in giving them an increase of twenty per cent.

Mr. Howard has been honored in an especial manner by the corporation of this city. In the Aldermanic Chamber to-day hangs a full length portrait of him as Engineer in Chief of the Fire Department, executed by order of the Common Council in recognition of his invaluable services; and "Harry Howard

Square," the open space located midway between Broadway and the Bowery, at the junction of Canal, Walker, Baxter and Mulberry Streets, is a further evidence of the gratitude of the municipality in perpetuation of Mr. Howard's name and fame.

Chief Engineer Harry Howard's long experience in the Volunteer Fire Department convinced him that the public did not appreciate the great personal sacrifices of the Volunteer Firemen, numbers of whom met death or became maimed and paralyzed in the performance of the onerous service of protecting lives and property, and extinguishing fires in this city by hand. He said they ought to be paid, and favored changing the Volunteer Fire Department to a Steam Fire Brigade, with horses to draw the fire apparatus and good salaries for the officers and men.

Of a herculean frame, iron constitution, and quick movement, he was able to go through enormous fatigues, and impart a nerve and vigor to the Department which, for the first time, gave reasonable security to the property and lives of New Yorkers. The losses by fires under his administration were less than under any other Chief. The expenses of the Department were reduced more than one-half from what they had been before, or ever have been since. The Chief then had entire supervision and control of all supplies, repairs and expenses, and no bill passed his scrutiny that was not a fair claim on the city. There was no atmosphere of corruption around him or his office; his hands were clean; nor could any contractor or company or private citizen induce him to receive any commissions, fees, perquisites, presents or rewards of any kind, outside of his salary, which he always declared was all he was entitled to.

Chief Engineer Howard arranged and was Grand Marshal of the two largest Firemen's Parades ever held in this city. First, the grand illuminated parade in celebration of the laying of the first Atlantic Cable, on the night of September 1, 1858; and second, the Department's last grand Triennial Day parade, October 17, 1859.

In February, 1885, Mr. Howard donated one thousand dollars to the burial fund of the Association of Exempt Firemen.

Ex-Chief Howard headed the firemen's division in the Bartholdi Parade of October, 1886, and received an ovation all along the line. Though the day was wet and the thoroughfares slippery, yet the veteran marched with a vigor that was remarkable.

CHIEF JOHN DECKER, for over a quarter of a century prior to 1866, attended fires as boy and man. To-day he is still stalwart, and seemingly as active as when in palmy days he was the proud leader of one of the finest bodies of men New York has ever seen, or, perhaps, will ever see again. He is a born fireman, is just as full as ever of the enthusiasm of his younger days, and will in all probability so continue to the end of his life. For it is a marked peculiarity or a distinguishing characteristic of such veterans as Chief Decker that to be a fireman once is to be a fireman forever. He was born next door to a fire house. Chief Decker was the last of the old Volunteer Chief Engineers. After him came the deluge that ingulfed the galant boys who served for glory and the love of the thing. The revolution found him an an irreconcilable, and, with his fellows, sooner than serve under strange masters he stepped down and out, relinquished his trumpet and retired to private life, to nurse thereafter as a cherished legacy the memory of those eventful and exciting times when to be a fireman meant hard knocks, plenty of work, scant thanks, and the sole recompense the consciousness of discharging a noble and humane public duty.

Born in this city (May 15, 1823), after passing through the evolutionary period of probation as a "Bunker," in 1840 he joined the Department, but did not get "time" for four years after. In 1848 he was promoted to be assistant foreman, serving in that capacity until 1852, when he was elected foreman, and one year later he went a step still higher—assistant engineer. He was re-elected in 1856, and again in 1859. He attained to the highest honor in the Department on the 7th of February, 1860, when he became Chief Engineer, serving as such until August 31, 1865. "I locked the door at 12 o'clock on that night," said Chief Decker, "because the commissioners did not appoint a man in my place when I had asked to be relieved. I was appointed by the commissioners with the stipulation that my successor would be speedily appointed.

JOHN DECKER.

This was about the end of June, and I served under the new régime until the last day of August, and, my successor not yet being appointed, I left in the manner I have stated. The commissioners and I could not get along together. They wanted to take the command out of my hands when at a fire, and I would not consent to this, for I desired to act independently of them, and in that way to be personally responsible for my action. There were four commissioners, and those, counting me in, would make five, whose authority would be supreme at a fire. I considered that five captains were enough to sink any ship, so I would not go on their craft. After I had locked the door at midnight, considering that my last official act, there came an alarm of fire in Mott Street. I turned out without my fire cap and put out the fire. That was my last official act as Chief Engineer."

Chief Decker has many exciting experiences to relate, but is reticent withal except when among his set. In the rooms of the Volunteer Association in Eighth Street are an oil painting and an engraving of Chief Decker, which the "boys" cherish as the counterfeit presentments of the John Decker who in many a firy foray has led and cheered them on to battle. Having his attention drawn to these portraits quite recently, the sturdy veteran said with some degree of pardonable pride: "Yes, that is what I looked like some thirty years ago. I then weighed one hundred and ninety pounds, and was a safe man to be let alone. I could hold my own with the best of them, and that is no mean boast."

Chief Decker's experience at fires goes back to the big fire of 1835. Since that memorable time he has attended every fire of note or otherwise in the city for thirty years. In referring to the fighting proclivities of some of the firemen of those days, Chief Decker said: "I never courted a fight and never shrank from one. Each and every member of the company," he added, "felt about as I did, and we were hard men to down." While Chief Engineer, Mr. Decker had to contend with the Draft Riots of 1863. Early in the month of July in that year he and his command were summoned to the corner of Forty-sixth Street and Third Avenue to quench the flames that were devouring the Provost Marshal's building. The rioters had begun their operations here, supposing that it was the source from which all their troubles emanated. Upon the arrival of Chief Decker his passage was blocked by the rioters, who refused to let him or his men approach the burning building. He appealed to the frenzied mob—told them to consider the consequences to innocent parties if the flames were permitted to spread to adjoining houses. Realizing the force of the argument, the mob gave way and allowed the Chief

DISCHARGE CERTIFICATE, CHIEF JOHN DECKER.

and his gallant boys to come forward with their apparatus, and thus valuable property was saved from destruction. The mob, as if repenting of their leniency, proceeded to Lexington Avenue and Forty-fourth Street and fired a building there. Here again they were met by the intrepid fire laddies. The mob was led by a man named Hunter, who incited them to all kinds of deviltry. Baffled here also, they next fired the Arlington House, and followed this up by burning down the Colored Orphan Asylum. Meanwhile the Volunteer Fire Department, in fighting the flames that the rioters had left in their path, had worked around to the Colored Orphan Asylum. They found the mob assailing the doors with axes, forcing an entry.

The chief did his best to stop the fiendish wreckers. Boldly thrusting himself among them, he snatched from the hands of those nearest him the implements they were using to demolish the doors. A blow of a cart-rung stretched him senseless. When consciousness returned he found himself in the hands of half a dozen infuriated rioters, who were firm in their determination to hang him from the nearest tree. That the miscreants meant business and were prepared to execute their threat was made evident by the fact that one of them carried a stout rope which he shook in the face of the partially stunned but undaunted Chief. A short shrift and a long halter, truly. It was a tragic looking group: the intrepid chief held in the grip of brawny hands; the waving arms of a gnarled tree overhead: the rope, the victim, the executioners: a background of smoke and flame, and human demons holding their saturnalia of crime: fleeing children, partially concealed by the clouds of smoke arising from the destruction of their common home, reared by philanthropic hands and sustained by charitable hearts—their swarthy faces lending to the general suggestiveness of pandemonum broke loose:—these were the startling accessories which, it need hardly be said, were sufficient to strike terror into the stoutest heart. How did it affect the man whose life was trembling in the balance? His nerve and mother wit alone saved him. Turning to the man who was adjusting the rope into a noose, Chief Decker carelessly remarked, drawing his hand suggestively across his neck:

"What good will it do you to hang me? You will only stop my *draft*, not the Government's."

The pun saved a good and a brave man's life.

Chief Decker took a leading part in the formation of the Fire Companies that went to the war. He was instrumental in recruiting the First Fire Zouaves, and assisting in raising thirty-one thousand dollars in the Fire Department to equip them. Also he recruited and maintained for several weeks at his own expense the Second Regiment of Fire Zouaves. He often visited the men on the battlefields, and never ceased to look after the interest and welfare of the brave soldiers at the front.

On one occasion he visited the battlefield of Williamsburgh, Va., recovered several bodies and removed them to their friends in this city. In a similar manner the graves of others were identified. Chief Decker was a most ardent Union man. The Chief says that the members of the Fire Department were the most loyal body of men in the country, the Department sending over two thousand seven hundred active members to the war.

The New York *Herald,* at the time, thus referred to the action of our firemen during the draft riots:

No class of men are more entitled to praise for heroism and self-sacrifice, as displayed in the recent uprising against the draft ordered by President Lincoln, than the firemen of New York, in extinguishing fires and saving valuable property that would have been destroyed had they not interposed their objections and determined to execute their functions at every hazard. * * * Hundreds of thousands of dollars were placed in jeopardy, and only saved by the prompt interference of the firemen. * * * Chief Engineer John Decker is especially entitled to the gratitude of the owners and occupants of real estate in the upper section of the city. That he absolutely saved to them their homes and contents is conceded by everybody. Never since the days of Gulick and Anderson has the Fire Department been managed with so much signal ability as during the time it has been controlled by Mr. Decker, and we sincerely believe it will be a great while ere the firemen will dispense with his valuable services.

In his last report (1865) to the Common Council Chief Decker protested against the contemplated abolishment of the Old Department and the substitution of the New. "The firemen of this city," he said, "are as intelligent, honest, sober, and industrious as any body of nearly four thousand men in the world. Some of our best merchants, bankers, mechanics, and tradesmen have been and are at present members of the Fire Department, and are proud to have it known in their social and business circles, and will always be pleased to remember that they belonged to the Volunteer Fire Department of this city."

At the fire in the Duane Street Sugar House, where Kerr and Fargis were killed, Mr. Decker held 14's pipe, and was talking to Mr. Fargis when the wall fell in and crushed him. "When the wall came," he says, "it came with a thud and a hissing. I looked up and saw steam and shavings pour out of the round windows of the top floor. Instantly a part of the cornice dropped beside me, killed Fargis, and broke part of 38 Engine. Fargis had started to run into the archway, and had just got on the sidewalk when he was struck on the head. You have no idea of the extent to which even business men of high intelligence who were firemen carried their enthusiasm. Fire duty was their religion; they sacrificed to it health, wealth, strength, wife's society, everything."

Chief Decker is president of the Volunteer Firemen's Association.

CHIEF DECKER IN THE HANDS OF THE RIOTERS.

CHAPTER XXV.

SOME PROMINENT VOLUNTEER FIREMEN.

Edward M. Hoffmire: His Varied and Interesting Career.—William Brandon: Fireman and Insurance
Surveyor.—John Baulch: At every Large Fire in New York from 1835 to 1862.—John T. Agnew:
Comes of a Family of Firemen.—Carlisle Norwood: "The very Ideal of the True Fireman."—
Richard P. Moore: First to Make Trial of a Steam Fire Engine in this City.—Clarkson Crolius:
At every Fire in the Sixth Ward.—William B. Dunley: The Best Informed Fireman in New York.—
John McDermott: An Art Connoisseur.—Richard Evans: Popular with the Boys.—Francis Haga-
dorn: Has filled Offices of Trust and Honor.—William L. Jenkins: Enamored of a Fireman's
Life.—Abraham H. Purdy: A Sturdy Veteran.—Anthony Yeoman: An Active Fireman.

EDWARD M. HOFFMIRE entered the old Fire Department when quite
a young man as a member of Fire Engine Company No. 6. Mr.
John MacMullen gives the following admirable sketch of him:

"Mr. Hoffmire rose to be assistant foreman and foreman of that company,
and was afterwards made assistant engineer of the Department, under James
Gulick as chief engineer. He was always very popular with the men, from
his daring, his manliness and his generosity. I presume that he never refused
to help any one if in his power, but I never knew except from others of any such
acts of his, for he never spoke of them. He made plenty of money in his
business, but he was too open-handed to keep it. His work as a carpenter had
developed him physically, in the best manner, and prepared him for his work as
a fireman. It was a pleasure to see him walking in the street with his erect
figure, his light elastic step, his square shoulders and his keen eye that noted
everything. My elder brother coming home one evening from Windust's, once
a celebrated restaurant, stated that Gabriel Ravel, one of the best of that
distinguished family of acrobats, was in the barroom, and when some one said
to him, 'It's all very easy for you to turn the somersaults you do because you
have springboards and all sorts of appliances upon the stage,' he said, 'That
makes no difference; I could do it right here;' and stepping out to the middle
of the floor he turned a somersault as neatly as possible, alighting on his feet
very nearly in the same place.

"'Well,' said Mr. Hoffmire, 'that isn't much to do. I could do it right
here on this carpet.'

"We all thought that he was joking, but he stepped out just as he was,
dressed in a light pair of boots and a dress suit, and turned a somersault,
coming down as lightly as a bird. His gold watch, which was worn, as usual
at that time, with a long gold chain that went around the neck, took advantage
of the occasion to fly out of his vest pocket and twist the chain around his
neck. When speaking one day about the softness of pine wood, he said that

one could make dents in it with his knuckles; and, when some disbelief was shown, he immediately demonstrated it, so that we had no difficulty in feeling the indentations with our fingers.

"Once in the course of conversation he stated that he had ordered a plate of turkey in an eating-house, and was eating it quietly in one of the small alcoves when some rowdies entered, and a big fellow coolly sat down opposite to him and, sticking a fork into a piece of the turkey, put it into his mouth, saying, 'Hey, bub, let's see how it tastes.'

"He said it was a foolish thing to do, since there were four of them, but he could not help striking square on the cheek where the turkey was. Then stepping out of the alcove, and putting his back against the partition, he stood there to take the consequences. Just at that moment, as luck would have it, the door opened and in came some firemen. They took in the situation immediately, and one of them said:

"'Why, Ned, what's up?'

"He told them what had happened, but the rowdies were so profuse in their apologies and assurances that it was all a joke and that they were ready to pay for the turkey ten times over that the firemen let them go without punishment.

"The daring he displayed at fires was a constant subject of remark. Many buildings were saved in consequence of it, and he received many tokens of gratitude from those whose lives or property he saved. I recollect seeing on his mantel-piece a small model of a fire-engine of those days, made by the pupils of a public school that he had saved from destruction by his exertions. He often

EDWARD M. HOFFMIRE.

risked his life without saying a word about it, and the first intimation that his startled wife received was usually from some outsider.

"A man came early one morning to ask if he were dead, and when his wife said no, that he was perfectly well, the man said, 'Well, I'm very glad to hear it, for they told me that he fell down a hoistway last evening, and I thought he must be dead.' On my asking Mr. Hoffmire about it afterwards, he said:

"'It was in a large store down town where they had the hoistway at the end against the wall, and as I was going along in the dark I walked right into the open hoistway, and fell down three stories. I struck on my feet, and was pretty well jarred, but not hurt seriously. I had the curiosity to go down the next day to see what it was that saved me, and I saw that it was my stepping forward so unhesitatingly that brought me square up against the end wall, and kept me from turning over so that I came down straight, and I could see where the toes of my boots had scraped against the wall.'

"On another occasion a large wholesale coffee store down town took fire in the rear basement, and the flames went straight up, leaving the front apparently untouched. The firemen had poured in plenty of water, which had run down and filled the cellar nearly full, though its ceiling was rather high. As they afterwards found out, some burning brands had floated, as they burned, on top of the water, which by that time was so near the ceiling as to enable them to set fire to the beams, so that when Chief Gulick and Assistant Hoffmire started in from the front to see whether the fire was sufficiently mastered, the floor was burned to a thin crust; and as Gulick was a heavy man, weighing over two hundred pounds, he broke through, making a large hole, into which Hoffmire followed him. When they attempted to catch hold of the floor the burning crust gave way, and their cries appeared to be unheard. Hoffmire, seeing that something desperate must immediately be done, jumped up on Gulick's broad shoulders, and thence made a sprawling jump upon the floor, spreading himself out as much as possible so as not to break through again, and lending

WILLIAM BRANDON.

a hand to Gulick as he came up from his involuntary plunge. By this time help came, and a ladder was run across by the ready firemen, who soon raised up their dripping Chief. Gulick was a good-natured and a reasonable man, who soon saw that what was done was best for both, and both often thereafter jokingly referred to this adventure, in which Hoffmire's prompt decision and successful execution certainly prevented some suffering, and may have averted a calamity."

WILLIAM BRANDON, ex-chief of battalion of the new Department, is well known, not only in New York, but throughout the whole country, as a capable fireman. He is a member of the Volunteer and Veteran Firemen's Associations, and is now in the service of the Home Insurance Company, of New York, as surveyor of that company. Few men have taken a greater interest in fire matters outside their native place, for Mr. Brandon has been instrumental in organizing or improving fire departments elsewhere. In June, 1873, he visited Boston, accompanying a committee of the National Board of Fire Underwriters, for the purpose of reorganizing the Department of that city. In November of the following year he visited Chicago with General Alexander Shaler, at the request of the Citizens' Committee of Chicago. The result of the visit was the reorganization of a Fire Department on a basis that has made it one of the best in the country. One of the most important works that Mr. Brandon has undertaken was the examining and reporting upon the Fire Departments of some of the leading cities. This was done at the request of the National Board of Fire Underwriters in 1876. The cities reported upon were: Philadelphia, Pa.; Baltimore, Md.; Louisville, Ky.; Nashville and Memphis, Tenn.; Indianapolis, Ind.; St. Louis, Mo.; Cincinnati and Cleveland, O.;

Milwaukee, Wis.; Detroit, Mich.; Albany, Syracuse, Rochester, Buffalo, and Elmira, N. Y.; Providence, R. I.; Boston and Springfield, Mass.; and Portland and Bangor, Me. These reports, which were the most comprehensive of the kind, were distributed among insurance companies doing a general agency business.

Mr. Brandon's experience as a fireman rendered him peculiarly fitted for this work. He was born in the city of New York on October 25, 1835. Before he was twenty-one years old he served as a volunteer with Peterson Engine Company No. 15; afterwards he joined Fulton Hose Company No. 15, and became its foreman. Next he joined Hook and Ladder Company No. 1, one of the oldest and most efficient companies in the service. In 1859 he was elected a fire warden. When the new Department came into existence, Mr. Brandon was appointed a foreman on September 8, 1865, and next year, in April, was promoted to the position of district engineer (now known as chief of battalion) and assigned to the "dry-goods district" (the third), one of the most important in the city. In January, 1870, he was promoted to be chief of the First Brigade.

In the Old Department he was once severely injured by the breaking of a ladder at a fire in Vesey Street. This was on August 24, 1858. He was laid up for some months.

In January, 1878, he went to Pittsburg, Pa., to examine the Fire Department there, and was presented with an elegant silver service. In September, 1882, he represented the National Board of Fire Underwriters at the National Convention of Fire Chief Engineers, held at Cincinnati, O.

JOHN BAULCH, at present the chief engineer of the Fortress Monroe

JOHN BAULCH.

Fire Department, whose robust form is well known to all old New York people, and generally throughout the country, is one of the oldest active firemen now living. He joined the "Good Intent" Engine Company, No. 39, when she lay in the park in the rear of the old Bridewell prison. In 1838, shortly after, the company moved to Doyers Street, near Chatham Square. Mr. Baulch was elected assistant foreman in 1840 and foreman in 1841, holding the latter position when the Common Council disbanded his company. The reason for the disbandment was this: One Sunday afternoon, at a fire in Peck Slip, Chief Anderson appeared without uniform or cap, and undertook to direct 39 to give water to 15 Engine. No. 15 was their natural enemy at this time, so they washed the "stranger" who "interfered" and gave the water to 12 Engine. Mr. Baulch next joined Bunker Hill Engine No. 32, and was soon elected assistant foreman. He held this position until 1847, when he resigned and immediately joined Eagle Engine Company No. 13. He was elected assistant foreman soon after, and at the following annual meeting was elected foreman, filling this office with credit until he was elected an assistant engineer in 1854.

John Baulch was an assistant engineer from 1854 to 1862. During the latter part of this time he was acting senior engineer, and chief during the absence of Chief Howard, who was unable to be present owing to illness. In 1862 Mayor Opdyke received an order from the Secretary of War, directing him to send two powerful engines and an experienced engineer to Fortress Monroe. Mr. Baulch was selected for this duty, and left New York within six hours after receiving orders, taking with him Mohawk Engine No. 16 and Peterson Engine No. 31. These two engines were considered the most powerful engines at that time. Mr. Baulch arrived at Fortress Monroe, and more apparatus was sent to him from Philadelphia, Baltimore and other points. He organized fire companies for each engine and carriage from the volunteer regiments stationed at the fort, many of them being old firemen from New York who had served under him before. Mr. Baulch was then made chief engineer of the division of the South, with headquarters at Fortress Monroe. His duty was to follow up the military and take charge of all fire apparatus in Southern towns occupied by our troops and to organize fire companies, with soldiers, for the temporary protection of the town. In this work he rendered valuable service in preventing the destruction of property and received many complimentary letters. With his corps of assistants he made many friends and ministered to the comforts of firemen as they lay wounded and dying on the field, or supplied them with clothing as they arrived at the fort as exchanged prisoners of war.

JOHN T. AGNEW.

Mr. Baulch was present at every large fire in New York from 1835 to 1862, and had many very narrow escapes. His grandchildren now admire the two beautiful silver trumpets presented to him as tokens of the esteem in which he was held. One was presented by the members of Engine Company No. 13, the other by the Volunteer Fire Department of Philadelphia ; also the cap, belt and lantern presented to him by the Norfolk (Va.) Fire Department for valuable services rendered while on duty in charge at that city. He was elected one of the vice-presidents of the Association of Fire Engineers of the United States. Mr. Baulch was elected for four terms as a member of the Board of Councilmen, representing the Fourth Ward, where he lived over thirty-seven years.

JOHN T. AGNEW comes of a family of firemen. His father, William Agnew, was a fireman and fire warden for twenty-one years, and served on the Floater. At the burning of Fulton Market Mr. William Agnew was conspicuous for his bravery. He was also conspicuous at the great 1835 fire, where he and others placed a keg of powder under Remsen's store in Hanover Square and blew up the building to arrest the progress of the flames. He preserved with care his fire warden's hat, and his son, John T., still has it. Mr. John T. Agnew's brother, Alexander M., likewise served with distinction in the Volunteer Department and was a member of Oceana Hose No. 36—a crack company. The fire hats of Alexander and his father are to be seen in Mr. Agnew's warehouse in Front Street. This warehouse is built within six feet of the spot where his grandfather had erected a dwelling house, at No. 313 Water Street, in 1793, and where he himself was born. Mr. Agnew's certificate of exemption (which is dated 1851) hangs in his office. He served for nine years in the Volunteers, and his courage, devotion to duty, and skill made him a remarkable man in the Department. With his father he was present at the fire of 1835, where he rendered great assistance and saved from the flames some valuable sets of books for his merchant friends. He was a member of Hose Company No. 1 for four years, then a fire war-den for three years, and finally a member of a hydrant company for two years. Associated with him in fire duty were Halsey R. Mead, a wholesale cooper, and two Mead brothers; the Ockershausens, sugar refiners, Van Nostrand, the hardware merchant, long at the corner of Beekman and Pearl Streets; Mr. Rich, of the firm of Taylor & Rich, shipping merchants; Edward Brooks, of the firm of Brooks Bros.; Peter H. Titus, Peter V. King, and Percy R. Pyne.

CARLISLE NORWOOD.

CARLISLE NORWOOD, who was President of the Lorillard Fire Insurance Company, was born at the corner of Vesey and Church Streets, New York, on February 12, 1812. His father, Andrew S. Norwood, was a friend of Lafayette and was well acquainted with the distinguished Frenchman before the latter's visit to New York in 1824. Among the interesting souvenirs which the son retains of the illustrious general is a letter of invitation to his father to attend the marriage of the general's daughter at the family château—La Grange, France. When Mr. Carlisle Norwood was attending school in France he was often invited to partake of General Lafayette's hospitality. At a very early age he evinced a love for the fireman's life—indeed he was only eight when he undertook to run with a machine and was severely reprimanded by his father for his ambition.

When eighteen his darling hope was realized, and he was admitted to membership in Engine Company No. 28. In 1830 he attached himself to No. 21 Engine, located on Tryon Row (where the *Staats Zeitung* building now stands). He was a fire warden in the Fifteenth Ward at the time of the Gulick disturbance, in 1836. In 1837 he raised Hose Company No. 5. This company was long regarded as the crack fire company of the city. It was organized at the house of George Woolredge, Chambers Street, on October 3, and Mr. Norwood was elected foreman. The company was composed of merchants and clerks, and among its members were Augustus W. Vanpell, assistant foreman, Richard K. Anthony, secretary and treasurer, John S. Winthrop, Abraham Van Nest, Robert S. Luqueer, Richard S. Williams, Robert D. Codington, Jonathan C. Ayers, and John Duer. General John Watts Depeyster was a volunteer. The only members now living, beside Mr. Norwoood, are Messrs. Luqueer, Livingston, Rutgers, and James M. Rankin, of Brooklyn. No. 5 had its headquarters at Firemen's Hall, in Mercer Street.

Mr. James F. Wenman said of Hose Company No. 5 and its organizer: " No. 5 was the best disciplined hose company in the service. Her men were not allowed to leave the rope when going home, nor the fire without permission of the foreman. Norwood was a strict disciplinarian." Mr. Norwood used to say himself that he considered it the duty of the foreman to see that all the laws were strictly obeyed. He refused several times to run as a candidate for engineer. Mr. Adam P. Pentz said: "To my mind Mr. Norwood was the very ideal of the true fireman; that is, his activity was never surpassed, his perceptions were quick, and his judgment cool, clear, and steady. He believed that ' the post of honor was the post of danger,' and exemplified the truth of the proverb in his own proper person."

When Mr. Norwood was on a visit to the town of Adrian, Mich., he saw from the character of the buildings, which were nearly all of wood, that in case of fire the whole town would run the risk of destruction. There were no fire engines or fire appliances. He suggested to the authorities that a fire department be organized and an engine purchased. His suggestion was thankfully received, and Mr. Norwood at once organized a fire department, that in time became one of the most effective in Michigan.

It may be mentioned that Mr. Norwood belongs to one of the oldest families in the city. His grandfather was a prisoner in the Sugarhouse during the Revolutionary War, and was often subjected to the insults and the bayonet points of the British who guarded that place. His father was one of the original incorporators of the Fifth Avenue Presbyterian Church in 1807, when the congregation was located in Cedar Street. Among his associates were Ebenezer Stevens, Selah Strong, Elisha Leavenworth, John Aspinwall, Archibald Gracie, Benjamin Strong, Theodore Ely, William W. Woolsey, Joseph Otis, Stephen Whitney, Hezekiah Lord, William Adams, Daniel Hosack, Nathaniel L. Griswold, Robert Weir, John Trumbull, and Lynde Catlin. The Rev. Dr. John Hall is the present pastor of the new and splendid edifice in Fifth Avenue.

RICHARD P. MOORE, surveyor for the German American Insurance Company, joined the Department in December, 1848, enrolling as a member of Liberty Hose Company No. 10. He remained only two years with that company, attaching himself in March, 1850, to Engine Company No. 42, the " Hay-wagon," so called from its likeness to that kind of vehicle. The company was then stationed at No. 2½ Murray Street. Mr. Moore left the Department in 1860, and when in 1861 the tocsin of war was sounded he enrolled as a member of the celebrated Irish Brigade, and under the gallant Meagher went to the front to do battle with the enemies of the Union. At a fire which occurred in French's Hotel in 1852 Mr. Moore received severe injuries, on account of which he was invalided for two months. He has the honor of having been the first man to make a trial of a steam fire engine in this city.

In 1857 Messrs. Lee & Larned completed, under contract with the corporation, two self-propellers. The firemen were opposed to the introduction of them, and meetings were held at which resolutions were adopted calling upon the Common Council not to accept them. Subsequently Mr. Moore was invited to make a test of their ability, and he took the "J. C. Cary" from the Novelty Works at Ninth Street and East River to the Battery, where the demonstration of her effectiveness was complete, and silenced all opposition. The then Street Commissioner, Mr. Edward Cooper, promptly accepted the engines. The "J. C. Cary" in after years became the charge of the Exempt Company.

Mr. Moore was born in the Second Ward of this city in 1830. He was elected assistant foreman of Engine Company No. 42 in 1854, and acted in that capacity until 1859, when he was elected foreman.

ALDERMAN CLARKSON CROLIUS is one of the most prominent names in the Croton Aqueduct celebration. No one is better identified with the history of New York than Mr. Crolius, who has lived eighty-five years in the city, and held public office for many years. While alderman of the Sixth and Seventeenth Wards he rarely missed being present at a fire. Mr. Crolius comes of an old Knicker-bocker family. The first of the family came from Germany in the beginning of the eighteenth century. This was William Crolius, whose male descendants were John Crolius, Clarkson Crolius, Sr., and Clarkson Crolius, Jr., now living, and who has survived all his con-

CLARKSON CROLIUS.

temporaries in the Common Council. His father was Colonel Crolius, a decided whig, who was compelled to leave the city after the defeat of the American troops on Long Island. When Sir William Howe took possession of the City of New York his property fell into the hands of the British, and did not again revert to the family till the peace of 1783. The two elder brothers of Colonel Crolius took part in the Revolutionary War. At the commencement of the war of 1812 Clarkson Crolius, Sr., was major in the Twenty-seventh Regiment, now the Seventh, but resigned his commission in the militia and received an appointment to the same rank in the regular service. In 1803 Colonel Crolius officiated at the laying of the corner stone of the City Hall in the Park, then called the "Fields." He was a member of the Common Council for many years, for ten years in the legislature, and in 1811, as a grand sachem of Tammany Society, laid the foundation stone of the old Tammany Hall in Frankfort Street. He died on October 5, 1843, at the age of seventy years.

The family records were lost during the Revolution, and it is not known from what part of Germany William came.   He was a manufacturer of stoneware, which occupation has been followed by a representative of the family in every generation of his descendants.   William Crolius' pottery was located in Reade Street near Broadway.   His son John acquired property on Reade Street, about one hundred feet west of Centre, where the pottery and the family residence were maintained for many years, until Clarkson Crolius, Sr., removed the works to Nos. 65 and 67 Bayard Street, the old home still remaining in Reade Street.   For one hundred years a ship could not sail to any part of the world without finding there some stone mug or jar bearing the stamp: " Clarkson Crolius, Manhattan Wells, New York."   Mr. Clarkson Crolius, Jr., discontinued the manufacture of stoneware in Bayard Street in 1845, and the pottery was afterwards demolished.

The subject of the present sketch was born in 1801, in the Sixth Ward, where the family residence has been for one hundred and twenty-seven years. As a boy he skated on the Fresh Water Pond, on the site of which now stands the Tombs.   He saw the workmen lay the foundation of the Tombs in the mire which formed the bottom of the pond.   The men placed three or four tiers of heavy timber crosswise in the mire, and upon these built the stone walls.   In 1838 the prison was finished, and it fell to the lot of Mr. Crolius, who was then chairman of the Joint Committee of the Common Council on prisons, to transfer the prisoners—about one hundred in number—from the old Bridewell, situated in the park between Broadway and the present City Hall, to the Hall of Justice, or the Tombs.   Mr. David Graham, then the alderman from the Fifteenth Ward, was a member of the Committee on Prisons, and High Constable Hayes also assisted.   In 1838 Alderman Crolius voted in favor of the act authorizing the construction of the High Bridge.   Mr Crolius was chairman of the Joint Committee of the Common Council on Receptions when General Scott visited the city on his return from the Mexican War, and when General Cass, General Quitman and Commodore Matthew C. Perry, who bombarded Vera Cruz, were publicly received by the municipal authorities. Mr. Crolius was also a member of the Reception Committee of the Common Council when Polk, Clay and other distinguished men were received.

Mr. Crolius, the present representative of the family, was assistant alderman from the Sixth Ward in 1838 and 1839, and alderman in 1842 and 1843.   He was also alderman of the Seventeenth Ward during four years from 1847, and State senator from the Fourth District in 1850 and 1851.   He was unanimously renominated as senator, but declined the nomination, and has since devoted his time to the management of public charities.   He is said to have been the only Republican ever elected from the Sixth Ward.   For thirty years he was a member of the Board of Trustees of the Seamen's Retreat at Stapleton, S. I., until the institution passed, in 1882, into the hands of the Government.   For twelve years he was a president of the retreat.

In 1842, at the aldermanic election in the Sixth Ward, Captain Mike Walsh, at the head of the " Spartan Band," attempted to destroy the ballot box.   It caused Mr. Crolius' election to be contested by " Hold-over Shaler."   The case was carried to the Supreme Court by a mandamus, subsequently by the advice of Mayor Robert Morris, to the Albany Court for the Correction of Errors, and in both places unanimously decided in favor of Mr. Crolius.

In 1848 the residents of the upper wards were indebted mainly to Alderman Crolius for the establishment of the first line of omnibuses up the Bowery. The outfit belonged to Hatfield, Bertine & McLelland.

Mr. Crolius was at every fire in the Sixth Ward.

WILLIAM BALLARD DUNLEY was born in Madison Street, formerly Banker Street, in the Seventh Ward of New York city, on the 12th day of February, 1831. The Dunley family had for many years been engaged in the shipping interests of the city. William's father and grandfather, both on his father's and mother's side, were shipbuilders, and his maternal grandfather was one of the firm of Ballard & Hart, of Boston, Mass., who assisted in the building of the frigate 'Constitution.' "Billy," as he is called by his numerous friends and acquaintances, followed in the footsteps of his ancestors, and has been engaged in the metal punching business for a long term of years, and always in the Seventh Ward, of which he was a resident until about twenty years ago when he removed to the Seventeenth Ward, where he now resides.

Mr. Dunley commenced running to fires at a very early age. When he was a boy living in Madison Street his whole interest was centered in old 26 Jefferson engine (then lying in the same street), and he was a volunteer of that company about the time that Ethan S. Blanck was the foreman and James (Kittens) Adams assistant foreman, when the Jefferson Blues target company was organized from 26 Engine. Mr. Dunley joined them, and was the first lieutenant of the company on their last two parades. When 26 Engine was disbanded for their constant troubles with Chatham Engine Company No. 2, who shared the same fate, Oceana Hose Company No. 36 took the house in

WILLIAM B. DUNLEY.

Madison Street, and "Billy" transferred his affections to them. Francis B. O'Conner and Lawrence Turnure were the foremen in those days, and Wm. M. Tweed was a member, being secretary of the company in 1845. When Americus Engine Company No. 6 was organized and took the house of Old Black Joke Engine Company No. 33 Mr. Dunley attached himself to them as a volunteer, commencing with their first fire, June 11, 1849. He became a member of the company March 9, 1852, being proposed by Tweed. He was soon elected assistant secretary, then assistant foreman and foreman, serving as such until 1860, and from that time on as treasurer and representative; he resigned as an active member in 1863, but kept up his interest in the organization until the disbandment of the old Volunteer system. In 1850 the "Americus Pleasure Club" sprang from Engine Company No. 6. The father of the club was John Betts. While in Greenwich in 1858, Mr. Dunley being at the time treasurer, Tweed joined the club, and their name was shortened to the "Americus Club." Mr. Dunley held the position of treasurer until 1873, and the club disbanded in 1874. He was also first lieutenant of the Gouverneur Blues (Captain W.

Gayte) and an officer in the Americus Guards, under Captain Joseph H. Johnson, both of these companies emanating from Engine Company No. 6. In 1854 Mr. Dunley, with Edward W. Jacobs, Richard Kimmons, John Buckbee and others, organized the famous City Club located at No. 253 Bowery, of which club he was the president for nine years, resigning the position in 1881, and afterwards accepting the position of secretary to further the interests of the club. This was a thoroughly social organization, keeping Liberty Hall on all holidays, free to their friends and visitors.

Mr. Dunley was one of the organizers and is also a member of the Volunteer and Exempt Associations. On Evacuation Day, 1883, Mr. Dunley, Ed. W. Jacobs, John Buckbee, David M. Smith, the first foreman of Americus Engine Company No. 6, he having held that office in 1849, took part in the procession. They procured the engine "Big Six" from Willett's Point, and paraded one hundred and ten men under Mr. Dunley as foreman and Mr.

RICHARD EVANS.

Smith as assistant. Mr. Dunley's knowledge of the old Department is vast, and he can place either from his vivid memory or his unerring records every person of prominence who has been connected with the organization.

JOHN McDERMOTT ("Old Time Enough") was born in Manchester, England, and was brought to this country by his parents in 1841. On August 4, 1852, he joined Excelsior Engine Company No. 2, which was then styled the Quaker Company because of the number of its members who belonged to that peculiar faith. In 1863 he was elected foreman and remained with it until it was disbanded. In 1854 Mr. McDermott was connected with the firm of Currier & Ives, and it was at his suggestion and under his personal direction that that house issued the well-remembered series of lithographs illustrative of a Volunteer fireman's life. They are known as "The Night Alarm" ("Start her lively, boys"); "The Race" ("Jump her, boys, jump her"); "The Fire" ("Shake her up, boys"). "The Ruins" ("Take up; man your rope"). The series, it is not generally known, contain many excellent portraits of prominent fire laddies, among others those of Carson, Howard and Cregier. In "The Night Alarm" are pictures of Mr. McDermott and "his left-handed Mascot," Sloper, who are represented as having hold of the tongue of the machine. Mr. McDermott is engaged in the picture business, and is known to artists of New York and other cities as a connoisseur.

RICHARD EVANS was born in New York on May 12, 1834. In 1854 he joined Hose Company No. 26, serving six years, part of the time as assistant foreman and secretary. Subsequently he joined Americus Engine Company No. 6, with which he remained for three years. In 1867 he was elected a school trustee in the Thirteenth Ward, in which ward he had been a resident for fifty years, and served six years. In 1882 he was elected trustee of the Exempt Firemen's Benevolent Fund, and re-elected in 1886 for another term of four years. Mr. Evans is also a member of the Veteran Firemen's Association, and Chairman of its Board of Trustees.

MICHAEL EICHELL was born on August 24, 1820. At the age of sixteen he began to run with an engine. On October 7, 1840, he joined Engine Company No. 19, served nine years, was elected assistant engineer, and twice re-elected, after having been successively foreman, treasurer and secretary of his company. He served six years as engineer and then re-entered his old company as a private. Altogether, he did twenty-four years' active duty in the Department, making an unusually good record. On October 11, 1849, at a large fire at Nos. 67 and 69 Forsyth Street, Assistant Engineer Eichell fell off a shed and was stumbled over by several firemen, who, in the dark, mistook him for a log, as he lay for some time unconscious. On picking him up, his head was found to be badly cut, and his knees severely injured, one of his knee pans being knocked out of place. He was disabled from fire duty for some time.

FRANCIS HAGADORN.

FRANCIS HAGADORN was born in New York city on January 1, 1820. He joined the Volunteers in November, 1843, becoming a member of Hose Company No. 8, which he left to reorganize Hose Company No. 10. In the latter company (where he finished his term of service) he was successively private, assistant foreman and foreman, after which he served as fire warden under the law for four years. For twenty-six years he was surveyor of the Columbia Insurance Company of New York, and is still engaged successfully in the insurance business. He has been re-elected annually since January, 1854. Mr. Hagadorn has served as the financial secretary of the Exempt Firemen's Association from 1854 to the present time— a term of thirty-three years. In addition, he has filled other offices of trust and honor, outside as well as inside the Department. To-day he refers with great satisfaction to the enjoyment (notwithstanding that the enjoyments were sandwiched in with the necessary hardships and deprivations of a Volunteer Fireman) of his term of service. He says that if he had his life to live over again and under like circumstances he would most assuredly be in the active ranks, as he was never happier than with his old associates and comrades in the discharge of their gratuitous and humane duty. His term of service commenced under Chief Anderson and closed under Chief Carson, both of whose funerals he attended. He speaks of the dead with the highest respect.

WILLIAM L. JENKINS, president of the Bank of America, became enamored of the fireman's life at an early age. He was enrolled in 1827 in Engine Company No. 13, then known as the "Eagle Company." Of the members of that period Mr. Jenkins believes that he is the only survivor. In 1833 he joined the Supply Engine, stationed in the Corporation Yard, which is the site of the Tombs Prison, and with the abandoning of the Supply he left the Department.

"The Volunteers, as a whole," says Mr. Jenkins, "were a fine set of fellows, spirited, manly, and self-sacrificing. I enjoyed the life hugely, but looking back from this age, nigh on eighty years, I cannot see where the fun came in; still the fun and excitement contributed not a little to keep very many in the ranks. When I remember that after returning from a fire, fatigued and wet, another call to duty had to be responded to within a brief interval, I cannot comprehend how it was so many survived the strain."

Mr. Jenkins was born in the Fourth Ward, and has been connected with the Bank of America, of which he is president, for the past forty years. Notwithstanding his great age he is wonderfully active, both mentally and physically.

Mr. ABRAHAM B. PURDY is one of the oldest firemen living. He was born in 1808 at Kensico, Westchester County. He came to New York in 1815. His father was a member of a regiment raised in Westchester County in 1812, and which was stationed in Brooklyn. Young Purdy learned the baking trade in the establishment of Joseph Van Varick, of 19 William Street. Van Varick was a fireman, and his apprentice wanted to be the same. Purdy joined Engine Company No. 11, then stationed in Old Slip, in 1825, but did not get his certificate until the following year. He remained in the service until the disbandment of the Volunteers. Mr. Purdy was elected foreman in 1828, and held that position until 1835. Purdy wanted to resign the foremanship before the year ended, as he saw there was a strong party in the company in favor of making his assistant, Robert Walker, foreman. Walker was eventually elected, and on his speedy resignation Mr. Purdy was again made foreman. In 1835 he had the engine removed from Old Slip to Wooster Street, near the barracks, next the station house. He remained there until he was made assistant engineer in 1836. After his term of service in 1839, Mr. Purdy went back to No. 11 as foreman again. In later years he served in the company as a private.

Mr. Purdy was a man of strong frame, and owing to his temperate habits is still hale and hearty. He is full of reminiscences. " I was in the '35 fire," said he to the writer, " although our engine was not, because we had been to a fire the night before. She froze up coming home, for it was a bitterly cold night, and she could not be thawed out, notwithstanding that we kept a fire in the engine house all day long. At the great fire our men helped other companies. I remained on the scene all night and the greater part of the next day. I was also present at the big '45 fire. At the burning of the Lorillard tobacco factory in Wooster Street, between Broome and Grand Streets, I was instrumental in checking the progress of the flames. No. 19 Hose was in the building, and, being notified of their danger, would not come out. I saved myself by jumping from a ladder." Of Mr. Uzziah Wenman, who was chief in his time, and was removed from that position on petition of the firemen, Mr. Purdy said: "At a fire you never knew where to find Mr. Wenman, because he was always working up somewhere out of our reach. He was so full of energy, dash, and courage he could not confine himself to a post in the street, where a chief should always be. When our company was down town our rivals were Nos. 4, 5, 9, 13, and 39. About 1835 No. 13 got a new engine and had it handsomely painted and everything about it in first-class condition. They declared that the first company that washed them its foreman should have a new suit of clothes. Well, at the Colgate fire in Dutch Street, near Fulton Street, we got the suction. No. 1 came from Duane Street and took our water, and the line was formed with No. 40 in it. No. 1 was the old 'Mosquito' float, and No. 40 belonged in the 'Holy Alliance.' Both companies had all the men they wanted. We worked away and got them right up to the rabbets, when they would stop. I went to Anderson and told him they

had better either work away or take all the water out of their boxes. If they would only work, we would wash them inside of five minutes. Anderson said to them, 'If you don't work I will wash you right away from the engine.' Finally No. 1 was ordered out of the line, and No. 13 was sent to take her place. I went back into the line. If I had one I had twenty men ready to hold the pipe. I said 'No' to them all. I had one of the best men to hold the butt—Cornelius Keef. I said to them: 'The first man who attempts to take it out I will knock him down.' There were lots of friends standing around waiting to help us. I told my assistant not to let a man work longer than ten or fifteen seconds. We had the old-fashioned goose-necked engine—our stroke was from one

ABRAHAM B. PURDY.

hundred and thirty to one hundred and fifty a minute. Many men would want to stay longer to show their powers. In less than five minutes we had No. 13 boiling over, and our suit of clothes was won. Then we let up. David T. Williams, afterward alderman of the Fourth Ward, was foreman of No. 13. When he saw that he was beaten he went into Fulton Market to hide his tears. That was the kind of enthusiastic men there were in those days.

"But our own engine also got washed once. It was at the time of the split in No. 11 Company. There was a fire near Maiden Lane, and we had not a dozen of our men left. No. 5 washed us. When I got to the engine I found my assistant foreman, William H. Baird, on top, shouting he would bet one hundred dollars they could not wash the engine again. Mr. Hoffmire ordered him down. Baird refused and was dismissed. I saw that every one was disheartened. I went to work, planked up so as to make it easier for the men, got help, and said, 'If you will go to work, boys, we can take all the water they can give us.' And so we did, although we were at it for three-quarters of an hour.

"While I was foreman of No. 11 I always managed to get the suction. I would often take the engine apart to make sure that everything was in good condition. I had made more experiments than any other fireman on engines. I even went so far as to have a large pair of cylinders put in, but I had to take them out and put the small regulation ones in, as the law required. Our engine house was a kind of primitive place. Our seats were the lockers in which the wood was stored. When the boys wanted a 'spree' they would go to a hotel, generally the old Shakespeare in Fulton Street. When I first joined we used to go to Burr's place in Washington Market, not that I ever took anything stronger than a cigar, which may account for the good health I enjoy to-day. Other rendezvous were Conklin Titus's, Dutch and Ann Streets, and Harry Ludlam's. (Harry was the machinist in the corporation yard.) Ours was the first company that ever turned out in fire dress on State occasions. That was in 1830 on the occasion of the celebration of the French Revolution. We all appeared in neat kersey suits.

"The first company that ever had a horse to run was Hook and Ladder No. 1. The introduction of horse power was owing to a squabble in the company, which resulted in the resignation of so many members that not enough remained to draw the truck to a fire. No. 11 was the means of killing that horse. There was a fire up in Broadway, and we and Hook and Ladder No. 1 ran side by side. Going up the hill at Canal Street was the proudest moment of my life. We beat the horse, and No. 1 did not get to the fire till some time after us. We winded the horse, which was no good after that. I recollect, by the way, that at that time Canal Street had numerous lumber yards. There was a horse market in Sullivan Street between Grand and Broome Streets—all open lots. There were lots of fun to be had with the old nags up for sale. How well, too, I recollect the playing matches at Cold Spring Garden! The first was between Nos. 27 and 36. Each had fifty feet of hose and worked five minutes, at the expiration of which that engine which was found to have the most water lost the match. The first time No. 27 won. It was asserted that No. 36 had a secret valve for letting out the water, but the boys would make any excuse to avoid the disgrace of being washed. The match was played over again with picked men. I worked with No. 36, and we won. The son of Seth Gear, the builder, was foreman of No. 36. The old man came along, looked at the fun and said, 'I will bet one thousand dollars to one hundred dollars that 36 wins.' There were no takers. The next contest was between Nos. 30 and 37, when No. 37 won. Going to the second burning of the Bowery Theater we got ahead of all the others at Chrystie Street. Having to come up from Old Slip we never knew where the fire was till we got to the City Hall, where the 'pointer' was.

"Some of the well known firemen of my time were J. D. Bedell, foreman of No. 4, a fine business man, afterwards assistant alderman of the Eighth Ward; Samuel J. Willis, foreman of No. 5, alderman of the Seventh Ward in 1838 and 1839; Robert Thompson, his assistant; Joseph Crossthwaite, foreman of No. 21; Peter McNamara, foreman of No. 22; Dwight B. Palmer, foreman of No. 41; John Goodwin (the butcher), foreman of No. 40; Bill Snell, foreman of No. 39; William Rhodes, foreman of No. 30; Jacob Brush, foreman of No. 29; James K. Rowe, foreman of No. 28; Ezeriah W. Ross (the builder), foreman of No. 27; Randolph Lowrey, his assistant; John Murphy, foreman of

No. 26, and John Cox, his assistant; Abraham Rich, foreman of No. 20, and David Beck, foreman of No. 19. Jim Bevans, also a foreman of No. 21, was a noted fighter and a betting man; he fought and beat 'Sandy' Graham, of No. 40, on the 'Island,' as we used to call Brooklyn. Bevans was at the time a runner with No. 11, and had he been beaten he would have run no more with us. We used to call a runner 'panfish.' Then, there was the Brennan family —Matt., Owen and Tim, the last two belonging to us. Matt. could run with his lame leg in a surprisingly swift manner. No. 30 used to have a lot of butchers. Among its members were John and Chris. Thiel or Theall, who were noted for their strength and fighting qualities. The boys then would take a civil knock-down and forget all about it afterwards. Abel K. Woolsey, of No. 15, was also noted for his strength, and Rawlinson M. Smith, a sailmaker, of the same company. Other names that recur to me are those of Manus Kelly, 'Johnny Ketchy,' and Seth Douglas. The last died a short time ago; his father was foreman of No. 27.

"Through my life I never had a week's sickness. I used to find the career of a fireman very hard. Up at a fire all night, I used almost to fall asleep at the bench during the day, and would swear that I would never go to a fire again. But in the evening when I made myself spruce I felt equal to anything that might happen. The life was especially hard for one who did his whole duty. The drones were soon weeded out of a company."

Anthony Yeoman joined Warren Hose Company, No. 33, December 7, 1852, located in Sullivan Street, Eighth Ward. Mr. Yeoman was a thoroughly active fireman. No. 33 was doing duty in the Third, Fourth, and Eighth Districts. He was elected assistant foreman, and afterwards foreman. Subsequently he retired from office, and resumed the more congenial, active duties of a "high private," and as such he remained with the company until the final disbandment of the Department, having served as a working member in one company with unflagging interest for thirteen years. He is one of the trustees of the Fire Department Fund, and is serving his twelfth year in that honorable and trustworthy position. That he has been for thirty-three years a trusted official in the New York Post-Office is a signal proof of Mr. Yeoman's capacity and faithfulness in public as well as private life.

VOLUNTEER DEPARTMENT EMBLEMS.

CHAPTER XXVI.

FIREMEN WHOSE DEEDS WILL LIVE AFTER THEM.

Adam W. Spies: One of the most Successful Merchants in the City.—Adolphus Borst: Has Signally
Served His Country.—James F. Wenman: First Used a Trumpet when a Child.—David Scannel:
Soldier and Public Officer.—Timothy Sullivan: Early Loved Fire.—John B. Miller: An Efficient
Assistant Engineer.—John K. Costigan: A Gallant Veteran.—Henry Wilson: His Generosity and
Self-sacrifice.

ADAM W. SPIES, one of the oldest New York firemen now living, is
eighty-six years old. He is one of the most successful merchants of
the city. He was a member of Engine Company No. 5, and was
made a fire warden. He and Thurlow Weed studied grammar together in
1817. Mr. Spies was born in the Second Ward, near Peck Slip, on September 4, 1800.

He is still quite vigorous in mind and body, and has lost none of his interest
in fire affairs. Quite recently he surprised the members of the volunteers by
entering their rooms in Eighth Street and hailing those present in a cheery,
hearty tone. After a pleasant chat, he went the rounds of the rooms and
curiously inspected the many interesting fire relics on the walls. He makes it
a point to drop in regularly to see "the boys."

The following interesting reminiscences of New York have been given by
Mr. Spies to the writer:

"I was born on the spot of ground now occupied by Clinton Hall, the
southwest corner of Beekman and Nassau Streets. At the time the place was
occupied by twelve little wooden stores and houses, and considered then pretty
nearly out of town. The City Hall was then at the head of Broad Street, where
George Washington was inaugurated. The new City Hall was not then
begun. Chambers Street was then the extreme limit of the graded streets,
west of Broadway. Division Street was the extreme limit of civilization on the
other side. I was sent to a madame's school in Ann Street in 1806, afterwards to S. Ely's and John Coffin's, in Nassau Street in the rear of the old Dutch
Church on Maiden Lane. In 1810 my grandfather, Adam Bergh (the present
Henry Bergh is a sort of second cousin of mine), and J. J. Astor, and many of
the old German residents, attended this church. German was regularly
preached there in the morning and the afternoon of every Sunday. Wall Street
was the great business street. Oswego Market then stood in Maiden Lane,
running down from Broadway about two hundred and fifty feet, and surrounded
by retail stores. At the foot of Maiden Lane was the Fly Market, reaching
from Pearl Street to the river to the ferry stairs. The sailboats to Brooklyn
used to start from this point. How the hundreds of thousands of travelers of
to-day by the big bridge and the capacious steamboats would smile could they

have seen the ferry of my childhood's days! Nothing larger than a yawl boat was then used. Only one horse at a time was carried over, after having been taken out of the gig or wagon, and all tumbled into the boat together, passengers and baggage. But horses rarely crossed the river. Horseboats or steamboats were not known in my early days. Soon, however, horseboats came into use, and an astonishing improvement they were. These boats continued for many years till displaced by steamboats.

"In my boyhood the Bear Market stretched along Greenwich Street from Vesey to Fulton Street. The Fish Market stood in Vesey Street, reaching from Greenwich to where Washington Street now is, the end facing the water, there not being any streets further west. Both these markets have disappeared, and a new market built where then was water. This is Washington Market.

"About 1812, or during the war, Market Street on the east side was called George Street, after the King of England. It was a great place for loose women. The street was afterwards bought by a Quaker, and made respectable. The unfortunate women were driven up to Corlear's Hook, the chief residents of which locality were sailors and girls of the town. The place was called simply the 'Hook,' and was away out of town. It was a broad, open, unsettled space, dangerous for decent people to pass through. At the foot of Catharine Street was located the only other ferry (besides the ferry from Maiden Lane) to Brooklyn. The ship yards began here, and the docks ceased. Division Street terminated among the hills of Rutgers Farm, as did also Harmon Street, now called East Broadway, leading to Corlear's Hook.

ADAM W. SPIES.

From Grand Street to the foot of Thirteenth Street was a salt meadow, considered then entirely worthless. It was a mere quagmire and useless for any purpose.

"About this time (1812) the City Hall in the park was finished. The Wigwam in Little George Street, kept by Martling, was removed to Frankfort Street, and became Tammany Hall. When I was a boy there was quite a number of houses of this description about Wall and Pearl Streets. Many of them were built of small yellow imported brick. The sides of the fireplaces were faced with small China tiles, five or six inches square, with sculptured subjects on them, painted in blue.

"In 1810 there were many citizens still wearing knee breeches, shoe buckles, and cocked hats. I was now a scholar of John Coffin at his school in Frankfort Street, in the rear of Tammany Hall. John and all his boys were Republicans, at that time the Democrats of to-day. On the Fourth of July we were conspicuous by wearing bucktails stuck in the front of our hats. The Fourth was then a great day. Our coppers were saved for at least two months ahead, and all our friends were levied upon for funds to buy powder and fire crackers. It was a grand sight to see four or five regiments, all with tall felt chapeaus, decorated with long stiff cocktail feathers, yellow leather breeches, and bobtail coats, marching through the streets, preceded by black musicians. The instruments were principally bass drums, French horns, and cornets—heart-scalding music, but which to us was divine. The musicians were almost all French West Indian negroes, and by profession barbers. By the way, at this time nearly all the hod carriers in the city were West India negroes. After the military came the Tammany Society, preceded by a band of yellow-stained men, fantastically dressed as Indians. Then came a great car with a tall temple, upon which was a throne, and sitting on the dais an elegant female appropriately dressed, representing the Goddess of Liberty. The streets being rough and badly paved, it required all the skill of the Goddess of Liberty to keep her seat on her trembling, tottering throne. Strong ropes, attached to flagstaffs on either side, prevented the affair from falling. Then came the big wigs, the professions, mounted ships, the firemen, and various societies. The fear of old Hayes and Sam Hazzard, who kept the Bridewell in the park, made the boys behave themselves. Thousands of flags hung from every conspicuous point.

"The Battery, Bowling Green, and Park were filled with booths, and there were sold principally liquors, hams, oysters in every style, pickled lobsters, mussels, pickled clams, roast pig, spruce beer, lemonade, and so on. It used to be a glorious holiday, and no one was found at home.

"At three o'clock in the morning we young fellows were aroused by a bell in the street, and by four we were off. Horse pistols were mounted on blocks, and when the pistols were exploded, the whole concern was kicked over and over again. By six A. M. we became hungry, and breakfasted at the booths at the Battery off pickled lobsters and spruce beer. By ten or eleven we were ready for dinner, when we dined off pig, oysters, pie, or fish, spruce beer, and cherries. An alarm of fire would take us away from everything else. At five or six o'clock we would return home, thoroughly used up.

"From 1812 to 1815 almost all the merchants lived over their stores. Pearl Street was mostly composed of dwelling houses. Greenwich Street and the lower end of Broadway and State Street held the residences of the "aristocracy." The churches were in Garden Street (now Exchange Place), Wall Street, and on the corner of Liberty Street. With the exception of St. John's, and the negro church in Church Street, corner of Anthony, there was not a church to the north of St. Paul's.

"The war of 1812 checked the growth of the city. The citizens that were drafted were drilled every morning in the park or in the forts newly built. All the New York boys were well drilled as soldiers. Hundreds of boys and mechanics turned privateers and returned home with three hundred dollars as their share of the prize money. I remember the detachments of country militia who used to pass through the city into the encampments on Long Island and Staten Island. A long line of fortifications was built by the citizens, stretching across the island at Bloomingdale, commanding the approach to the city from the north. The heights of Brooklyn were fortified in the same manner. From Fort Greene to Gowanus Bay, for two miles, there were block houses and batteries. The work was performed by the trades, the professions, and citizens generally, foremost among whom were the fire companies. Day after day lawyers, merchants, and others would assemble in the park, and, with flags flying and music and plenty of good cheer furnished by themselves, would march to Fort Greene or other forts, and would handle the pick and shovel like common laborers. There were to be seen digging, carpenters, tailors, shoemakers, blacksmiths, the association of clerks, clergymen, actors, doctors, indeed all the trades and professions under their special banners. They all did this without pay, and they fed themselves.

"I joined Engine Company No. 5 on October 16, 1818, located in Fulton Street (then Fair Street), near Dutch Street. I had been running with the machine for some time. Foster Nostrand was the foreman, and Samuel J. Willis the assistant. Willis afterward became chief engineer. Robert Thompson was the second assistant and secretary. All our members were first-class merchants and well to do. Thompson was a hardware merchant; Bob Glender a fruit dealer; Thomas B. ('Buck') Goelet was a brother of the rich Peter Goelet; Peter Vroom was the son of a bank president; there were also 'Buck' Gardiner, Sam Winterton, William Burger (afterwards a druggist), now living and whose age is eighty-nine; Wm. H. Smith (a partner of Henry Young & Co., hardware and military supplies), who died worth five millions of money. Other members of the company were R. Dunn, hatter; Hugh Taylor, a first-class fireman; Henry Lawrence, merchant; Thomas Vanderpoel; John Hyatt, jeweler; James Whitlock, merchant; Blaze Moore (his father was one of the best known chandler merchants); Isaac N. Townsend, merchant; James Bissett, Francis Hall, son of an editor, subsequently an editor himself; George Went, Robert Bage, hatter; and Richard Demill, merchant.

"Not one of these men has ever done anything to disgrace himself. Most of them were rich, and some of them very rich. For thirty years No. 5 maintained her position as a most respectable company. It was the crack company for duty and honor. We ran all over the city, but rarely had to go above Canal Street or Stone Bridge. Canal Street had not one house in it in 1819. We took our water from cisterns, pumps, or plugs. Our boys were so well posted that they could find any fire-plug, no matter how deeply it might be covered with mud or snow, in any part of the city. We kept memoranda books in which good cisterns and plugs were carefully and privately noted.

"Fires were not so frequent then, even comparatively, as they are now, but still our work was very hard, because we had no Croton. Ten companies would sometimes form one line, and thus carry the water from a distance. The stream was kept up by constant work at the brakes, we all the time standing in water. After which we had to take up, clean up, and slush our own hose. I took her out as often as any one, and consequently held the pipe oftener. The bell on the old jail was the fire signal. How well I remember its tones! How familiar they were! I resigned September 8, 1823, to go to England and travel in Europe as the agent of my firm. A peculiar thing happened to me in Liege, Belgium, in 1829. The voice of that bell on the old jail I knew as well as my mother's. Well, one night I was suddenly aroused from a deep slumber by the ringing of a church bell in Liege that had exactly the same tone as our old fire bell. I thought I was summoned to a fire in New York.

The incident recalled pleasant memories of home. In 1831 I returned to this city and rejoined my company. I was made a fire warden and served until 1836.

"I remember the Crane Wharf fire (1820), which was where the Fulton Market now stands. I took out the machine and held the pipe that night. I was knocked off a ladder. It was bitterly cold, and my clothes were frozen to my back, so that I had to go home to thaw out. The North River was frozen over for a week, and we could walk to Jersey City. The mails were carried over the ice in sleighs. I sleighed from New York to Albany.

"About the year 1821, at a big fire in Brooklyn, which burned seven hundred bales of cotton and many barrels of tar, No. 5 Engine crossed the river on a horseboat. My feet became almost as big as my head while I was walking through the melted tar. Clots of burning tar floated out of the docks. Brooklyn then had a population of about six hundred, and on Brooklyn Heights snug little farms hung over the river.

"I remember buying a hunting horn, which we used when at the drag-rope on the way to a fire to call the boys to the engine. As soon as they heard it they knew the machine had left the house, and they crossed lots and ran over to us, thus saving a useless expenditure of time in going to the engine house when the engine had already been taken out. A fire used to be like a battle to us. It aroused our spirits and made us eager to confront it. The deeper the mud and snow, the more we enjoyed it. My experience hasn't hurt me a bit.

"Did we ever have any fighting? Oh, no; there was nothing of that kind in our days, although we were all able to down our man. The only trouble the members of our company got into had more of a humorous than a serious side to it. Late one night I and ten or eleven of the company were returning home. We had been dining with our foreman, who lived up the Bowery. We were walking two and two on the sidewalk, and the foremost couple enlivened the march by singing. A watchman stopped us and raised his club to strike one of the men. Another man grasped it to prevent trouble. Then the watchman insisted upon taking us all to the station, and, like good citizens, we went. We all thought we had sufficient influence to get off. But what was our surprise to hear the policeman charging us all with conspiracy! A rough, crabbed, one-legged captain would listen to no explanation, and we were locked up. Imagine our chagrin. For the first time we found ourselves behind prison bars. Next morning we were taken to the City Hall and fined thirteen shillings and sixpence each. We were afraid to demur or demand a fair trial lest the affair should get into the papers.

"At this time (1832) Pearl Street was the great store center, the buildings renting at from three to six thousand dollars a year. Fortunes were rapidly made. The heavy dry goods importers were in Pine Street. The domestic commission houses were few and their sales moderate. The principal shoe and hat houses were in Water Street, and the grocers in Water and Front Streets up to 1840. Cortlandt Street, Dey, Fulton, Barclay, and Reade Streets were almost without an exception filled with dwelling houses. A steam engine or manufactory was unknown in any of the above-named streets. No country merchant would venture to buy his dry goods of any but a Pearl Street jobber. Nearly every bank was in Wall Street. Liberty Street was then all dwellings from Broadway to William Street. The old sugar house was then standing where once was a British prison, while the New York Dutch Church adjoining was once used as a riding school for the British cavalry. The Fulton Street Church was called the North Church, the Garden Street the South Dutch Church, and Liberty Street Church was called the New Model Dutch Church.

"Looking back, I have witnessed the introduction of the steam engine, steamboats, railroads, the wonderful telegraph on land and across the sea, the daguerreotype, photography, galvanism, electricity, the increase of cotton from one bale to six millions. It was in 1820 that coal was discovered in Pennsylvania. I took a specimen of it to England as a curiosity, and they did not know how to burn it. The first line of packets to Liverpool consisted of sailing vessels of only three hundred and fifty tons. Orders to merchants had to be sent six or nine months ahead to procure the goods in time for the spring or fall sales. Merchandise could not be sent into the interior after the close of navigation, from the ice. Hence New York was without much country trade from December to May, there being no railroads. We were about a month in getting an answer from New Orleans.

ADOLPHUS BORST.
["Bill Post."]

"When I was a boy muslin shirts were unknown, and coarse linens cost thirty or forty cents a yard. Better cotton has been sold for eight cents a yard, and savages can now be supplied with elegant printed cloths at from four to six cents a yard. I went out of business in 1865."

Mr. Spies had two children, and of his eight grandchildren one is dead.

FRANK PRINCE, of the old firm of Prince & Moon, ship painters in Lewis Street, near the old Mechanics' Bell, for nearly half a century, was a tall broad-shouldered, handsome man of light complexion, and as brave a fireman as ever carried a trumpet. He joined No. 32 Engine Company in June, 1849, and became foreman at the death of Jacob Cobanks in August, 1850, serving in that position until 1852. His name was a household word along the river front, when shipbuilding was at its zenith. While Prince was foreman of No. 32, Wm. M. Tweed was elected foreman of "Big Six," then lying in Gouverneur Street. Prince left 32 in October, 1853, and the same day joined No. 26 Hose. He served ten years as a member of Nos. 32 and 26, and thirty years as a volunteer. He was a warm friend of Dave Broderick. Asa Bogart and "Jim" Cooper, ex-foremen, did duty under Prince, as did John Nixon, who led a charge at Roanoke Island. Ben Wilt, a baker, succeeded Prince as foreman of No. 32.

ADOLPHUS BORST, better known to the "old timers" as "Bill Post," because of the variety of peculiar employments in which he has been engaged, is perhaps as reminiscent of the old days of the Volunteer Department as any one who belonged to it. He was born in the city of Strasburg, France, in

1820, and was brought to America by his parents when he was seven months old. His father's brother was chief of the Strasburg Fire Department for thirty years, and his maternal uncle, Charles Kullmann, constructed the famous clock of the Strasburg Cathedral. Borst began his fire duty in 1835 as a volunteer of 12 Engine, which then lay in Rose Street, and in the fall of 1841 regularly joined that company, then known as Knickerbocker Engine No. 12, having its quarters in William Street near Pearl Street. The engine, excepting the brass work, which the boys delighted in keeping highly polished, was painted green, giving it a rather unique appearance, and was built by James Smith, of West Broadway and Anthony Street.

Borst went to France with his father in 1842, and returning in a few months joined 14 Engine, in which he retained his membership until the disbandment of the Volunteer organization. In 1839 he was appointed special officer of the Old Bowery Theatre, and has many "yarns to spin" regarding the scenes and incidents which form part of the history of that noted place of amusement. This position he occupied until the building of the New Bowery in 1861, which he served in a similar capacity until it was destroyed by fire in 1866. But during this period—from 1839 to 1866—he was engaged in many other employments, which oftentimes required him to put a substitute (in most instances his younger brother) in his stead at the theatre for extended periods. In January, 1859, he was appointed a policeman, but resigned when the Metropolitan Force came in, having served only about a month. During the late war he was special agent of the War Department, and also Deputy U. S. Marshal under Marshal Robert Murray. Early in 1861 Borst captured, in New York City, Confederate bank note plates and with them over three hundred million dollars in Confederate notes of various denominations. The plates were destroyed, and a good sized bonfire was made of the notes in the yard of the U. S. Marshal's office. Shortly after this he arrested United States Senator Soulé, of Louisiana, and had him imprisoned in Fort Lafayette for treason. From the corps of agents of the War Department, Borst was selected by Secretary Stanton for an important and hazardous mission, which may best be told in his own words :

"I suppose it all came about," said old " Bill Post," "because I spoke both French and German—one about as well as the other—and both as well as an old rounder like me could be expected to do it. Besides, my life in the Bowery might have had something to do with having me selected for the job. To tell the truth, I didn't like the job for I saw that there was a chance at every turn of being tripped up, and once tripped—well, I wouldn't be chatting with you now. In some way—of course I don't know how—Secretary Seward got a commission for me from the Prussian Government. It bore my proper name, and I was actually working for the Prussian Government. Just now it occurs to me, however, that I never got any pay from Prussia all the same. Uncle Sam paid me and footed my bills. I was commissioned to visit all the Confederate prisons, and as far as possible look after the welfare of the subjects of Prussia, but, of course, that was only a blind. Our people at the North wanted to know how the Union prisoners were treated by the Confederates. I entered the Confederate lines at Fort Monroe—everything regular, you know, as an agent of Prussia—and, as carefully as I knew how, inspected every military prison in the South. I wasn't breaking my heart about the subjects of Prussia, although my papers came from their government. I got along remarkably well until I struck Andersonville. One day I went in there with a Colonel Lefevre of South Carolina, who at that time, I believe, was in full charge of the prison. I wasn't five minutes in the stockade until some of the old boys got on to me, and began shouting as well as they could, ' Hey, Posty, got you, have they? You'll have a jolly time, old man.' I couldn't, you know, recognize one of them. It would have been all up with me if my rôle had been discovered. Did I want to speak to them? You bet your sweet life I did. Of course my report was a verbal one. I remember well when it was given in. Seward and Stanton sat together and heard it all. I began at the beginning, and gave it all to them in my own way. They listened. Finally, when it came to the toughest part—Andersonville—old Seward got up quite excited and put his fist on the table we sat at, mad as a hornet. He hadn't

BORST RECOGNIZED BY PRISONERS   STANTON SAID:
IN ANDERSONVILLE.   " WE MUST RETALIATE."

got seated until Stanton was on his feet, and pounding the table (I'll always remember those words), shouted, ' We must—we MUST—retaliate !' Seward jumped up, and said, ' *No*, NO, NO '—just like a fire alarm bell—' we mustn't let it go out to the world ! It would never do.' Now I'll just say this, although I'm not much on history, that was a big scene in the big affairs of a big country."

JAMES F. WENMAN comes of a good old fire stock, and can be said to have been born a fireman, his father, Uzziah Wenman, being at the time of his birth (March 7, 1824) an assistant engineer, and living at that time in Fulton Street, just below Church. Mr. Wenman received his first ideas of the Fire Department in the house of Franklin Engine Company 39 (his father's old company), then located on the corner of Vesey and Church Streets, where his old colored nurse took him nearly every day. He says his *earliest* recollection of the Department is being seated on the front box of the engine with a firecap on, and the members telling him how to give orders through the trumpet. At the fire of 1835, although but eleven years old, he and his brother Thomas Franklin (two years his senior) went down at the early stage of the fire, and remained all night. One of 39's members, Samuel Maverick, found them almost frozen, and wrapping them up in blankets (of which there were an abundance lying around) placed them in the doorway of a house in Pearl Street, below Wall. They put in an appearance at their home (66 Elm Street) at seven o'clock the next morning, to the relief of their family, and were great heroes with their brothers and sisters. On the return of their father, who had remained three days at the fire, their glory departed for the time being, for, when he heard of the youngsters' night off, there was a "fire in the rear" of which they did not say much.

At the age of fourteen he commenced doing "active duty" (as he called it) with Victory Hose Company 15, then located in Cortlandt Alley, near Canal Street.

JAMES F. WENMAN.

On the organization of American Hose Company 19, they occupied Hose 15's quarters. Mr. Wenman attached himself to that company in 1841, where he served five years, then joined Engine 38, but served there but a short time. His father moving to Sixteenth Street and Eighth Avenue, he joined Hose Company 35, serving there three years, when he joined New York Hose Company 5—March 5, 1849. In October of the same year he was elected secretary and representative, and on September 4, 1850, assistant foreman and representative, and on December 2 of the same year was made foreman, and re-elected for six consecutive years. He resigned in May, 1856, having been elected an assistant engineer. On his retirement from his old company they presented him with a handsomely engrossed copy of complimentary resolutions and an elegant silver trumpet, on which were engraved a fac-simile of their hose carriage and their headquarters, Firemen's Hall. In 1853 he was elected Secretary of the Board of Engineers and Foremen, and was one of the committee appointed to build the "New Firemen's Hall." He held the position of secretary until his election as assistant engineer. On his retiring from the Engineer Board, in 1859, they presented him with a copy of complimentary resolutions, suitably engrossed (the first and only ones ever presented by the Board of Engineers to a retiring member).

At the Jennings fire in 1854 Mr. Wenman was foreman of Hose 5. In regard to that fire Mr. Wenman says, if he had had his trumpet with him, he might have saved the lives of some who were crushed by the second falling of the floors, as from his position, in the rear of the adjoining building, he saw the beams giving way, and called out to "back out quick." His brother

Uzziah Wilson recognized the voice, and jumped out into the rear, escaping with a slight bruise.

At the Kipp & Brown fire in May, 1848, there was a report that a sick man had been left in a small shanty back in an alley. Mr. Wenman and brother made their way in, just in time to seize the sheet on either end and bring the man out, more dead than alive.

Mr. Wenman became a member of the "Firemen's Ball Committee" in 1849 (when C. V. Anderson was its president), and is now its president, having been unanimously elected to that position for twenty-two consecutive years. He was also elected to the position of Treasurer of the Exempt Firemen's Benevolent Fund on the death of John S. Giles. On the organization of the "Veteran Firemen's Association" he was selected as their treasurer, and a few of his friends had a full length portrait of him painted in oil by the celebrated artist Mr. Joseph H. Johnson, and presented it to the association.

In 1876 Mayor Wickham appointed Mr. Wenman a park commissioner. He was elected president of the Board, and retained the position during his term of office. He always took a great pleasure in furthering the interests of the two museums in Central Park— the "Metropolitan Museum of Art" and "Museum of Natural History." On his retirement from the Board the trustees of the Metropolitan Museum of Art unanimously elected him an "Honorary Fellow for Life," a distinction very seldom bestowed.

DAVID SCANNEL, the present famous chief of the San Francisco Fire Department, earned his first laurels in that nursery of gallant men, the Old Volunteer Fire Department of New York.

DAVID SCANNEL.

Born in this city in 1820 he ran with the engines as a lad and early enrolled in Engine Company No. 5, lying in Fulton Street, of whose men it is related that on an alarm of fire they used to throw their boots out of the bunk room window and be downstairs as soon as the boots were. He soon earned a pre-eminent reputation as a man of absolutely reckless courage, ever foremost when any hazardous feat was to be undertaken.

On the call for troops for the invasion of Mexico in 1846 he was among the first to spring to arms. He offered his services to Colonel Ward B. Burnett, who had the honor of raising the first regiment of New York Volunteers, and was immediately gazetted second lieutenant. Such was his reputation as a gallant man that unaided he succeeded in a few days in recruiting his company to its full strength. Under General Scott he participated in the whole series of brilliant engagements that marked the advance of the American army on the City of Mexico, and was one of the first to enter the captured capital, the division, under General Quitman, to which he was attached, forming the advance of the army. Immediately after the capture of the city Lieutenant Scannel was promoted to the rank of captain. On the disbandment of the forces at the close of the war he was mustered out of the service and returned to New York. The greater part of the two ensuing years he spent in the South, returning to New York in 1850. The gold fever was then at its height, and Scannel's adventurous spirit prompted him to seek his fortune in the new El Dorado. He landed in San Francisco in March, 1851, and promptly joined Empire Company No. 1, whose house stood at Clay and Dupont Streets. In a few months he was elected assistant foreman and then foreman. His splendid services were rewarded in 1860 with the post of chief of the Department, to which he was re-elected in 1863 without opposition. On the organization of the paid Department in 1866 he was succeeded by Frank E. R. Whitney.

In 1871 he was again called to the post of honor, but retired for eight months in 1873, at the expiration of which time he resumed the command which he has

TIMOTHY SULLIVAN.

held with infinite credit ever since. In 1853 Mr. Scannel held an important office under Major Hammond, the collector of the port, and in the following year served as under-sheriff. In 1855 he was elected sheriff, a post in which he gained much honor during the terrible days of the vigilance committee.

Superb as was his record as a soldier and as a public officer it is as a brave and skillful fireman that his reputation is imperishable.

To his thorough administrative qualities, no less than his brilliant example as an intrepid leader, is due the present high efficiency of the Fire Department of San Francisco. His absolute contempt of personal danger has been marvellous. An arm thrice broken, two broken ribs, and a fractured collar-bone, to say nothing of minor injuries innumerable, attest the recklessness with which he has exposed himself in the public service. Fully a score of times, while urging his horse at full speed to the scene of some conflagration, he has been hurled from his wagon and seriously injured.

Age has dealt kindly with the veteran chief, whose erect, stalwart frame, showing unfailing vigor in every movement, give him the air of a man scarce fifty. His face is a kindly one graced by carefully waxed moustache and imperial that shade a mouth showing in every line indomitable determination. In manner he is genial and courteous. During the many years in which he has directed the affairs of the San Francisco Fire Department he has fairly earned the affection and confidence of his fellow-citizens due to the unceasing fidelity with which he has administered the duties of a position of unrivalled responsibility. There is in San Francisco to-day no more trusted official than the gallant soldier and fireman " Dave " Scannel.

TIMOTHY SULLIVAN was born in the Sixth Ward, New York, in the year

1839. In 1860 he joined Peterson Engine Company No. 31, which lay at that time in Christie Street, near Canal, in the house formerly occupied by Engine Company No. 15. It was not a new business to Tim, for he had been thoroughly schooled from childhood, and had run as a Volunteer many years with Hose Companies 14 and 15 and old Peterson Engine Company 15, known as "Old Maid." Tim lived in the vicinity of the Bowery, and was well acquainted with all the old-time "Bowery Boys" and fighters of those days, as they all congregated in that neighborhood, around the old Bowery Theatre. He performed duty with the old hand engine of 31 until 1863, when, in September of that year, the company received a small steam fire engine of the "Smith" build, and he was appointed the engineer. He continued in that position until May, 1865, when he received a paralytic stroke (while proceeding to a fire in the old sixth district), from which he has never fully recovered. President J. L. Perley in 1873 made Tim a night watchman at fire headquarters.

JOHN B. MILLER, one of the assistant engineers of the Old Department, was born September 12, 1817, his parents residing at the time on the corner of Chatham and Orange Streets (now Baxter). In his younger days he ran with Jackson Engine Company No. 24 — his liking for that peculiar life very early developing itself. He was at home in any position, whether on the rope, with the pipe, at the head of his company, or assistant engineer. He was elected a member of Engine No. 32 (Bunker Hill), located in Hester Street, back of St. George's Church, in 1836, and resigned at the time of the Gulick strike, the morning after the Bowery Theatre fire, in September of the same year. He

JOHN B. MILLER.

rejoined in May, 1837, was elected foreman and served till 1841, when he was elected engineer on the ticket with Chief Engineer Cornelius V. Anderson and Engineers Zophar Mills, Wells, Wilson, John Kenyon, Alfred Carson, Wm. A. Freeborn, George H. Rampen, George Kerr, and John T. Rollins. Later he became president of the Board of Fire Underwriters. At a fire in Grand Street, near the Bowery, Mr. Miller rescued an old man (a German) from suffocation. At the great fire of 1845 he discovered a fire in a large brick storage warehouse in Stone Street. A line of hose was stretched through to the roof, and at his direction Edwin Coe, of Hose Company 9, and a most daring man, was placed in charge until water could be obtained. Finding the line all broken up on account of the explosion and no water to be had, and fearing for Coe's safety, Mr. Miller returned to the burning building, found it full of smoke, and Coe in the upper part unable to get out. Determining that Coe should not suffer alone, he crawled up the stairway through the blinding smoke, calling loudly for Coe, but received no answer. On reaching the third story he found Coe nearly suffocated, and with difficulty got him out of the building to a place of safety. Soon after this the building fell, a mass of burning ruins. In 1850 he was elected President of the Board of Fire Wardens under the new law. In 1857 Mr. Miller organized Adriatic Engine Company No. 31, and was elected foreman. In 1859 he was one of the organizers of C. V. Anderson Hook and Ladder Company No. 10, and remained with her till the disbanding of the Department in 1865, after twenty-five years of active service. For the past thirty years Mr. Miller has been surveyor of the Old Firemen's Insurance Company.

When Mr. Miller resigned the office of assistant engineer on the ninth of April, 1851, owing to business arrangements, it was determined to present him with a testimonial. On January 12, 1852, the principal firemen of the day assembled at Odd Fellows' Hall, corner of Grand and Centre Streets, and

JOHN K. COSTIGAN.

presented him with a splendid service of silver in token of their esteem for him as a man and a fireman. Then the company sat down to a banquet, Robert McGinnis, assistant engineer and formerly foreman of old Southwark Engine Company No. 38, presiding, his assistant being Daniel D. Conover, of Amity Hose Company No. 38. Mr. Miller had a brother, J. L., who also did good service in the Fire Department.

JOHN K. COSTIGAN joined Lafayette Hook and Ladder Company No. 6 in 1857 and continued a member until 1862. At the outbreak of the civil war he, with other members of the company, enlisted in Company A, Ninth Regiment, New York State militia. Mr. Costigan has been a member of the Volunteer Firemen's Association since its inception, treasurer of the New Haven delegation and secretary of the last barbecue and picnic committee, and is at present a member of the Board of Directors.

Mr. HENRY WILSON was born in New York City September 10, 1810. He began running to fires at an early age, and on arriving at manhood was captain of the very large roll of volunteers connected with Union Engine Company No. 18. He joined the company June 20, 1832, but, the volunteers declaring that they could not succeed except under his leadership, he resigned and resumed his position as their captain. He shortly afterwards rejoined the company, becoming its foreman in 1834 and continuing until 1838, when he went to the South. He returned in 1839 and was again elected foreman, serving until 1844. He also served a term with engine companies Nos. 3 and 31. In 1849 Mr. Wilson, with James Booth, Isaac T. Redfield, and others, organized Niagara Engine Company No. 4. This was at the time one of the best organizations in the city. The members were nearly all old firemen and started under the most favorable auspices. Mr. Wilson was its first foreman and served the company faithfully until it was on a fair footing, and then retired to make way for the younger men. In 1859 Mr. Wilson was elected Fire Commissioner to fill the vacancy caused by the resignation of Andrew Craft. His election was unanimous, and he gave the greatest satisfaction in the performance of the unpleasant duties connected with the office.

In 1860 Mr. Wilson declined a re-election; but the firemen, knowing his worth, refused to receive it, and by a flattering vote again elected him. Mr. Wilson greatly benefited the Department. There was no meeting at which he was not present, and no fireman who had any complaint to make went away unheard.

Mr. Wilson did not give his time to the fire business only — the soldiers who enlisted from the Department had as much of it as he could spare. His work with the two regiments bearing the name of " Fire Zouaves " was beyond praise.

The " Harrington Guard " was a volunteer organization from Union Engine Company No 18, and Henry Wilson was its captain. This volunteer company was in existence for a number of years, and one act while Mr. Wilson was in command should not go unrecorded. We allude to their noble conduct toward the first of the New York Volunteers who died after that regiment returned from the Mexican War. The late Sherman Brownell was called upon to deliver the address at the dedication of a monument placed in Greenwood by the Harrington Guard. That gallant fellow George Struthers was one of

HENRY WILSON.

the first to enroll his name in Company I of the first regiment of New York State Volunteers. With them he went to Mexico, and remained among them until disbanded. He was one of the comparatively small number of the originals of the regiment that returned, and, although he escaped the ravages of the battlefield and returned to his friends, he was, like most of his companions, prostrated with the climate and exposure. He found, by disease contracted in Mexico, that he was fast failing. He went to the hospital, where his friends gave him all the attention that could be paid him. After remaining in the hospital for some time, he was called from his sufferings on earth. His sister hastened to the hospital, and wished the body of her brother to be kept two or three days, as it was cold weather, that she might send word to her sons, who lived out of town. The sons arrived, but to their inquiries for the body of their uncle at the hospital they were informed that he was buried at Randall's Island in the Potter's Field. Struthers died on the eleventh of January, 1849. Some ten days after his death the circumstances came to the ear of the

Harrington Guard. They immediately called a meeting of the company, and passed a resolution to appoint a committee to recover the body, if possible; and that they would invite the volunteers, and give him a soldier's burial. The committee, headed by Captain Henry Wilson, started on the mission, after surmounting many difficulties, and giving sureties to replace the bodies as they found them. They commenced on the twenty-third of January, 1849, at the morning's dawn. Captain Henry Wilson had two men, who were employed for the occasion, removing the dead in search of the body of the volunteer, and there they labored in this noble act until the day was almost finished, when, after removing and opening some three hundred and fifty coffins and returning them again, the body was found, and was brought to the city to Captain Wilson's house, re-coffined, and preparations were made for the funeral, which took place on the twenty-eighth of January, 1849. The funeral was a large one, and caused great excitement in the city at the time. Thomas Starr, the ex-foreman of 29 Engine, knew poor Struthers well, and a little anecdote in which his name is connected will not be out of place. Captain Wilson had worked very hard to get the body, and, as the bodies of paupers were then buried in ditches or pits, the job was no small one, and had he not known the deceased it would have been impossible to have gotten the right one. After the body had been carried to his house and laid out in the best manner, Mr. Wilson looked again at the face, and a doubt arose in his mind as to the identity. It was a terrible thing! A mistake was possible—yet, although he felt almost certain, the doubt was there. He had not called in any of the relatives of the deceased, and as the day began to fade he grew more nervous. He went to the door and watched for some one to whom the deceased was known, when who should come along in his butcher cart but Tom Starr? Wilson hailed him, and Tom stopped short. He went in the house on Wilson's invitation. "What's the matter here?" said he; "there ain't nobody dead, is there?" "Yes, Tom; look and see if you know him." The coffin lid was raised, and Tom exclaimed, "Why, its George Struthers!" Wilson said afterwards that those were the most refreshing words he had heard in a year.

While Henry Wilson was president of the Board of Fire Commissioners he and his colleague, Thomas Lawrence, were summoned to Washington by Edwin M. Stanton, Secretary of War, and consulted in regard to the protection of the vast amount of Government stores at Fortress Monroe from fire. They visited the fortress, and reported to the Secretary, and the result was the detail of Engines Nos. 16 and 31 to the duty of protecting the Government property, and these engines, under the command of John Baulch, senior assistant engineer, were sent to Fortress Monroe on April 17, 1862. They remain there to this day, and look very familiar to an old-time fireman.

Mr. Wilson continued in the Board of Fire Commissioners until 1864, when he retired. He is a thorough New Yorker, and proved his friendship for the Old Fire Department by years of active service, as well as in the honorary office afterwards held by him. He bears his years lightly, stands full six feet, and his eyes are still full of the old-time fire.

CHAPTER XXVII.

TALKS WITH SOME WELL-KNOWN VETERANS.

Alonzo Slote: Enthusiastic and Liked to be near the Pipe.—William A. Macy: Extravagantly Fond of the Life of a Fireman.—John A. Cregier: Rich in Reminiscences.—Carlisle Norwood: A Veteran with a History.—Zophar Mills: The Nestor of the Volunteers.—Thomas Boese: Crippled in the Discharge of Duty.—Christopher Johnson: Has seen Exciting Times.—Henry J. Ockershausen: Believed in Energetic Work.—John W. Degrauw: What he Considered the Pleasantest Part of a Fireman's Life.—James F. Wenman: Looks back to his Fire Days as the Happiest of his Life.—Theodore Keeler: Felt as if he'd Like to See the Boys again.—W. L. Jenkins: Gives him Pleasure to Recall the Old Days.—John S. Giles: Not Deserted by his Friends.—Peter R. Warner: True to his Post.—Edward Wood: Why he Never Became an Alderman.—W. B. Hays.

ALONZO SLOTE, of the firm of Tredwell & Slote, is another of the many members of the Volunteer Department who have attained commercial prominence and high social standing in the community. He was born in the Tenth Ward, on the corner of Orchard and Broome Streets, on September 13, 1830. In March, 1851, though not having quite attained his majority, he enrolled as a member of Hose Company No. 36, then located at No. 205 Madison Street. His brother, Daniel Slote, a very estimable gentleman, who died four years ago, was a member of the same company, as also were W.D. Wade, John R. Platt, William A. Woodhull, Elanson Tredwell, Lawrence Turnure, and Richard B. Ferris, president of the Bank of New York, and son of the distinguished Chancellor Ferris, of the Presbyterian Church. Messrs. Wade, Woodhull and Platt severally became presidents of the Fire Department, and altogether "Oceana's" crew were an exclusive set, who prided themselves upon possessing one of the finest looking carriages in the Department and in being able to make the most attractive appearance on gala occasions. Not unnaturally they were regarded with jealousy by some and with a feeling akin to contempt by others, who dubbed them "the quills," because they were mainly merchants and merchants' clerks. They were the "dudes" of the Department. Nevertheless the records show that for

ALONZO SLOTE.

effectiveness and strict attention to the line of duty the exhibit of Oceana Hose No. 36 is not excelled by any.

"We did everything up in style regardless," says Mr. Alonzo Slote, "on the principle that what was worth doing at all was worth doing well. At a parade we sought to excel, and we contended in a manly way for superiority in the line of duty. I liked the business. Even now I am full of it. Afraid that I might miss a fire I would not leave the hose house evenings to go to the theater or other place of amusement. Yet I never missed a day from business. I was a fireman in opposition to my uncle's wishes—in whose house I was a clerk—and my pride would not allow me to offer fire duty as an excuse for absence from business. I was enthusiastic and liked to be where the pipe was —nearest the fire, where the hardest work was."

Mr. Slote did fire duty for eleven years.

WILLIAM H. MACY, president of the Seaman's Bank for Savings, exclaimed: "Extravagantly, yes, I was extravagantly fond of the life of the volunteer fireman. I was born in Nantucket in 1806, and came to New York in April, 1823. On the 8th of February, 1830, I joined the Department, enrolling in the Supply Engine Company and remained with her until 1836, when I went to Europe and ceased my connection with the Department. The most startling event during my career as a fireman was the big fire in December, 1835. Gulick was then chief, and he and I entered the second building which caught fire. Subsequently I was stationed on the Tontine steps, corner of Water and Wall Streets, to assist in preventing the spread of the fire in that direction. The heat was so intense that my great coat was burnt through and the leather on the inside of my cap was crisped. Then it was found necessary to have Engine No. 13, which was at the corner of Wall and Pearl Streets, to play on me, although the thermometer was below zero, to keep me from being completely burnt. That was a terrible night. When I got home the next morning my fire clothes, which I had hastily pulled on over my business suit (and fortunately too) actually stood up stiff when I took them off. I suffered considerably from the exertion and exposure that night, and it was on that account I was obliged to take a trip across the Atlantic."

Mr. Macy bears his eighty years with amazing vigor. He has been vice-president and president of the institution over which he presides since 1851.

JOHN A. CREGIER, who is now in his seventy-first year, comes of a race of firemen, and it would be unnatural if he did not follow in the footsteps of his many generations of intrepid ancestors. He was born in the Fifth Ward on November 30, 1815, in a two-story and attic frame house on Chapel Street, which is now known as West Broadway. Notwithstanding the tearing down and obliteration of the antiquated structures, the very frame house where Mr. Cregier was born still remains, nearly opposite Lispenard Street. At the age of twenty John Cregier joined the Fire Department, being enrolled as a member of Engine Company No. 9, which was located in Beaver Street. Henry B. Cook was then foreman, and the members, twenty-six in number, were all unmarried men, principally cabinet makers, carvers, gilders, etc.

Speaking of the effectiveness of that company with a manifestation of pride, Mr. Cregier remarked: "I have seen that company with twenty men on the rope before she reached Wall Street. The way those men piled out of their houses was a caution—quick as a flash and ready for action. The jail bell was the principal alarm bell at that time, and we could hear it distinctly above every other bell. The fire of 1835 was the biggest I remember. No. 9 was stationed in Beaver Street, near Broad Street, and was called upon to do some lively work. I believe that Rynier Vechte, now residing at Plainfield, N. J., and myself are the only living representatives of the company as it then existed. About 1840 I retired from Engine Company No. 9 and joined No. 12, which was located in William Street, near Pearl Street. James Jackson was the foreman, and when he retired Alfred Carson took his place. No. 12 was called 'The Knickerbocker,' and its members, who were a very respectable class of men—merchants and mechanics—were regarded to a great extent as typical New Yorkers. In 1842 I retired from No. 12 and came up here to Greenwich Village, as this part of the city (the Ninth Ward) was then called. Old and young ladies made as much fuss in those days about taking a trip to 'Greenwich Village' as people nowadays would undertake for a trip to Europe. Omnibuses ran regularly twice a day from Niblo's Coffee House in Pine Street to the 'Village.'

JOHN A. CREGIER.

"Assisted by James L. Miller, who had been an engineer for many years, I organized Hose Company No. 40, of which Mr. Miller became the first foreman. I succeeded Miller, and after me came David Milliken, John Kettleman, and other men of prominence. I remained with 40 Hose until 1847, when I was appointed assistant engineer. We had no circumscribed limits for duty. The whole city was our sphere, and was not too extended for our enthusiasm. Why on one occasion, seeing the red glare in the sky to the northward, we started in search of the fire. We brought up at One Hundred and Tenth Street and Ninth Avenue, where the Lion Brewery was ablaze.

"I retired from the Department in 1860. I contemplate now with pleasure my term of service in the Department, and remember the many happy hours I spent in the company of those with whom it was my privilege to share the trials and dangers of a fireman's life.

"The chief feature in the effectiveness of a company was the alacrity with which the men responded to an alarm. No matter where they were, whether in church, in bed, visiting, or elsewhere, as soon as the bells rung out the warning notes all else was forgotten, and their hearts and souls seemed afire with enthusiasm to hasten and perform their duty. I knew a man belonging to Engine Company No. 9 who was taking his lady-love to Niblo's Theater one evening. When they had reached the corner of Prince Street and Broadway, a watch-house bell struck an alarm. Off the fireman started, leaving his astonished companion, who was a stranger in New York and had come from Elizabeth, N. J., that day, standing on the corner. After being about two hours at work, his thoughts reverted to the lady whom he had so unceremoniously abandoned. He hastened to the place, and there, trustful that he would return and fearful to move, not being acquainted with the neighborhood, he found the fluttering damsel, who would no doubt have overwhelmed him with reproaches but that she divined he must have been upon an errand of mercy and daring.

"I took my wife to Jenny Lind's Theater one evening. A policeman during the performance whispered to me that there was a big fire up-town. Hastily telling my wife to wait for me, I darted off to the fire—a big factory on East Twenty-ninth Street. After being two hours at the fire, I said to Carson, 'Chief, I left my wife at the theater two hours ago.' 'Go and take her home,' he replied. When I reached the theater it was closed.

"It appears to me now, when I look back, to be wonderful the endurance these men manifested and what deprivations they would willingly undergo in order to keep up their ends, maintain their superiority or claim thereto. There were two companies—No. 9 in Beaver Street and No. 5 in Fulton Street, near the Middle Dutch Church—between which great rivalry existed. The members lived in different parts of the city, and on Saturday nights they would come from different quarters and bunk in the rear of the grocery store kept by Miles Hitchcock, on the northwest corner of Liberty and Nassau Streets. Upon an alarm of fire the fun commenced. They rushed for their engines, and then raced to the fire. Every Saturday night there would be an alarm, and a watch was established on the cupola of the Middle Dutch Church to notify the boys. At times No. 9 would have a string of men stretched along Broadway to give the alarm, which was done by clapping the hands three times, which was repeated from one to the other. A careless fellow one night thought to scare off an unpleasantly attentive wandering dog by clapping his hands. He soon brought a host of contending companies around him, whose anger was only appeased by a genuine alarm which took place soon after.

"In 1833, 1834 and 1835 the personnel of the Department consisted of men whom it was a pleasure and a pride to know and be associated with. But beginning, say, at 1846, the class of men began to deteriorate. The proposition to introduce steam engines was perhaps a chief cause, as those who were opposed to the steamers, and they were many, regarded their introduction as the beginning of the end of the Volunteer Department. This tended to bring on demoralization, and a good many of the best men retired. The ambition to wear a red shirt and be a fireman seemed to pervade the young men thoroughly, although it was the ruin of many of them physically, and of not a few morally, because at all times the associations and the excitement led to excesses. Happily the instances of the latter effect were few. I endured a good deal of hardship; so did every man in the service, more or less. It was incidental to the life we led. Yet, although I am now suffering from the results of want of care at times from having got soaking wet and other self-neglect, if by some potent charm I could take forty years off my life, I would not hesitate a moment to undergo the same manner of life again. I remember some of the pranks the boys played when I was yet, I may say, an apprentice fireman, a boy who ran after the engine for the fun and exhilaration that came of it. Hook and Ladder No. 1 lay alongside No. 9's house in Beaver Street. Gabriel P. Disosway was foreman. In order to relieve his men and expedite their getting to a fire, he bought a powerful black horse, which was stabled in Mill Street. When an alarm was given one night for a fire in Chatham Square, Mr. Disosway was astonished upon the arrival of his coal-black steed to find that the harness was missing from the collar. The harness was resting at the bottom of Old Slip. On another occasion the horse's tail and mane were shaved; and on another the sight of his black horse with a white-painted stripe the length of his back, and his ribs all indicated with white paint lines, astonished and disgusted the enterprising foreman."

Mr. Cregier in 1861 assisted Colonel Ellsworth in raising the celebrated regiment of Fire Zouaves, as fine a body of men as appeared in the service of the Union, and accompanied it to the theater of war.

CARLISLE NORWOOD, president of the Lorillard Insurance Company, said:

"In old times, say 1820, and for a good while before that period, there was a bell in the cupola of the City Hall for ringing alarms of fire, and also one on the top of the jail which is the building now used as the Register's Office in the City Hall Park. This latter bell possessed a peculiar tone so that it could be distinctly distinguished above and among all the other alarm bells in the city which might be ringing simultaneously. It was taken from the jail and placed on the roof of the Bridewell, a prison for criminals which was on the Broadway side of the park, nearly opposite Murray Street. Thence it was taken to and placed on the top of the house occupied by Hose Company No. 16 in Beaver Street near Broad Street. Delancey Barclay was at one time foreman of that company—one of the distinguished Barclay family—and the company was mainly composed of the sons of old and respectable New Yorkers—the Schermerhorns, the Callenders, the Nelsons, and others of that class. There was no sacrifice that the firemen were not ready to make in the line of duty, and their discipline was perfect. For that matter it might be said that from the time of its organization up to 1849, when it ran down after the resignation of Anderson, the condition of the Department was most satisfactory, creditable alike to the city and to the members thereof who took pride in maintaining its efficiency and *morale*. Every chief engineer was a man of character and of undoubted respectability. Among them I will mention Ellsworth, Thomas Franklin, Jamieson Cox, Uzziah Wenman, James Gulick, John Ryker, and Cornelius V. Anderson.

"The first serious trouble in the Department arose during the career of Alfred Carson, who succeeded Anderson as chief engineer. He picked a quarrel with the Common Council, supposing that he could do with them as he pleased. He procured the publication of articles attacking the Common Council, and in his reports to that body, written by an eccentric and altogether untrustworthy character named Steve Branch, flung epithets and made insinuations against the Council which caused an angry rupture, and brought the Department into antagonism with them. About this time people began to move up town, which caused a thinning of the strength of the down-town fire companies, to offset which almost anybody without discrimination as to character or other fitness was accepted into the companies. Those persons became the rowdy element in the department and helped to give it the character of a rowdy institution. Indeed so marked was their misconduct that good citizens generally wished well to the project for disbanding the volunteers and establishing a paid department. The politicians began to use the Department for their ends, and the people and even the press were afraid to denounce them. The disagreeable duty of abolishing the offensive thing it was beginning to be was therefore undertaken by the Board of Fire Underwriters."

Speaking of the great fire of December 16, 1835, Mr. Norwood said: "James Gulick was chief engineer at that time. There was a good deal of feeling against him in the Common Council, who considered him to blame for the great destruction of property. It was a bitter cold night, the coldest we had had in New York for very many years, and thus the efforts of the firemen were badly handicapped, and the only way to prevent the spread of the fire was that which was finally adopted—by blowing up adjacent buildings. The Common Council determined to remove Gulick and passed a vote of censure upon him. They had no right to do that, for he did all that mortal man could do."

ZOPHAR MILLS was interviewed on his connection with the Volunteer Fire Department, and said:

"As a boy I began to run with the engines in 1820, and became a member of the Department in 1832, attaching myself to Engine No. 13, which was located in Fulton Street near Gold Street, and was afterwards in Dover near Pearl Street. The company consisted of twenty-six men, of whom eighteen are dead, three I cannot trace, and five are living: Hy. W. Flewry, at Prescott, Arizona; Josiah G. Macy, at Nantucket, Mass; Cornelius T. Nostrand, living in Connecticut; John T. Hall, Brooklyn, and myself, the only one living in this city. In 1835 I was foreman of No. 13 and acting at the great fire on December 16. We were stationed in Wall Street opposite the Merchants' Exchange (now the Custom House). We did great service. In 1838 was assistant engineer and served until 1842, when my business compelled me to sever my connection with the Department. I was a bookkeeper, and it was exceedingly severe on me, after serving for hours at a fire, to be obliged to go back to the office and post up my books.

"In 1845 we formed the Exempt Firemen's Company for the purpose of assisting in cases of the greatest emergency. We had two steam fire engines and one hand-engine (large size). These were, with one exception, the only steam fire-engines in the city; and they did great service, saving millions of dollars' worth of property. It was the opinion of Philip W. Engs—no mean authority—that at the burning of Barnum's Museum, corner of Broadway and Ann Street, one of these engines, the "John G. Storm," had saved a quarter million dollars' worth of property. Judge John J. Gorman was foreman of that company. The engines were self-propellers. We never got credit for what we did because there was a prejudice in the Department against that class of engines. But in a short time the other companies began to clamor for them. I lived in Rutgers Street in 1864, and in 1865 removed to Lexington Avenue, where I now live, and resigned from the Department.

"At the fire in Haydock's drug store in Pearl Street near Fulton, on July 1, 1834, two men were killed. I had a close call myself. The building had burnt down to the second story, and while four of us were engaged on that floor one of the side walls fell in, carrying us down to the cellar. Eugene Underhill and Frederick A. Ward were killed. I was foreman of Engine No. 13 at that fire. Wm. E. Crooker, who had formerly been one of the company and who was present giving assistance, was found buried amid burning bricks and his life was saved by Chief Gulick, who ordered one engine to play water on the bricks so that they might be cooled off, and the men could handle them and pick them off and another engine to pump in air. Crooker was buried up to his neck in the bricks. He was crippled for life, and was afterwards employed as bell-ringer at the City Hall. Two other men were in the building with us, but seeing the wall tottering they saved their lives by jumping out of the second story window. I saw the wall falling, recognized that I could not escape by running, and before I could think further down it came upon me, carrying me into the cellar. How I escaped unhurt, beyond a few slight bruises, was miraculous. When the dust had cleared away I came to consciousness, and, finding myself free, crawled out with only the loss of my cap, which was not found until after the men had been engaged in the work of rescuing Crooker and recovering the two dead firemen, a period of twelve hours.

"Eleven men were killed at the burning of Jennings's clothing store on Broadway, near Barclay Street, which took place on April 25, 1854. I was not a fireman at the time, but went there to give assistance. The fire was burning furiously, and Harry Howard, who was in command, ordered the men who were in the second story of an extension building in the rear to the roof. I intended to help them, and was climbing up a ladder, when down came the greater portion of the back wall of the main building, burying all who were in the extension building in the ruins. I got out I know not how, minus my cap. While I went around to 42's house, which was not far away,

ZOPHAR MILLS.

the remainder of the wall fell. The casualties numbered eleven killed (the greatest number killed at any fire in New York—of firemen I mean) and several wounded.

"Well, the fireman's work nowadays is mere child's play to what it was thirty years ago; for he rides to the fire, his engine is drawn there by strong, fleet horses, and steam plays the most important part, while in olden times all, everything, was done by main strength and wonderful endurance."

THOMAS BOESÉ, now clerk of the Superior Court, was maimed in the performance of duty as a fireman. "Ah!" said Mr. Boesé, "how different the system now from what it was in my time! Then our engines took suction from the docks and cisterns. On the roofs of buildings there were tanks containing water, which were utilized in cases of fire. When the ordinary supply failed the firemen, they used to break down the palings around the houses in their efforts to get at the tanks on the roofs. When the Croton was introduced it was a boon, but it was soon found that there were not hydrants enough for the firemen. I remember the introduction of the famous Philadelphia engines, large and powerful machines that required three times as many men to work them.

"At one time, I am sorry to say, our Department became somewhat demoralized, and charges were made against members. When a Paid Department was suggested, the Volunteers were dead against it. All the insurance companies were in favor of it. At that time I was secretary to the Board of Education, and at the instance of Mr. McLane I drafted the bill for the new Department substantially as it was passed. It was framed on the plan of the old Metropolitan Police force. It was proposed to appoint a commission to see that the Department should conform to the constitution of the State. So great was the influence of the Volunteers that no city official dared openly assist or countenance the scheme. One modification of the original draft was a clause requiring the new Department to attend fires out of the city limits. Reuben E. Fenton was then governor. The insurance people were very anxious about the bill. They very much desired to have the old engineers appointed in the new Department, as they were reliable men who thoroughly understood their work. Governor Fenton, however, disappointed them, by making it a political machine. In the second year of the new Department great loss was caused through incompetent management; the loss by fires, indeed, was greater than under the Volunteer system. This state of things was soon altered by better appointments and a change in the law.

"The present chief justice of the Superior Court—Justice Sedgwick—was counsel against the passage of the bill creating the paid Department, while Judge Abram R. Lawrence, now of the Supreme Court, was the counsel in favor of it. Mr. Acton, chief of the police, rendered great assistance in getting the bill through; so did Mr. Seth C. Hawley. The expenses were defrayed by the insurance companies of the city."

JOHN T. AGNEW is one of the best known survivors of the Volunteer Department, formerly of Hose Company No. 1. "Our company," said the veteran with just pride to the writer, "was a crack company as to time. We were as quick as lightning. We lay in Duane Street, and were always on the jump. Did we adopt the bunking system? Oh! no. Our men were of a different stamp, and we all lived within easy access of the engine house. Our rules were very strict. We had assistance to take down and put up our hose. Our foreman was Henry J. Ockershausen. Our company's reputation was such that we always had a large number of applicants on the list waiting for membership. Vacancies, however, were rare; at that time the Department was fully adapted to the requirements of the city; now, of course, it would not do at all. We had no such buildings then as are to be seen in the New York of to-day.

"In the same street with us was No. 13 Company, composed, like ourselves, of merchants and business men. We were friendly rivals, and though we beat them, so often we never had a quarrel at a fire. Although some of the companies on the east side used to quarrel, yet, take the Department altogether, it was composed of a respectable body of men. To be exempted from jury duty was a consideration. I was at the famous fire of 1835 all night. Two or three times I had to remove a set of books to places of safety. I was one of the men who helped to put the powder under Bailey's store to arrest the conflagration.

"Took part in the great fire of '35."

"Paraded and hurrahed for Jenny Lind."

"Was at the Hague Street Explosion."

"Ran into Big Six as we rounded the corner."

"Was in the hold of the Great Republic."

"Was with Ellsworth in Alexandria."

CHARACTER HEADS OF OLD FIREMEN.

After that night of terrible work I was compelled to rest for two or three days.

"At the fire in King Street I took a crippled woman out of the house. I remember well it was a very cold night. I carried her down from the second story. I was also lucky enough to get a child out.

"I never cared for military tactics, but it seemed to come natural to me to join the Fire Department. I never took cold, and could run up a ladder and along a gutter with much more nimbleness than I could now," added the old gentleman smilingly. "I was present at the disastrous fire in Duane Street, and I held the pipe at the Mulberry Street fire. We were in an alleyway, and were ordered to back out. Just as we did so the building fell, and one of our members was struck on the head and badly hurt.

"When I joined, it was understood that I should not go to fires in the day-time unless they were big ones. At night, of course, I attended all fires."

CHRISTOPHER JOHNSON, ex-member of the State legislature, connected with the Exempt Firemen's Association for the past ten years, and at present a member of the executive committee of that association, says : "I joined the Department in December, 1858, and was attached to Oceanus Engine Company No. 11, located in Wooster Street. The foreman was John Wildey, who afterwards became coroner, and the strength of the company was sixty men, mostly all mechanics of the best class. After being six months in the company I was elected its treasurer. In 1860 I was elected assistant foreman; and in 1861 foreman. We had quite an exciting time in 1864, when John Wildey contested the foremanship with me. He was then a coroner, and well versed in all the political maneuvers that could be brought into play; and how successfully he worked his points was shown by the fact that I beat him by only six votes. It was a tight race, and the majority small, but my victory was none the less one to feel proud of. I remained with the Department until it was mustered out in September, 1865. There was no rowdyism to speak of in the Department in my day. There was friendly rivalry among the companies for excellence in running and efficiency, and that was to my mind a commendable spirit. Now, as between the Company No. 11, I was foreman of, and Engine Company 16, located in West Broadway, we never ceased to contend with each other for the mastery, and the approval and recognition of the people. It was a sight worth witnessing to see these two double deckers hastening upon an alarm of fire. Often, I may say very often, on Sunday afternoons, a false alarm would be given on purpose somewhere on Eighth Avenue, so that 11 and 16 would be seen running in response. The people looked for these trials of speed and endurance, and lined the avenue on both sides, encouraging their favorite. They congregated there just as lovers of horse-flesh now assemble on the upper avenues, to see the trotters speeding. But, while at times some loud talk and angry words were bandied about, and threats perhaps indulged in, there were never any blows inflicted."

Mr. Johnson, besides being connected with the Exempt Firemen's Association, is also a member of the Volunteer and Veteran Associations.

MR. A. B. HAYS, cashier of the North River Bank, a few days before his death in 1882, said : "I look with pleasure upon my connection with the Fire Department. I often thought of proposing a meeting of Volunteer Firemen to celebrate the days of auld lang syne."

HENRY J. OCKERSHAUSEN, formerly assistant engineer in the Department, is credited with the aphorism that firemen generally gave the machine more praise for what was accomplished than themselves. "This fact," he said, "is evidenced by the minutes of the transactions of the engine companies, among which are to be found such entries as these:

Dec. 14, 1808.—The engine was taken to the place of action, etc., etc. *No. 13 did her part this night.*

July 5, 1819.—This morning about half past ten o'clock there was an alarm of fire, said to have originated in a house in Church Street. The engine was, with great expedition, taken out and made a fine display among the military, who, with the politeness inherent in soldiers, quickly made way for us, having perhaps an idea that No. 13, by coming too close to them, might spoil their "marking time" for a season.

Aug. 30, 1825.—Our men never worked better than they did this morning, and were well satisfied with the machine (No. 41).

Elisha Kingsland.
G. Jos. Rush.
John Decker.
John Baulch.
John Brice.

Wm. Hackett.
Dan'l Donovan.
Chief Harry Howard.
John A. Cregier.
N. L. Farnham.

W. T. Mawbey.
James F. Wenman.
P. N. Cornwell.
Timothy L. West.
Ed. W. Jacobs.

CHIEF HARRY HOWARD AND STAFF.

Oct., 1825.—No. 41 took water from the river and gave it to 29, who played on the fire. Of course our machine (No. 41) gave more water than she (No. 29) could make use of.

Mr. Ockershausen believed in energetic work. "I had rather go to a fire than anything else" are his words; "and when called out I was always a little vexed if we hadn't a good fire." Of Mr. Ockershausen it is said that he once ran all the way from the City Hall Park to the House of Refuge (where the Fifth Avenue Hotel how stands) to attend a fire; and on another occasion to Rose Hill (Twenty-seventh Street and Third Avenue).

JOHN W. DEGRAUW, for twenty years a fireman and once President of the Fire Department, expressed his estimate of the qualities necessary to be a fireman in this sententious sentence: "To be a fireman one must have a love for arduous duty." Hence it is not astonishing that as a corollary to that opinion he should remark: "And the pleasantest thing about being a fireman was to have a big fire and to go to work and put it out."

JAMES F. WENMAN said: "My life as a volunteer fireman was the happiest part of my existence. My service extended over a period of twenty years, and the associations then formed are among my pleasantest recollections."

THEODORE KEELER, surveyor of the Lorillard Insurance Company, was attached to No. 12 engine when about fifteen years old, and subsequently became connected with Fourteen, Twenty-one and Thirty-eight, in succession. Referring to older days in the Department, Mr. Keeler said: "Twelve engine lay in Rose Street. The house, now a tenement house, back from the street, is there yet. I often go there and stand and look at it, and feel as though I'd like to see the boys again." His death took place Monday, Jan. 10, 1887.

W. L. JENKINS, President of the Bank of America, and at one time foreman of No. 13 Engine, said: "I can't explain why we were carried away with a desire to do fire duty. I don't see where the fine times came in, for there was a great deal of hard work to be done, and not a little a risk to be undertaken. Yet it gives me pleasure to recall those days when, with commendable rivalry, we contended for the palm for doing the quickest and most effective work in saving life and property from the destructive element."

JOHN S. GILES, first treasurer of the Exempt Engine Company, said: "A fireman thought as much of his engine as he did of his family. He spoke of it in the feminine gender. He liked to see *her* look well, and hence his readiness to spend his money on the decoration of his engine. Mr. James N. Phillips lost all he had by being a fireman. He spent so much of his time attending to the affairs of the association that he failed in business. But the firemen did not desert him. They caused the creation of the office of Inspector of Unsafe Buildings, to which Mr. Phillips was appointed."

PETER R. WARNER, who was foreman of 23 Engine fifty-four years ago, ascribes the motives of the majority of men who served as firemen to a sense of public duty, and not as arising from a desire to get rid of jury or militia service. "Mechanics," he said, "who upon an alarm of fire would throw down their tools, leaving them exposed where they fell, lost half a day often, or a whole day, without remuneration. Frequently they ruined their clothes at a fire, and were compelled to buy new suits at their own expense. A large proportion of the expense of keeping engine and engine house in repair, and the entire expense of decorating them, fell upon the Volunteers. My company was allowed by the city one gallon of oil a month for torches, signal lanterns, and ordinary lamps, and we had to provide extra oil, which was often needed. Yet I would rather have lost a dozen teeth than resign from my company, or be rendered incapable of doing duty with it."

EDWARD WOOD, president of the Bowery Savings Bank, enrolled in Engine Company No. 2 (which had been organized out of Hose Company No. 21) in 1846. She was then located in Henry Street, near Catharine Street. The company name was "Excelsior," as distinguished from "Chatham" No. 2, which had been disbanded a short while before the organization of the "Excelsior."

"I was born in the Fourth Ward," said Mr. Wood, facetiously adding, "and that is the reason perhaps that I never became an alderman, as would inevitably have been the case if I had been born elsewhere. When I served my full term I retired from the Department. Although I had two objects in view in joining the Department, namely, to avoid military and jury duty, I was, nevertheless, all in love with the fire business. I was fond of the excitement and the fun. But I had no ambition to be other than a high private. I did not interest myself in the politics of the Department. I tried to attend strictly to my duty, and for three years never had to pay a fine for absence from a night fire. But when the old Essex Market bell cracked, upon which I used to depend for the alarms, I got frequently mulcted. During my career John Barry, Asher C. Havens, John H. Macy, and George C. Baker were at different times foremen of No. 2.''

WILLIAM B. HAYS, a popular member of Hose Company No. 24, has the honor of being the man who first discovered the great fire of 1835. "I was at that time,'' says Mr. Hays, "a member of the city watch, one of the old 'Leatherheads,' as they were called. I remember it was a bitter cold night, one of the coldest I ever remember to have experienced. As I was passing the corner of Exchange and Pearl Streets I smelled smoke, and summoned several other watchmen. We found that the building on the corner was on fire, and together we managed to force open the door. We found the whole interior of the building in flames from cellar to roof, and I can tell you we shut that door mighty quick. Almost immediately the flames broke through the roof, and in less than fifteen minutes I believe fully fifty buildings were blazing. It was the most awful night I ever saw.''

WILLIAM B. HAYS.

Mr. Hays joined Hose No. 24 in 1843, and served with that company for seven years, the last three as foreman. Having finished his term of service, he was elected fire warden, and served six years. As a member of the Governor's Guard, Mr. Hays did good service during the trying times of the abolition riots. Sprung from a sturdy New Jersey stock, his father having been a soldier in the war of 1812, while his grandfather carried a musket during the Revolution, he is still stalwart and hearty, at the age of seventy-five years. He is a member of the Association of Exempt Firemen.

CHAPTER XXVIII.

VOLUNTEERS WHO ARE DESERVING OF ALL PRAISE.

W. D. Wade.—J. S. Giles.—Peter Goelet.—A. Tredwell.—J. McGarrigal.—H. L. Slote.—J. Betts.—F. Harper.
—W. M. Tweed.—J. Tyson.—P. R. Warner.—J. Y. Watkins, Sr.—J. Y. Watkins, Jr.—J. R. Mount.
—W. H. Webb.—S. Willetts.—B. Strong.—J. P. Bailey.—J. S. Belcher.—J. J. Bloomfield.—W.
Boardman.—T. Cleary.—A. Craft.—J. W. Degrauw.—D. C. Silleck.—W. H. Philp.—P. J. Chappell.—
A. V. Davidson.—J. H. Johnson.—N. D. Thayer.—J. P. Teale.—F. R. Mott.—M. T. Green.—J. J.
Reilly.—D. C. Broderick.—T. Moloney.—N. Seagrist.—J. W. Walsh.—W. Lamb.—M. O. Allen.—
J. Barker.

WILLIAM DURAND WADE joined the New York Fire Department on March 15, 1845, and was enrolled a member of Oceana Hose Company No. 36. This company had just been reorganized, and Mr. Wade served with it for nearly eleven years. In May, 1848, he was elected assistant foreman. His service was so admirable and he became so popular by a thorough performance of his duties that he was elected foreman in 1850, and re-elected in the following year. Towards the close of 1851 Mr. Wade was compelled to resign in consequence of ill health. Although afterwards not able to continue in active duty as a fireman, the members of No. 36 still retained him on their roll and he still held his position as representative. He was exceedingly useful in the Department by his talent and experience. At the annual election in 1853 he was chosen secretary of the Department, and in the following year was advanced to the post of vice-president. In December, 1855, he was unanimously elected president. On this occasion his old comrades presented him with a handsome hat and a silver trumpet. The trumpet was inclosed in an elegant case.

WILLIAM D. WADE.

Mr. Wade did not enjoy his new honors long, for he died on Friday, Jan. 11, 1856. The next day a special meeting of the Representatives was held in Stuyvesant Institute. Mr. John S. Belcher, vice-president of the Department, presided. Mr. Carlisle Norwood offered a series of resolutions commemorating the energy, perseverance and fidelity of the deceased. Mr. Norwood said of his departed comrade: "As a fireman he was ever zealous and active, foremost at the post of danger, and rose through all the various grades of office to the highest in his company. As a representative he was faithful, energetic and diligent, always ready to take part in the proceedings of this body; never shrinking from duty, he labored assiduously and incessantly to promote the welfare of the department." Among others who eulogized the dead were Mr. C. L. Curtis, of Hook and Ladder No. 4; Mr. John A. Smith, of Engine Company No. 51; Mr. David Milliken, secretary; Mr. Zophar Mills and Mr. James F. Wenman, of Hose Company No. 5.

The Board of Engineers and Foremen also held a special meeting to take appropriate action on President Wade's death, and Mr. John Lynes, of Hose Company No. 9, Mr. John Slowey, of Engine Company No. 19, and Mr. John Gillilan made feeling speeches.

The Rev. Thomas Gallaudet, Rector of St. Ann's, preached a memorial sermon in that church on Sunday evening, Jan. 29. The discourse was remarkably eloquent, able and appropriate, and was listened to by a number of firemen. A very touching general address was made by the Rev. Isaac Ferris, D. D., LL. D,, Chancellor of the University of the city of New York.

Said the Rev. Dr. Gallaudet: "We recall the time when he stood before us in the full glory of health and strength and beauty; we see him as disease lightly touched the secret springs of life; we trace his gradual yet steady course, through encouraging and discouraging vicissitudes, towards the period of physical weakness and general prostration; we see him withdraw again from the duties of active life, and seek gentle, faithful nursing of maternal love; we call to mind those weeks of anxiety when our daily inquiries were made as to his welfare; we remember the pang which pierced our hearts when the word, passed swiftly yet gently from one to another, came to us that he was gone; we see once more the pallid, sunken features of the lifeless form —the casket from which the Almighty had taken the gem—laid out in the chamber of death; we set before us the solemn gathering at the home of our loved one; we behold the outward insignia of grief, and we hear the sobs which indicate that the deep places of the soul are broken up; we listen once more to those sublime strains which characterize a Christian burial; we bring back the word of the venerable man who spoke so appropriately of our brother; we picture the solemn procession of genuine mourners, slowly bearing the precious earthly remains to the house appointed for all living; we hear a voice from heaven proclaiming, 'Blessed are the dead who die in the Lord; even so saith the Spirit, for they rest from their labors,' and we bow our heads at the great, the mysterious truth, that man giveth up the ghost. Verily the passing away from earthly scenes of our friend and brother has been to us an impressive instance of the mortality which is inwrought into the race of which we are part and parcel."

The Board of Representatives and the Board of Engineers and Foremen appointed a joint committee to see to the suitable erection of a memorial. The committee was as follows: Messrs. Carlisle Norwood, C. L. Curtis, D. Reynolds Budd (Hose Company No. 36), H. B. Venn (Engine Company No. 14), J. Lynes, J. Slowey, D. Stanbury (Engine Company No. 28), Jacob Ostrom (Hose Company No. 38), J. F. Wenman and W. H. Blague (Hook and Ladder Company No. 1). The result was the placing of a tablet in Fireman's Hall, (on the building committee of which Mr. Wade had served), with the following inscription :

To the Memory of

WILLIAM DURAND WADE,

Born January 18, 1826; Died January 11, 1856,

Aged Twenty-nine Years, Eleven Months, Twenty-one Days.

This tablet is erected by the Fire Department of the city of New York, of which he was president at the time of his death, a graceful tribute to his faithful and devoted attention to its usefulness and prosperity.

MONUMENT TO WILLIAM DURAND WADE.

JOHN S. GILES, for many years treasurer of the old Department, was born in 1799. As a lad he ran with the engines. At the age of twelve he went to sea and made two voyages before the mast to India. When but fifteen years of age he was apprenticed to a builder and worked with such a will that two years later he was able to start in business on his own account. He had scarcely done so when he was burned out, and, being uninsured, lost every penny he had in the world. Nothing daunted, he set to work again as a journeyman and wrought with untiring energy at his trade until his thirty-second year, when by great self-denial he had accumulated funds sufficient to pay off all the indebtedness due at the time of his misfortune and leave a balance sufficient to re-establish himself on his own account. From that time his affairs prospered greatly, and at the time of his death, at the age of eighty years, he was in the possession of an independent fortune. Mr. Giles was one of the organizers of Hose Company No. 14. In the year 1849 he rendered invaluable services in securing the passage by the legislature of an act requiring all fire insurance companies, organized outside of the State of New York, to pay to the treasurer of the fund of the Fire Department two per cent. of the amount received for premiums.

Mr. Giles was for years the treasurer of the fund. On the outbreak of the civil war Mr. Giles was an active member of the committee appointed to recruit the famous Second Regiment of Fire Zouaves. When the famous Exempt Engine Company was organized on November 14, 1854, to run the heavy engine, known as the "Man-Killer," Mr. Giles was elected treasurer. He was an enthusiastic and intrepid fireman, and leaves on record the opinion that in his day "a fireman thought more of his engine than he did of his family."

FLETCHER HARPER.

PETER GOELET, the well known capitalist whose late residence at the corner of Broadway and Nineteenth Street is one of the landmarks of New York, was a prominent member of the old Volunteer Department. He died leaving an enormous fortune. Mr. Goelet served his time with Engine No. 9, and was for many years a Trustee of the Fire Department Fund. His brother Robert was also a famous fireman. Mr. Goelet bore an active part in raising the Charitable Fund.

ALANSON TREDWELL, now a member of the well known clothing firm of Tredwell, Slote & Co., at the corner of Broadway and Chambers Street, was born on November 24, 1828. In 1851 he joined Hose Company No. 6, and in 1857 was elected foreman of Oceana Hose No. 36, to which company belonged such solid citizens as Alonzo Slote, Daniel Slote, William A. Woodhull and William D. Wade, subsequently Presidents of the Department; L. H. Macy and John H. Waydell. Mr. Tredwell served long in the Department and has a gallant record.

JOHN MCGARRIGAL, formerly of the firm of Gayte & McGarrigal, who built the present Firemen's Hall, was born on February 22, 1829. Mr. McGarrigal was a brave fireman, and was at one time foreman of Americus Engine No. 6. He is a member of the Exempt Firemen's Association and still takes a great interest in everything pertaining to the old Department.

HENRY L. SLOTE, formerly of the firm of Slote & Janes, stationers, was born in 1828, and began his career as a fireman with Oceana Hose No. 36.

Subsequently he became a member of Americus Engine Company No. 6. **Mr.** Slote married a daughter of Alderman Griffiths of the Tenth Ward. He was well known in the Department as a brave, enthusiastic fireman. Mr. Slote died recently, deeply regretted by a large circle of old comrades.

JOHN BETTS, born in New York on January 11, 1823, was one of the organizers of Americus Engine No. 6, and went with the company on its famous excursion to Canada. Mr. Betts was the father and founder of the famous Americus Pleasure Club, which was organized in 1850, was its first president and remained a member of the club until it was disbanded in 1874. For many years Mr. Betts was a member of old Engine 33. No member of the Department was more popular than Mr. Betts. He formerly did a good business as head carman for Vanderworth & Dickerson, in Cliff Street. He now lives in Brooklyn.

FLETCHER HARPER, of the firm of Harper & Brothers, was one of the best

WILLIAM M. TWEED.

looking firemen of his time. He was a member of Engine Company No. 7, and became its secretary and foreman. He was a man of most affectionate disposition. Mr. Adam P. Pentz said that at the destruction of the Harpers' buildings in Franklin Square Mr. Fletcher Harper watched the fire and said to him (Mr. Pentz) that the great loss did not affect him as much as the recent death of a grandchild. "Property," said Mr. Harper, " we can restore, but life, never."

WILLIAM M. TWEED, whose parents were of Scotch descent, was as famous as the foreman of Americus Engine Company No. 6—Big Six—as he was as a politician. He was born on April 3, 1823, at No. 24 Cherry Street. He was apprenticed to a chairmaker, subsequently became salesman or clerk in various stores, and then set up in business for himself as a chairmaker at his father's old place, No. 5 Cherry Street. In turn he was alderman, school commissioner, deputy street commissioner, commissioner of public works, congressman, and practically " Boss " of the city of New York. He was first a member of Fashion Hose 25, next a member of Oceana Hose 36, then of Fulton Engine Company No. 12, and of Knickerbocker Engine No. 12. He organized " Big Six " in 1849, and was its foreman from 1852 to 1854. His fall from his political shrine is a matter of history. He died in Ludlow Street Jail, April 12, 1878, having been one of the commissioners who built that prison.

JOHN TYSON, now in charge of the horse hospital of the Jersey City Fire Department, has ever been a great collector of fire souvenirs, and possesses some very curious and rare relics of the olden time. He was a volunteer of Engine Company No. 21, and went to the war in Company A, Second Regiment, New Jersey Volunteers.

PETER R. WARNER belonged to a fire family. His grandfather, Peter Roome, was foreman of Engine Company No. 7, and Peter's sons were also firemen. Mr. Warner was born March 12, 1804; he joined Engine Company No. 23 in 1824, when less than twenty-one years old, and was six years its foreman. He was afterwards a fire warden. Mr. Warner was president of the North River Fire Insurance Company.

JAMES Y. WATKINS, SR., a successful merchant, was successively a member of Engine Companies Nos. 21 and 14, having joined the first in 1828. He was a trustee of the Fire Department. His sons were also firemen, James Y., Jr., of Engine Company No. 42, and John O., of Hose Company No. 38.

JAMES Y. WATKINS, JR., was born in the Fourth Ward in 1830. He joined Hose Company No. 10 in May, 1849, then located in Dover Street. He remained with her till the organization of Hose Company No. 50 in 1851, when he helped to launch the latter. On the first night of the meeting of Hose 50 Mr. Watkins was elected secretary. Subsequently he was assistant foreman of Hose 50 for five years. When Mr. Cregier ran for chief engineer he formed Engine Company No. 42, serving as active or honorary member till 1865. Mr. Watkins was a member of the Exempt Engine Company for many years. He was elected treasurer of the Association of Exempt Firemen, serving from 1869. When the New Department was inaugurated the first engine company was located in old No. 42's house, and the Volunteers had charge of it, and worked at the first fire till the new company was thoroughly organized, when old 42 was relieved. Mr. Watkins is in the furnishing business and still retains the same place his father had in the Fourth Ward.

JAMES R. MOUNT.

JAMES R. MOUNT was born in 1826 in New York in the Fourteenth Ward. In 1840 he began to run with Engine Company No. 15. On June 6, 1850, he became a regular member of the Department, joining Hose Company No. 14. When that was disbanded in 1857 he joined Engine Company No. 30. Subsequently he helped to reorganize Hose Company No. 15. He retired from the Department about 1860. On October 17, 1859, Mr. Mount received a compliment from the members and friends of Atlantic Hose Company No. 15. Since the inauguration of Chief Engineer Howard he had been foreman of the Corporation Yard, and his pleasant attentions to the wants of the firemen had made him many friends. The compliment took the form of a fine gold medal, valued at two hundred dollars, having engraved on one side the fac-simile of the Fireman's Discharge Certificate, and on the other an appropriate inscription. The medal was presented by John J. Tindale, ex-president of the Fire Department. Mr. Mount's exploits and experiences as a life saver are mentioned in a preceding chapter (pages 186 and 187.)

WILLIAM H. WEBB is one of New York's famous old shipbuilders who belonged to the Old Fire Department. Many are the runs he had with old Live Oak Engine 44 before he entered Engine Co. No. 47. He was also a member of Hose Co. 34, and a fire warden. When only fifteen years old he worked for his father, Isaac, as a journeyman, and so acquired a thorough knowledge of every branch of the shipbuilding business. In 1849 he built the three decker " *Guy Mannering* " for the American packet service. At the invitation of the Russian Government he built the " *General Admiral*," a first-class propeller frigate. The celebrated steam ram, the " *Dunderberg* " was also his design. It was launched in 1865, and sold to the French Government.

SAMUEL WILLETS as a boy ran with an engine. When twenty-one years old he joined Engine Company No. 18. He was born on Long Island on June 15, 1795, came to New York in 1812, and made a name for himself as a successful merchant.

BENJAMIN STRONG—born in 1770, died on January 27, 1851—was thirty-one years in the Fire Department. He first entered in 1791, and served until 1822. He joined Engine Company No. 13, and was its foreman for several years, was assistant engineer for nine years, and treasurer of the Fire Department Fund for eighteen years. He was the founder of the first savings bank in this city, and for sixteen years president of the Seaman's Savings Bank.

JOHN W. TOWT was the foreman of Hook and Ladder Company No. 1, who in 1830 bought a horse to draw the truck. He was formerly a merchant doing business at the corner of Old Slip and Pearl Streets. He had several miraculous escapes, and was noted for his bravery.

JOHN P. BAILEY, foreman of Engine Company No. 23, treasurer of the Fire Department, became prominent through his expulsion from office by the Common Council in 1828. Mr. Bailey refused to recognize at a fire an officious assistant alderman until the latter showed his badge. The company threatened to resign if their comrade was not reinstated; public feeling ran high on the injustice done, and finally Mr. Bailey was reinstated.

JOHN S. BELCHER was foreman of Hydrant Company No. 2 in 1850. In 1854 he was selected representative and secretary of the Board of Representatives. In 1855 he became vice-president, subsequently president, and was elected to the latter office three times without opposition.

J. J. BLOOMFIELD, a well-known statesman and member of the Firemen's Ball Committee, was foreman of Engine Company No. 42 at the time of the Jennings fire. He was born November 27, 1827.

WILLIAM BOARDMAN, of the firm of A. M. Pentz & Co. (Empire Cotton Press), was the engineer of the first steam fire engine ever used by the city. He was alderman and chairman of the Fire and Water Committee.

THOMAS CLEARY was born about 1826 in Ireland, his father, on account of his patriotism, being obliged to emigrate. He was foreman of Engine Company No. 20. He was elected engineer February 27, 1865, and was on that occasion presented by his company with a sixteen cone hat. In 1883 Mr. Cleary was elected to the Board of Aldermen for the First Ward, and was re-elected in 1884. He was an assistant engineer in 1864.

ANDREW CRAFT joined Engine Company No. 41 in 1829. He was in succession steward, secretary, assistant foreman, foreman, and finally fire commissioner. His connection with the company lasted until 1865. Mr.

Craft was present at the burning of the Lafayette Theatre in Laurens Street in 1829.

JOHN W. DEGRAUW was born a fireman, as he himself expressed it. His father, two uncles and three brothers, were members of Engine Company No. 16. He was born in the First Ward May 21, 1797. He used to play with the Ewings, the Goelets, the Roosevelts, General Morris and Mr. Drake, the poets, and Mr. Hackett, the actor. In 1816 he joined Engine Company No. 16, and served continuously for twenty-one years. Mr. Degrauw became foreman of his company. He was chairman of the Board of Trustees of the Fire Department for many years, and was president for several years. He was a most indefatigable fireman. After the fire of 1835 he organized two hose companies. At that time he was an assessor from the Third Ward, and raised in five hours one thousand seven hundred dollars to purchase the apparatus. When Lafayette visited the city Mr. Degrauw was instrumental in making a success of the ball tendered the great Frenchman. On resigning the office of president he was presented by the members of the Department with a large silver urn. It was he who rang the alarm for the big fire of 1811, which was so destructive. He was the father of the Fire Department Fund. In 1833 he was elected a member of the Assembly, and was instrumental in obtaining the city charter for Brooklyn. He was the recipient of many flattering presentations, among them being a handsome cane made from the timber of the first Methodist Church erected in this city in 1768. He has written a history of New York, held to be of high merit. Mr. Degrauw's son, Mr. A. J. S. Degrauw, was also a fireman. The young man, who had much capacity, and gave promise of great things, was president of the Brooklyn Volunteer Fire Department. His end was untimely; he was killed at a fire in 1856 while saving the lives of the occupants of a tenement. It was a great blow to his father.

DANIEL C. SILLECK was born in July, 1815, at Oyster Bay, L. I. In April, 1828, he came to New York, and in the spring of 1832 became associated with Columbia Engine Company No. 14, located at the corner of Church and Vesey Streets. In the fall of 1835 Mr. Silleck was elected assistant foreman, in the following year treasurer, and in 1837 assistant engineer under Chief Anderson. In the year 1838 he was re-elected to the same position and served up to the spring of 1841. Mr. Silleck, notwithstanding his great age, has a well preserved appearance.

WILLIAM H. PHILP, a well known portrait painter and quartermaster of the First New York Mounted Rifles during the rebellion, joined the Fire Department in 1850, becoming a member of No. 3 Hose. Mr. Philp decorated the panels of the hose carriage, painting "The Battle of Bunker Hill" on one side and "Washington at the Battle of Monmouth" on the other. This handsome carriage was different in its construction from any other in the Department at that time. By means of ingeniously contrived cog-wheels, it could be turned completely around within its own length. It was placed on exhibition in one of the American Institute Fairs, held in Castle Garden, and attracted great attention.

Some of the best American artists of that period did not consider it beneath their dignity to decorate the panels of the fire engines and hose carriages. The celebrated artist Henry Inman painted a beautiful allegorical design on the banner used at the general parade of the Department, and this design was engraved on steel and embellished the certificates of membership issued to firemen. Jos. H. Johnson and T. Pine painted many panels in elaborate style

PAUL J. CHAPPELL.

for various engine companies, and their work will compare favorably with more modern and renowned decorators.

Mr. Philp was born in 1828, and his recollections of the Department date back to the great fire of 1835, when he was but eight years old. He distinctly remembers accompanying his guardian to the scene of the disaster a day or two afterward when the smoke was still rising from the ruins. His guardian, Cornelius Cadle, was a fire warden, and three brothers of Cadle—Joseph, James and Richard—were all prominent firemen.

PAUL J. CHAPPELL first joined the Fire Department in 1856, going on the roll of Americus Hose Company No. 48, and served some two years, when he left the above company and joined Marion Hose Company No. 4, and was elected as a representative from that company to the Board of Representatives. He served in the company until the disbandment of the old Fire Department. In April, 1869, he joined the Exempt Firemen's Association; he is a life member. He was one of the organizers of the Veteran Firemen's Association on their return from Washington, and accompanied the association to Poughkeepsie. At a fire on October 7, 1886, at Nos. 63, 65 and 67 Bayard Street he saved the lives of eight persons by climbing out of an attic window of No. 69 Bayard Street, and climbing up a peak slate roof at the risk of losing his own life, for which act of gallantry he received great praise.

The members of the City Club and their friends gathered in their rooms at 253 Bowery on Saturday evening, November 14, 1886, to witness the presentation to Mr. Paul J. Chappell of an emblem of the club's admiration of his pluck and bravery. The gift was a gold bar and badge, to which was attached a tiger's head in gold, with diamond eyes. On the face of the badge was: "Presented to Paul J. Chappell by his friends of the City Club for his bravery in saving lives at the fire in Bayard Street, October 7, 1886." The venerable John Buckbee made the presentation speech, and Mr. Chappel made a hearty response. Among those present at the reception were William B. Dunley,

PRESENTATION MEDAL TO PAUL J. CHAPPELL.

Richard Evans, Frank Prendergast, James J. Donovan, John Rudman, Daniel Garvey, William Dunne, the Poet Geoghegan, W. P. Wall, John Dawson, and Ed. W. Jacobs.

ALEX. V. DAVIDSON was assistant foreman of Hose Company No. 53 in 1857 when it was established in Horatio Street near Hudson. It organized with twenty men, but by order of the Common Council the number was subsequently increased to twenty-five. In 1858 Mr. Davidson was appointed foreman, and remained foreman until the Volunteer Department broke up. He was also one of the assistant engineers, and under Chief Decker he was chief clerk of the Department. "Aleck" Davidson was a popular member of Engine Company 23. He took the full share of the work and the hard knocks, and always kept up a buoyant fund of spirits. He was the life of the company when they were off duty and passing the time in their own quarters.

ALEX. V. DAVIDSON.

There were in the same company with ex-Sheriff Davidson Police Justice Gorman, Peter Bowe and ex-Fire Commissioner Vincent C. King. Mr. Davidson was elected sheriff, his successor being the present popular incumbent, Hugh J. Grant.

JOSEPH H. JOHNSON, of No. 1 Great Jones Street, is one of the veteran firemen. He joined Engine Company 15 in 1841 in Christie Street near Bayard. He served a full term with her, consisting of seven years. In 1849 he became one of the organizers of Engine Company No. 6, called Americus, or more commonly known as "Big Six." He served three years with her as assistant foreman under Wm. M. Tweed. For a great number of years Mr. Johnson did painting for the Fire Department, decorating engine backs,

JOSEPH H. JOHNSON.

carriage reels, etc., and he also painted the big banner, ten feet by twelve, that was presented by the City of New York to the Fire Department January 20, 1858. It cost fifteen hundred dollars. It had a blue silk front, scarlet back, with heavy gold mountings, a massive eagle on top and flambeaux on either side. The design in front represented Protection and Benevolence surrounded by emblems of the Fire Department. The latest thing he has done in painting is the picture panels on the Veteran Association's engine. Mr. Johnson, before he became a member of Company 15, was a volunteer in that company for six or seven years, doing active duty previous to his being elected a member, as he was too young to be eligible.

NELSON D. THAYER was born on November 6, 1818. He joined Union Engine Company No. 18 on January 18, 1838, located in Amity Street near Sixth Avenue. This company was disbanded in 1846, and together with a number of old 18 Engine Company Mr. Thayer organized in 1849 Niagara Engine Company No. 4. It was located in Great Jones Street. Mr. Thayer was assistant foreman of 18 Engine two years, secretary four years, and treasurer three years. He was elected Fire Commissioner in 1858, serving until 1860, when he resigned. In 1862 he was elected representative by Engine Company No.

JOHN P. TEALE.

18. He served until the Department was disbanded in 1865. He took a active part in the demonstration made by the Old Volunteer Department on Evacuation Day, the twenty-sixth of November, 1883. He was elected vice-president of the Volunteers February 22, 1884. He is also an active member of the Veteran Firemen's Association, in East Tenth Street. He was chairman of the Ball Committee of the "Vets" Ball which was held at the Metropolitan Opera House on January 12, 1886. He is an active working member of the above association; also was chairman of the Ball Committee of the Volunteers' held at the same house in 1884.

JOHN P. TEALE, one of the oldest living Volunteer Firemen, was born November, 1812, in the Fifth Ward of New York. He was bound an apprentice to John G. Tibbets, in Grand Street near the Bowery, to learn the housesmith and ornamental iron work. In 1826 he became a runner or volunteer to Tradesman Engine No. 37, better known as "Old Sall." At that time Thomas Howe was foreman, and the engine house was a one story brick building situated in Christie Street near Stanton Street. At the age of twenty-one he attached himself to the above company, serving three years, after which he took out a certificate dated January 8, 1833, and was elected steward of the company. He was one of the most persevering of Firemen. He was the first man to enter the ruins of the fire at Haddock's drug store in Pearl Street in 1834, and the first to discover Eugene Underhill beneath its ruins. By his exertion the body was taken out and several lives were saved. Mr. Teale resigned from Engine Company No. 37, and joined Hope Engine Company No. 31, known as "Frogtown," located in old Chapel Street, now West Broadway. A strife soon arose between him and the foreman, Wm. Laurence, and Teale resigned and joined Hudson Engine Company No. 1. Cornelius V. Anderson was foreman, and they both roomed together. Mr. Teale was married December 6, 1835. On the sixteenth the great fire occurred, at which he held the pipe, the post of honor that put the first stream of water on that conflagration, No. 1 being at the head of the line. In May, 1836, he removed to Twenty-first Street, and was made a member of Jackson Engine Company No. 24, then located in Eighteenth Street near Ninth Avenue, Stephen Mead, foreman. Mr. Teale resigned from Nos. 1 and 24, and organized Engine Company No. 16 as Croton, and was its foreman. The company presented him with a splendid silver mounted trumpet in 1838. In the fall of that year he resigned from 16, and joined Guardian Engine Company 29, known as "Butt-Enders." Soon after he became sexton of the church corner of Prince and Thompson Streets, and, after serving three years with 29, resigned to organize in 1841 Hose Company No. 33 as City Hose, and was made its foreman. In 1842 the company presented him with a silver mounted trumpet. In April, 1843, the Common Council pre-sented the company with a handsome trumpet; afterwards the company pre-sented it to Mr. Teale. About the same time Liberty Fire Engine Company, of Baltimore, Md., presented No. 33 with a handsome banner and Mr. Teale with a handsome burnished axe with a suitable inscription thereon. Mr. Teale removed to Williamsburgh, L. I., in the spring of 1849, and on September 3, 1849, took up a certificate as a member of Good Intent Engine Company No. 3. On February 4, 1850, at the Hague Street explosion, he took a very active part, and soon after was elected foreman of his new company. He also assisted in organizing Putnam Hook and Ladder No. 2. Mr. Teale is now in the seventy-fifth year of his age, and is as active and in good health as though he were but twenty-five. He has received many testimonials for his valor and courtesy. One is a splendid mounted cane with calendar of 1842 and other devices thereon. He is the oldest Odd Fellow in Kings County, having joined April 12, 1836, and is now the standard bearer of the Veteran Firemen's Association and an energetic mem-ber of the Volunteers.

FRANK R. MOTT, a son of Dr. Valentine Mott, the eminent surgeon, served his time in the old Volunteer Department. He was at one time assistant fore-man of Harry Howard Hose No. 55. Mr. Mott died in Paris on April 24, 1885.

MATTHEW D. GREEN, at one time a prominent Whig politician and well known hotel keeper and sporting man, was born on July 9, 1815. His first service was performed with old Peterson Engine No. 15. Subsequently he joined Southwark Engine No. 38 and ran with her for several years. Mr. Green was at one time wealthy, but died on January 9, 1870, in reduced circumstances.

JOHN J. REILLY was born in the Seventh Ward on July 2, 1829. He was secretary and representative of Americus Engine No. 6. Mr. Reilly was for many years a prominent politician in the Seventh Ward, and served several terms in the Assembly. At the time of his death, June 14, 1886, he held a position in Father Drumgoole's Home at Lafayette Place and Great Jones Street.

DAVID COLBERT BRODERICK was a noble figure in the annals of the Volun-teers. He was educated in the public school and learned the trade of a stone cutter. A self-made man with the best attributes of manhood, he aspired to shine in politics, not for greed or gain, but to have an opportunity of doing good and to exercise the great gifts which nature had bestowed on him. In New York he was defeated for Congress in 1846. Three years later he determined to tussle with fortune in California. He was a member of Howard Engine Company No. 34, and his comrades gave him a farewell reception and a costly watch and chain. His ambition cropped out just before he went away. Meeting in the street Adam P. Pentz, in reply to his badinage that he supposed he would return a member of Congress, Broderick replied:

"I'll come back a United States Senator or I will not return."

Broderick kept his word. He sailed on the "*Crescent City*" on the seventeenth of April, 1849, and on his arrival at San Francisco went into the assaying business with Frederick D. Kohler, an ex-assistant engineer of the Volunteer Fire Department of New York and a member of Protection Engine No. 5. He was elected to the California Senate, and in 1856 became United States Senator.

DAVID C. BRODERICK.

He was an anti-slavery or anti-Lecompton champion, and as such the foe of Senator William M. Gwin. Ex-Chief Justice of the Supreme Court of California David S. Terry, who recently married his client (Sarah Althea Hill Sharon), at the Lecompton Democratic State Convention at Sacramento brought about an issue with Broderick by sneering at him as a "Douglas Democrat," because he knew well how sincere Broderick's friendship for Stephen A. Douglas was. He went on to brand Broderick as an "arch traitor." After a correspondence famous in the records of the "Code," a hostile meeting was arranged. Broderick's seconds were Joseph C. McKibben, David A. Cotton and Leonidas Haskell, and Terry's, Calhoun Benham, S. H. Brooks and Thomas Hayes. Their meeting at Laguna de la Merced, near San Francisco, on the thirteenth of September, 1859, is spoken of as one of "intellectual giants." At ten paces Broderick inadvertently discharged his pistol while in the act of aiming at "the word." Terry took an advantage, that might not have been, under such circumstances, an unfair one, and fired. Broderick's right breast was pierced to the left armpit, and he was carried from the field to die three days later at Leonidas Haskell's residence at Black Point. His last words were: "They have killed me because I was opposed to slavery and a corrupt administration."

In a public square in San Francisco the war hero General and Senator Edward D. Baker pronounced the funeral oration. It was worthy of the speaker and the illustrious man who lay in his coffin before him. Terry was not punished. Broderick's memory was honored in New York, and the drama, "Three Eras in the Life of a New York Fireman," was founded on his remarkable career. The duel in which he was killed was the second·in which he was engaged. His first was in 1852, on the east shore of San Francisco, with Judge Smith, son of Governor Smith of Virginia—"Extra Billy" Smith. The conditions were navy revolvers at ten paces, "go as you please," with six shots. Broderick's pistol became out of order at his first shot, and while he was bending over to get it into proper condition for continuing the fight, a bullet from Smith's pistol shattered to fragments the watch which the members of Howard Engine gave him. Fragments of the case lacerated his stomach, but the present saved his life. Ex-Police Justice William Dodge has the chain which was attached to the watch on this occasion.

THOMAS MOLONEY, a well-known citizen, now in his eighty-seventh year, who belongs to a family of firemen, did fire duty in 1822, and he knew well how to handle the buckets in those days. At the time of the great fire in 1835 he resided at 36 Wall Street. All of his sons and his two sons-in-law were members of the Volunteer Fire Department of New York. His son Michael C. Moloney was assistant foreman of Fulton Engine Company No 21, when she lay in Temple Street, and M. T. Brennan was foreman. He also fought under the Stars and Stripes as well as under the banner of the Volunteer Fire Department; he was aboard of the United States frigate "Potomac" at the bombardment of Vera Cruz. During the war with Mexico Thomas P. Moloney was a member of Protection Engine Company No. 5, and in 1857 lost his life at sea, going down in the steamer "Central America," which was commanded by W. L. Herndon, father-in-law of the late ex-President, Chester A. Arthur. Nearly all the women and children were saved, but Tom remained steadfast to duty, and, like her gallant commander, went down with the ship. John J. Moloney was foreman of Protection Engine Company No. 5, and secretary of the Volunteer Firemen's Association, and bears the scars he received in his devotion to duty. William H. Moloney, was also a member and representative of Protection Engine Company No. 5, and, like his brother Mike, rallied around the old flag in the hour ·of need. He was a member of the First Fire Zouaves, and secretary to Colonel Ellsworth. Charles A. Brown was his son-in-law. He was a member of Protection Engine Company No. 5, and in 1853 was elected an assistant engineer. He was a good fireman and much liked, not only by the Honey Bees, but by the Department. Matthew T. Brennan, foreman of Fulton Engine Company No. 21, was one of the sons-in-law.

NICHOLAS SEAGRIST commanded Empire Hook and Ladder Company No. 8, and was at one time sergeant-at-arms to the Board of Aldermen, and, what is more, kept them in the straight path. 8's boys thought he acquitted himself so well that he was deserving of a white cap, and they worked hard to get it for him. He was several times an independent candidate. However, the voters in the district elected him as member of Assembly, and afterwards as alderman of the district. He has been for many years a director in the Hamilton Fire Insurance Company, of which Mayor Whitney of Brooklyn is the president.

JOSEPH W. WALSH, Surveyor of the Williamsburgh City Fire Insurance Company, was a hard working, efficient fireman who quietly performed his duty and thought no more about it. In July, 1850, at the time of the great fire in Philadelphia, when aid was asked from this city, he, with David Conger,

Abraham W. Kennedy, and other members of Putnam Hose Company No. 31, went on to assist their brother firemen of the Quaker City. He was also active in working negotiations to receive the Philadelphia firemen when they

WILLIAM LAMB.

came on a pleasant trip to this city. In 1858, with A. W. Kennedy and others, he resigned from the hose company and joined Excelsior Engine Company No. 2. He always did good service as a member of the Department and of the Insurance Fire Patrol.

WILLIAM LAMB commenced service as a volunteer with Engine Company No. 30. In 1840 he became a member of the company. His service with No. 30 was short-lived. A difficulty arose between Nos. 30 and 40. No. 30 felt aggrieved at the issue of the controversy and determined to withdraw from the Department. Mr. Lamb in 1844 became a member of Engine Company No. 18 and served until 1846, when the company was disbanded; he then joined Engine Company No. 25, and in 1852 was

elected assistant foreman, and foreman in 1854. He served with No. 25 until 1861, when he was elected assistant engineer, and held that position until 1865. During the draft riots in 1863 En-gineer Lamb was incessantly on duty for three days and nights, and was constantly in danger. He was at-tacked and knocked down by the rioters, but was rescued by some friends. He escaped without serious injury. The newspapers gave special commendation to the firemen, and Engineer Lamb was highly praised. Mr. Lamb has been connected with the New Department for the past eight years as Superintendent of Repairs to Buildings.

JOHN BARKER was born Novem-ber 1819, in Tyron Row, and at an early age he was indentured appren-tice to James Ruthven, in Fulton Street, where he earned the art of brass, ivory and hardwood turner,

JOHN BARKER.

and became a proficient workman. In 1841 he was a runner to City Hose No. 33, and in April, 1843, became a certificate member of the company and was one of its most active members. His pride was to be the signal lantern bearer, which was a post of honor. He had experienced many hair-breadth escapes by his daring efforts at fires. One of the most notable was at the burning of

Niblo's Theatre (the first time).   He was a leading man with the pipe to direct the stream of water on the fire.   He is known as "Honest John." He entered the Fire Patrol March, 1859, and was energetic and persevering. In 1868 he was admitted into the Exempt Association, and is now a life member of the same.

MOSES O. ALLEN, a genial, kindly gentleman and an active fireman, though small of stature, was big of heart.   He served the Department well in many positions—as foreman of Independence Hose Company No. 3, member of the Jenny Lind Testimonial, Washington Monument, and other committees. Mr. Allen is now a prosperous merchant.   His son, Theodore L. Allen, was foreman of Geo. F. Larned Engine Company No. 2, of Pittsfield, Mass.   The company ran a steamer, and young Allen, like his father, was a popular and efficient officer.   At a Ladies' Fair, held for a benevolent object, he was voted a silver trumpet as being the most popular fireman of the city.   Mr. Moses O. Allen was conspicuous for the very energetic efforts he made to entertain his brother firemen of other cities during their visits to Gotham. The old Philadelphia firemen remember him with pleasure.

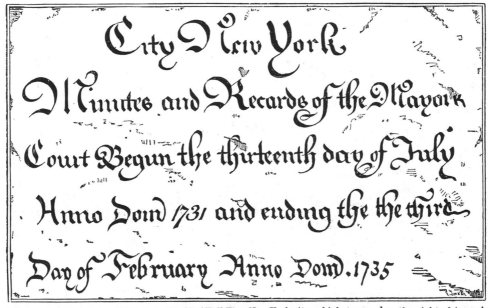

City Of New York

Minutes and Records of the Mayor's

Court Begun the thirteenth day of July

Anno Dom 1731 and ending the the third

Day of February Anno Dom. 1735

This parchment was recovered from the City Hall Fire, New York city, which occurred on the night of August 17, 1858, during the display of fireworks in commemoration of the laying of the Atlantic Cable. Presented by Mr. Robert J. Matthews to John Tyron, on July 26, 1886.

CHAPTER XXIX.

HEROES WHO DID BATTLE WITH THE FLAMES.

F. A. Ridabock.—J. Dawson.—W. Dunn.—D. Garrey.—F. S. Gwyer.—E. W. Jacobs.—Benj. J. Brown.—M. W. Duane.—C. Van Blarcom.—M. Franklin.—P. W. Engs.—Francis Hall.—John G. Hall.—C. H. Haswell.—S. T. Hoyt.- P. N. Cornwell.—J. M. Bennett.—W. H. Wilson.—B. Kenney.—Eugene Ward.—I. Williams.—W. M. Mitchell.—T. F. Goodwin.—W. E. Bishop.—L. Delmonico.—A. R. Jollie.—T. Keeler.—G. W. Lane.—E. R. Campbell.—David Milliken.—Zophar Mills.—T. Monahan.— O. A. Pesoa.—C. Forrester.—H. W. Taylor.—J. Quigg.—C. A. Childs.—E. Haight.—J. Kittleman.— J. and R. Kimmens.—W. H. Pegg.—D. C. Smith.—T. A. Ricard.—T. W. Adams.—W. L. Proch.

FREDERICK A. RIDABOCK, one of the best known of the Volunteer firemen of the city, was born in the Fifth Ward, at the corner of Broadway and Walker street, in 1816, where his father had kept a grocery store for forty years. The latter was also an old fire laddie, having served a full term with Engine Company No. 24, which lay in Fulton Street. His period of service extended from 1800 to 1815. Mr. Frederick A. Ridabock learned the trade of upholsterer. He joined Engine Company 31 in September, 1835, in which company he served for seven years. In 1852 he organized Hook and Ladder Company No. 12, the company's quarters being located in West Broadway, near Beach Street. Mr. Ridabock was elected foreman of the company—an office which he held for six years. In 1858 he was elected a representative from the company as a trustee of the Widows' and Orphans' Fund of the Exempt Firemen's Benevolent Fund. Mr. Ridabock is one of the organizers and also

FREDERICK A. RIDABOCK.

a trustee of the Veteran Firemen's Association.

JOHN DAWSON, of the firm of Joel Mason & Co., was born on March 3, 1839. He served his time with Eagle Hook and Ladder No. 4, of which company he was treasurer for several years. Mr. Dawson was formerly president of the Eckford Social Club of Williamsburg, and is now a very popular member of the City Club.

WILLIAM DUNN, affectionately known as "Old Father Dunn," saw over twenty-two years of service in the Old Department. Born on December 5, 1825, he early enrolled in Americus Engine No. 6. He also served with Bunker Hill Engine No. 32 and Jefferson Engine No. 26. Although one of the most popular men in the Department, Mr. Dunn repeatedly refused to accept office.

DANIEL GARVEY, at one time a well-known shipwright in the employ of Messrs. Steengraff & Co. of South street, has an honorable record of over twenty years in the Old Department. He was born on March 7, 1830, and on arriving at age joined Croton Hose. In 1857 he assisted in organizing Harry Howard Hook and Ladder No. 11, in which he served several years. Mr.

EDWARD W. JACOBS.

Garvey was a member of the committee in charge of the building of Firemen's Hall, and is an ex-president of the City Club. He is now one of the trustees of the Veteran Firemen's Association.

FREDERICK S. GWYER, a very popular fireman, served with Lafayette Engine No. 19 for ten years, joining that company September 5, 1857. He was born on November 4, 1833. Mr. Gwyer is a member of the Volunteer and Veterans' Firemen's Associations, and had the good fortune to win the engine drawn for by the Association in the summer of 1886. With characteristic generosity he presented the engine to the Veterans' Association, in appreciation of which the Association presented him with a handsome gold badge. Mr. Gwyer was one of the "old boys" of "19" when John Slowey and George W. Badger were killed at the fire at Goodwin's cracker bakery, February 3, 1863.

EDWARD W. JACOBS has the distinction of being the only private of the Old Department who was ever elected representative, a post which he filled with honor for four years. He was born on December 29, 1822, and joined Americus Engine No. 6 in 1850. He was an assistant engineer from 1856 to 1862. For three consecutive terms he was elected third vice-president of the Americus Club. Mr. Jacobs is now one of the trustees of the Exempt Firemen's Association.

BENJAMIN M. BROWN, as a fireman, was ever among the foremost to respond to the call of duty. He was largely instrumental in the erection of the Thirteenth Street reservoir. He held many offices : foreman, fire warden, trustee, alderman and commissioner of the Croton Water Works.

MARTIN W. DUANE, an old and popular member of Peterson Engine No. 15, was born on September 10, 1825. Mr. Duane lives in Brooklyn, and was at one time alderman in that city. He is now in the cooperage business.

CHRISTIAN VAN BLARCOM, who served as assistant foreman of Americus Engine No. 6 in 1862 and 1863, was born on July 5, 1832. Mr. Van Blarcom was an enthusiastic fireman. He is now a member of the Associations of Veteran and Volunteer Firemen.

MORRIS FRANKLIN, late president of the New York Life Insurance Company, son of Chief Engineer Thomas Franklin, attained a reputation as an intrepid and skillful fireman as great as that of his distinguished father.

Mr. Franklin early in life enrolled in Supply Engine Company, then stationed at the Corporation Yard, the present site of the Tombs Prison. From this company he went to No. 24, known as the " Brass Back Engine," of which he soon became foreman.

His reckless bravery frequently carried him into situations of extraordinary danger, from which, on two different occasions at least, he barely escaped with his life. At the first fire in the Bowery Theater he forced his way through flames and smoke to the third tier. Suddenly the word " All out !" was passed, and in a few moments he found himself the only man in the building. Finding no other way of escape he made a desperate leap to the ground floor, and although badly bruised and half stunned he managed to grope his way, crawling on hands and knees, to the great door which was just being closed, where he was caught up by his comrades and carried in a fainting condition into a neighboring house. As soon as he recovered consciousness he insisted on returning to duty, and manfully stood at his post until the fire was over.

At a fire in Park Place Mr. Franklin was holding the pipe in an attic when the blazing roof fell in on him so as to make escape impossible. In this fearful situation he was discovered by Chief Gulick, who gallantly went to his rescue and succeeded in extricating him, not, however, before he had been so terribly burned that he was confined to his bed for many weeks.

In 1837 Mr. Franklin was elected to the Assembly on the firemen's ticket, and in 1842 he took his seat in the Senate. In 1838 he was a member of the Board of Assistant Aldermen, and in the following year was elected President of the Board of Aldermen. He was also chairman of the Committee of Arrangements for the grand celebration of the Thirty-fourth Anniversary of the organization of the Department in October 15, 1827.

When John W. Degrauw was presented with a magnificent silver urn on the occasion of his retirement from the presidency of the Department, the presentation address was made by Mr. Franklin. On the occasion of the laying of the corner stone of the present Firemen's Hall Mr. Franklin delivered the inaugural address.

PHILIP W. ENGS, one of the most active of the old Volunteers in promoting fire matters, was born in 1789. He joined Engine Company No. 21 December 9, 1813. He became assistant engineer in 1824, and served in that capacity until 1833. In 1857 he was elected President of the Association of Exempt Firemen and thereafter for twenty-five years was annually re-elected. It was due to his exertions while in the legislature in 1866 that the Exempts obtained control of the Benevolent Fund of the Fire Department. He died May 19, 1875.

FRANCIS HALL, publisher of the *Commercial Advertiser*, was a member of Hose Company No. 1, joining the Department about 1813.

JOHN B. HALL, of the *Commercial Advertiser*, son of Francis Hall, was a chip of the old block, and was first a member of Engine Company No. 5, and then of Hook and Ladder Company No. 1. Once at a fire in Maiden Lane, below Gold Street, he had a very narrow escape of his life.

CHARLES H. HASWELL was in his time a member of many companies. At the age of twenty-one he joined Merchants' Engine Company No. 25. In 1822 he was a member of Columbian Engine Company No. 14, then of Union Engine Company No. 18. In 1830 he removed from North Moore Street, where he was born, to Clinton Street, and joined Jefferson Engine Company No. 26. In 1832 having removed to Crosby Street, he was invited to join Metamora Engine

PHILIP W. ENGS.

Company No. 3 as foreman. In 1835, having moved to Twenty-second Street near Ninth Avenue, Chelsea Engine Comapny No. 16 offered him the position, of foreman if he would join, and he did so. When Mr. Haswell obtained a position in the naval service he resigned from the Department.

STEPHEN T. HOYT was a member of Hudson Engine Company No. 1, was afterwards foreman of Hudson Hose Company No. 21, and was elected assistant engineer in March, 1850. He died on September, 17, 1852, at the age of thirty-seven. For some time before he expired he lay in a lethargy. The bell on the Twenty-second Street tower striking an alarm, the sound appeared to arouse him. He counted the district with his fingers, and a moment or two afterwards died.

PETER N. CORNWELL was every inch a fireman. He knew how to obey and how to command and to see that his commands were obeyed; and to fight and conquer a fire, always having due regard for the welfare of those who served under him, never ordering a man to take a risk that he would not readily take himself. In early life he joined Eagle Hook and Ladder Company No. 4, and in time was elected assistant foreman, in which office he served two years and a half, when he was elected foreman, and also served two years and a half in that position, when he resigned and could not be prevailed upon to serve any longer, as he wished to give the boys a chance to go up ahead. After his resignation the company presented him with a silver trumpet as a token of their esteem, and also elected him representative. While a member and officer he aided greatly to achieve and maintain for the company the reputation of being the quickest and hardest working truck company in the city. In 1853 he was elected an assistant engineer, in which office he served many years. He was several times injured and had many hair-breadth escapes at fires. He was prominent as a Fire Insurance Surveyor and was General Surveyor of the New York Board of Fire Underwriters. He died August 7, 1875, at the age of forty-five years. Funeral services were held at his residence and also at the church in Second Avenue, corner One Hundred and Nineteenth Street, and were attended by the Masonic fraternity, members of the Volunteer Fire Department, many gentlemen prominent in insurance circles, and a large number of the residents of Harlem.

JOHN M. BENNETT, one of the oldest living members of the Old Department, joined Protection Engine No. 5, of which Wilson Small was then foreman, in 1835, and served with her during the great fire of that year. Mr. Bennett remained with No. 5 until 1840, when he resigned, taking most of the company with him, and organized Protector Engine No. 22. She was the first piano engine ever built in New York. Samuel Waddell was foreman and Bennett assistant foreman. In the following year he was elected foreman. Mr. Bennett was at the big fire in Broad Street in 1845, when his engine was blown across the street by the explosion and burned up. Mr. Bennett remained with No. 22 until 1850, when he resigned and joined the Insurance Patrol. In 1857 he joined the Police force and is now attached to the Yorkville Police Court.

WILLIAM H. WILSON joined engine No. 18 in 1837, and ran with it for twelve years. She used to lie in West Third Street, where the repair shops of the present Department now are. Previous to joining No. 18 Mr. Wilson served for a short time with Engine No. 24, then in the house now occupied by engine No. 3 in Seventeenth Street, near Ninth Avenue. On the disbandment in 1865 Mr. Wilson was appointed captain of engine No. 14, a post which he held for six years, when he retired.

BERNARD KENNEY, a very popular member of the Old Department, was born in New York on February 2, 1830, and joined Tompkins Hose No. 16 on November 17, 1857. From 1859 to 1862 he was foreman of that company, and during the last two years of the existence of the Old Department he held the post of assistant engineer. At the time of his death, which occurred on March 27, 1886, Mr. Kenney was a member of the Board of Trustees of the Veteran Firemen's Association. His funeral was largely attended by his old comrades.

EUGENE WARD was born in New York on February 22, 1826, and joined Guardian Engine No. 29 in 1845. In 1849 he was elected assistant foreman, and during the next four succeeding years he was in command of the company. Mr. Ward was a trustee of the Exempt Firemen's Association, and is now a trustee of the Veteran Firemen's Association. When the members of this organization went to Washington to attend the inauguration of President Cleveland Mr. Ward acted as marshal. His portrait is on the next page.

ICHABOD WILLIAMS, one of the oldest surviving members of the Old Department, was born on December 6, 1807, and ran with the Engine No. 9 long before he was old enough to be enrolled. The engine lay in Marketfield Street. As he worked at his trade of cabinet-maker during the day it was only at night that he could spare the time to run to fires. He says that Saturday night was a time he looked forward to, for it was generally marked by a fire among the lumber yards in the "Hook." In 1829 Mr. Williams joined Hook and Ladder No. 1, of which William Disosway was foreman, then lying in Beaver near Broad. The first fire he went to was at the Lafayette Theatre in Laurens Street, now South Fifth Avenue. He remained with Hook and Ladder No. 1 for a year, when a split occurred in the company, and he and many others seceded to Engine No. 9, of which he became assistant foreman. In 1832 Mr. Williams joined Engine No. 15, and served with her through the great fire of 1835. In 1837 Mr. Williams's term was up, and he resigned to make room for another man, and moved to Elizabeth, N. J. His last fire service in New York was during the great fire in Broad Street in 1845, when he came over from Elizabeth with an engine and did good work in putting out the fire. Mr. Williams is a member of the Volunteer Firemen's Association. He is still hale and hearty, and keeps a hotel in Elizabeth.

WILLIAM M. MITCHELL joined Engine Company No. 24 on June 9, 1845, and in 1855 was assistant foreman under T. L. West, when he was elected engineer; was then made foreman and served in that capacity until 1860 and held connection with the company until the Paid Department was organized, and was then made foreman of Engine Company No. 26 and served three years; was then transferred to Engine No. 21 as foreman and served one year in that capacity.

THOMAS F. GOODWIN joined the Old Volunteer Fire Department May 25, 1849, and became a member of the old Fifteenth Ward Hose Company known as No. 35, and commonly spoken of as Curry's Hose Cart. Subsequently Mr. Goodwin was elected foreman of this company, in which position he served until the organization of Baxter Hook and Ladder Company No. 15, then lying in Franklin Street. In the latter company he served as

EUGENE WARD.

an assistant foreman, and finally was placed in the charge of that apparatus as foreman. During his many years of service Mr. Goodwin encountered his due share of the hardship and danger incident to the fireman's life. As one of the organizers of the Old Volunteer Firemen's Association, Mr. Goodwin came into prominence, being one of the board of directors during the first year of the existence of that organization. Mr. Goodwin is also a member of long standing of the Exempt Firemen's Association. Mr. Goodwin has shown latterly that there is yet some of the old-time vim left among the old fire "vamps" by his entering a foot race at the annual picnic and barbecue of the Volunteer Firemen's Association in September, 1886. He won the first prize—a handsome gold badge, Mr. Goodwin then being over fifty-five years old, and considerably over two hundred and twenty-five pounds avoirdupois. At the beginning of the civil war he enlisted as sergeant-major in Ellsworth's Zouaves, and was wounded at the first battle of Bull Run. He was mustered out in 1862 as adjutant and re-entered civil life for but a few weeks, when he enlisted as captain with a full company and was attached to the One Hundred and Thirty-second

Regiment New York State Volunteers, Spinola's brigade, with which command he served until the surrender at Appomattox, Virginia.

Mr. Goodwin is one of the charter members of Noah L. Farnham Post 458, G. A. R., Department of New York, organized in April, 1884. He is its first Past Senior Vice-Commander. On Decoration Day, 1885, this Post visited New Haven to decorate the grave of Colonel Farnham. Mr. Goodwin is a sculptor by profession and has erected many monuments in memory of those who were formerly prominent firemen, notably Chief Anderson and Andrew Schenck. He has also executed many fine life size-portraits of distinguished firemen and citizens.

WILLIAM E. BISHOP assisted in the organization of Washington Irving Hose Company 44 in January, 1849, and was appointed one of the firemen of the city of New York February 1, 1849. He was a member of Laurel Company No. 30 about 1854, but resigned his membership and joined Jackson Engine Company No. 24 and served as its secretary until 1857. Business matters caused him to resign about that time; subsequently he joined the Exempt Engine Company and served until 1863. He was one of the Committee of Arrangements for the Centennial of 1883 when the call for the old Volunteers was made. Subsequently he was appointed one of the committee to organize the Volunteer Firemen's Association of the City of New York. Mr. Bishop is a charter member of that organization, now numbering two thousand one hundred members, and has served as the Financial Secretary up to the present date. Mr. Bishop was Secretary of the Irving Guards, a notable organization of the period.

WILLIAM E. BISHOP.

The Irving Guards were composed of a fine body of men, and annually used to make quite a presentable turnout. They were attached to Hose Company No. 44. They went on their first annual target excursion to Tarrytown, N. Y., on Thanksgiving Day. This was the place of abode of our country's gifted author Washington Irving, in whose honor the company was named. He received them in a cordial manner, and in a short address returned his thanks to the company for the flattering compliment paid to him; he was then introduced to them all personally. The officers, May 6, 1850, elected for the ensuing year were: Leonard Myers, foreman; James R. Remsen, assistant; William E. Bishop, secretary; Alvah Spaulding, treasurer; William Simpson and John Maxwell representatives.

The Guards, in 1850, gave their annual excursion and invited the celebrated Washington Irving to be present. The following autograph letter of the distinguished author in reply to Mr. Bishop's note is now of much interest:

Sunnyside Oct 1st 1850

Dear Sir,

I cannot but feel highly sensible of the honor done me by the Irving guard in inviting me to meet and dine with them on their approaching annual excursion; but I regret to say that the loss I have sustained in the death of my Sister; and the languor resulting from a long and severe indisposition from which I am but recently recovered have totally unfitted me to partake of any public festivity. I beg you to communicate this to the Irving guard as my excuse for declining their very kind and flattering invitation I remain dear Sir

Your obliged humble Servant

Washington Irving

William E Bishop Esq
Secretary of I. G.

LORENZO DELMONICO, one of the brothers who are famous as caterers, was born in 1813, in the village of Marengo, Canton of Ticino, Switzerland. He joined his relatives in this country in 1832. In 1840 he entered the Fire Department as one of the organizers of Engine Company No. 42, of which company his brother Siro was also a member. Siro died in December, 1881. Another member of the family, Charles, belonged to North River Engine Company No. 30, and later of Metamora Hose Company No 29. Lorenzo died at Sharon Springs, N. Y., September 5, 1881.

ALLEN R. JOLLIE, who died in 1877, will long be remembered as the enthusiastic fireman who was invariably first at the engine house, and who used, single handed, to roll it along the sidewalk until help arrived. He was a man of considerable strength of muscle as well as of character. In 1826 he joined Engine Company No. 12, and in 1828 No. 29 in Greenwich village, to which locality he had removed. He served for several years as foreman and was then, in 1835, made assistant engineer. Subsequently he joined Hydrant Company No. 2, with which he served until 1842. Mr. Jollie had three brothers in the Department, and his son Edward was an active member of Hose Company No. 41.

LORENZO DELMONICO.

THEODORE KEELER was born on July 28, 1815. When only fifteen years old he ran as a volunteer with Engine Company No. 12. In 1835 he joined Engine Company No. 14, then No. 21, and next No. 38. He was surveyor of the Lorillard Insurance Company. Died January 10, 1887.

GEORGE W. LANE was a member of Pearl Hose Company No. 28, and treasurer for more than seven years. At his instance his company used the first steam fire engine ever seen in the city. Mr. Lane was chamberlain of the city, and president of the Chamber of Commerce.

E. R. CAMPBELL was born January 7, 1833, in the Thirteenth Ward. He joined the famous Engine Company No. 6 in Gouverneur Street on March 17, 1852. On September 8, 1855, he was nearly killed going to a fire in Grand Street. Near Lord & Taylor's his engine collided with a stage, and the big machine, weighing about four thousand two hundred pounds, threw the stage on the sidewalk. Half a dozen of the firemen went down, and the engine ran over Mr. Campbell, breaking his leg and injuring one of his arms. It was thought he would not survive, but he did, although he was laid up for seven or eight months. Charles B. Elliott, who afterwards became a justice in one of the Brooklyn courts, was also thrown down and injured, but he lived to tell the tale. In later years Mr. Campbell was a keeper in Sing Sing and Clinton prisons. He was instrumental in bringing prominently before the public the evils of the contract system, and had to leave the Prison Department.

DAVID MILLIKEN was secretary and vice-president of the Fire Department one year, and president three years; afterwards vice-president of the Association of Exempt Firemen. In March, 1840, he joined Engine Company No. 18, and was its representative for five years. In 1847 he was transferred to Hose Company No. 40, elected assistant foreman for one year, foreman for three years, and was its representative for six years. He was prominent in local politics, and his opinion always carried weight.

ZOPHAR MILLS has made one of the most remarkable records the Fire Department can boast of. He was born on September 23, 1809, and when only thirteen years old ran with Engine Company No. 13. But in time his ambition was satisfied, and he became a regular member of this company. In November, 1835, he was elected its foreman. On July 11, 1838, he was elected assistant engineer, and received the congratulations of all. Finally he became president of the Fire Department, and on his retirement in 1842 received from the representatives a beautifully engrossed testimonial. Again in August, 1853, Mr. Mills received another testimonial—a magnificent silver tea service, costing one thousand dollars, and subscribed for by the firemen. He became president of the Association of Exempt Firemen, an office which he has held for many years. In early days he was indefatigable in getting up balls, and still more zealous in attending fires. At the destruction of the Jennings building he with other firemen was buried beneath a collapsed wall. But he managed to crawl out of the rubbish and assist the unfortunates who couldn't get out. At the Hague Street explosion he also distinguished himself. No man was thought more of in and out of the Department than he, and his bravery, self-sacrifice, and generosity entitled him to the high esteem in which he was held. His views (of a most interesting character) on fire matters will be found on page 446; also his portrait.

THOMAS MONAHAN served for ten years, making an excellent record. He was first a member of Engine Company No. 4, and next of Hose Company No. 1. He was one of the men in 1835 fire. Mr. Monahan was president of the Fulton Bank.

OSCAR A. PESOA, assistant foreman of Engine Company No. 4, in the present Department, has been a fireman for the past thirty years, having joined the Volunteer Fire Department on June 2, 1856, attaching himself to Hose Company No. 41, which then lay in Watts Street. In 1857 Mr. Pesoa was elected assistant foreman, and after serving the full term of five years he was placed upon the honorary roll. Still he continued to do active service until the creation of the Paid Department, to which he immediately received an appointment, being assigned to Engine Company No. 18, then stationed on West Tenth Street. Mr. Pesoa is a fireman of acknowledged skill and daring, and he carries to-day upon his body honorable though unpleasant reminders of the fiery ordeals he has passed through. Hose Company No. 41 bore the reputation, and deservedly, too, of being hard to beat for quickness in getting to a fire, and for the efficiency of its members. But Mr. Pesoa, with becoming modesty, avoids all reference to their achievements. When interrogated he speaks glowingly of the excellent work done by the Volunteers generally.

CHARLES FORRESTER, for many years foreman of the celebrated Black Joke

Engine 33, lying in Gouverneur Street, and subsequently an engineer of the old Department, was born in New York on November 4, 1814. When a lad of eleven he became an assistant to his father, who was a clerk and letter carrier in the Post-Office. He remained in the service of the Post-Office throughout his life, rising to the position of superintendent of the City Paper Department, which he held up to the time of his death, which occurred on the twenty-first of February, 1886.

Mr. Forrester was a born fireman, and began to run to fires as soon as he could walk. At the great fire in the shipyard of Adam & Noah Brown at Stanton and Houston Streets, in 1824, young Forrester, then barely ten years of age, carried a torch. During this fire the men of Black Joke Engine were forced to abandon their machine, which was totally destroyed. The shipyard and a number of vessels on the stocks were consumed. Mr. Forrester was successively elected steward, secretary, treasurer, assistant foreman, and finally foreman of Black Joke. He served as steward but one year, and failed of re-election on account of his refusal to serve out liquor to the boys.

CHARLES FORRESTER.

Throughout a service of fifteen years Mr. Forrester never missed a day from his business, in spite of frequently being called out on duty as often as four nights in one week. It is related of him that on one occasion, while taking a vapor bath to check a cold, he threw off the coverings, and, hastening to the engine house in response to an alarm, worked bravely throughout a bitterly cold night. Next day he declared that he had discovered a new cure for colds. At the "Great Fire" in 1835 Engine 33 was run on the deck of a brig at the foot of Wall Street, and supplied water to the engine playing on the fire further up the street. The weather was bitterly cold, and the boys were frequently obliged to leave the brakes, and get into the brig's cabin to "thaw out." When their comrades on deck judged that their turn at the stove had come the expedient of placing a fire hat over the stove pipe speedily smoked out those below. After working all night the engine became so encased in ice that further work was impossible. At the great fire in West Street, near the Battery, Mr. Forrester, then engineer, entered the building to order out the men of Engine 33 and Hose 13, the walls being in danger of falling. The boys of Hose 13 lingered to save their hose, and three of them were instantly killed by the falling walls. A ludicrous adventure befell Mr. Forrester at a fire in a stove store at No. 231 Water Street in 1842. The stoves in the upper floor having fallen through to the basement, tearing away the staircase, the escape of the men on the roof was cut off. Finally some one found an old signboard which was placed at a steep incline against an adjoining roof. It proved to be coated with a preparation of smalts—a mixture of powdered glass. Man after man was obliged to slide down, and those who only ruined their trousers were considered lucky. Mr. Forrester said that it was many a day before he could sit down.

At the fire in the Buck's Horn Tavern, in 1842, at the junction of the Boston Post Road and the Bloomingdale Road, near the present site of the Fifth Avenue Hotel, Engineer Forrester formed a line of engines to the corner of Fourth Street and Fourth Avenue, that being the nearest point where water could be procured. In the same year a disastrous fire occurred near Fulton Ferry in Brooklyn. So rapidly did the flames spread that the chief engineer decided to dispatch a messenger to the Navy Yard to beg that a force of marines might be detailed to blow up a row of brick buildings in the path of the conflagration. Chief Engineer Anderson, of New York, and Engineer Forrester assured the Brooklyn chief that with the aid of the New York fire laddies the fire could be checked without help from the Navy Yard. In a few minutes Engineer Forrester was on his way to New York with orders to summon assistance. His first care was to hold the ferry boat in her slip, and then he rang an alarm on the Fulton Market Bell. This was taken up by the bells of the City Hall, the North Dutch Tower, and the old Brick Church Tower, and in an incredibly short space of time the ferry boat, heavily laden with engines, was on her way back to Brooklyn. The reinforcements got to work with a will, and soon got the fire under control, and saved the row of buildings which were about to be blown up.

JOHN QUIGG.

Mr. Forrester was a firm believer in the virtues of salt water for extinguishing fires. It could not be thrown so far, he said, but wherever it struck its effect was felt. In 1847, when Mr. Forrester applied to Chief Engineer Anderson for an honorable discharge, that officer complimented him greatly on his splendid record, and said, "You ought to have two—one for each term you have served."

HUGH W. TAYLOR was born in New York city in Beekman Slip, now called Fulton Slip, on July 28, 1800. He is now living at Mill Neck, Oyster Bay Township, Queens County, Long Island. On May 20, 1820, he joined Protection Fire Engine Company No. 5, Foster Nostrand being foreman, and Samuel Jones Willis assistant foreman; location in Fulton Street, at the rear of the old Dutch Church. He was elected foreman of the company on the fifteenth of January, 1828, and resigned from the office and the company on the twenty-second of June, 1830. At the time he joined the company a fireman had to serve ten years to clear him from jury and military duties. On December 21, 1821, he was at the fire that took place in Fulton Street reaching from Fulton on Front Street to Beekman Street, and on Fulton and Beekman to the East River, the block where Fulton Market now stands. It was a bitter cold night, and the engines had to work all the time to keep from freezing. He was also at the first burning of the Bowery Theater.

JOHN QUIGG was born in the Eleventh Ward. He joined Mechanics'

Hose Company No. 47, of the old Volunteer Fire Department, in 1854. He has held every position in the company, and was foreman at the dissolution of the Department. As a fireman he was always prompt in the discharge of his duty. He was a disciplinarian, and his company was second to none in fire duty. At one time he represented No. 47 in the Board. He became a member of the Exempt Firemen's Association in 1867, was one of the chartered members of the Volunteer Firemen's Association of New York, and is now one of the directors. He was president of the Mechanics' Association, composed of members of the Old Department on the east side of the city. This organization claims to be the spark which kindled the flame of enthusiasm among the scattered members of the Old Department which eventually brought the present Volunteer Firemen's Association into existence. As a testimony of the esteem and respect in which his comrades held him, they presented him with a beautiful fire trumpet bearing the following inscription engraved thereon: "Presented to John Quigg, foreman, by the members of Mechanics' Hose

CHARLES A. CHILDS.

47 of the Volunteer Department, for his ability as a fireman, his qualifications as a man, and his many acts of kindness to his fellow members. October 16, 1865." Mr. Quigg's ability as an artist is well known. He has been connected with the present Fire Department since its organization as master painter and decorator, a position which he still holds.

CHARLES A. CHILDS, like many members of the Volunteer Fire Department, in very early years evinced his love for fire life, and he ran with Atlantic Hose Company No. 14. In 1855, when he had attained his majority, he became a member. James R. Mount was then foreman of the company. He resigned in 1857 and joined Adriatic (afterwards Peterson) Engine Company No. 31. While a member of 14 he was elected secretary. He served his time in 31, and during his membership he was elected treasurer and also a representative. He was one of the organizers and members of the Baxter Light Guard (named in honor of Lieut.-Col. Baxter, who was killed in the Mexican War. He had been a member of the Volunteer Fire Department and also of the Peterson Guard. He likewise was one of the organizers of the Atlantic Light Guard and was elected the first captain.

Mr. Childs at an early age became connected with the express business. John Hoey and he were boys together in the Adams Express Co. For many years he was superintendent of the New York Transfer Company, and had charge of the transportation of the United States mail. He organized the Dodd & Childs Express Company, of Jersey City, and for several years has been baggage agent of the Fall River Line of steamers. He resides on Jersey City Heights and is a member of both the Veteran Firemen's and the Volunteer Firemen's Association. He was born in Albany, N. Y., and is a descendant of the Childs family that settled in Roxbury, Mass., in 1630, being of the sixth generation. Twenty-two of that family were of the first company of volunteers and minute men at Lexington, Mass., April 19, 1775, when the boys of those days taught John Bull's regulars what volunteers could do.

EDWARD HAIGHT, the president of the Commonwealth Bank, was an enthusiastic fireman. On one occasion he turned out with his engine thirteen times in six days, a feat that he was fond of citing in later years as an example of the amount of work that the old-timers could do. In order to insure being roused in case of fire, he had an ingenious attachment fitted to his front door by which the ringing of the door bell started an alarm bell in his bedroom. He was a member of the Association of Exempt Firemen. His five sons all served their time in the Department.

JOHN KITTLEMAN, affectionately known as "Old Kit," a member of Empire Hook and Ladder Company No. 40, was a very popular fireman. He was a mason by trade. No firemen's excursion was considered complete without the presence of "Old Kit." Mr. Kittleman died on June 14, 1861.

JOHN and RICHARD KIMMENS, twin brothers, were born on August 6, 1825. John Kimmens was a well-known member of Americus Engine No. 6. He died on April 27, 1882. His brother "Dick," at one time foreman of No. 6, was one of the most popular men of his day.

WILLIAM H. PEGG, a prominent member of Oceana Hose, was born in 1825. Few men in the Department could number more friends than "Billy" Pegg. He died on November 27, 1884.

DAVID C. SMITH, one of the organizers of Americus Engine No. 6, was born on April 28, 1829. He was for many years in the plumbing business in this city. He went to Rochester, where he is now connected with the firm of E. H. Clarke & Co. He was a brave and popular fireman. He served with No. 6 for over nine years.

T. AUGUSTUS RICARD, son of George Ricard, the millionaire who died in 1880, was born December 25, 1819. He was a member of Peterson Engine No. 15, and helped to roll her at the great fire at Woolsey's sugar house, at Montgomery and South Streets, in 1850. Mr. Ricard, who is quite wealthy, has retired from business and resides in Staten Island.

THOMAS W. ADAMS, an old member of Americus Engine, was born November 29, 1822. He was a carman by occupation, and was at one time Alderman of the Seventh Ward, being elected by the firemen's votes. He was at one time Commissioner of Public Works in Brooklyn. Mr. Adams used to be noted for his personal strength. He now resides in Brooklyn, where he is engaged in the house-moving business.

WILLIAM L. PROCH, of the firm of Drumgoole & Proch, died on October 7, 1876. He was a famous musician, and possessed the faculty of whistling like a flute. He was very popular, and on all occasions of social enjoyment used to contribute with his musical talent to the entertainment of the boys.

CHAPTER XXX.

OTHER FAMOUS FIREMEN.

G. W. Anderson.—J. J. Ferris.—J. Hayes.—H. P. McGown.—S. Burhans, Jr.—G. W. Wheeler.—N. Finch.—M. Fowler.—W. R. W. Chambers.—J. Galvin.—J. E. Colegrove.—J. P. Lacour.—A. Boese.—J. F. Gillin.—L. J. Belloni.—J. Harris.—A. C. D'Ozeville.-O. A. Farrin.—J. Fagin.—J. H. English.—J. Kavanagh.—J. Dailey.—E. P. Durham,—J. J. Slevin.—E. Bonnoll.—A. J. Allaire.—J. Mullin,—J. Buckbee—A. Franklin.—M. J. Keese.—J. L. Mott.—H. J. Ockershausen.—M. F. Odell.—J. R. Platt.—J. R. Steers.—J. Cornwell.—R. McGinnis.—F. E. Gibert.—A. P. Pentz.—E. Byrnes.

GEORGE W. ANDERSON was born in the Tenth Ward, on January 24, 1834. He joined Phenix Hose Company, No. 22, on March 20, 1854. In succession he was secretary, treasurer, representative, and foreman of the company, holding the last position when the company disbanded in 1865.

GEORGE W. ANDERSON.

He is a self-made man, having educated himself. He wanted to be a bookkeeper, and found a position at the Charleston Steamship Company, at Pier 26, N. R. He has been purser, and for the past twelve years has been in the city and harbor transportation business for the Charleston, Morgan, and Guion line of steamers. He was elected supervisor of Kings County in 1878, served four years, and was president of the Board in 1880 - 81. On retiring from the presidency he was presented with a handsomely framed set of resolutions, which grace the walls of the Washington Club of Brooklyn, of which has been the president since its organization, covering a period of five years. He was one of the organizers of the Volunteer Firemen's Association, of this city. He also belongs to and is a life member of the Exempt Firemen's Association, and a member of the Veteran Firemen's Association, and its president for the last two years. Mr. Anderson is a member of the Brooklyn Bridge Trustees.

JAMES J. FERRIS, first vice-president of the Volunteer Firemen's Association of the City of New York, is an old Fourth Warder, and is fifty-two years old. On attaining his majority he joined Eagle Engine Company, No. 13. He served upwards of ten years in the company, four years of which he was secretary. His record as a volunteer fireman in the New York Department is one that he may well be proud of. He is also a member of the Association of Exempt Firemen of the city of New York, and held in high esteem by his fellow members. At the commencement of the war he was among the first to subscribe his name on the roll of the "Ellsworth Fire Zouaves," insisting on entering the service as a private, although he had had considerable military experience previously, he being captain in command of the "Continental Blues" (an independent uniformed organization) for some five years before the war, and at the time of entering upon the roll of Company "G" of the Eleventh Regiment. While in active service he always held a position in the "front rank" of the bravest; promotion for meritorious

conduct and bravery was his reward. At the first battle of Bull Run—having been advanced to the rank of sergeant—he was made a lieutenant on the field by Col. Farnham, but never got his commission. He fought bravely, and was badly wounded, on account of which wounds he was finally discharged. He was one of the incorporators, or charter members, of Noah L. Farnham Post, No. 458, G. A. R., and still holds his membership. He served as adjutant of the post for two terms. His happy and genial disposition, coupled with his executive ability, make him a coveted and valuable member and officer of every organization having his name on its roll book. He is now (1887) holding the position of Deputy United States Shipping Commissioner for the port of New York.

JAMES J. FERRIS.

JAMES HAYES, a well-known citizen of the Fourteenth Ward, was one of the most active and stirring of politicians and firemen. He joined Marion Engine Company, No. 9, in 1856, was chosen foreman in 1857, and ably filled the position until the end of the Department, in 1865, a period of eight years. No. 9 had a long list of members, numbering seventy men, and the roll was constantly filled. Under the guidance of Mr. Hayes, the strictest discipline was maintained; his word was law, and the members of the company understood it. He held the position of councilman and supervisor, and was elected member of assembly in the years 1872, 1873, 1874, and 1878. Mr. Hayes is a member of the Veteran Firemen's Association, and, although an invalid for a long time, his flow of spirits remains, and he can relate many a story of old-time firemen and politicians with all the vigor of youth.

HENRY P. McGOWN was born and bred in Harlem; he joined Pocahontas Engine Company No. 49 on October 5, 1842, as private. Six months later he was made secretary, and the end of his first year of service found him foreman.

The quarters of the company were on Fourth Avenue, between One Hundred and Twenty-sixth and One Hundred and Twenty-seventh Streets, where Engine No. 36 of the present Department is stationed. It was the glory of 49's boys that they were never "washed themselves" and frequently washed their rivals. Once when the frozen surface of a stream had to be cut to let down the suction pipe, Foreman McGown himself stood for hours up to his knees in the icy water, holding the pipe under. He would not take a man from the engine, as he wished to "wash" the machine just ahead.

In racing to fires Hose 43 and Engine 35 were "Pocahontas's" chief opponents.

One bitterly cold night the mansion of John A. Haven, at Fort Washington, took fire. Mr. Haven was a commission merchant with an office at No. 7 Beaver Street. The alarm was carried from steeple to steeple, and 43 Hose and 49 Engine started for the rescue. Scarcely could a foothold be obtained upon the frozen roads, and Beekman Hill was a glacé of ice. Mr. Haven's house was on the river bank at the foot of a steep hill about four hundred feet long. The road into the merchant's grounds ran between two massive stone pillars. The hose company, which was slightly in advance of No. 49, dashed recklessly down this icy incline. In vain the men at the tongue strove to hold the carriage back. It shot like lightning down the hill, scattering the firemen right and left and running over one, named Wilson. He died from his injuries. Foreman McGown ordered his men to pass the ropes back under the engine, and hang on with all their might. They obeyed, and No. 49 passed between the pillars with but little damage. Mr. Haven's stately house was in flames from roof to cellar. His three young daughters had been rescued, but ran back to get some jewels. They had scarcely re-entered when the walls fell and buried them.

At daybreak, believing that he could be of no further service, Foreman McGown directed his men to "take up." Then Mr. Audubon, son of the famous naturalist, approached and begged him to assist in exhuming the bodies of the three girls. The family particularly desired No. 49 to remain. The men, cold, stiffened, and weary though they were, consented, and the foreman granted Mr. Audubon's request. After the best breakfast obtainable, the sad task was begun. Tools were improvised by some men, and others worked with their bare hands. Several hours passed before something white was seen beneath the blackened timbers. It was the skull of one of the girls, denuded of flesh and hair, and bleached by the terrible heat. The right hand had been burned away, and the head lay on the arm in the attitude of sleep. Within a radius of a few feet were the bodies of the other girls. It was after noon when No. 49 finally "took up." They had been at work eighteen hours.

Mr. McGown studied law, and was admitted to the bar in 1846. He is now justice of the Ninth District Court. He resigned from the Department May 4, 1857.

SAMUEL BURHANS, Jr., took hold of an engine rope as soon as he was old enough to drop his mother's apron-strings. 27 Engine was his first love. She used to lie in Watts Street, between Greenwich and Hudson. Her great rival was 34 Engine, lying in Christopher Street. Mr. Burhans relates, with great gusto, that when the two engines were racing to a fire down Canal Street 27's men would crowd to the rope furthest from their opponents so as to avoid a row, leaving him to carry the other side of the rope. "I was so little then," he says, "that I could hardly hold the rope up from the ground, but I managed to get along." On July 16, 1852, he joined National Hose No. 24, and in the following year was elected assistant foreman. On October 3, 1854, he was elected foreman and continued to command the company till November 3, 1857. In the following year he was again elected. He resigned his position as foreman on May 3, 1859, and was afterward elected representative. On January 28, 1861, he resigned from the Department. On the occasion of his resignation as foreman the company presented him with a handsome gold watch and massive fob chain and seal. While in command of this company Mr. Burhans was instrumental in obtaining a handsome hose carriage in place of the old-fashioned cart that the company had formerly used. He also designed the handsome house in Spring Street which was for many years the quarters of the company. The distinctive badges for Engine, Hose, and Hook and Ladder Companies, adopted in 1860, were also of his design. There used to hang in the house in Spring Street an immense frame containing the portrait of thirty members

of the company. It was the first thing of the kind ever made and attracted much attention. On the disbandment of the Department it was placed in the museum at Mount St. Vincent in Central Park, and when that was burned the picture was one of the few objects saved. It is now in possession of Richard L. Simonson, an old member of the company. Mr. Burhans was also vice-chairman of the Board of Engineers and Foremen under Chief Carson. For fifteen years he was president of the Coney Island and Brooklyn Railroad Company. He is also a life member of the Association of Exempt Firemen. Mr. Burhans is an enthusiast in all matters pertaining to the history of

SAMUEL BURHANS, JR.

the Volunteer Fire Department. He retired from business in 1867, and has for many years been librarian of the New York Genealogical and Biographical Society. He is a native of the Fifth Ward.

GEORGE W. WHEELER joined Clinton Engine No. 41, February 9, 1836, although he was far from robust. Mr. Wheeler was a drug clerk, 21 years old, when he joined. He was soon made secretary of the company, and might have held a higher office had he been of stronger frame. In seven years he was "out of his time," but remained three years longer in service. Then an injury to his leg compelled him to abandon the hard life he, with hundreds of others, loved so well. He was appointed bellringer at Essex Market, and held the position for fifteen months, when the municipal police were organized, and his occupation was gone. Chief Anderson, a firm friend of the young man, offered him the post of clerk, and Mr. Wheeler accepted. Shortly afterwards Mr. Wheeler was made foreman of the repair shops—a salaried post— and at the same time discharged the duties of clerk. He joined the

Exempt Engine Company, and is now secretary of the Exempt Firemen's Association.

Mr. Wheeler was injured three times while performing fireman's duty. Soon after he joined the Department, Truck 5 ran over his leg. In 1839 he fell under the brakes at the foot of Delancey Street, and his back was terribly hurt. It was two years before he completely recovered from this misfortune. A fortnight before his time expired Mr. Wheeler went with his company to a fire in Attorney Street. A sawmill was ablaze. While young Wheeler and a comrade were holding a pipe, the fire leaped across the street, as fires had a trick of doing in those days. The heat compelled the two men to abandon the pipe. They recovered it a few minutes later, and Mr. Wheeler sprang with it upon a pile of mahogany logs, which gave way beneath him. One massive trunk fell across his thigh, causing a compound fracture.

NATHANIEL FINCH, a prominent member of Hose No. 15, went to Pennsylvania at the outbreak of the oil fever, and settled in McKeesport, of which place he was elected mayor several years ago. Mr. Finch is a member of the Exempt Firemen's Association, and was at one time a member of the Executive Committee. He now resides at No. 79 Market Street, McKeesport.

MARK FOWLER joined Engine Company No. 4, in 1836, and served with her for seven years, during which time he was successively elected foreman and representative. He resigned from the Department at the close of his term of service with an excellent record for devotion to duty. Mr. Fowler is now in business in Front Street. He is a member of the Association of Exempt Firemen.

W. R. W. CHAMBERS is noted among firemen. Any of the old firemen who were in the habit of attending balls and soirees in the "forties" may remember a young, very young, man, who was a regular attendant at the best of those social gatherings. He was as light as a humming bird in his movements, and "such a love of a dancer!" He now weighs about two hundred and fifty pounds, is running over with good nature, fat and jovial, yet active. Mr. Chambers was born in New York city fifty-seven years ago, appointed recording clerk in the register's office January, 1855, by John Doane, register, and the same year elected delegate to the State Convention from the Seventeenth Ward. Appointed by George W. Morton, city inspector, as chief clerk and confirmed by the Common Council, January, 1856, he was reappointed by Daniel E. Develin, and again by F. I. A. Boole, serving in this very responsible position a period of eleven years. He was deputy sheriff under Sheriffs O'Brien and Davidson, sergeant at-arms of the Board of Aldermen during the years 1882, 1883, and 1884, and is now recording clerk in the county clerk's office. His fire record is as weighty as his municipal cares. He joined Hose Company No. 22 in 1849, served nearly three years, and resigned ; joined Hose Company No. 36, served nearly seven years, and resigned ; rejoined Hose Company No. 22, and was elected foreman two months later, and re-elected five successive years ; was secretary of board of engineers and foreman under Chiefs Howard and Decker ; was elected member of Exempt Firemen's Association, January 19, 1858, and served nearly ten years upon the executive committee with Engs, Ockershausen, Mills, Watkins, and other bright lights of the Department. The colonel is now a member of the "Veteran" and "Volunteer" Fire Associations. At the time of serving as a fireman he was attached to the military of the city, served five years with the "Washington Continental Guard," Captain Darrow, and two years with the celebrated "State Guard," Captain Joseph H. Johnson. He attended the meeting of firemen at the Astor House in 1861, where it was decided to form a regiment of "Fire Zouaves," under Colonel E. E. Ellsworth. Within three hours after the meeting adjourned Mr. Chambers's books at the city inspector's office were closed, and he was enrolling men for company E, Captain John B. Leverich, at the Old "Gotham," in the Bowery, owned by the veteran Harry Venn. Mr. Chambers kept open house there free to all, he paying the entire bill. Within three days two hundred and forty-three men had signed the roll. Only one hundred and five were chosen, of which number thirteen were from Hose Company No. 22. Thomas Chambers, a brother of the colonel, enlisted, and was one of the first killed at the first "Bull Run." Mr. Chambers was commissioned as first lieutenant of Company E, and was the only officer of that rank in the regiment chosen from the Fire Department, all others being chosen from the "Ellsworth Zouaves."

COL. W. R. W. CHAMBERS.

Colonel Chambers came home seriously ill, and was confined to his bed three months. As soon as he was sufficiently recovered he decided to raise a regiment, and he at once commenced recruiting. By his personal exertions five hundred and seven men were inspected and mustered into the service without cost to the city, State, or general government, and W. R. W. Chambers received his commission as the colonel. A stand of colors was presented to the regiment by the city and another by the State. Colonel Chambers has four commissions—first lieutenant, captain, major, and colonel; and has two honorable discharges. As the Colonel must have some military around him, he is a member of Kilpatrick Post, No. 143, G. A. R.

JOHN GALVIN was born in Kings County, Ireland, and came to this country as a boy. He early ran with the engines, but had no direct connection with the Fire Department until 1863, when he enrolled in East River Engine Company No. 17, then lying in Goerck Street, near Grand. His service in the Department was of brief duration, but marked by efficiency and great personal popularity. During a residence of over forty years in the Seventh Ward Mr. Galvin has been closely and honorably identified with politics. In 1868 he was elected a member of the legislature from the Fourth District, and was re-elected in the following year. He was again elected, and in the three succeeding years. In 1870 he was elected a member of the Board of Assistant Aldermen, and during the following year he was re-elected. During this time he was president of the Board for seventeen months. In 1885 Mr. Galvin received the County Democracy nomination for Congress, and made a gallant fight against Mr. Timothy J. Campbell, the nominee of the Republicans and Tammany Hall, who was elected by a small majority. Mr. Galvin is a strict temperance man, never having tasted either liquor or tobacco in his life. He has been in business in Grand Street since 1860.

JAMES E. COLEGROVE was born in New York city in 1826, and began his fire experiences as a volunteer with North River Engine Company No. 27. He became a member of Hose Company No. 33 December 11, 1845. The name was changed to Warren Hose in February, 1846, when he was elected assistant foreman, and in May following was made foreman. He continued in office during the years 1846, 1847, 1848, 1849, and 1850; and was an active and prominent member of the company thirteen years. He resigned in 1858. In 1856 he was elected councilman from the Eighth Ward, and is now surveyor of the Greenwich Insurance Company. He is a member of the Warren, the Exempts,' Volunteers,' and Veterans' Associations of this city.

JOHN P. LACOUR, a prominent member of the old Department, joined Hook and Ladder No. 5 in 1835, and served in that company thirteen years, during eleven of which he was foreman and representative. The company lay at Attorney and Delancey Streets. Having served two terms, Mr. Lacour resigned and received his discharge papers, but remained an honorary member and representative of the company. In 1847 he was elected assistant engineer, a post that he held with great credit for seven years. He afterwards joined Engine Company No. 8, which was the first company to run a steamer. This important step was largely due to the influence of Mr. Lacour, who was one of the first firemen to recognize the fact that the steamer was bound to supersede the old manual engine. Engine No. 8 lay at No. 91 Crosby Street. Mr. Lacour ran with her until the disbandment of the Department. In the early days of the war Mr. Lacour joined the Twenty-second Regiment and remained an active member for thirteen years. He is now an honorary member of the regiment. Mr. Lacour bore the reputation of being a brave and scientific fireman. He is now surveyor for the Pacific Fire Insurance Company and resides in Brooklyn.

ALONZO BOESE, of whom it used to be said that he had not an enemy in the world, was one of the most intrepid men who ever put his hand to a brake. He was born in the Fourteenth Ward in 1833, and attended old Public School No. 7, where he was known as an apt and industrious scholar. His father was a wealthy sugar refiner, but at the time of his death, which occurred when Alonzo was still a young man, his fortune had been so reduced by unfortunate ventures that his family were left in reduced circumstances. Finding that it was necessary for him to carve out his own fortune, Alonzo entered the law office of Burrell, Davison & Burrell. A few years of office work served to give him a distaste for the law, and he determined to enter the arena of politics. In this career his great personal popularity made itself felt, and led to his receiving the appointment from President Buchanan of clerk in the Brooklyn Navy Yard, a position which he filled with credit, and resigned at the beginning of Lincoln's administration. When Mr. Augustus Schell was Collector of the Port of New York, Alonzo Boese held an important position in the United States Bonded Warehouse. While there, Mr. Nathaniel Jarvis, Clerk of the Court of Common Pleas in this city, appointed him assistant clerk, a post that he held up to the time of his death, a period of eighteen years.

He became connected with the Fire Department at an early age, when he joined Engine Co. No. 9. He always bunked at the engine house, and by his genial disposition, no less than the enthusiasm with which he was always ready to respond to the call of danger, earned the sincere affection of all his comrades. His name will always be remembered in connection with one of the most desperate deeds recorded in the annals of the Old Department. A temporary hospital filled with small-pox patients, at the corner of the Bowery and Bond Street, was found to be on fire one night. Little shame was it to the firemen, brave as they were, to shrink from facing the double danger of pestilence added to flame. The fire was spreading rapidly, and the danger of the poor afflicted wretches in the pest house was imminent, and yet all hung back, when "Lon" Boese stepped forward and without a word began ascending the ladder. A storm of cheers arose as he began to descend a moment later, carrying a patient in his arms. He continued the ascent until the last poor wretch was in safety.

On the outbreak of the war "Lon" was foremost in organizing the famous Hawkins Zouaves. It was generally believed that his services would be rewarded with the colonelcy of the regiment, but nothing better than the command of a company was offered him. He felt the slight bitterly, and declined the proffered captaincy. Mr. Boese was almost as famous as a fisherman as he was as a fireman, and was known as one the most scientific and enthusiastic disciples of Isaac Walton in New York. With " Larry " Kerr and " Brooks " De Garmo, both old fire laddies, Mr. Boese helped to organize the famous Excelsior Fishing Club of Staten Island, one of the most prominent organizations of the kind in this country. Mr. Boese died October 4, 1881, of cancer of the tongue, after a long and agonizing illness. His death was in keeping with his life, his last words being, " I'm not afraid to die."

JEREMIAH F. GILLIN.

JEREMIAH F. GILLIN was born in the City of New York, May 7, 1836. He joined Croton Hose Company No. 6 July 10, 1857, and served his full time with that company. On January 3, 1860, the hose carriage had been laid up for repairs ; it was a bitterly cold night, and Mr. Gillin had visited the house for the purpose of being ready to take charge of a party of workmen early in the morning. He was sleeping on a chair at 3 A. M., when there came a sharp knock at the door and then a cry of fire. The sleeper was at the door in an instant. " Fire in Division Street near Clinton !" was shouted. Mr. Gillin started, and was the first one at the scene. It was an old-fashioned dwelling with a camphene store on the ground floor. The flames spread with marvelous rapidity ; the narrow staircase was ablaze. Fifteen human beings were in the upper part of the house. A few persons had gathered in front of the burning building. Mr. Gillin clambered over the top of the store window, and entered the second story. The smoke was dense and suffocating, and the heat overpowering. He stumbled against a woman with a child in her arms, both over-come by the smoke. He hurriedly, but carefully, carried the child to the window, and dropped it tenderly into the arms of those below, and returning to the mother performed the same act for her. Mr. Gillin then went to the rear of the building and rescued a boy thirteen years of age. While carrying the boy he heard cries from a rear room. He tried the door—it was locked— burst it open, and saved a family of four persons—grandmother, mother, and two chil-dren. It was now time for the rescuer to think of his own safety. He staggered toward the window, now a mass of flames. As he crossed the floor his foot struck against the body of an old man. He dragged him to the window, where friendly hands were ready to receive him. After this effort Mr. Gillin turned to look if there were any other inmates; not seeing any he prepared to descend, but the ladder had been removed. There was now only one way for him to escape, "a leap for life." The flames were circling about him. With-out hesitation he sprang from the window. His life was spared, but six weeks of medical treatment was necessary for him to recuperate. Eight lives had been saved by this courageous young man, but, sad to relate, seven others, residing on the upper story, were burnt to an undistinguishable crisp.

Mr. Gillin was appointed on the police force in the fall of 1863. While on post duty in the Twenty-first Precinct, December 13, 1865, during a fearful storm of snow and sleet, he discovered a fire at the corner of Second Avenue and Thirty-first Street. The store, a liquor saloon, was owned by a man named Kane, and the upper part was occupied by a Mrs. Webb, and Mrs. Foster and child. The fire had commenced under the stairs, and the flames cut off all means of escape in that direction. Mr. Gillin used every effort to reach the sufferers, but in vain. Mrs. Webb, clothed with only a night dress in that awful storm, swung herself from the front window on the fourth floor, holding on by the strength of her hands alone, and, nerved by despair and terror, she retained her grasp until the skin peeled from the ends of her fingers, and she fell. Mr. Gillin had prepared a mattress, and, with three others, held it to receive the falling woman. The force was too great, and Mrs. Webb fell to the cellar. No bones were broken, but the exposure and shock were more than she could bear. On the following morning she died at the hospital where she had been conveyed. Every effort was made to rescue Mrs. Foster and child, but with-out avail; they perished in the flames. On investigating the cause of the fire it was ascertained that it was a case of arson. The coroner's jury brought in a verdict of murder and arson against Kane. He was arrested, and tried three times, defended by James T. Brady. On each trial the jury disagreed; on each occasion they stood eleven for conviction and one for acquittal. Mr. Gillin was taken from this fire in Chief Perley's wagon. He was unable to move, being prostrated by the heat and over-exertion. The coroner's jury added to their verdict a recommendation that Mr. Gillin was well worthy of promotion for gallant service.

In April, 1861, Mr. Gillin enlisted in the First (Ellsworth) Fire Zouaves; was third sergeant of Company F, afterwards orderly sergeant of Company K ; took an active part at the burning of Willard's Hotel, Washington, D. C., where the Zouaves lent their valuable aid ; was present at several skirmishes, and in charge of his company at "Bull Run" when the historic "Black Horse Cavalry" charge was made. When the regiment was mustered out of service

Mr. Gillin was appointed chief detective to the Union Pacific Railroad, under direction of the United States. He was engaged in that service for over five years. His last public duty as a detective was under Colonel Whiteley, of the United States Secret Service Force. Mr. Gillin had charge of one of the most dangerous and delicate missions during his service—an investigation of the Ku-Klux organization when his life was momentarily in danger. Mr. Gillin is a prominent member of the "Veteran Firemen's Association."

LOUIS J. BELLONI was an active fireman. In the year 1851 John T. Rollins, Jordan L. Mott, Franklin E. James, Louis J. Belloni, and other prominent residents of what was then the beautiful but sparsely settled village of Harlem, and the extreme limit of the City and County of New York, organized for the protection of that remote district a hose company, christened the new-born nymph "Undine," and Undine Hose Company No. 52 became a part and parcel of the N. Y. F. D. Mr. Belloni was very active in forming the company, and an energetic working member, elected as representative of 52 at Firemen's Hall for nine consecutive years, a member of the company for twelve years, and only retired when the younger members resolved to change the organization to an engine company (Undine Engine Company No. 52). Mr. Belloni has been a member of the Exempt Firemen's Association for many years, was one of the Trustees of the Fire Department Fund, and is now the treasurer of the fund. Mr. Belloni is one of the old merchants of New York. The firm of Belloni & Company is a landmark among the large shipping houses of South Street.

JAMES HARRIS joined the Volunteer roll of Engine No. 1, then lying in Duane Street, in 1836. Mr. Harris was prominent among the organizers of National Hose No. 24 as a private company at the time of the "June Bug" excitement. He served his time with Hose 24, and then retired from the Department. He is a member of the Association of Exempt Firemen. While Mr. Harris was an enthusiastic fireman and one of the most popular members of his company, he resolutely declined to accept office, although frequently pressed to do so.

ANTHONY C. D'OZEVILLE performed his first fire service with Americus Hose No. 19, lying in Greene Street, near Broome. His connection with that company was of brief duration, and in 1857 he enrolled in National Hose No. 24, lying in the house now occupied by Engine No. 30 in Spring Street. During the first years of his membership he had the honor of being elected representative and then secretary. In the following year he was elected assistant foreman and shortly afterwards foreman. His efficiency as a commanding officer and his personal popularity are attested by the fact that during the three succeeding years he was re-elected by an almost unanimous vote. At the time when a strong effort was being made in the legislature to pass a bill reducing the number of men allowed to hose companies from thirty to twenty, with a proportionate reduction in engine and hook and ladder companies, Mr. D'Ozeville strenuously opposed the measure. It was evident to him that a reduction on such a large scale would have the effect of completely crippling many organizations. With the assistance of Mr. Samuel Burhans, Jr., a former foreman of the company, he drew up a masterly memorial, conclusively showing the inadvisability of the proposed step, which was forwarded to Albany. The document attracted much attention and led to a modification of the proposed measure. The bill as passed reduced the force allowed to hose companies by only five men, instead of ten. Mr. D'Ozeville was one of the first officers to recognize the danger threatening the Volunteer organization by the introduction of steamers, and resolutely opposed their use. He resigned from the Department shortly before the disbandment of the Volunteers.

His father was a native of France and a personal friend of Lafayette, by whose influence he was appointed to a responsible position in the New York Custom House. Mr. D'Ozeville is a life member of the Association of Exempt Firemen and one of the executive committee, a member of the Volunteer Firemen's Association, and secretary of the New York County Democracy of the Fifth Assembly District.

OLIVER A. FARRIN joined National Hose No. 24, then lying in Spring Street, between Greenwich and Hudson Streets, in 1844, and served with that company for five years, when he received his discharge certificate. For several years before that Mr. Farrin was on the Volunteer roll of Engine No. 27. As a brave and popular fireman Mr. Farrin has a fine record. He is a member of the Association of Exempts, and resides at No. 159 West Fifteenth Street.

JAMES H. ENGLISH.

JAMES FAGIN was born in New York city in 1838, joined Forrest Engine Company No. 3 in 1861, and continued in service until 1865. He was appointed a member of the Fire Insurance Patrol on the twenty-fifth of June, 1868. He is at present a member of Patrol No. 2. Mr. Fagin is a member of the Volunteer Firemen's Association.

JAMES H. ENGLISH, of Pearl Hose Company 28, joined the Fire Department in 1853, and served thirteen years with the company, and was representative for three years. He was one of the workers and one of the original ten bunkers who took pride in making the carriage one of the quickest in the Department. He is now in business as a blank book manufacturer.

JOHN KAVANAGH was born on the twenty-second of June, 1832, in the old "Eighth Ward of New York," and at an early age joined 34 Engine. Mr. Kavanagh was apprenticed to the boiler maker's trade and soon acquired a thorough knowledge of that business. In 1857 Mr. Kavanagh was elected assistant foreman, and so satisfactorily did he perform the duties that at the expiration of his term of office he was elected foreman, which honor he held from 1859 to 1862. Many instances of bravery and coolness at fires are told of Mr. Kavanagh. He was also representative of the company from 1863 to 1865. He was appointed in the present Department January 28, 1867, and assigned to Hook and Ladder 8, and in 1869 was transferred to Engine Company 30. He was promoted to be assistant engineer in 1871, and in 1878 was promoted to be engineer. In the year 1854, while running to a fire down Broadway, he was tripped by one of the men and caught under the engine, and was dragged for nearly a block before he could get free, and then he was run over and had his leg broken. In 1865, at a fire on the corner of King and Washington Streets, he was buried under a wall and was pulled out after much difficulty. On November 14, 1868, he saved two lives at the risk of his own at the fire in the Stewart House. In the same year he saved the life of Thomas Farrell, a brother fireman. The fire was on the dock of the Neptune line of steamers at the foot of Murray Street. Farrell slipped into the river, and Kavanagh caught the end of a coil of rope lying on the deck of a boat, jumped in after him and seized him just as he was about to go down. They were both pulled out by the members of their company. In 1869, at a fire in Church

JOHN KAVANAGH.

Street, near Canal, Kavanagh saved the life of Thomas Smith at the risk of his own. In 1873, at a fire in Crosby Street, in the rear of Howard Street, a back wall of a house fell outward into an alley, burying Foreman Martin Walsh, of Engine Company 30, and Foreman Wilhelm, of Engine Company 29.

JOHN DAILEY.

Kavanagh lifted Foreman Walsh out and took him to a store in Howard Street, and from there to a hospital. At another time, at a fire at Jackson Square, he again saved the life of Foreman Walsh. They were both on the second floor of a burning building when the floor gave way, and Foreman Walsh had just time enough to straddle a window sill until the arrival of Kavanagh so that he would not fall into the flames. They were both burnt about the hands and face.

JOHN DAILEY was born in the Eleventh Ward about fifty-three years ago. In his early youth he attended private schools, and prepared himself for an active business life. In his early manhood he served his apprenticeship with one of the extensive engineering and machine concerns on the east side. He became a master mechanic in practical engineering, etc. He was first identified with Atlantic Engine Company No. 18, being one of the active participants in organizing the company, of which he remained a member until its disbandment. In 1856 he joined Hose Company No. 34, was elected and served as foreman of that company until the growth of his business interests in Brooklyn necessitated his removal to that city. In 1859 he joined

Mechanics' Hose Company No. 2, of Brooklyn, E. D., and served with it until 1864, when he resigned. Mr. Dailey is an active member of the Exempt Firemen's Association, and of the Volunteer Firemen's Association of Brooklyn, E. D. He is also a valuable member of the Volunteer Firemen's Association of the City of New York, on all occasions taking an active part in every

JAMES J. SLEVIN.

movement for the interest of his old-time companions. He was chief aid to Marshal John Decker in the "Bartholdi" day parade of Volunteer Firemen, the success of which was, in a great measure, due to his exertions.

EDWARD P. DURHAM, born in 1826, is one of the "Old Vamps" whose progeny can point back with considerable pride to his record as a Volunteer fireman. He first joined Constitution Engine Company No. 7, of Brooklyn, E. D., in 1853, where he served his full time, after which he resigned and moved to New York City. At a fire in Talman Street, Brooklyn, in the winter of 1855, he particularly distinguished himself by saving the life of an aged man from the attic of a blazing frame building. Having deposited his almost lifeless burden in the hands of his companions on the street, he rushed back into the building in search of another decrepit old man, who he knew had been in the building, and in doing so very nearly lost his own life, the upper part of the building falling in. He was rescued by his comrades, but was badly injured. The aged man he was in search of was rescued through the rear of the building by another fireman. Mr. Durham performed many other acts of mercy. On moving to New York City he joined United States Engine Company No. 23, and served with that company until the disbandment of the Volunteer Department in 1865. Mr. Durham is now an active member of the Volunteer Firemen's Association of New York, taking an interest in everything pointing toward the benefit of his old-time companions.

JAMES J. SLEVIN, ex-Alderman and Register of this city, was a member of No. 9 Hose Company, and considered

EDWARD P. DURHAM.

the handsomest-looking man in the whole service of the Fire Department. On days of popular celebration—like the Fourth of July—the girls had eyes for him alone. The headquarters of the company were at that time in Mulberry Street. Mr. Slevin filled several offices, was representative, engineer, and foreman, and was connected with the company for a full term. The company had a stirring experience in its day, and had many prominent men connected with it, or at least who became prominent in after years.

EDWARD BONNOLL, born on October 20, 1826, performed his first fire service with Clinton Engine No. 4 in 1846. In 1857 he joined Tompkins Hose. He was at one time foreman of Hose No. 16. From 1862 to 1865 Mr. Bonnoll served as fire commissioner. He was also a member of the Board of Trustees of the Veteran Firemen's Association. Mr. Bonnoll died on December 17, 1885. Few firemen were more widely popular than he was. His funeral from the Club House of the Veteran Firemen, No. 53 East Tenth Street, was attended by hundreds of his late comrades.

EDWARD BONNOLL.

ANTHONY J. ALLAIRE is one of the celebrated family whose name was well known as the great iron workers and boiler builders. The "Allaire Works" built the boiler for the first steamship that ever crossed the Atlantic, the "Savannah," that sailed from Savannah, Georgia, for St. Petersburg (and successfully made the trip) years before the "Sirius" entered New York harbor. The last piece of work from the Allaires' hands was the boilers for the Collins steamship "Baltic." The work of the firm was familiar on all classes of steam vessels from the St. Lawrence River to the Spanish Main. Anthony J. was the last of the name engaged in the iron business. He joned Engine Company No. 41 in 1853. His first experience as a fireman was at the destruction of the Harper Brothers' buildings. Mr. Allaire served three years as assistant foreman, and as foreman one term, when an accident incapacitated him from active duty, and he resigned his office, but remained a member until 1864. Mr. Allaire was appointed on the police force August 24, 1860, has filled every position in the Police Department from patrolman to captain, to which position

ANTHONY J. ALLAIRE.

he was promoted May 23, 1867, and is now in command at the Tenth Precinct, having performed twenty-six years of active duty on the force.

Mr. Allaire's war record is one to be proud of. He went out with the Second Police Regiment (One Hundred and Thirty-third Regiment N. Y. Volunteers) as captain, was promoted to major and lieutenant colonel, and was mustered out of the service as brevet colonel and brevet brigadier general. He is too modest to talk much of "moving accidents by flood and field" where he was personally engaged. But there is one event that he takes just pride in. Our fleet at Alexandria, Red River, Louisiana, under Admiral Porter, was imprisoned. The water had fallen so low that the vessels could not move. Mr. Allaire was selected as one of the officers to build a dam. His mechanical education was here of service. The dam was constructed, and the general says it was one of the happiest moments of his life when gunboats, supply vessels, and transports passed safely through, making a marine procession of over one hundred and fifty vessels. Millions of dollars were saved to the government, and the officers and men were proud of their achievement.

JOHN MULLIN was a member of that once famous Hose Company No. 3, which was organized in 1832, and was called "Independence." It had a roll of thirty members, and its headquarters were in Hester Street. Geo. Spencer was foreman, and he went to the front, when the war broke out, in the New York Fire Zouave Regiment.

JOHN BUCKBEE was born on December 29, 1831, and became a member of Americus Engine No. 6 on February 16, 1854. He served as assistant foreman in 1860 and 1861, and in the following year was elected foreman, a post he filled with honor for two years. Mr. Buckbee is a member of the firm of Ash & Buckbee, plumbers, at the corner of Cedar and William Streets. He is an ex-president of the Eckford Social Club of Williamsburg, a prominent member of the City Club and member of the Associations of Exempt, Veteran and Volunteer Firemen. Mr. Buckbee is also a prominent Mason and one of the most genial and popular "fire laddies" in the city.

ABRAHAM FRANKLIN was the first secretary of the Fire Department, being elected on January 17, 1792, on which occasion a constitution for the Department was drafted and duly adopted.

The first written report of the proceedings of the Fire Department was made on November 4, 1791, at a meeting held in the house of Jacob Brouwer, in Nassau Street. Mr. Franklin, then a foreman, was elected secretary. On January 25, 1792, he was elected the first secretary of the Fire Department Fund.

MARTIN J. KEESE was a volunteer runner of Fulton Engine Company No. 21, and upon attaining his majority in 1858 linked his fortunes with the Matthew T. Brennan Hose Company No. 60. He was elected to the office of representative. In the meantime he went to the war in the Eleventh New York, Ellsworth's Fire Zouaves, and was severely wounded at the battle of Bull Run. On returning he was elected foreman of the company each year till the break up of the Volunteer Department in 1865. Mr. Keese is a member of Noah L. Farnum Post No. 458 of the G. A. R. and one of the organizers, a member of the Exempt Firemen's Association, and also one of the organizers of the Volunteer Firemen's Association, which numbers two thousand one hundred members. Mr. Keese was deputy sheriff with M. T. Brennan when the arrest was made at the Metropolitan Hotel of Wm. M. Tweed, and at the comptroller's office of Richard B. Connolly, and was in jail with the latter in Ludlow Street jail for about a month until he was admitted to bail by Judge Barnard, of the Supreme Court. Mr. Keese is now custodian of the City Hall, an office which he is well qualified to fill.

JORDAN L. MOTT was an active promoter of the Benevolent Fund and a member of the Ball Committee. Mr. Mott, who was a merchant at Beekman and Cliff Streets, was a member of Hose Company No. 52.

HENRY J. OCKERSHAUSEN, who died in 1882 at the age of sixty-six, was for twenty years vice-president of the Association of Exempt Firemen. He was foreman of Hose Company No. 1, and assistant engineer of the Department.

MOSES F. ODELL filled many important offices outside of the Fire Department. He joined Engine Company No. 15 in 1841. From 1861 to 1865 he was member of Congress from Brooklyn, was a member of the Joint Committee on the Conduct of the War, and in 1865 was appointed naval officer. He died June 14, 1866.

JOHN R. PLATT was a member of Engine Company No. 5, then of Hose Company No. 36, of Engine Company No. 28, and of Hose Company No. 29. He was foreman of the last three companies and finally president of the Department. He received a handsome testimonial from Hose 36. Mr. Platt often rolled out the engine alone, being the first to get to the house. He was considered the *beau ideal* of a fireman.

JAMES R. STEERS, a member of Live Oak Engine No. 44, was one of the most famous shipbuilders of his time. In 1851 he and his brother built the celebrated yacht "*America*," which was unfairly ruled out of the race for the Queen's Cup at the annual regatta of the London Royal Yacht Club, yet started with the others and beat them all.

JOHN CORNWELL was born in 1829, and at an early age was apprenticed to a gilder. Having learned this trade, Mr. Cornwell worked at it but a short time, and since his early manhood has been a contractor. On June 15, 1846, he joined Hook and Ladder Company No. 4, whose quarters were in Eldridge Street. Young Cornwell lived just opposite to the truck house. Many a time his sound, boyish slumber was broken by the clang of the Fulton Market bell, and the ringing " Turn out there! " of his comrades in the street below. Peter N. Cornwell, John's brother, was foreman of the company. At the end of his six years' service Mr. Cornwell rejoined the company as assistant foreman. This post he held until Peter was called to the Board of Engineers, when the younger Cornwell succeeded him as foreman. As though his duties did not keep him busy enough, the young man joined the Insurance Patrol as a private in 1852, still retaining his connection with Truck No. 4. Four years later he became captain, and subsequently succeeded Alfred W. Carson as superintendent of the patrol. This office was no sinecure during the war, when fires in warehouses of the kind called " free stores " were very frequent. The merchandise stored in these places was generally cotton and flour.

Mr. Cornwell often urged the necessity for horses to draw the patrol wagons, and for two months supplied teams at his own expense. The consequence was that the patrol made much better time than the firemen. When he became superintendent of the patrol, his force consisted of seventy men and three wagons. Superintendent Cornwell was expected to be present at all fires below Sixty-first Street. His heart and soul were in his work, and his success in saving property at big fires won for him the high regard of the insurance men. In addition to actual work at fires, Mr. Cornwell had a vast amount of routine business. For instance, a patrolman is stationed for ten hours in a building where a fire has occurred. His pay for that service is two dollars and fifty cents. Mr. Cornwell had to divide this amount among the several insurance companies, make out a bill for each, collect the money and pay the patrolman. In 1870 Mr. Cornwell left the Insurance Patrol, and Monmouth B. Wilson succeeded him. He had between 1846 and 1870 worked at all the large fires in the city.

When Mr. Cornwell joined No. 4 there were no bunks for the men on house duty, and they asked no more luxurious couch than the carpeted floor of the meeting room. The original insurance patrolmen walked the streets at night, and worked at different trades in the daytime. Mr. Cornwell was captain when Chittidere's dry goods store, at Broadway and Leonard Street, was burned. A few minutes after the fire broke out the walls fell inward. The loss was estimated at one million dollars, and the insurance presidents looked glum. They asked Capt. Cornwell if he would "work" the fire and save what he could. He modestly assented, and surprised the men in broadcloth by saying that he would give twenty thousand dollars for the ruins himself.

"You are dreaming," said the insurance men.

"We shall see," replied Capt. Cornwell.

At that time gangs had been working in the ruins for three days, but had saved nothing. Capt. Cornwell got men and derricks, and in a few hours had dug down to the iron doors of several big vaults under the sidewalk. The vaults were filled with cases of calicoes, ginghams, etc., which did not even smell of fire. Eighty cases, containing stock worth one hundred thousand dollars, were exhumed in a little more than two weeks. Mr. Cornwell was a valuable man at a cotton fire, and was frequently sent to Brooklyn, Philadelphia and other large cities, where the local firemen ruined more cotton than they saved. At his own request, Mr. Cornwell's bailiwick was limited to New York, by a resolution of the Board of Underwriters.

Mr. Cornwell is now a busy contractor. He belongs to the Veteran Firemen's Association, and says that he will never lose his interest in the Department.

ROBERT McGINNIS is among the best known members of the Old Department, and is noted for his suavity and uniform courtesy. He was always prominent in social affairs, and used to be deemed quite a ladies' man, and in fact was called "Gentleman Bob." His father, Hugh McGinnis, came from Londonderry, Ireland, to this city in 1799 in consequence of the rebellion in his native land of the preceding year. Here he married and began business, and about 1820 joined the Fire Department as a member of No. 11 Engine, serving for 14 years. His son Robert remembers that his father's company had its engine house in Old Slip. It was quite natural that the subject of this sketch was early imbued with an irresistible desire to run "wid der machine," and for some ten years he did do so before regularly joining, on May 5, 1846, Southwark Engine Company No. 38. He was shortly afterwards elected secretary, then assistant foreman and after a time foreman of No. 38. His promotions followed each other with great rapidity, affording a proof of his popularity among his companions, for on April 19, 1850, a little less than four years from the date of his original membership, he was appointed an assistant engineer. While in this office he was elected a representative from No. 38, and by his fellows was elected a trustee of the Firemen's Fund. Of that board of trustees, which consisted of eight, but two members are alive to-day—Zophar Mills and Robert

McGinnis. In July, 1857, Mr. McGinnis's health began to fail because of the exposure and hardships incident to the service, and at the urgent advice of his physicians he resigned as assistant engineer. A series of resolutions of the most complimentary character, expressing regret at his enforced action, were adopted by his associates July 10, 1857, and formally presented to him.

Mr. McGinnis was elected by the voters of the Nineteenth Ward, of which he had long been a resident, as a trustee of the Fire Department, in which capacity he served for four years. In 1863 he ran for alderman on the Mozart Hall ticket, against Terence Farley, the Tammany candidate, who was declared elected by a majority of 300. In 1865, in the same district (the Nineteenth Ward), he ran as the Mozart candidate against Charles Devlin, the well known contractor, who afterwards became Tweed's bondsman for a large sum, and defeated him by a handsome majority. During his term in the board he introduced a resolution returning thanks to Congress for its appropriation of $500,000 to purchase a site for a Post-Office in New York City, which led to his being made chairman of the Committee on Post-Office Site, and subsequently through his instrumentality the southerly end of the City Hall Park was sold to the Federal Government for the present Post-Office building. The same committee selected the site of the present Barge-Office. Upon the expiration of his term, Mayor Hoffman appointed him Inspector of Schools for the Seventh District (an unsalaried office), and after three years' service he was reappointed by Mayor Hall, December 20, 1871. He is at present, and has been for a number

ROBERT McGINNIS.

of years, a well known resident of Harlem, and largely interested in building operations.

FREDERICK E. GIBERT, the well-known capitalist and philanthropist, was a distinguished fireman. He was born in Newport, R. I., of wealthy parents in October 11, 1810, and graduated from Columbia College in 1830. For many years Mr. Gibert was a director of the Delaware, Lackawanna, and Western Railroad, of the Academy of Music, and of several prominent banks, and was also interested in the management of many charitable institutions. For twelve years Mr. Gibert was president of the New York Club. He was for years foreman of Engine Company No. 4, and served as fire warden of the Third Ward. His services in the Department were characterized by intrepidity and unswerving devotion to duty.

On the occasion of the famous duel between August Belmont and William Hayward, of South Carolina, in 1841, Mr. Gibert acted as second to Mr. Hayward.   His subsequent relations, however, with Mr. Belmont were of the most friendly character.   In May, 1882, Mr. Gibert succumbed to an attack of pneumonia at his residence, No. 298 Fifth Avenue.

ADAM P. PENTZ, for five years President of the Volunteer Fire Department, comes of a famous fire fighting family.   His father was a member of the Floating Engine Company during the last years of the Revolutionary War, was subsequently a member of Supply Engine and foreman of Engine Company 11, was one of the original representatives of the Department at its organization in 1798, one of the incorporators of the Benevolent Fund, and one of the founders of the old Mariners' Church in Roosevelt Street.   His service in the Department covered a period of over twenty years.

Mr. A. P. Pentz was born in New York in the early part of this century. While his father was endeavoring to decide on a second name for his son tidings

ADAM P. PENTZ.

arrived of Perry's glorious victory on Lake Erie, and the father instantly determined that the boy should bear the name of the immortal commodore.

Mr. Pentz's first service was done with Hydrant Company No. 1, in which he was enrolled in 1836.   Subsequently he served with Excelsior Engine No. 36.   Soon afterwards he was chosen representative, and was successively elected foreman of the Board of Fire Wardens of the Fourth Ward, treasurer of the Department Fund for four years, president of the Department for five years and secretary of the Firemen's Ball Committee.

As trustee of the Benevolent Fund he served three successive terms of three years.

Other members of Mr. Pentz's family who rendered distinguished service as foremen were his uncle, Frederick Pentz, representative of Engine Company 11; his brother, Alderman David C. P. Pentz, of Engine 42, and George W. Pentz, of Engine 17; his nephews, Enoch C. P. Pentz and John H. Pentz, of Southwark Engine No. 38, and his cousins, William A. F. Pentz, General Frederick Pentz and John Pentz, respectively, of Hook and Ladder No. 1, Hydrant Company No. 1, and Hook and Ladder No. 2.

Mr. Pentz was at one time a member of the Board of Education.   In 1845 he was appointed by President James K. Polk naval storekeeper at the Brooklyn Navy Yard, a post which he held during the war with Mexico, and from which he retired with great credit to himself and with the regret of all the officials and employees of the Yard.

For many years he was a member of the well-known house of Goin, Poole

& Pentz, in Burling Slip. Mr. Pentz's reminiscences of fire matters in the good old times would fill a respectable volume. One of his earliest recollections as a boy is of seeing Molly, a slave of John Aymar, who was quite a character in her day, helping the firemen to drag old 11 Engine through a snowdrift in William Street in the winter of 1818. It was Molly's boast that she belonged to "Ole 'Leben," and always ran with it. On one occasion Mr. Pentz ran with the old East River Engine No. 42, from Roosevelt Street to the Robin Hood Tavern, three miles up Third Avenue.

During the famous "June-bug" excitement Mr. Pentz helped to exclude the representatives of the bogus companies from the hall in which the regular representatives were in session. During the "Great Fire" of 1835 the warehouse of Pentz & Co. was blown up by order of General Swift to check the spread of the conflagration.

As an instance of the difficulties that old-time firemen had to contend with Mr. Pentz recalls the fact that at a fire in Hester Street water had to be pumped from the East River—a distance of over one mile.

EDWARD BYRNES, brother of Detective Inspector Thomas Byrnes, was a fireman in the true and heroic sense. In the year 1859, at a fire in Canal Street, he saved the life of a little girl, who was almost suffocated in the attic. After removing her from her perilous position, he bought new clothes for her and took her to a ball of the company that was held shortly after the fire, at City Assembly Rooms, where she was made the heroine of the occasion. Mr. Byrnes, in 1861, organized Company A of the Ellsworth Zouaves, and went to the war. He was a good fireman and a gallant soldier.

CHAPTER XXXI.

SOME OLD-TIME FIRE LADDIES.

R H. Ellis.—W. C. Conner.—S. Yates.—J. H. Bartley.—B. M. Sweeney.—S. Townsend.—M. Thompson.—J. P. Prote.—M. Fallon.—S. Lichtenstein.—J. A. Flack.—P. B. Van Arsdale.—J. W. Garside.—J. J. Blair.—J. M. Van Alst.—F. J. Twomey.—S. Waterbury.—C. Place.—Peter Vetter, Jr.—Peter Vetter, Sr.—J. H.Waydell.—W. H. Van Sickel, Sr.—W. H. Van Sickel, Jr.—W. W. Warner.—T. E. Howe.—G. H. Dunn.—J. H. Hughes.—Samuel Waddell.—T. Leavy.—W. Hitchman.—J. L. Miller.—A. B. Hauptman.

ROBERT H. ELLIS, ex-fire commissioner, was born in the Seventh Ward. The old Seventh in former days was, in point of intelligence, wealth, beauty, and Quakers, the peer of all wards in the city. East Broadway, as a street, was equal to what Fifth Avenue was in after years, a

ROBERT H. ELLIS.

continuous row of handsome private residences from Catharine to Grand Street. Millionaires were not as plentiful as they are now, and palatial dwellings were unknown, but the houses were large and substantial. Henry, Madison, Market, Pike, and Rutgers Streets were filled with the homes of solid business men, with a large sprinkling of the old school Quaker families. Mr. Ellis had a peculiar entry on fire duty. When about nineteen years of age he was troubled with palpitation of the heart. One hot July evening he visited the family physician, was given a dozen powders, and a strict injunction to keep perfectly quiet, no violent exercise, etc. He was wending his way homeward, had reached the corner of Grand and Essex Streets, when the Essex Market bell struck an alarm for the old Third District. A few moments after Hose Company No. 36 reached the corner; Mr. Ellis stood in the center of the street. "Major Wade" and "Dave Budd" had the head of 36's rope. They lifted it, Ellis slid under; he tried to escape, but without avail. Hose 6 was close behind 36, the pace was terrific, and was kept up until the fire was reached at Seventeenth Street and First Avenue. For eight years after that night Ellis was an active fireman. He has no knowledge what became of the powders or advice. For a year he was a volunteer with 36 (the only one they had, or would allow). In August, 1846, he joined Excelsior Engine

Company No. 2, called " Quaker Two," as a majority of her members were young Quakers. Mr. Ellis was a quiet duty-doing member, rarely missed a fire, served his full time with the ponderous old machine, was on three occasions in great jeopardy, but came out in good order and sound condition. In 1859 Mr. Ellis was elected commissioner, was twice elected president of the Board, was presiding officer when the case of Engine Companies 30 and 40 was tried, which resulted in the commissioner voting to disband No. 40. Mr. Ellis with three of his colleagues resigned. In 1861 Mr. Ellis was commissioned as first lieutenant in the Sixty-first regiment N. Y. Volunteers. He was with the army of the Potomac under McClellan, and served with " Little Mac " from the commencement until the General was relieved of command at Bolivar Heights.

SAMUEL YATES.

WILLIAM C. CONNER joined Fire Engine Company No. 5, May 26, 1845. The foreman of the company at the time was Charles A. Brown, carpenter, 103 Nassau Street, who resigned July 7, 1856. The assistant foreman was Joseph Smith, florist, 383 Broadway, who resigned August 7, 1855. William C. Conner was appointed in turn representative and treasurer of the company and remained with it till it was disbanded on the establishment of the new Paid Fire Department in 1865. In 1874 he ran for sheriff against John McCool, the well-known contractor and quondam friend and champion of ex-Mayor and ex-Congressman Fernando Wood. Conner was elected and made a creditable showing as sheriff for his term of three years, after which he retired from the active exercise of politics,

SAMUEL YATES' MEDAL.
[Presented as an award of merit]

and devoted himself to the more congenial and lucrative business of his type foundry.

SAMUEL YATES was born June 6, 1826. He joined Humane Hose Company No. 20, August 26, 1852, and was assistant foreman from 1852 to 1855. He was presented with a silver medal for bravery. He joined Southwark Engine No. 38, July 20, 1854 ; subsequently was in Protection Engine No. 5, January 30, 1856, and served with them six years.

He was appointed captain of Company No. 7 in the new Department by Commissioner Abby. He is now employed in the *Sun* office. He is a member of the Exempt, Veterans, and Volunteers.

JAMES H. BARTLEY was born October 5, 1857, in the Seventh Ward. Joined Eagle Hose Company No. 1, May 15, 1861, and served as assistant foreman in 1863, 1864 and 1865–1866. He was one of the first organizers of the Veterans' Association, and was secretary and now holds the office of financial secretary. Mr. Bartley's father, W. G. C. Bartley, was an old member of Mutual Hook and Ladder No. 1, and died March 15, 1855. James belongs to the Exempt and Veterans' Associations.

BERNARD M. SWEENY was born September 8, 1827. He joined Franklin Engine No. 39 December 27, 1853, was foreman in 1858, 1859 and 1860; representative in 1861, 1862, 1863, 1864, 1865, and treasurer in 1862. He was bell ringer at Thirty-third Street tower, between Ninth and Tenth Avenues, in 1861. He is now corresponding secretary of the Veterans, and is connected with the Manhattan Gas Company.

SAMUEL TOWNSEND was born November 4, 1815. He joined Engine No. 22 November 3, 1831, Engine No. 32, September 13, 1836, and Hose Company No. 22 June 13, 1842. He is connected with an insurance company.

MATTHEW THOMPSON was born June 19, 1835. He joined Neptune Hose No. 27 February 7, 1858, and was foreman in 1859. He did not like hose company duty, and joined Baxter Hook and Ladder No. 15, March 4, 1862, became treasurer and served his time in that company. He is a member of the Veterans and Exempts.

JOHN P. PROTE was born on Manhattan Island November 26, 1819. He joined Live Oak Engine Company No. 44, September 14, 1844, and served his time in that company, after which he moved to Yonkers, and is now the engineer there.

MALACHI FALLON, the fearless foreman of Black Joke Engine, the redoubtable politician and genial host of the famous "Ivy Green" tavern, will live in the recollection of the old-time firemen as long as memories of the Volunteer Fire Department last. He belongs to a type now well-nigh extinct, which was the peculiar outgrowth of the days when men lived to run to fires.

Born in the old Thirteenth Ward, he ran with the engines as soon as he could find his legs. His father, who was a deeply religious man—a trait for which young Malachi was not conspicuous—kept a harness store in Grand Street between Clinton and Attorney, and afterwards near Goerck Street. He used to attend St. Mary's Roman Catholic Church, on the corner of Ridge and Grand Streets, in the basement of which was the parish school in which Malachi received a rudimentary education. Augustin Daly, the manager, and his brother Judge Joseph F. Daly, attended the same school for a short time.

Fallon joined Black Joke Engine Company No. 33, then the crack company in the Department, as soon as he was of age, and was soon elected treasurer, then assistant foreman, and finally foreman.

As foreman he began to take an active interest in politics in the Seventh and Thirteenth Wards, and soon made Black Joke Engine Company a power of no mean importance. Among Fallon's particular friends in the Board of Aldermen were Cornelius B. Timpson of the Thirteenth Ward, who had formerly been treasurer of Black Joke Engine, and afterwards became police justice, and Alderman Abraham Hatfield of the Eleventh Ward, part proprietor of the Dry Dock line of stages, which ran through East Broadway and Grand Street to the South Ferry. Through their influence he received the appointment of assistant warden of the Tombs, under Warden James Hyde. Not long afterwards he was appointed warden, and held the position for several years. It was to him that John C. Colt, the murderer of Samuel

Adams, made his celebrated confession. Fallon was also one of the one hundred marshals who succeeded the old "Leatherheads" as guardians of the peace, and made a number of clever arrests, which earned for him considerable fame as a detective.

While foreman of Black Joke he performed many acts of heroism at fires, notably the rescue of Mrs. Dyott, the celebrated actress, at the destruction of the Park Theatre in 1848.

A writer of the time describes the famous fireman as being "a handsome fellow, weighing about one hundred and eighty pounds, athletic, wiry, fearless, and having the air of a man born to command."

The Black Joke Volunteers, parading one thousand men, armed and uniformed in red shirts, black trousers and leggings and glazed caps, were commanded by Fallon, who also led the "Baxter Blues," a crack independent military organization, which was named after Colonel Baxter, who fell at the head of his regiment during the Mexican war. Orange Street was re-named in honor of the gallant colonel.

When the great Polk and Dallas demonstration took place in 1844, Fallon, believing his power to be invincible, ordered Black Joke Engine Company to parade with their machine. She was brand new, and was considered the most magnificent specimen of the engine builder's art in existence, having just won the first prize at the American Institute Fair against several competitors. Glittering in all the bravery of burnished brass and bright varnish, she was paraded on a truck drawn by four milk-white horses, and escorted by the whole company in new uniforms, and formed one of the principal features of the procession. Fallon, however, had overstepped the bounds of discretion, for the next day Chief Engineer Cornelius V. Anderson reported what was considered a flagrant violation of the rules of the Department, and at the next meeting of the Common Council Black Joke Engine was disbanded.

After resigning his position as Warden of the Tombs, Fallon opened the celebrated "Ivy Green," in Elm Street, directly behind the Tombs. Up to that time a saloon on the northwest corner of Elm and Franklin Streets had been a favorite resort, but it soon succumbed to the popularity of Malachi Fallon, and the Ivy Green became the recognized rendezvous for politicians, firemen, and men about town.

Fallon's political influence became almost unbounded. In 1848, when the Democratic party was split into the two rival factions of "Old Hunkers" and "Barnburners," he was secretary of the Tammany Hall General Committee. He ran for sheriff, but suffered a defeat at the hands of John J. V. Westervelt. In 1849 he caught the gold fever and sailed for California with a band of argonauts, among whom was the famous David C. Broderick, who subsequently became United States Senator, and fell in a duel with Judge Terry. In San Francisco Fallon ran for sheriff, but was defeated by Jack Hays, of Texas. He was one of the earliest chiefs of police in San Francisco, and with Broderick opposed the formation of the Vigilance Committee, but was forced to succumb to the wave of popular sentiment. After retiring from office he opened a saloon, and through some fortunate speculations in real estate became very wealthly. He at present resides in Oakland.

Seaman Lichtenstein, the well known produce merchant, went to work in Washington Market just half a century ago, when he was but eleven years of age, and by dint of sheer hard work was in a position to start in business on his own account at the age of twenty-one, when he secured a good stand, and, by his great popularity and unrivaled reputation for square dealing, laid the foundation of the extensive business of which he is now the head. At the age of fifteen he began to run with Columbia Engine No. 14, and became a member of that crack company in 1849. Among his comrades were such famous firemen as Chief Decker, Owen Brennan, Harry B. Venn, John Baum and Augustus Tyler. Engine 14 then lay at Vesey and Church Streets, with the entrance on Vesey Street. The bunk-room was two doors away on Vesey Street, over the saloon of Enoch Smith.

"I was a 'bunker' for three years," says Mr. Lichtenstein, "and it wasn't very often that I wasn't the first man at the tongue when an alarm was rung. You see I had a little advantage over the boys, for my business made it necessary for me to get up at two o'clock in the morning, and of course I had to get to bed early; so that when an early morning fire came I had had my sleep, and was ready to jump at the first tap of the bell, while the others, who had only turned in a short time before, were deep in their first slumber. In this way I got the first start and never failed to make the most of it. True, I was never a laggard, but a man should be extra wide-awake and smart to get ahead in such trials as this. But despite all active competitors, as the boys say, 'I got there all the same.' "

SEAMAN LICHTENSTEIN.

Mr. Lichtenstein was never an officer of the company, simply because he felt that he could not spare the necessary time from his business, but he was active in committee work when the welfare of the company was at stake, or when entertainments were projected. He was a member of the committee appointed with power to erect a new engine house on the site of the old one, but with the entrance on Church Street. When it was finished it was pronounced a model of convenience, but Mr. Lichtenstein was determined to make it the finest house in the city, and, with this end in view, contributed out of his own pocket nearly four thousand dollars for extra furniture and embellishments, the funds originally set aside for the purpose being exhausted. The company took possession of its new quarters with great *eclat* and kept open house for three days, during which the premises were inspected by hundreds of admiring visitors. Soon after, the honorary members met and subscribed a sum sufficient to reimburse Mr. Lichtenstein for his generous advance.

At the balls given by the company in Tripler Hall and Niblo's Garden Mr. Lichtenstein was always on the committee. He remained an active member of Engine Company No. 14 till the disbandment, up to which time he resided in the Third Ward.

PETER B. VAN ARSDALE was just of age in 1856, when he joined Friendship

Hook and Ladder Company No. 12, then stationed in Thirteenth Street near Fourth Avenue. He served there five years, making the bunk room his headquarters. When his time had expired he joined Clinton Hose Company No. 17, and served for three years. During a great portion of this time he was a member of the Board of Representatives.

JAMES A. FLACK was born in Willsborough, Essex County, New York, in the year 1830. At an early age he came to the city of New York, and almost immediately identified himself with the Volunteer Fire Department.

He was a runner with Clinton Engine Company No. 41 (commonly known as "Old Stag") long before he became of age, and was elected a member and secretary of the company when he was only nineteen years old. On attaining his majority he continued his association with the old company, and remained with it until the commencement of the war, having served as an active fireman for over ten years.

During his connection with the Department he was the representative of his company for three different terms in Fireman's Hall. He was always an active and efficient fireman, and no duty was too arduous or danger too great for him to perform when occasion required.

Mr. Flack was (1885) elected clerk of the city and county of New York, running on the Tammany Hall ticket, and the respect in which he was held by his old associates in the Department was manifested by the flattering vote which he received.

JAMES A. FLACK.

JOHN W. GARSIDE was born at No. 13 Oak Street, New York city, November 27, 1818. At an early age he was a volunteer with Knickerbocker Engine Company No. 12. On the volunteer roll were the names of men who became famous in the history of the Fire Department: William Drew, William M. Tweed, two of the Pentz family, and many other equally well known fire names. August 18, 1840, he became a member of the company. About the time of the Croton celebration, October 14, 1842, a trouble occurred between C. V. Anderson, chief engineer, and the company, and after the parade the company never performed any duty. In 1844 the company was reorganized under the name of Tradsmen's Engine Company No. 12. Mr. Garside was a leading member, and was elected assistant foreman, and later on foreman. In 1847 No. 12 was disbanded. During 1847 he joined Columbian Hose Company No. 9; in 1849 was elected assistant foreman, in 1850 elected foreman, and resigned from No. 9 in 1860, after serving thirteen years in the company. On October 14, 1853, the members of No. 9, appreciating the valuable services of Mr. Garside, presented him with a handsome silver trumpet. On July 1, 1854, a fire occurred at noonday, in Grand Street, opposite Essex Market. Three persons were in the burning building unable to escape, the stairs having burnt away. Mr. Garside, by main strength and activity, clambered from the window of an adjoining building, lifted the imperilled persons from their dangerous position, and passed them to the next window : thus saved their lives, and received the hearty plaudits of an excited and enthusiastic throng. The papers published highly laudatory notices of the heroic deed, nor did the appreciation of the people end here. A few days after, a gentleman invited Mr. Garside to call at Henry T. Gratacap's store in Grand Street. When he entered the store he found a committee waiting for him. Among the party was Thomas Asten, John Slowey, Henry T. Gratacap, Frederick A. William, and James Ridabock. After hearty greetings Dr. Wilson presented to Mr. Garside a magnificent gold watch and chain. The Common Council passed a resolution directing the

JOHN J. BLAIR.

comptroller to draw a warrant for a gold medal to be presented to John W. Garside. The medal was made— a very elegant specimen of workmanship—the precious metal used in its manufacture costing over one hundred dollars in gold. The city's gift was presented to the brave fireman by Mayor Fernando Wood at his office in the City Hall. Mr. Garside was appointed bell ringer in 1849, and retained the position until 1860. When the Exempt Engine Company was organized he joined, and was elected second assistant foreman at the first meeting of the company, and afterwards first assistant foreman. He was on the police force, first and last, thirty years. He is now a member of the Volunteer Firemen's Association.

JOHN J. BLAIR, ex-fire commissioner, was born in New York city April 17, 1833. He joined Engine Company No. 6 in 1852, when William M. Tweed was foreman, and Joseph H. Johnson assistant foreman. Mr. Blair's life has been one of unusual activity. He was a constable in the Seventh Ward before he had reached his voting year. When he was twenty-two years of age he was appointed assistant captain of police, and held the position until the legislature passed the new police act; was "superintendent of repairs to gunboats and machinery" at Hilton Head in 1862, and was noted as one of the most skillful machinists in the service of the United States. When his labors for the government were finished he returned to New York, and for a time was connected with the Fifth Judicial District Court. He was the first president of the Workingmen's Union in this city. Mr. Blair was elected to the legislature in 1867, and defeated the ring candidate in a district that was supposed to be entirely in the hands of the bosses. He was returned to the legislature in 1870, '71, and '72. Was chairman of the " Committee on Engrossed Bills," and received from his fellow members a set of engrossed resolutions, expressing their personal regard and their appreciation of his parliamentary and legislative knowledge.

Mr. Alvord said in seconding the resolutions : " In my acquaintance with legislative duties I have never yet seen so prompt, punctual, and straight_ forward a chairman of the engrossing committee as Mr. Blair, and I pronounce him the noblest work of God, in this respect, that he is an honest man." In 1870 Mr. Blair was appointed fire commissioner, and made a valuable and efficient officer. During all his official years he never ceased to remember his old companions, the Volunteers He is now one of the directors of the Volunteer Firemen's Association. Mr. Blair studied for the bar, was called, but has not practiced to any extent. His practical mind turned to machinery, and at present he has entire charge of the machinery connected with the New York Post-Office.

JOHN M. VAN ALST ran as a boy with Engine No. 8, lying at 91 Ludlow Street, and joined her on July 15, 1846. He was then some months under the legal age, but, as he says now with a merry twinkle, " I think I'll be forgiven for a small fib in a good cause." After serving his time with Engine No. 8 he joined Hose No. 19 and ran with that company as an active and honorary member for nine years. In 1854 he became a member of the Exempt Firemen's Association. He is now a life member.

FRANCIS J. TWOMEY.

Engine No. 12 in Delancey Street was the principal rival of 8 Engine. " We never went out without meeting her," says Mr. Van Alst, " and we rarely met without a row. I always thought fighting was a bad business, and I'm not ashamed to say that I never struck a man in my life, although I was knocked down once and was pretty badly hurt. Those were rough times—fighting times and drinking times, but I kept away from the rows and the whiskey, and I'm feeling the benefit of it now." Mr. Van Alst is in his sixtieth year, but is as active as most men of forty. He thinks that if the Volunteer Department was in existence to-day he would join it.

FRANCIS J. TWOMEY, now clerk of the Common Council, was born in 1825 in Canada, not far from Montreal, and came to New York with his parents when he was eleven years old. After running with the engines as a lad he joined Aurora Engine Company No. 46, then lying on the northeast corner of Eighty-fifth Street and Third Avenue, on February 2, 1847. He served his full time with that company, and subsequently assisted in organizing Aqueduct Engine No. 10, lying in Eighty-second Street, near Third Avenue, and served with her for several years. He is a member of the Association of Exempt Firemen. Captain Twomey began life in the printing office of Francis L. Hawkes, D.D., of St. Thomas's Hall College, Flushing, L. I., where he served his apprenticeship. In the fall of 1844, his apprenticeship being over, he came to New York and went to work in the *Sun* job printing office, then at the corner of Nassau and Fulton Streets. Subsequently he worked as a compositor on the *Evening Mirror*, then owned and edited by General George P. Morris, Nathaniel P. Willis and Hiram Fuller, and on the *Home Journal*. In 1849 he entered the employ of Messrs. McSpedon & Baker, printers to the Corporation, at No. 25 Pine Street, and remained with them till 1855. For two years he had complete charge of their establishment. In 1855 he was elected one of the assessors of the Nineteenth Ward, and in the following year was appointed police captain of that Ward by Mayor Fernando Wood, Recorder James M. Smith and City Judge Sydney H. Stuart, who were then police commissioners. He continued in command until the organization of the Metropolitan Police Department in the following year. On October 1, 1857, he was appointed an assistant clerk in the office of David T. Valentine, then clerk of the Common Council, and in the following year he was made deputy clerk, a post which he held for ten years under Mr. Valentine, and for six years under his successors. In 1875 he was elected clerk of the Common Council, an office which he has held ever since, with the exception of a few months when he was deputy to Jacob M. Patterson, the present police justice.

SELLECK WATERBURY served his time with Dry Dock Engine No. 47. He was born in Connecticut, came to New York in 1831, and joined the Fire Department in 1836. Engine 47 was organized for the protection of the dry dock and adjacent shipping about the foot of East Tenth Street. The ground for the engine house was presented to the city by the Dry Dock Company, with the understanding that the engine should not be required to go to fires south of Grand or west of Essex Street. William H. Webb, the shipbuilder, was a member of the company. Mr. Waterbury is a life member of the Exempt Firemen's Association, and is now in the wholesale shoe business at No. 37 Warren Street.

CHARLES PLACE served his time with Engine No. 38, which was located in Ann Street, opposite Theater Alley. He was an enthusiastic fireman, and was, of course, a "bunker." Prior to joining 38 he was, as a boy, first with Engine 15 and then with Hose No. 1. Mr. Place is a member of the Exempt Firemen's Association, and one of the oldest members of the Firemen's Ball Committee. He is now president and treasurer of the Consumers' Gas Company of Jersey City, secretary and treasurer of the Consumers' Gas Works Company (Limited), and director in several other companies.

PETER VETTER, JR., now foreman of Engine Company No. 26 in West Thirty-seventh Street, is the eldest of the twelve children of Peter Vetter, Sr. He was born in Ludlow Street on December 13, 1838. His father was a member of Clinton Engine Company No. 41, and of course young Peter ran with that engine as soon as he was old enough to run at all. He relates that he got lost the first time he undertook to go to a fire, and was picked up and carried by a policeman to the station house at the Bowery and Third Street, where he was claimed by his father after the fire was over. He ran with 21 until the company was disbanded for fighting with 15 Engine, when he joined the runners with Manhattan Engine No. 8, which was a Philadelphia double decker and had the only four-wheel hose carriage in the Department. The boys who used to run with her organized themselves into a company, of which Peter Vetter, Jr., was assistant foreman. The runners used to congregate at the corner of Ludlow and Delancey, and the moment the Essex Market bell struck they would make for the engine house and man the ropes of the hose carriage.

" And a hard time we young ones had to keep up with the engine," says **Mr.** Vetter in talking of the old times.

Shortly afterwards Engine 41 was reorganized, and Mr. Vetter went back to his first love. On August 9, 1859, he became a regular member of the company, and in the following year was elected assistant secretary, a post which he held for the two succeeding years. In 1863, 1864, and 1865 he was secretary. On August 20, 1865, the company was again disbanded for fighting with " Big Six " in Ridge Street.

On the organization of the Paid Department, Mr. Vetter was appointed a fireman and assigned to duty with Hook and Ladder No. 16, which was organized on October 20, 1865. That evening the members held a meeting and informally elected Mr. Vetter secretary. He was soon afterwards appointed district inspector, and in June 1, 1868, he was made assistant foreman and placed in command of Hook and Ladder No. 6. On December 16, 1868, he was placed in command of Hook and Ladder No. 3, and on September 18, 1870, was transferred to Hook and Ladder No. 9. On May 1, 1872, he was appointed foreman and placed in command of Hook and Ladder No. 1. After successively commanding Engine No. 11, Hook and Ladder Nos. 11, 7, 15, 13, and 19, and Engine No. 4, he was given his present command on November 14, 1884. 26 Engine is a double company, and covers one of the most important districts in the city. Under Captain Vetter's command the company has been kept in a condition of the highest efficiency. The captain takes the deepest interest in everything pertaining to fire matters, and possesses a large and valuable collec-

PETER VETTER, JR.

tion of " fronts," trumpets, fire hats, and minute books, and other documents relating to the old Volunteer Department. He is a member of the Exempt Firemen's and Volunteer Firemen's Associations.

PETER VETTER, SR., the father of Captain Peter Vetter of Engine No. 26 of the Paid Department, was born in the Tenth Ward on February 7, 1815. After running with the engines as a boy he joined Live Oak Engine No. 44 as soon as he became of age. The engine lay on the north side of Houston Street near Lewis. Mr. Vetter then lived in Delancey Street near Essex. After serving two years with " Live Oak " he joined Clinton Engine No. 41, familiarly known as " Old Stag," in 1838, and served with her as an active and honorary member until the disbandment of the department. His total term of service in the department covered a period of nearly thirty years, during which time it is said that he never, even once, failed to respond to an alarm of fire. Although one of the most efficient and popular members of the company, he resolutely refused to hold office, remaining a private throughout his whole career. He was one of the earliest members of the Association of Exempt Firemen, which he joined on October 21, 1851. His son, Captain Vetter, is also a member, forming the only instance of a father and son being simultaneously members of the organization.

"Old Stag" used to lie at the corner of Delancey and Attorney Streets, occupying the first floor of the building, while the upper part contained the station house of the Thirteenth Precinct Police, commanded by Captain Devoy. No. 15 Engine, known as "Old Maid," and "Black Joke" No. 33, were the principal rivals of "Old Stag." Considerable ill-feeling existed between the firemen and Captain Devoy, who was disposed to be overbearing. On one occasion he took exception to the practice the firemen had of lounging in front of the engine house in warm weather and rudely ordered them into the house, alleging that they were annoying people on the way to church. The firemen were naturally furious at this attempted infringement on their rights and determined to "get even" with the captain.

Shortly afterwards the company went on a target excursion to Matt. Gooderson's at Flushing, L. I. They paraded as the "Clinton Guards" with Foreman John Brown as captain. The target, borne at the rear of the company by "Nigger Sam," who cleaned the engine, and three other colored men, consisted of a life size portrait of Captain Devoy in full uniform. On the shield over his head was the couplet:

"From thy heart the blood shall run
From the bullets of Forty-one."

When the company returned that night, they drew up in front of the station house, and displayed the portrait with the shield riddled with bullet holes, from which ran streaks of red paint. Captain Devoy was furious, and next day caused every member of the company to be arrested and bound over to keep the peace. Captain Vetter relates of his father, to illustrate the old gentleman's fondness for a dry joke, that one night when he was hurrying to the engine house a citizen in a night cap thrust his head out of the window, and excitedly cried: "Fireman, where's the fire?"

"I don't know, but I'll come back and tell you," replied Mr. Vetter, without stopping. About four hours later, on his way home, Mr. Vetter stopped at the citizen's door, and, seizing the knocker, delivered a perfect volley of raps. Out came the night cap again with, "Hello! What's the matter?" "I only wanted to tell you where that fire was. It's at" ——, began Mr. Vetter, mildly. "The fire be d——d," howled the night cap, and down came the window, and Mr. Vetter went chuckling home.

Among Mr. Vetter's fellow members in "Old Stag" were John Brown, Philip B. White, George W. Wheeler, Samuel Berrian, Thomas Haviland, Henry Lewis, Jesse Smith, Charles Ostrander, Arthur Britton and Joseph Hyde.

Mr. Vetter retired a few years ago with his wife to the enjoyment of his vine and figtree at Keyport, N. J., where, true to his old instincts, he is an active member of the local Fire Department.

JOHN H. WAYDELL is one of the "Old Knickerbockers" in the true sense of the word. He was born in the old Sixth Ward in 1826, and has lived all those years in his native city. He first joined Oceana Hose Company No. 36, in 1847. The boys had a good joke on "Old Boy Waydell," as they liked to call him. Just about that time one of his side partners, in a joking way, made a bet that Waydell would miss the first "working fire." The bet was taken up by another, and a few nights passed without their having a "working fire." The matter finally got to the ears of Waydell, and he made a vow (rather a rash one, as will be seen hereafter) that in no event would he miss that fire if alive and well. It so happened that just about the time named he got married, and on the nuptial night the test of his loyalty to the cause and his vow came. The groom, while yet the wedding bells were sounding in his ears, heard the clangor of that other bell calling for help to suppress the flames. Likewise he recalled his vow. The situation was embarrassing. In imagination he saw the smiles and heard the laughter of his mocking "chums." The neophyte groom and fireman felt himself placed in a dire dilemma. Should he abandon his bride—but now led from the altar—the wedding feast, the assembled guests? Or should he remain and brave the taunts and flings he knew would be his portion did he shirk that other duty which this brassy bell was clamorously proclaiming. Which bell, then, should he give his first allegiance to? Their sounds became intermingled and confused in his brain. There was no help for it; he would go. And he did go to that fire, and was among the first to arrive at the big blaze. This immortalized him in the estimation of his associates. It is recorded also that the bride generously forgave him.

JOHN H. WAYDELL.

Mr. Waydell served with Oceana Hose for about six years, during which time roll-call, hardly with an exception, never found him absent from his post of duty. The last fire he attended as an active member of the Old Volunteer Department was in the winter of 1852. It was a downtown fire. He got inside the rope on Engine No. 19; his side partner tripped and fell; the engine went over and killed him. This made such a sad impression on Mr. Waydell's mind that he retired from active duty, not by any means from lack of bravery, for no more fearless fireman could New York produce.

Mr. Waydell is perhaps one of the most active, and certainly one of the most popular of the Trustees of the Widows' and Orphans' Fund of the Exempt Firemen's Association. He has been for years a member of the Association. He is an active member of the Volunteer Firemen's Association of New York, and was unanimously requested to accept the treasurership last year, but declined. He is, perhaps, one of the wealthiest shipowners in the country. He has been a director in the Firemen's Insurance Company for the past ten years, a member of the Produce Exchange, and also of the Maritime

WILLIAM H. VAN SICKEL, JR.

Exchange, for fifteen and ten years respectively; is president of the Eastern District Dispensary, a position he has held for the last five years. He was president of the Mechanics' and Tradesmen's Society for several years. Yet of all the honors conferred upon him none have more charms for him than the recollections of his connection with the Old Volunteer Department.

WILLIAM H. VAN SICKEL, SR., was born in New Brunswick, N. J., on June 4, 1812. He joined Engine Company 30, May, 1829. He was assistant foreman for two years, and foreman for two years more. He resigned in 1836.

WILLIAM H. VAN SICKEL, JR., was born in this city October 11, 1837. He joined 26 Engine January 7, 1859, and was mustered out with the Old Department.

WILLIAM W. WARNER was born in the city of New York about 1830. In 1847 he was a runner with 5 Engine of Newark. In 1848 he moved to New York, where he served his apprenticeship as a printer. When he was twenty-one years of age he joined Marion Hose No. 4, afterwards No. 2 Engine. He is a veteran of the late war, having served as first sergeant in Company B, One Hundred and Twenty-seventh Regiment New York State Volunteers. He has been over twenty years with the Bradstreet Mercantile Agency, where he is in charge of the press room.

THOMAS E. HOWE is an old Tenth and Seventh Warder. Was formerly a carman and joined

WILLIAM W. WARNER.

Tradesman's Engine 37 on October 10, 1842, then located in Delancey Street near Allen. That was disbanded on March 1, 1843, and he then joined Tradesman's Engine 12, organized in 1844, principally by the former members of Engine 37. The engine lay at No. 74 Delancey Street.

The company disbanded April, 1847. Mr. Howe next joined Mayflower Hose 29, March 29, 1853, serving only a few months; he left to join Croton Hose No. 6, September 6, 1853, and served there two years. He is now in the insurance business as an out-door man. He is the eldest son of Thomas D. Howe, who belonged to old 37 Engine, and who was an assistant engineer from 1828 to 1837. His father was born August 8, 1796, and died September 12, 1865.

GEORGE H. DUNN was born in Queens County, L. I., in 1840. His family moved to New York City in 1841, and settled in the Eighth Ward. They subsequently moved to the Ninth Ward. Mr. Dunn joined United States Hose Company No. 25 in 1860, and was never known to have missed a fire. He served until the Old Department was disbanded in 1865.

JOHN H. HUGHES was born on March 6, 1828. He was a painter by trade. He joined Americus Engine Company No. 6 December 17, 1851, and was a member of the company for eight years. He was always out to fires. When the roll was called at the company's meetings to fine members for not being out, the secretary, when he came to his own name, had the pleasure of saying "John H. Hughes, four shilling dues," which was a great byword, and is yet so. John was a great friend of the late John Kelly. He is executor for many an estate, and a widower. He belongs to the Exempt Veteran Association, and is treasurer of the Americus (6) Engine Association.

GEORGE H. DUNN.

SAMUEL WADDELL was a good fireman and a very efficient foreman. He was also an assistant engineer. He also possessed strategic talent, and when he was foreman of United States Engine Company No. 23, before he was foreman of Protector Engine Company No. 22, he used to practice it on 6's boys. Neptune Engine Company No. 6, and United States Engine Company No. 23, and not forgetting Hudson Engine Company No. 1, used to have some very lively times. When 6 was gaining on 22 while going to a fire, Sam used to make his men take it easy to give them a chance to get their wind. He would keenly wait until the head of 6's rope lapped 23's leader jacket, and the Neptunes would be in fine spirits, with a sure thing of passing 23, when he would raise his trumpet and shout, "Let her go, boys!" and she went, much to 6's discomfort. Neptune's trident might be just the thing at sea, but it was not a daisy on land on such occasions, as it could not always carry his namesakes to the front—though they often got there.

THOMAS LEAVY was born in New York City in 1824. At an early age his name was a prominent one on the Volunteer roll of Howard Engine Company No. 34. He remained with the "boys" from 1840 until 1844. There is a legend, still extant, in Greenwich Village, that he was the original party who bore the title of the "fair one with golden locks." In 1844 he was old enough to become a full fledged member of No. 34, under the foremanship of David

C. Broderick, whose life and death became the subject of universal comment throughout the United States. He served seven years with No. 34. Some parties, envious of his golden locks, stated that No. 34 never carried a signal when Leavy had the head of the rope. Mr. Leavy resigned from No. 34 in 1851, joined Niagara Engine Company No. 4 immediately after, and was elected assistant foreman in 1852 and foreman in 1853. It is worthy of note that Mr. Leavy was re-elected foreman for over ten years, a very long period for one man to retain the command and respect of such a large and ever-varying number of men as No. 4 had upon their roll. He served until the department ceased to exist. Mr. Leavy very materially assisted in saving the lives of a woman and two children at a fire at Eldridge and Broome Streets; and at a fire on Broadway near Broome Street he carried out the janitor of the building in an unconscious state. A few moments' delay and the man would have perished in the flames. In the palmy days of base-ball he was a leading

WILLIAM HITCHMAN.

member of the Empire Club, and a good player. Mr. Leavy is a member of the Volunteer and Veteran's Firemen's Associations.

WILLIAM HITCHMAN.—Every old fireman in Yorkville and Harlem knows William or "Billy" Hitchman, as he is familiarly called, and even those who were in old days his political opponents consider him personally a friend. Mr. Hitchman is the son of a livery stable keeper, and was born in Pearl Street, November 18, 1830. Young Hitchman was apprenticed to carriage painter James Flynn, in Eighty-sixth Street near Third Avenue. He joined 45 Engine Company as a runner, and got his certificate when he was twenty-one years old. His comrades elected him secretary, and in this capacity he served until his term expired. Carriage painting injured his health, and he abandoned the trade to become a policeman under the old municipal system. He rose to the ranks of sergeant and lieutenant, and held the latter grade in the Nineteenth Ward when the fight between the Municipal and Metropolitan Departments began. Resigning from the force, Mr. Hitchman entered United States Weigher Dennis McCarthy's office as clerk, and remained there about a year. His next position, assumed in 1859, was that of engrossing clerk to the Common Council. Subsequently he was school trustee, commissioner of education, and secretary of the Tammany Hall General Committee. In 1864 he was made trustee of the Fire Department, and three years later he became a member of the Constitutional Convention. The next year found him Speaker of the Assembly. At present he is an invalid, and lives in Harlem.

JAMES L. MILLER was born in this city November 25, 1813, became a member of Jackson Engine Company No. 24 in 1831, served about eighteen months;

was one of the organizers of Hose Company No. 40 and first foreman in 1843, elected an engineer in 1844, served till 1850, was superintendent of buildings, was an extensive builder and associated with John S. Giles, treasurer of the Fire Department, under the firm name of "James L. Miller & Co., builders." He built Fireman's Hall, in Mercer Street, in 1854. Mr. Miller was one of the organizers of and foreman of the Exempt Engine Company ; also one of the organizers of Adriatic Engine Company No. 31, of which company his brother, John B. Miller, was foreman. He was an active member of the committee appointed by the Board of Representatives of the Fire Department to take charge of the division allotted to them by the Sanitary Commission in aid of the sick and wounded soldiers, which yielded the handsome sum of over thirty thousand dollars. The beautiful decorations and general arrangements were due almost entirely to his skill and good taste. He died November 26, aged sixty-three years and one day.

ARTHUR B. HAUPTMAN, son of Jacob Hauptman, Jr., and grandson of the Jacob Huffman whose name is recorded in the accompanying certificate, was

THIS is to certify, that the Bearer hereof *Jacd Huffman*

is a Fireman belonging to this

City.

NEW-YORK, 28th May, 1778.

Mathews
Mayor

for many years a resident of New York City, and was one of the original settlers of the village of Morrisania, now the Twenty-third Ward. He was elected to various positions in the village and town, and died September 29, 1885, in the seventy-eighth year of his age. Rev. T. R. Harris, of St. Paul's Episcopal Church, read the burial service at the residence, and paid an eloquent tribute to the memory of the deceased. He spoke of his genial nature, generous disposition, and of his marked traits of character, as an earnest friend of education, and particularly of his love for the little ones. Morrisania Lodge, No. 171, I. O. of O. F., of which he was a charter member, and members of Goethe Lodge, No. 193, I. O. of O. F., celebrated the rites of the Order of Odd Fellows at the grave at Woodlawn. Jacob Hauptman, Jr.'s, fire certificate dates back to the year 1801.

CHAPTER XXXII.

FAMOUS FIREMEN OF THE OLD REGIME.

Firemen who have run with the "Machines."—Their Companies and their Exploits.—Methods of Fire Extinguishing which have passed out of Vogue.—Very Lively Times when an Alarm was Rung out.—The kind of History which does not Repeat itself in our day and Generation.—Leading Spirits who Cherish the Memories of the Past.

GEORGE ROBERTSON joined the Department in 1828. He had known all the chief engineers from and including Thomas Franklin to John Decker. New York, when Mr. Robertson was a fireman, had not crept beyond Canal Street, through which ran a sluggish and malodorous stream, confined by a big ditch. The First, Second, and Third Wards were considered the fashionable districts. The first fire Mr. Robertson attended was the one at Crane's Wharf, where the Fulton Market now stands. It was a bitterly cold night. Mr. Robertson became a member of No. 9 Engine in 1829. The company was well known: Hon. James C. Millet, afterwards sheriff of New York; Hon. E. B. Hart, Robert and Peter Goelet, and others were members. Mr. Robertson says that he thinks the boys of the Old Department were as active and quick, all things considered, as they are at the present day.

PETER MASTERSON

JAMES A. MONAGHAN joined Marion Engine No. 9 April 1, 1858, and served until the disbandment of the Old Department in 1865. Born in the Fourteenth Ward, Mr. Monaghan was familiar and popular with the entire population, and he soon drifted into politics. In 1867 he was elected a member of the Board of Councilmen, and became its president. The next year he was elected alderman, and also became president of that body. He is a member of the Exempt and Veteran Firemen's Associations.

PETER MASTERSON, in 1850, joined Engine Company 36, then located at Seventieth Street and Broadway. The following year the company was disbanded. Mr. Masterson then organized, in 1852, Engine Company No. 33, which was popularly known as "Black Joke." The company's quarters were located at Fifty-eighth Street and Broadway, and Mr. Masterson for many years remained her foreman. "Black Joke" was one of the hardest working companies in the city, and was besides a power in the department. Mr. Masterson was likewise instrumental in organizing Hose Company No. 34, at Forty-first Street and Eighth Avenue; also Pete Masterson Engine Company 32, at One Hundred and Fourth Street and Bloomingdale Road. Mr. Masterson was elected one of the trustees of the Benevolent Fund. During the draft riots Foreman Masterson did some splendid service in the upper part of the city. On the first two nights of the riots Mr. Masterson kept up a full head of steam on the engine. His men were formed into a patrol, extending from Sixty-second Street to Fiftieth Street, and from Sixth Avenue to the Hudson River. For the protection so afforded to life and property, citizens presented Mr. Masterson with a case of beautiful pistols, and the company with a large purse of money.

DAVID DECKER was born at No. 38 Vesey Street, New York city, April 10, 1821. As soon as his legs would allow he commenenced to run to fires. In fact, the four Decker brothers (Chief John was one of the four) were all active firemen. When David was old enough he joined Columbian Engine Company No. 14, and served with the old engine many years, but, as No. 14 was only doing duty down town, he resigned to join Washington Engine Company No. 20, which company was running "all over." He served as a member and representative of No. 20 about two years, and resigned so as to have an opportunity to try hose company duty. He joined Hose Company No. 27, served with that company about three years, and having done active fire duty for over fifteen years, he resigned to take

RICHARD H. NUGENT.

a rest. When Mohawk Engine Company No. 16 was organized a number of his old friends and companions of No. 14 were on the roll, and Mr. Decker was induced to add his name to the list. He served with No. 16 until a difficulty arose, and the engine was placed out of service. Through Mr. Decker's influence the engine was returned to the company, and he remained until he felt it to be his duty to retire to private life. Mr. Decker had many offers to accept office, but always declined any position but that of representative, where he could do good service for his company, and aid in elevating the standing of the department.

RICHARD H. NUGENT was born in the City of New York. He joined Baltic Hose Company No. 35 (located in Mercer Street) February 22, 1859, and remained with that company until it was disbanded. In 1862 he joined Empire Hose Company No. 40. Mr. Nugent is a very quiet, unassuming man, never was ambitious of holding office, but preferred to do duty as a private. He is a member of both the Volunteer and Veteran Firemen's Associations, a trustee of the latter organization, and a hard and earnest worker.

JOHN J. FINN'S first experience in fire matters as a boy was attained in running with Old 14 Engine ("Jumper,") then located at Church and Vesey Streets, in the year 1853. At the breaking out of the civil war he enlisted as private in K Company, Eleventh New York Volunteers, known as Ellsworth's Fire Zouaves, on April 19, 1861, and did duty with the regiment until it was mustered out of service in June, 1862. On returning to New York he joined Columbian Engine Company 14, and acted as such until the Volunteer Fire Department was abolished and the present Paid Department substituted. He is a member of the Old Volunteer Fire Department Association, and is well known in Masonic circles, having been a member of the fraternity for twenty-two years. During that period he served four years as Master of Eastern Star Lodge No. 227, F. & A. M., and three as High Priest of Empire Chapter No. 170, R. A. M. He is also a member of the Masonic Veteran Association. In 1883, in conjunction with several old firemen, he helped to organize Noah L. Farnham Post No. 458, G. A. R., Department of New York,

JOHN J. FINN.

and was elected its quartermaster, a position which he has ever since retained. At the annual session of the International Typographical Convention of the United States and Canada, held at Detroit, Mich., in 1878, he represented Typographical Union No. 6, of New York City, and received a vote of thanks from the Union for services rendered.

THEODORE E. TOMLINSON was a favorite with the Volunteer firemen, and many a festive scene was made brighter by his eloquence. There were but few orators in the country equal to Theodore E. Tomlinson in his prime. He was an honorary member of Columbian Engine Company No. 14, and accompanied them on their trips to Washington. During their stay at Baltimore, while being entertained by their brother firemen, Tomlinson was called on for a speech, and he made one that electrified the Baltimoreans and carried them clear off their feet. He told them he had been looking for Mason's and Dixon's line ever since he started from home, but had not found it, nor any line that could separate the friendships of the Volunteer firemen. The word was soon passed among the Baltimoreans to hunt up the Demostheneese and Ciceros of the Monumental City, as they had not expected to hear such eloquence in pure classic style as that of the orator. The distinguished men came to welcome the New Yorkers with true Southern eloquence, but it was the general opinion that none could pass 14's orator.

DAVID CLOSEY, considered one of the best firemen in the department, was retired on July 1, 1883, on a pension of six hundred dollars. He enjoyed the distinction of being one of the quickest "bunkers" as well as one of the best pipemen on the force. Cool and quiet in his demeanor, and strictly temperate, he was ever prompt at the call of duty. In his day he was a noted athlete, being a well-known runner and oarsman. He is an exempt member of the Volunteer **Fire** Department, having served in Washington Engine Company No. 20. On a call for volunteers to go to the front, he was one of the first to respond, going out as a sergeant in Captain William Hackett's company. He came back as color bearer of the regiment (the First Zouaves).

He re-enlisted in the Metropolitan Police regiment, and was made sergeant in Captain James Lee's company, and he was also appointed color bearer of the regiment. While so serving he was wounded, losing a part of his jaw and a number of teeth. He was discharged at the General Hospital on the twenty-ninth of May, 1865, and on the twenty-ninth of September following was appointed a member of the Fire Department, and attached to Engine Company No. 17.

DAVID CLOSEY.

Mr. Closey experienced not a few painful accidents. While serving in Washington Engine Company 20 he was badly hurt. While a member of Engine Company No. 6 he received a severe cut in the head, necessitating seventeen stitches to close the wound. Afterward he was thrown from Hook and Ladder Company No. 12, and was taken to the New York Hospital. At another time he was struck by a falling beam ; and again he was crushed by a portion of a

ROBERT B. NOONEY.

wall falling upon him. Most of his injuries were received about the head, and these repeated hard knocks (including, as stated, the tearing away of part of his face by a Rebel bullet) in time told upon his general health. He had to retire from the service a scarred and pulverized veteran — a martyr to duty in the service of his country. Mr. Closey enjoys fair health now, and is a member of the Volunteers' Association and Farnham Post, G. A. R., of which he is color bearer.

ROBERT B. NOONEY, President of the Board of Aldermen of the year 1886, became a member of Red Jacket Hose Company No. 45, located in East Thirty-third Street near Third Avenue, in 1850. He was made secretary of the company the night that he was elected a member, and the following meeting night was elected representative of the company. He served about two years, when, with six other members, he resigned and joined Metropolitan Hose

No. 39, located on Third Avenue near Twenty-sixth Street. He was elected secretary of that company two months thereafter, and served in that capacity until he was elected foreman two years later, which position he was re-elected to the following year. He resigned his membership in the department in 1856, having served six years, and having been a member of the Board of Representatives nearly the whole time of his connection with the department. He took a very active part in sustaining Alfred Carson as chief engineer, and also in his canvass for re-election, when partisan spirit ran very high, for and against the chief, in every company in the city.

GEORGE T. PATTERSON, ex-foreman of Manhattan Engine Company No. 8, was born March 9, 1824, and joined Engine 8 (Manhattan) in October, 1843, an office which he resigned in March, 1846. He joined Southwark Engine 38 in May, 1846, and resigned November, 1849. In December he rejoined Manhattan

GEORGE T. PATTERSON.

Engine 8, and served until the disbandment of the company, October 14, 1865, making twenty-two years of continuous fire duty. Mr. Patterson was foreman of the company at the time it was disbanded. He is one of the originators and incorporators of the Volunteer and Veteran Firemen's Associations, and is also a member of the Exempt Firemen's Association.

SAMUEL W. ENGS was one of the early members of Neptune Hose No. 5, Carlisle Norwood, foreman, which was organized soon after the strike of 1836, when Chief Gulick was superseded by John Ryker, Jr. "In these days," said Mr. Engs, "we would be called a 'dude' company, for our membership included many merchants and their clerks. I joined in 1838, when I was twenty-one years old. But my recollection of the department goes way back of that. My father, P. W. Engs, was a prominent fireman, and his red-shirted associates came often to the house. When I was ten years old I saw Chief Thomas Franklin. The form and faces of Assistant Chiefs Tom Howe, Jamieson Cox and Uzziah Wenman were familiar to me. Wenman was so dashing and impulsive that his energy was supposed at times to get the better of his judgment. Cox kept a baker shop in Harmon Street, now called East Broadway.

"Neptune Hose No. 5 was located in Mercer Street, where the headquarters of the present department are. Our number was limited to thirty members, and our ranks were always full. We considered that we had the finest carriage in the city. At first we did not perform duty in our own district, but in the Fifth, which included the whole city below Chambers Street. Although we were a silk stocking company, we were well treated at fires, and never, as a body, got into a fight with another company. Marshall O. Roberts, then a West Street ship chandler, joined us, and pulled at the rope for some time, but I don't think he finished his term. Foreman Norwood was so full of vim that he always found work for us. In the usual order of things, most of us would have nothing to do after we had put a stream on the fire. Then came the familiar voice through the trumpet, 'Five—Hose Five!' A minute later we would be at hook and ladder duty, pulling down a wall, for example. We were particularly friendly with Hose Companies 8 and 9, and ran with them when our carriage was laid up for repairs. George Hope, called 'Tall George,' was foreman of No. 8. I had served four years with No. 5, when I joined Hydrant Company No. 1. In a short time I became assistant foreman, and was soon foreman. This organization had no quarters, and no apparatus except the wrench which each man carried in his pocket. Our monthly meetings were held in the old Second Ward Hotel, in Nassau Street, near Fulton.

At fires our duty was simply to tend the hydrant. The other firemen always welcomed us with 'Hallo, old boys! Glad to see you,' for we took the most tedious portion of the work off their hands. Often the hydrant would be so far from the fire that the man tending it had no excitement to compensate for his hours of watching and exposure."

CARROLL CUNNEEN was born in the City of New York in the year 1837, and joined Mohawk Engine Company No. 16, located in West Broadway, in 1860. He was noted as one who was always on duty, fearless, and hard working. No. 16 had several difficulties with other companies during Mr. Cunneen's membership, but his record stands clean and unspotted. He remained with No. 16 until the Old Department gave place to the New.

CARROLL CUNNEEN.

He is a member of the Volunteer and Veteran Firemen's Associations. Mr. Cunneen's family was fire all through. His father, Timothy, was a member of old Neptune Engine Company No. 6, located in Reade Street, for over twenty years, and his uncles, John and Michael Cunneen, were also members of the same company. All three were well known and appreciated in fire circles, when only "gooseneck" engines were used, and all night working fires were the rule and not the exception.

THOMAS D. HOWE was a picturesque figure at a fire. More than six feet tall, he was broad of shoulders and deep of chest in proportion. With his helmet on, he looked like a giant. He was as famous for his physical strength as for the gentleness and good-nature which endeared him to hundreds. But the gentleness was not weakness, as Tom Howe proved many a time. Being a man of peaceful instinct, Howe quelled all disturbances with unsparing vigor, and in this work he was equal to a whole squad of police. His only weapon was a massive copper speaking trumpet nearly a yard long. When it hit a man's head he dropped as if a steam hammer had fallen on him. Few men cared to tackle Tom Howe for the first time, and it is not known that any one braved him twice. His words were few, but he meant every one of them. Tom was satisfied with the post of first assistant (Engine 37), and never tried to be chief. He was as active in politics as in fire duty, and served several terms as alderman from the Eighth and Fourteenth Wards. He died eleven years ago, aged eighty-five years, and retained much of his surprising bodily strength to the last. The big trumpet, his helmets and his numerous medals, badges, etc., are treasured by his heirs.

ROBERT MCWINNIE was born October 8, 1828. He joined Jackson Engine Company No. 24 January 10, 1850. He is now in charge of the High Bridge aqueduct.

DAVID MCLEOD was born September 14, 1834. He joined Harry Howard Hose No. 55 on November 1, 1853, and was foreman in 1861 and 1862.

JOSEPH MCCURDY was born April 14, 1830. He joined Washington Engine No. 20 February 12, 1851, Eagle Hook and Ladder No. 4, April 19, 1852, and Lexington Engine No. 7, February 9, 1855.

LOUIS F. HALLEN, a retired merchant, was born August 9, 1830. On July 1, 1853, he joined Howard Engine No. 34. Mr. Hallen was treasurer for one year of the Volunteer Firemen's Association. He was the treasurer of the Veteran Firemen's Association when they went to Washington in 1885.

JACOB A. FORSHAY was born January 12, 1828. He joined Oceana Engine Company No. 11 June 28, 1853, and National Hose Company No. 24 February 4, 1859.

THOMAS JUDGE was born July 6, 1832. He joined Niagara Engine Company No. 4 on February 20, 1850. He is captain of Engine Company No. 15 in the present department.

JOHN C. PERRINE was born July 28, 1837. He joined Friendship Hook and Ladder Company No. 12 August 3, 1858, and on April 3, 1860, he became a member of Ringgold Hose Company No. 7. He is a member of the Veteran Firemen's Association.

CYRILLUS L. ROBINSON was born November 14, 1833. On October 15, 1852, he became a member of City Hose Company No. 8, and on November 6, 1836, he joined National Hose Company No. 24, and was foreman for the years 1854-'5.

HENRY WEBB was born April 3, 1838. He joined Mohawk Engine Company No. 16 March 8, 1858. He was foreman in 1860 and 1861. He went to Fortress Monroe with Chief John Baulch during the war.

ABRAM SLAIGHT was born October 15, 1857, in the old Ninth Ward. He joined Empire Hose Company No. 40 August 12, 1861, and served until the old Department went out of existence. He is a trustee of the Veteran Firemen's Association.

WILLIAM H. PEREGO was born November 28, 1814. He joined Equitable Engine Company No. 36 October 5, 1839, and Clinton Engine No. 41 March 7, 1838. He is a member of the Veteran Firemen's Association.

DAVID PROTHERO was born May 3, 1839. He joined Excelsior Engine Company No. 2 May 8, 1860, and afterwards became its secretary.

CHARLES J. SIMMONS was born December 17, 1827. He joined Empire Hose Company No. 40 April 17, 1854, and American Hose No. 19 July 22, 1859. He was the "boss" runner of both companies, a bunker, and full of information about fire matters. He is now in charge of the Essex Market Police Court.

EDWARD A. SMITH was born March 28, 1828, and joined Relief Hose September 1, 1851, being one of its organizers. He is a member of the Exempt and Veteran Firemen's Associations. His two sons are members of Tiger Hose of Long Island City. Mr. Smith always visits the "Vets'" house every night on his way home to Long Island City.

JOHN MOLLER, now vice-president of the Veteran Firemen's Association, in Tenth Street, was born in the Seventh Ward in November, 1838. He joined the famous "Big Six" on December 14, 1859. From that day up his record is one of the best. Indefatigable, courageous, always on the alert, he was a model fireman. Notwithstanding all the hard work he has done he looks hardly more than thirty now. His father was in the sugar business in the old Seventh Ward, and his sons, when they grew up, joined him. The firm, which many still remember, remained in existence at Montgomery Street and South Street from 1849 to 1868. Young John Moller, when only twelve years old, was always to be found around the engine house of "Big Six." He was born to be a fireman, and when he arrived at man's estate a fireman he became. He served with No. 6 Engine Company for three years, and left to join Harry Howard Engine Company, No. 11. With the latter he served only five or six months, and then he went back to his "old love," with which he remained until the department was disbanded. Mr. Moller has been vice-president of the Tenth Street Association from its organization, and is also a member of the Old Volunteer Association in Eighth Street. The big double-deck engine,

JOHN MOLLER.

built in 1838, that belonged to Hope Engine Company, of Philadelphia, and now in the possession of the Tenth Street organization, was purchased by Mr. Moller, repainted, and put in perfect order, at an expense to him of one thousand dollars, and was presented by him to his association. When the old firemen went to Washington on the occasion of President Cleveland's inauguration, they took this engine with them, Mr. Moller being one of the marshals. He was also prominent in the parades at Bayonne, Jamaica, and Poughkeepsie. At the burning of the ship 'John J. Boyd,' in the North River at the Ledger Building and Goodwin Crackery Bakery fires, Mr. Moller did good service.

AARON BURR HAYS was born on October 31, 1802. He served for eight years in Engine Company No. 25. He was also a fire warden. Mr. Hays was instrumental in making his company strictly temperate. He also introduced the novelty of making the men on one side of the engine to pump up and those on the other to pump down, thus saving the expenditure of much muscular energy. By this skillful way of working, his company on not a few occasions were able to remain a great deal longer at the brakes than companies composed exclusively of laboring men. Mr. Abraham B. Purdy was one of the first to introduce the same system. Mr. Hays was for a long time cashier of the North River Bank. He died in 1882.

THOMAS BYRNES, Inspector and Chief Detective, joined Hose Company No. 21 in 1862, and was one of its most active members under foreman Arnot Spence. When the company became, in 1863, Engine Company No. 53, under Terence Duffy, Private Byrnes went with the other members and left it December 10, 1863, when appointed a policeman. Fireman Byrnes was imbued with the *esprit du corps* common in those days, and was as lively as his comrades in a scrimmage. Once chatting with Cornelius Van Cott, president of the Paid Fire Department, about old "vamp" times, Van Cott related how in

INSPECTOR THOMAS BYRNES.

a little difficulty between two companies a scrimmage ensued and he, Van Cott, was laid out by "a lanky, black muzzled fellow" of the rival company. Byrnes was intensely interested, and when notes were compared it was discovered that Van Cott was placed *hors du combat* by the present head of the Detective bureau.

J. WELLS SANFORD was born August 9, 1825. He joined R. M. Johnson Hose Company No. 32 April 22, 1844, and Pacific Engine Company No. 28 September 15, 1859. He is now connected with the Fire Patrol.

THADDEUS SCOTT was born August 13, 1839. He joined Mohawk Engine Company No. 16, which lay at No. 7 North Moore Street. He made an excellent record as a fireman.

DAVID GRAHAM, an active and intelligent member of the Volunteer and Paid Departments, was born in this city January 25, 1841. When twenty-one years old he joined Hose Company No. 7 and was legislated out of service by the Act of the thirtieth of March, 1865. He was appointed a member of the Paid Department August 1, 1866, and became a clerk in the secretary's department July 20, 1870.

HUGH CURRY will long be remembered as one of the most enthusiastic firemen that ever lived. It is said of him that he was the only fireman who ever held on to his pipe till the nozzle was melted off. This, however, must be regarded as a pardonable bit of exaggeration on the part of Mr. Curry's admirers, for he strenuously denies that he ever did anthing of the kind. It is, nevertheless, incontestable that he was a skillful and brave fireman. He joined Hose No. 35, lying in Mercer Street, between Bleecker and Amity, in 1847, and was subsequently a member of Hook and Ladder 14 and the Exempt Engine Company. He was an active member of the department at the disbandment, and is ready to do fire duty to-day. He is a member of the Exempt Firemen's Association. His elder brother, Daniel, was a famous old-time fireman.

ALEXANDER MURRAY joined Engine Company No. 39 in the latter part of 1859. He served one year and then joined Hose Company No. 44. He continued in the service till the disbandment. He was foreman of Hose Company No. 44 from 1862 to 1863.

ANDREW ROGERS, of 40 Hose, made his first appearance as a fireman at the great conflagration of 1835, when, at the age of ten years, he attempted to run with Peterson Engine No. 15, an exploit that earned him an acquaintance with the maternal slipper when he got home. After running with Hose No. 40 for several years he became a member September 21, 1849, and served

as an active and honorary member until the disbandment of the Department. He was for a short time treasurer of the company. His brothers Joshua and William also belonged to the company. The latter was bellringer in the Spring Street tower. Mr. Rogers is a life member of the Exempt Firemen's Association. He is employed in the Dime Savings Bank.

ABRAHAM MYERS joined 40 Hose on July 4, 1845, and successively served as secretary, representative, assistant foreman, and foreman. After serving out his time he retired for a year and then re-joined, and served for six years more. He was

ALEXANDER MURRAY.

an honorary member of Hose No. 40 and Hose No. 19. Mr. Myers is one of the few firemen who achieved distinction who never ran a day as a "Volunteer" He is a member of the Exempt Firemen's Association.

JOHN W. TERHUNE joined Hose Company No. 40, then commanded by David Milliken, and lying in Barrow Street, between Hudson and Bedford, in 1850. After serving for twelve years he joined Hook and Ladder No. 14 in Charles Street, and served for two years. He was subsequently elected an honorary member of both companies. In 1862 he joined the Exempt Firemen's Association, of which he is now a life member.

CYRUS LORD, now seventy years old, was the youngest member of the Supply, and is one of the few survivors. He declares that he considers himself as much a fireman as anybody, and never tried to strengthen his position by running with a regular machine. The unwieldy contrivance in Centre Street was very useful, he says, and covered itself with glory when the Old Bowery Theater burned.

SAMUEL G. SMITH, THEODORE S. SMITH, and ARNETT G. SMITH formed a family of firemen. They are, in the order named, grandfather, father, and son. The first was born in 1790, died July 4, 1866, was foreman of Engine Company No. 13 in 1820, having joined on July 5, 1816, served ten years, and was discharged on July 15, 1826. His son, Mr. Theodore S., was born in 1823, died June 19, 1867, joined No. 2 Hose on November 4, 1841, No. 21 Engine on July 13, 1847, and was afterwards an honorary member of No. 30 Engine from 1858 to 1865. Mr. Arnett G., son of the latter, joined No. 28 Engine in 1862, and served until the department was broken up, when he was secretary. He is now in business in Fulton Street, and has a very fine collection of "fronts" of the Old Department and many other interesting relics.

JOHN L. VAN WART, although seventy-five years old, is hale and rugged as many a younger man. He was born in the Ninth Ward, and learned the carpenter's trade. In August, 1832, he joined Union Engine No. 18, and served there two years. Then he tugged at the rope of Howard Engine No. 34 for eight years, when he signed the roll of Guardian Engine No. 29. In

JOHN L. VAN WART.

this company he served until the disbandment of the Volunteer Department. He does not claim to be the senior survivor of the old *regime*, but believes that there are few of his comrades who served for thirty-three years with but one interruption—the strike of 1836. More than once Mr. Van Wart was offered an office, but he always declined, saying that he preferred to be a high private. From 1860 to 1865 he spent six hours a day in the bellringer's loft perch at Jefferson Market. Mr. Van Wart remembers answering fifteen alarms in one night. The little gooseneck engine was dragged downtown to work at the big fire of '35. She had already been to two minor fires, and the men were tired when they ran to the aid of their comrades at the historic blaze. No. 34 was known as the Van Wart Company, and at one fire it was said that there was nobody at the rope except members of that family. John, his father, Isaac Van Wart, and his brother Samuel and Lawrence were members. The Howard Insurance Company gave the boys a set of runners for their engine, which took the place of wheels in winter time. On one never-to-be-forgotten night 34 was at the cistern at Bleecker and West Tenth Streets. There was a fire in West Eleventh Street. No. 48, which took 34's water, was soon washed. No. 16 took her place with no better luck, and then No. 2, a new engine fresh from the painter's shop, tried her fortunes. On the back of this machine was a splendid picture of the unrivalled Forrest as *Rolla*. A yell of triumph went up from the Howards in a few minutes, when they saw water trickling over the tragedian's features. "Who washed *Rolla?*" was for a long time the bitterest taunt that could be flung at No. 2. Mr. Van Wart says that during his long service there were not half a dozen important fires at which he was not present. He took part in all the large parades, including the one which celebrated the introduction of Croton water, and that in honor of the Prince of Wales.

THOMAS SULLIVAN, assistant engineer, was born in 1838. He joined Friendship Hook and Ladder Company, No. 12, April 7, 1858, after serving two years as private. He was elected assistant foreman, and served one year in that position. In 1861 he was elected foreman, and for three subsequent yearly elections the members of the company deemed a ballot unnecessary, and elected Mr. Sullivan by acclamation. In 1865 Mr. Sullivan's friends placed his name before the department as a candidate for assistant engineer. His merits were recognized, and he was triumphantly elected. This was the last election held by the Old Department, and Mr. Sullivan remained at his post until the new force was in working order.

In the winter of 1862 a fire occurred at a tenement house in Thirteenth Street, between Avenues A and B. A distillery occupied the lower floor. The inflammable nature of the stock caused the flames to spread rapidly, and, as usual, the stairs were burnt away, causing a dozen human beings to be left to the mercy of the devouring element. Fortunately Hook and Ladder Company No. 12 were promptly on hand, and arrived at a critical moment. Foreman Sullivan displayed his usual cool-headed judgment. The ladders were raised; a number of brave fellows, headed by Sullivan, mounted to the crazed occupants of the upper floors. They were all saved; the last one rescued was a woman on the top floor; she was desperately sick, and had to be tied in blankets, and tenderly lowered, round by round down the swaying ladder. As she reached the ground in safety the assembled

THOMAS SULLIVAN.

throng gave vent to their feelings with rousing cheers for Foreman Sullivan and his gallant men.

When the Legislature passed the new fire bill creating "The Metropolitan Fire Department," Philip W. Engs was appointed one of the Board of Fire Commissioners. One of his first official acts was the appointment of Thomas Sullivan as engineer, which position he held until May 20, 1873. A new act of the law-makers at Albany was the cause of his being left out. On August 23, 1884, Fire Commissioner Henry D. Purroy reinstated Mr. Sullivan as foreman. He was placed in command of Hook and Ladder Company No. 11, stationed in Fifth Street, between Avenues C and D, where he is located to the satisfaction of his superior officers, and the safety of the public.

HENRY B. VENN, foreman of Engine Company No. 14, was quite a prominent fireman. In 1851 he was defeated by Moses Jackson for the office of assistant engineer. Mr. Venn was a very active worker, and a devoted and enthusiastic fireman. No man was better known or had a larger circle of friends. He has been referred to already in several parts of this book, leaving but little more to be said. He died suddenly March 16, 1879. Mr. Venn, although not a very religious man in the strictest sense, at one period of his life, at least, interested himself in a religious assemblage held (1858) in the Academy of Music, Henry M. Graham and John J. Gorman also taking a prominent part in the meetings. "Oh, for that Flame of Living Fire" was the title of one of the most popular hymns sung upon those occasions. His portrait will be found on page 167.

THOMAS RYAN, a well-known fireman, joined Mohawk Hose 39, May 10, 1859, resigned therefrom on the second of November of the same year, and joined Lexington Engine Company No. 7 on the same day. Mr. Ryan, whose portrait we print, has a most honorable record as a brave and active foreman of the Old Department. In common with a number of others of the Volunteer firemen, he cherishes old mementos and records of his company, a number of which Mr. Ryan has preserved with fostering care and an honest pride, because of the memories and associations they inspire, and of their historic value. Mr. Ryan pays as strict attention to his business as he ever did to the obligations appertaining to the duties of a fireman. Mr. Ryan joined the Masonic Order in 1865, and attained the Degree of Knight Templar. He is also a Knight Templar and a member of the Land League.

THOMAS RYAN.

JOHN F. McGOVERN joined Mohawk Hose No. 39 on February 1, 1862, when he was twenty-one years old. An enthusiastic fireman, he made the company's house in Twenty-sixth Street his home, and asked no better accommodation than the bunk-room offered. Though his term of service was short, it was eventful, including, as it did, the fearful days of the draft riots in the summer of 1863. Whoever remembers that awful time will not forget the gallantry of the firemen and the tests to which they were put. Hose 39 furnished her own quota of heroes, among whom Mr. McGovern was one of the most conspicuous and most modest. To this day he speaks of his exploit with reluctance, and only persistent questioning can draw the story from him. He can tell, if he will, of the days when his company did police as well as fire duty. When the lumber yards along the East River front were fired, the mob built a strong barricade of trucks, boxes, timber, stones, etc., across Fourteenth Street. But it needed a stronger barrier than this to keep back the Mohawks, and John McGovern was foremost as they grasped the ropes hard and dragged their carriage completely over the barricade.

Mr. McGovern's parents lived on the west side of Second Avenue, one door from Twenty-ninth Street. In the rear of the row, between Twenty-eighth and Twenty-ninth Streets was a courtyard upon which three frame houses opened. These houses were occupied by respectable colored people, who reached their homes by a narrow alley leading from the Twenty-eighth Street side. Back of the houses, on the north side of the court, was a small yard, separated by a high fence from the McGovern property. A gang of rioters entered the alley in the morning and set fire to the houses. Before the firemen could arrive the flames barred exit through the alley, and the negroes retreated to the little yard already mentioned. Hotter and hotter grew the fire; nearer and nearer it came to the frightened group, who believed that they were staring a horrible death in the face. Strong, active men, unencumbered, might scale the fences, but for the old and feeble, and women with babes in their arms, and little ones clinging to their skirts, there seemed no hope of rescue. McGovern, with Dan Rooney and Joe Twombly, ran into the former's yard and heard, above the crackling of the fire, the voices on the other side of the fence. Some of the colored people called frantically for help—made "a clamorous appealing to the mercy of the fire." Others had lost hope, and meekly prayed that God would receive their spirits.

The voices steeled the arms of the firemen, who in a few moments had bat-

MR. McGOVERN'S ADVENTURE WITH THE MOB.

tered down the fence, and drawn the imperilled group into the McGovern yard. But they had now to face another enemy. Filling the streets, and pouring into areas and hallways, was the mob, a foe more cruel than the deaf and frantic fire. When they saw the black faces, the rioters ran toward them, howling like the wild beasts they were. Bravely the three firemen defended their charges. With their helmets like shields in their left hands, and their hydrant wrenches in their right, they struck out fiercely, knocking down every wretch who came too near. Rooney and Twombly managed to get all the negroes to a place of safety, except a mulatto child, four years old, named Reed, who clung to McGovern. Strong and brave as he was, the stalwart fireman could not fight the mob alone. He snatched the child in his arms and ran up the avenue, pursued by a yelling crowd hurling sticks and stones at him. Near Thirtieth Street he ran into a brown stone house, and gained the back yard. The fences were moderately high, and surrounded by a narrow ledge, upon which a cool-headed person might walk with safety for some distance. At an angle of the fence Mr. McGovern climbed, while the child clung to his neck. He heard the mob shouting as he walked cautiously along the ledge. Having passed three or four yards he dropped into one, and ran to a window; where he saw a woman's face. He explained the situation to her in a few words, and asked her to take temporary charge of the child. The woman consented, and Mr. McGovern rejoined his company. Early the next morning he and Twombly borrowed a wagon of a German baker, named George Bauer. The disorder had partially subsided, and they had no trouble in reaching the house in which was David Reed. During the night the child had been restless. He had slept a little, then awoke weeping, and begging to be taken from the fire and the men in the street. Mr. McGovern wrapped a shawl about him and told him to be quiet, and he would see his mother. The child promised, and kept his word. He was put into a bread-box in the wagon, and a stick shoved under a corner of the lid for ventilation. Mr. McGovern drove to Police Headquarters, where he was told that several colored families had taken refuge. As he carried David to the top floor, he heard voices of prayer and lamentation. In a large room were many negroes. Mr. McGovern took the shawl from the boy and held him up.

" Whose child is this ? "

There was a wild, half-savage scream of delight, as two women sprang forward. They were David Reed's mother and grandmother. With hysterical sobs and laughter they embraced the fireman's knees, kissed his hands, and invoked on his behalf every blessing with which Heaven rewards those who risk their lives in defending the helpless. In a pamphlet written at the time, Rev. Stephen H. Tyng, Jr., mentions Mr. McGovern's gallantry. He called at the hose company's house to make the hero's acquaintance, and said he would be glad to serve Mr. McGovern at any time. When Henry Ward Beecher went to England during the war, he was quoted as saying that the instigators of the draft riots were mostly Irishmen. In answer to this a prominent Dublin journal spoke of the rescue of the Reed child, and suggested that there might be Irishmen on the side of law and order too, since McGovern was undoubtedly an Irish name. Mr. McGovern got an appointment as clerk in the Post-office, where his duties conflicted with those of a fireman. He resigned from the department December 5, 1864. Little David Reed never recovered from his awful experience, and died in a short time.

LAWRENCE TURNURE, foreman of Hose Company No. 36, representative of the company, treasurer of the Firemen's Monument Committee (Greenwood Cemetery) and late president of the City Bank, was quite an active fireman in his day. He was a member of the firm of Moses Taylor & Co.

D. LYDIG SUYDAM had a narrow escape from perishing beneath falling walls at a fire in Eldridge Street near Grand (1840). A stream of water was being played from the street upon the burning building, and he was holding the pipe, when the wall fell in, burying several firemen beneath the ruins. Had the wall fallen outwards, Mr. Suydam would have been mixed up with the débris, no doubt. He lived at No. 40 East Thirty-first Street, and was a member of Hose Company No. 5.

DANIEL MOONEY was born in the City of New York in 1819, and has lived in the vicinity of Spring and Varick Streets (Eighth Ward) for over sixty years. After serving on the Volunteer roll for four years, he joined **Hope Engine Company No. 31**, located in West Broadway, in 1841. Mr. Mooney served seventeen years as a certificate member, during which time he was assistant foreman for two years, foreman for two years, and representative for three years. When Hope Hose Company of Philadelphia, one of the handsomest carriages in that city, visited their namesake, No. 31, Foreman Mooney showed them every attention. Their carriage was placed on exhibition at the Crystal Palace, and Mr. Mooney assumed guardianship of their "pet" until it was returned to its birthplace. In return for the courtesy displayed by Mr. Mooney, Hope Hose presented him with a beautiful model of their apparatus and a set of engrossed resolutions, handsomely framed.

WILLIAM A. WOODHULL, in 1847, when twenty-one years old, joined **First Ward Hose Company No. 8.** He did duty for three and a half years; then transferred his allegiance to **Oceana Hose, 36,** stationed in Madison Street near

Rutgers. At the end of three years' service as foreman Mr. Woodhull resigned in 1855 to become secretary of the department. The company presented him with a small but rich and massive rosewood bookcase. On the top is a gracefully carved hose carriage. A brass plate informs the reader that the bookcase was "Presented to William A. Woodhull by the members and honorary members of Oceana Hose Company No. 36, November 7, 1855. D. Reynolds Budd, William D. Wade, Henry B. Clapp, W. R. W. Chambers, Alonzo Slote, committee." He did duty with his company at the Park Theater fire, the American Museum blaze, and the Harper Bros'. conflagration. Mr. Wood-

WILLIAM A. WOODHULL.

hull was also present in Hague Street a few minutes after the awful explosion. His resignation as foreman of Hose 36 was followed by his appointment as secretary of the department. This office he quitted for that of vice-president. After a year's service as president he left the department, retaining, however, his membership in the ball committee, which he holds to this day.

THOMAS COMAN was born in 1835, and in September, 1856, joined **Eagle Engine Company No. 13.** Almost immediately after becoming a member he was elected secretary and representative, and after serving two years in those positions, was elected foreman of No. 13 in 1859. He was re-elected in 1860-'61-'62-'63-'64, and was in command when the curtain fell on the last act of the Volunteer Department in 1865. During the draft riots in 1863 the members of No. 13, under the direction and command of Mr. Coman, performed police, military and fire duty, taking under their charge all the large storehouses in the vicinity of the engine house. This duty was performed day and night, until the riot was quelled and the city was in a peaceable condition.

In 1865 the people of the Second Aldermanic District, comprising the Fourth and Sixth Wards, elected Mr. Coman alderman, and re-elected him in the years 1867-'69. He was elected alderman-at-large in 1870-'71 and '72, and president of the board in 1867-'68-'69-'70, and twice in 1871. During these years he was three times legislated out of office, and on each occasion his constituency at once returned him to his position. On only one occasion was there any opposition to his election; at all other times he was indorsed by all parties. He was supervisor in 1871 and '72. When John T. Hoffman was elected governor Mr. Coman became acting mayor. In every position held by Mr. Coman he has displayed untiring energy and application. Mr. Coman is now connected with the Equitable Life Insurance Society of this city.

ENOCH C. PENTZ.—Enoch C. Pentz was born in 1822, and for several years was a Volunteer with Knickerbocker Engine No. 12. He was an early member of Southwark Engine Company No. 38, and served over seven years with the company. He was elected assistant foreman in 1843. His record in the

ENOCH C. PENTZ.

company was a fine one. Mr. Pentz belongs to one of the oldest families in New York. The cooperage establishment, No. 2 Gouverneur Lane, where he now carries on business, has been occupied by members of his family for over one hundred years.

THOMAS DUNLAP commenced his fire duty as a volunteer with " Black Joke " Engine Company No. 33, located in Gouverneur Street (the same house was subsequently occupied by " Big Six"), and after serving his apprenticeship was elected a member of the company in 1838. Four Dunlap brothers were members, viz.: Thomas, James, Samuel and William. Samuel was assistant foreman of the company at one period. In 1844, when C. V. Anderson was chief engineer, there was to be a great " Polk and Dallas" celebration and parade, and several fire companies had signified their intention to join in the Democratic jubilee. The chief engineer warned them against such a proceeding, and informed them that any company disregarding his command would be disbanded. Engine Companies Nos. 15 and 33 vowed they would turn out, and they did, but the chief kept his word, and both companies were disbanded. This closed Mr. Dunlap's career as an active fireman. During his service he had many narrow escapes, and on one occasion was run over by the engine and picked up for dead.

One of the most celebrated public houses in the United States was the "Pewter Mug," located in Frankfort Street, next door to old Tammany Hall (now the *Sun* Building). Thomas Dunlap was the proprietor, and during his popular management he received as friends and visitors the most distinguished men of the period. The highest officials of the country were in the habit of making the " Pewter Mug " the Mecca of their political pilgrimage. In the rooms of this out-of-the-way tavern names were made or unmade, the laurel crown was placed upon or snatched from the brows of aspiring statesmen, and not a nomination for governor, congressman, state legislature, or city or county office could be made unless the sanction of the "Pewter Mug" was first obtained. But Mr. Dunlap retired from the business, and the glory departed from the spot forever. When William F. Havemeyer was mayor, he appointed Mr. Dunlap to the responsible position of mayor's marshal. Sheriff Davidson secured Mr. Dunlap as a deputy, and several succeeding sheriffs retained him, appreciating his valuable services. Mr. Dunlap was one of the Commissioners of Emigration, a member of the Common Council in 1854-'55, deputy naval officer under the administrations of Franklin Pierce and James Buchanan, deputy collector of city revenue under Comptrollers Flagg and Hawes, collector of city revenue many years when nearly all moneys belonging to the city passed safely through his hands, and commissioner of jurors for several years, in which position he secured the hearty commendation of all the judges in the city. He was a delegate to almost every National, State or County Convention that has occurred for the past fifty years, and for forty-six years was on either the young or old men's Tammany Hall committee, a longer continuous term than any living man. Mr. Dunlap was the intimate friend and confidant of Governor Horatio Seymour. When the presidential contest was waging between Lincoln and McClellan, and it became necessary to secure an honest, trustworthy commissioner to distribute and collect the New York soldiers' vote, Thomas Dunlap was selected. He faithfully discharged the duty, and was the only one who brought the vote to New York City. He takes his title of colonel from

DANIEL DONOVAN.

his position on Governor Seymour's staff, and also his commission from Brigadier-General Spinola.

DANIEL DONOVAN was born in the Fourth Ward of the City of New York in the year 1830, and began life as a printer in the office of the *Journal of Commerce*. He joined Eagle Engine No. 13, of which the well-known fireman, John Baulch, was foreman, but his first service in the company only covered a period of four months, when, on account of some internal discord, he resigned, and immediately joined Fulton Engine Company No. 21, serving until the early part of 1852, when he rejoined No. 13. He was elected assistant foreman in 1852, and foreman in 1853-'54-'55. In 1857, when Harry Howard was elected chief engineer, causing a vacancy in the Board of Engineers, it was filled by the election of Mr. Donovan. His attention to rules so pleased the department that at two subsequent elections he was re-elected, leading all other candidates. In 1860 Chief Decker appointed Mr. Donovan foreman of the Corporation Yard—an office which he held until the time of his death, which occurred in August, 1862.

WILLIAM H. LANDERS was born in New York City in 1825, and joined Star Hose Company No. 34, then located at Tenth Street and Avenue D, on August 27, 1849, and served seven months, when he resigned and joined Live Oak Engine Company No. 44. He remained with No. 44 until September 29, 1865, and during his service was foreman for one year and representative for three years. On the date last mentioned the Volunteer Department went out of existence, and the same day Mr. Landers became a member of the Metropolitan Fire Department. He was made assistant captain November 15, 1865, and captain of Engine Company 39 December 24, 1870. He is at present captain of Engine Company No. 42, located in Fulton Avenue, between One Hundred and Sixty-Seventh and One Hundred and Sixty-eighth Streets (Morrisania). Mr. Landers's fire service covers a period of nearly forty years without a break, and to-day he is hale and hearty, and apparently able to survive forty years more of the hard work he has endured.

Two items of gallantry to Mr. Landers' credit must be mentioned, both occurring in 1858. The first was at a fire in Sixth Street, between Avenues B and C, in a building adjoining what was known as Jones's Brewery. A mother and two children had been left on the third story, and their position was perilous in the extreme, when Mr. Landers placed a ladder in position and succeeded in rescuing the family. The other event took place in Eighth Street, between Avenues B and C, when two children had been cut off from escape in a rear room on the third story of the burning building. Foreman Landers mounted a ladder at the front of the house, crawled through the window, and, though nearly suffocated, reached the panic-stricken group and bore them to the window, where willing hands were waiting to receive them.

LEWIS P. TIBBALS was born in Milford, Connecticut, in 1832. His ancestors were among the original settlers of the place, their names being on the State records in 1640. One of them married a beautiful Indian maiden, consequently Mr. Tibbals claims to be a genuine native American. The "Charter Oak" is no better known in Milford than the old family name of Tibbals.

Lewis P. Tibbals came to this city at a tender age, and joined Southwark Engine Company No. 38 in 1853. He was an ardent worker in the company. One night in 1854 the "Pearl Street House," in Pearl Street between Old Slip and Coenties Slip, was discovered to be on fire. Mr. Tibbals had the pipe of Southwark on the roof of the tall six-story building, when the engineer, deeming the position unsafe, ordered the pipe down. The smoke was dense, and as Mr. Tibbals was striving to obey the order he became bewildered, stumbled and fell from the dizzy height. He was missed in a short time, and, search being made, was found between the hotel and adjoining building. He was conveyed insensible to the New York Hospital, but in six days was discharged, lame of course, suffering only from the effects of shock and a sprained ankle. Few firemen have had a more wonderful escape.

DANIEL D. CONOVER was an active and influential member of the Volunteer Fire Department, and took a prominent part in all matters pertaining to its welfare. In 1853 he was foreman of Amity Hose No. 38, a company noted not only for its elegant carriage, but for the character and standing of its members in the community. He was also identified with municipal affairs.

He is still vigorous, and he does not neglect the recreation afforded by the Olympic Club at the new quarters down on Long Island, and in the season participates in the sports with such old fire laddies as John R. Platt, ex-foreman of Oceana Hose Company No. 36, ex-Assistant Engineer John H. Forman and Richard P. Moore, ex-foreman of Empire Engine Company No. 42, who, bye-the-bye, has recently made the grand tour of Europe and can enlighten the Olympics with foreign " yarns," and tell how Stanley got on with the last words of Marmion. Mr. Conover is a member of the Veteran Firemen's Association and threaded the terpsichorean muses at their grand ball at the Metropolitan Opera House in 1886, with all the sprightliness of other days. When Mr. Conover was in the Common Council he appreciated the necessity and advantage of a steam engine and introduced a resolution for the purchase of one.

WILLIAM P. ALLEN was born in New York City in January, 1843, in Chrystie Street, within a few doors of old Peterson Engine Company No. 15, which was more familiarly known as " Old Maid." He lived in that neighbor-

hood during the greater part of his life, and from boyhood ran as a Volunteer or runner with that old company and its successor, Adriatic Engine No. 31, which laid in the same location, and was afterwards known as " Peterson," until 1863, when, on arriving at his twenty-first birthday, he joined Manhattan Engine Company No. 8, located in Ludlow Street, between Broome and Delancey Streets. He immediately became a " bunker," and was known as a tongue rusher, as that post of honor gave the ones that obtained it the privilege of taking the pipe at the fire. While proceeding to the large fire in Pell Street, August

WILLIAM P. ALLEN.

12, 1864, and as usual at the tongue of the engine, and going down the Bowery in the railroad track, a large wagon was stopped directly in front of the engine. The engine smashed into the wagon, crushing Mr. Allen, and, as he fell, the engine passed over his body. The result was a broken thigh, ribs, hips, and a badly bruised condition generally. He was picked up by his comrades, taken in a coach to the engine house, and carried on his bunk room bed (which he still possesses) to his residence, where he laid for four months. He remained in active service until the organization of the Metropolitan Fire Department in 1865, when, on the thirteenth of October of that year, he was appointed driver of Engine 12. While driving to a fire one rainy night in 1867, the engine went into a large hole in Pearl Street, and threw him from the seat, but he managed to regain it, and continued driving to the fire with a badly injured back. He was unable thereafter to stand the jolting of the engine, and was transferred to Hook and Ladder Company No. 6. Abram C. Hull (now superintendent of the Fire Patrol) was foreman of Hook and Ladder Company No. 6 at that time, and was detailed to act as a district engineer (same as the present chief's of battalion), during which time Allen was placed in command of the company. Eventually he was detailed to headquarters, and in 1870 appointed clerk to the chief, which position, as the business of the Department developed, was made chief clerk of the bureau, an office which he still holds. While in active service he instituted the quick hitching, and drew the plans for the hitching drill for engine and hook and ladder companies, which were afterward made permanent rules of the Department. Has served continuously under every Board of Commissioners for twenty-one years. Has had charge of all collections made by the force for charitable or other purposes, and has collected over fifty thousand dollars, among which was five thousand dollars for the blind fireman, Eddie McGaffney, and ten thousand dollars for the widows of Firemen Reilly and Irving, who were killed in the discharge of their duty.

DENNIS HAYS, the inventor of the famous truck which bears his name, joined Engine No. 2 in 1852, and served with her until 1862, when he joined Engine 42 as engineer. On the organization of the Paid Department he was appointed engineer of Engine No. 1, but only served a few days. In the following year he went to San Francisco, where he was for many years in charge of the repair shops of the Fire Department. While thus engaged he perfected the details of his truck, which is now considered the best contrivance of the kind in use.

ANDREW M. UNDERHILL.

ANDREW M. UNDERHILL was born in New York City fifty-one years ago. He is descended of an old and honorable Warwickshire (England) family, who were among the first settlers of the New England States. He was educated at private schools in East Broadway, in Market and in Crosby Streets. He joined the Volunteer Fire Department of Brooklyn, and served his time with Mechanics' Hose Company No. 2, of which company he was foreman for over two years. When the war broke out he was commissioned first lieutenant of Company G of the Eleventh Regiment, N. Y. V. (the Ellsworth Fire Zouaves). At the first battle of Bull Run he distinguished himself by his heroism. At one time, on that day—when Rickett's Battery was left on the field—every man being killed or wounded, he said to Sergeant Ferris of G Company: "It's a pity to leave those splendid guns for the 'Rebs'; can't we get them off?" With three or four brave Zouaves to help, the guns were dragged off the field under a galling fire from the advancing columns of Rebs, which killed three, wounding Sergeant Ferris and a private. The rifle of Sergeant Ferris was shattered with balls, pieces of their clothing being shot away, yet strange to say, the tall, erect and muscular lieutenant escaped injury. Later in the day, however, he was captured, taken prisoner and held for over twelve months; during which time he had a variety of Confederate prison experiences, being confined, from time to time, in no less than eight prison pens. He was finally pardoned, and returned home, a skeleton of his former self. He made several offers of his services to the government subsequently, but each time received the reply that he was still a prisoner of war. He entered the employ of Williams & Guion as freight agent in 1863, and was promoted step by step until now (1887) he has succeeded the old firm, and is the senior of the firm (with his son as partner) of A. M. Underhill & Co., general agents of "The Guion Line, Liverpool Steamers." He holds a captain's commission in the Seventy-first Regiment, N. G. S. N. Y.; is commander of Alexander Hamilton Post G. A. R., and no old-time fire-laddie or war veteran was, or is, more popular than Andrew M. Underhill.

WILLIAM F. HAYES, now Captain of Engine 16, joined Protector Engine No. 22, on coming of age in the spring of 1859, and remained with that company until the organization of the Paid Department, when he was one of the first men to join the first company organized, Engine No. 1. While assistant foreman of Hook and Ladder No. 1, he assisted in rescuing several persons from a burning building in Bayard Street. In the same year he made several rescues during a fire at the corner of Montgomery and Cherry Streets. His name appears twice on the roll of merit.

MATTHEW MCCULLOUGH, when a mere child, began to run with the machine. He was born at Tarrytown in April, 1843, and came to New York at an early age. Though but eighteen years old, he went to the front with the Second Fire Zouaves, and took part in all the battles where his regiment was engaged up to Petersburg, after which he was discharged. No bullet ever touched him, although he was twenty times under fire. Only one other man in the regiment had similar good fortune. After he came home, Mr. McCullough joined Croton Engine Company

MATTHEW M CULLOUGH.

No. 47, where he served until the Volunteer organization was disbanded. He is president of the Veteran Association of the Second Fire Zouaves, and trustee of the Volunteer Firemen's Association. The Veteran Zouave Association, of which Mr. Matthew McCullough is president, is a pleasant company of old soldiers, who have a handsome room in First Street, decorated with trophies brought from many a hard-fought field. Twice a month the members meet, talk over old times, and drink a silent toast to those comrades who lie in Southern soil awaiting the last bugle call.

JOSEPH W. SANDFORD is a member of the Veteran Firemen's Association, and his good-looking countenance can be seen on the big picture of the "Vets" with their machine. He stands a little nearer the head of the rope than Judge Gorman. Mr. Sandford joined Richard M. Johnson Hose Company No. 32 as a youngster, and when the company merged in Jefferson Engine No. 26 he joined Friendship Hook and Ladder No. 12 when Frederick A. Ridabock was foreman, and afterwards became a member of Pacific Engine Company No. 28 under Foreman John Pettigrew. Later on he was assistant foreman of

Brooklyn Engine Company No. 17 of Brooklyn, known as the "Grasshoppers," a sterling company whose members occupied a high position as citizens and firemen. Before the war Mr. Sandford was a well-known carpenter and builder, and during the war was engaged as assistant master builder on Government work on Acquia Creek in Virginia. Afterwards he became connected with the fire insurance interest, and was for a while a captain of the patrol, and afterwards surveyor. His son, Jefferson M. Sandford, is captain of Patrol No. 4.

PETER P. PULLIS was born in this city in the year 1840. His father and uncle had been firemen away back in the year 1825, both of them serving their time with Howard Engine Company No. 34. Peter P. listened to their talk of midnight battles with the fire fiend, and determined to follow their example. When he was thirteen years old he commenced to go to fires, and kept up his Volunteer duty until July 15, 1862, when he joined Empire Hose Company No. 40, and served with that company until the New superseded the Old Department. During the years of his service he missed but two fires.

PETER P. PULLIS.

When it was decided to have a grand celebration on the centennial anniversary of Evacuation Day, Mr. Pullis determined to organize a procession on his own account. He secured the old hose carriage, induced nineteen of the members to join him, and on November 25, 1883, eighteen years after the company had gone out of service, Empire Hose Company No. 40 reappeared, as jaunty and saucy as ever, and was a marked and notable feature in the grand pageant. In December, 1883, Mr. Pullis was one of ten gentlemen who met and decided to form a Volunteer Firemen's Association. The result was the great success that may be appreciated when it is known that over two thousand firemen are enrolled as members of the association. Mr. Pullis was one of the original trustees.

Early in 1884 the Veteran Firemen's Association was formed; Mr. Pullis was also one of the originators of this successful undertaking. He is one of the trustees of the association, and one of the incorporators of the "Fireman's Home Association."

JOHN CARLAND was born in the City of New York in 1814, and commenced fire duty at such an early period of his life that he does not remember the date. On August 25, 1835, he joined Lady Washington Engine Company No. 40, better known by the name "White Ghost." After a short service as private he was elected assistant foreman. The company so appreciated his services that at the next election he was made foreman. Year after year rolled on, and at each successive annual meeting John Carland was re-elected. It is sufficient to state that from his first fire duty until he resigned, forty years had elapsed. His love for No. 40 never changed; it was No. 40 first, last and all the time.

When he retired from active fire duty, a new service was imposed upon him : he was twice elected "Commissioner of Appeals," served faithfully five years in that unthankful position, receiving the respect and esteem of the Department, and the lasting friendship of his fellow commissioners.

When Mr. Carland was foreman of No. 40, the old "gooseneck" fraternity were not noted for their peaceable habits ; in fact hardly a fire occurred without a skirmish or a battle. No. 40 was not backward to take a hand when necessity (or inclination) offered ; but John Carland was always a peacemaker, and the most violent of his opponents at all times respected him and his person. Peterson Engine Company No. 15 was at sword's points with No. 40, yet Carland's home was next door to the house of No. 15, and after many a hand-to-hand conflict Mr. Carland would return home and sit on his front steps with the volunteers and members of No. 15 around him, and discuss the merits of their engagements. It would not have been safe for any other member of No. 40 to have ventured within gunshot of Chrystie and Bayard Streets.

AUGUSTUS T. ANDERSON.

Mr. Carland was also a well-known military man. He was a member of the celebrated "Independent Tompkins Blues," a high-toned organization, second to none in point of drill and discipline. He was also captain of the celebrated Gulick Guards, named after James Gulick, chief engineer, a company almost entirely composed of firemen. It was equal in appearance and drill to any of the city militia companies. When the difficulties occurred with the Canadas, about the year 1837, the cry was "On to Canada !" and war seemed imminent ; the militia were held in readiness ; the Gulick Guards, fifty strong, armed and equipped, assembled in the City Hall Park ready to move toward the border. Happily the strife was averted by diplomacy, and the Gulick Guards returned to their homes.

AUGUSTUS T. ANDERSON has certainly had a varied fire existence. Born in New York City in 1829, he joined Phoenix Hook and Ladder Company No. 3 September 21, 1847, where he served two years; resigned; joined Niagara Engine Company No. 4; resigned; returned to Hook and Ladder No. 3; served a year; resigned; and immediately after organized Waverly Engine Company No. 23; was elected foreman; served one year; resigned; and again was at work organizing. At this time an event occurred that has no parallel in the history of company organizations : the petition for a new company was presented and passed by the Board of Aldermen; taken to the Board of Assistant Aldermen; passed there; taken to and signed by the mayor, and in twenty minutes' time from its first presentation, until the mayor's pen was raised from the official document, "Harry Howard" Hose Company No. 55 became a part and parcel of the New York Fire Department. Mr. Anderson was elected foreman of No. 55, and remained with the company three years, when he was forced to resign by removal to a distant part of the city. In his new location he was elected an honorary member of Valley Forge Engine Company No. 46. At a later date he became a member of the Exempt Engine Company under Zophar Mills. Mr. Anderson is a member of the Veteran Firemen's Association.

TIMOTHY J. CREEDEN was a member of Hook and Ladder Company No. 4. He was severely injured during his service by falling under the wheels of Engine Company No. 31. When the tocsin of war sounded in 1861 about one-half of the members of No. 4 responded. Mr. Creeden was an Irishman, whose family had suffered for their loyalty to the "Green Flag." On April 17, 1861, he enlisted in the Second Regiment, N. Y. S. M., and served until June 15,

SERGEANT CREEDEN AND BALITIMORE KEYS.

1864. The title of the regiment was changed to the Eighty-second New York Volunteers. The boys never accepted the alteration, but remained faithful to the "Old Second." During Mr. Creeden's service he rose to the position of first sergeant, and was recommended for promotion as first lieutenant. Sergeant Creeden was present in twenty-three engagements, escaping without a scratch in twenty-two of them. At the battle at Bristow's Station, a minie ball entered Creeden's left shoulder, passed over the shoulder blade, and came out at his back. At this late day the end of a finger can be inserted where the bullet entered. Mr. Creeden has been on the police force for twenty-two years, and is now sergeant at the Tenth Precinct, in Eldridge Street. He is a fine specimen of a man, of medium height, erect, vigilant and courteous.

JOHN H. FORMAN joined Peterson Engine Company No. 15 in 1843, when Nicholas F. Wilson, who was afterwards assistant engineer, was foreman. He was an active member, and was elected assistant foreman when John J. Tindale was foreman. Mr. Tindale in later years was chosen president of the Fire Department. About 1850 he became a member of Lafayette Engine Company No. 19, and was elected foreman of the company in 1851; he resigned, and in 1853 was elected an assistant engineer, which office he also resigned after a brief term of service. Later he organized Washington Hook and Ladder Company No. 9. William Tapper, of Lexington Engine Company No. 7 was chosen the first foreman of Hook and Ladder Company No. 9. Mr. Forman was afterwards elected foreman, in which office he served nine years. He has been a fire insurance surveyor for nearly a quarter of a century, but notwith-standing, found time to become a member of the Olympic Club, which is quartered down on "Long Island's seagirt 'shore," and numbers among its members many who were connected with the Volunteer Fire Department, among them, Daniel D. Conover, foreman of Amity Hose Company No. 38, and Richard P. Moore, foreman of Engine Company No. 42. Of course, John was not a "silent" member. His early experience in the United States Navy enabled him to see through the schemes of the gallant tars of the Olympic who discussed nautical questions, spliced the main brace, and manned the fleet, and he always kept his weather eye open for any tricks they attempted to play upon old sailors, leaving the marines to look out for themselves. Mr. Forman resides in Harlem, is still a surveyor, and a member of the Veteran Firemen's Association.

JOHN H. FORMAN.

The following is from the *Fireman's Journal* of October, 22, 1853:

A PRESENTATION.—On Thursday evening, thirteenth instant, Friendship Hook and Ladder Company No. 12 presented to Mr. John H. Forman, assistant engineer, an elegant fire-cap. The presentation took place at the saloon of Messrs. Slowey & Sickles, corner of Grand and Essex Streets. The cap was presented in behalf of the company by J. B. Leverich. The speeches were brief, but to the point, and the party partook of an oyster supper, after which many sentiments were drank, and the party enjoyed themselves finely until an alarm of fire put an end to the festivities. The cap has one hundred and twenty-eight cones, and was manufactured by H. T. Gratacap, and is a beautiful piece of workmanship. It has a silver plate with the following inscription :

"Presented to John H. Forman, by the members of Friendship Hook and Ladder Company No. 12, October 14, 1853."

JOSEPH W. WALSH joined the department August 8, 1849, and was appointed to Putnam Hose Company No. 31. He served with 31 Hose for two years and a half, and after that with Excelsior Engine Company No. 2, and finished his time with that company, leaving the department in 1856. He next connected himself with Fire Patrol No. 1, the only one in the city at the time, and under command of Henry Flender, who was captain. He remained with the Patrol for sixteen years, serving with Captain Flender, Franklin Waterbury, John Cornwell, Joseph W. Sanford, John Slowey, and Abram Hull, the present superintendent. Mr. Walsh is at present Surveyor of the Williamsburg Fire Insurance Company, a position he has held for the last fifteen years. He is also a life member of the Exempt Firemen's Association.

WILLIAM H. WICKHAM was born on Long Island in 1833. On the paternal side, the Wickhams date back their residence in New York to the early days when the Dutch residents emigrated from the neighborhood of the "Battery," and settled where the Ninth Ward is now located, otherwise Greenwich Village. On the maternal side his ancestors were the first settlers of Long Island. William H. joined Mutual Hook and Ladder Company No.

1 in 1850. Charles E. Gildersleve, Andrew Schenck, "Pony" Farnham, William H. Wickham, and a few others, aroused the old company from the Rip Van Winkle slumber in which it had been indulging. Their efforts changed No. 1 from a condition of "no good" to a state of eminent usefulness. There was not a truck company in the city that performed better duty than Mutual No. 1. After the new blood was infused in 1854, Mr. Wickham resigned, and organized Baxter Hook and Ladder Company No. 15, located in Franklin Street, between West Broadway and Hudson Street.

WILLIAM H. WICKHAM.

He was elected foreman and representative for several years. In 1858 he was elected secretary, in 1859 vice-president, and in 1860-'61 president of the New York Fire Department. In 1874 Mr. Wickham received the Democratic nomination for mayor; was elected by a large majority; served during the years 1875-'76, winning praise from all classes for the faithful and honest performance of his duties. Mr. Wickham is now president of the "New York Arcade Railway." He expects to beautify and benefit the city by the completion of his great project.

BENJAMIN L. GUION performed his first service in 1826 with Engine Company No. 15, and subsequently served three years with Hose Company No. 1. For four years he filled the responsible post of fire warden. When Chief Engineer Gulick was appointed in 1831 Mr. Guion was a member of the committee appointed to purchase a silver trumpet, to be presented to the chief on behalf of the department. While serving as a fire warden Mr. Guion rendered services of incalculable value at a fire at Houston and Second Streets in 1836. The fire was almost under control when news arrived that Chief Gulick, against whom charges were pending in the Common Council, had been removed from office. The moment the intelligence reached the chief he withdrew from the scene, after briefly announcing to his men that he was no longer their commander, and went to his office at Canal Street and Broadway. At once all order was at an end. At the most critical moment, Mr. Guion, realizing that something must be done to arrest a terrible catastrophe, hired a conveyance and hurried to the chief's office. His entreaties, joined to those of Carlisle Norwood, at last prevailed, and the chief hurried back to the scene of action, which fire, but for Mr. Guion's eloquent entreaties, would soon have spread beyond all bounds.

DANIEL PATTERSON, a native of New York City, was born in 1837, and was a volunteer with Live Oak Engine Company No. 44 for nine years; became a member of the company in 1859; served until the memorable month of March, 1865, when Volunteer organizations ceased to exist; was elected member of Assembly for two terms, 1877 and 1878. He is a member of both the Volunteer and Veteran Fireman's Associations. During the rebellion he was a member of the Eighth Regiment, and served with the regiment in the field. He is a member of Dahlgren Post No. 113. In the early days of baseball excitement he was a prominent member of the celebrated Mutual Club, an expert at the game, and considers himself one of the fathers of the diamond field. Mr. Patterson is now proprietor of the Oriental House, at Grand and Ludlow Streets. This house has a curious political history. Before, and during Jackson's time, it was the great Democratic headquarters for the east side of the city. A tall liberty pole stood in front of the door, and a portrait of the gallant general was the sign that indi-

DANIEL PATTERSON.

cated the political pulse of the frequenters of the old inn. That lasted until 1853, when the place was captured by the Native Americans (Know Nothings), and remained in their hands until 1875, when the Republicans stormed and carried the fortification and held possession for ten years. Mr. Patterson became lessee, and it is again the rallying point for the unterrified Democracy.

JOHN M. HARNED was born in New York City in 1833, and was elected a member of Fifteenth Ward Hose Company No. 35 in 1851. Young Harned had a very trying initiation. The night of his election there was a big fire at Erban's organ factory, in Centre Street, directly opposite Canal Street. This was before Canal Street was cut through; it was a fine opportunity for a new man to display his aptitude for fire duty. Later on, the same night, a fire broke out at the New York Hotel. No. 35 was quickly on hand; the new member had the pipe; he clung to it manfully; it could well be said that he received a "baptism of fire." No. 35 claimed the honor of saving the hotel. In 1854 he and a party of young men, all members, decided to organize an engine company. The result was the organization of "Lone Star Engine

Company No. 50." Ralph Barker was elected foreman, A. R. Whitney assistant foreman, and John M. Harned secretary. In 1857 Mr. Harned was elected assistant foreman; in 1858 made foreman; was in command during the years 1858, 1859, 1860, and 1861. Mr. Harned served over ten years with the company. He was also a member of the Exempt Engine Company, under Zophar Mills. At present he is a member of the Association of Exempt Firemen, the Volunteer Firemen's Association, and the Veteran Firemen's Association.

THOMAS FLENDER, one of the last Volunteer fire commissioners, known as "the lame man of 6 Engine" (house in Reade Street), for all his lameness, had the reputation of being the fleetest and "most long-winded runner in the department." He asked no odds of any one, and when inside the ropes of the engine, his crutch seemed to be a living part of himself.

JULIAN BOTTS was connected with 38 Hose in 1849 with all the privileges of

THOMAS FLENDER.

a member except having a vote, as the company was full; went to Engine 4 as one of its organizers from 38 Hose, and, after serving about a year, left with several others, and went back to 38 Hose, as above mentioned, the company being full. Left 38 Hose in 1850, and joined 38 Engine; was elected assistant foreman, and served in that capacity eight months, and was elected foreman.

During his connection with old Southwark 38 as its chief officer, he discovered the disastrous Jennings' fire at 231 Broadway, at which the lamented Andrew Schenck, foreman of Hook and Ladder Company 1, lost his life, as well as several others. On discovering the fire, while on the corner of Broadway and Ann Street, by seeing a flash of light, he started the engine, and consequently they were at the scene in a very few minutes. He sent the pipe down in the rear, through the first or store floor, as the fire seemed to be located chiefly at that point, although it had worked up through the rear, as was found on closer examination, and if Chief Carson had not arrived during Foreman Botts' temporary absence, and ordering 38's pipe up into the American Hotel, he would have shared the fate of the others.

C. GODFREY GUNTHER was born in Maiden Lane, New York City, in 1844. He joined Eagle Hose Company No. 1, was a very active, efficient fireman and a working member, who rarely missed a fire. He served his full time with No. 1.

In 1863 Mr. Gunther was elected mayor of New York City. His official acts will be remembered by old citizens as being always business-like, honest, prompt, and actuated by a sincere desire to forward the interests of the city of his birth. It was while Mr. Gunther was mayor that the city was under martial law, General Benj. F. Butler in command. The general sent a message to Mayor Gunther that he desired to see him at his headquarters at the Fifth Avenue Hotel. The mayor's reply was characteristic of the man: "Tell General Butler that if he has any business to transact with me, that I can be found in my official office at the City Hall."

Mr. Gunther was a member of the Firemen's Ball Committee for many years prior and up to the time of his death, and was chairman of the committee for two years.

ALFRED CHANCELLOR was born on July 15, 1815. He joined Columbian Engine Company No. 14 on February 21, 1831, and served in that company for twenty years. Mr. Chancellor has been the master baker on Blackwell's Island for a number of years.

JAMES J. BEVINS was born in Baltimore, Md., in 1814; came to New York when very young; was a Volunteer with Oceanus Engine Company No. 11 for three or four years when the machine laid in Old Slip, and became a member of No. 11 in 1834. George Brown was the secretary at the time; he was not attentive to his duties, neglected to send in the names of several parties who were elected members of the company, and in consequence Mr. Bevins lost three years of his service. About this time an exciting election took place for foreman. Robert Walker defeated "Abe Purdy." A split was the consequence; at the same time a severe break occurred in the ranks of Eagle Engine Company No. 13. In both companies a number of the best men withdrew from their respective companies and mutually agreed to join Fulton Engine Company No. 21. Upon being received in No. 21 an election was held. Robert Walker, seceder from No. 11, was elected foreman, and Peter F. Knapp, seceder from No. 13, assistant foreman. A few years after Mr. Bevins was elected foreman. He remained with the company for a number of years. In 1835 Mr. Bevins received an order from James Gulick, chief engineer, to bring the old engine from the corporation yard. He obeyed the order, and conveyed the machine to a stable in New Street, near Wall Street. The engine was put in good working order. A few nights afterwards the weather was fearfully cold; an alarm was given; No. 21 was rolled from the stable; went down New to Beaver Street, through Beaver to William, up William to Merchant Street; on turning the corner of Merchant Street (now Exchange Place) the fire was reached; it was apparently an insignificant affair, but from that little commencement sprang the great fire of December 16, 1835, which swept away nearly the entire business portion of the city. Mr. Bevins claims that No. 21 was first at the fire, notwithstanding what others have asserted to the contrary. No. 21 tried two hydrants, but both were frozen; next proceeded to the river, where a line was formed, but before ten minutes had elapsed the hose was frozen as rigid as bars of iron, rendering the firemen

ALFRED CHANCELLOR.

powerless. The flames spread with frightful rapidity, and for nearly twenty-four hours the fire held complete sway over the city. After completing his long term of fire duty, Mr. Bevins opened the Fulton House, No. 23 Nassau Street, which became a great resort of the down-town merchants, leading politicians, and veteran firemen. Hose Company No. 8 laid around the corner, on Cedar Street. One night the company elected Mr. Bevins a member, and proffered him the command of the company, but he declined. He was also urged to accept the position of assistant engineer, but his business would not permit him to accept. Mr. Bevins has held many positions of honor and trust, among which may be mentioned harbor master, deputy sheriff, boarding officer under the administrations of Presidents Harrison, Tyler, Taylor, Fillmore and Lincoln; also chief keeper of the old Eldridge Street jail. Mr. Bevins has lived in New York City nearly seventy years. In his earlier days he was a complete master of the "manly art of self-defense." It would take a very able young man to cope with him to-day. He was regarded as invincible as the redoubtable John L. Sullivan is to-day, having polished off such bruisers as Bill Poole and others of that school.

JAMES I. MURRAY.

JAMES I. MURRAY was born in 1827; was a Volunteer with Oceanus Engine Company No. 11, when she was located in Wooster Street, near Prince Street, next door to the old "Watch House"; became a member of No. 11 in 1847; served several years; was elected foreman, and remained in command until William W. Williams succeeded him. His brother, David Murray, had also been an officer in the company, having served four years as assistant foreman and foreman. Few companies can boast of as many veteran ex-foremen as old Oceanus; at least six living ones can be mentioned, viz.: Abe Purdy, David Murray, James I. Murray, William W. Williams, John Wildey, and Christopher Johnson.

GEORGE EVANS, No. 1 Jacob Street, joined Engine Company No. 13 in 1844, when it was stationed at Duane Street, between Rose and William Streets, adjoining the Shakespeare Hotel. The engine house is now used as a fuel depot for one fire engine company and two hose companies of the present department. Mr. Evans was elected representative of the company, and held the position for five years. He was a member at the time that Zophar Mills was foreman. The company organized on April 10, 1826, with James J. M. Valentine, clerk, 23 Fulton Street, as foreman, and George Timson, accountant, 18 Cherry Street, assistant foreman. Among the members were Sidney S. Franklin, who resigned September 22, 1828; Robert H. Haydock, resigned January 5, 1829; Peter Gordon, resigned November 13, 1829; Washington Van Wyck, John W. Shipley, William L. Jennings, William Jagger, Henry Dunham, William Gilder, Walter Titus, Jr.

WILLIAM ADAMS.—Born in Greenwich Village (Ninth Ward), New York City; joined Guardian Engine Company No. 29 in 1824; served as foreman for two years; remained with the company until his removal to the lower part of the city. Was elected alderman of the Fifth Ward. As alderman he was placed as chairman of the Fire and Water Committee. This committee had entire charge of all Fire Department matters. "Boss Adams" performed his duties with such tact and discrimination that the firemen united in praising his careful and unbiased actions toward them.

Sergeant JOSEPH DOUGLASS, of the Fifteenth Precinct, is an old Volunteer fireman. He joined "Nassau" (America) Hose Company No. 46 on October 20, 1853, then located in Nassau Street, near Fulton Street, in the house formerly occupied by Engine Company No. 42. He joined Fulton Engine No. 21, December 7, 1856, located in Worth Street, near Broadway. Sergeant Douglass was the first driver of the Metropolitan Fire Department, and was appointed by Commissioner Booth, and served in that position for about ten days. At a fire in a frame tenement in Mulberry Street, in 1868, Roundsman

Douglass saved the lives of two children. He was honorably mentioned by the Board of Police Commissioners for his devotion to the work of searching for bodies of victims of the Centre Street explosion, December 31, 1872.

JAMES YOUNG, deputy sheriff, joined Engine Company 38 in June, 1854. It was stationed at 28 Ann Street, and had seventy members on its roll at the time. The foreman was Julian T. Botts, an insurance agent, and the assistant foreman was James Taylor, a photographic artist; George Bevins was representative. He was the bellringer of the old City Hall bell, which used to ring for fires in the Seventh and Eighth Districts, to which Company No. 38 attended.

JOSEPH DOUGLASS.

It also rang for fires elsewhere throughout the city. According to Mr. Young, 38 Engine was called "Southwick," from being built at Southwick, Philadelphia, and was the heaviest engine in the city. It had double brakes, and took more men to man her than any other engine. She was purchased by a party of gentlemen of this city, among whom were Matt Green, Dave Pollock, John T. Schenck, and others, and became the private property of the company. It was purchased in 1840, and remained the property of the company until 1853, when it was sold to the city. The money received from the city remained in the old members' hands, and a quarrel arose between the old and the new members in regard to the disposition of the money, the new members claiming that they had as good a right to it as the old ones, because that when they joined the company, they were entitled to a joint share in the property and the proceeds of the sale of said property. The old members claimed an old oil painting of Harry Farges, their own assistant foreman, who was killed at a fire in Duane

Street about the year 1852, but the family of Farges finally got the picture on the breaking up of the Old Department. The young members of the company succeeded in finding out that old Joe, the colored man who used to clean the engine, got four hundred dollars of the money that was given in the purchase of the engine, but they never discovered where the balance went.

WILLIAM CAMPBELL, a prominent fireman, served with Engine Company 50 from 1861 to the end of 1863, and subsequently with Engine 24. Here he remained until the Old Department disappeared from official view.

JOHN S. CRAIG and CORNELIUS V. ANDERSON were boys together, and played their juvenile games in Provost (now Franklin) Street. They both learned trades connected with the building business. Anderson became a mason and Craig a carpenter. They both became members of the Volunteer Fire Department. Anderson joined Hudson Engine Company No. 1, became foreman, and afterwards chief engineer of the Fire Department. Craig became a

WILLIAM CAMPBELL.

member of Independence Hose Company No. 3 when James Elkins was foreman, and was afterwards chosen assistant foreman. He was for a short time a member of Friendship Hook and Ladder Company No. 12, and later joined Empire Engine Company No. 42. Anderson and Craig both became identified with the fire insurance interest. After Anderson retired from the office of register, he, together with a number of old firemen, organized the Lorillard Fire Insurance Company February 3, 1852, and was elected president of the company, which position he held until his death. Washington Smith was chosen vice-president, Carlisle Norwood secretary, and John Coger,

Jr., surveyor. After Anderson's death, Carlisle Norwood was elected president. Zophar Mills succeeded Washington Smith, and Theodore Keeler became surveyor. When Coger retired, Craig was appointed surveyor of the National Insurance Company, and was also selected as captain of the Fire Patrol, and served on alternate nights with Captain Samuel Smith. This was in the era before horses, wagons, and automatic valves, when the men pulled a cart containing the covers, etc., and rolled her on many a still alarm, and had lively races with the fire companies. There was no electricity in those days, but the men went as if they had it in their boots. They were quick, hard-working fellows, without discount. Smith was a member of the Volunteer Fire Department, an active, energetic worker, and was the surveyor of the Niagara Fire Insurance Company, and also of the Empire City Fire Insurance Company. Craig was also appointed surveyor of the Citizens' Fire Insurance Company, and, although he now carries a cane in his daily business walks, he was a lively and hardworking man in the Fire Department and on the Fire

Patrol, and always had a respect for a true fireman, without discrimination as to the color of his hair or the cut of his coat, or whether he had a coat; if he was a good fireman, Craig was ready to give him due credit. John S. Craig is no longer a young man, but he is still active, and has the respect of those who know him. He has long been a prominent figure in the fire insurance interest. Anderson, Smith, Coger, and Keeler have gone from among us, but Norwood, Mills, and Craig remain. They have witnessed many remarkable changes in New York, the city they loved and served so well. In memory of Auld Lang Syne, happy be their declining years.

DANIEL F. TIEMANN.

DANIEL F. TIEMANN, ex-mayor of the City of New York, had his first experience as a fireman when he joined Engine Company No. 43. Later on he was elected assistant foreman, John McArthur foreman. That was in 1836. Two years later Mr. Tiemann became the company's foreman, and remained as such for eight years. Mr. Tiemann held many offices as a fireman and citizen. He never, in fact, ran for a public office that he was not elected to. He was alternately representative in Fireman's Hall, alderman, State senator, and mayor of New York City.

THOMAS LAWRENCE. — Born in Haverstraw, Rockland County, N. Y.; joined Guardian Engine Company No. 29 in 1836; remained with No. 29 one year; resigned, and joined Columbian Engine Company No. 14; remained with No. 14 about one year, and returned to his old love, No. 29. He served with old "Guardian" for ten years. During those years he was elected foreman three times, first in 1840, and subsequently in 1844 and 1845. After having entirely retired

THOMAS LAWRENCE.

from active duty, he was elected fire commissioner; served the full term, five years. "Tom" Lawrence was an old resident of the Ninth Ward, a free-hearted, jovial man; was very highly esteemed by all classes, rich and poor, high and low, was liberal to a fault, and gathered around him hosts of friends.

SHEPHERD F. KNAPP, one of New York's most respected and successful merchants and well known citizens, was an enthusiastic fireman. He was one

of the old "Vets" who ran with the "machine," and in his day was the popular and efficient foreman of Engine No. 37. That was some thirty years ago, when "Shep." Knapp was a hardy, strapping young fellow, full of adventure and grit, like most of the manly fellows who were associated with him as firemen. He was born in Beekman Street, August 29, 1832, his father being one of the leather merchants of the Swamp, and also many years president of the Mechanics' Bank of this city. Shepherd F. was appointed street commissioner by Mayor Wood, and was also receiver of the Bowling Green Savings Bank. He died at his home in Audubon Park, Carmansville, December 25, 1886.

SHEPHERD F.-KNAPP.

MATTHEW J. SHANNON was born in 1831. On March 16, 1854, M. J. Read, Owen J. Kelly, Francis J. Twomey (clerk of the Common Council), ex-Alderman Thomas McSpedon, Matthew J. Shannon, and a number of citizens, organized Aqueduct Engine Company No. 47. M. J. Read was elected foreman, and Owen J. Kelly assistant foreman. The company was located in Eighty-second Street east of Fourth Avenue. The life of the organization was brief. For some cause the company was disbanded September 18, 1855. In 1861 Mr. Shannon joined Americus Hose Company No. 48, located in Eighty-fifth Street west of Third Avenue. After a short service Mr. Shannon was elected assistant foreman. At the next annual election he was made foreman, and remained in command until the dissolution of the Old Department.

MATTHEW J. SHANNON.

JOSEPH H. TOOKER, who is more generally known by his popular title of "Commodore," acquired by his position of manager of the mammoth Rockaway steamboats 'Grand Republic' and 'Columbia,' and previously as commander of the renowned Long Branch steamer 'Plymouth Rock,' is an old-time fireman. He was once, in 1852, assistant foreman of Rutgers Hose Company No. 26, and afterwards joined Victory Hose Company No. 15, when they occupied the house in Eldridge Street, by Division. In those days Mr. Tooker was frequently called upon to write obituary and complimentary resolutions for various fire engine and target companies, and his pen is kept busy even in these later days upon local reminiscences, which for the past year he has contributed to the columns of the New York *Times*. He wrote humorous letters over the *nom de plume* of "John Bolivar" for the Boston *Saturday Evening Gazette*, originated "Shipping Notes" in the New York *Herald*, and contributed semi-political articles over the signatures of "The Widow Rogers" and "Walton" for the old *Sunday Atlas*. He was first marshal under Mayor A. Oakey Hall, and for five years a school trustee in and for the Thirteenth Ward, where he was born, becoming the chairman of the board.

He was a member of the copper firm of Jones, Tooker & Co., 244 South Street, agents of the Revere Company of Boston, the silent company being the celebrated comedian, W. J. Florence, a brother-in-law of the commodore. Mr. Tooker was managing man for Col. James Fisk, Jr., at the Grand Opera House, Eighth Avenue and Twenty-third Street, and also for Baker & Cole and Augustin Daly, when they were lessees of the theater. He was with Mr. Daly at the Fifth Avenue Theater, Twenty-fourth Street, next adjoining the Fifth Avenue Hotel, and at the later Fifth Avenue Theater, Broadway, opposite the New York Hotel, which was leased after the destruction by fire of the Twenty-fourth Street

JOSEPH H. TOOKER.

building. He afterwards was Mr. Daly's business man at Daly's Theater, Broadway, near Thirtieth Street. He has been in the interest of Wallack's Theater, and managed the Bijou Opera House during the lesseeship of Harry M. Pitt. He was for one season of the management of Niblo's Garden, Edward G. Gilmore, lessee. His most prominent theatrical career, however, was his five years' service as business manager of Booth's Theater, under the lesseeship of Jarrett & Palmer, and for one season subsequently during that of Henry E. Abbey. For the three or four years last past he has been president of the Metropolitan Job Printing Company, of No. 38 Vesey Street, which was formerly the New York *Herald* job office, theatrical printers. He served his time at the case in the office of the *Literary American*, corner of Ann Street and Nassau. Mr. Tooker, in his *Times* reminiscences, frequently refers to his career as a Volunteer fireman, and is apparently proud of the association. He is, in this year of our Lord, 1887, in the fifty-sixth year of his age.

BENJAMIN J. EVANS commenced running with the machine when a boy in 1843, when he lived in Walker Street, near West Broadway. He ran with Hope 31, located in West Broadway, near Beach Street. Neptune 6 laid in Reade Street, Equitable 36 in Varick, near Vandam; Hudson 1 at the foot of Duane Street, where the Erie building now stands; 23 in Anthony Street, near Broadway. There was great rivalry between those companies. On the twenty-sixth of July, 1846, they all met in Broadway, near the Astor House, and had a great fight, for which they were all disbanded, August 5, 1846. Mr. Evans joined 5 Hose in 1850, under Henry Butler, foreman, and J. F. Wenman, assistant. 3 Engine was organized in 1847. She ran until 1852, when they got the old number, 31, back. Then he joined 31. In 1853 he was elected assistant foreman. The company ran until September, 1854, when she was disbanded again. He next joined 14 Hose, under James R. Mount, and ran with her until February 24, 1852, when Adriatic 31 was organized. He joined her, and

BENJAMIN J. EVANS.

was a member until the Paid Department went into effect. Mr. Evans was one of the first to go to the war under the president's first call. He enlisted in the New York State Militia, Company I, Captain Raynor. He is at present connected with the Jersey City Fire Department, Engine No. 9.

WILLIAM RAINER was born September, 1817. At a very early age he became a "runner" with Daniel D. Tompkins Engine Company No. 30. When he was sufficiently advanced, his name was placed on the Volunteer roll. Served six years with the junior firemen, wore a fire-cap at the great fire of 1835, and was elected a member of the company in 1837. William Van Sickel, of Washington Market, was foreman. Nearly all of the officers and many of the members of No. 30 were the leading butchers at the period mentioned. Mr. Rainer had a weakness for salt water, and after serving three years with the engine, he embarked upon the briny deep, and was away from the city for a long time. In 1850 he again appeared upon the fire record as one of the reorganizers of Lady Washington Engine Company No. 40, with Alderman James Bard as foreman and William Mehan assistant. He served two years with No. 40, resigned, became one of the principal and most influential organizers of Adriatic Engine Company No. 31, with John B. Miller (brother of James L. Miller) as foreman. In 1858 a great "Firemen's Tournament" was to be held at Albany, New York. A prize of five hundred dollars was offered for the highest and best stream of water. No. 31 determined to join the contestants. Mr. Rainer was elected foreman. Adriatic took part in the struggle; the engine was in perfect order, but the hose could not stand the strain that the muscle of the New York men brought to bear upon it; five times the hose was burst, and no new lengths could be obtained, bought or borrowed. Sorrowfully No. 31 was forced to retire from the arena when they felt that victory was within their grasp. Mr. Rainer was a prominent member of the "Independent Tompkins Blues," one of the leading military companies of the city in bygone days. At the breaking out of the Rebellion, Mr. Rainer was commissioned as captain of Company F, First Regiment Marine Artillery; was detailed on recruiting service for seamen, and stationed at Buffalo, and subsequently was placed in command of the post at Camp Arthur on Staten Island. In 1862 he was ordered to Newbern, N. C.; was captain of the United States gunboat '*Vidette*'; from Newbern was ordered to the Roanoke River, N. C., to act in concert with the fleet to intercept the rebel ram '*Albemarle.*' During Captain Rainer's varied service amid the Southern swamps, he contracted sickness that thoroughly disabled

WILLIAM RAINER.

him, and he was reluctantly forced to resign. Mr. Rainer is a member of the Volunteer and Veteran Firemen's Associations.

CHARLES F. ALLEN, soldier and fireman, who has won well-deserved distinction in both arms of the service, is at present connected with the Great Western Insurance Company in Wall Street. Mr. Allen served as secretary and representative of Baxter Hook and Ladder Company No. 15 for about seven years. Among his colleagues were ex-Mayor William H. Wickham, Daniel P. Steele, Samuel Archer, Thomas F. Goodwin, A. A. Jones, and R. H. Murray. Mr. Allen was always found at the front. Whether as fireman or soldier, whether holding the pipe or shouldering a musket, whether fighting fire or the enemies of the Union, Mr. Allen always acted the part of a brave man and a good citizen.

WILLIAM A. DOOLEY has been a resident of New York City for many scores of years. He was very successfully engaged in business in Fifty-seventh Street about half a century ago. He was a prominent politician when the Nineteenth Ward was made in 1851. Mr. Dooley was elected to represent the new addition to the city map in the Board of Aldermen. For five years previous he had served as a fireman with Knickerbocker Engine Company No. 12. In 1856 and 1857 he was a member of the Board of Assessment. Mr. Dooley is reputed to be one of the best judges of real estate in this city, and his knowledge has been the means of adding material aid to his coffers. He is the same unassuming gentleman now as he was while he ran with the "machine." He was a fireman in the Old Department, and a good one. He takes honest pride in the *role* he played as a member of the Volunteer Department.

DAVID M. SMITH was born in Cliff Street, New York City, in 1818. In 1840 he was one of the original members of the Southwark Engine Company No. 38; served four years with the big machine, No. 38 being the first double-deck engine used in the city. At the time Mr. Smith thought of resigning from Southwark he held a dual position. Lafayette Hose Company No. 4 laid in Attorney Street; the company was in a very weak conition, only two members remaining; those two had decided to dissolve the organization. David M. Smith came to the rescue; he, with a dozen more, joined the company, infused new life into it, and changed the name to Marion Hose. During this time Mr. Smith was a member of the two companies, doing duty with the Hose Company in the Third and Fourth Districts, and with No. 38 in the Fifth and Sixth Districts; finally he resigned from No. 38, devoting all his energies to the up-building of No. 4. He succeeded so well that the chief engineer, C. V. Anderson, stated that No. 4 had become one of the best and most reliable companies in the department. In 1844 Mr. Smith was elected assistant foreman, and was foreman in 1845. The roll being full, he resigned to make room for new members; but remained an active member on the honorary roll.

JOHN W. TIMSON.—The New York Volunteer Fire Department had many members who endeavored to discharge their duties in a quiet, unostentatious manner, without being anxious to attain office or notoriety, but were ambitious to do good duty and promote the welfare of their company and the department. Such a member was John W. Timson. He belonged to Manhattan Engine Company No. 8, in which he served his time. 8 was a strong company, noted for activity in hard work at fires and the respectable standing of its members in the community and for running the first fire steam engine, when Robert C. Brown was foreman. 8's members were men of nerve and character, and were not to be frightened from doing their duty when running a steam fire engine was not popular in this city. John W. Timson is a good type of the New York Volunteer fireman. He has been for many years a member of the Fire Insurance Patrol, and was assigned as clerk to the superintendent, and he has filled that position for a number of years. He is respected for his industry, integrity and manhood. Like most New York boys, John feels a pride in the city and her institutions, and he does not forget the days when "the Elephants" were on deck every time.

JOHN C. DENHAM was born in Newark, N. J., September 15, 1836. As a boy he ran with Hose Company No. 14. In 1859 he joined Hose Company No. 15, and did duty in the Fifth District, and was with his company in the draft riots of 1863. In 1861 he went to the war with the Eighth Regiment, N. Y. N. G. When the first shot was fired at Fort Sumter, and the declaration of war was made, Mr. Denham raised the Union flag on his engine house. At the burning of Barnum's Museum in the Chinese Assembly Rooms in Broadway, in March, 1868, Denham distinguished himself. At the time he was master stage carpenter at Booth's Theater. Barnum's animals broke loose, and among them was the tiger which appeared threateningly on the sidewalk, to the terror of everybody. Policemen banged away with their pistols at the brute, but without effect. Denham seized an axe, boldly confronted the beast, and struck him a terrific blow on the head. The tiger dropped dead. Denham then went into the burning building, carried out the fat woman, and afterwards two children, to a restaurant, making his way through water almost knee-deep. He returned and carried out the woolly-headed woman. The spectators cried to the red-shirted braves: "Good for the old fire laddies!"

CHAPTER XXXIII.

HISTORY OF THE ENGINE COMPANIES.

When They were Organized.—Where Located at Different Times.—Their Officers and Prominent Members.—Engines they Used, and How the most Famous were Painted or Decorated.—Changes in the Organizations.—"Hudson," "Excelsior," "Forrest," "Niagara," "Protection," "Big Six," "Lexington."

No. 1.—HUDSON ("Hayseed").—This is the first fire company of New York. It received its apparatus in the year 1731. Its engine was one of two brought over from London in that year.

Two small frame buildings were erected for the two engines in Wall Street on the north side of the City Hall. No. 1 house fronted on what was known then as King street. Peter Rutgers, a brewer, and assistant alderman of the North Ward, was appointed Overseer (a title given in those days for Foremanship). Every one was then supposed to act as fireman, buckets having been previously used. The two imported engines were looked upon with as much pride by the firemen of those days as were the silver mounted carriages by the boys who lived nearly a century afterwards. In 1735 Anthony Lamb was appointed Overseer. In 1738 John Mann was at the head of the engine, but in 1772 the engine was allowed twenty-one men, Johannes Vriedenburgh being made foreman. During the war the Department, numbering one hundred and sixteen men, was detailed as a home guard under General Washington, but Jacob Stoutenburgh was chief in command at fires. Few of the original twenty-one survived the Revolutionary war. As soon as the British evacuated the city— November, 1783—the question of reorganizing the Fire

SIGNAL LAMP OF ENGINE NO. 1.

Department was considered, and early in 1784 several new companies were formed, No. 1 at that time having at its head as Overseer Peter Van Doland. The company soon mustered twenty-five new men, and took the name of "Hudson," after Henry Hudson, the first explorer of the North River. At this time the engine was kept under a small shed in a lane running down to the North River which was then known as Reynolds Farm, now Barclay street. In 1795 and 1796 they moved to Barclay street, opposite to which, it was said, was a brewery owned by a man named Groshon. Henry J. Hardtwell was foreman. Previous to Hardtwell, Thomas Ash is reported to have served in the same capacity.

Among the members in those days were Theodorus De Forest, John Bedient, John Titus, Caleb Havilhand, Anthony Steenback, Henry Verveelen, John P.

Gooshen, Thomas J. Campbell, John T. Campbell, Jacob Evans and David Heckle. In 1810 the engine lay in a new frame house on Duane street, formerly Barley, opposite an alley. On March 8, 1827, Francis Joseph, who had been a member only about one year, was killed at a fire in Maiden Lane, and his funeral was one of the largest ever held by the Department in those days.

During 1829 there were found on the roll the names of Benjamin Abrahams, Robert Johnson, Charles L. Shriver, Caleb F. Lathrop, Josiah Foot, John Beam, Jr., and Cornelius V. Anderson. In 1830 Anderson was made foreman, and served in that capacity until 1837, when he was elected Chief Engineer of the Fire Department. During Anderson's foremanship John Beadell, Jr., Wm. W. McMullen, William Howard, and Peter B. Lawson became members. No. 1 had a new house built at the expense of the company and citizens of the Third and Fifth Wards on what was called Clinton Square, Duane Street. It was here they were dubbed the "Hayseed," and many of the leading citizens down town did duty with her. At the old Duane Street Methodist Episcopal Church all the firemen and their "young ladies" used to be in attendance on Sunday nights. When an alarm of fire was sounded, such a rush was made for old "One" that many a time the house was cleared and the services closed. The girls would turn out and wait on the sidewalks for the boys to come home.

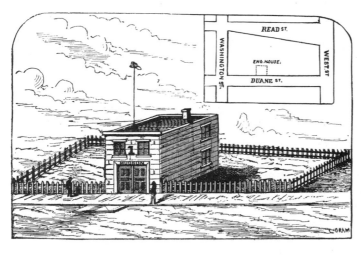

ENGINE HOUSE No. 1 (1810), DUANE STREET.

The volunteer roll was as large as the active. Among the volunteers were the McCoys, one of the Henry brothers, Henry Reynolds, Wm. McCrady, and James and Philip Burke.

At the Erie Canal celebration on November 4, 1825, this company made a magnificent display. On their banner was painted a view of the city of New York from the Jersey shore: buildings in the center of the city represented in flames to which the Genius of America is pointing to direct the firemen; over her head is seen hovering an eagle bearing the motto: "Where duty calls, there you will find us." On the reverse was a painting of Washington.

In the later years of the company their pugnacious qualities increased and continued until they were disbanded August 5, 1846.

HUDSON (the second company of the number and name) was reorganized on December 26, 1846, from Engine Company No. 9. It was located at the corner of Forty-eighth Street and Eighth Avenue, and afterwards in Forty-seventh Street, west of Eighth Avenue. It went out of service in 1865. William M. Guest, a former foreman of old No. 1, moved uptown and reorganized

Dolphin Engine No 9 as Hudson No. 1. Among those who assisted Mr. Guest were Leonard H. Rieger, Joseph Whiteman, Joseph Churchill, Samuel L. Cox, Theodore Myers, Richard M. Mott, Charles Simpson, William Holden, Augustus Rainer and James M. Burns. At the first meeting Wm. M. Guest was elected foreman and served for two years; following him came Leonard H. Rieger, for one year, Richard M. Mott for one year, James M. Burns for two years, John Lamberson for one year with John F. Feitner as assistant foreman. John Hammil was foreman for ten years; he had as assistant foreman Jacob Morgan for one year, and Michael Morrissey for one year; Charles Feitner and Michael Morrissey were the foreman and assistant foreman from 1863 until the disbandment in 1865. This company purchased the old engine and all appurtenances from the city for six hundred dollars.

No. 2.—CHATHAM Engine Company No. 2 was one of the two engines brought from London in 1731. Its foreman, or Overseer as it was termed in those days, was John Roosevelt, who was well known as a merchant, also as alderman of the East Ward. In 1748 his brother, Nicholas Roosevelt, at that time assistant alderman of the West Ward, became Overseer. The members in those days were the people at large. It was housed like No. 1 Engine, in Wall Street, on the north side of the City Hall. In 1762 one Hazleworth was in charge. He was superseded by James P. Ovendyke. In 1772 it was decided by the City Fathers to grant each engine a certain number of men—No. 2 being allowed twenty-one. At this time Jacob Stoutenburgh, soon after chief engineer, was overseer or foreman.

OLD ENGINE HOUSE, HANOVER SQUARE.

In 1776 the Department was organized into two military companies, with Chief Stoutenburgh at the head, but directly under the command of General George Washington.

In 1780 Jacob Delamontagne was in command, and so remained until 1784, when the Department was virtually reorganized; although steps were taken to place the Department on a solid basis immediately after the British evacuated New York. In the early part of 1784 the engine was removed to the head of the old Boston Post Road, now Chatham Square, and was called "Chatham," after Mr. Chatham, who owned a vast amount of property in that vicinity, and from whom Chatham Street derived its name. At that time John Lyng is reported to have been foreman. In 1796 Benjamin North was chosen as the head of the company, and they moved to new quarters in the rear of the old Methodist Church grounds, now Forsyth Street. James W. Dominick followed as foreman, serving several years; and in 1817 was elected an assistant engineer, serving until 1825. Among the members at this time were Pine Hopkins, John G. C. Lord, David and Richard Lewis, who were running an engine built in 1807. In 1825 and 1826 Samuel Johnson, C. E. Turnbull and William D. Lord joined; and the following year William D. Hunt, Charles R. Pearsall, Henry Boyce and Isaac Harrow were made members.

The company now proposed to build an engine at their own expense. Efforts were made to increase the roll as much as possible, and many names were added to the list. Among those joining were Ogden Price, Ed. Purcill, Edgar Morris, Matthew McBeath, Ed. Newkirk, William Tyson and John W. Adams. In 1832 the company removed to Eldridge Street. Many were the contests they had with Engine Company No. 19, playing over the cupola on the Eldridge Street Jail, the boys of No. 2 forcing cork in the nozzle of their pipe in order to throw a higher stream. About 1840 John C. Blake was elected foreman; he was followed by John Parsons, both serving several terms. Among the runners was Captain John Mount, who was foreman of the volunteer roll for several years. In 1845 they were continually in hot water with Engine 26, and hardly an alarm sounded but was a signal for a battle with their antagonists. This continued until July 18, 1845, when both companies were run in tongue first and locked up. This occurred the night before the great fire of 1845, and both were disbanded on September 22 of the same year.

EXCELSIOR.—Immediately after the holidays several of the old vamps assembled and proposed reorganizing No. 2, as an engine was very much needed in the vicinity of Henry and Catharine Streets, so, on the sixteenth day of January, 1846, Engine Company No. 2 was re-established under the name of "Excelsior," and located on Henry Street. Among the incorporators were, Erastus W. Brown, George E. Cowperthwait, John Barry, Asher E. Havens, Franklin Waterbury, Seth B. Kneeland, Joseph Baker, Richard M. Jessups, Samuel P. Titus, and Francis H. Macy. John Barry was elected foreman. They resumed duty with a double decker "hay wagon" built for them in the year of their reorganization by John Agnew, of Philadelphia. When they first received the engine it set very low, and the wheels were no larger than those on the old style New York engines, but the company afterwards had her running gear reconstructed and larger wheels put under her. The company received the nickname of "Quakes" owing to the fact that most of the members were from old Quaker families, Henry Street and its vicinity being noted for that class of people. In the meetings the Quaker members were conspicuous for their methodical manners and precise ways. One old citizen stated that he counted seventeen one Sunday morning going to a fire with canes. He wondered what they would do with them in case of a working fire.

Among the members in 1846 was Edward Wood, President of the Bowery Savings Bank. He was born in the Fourth Ward, and never had to pay a fine for absence from a fire day or night while serving out his seven years. Samuel P. Titus followed Barry as foreman, Barry having been elected assistant engineer, serving until 1850.

William A. Jennings was the third foreman of the company. He afterwards went to California, where he kept a saloon. One day a drunken miner came in, and after a little shouting drew a chalk line on the floor and said he would cut the man in two who crossed it. Jennings was out at the time, and on his return unconsciously crossed the line, and the miner kept his word by cutting him to death. Robert H. Ellis, who was afterwards President of the Board of Fire Commissioners, joined this company in 1847. Franklin Waterbury, afterwards captain of the Insurance Patrol, became foreman of the company in 1852. Adam P. Pentz, who was Treasurer of the Fire Department Fund for four years, President of the Fire Department for five years, and Secretary of the Fireman's Ball Committee, was a member of this company, as were many of the solid Quaker residents of the Seventh Ward, all of them being men of standing and character.

On February 14, 1853, Delancey W. Knevals was elected foreman, and on the same night John F. Sloper was presented with a handsome fire cap as a token of appreciation of his meritorious services as pipeman. Knevals held the office of foreman for several years and was followed by Edward J. Knight, in 1859, in which year the company abandoned their double deck engine for a

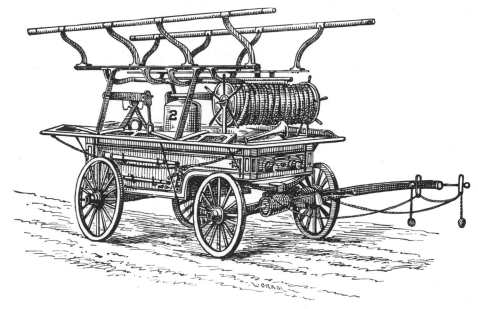

EXCELSIOR ENGINE NO. 2.
[Organized January 16, 1846.]

Shanghai style of apparatus built by James Smith. This engine carried a magnificent signal lamp that cost one hundred and fifty dollars, and was claimed to be the handsomest in the Department at the time. On Knight's retirement from the office of foreman, Delancey W. Knevals was recalled to that position again, serving two years. It was during this second term of his service that the company, in 1861, received a new steam engine built by the Amoskeag Company of New Hampshire. He was succeeded by John McDermott. Robert H. Jones succeeded McDermott and was the last foreman of the company.

While proceeding to a fire one night in 1854, a stranger who was pulling on the rope was run over and killed instantly. The company took charge of the body and buried it at their own expense, holding the funeral services at the engine house. It was not until some time afterwards that the identity of the stranger was discovered, and it was ascertained that he had a wife living in the Seventh Ward. His name was Michael Carvet. He had caught hold of the rope, when he tripped and fell. It was another death caused by the carelessness of the municipal authorities—the street being suffered to remain in a horrible condition, there being quite a deep hole where Carvet fell. He would have come into considerable property in Dublin when he came of age.

The engine house of Excelsior Engine Company No. 2 could boast of something very attractive. The meeting room was artistically furnished, and was ornamented by two beautiful paintings. One was a well-executed portrait of Mr. C. V. Anderson, who had been chief engineer, encircled by a magnificent gold frame, upon which was represented every emblem of the Fire Department and the coat of arms of the State—"Excelsior." The other painting was "Christ appearing before the Mary Magdalen." This last was purchased by the Art Union for three hundred and seventy-five dollars, and fell to the lot of the company through the liberality of Mr. Henry Griffen, a treasurer of the company, who presented them with the ticket. There (in 1850) was to be seen the cap of J. M. Forrester, who lost his life through the fire at the Woolsey Sugar Works in 1849. This company had in its posession a copy of the first Fire Department certificate issued in this city, and also a copy of the second.

Besides those already named as officers were : A. E. Havens, F. H. Macy, Joseph Baker and John McDermott, who were foremen, and Daniel Cosgrove, one of the assistants. In 1863 they had on the roll forty-three men, among whom were Hugh Gillen, David Prothero, Roday S. Brassel, Wm. A. Smith, George Gormley, Robert A. Jones, Patrick H. Keenan, who was councilman, George Corbett, John G. Harris, Thomas Healey, John Conway, James Waite, Terrence T. Tracey and Timothy Farrell. While among the last members were, John J. Harris, Dennis Dunn, Patrick H. Stewart, assistant foreman, Timothy J. Bergen, Jeremiah Toumey, Thomas and Patrick Loftus and John G. Burke. Robert H. Jones was the recipient of a silver trumpet and cap before retiring.

During the draft riots in 1863 their house afforded shelter to some of the unfortunate victims of the rioters, and the company did their share of duty in the downtown districts during those troublous times. Just before the disbandment of the Old Department the company took up their quarters in a new house that had been built for them at 55 East Broadway, but they did not have time to feel at home in the location before the organization of the Paid Department.

Excelsior Engine Company No. 2 will always occupy a front rank in the annals of the old Fire Department. Its steam engine was transferred to Engine Company No. 11 of the New Department.

No. 3.—NEW YORK.—This company was organized some time previous to 1783. In 1796 we find it located in Nassau Street, opposite the City Hall, and in 1813 in Beaver Street near Broad Street. The records of the Common Council show that it was disbanded in 1829.

"Old Brass Back" was the title of an engine, the first ever built in this country, by one Thomas Lote, in 1743, after the pattern of Nos. 1 and 2. Lote was a cooper and boat-builder, at the foot of Fair Street. Cornelius Bickers was the Overseer, afterwards a lieutenant, in the Continentals during the war. She lay near what is called "Kalch-Hook Pond," a body of fresh water abounding with fish, running along about what is now Warren and Chambers Streets.

In 1776 Isaac Bokea was the Overseer or foreman, and in 1780 they moved her to Dugan Street. In 1784 the company was reorganized and called Dugan Engine Company No. 3, after Thomas Dugan, owner of the property in that vicinity. It remained here but a short time. Subsequently it was temporarily located in 1795 on what is now Centre Street, near where stands the Tombs. Wm. J. Ellsworth, Abraham Dœnaire, Alexander Lamb and Peter Chapple were then members. In 1801 they received a new suction engine, and until 1812 had a light roll of members.

METAMORA.—This company was organized on March 22, 1830, by Frederick R. Lee, who was the first foreman, and who was afterwards alderman of the City and chairman of the fire and water committee, Wilson Wright, Thos. H. Hawks, Arnest Funk, Jr., John Raymer (from Engine Company No. 40), Andrew Storms, Wm. Anderson, James Ford, Edward Norris, Edward Vaughn, Wm. Allen, Wm. Jarvis and several others. At that time they were located in Mott street near Prince ; they afterwards moved to Marion street in

ENGINE COMPANY NO. 3 (1745).
[Kolch Hook Pond : Present Broadway and Warren Street.]

the house occupied after their disbanding by Engine Company No. 9. Charles H. Haswell, the eminent engineer, and who was a member of the Common Council of this city, belonged to this company when she lay in Marion street. The company was disbanded for fighting with 40 Engine on December 6, 1843.

HOPE.—This company was organized on July 16, 1847, and was located at 128 West Broadway. In 1852 it was changed to Engine Company No. 31.

METAMORA—NATIONAL—BRODERICK.—Organized October 25, 1852, and located at 390 Bleecker street, subsequently removed to 557 Hudson street. Disbanded on September 22, 1845.

FORREST.—On the fifth of March, 1860, No. 3 was reorganized from Lafayette Hose Company 34. The members proposed to form a new Hose Company, and were receiving more applications for membership than they were entitled to elect, and an engine being much needed in that locality, it was resolved to make application for a change, which they did, resulting in Forrest

Engine Company No. 3. They located at 211 East Eleventh street, between Avenues B and C, at present the location of Engine Company 28 of the Paid Department. Their first foreman was John Irwin, and they ran the little old gooseneck engine belonging to Oceanus Engine Company 11 until they received a new piano engine, which they used until the Department went out of service in 1865. James Mason, Jeremiah Heffernan and Wm. Donnelly were foremen in the order named, the last a captain in the Paid Department for a time. Engine Companies 9, 44 and 51, and 18 Hook and Ladder were rivals of this company during their term of service, and many a rush they had with each other. Engine Company 3 inaugurated a series of yearly picnics, engaging a steamboat and a number of barges and taking their families with them. On the outbreak of the rebellion several of their members joined the First and Second Fire Zouaves. Those who went with Ellsworth's regiment were in company I, Captain John Wildey's. John Gleeson was shot in the face at Bull Run and died in New York. James Hurley was killed at Bull Run. Robert Vreeland and Augustus Calhoun were also out with the First Regiment. In the Second Fire Zouaves Wm. Gleeson, Wm. Perkins, George Ramsey and others enlisted. During the draft riots in 1863 they formed themselves into a military company and did patrol and picket duty around the property in the neighborhood of Dry Dock, and so thoroughly was this done that that portion of the city was comparatively free from the outrages of the mob. It was while serving as a member of this company that Wm. Gleeson, formerly lieutenant in the Second Fire Zouaves, devised an ingenious contrivance for keeping the water in the engine boilers warm. It was an oblong form of gas pipe fitted up with twenty-four gas jets and shut up like a rat trap, but when opened would fit under the boiler of an engine, and could be attached to the gas pipe with rubber tubing. It was placed under the boiler of Washington Engine Company 20, which then laid in Cedar street, and was the first attempt made in New York city to keep the water in engine boilers at a certain temperature while awaiting an alarm of fire.

No. 4. AMERICAN.—The first engine of this company was built in 1749. It was located on a lot at the corner of Broadway and a lane leading to a windmill belonging to Peter Jansen, about midway between Little Queen Street, now Cedar, and Fair, now Fulton. It was proposed to purchase the lot, but the price asked, being five hundred and eighty dollars, was considered too great. The Vreedenburghs and De Kalbs were Overseers in its early days, and during the Revolution the engine was destroyed. When the Fire Department was re-established in 1784 No. 4 was reorganized, and in 1796 she is recorded as being located on John Street, opposite the playhouse, Thomas Bruen being the foreman. Among its early members we find the names of John A. Hardenbrook, broker, and John Colwill, grocer, the latter being foreman. In 1811 Colwill was appointed an assistant engineer, and Willett A. Robbins was chosen foreman, and John A. Hardenbrook assistant. The latter the very night he was elected was fined twelve shillings for going first to the fire on an alarm, in place of repairing immediately to the engine house.

In 1812 Henry Cowenhover, merchant tailor; Daniel Hawdhurst, iron monger, and John Sutphen, a whip maker, joined. On the roll were also Thomas Shotwell, Anthony Chapples, Michael Schoonmaker, William Revee, and Henry W. Peckwell. At this time the initiation fee was said to be ten dollars. Hawkhurst Smith followed as foreman, and then came one Weyman. During 1809 the company did most praiseworthy duty at the burning of the ship "Nancy," which was flatteringly commented upon in the papers. The company was accustomed to give an annual dinner, at which assistant engineers Van Antwerp, Tyler and Bruen were the company's guests. The last bill paid for a supper was nine pounds. In 1814 Jasper Corning, M. Mandeville, J. V. Varick and John Van Benschoten appeared on the roll, and from 1818 to 1820 the new members were Joseph Bedell, Abraham Warner, Cornelius Romain, John H. Giffing and William Winterton.

NIAGARA (Race horse).—This company was the result of a meeting called at Constitution Hall, December 9, 1848, to organize an engine company. Among those present were Messrs. John A. Baker, C. P. Dickie, Henry Wilson, H. W. Smith, J. G. Storm, M. E. Greene, A. Owens, Chas. Holder, Wm. Mount, J. A. Hammond, F. A. Long and C. W. Cornell, most of them having been members of Union Engine Company No. 18, which had been disbanded in November, 1846. John A. Baker was elected chairman, and C. P.

NIAGARA ENGINE NO. 4.

Dickie secretary. At this meeting it was resolved that a committee be appointed to select a suitable name for the company, and also resolved that their number should be eighteen. The next meeting was held December 18, and twenty-four members answered to the roll call. At this meeting they elected the following officers:

Henry Wilson, foreman; John A. Baker, assistant; H. W. Smith, secretary, and Nelson D. Thayer, treasurer, and again by a vote of thirteen to ten adopted the number of 18 for the company.

On January 5, 1849, another meeting was held at which by-laws were adopted, and committees on house and location were appointed. On January 11, 1849, a special meeting was held, and on Monday evening March 5, 1849, the first regular meeting of Niagara Engine Company No. 4 was held, when several new members were elected. At this meeting the following preamble and resolution were adopted.

Whereas, the fire and water committee, through the chief engineer, has decided that this company shall be No. 4, therefore, Resolved, that we accept and will do duty under said number.

John A. Baker, the newly-elected assistant foreman, having died while the company was organizing, it was also resolved, "that in token of esteem for his memory the office held by him remain unfilled during the term for which he was elected."

The location selected for the company by the Common Council, at 33 Great Jones Street, did not seem to please the company, but they were unable to alter the decision of the authorities, and accepted the situation. On May 7, 1849, the regular election of the company took place, and Henry Wilson was unanimously elected foreman, and John A. Hammond, assistant. At a special meeting held July 23, 1849, Henry Wilson resigned as foreman, and Isaac T. Redfield was elected to fill the vacancy. At this meeting thirteen of the members resigned from the company and two were expelled.

On July 27, 1849, the company turned out to their first alarm. There proved to be no fire, and the company stopped corner of Sixth Avenue and Sixth Street.

In this year the company received one of the three Philadelphia style of engines built by James Smith, the other two going to 6 and 7 Engine Companies. They were painted lead color when delivered to the companies and finished by them. That of No. 4 was painted by Thorp & Grenell. The box was white ornamented with gold with a delicate shadow, the wheels blue, full gilt, the levers blue, neatly ornamented. There were four paintings on the condenser case: on the front a volcano at sea, with vessels in the perspective; on the right side a view of the suspension bridge across the Niagara River, and of the little steamer "*Maid of the Mist*," the view being taken from the "Devil's Hole" on the American side; on the left a birds-eye view of Niagara Falls showing the whole cataract, with the "Table Rock," Horse Shoe," and the great current above, the view taken from the American side; on the back a scene of a prairie on fire, the carved work inlaid with solid gold. On the gallery of the condenser case were the following mottoes: "Duty our Pleasure;" "Ever Ready, ever Willing." It was a magnificent engine and was one of the decorations at the Fireman's Ball in the year it was finished.

On May 6, 1850, Isaac T. Redfield was re-elected foreman, J. A. Hammond, assistant, and John J. Morris was elected treasurer. In July of this year the officers all resigned their positions, but with a few exceptions were immediately re-elected, and on the fifteenth of that month eighteen of the members resigned from the company. On May 5, 1851, J. B. Foley was elected foreman and Thomas Leavy assistant, who were re-elected in 1852. During the latter year the company were out of a location and held their meetings at the house of Engine Company No. 26, they having stored their furniture while waiting for a location. On September 7, 1852, Mr. James B. Foley having resigned the office of foreman, Mr. Thomas Leavy was promoted to that office, and Cyrus T. Frost was advanced to the position of assistant foreman. In May, 1853, the company took possession of the house No. 220 Mercer Street, and Thomas Leavy was re-elected foreman, and George W. Lyon assistant. In May, 1854, Mr. Leavy was again elected foreman and Charles K. Hyde assistant. In May, 1855, Mr. Leavy was for the fourth time elected foreman, and Mr. John Kennard succeeded Mr. Hyde in the position of assistant. At this election the company presented Mr. Leavy with a gold watch as a mark of their esteem. In July of the same year Mr. Leavy resigned the office of foreman, and Mr. Charles K. Hyde was elected to fill his place, Robert W. Adams being elected assistant.

On the evening of November 26, 1855, while Wallace T. Vaughn, a member of this company, was passing Wallack's Theatre, the flagstaff on that building blew down, killing him instantly. The company defrayed the expenses of his funeral, and a benefit was given by them at Wallack's Theatre for the family of the deceased at which the company netted over five hundred dollars, which was invested in the interest of the widow and son. In May, 1856, the company, seeing no reason to change their officers, re-elected Messrs. Hyde and Adams, while L. De Garmo Brooks, the professor of dancing, was unanimously elected treasurer. These officers were continued in charge at the election in 1857. In 1858 Mr. Hyde declined a re-election to the foremanship, and Mr. Adams was promoted to fill the position, William Forbes being elevated to the office of assistant.

In 1859 the company had their engine rebuilt, doing duty in the meantime

ENGINE COMPANY NO. 5.

with a little old gooseneck engine. In the latter year Frank W. Robb and John Judge were elected foreman and assistant respectively. Judge was elected foreman in 1861, and held the office until 1863, when Thomas Leavy was recalled to that position, and the company procured a steam engine built by Joseph Banks. Leavy was continued in the office of foreman until the disbandment of the company in 1865.

No. 5.—PROTECTION (Honey Bee).—This company was undoubtedly one of the oldest in the Volunteer Fire Department. The old "North Dutch Church" was founded in the latter part of the year 1761, and in 1762 No. 5 Engine was located on Smith Valley, near Pearl Street, between wall and Beekman Streets, the locality being then a fashionable place of residence. It afterwards became Queen Street and was improved by handsome brick edifices. Here was found, identified with No. 5, Jonathan Black, who was a lieutenant in the second battalion of the Firemen's Military Organization. Associated with Black was John Somerendyck, Gerit Peterson and Henry Shut. For many years No. 5 did duty as a bucket company, carrying a number of the buckets in use in those days, which were filled at the nearest water supply, and passed from hand to hand in a line to the fire. The earlier minutes of the company have been lost or destroyed, making it impossible to obtain correct data of its younger days. It is on record, however, that Francis Arden, John Cole, and Abram and Frederick Easthart were members in 1786. The records for 1793 show that Frederick Acker was foreman, Garret Vandewater assistant, James Aymar secretary, and as privates Wm. McKenny, Peter Thompson, John Cole, Caleb Pell, A. Acker and Wm. Pinckney. They did not increase their membership for some years afterwards. John Leonard, Joel Sagers, and H. W. Rosenbaum joined about the year 1812, and later on Adam W. Spies, Thomas P. Goelet and David M. Prall became connected with the company.

Samuel J. Willis resigned the foremanship in 1824 to become an assistant engineer, and served until 1829. In 1829 the company received a new gooseneck engine which they were very proud of. This engine was in use continuously until 1856, when they procured a piano engine. A fire broke out on the early morning of December 29, 1859, and Five's company had both their engines to work on the fire, which was in Ann Street, near William. The wall of the building fell into the street, burying the engine and injuring some of the members. The engine was found to be almost a total wreck when dug out.

Wilson Small was one of the prominent members of this company; he left it when appointed an assistant engineer in 1837. Frederick D. Kohler succeeded Wilson Small as foreman of the company, and he too became an engineer in 1838, serving until 1841. Henry Heamstead, Bob Thompson and Harry Young were also members from 1835 to 1838.

In the year 1840 Ed. Floyd and his brother, Ira Floyd, the former then proprietor of a hotel at No. 58 Beekman Street, joined. At this time the company began to muster quite a crowd of runners, at the head of which was Chaff Storms. He was a son of old General Storms. The boys used to congregate at Leggett's in Chatham Street. Frank Leggett and Alfred Storms were heavy weights among the firemen in former days, and served up many a good hot cup of coffee to the men on a cold night. In 1842 we find Sheriff Wm. C. Conner on the rolls, and a quicker fireman never manned a rope. In 1845 nothing but printers were found on the roll. Among them were: Charles Bonnard, David Young, Thomas R. Morrison, M. C. Gray, Joseph H. Mink, Thomas L. Maxwell and David Demerest. In 1850 Chauncey M. Leonard, subsequently mayor of the City of Newburg, N. Y., and who was buried on the same day with Mayor Havermeyer of this city, united his fortune with the "Honey Bees." He rose to be foreman, and finally left the company, having returned to Newburg, where he went into business. Here he was chief engineer of the Fire Department for over ten years, was then elected member of assembly, and finally mayor. He died while in office.

In 1851 Wm. H. Griffiths, the celebrated billiard manufacturer, and ex-Fire Commissioner Joshua G. Abbe were added to the roll. During this year the company went to Bridgeport, and on their return John J. Mahoney (afterward foreman) and Tobias C. Connor, Jr., billiard maker, were found in the ranks. In 1859 Captain J. Murray Ditchett, who for several years was captain of the Fourth Ward Police, and until his death held a position in the Register's office, became a member. He was soon elevated to the foremanship. A better fireman never donned a red shirt.

At his side at many a fire, as a member of No. 5, stood Amor J. Williamson, editor and proprietor of *The Sunday Dispatch;* Thomas Campbell, the well-known lithographer; Fred. Collier, of late years one of the chief engineers of the San Francisco Fire Department; Smith, the clothier, of Fulton Street; Hiram Arentz, who once ran for chief engineer, and was defeated by Carson. Wm. H. Maloney, who was assistant clerk of the Board of Aldermen, was likewise a member. Toward the last days of the Volunteer Department but few of the old stock remained, Joseph F. Sartin and Wm. McAnneny being the last to join the organization. N. McCauley was the last foreman. He afterward became foreman of No. 4 in the Metropolitan Paid Department.

Many of the old vamps of "Protection" will remember the playing match at Reilly's Liberty Pole in 1862, when Engine Companies Nos. 5, 6, 9, 26, 30, 38, 40 and 50 took part, with No. 12 of Williamsburg, No. 7 of Brooklyn and No. 4 of Newburg; also the Centennial Ball g'ven at the old Apollo Rooms in the same 'year; and the Rainbow Hotel fire in Beekman Street. Foreman John J. Maloney was buried in the ruins at the Ann Street fire, and after two hours' hard work was dug out with several ribs and his left arm broken. When the thirty dollar prize was in vogue for the first company at a fire, the "Honey Bees" won twenty of the thirty dollar prizes in five years. The back of the old gooseneck engine of No. 5 now adorns the rooms of the Firemen's Association.

The company petitioned for and received an Amoskeag steam engine in 1861, and, being located in the midst of the paper warehouses, were greatly relied on during the extensive fires that occurred in that section. Charles A. Brown was elected an assistant engineer from this company in 1853. During the war of the rebellion more than fifteen of their members enlisted in the Union army. The company continued in service until the last, giving up their organization on the beginning of the Paid Department.

No. 6.—NEPTUNE (Bean Soup).—No. 6 was organized in 1765, and was stationed on Crown Street (now Liberty) near King (now Nassau). It was established by the East Warders, and among the members were John C. Prentiss and John Barrow. In 1778 they moved around on King Street, Peter Wilse being Overseeer of the company. They first did duty with buckets, until an engine could be built for them. Among the most noted members of No. 6 during the war was Jonas Addoms, who was born on March 26, 1753. He was one of the first five months men who enlisted whose term expired when the British army crossed from Long Island and took possession of the city. When New York was evacuated by the British in 1783 his regiment was the first to march in and take possession. Addoms fired the first salute of thirteen guns at Fort George at the Battery, and helped to reorganize his company in 1783, when it had twenty-one men on the rolls. Joseph Smith was foreman in 1793, and his son was the assistant foreman, and these two held their respective offices for several years. They were located at the college yard in Murray Street until 1832. While in Murray Street their prominent members were Moses Moore, John Shotwell, Wm. Civil, John Schenck, Edward M. Hoffmire, Joseph Gouge and Benjamin Brower, the last four being all carpenters. Hoffmire was elected foreman of the company in 1828, and advanced to the position of assistant engineer in 1831, serving until 1837. When he organized Thirty-three Hose Company he was afterwards elected Alderman of the Fifth Ward. In 1826 John Coddington and Wm. and James Hoffmire became members of the company, and were followed by Robert Barr, Thomas Baker, Henry Gaines, Joseph Moon, Richard McCottrick and Joseph Debaun, the company using at that time an engine built in 1805. From 1829 until they moved to Reade Street the following names appear on the company rolls: Wm. Baker, John Miles, Daniel E. Ruckle, Charles Hoffmire, Samuel Bennett and Robert Sanderson.

This company and Engine Company No. 1 were always bitter rivals, and their rivalry did not cease when the company moved to Reade Street. John Lyng, the old time sport, who is still living, and who has had as eventful an existence as it is possible for any one man to have, was a member of the company in Reade Street.

On May 26, 1836, the company lost one of their members, who was killed at

AMERICUS ENGINE NO. 6.
["Big Six" engine, built in 1851.]

a fire on that date. The company continued to get into hot water and finally were disbanded on August 5, 1846, with Engine Companies 21, 23, and 36, for fighting.

AMERICUS (Big Six—Tiger) was started at a meeting of citizens of the east side held at Mather's printing ink establishment in Front Street near Gouverneur, December 11, 1848. Wm. A. Freeborn, an old member of Hook and Ladder 4, and an assistant engineer from 1839 to 1842, aided the movement by his presence and advice. The next meeting was held at the Vivarambia, No. 3 Hester Street. At this second meeting it was formally announced that the city authorities had resolved to locate the company when organized in the house of old Black Joke Engine Company No. 33, in Gouverneur Street near Henry. On December 30, 1848, the following gentlemen organized the company: David M. Smith, carpenter; George D. Demilt, painter; Wm. M. Tweed, chair manufacturer; John B. Golder, accountant; W. H. Brown, accountant; David C. Smith, plumber; Ed. Phillips, Jr. plumber; Robert C. Brown, plumber; James H. Sturges, broker; Joseph H. Johnson, artist; Robert Darrow, carman; Isaac Bachman, hotel; John T. Clapp, calker; H. C. McDonald, joiner; Henry A. Burr, cooper; George Backus, clerk; Alfred Palmer, coachmaker; Lawrence Pridham, painter; W. H. Pratt, calker; Matthew Bradley, brush manufacturer; Chas. Schriver, oysters; Benj. G. Brown, merchant; Isaac Jenkins, accountant; W. H. Wilson, fire cap manufacturer; John T. Harding, carver; Edward S. Baker, merchant; Edward D. Moore, merchant; John Anderson, druggist; Jeremiah Morris, calker; Julius Frazier, calker; R. S. Jones, accountant; John Stratton, merchant; William Freshwater, merchant.

They adopted the name and number of "Americus Six," this name having received the approval of fourteen members, while that of Fredonia received four votes, and Franklin, Eureka, and Black Joke one each. David M. Smith was elected foreman and Geo. G. Demilt assistant; Robert C. and Wm. H. Brown were selected as representatives. On May 14, 1849, the first regular annual election was held, and Smith and Demilt were re-elected. On the ninth of July Smith resigned, and Demilt was made foreman, and Wm. M. Tweed assistant. On the evening of December 9, their first annual ball was given at the Apollo Hall, a favorite assembly room with the firemen in those and later days. On May 23, 1850, Demilt resigned and Wm. M. Tweed was elected foreman, with Joseph H. Johnson, the famous artist, as assistant. Tweed was re-elected May 12, 1851, but, Johnson declining, Alfred Palmer was chosen assistant. On July 14, the same year, Tweed resigned and Palmer was

TIGER CARRIED ON "BIG SIX."

elected his successor, with Edward Phillips, Jr., as his assistant. On August 1 a banquet was given to Wm. M. Tweed, at which he was presented with a magnificent watch and chain. On October 13 the new apparatus secured by the company was received from the hands of the painter, Joseph H. Johnson, and having been placed on exhibition at the Fair of the American Institute in Castle Garden gained the diploma. The engine was a "double decker," giving accommodation to firemen on the box to work the brakes, and being of unusual size—the other companies running the gooseneck pattern she soon received the *soubriquet* of "Big Six." February 9, 1852, Edward Phillips, Jr., resigned as assistant foreman, and Henry Close was chosen in his stead. On May 10 Alfred Palmer was re-elected foreman and Close his assistant.

On November 8 Frederick Best, one of the members, died, and Tweed presented the company with a lot in Greenwood, where their comrade was buried. On May 10, 1853, Palmer and Close were re-elected, and on January 28, 1854, the company took possession of their new brown stone front house on Henry Street, near Gouverneur Street. This house was really a beautiful one, and acknowledged to be the most sumptuously furnished engine house in the city. On May 8, 1854, Henry Close was chosen foreman, and Richard Kimmens assistant. May 14, 1855, Close and Kimmens were re-elected. May 12, 1856, Kimmens was elected foreman, and William Anspake assistant. May 11, 1857, William Anspake was promoted to the foremanship, and William B. Dunley made assistant. Thomas J. Shandley was also elected secretary. October 18, 1858, Anspake resigned and William B. Dunley was promoted to fill the vacancy, but no one was placed in the office made vacant by Dunley's advance. May 9, 1859, Dunley was re-elected, with John J. Blair assistant. May 14, 1860, John McGarrigle was elected foreman, John Buckbee assistant, and William B. Dunley treasurer and representative, who were all re-elected in May 1861. On October 11, 1860, the company participated in the torchlight parade

AMERICUS BADGE.

in honor of the Prince of Wales, and on November 20 received the Hibernia Company of Philadelphia, commanded by Col. James Page, since deceased. May 14, 1861, "Big Six" sent large supplies of food, clothing and delicacies to the First Regiment of Fire Zouaves, then stationed in the defences of Washington. While William B. Dunley was foreman the company made an extended excursion trip, visiting Niagara Falls, the British dominions, etc., being received wherever they went with marked respect and enthusiasm, the gallant " Tigers " being cheered to the echo, while the ladies filled the windows and waved their handkerchiefs in token of admiration. In the Canadas they were fêted everywhere. On their return home they were received by Hook and Ladder (Marion) 13, and a number of other companies.

The famous Americus Club was originated in 6 Engine Company. It has been the custom of some of the members for years to make a Fourth of July excursion up the Sound in a yacht, often going as far as South Norwalk, Conn. On one of these excursions they stopped at the beautiful grounds at Indian Harbor, at Greenwich, and when the Americus Club was founded they leased the ground from Augustus Mead and erected a building. William M. Tweed was the president of the club, Edward W. Jacobs vice-president; Charles H. Hall secretary, and William B. Dunley was treasurer.

In May, 1862, John Buckbee was elected foreman, and Christian Van Blarcom assistant. In May, 1863, Anthony Burke and John Whalen were chosen as foreman and assistant, and were re-elected in 1864. In May, 1865, Anthony Burke was elected the last foreman of the company, and John Sigerson the last assistant. The company had continued the use of the double deck engine until 1861, when they obtained a steamer of Silsby's build which they ran until disbanded in 1865.

Thomas Sweeney and John Cary of this company were severely injured at the fire in Goodwin's cracker bakery in Cherry Street, February 3, 1863, at which John Slowey, of Engine Company 19, was killed, and George W. Badger of same company, fatally injured. Edward W. Jacobs was elected an assistant engineer from the ranks of this company, the only man ever advanced to that position who had not previously served as foreman or assistant. In 1853 the company, under Henry Close as foreman, went to Albany, Saratoga, and West Troy, where they visited the arsenal, and in 1865, on the disbandment of the Volunteer Department, Anthony Burke took the company to Philadelphia, the company expending the proceeds of the sale of their effects for that purpose. They took with them the double deck engine the original "Big Six." This engine is now stationed at Willett's Point, and on Evacuation Day, 1884, the Americus Association and their old firemen friends including ex-Chief Harry Howard, and ex-Assistant Engineers G. Joseph Ruch, Edward W.

BUNK ROOM "BIG 6."
[269 Henry Street.]

Jacobs and Bernard Kenney, and numbering one hundred and ten men, under command of William B. Dunley as foreman, and David M. Smith (the first foreman of Americus Engine Company No. 6) as assistant foreman, obtained the engine and took part in the parade, the engine being drawn by eight large horses, and the members forming a square around it.

During the existence of Americus Engine Company No. 6 three hundred and eighty-nine members signed the roll. Of these, one hundred and sixty-one are known to be living and are members of the Americus Association, who each year celebrate the eleventh of June as the anniversary of the first fire the company ever ran to.

When 6 Engine Company was first organized they did duty in the Fifth and Sixth Districts. About 1855 they commenced to run down-town in the Seventh and Eighth Districts. Engine Companies 8 and 19 had begun to run down-town a short time previously, and No. 19 Engine was transferred to the Fifth and Sixth Districts, and 6 Engine took their place down-town. Then commenced the famous races between Big Six and the Elephant, when printers, binders, and in fact all classes would drop work to go and see or help "Six and Eight raise the hill." No. 6 and No. 41 were also great rivals, so much so that No. 41 had to be transferred to the upper districts, and in 1864, when they were returned to duty in the down-town districts, the rivalry was so great, and led to such serious troubles, that 41 Engine was disbanded. 6 and 41 Engine Companies, and 6 and 44 Engine Companies, had several serious encounters during their existence.

Engine Company No. 6, like their confrères, had several target companies, among which were the "Cudney Guards" under Captain Ed. W. Jacobs, the "Wm. M. Tweed Guards," under the command of Captain Jos. H. Johnson, and the "Young Americus Guard," for five years under John G. McGee, and next under John J. Blair as captains, Gouverneur Blues under John Casilear and William Gayte as captains. When the war broke out in 1861 many of the men who had shouldered muskets to shoot at wooden targets started off in defense of their country and went south to shoot in deadly earnest.

On September 8, 1855, the double deck engine, which weighed forty-two hundred pounds, ran over Elihu B. Campbell and Charles B. Elliott in front of Lord & Taylor's store in Grand Street. They had attended a fire at Hester and Allen Streets, and were going home with a full rope, when the bell struck for the Fifth, and they started off, and in going through Grand Street the men fell. Campbell was very severely injured. The engine passed over the middle of his body, crushing him fearfully. He lay eight months in bed, but finally recovered, and is an active man at this time.

No. 7.—LAFAYETTE—HAMILTON.—This company was organized in 1701, and located on Duke Street, called in former days High Street. Duke Street was just on a corner of a lane leading down to Fort George. William Crolius, John Miltenberger, George Janeway, Robert Berry, and Henry Sickles were among its first members. But little is known of the company till 1783, when the Department was re-established, and Stephen P. Trippall was at the head of No. 6. In 1798 they were housed in a small frame building in Beekman Street, where now stands Lovejoy's Hotel. In 1813 the company was located in Rose Street, about 1831 at 91 Henry Street, from 1832 to 1834 at the Corporation Yard, Leonard Street, and in 1842 again in Rose Street. On March 1, 1843, it was disbanded. On October 4, 1843, the company was re-organized and stationed at 6 Third Street, but on February 4, 1847, it was again disbanded.

In 1815, while the company was stationed in the churchyard of St. George's Chapel, on Cliff Street, its foreman was William L. Mott, merchant; first assistant, Eleazar Lundy, currier; second assistant, Gregory Snether, distiller; clerk, Peter Williams, bookbinder.

LEXINGTON was organized on December 26, 1849. The first regular meeting was held on February 4, 1850. The first officers and members were as follows: Richard Kelly, foreman (now president); William Tapper, assistant; Edmund Stephenson, secretary; William A. Bennett, Henry L. Jolly, William H. Hamford, Jeremiah Keyser, Garrett Shepherd, William H. Oliver, John Rosenbrook, Isaac Pierson, John McKeon, Seth W. Valentine, Andrew J.

Odell, Nathaniel B. Abbott, James Brown, William H. Smith, William Watson, George Joseph Ruch, Thomas McParlan, Lorenzo Milles, William Doubleday. In 1851 Mr. Kelly having been elected assistant engineer, William Tapper was elected foreman, William W. Bennett, assistant foreman, Edmund Stephenson, secretary. Mr. Tapper resigned May 8, 1854, and G. Joseph Ruch was elected foreman, Samuel Cheshire, assistant, and Henry Wilson, secretary. Mr. Ruch resigned May 14, 1856, having been elected assistant engineer, and Samuel Cheshire was elected foreman, Robert Ennever assistant, and Aaron J. Quimby, secretary. Mr. Cheshire resigned July 11, 1859, and John C. Fisher was elected foreman, John R. Barnes, assistant and Edgar T. Stewart, secretary. Mr. Barnes resigned May 14, 1860, and Edward Marrenner was elected foreman, Hans J. Gladney assistant, and Eugene D. Croker secretary. Mr. Marrenner resigned May 11, 1863, and Alden Wild was elected foreman, Hans J. Gladney assistant and Thomas Ryan secretary. Mr. Wild resigned May 9, 1864, and Hans J. Gladney was elected foreman, Lancelot W. Armstrong assistant and Thomas Ryan secretary. At the annual meeting held May 8, 1865, Hans J. Gladney was re-elected foreman, Lancelot W. Armstrong assistant foreman and Thomas Ryan secretary. The above officers served until September 24, 1865, when the company held their last meeting and were superseded by the present Engine No. 16 of the Metropolitan Fire Department. All the company's books and records were presented to Secretary Ryan.

LEXINGTON ENGINE NO. 7.

The company was originally quartered in the house formerly occupied by Engine 46, in Third Avenue, between Twenty-sixth and Twenty-Seventh Streets, but remained there but a short time before it was transferred to the present quarters of Engine 16 in Twenty-fifth Street between Second and Third Avenues. There it remained throughout its career. The first engine was built for Engine 15 in Christie Street near Canal, but on the disbandment of that company it was assigned to No. 7. This engine was in active service until March 5, 1860, when a steamer was procured.

Many of the members of Lexington in time became prominent citizens. For example: Richard Kelly, president of the Fifth National Bank; Edmund Stephenson, Commissioner of Emigration and president of the Home Bank; Charles E. Munson, the well-known baker; James L. Potter, popular builder; Robert Ennever, School Commissioner; Wm. H. Cochran; Peter Wood, assemblyman for the Sixteenth District; Charles H. Doremus, of the firm of Doremus & Corbett; William W. Rhodes, assistant engineer in the Paid Department; Alvin W. Gordon, Superintendent of Frankin Telegraph Company; Lancelot W. Armstrong, of the firm of Moran & Armstrong; J. P. Teller, engineer of the company's steamer; John M. Semler, director of the Third Avenue Railroad Company; George Fielding, Henry Bullwinkel, Jeremiah Keyser, the original "Keyser" of Chanfrau's "Mose;" William H. Hayward,

Harris Wines, ex-foreman of 39 Hose; John Taylor, Henry Saulspaugh, John Geary, Michael V. Caffrey, of calcium light fame; John Gannon, T. P. Brennan, now of Hook and Ladder No. 3; John and James Dalton, Thomas Corr, William Haggerty, superintendent for several years of Post Office Station A.

Among the principal fires attended by the company were: The fire in a tenement house on Elm Street, between Grand and Howard, on the night of February 2, 1860, when five persons were burned to death on the roof in sight of the firemen, who were powerless to reach them; the destruction of the Third Avenue Railroad Depot on June 27, 1861; the fire at the Empire Works on February 6, 1864, on which occasion Engineer J. P. Teller stood at his post for eighteen consecutive hours, and the great fire at D. D. Badger's iron works on April 24, 1864. The company participated in the great demonstration in honor of the laying of the Atlantic Cable in 1859; and on the occasion of the procession in honor of the Prince of Wales, on October 13, 1860, it turned out with not less than one hundred men.

On the breaking out of the war the following members of Lexington Engine sprang to arms and went to the front: Colonel John W. Marshall, Lieutenant-Colonel of the Tenth New York Zouaves; George Mings, enlisted in the Fifth New York Artillery, was captured at Winchester and died in Andersonville; Corporal W. F. Wilson, was wounded at Bull Run; H. J. Gladney and Theodore J. McDonough enlisted in the First Fire Zouaves, Frederick J. McDonald and Thomas Gillett enlisted in the Second Fire Zouaves, Albert J. Wilson entered the Navy, Nelson T. Wilson enlisted in the Thirtyseventh New York Volunteers, John F. Croker and William E. Sandbeg enlisted in the Eighth New York Volunteers, Emmerich Schneider entered the Fifth Artillery, Jacob Lowndes enlisted in the Duryea Zouaves, Patrick Murray enlisted in the Sixty-ninth Regiment, William F. Baker enlisted in Berrian's Battery, E. T. Stewart served in the United States Quartermaster's Department. John B. Brewer and Timothy Conron also enlisted.

Splendid service was done by the members of Lexington Engine during the Draft Riots, under the command of Secretary Thomas Ryan. On the breaking out of the riots on July 13, 1863, the company worked on the fire in the provost marshal's office, at Third Avenue and Forty-sixth Street, and, having extinguished it, made for the fire at the Bull's Head Hotel, at Fifth Avenue and Forty-fourth Street, where in spite of the attacks of the mob they succeeded in saving much valuable property. Next they were called on to work on the Colored Orphan Asylum near by, and from there they were hurried to Lexington Avenue and Forty-third Street, where a whole row of dwellings was in flames. Having assisted in extinguishing this conflagration the company hurried to the Armory at Second Avenue and Twenty-first Street, and worked till the fire was extinguished. By this time the city was in the hands of the mob, and all order was at an end. Secretary Ryan, with a few friends, went along Third Avenue, rallying the citizens and calling upon them to organize in defence of their lives and property. Lexington Engine House became the headquarters for the district, and in a few hours Secretary Ryan found himself in command of a formidable fighting force of citizens, regularly officered and provided with passwords and rallying signals. A series of desperate encounters with the mob soon followed, in which the men of Lexington

Engine punished the rioters severely, and succeeded in holding the mob in check until the arrival of troops from the front. In acknowledgment of the heroism displayed during these trying times, the ladies of the Eighteenth Ward presented Lexington Engine Company No. 7 with a handsome American flag embroidered with the name and number of the company.

No. 8.—MANHATTAN—ESSEX—MANHATTAN ("Elephant").—Engine Company No. 8 may be said to be the last company established before the Revolutionary War of 1776. We find the eighth company lying near the Tan Pits,

SECRETARY'S CARD OF NOTIFICATION OF MEETING.

at the foot of what is now Maiden Lane, at one time known as Shoemakers' Pasture. It was used in those days by one John Harpendinck. Little was known of the company till 1783, when they were reorganized with Herbert L. Proudfoot as Treasurer. Other foremen were Henry Riker (1783), John Post, David Morris (1793) and Thomas Browne (1796). In 1783 the company consisted of twenty-three men.

In 1793 Abraham Brevoort was assistant foreman, and on Morris's retirement Brevoort assumed the foremanship. Their early location was at the

jail yard in Chatham Street, with Joseph G. Dunell, David Note, Thomas
Hunt, Otis Harrington, Washington Ryder, John McBlair, John Welch, John
Phillips and George Enny as members. On April 4, 1831, Robert W. Piggott,
Dennis Cornell, John F. Butt and fifteen others joined the company, and had the
location moved to Essex Street, where the name was changed to " Essex," and
Piggott was chosen the first foreman, and from there moved to Ludlow Street.
He was succeeded by Daniel Coger, who was elected an assistant engineer
in 1835, serving until 1837, being followed by his brother, John Coger, Jr.,
who was foreman at the time of the Gulick trouble. At the fire where the
trouble occurred Coger wished his company to continue at work, but they were
driven from the brakes by the other firemen, and Coger was assaulted. After
their hose was cut the company discontinued their endeavors to extinguish the
fire. John Coger, Jr., also became an assistant engineer, serving from 1838
to 1841. Dewitt C. Mott was the next foreman of the company, and when he
also became an assistant engineer, which he did in 1842, he was succeeded by
Charles J. Harris, who held the office for three years, and was succeeded in
turn by Lewis D. Walters and James Tyler. Seth C. Douglass, afterwards

MANHATTAN ENGINE NO. 8.

deputy sheriff, Samuel Betts, John Boyle, Jesse Chase, Robert C. Brown, John C.
Hooper, Charles Nicolls and George T. Patterson, who remained until the disbandment of the Fire Department. Of this company, Jacob Smith served as
assistant engineer from 1803 to 1808; Edward Arrowsmith from 1825 to 1830;
Richard Kelly from 1851 to 1853; and Joseph G. Ruch from 1856 to 1862.

At a fire in Florentine's undertaking establishment on Mulberry Street this
company took the water of Twenty Engine, who took suction from the gas
house cistern and was washed. The chief engineer sent the company's engine
to the corporation yard on June 21, 1824, because the members permitted boys
in the regular uniform to run with them, contrary to law. The company made
an excursion to Washington at the inauguration of President Pierce in March,
1853, and received quite an ovation from the citizens of that city. They were
the first to run a steam engine, of which Edgar Laing was the engineer. This
steamer the company owned themselves, and encountered much opposition
from the other companies in the Department. They had a track of flag-stones
built from their house in Ludlow Street to Grand Street, where they could
strike the Belgian pavement.

At a fire in Rivington Street, June 10, 1859, the new steamer, under the management of this company, was given its first test in actual service. In seven minutes she had steam up and was ready to play. There was some little difficulty in supplying the engine with water, but when this was remedied she rendered great assistance, and, by the steady streams directed against the

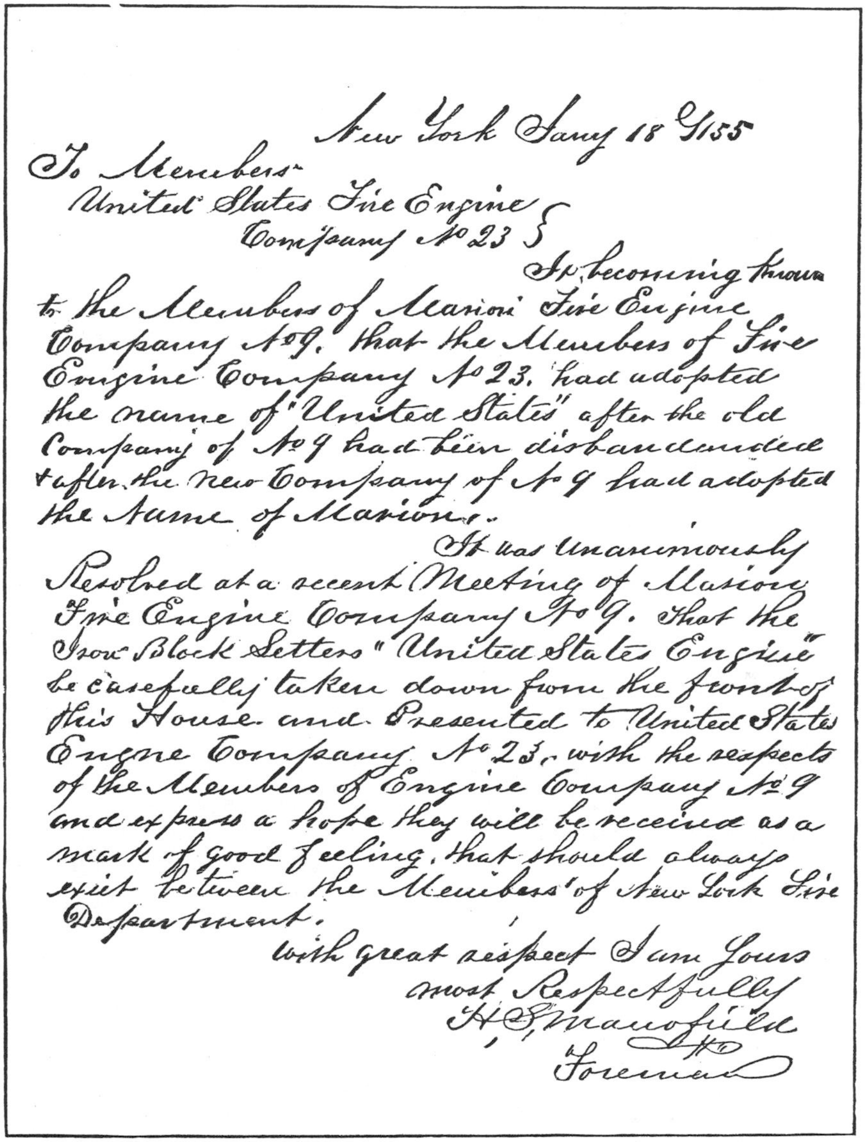

New York Jany 18 1855

To Members—
United States Fire Engine
Company No 23

It becoming known to the Members of Marion Fire Engine Company No 9. that the Members of Fire Engine Company No 23. had adopted the name of "United States" after the old Company of No 9 had been disbanded and after the new Company of No 9 had adopted the Name of Marion.—

It was unanimously Resolved at a recent Meeting of Marion Fire Engine Company No 9. That the Iron Block Letters "United States Engine" be carefully taken down from the front of this House. and Presented to United States Engine Company No 23, with the respects of the Members of Engine Company No 9 and express a hope they will be received as a mark of good feeling, that should always exist between the Members of New York Fire Department.

With great respect I am Yours
most Respectfully
H. J. Mansfield
Foreman

MARION ENGINE COMPANY NO. 9 TO ENGINE COMPANY NO. 23.

buildings, prevented the flames from spreading to the cabinet shop, 105 Norfolk Street, thus checking what threatened to be a vast conflagration.

Mr. Wm. P. Allen, now chief clerk to the chief engineer, Charles O. Shay, was badly crushed by a collision between their large steamer and a wagon, August 11, 1864, on the Bowery, near Pell Street. He had the tongue at the time, and was thought to be fatally injured, but after four months of suffering was able to leave the house, although he did not recover his strength for over a year.

No. 9.—BOLIVAR.—Engine No. 9 was the first additional company organized after the evacuation of the city by the British. The whole Department was, in 1783, reorganized, five additional engine companies being established, making thirteen engine companies, all told, and two hook and ladder trucks. Among No. 9's early members were Theophilus Beekman, alderman of Montgomerie Ward, Wm. T. Ellsworth, and Samuel Johnson, both assistant aldermen. They were located in the Swamp, in Leisler Street. John Clark was foreman from 1793 to 1796, when the company was located in Whitehall Street, near the Government House. From 1832 to 1834 the engine lay in Beaver Street, near Broad Street. In 1830 there was some dissatisfaction in the company, and the following members tendered their resignations on September 6:

Caleb F. Lindsly, foreman; E. B. Hart, Ichabod Williams, Archibald Reed, John D. Smith, Samuel Riddell, A. W. Hardee, George Robertson, Wm. Dobson, Edward Watson, Wm. Webber, Isaac H. Cogswell, George Dawson, Joseph R. Young.

The company was disbanded on March 1, 1843.

FIFTEENTH WARD was organized on October 27, 1840, and was located in Mercer Street, near Bleecker Street. In 1841 it ran a hose cart, and on June 22, 1842, was organized as Hose Company No. 35.

DOLPHIN.—Organized February 1, 1843, at Forty-eighth Street and Eighth Avenue; changed to Engine Company No. 1 on December 26, 1846.

UNITED STATES MARION (Rock) was organized under peculiar circumstances. The first attempt at organization was an effort on the part of certain members, a majority of Hose Company No. 9, to change their title to Engine Company No. 9, which failed from the continued efforts of a few members who were unwilling to give up the Hose Company. Thereupon, the majority succeeded on the fourteenth of August, 1849, in obtaining a separate organization under the title of United States Engine Company No. 9, and located at 47 Marion Street, near Prince, in old Third Engine House, leaving but five or six men in possession of the hose house and carriage. A very bitter feeling existed for a considerable time between the members of the two companies, which extended itself to those who afterwards joined either of them. The first officers of the company were Daniel W. Talcot, foreman, and John W. Morris assistant. They performed duty in all but the uptown (first and second) districts. Being located in a populous portion of the city, and in the same house formerly occupied by Engine Company No. 3, they soon had a great number of runners, who, under the title of "Rock Boys," kept the company in a continual excitement. At nearly every fire the runners would get the company into some difficulty, and one evening the company was twice attacked by the "Bowery Boys," most of whom were the runners of Hose Company No. 14. Mr. Talcot resinging his foremanship April 12, 1852, Charles F. Myers was elected in his stead, and Rudolph E. Abbey elected assistant in place of Archy McNaughton, also resigned. Mr. Myers had served some time in Engine Company No. 48, and was considered a good officer. Ex-Chief Carson had great influence with the company, and induced them to accept one of his patent engines. After some years of hard work and the expenditure of a large amount of money, besides the two thousand eight hundred dollars of their original estimate, the engine was completed and became the wonder of the Department, but not from her extraordinary performance as a fire engine. The wonder was how such an enormous weight could be compressed in so small a compass, and how any body of men could drag her through the streets. After a short service and the expenditure of a great deal of money in continual repairs and alterations, she was laid aside in the corporation yard and afterwards sold for old iron. While the engine was building, the company, being unable to keep away their "help," were in continuous quarrels.

The foreman, Charles Myers, resigned in February, 1854, and James R. Tate was elected in his place. Mr. Tate's foremanship lasted but a few months as Mr. R. E. Abbey was elected at the next May meeting. The new foreman had a stormy time of it. The company was incessantly in trouble, which only ended in December, 1854, by their disbandment, a number of the members being expelled at the same time.

Harry Mansfield, a fine fellow and excellent officer, who came from Hose

HARRY MANSFIELD.

Company No. 9, then took charge of the disbanded crowd, and by strenuous exertions and pledges that a different state of affairs should exist if they were again permitted to do duty, the company was reorganized as Marion Engine Company No. 9. The list of members was quite small at the beginning, and they did duty with a hose carriage. It was after this organization that the mammoth engine was first brought into use, and with this terrible load to start with they again went to work. They elected Harry Mansfield foreman and James McCully assistant foreman. After serving about a year, Mr. Mansfield resigned on account of ill health, and the assistant was promoted. In May, 1855, Patrick Cunningham was elected foreman. In 1856 William Gorman was chosen foreman at the annual election and served until February, 1857, when he was superseded by James A. Duncan. On May 12, 1857, Mr. James Hayes was elected foreman, and from that time until the Department was disbanded the fortunes of the company seemed to change, their roll of members increased until it was seldom that there was a vacancy, and they became one of the quickest and hardest working companies in their district. In 1859 they received a new first-class Shanghai style of engine, and in 1861 did duty from a temporary location, No. 52 Marion Street, while their new house was building at No. 47 Marion Street. They now had members enough of their own, and being independent of any "help" they kept free from any trouble or entangling alliances with any other company. In 1862 this company procured a steam engine with which they did duty until mustered out. Mr. James Hayes continued to be the foreman of the company until the end, serving as such for nearly eight years and having nine different assistant foremen under him. During his foremanship he was elected a councilman, supervisor, and assemblyman from the city.

At the Cable Celebration 9 Engine had made up their mind not to parade, as they said they had no suitable engine. Chief Howard, however, overcame their scruples, and gave them the right of the line and placed them in charge of the banner.

At the parade for the Prince of Wales it was the only company that did not parade, although all the members were bred and born in the Fourteenth Ward.

No. 10.—NIAGARA.—This was one of five companies organized about 1783 and until 1796 stationed at the top of Catharine Street, Chatham Square. The leader was Benjamin Blagge. In 1793 Robert Furman was foreman, in 1796 Leonard Fisher. In 1804 the engine was in Centre Street; in 1813 at the Bowery and Great Jones Street; from 1832 to 1834 at Fifth Street and Second Avenue; was disbanded on February 4, 1836. Among its earlier members were the following—all mechanics:

Moses C. Palmer (1820); Daniel H. Covert (1822); Daniel Horton (1822); Jacob M. Luff (1825); Stephen Jobs (1825); (Peter Brown (1826); Thomas Lawrence (1826); Joseph Applebee (1826); Robert Patterson (1827); Daniel Morton (1828); Samuel B. Good (1829); William A. Good (1829); Thomas Good (1829); George S. Kip (1830).

Niagara ran an old style New York engine built in 1824.

WATER WITCH was organized on January 4, 1837, and was located at 6 Third Street. Disbanded March 1, 1843.

WATER WITCH (Wren), organized March 24, 1843. Located Ninth Avenue and Twenty-sixth Street, and later in Twenty-seventh Street, west of Ninth Avenue. Kipp & Brown, stage proprietors, famous in their day, were members when the company was in West Twenty-seventh Street. Disbanded, August 7, 1855.

UNITED WATER WITCH—The last engine company with the number "Ten," was organized in Yorkville, September 28, 1855, and located in Eighty-second Street, between Third and Fourth Avenues. Their first officers were John H. Hoffman, foreman; A. O. Alcock, assistant; Cyrus T. Frost, secretary, and George J. Gregory, treasurer. They first ran a double-end brake engine, built for them by the Burnhams of Yorkville. The name of the company was changed the following year to Water Witch, and in that year John Warne was made foreman and Thomas E. Dey assistant. Warne was re-elected the two succeeding years, Wm. Banham, Jr., becoming assistant in 1859, in which year the company discarded their first engine as being too heavy, and took charge of a new piano engine just finished for them by Van Ness. At the next election of the company John R. Higbie was chosen foreman, with William Hay as assistant and William J. Kelly, whom many may remember as the famous catcher on the base-ball nine of the Yorkville "Champion" Club. Secretary Higbie was continued in office during the following year. When William Banham, Jr., was chosen foreman the company filled up rapidly, and applied for, and in 1864 obtained, a steam engine, which, after the reorganization, was transferred to the use of Engine Company No. 32 of the Metropolitan Fire Department. Banham was continued in the office of foreman until the disbanding of the company in 1865.

CHAPTER XXXIV.

MORE ABOUT THE ENGINE COMPANIES.

Their History and Exploits.—Fire Experiences in Company Quarters.—The Brave Days of Old.—Famous Fire Commandants.—Organization and Development of Companies.—Recalling many Interesting Episodes.—Scenes and Incidents in the Life of a Volunteer Fireman.

N0. 11.—OCEANUS.—The original records of this company are now in the possession of ex-Assistant Engineer A. B. Purdy. The company was organized on December 28, 1780, and located in Hanover Square (dock ward) with the following members : Daniel Ten Eyck foreman, Thomas Barrow assistant, Charles Phillips, Evert Wessels, Jacobus Quick, Benj. Mc-Dowl, Andrew Meyer, Adam Keyser, Wm. Meyer, Emanuel Rhinedollar, John Haskin, Abraham Ten Eyck, Jr., Samuel Wessels, Wm. Hazelton, Barrant Evers, James Moore, John Townsend, Jacob Moore, Dennis Coyl, Israel Bedell, Benj. Shepherd, Wm. Brown, Augustus Sidell, Samuel Clap, and Joseph George.

ENGINE NO. 11 (GOOSENECK).

At a meeting on November 9, 1784, at Doughty's tavern Haskin and Moore were struck off the list for non-attendance at washings, Bedell and Clap because they had moved out of the city, and Moses Smith, John Murray, Jas. McCullen and John Devine, were appointed in their places. The fines that were collected and the new members' entrance money were handed over to mine host to pay for the "supper and liquors." No. 11 seems to have been a jolly and sociable company. On November 8, 1787, we find them paying to a tavern keeper £7 18s. for "supper and liquors," for which Nicholas Van Antwerp receipted. In November, 1789, Evert Wessels was elected foreman and James Moore assistant, and on that occasion £10 6s. was paid "for supper and liquors." The company had a "moderator" to preside over its meetings, as we find Josoph Corré named in that capacity. The members solemnly signed their names on the book pledging themselves to conform to his rules. The following quaint extract will give an idea of the business :

That upon first call of silence by the Moderator the person refusing to keep silence shall pay one shilling, and upon second call of silence by the Moderator the person refusing to keep silence shall be fined two shillings, or be expelled the company if the majority shall so determine.

In 1798 a penalty of eight shillings was ordered to be paid by every member who did not provide himself with a fire cap within a month.

In 1811 it was resolved that the initiation fee be $10. The by-laws were ordered to be printed, the bill being $8. On November 1, 1813, it was resolved " that the company accept of twelve young lads as volunteers, and that the company furnish them with suitable hats. A committee of three, consisting of Wm. Brown, Andrew Murray and James Dunham, were appointed to carry the same into effect."

In 1816 the Corporation wanted to remove the company from Old Slip to Marketfield Street, and strong objections were made by the members and by the residents who petitioned the Common Council to suffer them to remain. The engine house had been begun by the Corporation, but was finished at the expense of the company. The following is a list of the members on November 6, 1818:

Abraham Van Nest, merchant; Andrew Murray, merchant; Robert L. Golby, hairdresser; Hugh McGinnis, cooper; Matthew Sharp, merchant; Benj. M. Brown, merchant; Francis T. Luqueer, saddler; Richard Duryea, Jr., merchant; Wm. P. Harris, merchant; States M. Mead, · cabinet maker; Isaac C. Holmes, merchant; John Watts, merchant; Wm. W. Lowere, carpenter; Horace S. Belden, merchant; John Miller, merchant; Charles Gregory, merchant; Hugh Munroe, merchant; Phineas B. Carman, accountant; Thomas B. Goelet, accountant; John D. Brown, chair maker; Charles Rosencrants, saddler; Peter Winants, block maker; John Van Nest, accountant; Daniel M. Lord, accountant; James Bloomer, merchant.

About 1835 the company removed to 118 Wooster Street, adjoining station house, and after 1854 was located at 99 Wooster Street. It went out of service in 1865. Abraham B. Purdy joined in April, 1826, and for many years was foreman. James Gulick was also one of its foremen, and was appointed assistant engineer from the company in 1824. Nicholas Van Antwerp was appointed assistant engineer from 1800 to 1818. Other prominent members at various times were as follows:

States M. Mead, 1820, Joseph Jamison, 1820, Hugh W. Harrol, 1825, Benjamin G. Miller, 1825, Frederick Hadley, 1826, John McCrea, 1826, Aaron Hallock, 1827, Laurence Vreeland, 1827, Charles Stewart, 1827, Abraham Van Duser, 1828, Samuel Turner, 1828, Jonas Colon, 1828, John McDougall, 1829, William McCrea, 1829, James P. Thompson, 1830, Henry R. Secor, 1830, Daniel Kerrigan, 1831. Christopher Johnson was the last foreman of the company.

This company was the first that had a carved back, the work being executed by John F. Miller.

No. 12.—KNICKERBOCKER ("Old Nick").—TRADESMAN'S—KNICKERBOCKER. —This company dates back its organization before 1783. In 1796 it is recorded as being located at the junction of Cherry and Pearl Streets, now called Franklin Square, with Daniel Hitchcock as foreman and James Prankland, Jr., as assistant. James Hopson, a foreman, subsequently became president of the Department. In 1832 they removed to Rose Street, and in 1841 to William Street near Duane. Alfred Carson was appointed an assistant engineer in this year from the foremanship of this company. During the Gulick excitement the company, like many others, withdrew from duty, but on the appointment of

Chief C. V. Anderson they resumed duty, taking the engine formerly used by Engine Company 25 and painting the number 12 on her sides. The first fire they ran to was in Greenwich Street, and when they returned to the house they called the roll on the panel of a door, not having any books ready. At the House of Refuge fire in 1838 they took suction from a mud pond called the "Sunfish Pond," about opposite where the Fifth Avenue Hotel now stands, or perhaps a little more to the east, and played into 33 Engine, washing her on that occasion, 33's folks claiming that the mud from the pond choked the engine. About the latter part of 1843 the company were disbanded, and reorganized on February 22d, 1844 (under the name of

FIREMAN'S CERTIFICATE, 1787.

"Tradesman's"), by some of the members of the old company and members of 37 Engine who had also been disbanded; among them were John Gildersleeve, William Drew, George Harsen and John W. Garside. Harsen was elected foreman, and they located at 74 Delancey Street, in the house formerly used by 37 Engine Company. They succeeded in obtaining the engine used by the old company, No. 12, which was painted green and yellow, with the numerals "XII" on the leader jacket, carved dolphins on the sides and a picture of Knickerbocker smoking his pipe on the back. John Gildersleeve followed Harsen as foreman. During the great fire of 1845 they took suction from the fountain at Bowling Green and played on the cotton in Marketfield

Street all next day. John W. Farmer, the Tenth ward philanthropist, was a member of this company at that time; he afterwards joined Manhattan Engine Company No. 8. Farmer opened a soup house on the west side of Ludlow Street, near Broome Street, where for many winters he furnished the poor of the ward with meals gratis. John W. Garside was the third and last foreman, the company being disbanded April 29, 1847.

A new company was formed under the number of 12 on the twenty-eighth day of the same year and took up their location in Fiftieth Street, near Lexington Avenue, adopting the name of Knickerbocker and doing duty with a little old gooseneck engine built in 1824. Wm. B. Rockwell and James W. Lawrence were among the early foremen of the company. In 1855 they elected Jacob W. Cooper as foreman and obtained a new style piano engine, removing to Fortieth Street, near Third Avenue. James O'Brien, afterwards sheriff, the Biglan Brothers—Bernard, James H. and John A.—with Bernard O'Neil, afterwards alderman, and Dennis Leary were members of the company about that time. Thomas J. Coutant followed Cooper as foreman and held the office for several terms. When 6 Engine Company got their steamer the members of 12 obtained the double deck engine belonging to that company, which they ran for a while. In 1859 they removed to 112 East Thirty-Third Street, near Third Avenue. In 1864 they received from the hands of James Smith, the builder, a new steam engine, Bartley Donohoe being the foreman. There was a great deal of rivalry between 12 and 28 Engine Companies, mostly on account of the political enmity between James O'Brien and Richard Croker, the engineer of 28.

No. 28 afterwards ran an old white piano hand engine, which was known as the "Arsenal," as it was supposed to be filled with revolvers. The Department being disbanded shortly afterwards, 28 were deprived of a chance to "get square." Bartley Donohoe was elected an assistant engineer in 1865, and Dennis Leary succeeded him as the last foreman of the company.

No. 13.—EAGLE.—This company was in existence at the time of the reorganization of the New York Fire Department in 1783. In 1790 she lay in Maiden Lane and was called "Continental Eagle Fire Engine Company No. 13." Wm. Bockay was the foreman at that time, and the company meetings were held at Jacob Brower's tavern in Nassau Street. In 1791 James J. Beekman was elected foreman, followed in 1797 by James Woodhull. At that time they changed their place of meeting to Crook's tavern. About this time they removed to a location near the "Ferry Stairs Fish Market," which is the Burling Slip of to-day. Benjamin Strong became foreman in 1798, and served as such until 1812, having for his assistants Wm. Allen, Thomas Stevenson, and David I. Hubbs. Strong was made an assistant engineer in 1812, serving until 1821, making twenty-three years of continuous service as an officer in the Fire Department. He was also treasurer of the Fire Department Fund in 1811 and 1812, and the report for those years showed twelve thousand one hundred and forty-eight dollars and three cents on hand. David I. Hubbs succeeded him as foreman in 1812, becoming an assistant engineer in 1815 and serving until 1824. Then came Valentine Vandewater, who served as foreman of the company from 1815 until December 10, 1822, when he, too, was appointed an assistant engineer, which office he held for two years. Samuel G. Smith was elected foreman in 1822, and followed by David T. Williams, who was an assistant engineer from 1832 to 1835. "In 1830," writes Mr. Zophar Mills, "the company was mostly Quakers of the highest respectability. They were generally merchants and merchants' clerks. They had their new engine—the first one in this city that was silver-plated, and probably the only one in this country whose brass work was silver-plated. The engine was painted black, gold striped, highly polished, and the back had Jupiter hurling thunderbolts painted on it in the best style of art. She was the most elegant engine ever seen in those days, and all this expense of decoration was paid for by the

A GROUP OF OLD FIREMEN.

| John Dennis. | Thomas Carlton. | James Burns. | W. Morenius. |
| Thomas McGuire. | | James McLoan. | Patrick McMahon. |

company and their friends. Mr. William L. Jenkins, late president of the Bank of America, and Mr. John S. Williams, late of the firm of Williams & Guion, were members of 13 Engine Company in those days. This engine did very important work at the great fire of 1835." On October 19, 1832, after an alarm of fire at the corner of Pearl and Elm Streets, Zophar Mills was proposed by R. S. Underhill and unanimously elected a member of this company. Wm. M. Haydock was the foreman in 1832, and Wm. S. Moore in 1834. Zophar Mills was elected foreman November 11, 1835, serving until July 11, 1838, when he was appointed an assistant engineer, which office he held until 1842, Henry S. Fleury succeeding him as foreman in 1838, and Wm. Williamson succeeded the latter in 1840. In 1817 the company moved their quarters to the Firemen's Hall in Fulton Street, and held their meetings in the engine house.

In 1830 the company was at 3 Dover Street, from 1857 to 1864 at 5 Duane Street, in 1864 at 261 William Street. Disbanded in 1865.

No. 14.—COLUMBIAN.—This company, which was undoubtedly one of the most efficient and best organized companies in the old Fire Department, was in existence before 1783, for in that year it was represented by its foreman, Benjamin Birdsall, in the report made by the officers of the Department to Governor George Clinton. They afterwards were located on the corner of Church and Vesey Streets, on the grounds of St. Paul's Church. When Engine Company 39 was organized in 1812, that company was also stationed on the church grounds, but on the corner of Partition, now Fulton Street. Later on the church wanted 39's location, and in 1825 built a double house on 14's location, which was used by both companies, 39 lying nearest Broadway, and after they were moved up to Doyers Street the church built 14 a house in Church Street, a little south of the corner of Vesey Street, the upper portion of which was used by the church as mission rooms.

Abraham Brouwer was one of the earliest foremen of this company, and John P. Roome was another. Roome was appointed an assistant engineer in 1808, serving until 1824. Ezra Dennison and Jacob Anthony, who followed Benjamin Haight as foreman, joined the company about this time, and Charles H. Haswell, who afterwards organized Engine Company 16 up-town, was one of the volunteers, and was in the procession in honor of General Lafayette, September 9, 1824. Owen W. Brennan carried one of the torches in the procession. Samuel Y. Coles and James H. McKenzie joined the company in 1825, and William Wallace and Conklin Titus, afterwards bell-ringer at the City Hall, joined in 1826. When Titus was bell-ringer at the Hall, "Bill" Demilt, one of 14's members, climbed up the lightning rod one evening to ask him over to Harry Venn's place, at No. 13 Ann Street, to have a drink. The boys had bet that he would not come down. Titus came down, however, and not by the lightning rod either, and took his favorite "gin and sugar" without winking. Titus afterwards kept the place at 13 Ann Street, when Harry Venn went up to the "Gotham," and afterwards moved around in Nassau Street.

In 1827 and '28 Andrew and Thomas Wallace, John Colgate, James Pine, Andrew Mount, and William L. Cisco, who is classed as a "news collector," became connected with the company, and in 1829 Samuel R. Mabbett, the west side coal merchant, and assistant alderman in 1853, joined with Henry T. Gratacap and James A. Chapple. Gratacap will be remembered as the famous fire-cap manufacturer, so long located in Grand Street, near Elm. When Ebenezer Silleck was elected foreman of Engine Company 14, Mr. Gratacap made for him the first "stitched front" made in this city. He afterwards made the first "raised letter" fronts used by the firemen, and continued in the business for many years. John L. Mills joined the company in 1830 with Benjamin G. Roe; and Theo. Mercer, and Peter M. Ottignon, and Richard H. Wentworth the following year; Cyprian L. Taillant, James Y. Watkins, and Theodore Keeler were also members of the company a little later on. When Engine Company 16 was disbanded at the Corporation Yard in Leonard Street, in 1833, 14 applied for and got the new engine that had just been built for them. This engine was run by the company until they got their double-decker in 1847. Captain James Lines and Joseph Venn, a volunteer of 14, and brother to Harry Venn, left this city on an expedition about the year 1840, and were supposed to have been shipwrecked, as they were never heard from afterwards.

In 1834, the company, to enable them to compete with rival fire engines, who were their chief opponents, hired rooms in Vesey Street for one of their members, a printer, named Tyrrell, and established a bunk room there. The company in the '40's made several excursions to Philadelphia, Baltimore, and Washington. On one of these excursions, under Harry Venn, in 1844, while in Philadelphia under escort of the Neptune Hose Company, the company got a little behind in the line, and while running to regain their place one of their members, James A. Chapple, fell, and was run over by their engine. From their frequent trips to the South, as well as from their numbers and high reputation, 14 usually had the honor of receiving the companies from that section, among others the celebrated Mechanical Engine Company, of Baltimore, who visited this city in 1853.

Alfred Chancellor, now and for many years past the master baker on Blackwell's Island, served thirteen years with this company as a member, joining in 1839, having been for a long time on the Volunteer roll. James W. Packer, foreman, and Andrew D. Purtell, assistant, were the last officers of the company. Purtell had been foreman of the company in 1860, and at the breaking out of the war commanded a company in Ellsworth's Fire Zouaves. In 1863 the vestry of St. Paul's Church wished to use the building occupied by the company, and they had to vacate their quarters. They were out of  service for two years, and just before the disbandment of the Department were furnished with a new house in Fulton Street, opposite Church Street. The paid system having been adopted, the company did not have a chance to become very well acquainted with their new location.

No. 15.—PETERSON (Old Maid)—WREATH OF ROSES.—The first Engine Company No. 15 was one of the typical companies of the old New York Fire Department. It was organized about 1785. The first record of her location is in 1796, when the company was known as "Wreath of Roses," and "lay" in Nassau Street opposite Federal Hall. They ran an old square box engine with a wreath painted on the back. In 1813 they removed to Chatham Square, and adopted the name of "Peterson," in honor of William Peterson, her foreman, who died from over exertion and injuries received at the great fire May, 19, 1811. This fire commenced on the northwest corner of Duane and Chatham Streets, and destroyed a large number of houses. Foreman Peterson expired in a few hours after being conveyed to his home, and was the first foreman in New York who lost his life in discharge of his duties. His name was revered by the members of 15 Engine Company during its existence, being handed down from member to member as a priceless heirloom, and on the back of their engine and on their banners the name and protrait of Peterson were the most prominent features. In 1830 they removed to No. 49 Christie Street, where they continued until disbanded

September 27, 1849. When in its prime this company had one of the largest volunteer rolls of any company in the Department. These volunteers were composed of young men who stood ready to become full-fledged members whenever a vacancy occurred on the regular roll, and most of them in after years did become members. At one time they were divided into two parties, the " Fly-by-nights " being headed by Joe Johnson and the " Bloods " by Nick Wilson. Among these volunteers were Sam Skinner, John McCleester, Country McCluskey, Sam Banta, who afterwards went to California with Yankee Sullivan, but who, unlike Yankee, returned to New York; Bill Ford, Ed. Sprague and others. Old Jim Kent says that at that time "they could lick any other fire company in New York." They were often called the Dock Rats, from their habit of making for the river to get their water first, and any engine who took their water was very liable to get washed. They claim to have "washed" more engines than any other company, and earned the name of "Old Maid" on account of never having been "washed" themselves. They always ran a gooseneck engine, and the last one of that style they ran was built by Harry Ludlam and was a very powerful engine for those days. They took her to Philadelphia under Nathaniel Bradford as foreman and Charles Colliday as assistant, on September 12, 1836, and participated in a playing match. They were the only company who succeeded in playing over the cupola of the Exchange building. Nathaniel Bradford, William Freeland, William Ford, N. F. Wilson, and John J. Tindale were members, who afterwards became foremen, and Wilson was elected assistant engineer in 1846. Harry Howard left this company to join Hose 14, which then lay in Elizabeth street back of the Bowery Theater. The Chanfraus—Peter, Henry, Joseph and Frank—the latter being the original "Mose" in "A Glance at New York," were also members, together with George R. Nicholl, afterward of 19 Engine and one of the organizers of Adriatic Engine Company 31, and Mart Cregier, the hard hitter. Four target companies were the outgrowth of this engine company, namely, the Peterson Blues, the Peterson Guards, the Freeland Guards, and the Wilson Guards, the latter being in two companies and under command of John J. Tindale. The Peterson Guards one year went to West Point under command of Col. William W. Tompkins, United States Army. The Pickwick Club was also organized from this company. They gave their first ball at Columbian Hall, in Grand Street between Allen and Eldridge Streets, and afterwards for many years at the Apollo Rooms. The members dressed in the costume of the club, the following being some of the most prominent characters: Mr. Pickwick, Elijah F. Purdy; Nathaniel Winkle, Joseph H. Johnson; Augustus Snodgrass, N. F. Wilson; Sam Weller, Martin Cregier; Fat Boy, William Work; Tony Weller, John Carland; Tracy Tupman, John Woods; Dr. Slammer, A. J. Fisher; Gardener, Joseph Chanfrau. They were a great success while they lasted, and invitations to their balls were eagerly sought for.

St. Stephen's Church, corner of Broome and Christie Streets, was a favorite place for the members of 15 to exercise their engine, after which they would adjourn to Toby Hoffman's, corner of Bayard and Bowery, or Pete Asten's, corner Hester and Bowery, for refreshments. The tavern of Peter Asten was one of the landmarks of old New York. He established it in 1826, when Hester Street was lined on both sides with poplar trees, and kept it as a hotel for fifty years. In 1848 the company, in violation of orders, took part in a political procession, and in 1849 was disbanded, principally on that account. Ben Baker, now treasurer of the Actors' Fund, and the author of "A Glance at New York," was a volunteer of old 15; he used to sleep curled up on the floor under the tongue and carry the signal, and many a time did he get whipped on reaching home for having oil on the back of his clothes, where it had dripped from the lamp.

After 1830 the company was located at 49 Christie Street; disbanded September 27, 1849; reorganized March 3, 1852; disbanded again on July 11, 1855.

CHATHAM—HIBERNIA.—Organized October 9, 1855; located temporarily in Ninth Avenue near Thirty-seventh Street, later in Thirty-sixth Street between Ninth and Tenth Avenues; disbanded in 1865.

No. 16.—ÆTNA—(Hounds)—CHELSEA — CROTON (Cit) — GOTHAM—MOHAWK.—Engine Company No. 16 (organized on April 19, 1786). John B. Dash, Jr., foreman; William Parker, Francis Child, John Peter Ritter, Daniel Boivie, Peter Ritter, Thomas Lawrence, Walter Frazer, Benjamin Haight, and Charles Stewart. She was located in Liberty Street in the rear of the old Dutch Church, which was afterwards used as the Post-Office; the same location was afterwards used by City Hose Company No. 8. John B. Dash, Jr., was elected an assistant engineer in 1803, serving until 1815. Their first new engine was built for them in 1806, and on the back of this they had painted a representation of Mount Ætna, the company having adopted the name of " Ætna Fire

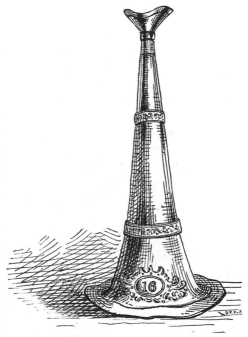

TRUMPET PRESENTED TO JOHN P. TEALE.

Engine Company." Among the other old members of the company appear the names of John W. Degrauw, William C. Titus, John Cobby, Joseph B. Bradshaw, Leonard L. Johnson, Henry B. Greenwood, Oliver Osborne, Edward F. Randolph, Samuel C. Titus, Henry McCaul, Andrew S. Titus, John W. Betts, Jared Williams, Thomas Halliday, Samuel Cox, David Theall— "Uncle David"—who, when he joined the company in 1830, was a grocer in Broome Street; Benjamin R. and John Guest. In 1832 the company moved to the Corporation Yard in Leonard Street. They did not prosper; they got a new engine at that time, but did not have it long enough to run it, and threw up the organization the following year.

In the early part of the next year, or to be more particular, on February 5, 1834, the company was reorganized as Chelsea Engine Company No. 16 by Chas. H. Haswell, who was the first foreman, and others, as a "silk stocking" company and located on Twenty-first Street just below Eighth Avenue in a little frame building. During the Gulick troubles this company, like many others, sent their engine to the Corporation Yard, and when matters were made serene for the firemen, the company reorganized as Croton Engine Company No. 16, with John P. Teale as foreman, George Styles, from 23 Engine, as assistant; Jacob Reise, Philip Ecker and James McCully; taking the old house as their location. They afterwards enrolled a number of 34 Engine men, among whom was Depeyster (Spice) Hopper, whom they elected foreman. They soon got in trouble, however, and were disbanded on May 6, 1841.

On May 10, 1842, the company was reorganized, the location having been for some time at 152 West Twentieth Street in a house built for them, and again commenced doing duty. They were more fortunate this time, and were free from any serious trouble for ten years. Moses Jackson was the foreman for several years, being elected an assistant engineer in 1851. Stephen Mitchell succeeded him in the foremanship. About this time the company got into hot water again, several companies, among whom were 34, 24, and 46 Engines being bitter rivals. On one occasion some of 16's members visited the house of 46 Engine Company and borrowed their engine for a little run. They got her to Bond Street, where the engine was broken. The authorities, thinking that 16 had carried the joke too far (from Twenty-fifth Street to Bond Street), disbanded the company on September 18, 1852.

On October 20, 1852, the company was again organized. This time under Mark R. Thomas as foreman and James Gregory as assistant, taking the location 165 West Twentieth Street. They did not run quite two years, for they ran foul of their old rivals, 46 Engine, and were again disbanded June 13, 1854, this time for good, as the next 26 Engine Company was organized September 29, 1854, in the lower districts, being first located at 126 West Broadway under the name of Gotham. Edward Beadle was the foreman, and Corra Osborne assistant. Thomas Flender, an old fireman and afterwards fire commissioner, was one of the organizers, as were Thomas Roe, David Decker, and Silas G. Butler. In 1857 the company elected Thomas Roe foreman, changed the name of the company to Mohawk and bought a new engine, which was placed on exhibition at the Crystal Palace and destroyed by the burning of that building October 5, 1858.

Anthony Carracciolo, one of the members of this company, was killed May 8, 1855, by being crushed between the front wheel of the engine and a heavy cart. Thomas Roe was elected an assistant engineer in 1860, and John J. Glass was elected as foreman to succeed him, and the company moved to their new house at 7 North Moore Street, receiving at the same time a new first-class double deck, Jeffers engine. The company was then placed in charge of the piano engine formerly used by Engine Company No. 2, and afterwards the engine which 13 had been running. Edward Byrnes (brother of Inspector Thomas Byrnes) was elected foreman in 1860. He went to the war in 1861, as captain of Company A of Ellsworth Zouaves. He was succeeded in the foremanship by Henry Webb, who took the engine to Fortress Monroe. Then came Walter J. Young, Jr., who held the office of foreman for several terms, being the last foreman of the company.

Sixteen members of this company enlisted during the war of the rebellion, John J. Glass, ex-foreman, a lieutenant in the Second Fire Zouaves, being killed at the battle of Williamsburg, Va., and Andrew Nesbit, Jr., being killed at the naval fight at Hampton Roads, he being at the time an engineer on the gunboat "*Whitehall.*" His remains were brought to this city and buried with honors by the Fire Department.

The company went out of service in 1865.

No. 17.—SCOTT-MUTUAL.—Archibald Kerley, in behalf of himself and neighbors residing in Cherry Street, petitioned the Common Council in December, 1787, setting forth that they had purchased a fire engine which they were willing to appropriate to the public use, and to erect a house and furnish a piece of ground therefor, and praying the Board to accept their propositions and appoint a proper number of men to take charge of the same. The petition was granted, and the engineer directed to report the names of ten men in accordance with the petition. At the meeting held on January 12, 1788, the engineer presented the following names to comprise the new company : Archibald Kerley, Theophilus Beekman, Peter Bogert, Peter R. Kissam, John Collet, Samuel Ackerly, Andrew Morris, William Fosbrook, Francis Jans and Robert Gosman.

EAST RIVER was organized February 13, 1852, located at 38 Mangin Street, and after 1858 at 7 Goerck Street. Went out of service 1865. The company was organized through the efforts of Wm. P. McCormack, John Gunson, and C. H. Reynolds and several others, after a large fire which had occurred in the neighborhood. Carson was then chief engineer, and the company was known as an anti-Carson one. They did duty in the Sixth and Seventh Districts. Chief Carson being opposed to the company, he had them transferred to do duty in the Fifth and Sixth Districts, but, owing to the efforts of William P. McCormack, the Common Council passed a resolution causing them to do duty in the Sixth and Seventh Districts, thus obtaining a victory over Carson. The foremen were as follows, serving in the order named : William P. McCormack, John Gunson, Christopher H. Reynolds, Charles Doane, Patrick F. Russell, Joseph Sellick, Stewart Carson and Christopher H. Reynolds (his second term). Mr. Reynolds joined the New Department as foreman of Hook and Ladder 11, and in 1870 was made chief of the Second Battalion. After twenty years' service he was relieved from duty.

No. 18.—UNION (" Shad-Belly").—UNION (" DryBones ").—ATLANTIC.— Mr. N. Kelsey in 1787, in behalf of himself and his neighbors, made a proposal to build an engine house and to provide ground for it. The site was in Water Street, near Fulton, and the company so referred to is believed to have become No. 18. Be this as it may, the authentic records show that " Union " Engine Company No. 18 was organized on April 30, 1792, and was located in 1796 on the hill at John Street, near Pearl Street. Its first members were : Abraham Franklin, foreman ; William Bowne, assistant ; Nathaniel Hawxhurst, Thomas Demilt, Alexander Mowat, John Vernon, John Mowat, Jr., Ezek White, James Hawxhurst, Richard Seaman, Robert Wardel, Walter Bowne, Richard Hallett, George Fox, Peter Talman, Albert Ryckman, Isaac Sharpless, Daniel Hawxhurst, James Harvey, Orange Webb, Robert Mott, Alexander Masterson, Christopher Lot, and James Parsons, Jr. In 1813 its location was changed to No. 228 Water Street, and later to Fireman's Hall in Fulton Street. The company was disbanded in 1828, and the engine was sent to the Ninth Ward, and stored there in a stable in Cornelia Street, between Bleecker and Fourth Streets. On August 6, 1829, a company was organized, resuming the old name and number, namely " Union No. 18," and was located at the junction of Waverley Place and Christopher Street on the ground now occupied by the Northern Dispensary. While the company was down town it was nicknamed the "Shad-belly"; but upon the reorganization, this name was dropped, for the more suggestive one of "Dry Bones," in consonance with the boast of the members that their engine had thus far never been "washed."

In 1831 another change of base was made to No. 132 Amity Street, near Sixth Avenue, to a new house built for the company, where it remained until 1846, when it was again disbanded, on account of a difficulty with Hook and Ladder No. 3, on the same block, the members of which were "a split" from the original No. 18, and with whom it seemed to be difficult to establish friendly relations after the separation. About 1836 Henry Wilson was foreman, William McClelland, assistant, and among the members were Charles W. Cornell, Nelson D. Thayer, John Kettleman, Martin B. Wallace, William H. Wilson, William E. Noble, David J. Chatfield, and John Youmans.

Again the company was reorganized on March 2, 1852, under the name of "Atlantic" Engine Company No. 18, and was located at No. 421 East Tenth Street. For the third time it was disbanded on December 27, 1854.

Another reorganization, under the name of "Union," took place on September 3, 1856, and the location was at Thirty-eighth Street and Broadway. James Connelly was foreman. In 1859 the company removed to a house built for it at 78 West Fortieth Street, where she remained until the general mustering out of the Department in September, 1865.

The services rendered by this company during its last term of existence were of such a satisfactory nature as to almost obliterate the disagreeable experiences and unpleasant reminiscences of former days. Looking over the company's rolls, we find men among their members who were prominent in their day, and many of whom became leading citizens at later times. For instance: John R. Willis, Townsend Cox, Samuel Leggett, John L. Embree, Effingham L. Embree, and Cornelius W. Lawrence, Mr. Lawrence being the first mayor of New York elected by the people. Again in 1829 Samuel J. Gillespie, foreman, Sylvester H. Jones, Peter Westervelt and John Westervelt, Azel McCannon, and Jacob N. Bates.

The Harrington Guards emanated from this company in 1849.

No. 19.—LAFAYETTE.—Was organized on June 25, 1792, and was located in Hester Street near Bowery Lane. In 1813 she lay in First (Christie) Street; from 1823 to 1832 at Eldridge and Division Streets; in 1834 in Elizabeth Street near Grand, and after 1844 at 199 Christie Street. Among the first names on the roll in 1793 are those of James Bartine, George Brown, W. A. Hardenbrook, Smith Hicks, John Keyser, David Marsh, William Messerre, William Perrin, Cornelius Tier and Isaac Varian, Junior. At other times there were Thomas White, Zeno Weeks, 1793; John Whitehead, 1796; Simon Demarest, 1793; George T. Dominick, 1794; Thomas Johnson, 1796; John Pell, 1794; Joseph Owen Bogart, 1798; Albert Kennard, 1799; Robert Leaman, 1797; William D. Vermilyea, 1797; Jacob Freeman, 1800; Thomas Bashford, 1805; James Bowen, Josiah Cox, George Hyde, Jacob Lobb, Henry Lownsbury, John Ricard and William Ryan, 1800; Thomas Austin, 1807; John Enikis, 1806; Andrew Pessenger, resigned 1807; Oliver Hicks, 1807; Leonard Kline, resigned 1807; Charles Nash, Hyer Somerindyke, Richard VanVoorhis, Jacob

Weeks, 1807 ; Edmund Fisher, George Aaron Fritz, Michael Crawbuck, 1809 ; Elnathan Underhill, 1808 ; Thomas Winship, 1809; Dennis Croft, 1810; William Doughty, 1810 ; Thomas Holmes, 1811 ; Thomas Truslow, George Armpits, Abraham Fisher, Thomas Foster, George F. Harper, Joseph Hyde, James Reynolds, Jacob Van Pelt, 1812 ; and Henry Willett, 1812; William Matthews and Henry Pessenger, 1815.

On December 16, 1793, the company petitioned the Common Council for an increase of two members, on the ground that "from the remote situation of the said engine from the body of the city they find it difficult to transport the engine." The petition was granted.

In 1823 we find the company with twenty-six men on the roll. In later years there belonged to No. 19, Philip E. Heiser, broker, 1850 ; George R. Nicholl, attorney, 1850 ; Robert A. Coffin, who kept a hotel in Division Street in 1850 ; Isaac B. Ostrander, accountant, 1850 ; John B. Miller, merchant of 22 Stanton Street, 1852 ; Jesse Rodman, merchant of 59 Hester Street, 1852. The company was disbanded in 1865.

No. 20.—Washington.—This company was organized on June 25, 1792, and first located in Greenwich Street, at what used to be called the New Albany Pier. Among its first members were the following : Jacob Abrams, William Barton, Peter Black, Daniel Burges, John Dawson, John Ellsworth, Abraham Labagh, Mi-

HOSE CARRIAGE.
[Lost on Steamer "*Andalusia*," March, 1867. See page 189.]

chael Lavrere, William Post, Moses Roff, Thomas Smith, Isaac J. Stagg, Isaac Torboss, Paul Vandewater, Peter Van Houten, George Walgrave, Joseph Webb, Peter H. Wendover, Israel Wood, John Woodward, Nathaniel Woodward, George Smith, William Alburtis, Alexander Campbell, Abraham Rich, Henry Ridabock, Arthur Smith, Jacob Berry. Amaziah Dusenburg, John Evans, Benjamin Everston, Anthony Glean, Elias Hatfield. Also Edmund Livingston, Thomas Rich, Thomas Taylor, Joseph Thompson, Cornell Compton, David Covert, John Day, John Evans, Isaac Little, Geo. Lord, Geo. Smith, Paul Vandevoort, Gideon Tucker, John Van Norden, Tunis Van Winkle, Stephen Callow, John Disbrow, Nevington Greenard, Henry J. Kip, John J. Labagh, David Pullis, John Webb, Jacob Crigier, Louis Decker, Benjamin J. Hendrickson, Gilbert B. Mott, Luke Torboss, William J. Van Allen, Peter Aymar, Peter Ely, William Timpson, William Guest, William McKinney, Samuel Ward, Garrett Cosine, and Allen Frost, Thomas Chisholm, Jac. Cram, Reuben Knapp, Robert Gordon, Charles O'Neil, Samuel G. Pearsall and John M. Reed, Wm. Brown, Thomas Rose, Jacob Day, Thomas Joralemon, Richard Ryan, Robert Stewart, John Tallman, Henry

Banker, Peter Bushes, William Cooper, and Henry Buckle, William Torboss, William Bull, William Butler, William Blakely, James Durbrow, John Guest, Peter Aymar, Thomas Ronalds, Alex. Wiley, Thos. Hopper, Peter Wilson, Thos. Kidney, B. Sanford, Robert Wiley.

In 1813 the company was located "at the Albany Basin;" in 1832, at 126 Cedar Street; in 1846, at 3 Temple Street; after 1861, at 100 Cedar Street. The company was disbanded in 1865.

No. 21.—FULTON.—Fulton Engine Company No. 21 was organized in June 1795, and was first located on Burling Slip. After a short time it was removed to "Fireman's Hall" on Fulton Street, where Nos. 13, 18, and 24 were then housed. In 1802 Philip W. Engs joined the company, which held its meetings in what was known as "Crook's Tavern." In 1810 John Bedient was elected foreman and Brigham Howe assistant. In 1811 Mr. Bedient was re-elected, and J. H. Todd was elected assistant, and Philip W. Engs secretary. Among the members was William Colgate, the soap manufacturer. In this year the company was stationed at the North District meeting house in Duane street. In December, 1815, the location was changed to Duane Market, on the same

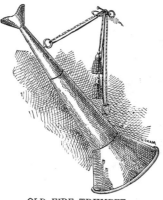

OLD FIRE TRUMPET.

street. The foreman then was Thomas Whitechurch, carpenter, 142 Chambers Street; the assistant, James Young, cabinetmaker, 58 Reade Street, and the secretary, Albert Journeay, grocer, 64 Provost Street. In 1818 she was moved to Marketfield Street.

During the war of 1812 the company promptly tendered its services to do duty in case of an assault upon the city. In 1815 Philip W. Engs was elected foreman and re-elected from year to year up to and including 1820. In 1821 John A. Mitchell became foreman, and remained in command two years. During 1823 the company got into trouble for running on the sidewalk at the corner of Anthony and Chapel Streets. At this time Carlisle Norwood, J. K. Sylvester, J. B. Rich, Charles J. Howell, Thomas Thomas, F. W. Leeds, Samuel Low, William H. Earle, C. C. Pearsall, W. M. Vermilye, and John J. Earle were members. In 1830 the members sold their old engine, which was shipped to Russia. They got a new machine which they boasted would beat anything in the Department. But they were humiliated, their engine being very often " washed," and the company began to diminish in numbers.

A split took place in No. 4, and some of their members ran with No. 21 for a while. At this time they lay in a frame building at the junction of Centre and Chatham, in front of where the *Staats Zeitung* building now stands. In 1834, owing to a dispute with Chief Engineer Gulick at a fire in Pearl Street near Maiden Lane, the company threw up their apparatus. In 1835 the company was reorganized by some of the members of Nos. 11 and 13 Engines. Robert Walker, of No. 11, was made foreman of No. 21, and John T. Moore, of No. 13, was made assistant.

Three times within the month of January, 1831, attempts were made to set fire to the house of Engine No. 21 in Tryon Row, and the mayor offered a reward of one hundred dollars for the apprehension of the offenders.

From Tryon Row No. 21 went to New Street, and in 1826 they again resigned on account of the Gulick difficulty. Joseph E. Jackson, pawnbroker, was then a member, and he took the engine up to the house of No. 19 in Elizabeth Street. A new party was got together and reorganized the company, running a hose cart. In 1837 they moved to Cedar Street, and in 1840 to Beaver Street, where they remained only a few days, thence going to the old house of No. 42 in John Street, where they stayed about three months, finally locating in Temple Street, near Liberty Street. In 1842 Michael Rupp became foreman; then came Robert Lota, next Charles Daly and James Torboss. In 1847 William Drew was elected foreman. In 1848 the company was located in Anthony Street, near Worth Street, on the north side of the old New York Hospital grounds alongside of Hose No. 25. Matthew T. Brennan was then foreman.

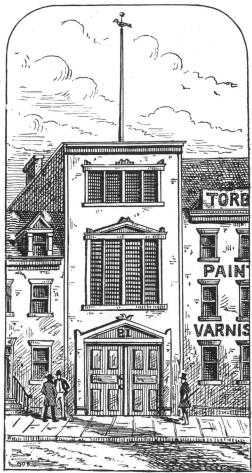

HOUSE OF ENGINE NO. 21.
[Temple Street between Cedar and Liberty Streets, 1865.]

In 1850 we find on the roll Samuel C. Millbank, the brewer; John Boyd, soap-chandler, who died a few years ago, a very wealthy man; Joseph Keefe, one of Matsell's detective force; James Leonard, and Luke C. Grimes, well known in social and political circles, and who for several years held the position of city librarian, was clerk of the court at Jefferson Market, school trustee in the Eighth Ward, and is now one of the directors of the Volunteer Firemen's Association.

In 1852 Thomas W. Constantine was elected foreman, and was re-elected in 1853. In 1854 Charles Neary became foreman. In 1856 James Leonard was foreman. He served until 1858, when he was succeeded by James McCollough, who was twice re-elected. He had in his command P. Fitzgerald, Mortimer Sullivan, Bryan Gaughan, Edward Coppers, M. Tanneau, James Meehan, Patrick Feeney, the old City Hall bell ringer; John and William Conner, Thomas Bowlan, and the Banks brothers. In 1861 Thomas Dunn was elected foreman, and in 1862 and 1863 Michael Fitzgerald was honored with that position. Patrick Garighan was the last foreman, and John McGowan the last man to join the company. In 1864 the company moved to Leonard Street into a new house, now occupied as a storehouse by the Fire Department. The popular name of the company was the "White Ghost," which originated with the failure of the new engine before referred to, which was designed to excel all others, but could not. The company was disbanded in 1865.

No. 22.—Phenix.—This company was organized in 1796 and located in a small frame building in George's (Market Street) Slip. Thomas Drake was the first foreman, and Jacob Carpenter his assistant. The house was afterwards replaced by a brick building for the use of the company, which was mostly composed of shipwrights and calkers, and who would turn out to an alarm with their hands and clothes full of the tar they had been working in. The floor of the engine house was generally covered with a coating of tar tracked in by the members. James Scott was appointed an assistant engineer from this company in 1817, serving until 1822. When the company lay in the slip it was very strong in numbers, but in 1832, when William Ruck was foreman, it was removed to Hester Street, between Eldridge and Allen Streets, and a great number of its members left and joined Engine Company 33. Their new location was next to Engine Company 32.

The company did not thrive well after their removal to Hester Street, and in 1839 a majority of the company organized themselves into Phœnix Hose Company No. 22. Among the earlier members of this company were the following:

John Robbins, 1820; Thomas Megson, afterwards bell ringer, 1824; Benjamin Fuller, 1825; Thomas Nourse, 1825; John Davis, 1826; George Monroe, 1826; Henry Bloodgood, 1827; Peter McNamara, 1827; John Valentine, 1828; Joseph Monk, 1828, Simeon Abrahams, 1829; Henry Ruck, afterwards foreman, 1829; Peter Powless, 1829; Joseph H. Hobby, 1830; Gilbert G. Smith, 1830; John Davis, 1831; Sylvester S. Townsend, 1835; Samuel P. Townsend, 1835.

Protector Engine Company (Old Junk).—Was organized June 25, 1840, and located in connection with Hook and Ladder Company No. 1 in a building in Chambers Street on the site of which now stands the Court House or General Sessions building. About 1849 or '50 the house on Chambers and Centre Streets was built for Engine 22, Hook and Ladder 1, and Hose 28. After the Big Engine (Old Junk) was destroyed by an explosion of saltpetre at the fire corner of Broad Street and Exchange Place, a new engine was built for the company by James Smith. She was of the piano style, and the company ran her until about 1856, when she was sent to the shop of James Smith, in West Broadway, near Duane Street, for repairs. The shop was demolished by fire, and Engine 22 and several other apparatus belonging to the city were destroyed. It was then that Torboss, of Essex Street, built the new craneneck piano engine, which the company ran until replaced by a steamer, built by Jeffers of Pawtucket, R. I., in 1863, and continued in use until the organization of the present Department. Among the prominent members of the company were, besides those already mentioned, L. P. Murray, afterwards foreman of Hose 28; John Bennett, now of the Fifty-seventh Street Police Court; Timothy Waters, Patrick Nealis, Dan and Hugh Friel, David Freeman, of Fulton Market, and Edward Hogan, now engineer of Engine 29, present Department.

No. 23.—United States.—After the fire at the New York Hospital in 1797, there being no fire company in that section of the city, the citizens of that locality organized United States Engine Company No. 23 with twenty-five members. Their engine was one of the old style of New York engines, and their house was on the hospital grounds, just north of the Broadway entrance gate to the hospital, about where the northwest corner of Thomas Street is now, or nearly opposite Pearl Street. Here they remained until 1826, when, the hospital authorities wishing to improve their grounds, the company was moved to Anthony (now Worth) Street, just west of Broadway, being still on the grounds belonging to the hospital. They used the same engine until about the year 1834, when the company ordered a new one built, which they used until their disbandment—about 1849. This company had the reputation of being one of the most efficient and harmonious companies of those days. Peter R. Warner, ex-president of the North River Insurance Company, still living, hale and hearty, in West Twelfth Street, was also a member at that time. Among the earlier members were the following:

John L. Smith, 1820; John P. Bailey, afterwards foreman, 1824; John Ryker, Jr., afterwards assistant engineer and chief, 1824; John Westervelt, 1825; James Smith, 1826; Richard Ackerman, 1827; Frederick G. Sprigg, 1827; William Bleakley, 1827; Edward D. Cooper, 1828; John W. Stryker, 1828; Edgar Ryker, 1828; Daniel V. H. Bertholf, 1829; Samuel Waddell, 1829, afterwards foreman and assistant engineer; Henry Valentine, 1830; Francis McKeon, 1830; Andrew S. Calder, 1831; Peter Thompson, 1831.

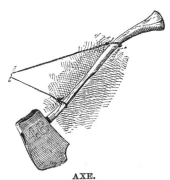

AXE.

[Used by Valley Forge Engine 46 during the riot of 1863; also to cut down "Nigger" Franklin, corner Thirty-second Street and Sixth Avenue, July 15, 1863, and on door of Colored Orphan Asylum, Fifth Avenue and Forty-fourth Street. Presented to assistant foreman J. Dunn, February 7, 1881.]

WAVERLY.—On March 2, 1852, the company was reorganized, being located at No. 193 Twelfth Street, east of Broadway. At a regular monthly meeting held on December 4, 1854, Mr. James Cogan in the chair, and the following members present: McLaughlin, Coyle, Idemiller, Benner, Doran, McGinn, Sammon, and Walsh, it was moved and seconded "that we change the name from Waverly to United States." On consideration the motion was carried. After 1864 the location was changed to No. 186 East Fourteenth Street.

No. 24.—JACKSON.—The company was organized in 1798, and had its headquarters at No. 2 Hook and Ladder House, Tryon Row, the company numbering thirty men. It was reorganized December 11, 1813, with Peter Targee, foreman, Stone Street, First Ward; and Stephen Young, cabinet-maker, Broad Street, assistant, resigned November 15, 1819. Targee died six months after being appointed foreman, and was succeeded by John Declew, confectioner, Nassau Street, who resigned May 22, 1820. Among the members were Ahasuerus Turk, grocer, corner Church and Duane Streets, resigned March 18, 1822; Lawrence Meyer, measurer, Lumber Street, treasurer, resigned July 31, 1815.

At a meeting of the Common Council, October 11, 1802, the committee to whom was referred the application of the members of Fire Company No. 24 reported that it would be proper to allow them the sum of five hundred and fifty dollars towards the purchase of a new engine that had been lately built by Mr. Hardenbrook, ordered that the said report be confirmed, and that the

mayor be authorized to issue a warrant on the treasurer for the sum of five
hundred and fifty dollars to be applied to that purpose accordingly, and that
the alderman and assistant of the Seventh Ward be directed to report a
proper place for the reception of the engine then used by the company with a
view to the formation of a new company in that ward, and to recommend
proper persons for the same. The old engine of Company 24 was supposed to
be good enough for the new company.

Among the names on the roll were Andrew M. Arcularius, time clerk and
grocer in John Street, resigned September 12, 1825; John Daddy, sailmaker,
Vesey Street; John Vandenberghs, carpenter, Thomas Street, time expired
October 10, 1825; Michael Funk, elected to company July 31, 1815; occupa-
tion, accountant; residence, 56 Fair Street; John C. Hegeman, elected Novem-
ber 11, 1819, attorney-at-law, Beekman Street. Stephen Bonner, father of
Robert Bonner, was elected January, 1829, brass founder, Broome and Queen
Streets; resigned September 7, 1829.

The company was again reorganized on January 29, 1836, was stationed at
Seventeenth Street, west of
Ninth Avenue, and went out
of service in 1865.

ENGINE COMPANY 25, 1809.
[Tryon Row, City Hall Square.]

No. 25.—MERCHANTS'—
CATARACT.—Merchants' was
organized in 1801, was located
at the Bridewell from 1832 to
1834 in Tryon Row. It was
disbanded in September 24,
1836. Three years later—
1839—"Cataract" was or-
ganized January 31, and located in a little frame building
with a bell on it on the House
of Refuge grounds at Bloomingdale Road and Twenty-
third Street, about opposite where the Fifth Avenue Hotel stands now, in the
house formerly occupied by old 38 Engine Company. They afterwards moved to
1006 Broadway, and in 1850 again moved to 1146 Broadway. They commenced
doing duty with a New York style of engine, and in 1851 procured a Carson Piano
Engine, which was replaced by a Sickles Piano Engine in 1857, which the
company used until they went out of service in 1865. Henry C. Dater was
foreman in 1849, Geo. W. Varian followed in 1850, and resigned to become an
assistant engineer; John Noakes succeeded him, and he was followed by Wm.
Lamb, who retained the position for two years, and who was elected an assistant engineer in 1862. Lamb was followed by Hugh T. Powers, James J.
Mooney (afterwards alderman), and Richard Flanagan. Henry Wilson was
one of the last representatives of the company, and Daniel F. Tiemann one of
the organizers and first foremen. During the great fire of 1845 the engine
was stationed at the Bowling Green, where she took suction from the cistern
there. In 1858, while Wm. Lamb was foreman, the company made an excursion to Newburgh, taking with them their new engine and being the guest of
Washington Engine Company No. 4 of Newburgh. The company was composed mostly of mechanics and generally ran a full roll.

CHAPTER XXXV.

FIREMEN OF THE BRAVE DAYS OF OLD.

Who the Men were who Ran with the Machine.—Life that was Exciting and Eventful.—Famous Volunteer Engine Companies.—Their Methods of Fire Extinguishing.—Vivid Descriptions of Stirrin Scenes and Incidents of New York Life.

NO. 26.—JEFFERSON—("Blue Boys").—The company was organized in 1803. The first record of its location is when she lay in Henry Street near the Presbyterian Church in Rutgers Street in 1813. During the year 1832 No. 26 moved to Madison Street, near Rutgers, in a frame building on the side of the brick building afterwards used by the company, and after 1845 by Oceana Hose Company No. 36. When the brick house at 205 Madison Street was finished, the company commenced to run the Blue Box Engine, calling themselves the "Blue Boys," with the rallying cry of "True Blue never fades." This engine was one of the handsomest, and at the same time the best geared, the lightest running and fastest engine of its day. Joseph Perkins, Elijah King (who afterwards kept the St. Mark's Place Hotel, and, later on, the Fire Island House) and Ethan S. Blanck were the foremen in those days, and in their little disputes with the "skivers" crowd (No. 39 Engine Company) Dave Phillips, and Jim or Puss Adams, were among the foremost in delivering striking arguments to their opponents. Jamieson Cox, chief engineer of the Department in 1824–28, was appointed an assistant engineer from this company. At the time of the Lorillard fire in Chatham Street, about where Leggett's Hotel now stands, Cox, then a member of 26 Engine, was on a three story ladder that was resting on the front of the building having 26's pipe. Some of the members noticed that the wall was shaking and called to Cox to come down. He had himself recognized the danger of his situation, and by a sudden and powerful effort jumped the ladder from the front of the building over to the front of the next one just as the wall fell in with a crash. Had he not moved the ladder over as he did, nothing could have saved him.

About May, 1836, the men were having some repairs done to their house in Madison Street, and ran from a little wooden shanty on the north side of Rutgers Street one door from Madison Street. While in this temporary location the building was discovered to be on fire one day, and on Mr. Charles J. Harris, one of the members, and Thomas Coger, a volunteer, arriving at the house and opening the doors, they were unable to draw the engine from the house, the machine having either been fastened to the floor, or the wheels so chocked that the engine could not be moved. The engine, which was a very handsome one with polished iron work, and a great deal of elaborate carving on it, was partially destroyed. It was a comparatively new machine, having been in use but about three years. This did not prevent the company from continuing their fire duty. They immediately applied for and obtained the engine that had been turned in by Hudson Engine Company No. 1, and commenced to run from their house in Madison Street.

At the fire in the *Tribune* building which occurred February 5, 1845, during a heavy snow storm which had lasted twenty-four hours, the streets being impassable for their engine, the members of 26 Engine Company put their hose on a wood sled belonging to Hecker, the flour merchant, and drew it to the fire, Zophar Mills and Charles Forrester being on the rope going down. The members then went and helped Engine Company No. 23 across the City Hall Park, they not having yet reached the fire from Anthony Street.

On the occasion of the obsequies of ex-President Andrew Jackson in New York, June 24, 1845, a great many of the New York fire companies turned out without their apparatus, and among others were Engine Companies Nos. 2 and

EMBLEMS OF THE OLD DEPARTMENT.

26. They had just reached the City Hall, where they were to be dismissed, when the Hall bell struck for the fifth district. Both companies started after their engines, and on reaching Chatham Square No. 26 Engine could be seen coming down East Broadway, and No. 2 Engine coming down Division Street. After a little parley about "going out first," No. 2 Engine started over toward Oliver Street, and John Harden, foreman of No. 26 Engine, headed his company over towards Mott Street. This "skinned" No. 2 Engine's rope, and the fun began. Both companies were halted at Chatham and Chambers Streets, where some lively hitting out was indulged in until stopped by Chief Anderson, and both companies sent home. They went back side by side, stopping a few moments before the Chatham Theater to exchange compliments, and as No. 2 Engine men hooted at No. 26 as they separated at Chatham Square, they were obliged to continue hostilities in front of old Johnny Pease's candy store in Division Street, which ended in No. 2 Engine being tied up to a lamp post, corner of Rutgers and Henry Streets.

On the night of July 16, 1845, there were several alarms struck and one of them was for the fire in the old Dispensary, corner of White and Centre Streets. On their way home, when in Walker Street near Eldridge Street, and about opposite the old Sawdust House, kept by "Yankee" Sullivan, No. 2 Engine ran into No. 26 Engine, and they struck out right and left. The companies were ordered to turn in "tongue first," and the next night the houses were locked up, neither company being present at the great fire which took place down town shortly afterwards. The Blue Engine which No. 26 ran was taken away, but is said to be still in existence. It had a picture on the back of it of Jefferson writing the Declaration of Independence. The company was disbanded on September 22, 1845. A company bearing the same number and name, organized on December 2, 1851, by the company formerly known as Hose Company No. 32, was stationed at No. 6 Third Street, and later in Fifth Street near First Avenue. It went out of service in 1865.

No. 27.—NORTH RIVER.—This company was organized in 1803, with twenty-four men, was located at Watts and Greenwich Streets, and disbanded March 1, 1843. Among the early members were Abraham Bogert, carpenter, Hudson Street. He resigned November 24, 1823 ; Assistant Foreman Henry Howard, familiarly known as "Harry" ; Frederick C. Havemeyer, sugar refiner, 16 Van Dam Street, elected to the company November 24, 1813, resigned June 9, 1823, his time having expired ; Wm. Havemeyer, sugar refiner, 14 Van Dam Street, resigned May 22, 1815, after two years' service; and John McClave, father of Police Commissioner McClave, who joined November 20, 1815 (lived

PACIFIC NO. 28.

at 17 Desbrosses Street), resigned December 18, 1826, as his time had expired.

FORT WASHINGTON was organized November 18, 1852, and was located at Carmansville. Disbanded in 1865.

No. 28.—MECHANICS'.—It was organized in 1805, and was located at One Mile Stone in the Bowery, and had twenty-two members. Thomas McGuier, carman, 366 Broadway, was foreman, and resigned in August, 1817 ; John A. Ten Broeck, butcher, was assistant foreman, resigned May 10, 1819 ; John Delamater, carpenter, Grand Street, expelled September 6, 1830, for not reporting himself to the Common Council ; Wm. A. Dodge, tavern keeper, 592 Broadway, resigned September 6, 1830, by order of the Common Council. Other members were John Frost, butcher, Spring Street, foreman ; John Vanderhoof, shoemaker, Elizabeth Street ; Henry Jerolomon, butcher, Spring Street ; Zebulon Brundage, grocer, Pike Street corner Henry, and Stephen Cleveland, carpenter, 25 Leonard Street, resigned June 5, 1815.

PACIFIC was organized January 27, 1852, located at 377 Fourth Avenue, and went out of service in 1865.

No. 29.—CONSTITUTION.—TRIDENT.—GUARDIAN ("Rooster"), No. 29, was organized in 1803 and located on the west side of a hill on Washington Street near Perry. When Washington Street was graded it left the house ten feet high on an embankment. The adjoining grounds were used by the old State Prison. Jesse M. Chaple, Jas. Van Norden, Joseph N. Blamm, and Garret Tinkey were among the organizers of this company. In 1816 they moved to the northwest corner of Hudson and Christopher Streets, Engine 34 and Hook and Ladder 3 being located in the same building, the upper part being used as a school and watchhouse. A liberty pole stood on this corner, which the members utilized to ascertain the location of fires. David Darrow, Matthew Armstrong and John Van Houten were among the members at this time. Among the runners was Armstrong's horse "Skinny," who did good service when the members were scarce or the mud very deep. In 1827 Allen R. Jollie joined the company, becoming its foreman in 1829, and after serving as such for several years was made an assistant engineer. It was claimed that he was one of the best runners in the Department in his day, and had the record of not missing a fire in seven years. In 1836 Thomas Lawrence and Martin Okie, well known Ninth Warders, were made members. About that time the establishing of a Paid Department was agitated, and Allen R. Jollie was the first man to submit a plan for the paid system, but it met with no favor.

Engine 29 was first known by the name of "Constitution," afterwards as "Trident," and in 1836 they changed their name, after some opposition from some of the members, to "Guardian," which they retained until the end. In 1838 the company visited Paterson, N. J., where they had a pleasant sojourn of three days. In 1841 they removed to Horatio Street near Hudson with Hook and Ladder 3. In 1845 Abraham D. Carlock, Jas. W. Booth (afterwards State senator), and Eugene Ward (afterwards alderman of the Ninth Ward) were members, and in 1846 John H. Brady (afterwards alderman) became connected with the company. In 1843 the company took up their quarters in Amos, now West Tenth Street. In 1846 Eli Bates joined the company, and Jas. W. Booth was elected foreman, and De Witt Forshay assistant foreman. In 1847 Forshay became foreman and Booth assistant foreman. In 1849 Stephen Messereau was elected foreman, but only served a short time, Eugene Ward taking his place. In 1851 they visited Albany under command of Ward as foreman and George C. Brown assistant. They were received by Neptune Engine Company 10, while Chief Engineer Gould turned out the whole Department in their honor, the Governor, Hamilton Fish, delivering the address of welcome. Captain De Groot's steamer "Reindeer," one of the finest and fastest boats on the river, conveyed them to and from Albany. Harry Bridgeman was the leader of 29's volunteer roll, which numbered over seventy young men, and Dave Broderick, afterwards of 34 Engine, was also a runner with 29 Engine. In 1857 the company made an excursion to Boston and Providence, receiving an ovation at each place. The company carried with them as fine a looking body of men as ever manned an engine rope. In 1858 Eli Bates was elected foreman, and in 1863 the company removed to their new house, 26 West Tenth Street. In the early days of the company they received the nickname of "Rooster Boys," but in later years this was changed to "Old Jeff" and "Iron Horse." The history of this company from 1803 until 1865 is a creditable and honorable one.

No. 30.—TOMPKINS.—This, the first company of that name and number, was organized in 1804, and in 1813 was located in Rivington Street, between Forsyth (then Second) and Eldridge (then Third) Streets, and in 1830 moved to 199 Chrystie Street near Stanton, the same location that Lafayette Engine Company 19 used in later years. The greatest rivals of 30 Engine Company were Engine Companies 15, 40 and 37. No. 44 Engine Company was also a rival of 30 Engine, and during a race in 1841 the companies became seriously engaged, and charges were preferred against both companies. John P. Teale, a ship carpenter, was foreman, and he called the company together, and tendered his resignation as an officer and also as a member of the company. The members were taken by surprise and asked the reason why. Teale said the company could not bear the blame of all the disasters, and the members thereupon sustained their foreman and resigned in a body with the exception of Mr. John Boyd. He was for retaining the organization and fighting down all opposition. He was, however, prevailed on to go with the rest, and the engine was left without members. The trial went on before the Fire and Water Committee, and Frederick R. Lee, alderman of the Seventeenth Ward, well known as the foreman of old No. 3 Engine, was the chairman of the committee. No. 30 Engine Company was exonerated, and the blame placed principally on 44 Engine Company. Alderman Lee waited on Mr. Teale, and endeavored to get the company to resume duty, but in vain. The engine was taken out of the house and given to Engine Company 20, and the doors of the house locked up on October 6, 1841. William Rainer, afterwards of Engine Company 40 and Engine Company 31, and William Lamb, afterwards of Engine Company 25 and an assistant engineer from 1862 to 1865, were members at the time of disbandment, as was James R. Mount, afterwards of Atlantic Hose Company 14.

TOMPKINS (second of the name).—Was organized December 28, 1847, and located in Twenty-second Street near Second Avenue; was afterwards located temporarily in a stable on East Twenty-fifth Street between Second and Third Avenues. While located here a fire took place on the corner of Hester and Christie Streets, on May 9, 1854, for which a general alarm was struck, and which destroyed a whole block of buildings. At this fire Chief Alfred Carson ordered the company to give their supply stream to another engine company. The members refused to obey the order, and one of them, named Gay, assaulted the chief. For this they were disbanded.

NORTH RIVER was organized July 15, 1858, by B. F. Grant, William F. Searing, William McGrew, and others from Eureka Hose Company No. 54, and ran an old engine from the yard until 1860, when it received a new piano style of engine which was used until the company commenced running a steamer in 1863. This company had a fight with 40 Engine Company in the City Hall Park in 1859. Charges were preferred against 40 Engine Company, and they were disbanded by the Board of Fire Commissioners. The company procured an injunction restraining the Board of Fire Commissioners from carrying their sentence into effect, and this led to the resignation of the entire Board, with the exception of Henry Wilson, the retiring members being Nelson D. Thayer, Robert H. Ellis and William Wright.

No. 31.—HOPE—Was organized in 1805, was located at Church and Leonard Streets, and after 1834 on Chapel Street (now West Broadway) near Beach

Street. The company was disbanded on August 5, 1846 ; was reorganized on July 16, 1847, by the members of Engine Company No. 3 (at No. 128 West Broadway), which number it assumed, and was again disbanded on September 11, 1854.

ADRIATIC—PETERSON—Was organized February 24, 1857, by James L. and John B. Miller, Geo. A. Perry, Geo. R. Nicholl, Geo. and Martin Braitmayer, Howard E. Coates, Wm. Rainer, and other old firemen, mostly of Engine Companies 15 and 19, and a number of the younger residents of the Tenth Ward, among whom were John McCauley and Frank Mahedy, both of whom afterwards became foremen. John B. Miller was the first foreman of Adriatic, and James L. Miller one of its first and last representatives. The company located in the old quarters of 15 Engine at 49 Christie Street, and within a year after their organization changed their name to that of Peterson. During the first year of their existence they received a first-class double deck,

ADRIATIC ENGINE NO. 31.

Jeffers style of engine, probably the finest piece of mechanism in the way of a fire engine ever seen in New York. It was placed on exhibition at the Crystal Palace, and was totally destroyed in the burning of that structure, October 5, 1858. Orders were immediately given to Jeffers & Co. for another engine, and in 1859 the company received from their hands a first-class side stroke engine of great power, which they ran until April, 1862, when it was taken with Mohawk Engine No. 16 to Fortress Monroe by Assistant Engineer John Baulch under a requisition from the United States Government for the protection of the stores of army materials at that point, and where it still remains. Cornelius Gillen was foreman at the time and accompanied the engine to Fortress Monroe. In 1863 the company commenced running a steamer which they used until the Paid Department came into existence. After Eagle Hook and Ladder Company 4 was disbanded in 1864, 31 Engine Company took up their quarters in their house at No. 20 Eldridge Street. John J. O'Brien was a runner with this company.

No. 32.—BUNKER HILL.—This company was founded in the summer of 1807 with Thomas Pennell, wheelwright, 128 Broadway, as foreman; Adam Hartell, butcher, North Street, as assistant; and twenty-three firemen, fifteen of whom had been transferred from other companies. The engine was located in 1813 in Grand Street, near the Bowery; about 1820 at Christie and Broome Streets; and after 1830 in Hester Street, near Allen. The company was disbanded on May 6, 1858.

PETE MASTERSON was organized December, 20, 1859, by John Quinn, Harrison H. and Geo. W. Ferguson, James Daley, James Hart, and others, and located first temporarily in a stable, corner of One Hundred and Fourth Street and the Bloomingdale Road, and in 1864 removed to a new brick house built for it at Bloomingdale Road and Ninety-sixth Street, and which is now occupied by Engine Company No. 47 of the Paid Department. The company first ran an end-brake engine, but soon replaced it for an old gooseneck, formerly used by Engine Company No. 35, and after this they obtained the little old gooseneck of No. 40 Engine Company, which they ran until the Department went out of existence. The company had applied for a steam engine, and would have procured one had not the paid system been adopted.

John Quinn was the foreman until 1864, when John J. Ferguson was elected foreman and Edward Gilbert assistant foreman. The Pete Masterson Guards originated in this company, and made an annual parade under Captain John Quinn.

"BLACK JOKE" NO. 33.

No. 33.—BLACK JOKE.—The company, organized in 1807, were located at Grand Street Market in 1813, and in 1820 they removed to a little one-story frame house on the north side of Cherry Street, between Jackson and Corlears. The house was still standing in 1886. In 1828 they removed to Gouverneur Street, near Henry, and located in the house afterwards used by Engine Company No. 6 on its organization in 1849. The first name of 33 Engine Company was "Bombazula," and when they moved over into the Seventh Ward a lady, who then lived in the large house on the corner of Gouverneur and Henry Streets, and who was a descendant of the Gouverneur family, was anxious that the name should be changed to that of "Lady Gouverneur," offering the company a golden trumpet to so name it, and the question of a change was agitated. The exploits of a certain privateer, called "*Black Joke*," which had performed some wonderful deeds during the war of 1812, was the talk of the men near the docks in those days, and a vote being taken the name of "Black Joke" was adopted, and on a later engine the leader jacket had a picture of the vessel in an action in which she had captured two merchantmen. The same engine had a picture of the Three Graces on the back at the fire in the shipyard of Adam & Noah Brown at the foot of

Stanton and Houston Streets, East River, in March, 1824. The engine belonging to the company—old "Bombazula"—which had a square box with solid wooden wheels, was destroyed by the flames. James P. Allaire was the first foreman of 33 Engine, and S. P. Allaire, his son, Edward Winship, Philander Webb, Edward Penny, Harry Andrews, Tom Primrose, Malachi Fallon, Edward Fernon, Samuel Dunlop, and Thomas McIntyre were all foremen in later years.

33 BLACK JOKE.

[Showing old engine house on Gouverneur Hill, as it appeared about the year 1820. The original (worked in worsted) is now in possession of the Jackson Club, foot of Jackson Street.]

Engine Company 33 was the first fire company to start a target excursion, which practice they continued for many years, and which was soon afterwards followed by the other engine companies. In 1843 Samuel Dunlop opened a place at the junction of East Broadway and Grand Street. This was a great resort for 33 Engine's followers. He had a lunch between the hours of ten and one o'clock, and the boys christened it the "Ten to One." In the latter part of that year some of the opponents of 33 Engine, who were connected with Nos. 6, 15, and 44 Engine Companies, gave out that they were going down to take off the "eagle," a wooden figure which decorated the front of 33 Engine's house, and on Christmas Eve down they came through Sheriff Street, tooting horns and making demonstrations towards Gouverneur Street. The boys at the engine house had no notion of having their eagle taken down, and had prepared a warm reception for their visitors. They had a howitzer loaded with slugs, chains, and bolts. The crowd first turned their attention to the "Ten to One" house, and a man on that building leveled his musket at them, but before he could pull the trigger Tom Primrose, of 33 Engine, hit him and knocked his musket up, the ball going through a doctor's window opposite, and just passing over the nose of that gentleman, who was lying in bed. The shot soon brought the constables, and the crowd quickly dispersed. The officers turned their attention to the "Ten to One," from the roof of which they took thirteen muskets to the Tombs. They were so heavily loaded that the charges had to be drawn. Some of 33 Engine members were arrested. During the presidential campaign of Polk and Clay in 1844, 33 Engine Company took part in a Polk and Dallas procession against the rules and orders of the Department, and a few days later the Whigs turned out, and the parade was headed by a number of horsemen, among whom was Tom Hyer. They had with them a bell belonging to the Allaires, and on coming through

East Broadway some one struck the Fourth District on it. Whether this was done because they were going through the Fourth District, or in a spirit of mischief, cannot now be determined; at any rate 33 Engine Company, always ready for an alarm, turned out, and as they met the procession, and saw the cause of the alarm, they swung around to return to their house. Some of the horses shied at the engine, and the rope upset others, and nearly upset the procession. This, in addition to other charges already in, caused the engine to be taken to the Corporation Yard, and the company was formally disbanded November 6, 1844. Thomas Conner was elected alderman of the ward that year on the issue that he would get the engine back. He was never able to do so, and Black Joke Engine Company 33 of the East River was a thing of the past.

BLACK JOKE (second of the name).—Was organized March 6, 1852, by Peter Masterson and others, and located in a little shed next door to his house at Fifty-eighth Street and Bloomingdale Road. James Masterson was the first foreman elected, and the company commenced doing duty with a New York style of engine built in 1827, which was painted black, and which they ran until 1855, when they received a Carson monument, and having bought the old engine, placed it on the top of their house. The fire commissioners objected to placing the engine there, and the trouble grew serious, but it finally ended in a victory for the company, who retained the engine in that position until the Department went out of exist-

SIGNAL LAMP OF BLACK JOKE.

ence. In 1854 the city bought ground, and erected a brick building for the use of the company, taking the plan of No. 7 Engine House in Twenty-fifth Street, then one of the largest and finest in the city. It was afterwards raised to three stories, and extended back to a depth of sixty feet, and is now used by Engine Company No. 23 of the Paid Department. At that time a bell, weighing eight hundred pounds, was placed on the rear of the building which some members would ring on, receiving an alarm, they having an independent telegraph line running from the bell tower in Thirty-third Street. In the daytime if an alarm came in on the wire, and no member was in the house, Mrs. Masterson would man the rope and call them together. Having this telegraph in the house was of great benefit to the company, and was the means of rendering them the quickest company in the upper districts. They ran the Carson Engine until

1862, when they applied for, and received, the first steamer built by order of the Common Council for use in the Department. Peter Masterson was foreman for ten years, during which time he served in the Legislature two years and in the Board of Aldermen four years. In 1863 they visited Newburg, N. Y., and received quite an ovation. The bunk room held twenty-four beds, which were all occupied.

The Black Joke Guards originated from this company, their first captain being ex-Judge Michael Connelly; Constantine Donoho was the second captain, after which Peter Masterson was captain for several years.

When the company first got the steamer, some of the members growled terribly, and at the first fire it was run to would not man the rope, leaving the runners to do it. The second alarm proved to be a five hours' working fire, and the "kickers" were convinced that steam was superior to muscle, and from that time until the end of the Department there was no more opposition to the steamer. Robert Gamble, a coroner, afterwards one of

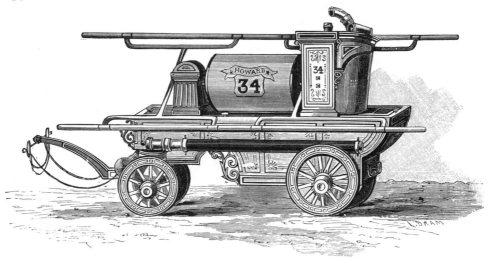

ENGINE NO. 34.

the organizers of Hook and Ladder 16, and Wm. A. and Jas. H. Turnure were members of this company in 1855, and Alderman Peter B. Masterson was a member from 1861 until it was disbanded in 1865.

No. 34.—HOWARD ("Red Rover").—This company was organized in 1807. In 1813 it was located in Amos Street, in 1820 in Gouverneur Street, in 1830 at Hudson and Christopher Streets, and in 1864 at 78 Morton Street; went out of service in 1865. It started with twenty-six men on its roll. Among the earlier names we find Barnard Smith, house carpenter, Essex Street, foreman; Ebenezer Winship, foundry, Cherry Street, assistant foreman, (resigned February 12, 1832); Abraham G. Depew, blacksmith, Vandam Street, foreman, 1824; and William Hedden, blacksmith, Spring and Sullivan Streets, assistant, 1824. Among other members about 1824 were Moses Springer, painter, 235 Hudson Street; John V. L. Hoagland, carpenter, Sixth Avenue; Joseph S. Shotwell, blindmaker, Minetta Street; and Jacob A. Roome, carpenter, Bedford Street (appointed engineer December 27, 1830). Bill Poole, the Washington Market butcher, who was shot in Stanwix Hall on Broadway by Lewis Baker at one o'clock Sunday morning February 25, 1855, was a Volunteer of this company. The famous Dave Broderick joined 34 Engine Company May 13, 1844, and resigned April 17, 1849, to go to California.

No. 35.—COLUMBUS.—This was the first engine company that was organized in Harlem, then called the village, and was placed in service in 1807. Their first location was in what is now One Hundred and Eighteenth Street and Lexington Avenue. The only connection then, and for many years after, between the east and west sides of the upper portion of the city, was by way of One Hundred and Twenty-fifth Street, or by Chauncey's Lane, which ran diagonally through the grounds of the present Central Park. In 1812 the engine with which they were doing duty was classed as "unknown" as to the date of its construction, and as it was the only engine so classed with the exception of 28, it is safe to conclude that it must have been one of the earliest engines known. In 1823 Abraham Vermilyea, butcher, was foreman, and Benson McGown, farmer, assistant. In 1827 the company prepared their first gooseneck engine and afterwards removed to a little shanty on One Hundred and Twenty-first Street, near Third Avenue, in the rear of the Harlem Market, and about 1850 moved to Third Avenue, between One Hundred and Twentieth and One Hundred and Twenty-first Streets, in a two-story brick house with 43 Hose. In 1861 they again removed their quarters, this time to One Hundred and Nineteenth Street, between Second and Third Avenues, the location of the present Engine Company No. 35. Among the old foremen of the company were William H. Colwell, the lumber merchant; Samuel Cross, William Graham, John H. Pain, Robert Crawford, and E. V. Graham. In 1850 Mr. Graham resigned the office of foreman, and John Gillelan was elected foreman in order to allow him to run for the office of assistant engineer, and on his election to that office Mr. Graham was again elected foreman of the company, and held the position until 1853, when the term for which Gillelan was elected an engineer having expired, he returned to the company, and was again elected its foreman, serving until 1858, when John Hart was elected. David Fitzgerald followed Hart as foreman, and he was succeeded by William Daily, who was the last foreman of the company. Samuel L. Liscomb, who was foreman of this company, and elected assistant engineer in 1842, started for California with John J. Audubon, the naturalist, and was killed in crossing the plains in 1849. Garret Dyckman, who was major of the First Regiment of New York Volunteers in the Mexican war, and colonel of the First New York Volunteers in the war of the Rebellion, was a member of this company from 1857 to the breaking out of the last war. The Common Council, by special committee, awarded to Dyckman the gold snuffbox that was left by Andrew Jackson to be presented to "that patriot residing in the city or State from which he was presented, who shall be adjudged, by his countrymen or the ladies, to have been the most valiant in defense of his country and our country's rights." The committee, after several sessions, at which much testimony was taken, declared in their report of August 8, 1857, that Garret Dyckman was entitled to the gold snuffbox for having been the bravest man in the Mexican war. Some difficulty arose, and Dyckman never received the box, but he was afterwards elected register of the city.

No. 36.—EQUITABLE.—It was established on August 13, 1810, and its location fixed at Spring Street, near Varick Street. The members of the company

who were appointed on August 22 consisted of John Targay, carpenter, Greenwich Street; B. C. Stevenson, inspector, Spring Street; Elkannah Mead,
carman, Hudson Street; Alexander Allaire, carman, Budd Street; Daniel
Martling, grocer, and Lotion Quick, carman, Budd Street; Silas Parklow,
carpenter, Spring Street; Frederick Glasham, butcher, Spring Street; David
Hartshorne, carpenter, Budd Street; John Goodheart, laborer, Macdougal
Street; Duncan Douglass, carpenter, Spring Street; John Lambert, gentleman, and Smith Valentine, grocer, Greenwich Street; Enoch Miller, carpenter, Varick Street; John Tompkins, milkman, Sullivan Street; James Clark,
milkman, Greenwich Street; Richard Worsburn, carman, Hetty Street;
Peter Roodeback, mason, Spring Street; John Freeman, carpenter, Spring
Street; A. J. Westervelt, carpenter, Greenwich Street; John C. Parmerly,
carpenter, Thomas Street; Thomas J. Booles, Spring Street; Elias B. Coy,
carpenter, Greenwich Street; Garret Smith, mason, Greenwich Street, and
Thomas Rockhill, mason, Spring Street. The company was disbanded on
August 5, 1846.

EQUITABLE—HARRY HOWARD—EQUITABLE.—No. 50 Engine Company was
changed on March 10, 1848, to No. 36, and was located at Sixty-eighth Street
and Bloomingdale Road. Went out of service in 1865.

No. 37.—TRADESMAN'S.—The company was organized in 1811, and was first
located in Orchard Street, between Rivington and Stanton Streets. Second
location Christie Street, between Rivington and Stanton Streets. Third
location Orchard Street above Delancey Street, and final home in Delancey
Street near Allen Street. Was disbanded in 1844. Thos. D. Howe joined the
engine in 1820. Within six months he was elected assistant foreman, served
two years in that position, when he was elected foreman, served five years,
when he was appointed assistant engineer, which office he filled for fifteen
years. In 1813, when thirty men were on the roll, the foreman was Gideon
Carstang, Jr., ropemaker, Third Street, near Stanton (resigned Sept. 18, 1820);
assistant foreman, George Howard, ropemaker, Sixth Street, near Rivington,
(resigned May 26, 1817); clerk, Thomas Willett, merchant, 47 Third Street,
(resigned July 27, 1818). In 1814 it was re-established with twelve men
on the roll. The foreman was John R. Thomas, clerk, of the Cross Roads
(resigned April 24, 1815); assistant foreman, Aaron B. Jackson, grocer at the
Cross Roads (resigned December 21, 1818). Among the members in 1823 were
Aaron Keyer, milkman, Bowery and Bond Street, foreman, and Joseph
Brewster, hat manufacturer, Third Avenue, assistant; Simon Van Winkle,
innkeeper, Broadway near Twelfth Street; William Ransom and Jonathan
H. Ransom, shoe dealers, Washington Square; Commodore T. Williams, Jr.,
Fifth Avenue; Wm. B. Bohn, painter, corner Essex and Worth Streets; Wm.
N. Romaine, butcher, 287 Houston Street; Robinson Whitlock, brass founder,
243 Houston Street; Peter G. Vandrough, cordwainer, 47 Suffolk Street.
In 1825 Joseph Brewster, hat maker, Third Avenue, was foreman, and Joseph
Whaley, milkman, Bowery, assistant; other members were Simon Van
Winkle, innkeeper, Bowery (resigned May 21, 1827); Samuel Van Norden,
wheelwright, Cross Roads and Bowery (resigned April 24, 1815). The company
disbanded on March 1, 1843, and another under the same name (Tradesman's)
was organized on September 26, 1853. It was located in Fifty-ninth Street near
Third Avenue, and went out of service in 1865.

No. 38.—This company, which is remarkable in not having a name, was organized in 1811. It was located at the Cross Roads, Bowery; next in Love Lane (Twenty-first Street), near Bloomingdale Road, and in 1833 at the junction of Bloomingdale Road and the Boston Post Road. It was disbanded on July 9, 1838.

SOUTHWARK was organized on February 10, 1840. The company was stationed in Nassau Street near Cedar, and after 1843 at No. 28 Ann Street. It was disbanded in 1865. At the burning of the Park Theater, Saturday

ASSOCIATION AND COMPANY BADGES.

evening, December 16, 1848, Engine Company No. 38 got first water on the fire. They soon discovered that the theater was doomed, and that their efforts could not save it, and, backing down their pipe, they turned their attention to saving the buildings of the American Bible Society, which stood in the rear opposite the theater. This they succeeded in doing. The society presented the company with a costly edition of their family Bible, on which was inscribed, "Presented to Southwark Fire Engine Company No. 38 by the American Bible Society for valuable services rendered in preserving their premises at the burning of the Park Theater, December 16, 1848." The gift was accompanied by a very flattering letter. When Southwark Engine Company was disbanded in 1865, Mr. Thomas F. Riley, who had rolled the engine and had the pipe at the above fire, was presented by the company with the Bible and the letter.

No. 39.—FRANKLIN—GOOD INTENT ("Skiver.").—Upon the petition of Gilbert B. Mott and others, Fire Engine Company No. 39 was established on April 6, 1812, among whose officers and men were: Gilbert B. Mott, foreman; John M. Read, assistant foreman; Thomas N. Stanford, secretary; Jacob Stoutenburgh, William McKenny, Thomas W. Hoyt, Nathaniel Merritt, John Sutherland, Elkanah Talbot, William B. Reed, William Leary, Peter Aymar, Jediah Morris, Uzziah Wenman. This company used the "Crosby Patent," but it proved to be a failure, and in January, 1814, it was decided to abandon that system of construction and revert to the old plan, to conform with which it was found necessary to alter No. 39. The company was first located in Partition Street (Fulton), corner of Church, next in Vesey, near Church Street, in 1834 at the old Bridewell Park, and in 1840 in Doyer Street. The company was reorganized at St. Paul's Churchyard in Vesey Street, on

LADY WASHINGTON NO 40.
[In Engine House 33. Owned by Assistant Chief Bonner.

March 20, 1820, with twenty-six men, and among the members were William Snell, accountant, foreman, and John Post, druggist, of Greenwich and Cortlandt Streets, assistant foreman; Abraham H. Kipp, merchant, Barclay Street; John Dupont, merchant, Hester Street; Frederick Pentz, merchant, 49 Vesey Street; Edward Williams, merchant, Fifth Avenue; Charles Ellet, merchant, 26 Howard Street. The company was disbanded on March 1, 1843.

FRANKLIN (second of the name) was organized December 27, 1853, and was located in Thirty-first Street, near Seventh Avenue, going out of service in 1865. At an alarm of fire, on January 24, 1864, in Thirty-first Street, between Seventh and Eighth Avenues, the second district apparatus were all present, although the bells did not ring. While Hibernia Engine Company No. 15 were on their way up, the engine ran over William Fanning a member of Franklin Engine, who was about getting on the rope of 15 Engine. He was removed to Eighth Avenue and Thirty-first Street, where he died in forty-five minutes.

No. 40.—LADY WASHINGTON ("White Ghost," "White Gal").—This company was organized in 1812, and was located at 174 Mulberry Street, near Broome, in the same house that Columbian Hose Company, No. 9, shared with them in later years. They were known as the "Ghosts," and were a lively crowd, being composed mostly of Centre Market boys. They had many enemies, the principal ones being Peterson Engine Company, No. 15, Black Joke Engine Company, No. 33, Forrest Engine Company, No. 3 (which lay in Marion Street at that time , and Tompkins Engine Company, No. 30. But they had some good friends, among whom were Clinton Engine Company, No. 41, and Live Oak Engine Company, No. 44. 30 and 40 never came together without having a fight, and some of them were very severe ones. The most famous we have already described.

Fire Engine 40 was organized at Mulberry Street, between Broome and Grand Streets, June 9, 1822, with twenty-six men, and John M. Sands, grocer, corner Spring and Crosby, was foreman, and Absalom Traver, grocer, 225 Mulberry Street, assistant. The company was located at 174 Mulberry Street, and later at 173 Elm Street. It was disbanded on December 6, 1843, reorganized on December 19, 1853, and went out of service in 1865.

No. 41.—CLINTON ("Old Stag").—Clinton was organized March 8, 1813, and had its quarters at the corner of Rivington and Arundel (now Clinton) Streets. The membership included sturdy mechanics, and a few clerks, etc. Here is the original roll: John Bayley, William Brown, Chauncey Carter, Joseph Collins, Casper Corley, John Garrett, John Grantz, Edward Grimes, William Haley, John Hallock, Abraham Halsey, C. M. Hamstead, Samuel Hopping, William Horsely, A. C. Hoyt, D. B. Hoyt, Walter Hyde, Samuel James, George Kirk, James T. Palmer, Joseph Parker, Robert Parker, William Place, Peter Marks, William Sherwood, James Stackburn, Henry T. Stiles, John Vincent, Solomon Williams, and John D. Webster. After a few years in the Rivington Street house, the company moved into a one-story building erected for them on the rear of the lot at Attorney and Delancey Streets, where the Thirteenth Precinct Police Station is to-day. In those times the city was not liberal in its treatment of the fire companies. It would furnish them with one-story houses only, and those of the plainest sort. If the boys wanted a fancy window over the front door, or any other ornament, they paid for it themselves. In 1825 Drake B. Palmer was foreman, Henry Bowran and Benjamin Defries, his assistants, Gilbert Lewis, secretary, and James Sands, treasurer. There were fourteen other members. Palmer was promoted to be assistant engineer in 1829. He served in that capacity until 1834. Later, he became successively president, vice-president, secretary and treasurer of the Department. Other foremen, in the order given below, succeeded Palmer at the head of No. 41: Edward Underhill, Henry C. Bowran, Randolph C. Laing, Andrew Craft, Benjamin C. Whitmore, Philip B. White, John Brown, John D. Halsted, Alonzo Hawley, Henry Lewis, Anthony J. Allaire, James Little, Thomas Cheevers, Joseph Swinerton and William Hennessey. A new engine, purchased in 1829, was long the pride of the company, and had the honor of washing half the engines in the department. During the Gulick trouble in 1836 the company voted to resign in a body. They appointed a committee to strip the engine of ornaments belonging to them. During the brief rule of Ryker, a company of "citizen firemen," as they were called, used the engine. Thomas Connor, afterwards alderman of the Seventh Ward, was foreman.

The old hands returned to the brakes when Cornelius V. Anderson became chief and continued to perform duty until 1852, when they were disbanded for fighting. Reorganized soon after this episode, No. 41 got a new piano engine with an eight-inch cylinder and nine-inch stroke. In 1859 they moved into a house in Clinton Street, near Grand, now used by the Fifth District Civil Court. Six years more of faithful service passed, and their career ended.

Mr. G. W. Wheeler, formerly secretary of the company, has some of its old records. One, containing the earlier minutes, is a ponderous volume with a leather binding almost thick enough to be bullet-proof. In this yellow, musty tome are accounts of fires where 41 covered herself with glory, and her rivals with confusion and water. Very seldom is an attempt made to estimate the actual damage by the fire, but the engine's place in the line, her hours of service, and the machines she washed, are all carefully noted. It was an era of wooden buildings, and a fire which destroyed two Tenth Ward blocks is succinctly described in half a page. No. 41 was late because the hose had been hung on the fence to dry. Afterwards the generous aldermen gave two sets of hose to each company. December 15, 1825, there was a fire in Thompson Street near Broome. Fourteen engines in line brought water

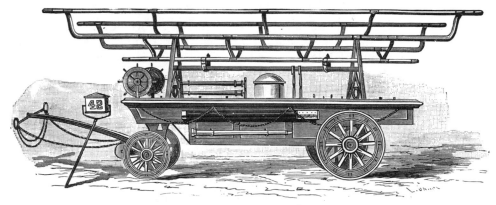

OLD "HAY-WAGON."

from the North River. "We sucked on 25," says the minute-book. That is, they pumped so fast that 25, just behind them, could not keep them supplied with water. The company worked from five in the afternoon until 12:30 A. M. Mr. Wm. Underhill and Mrs. Mason, of Spring Street, furnished refreshments to the boys, and were officially thanked. A fire on October 3, 1830, destroyed seven buildings on the Bowery, between Spring and Prince Streets, and four on Elizabeth Street. The minutes show that 41 washed 18 and 31 successively.

During the great fire in 1835 the cold was awful. Beside the engine stood a keg of brandy with the head broken in, and a copper kettle. Old firemen's eyes sparkle as they declare that the liquor was poured into the engine to keep her from freezing. It must have been poor brandy, for she froze in spite of it. The next morning she was on duty again. The company disbanded in 1865.

No. 42.—EAST RIVER.—Formerly Floating Engine, had its headquarters at Roosevelt Street, between Cherry and Water Streets, and was organized June 21, 1824, with thirty men: William Hawk, boatbuilder, of Water Street, was foreman; William Johnson, assistant foreman; other members were Thomas

Vredenbergh, Philip Snyder, Levi B. Devoe, Benjamin H. Chapman, foreman, Anthony Klopper, assistant foreman (resigned), Paschall Michaletta, John Van Horne.

On June 20, 1835, Anthony Klopper and other members of the company memorialized the Common Council for permission to remove from the foot of Roosevelt Street to Vandewater Street. The company was disbanded on July 9, 1838.

NORTHERN LIBERTY.—EMPIRE ("Hay-wagon," "Mankiller").—A new No. 42, was organized on March 5, 1840. First it was located in Beaver Street, near Broad, next at 45 John Street, then at 88 Nassau Street, afterwards at 2½ Murray Street, and after 1860 at No. 4 Centre Street. It went out of service in 1865. On July 18, 1850, a grand entertainment was given to the company in its engine house, the occasion being to celebrate the elaborate painting of its machine. Among the ladies present were Madame Antoinette Otto (an "honorary member"), Miss Mary Taylor and Mrs. Dr. Traphagen. On the next evening the gentlemen friends of the company were exclusively entertained, and about one thousand partook of the hospitality proffered. The engine house had been superbly decorated.

No. 43.—MANHATTA.—Engine Company 43 was organized October 29, 1821, and located first on Lawrence Street west of Broadway, Manhattanville, in a shanty which is still standing. They had a bell on the building which they took with them to their new house, a two-story frame building, which was built for them in 1843, on the same street, but nearer Tenth Avenue. The quarters of Engine 37 of the Paid Department are on the same site to-day. This company ran an old New York style gooseneck engine painted red; after this an old engine formerly used by 40 Engine, and in 1853 received a Carson style piano engine which they ran until the Department was mustered out. No. 43 ran several months longer than the down-town companies at the request of the Commissioners, as the organization for the upper part of the city was not perfected as early as the down-town portion. Abe Horn, who was foreman from 1851 to 1860, was elected assistant engineer in 1865, and continued under the New Department until January 1, 1868. Ex-Mayor Daniel F. Tiemann joined this company in 1839, and was afterwards elected as foreman, and served as such for eight years. James Pettit, who was assistant foreman under Mr. Tiemann, succeeded him as foreman. In those days they did duty all over the ward, and that extended from Kingsbridge to Fourteenth Street. Other members at various times were William Crawford, blacksmith, foreman, died June 15, 1831, after ten years' service; Peter Myers, Sr., and John Myers, Jr., both famous (1823).

No. 44.—LIVE OAK ("Old Turk").—This company was organized August 2, 1824, by the master shipbuilders of the Dry Dock for the protection of the shipyards in that vicinity. Jacob Bell, Isaac Webb, John Demon, Edward Merritt and Foster Rhodes were the organizers and Isaac Webb the first foreman. They located in a small frame house, built by themselves, in Columbia Street, near Houston, the river at that time coming almost to Goerck Street. They were not attached to the Fire Department for some years, but about 1828 they received the number 44, and had a brick house, one story with peaked roof, built for them in Houston Street, between Lewis and Manhattan Streets, about one hundred feet west of Lewis Street. In 1830 Henry Eckford, the shipbuilder, took a gang of ship carpenters with him to Constantinople to work on a contract he had over there, several of the men being members of No. 44. Eckford died in a very short time after reaching Turkey, and the men were called Turks on their return. One of them, named Russell, had let his beard and hair grow long and was dubbed by his companions as the "Old Turk." The name afterwards extended to the company and remained with them ever afterwards. On their gooseneck engine they had two Turks carved standing upright and full dressed in their costumes and wearing sabres. On the back of the box they had a painting of a female figure with outstretched arms. Edward Penny, Jr., was foreman of the company in 1836, and was elected an assistant engineer in 1837, Nicholas Fisher being elected foreman in his place. Isaac Selleck, Enoch J. Radley and Frank Clark came afterwards as foremen of the company.

The company was always composed of active, tough men, abundantly able to take care of themselves, and at the same time full of animal spirits. They had many enemies, 41, 33, 15, 30 and 18 being at different times the principal rivals. In 1851, under Frank Clark as foreman, this company got their double deck engine, and in connection with this engine the following story is told of the efforts of the company to get her painted.

HOUSE OF LIVE OAK.
[Houston Street, between Lewis and Manhattan Streets.]

In 1852 the "Quills" were in a majority in the company, but one night at a special meeting they were short-handed, and Frank Clark and his party passed a resolution to have the engine painted. She was sent to Van Ness to have the works taken out first, and while there the "Quills" sent a communication to Chief Alfred Carson saying that a majority of the company did not want her painted, and the chief ordered the engine back to the house. When she got there some of the members found that the end brake straps were missing, and concluded that it was not safe to run her over the large gutters in the streets at that time, and turned her in tongue first. A day or two afterwards Bill Landers, Jack Murdock and Charlie (Bangs) Ludlam happened to meet in the house and concluded that the engine ought to be painted anyhow. They got a painter, and he began painting one side a pure white, with the bolts and bolt heads touched up a bright red, leaving the other half a Quaker brown color. The "Quills" were furious, and Mr. Carson was again appealed to. This time he took the engine over to his office in Elizabeth Street, and preferred charges before the Fire and Water Committee, who summoned Messrs. Ludlam, Landers and Murdock before them. Landers was the only witness called. The complaint was dismissed, and the engine sent to the company, who next time had her painted all over. Afterwards one of the members, Charles Wykoff, carved a very handsome box out of solid mahogany for the condenser, the corners surmounted by Turk's heads, and live oak trees with the branches running over and intertwining with each other, with squirrels perched on the branches. On the panels were two pilot boats, one outgoing and the other incoming, which, like the trees, were carved out of the solid wood. This engine the company afterwards owned. The box of the engine was painted a blue color about a shade lighter than ultramarine, and on the front panels was a picture of the Woolsey sugar house fire at Montgomery and Front Streets in November 1849, and on the back panel a portrait of Lady Jane Grey.

John S. Green, one of their members, was run over in 1851 while going to a fire in Houston Street, near Ridge, and killed. The company gave a ball for the benefit of his family. Wm. H. Van Ness, the engine builder, was a member of this company, and Nelson Sampson, who afterwards helped to organize 13 Hook and Ladder, also belonged here. Wm. H. Landers, now foreman of Engine Company No. 42, of the Paid Department, and stationed in Morrisania, followed Clark as foreman, being succeeded by Julien C. Harrison, James Garry, Jeremiah Keeler and John Murdock, and the company laid aside their double-decker for a new piano style of engine built by Van Ness.

In 1851 the company moved to Houston Street, near Columbia, which quarters they retained until they went out of service. Joseph L. Perley, formerly assistant foreman of this company, was elected an assistant engineer in 1862, while a private, and re-elected in 1865. He was appointed an assistant engineer in the Paid Department, afterwards made chief, and finally one of the fire commissioners. James M. Flynn followed as foreman of the company, then Charles L. Miller and William F. Squires, the last foreman. The company were always bitterly opposed to steam engines in the Fire Department, and fought hard against their introduction. Five of their members went to the war with Ellsworth's Zouaves.

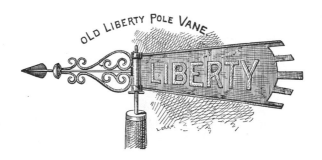

OLD LIBERTY POLE VANE.

CHAPTER XXXVI.

RING OUT THE OLD, RING IN THE NEW.

The Last of the Volunteer Fire Companies.—Dates of Organization and Names of Foremen.—Some Quaint New York History.—Hand and Steam Engines.—New York Grows too Large for Old Time Appliances and Methods.—The New Regime Takes Charge.

N**O. 45.**—YORKVILLE.—AURORA.—This company was organized on September 11, 1826, by Milne Parker, Samuel Parker, Alexander Parker, the coach builders, Edward Prince, Edward Wells, and Jefferson Brown, Milne Parker becoming the first foreman. On May 21, 1827, the company were reinforced by the following members: John G. Kip, Joseph Tricker, Robert Kilpatrick, Stephen Huestis, James Bell, Stephen Harris, Augustus J. Flanagan, and others. Their first location was on the northwest corner of Eighty-fourth Street and Fourth Avenue, and when the tunnel was cut through Fourth Avenue, about 1836, they moved up to the old frame house of No. 16 Engine Company, and placed it on the lot on the northeast corner of Eighty-fifth Street and Third Avenue. A two-story brick house was afterwards built for them and Hook and Ladder No. 10, the company doing duty from a shed in Eighty-fifth Street. The house was afterwards made three stories high. About 1845 the company had their engine painted white and gold with a picture of Aurora, the goddess of day, on the back of the condenser case. She was then christened "Aurora," which name she retained. Philip Grimm, Eli Budd, Alonzo A. Alvord, Rufus Prime, Wm. Fulmer, Frank B. Ball, William Mead, and Frank Bazzoni were the different foremen of the company, Bazzoni serving as such from 1853 until 1865, the longest continuous service of any foreman in the Old Department. Joseph M. McDonald, the colonel of the Forty-seventh New York Volunteers during the late war, was a runner with this company, and John Shelly, brother of Assemblyman Edward J. Shelly, was at one time an assistant foreman and a prominent candidate for assistant engineer. Went out of service in 1865.

No. 46.—RELIEF ("Bull's Head").—It was organized on October 8, 1827, by Lodowick Fick, Jacob Smith, John K. Van Houton, Isaac Kenard, Isaac Van Horn, Joseph Fick, Henry Townsend, Peter Allen, Robert Davidson, John F. Nunn (the pianoforte maker of that time), John Fick, and Henry Smith. The company were composed mostly of pianomakers. They located at Rose Hill (East Twenty-fifth Street), and had a new engine built for them, which they ran until 1835, when it was replaced by another New York style of engine which they used until they were disbanded, October 17, 1849. In 1840, under the foremanship of Charles H. Smith, they were located at 349 Third Avenue, near Twenty-sixth Street. After their disbandment the company were out of service until May 5, 1852, when they were reorganized by Wm. Haw, Jr. (afterwards a member of the Board of Appeals of the New York Fire Department), John Nesbit, the brick maker (the candidate against Florence Scannell for alderman the year that Scannell was shot and fatally wounded in Donohue's saloon), Oliver S. Hibbard, who used to keep the Mansion House on Fourth Avenue near the tunnel, Maurice Daly, father of the celebrated billiard player, Robert Foster, Wm. Wines, John Kennedy, and others. They took the same location, and commenced doing duty with one of the goosenecks built in 1827. Wm. Haw, Jr., was the first foreman, and John Nesbit assistant. John Nesbit succeeded to the office of foreman, and during his term the company was disbanded, October 7, 1854, having been in existence a little over two years.

VALLEY FORGE was organized April 21, 1860, from the company known as Valley Forge Hose Company No. 46. This company was among the first to recognize the value of steam, and purchased one of Lee & Larned's steam engines. The company used the same location as the Hose company, at 138 West Thirty-seventh Street, and commenced doing duty under the foremanship of George A. Nurse. The first working fire the steamer ran to was in Thirty-fourth Street, between Ninth and Tenth Avenues, at which fire she had two streams on the burning building. Wm. J. Peck, at that time president of the Board of Aldermen, was present at the fire, and was so pleased with the working and power of the engine that he offered a resolution in the board to purchase the machine, which was subsequently done. The company had up-hill work of it, however, for nearly a year; the opposition to steam engines in the upper districts was very great, and the company were notified by some of the up-town companies that the engine would certainly be taken away from them, and dumped in the river. The good work of the company soon convinced the firemen, and it was but a short time before Engine Companies 33 and 48—their strongest opponents—applied for steamers themselves. Nurse held the foremanship for several years, during which time the company rapidly increased in membership. They did duty not alone in the First and Second Districts, but held themselves in readiness for special calls. At the fire at Pier 6 in 1860 the company were telegraphed for on a request from assistant Engineer John Baulch to James Millward, who was then assistant foreman of the Exempts, and in twenty-seven minutes afterwards the engine reached the dock from their house in Thirty-seventh Street. Baulch had bet Millward a bottle that they would not get down in half an hour. They got to work and stayed there ten hours. Frank E. Skelding, who was foreman of the company in 1864, afterwards became chief engineer of the Stamford, Conn., Fire Department. James E. Dunn succeeded Skelding, and was the last foreman of the company, which went out of existence on the incoming of the Paid Department. Edward L. Cobb, Geo. W. Da Cunha, Samuel H. Tucker, Elias H. Platt, Alexander McFadden, and William A. Brickhill enlisted in the Union army from this company.

No. 47.—MECHANICS'.—This company was organized March 10, 1828, about the time that Engine Company No. 24 moved from the Dry Dock over to Columbia Street. The first names on the old roll are: Jesse Woods, Jonathan H. Gedney, Jacob H. Strever, Jeremiah Jennings, Benj. R. McCord, John Fallon, Benjamin Perry, James Weeks, Wm. Humes, Henry Worley, and Adam Atchison. These members were all master shipwrights or builders, and the company was specially organized for the protection of the shipyards. They located on the Dry Dock, and in March, 1829, took in the following well-known eastsiders as members: Jacob Bell, Isaac P. Smith, Stephen Smith, John English, and David Brown. Their duty was just about hard enough to clear the members from jury duty. Their house was a small one, which had a bell on it, and a hole cut in the front door through which the rope attached to the bell could be reached, to summon the firemen in case of fire. It was said of the company that they used to "grease their wheels with butter," being too high-toned to use anything more common. They never ran a very large roll, and June 22, 1842, they were organized into Hose Company No. 34.

AQUEDUCT (the second No. 47) Was organized March 6, 1854. It was located in Eighty-second Street, near Third Avenue. The company was disbanded September 18, 1855. Matthew J. Shannon was one of the organizers of Aqueduct with Captain Thomas Beatty, of Central Park Police, and Judge Thomas Pearson and others. Shannon afterwards joined Americus Hose Company 48, was elected assistant foreman, and then foreman.

NEW YORK (the third No. 47.—Was organized on June 4, 1860, the members of New York Hose Company No. 5 having resolved to form themselves into an engine company, and on November 14 of the same year organized New York Engine Company No. 47. They remained in the same location, in Fireman's Hall, and their first officers were, Frank W. Raymond, foreman, and U. W. Wenman, assistant, with James F. Wenman as representative. They commenced doing duty immediately with a new steamer, built in 1860 by Lee & Larned, and rapidly increased their number of members at the next election. Raymond was re-elected foreman, John A. Phillips taking the place of U. W. Wenman as assistant. In the following year Raymond and Phillips were again elected. After this time the company had mutual troubles, which ended in their abandoning their organization March 23, 1864.

CROTON (the fourth No. 47—Was organized on May 26, 1864, Philip Cosgriff foreman, James L. Ewing, assistant, and John D. Smith, secretary. Among the organizers were James Harris, Benjamin C. Bogert, George A. Mott, Benjamin W. Palmer, and E. J. Montague. They were stationed at 165 West Twentieth Street, and did duty with the Shanghai engine of Marion Engine Company No. 9, which they had abandoned for a steamer. The company did duty in the third and fourth districts. In the election of May, 1865, Benjamin W. Palmer was elected foreman, and John Wilkinson assistant. These were the last officers of the company, which was mustered out by the Paid Department. They were in existence but little over a year.

No. 48.—MAZEPPA.—Fire Engine Company No. 48 was organized and established at Fitzroy Road near Nineteenth Street, November 17, 1828, and had eighteen men. Robert Simpson, grocer, corner of Eighth Avenue and Fourteenth Street, in the Ninth Ward, was foreman, and Stephen Merritt, dyer, Factory Road, assistant foreman. Among its members at various times were Alfred Mead, John Mogier, James R. Howell, carman, Henry May, foreman in 1837, William Lawrence, carpenter, Abram Van Orden, John Pennycook, Adam V. Varick. The other locations of the company were: Thirteenth Street and Sixth Avenue; after 1843, at 152 West Twentieth Street; after 1851 in Twenty-fourth Street near Seventh Avenue; after 1864, in Twenty-fifth Street near Ninth Avenue. Disbanded in 1865.

EVERY STEAM ENGINE IN USE AT THE DISBANDMENT OF THE DEPARTMENT IN 1865.

No. 49.—The first company of this number was organized on April 4, 1832, was located in Cherry Street near Walnut, and disbanded about 1835.

POCAHONTAS (the second No. 49).—After the great fire of 1835 the residents of Harlem, feeling themselves not fully protected by the one Engine Company—No. 35—stationed in their section of the city, set to work to organize another engine company, and No. 49 came into existence and located in One Hundred and Twenty-sixth Street, between Third and Fourth Avenues, under the old station house. This house had a fire bell on it, as had the next house to which they removed in 1857. This was a new brick building on the east side of Fourth Avenue, between One Hundred and Twenty-sixth and One Hundred and Twenty-seventh Streets, and is now used by Engine Company No. 36 of the Paid Department. At the time of their organization Gouverneur Morris ran a milk dairy in Harlem, which he called the "Pocahontas Dairy," and their little old gooseneck engine, which was built in 1826, and was painted white, was christened "Pocahontas." They had the back painted with a representation of Pocahontas saving the life of Captain John Smith, and did duty with this engine until 1854, when they received a new Carson piano engine of third-class caliber. The old engine was laid aside, and now graces one of the upper floors of the repair shops of the present Fire Department in West Third Street. The back remains the same, but the box has been painted a dark color. John S. Kenyon was the first foreman, and was elected an assistant engineer in 1840; Warren Brady followed him as foreman. At a fire in Astoria at a tar factory in 1842, one of the former members of this company, William R. Kilpatrick, contracted a severe cold, from which he lost his eyesight, and, although alive and well at this time, has never regained his sight. The trustees of the Benevolent Fund have for years stood by him. Wm. E. Pabor, Wm. Tabele and Epenetus Doughty were among the early foremen of this company, and Henry P. McGown, now civil justice, held the position of foreman for ten years, being succeeded in 1858 by E. W. Gardner, who had been assistant foreman. Wm. T. Mawbey, of this company, was elected an assistant engineer in 1855, serving until 1859. Thomas C. Freeborn, the Harlem undertaker, and George W. Brown, alderman in 1885, and brother to Robert C. Brown, of No. 8 Engine, were also members for a number of years. The Harlem Base Ball Club (celebrated from 1857 to 1860) contained several members of this company. Michael Kennedy succeeded Gardner as foreman, with A. A. Liscomb as assistant. In 1861 the company discarded the Carson engine, and took in its place the engine that had been used by No. 26 Engine Company, and replaced by a steam engine. It was of a piano style, but of a much lighter build than their former engine. Wm. H. Waterson and A. J. Walsh were at that time elected foreman and assistant of the company. Cuthbert W. Ridley followed in 1862 as foreman and was elected an assistant engineer in 1863. Thomas C. Kennedy, who was assistant foreman, was elected foreman, and held the office till the company went out of service in 1865.

No. 50.— MOHEGAN.—Was organized April 1, 1840, was located at Harsenville, and changed to Engine Company No. 36 on March 10, 1848.

LONE STAR—LIBERTY (the second No. 50.—Was organized as an American Company, in the Ninth Ward, on September 1, 1854. The organizers were Ralph P. Barker, Alexander McCune, A. R. Whitney, John M. Harned, George Merritt, and some others. Mr. Barker was the first foreman, Mr.

Whitney the first assistant, and Mr. Harned the first secretary. In 1856 William P. Daniels was elected foreman, with R. Van Houten as assistant. In 1857 Mr. Van Houten became foreman and Mr. Harned assistant. The name of the company was changed to that of " Liberty Engine Company " in 1858, and Mr. Harned was elected foreman, and Jacob R. Riley assistant. A disagreement arose over the election of Mr. Harned, who was opposed by Mr. Van Houten, the outcome of which was that thirteen members resigned. John M. Harned served as foreman for four years, and was succeeded by Richard Dougherty, who, however, resigned before the expiration of one year, and was succeeded by P. Gibney in 1864. On the eleventh of February of that year, about three months after Mr. Gibney's election, the company was disbanded on account of a difficulty with the members of Engine Company No. 54 (previously known as Hose Company No. 57). The company was subsequently reorganized as Croton Engine Company No 47.

Among the prominent members in the early days of No. 50 besides those already mentioned, were George C. Kibbe, Frank T. Baker, Gilbert G. Butler, J. Hogencamp, James Lounsberry, Peter Vanderbilt and John Frink. The social name of the company was at one time " The Liberty Boys" and later " The Dashing Half Hundred," and a right lively lot they were. The company was largely composed of carmen and masons. During the war of the rebellion Thomas Hendricks, William H. Covert,

[ENGINE, ETC.—From Policy of the Firemen's Insurance Company, New York, 1838. Anderson, first American wood engraver in this country, executed this sketch for Firemen's Insurance Company.]

John L. Conry, William A. Wood, and some fifteen other members of the company volunteered into the Union Army.

No. 51.—MUTUAL.—Shortly after Engine Company No. 30 was disbanded in 1854, a number of their members, with many other companies, among whom were Andrew P. Sutton, John A. Smith, John F. Sloper, Geo. McGrath and Wm. H. Swords, met together, and on December 29 of the same year organized Mutual Engine Company No. 51, taking up their quarters in No. 30's old house on the north side of Twenty-second Street, between First and Second Avenues, next door to where the police station now stands, John F. Sloper becoming their first foreman. They ran an old gooseneck engine during their first year, and in 1856 received a new second-class Shanghai engine, which they shortly afterwards, in 1857, took with them to the State fair at Elmira, and carried off the first prize at a playing match, beating seven other engines, and being the first New York City company to win and get an out-of-town prize. While at Elmira an opportunity occurred in the burning of a building for the New Yorkers to exhibit their skill, and they did so creditably, Sloper " borrowing " the butt out of a country engine that had got to work, to put into No. 51. The members of 51 Engine Company, 29 Hose, and some other companies, were greatly annoyed at being assaulted and stoned by the hangers-on at the dog-pit on Second Avenue, and this the members of 51 determined to put a stop to. So on the night of the fire at the Second Avenue stables in 1856, and after being stoned on their way to the fire, 51's boys "dropped in" on them as they were on their way home and thrashed them. The latter complained to Mayor Wood the next day at the City Hall, but the mayor took a common sense view of the matter and told them that they had this time woke up the wrong customer. After Sloper's term expired John A. Smith was elected foreman, and he was succeeded by Geo. McGrath, who was elected assistant engineer in 1865.

One afternoon, as Nos. 51 and 7 Companies were racing down Broadway, having met at Astor Place, a lot of No. 9's men jumped in on the rope of No. 51 Engine near Prince Street to rather offset the help that No. 4 Engine had given No. 7 Engine just above. One of them, in his haste to be of assistance, got between the tongue and front wheel. That was no place for him, so he rolled up in a heap and went under the wheels of the engine. Jack Sloper, who had command of No. 51 Engine, had the man picked up, and, thinking him mortally wounded from the quantity of blood, conveyed him to the New York Hospital, then on Broadway near Anthony Street. A few days afterwards, as Sloper was passing the building, he thought he would stop in and see if he was yet living. At the hospital gate were Alfred Carson, chief, and Elisha Kingsland, assistant engineer, who were trying to gain admittance to see a member of No. 5 Engine Company who had broken his leg at a fire a short time previously. As Sloper had on his best clothes, he pretended not to notice the chief and assistant engineer, but stepped up and also put in his plea for admittance. The keeper asked if he wanted, like the others, to see the wounded fireman. Sloper, seeing that his predecessors were unsuccessful in gaining entrance, it not being visiting day, said indignantly that he knew nothing and wished to know nothing about any fireman—that he wished to see one of the doctors. But his efforts were of no avail, and all three had to leave without entering the front gate. Sloper did not give it up so easily. Going around to No. 21 Engine house he asked one of the members how he could get into the hospital when they wouldn't let him in by the front gate. Upon advice Sloper went to the back gate, where they were getting in coal that day, and asking the old Irishman who was doing the shoveling "Who's in charge here?" "I am, sorr," said the old man. "Well, then," said Sloper, "see that you stay here and attend to it," and walked into the building. He very soon came to the bed of the wounded member of No. 5 Engine and stopped to offer him a few words of comfort, saying that he must keep up a good heart and that his friends did not come oftener on account of not always being able to get there on visiting days, and added that he would have had two more visitors that day had they been able to gain admittance. He then asked him if he knew where the member of No. 9 Engine was that No. 51 had run over and so severely injured a few days before. "What, that fellow!" said the sick man;" "why, Sloper, he's the worst man I ever knew; he is down in the yard now; just look here!" and turning down the coverlid disclosed to the astonished eyes of Sloper oranges, apples, jams, jellies and other delicacies, and said, "That fellow prowls around the ward, and whenever he sees anything nice, no matter where it is, he steals it and brings it here. I can't eat all of these, and I don't want them found here." Sloper guessed that it couldn't be the same man, for his man was very badly hurt. "Oh, no, this one is down in the yard now," said the member of No. 5 Engine. Sloper went down, and, sure enough, there he was. He told him he ought to be in bed, as he was hurt worse than he imagined, and besides he wanted him to go up and take away those things from that bed and not get No. 5's member into trouble. "Oh, that's all right; I ain't hurt, and that poor fellow up stairs shall have anything he wants; mind, now, I say so. I am only waiting here a day or two longer to make a stake and I'll see you." Two days afterwards Sloper, who then lived in Twenty-third Street, back of the engine house, was called to the door, and there was the No. 9 Engine man. "Sloper," he said, "come round to the engine house. I've got lots of money, and we'll have a bully time." Sloper told him he had company, but if he would go around he would join him in an hour. The fellow went off, and Sloper did not go near the engine house that day. He had had enough of badly wounded firemen for a while.

No. 52.—UNDINE.—This company was organized on February 19, 1863, by the members of Hose Company No. 21, and located at 304 Washington Street. It went out of service in 1865.

No. 53.—HUDSON RIVER.—Was organized by members of Hose Company No. 21 February 19, 1863, and elected Terence Duffy foreman, and Thomas McGrath assistant foreman. On March 23 the company was suspended from duty for six months, and was disbanded December 17, 1864. An appeal was made to the courts, and on June 13, 1865, the Supreme Court reversed the decision of the fire commissioners, so that No. 53 was in good standing when the Volunteer Department ceased to exist.

No. 54.—PAULDING.—Was organized February 19, 1863, by members of Hose Company No. 57, stationed at No. 162 West Eighteenth Street, between Seventh and Eighth Avenues. The officers elected were: Robert Williams, foreman; James McEntee, assistant foreman. The existence of No. 54 was very brief. The company was disbanded February 11, 1864, inside of a year of their organization.

FLOATING ENGINE.—The mist of years appears to wrap this company with an almost impenetrable cloud. As near as can be ascertained, some time in the year 1800 the city had a boat constructed after the model of a scow, skiff-shaped, sharp bow and square stern. On board this vessel was placed the works of an ordinary fire engine, with all the paraphernalia for extinguishing fires—hose, pipes, etc. The motive power was twelve strong, willing men, and long man-of-war's sweeps, or oars. The vessel was located at the foot of Roosevelt Street, and was to be used for the purpose of aiding the Fire Department at fires occurring on vessels at shipyards, wharves, and adjacent property generally. The company did not remain in service many years, was finally broken up, and the engine became the "Supply Engine," and was located at Leonard Street, between Centre and Elm Streets, where the Tombs now is.

In the Common Council, January 7, 1805, a report was received from the select committee to whom was referred a report of the city inspector, dated 24th ult., upon the subject of fire, and a letter upon the same subject from the street commissioner to the mayor, under same date, and also a report of the engineer of the Fire Department. The select committee reported as follows:

That the means employed in the extinguishment of fire are susceptible of considerable improvement, that the increasing extent and population of the city increase the chances of frequent and dangerous fires, but at the same time afford the means, and indicate the propriety, of putting the Fire Department upon a more efficacious and systematic footing. It is now known that experience has fully proved the superior utility of the Floating Engine. But as that engine cannot always be moved in due season to the place where it may be wanted, the committee propose that another of the same kind should be procured. For a like reason, and also because at some seasons the ice or other causes may prevent the floating engines from moving, the committee recommend that two other engines be procured of similar powers, but to be placed on wheels, and to be kept within the city. These, however, are not proposed merely as substitutes for the floating engines, but because it is thought that four of this species are not more than can be usefully employed on many occasions. It appears also to the committee that certain of the engines now in use are both entirely too small and greatly out of repair, that they accede more readily to the proposal of selling these because they are of opinion that in future all the engines except those before mentioned should be of about equal size and power. The committee is also of opinion that the screws of all the leaders should be made of uniform size, so that each one may fit all the rest, by which means the accidental failure of a leader, when in use, may be supplied if necessary, from another engine. Upon this subject, too, an improvement upon the method of fixing the leaders to each other has been suggested, which is submitted to the Board among the resolutions subjoined :

Resolved, That one floating engine of like power with that now in use, and also two other engines of like power to go on wheels, be constructed in this city for the use of the corporation, and that the same be contracted for by the chief engineer, and built under his direction. That Engines Nos. 2, 5, 6, and 16 be sold at auction, or otherwise, under the direction of the chief engineer ; and that he cause their places to be supplied by an equal number of new engines of equal power with the largest now in use except the floating engine.

That in future there be but two sizes of leaders and of the screws wherewith they are fitted, viz.: The first size for the engines of the like power with the floating engine, and the second size for the others. That to every common engine there be at least four leaders of forty feet each, and that the chief engineer procure and always keep at such places as he shall think proper a number of spare leaders, sufficient to supply the probable deficiencies that may suddenly happen. That the leaders be connected with each other by screws of such construction that they may be joined without twisting, and that each leader may be fitted to any other of the same class of engines, and for this purpose new screws be added to all the leaders now in use, which will admit of screws of the size that may be determined on as the standard, and that the chief engineer cause this resolution to be carried into effect.

That it be the duty of the chief engineer, whenever any engine leader or other fire machinery or utensil belonging to the Board is out of repair, to have it repaired immediately at his discretion and at the expense of the Board.   *   *   *   *   *   *   *   *

WYMANT VAN ZANDT, ABRAHAM KING, ABRAHAM BLOODGOOD, SAM. M. HOPKINS, JACOB MOTT,   *Members of Select Committee.*

The Floating Engine was changed to Engine Company No. 42 in 1824.

SUPPLY ENGINE.—This company was organized in 1827. Among the earliest members were William L. Jenkins, Robert S. Barnes, Thomas C. Shipley, James M. Tilley, Robert H. Haydock, Leffert Schenck, Edmond Penfold, William W. Macy, John H. Robins, and James B. Townsend. These men were all merchants or accountants, and their fire duty with this company was not very arduous. The Supply Engine stood on the Franklin Street side of the Corporation Yard, in the middle of the block between Elm and Centre Streets.

It was in a frame building about seventy-five feet long, and about twenty feet deep. The engine was stationary, and drew the water from the well underneath. It was only used when a fire occurred in the neighborhood, and then only for the supply of the engines, the well being too deep for them to take suction from it. It was on the site of the old Collect Pond, and, as the saying went, "had no bottom." The engine could not throw a stream, being only a suction engine, and its utmost capacity was the supplying of three engines at one time. It was worked by a revolving shaft running the whole length of the building, the pump being in the center, and whenever occasion required the assistance of this company they were helped out by the citizens, and boys of the neighborhood, who would flock to the house when the engine was at work for the fun of having the chance to turn the crank. There was always an opposition to this company among the firemen, on account of its having so little duty to perform, but it remained in existence until February 26, 1841, when it went out of service. The placing of hydrants around the city had rendered the use of the engine needless, and, the Corporation Yard being moved away, the pump was laid aside.

EXEMPT ENGINE COMPANY.—This company was organized by the Common Council as a reserve corps, December 27, 1854. It was composed exclusively of exempt members of the Fire Department, and only performed duty in the case of a general alarm, or when directed by the engineers. The first officers were James L. Miller, foreman; Floyd S. Gregg, first assistant; John W. Garside, second assistant; John B. Leverich, third assistant; James Gilmore,

SUPPLY ENGINE NO. 1.

secretary; Charles E. Gildersleve, assistant secretary, and John S. Giles, treasurer. They took charge of the large first-class haywagon style engine, that was built by Waterman in 1842 for the use of 42 Engine Company, and which had been abandoned by them on account of its great weight. They organized with one hundred and fifty names on their roll, including at least seven ex-assistant engineers, any number of ex-foremen, and one ex-fire commissioner. On the ninth of February, 1855, the Exempts had a trial in the City Hall Park between their old "Man-killer" Engine and a new steam engine built in Cincinnati. The Park was thronged with spectators all interested in the exhibition. The engines took suction from a cistern, and each played through four lengths of hose (two hundred feet). On the first trial, playing horizontally, the steamer threw a stream over one hundred and eighty-two feet, while the exempts reached one hundred and eighty-nine feet. The second trial on the same conditions had the same result. Preparations were made for a third trial, this time perpendicularly, and when the streams were directed to the figure of Justice on the cupola of the City Hall, Zophar Mills and John W. Garside, assistant foreman of the Exempts, ascended to the roof to watch the progress of the playing. The "Haywagon's" stream was the highest, but after the men had dropped exhausted from the brakes, the steamer's stream kept steadily on.

"John," said Mr. Mills, "that stream stays there."

"Yes, it does," said Mr. Garside.

"Well, that settles it," said Mr. Mills, and both these old firemen then felt convinced that the steamer was the engine of the future.

Zophar Mills followed James L. Miller as foreman of the company, and held the office several years. In 1859 this company was given charge of two steam fire engines which were stationed in the Park, the hand engine being still housed at 202 Centre Street. One of the steamers was the large self-propeller, a very powerful engine, but hard to get to and from fires, its liability to break down of its own great weight causing considerable trouble. Once at work at a fire, it was worth a dozen hand engines in its capacity for throwing water.

John J. Gorman followed Zophar Mills as foreman of the company, and remained as such until the reorganization of the Department in 1865. Shortly before that time the company had given up their location in Centre Street, housing both their engines in the house in the Park—the John G. Storms and the Haywagon; the Cary had been taken from their charge previously. At the fire at Pier 6, N. R., January 28, 1860, the Exempts had the "Storms" to work, and after the fire, and while coming up Broadway, the alarm struck for the *Ledger* building fire in Fulton Street. The company proceeded there and again got to work. It was Friday evening when the company went to the ship fire, and they did not again house their engine until Sunday morning.

In 1860 the following officers were in command : Zophar Mills, foreman; John W. Garside, first assistant foreman; James Millward, second assistant foreman; Charles E. Gildersleve, third assistant foreman; James Y. Watkins, Jr., secretary; Thomas L. Talman, assistant secretary. The company continued in active service until the time of the absorption of the Old by the New Department. The officers at the time of the final act were as follows: John J. Gorman, foreman; James Y. Watkins, first assistant foreman; E. F. Lasak, second assistant foreman; George R. Connor, third assistant foreman; John M. Harned, secretary; Joshua Isaacs, assistant secretary. The insurance interests and the public generally were profuse in their thanks to those old firemen, who, after serving their many years of toil, exposure and danger, were willing to sacrifice family ties and home comforts to secure safety to their fellow-citizens.

In 1853 Seth R. Abrahams, Peter Hoffman, W. J. Holmes, Wm. Hardy, John A. Leonard, W. J. Roome and John A. Tucker were members, and Neptune Hose, of Philadelphia, presented the company with a massive silver trumpet. This, by a unanimous vote, was presented to Mr. Garside as a token of their esteem for him as an officer and fireman. In 1855 Philip Farley was elected foreman, and the company brought home another new carriage. In 1862 still another one was built by Van Ness, when John Lynch became foreman. He was followed by John L. Herbell. The company in 1863 elected James Cook foreman and John Kennedy assistant. The last foreman was John Kennedy, the company going down with colors flying at the disbandment of the Old Department.

CHAPTER XXXVII.

HISTORY OF THE HOSE COMPANIES.

From No. 1 to 25, inclusive.—The Dates of their Organization and Disbandment.—The Men who Rendered Conspicuous Services.—Their Foremen and other Officers.—Services Rendered and their Story Narrated.—Some Incidents worth Recording.—Heroic in all Things.

NO. 1.—EAGLE.—This company was organized on September 7, 1812. Its various locations were as follows: In 1813, at the Bridewell on Broadway; in 1823, in the Corporation Yard; from 1832 to 1834, in Mulberry Street, near Broome; later in Tryon Row; in 1837, at 5 Duane Street; in 1847, at 156 Madison Street; in 1863, at 3 Pike Street; went out of service in 1865. Among the members in 1813 and later were William Stone, foreman; Joseph H. Horton, assistant; Simon Van Ness, steward; Wm. W. Halsted, Sinclair Tousey. On Sunday morning in January, 1850, Joseph S. Taylor and Comptroller Taylor (the son subsequently becoming well known in municipal affairs as the head of a department), while running to a fire caught hold of No. 1's rope. He tripped and fell, and, his face coming in contact with some sharp substance, his nose was split in the center from the forehead down. The scar remained for life. At the time there were in the company E. P. Morris, Charles Aikman, Geo. C. Webster, John S. Beers, John A. Seaman and William A. Boyd. The company, while located in Madison Street, near Pike, were called " Mutton Hose." The name (" Mutton Hose ") came about in this manner: at an annual meeting, after the officers were elected, the newly-elected officers took the boys down to an old-fashioned English ale house in Madison Street near Catharine Street, and were eating English mutton pies, when an alarm of fire occurred and they rushed out with pies in hand—hence the name.

The company was one of the last companies disbanded by the Metropolitan Commissioners, in October, 1865. The last fire attended was in a grocery house, corner of Warren and Greenwich Streets. The rope was filled with not only their own members, but with members of most all companies running in the Seventh and Eighth Districts, they having been disbanded but a short time previously. The last officers were Lewis Hopps, foreman; James H. Bartley, assistant foreman. Among the firemen of No. 1 were Henry J. Ockershausen, Halsey M. Mead, James Connor and Thomas Truslow (an old Quaker).

At the annual meeting of Eagle Hose on Monday evening, May 12, 1851, the following were elected officers for the ensuing year: Charles Aikman, foreman; George C. Webster, assistant; Joseph S. Taylor, secretary: William A. Boyd, treasurer; and Joseph S. Taylor and Charles Aikman, representatives.

On Monday, June 14, 1852, the morning of the second annual parade of the

Department, the members of Eagle Hose called a meeting to witness a presentation. The presents were a pair of handsome trumpets—one to Mr. Charles Aikman, the foreman of No. 1, by Messrs. Joseph Canning, Joseph S. Taylor and Henry A. Kendall; and one to the assistant, Mr. G. C. Webster, by Mr. James W. Conner, as a slight token of the respect and esteem of the company.

No. 2.—NIAGARA—KNICKERBOCKER.—This company was organized on December 5, 1831, and located in Rose Street; in 1841 it was at 262 William Street; after 1847 at 5 Duane Street; went out of service in 1865. Among the earlier members of the company were John Ryan, clerk, foreman; Peter McAvoy, carman, assistant; Daniel Brady, merchant; John Monahan, cooper; Charles Kirchhoff, currier. Some time after the organization of "Niagara," J. Munroe Russell and Richard Davis were appointed a committee to ask the Common Council for an increase of members, to make the total thirty men, which request was granted.

No. 3.—INDEPENDENCE — INDEPENDENT.—This company was organized November 19, 1832, by some of the members of Engine Company No. 24, and located at the corner of Beach and Chapel Streets. Joseph Stanton, cordwainer, was the first foreman, and Charles Copping, cordwainer, assistant.

STYLE OF FIRST HOSE CARRIAGE IN NEW YORK.

John S. Giles, afterwards treasurer of the Fire Department fund, was one of the early foremen of this company, and Charles H. Innes, who was a captain in the Mexican war, and was distinguished for his bravery, was a member of the company. After the Gulick trouble Mr. J. Rogers was foreman, and he was followed by William Taylor, who died in Mexico, and after him came James Elkins and George Whitehead. About this time they changed their location to 202 Centre Street. At the fair of the American Institute, held at Castle Garden in the fall of 1849, this company had their new carriage, just built by Pine and painted by Thorp and Grinnell, on exhibition. It was a beautiful piece of workmanship, and all the paintings were patriotic. The body and running gear were painted black, with gilt stripes. On the right of the reel was a magnificent representation of the Boston Tea Party. On the left of the reel was a stirring picture of the Battle of Bunker Hill. On the back box was a painting of the signing of the Declaration of Independence; on the right panel was represented the Stamp Act Parade in New York, in 1765. On the left panel Col. Ethan Allen demanding the surrender of Fort Ticonderoga, May 10, 1775. On the front box was a beautifully painted landscape representing the Goddess of Liberty in the foreground and civilization in the perspective. Each end of the panels was ornamented with a neat silver shield bearing a figure 3 in gold. The whole was topped by a handsome signal lamp with the name and number of the company. The carriage was one of the most beautiful of the several apparatus on exhibition at the fair that year. In 1850 Moses O. Allen, an active and efficient officer and fireman, was foreman of the company, and in 1852 they again removed their location, this time to 211 Hester Street, near Centre, and Nicholas W. Mooney was chosen as foreman. He held the office until 1856, when his assistant, James McKelvey, was promoted to the position. George W. Spencer, Owen Campbell and H. K. Woodruff subsequently filled the position, the latter being foreman when the company went out of service in 1865. The carriage previously mentioned was run by the company until 1855, when it was laid aside for a new and improved Pine & Hartshorn, which was disabled in 1861, and after doing duty for a time with a jumper, they procured a carriage built by Van Ness, which they ran until the Department was disbanded.

The later records of the Department have the name of this company as "Independent," but Mr. Moses O. Allen states that her name was always Independence, "first, last and all the time."

Mr. Allen seems to have been a popular foreman, for he received many presentations. On November 19, 1850, the company went on a memorable excursion to Philadelphia, where they were right royally received. Thousands turned out to welcome them. The Philadelphians paraded in the following order:

Chief Marshal and two Aids mounted. Representatives of each company in the parade mounted. Members of the Buffalo Club mounted. Pennsylvania Cornet Band, Hibernia Engine Company, Good Intent Hose Company, Northern Liberty Engine Company, Resolution Hose Company, Reliance Engine Company, Pennsylvania Band, Columbia Hose Company, Mechanics' Band, American Engine Company, Diligent Hose Company Band, Kensington Engine Company, Philadelphia Greys' Brass Band, Northern Liberty Hose Company, Navy Yard Band, Franklin Engine Company, Committee of Humane Hose Company, Washington Brass Band of New York, Independence Hose Company of New York, Beck's Philadelphia Brass Band, Humane Hose Company, with New York apparatus, Washington Band, Washington Hose Company, Independent Greys' Band of Baltimore, Howard Engine Company of Baltimore, Friendship Engine Company, Union Band, Independence Hose Company Band, Good Will Engine Company, Good Will Hose Company, Kensington Hose Company, Fairmount Engine Company, Carroll Hose Company, Southwark Engine Company, Martial Music, Spring Garden Hose Company, Western Hose Company, Fairmount Hose Company. The line moved with difficulty along Delaware Avenue to Dock Street, where it met the Howard of Baltimore; and here again the fraternal feeling was manifested, each company, the Independence of New York, and Howard of Baltimore, passing each other uncovered, while the surveying mass rent the welkin in huzzas. The engine and hose houses were festooned with colors, the apparatus exhibited in front, and the fire bells tolled. On account of the lateness of the arrival, the route being very long, the parade was finally made by torchlight, and as the line neared, bonfires were kindled and variegated fireworks displayed. As it passed the Humane Engine House (the steeple illuminated) the display was grand, specimens of the whole pyrotechnic art being exhibited. M. O. Allen, E. M. Conklin, J. J. Poillon, T. W. Timpson, J. H. Ridabock, M. Toumey, and W. H. Smith were the committee to prepare a card of thanks to the Philadelphians.

Hose Company No. 3 contributed more men than any fire company in this city to the New York Fire Zouave Regiment when the war broke out. Their number was so reduced by members catching the patriotic frenzy of the hour and going off to the field of battle for the sake of the Union, that the Common Council considered the advisability of either disbanding the company or consolidating its remaining members with some other hose company. After the war, however, the members who survived and who served in the Fire Zouave Regiment, belonging to Hose Company 3, came back to their first love, and the company had its existence prolonged, but only for a brief period, for in 1865 the new order of things came into existence.

No. 4.—LAFAYETTE.—MARION (" Veto").—Lafayette was organized February 5, 1833. It was located at the corner of Delancey and Attorney Streets, and after 1860 at 84 Attorney Street, going out of service in 1865. Among its members were: John W. Slocum, grocer, foreman (1839); James H. Sutton, carpenter, assistant (resigned 1838); Dave Smith (1848), Abe Brown (1849), Joe Buckman (1851), "Bob" Smith (1853), Theo. Hillyer (1856), "Ed." Lewis (1860), George Smith (1861-1865), John Dean, John Sutcliff, John Eldridge, James Hinchman, "Al." Jeffray, and John Hall. In 1850 the following officers were elected: Joseph Buchman, foreman, vice A. F. Brown, declined; William Swenarton, assistant, vice E. Prince, declined; William H. Anderson, secretary, vice William Swenarton, promoted; Theodore H. Abbott, treasurer, re-elected; Abram F. Brown and William H. Willmott, representatives. In 1850 the company had their new carriage built by Van Ness, ornamented in a superb manner. They brought her home from the painter's on the fourth of April, upon which occasion they gave an entertainment to their friends at the carriage house. The running gear was an ultramarine blue, boxes and arch purple, reel carmine, with rich gilt carved work; the wheels had a gilt and red stripe. On the front box was a beautiful painting, entitled, "The Spirit of '76." It represented the interior of a farmhouse, and a young American was preparing to hasten forward to join his countrymen in arms to resist the tyranny of Great Britain; the family were busily engaged about him in assisting him in his preparations, and taking a fond farewell. On the back box was a splendid illustration of Marion's swamp encampment, and the general inviting the British officer to a dinner of sweet potatoes. On the side panel was an illustration from Washington Irving's "Legend of Rip Van Winkle." The back panel represented old Rip just as he returned to the village after taking his long nap, clothed in rags, with his old rusty firelock in his hand. The designs were the same on each side. On each side of the reel was a handsome silver-plated shield, with "IV" engraved on it. On the front there were two figures supporting a shield bearing "IV." The tongue was silver-plated, and there was a considerable amount of silver-plating on the carriage. The painting was done by E. Weir, the picture by J. Quidor, and the silver-plating by J. Johnson.

In September, 1850, Marion Hose embarked for Philadelphia. They turned out thirty-six caps, and were accompanied by Dodworth's Band, comprising sixteen pieces. Mr. John P. Lacour, assistant engineer, acted as marshal. The company looked exceedingly well: dress – black pants, red shirts, black belts, and fire caps. Their beautiful carriage was ornamented with two splendid wreaths. They received a true Philadelphia welcome, and were received at Burlington by the Hope Hose Company and a delegation from the Hope Hose Company of Philadelphia, whose guests they were to be, **Mr. C.**

W. Hepburn acting as chairman of the Committee of Arrangements and chief marshal of the Hopes. After an exchange of courtesies on the part of the committee and their guests, Wm. Moran, Esq., received the New Yorkers in a neat speech in the cars at Burlington, welcoming them upon the soil of New Jersey, but more particularly upon the spot made interesting in our history by the landing of Penn. In the "City of Brotherly Love" they were received by the following companies: Reliance Engine Company, Humane Hose Company, Assistance Engine Company, Beck's Philadelphia Band, Hope Hose Company, Dodworth's Cornet Band, Marion Hose Company No. 4, of New York, with their carriage handsomely decorated with wreaths, Franklin Engine Company, Bayley's Independent Brass Band, Columbia Hose Com-

HAT AND TRUMPET OF DAVID C. BRODERICK.

pany, Good Will Engine Company, Washington Brass Band, Diligent Hose Company, Northern Liberty Hose Company, Marion Hose Company, Pennsylvania Hose Company, Schuylkill Hose Company. The procession was under the direction of the following gentlemen: Colonel Thomas B. Florence, chief marshal; Samuel Van Stavoren and John Chambers, aids; Samuel Freas, John F. Gibson, John Porter, and George Robbins, assistant marshals.

No. 5.—NEW YORK.—The first New York was organized March 20, 1833, was located in Eldridge Street, near Division, and was disbanded on September 23, 1833. Its foreman was Walter Welsh, with John Peach, assistant.

NEW YORK.—On September 26, 1836, three days after the disbanding of the company of the same name and number, another was organized by the following:

T. C. Sherman, Chas. E. Wardell, Carlisle Norwood, A. W. Vanpell, John S. Winthrop, William H. Townsend, A. G. Norwood, Richard K. Anthony, Charles C. Walden, F. W. Macy, Charles P. Williams, Richard Williams, James Daily, Wm. H. Hays, and Eccles Gillender. On October 3 they met at the house of George Wooddredge in Chambers Street, and elected the following officers: Carlisle Norwood, foreman; Augustus W. Vanpell, assistant; and Richard K. Anthony, secretary and treasurer. The company was composed of the best material, most of the members being merchants, and all of them men of high character. They located in Fireman's Hall, then a frame building on the site of the present hall on Mercer Street, and commenced their career with a two-wheeled jumper. Their first duty was on the night of October 16, the fire being on the corner of Christopher and Washington Streets, where they took the water of 8 Engine and had a pipe on the fire. On May 1, 1837, the first regular meeting of the company was held at Constitution Hall on Broadway, and the officers were re-elected. In the following month Mr. Norwood, the foreman, called a special meeting and tendered his resignation, feeling that much of the hostility that had been shown to the company on the part of some members of the Common Council had been directed towards him personally, and he did not care to embarrass the company. The company, however, refused to accept the resignation, and passed resolutions sustaining Mr. Norwood. In the following year Carlisle Norwood was again elected foreman, R. K. Anthony being chosen assistant. On May 6, 1839, Mr. Norwood was unanimously re-elected foreman, making the fourth time, and Mr. Anthony re-elected assistant. At a special meeting held June 18, to discuss the Gulick trouble, the company resolved to continue to do duty, while deprecating political strife.

In October, 1839, the company had the carriage with which they had been doing duty rebuilt and painted. The cost was two hundred and fifty dollars, of which the company paid two hundred and twenty-five dollars. It was a very elaborate affair for those times. The design on the front box represented the city coat of arms, while to the left were seen snow-capped mountains, forest trees, streams leaping over rocks, etc., descriptive of the rude state of our country when in possession of the Indians. On the right was a view of the City of New York, its bay and harbor, emblematic of the improvements of civilization. The rear box had a view of Neptune and Amphitrite riding over the sea, drawn by sea horses, in the distance a fire which Amphitrite is seemingly imploring Neptune to extinguish. The paintings were executed in the finest manner by Joseph H. Johnson. In May, 1840, Mr. Norwood was again re-elected foreman, with J. S. Winthrop, Jr., as assistant, and on September 21 Messrs. Norwood and Winthrop and eight others resigned from the company, which thereupon, after passing a vote of thanks to the officers for the faithful discharge of their duties, elected Mr. Reuben B. Mount as foreman, and John Orde Creighton assistant, to fill the vacancies. In May, 1841 and 1842, Mount and Creighton were re-elected. The winter of 1842-43 was a particularly severe one, and in February, the snow being almost impassable, the company bought a sleigh, to which they attached their hose reel, and with it did duty. In 1844 the same officers were continued in their respective positions, and the carriage that the company had been running broke down. It had been repaired and rebuilt so often that, like the boy's pocket-knife, only about a spring remained of the original, and the company went back to their two-wheeled carriage. The company considering themselves favored in their choice of officers, retained Messrs. Mount and Creighton at their election in 1845, and on Christmas Eve Mr. Howard Havens, on behalf of the company, presented Mr. Mount with a silver trumpet, as a mark of their regard and esteem. In 1846 Mount and Creighton were again chosen as officers, Creighton resigning in October, and J. C. Ayers taking his place. The election of 1847 resulted in Mount and Ayers being again selected, and in November the company housed a new carriage built by Pine. This was considered one of the finest carriages in the Department, and the company went to considerable expense in embellishing it. The running gear was painted a lake color striped with gold, the hose reel was elegantly carved, the iron work entirely silver-plated, and the side shields with the city coat of arms of solid silver.

In May, 1848, Mr. Mount declined re-election and Mr. J. C. Ayers was promoted, and Mr. H. L. Butler advanced to the position of assistant. Ayers resigned the following month, and Mr. Butler was elected foreman, and H. W. Banks made assistant, they being re-elected in 1849 and 1850. In the latter year Mr. James F. Wenman was elected secretary. During this year the company took charge of the reception of Phenix Hook and Ladder Company No. 3,

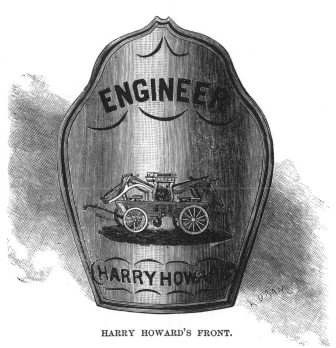

HARRY HOWARD'S FRONT.

which returned from a visit to Baltimore, and also took part in the parade in honor of Diligent Hose Company of Philadelphia, Messrs. Butler and Gowers of the company entertaining them with a collation. Mr. Banks resigned his position as assistant foreman on September 4, and Mr. J. F. Wenman was elected to fill the vacancy, holding the office until December, 1850, when, on Mr. Butler resigning, he was elected foreman. In May, 1851, Mr. Wenman was re-elected foreman, and Mr. S. J. Sullivan made assistant. On August 9, of this year, the company received an accession of twelve new members from Engine Company No. 4, and in November the company abandoned the gilded cap fronts they had worn and adopted a stitched front style with golden figures stitched on. Messrs. Wenman and Sullivan were re-elected in 1852 and 1853, and on July 22 of the latter year the company attended the annual parade of the New Haven Fire Department. They also took part in the reception of Engine Company No. 10

of Albany on September 1. While Fireman's Hall was being built the company did duty from the old house of No. 11 Engine Company, 118 Wooster Street. In May, 1854, Messrs. Wenman and Sullivan were re-elected, but Mr. Sullivan resigned in June and John H. Lyons was elected in his place. At the election of 1855 Mr. Wenman again received the vote of his company, W. H. Colwell being elected assistant. In May, 1856, the company accepted the resignation of Mr. Wenman, he having been elected an assistant engineer, and passed the following resolution:

Resolved, That in accepting the resignation of Mr. James F. Wenman, we take occasion to express to him our unanimous appreciation and approval of the prompt, efficient, and fearless manner in which he has discharged the duties of chief officer of this company for the past six years.

They elected him an honorary member of the company, and Mr. Sullivan, on behalf of the company, presented Mr. Wenman with an elegant silver trumpet as a token of their respect and esteem. At the election held that month, W. H. Colwell was made foreman and Geo. A. Harriott assistant. The resolutions passed by the company were handsomely engrossed and presented to Mr. Wenman. In May, 1857, Mr. Harriott was elected foreman and E. Yerks assistant; in 1858 Frank W. Raymond and W. H. Lamb; in 1859 Raymond and U. W. Wenman; in 1860 Raymond and James Murray. Henry Wilson, who, from his long connection with the Department, and especially with west side companies, is good authority, says of them: "5 Hose was as fine a company as belonged to the Department. There was no better duty doing company than they were, and they were all a fine class of men."

On June 4, 1860, the company resolved to organize themselves as an Engine Company, selecting the number 47, and succeeding 5 Hose in location, etc. This was consummated in the fall of the year. In the meantime they continued to do duty, and on November 16, 1860, they ran to their last fire as New York Hose Company No. 5, which was in Grand Street, near Elm Street, when they stretched hose, and gave their water to 9 Engine.

EDWIN FORREST (the third No. 5) Was organized on December 19, 1860, having been changed from Hose No. 58. It was located at 18 Burling Slip, and went out of service in 1865.

No. 6.—CROTON.—Was organized July 6, 1837, located at Gouverneur Street, near East Broadway, and went out of service in 1865. Among its members were David Kelton, foreman; John Smith, assistant foreman; Wilson H. Hendershot, Francis J. Kearns, John Brophy, Philip Reilly, Wilson Small, Jr., Charles Fostick; John B. Parker, foreman; Wm. A. Walker, David Van Buren, and Wm. E. Dusenbury.

No. 7.—WAVE.—Organized December 5, 1836, located at 199 Christie Street, disbanded April 2, 1845. Among its members were William K. Tattersal, foreman (resigned 1837); Joseph Hendrick (resigned 1837); William H. Van Wagener, Abraham Van Nest, W. H. B. Van Nortunck and John L. Vandewater.

RINGGOLD (second No. 7) Was organized September 22, 1845, located in Thirteenth Street, near Fourth Avenue; went out of service in 1865. Among its members were Ely A. Horton, foreman; Edwin W. Ryerson, assistant; John C. Perrin, Edwin A. Lopez, Charles S. Hunt, Samuel B. Seaman, James S. Kent.

No. 8.—First Ward.—City.—Organized October 15, 1836, located at 74 Cedar Street, and after 1859 at 39 Liberty Street; went out of service in 1865. Among its members were Abel Foster, foreman (1837); Augustus Brett, assistant foreman (1837); John D. Ammerman, George R. Rollins, R. M. Folger (subsequently chief engineer of the Fire Department of Sacramento); and Charles H. Cornell, foreman, (1853). The company changed its name to "City" on October 15, 1852. In the next year they put a fine new engine on exhibition at the Crystal Palace, the old one (a heavy machine) having been in use for eight years. The new apparatus was designed expressly for the company by Mr. Joseph Pine, hose carriage builder, and built by Pine & Hartshorn. The carriage was extremely light, and presented a frail appearance, but was substantially constructed. The company tried her for two months before she was sent to be ornamented, and they tested her in every manner, and were well satisfied with the result. The carriage was quite a triumph for Messrs. Pine & Hartshorn, and other companies were anxious to obtain one like her. She was painted a light tan color, handsomely striped with gilt. The painting was done by A. P. Moriarty. The springs and fifth wheel were polished. The reel was open with silver-plated work. On the front box was a large silver plate with the word "City." On the side panels a silver figure 8. On the back box was a figure 8 in a sun, struck out of solid silver, and "Organized October 15, 1836"; on the end panels was the city coat of arms in silver. The lifters were eagles with a figure 8 in their bills. The lamps were probably the most beautiful ones ever made in the country. The glass was stained red, and upon it was engraved the city coat of arms. On the top of the lamps was a silver cedar tree (Cedar was the soubriquet bestowed upon the company in consequence of being located in Cedar Street). The lamps were manufactured by Parker, DeVoursney & Tucker. The designs on the ends of the boxes and engravings were by Jamison & Guyer, and the lifters by James McKenna, the silver plates by James Collard. The committee on building the carriage consisted of John Black, Charles H. Cornell, J. S. Hallenbeck, Joseph Black and James F. Halsey.

John A. Keyser of this company was the first man known to be killed after the falling of the walls at the Jennings fire on Broadway. Nich. W. Mooney, foreman of 3 Hose, had gone into the cellar, and, in groping around, had found the body with the fire cap lying near it. On bringing the cap out, it was found to bear the front of City Hose No. 8 with the initials J. A. K.

On Tuesday evening, December 9, 1851, the members of First Ward Hose presented their late worthy foreman, Joseph Black, with a massive and elegantly wrought gold chain, as a slight testimonial of their regard. The presentation took place at Mr. Black's residence, and the company partook of a splendid entertainment. Attached to the chain was a plate in the shape of a frontispiece of a fire cap. On the reverse side are the names of the committee: Chas. H. Cornell, Chas. Smith, Jr., E. T. Proudhomme. Mr. Black was for a long time secretary of the Board of Engineers. At the annual meeting held on Monday evening, May 10, 1852, the following were elected officers for the ensuing year: John Black, Jr., unanimously re-elected foreman; Chas. H. Cornell, re-elected assistant; Benjamin White, secretary, vice James W. White, resigned; George W. Lowerre, re-elected steward; Isaac S. Hallenbeck, vice Charles Smith, Jr., resigned, and Joseph Black, representatives.

At the annual meeting of City Hose Company No. 8 held on Monday evening, May 9, 1853, the following were elected officers for the ensuing year: Chas. H. Cornell, foreman, vice John Black, who declined re-election; Chas. A. L. Mignard, assistant; Isaac S. Hallenbeck, secretary, re-elected; George W. Lowerre, steward, re-elected; Joseph Black, re-elected, and John Black, representatives. At the annual meeting of City Hose held Monday evening, May 8, 1854, the following officers were elected: Chas. H. Cornell, re-elected foreman; Theron Kidd, assistant, vice Chas. A. L. Mignard; James W. White, secretary, vice C. L. Robinson; John Letson, steward, vice James W. White; John Black, Jr., representative, vice Charles Smith, Jr.

No. 9.—COLUMBIAN.—This company was one of the most active in the central portion of the city, doing duty in the Fifth and Sixth Districts. It was organized January 17, 1837, by Edgar Brown, Eugene Thompson, and Jefferson Brown. Other early members were James M. Clark, assistant foreman (1838); Wm. H. Mosher (1838); Nehemiah S. Zimmerman and Nicholas Groesbeck (1838). They located at 174 Mulberry Street, adjoining Engine 40, where fifteen years afterwards they erected a new three-story building, and where they remained until mustered out of service in 1865. Shortly after they were organized they purchased at their own expense a new carriage, but, finding it too heavy, they finally sold it to a company at Newburg, N. Y. In 1849 they received the new carriage they had ordered built, one of the most attractive in the Department. It was silver mounted—the signal and lamps being of a novel pattern, and plated tongue. The company was immediately dubbed " Silver Nine," which name they carried until they passed out of existence. At a fire one could always tell when she was coming, as the old cry of " Come, ye old Silver Nines!" could be heard blocks away. In the days

BADGE OF ED. W. JACOBS.

when the new silver carriage was housed for the first time, Harry Mansfield and Thomas Boese were members, and a more downhearted set could not have been found in the City of New York than the Columbian boys on the first alarm they turned out to. It seems that some two or three companies had conspired together to give the new carriage the " go by," and a false alarm was sounded for an up-town fire. The story is related in detail in an earlier chapter. No. 9 was called the " Quill " and " Silk Stocking " Company of the Fourteenth Ward, but there was no silk stocking work about them when on duty. Many had narrow escapes at fires. At a fire on Broadway, Tom Boese and Harry Mansfield had a narrow escape by the falling of a wall. Thomas Cochran fell off a roof corner of Broadway and Broome Street in 1848, and was seriously injured. In 1849 George T. Hopper and Joseph M. Harper were added to the roll, and during the fall of this year they went on an excursion to Albany, Utica, Auburn, Rochester, Buffalo, Niagara Falls, and Canada. They were absent thirteen days, parading twenty-six men and accompanied by Dodworth's Band. Their reception at these places was one continuous ovation along the route, and on their return some twenty companies turned out to bid them a welcome home. Early in 1850 some dissatisfaction arose, when all but six members resigned and reorganized Engine Company

No. 9, which had been disbanded. During this year John W. Garside, better known as "Johnny Garside" and "Dandy Gig," was elected foreman, and he succeeded in working the company up to its former standing.

On Friday, May 28, 1851, the company brought home their new carriage from the painter's. The body was a plum color, the running gear brown, with gilt, red and white stripes. On the reel were two beautiful paintings; on the right panel was a very pretty design, entitled "The Guardian Angels," representing a child slumbering on a couch and an angel leaning over the head of the couch, and another watching at the side. On the left panel was an elegant and chaste design, entitled "Repose," representing a group of females reposing under the shade of a cluster of trees. The pictures on the reel were encircled by a silver rim, and the outer edge of the reel by rich carved work. On the front box was a large silver plate, with "Columbian" neatly engraved on it. On the back box was a representation of the Firemen's Monument at Greenwood, with the motto, "We Cherish their Memory." Underneath the front and back boxes were two carved dolphins, richly gilt. On each of the side panels was a large silver figure "9," surrounded by rich carved work. The springs and tongue were polished in a superb manner. The lifters were very handsome, representing a boy shooting marbles. On the lid of the front box was the following unique inscription:

> "They who steal our purse steal trash;
> But they who basely steal our books, torches, etc.,
> Rob us most villainously."—[See minutes of 9
> Hose, and when found make a note of it.]

The carriage was painted by A. P. Moriarty.

No. 10.—East River.—Liberty.—Organized February 1, 1837; located in Roosevelt Street, and after 1846 at 3 Dover Street; went out of service in 1865. Among the members were Chas. H. Lyons, foreman; Jacob M. Small, assistant; Bartholomew J. Broderick, James Corrigan, Chas. Collins, and Robert Cottrell. At the annual meeting of Liberty Hose, held on Monday evening, May 12, 1851, the following were elected officers for the ensuing year: Thomas Woodward, foreman; William M. Randell, assistant; Thomas L. Thornell, secretary; Joseph Hilton, treasurer; M. Shaffner, steward; George A. Buckingham and James Y. Watkins, Jr., representatives. On May 10, 1852, the following were elected officers for the ensuing year: Thomas Woodward, foreman; William Hagadorn, assistant; Charles L. Brower, secretary; John T. Southwell, treasurer; John Nichols, steward; Wm. De Lander and Israel C. Lawrence, representatives. On Monday evening, May 8, 1854, Liberty Hose presented Thomas Woodward, ex-foreman, with a handsome gold hunting watch as a testimonial of their esteem. It was presented by the foreman, Charles L. Brower, which Mr. Woodward responded to. At the same meeting the following officers were elected: Charles L. Brower, re-elected foreman; Chas. H. Lyons, re-elected assistant; Lewis Sylvester, secretary, vice Geo. Randell; Andrew Cusack, treasurer, vice Theodore Ward; Thomas Woodward and Geo. Randell, representatives. At the annual meeting held May 14, 1855, the following officers were elected for the ensuing year: Charles H. Lyons, foreman; Lewis Sylvester, assistant; Stephen J. Jennings, secretary; Charles L. Brower, treasurer; Chas. L. Brower and John Mills, representatives.

No. 11.—Gulick.—Organized March 25, 1837, located at Amos Street, went out of service in 1865. Among the members were Henry M. Van Wart, foreman; David G. Robinson, assistant; Geo. Brettel, Charles E. Findlay, Allen J. Cumming, Schuyler Westervelt, Robert M. Halliday, James Bogardus. In November, 1850, the company presented their retiring foreman, Mr. Jacob Varian, with a beautiful silver trumpet. Mr. V. L. Buxton made the presentation. John Wesley Stinman was foreman, and Alderman Jacob L. Dodge assistant foreman, until 1847, in which year they received a new hose carriage, one of the most beautiful in the service, all the metal work being silver-plated and the wood work handsomely painted; on the back panel was painted a beautiful picture of the capture of André. It was always one of the most respectable companies in the service.

Jacob Varian was foreman and Thomas H. Vantine assistant foreman until May, 1850. Thomas H. Vantine was elected foreman and John J. Gorman assistant foreman, May, 1850; John J. Gorman resigned his office, also membership in the company, July 17, 1851. Thomas H. Vantine was foreman and Robert R. Colfax assistant foreman until May, 1854; Robert R. Colfax

WASHINGTON HOSE NO. 12 ("YELLOW BIRD.")

was foreman and James B. Hunt assistant foreman until May, 1855; James B. Hunt was foreman and John H. Westervelt assistant foreman until May, 1856; John H. Westervelt was foreman and David G. Robinson assistant foreman until May, 1858; David G. Robinson was foreman and Henry M. Van Wart assistant foreman until May, 1861; Henry Van Wart was foreman and Wm. H. Spear assistant foreman until May, 1862; Wm. H. Spear was elected foreman and James W. Groome assistant foreman, May, 1862; in May, 1864, Wm. H. Matthews was elected assistant foreman, Spear still continuing foreman and Matthews assistant foreman until the disbandment of the company in 1865.

No. 12.—WASHINGTON.—Organized March 24, 1837, located at 244 West Seventeenth Street, and after 1847 in Horatio Street near Hudson; disbanded January 21, 1858. Samuel Wooley was foreman, Freeman Campbell, assistant. Other members were James Berrian, foreman, Wm. D. Wallace, assistant, Ezra Woodruff and Samuel S. Carman.

MINUTE—WASHINGTON—(the second No. 12).—Organized under the name of "Minute" on January 20, 1859, having changed from Hose Company No. 62. The name was subsequently changed to "Washington," located in Forty-third

Street near Tenth Avenue, and went out of service in 1865. Robert B. Lecte was foreman, and Samuel Wooley assistant.

In May, 1852, the Washington Volunteers attached to Washington Hose Company No. 12 held a meeting at the carriage house for the purpose of showing their respect and esteem for the foreman of the company. Mr. P. W. Black, secretary of the Volunteers, presented on behalf of the Volunteers a magnificent ring to Wm. P. Daniels.

At the annual meeting of Washington Hose, May 14, 1850, the following officers were elected for the ensuing year : Wm. P. Daniels, foreman, vice Abram Ackerman, declined ; John F. Giraud, assistant, vice Wm. P. Daniels, promoted ; John W. Bartine, secretary, vice John W. Jacobus, declined ; E. K. Adams, treasurer ; Robert Dickson and John W. Jacobus, representatives. On May 11, 1852, the following officers were elected for the ensuing year : Wm. P. Daniels, re-elected foreman ; John F. Giraud, re-elected assistant ; A. C. Coquillett, re-elected secretary ; John Nicholson, re-elected treasurer ; Wm. A. Harrison, steward : John W. Bartine, recorder ; Wm. Wray and James Graham, representatives. On May 10, 1853, the following were elected for the ensuing year : John F. Giraud, foreman ; Abram C. Coquillett, assistant ; Robert Kiernen, secretary ; John Nicholson, treasurer ; Miles W. Standish, steward ; Wm. P. Daniels and James Graham, representatives. On May 9, 1854, the following were elected officers for the ensuing year : Abram C. Coquillett, foreman ; Joseph De Shay, assistant ; James A. Fenning, secretary ; John Nicholson, treasurer ; Robert Dixon and Samuel Galloway, representatives.

No. 13.—EXPRESS.—Organized May 6, 1837, with Zophar Mills foreman, Cornelius C. Glashan assistant foreman. "Express" was organized by some of the former members of No. 13 Engine ; located in Rose Street, and next in Eldridge Street near Division. Disbanded December 6, 1843.

JACKSON (the second No. 13).—Was organized on February 7, 1844, located at 34 Mangin Street, went out of service in 1865. Among the members were Peter Boyce, foreman ; Floyd W. Patrick, assistant, William Barnes, Jacob E. Terhune and Jacob M. Fenn. On November 4, 1852, the members of Jackson Hose assembled at the hose house and presented an elegant fire certificate frame to Stephen Hallick, retiring foreman. The frame was presented by James H. Johnson, and was gotten up by A. J. Martin. The presentation committee were John H. Blake, James H. Johnson and Thomas Jarvis. At the burning of the Althouse Iron Works, corner of Houston and Greene Streets, on November 16, 1862, the fire went across the street and burned a church on the southwest corner of the above streets. At this fire Theodore Mangum, a member of the Insurance Patrol, was killed while in the back room of an adjoining house by the walls crushing through the roof upon him. Mangum was an exempt member of Jackson Hose.

No. 14.—ATLANTIC ("Lady Suffolk").—Organized May 3, 1837, by John S. Giles, Henry A. Burr, Wm. W. Corlies and others, and located first at 2 Elizabeth Street in a little two-story building still standing, and commenced doing duty with a two-wheeled jumper. Messrs. Giles, Burr and Corlies were each of them afterwards foreman of the company, Mr. Corlies becoming assistant engineer in 1848. When Engine Company 15 was disbanded in 1849 No. 14 Hose Co. moved into their house at 49 Chrystie Street, where they remained until Engine Company 15 was reorganized in 1852. As No. 15 went back to their old quarters, this left Hose Company No. 14 without a location, and the carriage was housed at the Corporation Yard in Mangin Street until 1853, when they removed to their new house, 19 Elizabeth Street, next door to the chief engineer's office, where they remained until disbanded in 1857. James R. Mount was foreman when they removed to their new house, and continued so until 1857. Arthur J. Evans, of this company, was killed at the fire in Palmer's chocolate factory, in Duane Street, near Centre, September 25, 1852, by the falling of the hoisting wheel. He was just going in the hallway with the pipe of 15 Engine when the wheel fell and nearly severed his head off. Another member, Patrick O'Brien, contracted a heavy cold at the foundry fire in Lewis Street, and died from its effects August 20, 1851.

When No. 14 lay at 19 Elizabeth Street they erected a pole on their building, which was surmounted by a weather vane representing the famous trotting horse "Lady Suffolk," then queen of the turf, the company having adopted her name after her then remarkable feat of trotting a mile in 2:26 on June 14, 1849. When the Volunteer Department was disbanded this vane was transferred to a pole on the southeast corner of Third Avenue and Fifty-first Street, where it still remains. They ran the jumper until 1850, when they received a new carriage with Pine's patent running gear, which was a very heavy solid carriage, and had the picture of "Lady Suffolk" on it. This was replaced in 1856 by a new carriage painted white and gold, built by J. H. Ludlum, and which was used by 29 Hose Company after No. 14 was disbanded. Harry Howard was foreman in 1851 and resigned to take the position of assistant engineer, to which he had been appointed. James E. Kerrigan, afterwards member of Congress and also colonel of the Twenty-fifth Regiment N. Y. S. Volunteers during the rebellion, was a volunteer with the company before he went on the filibustering expedition of Capt. Walker to Central America; and Manuel Silva, afterwards of Peterson Engine Co. 31, was assistant foreman at the time of their disbandment.

EXCELSIOR (the second No. 14).—Was organized March 11, 1858, with Wm. H. Ely foreman, and Alex. M. Eagleson assistant. Among the members were J. Wentworth Braine, Chas. E. Findlay and Jonas H. Sayre. The company was located at 160 West Thirteenth Street, and went out of service in 1865.

No. 15.—VICTORY.—FULTON.—PETERSON.—This company was organized May 13, 1837, and located in Cortlandt (Tin Pot) Alley, in the house afterwards used by 19 Hose. James Gulick was foreman, John M. Valentine assistant, and John McBraw secretary. Their carriage was one of the two-wheeled affairs then in use, and which they ran for ten years. In 1839 they were located in the alley in the rear of Essex Market, and in 1847 they removed to the house No. 1½ Eldridge Street, the former location of Chatham Engine Company No. 2 and Lafayette Engine Company No. 19. This building had a wooden figure of a fireman on the roof. In 1847 the company got their first four-wheeled carriage, George Baker being the foreman. In 1849 John P. Hopkins became foreman of the company, followed in 1851 by Andrew H. Mitchell. In 1852 the company was disbanded, and reorganized the same night as Fulton Hose Company No. 15, and in the following year got a new carriage, which was painted the same colors as Fulton Engine Company No. 21—yellow running gear and white boxes. The paintings were a scene on the

North River, Robert Fulton, and a representation of one of the "Lindsey Blues," a famous militia company of that day. This carriage killed two men while going to fires, at one time while racing down Columbia Street, with 4 Truck on the crown of the street and 9 Hose on the left. 15 turned to the right to go by them, and a blacksmith named Wall jumped on the rope, but, before going far, tripped on a pile of rubbish and fell under the wheels. He

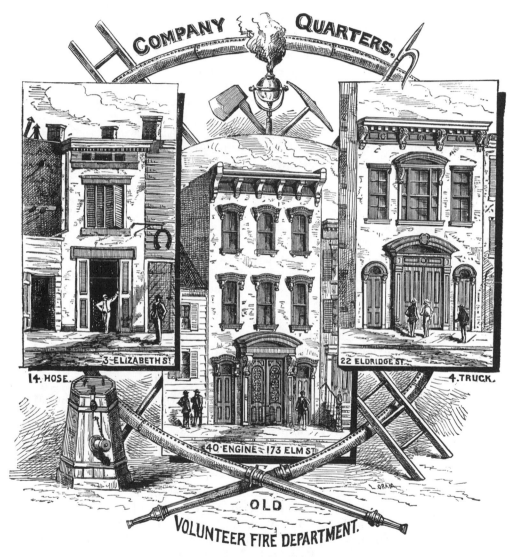

OLD COMPANY QUARTERS.

was carried into a neighboring drug store, where he soon after expired. At another time, while turning into Pearl Street, near William Street, Robert McCausland, a runner, and brother-in-law to Thomas Bonran, one of the members, fell from the rope as the company turned out to pass 2 Engine, and was instantly killed. On the morning of April 15, 1840, James Glasgow, of this company, lost his life by the falling of the walls at the fire of a match factory in Eldridge Street, north of Grand Street. James S. Wells, an assistant engineer, formerly a member of Engine Company No. 36, was also killed at this fire.

In 1850 the officers of Victory were : John P. Hopkins, foreman ; Jesse Rodman, assistant ; Benjamin F. French, secretary ; Joseph H. Weed, treasurer; J. P. Hopkins and B. F. French, representatives. In 1851 Andrew H. Mitchell, foreman ; Owen McCollough, assistant, vice Wm. H. Overton, resigned ; Wm. P. Driver, secretary ; Chas E. Ridgeway, treasurer ; A. H. Mitchell and Daniel H. Carnes, representatives. In 1852 the officers of the Fulton were: James Hopkins, foreman; Wm. O'Shaughnessy, assistant ; William Woods, secretary ; Andrew H. Mitchell, treasurer; Josiah McCord and Edward J. Riley, representatives. At a previous meeting of this company they adopted the name of " Fulton," and were henceforth to be known as Fulton Hose Company No. 15.

William O'Shaughnessy was foreman of the company in 1853, and Andrew H. Mitchell in 1854 and 1855, the latter having previously served as foreman of the company. In 1856 Daniel McLaren was elected foreman, and re-elected the following year with William Brandon as assistant. At that time the company adopted the name of Peterson. After McLaren, William Brandon was elected foreman, and on April 6, 1859, the company was disbanded.

ATLANTIC (second No. 15).—Was reorganized July 4, 1859, at the house of William Rainer, an old member of 40 Engine, and for many years captain of the Third Company Continental Guards, an independent militia company, which was about the last of those organizations to disband. Among the organizers were A. McDonald, George Cramer, William Rainer, and Henry B. Clark. James R. Mount was elected the first foreman, and they commenced doing duty with an old carriage. In 1860 John Kerrigan, brother to Col. Jas. E. Kerrigan, was elected foreman, and they secured a new hose carriage the following year. The location of the company was in the quarters vacated by Hose Company No. 14, whose name, " Atlantic," they had also adopted. Henry Clark was a sergeant in the Twenty-fifth Regiment, New York State Volunteers, during the rebellion, and lost his life at the battle of Hanover Court House, in Virginia, in 1863. This company continued in service until the Department was disbanded. The Adema brothers, Frank, William, and Thomas, were prominent members of this company. Went out of service in 1865.

No. 16.—NAIAD.—Organized November 21, 1837 ; located at 24 Beaver Street, and disbanded January 10, 1848. Among the members were : John S. Giles, foreman ; A. Mather, assistant ; and Alfred A. Mott.

TOMPKINS (the second No. 16).—Was organized May 23, 1848, by Geo. W. Trenchard (then an officer in Purdy's old Chatham Street Theater), Wm. H. Mansfield, afterwards Judge Mansfield, E. A. Hopkins, and others, and located at the junction of First and Houston Streets, where they remained until 1855, when they removed to 154 Norfolk Street, which was their last location. Geo. W. Trenchard was their first foreman and served several years, being succeeded by Wm. Bell and N. Lockwood. In 1853 Mr. Trenchard was re-elected foreman, and on May 31, 1853, while in command of the company at a fire in Essex Street, between Rivington and Stanton Streets, he fell through the back area into the basement where the fire was burning fiercely, and sustained injuries and internal burns, from which he died June 2, 1853. He was buried on the following Sunday, the Department generally turning out in mourning for the occasion. The company first ran a small "jumper," and afterwards the larger one of 36 Hose, dark green with gold stripes and very high wheels. In 1855 they ran a new carriage, built by Torboss, and in 1860 they received a new carriage from Van Ness with an elliptic perch, which they had painted green, and which carriage they claim was never passed. They used this carriage during the remainder of their service. Many old timers will remember Wm. H. Brower (old 40), at one time foreman of the company, and who was suspended for six months for disobeying the orders of Assistant Engineer John A. Cregier at a fire. Brower always claimed that he did not know Cregier (he not being in uniform at the time) when he gave the order. At the Hague Street explosion, February 4, 1850, this company responded to the call, although out of their regular districts, and worked faithfully all day. Hose Companies Nos. 16 and 17 were bitter rivals, as were Nos. 16 and 9 Hose. Tompkins Hose Company had an old white dog which some of No. 15 Engine boys had given them, and he acquired quite a reputation for his peculating qualities, as he would endeavor to steal anything that was shown him, from a codfish to a watermelon. The carriage was known by the appellation of "Old Hump," and the company was certainly a very efficient, hard-working one. Timothy Donovan, Edward Bonnell, and Bernard Kenney were foremen, and all of them achieved distinction outside as well as in the Department.

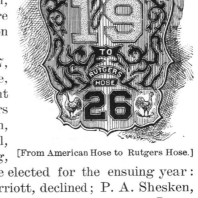

[From American Hose to Rutgers Hose.]

No. 17.—CLINTON.—Organized January 27, 1838, located at Fifth Street, near Second Avenue, later at Fifth Street and First Avenue, and went out of service in 1865. Among the members were: Patrick Martin, foreman; James O'Brien, assistant; S. Livingston, Jr., Benjamin Gicquel, and Bernard Sheridan. At the annual meeting, held May 13, 1850, the following officers were elected for the ensuing year: John McMahon, foreman, vice James A. Harriott, declined; P. A. Shesken, assistant; James A. Harriott, secretary; Abraham Lowere, treasurer; James A. Harriott and Abraham Lowere, representatives.

No. 18.—FRANKLIN.—Organized April 11, 1838, located at Franklin Market, Old Slip; after 1848 at 24 Beaver Street; went out of service in 1865. Among the members were: William Farrel, foreman; Charles Asher, assistant; Matthew F. Beirne, Charles Kallenstroth, John Bacterbury, and William J. Dagan (killed in the Jennings building fire). No. 18 Hose, with other companies, organized a patrol during the draft riots of 1863 for the protection of the First Ward.

No. 19.—AMERICAN.—Organized January 29, 1839, located in Cortlandt Alley; next at 52 Greene Street; after 1862 at 83 Greene Street; went out of service in 1865. In 1851 Richard Burnton was elected foreman, but, declining to serve, Henry W. Banks was elected to fill the office; A. P. Silloon was elected assistant foreman; S. B. Thomson, secretary; and Messrs. Silloon and

Thomson, representatives. In this year, when the engine lay at 52 Greene Street, the company was in a prosperous condition, due mainly to the exertions of Mr. Banks. Among other members of the company were Wm. Van Deusen, foreman; Richard Kidd, assistant foreman; James G. Weaver, Henry R. Williams, Lawrence H. Bogert, and Jacob H. Dawson.

No. 20.—SECOND WARD.—HUMANE.—Organized October 1, 1836, under the name of "Second Ward Hose Company." On June 22, 1842, it received the "No. 20." It was located in John Street, near Nassau, and after 1843 at 30 Ann Street. Went out of service in 1865. Among the members were John Schumagel, foreman; Ferdinand Rath, assistant; Bernard Leddy, Daniel Sullivan, and Wm. F. Scott.

No. 21.—PROTECTION.—This company was organized on February 13, 1839, was located in Henry Street, near Catharine, and on March 20, 1846, organized as Engine Company No. 2.

HUDSON (the second No. 21).—Was organized from Hose Company No. 27 on October 21, 1846. It was located in Duane Street, near West, and later in Washington, near Duane. On February 19, 1863, it was organized as Engine Company No. 53.

HUDSON (the third No. 21, and the second bearing the same name).—Was organized on February 19, 1863, by William T. Mawbey, an ex-assistant engineer, and an old member of 49 Engine Company, John Hart, the ex-foreman of 35 Engine, Sidney P. Ingraham, nephew of Judge Ingraham, George H. Egleston, Henry S. McDowell, William Seaman, Henry G. Sherman, George J. Storoter, William R. Pettigrew, now superintendent of Appleton's factory in Brooklyn, and others, all active men. They began with a full roll, and it remained so until the company went out of service in 1865. They commenced duty with a four-wheeled crab formerly in use by Hose Company No. 52, who had procured a steamer and been organized as an engine company. The first officers were: William T. Mawbey, foreman, and John Hart, assistant, and their location was on the rear of the lot on the southwest corner of One Hundred and Twenty-seventh Street and Third Avenue in a one-story frame building. It was a very quick, active company, composed mostly of young men, who took great pride in their fire duty. John Hart, as foreman, and R. M. Carlock, as assistant, were the next and last officers of the company, and Robt. C. Brown, formerly foreman of Manhattan No. 8, was one of the last representatives. In 1865, when the Metropolitan Fire Commissioners took charge of the Department, this company was placed in charge of No. 49 Engine, and took their house in Fourth Avenue, near One Hundred and Twenty-seventh Street, being known as Engine Company No. 36 of the New Department. Robert C. Brown was made foreman, and John Hart was appointed an assistant engineer. They served thus for a little over two years, and by that time, the Department being well organized in the lower districts, the commissioners turned their attention to the companies up town. A steamer was procured, and the company placed on the same footing as the others in the Department.

No. 22.—PHENIX.—The members of Engine Company No. 22 organized Hose Company No. 22 about August 1, 1839. They were located in Hester Street, near Allen, and after 1864 at 77 Canal Street. The company went out of service in 1865. This company carried the Fire Department banner in 1863 on the occasion of the funeral of George W. Badger, who was killed at a fire.

C. C. Pinckney, of Hose 22, was one of a committee of seven appointed in 1851 to present Jenny Lind with a testimonial for her gift to the Fire Department. Colonel W. R. W. Chambers was a member, and while serving his country in the time of the war was re-elected foreman. Among other members were Schuyler Stymers, foreman in 1854, George Anderson, assistant foreman in 1854; Kendall F. Knowles, Zabriskie H. Mullen and Nicholas V. Eberhard.

No. 23.—TRITON—PERRY.—This company first organized under the name of "Triton" on April 1, 1839, and subsequently changed the name to "Perry," in honor of the celebrated Commodore. Two round panels of Perry Hose, illustrating Commodore Perry's victory, and which were owned by ex-President King of the Fire Department, are preserved at the Volunteer Firemen's Headquarters. No. 23 was located in Charles Street, near Hudson; after 1847 in Horatio Street, near Hudson, and went out of service in 1865. Among the members were Alexander V. Davidson, who became an assistant engineer in 1865, and in later years was sheriff; John J. Gorman, who was president of the New Department, and is now a police justice; John Cavana, assistant foreman about 1855; John Osborne, Wm. H. Ambury and Robert Brien.

No. 24.—EIGHTH WARD.—This company was organized on October 3, 1836, as "Eighth Ward Hose," and was located for some time in "Dave" Vanduzer's carpenter shop, in Renwick Street near Spring. The first foreman of Eighth Ward Company was John T. Smith, who was succeeded by Peter Silcox, Jas. Plant and Samuel Freer. Other members of the company were, O. A. Farrin, John Van Riper, Lawrence Hampton, Charles Wilcox, W. B. Hays, William Kennedy and John Woerum. The company was reorganized in 1842.

HAT.

[Presented by Wm. P. Kirk to John Tyson, March 10, 1884. One of the first adopted by the New York Volunteer Department on the twenty-ninth day of November, 1813.]

NATIONAL (the second No. 24).—Was reorganized from Eighth Ward Hose on June 22, 1842. Peter Silcox was the first foreman after the reorganization, and John S. Fletcher, John Van Riper, Wm. B. Hays, C. C. Ross, Wm. Hayes, Oliver Farrin, Lawrence M. Luther and Alonzo Hampton, members. Charles Wilcox and James Harris joined the company during the first year of its existence. Wm. B. Hays was elected assistant foreman in 1844, and resigned to take the position of fire warden, which office he held for six years. At the fire corner of King and Washington Streets in 1844 the carriage was laid up, and the members of the company carried their hose to the fire, and did good duty in checking the progress of the fire. Joseph W. Robb was elected foreman of the company in 1851, followed by Abraham L. Brewer, Samuel Burhans, Jr., Richard L. Simonson, A. C. D'Ozeville, the last named being re-elected for several terms. In the latter part of 1845 the company removed their location to the rear of Lowry's hardware store, in Spring Street near Greenwich Street, and in 1856 had a new house built for them at 253 Spring Street. This company went on an annual chowder excursion to Sheepshead Bay, making their stop at the "Widow's," then a famous headquarters for chowder parties.

The last carriage run by "National" was built in 1861 by C. E. Hartshorn. It was owned by No. 24, and was sold to a company in Bergen, N. J., on the disbanding of the Old Department. Mr. John Garrie was foreman of the company in 1864, and was re-elected in 1865, being the last foreman in the service of the company. National Hose Company No. 24 enjoyed a first-class reputation among the citizens of their own ward and in the Department generally; their roll was large, and they were never mixed up in any broils or trouble. The company comprised many of the solid citizens of the west side, and they stood among the first for their record of fire duty. John McCool, Daniel Cruger, Michael B. Terhune, D. D. Tullman, and John J. Vanderbilt were among the members. Hose 24 was in line at the Prince of Wales' procession, and was on that occasion dubbed "The Giraffe," on account of its seven foot wheels.

No. 25.—United States ("Fashion").—Organized May 27, 1839, located in Anthony Street, near Broadway, and after 1864 at 128 Worth Street. It went out of service in 1841, and was reorganized on July 13, 1843, doing duty till the end of the Old Department. Among its officers were Wm. McDonough, foreman, and Wm. Barrett, assistant. On May 8, 1850, the members of No. 25 presented to Mr. James H. Ridabock, their newly-elected foreman, a beautifully wrought silver trumpet in appreciation of the services which he had rendered. The trumpet, a fine specimen of workmanship, was manufactured by J. W. Faulkner, of Broadway. The same evening the following officers were elected for the ensuing year: James H. Ridabock, foreman, vice George McKinley, declined; William S. Kirby, assistant, vice James H. Ridabock, promoted; James R. Dunscombe, secretary; John Curson, treasurer; James H. Ridabock and George McKinley, representatives. In 1852 the company housed a new and beautiful carriage, and entertained their friends in honor of the occasion. The carriage was entirely different from any other in the city. She was built by Cizelmen & Sickles. The reel was polished mahogany, with a small carved rim, and was ornamented with a wreath of flowers; on each arch was an easel; the boxes were polished mahogany, the panels plain; on the front box was a silver plate with the following: "Organized 1843"; on the back box was the name of the company in silver letters. The wheels were polished oak; the springs were polished, as were also all the iron work exposed to view. The lifters were new and unique. This company had the name of "Fashion," after the celebrated racer. The lifters represented a horse's head, and the jaws moved as the lids rose. The tongue was a piece of polished hickory. There was much silver plating about the carriage. The painting was done by Moriarty. At the annual meeting held at the house of Perez S. Whiting, No. 75 Anthony Street, on Wednesday evening, May 11, 1853, the following were elected officers for the ensuing year: John Henry Evers, foreman, re-elected; Daniel Rooney, assistant, re-elected, Frederick S. Whiting, secretary, re-elected; Wm. H. MacDonough, treasurer; John Crossin and George Shannon, representatives.

CHAPTER XXXVIII.

MORE VETERAN HOSE COMPANIES.

Nos. 26 to 46, inclusive.—Names that are Familiar as Household Words.—Location and Changes.—Nomenclature of Companies: Rutgers, Neptune, Mayflower, Metamora, Laurel, Putnam, Oceana, Amity, Mohawk, Mazeppa, Pioneer, Red Jacket.

NO. 26.—VAN BUREN—RUTGERS.—Organized June 1, 1839; located at 166 Monroe Street, and later at 6 Norfolk Street. Went out of service in 1865. In 1850 the company gave a grand entertainment to the ladies at their carriage house. The machine was much admired. The running gear was red, with gilt stripes; the reel was very tastefully done. It was red, ornamented with beautiful gilt carving, representing an olive and oak vine, indicative of peace and strength. On the arch on each side of the reel was a neat little equestrian statue of Washington. On the front box was a representation of the Rutgers mansion and the motto of the company: "The noblest motive is the public good." On the side panels was a shield, a beautiful ornament; on the back boxes was a well-executed likeness of Colonel Rutgers; on the side panels was a small fancy sketch of a female peeping through a lattice. The boxes were decorated with rich scroll work; the lifters were made to represent sea horses; the lamps on the carriage were about the neatest of the kind in the city. The carriage was built by Van Ness, and painted by Moriarty. The company gave to their late foreman, Mr. David H. Hempstead, as a slight token of esteem, a complimentary certificate. No. 26 possessed an excellent library. At the annual meeting, held May 8, 1850, the following officers were elected for the ensuing year: J. Henry Wilkinson, foreman, vice John E. B. Fick, resigned; Thomas G. Mason, assistant; Samuel M. Farran, secretary; Geo. W. Knapp, treasurer; John S. Farran and George W. Knapp, representatives. On July 6, 1852, the following officers were unanimously elected for the ensuing year: Thomas G. Mason, foreman, vice John F. Buckley, resigned; Samuel H. Heartney, assistant, vice Joseph H. Tooker, resigned; B. J. Gallagher, secretary, vice James B. Smith, resigned; John S. Farran, treasurer, vice James H. Wilkinson, resigned; John E. B. Fick and William H. Christie, representatives.

No. 27.—THIRD WARD.—Although this company organized in February, 1836, it did not receive a number until June 22, 1842. It was located at Vesey and Church Streets. It was changed to Hose Company No. 21 on October 21, 1846.

NEPTUNE was organized on November 16, 1847, located at 106 Reade Street, and after 1859 at 179 Church Street. It went out of service in 1865. John Corballis was one of her foremen, and James D. Hall an assistant foreman.

No. 28.—FIFTH DISTRICT—PEARL.—"The Fifth District" Hose Company was organized on May 25, 1839, received its number, No. 28, and was designated "Pearl" on June 22, 1842. The late George T. Hope, ex-president of the Continental Insurance Company, was the first foreman of this company. It was located in Chambers, above Centre Street. Edward W. Wilhelm, ex-chief of the battalion in the Metropolitan Fire Department, was foreman of Pearl Hose Company No. 28 in 1864 and 1865. A good many big merchants belonged to the company. At the Jennings fire on Broadway Mr. Wilhelm narrowly escaped death. He held No. 8 Engine's pipe, which, on account of want of hose, kept him from entering the house and being buried in the ruins when the building fell. At the annual meeting of Pearl Hose, held at the carriage house on the first Monday in May, 1850, the following gentlemen were elected officers for the ensuing year: Albert J. Delatour, foreman; John Clancy, assistant, vice George O. Depew, declined; Abraham Halsey, Jr., secretary; John C. Thompson, treasurer; George W. Littell and John G. Fisher, representatives. In 1851 Augustus Hurd was elected foreman; Stephen Burkhalter, Jr., assistant; James G. Sweeny, secretary; George P. Ockershausen, Jr., treasurer; John C. Thompson and John G. Fisher, representatives. In 1852 the company removed to Centre and Chambers Streets, and continued in that house till the company was disbanded in 1865.

No. 29.—ELEVENTH WARD—MAYFLOWER—UNION.—This company, which was organized from Hose Company No. 44, on June 22, 1842, first took the name Eleventh Ward, subsequently changed to Mayflower, and then to Union. It was located at 77 Willett Street, and disbanded on September 18, 1854. At the annual meeting of Union Hose Company held at their house on May 2, 1851, the following gentlemen were elected officers for the ensuing year: Joseph Goldie, foreman, vice Thos. Stack, resigned; A. Phillips, Jr., assistant, vice Treadwell Pearsall, time expired; Thos. Stack, treasurer, vice Geo. H. Covert, time expired; John Robertson, secretary; S. B. Strickland, steward; and John J. Kelly and John Ryan, representatives.

METAMORA—CONTINENTAL.—Organized December 27, 1854, and located at Twenty-first Street and Broadway; after 1863 in Eighteenth Street, near Broadway. It went out of service in 1865. At the annual meeting of Continental Hose Company, held at the carriage house on Monday evening, May 1, 1854, the following were elected officers for the ensuing year: Thomas H. Skelly, foreman; Joseph Hoffman, assistant; Richard Evans, secretary; Philip Farley, treasurer; Jacob Coons and Geo. V. Dale, representatives; P. H. Lauchanton, foreman; B. Rhinelander, assistant foreman; Albert B. Stanton, John R. Platt, H. L. Field, John Sidell, Thos. W. Conkling, and F. E. Ostrander.

No. 30.—The first Hose Company No. 30 had no special name. It was changed from Hose Company No. 42 on June 1, 1840, located at Bowery and Thirteenth Street, and disbanded on February 5, 1843.

EDWIN FORREST—LAUREL—GEORGE B. McCLELLAN.—This company had the honor of bearing no less than three names—Edwin Forrest, Laurel, and George B. McClellan. They were organized July 6, 1847, and located on Twenty-seventh Street, between Ninth and Tenth Avenues, in a two-story building, which was purchased by the city, and altered for them and Engine Company No. 10. Jacob Miller was chosen the first foreman, and served one year, and then gave way to Edward Esler, who had the honor of being at the head of the company for five years. In 1849 they brought home a neat carriage, built in a most substantial manner, and with which they performed duty until 1856. In 1850 some opposition arose among the members over the name of "Forrest." Several new names were presented, when finally they selected that of Laurel. In 1854 Daniel Townsend was elevated to the foremanship, and the roll immediately swelled to the full complement of men. In 1856 John T. Williams, Jr., became foreman, and another new carriage was brought home. Then came James H. Arnold as foreman, who was followed by Louis S. Richards. The latter took a deep interest in the company, so much so that he was re-elected for five consecutive years. John Brown was advanced to the foremanship after Richards. He held the post until the last day of the company's existence in 1865. Mr. Brown proved a most efficient fireman. He saved several lives at a large fire in Seventh Avenue and Twenty-ninth Street,

for which he received a silver trumpet from the Common Council. During the early part of 1861 they purchased a new carriage at their own expense, and when they disbanded presented it to Independence Hose, of Philadelphia. Several members of the company enlisted in the war, Henry W. Dale, Jabez C. F. Lockwood, Samuel H. Jollie, John Wilkinson, John R. Auten, and James H. Bird being among those who served the full term at the front. In 1863

CAP OF FOREMAN HUNT OF CALIFORNIA.
[Cost thirteen hundred and fifty dollars, and made by Gratacap, New York City.]

they hauled down the name of Laurel, and hoisted that of George B. McClellan, who was then talked of as Democratic candidate for President of the United States. Among the many members of note at this time were Wm. H. Chapman, Charles Cusick, Richard H. Bell, Abram Vanderbilt, Hugh W. Paul, L. M. Starrete, Wm. H. Morgan, John J. Evans, Alex. T. Smith, James H. Bird, Charles H. Boardman, Andrew J. Rhine, John Wilkinson, George W. Armstrong, Philip Cusick, Samuel Hays, John McDermott, Wm. J. Gardner, and Wm. M. Vose.

On Wednesday, May 28, 1851, Forrest Hose Company received a new carriage from the painter. The carriage was one of Pine's patent, painted a rich plum color, with carmine running gear, and blue panels; on one side was a figure of Diana, the Goddess of the Chase, on the other the Nymph of the Waterfall, the side panels filled in with a wreath of flowers. On the front box was the motto, "Fearless of Danger," surrounded by the implements of the department, and on the back the date of the organization; on the back panel box the portraits of the foreman and assistant, and on the front figures representing the seasons; suspended between the bells was a splendid lamp, with the number cut in blue and red glass, made by Edwards, of Nassau Street; the deck lifters represented a girl sitting down with a basket on her arm, into which she is putting a fish. The figures were of bronze, got up by Tiffany, of Broadway. The painting, both plain and ornamental, was executed by Moriarty. The carriage was further decorated with a splendid wreath, made and presented by Miss M. L. Moriarty, and was drawn by thirty men, in citizen's dress, of whom twenty-seven were members of the company.

They visited the Institution of the Blind, by invitation of Mr. Chamberlain, the superintendent. On their arrival at the Institute they were introduced to Miss Frances J. Crosby, who welcomed them by reciting an address in verse.

No. 31.—PUTNAM.—Putnam was changed from Hose Company No. 43 on April 28, 1842, located at 7 Walnut (Jackson) Street, and went out of service in 1865. Among the members were Andrew Hill, foreman; Charles Daley, assistant; Nicholas Kent, Peter L. Thompson and Philip Smith. At the annual meeting on the evening of May 6, 1851, the following were elected officers for the ensuing year: David P. Conger, re-elected foreman; Abraham W. Kennedy, assistant, vice J. B. King, declined; Wm. J. Jessup, re-elected secretary; J. B. King, re-elected treasurer, and Jesse Thomas and Wm. H. Jones, representatives. About August, 1851, Putnam brought home a new hose carriage. She was different in construction from any other apparatus, and was a very handsome carriage. She was built by Pine & Pearson. At the annual meeting on May 4, 1852, the following were elected officers for the ensuing year: Jesse Thomas, re-elected foreman; Thomas Sullivan, re-elected assistant; Wm. J. Jessup, re-elected secretary; John Boyd, treasurer, vice J. B. King, resigned; Jesse Thomas and John Boyd re-elected representatives. On May 3, 1853, the following were elected officers for the ensuing year: Thos. Sullivan, foreman, vice Jesse Thomas; John Boyd, assistant, vice Thomas Sullivan; Wm. J. Jessup, secretary, re-elected; Archibald Armstrong, treasurer, vice John Boyd; Thomas Sullivan, vice Jesse Thomas and John Boyd, re-elected representatives. On May 2, 1854, the following officers were unanimously elected: Thomas Sullivan, foreman; Charles J. E. Spring, assistant; Wm. Gamble, secretary; Archibald Armstrong, treasurer; John McCarthy, vice Thomas Sullivan, who declined re-election, and Thomas K. Coultors, representatives.

No. 32.—RICHARD M. JOHNSON.—Organized June 1, 1840, located at 6 Third Street, and organized as Engine Company No. 26 on December 2, 1851. Among the members were Clark Vanderbilt, who was assistant engineer from 1848 to 1853; Oliver Charlick, foreman; S. R. Harris, assistant foreman; Alfred S. Wright, R. Putnam, Daniel L. Carpenter and Reuben S. Munson. At the annual meeting in 1850 the following officers were elected for the ensuing year: Geo. A. Jeremiah, foreman; George F. C. Tufts, assistant; Samuel H. Doty, secretary; Elisha Kingsland, treasurer. On May 12, 1851, the following were elected officers for the ensuing year: George A. Jeremiah, foreman; G. F. C. Tufts, assistant; E. A. Tewes, secretary; E. Kingsland, treasurer; and Messrs. Kingsland and Peterson representatives.

INDEX (the second No. 32).—In 1852 William Halden resigned from Hudson Engine Company No. 1, and organized Hose Company 32. The headquarters were in Forty-eighth Street, east of Eighth Avenue. The house is now used as a stable by Hook and Ladder Company No. 4. This company continued in active service until 1865. The organizer, William Halden, was a very popular man in the Twenty-second Ward, having held several prominent political positions in his time. He joined the Fire Department in 1840, and continued an active member until 1865; he died in April, 1875. The Exempt Firemen's Association attended his funeral in a body. The last foreman of this company was Benjamin Martin, and the last assistant foreman John Linder.

No. 33.—HOFFMIRE—CITY—WARREN.—("Kentuck")—("Blackbird").—This company was first organized as a "June Bug" in 1839, under the name of Hoffmire Hose Company No. 33, taking its name from Edward M. Hoffmire, an ex-assistant engineer from Neptune Engine Company No. 6. They procured a two-wheeled jumper, and located in a one-story frame building which was formerly used as a stable, on the east side of Sullivan Street, between Prince and Houston Streets. John Ely, formerly of Engine Company No. 37, and an ex-assistant engineer, was foreman of the company. They did not do any duty, however, and on February 3, 1841, the company was reorganized as City Hose Company No. 33, with John P. Teale as foreman, Theodore P. Trumpore, assistant, and John Barker, Levi Guernsey, Jacob May, Robert R. Lawrence and others, members. They took the location and apparatus of the former company, but added a story to the building, and in a short time procured a new carriage. This, like its predecessor, was a two-wheeled machine. In fact, there were but four or five four-wheeled hose carriages in the city at that time, but it was tastefully painted and ornamented by the company, being painted red with gilt stripes. On January 4, 1842, the company in a body joined the Washingtonian Temperance Society, of which Nicholas Duff was the president. The ladies of the society presented the company with a handsome banner. Mr. Wm. W. Adams, a silversmith, who kept his place in Church Street, between Franklin and White Streets, and who was the assistant alderman for the Fifth Ward, made the trumpets given by the city to temperance companies, and they were presented by Alderman Simpson, chairman of the Fire and Water Committee. They were received on behalf of the engine companies by Henry Wilson of Engine Company No. 18, and on behalf of the hose companies by John P. Teale, of Hose Company No. 33. About this time a committee from 33 Hose Company proceeded to Washington to present to Thomas F. Marshall of Kentucky, then a member of Congress, a gold badge for his efforts in the temperance cause. When they returned they adopted the nickname of "Kentuck," and had this name painted on their back box. On October 14, 1842, the Liberty Company No. 5, of Baltimore, were the guests of Hose Company No. 33 on the occasion of the Croton Water celebration. They brought with them and presented to the company the double silk banner carried by them that day. It was a very handsome and costly affair, suitably inscribed with the names of the donors and recipients. Robert R. Lawrence succeeded Mr. Teale as foreman, and Henry Colgrove followed him. About the year 1849, the company having dwindled down considerably, was reorganized as Warren Hose Company, and they procured a new two-story brick house on the west side of Sullivan Street, between Spring and Prince Streets, in 1851. James E. Colegrove was foreman in 1849 and 1850, and during his service the company had obtained a new hose carriage. Joseph C. Devine was the next foreman, and he held the position for several years, being succeeded by John Rayney. In 1855 the company elected Robert A. Johnson, foreman, and John Riley, assistant, and housed a new carriage built by J. H. Ludlum. John S. Craft and

BANNER PRESENTED BY THE MARTHA WASHINGTON TEMPERANCE AND BENEVOLENT SOCIETY TO CITY HOSE COMPANY NO. 33 (FRONT).

[Original in Volunteer Firemen's Association, Eighth Street.]

Anthony Yeomans succeeded to the positions of foreman and assistant, and when the law was passed allowing hose companies thirty members, No. 33 had no trouble in keeping their roll full. In 1859 Anthony Yeomans was elected foreman of the company, and was succeeded by Henry C. Dennett, Charles H. Denman being elected assistant foreman. These two gentlemen were re-elected for several years. When Denman was promoted to the foremanship, a new carriage of Hartshorn's build was obtained by the company. Chas. E. Bacon and Peter Keenan were the last officers of the company. No. 33 Hose obtained the nickname of " Blackbird," from a carriage they ran which was painted black and gold. They were one of the quickest companies on the west side of the city, and enjoyed a good reputation for their duty-doing qualities, and they

REVERSE SIDE OF BANNER OF CITY HOSE COMPANY NO. 33.

[Original in Volunteer Firemen's Association Rooms.]

were certainly famous for their " chowders," which were served up on Saturday evenings, at which times they would always have a number of guests, and passed the evening in a very enjoyable manner. They went out of service in 1865.

No. 34.—STAR—LAFAYETTE.—Organized on June 22, 1842, by the members of Engine Company No. 47; located in Tenth Street near the Dry Dock ; after

1858 at 211 East Eleventh Street; organized on March, 5, 1860, as Engine Company No. 3. On May 13, 1851, the company gave a grand entertainment to afford their friends a view of their newly painted machine. The carriage was built by Pine, and painted by Moriarty. The running gear was ultramarine blue with rich gilt stripes; the springs were polished, the reel was ornamented with two paintings. On the right panel was a view of a ship on fire at sea, and the passengers and crew are seeking safety in the boats; on the left panel was a scene at a fire; in the background a dwelling on fire, and in the foreground a figure of a fireman who has just rescued two children— one he is leading by the hand, and the other has clasped its tiny arms around his neck. It was a very expressive picture. The pictures were encircled with handsome carved work, which was decorated with stars. The boxes were a plum color; on the front box was the Brooklyn Fire Department certificate, and on the back box the New York Fire Department certificate, with the motto "Protection and Benevolence." On each of the side panels were neat little paintings. The Star Volunteers have presented to Mr. S. Gunyan, assistant foreman, a beautiful trumpet as a token of their respect and esteem. It was presented by Mr. David Kerr, captain of the company. At the annual meeting of Star Hose Company No. 34, held on May 14, 1850, the following officers were elected for the ensuing year: Wesley Smith, foreman; Scott Gunyan, assistant; William Foulks, treasurer; David Kerr and John Wood, representatives.

HIBERNIA (the second No. 34).—Was organized May 25, 1863; located in Forty-first Street, east of Eighth Avenue, and disbanded February 8, 1864. Among the members were Thomas McCarthy, foreman; David Anderson, assistant foreman; Edward S. Lord, Thomas D'Arcy, Geo. W. Osborne, Henry Clifford, and Peter Hanlon.

No. 35.—FIFTEENTH WARD—BALTIC.—This number was first taken up by several of the citizens of the Fifteenth Ward, among whom were Carlisle Norwood, A. W. Van Pelt, J. S. Winthrop, Jr., L. S. Foreman, Wm. M. Calhoun, E. P. Willetts and John S. Kelso, a split from Hose Company No. 5. They adopted the name of the Fifteenth Ward Hose Company No. 35, and on the evening of October 27, 1840, elected J. S. Winthrop foreman. The company succeeded in filling up with good duty-doing men, and in 1849 James F. Wenman, in after years an assistant engineer, became a member. About this time they changed their name to "Baltic." L. S. Foreman and John K. Bowen both served several terms as foreman. The company was located at 199 Mercer Street. After 1840 Hugh Curry (the champion pipeman) became an active member, and was soon elected foreman, which position he filled for several terms. At each election, however, he was a candidate for a white hat. While under his administration they received a new carriage, which was shortly after disabled, and in 1854, they secured another new one. The company had now changed considerably, many of the old members having resigned During the sugar house fire in 1848, in Duane Street, one of the members, Charles J. Durant, was fatally injured. In 1854 E. P. White was elected foreman, having succeeded T. F. Goodwin. In 1857 John W. Slater was promoted to the foremanship, and James H. Bell made assistant. Bell was the last foreman. At the Tripler Hall fire, as well as on several other occasions, the men of the company distinguished themselves, but they were continually in trouble, and were finally disbanded June 30, 1859.

CRYSTAL (the second No. 35).—Was organized June 25, 1863, by Gustavus Isaacs, Geo. S. Wickham and Wm. T. Worrall, from Amity Hose Company No. 38, and fourteen others, among whom were Charles Delmonico, Seneca M. Bell and Henry L. Faris. Gustavus Isaacs was chosen foreman, and Wm. Mead, Jr., assistant. They were assigned to duty in the Third and Fourth Districts, but for quite a while without an apparatus or location. They succeeded in getting a location in 101 West Fifteenth Street, near Sixth Avenue, where they remained until the department was reorganized. Isaacs and Mead continued to be the officers of the company during the course of its existence.

OCEANA HOSE.—Was organized on March 5, 1845, at a meeting held at the residence of Francis B. O'Connor, No. 94 Madison Street. There were present Messrs. James H. Rich, Daniel B. Jenkins, Lawrence Turnure, Charles A. Coe and Francis B. O'Connor. Messrs. James Gillan, Benjamin Cartwright and Charles Rose, who were absent, had signified their intention of joining the new company and were duly enrolled.

Messrs. O'Connor, Turnure, and Coe were respectively elected foreman, assistant foreman and secretary. In the following December the company was comfortably quartered at No. 189 Madison Street. Benjamin Cartwright and W. D. Wade were the two fire representatives.

The hose carriage, built for the company in 1848 by Van Ness & Co., and painted by Edward Weir, Jr. and W. Hamilton, was a very elaborate affair, and cost with its embellishments fifteen hundred dollars, of which the company paid twelve hundred. On the front panel Oceana was represented with her attendant nymphs rising from the sea. On the back was a finely executed view of the High Bridge at Harlem, with a group of Indians; on the back ends the Park and Bowling Green fountains, and on the front a painting of a little girl washing her feet at a hydrant and a little boy playing the hose.

William M. Tweed was elected secretary of 36 Hose on December 19, 1845, but only held the office till the following April, when he resigned. He aspired to reach the position of assistant foreman, but he had evidently not yet learned the art of manipulating the political machine, at which he became so expert in after years, and his plans were frustrated. Seeing no chance of advancing his ambition in the company, he betook himself to Engine Company No. 1.

On resigning from the company on May 1, 1850, Mr. John R. Platt presented it with a handsome silver trumpet and a fine engraving.

The minute books of the company, from the time of its organization to its disbandment in 1865, were in the possession of Mr. Alonzo Slote, for many years a prominent member, and are remarkable as being probably the best kept set of books of the Old Fire Department now in existence.

No. 37.—This company (without a name) was organized by ex-members of Engine Company No. 37 on June 22, 1842, at Grand and Monroe Streets. The material of which the company was formed was not as smooth as was necessary for success. The consequence was internal and external strife, which was terminated by the company being disbanded on February 29, 1843.

MADISON (the second No. 37).—Was organized in 1848; located first at Twenty-first Street and Fifth Avenue, subsequently at Broadway near Twenty-sixth Street, and completed her career at Twenty-ninth Street, near Seventh Avenue, in 1865. In 1850 Madison gave a sumptuous entertainment to their friends in commemoration of their new carriage, which they had just received from the painters. The body was an ultramarine blue, with a gilt and pure white stripe. The reel was handsomely ornamented with rich gilt carved work, and two paintings; on the right was the Firemen's Monument at Greenwood, and on the left a scene on the Grecian coast, representing a storm. In the foreground was represented the mariner's family, and the wife attempting to wave a signal, in hopes of attracting the attention of those on board her husband's vessel, which is seen in the distance struggling with the waves, to warn them off a dangerous part of the coast. On the front box was " Madison Hose Company No. 37, organized January 25, 1848," in gilt letters. On the side panels were the emblems of the Fire Department. On the right a hook and ladder crossed with axe and trumpet; on the left two torches, two pipes and a fire-cap. On the front box was a silver plate on which was inscribed " Alfred Carson, Chief Engineer." On the back box was a neat landscape; on the panels, right, a fountain; left, a hydrant. The lifters were sea-horses. The running gear and wheels were carmine with a gilt and bright red stripe. The carriage was built by Joseph Pine and painted by E. Weir. At the annual meeting of Madison, held on Wednesday evening, April 9, 1851, the following were elected officers for the ensuing year: Tobias Lawrence, foreman; William Wilson, assistant foreman; George Kass, secretary; Sylvester Sparks, treasurer; and Tobias Lawrence and James Parish, representatives.

No. 38.—AMITY.—Was organized March 8, 1842, and located at 130 Amity Street, next door to Union Engine Company No. 18, and a few doors from Phoenix Hook and Ladder Company No. 3. John Gillilan was one of the organizers and the first foreman of the company; he afterwards joined Engine Company No. 35, and became an assistant engineer in 1850, serving until 1853. Samuel Conover, afterwards park commissioner, was also foreman of the company in its later days. In 1849 Wm. J. Lippincott was foreman, Samuel E. Belcher assistant, and Daniel D. Conover, George D. Crary, Julian Botts, George T. Alker and Geo. W. Engs among the members. This was in every respect a first-class company, and did service in the First and Second Districts, which comprised that part of the city lying north of Canal Street on the west side of the city, and they also took occasional runs into the lower districts. The " Amity hops," which were given each season by this company either at the Apollo Rooms, on Broadway near Canal Street, or at Niblo's Saloon, were quite noted at the time and were remarkable for the beauty of the ladies' toilets, and were altogether very enjoyable affairs. This company never engaged in street brawls, and about the only serious trouble of that kind they ever had was with Union Engine Company 18 in 1845; there was, however, a friendly rivalry between them and Empire Hose Company No. 40 in racing to fires. The company was noted for owning the finest and most expensive Hose carriage in the United States. It was of hard wood, painted snow white, very heavily silver mounted, and with red glass lamps mounted in gold on the sides, and shaped to represent pineapples. The cost of its construction was eight thousand dollars, a very high price for those times. Jacob Ostrom was foreman of the company in 1856, and Lawrence Taylor succeeded him in that position. No. 38 was the first company that ever paraded with Dodworth's full band, the parade taking place in 1851. In 1863 Gustavus Isaacs, Geo. S. Wickham and Wm. T. Worrall left this company, and, with others, organized Crystal Hose Company No. 35. In 1864 Jacob Bogart was eiected foreman, and in 1865 Charles W. Veitch was chosen as their last first officer. In the matter of fire duty No. 38 Hose stood second to none, and in the turning out of the men and their rapidity in getting to work was highly complimented by the officers of the Department. Their discipline also was of the best, they never having been suspended from duty nor had their carriage turned into the house " tongue first," a mark of suspension and disgrace; but, on the contrary, on several occasions they were highly spoken of by the officers of the department for their general good order, neat appearance and untiring vigilance.

No. 39.—METROPOLITAN—MOHAWK.—Organized in May, 1842; located at Third Avenue near Twenty-sixth Street, removed to Twenty-sixth Street, between Third and Fourth Avenues, where the company remained until the closing years of the department. During the lifetime of the company the name was changed to Mohawk. In the summer of 1850 the company brought their new carriage home from the painter's. She was plain but prettily ornamented. The running gear was a light cream color with blue and red stripes; boxes and arch blue; reel, red with gilt stripes. On the front box was the following inscription: "Organized May 8, 1842," on the side panels was the number of the company, on the back box the name of the company, on one panel

AMITY HOSE NO. 38.

a painting of Neptune, and on the other a fancy sketch of a female. On the arch on each side of the reel was a neat figure of an eagle, and on the front framework a figure of a fireman in full costume. The carriage was decorated with a splendid pair of lamps. She was built by Van Ness, and painted by Moriarty. The company gave a grand entertainment to their friends upon the occasion. At the annual meeting in 1850 of Metropolitan Hose the following officers were elected for the ensuing year: Joseph C. Davison, foreman; John Rogers, assistant; Wm. W. Seaman, secretary; Wm. H. Bowen, treasurer; Wm. J. Minard and Wm. Wines, representatives. At the annual meeting in 1853 the following officers were elected for the ensuing year: Robert B. Nooney, foreman; John Meighan, assistant; Henry Allman, secretary; John Mason, treasurer; Alonzo Forbes and George Carr, representatives. At the annual meeting on May 8, 1855, the following officers were elected: Henry Allman, foreman, vice Robert B. Nooney, declined; Wm. F. Harned, assistant, vice John Meighan, declined; Alex. N. Murray, re-elected secretary; George Carr, treasurer, vice John Mason, declined; Benjamin Hyde, steward, vice Abram Jones, declined; Charles E. Cannon and Robert B. Nooney, representatives, vice Henry Allman and P. H. Brody, declined.

No. 40.—EMPIRE—("Redbird").—Empire Hose Company No. 40 was organized in 1843. Its organization was mainly due to James L. Miller, and one of the original members was Cornelius R. Campbell, now janitor of the Jefferson Market Police Court building. It had a four-wheeled carriage painted white and lavishly gilded, and first lay at No. 2 Leroy Street. A new carriage, built in 1848, was at the fatal Duane Street sugar house fire. It moved to a miserable shed in Barrow Street, between Hudson and Greenwich Streets. On the night of the disbanding of Engine Company No. 34 "the boys" ran their carriage into No. 34's quarters. Next day they found that it had been taken to the Corporation Yard, but that night they took her out and put her back in Barrow Street. Soon after new quarters were erected at No. 70 Barrow Street, and in 1851 a new carriage was built by John Sickels. A later one, constructed (1857) by Pine & Hartshorn, lasted until the company was disbanded in 1865. Its rivals were Hose No. 38 and Hose No. 33, but it was rarely beaten. Among the foremen of this company were James L. Miller, Abraham Myers, S. V. W. Jones, John A. Cregier, Wm. Evans, and W. C. Rogers; and the following were permanent members of the company : John Kettleman, Andrew Owens, Deacon Edward Wright, Alanson and Ellis Finch, Robert Wright, David Milliken, David Walker, Thomas J. Forbes, Isaac P. Lockman, John T. Lockman, E. H. Brinckerhoff, John C. Brinckerhoff, C. P. Buckley, Clarence A. Burtis, Peter P. and Abraham W. Pullis, Charles A. Hilliker, Andrew Bleakley, Montgomery Maze, James B. Mingay, Abraham R. and William A. Auten, Warren Chapman, Charles P. Buckley, John A. Loinherr, De Witt C. Hammond, Abraham Tallman, Charles L. Gowdey, James Bambrick, D. P. Beers, G. W. Quick, J. L. Forbes, R. A. McFarland, and G. W. Waterbury. Mr. Cornelius R. Campbell went to California in 1850 to become in San Francisco a member of Engine 3. He there saw among other New York firemen, Dave Broderick, Chief Dave Scannel of New York Engine No. 5, Recorder George Green of New York 34 Engine, Alexander Devoe of New York 14 Engine, a member of San Francisco 3 Engine, who was frightfully injured at a fire in Commercial Street, San Francisco, by falling from a cornice and, refusing to have a leg amputated, died of gangrene; Dave Roberts of New York Engine 38, who died insane in California, and Malachi Fallon, foreman of New York Engine 33, keeper of the Ivy Green at the rear of the Tombs and warden of the Tombs, afterward chief of police at San Francisco. On Mr. Campbell's return from California he joined Engine 23. The company went out of service in 1865.

No. 41.—ALERT.—Hose Company No. 41, known as the Alert, and among the "giddy boys" variously as the "Blackbird" and the "Bucky-boys," was organized on March 24, 1843, by some of the members of Engine Company No. 27, the "North River," which had been disbanded a little while previously. In 1861 the Alert was transferred to a new house, No. 18 Renwick Street, where she remained until statutorily disbanded in 1865. Alert Hose petitioned in 1862 to be organized as an engine company to run a hand engine. The request was strange at that time, as most of the companies wanted steamers.

They continued, however, to do duty as a hose company, until the end of the department.

No. 42.—This company was organized on June 1, 1839, located at Third Street and the Bowery, and changed to Hose Company No. 30 in June 1, 1840.

MAZEPPA—MOUNT PLEASANT (the second No. 42).—Was organized on October 12, 1848, located in Thirty-third Street, near Ninth Avenue, and went out of service in 1865. At the annual meeting of Mount Pleasant Hose Company, held May 14, 1850, the following officers were unanimously elected for the ensuing year: Oscar Taylor, foreman; Alfred Reed, assistant, vice James T. Austin, resigned; E. Harrison, secretary; Philip Agnew, treasurer; John D. Revere and James Odell, representatives.

On Friday, October 24, 1851, Hose 42 brought home a carriage from the fair at Castle Garden. They were accompanied by a band of music, and presented a fine appearance. The boxes and upper works were painted a dark plum color, striped with gold, edged with a fine blossom-colored stripe; the gilding was connected by gold scrolls at the corners. On the front panel was a rich scroll with the words "Mazeppa Hose 42," and the date of the organization of the company. On the back box panel was a small picture of Washington's Camp at Valley Forge, and a scroll with the motto "Fearless and Faithful." On the right hand reel panel was a painting of Mazeppa, at sunset, where his horse has fallen, and he is surrounded by a group of wild horses. On the left reel panel was another scene from Mazeppa, where he is rushing through the forest pursued by a flock of wolves. On the right end of the front box was a fireman standing at a hydrant, while his associates are

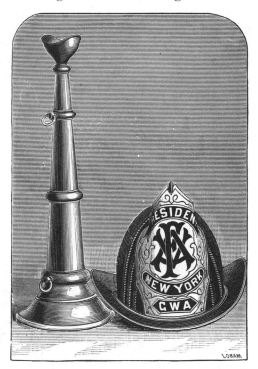

HAT AND TRUMPET OF G. W. ANDERSON.

conducting the hose to a fire in the background. On the left end was a miniature view of the Institution for the Blind. On the right end of the back box was the coat of arms of the city, and on the left was a figure of Hope. The wheels and running gear were painted carmine, striped full with gold, relieved by a delicate lilac stripe. The back and front plates on the running part were ornamented with rich gold scroll work. The carriage was painted by A. P. Moriarty, and he received a medal at the fair for the superior manner in which the painting was executed. The company visited the Institution for the Blind and were welcomed by Miss Crosby, who delivered a pretty address, to which Foreman Read responded.

The house of this company caught fire under the stairs at 11.30 P. M. September 10, 1862. It was believed to be the work of an incendiary, from the fact of the bunkers being all in bed, and the lights having been out in the carriage room. While this fire was burning, Mr. John Bathe, a member of No. 42, showed remarkable presence of mind. Instead of running down stairs at the risk of being burned, he invented a fire escape by detaching the rope which was used for hoisting hose to dry, and, getting "Billy" Timms to hold one end while he threw the other end out of the rear window, he then "shinned" down the rope safely to the yard. This was all very nice for Bathe, but after he got down, Timms had no one to hold the rope for him, so he had to take his chances down the stairs.

No. 43.—This company was organized on May 20, 1839, located in Willett Street, near Rivington, and changed to Hose Company No. 31 on April 28, 1842.

PIONEER (the second No. 43).—Was organized September 28, 1848, and was first located on Third Avenue, north side, between One Hundred and Twenty-first and One Hundred and Twenty-second Streets. This company removed their quarters in 1860 to their new house on One Hundred and Twenty-first Street, corner of old Harlem Lane, now the corner of One Hundred and Twenty-first Street and Lexington Avenue. They first ran a carriage painted drab, with gold stripes, and in 1851 received a new carriage, painted red, and which they christened "Little Red Bird." They ran it until the company went out of service in 1865. During the entire service of Pioneer it had but three foremen, John D. Jones being the first, and John R. Farrington the last, the latter serving in that capacity for eleven years and six months. It was while proceeding to a fire at Fort Washington, and while descending a hill, that J. Wilson, of this company, had his leg so badly injured by being crushed between the wheel of the carriage and a tree that he afterwards died from the effects of the wound. This company ran from Harlem to the Tripler Hall fire in January, 1854, and did good work. At the annual meeting of Pioneer, held on Monday evening, May 3, 1852, the following gentlemen were unanimously elected officers for the ensuing year: John DeWitt Jones, foreman; Wm. Wilson, assistant; Wm. Skinner, secretary; James L. Mason and Aaron Hosford, representatives.

No. 44.—ELEVENTH WARD.—Organized June 1, 1839, located at 77 Willett Street, and changed to Hose Company No. 29 on June 22, 1842.

WASHINGTON IRVING.—This company, which performed duty in the First and Second Districts, was organized February 1, 1849, and was located in Thirty-first Street, west of Seventh Avenue, and next door to where Franklin Engine Company No. 39 was located in 1853. They commenced service with a hose tender, having a new carriage built for them in 1851, and when this carriage was disabled in 1856, they obtained another which they ran until 1860. Pending the procurement of the last carriage they used in 1864, they appropriated for a while the old carriage of Hose Company 17. Wm. Simpson was foreman of the company in 1852, followed by Wm. J. Wilson, Jacob Tooker, Geo. Hook, Edward Craddock, and George A. Campbell. At the annual meeting held on Monday evening, May 6, 1850, the following officers were elected for the ensuing year: Leonard Myers, foreman; James R. Remsen, assistant; William E. Bishop, secretary; Alvah Spaulding, treasurer; William Simpson and John Maxwell, representatives. Mr. Simpson was elected assistant foreman in 1853, and served for three years. September,

1852, was a memorable year for the company. They went on an excursion to Poughkeepsie, and were treated to a banquet, parade, and the best of everything.

During the riots of July, 1863, this company did most faithful duty. They were located in the midst of the troubled districts, and some of their members were on duty during the whole of that memorable week, and either the foreman, Geo. A. Campbell, or the assistant, John A. Ripple, were in command at all of the many incendiary fires in their district. The members of the company who were " bunkers," brought their mattresses down to the carriage room, and slept there, and some of the members staid there night and day until quiet was restored to the city. At many of the fires the company encountered serious opposition from the rioters, and their hose was cut in Twenty-seventh Street, near Seventh Avenue, and also at the ferry house, and at the fire in Allerton's Hotel, Forty-first Street and Eleventh Avenue. At the latter place the company had taken a hydrant in Forty-second Street, and stretched in, but were not allowed to get to work. The company were instrumental in saving a colored family in Thirty-second Street, whom they harbored next to the carriage house until the police were able to get them to the station house. Any account that fully describes the incidents of riots in the upper districts must necessarily mention Washington Irving Hose Company 44 and the bravery of its members.

RESCUE OF A CHILD.

No. 45.—RED JACKET.—Organized December 10, 1849, located in Thirty-third Street, near Third Avenue, disbanded July 19, 1858. In April, 1850, the following officers were elected for the ensuing year: John M. Manolt, foreman; Henry Allman, assistant; Jacob W. Cooper, secretary; Hiram L. Frost, treasurer; Thomas W. Bennett and Henry Allman, representatives.

In October, 1851, the company brought home a new carriage from the Fair at Castle Garden, where she had been placed on exhibition. The company turned out strong, accompanied by a band of music, and presented a good appearance, attracting much attention as they passed through the streets on their route homewards. The carriage was one of Pine's build, and was ornamented in superb style. The running gear was carmine with a gilt stripe; on the right panel of the reel a painting of an Indian chief and an Indian maid leaning upon him for support, while he is casting his eye over the plain beneath him where his enemies are in pursuit. On the left is a representation of an interview between Red Jacket and Washington. The paintings were encircled in richly carved wood. On the front box was a scene representing the early settlement of the country; a settler and his family have just escaped across a river and are looking back at the log house which a short time before was their home, but is now being destroyed by fire, the work of Indians. On the side panels were two very neat female Indian figures. On the back box was a scene at Fort Hamilton; on the side panels two figures of Indian hunters. The carriage was adorned with a handsome bell arch, which was silver-plated; the signal was in the center of the arch, on the top a figure of an Indian. The lifters were of an entirely new pattern, representing an Indian maid. The tongue was silver-plated. The painting was done by E. Weir; the pictures by L. Ryer, 151 Charles Street. In the evening the company, with a large number of invited guests, partook of a supper. At a meeting of Red Jacket Hose held on Monday evening, December 7, 1852, the following officers were elected: Adam Keifer, foreman, vice A. M. Manolt, resigned; John Golden, assistant; Michael Wallace, secretary; John McBride, treasurer.

C. GODFREY GUNTHER (the second No. 45).—Was organized on June 25, 1863, located at 278 Avenue A, and went out of service in 1865.

No. 46.—NASSAU.—At "Windust," corner of Ann Street and Park Row, one of the most famous resorts in the lower portion of the city, there congregated a number of young men in 1849, who proposed the organization of a hose company. On the fifth of November of that year they again met, and after some twenty signing the roll, they elected Andrew McNicol foreman; Christian A. Borras, assistant; Francis McKennon, secretary; James Hawkins, treasurer; John Spittle and John McNicol, representatives. They adopted the name of "Nassau," after the street they were located on, which was Nassau (No. 83), between Fulton and John. They ran a "jumper" till 1851, when they received a new carriage. The company did not seem to fill up very fast, although they were very quick at fires, and did excellent work. From 1851 till 1854 Daniel Meehan was foreman, when in the latter year they became involved in some trouble, and were disbanded September 18.

VALLEY FORGE.—On the twentieth of December, 1854, just two months after the Nassau boys threw up No. 46, James Millward, Jr., Wm. W. Jacobus, Alexander Gedney, John C. Wandell, James Finch, Wm. J. Minard, John W. Jones, Abram Odell, Edward Dobbs, George W. Lowerre, John Warren, Alfred T. Serrell, James Richmond, and others met on Eighth Avenue, and formed a new hose company, taking up No. 46, and selecting the name of "Valley Forge." They obtained a location on West Thirty-seventh Street, one door from Eighth Avenue, and, securing the old carriage, elected as officers James Millward, Jr., an old fireman from Engine 39, as foreman; Wm. J. Minard, assistant; Edward L. Cobb, secretary; and John Cross, treasurer. In 1855 they removed to more comfortable quarters, 185 West Thirty-seventh Street, and in 1856 received a new carriage, built by Sickles, and painted by A. P. Moriarty. The panels were finely finished. On the one side was "Washington at Valley Forge," and on the other "Washington crossing the Delaware." In 1858 Edward L. Cobb was elected foreman; J. Elias Whitehead, assistant; and Frank E. Skilding, secretary. These gentlemen remained in office till 1860, when the company petitioned for a steamer, which being awarded them, they resolved themselves into an engine company, retaining the same number. Thus ended Hose Company No. 46. James Millward, Jr., the first foreman of Valley Forge, was for many years a port warden and commissioner of exchange at Fortress Monroe during the war, and, under the second term of U. S. Grant as President of the United States, was appointed Minister to Belgium. While there he escorted General Grant through that country during the latter's tour around the world. Jonas A. Bryant, at one time assistant foreman of the company, enlisted in the Fifth New York State Volunteers, and was killed at the battle of Williamsburg, Va. In April, 1860, the company organized themselves as Valley Forge Engine Company No. 46. The company was composed of good material, and had a good reputation for fire duty.

TO OCEANA HOSE COMPANY No. 36.

[Air :—"LIFE ON THE OCEAN WAVE."]

Huzza for brave Thirty-six,
  Ever prompt at the fire-bell's call,
Three cheers for brave Thirty-six,
  Huzza for the Firemen all.
When the red flames wildest flash
  On the startled midnight air,
Where the crackling embers crash,
  Oceana's men are there.
                    Huzza, etc.

Secure may the mother sleep,
  With her babe upon her breast,
Brave hearts her vigils keep,
  To guard them while they rest.
Though sudden flames alarm them
  In the dwelling where they lie,
The fires shall never harm them,
  Oceana's men are nigh.
                    Huzza, etc.

Then, laborer, cease thy toil
  And want, forget thy woes ;
Though fiery serpents coil
  'Round you in your repose,
No fatal fang shall wound you,
  The Fireman's wary eye
Shall be a guard around you—
  Oceana's men are nigh.
                    Huzza, etc.

CHAPTER XXXIX.

CONCLUSION OF THE HOSE COMPANIES.

No. 47 (Mechanics' Own, Howard, Mechanics).—No. 48 (Carson, Americus).—No. 49 (Lady Washington).—No. 50 (Corlies, Hope).—No. 51 (Relief).—No. 52 (Undine).—No. 53 (Naiad).—No. 54 (Eureka).—No. 55 (Harry Howard).—No. 56 (Equitable, Nassau).—No. 57 (Paulding).—No. 58 (Merchant, Forrest).—No. 59 (Ion, Manhattan).—No. 60 (M. T. Brennan).—No. 61 (Zephyr).—No. 62 (Minute).—Fifth Ward Exempt.

N O. 47.—MECHANICS' OWN—MECHANICS.—Although this company was organized on "All Fool's Day," it was no fool of a company, for it proved one of the most active on the east side of the city. Their organization dates from April 1, 1850, and was started mostly by shipbuilders and foundrymen, among whom were David Coleman, Robert Johnson, John Sperry, Harvey M. Weed, and Asa H. Leonard. They adopted the name of "Mechanics' Own" after a noted clipper ship that had recently been launched at one of the shipyards for the California trade, and upon which several of the members had worked. Shortly afterwards the word "Own" was dropped, making it plain "Mechanics." Securing a temporary location in a small shanty on Fifth Street, near Avenue C, they elected Robert H. Johnson foreman, and commenced doing duty with a two-wheeled "jumper." Robert B. Herring followed as foreman, and in 1853 Joseph Radley was elected. This year they had a house in Fourth Street, near Lewis, altered, and moved in, when they brought home a new carriage built by Pine. It was double-reeled and richly painted by John Quigg. On the one side was a representation of the famous clipper ship 'Contest,' and on the other side the yacht 'America;' on the front box was a marine view of a shipwreck and rescue, and on the rear box a fine view of a shipyard with vessels on the stocks and the men at their work. In fact the whole was a very superior piece of workmanship, and reflected great credit on the artist. Shortly before they removed to Fourth Street they changed the name to "Howard" (the philanthropist—not Harry). They had run under the name of Howard only a year when it was changed again to "Mechanics," dropping the word "Own." During 1855, 1856, and part of 1857, Jacob H. Miller was foreman, and in 1857 Cornelius N. Rice was chosen. The company had a favorite dog called "Major," who knew the stroke of the fire-bell as well as any one of the members, and he seemed to take as much delight in a race with Engine 44 or Hook and Ladder 13 as the boys themselves. When the company went out of existence they gave him to Engine Company No. 3, of Elizabeth, N. J., where he died a few years after. About this time Alderman Francis I. A. Boole, of the Eleventh Ward, afterwards defeated for mayor, and who died in an asylum, was elected a member. In 1858 we find John J. Whyte foreman, who remained in charge till 1860, when Daniel Kelly took his place. Kelly, as related elsewhere, subsequently entered the monastery at West

Hoboken, and took the name of Brother Bonaventure. Samuel Lynch succeeded Kelly as foreman, and John Quigg was elected assistant under Lynch. About this time they brought home another new carriage built

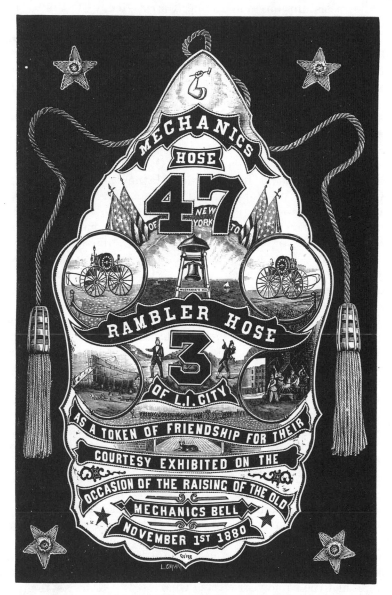

RAMBLER HOSE.—PRESENTATION FRONT.

[Painted by John Quigg. This Front was presented to Rambler Hose Company No. 3 of Blissville, Long Island, August 20, 1881, by the members of Mechanics' Association of New York. The party were conveyed in special cars to the quarters of Rambler Hose. The presentation was made by the president, Mr. John Quigg, in a neat speech in behalf of the members of the Mechanics' Association, which was responded to by Patrick Hughes, foreman of Rambler Hose Company.]

by Torboss, painted maroon color tipped with gold. On the four ends of the front and rear boxes were the portraits of Patrick Brown, a deceased member, Andrew Mills, George Steers, and Wm. H. Webb, all boss shipbuilders. On the top of the carriage they used to carry an "Ox Tail" of immense size, which resembled a high bunch of flax, and when it was worn out they ran an elegant plume till disbanded. In 1862 Wm. A. Nelson was elected foreman, and re-elected in 1863, while among the members were Thomas Lane, assistant foreman; James Clark, Henry H. Wells, George G. Cornell, John Clark, Lewis H. Lanman, F. W. Adams, George Frelich, Mathew Curran, and Jacob Couterie. In 1864 John Quigg was elected foreman, and while under his command they moved to their new house, 548 Fifth Street, where they held a grand entertainment. On the fourth of July, 1865, just before the Old Department disbanded, they paid a visit to Elizabeth, N. J., where they were received by Engine No. 3 and the members of that Department. After they had sold out and divided up the old relics of the company, they presented their last foreman, Mr. Quigg, with a silver trumpet as a token of their esteem for him as a man and a foreman. Towards the close of the company we find among its members Henry G. Hellthaler, Lyman F. Green, Jacob Wool, Wm. G. Clark, John Stehle, Mathew J. Montgomery, Joseph Stumpf, G. Reeves, M. W. Roberts, C. F. Patten and H. Goube. A few of the old boys can still be found around the old Eleventh Ward. Nathaniel K. Thompson, a former member of this company, afterwards became chief engineer of the Fire Department of Elizabeth, N. J., and afterwards sheriff.

No. 48.—CARSON—AMERICUS.—In November, 1850, at the house of George B. Over, in Third Avenue, between Eighty-sixth and Eighty-seventh Streets, the subject was agitated of organizing a hose company for the Yorkville district. On December 11, 1850, the company was organized by Frank B. Ball, William Granger, James Lynch, William H. Karr, Abram Quackenbush, Charles Quackenbush, Benjamin Pine, Charles Abel, Thomas Pearson—afterwards councilman and district judge, M. A. Read—for many years past Superintendent of Station D Post-office, John Singer, and others. They started with eighteen men, and elected Frank B. Ball foreman, and William H. Karr assistant foreman. Ball was a runner with Lafayette Engine Company No. 19 when she lay corner of Eldridge and Division Streets, and for five years foreman of No. 45 Engine. The company adopted the name of "Carson," and commenced doing duty with a tender belonging to No. 44 Hose, the wheels of which were very high, so the company applied and received a new four-wheeled carriage in 1851. They had it painted black and gold with red running gear. When the apparatus was finished, the company adopted the name of "Americus," which name they retained until disbanded. Their location was in a two-story brick building on the northeast corner of Eighty-fifth Street and Third Avenue. After Ball had succeeded in getting the company well under way, he retired from the office of foreman, and William H. Karr was chosen to succeed him, Abram Quackenbush followed, and in 1856 the company procured another new carriage, and the same year elected Charles W. Keip as their foreman. Seth W. Valentine and James R. Dalton followed, the latter holding the office for several years. Michael Hallaran was elected foreman in 1863, and elected an assistant engineer in the Spring of 1865. Mr. J. Shanahan, at one time assistant foreman, was elected the last foreman of the company, which went out of service when the Metropolitan Fire Commissioners assumed control. John O'Donnell was assistant foreman in 1863, and Daniel H. Griffith, secretary. Among the many members this company had were Thomas Beaty, James J. Gilmore, John H. Bradbrook, S. Otis Clapp, John F. Twomey,

William E. Marshall, James R. Dalton, Thomas Webster, Moses Marsh, and Mathew Shanahan.

No. 49.—LADY WASHINGTON.—Hose Company No. 49 was organized by Jacob L. Smith in 1851, and was located at 126 Cedar Street. Among the members were Andrew Seeley, Henry Beck, Cornelius Flynn, and James McGlynn. Most all were residents of the First and Third Wards, of various occupations, mechanics, liquor dealers, boatmen, and a few were merchants. Cornelius Flynn, who is to-day a well-known figure in First Ward politics, succeeded Mr. Smith as foreman. Mr. Flynn resigned in 1864, after seven years' service, and he was elected to the Legislature. "The company" says Mr. Flynn, "was a very quiet, easy-going lot, no trouble, only now and again a little brush in contending with rivals for the honor of being the first to get to a fire." The pet name of the company was "Lady Washington," and she was decorated in gorgeous array on all occasions of public display. All the works of the carriage were silver-mounted and the panels decorated with a likeness of Lady Washington and of the General crossing the Delaware. Went out of service in 1865.

No. 50.— CORLIES—HOPE. —Organized September 8, 1851, and was officered as follows : William A. Tyson, foreman ; James Y. Watkins, Jr., assistant foreman ; John G. Tibbets, secretary ; Joseph Hilton, treasurer ; Henry A. Burr and James Y. Watkins, Sr., representatives. This company was located at 10½ Mott Street, between Chatham and Pell Streets, and was formed by members of Hose Companies Nos. 10 and 14. The company

OLD JAIL.
[City Hall Park.]

retained the name of " Corlies" but a short time, when the name was changed to "Hope." William W. Corlies was the founder of the company, and gave his name to it. Among the original members the name of James Y. Watkins, Sr., stands prominent; he was an old fireman, having been a member of Engine Companies 21 and 14 ; he was also a trustee of the Fire Department Fund, serving faithfully from 1853 until the time of his death in 1883, a period of thirty years. Henry A. Burr was also prominent in the department, serving as treasurer of the fund, and chairman of the Firemen's Ball Committee. The Watkins family were well represented in this company. James Y., Sr., mentioned above, and James Y., Jr., the assistant foreman, were well known members of Hose Company No. 10, Engine Company 42, and the Exempt Engine. Another member of the family, John O., served his time in this company. Two other members of No. 50, John Feeney and Matthew Stewart, served in the Second Fire Zouaves. Both of them were honorably mentioned. Captain Feeney was severely wounded. No. 50 remained in the department until the end, and and was always known as a quiet, duty-doing company.

No. 51.—RELIEF.—Organized September 1, 1852; located in Fiftieth Street, near Second Avenue, and went out of service in 1865. Among its members were John E. Flagler, foreman; Thomas Harrison, assistant foreman; Geo. Nixon, Stephen McCoy, Henry Brickall, John Johnson, William Duane, and James Dorsey.

No. 52.—UNDINE.—Was organized October 27, 1851, by John T. Rollins, from old 8 Hose, and who was assistant engineer in 1840. Wright Seaman, Jordan L. Mott, George H. E. Lynch (who was afterwards foreman), and others of Harlem. They located in One Hundred and Twenty-second Street on the north side, between Second and Third Avenues, and continued in the same location until organized as Engine Company 52. They received a new carriage the year following their organization, and in 1856 received the carriage that they ran until 1862, when they obtained the steamer, which was one of the first to make its appearance in the Harlem River District. John A. McCosker was elected assistant engineer from this company in 1860, having been its foreman in 1858. Louis J. and Charles Belloni, Jordan L. Mott, and William Tabele were among the prominent members of this company. When old Tripler Hall was destroyed by fire on the night of January 8, 1854, this company ran their carriage from Harlem to the fire, and did good duty, not reaching home until the next day at noon. There was no general alarm struck, but, as one of the members expressed it, "we saw a big light and started for it, and just kept a running till we got there." At the annual meeting held Monday evening, May 3, 1852, the following were unanimously elected officers for the ensuing year: John T. Rollins, re-elected foreman; Wright Seaman, re-elected assistant; Franklin S. James, secretary; Elisha Morrill, re-elected treasurer; William V. McDaniels and Louis J. Belloni, representatives.

No. 53.—NAIAD.—Organized on January 21, 1852; located at 179 Church Street, and voluntarily disbanded on December 1, 1858. Among its leading members were John Garcia, William Thompson, Samuel R. Brown, Lew Van Boskerck, James L. Miller, William H. Shumway, Josiah Hedden, E. L. Garesche, William Baker, P. V. Z. Lane, George Schott, Edward Wheelock, Silas G. Butler, William M. Randell, R. M. Hedden, E. M. Schaffer, I. E. Zimmerman, J. L. Mathez, Siro Delmonico, George Randell. The company was reorganized under the same name and number in September, 1859, located at 142 East Fortieth Street, and went out of service in 1865. Among its members at various times were John P. Flender, foreman; John McCann, assistant; David Montgomery, Joseph Dixon, Thomas Barrett, Henry Neville, Adam Kohl, Martin Kalb, George F. Uhl, and Francis Mannix.

No. 54.—EUREKA.—This company was short-lived, remaining in service as a hose company a little over six years. They were organized February 19, 1852, securing a temporary location at 105 West Broadway. John D. Dixon was the first foreman, and Daniel Horrigan assistant; the company doing duty in the Seventh and Eighth Districts. Among its members at the outset were Alexander M. C. Smith, the hose manufacturer; William H. Board, George S. Crary, Robert McDonnell, Joseph R. Candee, William F. Searing, B. F. Grant, Frank Johnson, James Craft, William H. Burras, William E. Crary and William H. Johnson (the two latter being representatives), and Benjamin Johnson, secretary. In 1853 they moved to 153 Franklin Street, adjoining Hook and Ladder 15. Here they remained until 1858, when they disbanded and formed themselves into Engine Company No. 30.

No. 55.—HARRY HOWARD.— Organized September 17, 1853. Harry Howard Hose Company had an elegant brown stone front house erected for them at 115 Christopher Street, upon the roof of which was a carved statue of Harry Howard in full fire rig. Upon the disbanding of the company in 1865 this statue was presented to Neptune Engine Company No. 2, of Paterson, N. J., and afterwards passed into the possession of Protection Engine Company No. 5, of the same place, where it yet remains. Among the members of No. 55 were Fred. Vredenbergh, foreman; John A. Van Buskirk, assistant; Jas. Van Riper, R. D. Wehman, Minturn Van Heusen, John M. Bogart, Samuel Stingerland, and John H. Froelegh.

No. 56.—EQUITABLE.—Organized March 5, 1853. located at 123 Wooster Street, disbanded December 20, 1855.

NASSAU (the second No. 56) organized November 27, 1856, located in Theater Alley, and after 1861 in City Hall Park; went out of service in 1865. Among the members were Patrick McGurick, foreman; Jas. Whalen, assistant; Leopold Schmidt, James Griston, Thos. Downey, Denis O'Connor, Thos. Goodwin, Joseph F. Reed, Richard Norris, Thomas McCook. John Boyle, Alexander Wilson and Joseph Gregory.

James Whalen was so severely injured while going to a fire in the Eighth District on Monday afternoon, November 28, 1859, that he died of internal injuries on the following Wednesday at the New York Hospital. He had the tongue of the carriage, and on descending the hill leading to Trinity Place, placed himself in front of the tongue in order to keep the carriage from going down too fast. While thus running backward a cart turned the corner, the shafts of which struck him in the back, and at the same time the iron nut on the end of the tongue struck his breast, knocking him under the horses' feet. He was representative and treasurer of the company when he died, and the Fire Department turned out on Sunday, December 4, 1859, at his funeral.

No. 57.—PAULDING.—Organized October 27, 1854, located in Eighteenth Street, between Seventh and Eighth Avenues, organized as Engine Company No. 54 on February 19, 1863. Among the members were James Burtes, foreman; Peter P. Ackerman, assistant; Wm. B. Parkerson, James G. Lindsay, Robert Borlane, Joseph Wilkinson, Henry James Potter, Townsend Clark, Walter Ryer, Jacob Duckhardt, James M. Barber, Jas. L. McEntee, Jr., Elias T. Hatch, and Robert W. Karle.

No. 58.—MERCHANT—FORREST.—Merchant Hose No. 58 was organized on May 14, 1856, and lay in Burling Slip. The first officers of the company were William H. Bulteel, foreman; James Sullivan, assistant foreman; and Cornelius Downey, secretary. Its members were almost exclusively oyster dealers and boatmen. In 1860 New York Hose No. 5, lying in Firemen's Hall, was supplied with a steamer and became Engine Company No. 47. Hose No. 58 then received the number 5 and became Edwin Forrest No. 5. The first officers of the reorganized company were Cornelius Downey, foreman; Richard Wilson, assistant foreman; and James Sullivan, secretary.

No. 59.—ION—MANHATTAN.—Ion Hose Company 59 was organized September 22, 1856, in James Pettit's carpenter shop, 86 Lawrence Street, Manhattanville, by Alfred Lyon, James Pettit, James Richmond and others, and first located on the first floor of the same building, opposite No. 43 Engine House. They remained here until 1860, when they removed to their new two-story brick house, 58 Lawrence Street, where they remained until mustered out in 1865. The company first ran a "jumper," then an old carriage, and in 1862 received a new carrige, painted a rich dark brown, ornamented with gold striping and silver plating, and which the company claimed was the handsomest carriage in the city, or at least in the upper section of it. Pettit had been formerly assistant foreman of 43 Engine under Daniel F. Tiemann, and succeeded Mr. Tiemann as foreman of that company. He was also foreman of No. 59 Hose, and when he left the company had been connected with the Department twenty-two years. James Richmond, now in Girard, Kansas, was secretary from its organization until 1863. They were a good duty doing company, and before the streets were cut through and graded had many a tough pull with their carriage over the hills. In 1859 the company changed

M. T. BRENNAN.

its name to Manhattan Hose Company, and continued under that name until the last. Robt. Prior, who was the secretary of the company in 1864, was the proprietor of the large stables in One Hundred and Twenty-ninth Street, Harlem, and also in Manhattanville. He and his widow, who survives him, were the parents of nineteen children. Wm. Crawford, assistant foreman; Robert O. Glover, secretary Fire Insurance Company; James Hedemath, Garrett Dardass, John McArthur, Patrick McKenna, John Lynch, Michael Lanihan, Paul Schwapper, John McArthur, Edward Roach, foreman, and James Murray.

No. 60.—M. T. BRENNAN.— Organized March 28, 1854. It had its headquarters in the Tombs, on Leonard Street, corner of Elm, and did duty in the Seventh and Eighth Districts. The men removed in 1858 to the corner of Manhattan Alley and Elm Street, into new quarters specially erected for their accommodation. They remained here till the disbandment of the Volunteer Department in 1865. The late county clerk, John Clancy, who was for a number of years editor of that popular paper, the *Leader*, and foreman of the company, was one of its originators, and also Supervisor Walter Roche, who was foreman, and Congressman Morgan Jones; also Denny Burns, known as "the member from Sligo," Johnny Stacom, and James M. Sweeney (brother of Peter B.), were representatives from it. It had a good many noted men in the down-town districts on its roll. Larry Clancy, brother of John and clerk of the Marine Court, was a member of No. 60 Hose. John R. Lyng, the old-time sporting man of New York, was an honorary member, and did good duty. James Hogan, better known as "Jumps" was a doorkeeper in the Sixth Ward when Captain Jourdan, afterwards Superintendent Jourdan, was in charge. Hogan was at one time foreman of No. 60 Hose Company. Matt. Brennan, according to Martin Keese, did good fire duty, and was many a time to be found at the head of the rope notwithstanding the infirmity that he suffered from in one of his legs. At all of the gatherings in the house, such as chowder parties or receptions to other companies, the familiar face of Matt. was always to be seen mingling in the throng in company with Clancy and Harrington, who writes the dramatic column in the *Dispatch*. Other members were Sweeny, Jones, Dowling the judge, and more old-timers of the Sixth and the surrounding vicinity. Poor Matt. Brennan, it is said, died of a broken heart, owing to the failure of his suit against the city for moneys legitimately due to him for his services as sheriff.

No. 61.—ZEPHYR.—Organized December 31, 1856, located at 379 Fourth Avenue, went out of service in 1865. Among the members were John H. Whitney, foreman; A. L. Thomas, assistant foreman; George L. Jordan, Henry L. Chichester, T. L. Hewitt, Nelson H. Oakley, M. V. B. Smith, George W. Fanning, Philip C. Benjamin, William Snectner, and George F. Nesbitt, Jr.

No. 62.—MINUTE.—Organized February 23, 1857, located at 380 West Forty-third Street, changed to Hose Company No. 12 on January 20, 1859. Samuel Woolley was foreman, Daniel Wanamaker, assistant foreman, and other members were Franklin C. Favor, John H. Tutgen, Freeman Campbell, Robert B. Leete and Charles Fanning.

FIFTH WARD EXEMPT.—This company was organized on the west side of the city in February, 1860, for the purpose of doing duty only in the Fifth Ward and vicinity when their services were needed. It was composed entirely of exempt firemen, and among the organizers were Christian B. Woodruff, ex-fire commissioner; Thomas Flender, his brother Henry Flender, Benjamin B. Johnston, James A. Johnston, Theo. A. Ward, John Hewitt, James Dupignac, Samuel Wykoff, William H. Board, and others, merchants, lawyers and manufacturers. They procured a hose tender, and located at 128 West Broadway, selecting as officers Robert C. McIntire, foreman; William H. Johnston, assistant foreman; and Samuel P. Smith, secretary. The number of men that were allowed to the company was thirty, and this number they always had on their roll, filling the vacancy when one occurred from a number of applicants who stood ready to join them. The officers were re-elected each year, and the same officers with which they started in 1860 were mustered out with them in 1865.

CHAPTER XL.

HOOK AND LADDER AND HYDRANT COMPANIES.

No. 1 (Mutual).—No. 2 (Chelsea).—No. 3 (Phoenix).—No. 4 (Eagle).—No. 5 (Union).—No. 6 (Lafayette).—No. 7 (Mechanics).—No. 8 (Empire).—No. 9 (America, Washington).—No. 10 (Narragansett).—No. 11 (Knickerbocker, Harry Howard).—No. 12 (Friendship).—No. 13 (Marion).—No. 14 (Columbian).—No. 15 (Baxter).—No. 16 (Manhattan and Liberty).—No. 17 (John Decker).—No. 18 (Hibernia).—Hydrant Companies.—The Hydrant Company that Never was Passed.

N0. 1.—MUTUAL.—This company was organized in 1772, although there had been in existence two Hook and Ladder trucks, but bearing no name or number. In this year (July 10, 1772,) a company was formed with George Brewerton, Jr., as overseer, Mr. Brewerton at that time being an alderman from the West Ward. They classed themselves as Hook and Ladder Company No. 1, and were located on Fair (Fulton Street) near Nassau. In the following year Jacob Stoutenburgh was elected the foreman, and in 1776 he was made chief of the department. In 1780 Jacob Montague, who was appointed one of the committee for the introduction of water into the city, was chosen foreman, and served till 1782. In 1784 the company was reorganized by Andrew Mather, grocer; E. T. Badeau, hatter; Frederick Pentz, shoemaker; James Sterling, merchant; William Gibbins, grocer; William Merrill, carpenter, and ten others. On June 16 they met and elected Frederick Pentz foreman, and took the name of "Mutual." In 1791 David Contant was chosen foreman, and was one of the early advocates for a benevolent fund. In 1796 Garret De Bow assumed command, and remained at the head of the company till 1800. At this time they were located at the head of Whitehall Street, opposite the Bowling Green. The manuscript records of the company date from December 23, 1799, but the first minutes of proceedings and duties performed date only from November 20, 1817, when a meeting was held at Hodgkinson's tavern, at which Thomas Shapter was elected foreman; Robert Spier, assistant; Hugh Aikman, clerk; and Lawrence V. Deforest and William Scott, representatives. At an extra meeting held January 3, 1818, David Keyes, cooper, 20 Bancker Street, Duncan McKeckney, cooper, 14 Cliff Street, and Donald McLeod, grocer, corner of Wall Street and Broadway, were elected members. On May 13, 1819, Robert Spier, having served the time required by law as assistant foreman, resigned, and Hugh Aikman was elected in his place, and Wm. A. F. Pentz was elected secretary.

At the annual meeting held November 11, 1819, Mr. Thomas Shapter and Mr. Aikman were re-elected as foreman and assistant; James Patterson, cooper, 9 Front Street, was elected clerk; and William Smith, merchant, 7 Old Slip, and Alexander Wiley, cooper, 92 Greenwich Street, were elected representatives. Mr. Shapter resigned on May 11, 1820, having served his term, and Hugh Aikman succeeded him, with Alexander Wiley as assistant. About this time the question of forming a new association of firemen was discussed at a meeting of delegates in Harmony Hall, who referred the matter to a committee which met in Firemen's Hall, and decided that it was inexpedient to form another association. In 1821 Wm. A. F. Pentz and William Van Antwerp were elected representatives. A circular letter from the representatives of the Fire Department was read at an extra meeting held at Hodgkinson's, on February 6, 1822, setting forth that the department was short of funds, and calling for aid. The sum of twenty dollars was immediately voted to the fund. Daniel Ayres, merchant, 94 John Street, was elected secretary on May 9, 1822. On May 13 of the same year the complete return of the members of the company was as follows: Hugh Aikman, foreman; Alexander Wiley, assistant foreman; William A. F. Pentz and Wm. Van Antwerp, merchant, representatives; Daniel Ayres, Allen McDougall, William Smith, John Heath, Hugh Spier, John Shay, James Patterson, Martin Reeder, Jesse McLaughlin, Ralph James Saddler, John Rossiter, John Davison. At the quarterly meeting held February 13, 1823, the representatives reported that their annual meeting was held in Fireman's Hall on December 9, 1822, and the following officers were elected for the year 1823: O. T. Hewlitt, president; J. M. Tuthill, vice-president; John P. Bailey, treasurer; J. A. Mitchell, secretary, and William Willis, collector. David Seaman, J. V. Varick and B. M. Brown were elected trustees. The com-

mittee of five appointed to petition the corporation to admit young men at the age of eighteen as firemen, reported that their petition had met with disfavor, and that the State law

OLDEST HOOK AND LADDER IN NEW YORK.

prohibited such permission. At an extra meeting of the representatives, held on January 7, 1823, Jamieson Cox and Philip W. Engs were elected trustees in place of David Seaman and Cyrenius Beers.

The officers of the Fire Department elected on December 8, 1823, for the year 1824, according to the report of the representatives of this company, made at the quarterly meeting held on February 12, 1824, were: J. W. Dominick, president; J. M. Tuthill, vice-president; John P. Bailey, treasurer; J. A. Mitchell, secretary, and W. Willis, collector. J. Quick, P. W. Engs, William Vouck, and Edward Arrowsmith were elected trustees. On May 13, 1824, Alexander Wiley was elected foreman, and Hugh Spier, assistant. Mr. Aikman declined to be a candidate. At an extra meeting held on December 6, 1824, the company gave expression to their choice for chief engineer to be recommended to the corporation to succeed Thomas Franklin, who had resigned. They cast ten votes for P. W. Engs, and three votes for Uzziah Wenman. Further, the sum of ten dollars was subscribed towards procuring a service of plate to be presented to Mr. Franklin. Jamieson Cox was appointed to succeed Mr. Franklin, and the "Mutuals," at a meeting held on December 16, petitioned the Common Council to rescind their action and appoint either Mr. Engs or Mr. Wenman. William P. Disosway, merchant, of 45 Pearl Street, joined the company on December 27, 1824, and was elected representative on August 11,

1825, in place of William A. F. Pentz, who had been appointed fire warden. On May 11, 1826, Alexander Wiley was elected foreman, and W. P. Disosway, assistant. Mr. Wiley resigned on October 9, and one month later, John Wright, Jr., was elected in his place. At a fire in Maiden Lane, on March 8, 1827, David W. Raynor, a member of the company, lost his life. On March 17 of that year, Gabriel P. Gratacap joined the company.

Messrs. Wright and Ayres being appointed fire wardens, Wm. P. Disosway was elected foreman at a meeting held on June 25, 1827 ; Richard F. Carman, assistant foreman, and James N. Van Antwerp, secretary. In the arrangements made for the celebration of the anniversary of the Fire Department on October 14, it was decided that Mr. De Anterisches take the tiller, Davison and Van Antwerp the tongue, and Gratacap the emblem. W. P. Disosway was elected foreman on May 8, 1828 ; C. T. Lindsley, assistant foreman ; J. M. Van Antwerp, secretary ; and G. De Angelis and J. M. Van Antwerp, representatives. Samuel C. Hawks was elected secretary on May 14, 1829 ; Thomas Williams and William Cook, representatives; and Jacob H. Dawson, steward. On May 13, 1830, Mr. Williams was made assistant, and James A. Coffin, secretary. They resigned on February 10, 1831, and Thomas Schiefflin and Sylvester Philips were elected in their stead respectively. In October of this year several members sought to get Mr. Schiefflin to resign, alleging that he was becoming incapacitated through ill health. In a letter to Foreman Disosway, read at an extra meeting held on October 13, Mr. Schiefflin repudiates the innuendo that he is not fully as capable of duty as any member of the company, and he severely castigates the gentlemen who exhibited so much pretended solicitude for his welfare. On May 9, 1832, however, he having served his full term, resigned, and John W. Towt was elected in his place. A horse was purchased by the company for eighty-eight dollars, on November 8, 1832. Mr. Disosway resigned the foremanship and his membership on February 14, 1833, and John W. Towt succeeded him, with Samuel C. Titus as assistant. April 3, 1833, it was decided to sell the horse. At the annual meeting on May 9, 1833, Samuel Turner was made assistant foreman, and Edward Tunis secretary. Mr. Turner resigned on November 14, and Warren Kimball was made his successor. Hook and Ladder Company No. 4, located in Eldridge Street, attended a fire in Mill Street on the evening of November 8, 1833. The " Mutuals " entertained their " up-town " friends after the extinguishment of the fire, and, besides, gave them the use of their horse to convey home their truck and implements, for all of which No. 4 passed the usual resolutions. The horse was the occasion of much anxiety to the company, and a man was hired to take care of him. At the funeral obsequies in honor of General Lafayette, held in July, 1834, Smith Burtt carried the company's banner, and George McKenna bore the emblem. Mr. Kimball resigned the assistant foremanship on November 13, 1834, and Edward Tunis was elected thereto, Warren Slover becoming secretary.

The minutes regarding the great fire of 1835 read :

December 15, 10½ P. M., fire in Water Street. Did duty and watch.

December 16, 3½ A. M. Went to the old fire.

December 16, 9 P. M. The largest fire New York ever saw in Merchant, Pearl, Water, Front, South, William, Wall, Hanover, Exchange Place, Beaver Street, Coenties Slip, Gouverneur Lane, Jones Lane, Stone Street, the Exchange, and the South Dutch Church. Absent, none.

May 11, 1836, the horse was reported as being unfit for duty, and a committee was appointed to dispose of the animal to the best advantage. An expression of opinion was evoked at this date on the subject of the reinstatement of James Gulick as chief engineer, and an affirmative resolution was defeated by a vote of twelve to six. The officers elected for the year 1836-'37 were: Edward Tunis, foreman; John S. Winthrop, Jr., assistant foreman; Alexander Morrisson, secretary; Thomas Kennedy, steward; and George F. Randolph, representative. The committee on "horse" reported on August 12 that they had "traded" for another quadruped, giving sixty dollars to boot.

The trouble in the department in the fall of 1836, when breaches of discipline and disorganization seemed about to become general, caused the "Mutuals" to adopt a resolution that they would continue to discharge their duties as formerly, and on September 27 John Ryker, Jr., chief engineer, sent them a complimentary letter therefor. It should be mentioned that the vote on the resolution was thirteen yeas to eleven nays. In April, 1837, it seemed to be the determination of the Common Council to remove John Ryker, Jr., from the office of chief engineer, whereupon the "Mutuals" passed a series of resolutions setting forth that such action was prompted by malicious persons who desired rather the ascendency of political party principles than the good of the Fire Department, and expressing the fullest confidence in Mr. Ryker's ability and honesty. At the annual meeting in May of this year, Mr. Tunis was re-elected foreman, Thomas Kennedy was elected assistant, and Hopkins P. Hall was made a representative; and a resolution was adopted stigmatizing the removal of Mr. Ryker as an outrage tending to the destruction of good order, efficiency, and harmony. Cornelius V. Anderson was appointed chief to succeed Mr. Ryker.

The business complexion of the company had by this time completely changed, for, whereas in years past, as may be seen by the roster, the majority —in fact, nearly all the members—were coopers, we now find not a single follower of that honorable occupation, the members being principally accountants and merchants. On June 13, 1837, John A. Hughes, accountant, was elected foreman, whereupon seven members resigned. On August 7 he was petitioned to resign in the interests of the harmony, efficiency, and prosperity of the company, which Mr. Hughes did, and Smith Burtt, grocer, was elected foreman. At a special meeting held November 14, Thomas Kennedy was removed from the position of assistant foreman, and from membership. Warren Slover was elected to succeed him as assistant foreman. Mr. Edward Tunis was again elected foreman in 1838, and re-elected in 1839, with William H. Tunis as assistant, Hopkins P. Hall as secretary, and Augustus Campbell as steward. The company consisted of only thirteen members at this time. On May 4, 1840, Hopkins P. Hall was elected foreman, Augustus Campbell assistant, and William King secretary. In 1841 Mr. Hall was re-elected, Alexander Morrisson made assistant, Oliver H. Hick secretary, and J. L. Carew steward.

The following is a list of the members elected during the year from May 1, 1843, to May 6, 1844: George W. Phyfe, S. F. Jenkins, James Irwin, S. McCamley, J. D. Ayman, August Brown, Le Grand Lockwood, J. W. Bradley, H. Bradley, J. Corse, Jr., William Q. Clark. The following resigned during that year: Alexander Morrisson, A. M. Sayre, J. R. Whelpley.

August 5, 1844, Mr. Hall resigned the foremanship which he had so long and honorably held, and William H. Geib was elected as his successor. In May, 1845, the company consisted of twenty members, among whom were the Messrs. Charles W., Isaac E., Edward C., and Henry S. Cotheal. On the fifth of May, Mr. H. P. Hall resigned from the company. Mr. Geib resigned the foremanship in September, 1845, and S. F. Jenkins, merchant, 188 Front Street, succeeded him. May 3, 1847, G. R. Smith, clerk, 18 Ferry Street, was elected foreman. He was re-elected in 1848, with T. Gentel as assistant, and P. S. Hine as secretary, who resigned in October, and S. F. Jenkins was elected to his place. At this time the company had received a new truck, of which they felt very proud, considering it the "handsomest truck in the City of New York." On November 28 the company cast fifteen votes in favor of Alfred Carson for chief engineer, and on December 13 gave the same number of votes in favor of Clark Vanderbilt as assistant engineer, rendered vacant by Mr. Carson's election.

In 1849 the brass work on the truck was silver-plated. At the annual meeting, May 7, Mr. Smith was again elected foreman, with Robert M. Bruce, merchant, as assistant, and William E. Rose, surgical instrument maker, as secretary. May 29 Mr. Smith resigned, and Michael Eichells received fourteen votes for the office of assistant engineer. In June Mr. Bruce was made foreman, and William E. Rose assistant, and James L. Kennedy secretary. In November Mr. Kennedy resigned, and E. W. Safford was elected. In February, 1850, petitions were circulated in favor of the enactment of a law prescribing the election of engineers once in three years. March 19 the company voted against the passage of such a law. The company stood by Chief Engineer Carson in his fight with the Common Council, in September, 1850, passing resolutions of confidence in him, and condemning the Common Council.

In October, 1850, upon the information that Jenny Lind, the nightingale, had donated a large sum to the fund of the Fire Department, the company passed appropriate resolutions of thankfulness, in which, after giving testimony of their deep sense of gratitude, they assured her that "when her voice should cease to charm the ear, her memory would be affectionately cherished, not only in their own hearts but in the heart of every widow and orphan, whose prayers for her welfare already ascend in grateful invocation to heaven." Mr. Bruce resigned the foremanship in March, 1851, and at the annual meeting, held in May, J. L. Kennedy was elected to the position, with A. C. Schenck as assistant, and George Hickok as secretary. Mr. Kennedy served only two months when he resigned, and Charles E. Gildersleve was elected. Ex-mayor William H. Wickham was an active member of the company at this period. On January 5, 1852, he resigned, and was elected an honorary member. The annual meeting of that year was held in the office of the Clinton Fire Insurance Company, No. 52 Wall Street. Mr. Gildersleve was re-elected foreman. On June 14, 1852, the company moved into their new house on the corner of Centre and Chambers Streets. In 1853 the company was fortunate in possessing "a recorder," John A. Smith. In April of that year (according to the recorder) there were twenty-four active duty-doing members on the roll, although by law the membership might be raised to forty, but the location, and "other causes," prevented the accession of such members as it was desired to secure.

In May, 1863, Douglas Cairns was elected foreman, Thomas Langan assistant, and Luke W. Rees secretary.

This company never lost their organization for a single day during the existence of the Old Fire Department, and on the organization of the Paid System, Hook and Ladder Company No. 1 was created September 8, 1865, using the same location, the same truck and the same red cap fronts as Mutual Hook and Ladder Company No. 1 did, and nine of her twelve members had served in the old company. It was the only company that was continued with the same number and location, and it might be said that Hook and Ladder Company No. 1 has had a continuous existence since the sixteenth day of June, 1784.

The famous Mutual Base Ball Club was named after this company and was organized in their house. John Carland was its first president, and John Wildey followed him. They had their grounds at the "Elysian Fields" in Hoboken, and their contests in 1859 and 1860 with the Atlantic, Eagle, Empire and Gotham Clubs will be remembered by all old-time lovers of the game.

No. 2.—Originally organized in 1782; was located at where is now the corner of Chambers and Centre Streets. It was the custom in those early days to have the ladders hung up on the fence of the City Hall Park, near the truck house, that plan being found handy for the first comer, citizen or fireman, to carry the ladder

FOLDING LADDER TRUCK.
[Run by Hook and Ladder Company No. 1 along in 1855.]

the short distance required at the time. In 1842 the company was stationed in Beaver Street, near Broad; they performed but little duty, and were disbanded August 1, 1850. On September 13, 1851, Isaac L. Seixas, with eighteen ex-members of Croton Engine Company No. 16, and a number of citizens, reorganized the defunct company, secured a house in Twenty-fourth Street, between Seventh and Eighth Avenues, procured a truck from the city, and christened the new-born child

CHELSEA HOOK AND LADDER COMPANY No. 2, in honor of the old village where they were located. Isaac L. Seixas was elected foreman, and a Mr. Dean assistant foreman. Mr. Seixas remained in command for two years, when Stephen Mitchell was elected foreman, and continued in command a number of years, until he was elected assistant engineer. During these ten years of service No. 2 was considered a first-class duty doing company, quick, skilled in their line of service, and of great benefit to the community. The members boasted of their long-winded capabilities, and offered wagers that they could beat any company in New York racing from Eighth Avenue and Twenty-fourth Street to the Battery. About this time matters became mixed with No. 2; their house became untenantable; the city refused a new one; old members resigned; no new recruits were enlisted; a new location was forced upon them at the junction of Sixth Avenue, Broadway and Thirty-third Street;

the building was nothing but a shed. Shortly afterwards their humble home was destroyed by fire; the company was homeless. The last seen of the once famed and fleet truck was at the corner of Eighth Avenue and Thirty-first Street, standing in the gutter, a sad monument to fallen greatness.

No. 3.—PHOENIX.—This company was organized on the twelfth of September, 1804, by Harvey Turner, Wm. Bruce, and James Curran, the latter being foreman. About the year 1810 they were located on Greenwich Street near Barrow, and in 1832 at Hudson and Christopher Streets, and about 1840 moved to Horatio Street near Hudson. Cornelius V. Anderson, then chief engineer, recognizing the need of a Hook and Ladder Company in that section of the city, lent his aid in reorganizing the company. About 1845 a new location was obtained at No. 126 Amity Street near Sixth Avenue, and adjoining Engine Company No. 18 and Hose Company No. 38. Among the new members were Edgar E. Holley, Samuel T. Rogers, Lawrence Van Wart, Harrison Redfield, Thos. B. Oakley, David W. Anderson, John W. Griffin, Augustus T. Anderson, Stephen D. Thatcher, Wm. P. Thatcher, Geo. G. B. Irish, C. Whingates, and others. Edgar E. Holley was the first foreman in Amity Street. He held the office for four years, being succeeded by his assistant foreman, Harrison Redfield. Edgar E. Holley was independent in his actions and a capable foreman. Like most New York boys, he took to fire life early, and was assistant foreman of Union Engine No. 18 before he had attained his majority. On the reorganization of Hook and Ladder No. 3, the independent and original traits of Mr. Holley's character were displayed by his introducing an improved hook and ladder truck to the New York Fire Department. He thought the trucks then in use could be greatly improved, and accordingly made plans for the construction of a truck that would better satisfy the wants of the department. Encountering difficulties in having his designs carried out in this city, he, not to be thwarted, made arrangements to have the truck built in Newark, N. J., and when it was finished and she first struck the New York pave, the boys voted her a success, and very soon other trucks were built on the same model. He was the first to apply elliptic springs in the construction of hook and ladder trucks, and his inventive genius was also displayed in making designs improving the construction of hose carriages. At a fire in West Seventeenth Street about the year 1847 the house, a four-story frame, caught fire from a stable in the rear. Holley was in the building, and, while making his way out, came across a woman lying in bed. She was blind and helpless. His rescue of her was a gallant act. An oil painting of the scene hung in the house of Hook and Ladder Company No. 3 for many years, and it seemed the opinion of many at the time that the woman had purposely been abandoned to her fate. A little over a year after the above he carried two small colored babies from a burning dwelling in Little Twelfth Street, and on returning to continue his search, found the burned body of the mother.

The company, on New Year's Eve, December 31, 1849, presented to Mr. David W. Anderson, their late secretary, a massive silver tobacco box and a superb gold pen and pencil, as a token of their esteem for him as a man and a fireman, and a slight tribute for the faithful manner in which he had always discharged the duties of his office. The box was exquisitely wrought. On the front is a beautiful wreath of chased work surmounted by a Phoenix, and enclosing a figure 3 crossed with a hook and ladder. On the back of the box was the inscription.

On Monday morning, April 8, 1850, the company left New York on a visit to Baltimore and Washington, turning out sixty-one caps. James L. Miller, assistant engineer, was grand marshal; Edgar E. Holley, foreman; and Harrison Redfield, assistant foreman. The truck was gaily decorated, the hooks polished, and presented a fine appearance. Dingle's band furnished the music, and on the rope were, among others, William N. McIntyre, of old Hope Engine Company, No. 31; James B. Mingay, of Empire Hose 40; William M. Tweed and Joseph H. Johnson, of Americus Engine Company No. 6; T. L. Thornell and William M. Randell, of Fourth Ward (Liberty) Hose No. 10; C. Banta and T. Dugan, of Neptune Hose Company No. 27; T. F. Riley and J. F. Kirby, of Southwark Engine Company No. 38; Wesley Smith and J. W. Price, of Star Hose Company No. 34; Charles Miller and W. B. Ripley, of Howard Engine Company No. 34. They were received with great enthusiasm on their arrival in Baltimore and Washington, and one result of their trip was the organization in Baltimore of a hook and ladder company, which took the name and number of Phoenix Hook and Ladder Company, No. 1. In May, 1850, Mr. Holley resigned. The company passed very complimentary resolutions, and elected him an honorary member. The Committee on Resolutions were Samuel T. Rogers, Alonzo H. Perrine, Lawrence Van Wart, Harrison Redfield, and John H. Brady. The exempt members, feeling that the occasion called for some action on their part, held a meeting at the residence of Mr.

HOUSE OF HOOK AND LADDER NO. 4, 1860.
[Eldridge Street.]

Thomas B. Oakley. It was largely attended, and among those present were David W. Anderson, John W. Griffin, Augustus T. Anderson, Stephen D. Thatcher, William P. Thatcher, George G. B. Irish, and C. Whingates. Harrison Redfield succeeded Mr. Holley to the foremanship, and was followed in turn by John H. Brady, an excellent fireman, who fully sustained the reputation of his company. William E. Berrian, Isaiah Rodgers, Abraham Cooper, Alonzo W. Hadden, were the foremen in later years, Hadden being the foreman at the time the Paid Department came in vogue in 1865. John H. Brady was elected from the foremanship of this company to the post of assistant engineer, serving from 1853 to 1856.

No. 4.—EAGLE.—The first No. 4 was established on October 21, 1811, and located at Chatham Square. Subsequently it was located in Third (Eldridge) Street, near Walker, and disbanded in 1864. Among the members were

Daniel M. C. Mills, foreman; Peter Cullen, assistant foreman; Charles Monell, John Douglas, George Hauptman, and Francis Raymond.

On Monday evening, May 10, 1852, the members of Eagle Hook and Ladder Company presented to Mr. Peter N. Cornwell a magnificent silver trumpet. The trumpet was presented in behalf of the company by W. R. Goodall, the young American tragedian. Before presenting it he called upon his friend Mr. Hamilton, a very clever actor of the Bowery Theater, to sing "The Ship on Fire." Mr. Hamilton complied. Mr. Goodall then proceeded in a brief but eloquent speech to present the trumpet. He alluded to himself being a fireman in the "City of Brotherly Love." He spoke of the universal praise with which he always heard the members mention Mr. Cornwell, and concluded by wishing them a long, happy and prosperous life.

GEORGE B. McCLELLAN (the second No. 4).—Was organized in 1864; had no special location, and went out of service in the following year. Michael Loftus was foreman, Thomas Flynn assistant, George W. Sanders secretary. Among the members were P. Murphy, James Toohill, J. J. Hogan, J. McKron, L. Loftus.

SIGNAL LAMP OF HOOK
AND LADDER NO. 6.

No. 5.—UNION ("Screamer)."—Organized in 1826; located at Delancey and Attorney Streets; after 1847 at 91 Ludlow Street; after 1856 at 152 Norfolk Street, and went out of service in 1865. Among the members were Andrew Grogarty, foreman; Floyd Palmer, and James Myers.

No. 6.—LAFAYETTE.—By a special resolution of the Common Council, Lafayette Hook and Ladder Company No. 6 was organized on the twenty-seventh of July,1829. Among its first members were David G. Winkle, Jacob L. C. Roome, Laurence Crumb, John C. Franklin, Henry Johnson, Ed. Moore, and John Leander Spinella. They were located on Mercer Street, between Prince and Houston, which location they maintained until disbanded by the overthrow of the Volunteer Department. They ran a rather old-fashioned truck until they could have a new one built. David G. Winkle was elected their first foreman, and on the night of the first election they had a grand jubilee at Lafayette Hall. There were present over one hundred delegates from other companies to wish them success as a new company. The following year they added to their roll Archibald Reid, William Sherwood, George and William Cowen, and Jacob Lozaba. At the great fire in 1835 the members to a man never left their post—in fact they were the last truck to take up and go home. The citizens gave them great credit for their efficiency, and the proprietors of the Astor House entertained them by furnishing them a sumptuous collation. The first new truck they ever brought out was with the new patent running gear of Pine & Hartshorn, which was adopted by many of the other companies afterwards. It was certainly a great improvement on the former style, as men upon the rung and tiller could buck the sidewalk with impunity, and not be thrown. About the time they received their new apparatus, Henry Hardenbrook, William H. Smith, and Alfred A. Judah joined, and were followed by James M. Murray, formerly clerk of the Jefferson Market Court, James L. Kellogg, Tunis Miller, George Boyd, Samuel A. Moore; then came Mortimer Marsh,

George Lightbody, George L. Mather, Charles P. Haviland, John Creighton, and Edward Portinger. At the fire in 1845, the company again distinguished itself by saving thousands of dollars' worth of property. There was probably no company in the department that was more particular in the selecting of members than No. 6. They never aspired to full rolls, and were contented with small numbers; but those they had were, however, good firemen.

In the years 1848, 1849, and 1850, there were among the members David Underhill, Silas S. Furbush, John K. Evans, Washington Barton, C. A. W. Ryerson, David Brower, and Ellis N. Crow, the well-known stableman, one of the best supporters the company ever had. Then, in '52, were James P. Decker, John J. Ferris, James Kellock, George W. Williams, and Charles H. Egbert. At the laying of the corner-stone of Fireman's Hall many will remember the grand reception No. 6 gave. A large platform was erected over the sidewalk, and here the ceremonies took place. When the building was completed, Hook and Ladder No. 6 took the north side of the first floor for their location, and Hose Company No. 5 the south side. About this time Gus. Hamilton, Jacob Larrick, and William J. Harkins joined. Then came the organization of the celebrated "Knights of the Round Table," composed of all the members of Hook and Ladder No. 6, and many of the leading members of the Fire Department and theatrical profession, among whom

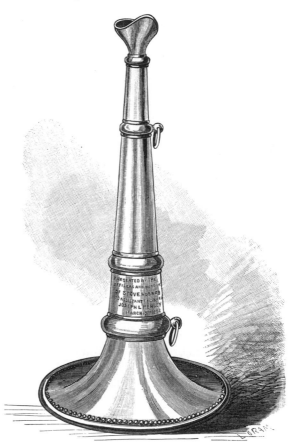

TRUMPET PRESENTED TO JOSEPH L. PERLEY.

were Lester Wallack, Dolly Davenport, Blake, Nelse Seymour, Jerry Bryant, Ed. Lamb, Harry Benson, the Buckley Brothers, Bob Hart, Tom Pendegrast, Charles Parsloe, together with Inspector Daniel Carpenter, Capt. Turnbull of the Eighth Ward police, Sandy Spencer, Campbell N. Gole, Thomas Parker, and Charles Dobbs. They held an annual feast every Christmas Eve at the truck house, which commenced after all the theaters were closed at night.

In 1859 the company visited Albany in a splendid new yacht, and had a most delightful visit. They were gone about a week, but took no apparatus with them. During the breaking out of the war there were added to the roll James Timony of Wallack's Theater, Harry W. Peck, George W. Wilson of

Winter Garden, Howard O'Hara, Joseph R. Wheeler, F. W. Melvin, James Moffatt, C. K. Bills, Henry O. Baker, Assistant Fire Marshal Charles H. Nesbitt, and, toward the closing up of the organization, Jacob Zimmerman of Niblo's Garden, Fernando Wood, Jr., and John Reilly, who was the last man. About 1862 they brought home one of the handsomest trucks ever connected with the Old Department. It was gold plated from tongue to tiller, while the signal was of new style, bearing a shield on four sides—two with the stars and stripes on glass plates, and the other two with the figure and name of the company. The following gentlemen commanded the company as foremen from its organization: David G. Van Winkle, Lawrence Crumb, Jacob Lozaba, James N. Murray, John Lightbody, John Creighton, George Boyd, S. F. E. Kirby, John K. Evans, Washington E. Barton, James K. Kellock, Augustus Hamilton, and Frederick Melvin. Among the assistants were George W. Williams, James Timothy, and C. A. W. Ryerson; while among the most efficient secretaries and treasurers were Charles H. Egbert, Mortimer Marsh, John Underhill, and George W. Blanchard.

In 1861 this company gave an exhibition in the park of the first extension ladder and truck ever brought out. It was patented by Mickle & Carville, Mickle being an exempt member of Hook and Ladder 1, and son of ex-Mayor Andrew H. Mickle. At the Prince of Wales' review they paraded the two trucks, decorated with over one thousand dollars' worth of new flags. The company sent ten members to the war, most of whom were killed on the battlefield. In 1864 Augustus Hamilton, of Wallack's Theater, was chosen foreman, he having also served as assistant the year previous. During the riots this company did most efficient duty, and when a band of conspirators attempted to destroy the principal hotels, Mr. Hamilton stationed his men in the Metropolitan, St. Nicholas, Revere, Commercial, and St. Clair Hotels, and kept them there for several nights. George Wilson, head carpenter at the Winter Garden, walked off the three-story frame building at a fire on the southwest corner of Broadway and Bleecker Street in 1863, falling in the yard, but, strange to say, none of his bones were broken, and in ten days he was up again and reported for duty. Edward Deacon was injured at a fire in Wooster Street in 1854. In 1865 Frederick W. Melvin was elected foreman, who remained until the company was disbanded. This company was noted for their chowder parties and suppers. Every Saturday night they would give an entertainment, and received a great many visiting firemen. Among the many companies they welcomed to their house were Hose Companies No. 7, 24; Engines 21, 34; Engine Company No. 13 of Williamsburg; and Hook and Ladder 1 of Hoboken.

No. 7.—MECHANICS.—Was organized September 7, 1837; located at One Hundred and Twenty-sixth Street and Third Avenue; removed in 1861 to One Hundred and Twenty-fifth Street and Third Avenue, and remained there until the camp fires of the Old Department were extinguished. About the time of the organization of No. 7, there was a "road house" at the northwest corner of One Hundred and Twenty-fifth Street and Third Avenue, known as "Bradshaw's," a favorite stopping place for fast trotters. Bradshaw was one of the early foremen of No. 7. John Kenyon, postmaster of Harlem for sixteen years, was foreman for a long time, also John Prophet, Samuel Christie and Henry A. Southerton. Many of the best citizens of Harlem were members. Colwell, the lumber merchant; George W. Thompson, an old settler and business man, and Frederick Goll, who was the last foreman. When the Metropolitan Department took control, No. 7 was invited to remain; they accepted, and each received at the rate of one thousand dollars per year; served with the New Department about fourteen months, and then passed away. Afterwards the remaining members claimed full pay, and put their claims in the hands of "Tom Fields." He collected the money, and, it is alleged, reimbursed himself like the generous soul he was.

No. 8.—EMPIRE.—Organized September 6, 1848; located at Eighth Avenue and Forty-eighth Street; and went out of service in 1865. Among the members were Nicholas Seagrist, a prominent character uptown, and known as the "Sage of Bloomingdale"; Lewis P. Guther, foreman; Peter Fleck, assistant foreman, (the foreman resigned August 6, 1862, and the assistant February 6, 1861); Henry Leber Mason, John Butcher, Peter Hudson, and Havier Hartwick.

No. 9.—AMERICA.—This company was organized on Tuesday evening, October 7, 1851. The following were elected officers: Alexander W. Murray, foreman; George H. Tinsdale, assistant; Edward Stevenson, secretary; James Thompson, treasurer; James E. Watson and Jacob Smith, representatives. This company was located in the house occupied by No. 7 Engine in Third Avenue, and proved a great benefit to the up-town portion of the Fire Depart-

OLD HOOK AND LADDER FRONTS.

ment. At the annual meeting held at the Bull's Head Hotel, May 11, 1852, the following were elected officers for the ensuing year: Robert V. Davis, foreman; James Province, assistant; William C. Tallmadge, secretary; James H. Thompson, treasurer; James E. Watson and Jacob Smith, representatives. The company was disbanded on December 26, 1855.

WASHINGTON (the second No. 9).—Was organized July 19, 1856, by William Tapper, Anthony A. Oliver, John H. Forman, John D. Ottiwell, John L. Tapper, John McCann, John B. Young, P. Henry Brady, Charles F. Lovejoy, Charles Norman, Samuel Oscar, Robinson W. Smith, and Abraham L. Dixon. They located at 337 Fourth Avenue, and William Tapper was elected the first foreman, and John H. Forman subsequently held this office. Their next location was at 132 East Twenty-sixth Street; after 1859 in Twenty-eighth Street, near Third Avenue; and went out of service in 1865. Among other members were Robert Amos, John K. Finck, Valentine Heiner, George B. Nicholson, Ferdinand Heigmann, Francis Dinsmore, and Isaac H. Archer.

No. 10.—NARRAGANSETT—CORNELIUS V. ANDERSON.—This company was organized on July 1, 1839. For a number of years previous to 1857 old Narragansett lay in Yorkville—at that time hardly more than a suburban village, although within the corporate limits of the city—at the corner of Eighty-fifth Street and Third Avenue. In the year mentioned, the company was by no means an alert or active one, its list of membership being made up very largely of those who enrolled as firemen in order to have a plausible excuse whereby to escape jury duty. Many of the members lived miles from the company's headquarters, and were never seen except when an election for officers was being held, or on some other special occasion. A majority of them would have been puzzled to identify the truck, and so seldom was it used that a rumor to the effect that a hen had hatched a brood of chickens under it entirely undisturbed, gained general credence in Yorkville about this time. In the spring of 1858, a number of members of Water Witch Engine Company No. 10, also stationed in Yorkville, joined the Narragansett Company for the avowed purpose of instituting a reform, Yorkville, with its many frame buildings, being greatly in need of a reliable company. Among these new members were A. O. Allcock and G. C. Hebberd, Jr., soon afterwards elected respectively foreman and assistant foreman of the company by the efforts of the reform element, and greatly to the discomfiture of the "dead heads." The infusion of new blood produced good results, the discipline of the company was greatly improved, and the truck was always out at the clang of the bell, doing duty in the First and Second Districts. During the year which ensued until the next election, the "dead head" element became greatly dissatisfied at being required to do active service, and in the spring of 1859, at the annual election, mustered in full force, and being numerically stronger than the opposition, elected their own officers, and took control of the company again. Complaint was made to the Fire Commissioners, Wm. M. Tweed being president at the time. Both sides were heard, and after considering the matter for some weeks, the commissioners decided to disband the company, it being impossible to reconcile the conflicting elements. The organization of a new company was thereupon recommended by the Board. Two petitions were presented to the Board, one headed by John B. Miller, ex-assistant engineer of the Department, new to Yorkville at that time, but old in experience relating to fire matters. The other was headed by William H. Johnson. The petition headed by Mr. Miller was granted, and a company of thirty-five active firemen was organized, including many from the Narragansett Company. Mr. Miller was elected foreman, and William Hunt, better known in Yorkville as "Daddy Hunt," and who, though very active, was, according to his own account of the time he had spent in various localities, nearly two hundred and seventy-two years old, was elected assistant foreman. The foreman only accepted the office after much persuasion, with the understanding that he would only continue to fill the office until the company was thoroughly organized. In June, 1859, the company chose the name of Cornelius V. Anderson No. 10, and took possession of the truck and house vacated by the Narragansetts. It continued to grow in numbers until the full complement of sixty men was reached, and the service of the company became so much improved as to win praise from the officers of the department. In recognition of the zeal of the company, the Common Council, in January, 1860, gave to it a new and handsome truck built by William Williams. After the truck was received it was felt that a new truck house would be in order, the old one being entirely too small. A petition was presented to the Common Council in February, 1860, asking that a new house be erected in Eighty-seventh Street, on a lot belonging to the city. The request was granted, and the building was ordered erected as soon as an appropriation could be procured for it. The house was finished, and the company occupied it for the first time December 13, 1862. On this occasion a grand ball and entertainment was given. The parlors and gymnasium were crowded with representative citizens of Yorkville and their families, and delegations were present from nearly all the fire companies of the city. A fine supper was supplied by a popular caterer of the time, and dancing was kept up until morning. In the midst of the dancing the old tower bell in Eighty-fifth Street sounded the alarm for the Harlem District, and the fire laddies left in their swallow-tails for the scene of the fire, telling the guests to go on and enjoy themselves until their return. It proved to be a false alarm, and the members were soon back enjoying the festivities. During an intermission, the secretary of the company, R. N. Hebberd, arose, and in a neat speech, on behalf of the company, presented the foreman, Mr. Miller, with a solid silver trumpet, elegantly engraved, and a full-sized oil portrait of himself in uniform. It was a complete surprise to the foreman, who, as soon as he could recover

FRONT OF JAMES WALSE.

his speech, thanked the company most heartily. At the next meeting of the company Mr. Miller insisted upon the acceptance of his resignation as foreman, to the regret of all. He still continued as a member, never losing his interest. G. C. Hebberd, Jr., was then chosen as foreman, and continued to hold the position until the disbandment of the Old Department in 1865. During the "draft riots" this company alone, of all those up-town, did continuous duty from Monday, July 13, 1863, to the following Saturday, when order was again restored. Patrol duty was continued for several days thereafter, and many expressions of thanks were received from the citizens up-town who had property at stake. The headquarters in Eighty-seventh Street is still used by the New Department.

No. 11.—KNICKERBOCKER.—Organized March 23, 1852, located at 153

Franklin Street, and disbanded July 12, 1855. In the second year of its organization Michael O'Brien was killed at a fire on the corner of Fulton and Nassau Streets.

HARRY HOWARD (the second No. 11) Was organized on August 26, 1857. It was located at 295 East Broadway, and after 1859 at 180 Clinton Street, and went out of service in 1865. Among the members were Charles L. Kent, foreman; John Brown, assistant; John B. Bassford, Daniel Brown and Thomas H. Beebe.

No. 12.—FRIENDSHIP.—Was organized February 26, 1852. F. A. Ridabock was foreman from 1852 to 1856, Edward Marriner, assistant. They served in Fifth Street. The truck was a small one, a hose carriage lengthened, so that they had to have ladders hung from them. The company moved to Thirteenth Street in 1856. E. Marriner was then foreman, James A. Caroline, assistant. In 1858 Thomas Sullivan was foreman, and Patrick Fagan assistant, to 1860. In 1861 Thomas Sullivan was elected assistant engineer, remaining as such up to 1865. Among the members were John Garvey, Peter Delancott, Joseph J. McDonnell, Joseph B. Clancy, Patrick W. Hennessy, J. Coyle, John Cahill, George Delaney, John Stacey, Peter J. Gillen, John A. Thompson, Thomas W. Kennedy, George Cooney, Bernard M. Tully and Calvin A. Simons. At the torchlight procession in 1860 in honor of the Prince of Wales, No. 12 was conspicuous with a calcium light, then considered a curiosity. The company temporarily located in Fifth Street and Second Avenue, and after 1856 in Thirteenth Street, near Fourth Avenue. At the World's Fair in the Crystal Palace, Friendship's truck, with two others, was on exhibition, the apparatus attracting much attention in those days. When the Palace was burned this truck was the only one of the three saved. When the company went out of service in 1865 it resolved itself into a social club, admitting old firemen of other companies to membership. John R. Farley was president; Charles A. McManus, vice-president; and Frank McNicol, secretary. Its annual balls were most enjoyable affairs.

No. 13.—MARION.—On the seventeenth of August, 1852, Robert Place, Charles Wakefield, James R. Davies, Nelson Sampson, Michael H. Fisher, John H. Hicks, William H. Manning, John Harding and others, from Engine Company 44, organized this company and located in a new three-story brick house on the north side of Third Street, between Avenue D and Lewis Street. They were the "Quills" of 44 Engine Company, and being somewhat dissatisfied with the election just held, started off for themselves. Michael H. Fisher was the first foreman. He afterwards went to New Orleans, and was presented with a gold watch and chain by his comrades before leaving. In 1855 they received a new truck built by Torboss. During the year 1856 this company saved lives at two fires—one in Sixth Street, near Avenue C, and again in Elizabeth Street, near Grand. At the latter fire John A. Cregier, assistant engineer, met the company on the Bowery, corner of Grand Street, and hurried them around to the building, where a ladder was soon raised, and the members succeeded in carrying down an old man and two children and placing them in safety. John H. Hicks was elected foreman in 1857, and he was succeeded by John Angus, James M. Grey, Abram C. Hull (now superintendent of the Insurance Patrol and an excellent officer and fireman), and John H. Roberts, who was their foreman at the time of their disbandment in 1865.

This company received Americus Engine Company No. 6 on their return from their Canada trip, and the reception was without doubt the largest and finest ever gotten up for a returning company. The excursionists arrived at the Twenty-seventh Street Depot at 9 o'clock, P. M. During the evening Fourth Avenue was lined with red shirts and resonant with the sound of martial music. The scene was exceedingly picturesque. The torches, the colored lights, and the various beautiful machines made a most attractive ensemble. As the train arrived, and the white coats of "6's fellows" were seen, cheers were given, and they were warmly welcomed home. Fireworks were let off, and the old Empire Club gun was called into requisition to salute the guests. There was no speech-making at the depot (firemen are not apt to indulge in long palavers on such occasions), but as soon as was practicable a line was formed, and the procession filed down the avenue in the following order :

Detachment of Policemen—Band—Marion Hook and Ladder Company No. 13—Band—Assistant Engineers of the New York Fire Department, in white coats and caps, and each carrying a lighted

OLD SIGNAL LAMPS : HOOK AND LADDER.

lantern—The guests—Americus Engine Company No. 6, dressed in white overcoats, red shirts, black pants, numbering one hundred men, and with the engine neatly decorated—Band—Lady Washington Engine Company No. 40—Band—Adriatic Engine Company No. 31, with their new first-class engine, which was much admired. Inside the rope were lads drawing a cannon—Phoenix Hose Company No. 22—Band—Putnam Hose Company No. 31—Union Hook and Ladder Company No. 5—Manhattan Engine Company No. 8—Liberty Hose Company No 10—Band—Empire Hose Company No. 40, with Drummond light mounted on top of their carriage—Jefferson Engine Company No. 26—Independent Hose Company No. 3 — Band — Clinton Hose Company No. 17—Guardian Engine Company No. 29—Band—Victory Engine Company No. 13, of Williamsburg—Continental Hook and Ladder Company No. 1, of Williamsburg, dressed in blue shirts—Valley Forge Engine Company No. 11, of Greenpoint—Band—Washington Hook and Ladder Company No. 9, with a detachment of Gulick Hose Company No. 11—Band—National Engine Company No. 3—Band—Lexington Engine Company No. 7—Zephyr Hose Company No. 61—Band—Rutger's Hose Company No. 26—United States Engine Company No. 23—Band—Fulton Engine Company No. 21—Franklin Hose Company No. 18—Peterson Hose Company No. 15—Jackson Hose Company No. 13—Band—Neptune Hose Company No. 27—Lafayette Hose Company No. 34—Band—Washington Engine Company No. 20—Nassau Hose Company No. 56—Band—Harry Howard Hook and Ladder Company No. 11—United States Hose Company No. 25—Band—Pacific Engine Company No. 28.

The procession moved down Broadway to the City Hall Park, to Chatham Street, to the Bowery, to Grand Street, and finally to 6's house in Henry Street, where extensive preparations had been made for giving the company a magnificent and fitting reception on their return. The engine house, together with the residence of Wilson Small, immediately opposite, was brilliantly illuminated both in front and rear, one hundred and fifty-four candles being placed in the windows of Mr. Small's house, and one hundred and fifty-eight in those of the engine house, which were lighted soon after eight o'clock and kept burning until the arrival of the firemen. These, with the thousands of blue lights, sky-rockets and other pieces of fireworks which were set off from the roofs of the two houses on the arrival of the company, presented a peculiarly brilliant and imposing spectacle. It was after eleven o'clock when the procession arrived at the house of No. 6, at which time there could not have been less than three or four thousand people on the ground, who gave the firemen, as they passed through the passageway that had been cleared for them, a most enthusiastic welcome home. After housing the engine, the members of No. 6 were mustered in the meeting room, where the foreman returned his thanks for the courtesy that had been manifested. The company was then formed in line and escorted by the members of 13 Truck to their house, where they found a feast awaiting them.

No. 14.—COLUMBIAN ("Wide Awake").—This company was organized May 11, 1854, with Robert S. Dixon as foreman, Kinloch S. Derickson as assistant, Robert Wright as secretary, William Hutchings as treasurer, and ten others as members. They commenced doing duty from a temporary location, erected at their own expense, in Greenwich Street, near Amos Street, June 3, 1854. In July, 1854, the assistant foreman resigned, and Edward Le Bas was elected and served until October, 1854, when he retired from the position, and Robert Wright was elected assistant, and served until May, 1856, when he was elected foreman in place of Robert S. Dixon, who died February 5, 1856, from injuries sustained while going to an alarm of fire December 25, 1855. Dixon had been struck in the back by the tongue of Engine No. 29. In May, 1855, Howell Vail was elected assistant foreman, and continued until May, 1858, when John L. Gulick was elected. He continued in office up to May, 1860, when Abraham H. Brown was elected. In October, 1855, the company removed to an old building, 96 Charles Street, on the site of the new building afterwards erected for them, and performed duty from there until May, 1856, when they were compelled to retire from active service until their new house was completed, which was in January, 1857, when they took possession, housing a new truck just finished by Pine & Hartshorn. The house and apparatus were among the best in the city, and the former was thoroughly furnished in the finest style. It contained a splendid meeting room and parlor, a neat and well-appointed bunk room and truck room. There was a beautiful little garden attached to the house, where on summer evenings the members would while away their leisure time; and if the duties of a fireman had difficulties it also had charms in an evening spent at such a resort as the truck house of Hook and Ladder Company No. 14. There was a large and excellent library in the truck house, the contribution of friends of the company. Robert Wright and Abraham H. Brown were re-elected foreman and assistant for several years, when Brown was promoted to the foremanship, and Charles O. Shay, the present Chief of the Paid Department, was made assistant foreman. The last foreman of the company was James C. Gregory. John Kennard was a representative for many years, as were also Charles F. M. Church, and Robert Wright, after his retirement from the foremanship. Also on the roll were Hugh Curry (the champion pipe holder), David M. Cooper, Kenneth McKenzie, John T. Hall, Wm. E. Laurence, John T. Rogers, Stewart Pierson, John H. Bowman, F. C. Hamilton, Wm. H. Ingraham, William Paulscraft and Philip Vores; and among the many who served their time out were: Charles E. Clearman, George S. Brant, Jacob Van Orden (a model fireman), E. G. Newman, James Wright, George C. Goeller, Daniel A. Anderson, John Fulton, Amzie L. Camp, Oscar Lyon, Lewis Mason, Jesse W. Ramsey and James H. Mabie. During the war of the rebellion the records of the company show that fourteen active members enlisted in the various volunteer regiments of the city; five went with the First Regiment Fire Zouaves, one of whom, James R. Tappan, was instantly killed at the first battle of Bull Run.

OLD HAT FRONTS: HOOK AND LADDER COMPANIES.

No. 15.—BAXTER.—This company was organized August, 1855, by Benjamin F. Brady, Samuel A. Besson, Isaac M. Moore, J. B. Zimmerman, J. H. Whitmore, and about fifteen others. They located at 153 Franklin Street, and the following were elected as their first officers: John H. Steele, foreman; Wm. H. Wickham, assistant; Daniel P. Steele, secretary; and Samuel Archer and Thos. F. Goodwin representatives. At the following election Wickham was made foreman, with Goodwin as assistant, both being old expert firemen. At the next election Wickham was re-elected foreman, and John Andrews elected assistant. The company had been using a truck that had been built for No. 11 in 1853, and which fell to the lot of No. 15 when No. 11 was disbanded in December, 1855, and this truck the company had rebuilt in 1856. At the election of 1858 John Andrews was elected foreman and A. A. Jones assistant, and in 1859 the company had their truck again rebuilt. In 1861 A. A. Jones was elected foreman and Wm. H. Runnett assistant, and they were re-elected in the two following years. In 1863 the company housed a new truck, built by Charles E. Hartshorn. In 1864 they elected John Andrews (who had held the position in 1859) as third foreman. From their first organization this company was in cramped quarters, and, although they petitioned for a new house and tried hard to obtain one, they were not as successful as some companies who did far less duty than they did. Andrews was re-elected foreman, and R. H. Murray was re-elected assistant, and were the last officers of the company which was mustered out by the Metropolitan Fire Department. Wm. H. Wickham, after leaving the foreman-ship, was elected a representative of the company, his colleague being Charles F. Allen, both of whom served for many years, and until the last. During the war of the rebellion Messrs. Allen, Ames, Parks, Belknap, Vigar, the two Whitings, Barnes, Crolius, Chamberlain, Neale, Colburn, Hogan, Goodwin and Connolly volunteered in the Union army from this company. Joseph Skillman, who was killed in 1861 at a fire in Fulton Street, near Greenwich Street, belonged to this company. The company was assigned to duty in the Seventh and Eighth Districts, and were located in the old house of Hook and Ladder Company No. 11, at 153 Franklin Street, which was disbanded in 1855. Mr. Wickham was elected secretary of the New York Fire Department in 1862, and president in 1863.

No. 16.—MANHATTAN.—LIBERTY.—This company was organized on Mon-day, October 10, 1859, by a number of old fire vamps of the department, among them James M. Macgregor, superintendent of buildings, coroner and health warden, Robert Gamble, Geo. Mountjoy, sergeant-at-arms of the Board of Aldermen, Isaac Keyser, George Whitfield, S. McBride, Patrick Russell, Wm. H. Rich and half-a-dozen others. They secured a location on the corner of Lexington Avenue and Forty-ninth Street, and obtaining a second-hand truck, elected the following officers: Foreman, Robert Gamble; assistant fore-man, James M. Macgregor; secretary, George Winfield; representatives, George Mountjoy and S. McBride. They took the name of "Manhattan," and on going into their new quarters they held a regular old-fashioned reunion, inviting all the members of the department to call. It was a great night for "Bob" Gamble, for such he was called among all the boys; he never felt so proud as he did on this occasion; George Mountjoy and Gamble were the life of the crowd. James M. Macgregor presided over the viands, surrounded by Chief Howard, Assistants Brice, Decker, McGrath, Tim West, any number of officers and members of the various companies, not forgetting old Davy Theall. In 1860 Gamble was re-elected foreman, but some little dissatisfac-tion arose over the name of "Manhattan," and finally, on a close vote, it was changed to "Liberty." In 1861 they moved into their new house, corner Lex-ington Avenue and Fiftieth Street, and in 1862 brought home their new truck, built by Charles E. Hartshorn. This was an occasion for another grand fes-tival, and none forgot the night the new truck was housed. The following year Gamble was again elected as leader of the company. Among its mem-bers at this time were John Rourke, Henry Murphy, Matthew Dale, William Ellicott, John Hogan, James Talilu and James Garry. During this year Macgregor resigned, and John H. Noakes was elected assistant. He was soon followed by John Rourke. M. D. Tompkins, the first recipient of the "Ben-nett Medal" given for bravery at fires, was a member. He finally moved to Connecticut, where he was elected to the Legislature. At the breaking out of the war several of the members joined the army. In 1863 Michael and James Garry, Ed. J. Hackett, John H. Pentz, Wm. Moss, John Conarton, James Halpin and Thomas Hart were on the active roll. The "Liberty" boys had but one foreman from its organization down to the time it was mustered out of service in 1865, and Robert Gamble was beloved by all. Another great feature about this company was that they never had a split; they were always harmonious, and continued in active service down to the last day of the Old Volunteers.

No. 17.—JOHN DECKER.—Organized March 5, 1860, located at Tenth Avenue and One Hundred and Fifty-ninth Street, and went out of service in 1865. Among the members were Patrick McDade, foreman; Wm. P. Smith, assistant; Samuel King, Peter Golden, John Conway, Peter Brady, Charles E. Carman, and Bernard Reilly.

No. 18.—HIBERNIAN.—The Hibernians were the last truck company organized in the Old Department. It originated in the Fourteenth Ward, a large number of the members being butchers in Centre Market. No. 18 dates from August 8, 1860. Alderman Peter Moneghan, James Barry, Sr., Thomas McCauley, Cornelius Desmond, John F. Dowling, James Barry, Jr., James Carty, Francis C. Gilmore, Daniel Keeley, John Clancy, Thomas Doyle and William Morris were among the first to sign the roll. In two days over fifty names were handed in, asking to be elected members of the company. They secured a temporary location at 270 Mott Street, near Prince, opposite St. Patrick's Church, and here they elected their first officers, viz.: James Carty, foreman; James Barry, Jr., assistant foreman; F. C. Gilmore, secretary; and Alderman Peter Moneghan and Cornelius Desmond representatives. An old rebuilt truck was furnished them from the corporation yard, which was painted green, and mounted with a double deck signal; they started out with a full complement of forty men, and were assigned to the Fifth and Sixth Districts. The first night the truck was housed a grand reception was given their friends, Foreman Carty, with Desmond, Barry, Clancy and Condon acting as the committee. Chief Decker, Assistants Kingsland, Perley, McGrath, Lewis, Commissioner Henry Wilson, Hon. John Morrissey, Alderman Moneghan, Alderman Twomey and others being among the visitors. The following year Carty was re-elected foreman. John Hoare, David Callaghan, P. M. White, P. M. Reilly, Wm. Casey, Patrick Scott, John Feeley, Hugh Carey and Owen Kehoe were among its members. In 1862 they brought home their new truck, built by Van Ness, and, it is needless to add, that she was the finest hook and ladder truck on the east side. They had a grand reception the day they brought it home, especially by the citizens of the Fourteenth Ward. Every man, woman and child in the old Fourteenth seemed to be a member of Hook and Ladder 18 that night. About 1863 were found as members Peter Ryan, C. M. Clancy, Wm. Heaney, Thos. McGinness, Richard Condon, Francis Margin, Robert Elf, John McCauley and Timothy Donovan. The company bunked over twenty men, and was never known to get a block away from the house before their rope was lined, and with never less than thirty caps. In 1883 James Barry, Jr., was elected foreman, and Thomas McCauley assistant. Barry was re-elected the following year, and Cornelius Desmond assistant, both serving until the close of the Department. In 1864 they moved into their new house, 195 Elizabeth Street, at which a regular old-fashioned housewarming took place. Here were found as members John Creegan, James Heaney, Joseph Evers, Thomas Bolen, John A. Gardiner, John Carty, James Dowling, William McNalley, Thomas Burcell, John Cull and John Barry. No company could show a better roll than the Hibernians.

HYDRANT COMPANIES.

No. 1.—Was organized in 1832. Among the members were : Charles A. Macy, foreman, resigned February 26, 1841 ; George S. Cock, Eagle Insurance Company, assistant, resigned February 26, 1841 ; Edmund Penfold, Henry Stanton, Walter Titus, Jr., Wm. C. Taylor, Wm. Marshall, Sila R. Bebee, S. J. Leggett, Silas Lord and J. H. Voorhees, merchant.

No. 2.—Was organized on June 1, 1839. Among the members were : Henry W. Belcher, foreman, resigned September 18, 1854 ; John S. Belcher, assistant foreman, resigned November 7, 1854 ; Herman Van Rensselaer, David M. Turnure, John R. Willis, Jordan Woodruff and George W. Elder.

No. 3.—Was organized on June 1, 1839, with Alexander Makim, foreman ; John Thompson, assistant ; Stephen Pell, Howard R. Martin, Francis P. Freeman, B. Strang, Samuel Saunders, and John D. Robbins.

No. 4.—Was organized April 18, 1853. Among the members were : Hiram Engle, foreman ; James W. Smith, assistant foreman ; Garret L. Schuyler, Bernard Kelly, Wm. H. Taylor and Edwin A. Gregory.

On March 19, 1855, the Board of Aldermen adopted the following resolution, which was approved by the Mayor on April 21, 1855 :

Resolved, That the chief engineer of the Fire Department be, and he is hereby directed, not to receive the returns of any members of Hydrant Companies who may join after the passage of this resolution.

Consequently this order terminated the existence of the Hydrant Companies.

Mr. E. B. Child, old-time editor of the *Firemen's Journal*, has penned the following graphic and humorous sketch of

THE HYDRANT COMPANY THAT NEVER WAS PASSED.

The writer regrets that all the histories treating of fire matters are deficient, for they do not tell the present generation about " the hydrant company that never was passed." To remedy in a great measure the injustice of this omission, the writer jots down from memory his recollections of a famous race of that same hydrant company. It was a race that stirred the heart, and the remembrance of it causes the blood to tingle in the veins of even such an old fogy as the writer.

It was a night in October : 40 turned from Mulberry Street into Grand. Old New Yorkers remember 40—Lady Washington Engine Company No. 40— a solid company of solid citizens who knew how to do fire duty. They were

Firemen with pleasure,
Soldiers at leisure,

and the Gulick Guards were celebrated not only for their fine appearance, but for the way they went through the manual of arms, and the writer is doubtful whether any of the crack military companies of the present day could excel them.

Whether it was David Garthwaite or John Carland who had 40's trumpet that night the writer is uncertain, but Mose Humphrey had the head of the rope. Old firemen recollect Mose—not the Mose represented on the stage by Frank Chanfrau, who pulled on 15's rope, but Mose Humphrey of Lady

Washington Engine Company No. 40. He was tall and slender, had red hair, and could hold his own well, express himself forcibly when excited, and down many a heavier weight; but it was his pride to be at the head of 40's rope. The last heard of Mose he was at Honolulu, Sandwich Islands. The King took a fancy to Mose and doubtless listened attentively to his narrations of fire life among the boys in New York, and the exploits of Old Hays, A. M. C. Smith, Prince John Davis, Bowyer, Stanton, Matsell, and others prominent in police history before the era of stars or blue coats and brass buttons, not excepting the M. P.'s of Mayor Harper's reign. Mose was made chief of police, and was never timid about going in himself when occasion required. No Sandwich Islander or imported tough had any terrors for Mose; he could lay them out without turning a hair, and give Captain Williams points how to deal with a crowd without being euchred. He had been educated among the New York boys who struck straight out from the shoulder, at a period when a knife or a pistol was never dreamed of being used. Their motto was to "go in if you get squeezed," and they went in every time. Mose became owner of a hotel, and was looked upon as one of the solid citizens, but he never went back on the "White Ghost."

As the engine swung into Grand Street, more rope was let out and eagerly seized by the men who darted out from Centre Market Place, and she went round the corner of Orange Street (now Baxter—name changed in honor of Lieut. Colonel Baxter, an old member of the Volunteer Fire Department, who was killed in the Mexican war) with a whiz. From the trumpet came a firm, determined shout, "Get down to your work, boys! Lively! lively, now! Give it to her!" It had been whispered that 15 was to be passed that night. Down Orange Street the "White Ghost" hummed. The signal was well ahead of the rope, and the glare of the torches illuminated the street as they dashed onward. As the head of the rope reached Bayard Street the invincible Hydrant Company was discovered thundering down the street. "Now, boys! she's

OLD FIRE HY-DRANT.

after you?" was the shout from 40's trumpet, and the little gooseneck engine just skimmed the cobblestones.

The Hydrant Company struck Orange Street, bucked the curb and took the walk. Who had command? It was a tall man, and of course could not have been Alfred H. Webster, neither was it John S. Belcher, F. Westray, Alexander Meakim, William Neilson nor David Rowland. Hiram Engle had not graduated into a Hydrant Company in those days. It may have been Stephen Barker, the well-known dry goods merchant. The writer is uncertain who commanded the Hydrant Company that night, but through the trumpet rolled out a bright cheering shout, "Old Smoky is after you, and the White Ghost is ahead! Lively, now!" Each man firmly grasped his wrench, as with increased energy he pushed onward. The crowd that had assembled on the walk in front of Pete Williams' noted dance house, opposite Leonard Street, scattered like chaff before a blizzard as the Hydrant Company reached 40's tail screw. A soiree at this dance house was one of the sights that Dickens beheld during his first visit to New York. Charles Dickens spoke well of the Volunteer Firemen of that period. He said New York had "an admirable fire department."

Con. Donahue's Democratic headquarters reached, and Mose began to see the heels of the Hydrant Company. Old-timers will recollect Con., and also the war cry of one of his followers : " Citizens of the Sixth Ward, turn out ! turn out ! Con. Donahue lies bleeding on the pave foreninst his own door." As Mose turned Vultee's corner into Chatham Street he saw 15's back, and heard the shout from her trumpet ring clear in the night air : " Come you now, Old Peterson ! Now you've got 'em ! " If Wilson, Foster or Freeland had command that night they never made better time. John J. Tindale, John H. Forman, William Charlock, Ed. J. Lappin, Geo. R. Nicholl, Robert A. Coffin, Phillip E. Heiser and John Slowey were probably on 15's rope, and with other youngsters were doing their level best, but that Hydrant Company passed the " Old Maids " at the corner of Pearl Street.

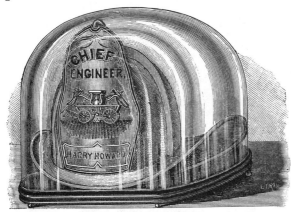

Neptune Engine Company No. 6—not " Big 6," for this was before the Tiger's time— and United States Engine Company No. 23, shot out of William Street nearly neck- and-neck ; they had met in Broadway, near Duane Street, and they "went for the fire." It is needless to tell old firemen how these two com- panies went, for they were boys who knew what quick time was, and made it every run.

(Continued from page 405.)

[CHIEF HARRY HOWARD, at the request of many old firemen, gave his old fire-cap to the city—a gift which the Board of Aldermen apprecia- tively accepted and acknowledged as follows, December 17, 1886 :

RESOLVED, That the fire-helmet of the Veteran Fire-Chief Engineer Harry Howard be accepted and kept, with other valued relics of the city, in the Governor's room in the City Hall.

INSCRIPTION ON FIRE-CAP : Fire-helmet worn twenty-five years in active service by Harry Howard, Chief Engineer New York Fire Department.

At a quarterly meeting of the Association of Exempt Firemen, April 22, 1885, the following was received from Harry Howard, 94 Elm Street :

JAMES Y. WATKINS, JR., Treasurer : DEAR SIR—While a cabinetmaker's apprentice and Sunday-school boy, I saved a little donation intended for the Exempt Firemen's Burial Fund, which is now grown to the en- closed one thousand dollars. Very respectfully, HARRY HOWARD.

The following resolution, thanking Chief Howard for his generous donation, was unanimously adopted :

RESOLVED, That the Association of Exempt Firemen of the City of New York, in accepting the gift of one thousand dollars donated by Harry Howard, is deeply sensible of the generosity that prompted it and the unswerving fidelity to duty that characterized his connection with the Old Volunteer Department, and which his recollections perpetuate.

GEO. W. WHEELER, Rec. Sec. ZOPHAR MILLS, Pres.

Pearl Street was now the scene of great excitement— signals dancing in the air, the glare of torches, the shouts of men eager to be at the front, and the clarion-like notes of the foremen, each determined to bring out all the mettle of his men while urging them on to achieve victory. It was a scene that would have defied the best efforts of the graphic pen of an 1887 reporter to portray, hence it would be presumption for the writer to attempt it. 40 was doing her best to pass 15, but the "Old Maids" were too lively for the " White Lady."

The present generation can hardly imagine the spirit and endurance exhib- ited in a race between fire companies in those days. Talk about horse races or rowing matches—they vanish like bubbles into thin air, in comparison with the race of the firemen, each endeavoring to outdo his fellow in the strife to be first at the fire, first at work, and have first stream on. Lives and prop- erty to be saved—that was the chief aim. When ladders were too short, or not on hand in time, packing boxes and barrels were brought into use. Water lead- ers on the houses were mounted ; buildings were scaled by climbing up the front without scaling ladders, using doors, shutters, sills, and lintels to rest the foot, as the intrepid spirits went up bound to win, knowing no such word as fail. What reward? Often abuse, misrepresentation, and an early grave at Greenwood. Who were these Old Volunteer Firemen? They represented New York's best citizens, men engaged in manufacturing and mercantile pursuits, all branches of trade, banking, the legal, theatrical, artistic, and other professions.

This article was intended to be about the Hydrant Company, but old memories rushing through the brain cause the pen to wander. The Hydrant Company that night won against the field, and was ready to give the field water, did not back down from any company, and had no fear of being washed. The chief congratulated the company, as did also a delegation from " Old Smoky," after the order was given to take up. Old firemen know " Old

Smoky," (Bunker Hill Engine Company No. 32); she swam the East River to reach a fire in Brooklyn, with Peter Burns as chief navigator. Among the delegation that night may have been John B. Miller, who was elected assistant engineer in 1841. He was foreman of 32, and was ever an active fireman; was president of the Board of Fire Wardens. He organized Adriatic Engine Company No. 31 and Hook and Ladder Company No. 10, and is a lively young man yet among the Veterans. His brother, James L. Miller, of Jackson Engine Company No. 24, and one of the organizers of Empire Hose

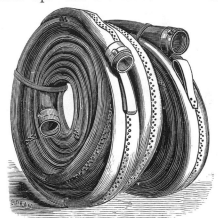

COIL OF HOSE.

Company No. 40, and afterwards assistant engineer, passed to the other side a few years since. "Should old acquaintance be forgot and never brought to mind?" He was every inch a fireman, took to fire life in very early years, and served with zeal till his brow bore a wrinkled front, tinged with gray. He received a very rich silver service from his friends in the department when he resigned the office of assistant engineer. But of "Old Smoky's" delegation, probably there were Neil Gray, alderman of the Tenth Ward when Wilson Small, of Protection Engine Company No. 5, represented the ward in the Board of Assistants. Neil was a member of Eagle Engine Company No. 13, but 32 was in his ward, and, of course, he took a lively interest in the boys. He was for many years secretary of the Firemen's Insurance Company, of which John B. Miller is the surveyor. This company has had but two surveyors in sixty-one years. Pine Hopkins, a member of Chatham Engine Company No. 2, was the first surveyor, and he filled the office for over thirty years; after his death, John B. Miller, who was the surveyor of the Hanover Insurance Company, succeeded him, and he also has occupied that position for over thirty years. Mr. John F. Halsted, an old and respected member of the Brooklyn Volunteer Fire Department, is now, and has been for a number of years, president of the company. It is one of the sturdy old landmarks of fire insurance that survives the reckless competition of late years. Wilson Small was assistant engineer when John Riker was chief, and was for many years one of the trustees of the Fire Department, and was long an earnest advocate of the public schools. His recent death is fresh in the minds of many. May his memory be ever green. But in 32's delegation could probably have been seen John Cobanks, John Treanor, Sam. Dougherty, able to have taken care of Boston's pride if he had been around in those days and cut up any of his antics about "Old Smoky." William Burnton, a good second, Jacob Joseph and Nicholas Theal, George Snyder, the well-known lithographer in William Street, Samuel Townsend, now president of the City Fire Insurance Company, which has celebrated its half century of an honorable business career, and his brother, Sylvanus, as enthusiastic a firemen as ever wore a fire-cap, William Smith, Cornelius Garrison, who was killed at a fire in Elm Street, William J. McLaughlin, John Tipper, who was able to defend "Old Smoky" on all occasions, John Lee, William Bell, and James Magee, one tall and the other thin, but good firemen, William Ackerman, Anthony Carroll, Thomas and James Cooper, John Nixon, William Cobanks, and William C. Glover, at one time coroner, and a well-known writer for the Sunday *Atlas* when under the editorial control of Deacon Herrick. John Boice must not be forgotten, as he doubtless was present. He is the oldest member of Bunker Hill Engine Company No. 32 living, being eighty-three years of age, and is as active as many men many years his junior. He resides over in Bayonne, but occasionally comes over to look after his real estate in this city. He takes a lively interest in the boys of olden times. The members of Bunker Hill Engine Company No. 32, knew what fire duty was, and never shirked it. If the writer is in error, see the ex-coroner at the High Court in Fifty-seventh Street, and get his opinion. George McKinley, of United States Engine Company No. 23, also congratulated the Hydrant Company, and John Crossin of the same company can tell all about the excitement in James Smith's (the celebrated engine builder) the next day, when the race was discussed. Many of the old boys know Crossin—he was a good fireman, and was afterwards a member of United States Hose Company No. 25, when James H. Ridabock was foreman. Crossin was elected at Firemen's Hall one of the fire wardens; later on he was captain on the Insurance Patrol, and for many years an insurance surveyor.

There is a model of Lady Washington Engine No. 40 at the rooms of the Volunteer Firemen's Association in Eighth Street. A son of David Garthwaite, who was a popular foreman of this company, is secretary of the Stuyvesant Insurance Company, of which Geo. B. Rhoads, captain of Company E, Seventh Regiment, is president. The Stuyvesant is another one of the old New York fire insurance companies which, under prudent management, has weathered the storms that have wrecked so many companies. Frederick R. Lee, foreman of Engine Company No. 3—Veteran firemen will recollect "Old Sea Bass"— was formerly president of this company. Mr. Lee was several years an alderman and a member of the fire and water committee. Ex-alderman James Kelly, formerly postmaster, member of Empire Engine Company No. 42, and for many years a trustee of the Fire Department, was also president of the Stuyvesant.

The Hydrant Companies evoluted many years ago. They had good citizens on their rolls—men who turned out to fires and endeavored to do their duty in a quiet way, creditable to themselves and to the Volunteer Fire Department.

CHAPTER XXXXI.

THE EXEMPT FIREMEN'S BENEVOLENT FUND.

Organization and Incorporation of the Fund.—The First Beginnings.—Quaint and Strange Methods Adopted to Create a Fund.—Names of the Early Officers.—Legislation Looking to the Creation of a Charitable Fund and its Distribution.—The Beneficiaries.—The Amount of Money Received each Year.—Revenue Derived from Annual Balls.—A Tax of Two Per Cent. License Fees Exacted from Insurance Agents.—The Metropolitan Fair.—Firemen's Monument.—Fire Commissioners.

AT a meeting of the engineers and foremen of the Fire Department, held on the twenty-ninth of October, 1789, it was resolved that the balance of the fund on hand, received from fines for chimney fires, should be divided among the members of the department. It was accordingly done, two hundred and eighty-three men receiving one shilling and four pence each. In May, 1790, a resolution was adopted by the same body to deposit the funds (£20) in the hands of a treasurer, who invested that sum in the purchase of ten tickets of the New York City Lottery for the benefit of all the firemen. Those who joined the department after this period were by resolution excluded from any participation in the advantages of this lottery scheme. The committee in charge of the matter reported at a meeting held in October that one of the ten tickets had drawn a £38 prize. It was then resolved to invest the balance in the hands of the treasurer (£4) in the purchase of two more lottery tickets, for the benefit of the engineers and firemen. It appears that the net profits of the investment amounted to £8 00s. 10d., which, with a balance in the treasury of £6 7s., was divided among two hundred and ninety-three men, at the rate of one shilling and one-half farthing per fireman. Afterwards the fines arising from chimney fires were deposited in a common fund for the purpose of assisting such firemen or their families as might be in straitened circumstances. These were the preliminary steps taken to form a charitable fund.

In 1791 representatives of the Fire Department convened at the house of Jacob Brown, in Nassau Street, for the purpose of raising a fund that might be beneficial to indigent, sick and disabled firemen, and their widows and orphans. At that time, owing to the limited extent of the city, the Fire Department was in consequence comparatively small; but even then the founders of the fund foresaw the necessity of an institution of some kind to afford relief to those of their unfortunate associates, a majority of whom were recruited from the hard working class of the community.

The minutes of this meeting furnish an account of the proceedings, from which is copied the following: Persons elected, viz.: John Stagg, president; Ahasuerus Turk, vice-president; William J. Elsworth, treasurer; Abram Franklin, secretary; Thomas Hazard, Christopher Halstead, James Beekman,

Gabriel Furman, James Tyler, Isaac Mead, John B. Dash, George Warner, and Peter Cole, trustees.

This voluntary organization continued until the Fire Department was chartered in 1798.

The first report of the treasurer of the Fire Department Fund was made by William J. Elsworth, at a meeting of the representatives held at the house of Edward Bardene, on the twelfth of April, 1793, when the following report of the state of the fund was made:

On loan on approved security....................................... £130.00
In hands of the treasurer.. 110.00
                                                                 ————
    Total..£240.00

At this meeting John Fabley was appointed collector of chimney fines. These fines appear to have been an important source of revenue:

"At a meeting of the Representatives from the Fire Department in the City of New York, on the twentieth day of December, 1791, authorized by their different companies, they proceeded to form a constitution for the purpose of establishing a fund for the relief of unfortunate firemen, whose misfortunes may be occasioned while doing their duty as firemen."

The following gentlemen composed the meeting, of which John Stagg was appointed chairman, viz.: James Tyler, Jeremiah Ackerly, B. Skaats, Sylvester Buskirk, Frederick Eikert, James Smith, William Mooney, Gabriel Furman, David Morris, John Clark, Jacob Sherrod, Richard Furman, Wm. Bush, Stephen Smith, Willett Seaman, Daniel Hitchcock, James Beekman, James Woodhull, Abraham Brown, Peter Cole, A. H. Turk, George Warner, John B. Dash, Jr., Archibald Reilly, Abraham Franklin, Wm. Bowne, Daniel Contant and Christopher Halstead.

At this meeting it was decreed to establish a fund, which shall be called the "Fire Department Fund," said fund to consist of the money arising from chimney fines, certificates, donations, and with such other moneys as may hereafter be agreed on by such fire companies as have already agreed or may hereafter agree to fund the same.

"The trustees shall have the sole disposal of the moneys in the funds, which shall be for the relief of such disabled firemen, or their families, as may be interested in the fund, and who may, in the opinion of a majority of trustees, be worthy of assistance."

The first annual report, presented by the treasurer in 1793, showed an accumulation of funds of £293 15s. These sums were collected for the years specified:

In 1794, £344 2s. 4d.
In 1795, £382 10s. 4d.
In 1796, £429 5s. 4d.
In 1797, £592 18s. 11d.
In 1798, £719 9s. 5d., equal to about $1800. The accounts were made under the State currency of the day, a pound being equal to $2.50 of present currency.

Wm. I. Elsworth was treasurer from 1793 to 1797.

Nicholas Van Antwerp, 1797 to 1798.

At the fifth annual meeting Nicholas Van Antwerp was elected treasurer in place of William I. Elsworth, who resigned on the thirteenth of October, 1797.

At this meeting a committee was appointed to draft a petition to the Legislature for an act of incorporation. These are the names of the committee: James Van Dyck, Joseph Newton, James Robinson, Mathias Nack and James Parsons, Jr. At a special meeting held at Hunter's Hotel, December 18, 1797, the committee submitted a petition, which was read and agreed to unanimously, and the committee instructed to lay the same before the Board of Corporation for their inspection, and afterwards to forward the report to the Legislature at Albany. At a special meeting of the representatives held at the house of Joseph Crook, No. 259 William Street, on the thirtieth day of April, 1798, the new act was considered and approved. This was entitled "An Act to incorporate the Firemen of the City of New York." A charter was at the same time granted, to continue in force until the first Tuesday in April, 1818, and limiting the capital to $20,000. The corporation thus created was authorized to receive certain fines, penalties, certificates and donations arising from violations of the corpora-

PROTECTING THE WIDOWS AND ORPHANS.

tion ordinances relative to fires, and the fund thus obtained was directed to be applied towards the relief of indigent or disabled firemen or their families, and was designed as a recognition of an equitable claim grounded on the faithful discharge of a highly meritorious public service, and at the same time as an inducement to secure the co-operation of reliable citizens. Subsequent acts of the Legislature continued the Fire Department of the City of New York until March, 1865, when an act was passed to create a Metropolitan Fire District and to establish a Fire Department therein. In 1849, however, the Legislature gave to the Fire Department then existing certain two per cent. tax license fees exacted from insurance agents, and which became a part of the benevolent fund which was commenced in 1798, and was designed for the benefit of disabled or indigent firemen and their families.

In 1820, Isaac Hatch, James Hopson, Edward Dayton, Valentine Vandewater and Oliver S. Hewlett were appointed a committee to devise and report such ways and means as they should deem proper to increase the funds of the Department. The first bequest to the Fire Department was made July, 1821, by the will of Dr. John Charlton, dated June 23, 1804, (Frederick de Payster, acting executor) amounting to two hundred and fifty dollars. The above bequest elicited a lengthy notice in the *National Advocate*. This notice was directed to be copied in full upon the minutes.

Application was made in 1831 to the Legislature to extend the charter to 1860, and to increase their right to hold real estate on foreclosures to $50,000, which was granted.

It was deemed expedient also to devise some plan for increasing the fund. The number of widows had trebled in fourteen years and doubled in ten years. A committee was appointed, who reported a proposition to tax every member of the department two dollars per annum. It was voted down. The committee also suggested an application to the Legislature to incorporate a fireman's bank. A clause was to be inserted in the charter securing an annual appropriation of fifteen hundred dollars to the Fire Department fund. Before the bill came up for final action the committee was apprised that the Legislature would refuse to grant the application embracing in the charter the proposed clause, thereby defeating the object and benefit intended. A subsequent meeting of the representatives was convened, and resolutions were adopted instructing the committee to withdraw the application, which was accordingly done. The great fire of 1835 nearly exhausted the widows' and orphans' fund, their surplus being invested in the insurance companies of that time, most of which were swept out of existence by their losses from that fire, and the leading members of the Fire Department, whose hearts were wrapped up in the benevolent fund, undertook to resuscitate its fallen fortunes. Adam W. Spies, of Engine Company 5, and James Russell, of Engine Company 2, started a subscription among the merchants of the city, and succeeded in raising about $14,000.

It was reported at the forty-fourth annual meeting, December, 1836, that the fund was reduced to the extent of $5,750, as the calls for charity had increased to a very great extent. By dint of redoubled exertions the following year the permanent fund was not only restored to its original amount, but was increased by $7,500, for which result the department was chiefly indebted to the indefatigable exertions of Messrs. Y. M. Russell, A. W. Spies and other members of the department, in obtaining in the manner above related, donations to the fund.

On the sixteenth of December, 1850, a committee was appointed at a meeting of the representatives of the Fire Department, to apply to the Legislature to amend the charter increasing the right to real estate to one hundred thousand dollars. Various donations had been made from time to time to the charitable fund of the department, embracing public benefits, contributions from fire insurance companies, as also many munificent gifts from private individuals. The number of widows and children who at this time depended upon the fund for assistance was in the aggregate of about 1,300; and notwithstanding the incessant and increasing calls for aid, the fund had by no means lost ground, but, on the contrary, had steadily increased, owing to its having been from the beginning faithfully guarded and correctly administered.

The act of 1849, to which reference has been made, directed that there should be paid to the treasurer of the Fire Department of the

City of New York for the use and benefit of the department the sum of two dollars upon the one hundred dollars, and at that rate upon the amount of premiums which during the year or part of a year ending on the next preceding first day of December, should have been received by such agents, and it was provided also that sections one, two and three of the act should apply to every city or incorporated village in the state where a treasurer of the Fire Department existed, and where no such officer was known by the laws of such city or village, the treasurer of such city or incorporated village should exercise the powers and perform all the duties, for the purposes of the act, of the treasurer of the Fire Department of the City of New York, as far as related to the city or village of which he was treasurer, and that he should, under the direction of the Common Council of the city or the trustees of the village, pay over all the moneys received or recovered under the first, second and third sections of the act to the Fire Department of such city or incorporated village.   By this act, although the license fee or tax upon the agents of insurance companies was continued, the mode of payment and

A NOBLE CHARITY.

disposition of the fund which would be created by its receipt was changed.   It was thereafter to be paid not to the treasurer of the state, but to the treasurer of the Fire Department and to the treasurers of the other Fire Departments throughout the State or to some one on their behalf.

In 1854, and while the act of 1849—without amendments—was still in force, a contest arose as to the constitutionality of this act, which imposed the payment of a certain percentage by every person who should act as an agent for individuals or associations of individuals not incorporated or authorized by the laws of this State to effect insurances against losses by fire or against marine losses and risks, and the question mooted was twice argued in the Court of Common Pleas of this city, and all the objections against the legislation which could be drawn either from the Federal or the State constitutions of 1846 were ably argued ; but they were overruled decisively, and the judgment of the Common Pleas affirmed by that of the Court of Appeals.   By the act of 1865 it was provided that the members of the old Volunteer Fire Department, if discharged by the new commissioners named in the act, were to be entitled to all the privileges and exemptions allowed by the laws as if they had served out the full term, and it was declared that nothing therein contained should be construed to deprive any such persons of their right to or effect their interest in the fund known as the New York Fire Department Fund, or any part thereof, and that the fund should continue to be held and administered by the then present trustees of the Fire Department or their successors.

By a supplementary act, passed on May 12, 1865, a board of trustees was created to take charge of the Fire Department Fund, and the income was required to be appropriated by the trustees to the relief of the widows and orphans of deceased firemen and other applicants for relief from among exempt firemen and their families, who should have served in the Volunteer Department of the city or should have received proper certificates of discharge from such service in the city from the Metropolitan Fire Commissioners, and it was

HOPE ON, HOPE EVER.

provided by the ninth section that the trustees were entitled to receive, and that there should be paid to them all duties, taxes, allowances, penalties and fees to which the Fire Department of the City of New York as theretofore established had been entitled. This seems to have been a temporary act, for in April, 1866, an act was passed creating a corporation under their present title, to exist for twenty years. By the first section it was declared that the president, two vice-presidents of the Exempt Firemen's Association of the City of New York, and the then present board of trustees of the Fire Department Fund of the City of New York were thereby constituted and appointed a body corporate and politic by the name and style of the trustees of the Exempt Firemen's Benevolent Fund of the City of New York. And by the third section of that act it was declared that the existing Fire Department Fund was transferred to the corporation thus created, and the surplus revenue derived from investments and from other sources, or so much thereof as should be required, should be appropriated by the trustees to afford aid and relief to such persons and their families as should have been lawfully discharged from the Volunteer Fire Department of the City of New York, who were in indigent circumstances, and to the families of members of that department who had been maimed or killed in the discharge of their duties as Volunteer Firemen. And by the seventh section it was declared that this corporation was entitled to receive, and that there should be paid, a percentage or tax on the receipts of foreign fire insurance companies doing business in the City of New York for five years from the passage of the act.

One of the principal sources of revenue received by the trustees of the Benevolent Fund was the proceeds of the Fire Department balls, under the management of a voluntary organization known as the Firemen's Ball Committee, which was organized in 1829. The amount of money paid into the Benevolent Fund by that organization up to 1873 exceeded the sum of one hundred and twenty-five thousand dollars.

Another source of income, and the principal one, was the revenue derived from the two per cent. tax on fire insurance companies not chartered by the laws of this State, or of the United States. The income from this source exceeded the sum of eight hundred and fifty thousand dollars since the year 1849, when the tax was authorized by the Legislature. This tax is still in existence, notwithstanding the Volunteer Department was disbanded twenty years since, and the whole system of state and city taxation upon other State and foreign insurance companies remodeled and placed upon an equality with State companies, and in face of the fact that, of the whole number—some eighty-two companies, but fourteen of them were in business in the City of New York at the time of the Volunteer Department.

The Firemen's Ball Committee was organized in 1829, under the following resolutions :

BEFRIENDING THE WIDOWS AND ORPHANS.

Whereas, The Fire Department Fund was instituted for the purpose of affording relief to such members of the Fire Department and their families as may stand in need of assistance, and to alleviate the wants and distresses of the widows and orphans of deceased firemen ; and,

Whereas, The ordinary receipts of the fund have been found to be insufficient to meet the increasing demands upon it, a number of individuals, impelled by feelings of philanthropy and benevolence, having formed themselves into a committee for the purpose of giving an annual ball for the benefit of the Fire Department, and with a view of perpetuating it, and for the government of the committee, the present members have found it advisable to form the following code of by-laws.

In 1883, at a meeting of the members of the committee, the following was passed :

Whereas, The Firemen's Ball Committee of the City of New York was originally organized for the purpose of augmenting the fund for the benefit of the widows and orphans of deceased members of the Volunteer Fire Department ; and,

Whereas, The circumstances that caused the formation of the committee no longer exist, it is still the desire of the surviving members to maintain their organization as a social institution in order to keep alive, foster, and cherish the friendships that have been engendered in the past years, and, should occasion require, give their best efforts in behalf of the fund. With this end in view, and for their better government, they subscribe to the following code of by-laws.

The greatest amount ever realized by one of the balls, six thousand two hundred and forty-four dollars and eight cents, was in 1868. The last ball was in 1873.

The by-laws of 1883 decided that the officers should consist of a president, two vice-presidents, a secretary, and a treasurer, to be elected anually.

The members at that time were:

James F. Wenman, Samuel A. Benson, Owen W. Brennan, Wm. A. Randell, Daniel D. Conover, George F. Nesbitt, James Y. Watkins, Thomas H. Jenkins, Robert McGinnis, Nathaniel D. White, Daniel Stanbury, Edward Smith, John Garcia, James Y. Watkins, Jr., William A. Woodhull, John J. Donnelly, John J. Westray, James J. Kelso, Alonzo Slote, Frederick A. Ridabock, William H. Wickham, Joseph L. Perley, C. Godfrey Gunther, John C. Bailey, William H. Stoddard, John R. Platt, Jordan L. Mott, John J. Bloomfield, Frederick White, John S. Davidson, James Cameron, James E. Morris, Charles Delmonico, Charles Place, John C. Perrin, Jr., Gustavus Isaacs, Martin V. B. Smith, J. Nelson Tappen.

And the following honorary members:

John Coger, Peter H. Titus, Adam P. Pentz, Charles McDougal, Henry A. Burr, and Viscount Mandeville.

The committee have continued their social entertainments, and have occasionally a summer excursion. They dine annually at Delmonico's on December 16, the anniversary of the great fire of 1835.

The following is the treasurer's report of the Yellow Fever Relief Fund:

At a meeting of the New York Firemen's Ball Committee of the old Volunteer Fire Department, held October 2, 1878, at the office of James F. Wenman, Esq., the treasurer submitted his financial report of the result of the concert in aid of the yellow fever sufferers at the South, given at Gilmore's Garden, September 23, 1878, under the auspices of the committee, as follows:

FIREMEN'S BALL COMMITTEE OF THE OLD VOLUNTEER FIRE DEPARTMENT OF THE CITY OF NEW YORK, *in account with* ALONZO SLOTE, TREASURER.

Tickets sold by New York Fire Department	$1,263.00
Tickets sold by New York Police Department	529.00
Tickets sold at Garden	1,673.00
Tickets sold by members Ball Committee	3,257.00
	$6,722.00
Donation, Mutual Gas Company, through John P. Kennedy	100.00
	$6,822.00

Paid Messrs. Shook & Gilmore, rent for Garden, and Thomas' orchestra, as per agreement	$1,000.00
Paulding & Moore, posting bills	30.00
Metropolitian Printing Company	45.00
John J. Bloomfield, tickets and bills	85.00
Premium, George Quackenbos, Captain Engine Company No. 10, New York Fire Department, for sale of tickets	200.00
	$1,360.00

Net proceeds...$5,462.00

DONATIONS ON YELLOW FEVER SUFFERERS.

New Orleans Young Men's Christian Association........................$500.00
Howard Association, Baton Rouge.................................... 500.00
Greenville, Miss., to E. S. Butts, Vicksburg............................. 500.00
Refuge Landing, Miss., to E. S. Butts, Vicksburg......................... 500.00
Canton, Miss., through Robert Powell................................... 500.00
Jackson, Miss., through J. L. Powers................................... 500.00
Lake Station, Miss., through J. L. Powers.............................. 500.00
Chief Engineer, New Orleans Fire Department.......................... 500.00
Chief Engineer, Memphis Fire Department............................. 500.00
Howard Association, Donaldsville, La.................................. 200.00
St. Vincent's Orphan Asylum, New Orleans........................ 100.00
St. Alphonsus Orphan Asylum, New Orleans.......................... 100.00

$4,900.00

Balance...$ 562.00

The balance of money on hand is held for another institution.

JAMES F. WENMAN, President.
ALONZO SLOTE, Treasurer.
JAMES CAMERON, Secretary.

On motion of James J. Kelso, Esq., the following resolution was adopted :

Resolved, That the New York Firemen's Ball Committee of the Old Volunteer Fire Department hereby tender their sincere thanks to all who aided them in giving success to their concert at Gilmore's Garden on the evening of September 23, 1878, in aid of the Relief Fund for the benefit of the yellow fever sufferers. The committee more especially express their obligations to Mlle. Ilma di Murska, Signor Tagliapietra, Wm. J. Levy, General C. S. Grafulla and the members of the Seventh Regiment National Guard Band, Harry B. Dodworth, Esq., and the members of Dodworth's Band, and Messrs. Oliver S. Dorlon and Edwin Coe for their services, tendered gratuitously on that occasion, and also to Mrs. Emma Watson Doty, Mrs. George Warrenreth, and Samuel H. Crooks, Esq., and the members of Crooks' Band, and the others who volunteered, and all whose noble efforts assisted our brethren who are suffering under the affliction of the terrible scourge which has been devastating the South. No appeal was responded to more kindly, promptly, and satisfactorily than that made by this committee, and feeling that this success was very largely due to those above named, the committee take this opportunity to make public recognition of their services, though aware that each and every one will find a greater reward in the knowledge that their charitable act will carry comfort to many a sorrowing home, and always remembering that

"No radiant pearl that crested fortune wears,
Nor gem that twinkling hangs from beauty's ears;
Not all the blue stars that night's blue arch adorn,
Not e'en the rising sun that gilds the vernal morn,
Shines with such luster as the tear that flows
Down Virtue's manly cheek for others' woes."

THE NEW YORK FIRE DEPARTMENT BALL COMMITTEE OF THE OLD VOLUNTEER FIRE DEPARTMENT :

James F. Wenman,	John Fox,	William C. Conner,
Daniel D. Conover,	Gustavus Isaacs,	William M. Randell,
John J. Westray,	Daniel Slote,	Thomas H. Jenkins,

William H. Wickham,
William H. Stodart,
Nelson Tappan,
Charles Delmonico,
J. Corbey Perrin, Jr.,
Samuel A. Besson,
George F. Nesbitt,
Nath. D. White,
Joseph L. Perley,
John R. Platt,
John S. Davidson,

Frederick White,
James Y. Watkins, Jr.,
James J. Kelso,
Aaron J. Westervelt,
Henry B. Venn,
Robert McGinnis,
Alonzo Slote,
Robert C. Brown,
Jordan L. Mott, Jr.,
James Cameron,
Wilbur F. Kirby,

Frederick A. Ridabock,
John C. Bailey,
John J. Bloomfield,
James E. Morris,
Charles Place,
C. Godfrey Gunther,
Cornelius C. Poillon,
Edward Smith,
John J. Donnelly,
M. V. B. Smith.

HONORARY.

John Coger, Jr.,
James Y. Watkins,
Daniel Stanbury,
John Garcia,
Lorenzo Delmonico,

Henry A. Burr,
Adam P. Pentz,
Peter H. Titus,
Owen W. Bruman,
Charles McDougal,

Daniel D. Conover,
James F. Wenman, *President.*
Henry B. Venn, *Vice-President.*
James Cameron, *Secretary.*
Alonzo Slote, *Treasurer.*

The amount of funds held by the trustees, as reported, from 1798 to the close of the year 1885, was as follows:

1799, £823 17s. 5d.	1821, $11,524.12.	1843, $34,467.93.	1864, $100,588.85.
1800, £870 7s. 7d.	1822, 12,154.22.	1844, 36,240.38.	1865, 90,497.90.
1801, £1126 19s.	1823, 12,619.40.	1845, 38,630.57.	1866, 93,533.37.
1802, £1151 2s. 2d.	1824, 12,700.22.	1846, 38,136.35.	1867, 103,063.08.
1803, £1383 16s.6d.	1825, 13,339.68.	1847, 38,495.12.	1868, 120,074.48.
1804, £1725 10s.3d.	1826, 13,157.15.	1848, 39,745.39.	1869, 135,365.87.
1805, £1831 13s.	1827, 15,917.77.	1849, 41,303.10.	1870, 145,029.02.
1806, £2078 10s.	1828, 15,419.97.	1850, 53,216.85.	1871, 146.823.73.
1807, £2537 16s.7d.	1829, 15,082.77.	1851, 59,480.22.	1872, 146,191.12.
1808, £3052 6s. 2d.	1830, 18,541.93.	1852, 72,701.53.	1873, 144,587.04.
1809, £3306 3s. 4d.	1831, 18,366.61.	1853, 85,439.89.	1874, 146,405.11.
1810, £9095 3d.	1832, 17,958.45.	1854, 95,963.34.	1875, 147,151.86.
1811, $10,036.36.	1833, 18,891.84.	1855, 93,788.45.	1876, 153,321.17.
1812, 10,241.96.	1834, 19,915.50.	1856, 95,963.34.	1877, 146,238.08.
1813, 10,350.26.	1835, 20,080.00.	1857, 98,002.34.	1878, 141,332.24.
1814, 10,419.76.	1836, 28,369.89.	1858, 97,144.48.	1879, 129,307.89.
1815, 10,622.38.	1837, 29,908.82.	1859, 100,475,82.	1880, 129,959.82.
1816, 10,364.17.	1838, 28,840.25.	1860, 97,934.73.	1881, 135,686.81.
1817, 11,956.02.	1839, 31,437.54.	1861, 97,434.08.	1882, 129,841.91.
1818, 10,264.72.	1840, 35,573.95.	1862, 101,569.00.	1883, 173,140.88.
1819, 10,537.85.	1841, 31,120.79.	1863, 103,658.47.	1884, 204,038.31.
1820, 11,398.98.	1842, 34,054.30.		

Nicholas Van Antwerp was treasurer from 1798 to 1801; Benjamin Strong from 1801 to 1819; David Bryson from 1819 to 1821; William Colgate from 1821 to 1823; John P. Bailey was treasurer from 1823 to 1829; Drake B. Palmer from 1829 to 1835; Henry B. Greenwood from 1835 to 1836; Elias G. Drake from 1836 to 1837; H. B. Cook from 1837 to 1839; A. P. Pentz from 1839 to 1841; John S. Giles from 1841 to 1881; James F. Wenman from 1881 to 1884; Robert C. Armstrong from 1884 to 1885.

Through the strenuous efforts of certain members of the Fire Patrol Committee of the New York Board of Fire Underwriters, viz., Messrs. Charles M. Peck, J. A. Silvey and George T. Patterson, Jr., an agreement was reached (March 26, 1866,) for the more equitable distribution of the two per cent. tax levied on other State and foreign companies' premiums received in this State. The Exempt Firemen's Benevolent Fund of New York City had renewed its charter (which was about expiring) for the term of thirty years. This fund has been accumulated by a two per cent. tax on the fire premiums received in New York City by insurance from other States and countries during the past twenty years, and now amounts to about two hundred and twenty-five thousand dollars. The new agreement was made between the trustees of the Exempt Firemen's Benevolent Fund of the New York Paid Fire Department and the New York Board of Fire Underwriters, that a bill should be passed, by which the proceeds of this tax, amounting to about sixty thousand dollars per annum, should hereafter be divided in the following proportion, viz.: for the first year, to the Exempt Firemen's Benevolent Fund, 46¼ per cent.; to the New York Paid Fire Department, 46¼ per cent.; and to the New York Fire Patrol, 7½ per cent.; and for the twenty-nine succeeding years, as follows, viz.: To the Exempt Firemen's Benevolent Fund, 42½ per cent.; to the New York Paid Fire Depart-

LADIES' METROPOLITAN FAIR.
[Firemen's Department.]

ment, 42½ per cent.; and to the New York Fire Patrol, 15 per cent., as a basis for a benevolent fund for widows and orphans of the Fire Patrol. The is a more just apportionment of this fund than heretofore, and, in fact, without such an adjustment, there would be no justice whatever in continuing this tax.

THE LADIES' METROPOLITAN FAIR.

The Ladies' Metropolitan Fair, in aid of the noble United States Sanitary Commission, which did such excellent work in relieving National sufferers, was opened in New York, April 4, 1864. The main building was the Twenty-second Regiment Armory. There was a cattle show at Fifteenth Street and Seventh Avenue, and International Hall, Knickerbocker Kitchen, Music Hall, and Children's Department in Union Square. The splendid exhibit of the Volunteer Fire Department was in the armory, against the east wall, of which it occupied one-half the length, and was in charge of the following committee: William H. Wickham, chairman; Lawrence Taylor, A. J. Delatour, James

L. Miller, Josiah Hedden, C. Godfrey Gunther, William M. Randell, Sylvanus J. Macy, John Gracie, Alonzo Slote, John Decker, John R. Platt, Robert McGinnis, Charles McDougall, E. D. Garesche, Francis H. Macy, George T. Hope, George W. Lane, James F. Wenman, Z. H. Jarman,

The opening address, made by General John A. Dix, placed the Fair in the hands of the Ladies' Committee, for whom Mr. Joseph H. Choate responded. The Fair lasted until the twenty-third of April, and netted one million one hundred and seventy-six thousand six hundred and seventy-one dollars and ninety cents, the contribution of the Volunteer Fire Department being thirty thousand two hundred and fifty dollars.

FIREMEN'S MONUMENT.
[Greenwood Cemetery.]

THE FIREMAN'S MONUMENT AT GREENWOOD.

Several years have passed since the New York Fire Department bought a handsome lot on Tulip Hill, Greenwood Cemetery, for the interment and commemoration of those who had lost their lives in the discharge of a laborious, and often perilous duty. The spot selected is one of the finest in the country. The Fireman's Monument is a pyramidal column of marble, resting on a massive pedestal of the same material, with a granite base below. The fireman on its summit is a well-executed figure. One arm surrounds and supports a child, just rescued from the flames, which still pursue it. His right hand holds a trumpet. The attitude is spirited, and the general effect very good. Upon four of the pilasters of the pedestal, and upon its upper surface, appears various representations in relief, or in full, of implements and articles appertaining to the fireman's calling. His swinging engine lantern, his trumpet and cap, his hose and hydrant, the hook and ladder—all are sculptured there. The workmanship of the structure is admirable. The monument occupies the center of a large circular lot, and its position is commanding. The eminence upon which it is built is some distance from the entrance. The view from this will detain the visitor a moment; the little dell which he has just passed, with its shady water, is immediately below. Here, with a city of the living before him, and another of the dead growing up around, is a striking contrast. From the loftiest height of charming Greenwood the marble monument rises, severe in beauty, and grand in its proportions. It is emblematical of the men, and their works will be a perpetual remembrance of the fireman's name.

The monument is surrounded by a neat iron railing. On each side of the gate, or entrance to the plot, is a hydrant, and on the top of the railing at different points are lamps. Through the openings of leafy trees the churches of Flatbush are to be seen. The prospect is one of peculiar peacefulness, and suggestive of heavenly rest. On the right is a monument erected to the memory of Henry Fargis, assistant foreman of Engine Company No. 38, and on the left another to the memory of George Kerr, engineer.

On the tablet at the base of the column, and facing the lake, is the following inscription :

THE FIRE DEPARTMENT

OF THE CITY OF NEW YORK

HAVE CAUSED

THIS MONUMENT TO BE ERECTED

IN MEMORY OF

THEIR COMPANIONS WHO PERISHED IN DISCHARGE OF THEIR DUTY,

A. D. 1848.

The names of the deceased firemen cover the remaining three sides of the base, and three sides of the first section of the pyramid next to the base. The chronological order has not been preserved, but we give here the names of the deceased in the order in which they died :

William Peterson, foreman Engine Company No. 15, May 19, 1811.
David W. Rayner, Engine Company No. 10, March 8, 1827.
Francis Joseph, assistant foreman Engine Company No. 1, March 8, 1827.
Cornelius Garrison, Engine Company No. 32, July 5, 1832.
Nathan Brown, Engine Company No. 42, September 25, 1832.
James Hedges, Engine Company No. 42, September 25, 1832.
John Knapp, Engine Company No. 32, March 6, 1834.
Engineer Underhill, Engine Company No. 13, July 1, 1834.
Frederic Ward, Engine Company No. 13, July 1, 1834.
Richard S. Richie, Engine Company No. 6, May 26, 1836.
Thomas Storton, Hose Company No. 13, June 3, 1837.
John Buckloh, Engine Company No. 19, February 6, 1838.
James S. Wells, engineer, April 15, 1840.
James Glasgow, Hose Company No. 15, April 15, 1840.
Augustus Cowdrey, Engine Company No. 42, July 19, 1845.
George Kerr, engineer, April 2, 1848.
Henry Fargis, assistant foreman Engine Company No. 38, April 2, 1848.
Charles J. Durant, Hose Company No. 35, April 2, 1848.
John L. Guire, engineer Engine Company No. 14, April 24, 1850.
Arthur J. Evans, Hose Company No. 14, September 25, 1852.
George W. Trenshard, Hose Company No. 16, June 2, 1853.
John S. Carman, Engine Company No. 5, October 30, 1853.
Michael O'Brien, Hook and Ladder Company No. 11, October 30, 1853.

Andrew C. Schenck, Hook and Ladder Company No. 1, April 25, 1854.
John A. Keyser, Hose Company No. 8, April 25, 1854.
Alexander McKay, Engine Company No. 21, April 25, 1854.
James McNulty, Engine Company No. 20, April 25, 1854.
Anthony Caraccioli, Engine Company No. 16, May 8, 1855.
James T. Laurie, Hose Company No. 7, December 20, 1855.
Lewis Barker, Hook and Ladder Company No. 3, April 20, 1860.

BOARD OF FIRE COMMISSIONERS.

(Authorized by "Act of the Legislature," March 29, 1855).

1855 and 1856.

CHAS. McDOUGALL, *President.*

Edward Brown, Benj. Cartwright, Wm. Wright, Wm. A. Freeborn.

1856 and 1857.

EDWARD BROWN, *President.*

Benj. Cartwright, Wm. Wright, Wm. A. Freeborn, Andrew Craft.

1857 and 1858.

WM. WRIGHT, *President.*

Edward Brown, Andrew Craft, Robert H. Ellis, John W. Schenck.

1858 and 1859.

ROBERT H. ELLIS, *President.*

Wm. Wright, John W. Schenck, Nelson D. Thayer, Henry Wilson.

1859 and 1860.

HENRY WILSON, *President.*

Wm. M. Tweed, John J. Gorman, Thomas Lawrence, Erastus W. Brown.

1861 and 1862.

HENRY WILSON, *President.*

Wm. M. Tweed, John J. Gorman, Thomas Lawrence, Erastus W. Brown.

1862 and 1863.

HENRY WILSON, *President.*

Wm. M. Tweed, John J. Gorman, Thomas Lawrence, Erastus W. Brown.

1863 and 1864.

HENRY WILSON, *President.*

Wm. M. Tweed, John J. Gorman, Thomas Lawrence, Edward Bonnell.

1864 and 1865.

JOHN J. GORMAN, *President.*

Wm. M. Tweed, Thomas Lawrence, Edward Bonnell, Thos. Flender.

1865.

JOHN J. GORMAN, *President.*

Wm. M. Tweed, Thomas Lawrence, Edward Bonnell, Thos. Flender.

BOARD OF COMMISSIONERS OF APPEALS.

(Organized by "Act of the Legislature," 1864).

JOHN GILLELAN, *President.*

Wm. Haw, Jr., John Carland, Vincent C. King, Ralph Trembly.

CHAPTER XLII.

THE FIRE ZOUAVES.

(Eleventh N. Y. S. V.)—Brave Deeds that have gone into History.—The Firemen Gallantly Respond to President Lincoln's Appeal for Men.—Formation of the First Regiment of Fire Zouaves.—On to Washington.—Death of Colonel Ellsworth.—Colonel Farnham taken from the field in a Dying Condition.—Captain Jack Wildey.—Colonel Leoser.—Lieutenant Divver.—The Second Regiment of Fire Zouaves.—Their Valiant Services in the field.

WHEN the gun was trailed on Sumter from which was fired the shot that, in no very metaphorical sense, may be said to have been "heard around the world," like that which woke the echoes of Bunker Hill when the "embattled farmers" stood in array for the defense of their rights, no class of our citizens more quickly rose to the level of the great occasion, or more heartily responded to President Lincoln's appeal for men, than did the Volunteer firemen of New York City. Nor was there anything in their subsequent record that indicated, at any period of the war, the slightest diminution in the earnest patriotism which inspired them at the beginning of the struggle. Although early deprived of their especial military organization, they were ever ready, around whatever regimental flag they may have rallied, to use their best efforts towards the suppression of the rebellion. Thus, as will be seen, the record of the Volunteer Firemen of New York, wherever made, and led by whatever officers they may have enlisted under, was one which both

COL. ELMER E. ELLSWORTH.

they and their fellow-citizens may contemplate with unmixed satisfaction. The First Fire Zouaves, officially known as the Eleventh New York, was recruited amid a tempest of enthusiasm, and with a celerity that will hardly be credited in less heroic days, a quarter of a century after the event. Colonel Ellsworth seemed to have infused some of his own restless energy into the firemen of that time, and every engine house was turned into a recruiting station. In some cases as many as eighteen and twenty men volunteered out of a single company, and the question was not who were to go, but who were to be so unfortunate as to be left behind. It thus took but a few days to rally the eleven hundred men that pushed on to Annapolis, but it was not the number so much as the extraordinary spirit and dash of its members that characterized this representative regiment. Colonel Ellsworth, breaking through the red-tape regulations that would have retained him in the vicinity of New York until a more convenient season, and having obtained the necessary arms directly from Washington instead of through the state officials, ignoring all obstacles, marched his men to the defense of the national capital in advance of its other defenders. Arrived in Washington, the first duty to which the regiment was assigned was the extinguishing of a fire in that well-known hostelry, Willard's Hotel. They went into camp on the Maryland side of the Potomac, and captured Alexandria May 24, where the gallant Ellsworth met his glorious fate. On the twenty-ninth the regiment moved to Shooter's Hill. About June 5, a picket-guard was detailed for duty at McCloud's Mills, when one man was killed and one wounded. This was the first loss in the field.

These were the officers in command of the First Regiment of First Fire Zouaves (Eleventh Regiment, N. Y. S. V.):

Elmer E. Ellsworth, Colonel,

Noah L. Farnham, Lieutenant-Colonel, Assistant Engineer Hook and Ladder Company No. 1.

John A. Cregier, Major, Assistant Engineer Hose No. 40.

Charles McK. Leoser, Adjutant.

Company A, John Coyle,	-	-	-	-	Hose 22
" B, Edward Byrnes,		-	-	-	Engine 16
" C, Michael C. Murphy,	-	-	-		Hose 41
" D, John Downey,	-	-	-	-	Engine 34
" E, John B. Leverich,	-	-	-		Hose 7
" F, William H. Burns, -	-	-	-	-	Engine 6
" G, Michael Teagen,	-	-	-		Engine 13
" H, William Hackett, -	Assistant Engineer				Engine 20
" I, John Wildey, -	-	-	-		Engine 11
" K, Andrew D. Purtell,	-	-	-		Engine 14

When the First Zouaves left the city they left it as a "three months' regiment" (sworn in April 20, 1861). On the seventh of May they were sworn in to serve during the war. The Zouaves performed picket duty in the vicinity of the Mills until July 16, when orders were given to march on to Bull Run. The command, on the death of Colonel Ellsworth, had devolved upon the brave Farnham, who was serving as lieutenant-colonel, and who at the time of enlisting was one of the engineers of the New York Fire Department. On the night of the seventeenth the regiment encamped at Fairfax Station, and in a brisk encounter with the enemy captured a sergeant and several men belonging to a South Carolina regiment, together with the first Rebel flag that came into its possession. On the morning of the eighteenth orders came to push forward to Centreville, and when within five miles of that place the men were ordered, at double-quick, to the support of the Sixty-ninth, Seventy-ninth, and Twelfth New York, then in action. In this brush only three or four men were wounded, and none killed. On the morning of the twenty-first another start was made for Bull Run. Colonel Farnham had been in hospital, but left his sick bed to assume command. During the battle that ensued he was shot behind the left ear and taken to Washington, where he died. The record of the regiment in this, its first engagement of any consequence, was a noble one: from seventy-five to one hundred killed, two hundred wounded, and one hundred and twenty-five taken prisoners. But this was not all. Before falling back on Centreville, the well-known Captain Jack Wildey and a few men performed one of the most

FIRE ZOUAVES LEAVING FOR THE SEAT OF WAR, ESCORTED BY THE FIRE DEPARTMENT.

gallant deeds of the war. Reckless of his own fate, Captain Wildey threw himself upon a party of the Confederates, and recaptured from them the colors of the Sixty-ninth New York, which he restored to their owners.

The next encampment of the regiment was at Shooter's Hill (Fort Ellsworth). Two weeks later, orders were given to return to New York, that the depleted ranks might be filled up to their original strength. While there, the regiment was stationed at Scarsdale, Bedloe's Island, and the Battery. In September, being again ready for duty, and now under command of Colonel Leoser, the Zouaves were ordered to Newport News. In the meantime the regiment had been largely reofficered: Major John A. Cregier, assistant engineer of the Fire Department and the first major of the regiment, had resigned on reaching New York, Captain McFarland, of Company H, being promoted to be major in his stead. He was a Seventh Regiment man, as were the majority of the new officers. After reaching Newport News the regiment was engaged in

several skirmishes, among them one near Young's Mills while on a foraging
expedition, when twelve of the Zouaves were taken prisoners, among them
Corporal Richard Gleason, of Company A, who was afterwards shot dead by a
sentry at Libby Prison for looking out of a window.

Colonel Leoser now asked permission for the regiment to join the expedition
to Norfolk, but the request was denied. This seemed to throw a damper upon
the entire organization, as it was evidently the intention of the authorities to
keep the men engaged in garrison duty, while all the fighting was to be done,
all the chances of promotion taken, by the more fortunate members of other
commands. The result of such a policy, when the spirit of patriotism and
adventure which characterized the First Fire Zouaves is taken into consideration, may be readily imagined. Colonel Leoser and a majority of the officers

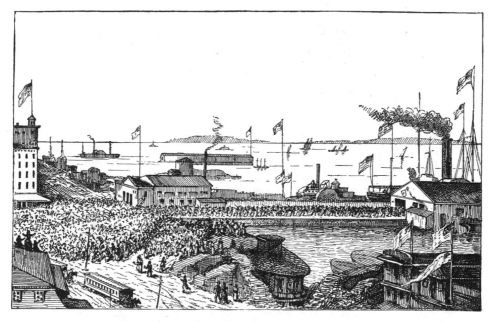

EMBARKATION OF THE FIRE ZOUAVES ON BOARD THE 'BALTIC,' APRIL 29, 1861.
[Foot of Canal and Spring Streets.]

resigned, and numbers of the men when mustered out enlisted in other
regiments, many going with Banks to New Orleans.

While on the Peninsula, however, the men were not allowed to be idle.
The regiment participated in a couple of skirmishes at Newmarket and Big
Bethel, while encamped at Newport News. During the famous engagement,
March 8, 1862, between the ' Merrimac ' and the ' Monitor ' and the ' Cum-
berland,' the regiment occupied rifle pits on shore with a view to repel any
force the enemy might attempt to land. One company, under command of
Colonel Leoser, had charge of a 12 lb. rifled gun, which he himself sighted and
fired from the bluff.

The First Zouaves were soon sent home, and mustered out of the service, June 2, 1862, at Fort Columbus, New York Harbor, by order of the
War Department. Lieutenant-colonel McFarland (one of the Seventh Regiment officers), after Colonel Leoser resigned his command and joined the

regular service, took command of the regiment at Newport News, and came home with them to be mustered out at Governor's Island.

Having thus no longer any regimental organization, the identity of tne First Fire Zouaves became merged, in the persons of its original members, with that of other corps during the remainder of the war. As soldiers serving under other colors, the New York "fire laddies" never failed to give a good account of themselves, and wherever the fighting was hottest, the danger greatest, they were sure to be found; thus proving how great a mistake the authorities of the War Department had made when they mustered out of service a body of men like the First Zouaves and condemned them to the monotony of doing garrison duty. On the other hand, had the matter been decided by those possessing ordinary discernment and common sense, and had not adverse influences been at work, a regiment composed of such material would have been pushed to the front, given work worthy of it to do, and afforded an opportunity to reflect credit upon the organization that under such circumstances would have been so dear to them. Among those who cast in their lot with other regiments, when they found the opportunity for promotion denied them in their own, may be mentioned, Thomas Riley, who served as an adjutant in General Spinola's brigade, and was killed at the Battle of the Black Water. Captains Coyle and Murphy

SHOOTING OF COLONEL ELLSWORTH.
[Marshall House.]

enlisted in the Irish Legion, and served until the end of the war. Captain Byrne joined the Eighteenth New York Cavalry and came home a brigadier-general, Captain Murphy returning as colonel. Sergeant Garvey, Company A, went out as lieutenant and returned as captain in the Fourth New York. He was wounded in the last engagement of the war at Appomattox Courthouse. Lieutenant Powers, originally of Company A, and afterwards transferred to Company I, served throughout the war. Corporal Donnelly, Company A, enlisted in the Seventy-second New York, and was killed in the Battle of the Wilderness, in which Private Meek, who had joined the same regiment, also lost his life. Corporal Ebling, of Company A, was among the killed at the first battle of Bull Run. Private Kane, of Company G, also went out in the Eighteenth New York Cavalry, and returned as first lieutenant.

Of those who fought through the war and are to-day still doing yeoman work in the Fire Department, must be mentioned Private O. O'Rorke, who volunteered in the Eighty-fourth New York, and returned in 1864. Sergeant-Major Goodwin went out in another regiment and came home captain. William Kennedy and Thomas Curtis returned respectively captain and lieutenant of the One Hundred and Sixty-second New York Volunteers.

ELLSWORTH ZOUAVE.

Many of the old firemen of twenty-five years ago are to-day buried in the soldiers' cemeteries at Gettysburg and Antietam. After the glorious fever of that time " they sleep well ; " scarcely a battle ground of the old Army of the Potomac but is reddened with the life blood of some of them, who in spite of the obstacles placed in the way of their patriotic efforts to serve their country, at last achieved the renown that must ever attach to those who have fought and died for " God and native land."

In fact, not over two hundred of the old regiment that left New York on the twenty-ninth of April, 1861, are still living. Many of the survivors have been reunited in the Farnham Post of the Grand Army of the Republic, which was organized, with the approval of Col. Leoser, by Private O'Rorke mentioned above. It counts to-day two hundred and twenty-five members in good standing, with Col. Leoser in command.

Among the prominent members are Gen. Newton, Brig.-Gen. Fitzgerald, now commanding the First Brigade, Police Superintendent Murray, Order of Arrest Clerk Martin, Alderman Cowie, of the present board, and Chief Engineer George W. Magee, now on duty in the Brooklyn Navy Yard, Colonel Clark, Seventh Regiment, Colonel Gilon, tax assessor, General Ferrero, Colonel Farnham's two brothers, etc. The rosters of but few regiments can make a better showing of its old members who have achieved distinction in civil life.

Of the First Fire Zouaves as a whole, nothing worse could be said when they took the lead in that grand military advance on Washington—the first fruits of one of the most remarkable national uprisings known to history—than that, in the words of one of their number, they were " a reckless harum-skarum lot." Although mostly very young men, they were thoroughly imbued with the *esprit du corps* that distinguished the Old Fire Department of New York to an extraordinary degree. If they were good for service of any kind, it was to be pushed to the very front of the fighting as soon as they had been accustomed to the routine of army life and their duties as soldiers. To select such a regiment, composed of elements so peculiar and so thoroughly permeated with the spirit of intrepid bravery—a spirit that regards the most heroic deeds in the light of everyday achievements—for the dull routine of permanent garrison duty, was a blunder as great, in the opposite direction, as that which was responsible for the famous, but fatal charge at Balaklava.

In referring to the Zouaves, Col. Leoser said recently that were he called upon to recruit a regiment to-morrow, he would prefer, had he his choice of material, to recruit it from the old firemen of New York. It was also his opinion that if they made any failures during their brief regimental existence, it was due to the mistakes of the officers and not to any lack of bravery on the part of the rank and file. Col. Leoser's relations to the regiment were of the most agreeable character, and he was both esteemed and beloved by his men.

Frank E. Brownell, who so gallantly avenged the killing of the heroic Ellsworth, has given this account of the tragedy:

"It was on the night of the twenty-third of May, about ten o'clock, that Colonel Ellsworth called the regiment out, and he said: 'Boys, I heard this morning that a movement was to be made on Alexandria. I went to General Mansfield and told him that, as we were the first volunteer regiment mustered into the service for the war, we would consider it a deep affront if we were not allowed the right of the line. Prepare yourselves for a night ride, with perhaps a skirmish at the end of it. When we arrive in Alexandria, I want you to act like men, and show the enemy that we are gentlemen as well as soldiers. Not a shot must be fired without orders.'

HEAD OF ZOUAVE.
[Showing style of cap first worn.]

"We were camped at Giesboro Point, and between two and three o'clock next morning the boats to convey us to Alexandria arrived. As we approached Alexandria, we found the gunboat 'Pawnee' lying off the town, and as our steamers moved up to the wharf, a boat put off from the 'Pawnee' with a white flag flying. Upon the landing, the officer in command of this boat had a consultation with Colonel Ellsworth, and I have always understood, informed him that the city had been placed under a flag of truce, or at least been given a certain time to surrender. At all events, the town was under a flag of truce from the officer commanding the 'Pawnee,' and for that reason it was not deemed imprudent for Colonel Ellsworth to leave his regiment and go up into the city. We landed at the foot of Cameron Street, and as the regiment disembarked, Colonel Ellsworth started up into the town accompanied by our chaplain and the correspondents of the New York *Times* and *Tribune*. As he passed the right of the regiment it was suggested by some one that he take a guard with him. He called for the first group on the right of the first company to follow him, which was made up of a sergeant, two corporals and two privates. As we turned into King Street, the first thing that met our gaze was the Rebel flag floating over the Marshall House. When he saw the Rebel flag, Colonel Ellsworth turned to the sergeant and told him to hurry back to

Captain Coyle, who commanded Company A, and tell him to hurry up there with his men as soon as possible. We were on the opposite side of the street from the hotel; and after passing the house, however, the colonel stopped for a moment or two, and then turned across the street and entered the building. There was a man behind the office counter, and Colonel Ellsworth asked him if he was the proprietor. He replied that he was not. Colonel Ellsworth then started up the stairway for the roof followed by the whole of our party. We pulled down the flag and started back. I was in advance, and as I made the turn between the third and second stories, I saw Jackson standing at the head

[Lieut.-Col. Noah L. Farnham, Adjutant Charles McK. Leoser (afterwards Colonel), Quartermaster Stetson (of Astor House fame), of the Eleventh Regiment (Ellsworth Fire Zouaves) in conference immediately following the killing of Colonel Ellsworth in Alexandria. This conference was held in the Marshall House, where Ellsworth was killed, and for which deed, Jackson, his slayer, paid the penalty of death on the spot.]

of the flight wing to the next story. I jumped towards him, and with my musket struck down his gun. As my weapon slid off his, I sprang backward and lost my footing, and just at that moment Colonel Ellsworth appeared around the turn of the stairs coming down. Jackson raised his gun and turned to give me the other barrel. I had recovered my feet, however, and fired upon him first, immediately following up my shot with the bayonet, my thrust pushing him down the stairs, the other barrel of his gun going off as he fell."

"What do you think prompted Colonel Ellsworth to undertake to pull down that flag himself?"

"I have always been under the impression that he did it to prevent any outbreak, and that he was afraid to allow the regiment to see it."

"Do you know anything regarding Colonel Ellsworth's personal character."

"I don't believe, if history were searched through to find a life to hold up for the emulation of the youth of our country, that you would find one that better illustrates the character of a true patriot and gentleman than that of Colonel Ellsworth. I have a number of his letters, and what is perhaps the best evidence of his character, his private diary."

Captain Brownell produced a small book bound in red leather. Turning

over the leaves, which were filled with neat round handwriting of the dead
hero, he read numerous extracts. It was a concise history of the daily life
of the young soldier when he was a law student in Chicago, struggling for an
honorable position among men, living upon bread and water, and sleeping
upon the bare floor of his employer's office. Pages were filled with affectionate
allusions to his aged parents and his fond hopes for a future that would shed
happiness and comfort over their declining years.

This is an extract from a letter written by President Lincoln to the bereaved
mother of Colonel Ellsworth :

" My acquaintance with him began less than two years ago, yet through the
latter half of the intervening period it was as intimate as the disparity of our
ages and my engrossing engagements would permit. To me he appeared to

THE FIRST FIRE ZOUAVES AT THE BATTLE OF MANASSAS.

have no indulgences or pastimes, and I never heard him utter a profane or
intemperate word. The honors he labored for so laudably, and in the sad end
so gallantly gave his life, he meant for them no less than himself. In the hope
that it may be no intrusion upon the sacredness of your sorrow, I have ventured
to address this tribute to the memory of my young friend, and your brave and
early fallen child. May God give you the consolation which is beyond earthly
power. Sincerely your friend in a common affliction,

A. LINCOLN."

THE FIRE ZOUAVES AT THE BATTLE OF MANASSAS.

John Wildey, an active fireman from 1844 until the dissolution of the Volunteer Department, was foreman of 11 Engine at the outbreak of the Rebellion.

He assisted in organizing the Eleventh Regiment, Fire Zouaves, and went to the front as captain in that command.

Captain Wildey says that while the regiment was forming in line on King Street, news came that Ellsworth was killed. The regiment then marched through the city to the railway station. The captain went to the Marshall House and took charge of Ellsworth's remains, and held possession of the Rebel flag and the double-barreled shotgun used by Jackson. These trophies were sent North with the colonel's body.

Wildey was with his regiment at Shooter's Hill (where a fort was constructed, and named after Ellsworth,) when the order to advance on Manassas was received. For weeks previous to this advance the regiment had been constantly drilled and disciplined by competent officers. Colonel Noah L. Farnham, who succeeded Ellsworth, had been a member of the Seventh N. Y. Regiment, and Adjutant Leoser was a graduate of West Point. In fact, when the regiment started out for Bull Run, it was in a high degree of efficiency, considering its short service; it was easily manœuvered, thoroughly equipped, and possessed of an *esprit du corps* that would have proved irresistible in any ordinary combat.

In the engagement at Manassas the regiment held the extreme right of the line in the brigade of General Wilcox, and first came under the fire of a Rebel battery and a corps of sharpshooters concealed in rifle pits. On hearing the first "whizz" of bullets, Wildey says he experienced a sensation similar to that felt years before when going into an old-time firemen's fight in front of the Astor House. The Zouaves charged under a murderous fire, drove the enemy out of the rifle pits, and cleared the field in front of them. Their loss, however, was severe. Among the fatally wounded was Colonel Farnham, who received a shot in the head above the ear. Captains Wildey and Purtell carried his body to the rear. He was sent to the hospital, where he died two weeks afterwards. Wildey returned to the front in time to see a body of cavalrymen coming swiftly down towards the right of the line, shouting and waving an American flag. At first it was thought the cavalrymen were friends, but an order rang out to "lie down and prepare to receive cavalry." The Zouaves instantly dropped to the ground, and the Rebel cavalry, waving captured flags, and yelling like demons, came down at a charge. Suddenly Rickett's Union Battery, in rear of the Zouaves, opened on the mounted Rebels, killing many men and horses, and throwing them into confusion. Wildey fired his revolver at the leader of the Confederates, and saw him fall. He was Colonel Ashby, of the famous "Black Horse Cavalry." As the Rebels turned to flee, the Zouaves jumped to their feet, and charged furiously into the midst of them. One of the Rebels bore aloft the green flag of the Sixty-ninth Regiment, captured a short time before. His horse was shot and tumbled. As the Rebel sprang off, Captain Wildey was upon him with his sword, and snatched the glorious flag away. This was one of the most brilliant individual exploits of the great battle. The flag was returned to the Sixty-ninth, and is still proudly held by that organization.

Wildey says that after the dispersion of the "Black Horse Cavalry," the Zouaves were elated with their victory, and thinking the battle was over, some of them began picking up trophies from the field to send to their friends at the North. But they were suddenly called into the ranks again upon the approach of a fresh force of the enemy. It proved to be General Joe Johnston's command, just arrived by rail from Winchester, where General Patterson had been vainly sent to detain him. These fresh troops resumed the battle, and turned the tide of victory. Our men were now thoroughly exhausted with long marching, excessively hot weather, and severe fighting. Their canteens were empty, and rations wasted or consumed; for they had not yet acquired the foresight of veterans in carefully husbanding supplies of food and water. All were suffering from thirst. Besides these great disadvantages, the moral effect upon young soldiers in discovering that their hard-fought vic-

tory was not a victory at all, but only the prelude to another mighty encounter, could not fail to be disastrous. Considerable confusion ensued upon the renewed onset of the Confederates, but Wildey avers that, so far as the Zouaves were concerned, there was no breaking of ranks, as reported at the time. The regiment, or what was left of it after losing two hundred and eighty men in killed, wounded, and prisoners, retired in good order, maintaining its company formation, firing and retreating slowly. The Zouaves, in fact, formed the rear guard of the whole Union army in its retrograde movement as far as Centreville, where they slept that night, retiring the following day to Fairfax Court-house.

NOAH LANE FARNHAM.
[From the original in possession of Farnham Post. Painted by J. Harrison Mills.]

Shortly after this battle Captain Wildey was ordered to New York, on recruiting service. While so engaged, he was nominated for coroner on the Union ticket, and elected. This closed his army career. He served as coroner six years.

NOAH LANE FARNHAM, eldest son of George W. and Caroline (Thompson) Farnham, was born at New Haven, Connecticut, on the first day of March, 1829. When he was about two years old his parents removed to the City of New York. When about eight years of age he was sent back to New Haven to one of its best schools, now the celebrated Collegiate and Commercial Institute of that city. After spending three years at that institution, he was sent to the Episcopal Academy at Cheshire, Connecticut, then, as now, one of the best church schools in the country. At the age of fourteen he was taken from there and placed in the then well-known dry goods commission house of Clapp, Kent & Beckley, of New York.

At the age of eighteen he joined the City Guards, a well-known and popular military organization of the time. Shortly after the celebrated Astor Place riot took place, and his company, having been called upon to take part in suppressing it, he participated with them in the duties and dangers of the hour. The alternation of drill and festivities which characterized the " crack " companies of the day did not suit his restless and energetic spirit, so that as soon as he came of age he joined Empire Engine Company No. 42, in which he served for about two years, when he resigned and joined Mutual Hook and Ladder No. 1, located in the same house now occupied by the company of the same number in the present department. His merit soon promoted him to the command of the company, from which position he was afterwards elected to be one of the assistant engineers of the department, serving as such under Chiefs Carson and Howard. While in the hook and ladder company he was associated with ex-Mayor Wickham, Andrew C. Schenck (killed at the Jennings fire), and others who did concurrent duty in the Seventh Regiment, and his military tastes reasserting themselves towards the close of his term of service in the department, he was elected a member of the second company of the Seventh Regiment. From the ranks he was promoted to second sergeant, and from that office to those of second and first lieutenant in rapid succession.

At the breaking out of the rebellion he held the last-named position, under Captain (now Colonel) Emmons Clark. On the memorable nineteenth of April, 1861, he marched down Broadway for the last time, in command of a platoon of his company, arm-in-arm with Colonel Ellsworth, whom he was so soon, by the fatal fortunes of war, to succeed. The history of the Seventh's campaign is familiar to the world, and need not be repeated here, but it may be noted that Lieutenant Farnham commanded the first detail of skilled skirmishers which was ever displayed in the war of the rebellion. While in camp with his regiment at Washington, his commission as lieutenant-colonel of the Fire Zouaves was sent him from Albany, which he immediately accepted, and bade farewell to his comrades of the Seventh, reporting without delay to Colonel Ellsworth. Immediately upon the tragic death of that gallant officer Colonel Farnham assumed command. The history of those trying hours is told elsewhere in this book. Some weeks after his promotion he was prostrated with typhoid fever, and had hardly passed the crisis of the disease when the advance which resulted in the Bull Run disaster was ordered. Weak, ill, and physically unfit, he insisted on accompanying his regiment, and against the remonstrances of his surgeons and officers, was lifted on his horse, and led his men into the battle, where he received his death wound. He was taken to the Washington Infirmary, where he lingered under faithful treatment until the fourteenth day of August, 1861, when he died peacefully and without a struggle. His brothers, who were present at his deathbed, caused the remains to be taken to his father's house in New York City. Funeral services were held on Saturday, the seventeenth, at Christ Church on Fifth Avenue. The remains were taken to New Haven, which was a city of mourning on that day, with stores closed and buildings draped. A long procession of the military, local Fire Department and delegations from the Seventh Regiment and Fire Department of New York, followed the remains to the grave in the family plot in the Old Grove Street cemetery, where the committal services were read by the rector of Trinity Church, the church of his fathers.

Colonel Farnham was a man of great force and energy of character. Descended from a long line of New England ancestors, fighters in all the wars from the colonial Indian battles, on through the French War and wars of the Revolution and of 1812, he inherited an abiding love of country, and of liberty for every man of whatever race or color. He was the soul of honor, pure in heart and life, unselfish to a fault, and in all respects a model for the young men of America to admire and imitate.

COLONEL CHARLES McKNIGHT LEOSER was born in Reading, Pa., in 1839, and graduated at West Point in May, 1861. He was at once commissioned in the Second United States Cavalry and was orderd to drill the First Fire Zouaves (Eleventh New York Volunteers) in July. On the death of Colonel Noah L. Farnham he was chosen to serve in his stead. He remained in command of the regiment until April 18, 1862, when he resigned and rejoined his own regiment, with which he remained until the end of the war. Colonel Leoser's record with his own command was an exceedingly brilliant one, he having taken part in over forty engagements. Among them may be mentioned those at Spottsylvania Court-house, Hanover Court-house, Fair Oaks, White Oaks Swamp, and Cold Harbor. He was with Sheridan in his raid to Haxall's Landing, and was present at Beaver Dam, Yellow Tavern and Hawes shop, his command having had nineteen distinct encounters with the enemy in seventeen days.

CHARLES McK. LEOSER.

At Trevillian Station, June 11, 1864, Colonel Leoser was wounded and captured. He remained a prisoner about three months, and so did not take part with his regiment in the battle of Gettysburg. He resigned from the army in October, 1865, since which time he has been engaged in business in this city.

He is now president of the Wine and Spirit Traders' Society, first vice-president of the American Institute, and a member of the Chamber of Commerce. Colonel Leoser is an ideal cavalry officer, bold, dashing, and as fearless as a lion. Of all the contests in which he engaged during the war he is of opinion that his experience at Bull Run brought him into closest quarters with death, the Zouaves having been for some time on that disastrous day exposed to a cross fire, and that the officers escaped alive is considered little less than a miracle. Whoever is responsible for the untoward result of that engagement, it is certainly neither the Fire Zouaves nor their gallant colonel.

LIEUTENANT DANIEL DIVVER, of Company G, Eleventh New York Volunteers (First Fire Zouaves), was born in Ireland in 1839, came to this country when he was a child, and resided in the Fourth Ward with his parents. He attended the public schools and learned his trade of tanner in the "Swamp," where he was well-known and popular. At the breaking out of the war of the Rebellion he was, and had been for two years previously, an active member of Eagle Engine Company No. 13, his record as a fireman being unexcelled. When Colonel Ellsworth called for recruits from our Old Volunteer Fire Department, Lieutenant Divver was among the first to subscribe to the roll of membership of Company G, in which command he was unanimously elected second lieutenant.

In camp, before the regiment crossed the Potomac to take Alexandria, he became endeared to all his comrades by his genial disposition and his untiring efforts for the comfort of the rank and file. With his fellow-officers he was a great favorite.

On the march to the battlefield of Bull Run he divested himself of all super-

LIEUTENANT DANIEL DIVVER.

fluous garments, entering the field with his gallant comrades in his shirt sleeves, and they rolled above the elbows, sword in hand, and, with the familiar yell of the old engine company, "Get down, Old Hague!" he rushed forward to his death. When the excitement of the charge (the Rebels being driven back into the woods) was over, Lieutenant Divver was found on the field, his life blood ebbing away from over a dozen fatal wounds. He was carried off by some of his faithful comrades and was taken into a wheelwright shop by Paul Chappell and others by direction of Surgeon Gray of the regiment, where he expired almost immediately. The Rebels, being reinforced, made another sally, and all those in and around the wheelwright shop who were able to do so, were off to resist the charge. Those who were left behind were eventually taken prisoners. Lieutenant Divver's body was never recovered, though many efforts were made by his family. He met the death of a gallant soldier at the head of his men, and lies in an unmarked grave with his fallen comrades. Lieutenant Daniel Divver was the brother of Alderman Patrick Divver.

THE SECOND FIRE ZOUAVES.

Of all the regiments which the Empire State sent to the front during the Civil War, none made a more honorable record than the Second Fire Zouaves. It was organized May 3, 1861, and consisted almost entirely of firemen and runners. At first Governor Morgan declined the services of the regiment, since it was supposed that enough troops to suppress the rebellion had already been raised. Not until the early part of July did the Zouaves go into "Camp

Decker," on Staten Island. The camp was named in honor of Chief Decker, of the Fire Department, who was very active in recruiting the regiment. Even when the boys, eight hundred and fourteen strong, started for the front, August 23, 1861, they had not been recognized by the Albany authorities, and had no State number. Private enterprise had organized and equipped the regiment, which was at first known simply as the Fourth Regiment of the Excelsior Brigade. Fire Commissioner Henry Wilson, Thomas Lawrence, Henry Graham and Judge Dusenbury were among the public-spirited men who aided in the work of Gen. Sickles' Excelsior Brigade. They were mustered into service as United States volunteers.

Colonel James Fairman, who had been organizing a regiment for the Sickles Brigade, agreed to take the companies as they were formed, company by company, and turn over his companies to the other regiments in the same brigade. He eventually did so, and mustered in eight companies of the

FIRE ZOUAVES IN CAMP.

Second Fire Zouaves at Camp Scott, on Staten Island. The other two companies being mustered in at the camp in Maryland, there was an agreement with the officers of the regiment that they would elect Fairman to the colonelcy, and he started with the regiment. He was, however, relieved of his command on the way to the boat, and Major Moriarty placed in command, which he retained until the regiment was encamped at Mendian Hill, on the outskirts of Washington. The privates of the regiment were in favor of Fairman, and for a time the excitement ran high. When the regiment went into Camp McClellan, in Maryland, just across the river from Washington, the officers held an election for colonel, and William R. Brewster, of Brooklyn, was elected, receiving the votes of all the commissioned officers of the regiment, excepting those of Capt. Daniel Crowley, Company D, formerly member of Engine Company 20; Lt. Wm. Gleeson, Company D, formerly member of Engine Company 3; Lt. John Skelin, Company D, also of Engine Company 20; Lt. J. Hamilton, Company 16, member of Company 14; and Lt. Evans.

Col. Brewster proved himself to be an honorable gentleman and a brave soldier, and continued in command of the regiment until the end of the war. The regiment went from Camp McClellan to Point Matthias, and afterwards to Port Tobacco, Md., and from there to join the Army of the Potomac. Below are the names of the other officers: Field and staff—Lieut. Colonel, Louis Benedict; Major, John D. Moriarty; Adjutant, George Le Fort; Surgeon, Henry P. Bostwick; Assistant Surgeon, Frank Ridgeway; Quartermaster, John A. McCosker; Chaplain, Rev. Joseph B. O'Hagen.

Non-Commissioned Staff.

Sergeant-major, Henry H. Lewis.

Quartermaster-sergeant, James T. Brady.

Drum-major, John Ross.

Fife-major, John McIntyre.

Company Commanders.

A, M. W. Burns,	- - . - - -	Hose 21.
B, Thomas Smith,	- .. - - -	Hose 56.
C, A. Gibson,	- .. .. -	Hook and Ladder 15.
D, Daniel Crowley,	- .. .. - -	Engine 20.
E, William M. Fisk,	- .. - -	- Engine 32.
F, Alfred A. Donald,	.. .. - -	Engine 17.
G, John Feeney,	- - - -	- Hose 50.
H, William McCaully,	.. .. - -	Engine 40.
I, Charles B. Elliott,	- .. -	Hose 7, Williamsburg.
K, Michael D. Purtell,	- - - -	————

Among the minor officers may be mentioned: Lieutenants William Gleeson, Engine 3; John J. Glass, Engine 16; Eugene C. Stine, Engine 31; John Phelan, Hose 10; Michael Feeny, Hose 6; Matthew Stewart, Hose 50; John T. Lawrence, Hose 11; Washington Mullen, Hose 22; John P. Skehan, Engine 20.

The State gave the regiment a tardy recognition, and, on November 27, 1861, issued commissions to the officers, and thenceforth the corps was known as the Seventy-third New York Volunteers. But the boys called themselves the Second Fire Zouaves to the end of their service. While they were at Camp McClellan, Good Hope, a delegation of New York firemen, headed by Chief Decker, visited them, and on October 17, 1861, presented them with a handsome stand of colors, the gift of the department. Early in November the regiment was ordered to Lomer, Maryland, about fifty miles below Washington, and detailed for picket duty on the banks of the Potomac. They crossed the river April 2, 1862, and made a raid on Stafford Court-house, where they destroyed a large amount of rebel stores. Closely pursued by the enemy, they recrossed the Potomac in good order under cover of their gunboats. Four days after the affair the regiment embarked in the steamer ' *Vanderbilt* ' for Yorktown. From Cheeseman's Creek, Virginia, they went to the front, and did picket duty in the trenches until May 4. It was a quiet Sunday morning when a negro clambered over the enemy's breastworks and told the Second Fire Zouaves that the greycoats were evacuating the town. The New York men dashed forward, and entered Yorktown in time to see the enemy retreating. Thomas

Madden, of Company H, secured the garrison flag, which the rebels had forgotten to take away. The trophy was sent to New York, where it remained for many years in the possession of Mr. Henry Jones, foreman of Engine No. 40. It is now the property of the Regimental Veteran Association, having been presented to them by Mr. Jones. In Townsend's "Records" of the First and Last Events of the War is the following:

"The first regiment to enter Yorktown and plant the Stars and Stripes on ramparts of the rebel works was the Seventy-third New York Volunteers, known as the Fourth Excelsior Regiment. Written on the wall of a deserted house in Yorktown was the cheering message, 'Yanks! we evacuate Yorktown to-day by order of our commander, but we will meet you to-morrow at Williamsburg.' Our heroes were on hand in Williamsburg the next day, and lost one hundred and fifty men on the field. Captain Feeney and Lieutenant Glass were among the killed. From that time until Lee's surrender

FIRE ZOUAVES: THEIR ENTRANCE INTO YORKTOWN.

the regiment got its share of every hard knock the Army of the Potomac received. They made a brilliant bayonet charge at Fair Oaks, June 1, which is thus mentioned in General McClellan's report:

"'General Sickles, having been ordered to the left, formed line of battle on both sides of the Williamsburg road and advanced under a sharp fire of the enemy deployed in the woods in front of Union. After a brisk countercharge of musketry fire while crossing the open ground, the Excelsior Brigade dashed into the timber with the bayonet, and put the enemy to flight. At Fair Oaks, June 15, the regiment was vigorously attacked during a severe thunderstorm. Company H bore the brunt of the rebel charge, and Captain McCaully was taken prisoner. Ten days later the Zouaves, who were in Hooker's division took part in the action at Oak Grove, which was brought about by the general advance of the Union lines."

McClellan's report contains these words: "If we succeed in what we have undertaken, it will be a very important advantage gained. Loss not large for the fighting up to this has been done by General Hooker's division, which has behaved as usual—that is, most splendidly." During the retreat from Richmond the regiment was engaged at Savage Station and Glendale. While the army was in camp at Harrison's Landing, the Zouaves fought under Hooker at Malvern Hill, August 5, 1862. During the night, Hooker, finding himself confronted by a superior force, withdrew. The Zouaves remained at Harrison's Landing until the army left the Peninsula, and on August 21 they embarked at Yorktown for Alexandria. Immediately they were sent to Pope; arrived in time to fight at Bristol Station on August 27. Here a third of the regiment fell. Captain Donalds and Lieutenant John McAllister (Engine No. 1, Williamsburg) were killed. At the second battle of Bull Run, (August 29, 1862), the battered regiment again crossed bayonets with the rebels. While they were advancing through the woods, the enemy fell upon their left flank and drove them back. The colors would have been taken had not Color-sergeant George Ramsay torn them from the staff and wrapped them about his body. Many Zouaves were taken prisoners. After the battle of Chantilly, September 1, the regiment went into camp near Alexandria, where several recruits from New York helped to fill the decimated companies. The muster rolls of November 1 show four hundred and eighteen men present for duty. From Alexandria the regiment was ordered to Falmuth, Va. It took part in the slaughter in Fredericksburg, and was stuck in the mud with the rest of Burnside's command during his famous march. Fredericksburg had again thinned the ranks, and at Falmuth on January 20, 1863, the One hundred and Sixty-third New York Volunteers were incorporated with the Fire Zouaves, bringing the strength up to five hundred and sixty-nine, as the muster rolls of March 1 show. On May 2 the fire laddies fought stubbornly at Chancellorsville, holding a position in the wood where Stonewall Jackson received his death-wound. Among the killed was Lieutenant Thomas Dennin (Engine 47).

After the battle the regiment went back to the camp at Falmuth, where it lay until the Pennsylvania campaign. At Gettysburg Colonel Brewster commanded the brigade, which was in the left of the line in Humphrey's division. The One Hundred and Fourteenth Pennsylvania was attacked by the Barksdale, Miss., brigade. Brewster ordered the Zouaves to support the Pennsylvanians at the Peach Orchard. The boys dashed forward into the smoke with a cheer. They went into the combat three hundred and twenty-four strong, and lost fifty-one killed, one hundred and three wounded, and eight prisoners. Captain E. C. Shine and Lieutenant W. L. Herbert, James Marksman and George C. Dennin were killed. July 23, 1863, found the Zouaves at Manassas Gap, where, with the rest of the Excelsior Brigade, under General Spinola, charged Wapping Heights. The regiment was on picket duty in the Rapidan until Lee forced Meade to fall back to Fairfax Court-house. November 7 the boys crossed the Rappahannock, and fought at Kelly's Ford. There they went into winter quarters at Brandy Station, and met the greycoats at Mine Run, November 27. After the action the regiment went back to winter quarters, where it remained until Spring. On January, 1864, three hundred and eighteen men were present for duty. Many of them re-enlisted, and went on furlough to New York, where their fellow firemen gave them a rousing reception.

The camp at Brandy Station was broken up May 1, 1864, and the regiment crossed the Rapidan. Grant was at the head of the army, and between the Wilderness and Cold Harbor the Zouaves saw plenty of hard fighting. Captains John Phelan, James McDermott, Michael D. Purtell and George L. Fort and Lieutenant B. Leonard were killed during the campaign. On the evening of June 15, the regiment entered the trenches in front of Petersburg, and were hotly engaged the next morning. Patrick Stack, of Engine 53, was the first man to fall. During the siege of Petersburg the regiment was continually on the move, taking part in most all the skirmishes in front of the stronghold. At Bull Run half of the regiment fell into the hands of the enemy, and the colors would have been taken had not the Color-Sergeant, Patrick Doyle, hidden them under his jacket. While the little band of Zouaves was returning through the mud to camp, the flag slipped unobserved from Doyle's person. He went back after it, and walked two miles without finding either the colors or any one who had picked them up. The cavalry picket refused to let him go further, as the enemy was close at hand. With a heart heavy as lead, Doyle walked towards the camp again. He had not gone five hundred yards, when, to his boundless joy, he found the dear blackened, tattered old flag buried in the mud, where one thousand soldiers had trodden it down.

On March 25, 1865, the regiment captured three officers and one hundred and twenty-four men at Hatcher's Run, while the One Hundred and Twenty-fourth New York and One Hundred and Tenth Pennsylvania and the Zouaves made a night attack April 1 and took many prisoners. They had their last march with the Rebels on the sixth. Three days later came the news of Lee's surrender. On June 29, the regiment, two hundred strong, was mustered out of a service in which it had spent four years, one month and seven days. It had fought gallantly at Stafford Court-

WILLIAM A. HACKETT.

house, Yorktown, Williamsburg, Seven Pines, Fair Oaks, Oak Grove, Savage Station, Glendale, Malvern Hill, Bristow Station, Second Bull Run, Chantilly, Fredericksburg, Chancellorsville, Gettysburg, Wapping Heights, Kelly's Ford, Mine Run, Wilderness, Spottsylvania, North Anna, Tolopotomy, Cold Harbor, Petersburg, Strawberry Plains, Deep Bottom and Boylston Road.

WILLIAM A. HACKETT.—At the breaking out of the War of Secession, William A. Hackett was among the first to volunteer his services to the Government as a soldier; was accepted, and assigned to the command of Company H, First Regiment, New York Fire Zouaves (afterwards known as the Eleventh New York Volunteers), under Colonel Elmer E. Ellsworth, which regiment left the city for the seat of war April 29, 1861.

William A. Hackett was born on the corner of Nassau and Liberty Streets, in the City of New York, on March 16, 1834, and became a member of the New York Volunteer Fire Department in 1851, having at that time joined Washington Engine Company No. 20, to which company he was strongly attached from early boyhood, an attachment he ever retained to an enthusiastic degree throughout his entire career as a fireman. His untiring devotion, never-failing attention to duty, and good judgment of fires, soon commanded the admiration of his associates, and he was unanimously elected to the foremanship while yet the youngest man among those on the roll of his company. Fire duty was his all-absorbing study through life, and were it not for his close application to fires, there is little reason to doubt he would have remained among us to this day in some active capacity not far removed from the present department. To enumerate the many noteworthy escapes, accidents, and incidents he experienced during his service would make a volume in itself. At the Jennings' fire on Broadway, where some thirteen firemen were killed by the falling of a heavy safe from one of the upper floors of the burning building, his escape was most miraculous. His labors at Penfold, Parker, and Moore's fire, in Beekman Street, where he was confined within the burning building for several hours, was an exhibition of endurance very few, if any, of his associates could have withstood ; and at the explosion during the progress of the fire in the bonded warehouse on Pearl Street, near State, where he received an injury of which he ever after complained, and it is believed was, to a great extent, instrumental in his untimely death. Mr. Hackett was elected in 1859 to the Engineer Board by a very flattering vote, a like honor being extended at every subsequent election up to the close of the Volunteer system.

"FOREVER FLOAT THAT STANDARD SHEET."

CHAPTER XLIII.

VARIOUS OLD FIRE HEADQUARTERS.

House in Fulton Street.—Old Building.—Site of Fireman's Hall.—Mercer Street Headquarters.—Laying of the Corner Stone.—Imposing Ceremonies.—Speech by Thomas Franklin.

THE first Fireman's Hall stood in Fair (now Fulton) Street, on the north side, just east of Gold Street. The entrance to the lot on which it stood was about twenty-five feet wide, and the building was located on the rear of the lot, and was one hundred feet deep, was much wider at the rear, tapering down to the entrance, and leaving a large courtyard in front. The building was very shallow, the engines not having much more than room to be run in. The companies had seats along the sides of their rooms, and when they held a meeting they would run their engine out in the yard. Two companies lay on each side of the entrance hall—Union 18 and Eagle 13, Jackson 24 and Fulton 21.

The corner stone of Fireman's Hall, Mercer Street, was laid on the twenty-first of August, 1854. Messrs. Field and Carreja drew the plans, under the direction of Mr. James L. Miller. The Building Committee were, James L. Miller, James F. Wenman, William D. Wade, John S. Belcher, and James Donohue. The occasion was observed as a holiday, and the order of the day was as follows:

The line formed four abreast at 2 P. M. in the Park, opposite the City Hall, the right on the east gate, and marched through Park Row, Broadway, Houston and Mercer Streets, to Fireman's Hall, in the following order: Grand Marshal, Zophar Mills; Special Aids, William A. Freeborn and Allen R. Jollie.

First Division.—John Barry, Marshal; Committee of Arrangements; Dodworth's Band; Fire Department Banner, in charge of Lafayette Engine Company No. 19; Officers and Trustees of the New York Fire Department; Chief and Assistant Engineers and Representatives of the New York Fire Department.

Second Division.—John T. Rollins, Marshal; Chairman of the Day, Adam P. Pentz; Chaplain, Reverend Isaac Ferris, D. D., Chancellor of the New York University; Orator, Hon. Morris Franklin; His Honor, the Mayor, Jacob A. Westervelt; Exempt Firemen's Association.

Third Division.—Samuel Waddell, Marshal; the Honorable, the Board of Aldermen, with their officers; the Honorable, the Board of Councilmen, with their officers; the Architects and Builders of the Hall.

Fourth Division.—Daniel Cogar, Marshal; Governors of the Alms House; Commissioners of Emigration; Heads of Departments and their Bureaus; County Officers; Members of the Press.

Fifth Division.—Owen W. Brennan, Marshal; Collector of the Port; Surveyor; Naval Officer; Assistant Treasurer of the United States; the United States District Attorney and Marshal; Members of Congress; Judges of the United States Courts; Judges of the Supreme and Superior Courts of Common Pleas; Judges of Marine, Police and District Courts.

Sixth Division.—John P. Lacour, Marshal; National Guard Band; Ex-Officers and Trustees of Fire Department; Ex-Chiefs and Assistant Engineers of Fire Department; Foremen, Assistant Foremen and Secretaries of the various Fire Companies.

Seventh Division.—Samuel M. Phillips, Marshal; Board of Fire Wardens; Members of the New York Fire Department, citizens, etc.

Committee of Arrangements: From Representatives—David P. Nivin, James L. Miller, Isaac G. Seixas, John S. Belcher, John B. Miller, Charles McDougall, president; John J. Tindale, vice-president; William D. Wade, secretary. From the Board of Foremen —John B. Leverich, Daniel Stanbury, John Gilleland, Daniel McGarvey, Henry Barrow, Alfred Carson, chief engineer; James F. Wenman, secretary.

Firemen's Hall was erected on lots Nos. 127 and 129 Mercer Street. These lots were formerly occupied by the old Firemen's Hall and the city oil house. The building from front to rear is ninety-five feet, the breadth forty-one feet, height of front elevation, fifty-five feet from the level of the sidewalk. The building is three stories high above the cellar. The

FIRST FIREMEN'S HALL.
[Fulton Street, 1824.]

first story was originally appropriated to the use of Hose Company No. 5 and Lafayette Hook and Ladder Company No. 6—the former on the south side and the latter on the north side of the main entrance. Each company occupied a space fifteen by ninety feet, which was divided into three rooms, the front room for the apparatus, the center room for their meetings, and the room in the rear for sitting and reading. The main entrance hall is eight feet in width, and is divided from the stairs by a pair of folding doors, which form a large receiving vestibule.

The second story is thirty feet in heighth and contains three rooms. One large room is for the meeting of the representatives, the engineers and foremen, and the Exempt Firemen's Association; this room is thirty-eight feet wide and seventy-one feet deep; it is ventilated, having large windows on all sides, and the side walls recede from the adjoining buildings three feet. On each side of the stairway is a room fifteen feet by twenty feet for committee rooms. The third story is fifteen feet in heighth, and contains the same number of rooms, and of the same size as the second story. The large room was used for a library and reading room, and the small rooms for the librarian and committees. All the rooms above the first story are heated with hot-air furnaces. The front of the building is Connecticut brown stone, cut in the best manner. The style of architecture is Italian, or in other words a composition of Greek and Roman details applied by the Italians to modern buildings. The outer angles are formed with rusticated quoins. The doors and windows are trimmed with architraves, pilasters, and cornices, supported on ornamental brackets.

SECOND FIREMEN'S HALL.
[Site of Mercer Street Headquarters.]

The two vertical lines of pillars extend the height of the elevation on each side of the entrance doorway and the center windows. Upon the face of these autaes on the first story is cut in relief the emblems of the Fire Department, such as hooks and ladders, torches, axes, trumpets, etc., and the tops of these autaes are surmounted with a fire hydrant. The name of the building, "Firemen's Hall" is cut on the stone over the second story windows.

The main corner of the front is an elaborated pattern, and is supported by heavy truss brackets. On the top of the cornice is a blocking course with three pedestals, the two side ones surmounted with a cluster of torches, and the center one with the full size statue of a fireman, the same one that had stood so many years in front of the old hall.

In a semi-circular arch over the front entrance door there is carved in *bas relief* the figures of Protection and Benevolence, as represented on the imitation certificate of the Old New York Fire Department, and upon the keystone of the arch is cut a full-size fire-cap. The whole building is constructed in the most substantial manner.

The plans for the building were drawn under the direction of James L. Miller, the chairman of the Building Committee, for the Board of Representatives, by Messrs. Field and Correja, architects, the same gentlemen to whom was awarded the first premium for the plans of the new City Hall, by the unanimous vote of the Common Council Committee.

The estimates were advertised for and awarded to the lowest bidder, as follows:

Messrs. Platt & Fisher, for the mason work..............$13,311
Mr. James L. Miller, for the carpenter work.............. 11,500
————————
Total...$24,811

The stone cutting was sub-contracted to Messrs. Gayette & McGarigal, two enterprising young firemen who had been but a short time in business, but who had given evidence of their superior ability on several engine and hose houses previously erected.

The iron work was from the works of Messrs. Cornell, the painting by Mr. James Gilmore, the carved work by Mr. Dewitt C. Mott, and the ornamental plastering by Mr. Andrew J. Garvey.

After the establishment of the Paid Fire Department, the Fire Headquarters at various times underwent many alterations in its interior construction, leaving it, when it was vacated for the new up-town building, a different structure to what it was at the beginning of its history.

Mr. Morris Franklin, the orator of the day, was foreman of Engine Company No. 25, son of a chief engineer of the department, and at various times had been a Whig assemblyman and senator, assistant alderman, alderman, and president of the Board of Aldermen. His oration covered many pathetic historical incidents of the department, of which the following are extracts:

" The laying of the corner stone of this building is an interesting era in the history of the department, and I am glad to be informed that accommodations are now to be provided adequate to the wants of those to whose services it is hereafter to be dedicated; yet there are associations which force themselves upon the mind upon such an occasion, mingled with emotions of pleasure and pain; for when we look back upon the old Firemen's Hall in Fulton Street, and that which has given place to the present structure, and call to our recollection the countenances of those whom we have so often met within their halls, and taken sweet counsel together, it seems like parting with an old friend, and we can but drop a tear over the knowledge of the fact that, while in our daily walks we meet many of those who, with us, occupied the former, yet how many have long since paid the last debt to nature, while others are scattered over the world, far distant from the familiar scenes of their early life, and perhaps, forgetful of those who were once their associates and friends. In those days, party politics disturbed not the deliberation of the representatives, nor entered into the considerations of their conclusions, but with one heart and one mind connected the general interest with the public good, and cemented together the ties of mutual responsibilities, determined to be foremost in the discharge of their respective duties. Let but such feelings as these continue to animate your exertions, and we shall no longer be pained with the reports which too often reach our ears, emanating from the chief of the department, of the bitter hostilities which so often prevail between the members of different companies. Then the reputation of the association would resume its former proud prominence, and the badge of a fireman be a sure and certain passport to the confidence and respect of all classes of the community. Then the spirits of our departed associates, if permitted to mingle in the things of life, and to watch the movements of the lower world, would rejoice over the prosperity of an institution which in the day of their pilgrimage constituted their ambition and their pride. With such feelings and desires, I most ardently commend the members of this department to the care and protection of the Almighty Power, without whose sleepless eye the watchman waketh but in vain, and who, through your instrumentality, can alone stay the progress of destruction, and say to the devouring element, ' Peace, be still !' "

" Among the most pleasing recollections of my early days are those which are connected with the Fire Department of our city, and although many of those who were then my companions and friends have long slumbered beneath the cold clods of the valley, and but few, if any, are now in the ranks of active duty, yet I rejoice in the opportunity of renewing my association with those who are emphatically the guardians of our safety and the bulwark and boast of our city.

" My earliest recollections of the department carry me back to the time when the bright calmness of a Sabbath morning was interrupted by the shrill sound of the old Bridewell bell, and the thickening smoke which gathered over the city, betokening the origin of that destructive conflagration which, in a few short hours, laid waste upwards of one hundred buildings in Chatham Street and vicinity, causing a vast amount of suffering among the poorer classes of our population, who at that time occupied that section of the city. Upon that occasion many of our valiant firemen, under the oppressive heat of the weather and continued exertion and exposure during the entire day and part of the succeeding night, became utterly exhausted, and were carried to their homes by their more fortunate companions, and some of them laid the foundation for a premature and early grave. It is true that at that time I was but a child, but it is impressed upon my memory by the fact that my venerated parent was among the number of those who, in the hour of their enthusiasm, forgot everything connected with personal safety in the faithful discharge of an arduous duty, and who, in an effort to pass through one of the narrow streets, the buildings on either side of which were then on fire, fell exhausted in the attempt and must inevitably have perished had not some kind and faithful friends rescued him from impending death by conveying him safely from the scene of danger and laying him upon his couch at home. In looking back upon the past, fond memory recalls to mind the names of some of those who, having occupied prominent positions in the front ranks of the department, and performed well their parts, have been gathered to their fathers, where no bell disturbs their sleeping and no alarm breaks upon the stillness of their graves; some have passed away by the gradual decay of nature in a good old age, some have prematurely ripened for an early tomb, and some have fallen victims at the post of danger.

" We can sigh over the mouldering remains of a Brown, a Franklin, a Strong, a Hobbs, and a Cox, and drop a tear or two over the too early graves of a Ryker, a Hoffmire and a Williams. We can refer to the sad calamity which caused the death of Peterson, whose banner, dedicated to the memory of departed worth, yet holds a prominent position in every parade of the department ; to the period of 1827, when a Raynor and a Joseph fell ; to the fires of 1832 and 1834, which resulted in the sudden deaths of Garrison, Brown, Hedges and Knapp ; to the sad disaster when an Underhill and a Ward were buried beneath the ruins of the Pearl Street fire ; to 1835, 1836 and 1837, when Ritchie, Horton and Bucklow were numbered among the victims of those years; to the excitement of 1840, when Wells and Glasgow sacrificed their lives ; to 1845 when Cowdrey died ; to 1848, when the deaths of the lamented Kerr, Farges and Durant cast a solemn gloom over our city, as in one sad procession

we followed two of them to the tomb ; to the times when Evans and Trenchard swelled the number of the victims at the shrine of duty; and I might lift the veil and point on to the mangled remains of those who were so recently sacrificed at the falling of the Broadway building, but I will not open afresh the yet bleeding wounds of the survivors, who will never cease to remember the agony of that dreadful night, and who should hold to strict accountability the authors of their calamity. The names and memory of those who have just fallen while in the service of the department are perpetuated upon the marble monument which stands as a conspicuous object upon the heights of Greenwood. Among the many interesting incidents connected with the early history of this department, the mind dwells with peculiar pleasure upon one which those who were witnesses of the scene will never cease to remember—I refer to the visit of the venerable and beloved Lafayette, who fre-

FACE OF PANEL ON OLD FIREMEN'S HALL, MERCER STREET.

quently recounted as among the gratifying circumstances of that visit his review and examination of the firemen and apparatus, and I well remember as he walked with slow and measured steps along the line, leaning upon the arm of our chief, and receiving the cheers of those who were arranged around the park in anticipation of his approach. The tear of affection kindled in his eye as he grasped the hands of those who stood in advance of their respective companies, and bade him welcome to our shores. When the review was ended, and the gallant general retired from the ranks, the cheers of the united multitude made the welkin ring, while streams from every engine presented a hydraulic display worthy of the occasion and the man. Carry your thoughts back, my friends, but a few short years and visit the field in which this department has been called upon to operate in contending with some of the most disastrous fires recorded in the annals of our history. Among the temples dedicated to our holy religion which have been swept away by the devouring element even within our own time, you may remember the fall of the Beekman Street Church, the burning spire of Wall Street, Zion's Church in Mott Street, the South Dutch in the memorable fire of 1835, the French in Franklin, the Synagogue in Canal, the Baptist in Oliver, Christ Church in Anthony, the Methodist in John Street, Thomas in Broadway, and recently the Central Presbyterian in Broome Street. Among the favorite and popular places of amusement, too, the fires within our recollection have been disastrous. Most of us can remember the destruction of the Mount Pitt Circus, the Laurens Street Theater, the Bowery upon several occasions, the Park, twice Niblo's, the most new and splendid opera house on the corner of Church and Leonard Streets, and though last, not least, the favorite temple within whose walls astonished thousands have so often listened to the sweet warbling of the Northern Nightingale. Besides these, and many others which may have escaped my recollection, almost innumerable have been the fires against which the department have had to contend, and how well and effectually they have performed their duty the universal applause of an appreciating and grateful people most abundantly testifies.

It is true that instances occurred in which the help of man seemed almost powerless for a time to arrest the progress of destruction and to stay the fury of the devouring element, but they have generally been owing to a combination of peculiar circumstances over which the firemen had no control, and for which they could not be held responsible; for it is not too much to say that there is no class of our fellow citizens to which we are more largely indebted for the preservation of our firesides and our homes than to these most valuable of men who this day celebrate the laying of the corner-stone of a building to be devoted to the services of the Fire Department of our city. Previous to the introduction of croton water, in 1842, our only resource was to the very inadequate supply of the fire-plugs, which were scattered throughout the densely populated portions of the city, and connected with the old Manhattan Works in Chambers Street, and subsequently with the reservoir in Thirteenth Street; the comparatively small cisterns in front of many of the public buildings; the old supply engine upon that part of the grounds now occupied by the Tombs; the float at the foot of Roosevelt Street, and our two noble rivers. In those days no district bell announced the location of the fires, and no boundaries short of the entire island marked the calls of duty; but when the alarm was sounded the whole department was aroused, and from one extreme of the city to the other, from the Battery to Harlem, and from the North to the East Rivers, they were required, promptly, to respond, frequently running many a weary mile, and exhausted long before arriving at the cause of alarm, for then no index but the pointing from the City Hall and the cupolas of the few remotely scattered watchhouses guided their nightly wanderings, and during the day they were obliged to rely upon the best information which could be obtained, oftentimes very contradictory and uncertain. Then, as was not unfrequently the case, it required nearly one-half of the strength of the

Department to force a single stream upon the fire, and I now recollect one instance in which water was conveyed, through a line of about fifty engines, from the East River to the vicinity of the Bowery, calling into requisition the services of nearly one thousand men, and requiring an immense amount of labor

FIREMEN'S HALL.
[155 Mercer Street.]

to stay the progress of destruction. It was in times like these, and during the intense cold of a December night, that the destructive fire at Crane's Wharf, the present site of Fulton Market, swept with fury the buildings in that neighborhood; and many of you may remember that the large and valuable stock of good old Bloodgood's wines furnished fuel for the flames. The burning of the cotton stores on South Street was also in the midst of winter, requiring nearly thirty-six hours' labor of the firemen before the entire department was dismissed. The ropewalk fire, in the far suburbs of the city, broke out during the meridian sun of a summer's Sabbath day, and many who started at the alarm fell

. exhausted ere they reached the scene. The chemical works in Broadway, then far beyond the limits of our thickly populated streets, the Exchange Buildings on William Street, and many others which might be referred to, will call to your minds an association of ideas which neither time nor the occasion will permit me to dwell or enlarge upon; but they will tend to show the impediments under which the firemen labored before the organization of the present system. The more recent conflagrations of 1835 and 1845, in which twenty-seven million dollars' of property was destroyed; the burning of the Harper's mammoth establishment, and the sad destruction of the '*Joseph Walker*' and the '*Great Republic*,' and the yet more awful tragedy at Jennings', are of such comparatively recent occurrence that I need only refer to them to recall vividly to your minds the circumstances connected with the disaster. But it is not only in the hour of danger that the department is the subject of comment and admiration, for in all the prominent civic proceedings for which this city is justly celebrated, it has always formed a prominent and important part, and is relied upon by the municipal authorities to swell the pageant and increase the enthusiasm upon such occasions. Among the many thousands who participated in 1825 in the celebration of the completion of the Erie Canal, no class of our fellow citizens entered more ardently into the popular feeling consequent upon the complete success of that mighty work, which mingled the waters of the ocean with the lakes, and none contributed more to give an *eclat* to the occasion than the firemen of our city. When in 1842 the waters of the Croton were introduced into our metropolis, all classes of its population participated in the celebration of an event so intimately connected with the prosperity of our city; but to none did it present more pleasing anticipations than those who had so often realized their entire dependence upon a full and permanent supply in the prompt and efficient discharge of their hazardous and important duties. It was, therefore, justly expected that, upon such an occasion, not only the strength, but the beauty of the department, would occupy a prominent position in the line of procession, and such expectations were more than realized, for the mounted engines, handsomely decorated, drawn by horses richly caparisoned—the numerous appropriate banners belonging to the various companies, including the one which had been presented them for the occasion, the bands of music dispersed throughout the line, but above all the general appearance and perfect order of the men, presented a display which was the admiration of strangers and the justly boasted comments of our citizens.

VOLUNTEER APPARATUS.

CHAPTER XLIV.

BALLS AND ASSOCIATIONS.

Some of the Brilliant Annual Entertainments of the Old Department.—Wealth, Fashion and Beauty at the Terpsichorean Entertainments.—All for Charity.—Organizations that were Concurrent with the Fire Companies.—Target Practice.—The Gulick Guards and Others.—Chowder Parties.—What the Old Boys did with Themselves after their Disbandment.

AT the beginning of the present century the Fire Department was in very fair working order, so far as the men and discipline were concerned. Soon the members followed the example of military and other organizations and celebrated annually the establishment of their Department. The ball was considered the best form of celebration, and in time became one of the most notable events in city life. The Benefit Fund was the beneficiary of these entertainments, which were got up in the very best style. Ladies and gentlemen of wealth and position attended, and often the reunions were quite exclusive in character. Some of the finest entertainments the city has seen took place at various times in the Park Theater on Park Row, Niblo's, the Academy of Music and the Astor Place Opera House. The world of fashion, which is seldom or never eager about anything, seemed to be eager to attend these gatherings, and often thirty dollars were paid for the price of a ticket. The price at the first ball was two dollars, afterwards it was twelve dollars. Every one had to pay—there was no complimentary list. As one of the newspapers remarked in 1859, these balls were gotten up by a committee of the oldest and most respected firemen, who carefully guarded "against the slightest possible indecorum." Every gentleman came in full evening dress, and as a matter of course the ladies endeavored to outvie each other in the brilliancy of their toilet. The first ball took place in the Bowery Theatre in 1828, and the magnificence of this entertainment was a fitting beginning to a long series of brilliant events of the same kind. Every company was eager to contribute something, and on the night previous the decoration committee used to take possession of the theater, and worked incessantly almost up to the opening hour of the ball. The ball tickets were very elaborate cards of artistic design. One of the handsomest was printed on the occasion of the ball which took place at the National Opera House on January 25, 1841.

The twenty-fifth annual ball, which took place at Niblo's on January 23, 1854, was one of the brightest and most beautiful of these events. The parquet of the opera house was boarded over for the dancers, and around the wall flowers and Venetian mirrors were arranged in an artistic and tasteful manner—the whole covered by an immense parti-colored tent. On ascending the staircase another large ballroom was to be found. To this room other and smaller ones adjoined, forming suites of elegantly furnished apartments, affording rest and quiet to those weary of dancing. The galleries were thronged with visitors, and it was estimated that three thousand persons were present. The supper was said to satisfy even the most fastidious. The proceeds of the ball amounted to three thousand eight hundred and thirty-nine dollars and five cents.

The twenty-ninth annual ball was held at the Academy of Music on January 25, 1858. The house was handsomely decorated. At the extreme end of the stage, within an enclosure, were arranged the apparatus of No. 1 Eagle Hose Company, No. 1 Adriatic Engine Company, and No. 7 Ringgold Company. In front of these upon one side were a splendid model of Engine No. 19, a miniature engine, hose carriage, hook and ladder, firemen's caps, trumpets, etc., worked in gold. On the other side was a statue representing a fireman in the act of rescuing a child from a burning building, and a model of Hook and Ladder No. 9, wrought in ivory. Just beyond the rail enclosing these were handsome gas decorations, with the sentence in blazing letters, "New York Fire Department." The stage was canopied over, and in the center, suspended

from the ceiling, was the banner of the department. The fronts of the galleries were tastefully festooned with wreaths of flowers, interwoven with groups of trumpets, axes, torches, trucks and other apparatus of firemen. From the upper tier were suspended numerous banners belonging to various companies. The floor and the private boxes were crowded. Dodworth's band furnished the music. The

BALL TICKET.

receipts amounted to four thousand seven hundred and forty-four dollars and ten cents. The following are the names of the officers: Door and Police Committee (pink badge)—Henry A. Burr, chairman, C. V. Anderson, A. P. Pentz, John Coger, Jr., O. W. Brennan, Peter W. Titus, J. G. Keater, H. L. Butler, Lorenzo Delmonico, A. J. Delatour, Daniel Stanbury, Daniel T. Willets, C. McDougall, W. A. Woodhull, C. C. Pillow. Floor Managers (white badge)—Robert McGinnis, chairman, Henry B. Venn, D. D. Conover, C. H. Ring, James Y. Watkins, Edgar E. Holley, John G. Fisher, Jacob Ostrom, W. S. O'Brien, H. M. Graham, Samuel Waddell, James F. Wenman, W. D. Baker, S. Burkhalter, Jr., Lawrence Taylor, Alonzo Slote, Noah L. Farnham, and T. S. Thornell. Saloon Committee (blue badge)—William S. Bates, chairman, James L. Miller, John S. Belcher, John Garcia, Ralph Trembly, J. J. Westray and Josiah Hedden.

In the following year the annual ball was held at the same place on Monday, January 24. The stage was enclosed in an immense marqué, with spacious balconies on three sides. There was on exhibition, among the ornaments, the engine of Columbia Company No. 14, just as it was received from Philadelphia a few days previous, whither it had been sent to be rebuilt. It was held to be a splendid specimen of mechanism, the brass and iron work glittering in the gaslight, and the polished panels resplendent with the limner's art. Among the decorations center pieces of radiated hose pipe shone like rays from the various points. Up in the second tier of boxes one hundred musicians were placed, but the music of their brazen instruments sounded soft and sweet through the vast auditorium. At ten o'clock there were nearly five thousand persons in the building. It was calculated that nearly five thousand dollars were realized. The *Tribune* next morning said: "The floor was full of stalwart, robust men, and healthy, roseate women, and the galleries were crowded with spectators. What with flashing lights, bright-hued dresses, ruddy cheeks and sparkling eyes, brimful of hope and happiness, it was truly a scene to kindle the warmest emotions."

The ball that took place on February 28, 1867, at the Academy of Music, was among the most notable. The *Herald*, describing the decorations, said: "The background of the *mise-en-scene* was formed of an appropriate painting, of rather Gothic, *ensemble*, representing a solitary castle upon the top of a lofty crag, and lighted at the windows as if cataracts of fire were about to burst therefrom and flood the Academy within. Beyond this the whole decorative system was conceived and carried out upon the single idea of the modulation of light and the compelling of the gas imp to wreath fantastic forms and mottoes in red letters, which should be expressive of the purpose of the ball and the benevolent aim which had called the guests together. It was in front of this painting over the stage that the principal device of illumination was located. From beneath a huge gas pipe had been caused to rise, like the body of a serpent, through the flooring, and as if for the head of this serpent, at a point ten feet above, where the flooring had been broken into, numerous small pipes, out of which, wreathed and twisted together, was formed an engine of gas jets, which, an hour later, flickered and blazed uneasily upon the moving forms of the dancers beneath them." The crush at this ball was almost unprecedented, and was the talk of the town for days after. Five thousand three hundred and seventy-two dollars and eighty-three cents were netted.

The fortieth annual ball was held on January 25, 1869, at the Academy of Music. In front of the balcony was a well-designed representation of a hose carriage brightly gleaming and typifying the machinery and brilliancy with which the working of the Old Department was accompanied. In elegance and tastefulness it was said this ball surpassed any of the season. The "Vets" came in large numbers. The floor committee were Messrs. Frederick White, Daniel D. Conover, James Y. Watkins, J. Guion Fisher, James L. Miller, John J. Westray, Martin V. B. Smith, James Cameron, John W. Cox, Wm. H. Blague, Wilton F. Kirtz, Wm. H. Pegg, Wm. S. O'Brien, Frank Foster, Wm. M. Randell, Geo. F. Nesbitt, Jr., Adolphus F. Pohle, and Thos. H. Jenkins. The guests were attended to by Messrs. William H. Wickham, Henry B. Venn, Charles Delmonico, Joshua S. Morley, Robert McGinnis, J. Corbey Perrin, Jr., and Sam. A. Besson. The order committee consisted of Messrs. James F. Wenman, Owen W. Brennan, Lorenzo Delmonico, Wm. S.

Bates, Albert J. Delatour, Dan. F. Willets, Alonzo Slote, Robert C. Brown, Wm. H. Stodart, Jordan L. Mott, Daniel Plole, C. Godfrey Gunther, Cornelius C. Poillon, Edgar F. Lasak, and Wm. C. Conover. Five thousand four hundred and sixty-six dollars and sixty-one cents were realized.

The Academy of Music was crowded again on January 31, 1870, with the wealth, industry, intelligence, and enterprise of New York, on the occasion of the forty-first annual ball. Almost all of those mentioned above were present. The decorations were handsome, and among them was a full view of the museum near Spring Street on the morning after the fire, the front covered with icicles, and sheets of crystal hung as a drop at the rear of the stage. In front of this, in jets of fire, was a ribbon enclosing the title of the ball, and below a representation of the old style hose carriage. About eleven o'clock Prince Arthur (who was visiting America) arrived with his suite: Messrs. Thornton, Archibald, Thane, French, and Elphinstone, all in full evening dress. They were escorted to the chief proscenium box at the right of the hall, and as they entered, the word went like wildfire through the house that the prince was present. All eyes were turned toward the box, and as he approached the front a general and spontaneous reception was given, the gentlemen clapping their hands and the ladies waving their handkerchiefs. He acknowledged the salute by kissing his hand and bowing, and then sat down and gazed awhile on the merry dancers. At the close of the dance the prince descended to the floor and took part in the promenade. Grafulla's orchestra struck up " Love among the roses." Shortly after midnight he retired. The following was the form of invitation sent to the prince :

NEW YORK FIREMEN'S BALL COMMITTEE.

Compliments to his Royal Highness, Prince Arthur, and respectfully invite him to their Forty-first Annual Ball in aid of the Widows' and Orphans' Fund, at the Academy of Music, on Tuesday evening, January 31, 1870.

JAMES F. WENMAN, FRED. WHITE, JORDAN L. MOTT, ALONZO SLOTE, *Committee.*

The highest amount netted by these balls was six thousand two hundred and forty-four dollars, in 1868. After this year the receipts steadily declined until in 1873 only one thousand dollars were realized. In forty-three years, from 1830 to 1873, the total net receipts were one hundred and twenty-five thousand, nine hundred and twenty-eight dollars and thirty-seven cents. The last ball took place in 1875 at the Academy of Music. Mr. James F. Wenman had always been conspicuous on these occasions, and he, on the last, led the grand opening march. The dresses of the ladies were remarkable for beauty, and the whole scene was one of unusual brilliancy. Banners that had figured for years in many a parade adorned the proscenium boxes, and here and there were firemen's axes, trumpets, and other apparatus, all intertwined with fragrant flowers and handsome vases. One of the striking features of the event was the illumination by thirty-five thousand gas jets, which illumined the representation of a hose carriage and truck in front of the stage. In the background was a painting of the 1835 fire. Although it was the night of a blinding snow-storm, the number present was unusually great.

The ball committee was composed of the gentlemen whose names are given above. After 1873 the committee gave other entertainments, such as excursions and concerts. The concert they organized in the Academy of Music on October 2, 1878, for the benefit of the yellow fever sufferers, was attended by eight

thousand persons.   Nearly five thousand five hundred dollars were realized.
Dodworth's and Grafulla's bands assisted, and among the singers and instru-
mentalists were Mlle. Ilma de Murska, Signor Tagliapietra, and Levy, the cor-
netist.

Besides the grand annual ball of the department, the individual companies
gave balls, to the expenses of which the members contributed ten dollars, five
dollars, or three dollars, as they were able.

One of the notable features of the Old Department was the number of social
organizations which sprang from it.   The men were not merely satisfied with
being banded together for the protection of life and property from fire, but
desired to form clubs and societies outside of the jurisdiction of the department.   These organizations took the form of target companies, chowder clubs,

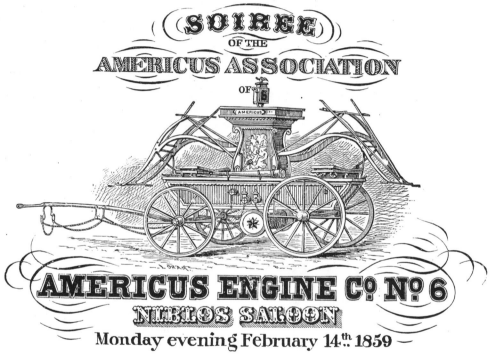

SOIREE OF THE AMERICUS ASSOCIATION OF
AMERICUS ENGINE Cº Nº 6
NIBLOS SALOON
Monday evening February 14.ᵗʰ 1859

BALL TICKET : AMERICUS ENGINE COMPANY NO. 6.

and so on.   The idea was to perpetuate the good fellowship which arose in the
engine house.   The associations gave opportunity for agreeable relaxation
after the arduous duties of the department had been attended to, and the
excursions and parties were participated in by friends of the members.   They
are by no means an insignificant part of the social history of the people of New
York, and therefore should have some notice in a work of this kind.   Below is
a pretty full list of these clubs, with the name of the captain or leader who has
been identified with them.   Engine Company No. 33 (Black Joke), be it noted,
has the honor of having been the first company to inaugurate a target
excursion :

From Engine Companies.—No. 1, Hudson Guards, John K. Oliver ; No. 2,
Excelsior Guards, John McDermott ; No. 3, Metamora Guards, James Martin ;

No. 3, Forrest Guards, John Gaville; No. 3, Hope Guards, F. Breman; No. 6, Americus Guards, J. H. Johnson; No. 6, W. M. Tweed Guards, Augustus Oliver; No. 6, Gouverneur Blues, John Casilear and Wm. Gayte; No. 8, Manhattan Guards; No. 9, Marion Volunteers, John A. Dunn; No. 9, Marion Guards, James Hayes; No. 9, Talcott Guards, Seth R. Abrams; No. 11, Oceanus Guards, John Wildey; No. 12, Knickerbocker Guards, G. J. Brown; No. 12, Tradesmen's Guards, A. H. Mitchell; No. 13, Eagle Guards, Con. Donovan; No. 14, Independence Guards, A. H. Tyler; No. 15, Wilson Guards; No. 15, Petersen Guards, Sam. Jackson; No. 16, Croton Guards, Mose Jackson; No. 16, Mitchell Guards, Stephen Mitchell; No. 16, Wilson Guards, John Slowey; No. 19, Edward Walsh Battalion, James Flood; No. 19, Lafayette Volunteers, George Borstman; No. 20, Clayton Guards, Wm. Hackett; No. 20, Washington Guards, —— Hasson; No. 24, Jackson Guards, Timothy Carroll; No. 26, Jefferson Blues, Robert Smack; No. 29, Guardian Guards, Eugene Ward; No. 30, Tompkins Blues; No. 30, James Irwin Guards; No. 32, Bunker Hill Volunteers, Wm. Fiske; No. 32, Subterranean Guards, Wm. McKibben; No. 33, Black Joke Volunteers, James Buckridge and John Quinn; No. 34, Red Rover Guards; No. 34, Howard Guards, Charles Miller; No. 34, Broderick Guards, S. M. Phillips; No. 39, Franklin Guards, P. Black; No. 40, Gentlemen's Sons, Joe Hutton; No. 41, Clinton Guards, Dennis Kehoe, James Little and Henry Lewis; No. 44, Live Oak Volunteers, Robert Gray and J. C. Harrison; No. 44, Turk's Island Guards, Henry Munn; No. 46, Relief Guards, J. Irving; No. 46, Independent Relief Guards; No. 46, Valley Forge Guards, James Brown; No. 49, Pocahontas Guards, Stephen L. Finley.

From Hose Companies.—No. 1, Eagle Guards, Joseph Cannon; No. 1, Eagle Cadets; No. 6, Independent Gouverneur Blues, Daniel Sarven and James Brown; No. 7, Ringgold Guards; No. 11, Varian Guards; No. 12, Washington Guards, Larry Orson, Joseph R. Riley, and S. Duffin; No. 13, Jackson Volunteers, Andrew Gloar; No. 15, Lindsey Blues, Edgar Roberts; No. 15, Hopkins Light Guards; No. 16, Tompkins Guards, Ed. Bonnoll; No. 17, Clinton Guards, Silas Lyng; No. 17, Anderson Guards, E. Malaly; No. 21, Hudson Guards, Wm. Cullen; No. 21, Hudson Blues, —— Hoyt; No. 22, Phenix Guards, W. R. W. Chambers; No. 24, National Guards, C. L. Robinson; No. 25, McKinley Guard; No. 26, Rutger and Van Buren Guard, James Wilkinson; No. 26, Tremendous Curbstone Light Infantry Fantasticals, Ed. Shandley; No. 29, Union Volunteers, Chas. E. Bell; No. 31, Putnam Guards, Jesse Thomas and Thos. Sullivan; No. 32, Johnson Guards; No. 33, Independent Warren Guards, A. S. Barnett; No. 33, Warren Guards, H. Dennett; No. 34, Star Volunteers, Scott Gunyon and L. Kerr; No. 35, Britton Guards, M. J. Conley; No. 39, Carson Guards, Gilbert C. Dean; No. 40, Empire Guards, Wm. C. Rogers and John Kettleman; No. 41, Alert Guards, Thos. Mitchell; No. 44, Washington Irving, Alex. Smith.

From Hook and Ladder Companies.—No. 1, Chelsea Guards, Stephen Mitchell; No. 3, Redfield Guards; No. 4, Eagle Guards, Harry Morris, Joseph Curtis, W. Rice, and Thos. Wilding; No. 5, Union (German), Peter Wannemacker and Geo. Kelling; No. 8, Empire Guards, John Seupert; No. 14, Columbia Guards, —— Wright; No. 15, Baxter Guards, John McCauley and Mark Thomas.

Handsome and often costly prizes were given for the best marksmen, and a degree of efficiency and discipline was attained that would do credit to the regular soldiers of an army.

The Gulick Guards were organized October 17, 1835, and during their existence sustained a high reputation for their drill and discipline. They first paraded in firemen's uniform, but later, in 1838 and 1839, they adopted a different uniform, and were finally attached to the Second Regiment N. Y. S. M., as an independent company. They numbered from one hundred to one hundred and twenty-five men, and were the outgrowth of No. 40 Engine Company. They had their yearly encampment, and were famous among the militia companies of the day. The first captain was John C. Helms. John Carland, the popular foreman of Lady Washington Engine Company No. 40, was his successor, and Gilbert C. Deane was the last captain of the Gulick Guards. The well-known Henry S. Mansfield, of Columbia Hose Company No. 9, and afterwards one of the organizers of United States Engine Company No. 9, was a lieutenant; and James Elkins, who was assistant foreman of Lady Washington Engine Company No. 40, and later foreman of Independence Hose Company No. 3, was also a lieutenant. James Bostwick, of Lady Washington Engine Company No. 40, was orderly sergeant. Moses O. Allen, of Hope Engine Company No. 31, and afterwards foreman of Independence Hose Company No. 3, was a sergeant; and James F. Wenman—a son of Uzziah Wenman, formerly chief engineer of the Fire Department, a gentleman of the old school, an associate of Thomas Frank-

BALL TICKET OF FULTON ENGINE COMPANY.

lin, Jamieson Cox, and firemen of the like stamp—who was foreman of New York Hose Company No. 5 and afterwards an assistant engineer, was likewise a sergeant. He was ever an active fireman, and is to-day a member of the Veteran Firemen's Association. Mr. Wenman and Mr. Allen were secretaries of the Gulick Guards. Nicholas Bello was also a sergeant. The Gulick Guards were not mere sunshine soldiers—they exercised not only in the drill room and streets, but camped out for a week in each year, and were thoroughly instructed in the practical life of a soldier. These encampments were in various sections; they went into camp at New Rochelle, Catskill, Hyde Park, and Keyport. During these encampments they were visited by many Gothamites, who wanted to see how the boys looked under canvas. The visitors were hospitably entertained—put through the awkward squad, and given to understand that they could not play off any of their practical jokes on old soldiers. The Gulick Guards paraded on all military occasions, with the Second Regiment, and Colonel Spicer considered them the crack company of the regiment. At the time of the anti-rent war they volunteered their services to the State, and held themselves in readiness to march with the regiment. They were not called into the field on this occasion, as the order for the military was afterwards countermanded. Their first uniform was, fire-coat of blue pilot cloth, with pants of the same material, white cross-belts, fire-cap skull with brass peak and frontispeice, with a silver G. G. The second uniform was double-breasted blue frock coat with gilt trimmings, blue pants with red stripes, white cross-belts with G. G. on the breast-plate, the cap the same as that worn by the Seventh Regiment at that period, with white pompon with red ball.

They went on an excursion to Philadelphia, making the entire trip by water on board of a schooner chartered for the occasion. The pleasure of this trip was saddened by a most melancholy accident. One morning, while the vessel was at Philadelphia, David Heulet and Frank Newman indulged in a little sportive "skylarking." In the course of their play they slipped on the deck, and while endeavoring to recover themselves, lost their balance and fell overboard. Newman was a good swimmer and was rescued, but Heulet did not come to the surface. Search was made for him, but the energetic efforts proved fruitless—it was supposed that his head must have struck against some hard substance, stunning him, and that he was swept away with the current. Much to their regret, his comrades were obliged to return home without his body. Some time after it was discovered several miles below the city, and kindly cared for and brought on to New York by a delegation of Philadelphia firemen, and was interred in Greenwood. The balls given by the Gulick Guards were features in the social life of the Metropolis, and were invariably looked forward to with pleasure by the belles of Gotham.

There were other organizations made up of members of different companies, and among them were the following :

The "P. G.'s" Sharpshooters, Captain John N. Hayward, organized 1841. All of the best shooters in the city accompanied them to target practice. Dave Pollock, of No. 22 Engine, and Joe Hannas, of No. 14 Hose, were among the leaders.

The Growler Guard, Captain Thos. O'Brien, from the Seventh Ward. Captain O'Brien was never known to smile or laugh. The men generally went to Thatcher College, New Jersey. It was a fantastical company, and gave large balls every year, and an extra street parade.

Island City Guards, Captain McConnell; Willet Guards, Captain Buckbee; Olive Guards, Captain Sweeney; Gotham Guards, Captain Perry; The Downing Guards, Captain McGee; Carlan Guards, Captain Carlan; Gulick Guards, Captain W. Lloyd; American Guards, Yellow Metal Musketeers, Captain Jos. H. Tooker; Batavia Guards, Captain Rohan; The Ward B. Smith Rangers, a fancy company; Caulker Guards, Captain Callahan; Fashion Guards, Captain Donohue; Bull's Head Guards, Captain Shandley; The Legion (November 25, 1870), Wm. M. Tweed in command; Colonel W. Kipp and Hawes, and Captain John Rudman, Eugene Durnin, Daniel Garvey, Michael Whalen and E. H. Hall. In this year they made a grand parade on Broadway and Fifth Avenue, eleven thousand turning out. At Irving Hall a dinner followed.

The chowder clubs were also important factors in this kind of sociability. Among them were the following :

"Big Six," (famous in all things), was located in Henry Street. They had there the cellar dug out at an expense of two hundred dollars and fitted up for that purpose, having the finest apartment of any company in the city. They were famous for chicken and oyster chowder, also salmon and clam chowder; and fish and eel chowders, distributed every Saturday night to hundreds. They had lots of fun in singing, dancing and telling fine "yarns." They never forgot Sunday morning, and always broke up at 12 o'clock on Saturday night. No. 33 Hose, Warren Association, in Sullivan Street, were visitors of "Big Six." No. 29, Metamora Hose, "Rich Men's Poor Sons," was also a great crowd. No. 40, Empire Hose, over in Morton Street, used to have lots of chowders, pigeon pies and pullets broiled. No. 36, Oceana Hose, caroused on wine and turkey *a la* Woodhull and Slote. No. 38, Amity Hose, nothing less than wine and turkey *a la* Connover. No. 9, Marion Engine, chowders. No. 14, Columbian Engine, veal pie. No. 16, Mohawk Engine, venison, stew and roasts. No. 24, Jackson Engine, mostly fish and eels and rapper cooked *a la* McWinnie. No. 7, Ringgold Hose, lots of good singing and music. No. 53, Naiad Hose, generally supper, very stylish. No. 55, Harry Howard Hose, much the same. No. 29, Guardian Engine, chowder *a la* Eugene Ward, head cook. No. 58, Merchant Hose. No. 15 Hose (Morris), famous for crackers and cheese, ale and herrings.

DESIGN OF BALL TICKET: EAGLE FIRE COMPANY.

After the Old Department was disbanded in 1865, the boys did not know where to congregate. Many a club was organized, and many a first floor and basement were rented and nicely fitted up. Among the new clubs was the Washington Club, located in Greenwich Street, giving its annual balls and picnics every year. Messrs. Thos. Cleary and James Hasson were at the head of it. The Warren Association, from No. 33 Hose Company, located in Sullivan Street, gave annual balls and chowder parties every Saturday evening to many old-timers. Its officers were Thomas Yeomans, Charles Denman, Jack Stoudhoff and H. Webb. Valley Forge Association, from Engine Company No. 46, J. H. Terrell, president; Dr. W. H. Boyd, secretary; Geo. A. Nurse, W. S. Hick, Ed. Cobb and J. W. Jacobus. They have their annual suppers at Martinelli's. Clinton Engine Company No. 41 Association, Geo. W. Wheeler, president. Live Oak Engine Company 44 Association has balls and picnics, and the profits go to the burial fund; Peter Maloney, president. Americus Engine Company No. 6 Association—W. B. Dunley, president; David M. Smith, vice-president; W. H. Burns, secretary; John H. Hughes, treasurer—was organized to have an annual supper to celebrate the first fire the company attended on June 11, 1849, and to bury the dead and visit the sick. This association has a lot in Greenwood Cemetery, close to the Firemen's Monument; they have one hundred and fifty-three living members, and at every supper about ninety attend.

CHAPTER XLV.

WHERE OLD FIREMEN CONGREGATE.

Their Headquarters and Association Rooms.—The Association of Exempt Firemen.—New York Firemen's Association.—Volunteer Firemen's Association.—Veteran Firemen's Association.—A Noble
Charity.—Reception Tendered to the Old Guard.—Volunteer Firemen's Sons' Association.

THE ASSOCIATION OF EXEMPT FIREMEN.

IN the fall of 1842 there was a scheme conceived to establish a Paid Fire Department, and at a meeting held in Monroe Hall, in Centre Street, over which Mr. Edward Dayton presided, the Exempt Firemen's Association was started, with Uzziah Wenman as president; James Gulick and John Ryker, Jr., vice-presidents; Neil Gray, secretary; C. Conklin Titus, sergeant-at-arms. Next year the title of the association was changed to the present one. The year after the disbandment of the Volunteer Fire Department, the Legislature enacted that the president and two vice-presidents of the association, and the trustees of the Volunteer Fire Department Benevolent Fund, should be a body corporate and politic, by name and style, to have control of the fund, and power to remove trustees and fill vacancies. On the fifteenth of February, 1886, the Act which incorporated these officers was amended by the Legislature, as follows:

SECTION 1. The President, two Vice-Presidents of the Exempt Firemen's Association of the City of New York, and the present Board of Trustees of the Exempt Firemen's Benevolent Fund of the City of New York, and their successors in office, are hereby constituted and appointed a body corporate and politic by the name and style of "The Trustees of the Exempt Firemen's Benevolent Fund of the City of New York," and by such corporate name may sue and be sued in any of the courts of this State. The said corporation created by the said Act hereby amended, shall continue to exist for thirty years after the passage of this Act.

SEC. 2. The existing trustees and officers of said corporation shall hold their respective offices for the unexpired terms for which they were respectively elected; and thereafter, upon the expiration of their present terms of office, there shall be elected by the Association of Exempt Firemen of the City of New York, at their annual meeting, to be held in the City of New York on the third Tuesday in January in each year, from their own members, three trustees of the said Exempt Firemen's Benevolent Fund, to hold office for the term of four years, and a treasurer of said fund, to hold office for the term of one year, and who shall be ex officio a member of said corporation. And in case any election herein provided for shall not be made on any day when pursuant to this Act it ought to have been made, the said corporation shall not, on that account, be deemed to be dissolved, but it shall and may be lawful on any other day to hold and make any such election in such manner, at such time as shall have been regulated by the by-laws and ordinances of the said association.

SEC. 3. The funds of said corporation, as now existing, shall be kept invested as directed by said trustees of said corporation, and with the revenue derived therefrom, and from all other sources, or so much thereof as shall be required, shall be appropriated and used for the aid and relief of such persons and their families as shall have been lawfully discharged from the late Volunteer Fire Department of the City of New York, who may be in indigent circumstances;

and to the families of members of said department who have been maimed or killed in the discharge of duty as a volunteer fireman.

SEC. 4. The said corporation is hereby empowered to make by-laws for its own government; to annually elect, from its own members, a President and Secretary; to provide a suitable place for its meetings, and, if necessary, an office for the Treasurer, and may employ a clerk for the Treasurer, at a salary not to exceed the sum of two hundred and fifty dollars per annum. It shall also have charge of the firemen's grounds and monument at Greenwood Cemetery, and shall pay these and all other necessary expenses. The President and two Vice-Presidents of the Association of Exempt Firemen, for the time being, shall be notified of all the meetings of said Board of Trustees, and may take part in and vote upon any business before said board. The Treasurer shall give security for the faithful discharge of his duties, in a bond or bonds, to said corporation, in such form and amount as it may prescribe or approve, and he shall, at every annual meeting of the corporation, and also to "The Association of Exempt Firemen of the City of New York," render an account of the state of the funds, how invested, the amount and sources of revenue of said corporation, and the disposition thereof. The officers, trustees and Treasurer, shall none of them be entitled to or receive any compensation for services in any such capacity.

SEC. 5. The said corporation may purchase and hold, in its said corporate name, any real estate sold under foreclosure of any mortgage held by it, and may sell and convey the same. It shall not hold, at any one time, real estate which shall exceed in value the sum of fifty thousand dollars.

SEC. 6. The Association of Exempt Firemen of the City of New York shall have the right to inquire into the investment, the revenue and disposition of the funds herein provided for; and to displace any member of the corporation guilty of misconduct, and to elect another in his stead, and in case of any vacancy occurring in said corporation, the said Association of Exempt Firemen of the City of New York, shall, at a regular meeting, elect another or others for the unexpired term of the person or persons in whose office such vacancy shall exist.

The rules of the Association of Exempt Firemen were remodeled in October, 1867, by P. W. Engs, president; Zophar Mills and A. F. Ockershausen, vice-presidents; and George W. Wheeler, secretary.

The benefits of the Association are fellowship, sixty dollars funeral expenses, and a delegation at funerals. The present officers are: President, Zophar Mills; Vice-presidents, David Milliken and John R. Platt; Recording Secretary, George W. Wheeler; Financial Secretary, Francis Hagadorn; Treasurer, James Y. Watkins, Jr.; Sergeant-at-Arms, Joseph D. Costa; and Executive Committee, J. D. Costa, Hugh Curry, Elisha Kingsland, H. R. Roome, Daniel Mooney, Chris. Johnson, R. L. Lomas and A. C. D'Ozeville. The Exempts meet at Caledonia Hall, but much of their business is transacted at No. 174 Canal Street.

The officers of the Association from October 13, 1842, to date, were:

Presidents: Uzziah Wenman, from October 13, 1842, to January, 1847; Samuel B. Warner, from January, 1847, to January, 1849; Adam W. Turnbull, from January, 1849, to January, 1851; Philip W. Engs, from January, 1851, to January, 1876; Zophar Mills, from January, 1876.

Vice-Presidents: James Gulick and John Ryker, Jr., from October 13, 1842, to January, 1847; Adam W. Turnbull and John Coger, from January, 1847, to January, 1849; Philip W. Engs and Allen McDougall, from January, 1849, to January, 1851; John Weeden and Hugh W. Taylor, from January, 1851, to January, 1852; Cornelius V. Anderson and John Coger, from January, 1852, to January, 1853; Daniel N. Lord and John Coger, from January, 1853, to January, 1854; Zophar Mills and James Y. Watkins, from January, 1854, to

January, 1856; Zophar Mills and Adolphus F. Ockershausen, from January, 1856, to January, 1876; Adolphus F. Ockershausen and David Milliken, from January, 1876, to January, 1878; David Milliken and John R. Platt, from January, 1878.

Secretaries: Neil Gray, from October 13, 1842, to January, 1846, (Recording and Financial); Jonas N. Phillips, from January, 1846, to January, 1850, (Recording and Financial, and afterwards Recording); George W. Wheeler, (Recording Secretary), from January, 1850; Thomas Boese, (Financial Secretary), from January, 1851, to January, 1854; Francis Hagadorn, (Financial Secretary), from January, 1854.

Treasurers: Joseph M. Price, from January, 1848, to January, 1869; James Y. Watkins, Jr., from January, 1869.

Sergeants-at-Arms: Conklin Titus, from October, 1842, to January, 1849; David Theall, from January, 1849, to May 6, 1868; John N. Clements, from July 21, 1868, to April 10, 1869; John K. Lyon, from April 20, 1869, to April 20, 1885; Joseph D. Costa, from April 20, 1885.

NOTE.—Secretaries Gray and Phillips were acting Treasurers until Mr. Price was elected.

NEW BANNER, VOLUNTEER FIREMEN'S ASSOCIATION.

During the past year the Volunteer Firemen's Association felt that as they were the representatives of the Volunteer Firemen it was meet that they should have a fitting emblem to display to the public on occasions of parade, etc. Early in October, 1886, a committee of the Association intrusted to Joseph H. Johnson, the artist, the order to prepare a banner to be worthy of the city, the Old Department, and the Association. Mr. Johnson, as an old fireman, took especial pride in his labor. Very soon after the work had been commenced the Volunteers decided to take part in the Bartholdi parade, October 28, 1886. There was but little prospect that their banner could be finished in time. The artist, whose heart was in the work, labored assiduously. The result was that the Association marched with their banner in an incomplete state, but sufficiently finished to show its beauties. The banner is now finished. It is 5 by 7 ft., made of heavy double blue and scarlet silk. On the front is depicted a classic figure of Protection standing upon a pedestal, her right hand grasping a spear, her left hand resting upon a shield emblazoned with a phoenix; below, on the left, is a widow, arrayed in her emblems of mourning, with her little daughter, bathed in tears, resting upon her knee; on the ground, near the widow's feet, are the sad mementos of her lost fireman husband: a fire-cap, trumpet, and coat; immediately in front of the mourning pair stands Benevolence, proffering aid and assistance; on the right is the figure of a stalwart fireman, in full fire costume, holding two orphan boys by the hand; in the rear of this scene is the view of a placid river, in the distance a glimpse of the city, and a perfect representation of the Firemen's Monument at Greenwood Cemetery; at the bottom, a picture to make an old fireman's heart beat faster—a night race between an old-time gooseneck engine and a hose carriage. The only drawback is that you are unable to "lay in" on either of the ropes. Across the top is inscribed: "Volunteer Firemen's Association;" at the bottom, "City of New York."

On the reverse is a large circular painting of the city coat-of-arms; below this, two exquisite gems of art, representing the initiation and discharge certificates of the Old Department; as a base, the old paraphernalia, hydrant, hose, ladders, hooks, etc., artistically arranged; across the top, the familiar legend, "Volunteer Firemen's Association," and below, the date of the organization and charter.

The banner is trimmed with heavy gold lace, bullion fringe, and elegant

OLD BANNER OF VOLUNTEER FIREMEN'S ASSOCIATION.

gold tassels. When used for parades it will be mounted upon a frame of polished ash, with scroll iron-work burnished. The whole will be surmounted by a large gold eagle, with silken festoons, and will be borne by six men. Altogether it is an admirable work, a "thing of beauty," and will be "a joy forever" to those who remain to cherish the pleasures and sorrows of their idol—the Old New York Fire Department.

THE NEW YORK FIREMEN'S ASSOCIATION.

Soon after the Volunteer Fire Department was disbanded, a number of the old officers assembled at the house of ex-Fire Commissioner Thomas Lawrence, under Jefferson Market, and formed the New York Firemen's Association, with

NEW BANNER—VOLUNTEER FIREMEN'S ASSOCIATION (FRONT).
[Painted by Joseph H. Johnson.]

ex-President Henry Wilson, of the old Board of Fire Commissioners, as president; ex-Assistant Engineer Wm. Lamb, as first vice-president; Lewis J. Parker, second vice-president; Robert Wright, secretary; and Frederick A. Ridabock, treasurer. Over three hundred names were enrolled, among them Thomas C. Burns, Alderman Eugene Ward, Dearborn G. Piper, Abraham Clearman, Colonel W. R. W. Chambers, William J. Smith, Charles Miller, Jonas L. Coe, George W. Williams, John Underhill, Judge Alfred A. Philips, Frank Byrns,

Andrew Holly, William Spear, Tobias Lawrence, Timothy L. West, Thomas
Lawrence, and others. During the month of October, 1865, they visited Philadelphia, and took part in the last parade the Volunteer Department of that
city held. The same year they fitted up fine quarters on the northwest corner
of Sixth Avenue and Fourth Street, where they received many visiting companies. In 1870 they removed to No. 5 Sixth Avenue, having secured the

NEW BANNER—VOLUNTEER FIREMEN'S ASSOCIATION (REVERSE).
[Painted by Joseph H Johnson.]

entire building. Here they received delegations of firemen from all sections of
the United States. In 1873 they removed to the "Bleecker Building," corner
of Bleecker and Morton Streets, where they remained until they broke up,
along in 1876. The members, it seems, became lukewarm, and, soon after, the
organization quietly passed out of existence.

VOLUNTEER FIREMEN'S ASSOCIATION.

On Sunday, November 18, 1883, the following advertisement appeared in the newspapers:

A GENERAL ALARM!!

TURN OUT! TURN OUT! TURN OUT!!

"All the members of the Old Volunteer Fire Department are requested to attend a meeting at Military Hall, No. 187 Bowery, on Tuesday night, November 20, 1883, to take action in relation to participating in the parade on Centennial Evacuation Day.

JOHN DECKER."

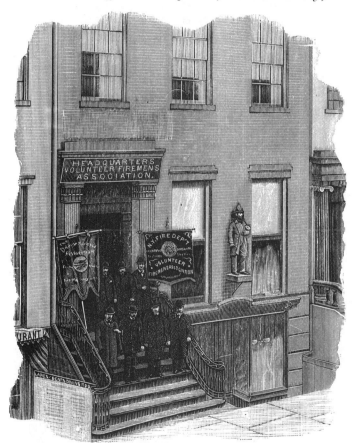

HEADQUARTERS OF VOLUNTEER FIREMEN'S ASSOCIATION.

[143 Eighth Street.]

This call was responded to by a host of old firemen—ex-chiefs and ex-assistant engineers, ex-foremen and ex-assistant foremen, together with a multitude of the rank and file. One hundred and thirty-one companies were represented. John Decker presided; H. H. Cummings, of Hose Company No. 22, was Secretary, and George T. Patterson, of Engine Company No. 8, Treasurer. On motion, a committee of ten was to be appointed by the chairman, said committee to make arrangements for the Centennial Evacuation Parade. The chair appointed Martin J. Keese, Hose Company No. 60; P. Bullard, Hose Company No. 39; James Higgins, Hook and Ladder Company No. 12; William E. Bishop, Engine Company No. 24; Gilbert J. Orr, Engineer; George W. Anderson, Hose Company No. 22; George T. Patterson, Engine Company No. 8; Frank Mahedy, Engine Company No. 31; Peter P. Pullis, Hose Company No. 40; David Decker, Engine Company No. 16.

Other committees were appointed in connection with the projected celebration. A meeting was held on the following Friday evening, November 23, to transact business, when four hundred and thirty-two firemen signed their names, requiring the appointment of several deputy secretaries. The committee of ten met until the twenty-sixth of the month. This was the inception of the Volunteer Firemen's Association.

In December, 1883, this unnamed association received an invitation from the Volunteer Firemen's Association of Philadelphia to attend their annual banquet on December 14. The invitation was accepted. Twenty-three firemen proceeded to the "City of Brotherly Love," were received, and feted to their hearts' content. While in Philadelphia a close examination was made of the workings of the Volunteer Association of that city. The New York committee was highly pleased with all the rules, by-laws, etc. The information they received was of vital importance at a later day.

A meeting was held at Military Hall December 22, 1883, Chief Decker presiding. The report of the committee of ten was read and approved. Additional names were added to the committee, as follows: E. W. Jacobs, Engineer; W. H. Arreson, Engine Company No. 25; Frank Bazzoni, Engine Company No. 45; Charles Miller, Engine Company No. 34.

This committee of fifteen met in the City Hall Library, transacted some unimportant business, and adjourned to meet at Hall's Hotel, where an election was held. John Decker was chosen as the first president of the association. A committee of three on by-laws, consisting of William E. Bishop, George W. Anderson and Peter P. Pullis, was appointed. The next meeting was at the Village House, Hudson and Bank Streets. Sixty members were enrolled and permanent organization agreed upon.

On February 14, 1884, the "Act of Incorporation" (or charter) was issued by the State of New York to the Volunteer Firemen's Association, signed by John A. McCall, Jr., Superintendent of the Insurance Department, Albany, New York.

On February 22, 1884, a meeting was held at the Village House to elect officers for the ensuing year. The result was as follows:

John Decker, president; George R. Connor, first vice-president; Nelson D. Thayer, second vice-president; William E. Bishop, financial secretary; Charles E. Benedict, recording secretary; George T. Patterson, treasurer; Patrick Connory, sergeant-at-arms. Board of Directors—George W. Anderson, Joseph Noble, Martin J. Keese, James Higgins, Peter P. Pullis, Edward Gilon, Thomas Goodwin. In July, 1884, the association took possession of the house in Eighth Street, opposite the old "Astor Place Opera House" (now the Mercantile Library). A brief description of the place may be interesting. The business room, or office, is dedicated to the board of directors and the financial secretary; the latter, Mr. William E. Bishop, does not find time falling heavily on his hands, as he is actively engaged from early morning to late in the evening. He has to transact business with over two thousand members, keep the accounts of each individual member, issue notices, receive dues · in fact, he transacts as much business as two or three ordinary bookkeepers. A huge safe is suggestive of the large amount of money received and disbursed by the association. The directors' table, the desks, account books, etc., give an accurate idea of the business transacted. The walls are hung with banners. The first is the one originally used by the association. Also old banners of Manhattan Engine Company No. 8, Americus

Engine Company No. 6, Mechanics' Hose Company No. 47, two guidons used by the Wilson Guards (Peterson Engine Company No. 5), a number of certificates, some dating back to the last century, engravings, etc., complete the furniture of the apartment.

The main room is a perfect fire museum; everything connected with the Old Department is represented, pipes of polished copper and brass, long and short, torches, lamps, ladder-jackets, trumpets and signals, paintings of old-time firemen, engravings of celebrated fires, photographs of members of almost every old company, fire-caps of old chiefs and assistant engineers, fire-cap fronts with such a variety of numbers that the eye wearies dwelling upon them. There is also a number of models of fire apparatus, beautifully made, and faithfully reproduced. The names of but a few can be mentioned : Empire Hook and Ladder Company No. 8, Mazeppa Engine Company No. 48 (old goose-neck), Cataract Engine Company No. 25 (piano), Mazeppa Hose Company No. 42, Peterson Engine Company No. 31 (double-decker). Among the antiques may be found the beautiful backs and panels painted by eminent artists. The first in order is from Neptune Engine Company No. 6, with Neptune surrounded by water nymphs ; Eagle Engine Company No. 13, a mother rescuing her child from the eagle's nest; D. D. Tompkins Engine Company No. 30, a portrait of Governor Tompkins ; Fulton Engine Company No. 21, the witch of the water, a scene from Byron's Manfred ; Washington Engine Company No. 20, Washington delivering his Inaugural; Howard Engine Company No. 34, Howard, the philanthropist, visiting the distressed ; Perry Hose Company No. 23, two views of Perry's victory on Lake Erie ; Forrest Engine Company No. 3, portraits of Edwin Forrest and John Decker. All of these backs show unmistakable evidences of age and exposure; some of them are scarcely discernible ; in one case the back was burned from too close proximity to a burning building. It is useless to attempt to describe the remainder of the articles, but it is very apparent that the association is in need of a larger building to transact its business and display its unique and valuable collection.

Board of officers, 1886-'87 : John Decker, president; James J. Ferris, first vice-president ; William Lamb, second vice-president; William E. Bishop, financial secretary ; Joseph S. Beer, recording secretary; and James B. Mingay, treasurer. Board of directors : John J. Blair, chairman ; Andrew J. Brush, John Quigg, George F. Haller, John K. Costigan, Martin Senger, Michael Loftus, William F. Searing, Matthew McCullough ; and Isaac Mills, sergeant-at-arms.

THE VETERAN FIREMEN'S ASSOCIATION.

While it must be admitted that the old Volunteer Firemen are rapidly passing away, a visit to the Veteran Firemen's Association headquarters, No. 53 East Tenth Street, indicates that they maintain the remembrances of the days when they were the young and active protectors of the lives and property of the people of the great metropolis. Just previous to the presidential election in 1884, a number of the old veterans decided to visit Washington and attend the inauguration of President Cleveland. During the latter part of September, just previous to the election, they organized as the

Veteran Firemen's Association, with the following officers: Foreman, Geo. T. Patterson; first assistant, William B. Dunley; second assistant, Peter P. Pullis; grand marshal, George B. Conner. On the third of March, 1885, they left the Grand Central Hotel, one hundred and sixty-eight men, equipped in full fire-rig, and taking with them an old Philadelphia style of engine built in the year 1838. On their arrival at Baltimore they were the guests of the firemen of that city, and were presented by the mayor, the Hon. F. C. Latrobe, with a full set of twelve keys of the public buildings and parks of the city, neatly arranged on a solid shield of copper, and also tendered a banquet. The shield consists of highly burnished copper, 20 x 15 inches, in the center of which is another shield, silver-plated, with the following inscription:

KEYS OF THE CITY OF BALTIMORE,
Presented by the HON. F. C. LATROBE, Mayor,
To the VETERAN FIREMEN'S ASSOCIATION,
On their visit to Baltimore and Washington,
March 3d, 4th and 5th, 1885.

Surrounding this are twelve keys, fac-similes of those of the public institutions of Baltimore, viz.: City Hall, engine houses, station houses, parks, theaters, monuments, churches, penitentiary, jail, Bay View, night key and the key of the buildings of the Pennsylvania Railroad Company, to which is attached a five-cent nickel piece. At each corner of the main shield is a model of the Baltimore Monument, and at the top is a pair of clasped hands. A silver-plated American eagle, perched on a globe, with red, white and blue streamers floating from its beak, surmounts the brass standard to which the shield is attached.

After the presentation by Mayor F. C. Latrobe, ex-Fire Chief Harry Howard responded, and said:

"Mr. Mayor, it is my happy privilege to respond in behalf of the Veteran Volunteer Firemen of New York, to your very flattering address of welcome, accompanying it with these ancient and beautiful symbols, the keys of your old and magnificent monumental city. We have command of words, but they are inadequate to express our heartfelt thanks and gratitude; our hearts are filled with what the clergyman terms a halo of rapture in listening to your grand oration and witnessing this enormous gathering of your citizens, who have waited patiently for five hours after the time set for our arrival, to cheer us on our way to Washington to take part in the inauguration of the new government. We have always heard that Baltimore was more like New York than any other place on earth, and to-night proves the assertion to be true. Your Honor says you were proud to have been a Volunteer Fireman, but steam fire engines have superseded them. Sir, we admit that it is partially true, but everything that is now accomplished by steam fire engines, horse power, and paid firemen, was all cheerfully done by the Volunteers with a scant water supply, cumbrous fire apparatus, limited supplies, and the want of nearly all necessary implements for extinguishing fires. The Volunteers rendered all this vast service without pay and without complaint. Imagine the present fireman without steam fire engines and horses, and you have our case. It is wonderful how we so successfully extinguished fires under all these disadvantages. There was great prejudice in the New York Fire Department to any change. I was one of only a few who favored paying the officers and men and declaring for steam fire brigades in large cities. I knew the people were as favorable to paying the firemen as they were to pay the military and police. I believe the firemen should always have been paid. When there is no active duty they have to remain in quarters, which is more confining and tiresome than doing hard work. We hope your firemen will visit New York. Then we will try to reciprocate all your kindness and generosity. Your beautiful symbols we will treasure while life lasts.''

On their homeward trip they became the guests of the Veteran Firemen's Association of Philadelphia, where they remained for two days. On their return home they reorganized, the following gentlemen being selected as officers: president, Geo. W. Anderson; vicepresident, John Moller; secretary, Bernard M. Sweeny; financial secretary, J. H. Bartley; treasurer, James F. Wenman; trustees, Frederick A. Ridabock, Eugene Ward, John Twomey, George T. Patterson, Sr., Thomas Barrett, Richard Evans, Thomas Cleary, Abram C. Hull, Abram Slaight, Henry Gunther, Daniel Quinn, Patrick Daily, William Oxford, Daniel Garvin; and Henry Jones, sergeant-at-arms. They leased the old Lorillard mansion, No. 53 East Tenth Street, and fitted it up in a most expensive manner. The basement was turned into one grand

VETERAN FIREMEN'S ASSOCIATION HEADQUARTERS,
[No. 53 East Tenth Street.]

meeting room, at the rear of which is a private wine chamber. The walls of the main room are covered with old fire certificates, resolutions, models, trumpets, and emblems of the Old Volunteers.

The first floor or parlors are richly furnished with French Brussel and velvet furniture, while the walls are hung with oil paintings of ex-Chief Engineers Harry Howard, James Gulick, ex-Comptroller Matthew T. Brennan, Harry Mansfield, and W. A. Woodhull. A fine painting of President George W. Anderson and Vice-President John Moller, and a life-size crayon of

Alderman Eugene Ward ; and an oil painting of ex-Assistant Engineer James F. Wenman were also added to the rooms by their personal friends. The second floor is set apart as a billiard room, containing two tables, the walls being encircled with the fire-hats of the members. Projecting from the folding doors are the hose-jackets of Engines 24 and 28, while the walls contain the panels of several engine and hose carriages, the backs of old gooseneck engines, and the likeness of David C. Broderick of Engine 34, at one time United States Senator from California. The rear extension contains a fine picture of old Firemen's Hall, an old painting of Engine 34, and a model of Putnam Engine 21. On this floor is also a bath-room and closets. The top floor is set apart for whist parties. The front room, however, is used more readily as a reading

ENGINE OF THE VETERAN ASSOCIATION.

[This double-deck engine was built in 1838, and belonged to Hope Engine Company, of Philadelphia ; it was bought by Mr. John Moller, repainted, and put in perfect order, at an expense of one thousand dollars, and was presented by him to the Veteran Association. It was raffled in the rooms of the association, and the winner was to receive a fifty dollar gold badge. Mr. Frederick S. Gwier, of Lafayette Engine, No. 19, was the winner. The association took this engine with them to President Cleveland's inauguration. It was again repainted and decorated for the parade in honor of the unveiling of the statue of " Liberty Enlightening the World," October 28, 1886.]

room, as it contains a fine library, a large writing desk, and tables for that purpose. In the library, in a large case, encircled in crape, is the fire-cap of Thomas I. Banks, of Hook and Ladder 11, killed July 1, 1862, at a fire in Mott Street. There are also several private rooms in the building, used by the single members, who make this their home.

On the twelfth of September, 1885, the association visited Jamaica, L. I., to attend the agricultural fair, and were received by the firemen of that city, delegates from Greenpoint, Flushing, Hempstead, Riverside and Long Island City. During the month of October, 1885, they visited Bayonne, N. J., where they were received by the Common Council and the Fire Department, John Wildey, an old New York firemen, acting as grand marshal. During their stay they were the recipients of no less than four presents : of a splendid silk banner from the " Argonauta " Boat Club, one from the Bergen Point Athletic Club, a handsome banner from the ladies of Bayonne, and a set of colors from the Fire Department. On Thursday, October 15, 1885, they received Phoenix Hose Company No. 1, of Poughkeepsie, while en route home after a most delightful visit to Albany, Boston and Salem, Mayor Ezra White and Chief Engineer William Kaess, of Poughkeepsie, accompanying them. On the twelfth of January, 1886, they gave their first annual ball at the Metropolitan Opera House, delegates from all the leading Fire Departments this side of the Alleghanies being present. The double deck engine that they took to Washington, and the silver carriage of Phoenix Hose No. 1, of Poughkeepsie, that cost about four thousand dollars, were conspicuous at one end of the ball-room. On the twenty-fourth of June, 1886, they visited Iona Island, and on the fourth

Matthew T. Brennan.   PARLORS OF VETERAN ASSOCIATION.   Fred. A. Ridabock.
[53 East Tenth Street.]

of October, 1886, they went to Poughkeepsie to take part in the annual parade of the Fire Department of that city. President George W. Anderson was, as usual, in command, ex-Assistant Engineer James F. Wenman acting as grand marshal. They were received on the evening of their arrival by the whole Fire Department, under Chief Engineer W. Kaess, but were the special guests of Phoenix Hose No. 1. They were escorted through the leading streets of the city, amid a blaze of fireworks, six blazing barrels lining both sides of the streets for over two miles, while the people turned out in a mass to bid them welcome. A banquet was given them at Armory Hall, and after the parade on the following day they were again entertained, the Phoenix boys doing special honors at their carriage house before their departure home. On the twenty-eighth of October, 1886, they took part in the unveiling and dedicating of Bartholdi's Statue of Liberty, turning out over two hundred and fifty men.

The following are some of the leading members of the association : ex-Superintendent of Police James J. Kelso ; Nelson D. Thayer and Joseph H. Johnson, the artist; ex-Chief Engineer Harry Howard, ex-Chief Engineer Elisha Kingsland, Chief of Battalion Benjamin J. Gicquel, Hon. Jordan L. Mott, ex-Fire Commissioner Martin B. Brown, Commissioner of Parks Thomas E. Crimmins, Captain of Police Anthony J. Allaire, Colonel W. R. W. Chambers, ex-Assistant Engineer E. W. Jacobs, Alderman Thomas Cleary, Thomas E. Tripler, John Buckbee, Denis Leary, Christopher Johnson, Anthony Yeomans, and four hundred and eighty more.

Under the auspices of the Veteran's Association a home for the poor and distressed Volunteer Firemen has been chartered, to be known and designated as the " Veteran Firemen's Home Association of the City of New York."

The incorporators are: George W. Anderson, John Moller, Bernard M. Sweeny, James H. Bartley, James F. Wenman, Frederick A. Ridabock, Eugene Ward, Abraham Slaight, Abram C. Hull, Richard Evans, Daniel Garvey, Thomas Cleary, Henry Gunther, William Orford, Thomas Barrett, John McCauley, Peter P. Pullis, Timothy Donovan, Robert McWinne, Richard H. Nugent, George T. Patterson, William H. Boyd, William Brandon, Daniel D. Conover and Henry Jones.

The management of the institution, by the charter, is vested in seven

VETERAN'S RECEPTION TO OLD GUARD, DEC. 31, 1886.

[President Anderson and Major McLean.]

PAINTING BY JOSEPH H. JOHNSON.

gentlemen, to wit: George W. Anderson, John Moller, James F. Wenman, Henry Gunther, George T. Patterson, Daniel D. Conover and William H. Boyd.

The management above named have already appointed a committee to select a site in a convenient locality upon which to erect buildings suitable for the object mentioned, and it is expected ere long the designs of the corporation will be consummated, and the Home established.

MAJOR GEORGE W. McLEAN.—Not long ago the major stated that when he was young he had a leaning toward fire duty, and loved to follow the machine, but an early experience in the financial world obliterated all tendencies of such youthful fancies. He became a power in Wall Street; his name represented vast amounts, and his word was as good as his bond. By an almost unanimous vote, he was elected President of the Stock Exchange, the greatest financial position on this continent. Upon retiring from the street, he was proffered, and accepted, the position of Street Commissioner of this city. Although occupying the office at a time of great peril and general distrust, yet on his retirement he was congratulated by our best citizens for the faithful and honest discharge ·of his duty. The major now fills the very important position of Receiver of Taxes.

THE VOLUNTEER, VETERAN AND EXEMPT FIREMEN'S SONS' ASSOCIATION.

The corporate existence of this association dates from August 1, 1886, when the charter received the signature of the Governor.

Its objects were declared to be "the promotion of friendly feelings and social intercourse, to provide a headquarters for the transaction of business connected with the association, together with a reading room where members can meet and extend the friendship now existing among their fathers, to take proper care of the members when sick, or in case of death, as provided in the by-laws of the association, and to allow members of the association, under proper restrictions, to provide a uniform to represent the association in all public parades, etc.; such parades to be made only after obtaining permission of the association.

The first regular meeting was held at Runk's Assembly Rooms, No. 73 Ludlow Street, on Sunday, August 9, 1885, when several members were initiated. Since then, the association has grown rapidly and prospered greatly. It now numbers 150 members. For the past year meetings have been held on the first and third Tuesdays of each month in a commodious hall at No. 295 Bowery.

The present officers of the association are: C. H. Throckmorton, president; W. H. Pardee, first vice-president; E. J. Blair, second vice-president; James J. Pardee, treasurer; J. E. Purdy, financial secretary; P. E. Ward, recording secretary; W. E. Gage, sergeant-at-arms.

The association owns a handsome hose carriage, with which it turns out on parades.

RESPONDING TO AN ALARM.

CHAPTER XLVI.

A FAREWELL TO THE VOLUNTEERS.

George Washington An Active Fireman.—His Great Interest in Fire Matters.—The Growth and Progress of the City.—Some Quaint Fire Ordinances.—Fires and Fire Bugs.—Life Saving Firemen.—Gallant and Devoted.—Brave Men; Honest Men.—We May Not Look Upon their Like Again.

IF we have carried the reader along with us thus far he will have noted that our assertion at the beginning—that the history of the Volunteer Fire Department meant the history of the rise and progress of New York—has been borne out by the facts we have presented. We have brought to light, among other important things, one interesting fact that had been forgotten or not generally known—the fact that the Father of his Country had enrolled himself as a Volunteer fireman. George Washington, who was as zealous in the discharge of his duty as a private citizen as he was eminent and efficient in public life, became an active fireman in Alexandria, Virginia, about the year 1750. He was then but eighteen years of age, and resided with his brother Lawrence at Mount Vernon, several miles from the town, which he visited "on horseback as often as ten times a week."

OLD FIREMAN OF ALEXANDRIA, VA.

As a young man he took an active part in all the affairs of the growing place until it became an important colonial city. Besides his firmness of character, his love of active pursuits, his passion for horsemanship and all manly sports made him a natural leader among the young men of the town. It is related that he was always one of the foremost to assist in putting out fires, riding even from Mount Vernon to be present at one. As Alexandria increased in size, the principal citizens began to organize for protection against fire, and the town record shows that they each agreed, out of "mutual friendship," to carry to every fire "two leathern buckets and one great bag of oznaburg or wider linnen." This was the primitive colonial mode of extinguishing flames.

The watchmen were also enrolled as firemen, and sounded an alarm by sending forth a blast from a huge trumpet which they wore slung about their shoulders. Instead of billies they carried quaint-looking weapons called spontoons, something between a spear and a halberd. These antique weapons were left behind in store at Alexandria by General Braddock's troops in 1755, when they marched on their disastrous expedition to the West. The spontoons were appropriated by the municipal authorities, and, strange to say, were still in use by the watchmen when the provost guard of a Michigan regiment in the summer of 1861 relieved these obsolete guardians from further duty.

The Friendship Fire Company of Alexandria, which still survives, was organized in 1774. At that time Washington was a delegate to the Continental Congress in Philadelphia, but the members of the new company evidently remembered his former services as fireman, for at one of their first meetings they unanimously elected him an honorary member, and forwarded him a copy of the minutes. To show his appreciation of the compliment, he at once made a thorough inspection of the different kind of fire engines in use in Philadelphia, and upon his second return there, in 1775, he bought from one Gibbs a small fourth-class engine for eighty pounds and ten shillings, and just before he set out for Boston to become Commander-in-chief of the Continental Army, he sent this little engine as a present to the Friendship Fire Company.

GEORGE WASHINGTON AS A FIREMAN.

The great Chieftain did not lose his interest in fire matters through his elevation to position and power. Upon his retirement to Mount Vernon, after his second term as president, and when his fame had spread round the world, he continued to take an active interest in the municipal affairs of Alexandria. It is related that in the last year of his life he was one day riding down King Street, when a fire broke out near the market. He was accompanied by his servant, also on horseback, and noticed that Friendship Company engine was poorly manned, though a crowd of well-dressed idlers stood about. Riding up to the crowd he employed very vigorous language in rebuking their indifference at such a time. He ended by calling out, " It is your business to lead in these matters," and throwing the bridle of his horse to his servant, he leaped off and seized the brakes, followed by a crowd that gave the engine such a " shaking up " as it never knew afterwards.

Washington voted for the last time, in Alexandria, in 1799, a few weeks previous to his death, which occurred just before the dawn of the nineteenth century.

How the Old Volunteers of New York would have enjoyed the spectacle! The great General pulling on a rope! The survivors must feel a greater pride in their profession, knowing that Washington had been one of their number.

The rapid rise of New York is unprecedented in history. Nearly two centuries and a half ago the island was a wilderness north of the Battery. In 1651, Indians, in canoes, paddled about the waters of the Hudson and the East River. About twenty years before, the whole island had been purchased from the Manhattans for the sum of twenty-four dollars. Think of it, ye rich New Yorkers of to-day, who willingly pay thousands of dollars for a few yards of this same land! Two hundred and fifty years back a fire alarmed the colonists, and because it destroyed much of their property, set them thinking about finding ways and means to prevent such occurrences. Wooden chimneys and thatched roofs were often the cause of fires, and in 1648 an ordinance was passed to abolish this kind of chimney and roof. In those days there was no lack of water for the extinguishment, for all the buildings comprising the city were confined to

GEORGE WASHINGTON RIDING TO A FIRE.

the neighborhood of the Battery. Proper appliances alone were needed to use the water for putting out the many fires that occurred. Some time elapsed before even the rudest machinery was obtainable for the primitive Fire Department. Naturally, buckets were the first things thought of, and, as we have seen, had very little effect upon a fire.

But as New York extended, the water supply diminished, or, in other words, was inadequate to meet the needs of the people. This was one of the most puzzling problems the inhabitants had to deal with. We have laid before the reader the schemes of individuals and corporations to remedy the evil. No sooner had a system been elaborated and adopted, than the still further growth of the city, in a few years, rendered the new system obsolete. Then another plan had to be devised to satisfy the firemen and the citizens, and when matured, became, like the preceding, in a short time, antiquated and inadequate. This struggle with a difficult question has continued right up to our own day. At last a gigantic project has been undertaken, and when accomplished, will, it is thought, solve the difficulty. The new aqueduct, as it is described in this book from official sources, will, to all appearances, satisfy the mind of the investigator that, at last, the city is furnished with a water supply that will prove ample for all purposes for many and many a year to come. But, if we bear in mind the lessons of the past, we may argue, from what we find in them, that our children will be looking upon the new aqueduct as an old system, unable to furnish the still greater New York with all that it wants for its Fire Department and other purposes. We have seen how New Yorkers have, at various times, prided themselves upon their splendid wells, have rejoiced over the opening of the Erie Canal, celebrated the introduction of the first stream of the crystal Croton, and viewed, with immense satisfaction, the construction of the new aqueduct. Mayhap, some other grand water scheme will, ere the lapse of another half century, occupy the attention of the citizens, and give occasion for another display to honor the event. Who knows? The growth of New York is held to be almost illimitable.

The rise of our city is one of the astonishing facts that strikes the mind of the inquiring foreigner. Nay, there are hundreds and hundreds of old firemen still living, who, though natives, are no less impressed by what they have seen and contemplate. We have men still with us who have known Chambers Street to be the northern limit of the city—men who have wandered among fields and meadows which are now the centers of the busiest neighborhoods in the world. These veterans are, to the younger generation, objects of venera-

THOMAS DUNLAP.
[Biography, Page 536.]

tion. These "old boys" are living links between the generation that tumbled buckets of water into what were little better than tubs worked by cranks, and the generation that mans the finest fire machines that modern science can devise. Let the reader turn to the illustrations we have given of those quaint boxes worked by firemen in pig tails, and then take a glance at the magnificent engines of to-day, manned by athletic fellows in neat fitting and appropriate costumes, and he will first be amazed, and then smile, at the thought that those bygone appliances could ever be of the slightest use. We have grown visibly.

Step by step the Volunteer Department became a great institution. Year by year it advanced in public estimation. Its every act was noted and placed on record. As an illustration, in addition to what has already been said on the subject, we give a few quaint extracts from the aldermanic proceedings:

At a meeting of the Common Council held Friday, October 23, 1789, "It being represented to the Board of Aldermen that the law of this corporation to prevent the danger of fire is inadequate, especially with respect to the danger arising from the use of iron stoves in joiners' workshops and other places, be it ordered that the recorder be requested to revise the law in the matter of fires, and to prepare a law with such further provisions as he may deem necessary."

At a meeting of the Common Council held Wednesday, December 5, 1787, a petition of Archibald Kesler was presented on behalf of himself and several of his neighbors in Cherry Street, setting forth that they had purchased a fire engine, which they were willing to appropriate to the use of the public, and to erect a house and purchase a piece of ground for its reception, and they "pray the board to accept it for that purpose, and to appoint the proper number of firemen to take charge of and to work the same." It was ordered that the engineer return the names of ten proper persons to be appointed to said engine.

At a meeting of the Common Council held Friday, November 13, 1789, a petition of the foremen of several of the small fire engines, praying that the number of men to each of said engines may be ten, as formerly, was read and referred to Alderman Stoutenburgh and Messrs. Elsworth and Curtinius, and on reading a petition of the company belonging to Engine No. 13, in favor of Nicholas Brevoort being appointed to their company, it was resolved "that the resolution of this board of August 12, that no person under the age of thirty years be appointed to the office of a fireman of this city, be repealed."

On reading a representation of the company of Engine No. 5 by Frederick Echert, their foreman, that Francis Arden and George Peck, members of that company, "had neglected their duty as firemen, and hoping that this board would order their names to be struck off the list of firemen," it was ordered "that the said Francis Arden and George Peck attend this board at the next meeting to show cause why the request of said company should not be complied with, and that Mr. Echert also attend to support the accusation." The firemen in those days were very particular as to their companions.

The first Fire Department numbered fifty members. In 1865 it had swelled to about four thousand. Year by year its members grew to keep pace with the requirements of the city. When the British took possession of "New Netherlands," the fire question was agitated. The fire wardens demanded more implements. Ordinances were passed compelling every citizen to furnish one bucket or more. Long after the introduction of fire engines, buckets were in general use. Towards the close of the seventeenth century a night watch was instituted to guard against fires, and a strict supervision of hearths and chimneys was maintained. Then bells were brought into use for the purpose of giving the alarm, and finally watch towers were erected. When Newsham's engines were brought from London in the beginning of the eighteenth century, the whole city heaved a sigh of relief—now it had really something scientific and effective to protect property from the ravages of fire, so it thought. Now were formed the first fire companies, and now began the fireman's manifestation of his love for the machine—a love which became so conspicuous in after years.

Very soon the Board of Aldermen began to take an active interest in fire matters, as the following facts will show: At a meeting of the Common

Council, January 12, 1801, a petition of Thomas Howell, praying for the reasons mentioned therein, that the board would grant him an additional sum of money towards indemnifying him for his loss on the importation of the new fire engine for Company No. 24 from London, and lately sold to the board, was read, and it was determined that no further sum ought to be granted. He had been allowed five hundred and fifty dollars for the engine, which appears a high price for the old-fashioned engine of those days. It was ordered that "Matthew West, fireman, heretofore belonging to engine No. 23, be removed to do duty with Company 1, and that Abm. Moore, Sixth Ward, carpenter, David Secor, Sixth Ward, carpenter, be appointed additional firemen to the same company, and that the following persons be also appointed firemen, viz.: John Westervelt, Fifth Ward, sailmaker; Henry Brevoort, Sixth Ward,

STADT HUYS (CITY HALL).
[Pearl Street and Coenties Slip, 1679.]

coach painter; John Leacraft, Sixth Ward, cordwainer; Joseph Ogden, Sixth Ward, cordwainer, to Engine No. 8; Isaac Parker, Seventh Ward, shipwright, vice Thomas Drahedee, to No. 22, and George Burras, First Ward, shoemaker, to No. 3, vice Thomas Gosman, resigned. A petition of the firemen for the appointment of a person as chief engineer "in the place of the person now exercising that office," was read and referred to the aldermen of the Sixth Ward, and the assistants of the Second and Fourth Wards, to inquire into the facts stated in the said petition. At a meeting of the Common Council, May 23, 1803, a resolution was passed that "Aldermen Barker, Morris and Stevens be a committee to confer with the engineers and firemen of the respective engines in this city respecting the best mode of keeping the fire engines in good repair from time to time as the same may be required, and also to confer with them and the fire wardens jointly, whether some more effectual means cannot with propriety be adopted than the present rules and order for the government of the Fire Department, and the compulsion of the citizens to assist on such occasions, under proper penalties for neglect or refusal when thereunto required, and the same committee be directed to report with all convenient speed."

A report of the inspector and a letter of Dr. Browne in relation to a big fire in 1804, recommending measures proper for the prevention and extinguishment of fires, was received in Common Council on December 24, De Witt Clinton, mayor, being present. It was ordered, "that such part of the said papers as relates to future improvements in the Fire Department be referred to Aldermen Van Zandt, King, Mr. Bloodgood. Mr. Mott, and Mr. Hopkins. Ordered that the mayor be authorized and requested to issue a proclamation in behalf of this board, and to offer a reward of five hundred dollars for the discovery of any conspiracy to set fire to the city, and a like reward for the discovery of any persons who may have willfully perpetrated the fire on December 18, and also a like reward for the discovery of any person who may have set fire to buildings since that period, and that such reward be paid on the conviction of the offender or offenders respectively." It was likewise ordered "that all officers be vigilant and attentive, as well in the detection of offenders as in preventing the execution of their designs, and that all persons be requested to communicate such information which they may possess in relation to the origin of the late fire, or in regard to future attempts, at the inspector's office. Ordered that the augmentation of the city watch directed by the mayor be continued until the further order of the board, and that the captain of watch of the First District be directed to be particularly attentive to the neighborhood of Burling Slip."

The corporation of the Presbyterian Church, having requested in the latter part of 1805 that the engine house standing on their ground in Nassau Street may be removed, "it is ordered that the engine house in the City Hall Yard be extended so as to admit the deposit of the engine on the said ground belonging to the Presbyterian Church."

In Common Council, March 23, 1807, the chief engineer represented the necessity of moving Engine No. 29 from the house of that number, standing on ground heretofore allotted to that purpose, "but now rented to Mr. Francis De Flyn, who wishes for the removal of said building." It was ordered, "that the alderman and assistant of the Eighth Ward do provide some proper place for Engine No. 29." The following were appointed firemen: George Griffin to Engine No. 14; Sewell Dodge to Engine No. 8; Ely Emmons to Engine No. 11; John Shaden to Engine No. 32; John H. Fisher to Engine No. 30.

The early engines were located in structures little better than sheds. Bye-and-bye the corporation voted sums of money to provide better accommodation, and it was not long before very respectable houses were provided. It was not till about the period of 1840 that regular dwellings were provided for the men who lived at a distance from their engine. At first the expense was borne by the men themselves. Many of the hardy Volunteers were content for years with a straw mattress. The "bunking" system enabled the firemen to have a watch all night, and the consequence was that a quicker service was obtained.

Never at any time was there the slightest intimation of a desire for a remuneration. The men gloried in working for nothing. "The Voluntary system," wrote ex-Judge Charles P. Daly, "was upon its introduction a most desirable one, and continued to be so for more than three-quarters of a century. For alacrity, intrepidity, skill, and courage, the men who composed it would compare with any body of firemen in the world. At its institution, and for many years, it consisted almost exclusively of the most influential and prominent citizens, who discharged their arduous labors at a great sacrifice of time, and frequently of health, from a high sense of public duty, and the example they set infused into the whole community a zeal and willingness to lend their aid and assistance upon the breaking out of a fire almost without precedent in the history of cities. The effect upon the rising generation was especially marked, and the young were made to feel that to be a fireman was an honorable distinction."

The old engines moved with difficulty, and were cumbrous and rude in construction. They, however, gave place to better machines, and the service improved as the demand upon it grew. The danger of the work was obvious, and a courage and daring which has gone into history began to leave behind it men who were maimed and crippled in the public service, and widows and orphans deprived of their natural protectors and reduced to poverty and want. The firemen themselves were the first to see the growing difficulty, and with characteristic unselfishness sought to provide a remedy.

It took the firemen a long time to find out that their beloved hand engine was not the most perfect machine possible. Really they had done excellent service with it, and no wonder it was hard to wean them from their darling. Steam fire engines were introduced in London in 1832 with a marked increase of efficiency and economy ; but it was nearly thirty years afterwards before they were introduced in New York. The influence of the firemen on public officials postponed the adoption of the steam engine long after its practicability had been established. In like manner horses had long been used in London to transport the engines and other fire apparatus more expeditiously. This, too, was regarded as an innovation by the Volunteer firemen of this city, who had a strong preference for dragging the engines themselves by hand. But steam and electricity, twin giants, could not long be put down by such puny efforts. They had taken a front place in the van of civilized life, and were soon to revolutionize the world. The Fire Department, it is true, were slow to appreciate these potent facts. Many held that New York was by far more progressive than the Fire Department. It had grown, and was growing apace, while the firemen, seemingly unconscious of this self-evident fact, had stuck to the old time methods of fire extinguishing in vogue when the city was comparatively a village. "When the city," says ex-Judge Daly, "was embraced within moderate limits, the occasional duty of acting as a fireman was not a very onerous one, but when the city had expanded miles in extent it exacted an amount of time which few were able to give who had their business to attend to, and consequently this class was gradually withdrawn from the department, which was filled by those who could give more time to it. The increasing extension of the city demanded, moreover, a constant augmentation of the force of the department, and as it increased in numbers it degenerated in quality."

A newspaper writer, with a spice of humor, once began his account of the old firemen with the remark : " We don't mean those redoubtable old chaps who had inserted in the by-laws of their company a clause to the effect that it was legitimate for a member, upon arriving at the engine house, after hearing an alarm of fire, to grease his boots at the expense of the corporation before he rolled the machine, or endeavor to catch her if she had rolled." But those " old chaps," nevertheless, were brave as lions. We have given many an instance of the bravery of the Volunteer firemen. Saving lives at fires was characteristic of them, and it is to be regretted that more records of their daring acts have not been preserved. Many gallant deeds in the cause of humanity have been forgotten, for no note was made of them at the time. The activity of the firemen in this respect, considering the facilities they possessed as compared with those of to-day, was remarkable. The assistance they rendered operatives and inmates of burning buildings, and the desperate chances they often took to save lives, seem to belong more to the days of knights-errantry than to an era of dollars and cents. In July, 1855, the *Tribune* had the following :

ENGINE CO. 21 (FULTON), 1855.

[Located adjoining Old New York Hospital, Anthony St. (now Worth St.), near Broadway. Original painting in possession of John Tyson, Jersey City.]

" GALLANT CONDUCT.—About twelve o'clock on Wednesday night, the fourth instant, a fire broke out in the building, No. 138 Prince Street, occupied by J. C. Stone on the first floor as a store for the sale of fancy articles and fireworks and dwelling, upper part as a dwelling by Jas. Nagle and family and Mr. Beebe and family. The fire originated among a quantity of fireworks, and in a short time the building was densely filled with smoke. The flames spread rapidly, and for some time defied the efforts of the firemen, who were promptly on the ground after the alarm was given. A large crowd gathered in the street, among whom the greatest excitement prevailed. The occupants of the building had not yet made their appearance, and it was not known whether or not they had escaped, although it was rumored that they were still in the building. A ladder was soon brought and placed against the second story window, when Thomas O'Brien, Charles Wilson, Levi D. White, of Hose Company No. 56, and Gardner Van Brunt, of Engine Company No. 2, four daring souls, made their way through fire and smoke into the second story. Crawling upon their hands and knees over the floor, they at length found the beds in the different apartments, all of which were occupied. They sought to arouse the occupants, but they were unable to do so, as nearly all of them were about half suffocated and unable to help themselves. No time was to be lost, as the smoke was becoming denser and denser every moment. The gallant fellows seized Mr. Beebe and his wife, and carrying them to the windows, passed them down the ladders to the street. They then returned and brought three young women, Margaret Nagle, Ellen Nagle, and Mary Ann Shannon, a niece of Mr. Nagle, also two sons of Mr. Nagle. Margaret, half crazed by the smoke, leaped from the fireman's arms through the window and fell heavily upon the sidewalk, injuring her back and ankles. Mary Ann was badly burned upon the head and shoulders. Ellen Nagle, while being lowered to the street, had her ankle sprained, and was somewhat burned. Mr. Nagle and his wife were almost gone, and it was only by the kindest attention that they recovered. The sons were also somewhat injured. The parties were conveyed to the Eighth Ward Station House, where they were attended personally by Captain Turnbull and Lieutenants Kohler and Stage, and several physicians. Mr. Stone and his wife escaped by the rear door, first floor. Mrs. Stone, on reaching the door, missed her child, and returned through the smoke to her room, where, recovering her child, she succeeded in escaping without injury."

Indeed, the words courage and fireman were synonomous. The bravery and devotion of the Department amply compensated, in the opinion of the public, for whatever shortcomings it had. The companies had quarrels, to be sure; but they were quarrels arising from a noble rivalry to be the first at a fire or a rescue. In later years the Department was an immense organization. What wonder that evil-disposed persons—big and little—took advantage of it, either to discredit or use it for their own purposes. It was seen that a new era was dawning—that the city wanted a simpler, more effective, and more compact organization. New York was immensely rich. It could afford to pay for this arduous service, and it was resolved to do so. Good citizens generally wished well to the prospect of disbanding the Volunteers and establishing a Paid Department. The politicians began to use the Department for their ends, and the people and even the press were afraid to denounce them. The disagreeable duty of abolishing the Volunteers was therefore undertaken by the Board of Fire Underwriters.

The work of disbandment went on slowly at first. The new regime was not yet organized, but the transfer of authority was effected with very little friction, all things considered. The disbanded Volunteers, by their dignity and forbearance, and their adherence to duty during the last trying hours of their organization, sustained their historic and well-earned reputation as brave men and devoted citizens. The New York *Herald,* editorially, (April 3, 1865), said:

"The conduct of the firemen under the present circumstances—which must be regarded as a great crisis in the history of their organization—is worthy of all admiration. There were many who supposed that upon the passage of the bill abolishing the Volunteer Department, there would have been resistance, and perhaps riotous conduct, on the part of the firemen. So far from that, they have exhibited the finest spirit, submitting cheerfully to the change, and consenting to fulfill their duties to the last in the protection of property and life. Their action proves, what we have always believed to be true, that the Fire Department proper was composed of a gallant, fearless, and honorable body of our citizens. The course which the members of the Department are now pursuing entitles them to the highest praise which is due to law-abiding citizens; and although the Volunteer Firemen's organization is no longer to comprise one of our local institutions, to have been a member of it will be a lasting honor."

On the twenty-ninth of July the work of retiring the Volunteers was begun, and by the first of November three thousand eight hundred and ten of their number were stricken from the rolls. That they had "continued faithfully to perform the duties which their obligations imposed," was their crowning glory. Their services could not be entirely dispensed with, however, and the services of the leading officers—engineers and foremen—were retained by the new Board.

At last the hour drew nigh. The Volunteers were to be numbered with the past, but their great services were not to be forgotten—they had made history, and they will live in it. Sorrowfully, regretfully, notwithstanding the promise of better things to come, the city said farewell to their old protectors. This book is a tribute—though an insufficient one—to the memory of their gallantry. Take them for all in all, they were brave men, honest men, devoted men—we shall never look upon their like again.

CHAPTER XLVII.

ORGANIZATION OF THE PAID DEPARTMENT.

New York Overtakes the Provinces in 1864.—Paving the Way to a Paid Department.—The only way to
Rescue the Volunteers was to Reorganize Them.—The Police, Insurance Men and Citizens
Take a Hand to this End.

THE establishment of Paid Fire Departments in several cities of the Union,
notably Boston, Cincinnati, St. Louis and Baltimore, and their success
and advantages had been watched and noted not only as a matter of
business by fire insurance underwriters, and citizens whose property was
exposed to accident or crime—for near the close of the war arson was resorted
to by allies of the South—but by the Volunteers and their friends and the general
thinking public. The way to the establishment of a Paid Fire Department in
New York City had been often paved, but the time for its legalization had not
come and the schemes were abandoned when only partially planned. Still it
was a striking commentary on New York's pre-eminence in advanced municipal
affairs that, in methods of dealing with criminals, the management of the
streets, the care of the indigent and criminal classes, etc., she was faithfully copied in every large city of the Union. A few cities, whose population
was comparatively a fraction of hers, had looked ahead and provided for the
time when buildings should be higher and more numerous, and when little less
than a quasi-military organization would be suitable. Citizens had wearied of
the noisy enthusiasm of the camp followers of men wedded to an old, slow
system, with inadequate apparatus—often so old as to be venerable. It necessitated the services of an average of fifty men to a company, and the firemen,
without fee, or hope of other reward than the gratification of a desire for
excitement and muscular exercise and the performance of their duties as
citizens, did service that well merited substantial recognition in the shape of pay
and permanent employment. Volunteer fire duty, it is true, was done as well as
possible under the circumstances, all cavil and innuendo to the contrary notwithstanding. It is just to say here that, as a whole, the Paid Department of this
city has not, in heroism, intrepidity or disinterestedness, excelled the active
Volunteers, when all things are taken into consideration. The same company
rivalry which, under the old system led to racing and sometimes brawls, still
exists, and despite iron-clad rules and public sentiment, crops out now and then,
showing that, after all, all firemen are human. The very rivalry which existed
between the Volunteer companies was in the end an advantage. Had they
been apathetic, few apparatuses would have reached a fire in time to prevent
serious loss. The racing was based on a point of honor, a test of endurance,
skill and strategy. It kept up the *esprit de corps*, and left laggards in the
rear. The anxiety in running to a fire to prevent a rival company from passing

was that of an English or American university crew of oarsmen to avoid getting "bumped." The system of competition taught firemen that the shortest distance between two points is a straight line, and that the alert and fleetfooted get to the goal first. So that in these days the company which has the "hitching up" drill well mastered, and leaves the quarters the moment a home signal is ticked off, may reach the station indicated before a less well drilled and not so wide-awake a company much nearer to the rendezvous, and so shame the laggards into better performance of duty another time. The Volunteers, once the members of the company assembled and the rope manned, made as good time as bipeds could. Taken as a whole, the active members of the Volunteer Fire Department—not the "runners" and hangers-on—were as brave, honest, efficient and earnest, without pay and with antiquated apparatus, as are the active members of the present Department, who are well paid and have the best fire extinguishing appliances that science and mechanical ingenuity can devise or that money can command. Such Volunteers, or such of them as would, for proper remuneration, do what they did gratuitously out of a sense of the highest duties and obligations of citizenship, apart from any love of excitement and peril, were worth saving from politicians and the rabble, and the only way to save them, it was asserted, was to destroy the Volunteer organization.

This enigmatical assertion is based on facts. Putting aside the question of the injustice of permitting able-bodied men, the majority of them working for their daily bread, to abandon work and risk their lives and expose themselves to the elements and severe toil, to save municipal and private property, and protect the lives and limbs of the community, without substantial reward—the time had come when a line had to be drawn between the Volunteers, who were already cursed with political manipulation from their camp followers and the dry rot of expediency which, to serve the purpsose of a few intent on using the Volunteers as political factors, had discountenanced the introduction of steam fire apparatus and the consequent and inevitable reduction in the number of companies and the working force of such as were retained ; the system saddled on the Volunteers was virtually at an end with the introduction of the first fire steam engine. This and many which followed were not built as strongly as those of later years, but—taking the complement of a hand engine at fifty men—it pointed a way to relieve six-sevenths of those doing duty with the hand engine, if horses were employed to draw the engine. At the same time, the time required to take an engine from quarters to a fire was so reduced that the necessity of having many companies in each district was obviated, while the employment of an engineer at a salary, although he was elected by the company, insured the strict and interested attention of at least one member of such company to details on which depended the prompt starting of the apparatus from quarters when a signal was struck. The old hand apparatus, made as light as possible to permit of quick hand transportation and elegance of construction, had to hug a fire to permit of a proper stream being thrown on the flames by ordinary exertion, which, as a rule, was no light work, under extraordinary exertion, and the stimulus of rivalry with the iron-lunged innovation, streams were thrown which equaled, if they did not excel, those thrown by steam power. But it was at once seen that as a rule the steam machine could take a remote hydrant and do as good service as a hand machine, until the men who manned the brakes became exhausted, and then continue to do equally good service as long as fuel lasted. Besides, it was evident that the resources of science and mechanism had not been exhausted in the construction of the first steam fire engines. The horses attached to the engine did away with the rope, and with it the yearning of the rabble to take a hand and "jump her," and the horses did not yell and urge each other to exertion on the way to a fire, but attended strictly to business and left the camp followers who were not the fleetest of foot in the lurch, so that the pranks and depredations of the "sidewalk committees" were done away with. The horses, too, had no fancy for hurrying to rush past a rival company, or halt and fight out a rancorous sentiment, partly jealousy, partly rivalry, while the fire which had started was getting ahead. All New York did not frown at their encounters and jealousies. If the naked truth were told, few outside the Department were gravely anxious about them at all times. To many it appeared that until New York paid for fire service it would be impossible to have such service at all efficient without at least winking at the competition which pitted one company against the other, and resulted generally in a gain in point of speed in reaching a fire. Men who did their utmost to create a Paid Department were members of companies whose reputation for zeal in distancing or vanquishing rivals by feet or hands was the best or worst, as the partisan or critic may determine, and were as eager as their comrades when the apparatus was rolled out and the race began, or when the goal was reached and others were found to have the ground of vantage. How many staid citizens of the Volunteer time who yet live will affirm that, even on Sunday, when the races either ·on genuine or false alarms, were along Broadway or the Bowery, and the ragamuffins ran to see them, and the often consequent unpleasantness

SEAL : METROPOLITAN FIRE DEPARTMENT.

between companies, they did not gird up their loins and become interested spectators? And how many, under the pressure of conscience, will fail to admit that at a pinch they vented their preferences, antipathies or interest in a shout or an exclamation, if they did not take a hand in the results of a collision after a war of words? Few citizens but had a tie or an interest of some sort in some engine, hose, or hook and ladder company. Many were impelled to vexation, and so on to exasperation, when their ox was gored, that is to say, when, often for trivial cause, such as a chimney fire or a false alarm, the streets in the neighborhood of their houses or counting rooms were invaded by apparatusses and crowds of excited, wrangling men and the hangers on at their company quarters, and business and traffic stopped until excited passions were calmed and temper improved. Storekeepers grinned, shouted and lost themselves in excitement in the business avenues until an apparatus cleared the sidewalk, as the malicious practical jokers who followed the regulars upset the goods displayed in front of stores and made havoc of them, if they did not plunder. It is to be doubted if the enemies of the Volunteer firemen proper, the active members of companies, were legion, because men of all ranks belonged to it, and persons of all walks in life did duty as "bunkers," "home sleepers" and "Exempts." But those who had dealings with the insurance companies, whose rates were high, were financially interested in any scheme which would put the Fire Department on any footing which would make it independent of those who were beginning to turn it into a political factor, and enable it to squelch the hangers-on or "runners," who were mainly an undesirable class, from the boys to depredators who waited for a fire alarm to run with the apparatus for no good purpose. In this and other ways the Volunteers had a bad name with the Paid Police Department, whose members lost no opportunity of exaggerating wrangles or brawls, and making insinuations or flat charges when property was damaged or outrage occurred. The patience of the police, it must be admitted, was often sorely tried. There were few alarms of fire that did not call for action, from especial vigilance to interference, and now and then a policeman got hurt in an encounter, and the blame was always laid on the Volunteers, although in the majority of instances the rabble had a hand in the melée, and it was fair to infer would be more likely to surreptitiously injure a policeman than an active fireman. The Hon. Thomas C. Acton and the late John A. Kennedy, superintendent of police, were prepared to encourage any plan to put the Volunteers on an independent footing or create a new Department in which Volunteers who chose to devote themselves to the service for proper remuneration could be enrolled. The chief engineer of the Volunteers in later days was but little better than a creature of the street commissioner, and had to mind his Ps and Qs. The district engineers were in a worse predicament, as had the chief engineer been a martinet, a crank, or a rascal, they could have been harrassed between him and the companies over which they had jurisdiction. The Commissioners owed allegiance to the companies because of their suffrages, and the Common Council's supreme influence was baneful. Proper discipline was out of the question. For excellent political reasons, any black sheep expelled or disciplined could, if he had " a pull," be reinstated, and snap his fingers at discipline.

Such was the condition of affairs in a department whose members had shown what stuff they were made of, and their leaning towards law and order against mob rule and anarchy in the riots of 1863, when it became certain that in the Legislature of 1865 an opportunity to pass a Paid Fire Department measure would be seized upon.

Preparations for the legislative campaign of 1865 were begun early in 1864. On the seventeenth of March of that year the following resolution was passed at a meeting of the Board of Fire Underwriters:

Resolved, That the subject of promoting the greater efficiency of the Fire Department be referred to a special committee to inquire into the same, and report to a subsequent meeting of this Board.

The committee was James M. McLean, president of the Citizens' Fire Insurance Company; Carlisle Norwood, president of the Lorillard; James M. Rankin, secretary of the Fulton; Rudolph Garrigue, Richard A. Reading, T. J. Glover, and T. G. Churchill. With them was associated Le Grand B. Cannon, director of the American. All were men of the greatest experience in fire matters, not only because the majority of them had been members of the Volunteer Department, but because they were experts in insurance business, and had studied European fire extinguishing methods, and the Paid Departments as they were successively established in this country.

Police Commissioner Acton and Superintendent John A. Kennedy furnished the committee with police reasons for a change. The underwriters' committee had for legal advisers Dorman B. Eaton and Abraham R. Lawrence, and much of the legal work was done by Mr. William C. Whitney, Secretary of the Navy under President Cleveland. The police contribution was in the form of affidavits from Captains Helm, Speight, Cameron, Williamson, Jordan, Todd, De Camp, Davis, Mount, Sebring, and others, who told of the disturbances, Sabbath desecration, pilfering, and general nuisances, of which they accused the Volunteers and their followers. The underwriters' committee mastered the legal feature of the proposed change, shaped a course from reports from Baltimore, Boston, St. Louis, and Cincinnati, and the first draft of the Paid

Fire Department Bill was made by Mr. James M. Rankin, in his house at Second Avenue and One Hundred and Twenty-fourth Street. The late Senator William Laimbeer, who was to father the bill in the Senate, did not trust to theories or reports, but visited the cities in which Paid Departments existed. He was accompanied by the Hon. Hugh Gardner, and profited not a little by that sturdy Scot's shrewdness, common sense, and practical views. The Volunteers got an inkling of what was contemplated, and to offset the iconoclasts, and to put the

WILLIAM LAIMBEER.

Volunteers in a better light before the public, and to render them independent of many alliances that had militated against their prestige and usefulness, concurred—rank and file—in the drawing up of the ordinance of the thirty-first of December, 1864, which was intended as an offset to action at Albany. It was entitled "An ordinance for the better regulation of the Firemen of the City of New York." It provided for a chief engineer, to be elected every three years by the votes of the members of the Volunteer Fire Department, the first election to be in February, 1866; but the election was simply a nomination to the Common Council for "appointment," and the salary was fixed at five thousand dollars per annum. No chief engineer could serve a second term. Nineteen assistant engineers, two for each district, except the Ninth, which was to have three, were to be elected in a precisely similar manner in February, 1865, and to serve three years. Vacancies were to be filled by ballot within thirty days. The working force of the department was to consist of "such members of fire engine men, hose men, and hook and ladder men   *   *   *   as now are or hereafter may be from time to time appointed in the manner required by law." Thus the Department was left in the hands of the voting firemen and the dominant Common Council, and the system that had been the bane of the Volunteers was continued. Apart from these provisions, the ordinance pursued the best features of the old regimes, and introduced some new regulations calculated to improve the efficiency of the Department. Discipline and deportment were insisted on. The assistant engineers were to choose one of their number as senior, and he was to take the place of the chief in the event of disability or a vacancy. The Board of Engineers and Foremen had the power to make elections for holding and conducting the elections. The companies chose their own foremen, assistant foremen, and secretaries, by such means and at such times as they considered proper, but the commissioners of the Fire Department decided in cases of irregularity and dispute. Stringent rules were in the ordinances against the admission of persons not members of the department entering company quarters, and boys and disorderly characters lounging in their vicinity, and no boys or improper persons were to be allowed to take hold of the drag rope. No racing was to be countenanced. The fire commissioners could reprimand, suspend, or disband any company, and any company could vote for the expulsion of a member, while the fire commissioners could reverse, modify, or confirm such act. Sections 37 and 38 provided as follows:

"Any person who may in future be elected to fill a vacancy to any fire company shall present to the Chief Engineer within thirty days thereafter a certificate of such election, signed by the foreman and secretary of the company in which he has been elected, stating his name, residence, and business; and said candidate, before the Chief Engineer presents his name to the Commissioners of the Fire Department, shall make affidavit that he is a citizen of the United States, is twenty-one years of age and upwards, that he is physically able, and that it is his intention to perform active and actual duty as a fireman with the company in which his name is enrolled, and that he will promote subordination in the Fire Department and the company to which he belongs, and it shall be the duty of the Chief Engineer to certify on every return whether a vacancy exists in the company. Applicants for appointment as members of the Fire Department must be of good moral character and actually engaged in some lawful business, and must be recommended to the Fire Commissioners as honest, sober, and industrious men, by their employers and three citizens of known respectability, and the Commissioners may confirm or reject any or all such applications."

Proper returns of duty performed were expected from all officers. The chief engineer was given authority to remove any apparatus or Corporation property to the Public or Corporation yard. Such removals were to be made if the company was short-handed, was not useful, or became disreputable or riotous. In case of disbandment, facilities were given for members of a company to join another. The Chief Engineer, Presidents of the Department, Board of Trustees, Fire Commissioners, and Board of Commissioners of Appeal were made a Commission of Construction and Repairs of the New York Fire Department, to inquire into applications for changes in locations, for apparatus, or for new companies, or new houses, or for alterations or repairs to houses, or for new apparatus, or for alterations or repairs to apparatus, costing seventy-five dollars or more. The police were required to report any fireman or company violating any law or ordinance of the Fire Department, and it was made their duty to wake up members of the Department who might reside on their beats on a fire alarm being given at night, and the firemen were to supply the police with their names and residences. It was also the duty of the police to form lines at fires and prevent unauthorized persons from invading the territory thus environed. The mayor was empowered to select three bellringers for each signal station at one thousand dollars a year each. Engineers for steam engines were to be appointed by the Board of Engineers on the recommendation of a majority of the members of the company in which the appointee was to serve. Such appointees were to be competent and properly recommended. The uniform of the different members and officers was designated, and the wearing of it insisted on. The following section will be read with interest by the present generation :

"If any of the fire companies shall embellish their apparatus by painting, silver or other plating, polishing or any other embellishment, the chief engineer or other authorities of the City of New York shall not have replaced at the expense of the said city any such embellishment on any fire apparatus which may need rebuilding, alteration, or repairs, but shall only have such apparatus put in good working order without such embellishments, and when any embellishment is placed on any fire apparatus by any person or persons, or fire company, so that the same shall become a fixture to said apparatus, the said person, or persons, or fire company, shall not displace or disfigure said embellishment, and the said embellishment shall belong to the Corporation of the City of New York."

The ordinance embodied such regulations as are now within the province of the Superintendent of Combustibles and the Bureau of Inspection of Buildings. It prescribed the amount of fines for various breaches of discipline and violations of its provisions, and how they should be disposed of.

Chief John Decker, throughout the excitement caused by the legislation at Albany, the testing of the constitutionality of the law, and the merging of the Volunteer System into the Paid System, while he never for an instant swerved from his allegiance to the comrades whose votes placed him at their head, displayed qualities that characterize the law-abiding citizen and conscientious official. The " Ordinance for the better regulation of the Firemen of the City of New York," which became a municipal law on the thirty-first of December, 1864, was prepared at the instance of Commissioner John J. Gorman, with a view of improving the Volunteer service. The first steps were taken at Firemen's Hall, on the twenty-seventh of September, 1864, when the Board of Representatives, Fire and Appeal Commissioners, Trustees, Engineers, Foremen, and Assistant Foremen met, discussed the reorganization of the Volunteer system, appointed a committee of twenty from all branches of the Department, of which President Gorman was chairman, and left it to devise a plan to meet the requirements of the law, and satisfy the Department and the public. Over his own signature Chief Decker said that this ordinance was all that was necessary for the government of the Department. He went on to say that neither the Department nor its officers were, until the passage of the revised ordinance of December, 1864, responsible for the expenditure of its moneys, and he yet says that Tweed, Cornell, and others, killed the ordinance bill, which was taken to Albany to be passed as a state law. Nearly all the funds charged to the Fire Department, he said, were disbursed lavishly by the Common Council and Street Commissioners' Department, of which he was a subordinate, without consulting any officer of the Fire Department. It was acknowledged by the officers of the Fire Department that two-thirds of the hose companies could be dispensed with ; but until the ordinance of 1864 was passed this could not be done, unless the companies violated a law or ordinance. In five years and a half only three out of fifty-seven hose companies were abolished, but under the new ordinance, in Chief Decker's opinion, more than forty could have been done away with in a year. When the presentation of the Paid Fire Department Bill was announced, Chief Decker did all he could for the Volunteers; and he says that the arguments in their favor before the Assembly committee were so powerful, that the Metropolitan Bill would not have been passed had not "some of the insurance companies of this city submitted to a tax on their capital amounting to fifty thousand dollars, and placed it in the hands of a committee who were urging the passage of the Metropolitan Fire Bill, after which arguments were in vain."

The legislation which created a Paid Fire Department was in stirring times. It was while all who could think or read watched the end of the struggle between North and South, and the proceedings at Albany attracted less of general attention than would have been paid to them had they been before the Legislature a year later or a year earlier. Had the measure been introduced in 1864 it is hardly possible to estimate what the result would have been had it become a law. A year later might have seen the innovation put off to another or a still later session by lobbying and influences of various sorts. But the Senate and Assembly were Republican; Reuben E. Fenton was Governor; Thomas G. Alvord, Lieutenant Governor; and G. G. Hoskins, Speaker. James Terwilliger was Clerk of the Senate; and Joseph B. Cushman, Clerk of the Assembly. The Hon. William Laimbeer, on the fourth of January, 1865, gave notice in the Senate of a bill to incorporate a Paid Fire Department for New York City, and in the Assembly a week later Mr. Thomas B. Van Buren gave notice that at an early day he would ask to introduce a similar bill. On the sixteenth of January Senator Laimbeer introduced " An Act to create a Metropolitan Fire District and establish a Fire Department therein," which was read a first time, and referred to the Committee on Cities and Villages, which consisted of Messrs. Laimbeer, Strong, Shafer, White, Dutcher, and Andrews. Mr. Thomas E. Stewart, on January 20, gave notice of the bill in the Assembly. It was introduced there January 23, and read a first time. On the thirty-first of January, on motion of Senator Laimbeer, the Committee on Cities and Villages was empowered to send for persons and papers to aid in considering the bill, but next day an amendment to send for the clerk of the Fire Commissioners and such books, papers, etc., as he might have in charge, prevailed. The Committee heard testimony from all interested persons. On the seventh of February Lenator Laimbeer presented a petition for a Paid Fire Department from Exempt Firemen, and two years later the bill was taken from the Senate Committee on Cities and Villages—because of the resignation of six of the members, who were disgusted with Senator Field's eccentricities— and referred to the following Select Committee: Dennis Strong, G. H. Andrews, William Laimbeer, John B. Dutcher, Ira Shafer, Andrew D. White, and Saxton Smith.

On the fifteenth of February Mr. Andrews reported in favor of the bill, and it was referred to the Committee of the Whole. On the twenty-fourth of February, in the Assembly, Mr. S. C. Reed presented a petition for a Paid Fire Department from residents of Brooklyn. Next day Senator Laimbeer's motion to make the bill the special order for March 2 was adopted. That day Senator

Allen reported in favor of passing the bill without amendment. Senator Chrystie's motion to recommit the bill to the Committee on Municipal Affairs, and to strike out the enacting clause, was lost, seven to twenty-one. Senator Cozans moved as a substitute, "An Act for the better regulation of the Firemen of the City of New York," Chief Decker's Volunteer measure; rejected, seven to nineteen. After a little more filibustering the bill was ordered to a third reading. Next day Senator Fields moved that the Supervisors of New York assess on the capital stock of the insurance companies (the framers of the Paid Fire Department measure) a sum sufficient to pay the expenses of the Fire Department. This motion was buried, as was a motion from the "Torpedo" to pay each fireman one thousand dollars a year, and each engineer one thousand five hundred dollars a year. Henry C. Murphy moved that at the next general election four Metropolitan Fire Commissioners be elected, but this and several minor and dilatory motions were lost, and the bill was read a third time and passed.

AYES—Allen, Ames, Andrews, Angel, Beach, Bell, Cole, Cook, Cornell, Dutcher, Folger, Havens, Hayt, Hobbs, Julian, Laimbier, Low, Mauger, Strong, White, and Williams—21.

NAYS—Allaben, Chrystie, Cozans, Fields, Murphy, and Woodruff—6.

On the fourth of March the Assembly received a message from the Senate asking concurrence in the bill, which was read a first time, and sent to the Committee on Cities. A week later the Speaker presented a

SCENE AT A BROADWAY FIRE.

communication from the General Society of Mechanics and Tradesmen in favor of a Paid Fire Department. On March 15 Assemblyman Perry, of Kings, for the Committee on Cities—J. C. Perry, Kings; T. E. Stewart, New York; W. P. Angel, Cattaraugus; Alexander Ward, New York; G. M. Holles, Otsego; Alexander Robertson, Albany; and J. B. Morey, of Livingston—reported in favor of the measure, which was referred to the Committee of the Whole. March 16, in Senate, the Hon. T. G. Alvord presented the petition of the General Society of Mechanics and Tradesmen as sent to the House. Assemblyman Wood, on the twenty-third of March, presented the report of the minority in the Committee on the Affairs of Cities against the measure. Its conclusions were, in substance:

1st. That the present system is in actual operation with beneficial results.

2d. That the proper mode of legislation on the subject is to improve the present system without making an entire and untried change.

3d. That as a matter of fact, the present system had from time to time adopted such practical reforms as were demanded by the progress of society and special contingencies.

4th. That the abuses alleged to exist were greatly exaggerated in the heat of an oral argument.

5th. That the economy of the present Department is equal to the average of the Paid Departments cited.

6th. That the Metropolitan Fire Department Bill, by its form and terms, was unjust to the people in not providing, either by specific sections or the establishment of any organization for economy or efficiency, or the introduction of any reforms.

Messrs. Creamer, Lyons, Keegan, and Smith spoke against the bill and in favor of the Volunteers, and Mr. Van Buren supported the measure, which was ordered to a third reading; Messrs. Angel, Bemis, Crowell, Kimball, Lewis, and Strong, Republicans, and Messrs. Blauvelt, Creamer, Gaughan, Keegan, Loutrel, Lyons, Maloy, McDonald, Murray, Seebacher, Smith, and Ward of the New York delegation voting nay, while their fellow-citizens, Van Buren, Stewart, and Reed, voted for it. Messrs. Ingraham and Salmon did not vote, the former being absent and the latter excused. The bill hung by a thread in the House, but on the thirtieth of March it came up for a third reading, and was passed amid some excitement. The ayes were (Democrats marked "D"):

Andrews, Bonham, A. A. Brown, Barkley, Bookstaver, D. J. W. Brown, Carpenter, N. Clark, Crowell, Cole, Close, Eldridge, D., Gleason, Hasbrouck, Hulse, Kellogg, Lefever, Lord, Mersereau, Oliver, J. L. Parker, Pitts, Rankin, Richardson, Rouse, Severance, Shepherd, Shutte, D., Stafford, Strong, Topliff, Wilber, Edgerton, Fonda, D., Green, Hollis, Humphrey, Kimball, Lee, McCall, Nolan, D., Palmer, Perry, Platt, D., Redington, Ridgeway, D., Root, Sumner, Sherman, E. S. Smith, Stanford, Tillinghast, Van Buren, Wood, Biddecour, Brandreth, Brunson, Collins, Crandall, Edwards, Godfrey, Hallenbeck, D., Howard, S. H. Hungerford, Lapham, Lewis, McNeil, D., Olcott, G. Parker, Pickard, Post, Reed, Rogers, Sanford, Shaw, Speaker, Spoor, Steward, Talman, Weller, D., and Worth—81.

The nays were (Republican marked "R"):

Bemis, R., Boswell, Blauvelt, Burdett, Burns, Cooper, Cutting, Chapman, W. N. Clark, Creamer, Daniels, Gaughan, Haynes, Keegan, Langner, Lockwood, Loutrel, Lyons, Maloy, Matthews, McConvil, McDonald, Murray, Nickerson, Penfield, Robertson, Salmon, Sammons, Seebacher, Sherwood, J. L. Smith, Stanard, Talman, Veeder, Ward, Weaver, Weed, and Whitman —39. Mr. Angel was excused from voting.

The Bill as passed was as follows:

CHAPTER 249.

AN ACT TO CREATE A METROPOLITAN FIRE DISTRICT AND ESTABLISH A FIRE DEPARTMENT THEREIN.

Passed March 30, 1865; three-fifths being present.

The People of the State of New York, represented in Senate and Assembly, do enact as follows:

SECTION 1. The Cities of New York and Brooklyn shall constitute and they are hereby united into a district to be known as the Metropolitan Fire District of the State of New York.

SEC. 2. The governor shall nominate, and by and with the consent of the Senate, appoint four citizens, residents of the said district, to be "Metropolitan Fire Commissioners" (which office is hereby created with the duties and powers herein contained and imposed), who shall form a Metropolitan Fire Department, to take and have, as provided by this act, control and management of all officers, men, property, measures and action, for the prevention and extinguishment of fires within the said district, to be organized as herein provided, and to be known as the "Metropolitan Fire Department." Said commissioners shall hold the said office respectively for the terms following, to wit: One for two years, one for four years, one for six years, and one for eight years; and at the expiration of each term respectively a successor shall be appointed in the manner above provided, who shall hold said office for the term of eight years. Vacancies in said office shall be filled by temporary appointments by the remaining members of said Department, to hold until the same are filled by the Senate on nomination by the governor. Said commissioners shall be subject to removal by the governor, as is provided by the law applicable to the removals of sheriffs, which are hereby extended so as to relate to each Department, but no removal shall be made until the commissioners contemplated to be removed shall have been served with written specific charges stating the derelictions complained of, and have been afforded an adequate opportunity to publicly answer the same and make his defense thereto.

SEC. 3. Immediately after the appointment of such commissioners they shall meet in the office of the Secretary of State and proceed under his direction to determine by lot which of such commissioners shall hold such office for each of the respective terms of two, four, six, and eight years; whereupon they shall take and file with said secretary the oath of office prescribed for State officers, and the Secretary of State shall give to each a certificate of appointment for the respective terms of office so determined as aforesaid.

SEC. 4. Said commissioners, on being qualified, shall meet and organize "The Metropolitan Fire Department," by electing one of said commissioners as president, and appointing a person as secretary, whereupon they shall possess and have all the power and authority conferred upon or possessed by any and all officers of the Fire Department of the City of New York, and to the exclusion of all such officers, and such other powers and duties in said district as are hereinafter conferred. Three of said commissioners shall constitute a quorum for the transaction of business, but the surviving members may at any time fill a vacancy, as provided in the second section of this act.

SEC. 5. The said "Metropolitan Fire Department" is hereby empowered and directed

BADGE: METROPOLITAN FIRE DEPARTMENT.

to possess and exercise fully and exclusively all the powers and perform all the duties for the government, management, maintenance, and direction of the Fire Department of the City of New York, and the premises and property thereof which at the time of the organization of said Department are possessed by or under the control of the boards and officers of the Fire Department of said city, or the officers or employees of said city, said powers and duties to be exercised and performed, and said property used in the said city or otherwise, as hereinafter provided, and the said Department shall hereafter have sole and exclusive power and authority to extinguish fires in said City of New York; and all acts conferring upon any other officer and officers any power in relation to the extinguishment of fires in said city are hereby repealed.

SEC. 6. The Board of Commissioners shall have full power to provide in and for the City of New York, supplies, horses, tools, implements, and apparatus of all kinds, (to be used in the extinguishing of fires), and fire telegraphs, to provide suitable locations for the same, and to buy, sell, construct, repair, and have the care of the same, and take any and all such action in the premises as may be reasonably necessary and proper.

SEC. 7. The Department hereby created is hereby empowered and directed to possess and exercise full and exclusive power and discretion for the government, management, maintenance, and direction of the several buildings and premises and property and appurtenances thereto, and all apparatus, hose, implements, and tools of any and all kinds which at the time of the appointment of the commissioners aforesaid were under the charge and control of any and all city officers, or officers of the Fire Department in said city for the use and benefit of the Fire Department of the City of New York; and it shall be the duty of all persons and officers in possession of any property, real and personal, belonging to, or set apart for, or in use by, or for the Fire Department of said city, to deliver the same to the possession and control of said "Metropolitan Fire Department."

Section 8 provided that any commissioner accepting or holding any other political office, or who, holding office as fire commissioner, should be publicly nominated for another elective office without declining the same, should be deemed to have forfeited his office. Section 9 provided for the selection of one of the commissioners as treasurer, on a bond of fifty thousand dollars.

Section 10 provided as follows:

SEC. 10. The "Metropolitan Fire Commissioners" and the comptroller and mayor of the City of New York, convened as a Board of Estimate, five of whom shall form a quorum for business, shall, annually, on or before the first of July, make up a financial estimate of the sums required annually for the payment of salaries, compensation, and rents, for the purchase of supplies, horses, apparatus of any and all kinds, tools, hose, implements, and keeping all of the same in repair; and generally for the purposes of this act, and such general and contingent expenses as may from time to time in the judgment of said Board of Estimate become necessary and proper, with the enumeration thereof. The said estimate shall then be submitted to a Board of Revision, composed of the Board of Supervisors of the County of New York. If the said Board of Revision, on or before the second Monday of October, shall object, in writing, to such estimate, or any portion thereof, and so notify the said Board of Estimate, it shall be the duty of the latter to immediately and carefully revise the same, and consider the said objections. If such Board of Estimate shall adhere to their original action of estimate, or if they shall modify the same without increasing the said estimate, then their final determination shall be binding upon the City of New York.

SEC. 11. The Board of Estimate created by the tenth section shall immediately after the organization of the said "Metropolitan Fire Department" meet, and make an estimate of the probable expenses of the Department in all branches of expenditure which will be required for the year one thousand eight hundred and sixty-five, before money can be realized under the tax levy for that year. They shall specify, as far as may be, to the several objects and purposes of expenditure. This estimate shall be immediately submitted to the Board of Revision, above provided in Section 10, for consideration. Said Board of Revision shall within ten days act upon said estimate, and return the same to the Board of Estimate with their objections, amendments, or approval, and said Board of Estimate shall take final action thereon, in the manner provided in Section 10. Whereupon the amount so estimated shall be levied and collected by the Board of Supervisors of the County of New York, in the same manner as is herein provided in relation to annual estimates for the expenses of the said "Metropolitan Fire Department."

SEC. 12. The comptroller of the City of New York shall have power, and it shall be his duty to borrow on the credit of said city, the amounts of said estimate for the year one thousand eight hundred and sixty-five, in anticipation of the receipt of said sum from the levy, and pay the same to the chamberlain of said city, to be drawn and used by the Metropolitan Fire Commissioners on their requisitions, from time to time, in such sums as they shall deem necessary, and for the purposes specified in this section. The said comptroller shall have the power to issue bonds in the name of the mayor, aldermen, and commonalty of the City of New York, which bonds shall be signed by the said mayor and comptroller, and authenticated by the seal of the corporation of the City of New York.

The remaining sections of the Act provided for officers and employees, a salary of three thousand five hundred dollars a year for the commissioners, the selection of firemen and employees, as far as possible, from the active and exempt members of the Volunteer Fire Department, giving the right of way to fire apparatus over all vehicles except the United States Mail, the raising of money by the Board of Supervisors for the annual expenses of the New Department, the transfer of all apparatus, etc., to the New Department by those having it in charge, the surrender to be to the Mayor, Aldermen and Commonalty of the City of New York, the designation of all real estate occupied by the Volunteers and not needed by the New Department, the return of all members of the Volunteer

Fire Department to the County Clerk, the same to be honorably discharged as exempt firemen if they continued to do duty until discharged by the new commissioners into whose control they passed by this Act, the guarantee of all benefits from the New York Fire Department Fund to those who up to the time of the passage of the Act were entitled to them, the continuance of the functions of the trustees of the fund, the return by the Clerk of the Common Council of the rolls of the Volunteers to the new commissioners, the punishment of those wearing in whole or in part the uniform or insignia of the New Department without authorization, or interfering with its apparatus, the adoption of a common seal, the power to institute and maintain suits in the name of the president for the enforcement of its rights and contracts, and for the possession and maintenance of the property under the control of the department, and the recovery of fines and penalties under Chapter 356 of the Laws of 1862; the transmission of an annual report to the Governor of the State of the condition, management and progress of the department, setting forth its needs, the selection of uniform and insignia, co-operation in case of need between Brooklyn and New York, and the continuance of the Volunteer Department until the new commissioners organized and entered upon their office.

JAMES M. RANKIN.

During the debates in both houses comparatively little acrimony was exhibited. Those in favor of the bill, which was at first a municipal measure and was changed to include Brooklyn to avoid a quibble in regard to its constitutionalty, evinced a disposition to treat the committees fairly, and the understanding that such of them as desired to become members of the New Department could do so, if eligible, was carried out eventually. In making the Senate report, Mr. Andrews said :

"The majority of the members of the New York Fire Department are men whose connection with it is prompted by a laudable devotion to the public interest, stimulated by that love of adventure and fearlessness in the face of danger, which would be accepted as the type of the loftiest heroism."

Senator Andrews also said he had not an unkind word for the New York Fire Department. One of the strong arguments, and in favor of the bill, was the reduction of rates of insurance in Baltimore under a Paid Department of from twenty-five to thirty per cent. The opponents of the bill were denounced as prejudiced, and it was represented that the New system would cost but little more than the Volunteer system, for which nearly five hundred and fifty thousand dollars were spent in 1864. Some harsh language was indulged in against the laxity of discipline in certain companies of the Volunteer Department, and habitual violation of rules, notably that against persons not members of a company "bunking" in their quarters; and the number of men in the Volunteer Department, four thousand, was ridiculed as excessive. The new measure was called "a dangerous though interesting experiment." Brooklyn was put in the bill to avoid any constitutional objection. One of the opponents of the innovation said it was "a blow to the liberties of the people of New York." The presence of Police Superintendent John A. Kennedy, who favored the bill, in Albany, was a signal for all sorts of comment on the interference of the police with the privileges and traditions of the public. Advocates of a Paid Department said that New York was no longer a village or a town. It had outgrown its former tastes, and its citizens should no longer be disturbed at all hours by "the rush of thousands of excited men and the clangor of bells and apparatus." Senator Andrews' harshest comments were: "It cannot be denied   *   *   *   that the luster of its early days has been tarnished by a spirit of insubordination and violence, which has so often led to a breach of the public peace." The advocates of the change were alive to the heroic nature of the measure. One of them admitted "It is the great change of the times if it becomes a law. Out goes the institution of an age so great that only Mr. Valentine can excavate it out of the dust. It is a revolution." It was "a revolution," in face of the sentiments of Mayor C. G. Gunther, as expressed in his message of January 9, 1865:

"The apparatus of the Fire Department is under the supervision of the street commissioners, together with the numerous houses for its accommodation. No city in the world possesses a more complete fire organization in the number of engines, the effectiveness of the recently-introduced steam machines, the copious supply of water, or the gallant army of volunteers that direct these means, for the preservation of property. No one appreciates more highly than myself the generosity and public spirit of our firemen, and nothing can efface the glorious records of their past history, so full of instances of heroic daring and unselfish toil. Many of its friends are of opinion that the system so admirably adapted to a small city is not suited to a metropolis, and that economy, as well as the new machinery, will compel a change. No one will cling to the old associations more firmly than myself, or surrender them with more reluctance, and nothing but the welfare of the city, and especially of that class whence our firemen are recruited, would reconcile me to the adoption of new ideas."

The last scene in the Assembly was a charge by Mr. Turner that he had been offered five hundred dollars for his vote in favor of the bill, but the accusation was withdrawn, and was without foundation.

It is just as well not to repeat here what was said in the Assembly and Senate when the bill came before the committees. Prominent among those advocating its passage were A. R. Lawrence, for banks, insurance companies, merchants, and property holders; Dorman B. Eaton, for the Citizens' Committee; Police Commissioner Thomas C. Acton, Superintendent John A. Kennedy, and minor police officials, and Messrs. Rankin, Norwood, McLean, Stansbury, and Curry, from the New York Board of Fire Insurance Companies, and Le Grand B. Cannon. Arranged against the measure were John Sedgwick, who supported the Ordinance Bill got up by Chief Decker and Commissioner John J. Gorman, Senator T. C. Fields, William Hitchman, a committee from the Volunteer Fire Department; Chief Decker, John R. Platt, of the Volunteers' Committee; Assemblyman T. J. Creamer, Senator Luke F. Cozans, and others. The police gave the strongest testimony. It did not appear fair, as the broadest of the charges made were not properly substantiated. Once, on the fifteenth of March, 1865, in the Assembly, it appeared as if the Paid Bill would be killed, as an adverse report on the Ordinance Bill was laid on the table by a vote of seventy-six to thirty-five. Twenty-three banks, one hundred and nine insurance companies, and thirteen thousand citizens petitioned in favor of the Paid Bill. Sweeping charges of bribery were made. Most of them were based on such incidents as this: Chief Decker was in Congress Hall bantering James M. Rankin, of the Underwriters' Committee, and said: " See that safe? I've twenty-five thousand dollars in there to beat your bill." " Pshaw," replied Mr. Rankin, " I've two hundred and fifty thousand dollars in my vest pocket to push ours through." How many votes were bought will probably never be known. It is as certain that both sides used money for some purpose, so that no member of any committee profited financially by his efforts, or the provision of a corruption fund.

There were other schemes for a Paid Fire Department. The insurance companies were ready in case of emergency to sustain a fire brigade if they could have its appointment and management, and the police commissioners were prepared to take control of the paid firemen and the Croton Board. A newspaper suggested that the Croton Board, having the water, should enter the list, petition for the empty engines, and with as much justice and consistency as was entrusted them, prevail on the superintendent of the police to have an effective force to work them.

The Police Commissioners, in advocating a Paid Fire Department, said:

" Steam engines with a small force to manage them are the best Fire Department. The voluntary system is unjust, oppressive upon its members, and not entirely trustworthy. The members do good service, perform prodigious labor, and encounter risks and dangers of the gravest character to save life and property from destruction by fire. For this they formerly enjoyed some degree of compensation through exemption from militia service; but even this has ceased, and the public has no right to demand or enjoy their services without pay. They should be paid like other public employees."

Some of the newspapers were very severe. The following savage and intemperate attack, in which not a few truths are buried in abuse, appeared in one of them:

" The Fire Department ought to be reorganized for the following reasons:

" 1st. Because, though a voluntary organization, it is unnecessarily expensive, and because the public do not know how expensive it is. Parties who render valuable public service ought not to be expected to render it without compensation, and will not do so for any considerable period without some motive; if the motive is not the compensation, it will be a less laudable one—say the interests of a political party or indirect benefits of an even less reputable character.

" 2d. Because being a voluntary organization there can be no penalty imposed greater than dismissal for misconduct. That merely deprives them of the right of serving the public for nothing.

" 3d. In effect, the rank and file of the Department appoint all the officers; therefore the officers have no legal or practical authority. The conduct of the officers must be satisfactory to the men; their tenure of office depends upon that. This is a fatal obstacle to all discipline and subordination. Every legislator should have known that a Fire Department so constituted would become, in time, unmanageable, vicious, and dangerous. It is a wonder that it did not become so much earlier.

"4th. Because associations of young men from the class that supplies volunteer firemen in a great city are removed from the restraints of family and well-ordered society; become proud of vices, and popular with their fellows because they possess them. Being organized and acting under a semblance of command, they feel a degree of strength that impels them too often to defy the law and disturb public order. Their calling as volunteer firemen requires them to turn out at any hour of the day and night, and is incompatible with any steady pursuit of industry, and renders impossible the earning of an honest support by labor. For this reason they are driven by their wants to exercise their wits to supply the deficiency of wages.

"5th. They are four thousand strong; inevitably they will control a political party or a political party will control them. Having sufficient numbers and ample unoccupied time, this body is able to control all the caucuses of the party. There is not a man in that party so strong as to be able to resist them in party nominations. They are therefore able to dictate terms to the city officials who hold the keys of the treasury; and it enables those who stoop low enough to be popular with the firemen to control and override the better members of their party. The effect of this is to reduce the grades of men that hold the public offices of the party. Being, to a large extent, without homes, they are able to vote early and often, without regard to the penalties for fraudulent voting. This may explain why so large a share of firemen are in the Common Council.

"6th. Because it involves an immense waste of time and labor. Four hundred men would be more efficient than four thousand can be. The time of three thousand six hundred men would be saved by a reorganization, and might be, if the men were willing, devoted to valuable productive uses.

"7th. The present system involves the awakening and alarming of a whole city by unnecessary bell ringing, and by the charge and rush of firemen and their ragged followers through the streets; again, the ringing of the fire bells is a signal to every robber in the city that there is an opportunity for him to ply his villainous calling—an opportunity he never omits to improve; all this will be completely remedied when a telegraphic apparatus calls the organized and disciplined firemen to the point of duty.

"8th. Every fire is a mob and a riot under the present system.

"The remedy is in the hands of the Legislature!"

These extracts afford an intelligent insight into the temper of the times. Party passion was running high. The Volunteers died hard. They fought to hold their Organization with that tenacity of purpose and grim resolve which so characterized them as firemen.

While the matter was being pushed through at Albany, a newspaper undertook to estimate the cost of the Volunteer Fire Department, and to compare it with other systems, as follows:

"The city furnishes one hundred and twenty-five engine houses at an estimated cost of $10,000 each. This is entirely too low an estimate, but taking it as correct, this is an investment of $1,250,000, on which no interest or taxes are paid to the city, as it cannot tax its own property.

The interest on $1,250,000, and loss of taxes, are a part of the annual expense, say............................. $150,000

The chief engineer estimates the expense for the present year for new apparatus, repairs, hose, salaries, arrears, etc., at 205,000

New buildings and repairs ordered by the Common Council 142,500

For bells and bell towers................................. 22,000

For bellringers... 39,000

Supplies of gas $9,500; wood, etc., $15,000; supplies, $15,000 39,500
                                                          ─────────
                                                          $598,000

"There are a number of smaller items, some arrearages, etc., not reckoned in the above, but which properly belong to the expenses of the department, and the Common Council takes the liberty of ordering our expenditures at its pleasure, whether there be an appropriation or not, so that it is difficult to say what the service will cost in any year. The item of fitting up kitchens, drawing-rooms, etc., in the engine houses, now very fashionable, at $1,000 each, is an example of frequent occurrence.

"Take now the expense of paid Fire Departments in other cities:

In London, with a population four times greater, it cost.... $75,000

Cincinnati, with 161,000 population, expense of Fire Department... 94,000

Baltimore, with 212,000 in 1864, expense of Fire Department 63,000

Boston, with 178,000 population, expense of Fire Department 105,000

St. Louis, with a population of 160,000, expense of Fire Department... 79,000
                                                          ─────────
                                                          $416,000

"All these five great cities, including London, cost less for paid services by nearly $200,000, than this one City of New York, where the firemen work for nothing, and yet the service here is so defective that insurance is double what it is in Boston, Baltimore and Cincinnati, and four times the price of London. We speak, in the above comparison, of the ascertained or publicly vouched for expense of the New York Fire Department. But there are drippings and contributions and stealings, which, if fully accounted for, would, in the judgment of persons who ought to know, swell the total from a million to a million and a half annually.

"Then the enormous waste of human exertion and life is against the voluntary system. We have four thousand regular firemen and six thousand or seven thousand runners and hangers-on, engaged in this exciting and wearying work. Baltimore employs one hundred and twelve officers and men, seven steam engines, and thirty-four horses. Cincinnati, one hundred and fifty-five officers and men, eleven steam engines, and seventy horses. Boston employs thirty-nine men constantly, and two hundred and fifteen who do duty on alarm. St. Louis employs fifty-nine men and seven steam engines. In all these cities less than five hundred and fifty men, while in this city seven thousand or eight thousand men are called out at every serious fire."

Another article, an appeal to the State Legislature, says, " If we except a few decent young men, sturdy and honest workmen, the bulk is composed of rude fellows without any regular calling, lazy clerks, street loungers, bruisers and sportsmen who have their pockets full of money though they never work. * * * There is no actual fire in the City of New York which does not attract at least one thousand two hundred firemen and about as many ex-members with the different companies, the children, the nincompoops and the thieves. * * * We emphatically affirm—because we have seen several fires in both London and Paris, and know how they were disposed of, that the Fire Department of New York is a costly and ridiculous farce."

When the bill was before the Assembly the following comments were made in a prominent newspaper :

The bill transforming our city's Fire Department into Paid one, having passed the Senate by a very large majority, is now before the Assembly on its third reading. There is said to be danger that it will be beaten by bribery. We do not credit the imputation, though *without* bribery we are sure it cannot be defeated. And for these reasons :

I.—The insurance companies are necessarily and intimately acquainted with fires and their extinguishment, and know what methods prove effective and what are conducive to needless loss, waste and robbery. And those companies, with scarcely an individual dissenter, are praying for the change proposed. Their officers are of all parties and of none, but on this question they are substantially unanimous. They originated the movement for a Paid Department; we are but deferring to their judgment in the premises.

II.—The precedents and analogies are all in favor of the measure. A village or small city, in which a fire occurs but seldom, adheres naturally and properly to the Volunteer system ; but wherever fighting fire becomes a business, requiring constant vigilance and the devotion of a large share of the firemen's time, it is simply honest and just that they should be compensated. The very worst way of paying them is to incite them to pay themselves.

III.—Under the present system five times as many firemen are enrolled as are actually needed. They thus secure exemption from onerous public duties, and become members of a powerful organization, which controls nominations and elections, rewards favorites, and takes vengeance on adversaries. The engine houses are dens of political intrigue, wherein primary meetings are rehearsed and regular nominations " fixed "—for a consideration. It is this fact which incites the fierce hostility which the proposed reform encounters. The firemen are the Janizaries, the Prætorian Guard, of our ruling politicians. They make our aldermen and councilmen—a bad lot, but this is owing in good part to the badness of the raw material. To abolish the Volunteer Fire Department is to derange the machinery whereby our city is made to pile up such atrocious copperhead majorities. We do not suppose this will make much difference in the long run, yet the terror and rage of our governing classes argue that the *placer* thus disturbed is a very rich one. But we want no votes for a Paid Fire Department on any other ground than that of its intrinsic right.

IV.—The very men who make the most ado in Albany against it are themselves paid firemen now, and anxious to remain so. The engineers who insist that firemen should not be paid take good care to be well paid themselves.

The cost of having our fires put out for nothing, including ground rent, engine houses, engines, trucks, hose, salaries, etc., etc., amounts to several hundred thousand dollars per annum; yet we are asked to consider this an *unpaid* service.

V.—Our firemen now choose their superiors, who of course cannot control them. The chief and assistant engineers are made so by votes cast in the engine houses. This proves fatal to subordination and discipline. If the chief should prove stern, he will be superseded at the next election. Hence lawlessness and crime, which are winked at from interested motives.

VI.—Notoriously, our Fire Department is a nursery of dissipation and vice. Large numbers of the firemen sleep or " bunk " at their respective engine houses. This cuts them off from all home or virtuous female influence, while exposing them to peculiar and urgent temptations. Our city is far more debauched and corrupt than it would be but for the deadly influence which centers in and emanates from our engine houses.

VII.—With a Paid Department we may reduce the number of firemen four-fifths, while the commissioners, being independent of the firemen, could enforce discipline, punish rowdyism, and expose theft. We shall no longer squander on fire extinguishment five times the force actually needed therefor. Vicious boys and rowdies will no longer "run with the machine" on purpose to steal whatever they can surely hide. We shall save, by the change proposed, time, money, muscle and morals. And, while the whole community is signally benefitted, nobody will be injured, unless it be such as clearly ought to be."

EX-MAYOR GUNTHER.

Legislators at Albany! What valid reason, not of the greenback persuasion, can be given for hesitating to pass this bill?

Mayor C. Godfrey Gunther's sympathies with the Volunteers in the legislative crisis were evinced by the following preamble and resolutions prepared by him, which were adopted by firemen at a meeting at Firemen's Hall:

Whereas, the threatened passage of the act no wpending before the Legislature of the State, which contemplates the establishment of a Paid Fire Department in lieu of the present Volunteer system, demands at our hands an expression of our sense of the unmerited degradation that is about to be put upon those comprising the present Volunteer system—a system that now is, and from time immemorial has been identified and most intimately connected with the best interests, the development, progress, and prosperity of the City of New York; and

Whereas, it is evident, in the opinion of this meeting, not only by the arguments or statements used before the Legislature, by the advocates of the new system, but by the fact that, without any previous intimation of the intention to supersede, violently and suddenly, the present system, without any consultation with its officers as to the best means of improving it, where improvements are needed; without even allowing of an opportunity to test the relative value or efficiency of the two systems, as well as entirely ignoring the opinions or wishes of the people of this city, who are the most directly and the most really interested parties, that it is intended to degrade the present Department, and, through it, the people of this city. Be it therefore

Resolved, That we regard the passage of the proposed act as an unmerited rebuke to men who have, on many occasions, voluntarily periled their lives in protecting the lives and property of their fellow citizens; that we regard it as unwise in forcing a new and untried experiment upon the city, when a failure is certain to be followed by consequences that may involve a fearful loss in life and property. We contend that, if intended for the good of the city, and if destined more effectually to guard its property and its interests, a gradual introduction of the new system should be provided for, whereby a test of its advantages over the old one could be made, a decisive comparison would be instituted, and the best one of the two be ultimately adopted; we are clearly of the opinion that it is a willful, positive, and direct interference with, and usurpation of, the rights of the people of this city, who, if they desired a change, have the power in their own hands, through their immediate representatives in the city government, to inaugurate a system similar to that now proposed by the State Legislature; and be it further

Resolved, In consideration of the above and many other equally cogent reasons, that we hereby earnestly and fervently yet respectfully remonstrate against the passage of the proposed bill now before the Assembly; more particularly at this time, when the present system was never more efficient, was never better governed or disciplined, and was never in a more advanced state of subordination to duty; and we also fervently and sincerely yet respectfully remonstrate against any change in the present system until it is satisfactorily proven that it cannot be improved in character and efficiency, and until the change shall have been asked for by those who are the most intimately and directly interested—the people of the city—who alone should be consulted and their consent obtained before making the proposed or any other change in any department of their own local government.

The Volunteer organs replied sharply to the attacks made on them at Albany and by the press. One article says:

"So long as the opponents of our present Volunteer Fire Department system confined themselves to facts, and admitted the sole intention they had in view was to benefit the existing organization while they did not expect to make any changes, except perhaps to reduce the force, and confine it within certain limits, we let them go on, and remained silent. Since these opponents have taken themselves to argument, and added to argument vituperation and falsehood, we think it is but just for us to say a few words about the matter.

"The insurance men have testified to but little. They make sweeping assertions against the present organization; say that it is cumbersome, expensive, and inefficient, and they believe "the citizens at large are in favor of a change." * * * These very insurance men, when steamers were first introduced, were the loudest in praise of the same. Notwithstanding we foresaw the trouble, and protested against the introduction of too many machines of the kind, these same exempt firemen, who had gone into the "policy" business, expected that as steamers were introduced, fires would decrease, and the losses must consequently be quite light. * * * They wanted steamers—steamers—steamers. They have got them; and what is the result? The damage done by water at fires in New York amounts to more than that caused by flame and smoke. * * * In just the same light we regard some of these insurance men, who, because they cannot be elevated to positions of trust and responsibility in the present Volunteer Fire Department, turn around and villify it. As investigation is demanded. We can give these insurance company gentlemen all they ask—and more too.

"A word to the Police Department, who seemed to have joined issue with the insurance companies. It is a well-known fact that Police Commissioner Thomas C. Acton, instead of attending to the business he was appointed to look after, has been bothering his brains over this Paid Fire Department scheme all last summer, and has asserted he can command two hundred and fifty thousand dollars, if necessary, to break up the present organization, and substitute some other plan in its stead. While himself, Superintendent Kennedy, Inspector Carpenter, and "a number of policemen" are in Albany, lobbying for this Paid Fire Department Bill, the good people of the City of New York who pay those individuals most liberally for what little they do, are almost afraid to walk the streets after dark for fear they may be robbed or murdered. * * * When the violence of the mob was at its height, and not a policeman dared show his face, did not these gentlemen, assisted by certain citizens whom we can name, drive back the mob, so that the different apparatus could get to work? Who patroled the city at night, as a special police, when those paid for the duty could not be seen? Who drove the thieves and rioters out of the stores in the principal streets? Who protected the shipping, the banks, the gas houses, the croton waterworks, the different factories, and other public buildings, before the National Guard belonging to the city reached home? We answer, the firemen. * * *

"So far as reducing the cost and force of the New York Volunteer Fire Department is concerned, of improving it in every shape and way, of making all reasonable and necessary rules and regulations to control the organization, and make every officer and man in it know his proper place, we are with the police commissioners, insurance folk, and everybody else. * * * We admit the mistakes or misdeeds of certain firemen. We stand up as no apologist for them, believing that the time has come when these mistakes can be corrected, and the organization may be improved and perfected. We feel satisfied that the community at large will sustain us in trying to retain the present organization rather than inaugurate an expensive political machine (for such it is intended to be) to gratify a few men who want office and pay.

"As for the doings in Albany, of which too much has already been said, we care nothing. The business there done may be summed up in a few words. Some of the metropolitan police went up (we don't know who paid their expenses) and testified, to what? They thought and believed we had bad men and bad companies in the Fire Department. The clerk of the Board of Fire Commissioners was ordered to read, before the committee, in the case of Engine Companies No. 40 and 53—both wiped out of existence long ago by the fire commissioners—as evidences of rowdyism. Why did they not go back to 1840, when fights among fire companies were of everyday occurrence in New York? * * * Now that a check is placed upon the appropriations, so that hose companies cannot build three-story brown stone houses to contain a reel with eight lengths of hose, and foremen cannot go to this or that alderman and councilman and obtain, through political influence, buildings and machines which are unnecessary, there is a prospect of curtailing expenses and securing economy for the future.

"We have yet to learn who authorized the Police Department, the insurance companies, or the Citizens' Association, to go to Albany and declare war against a body of men who have sacrificed their health and time to save the lives and property of their fellow-citizens. We have yet to learn if the people pay the police for doing such work, or whether the insurance companies expect to reap extra dividends in consequence, or if the Citizens' Association is about to resolve itself into a committee of the whole for the purchase of political patronage. One thing we do know, and that is, the firemen of New York have yet to be heard from." * * *

Mr. Philip W. Engs, afterwards a member of the first Paid Fire Department Board, resented the attacks on the Volunteers. In a speech at Firemen's Hall, on the fourteenth of February, 1865, before the Board of the New York Fire Department, he said:

"You have been contending with the Legislature of the State regarding the conduct of the firemen of this city. Instead of meeting that issue, we should go before them with this ordinance, which we have passed for the better regulation of the department. They have now become the rules for the government of this department, and we propose by these rules to avoid all the objections that are made against the character of the department. Then all that matter is at an end, no matter what Mr. Acton or anybody else says. It appears to me that we should appear at Albany once more in some shape, and show to these gentlemen that here are the rules under which we propose to act, and under these we can keep the Fire Department together, and still sustain our noble charitable institution, which has such an important bearing upon the proper conduct of the department. I hope that some means will be adopted here to-night by which we shall have this opportunity, and that the chief engineer, the chairman, or some one else, will be authorized to telegraph to Albany, and say that on a certain day we will meet them and see whether we cannot be able to settle this matter. I am very well pleased with the disposition manifested by Mr. Platt, who has appeared before these gentlemen, as did certain gentlemen who went from Washington recently to meet certain other gentlemen from Richmond, not pretending to be clothed with authority, but merely having a friendly conference with them, with the expectation and hope of bringing about some compromise in the affair. I do not see that it can be done here. We want to go to the fountain head at Albany. That is the place where the mischief commences, and this bill will be carried through—for what? To give four certain gentlemen somewhere four places; and I do not see, as I read the bill, but they will have to fix the salaries. It appears to me to be about as improperly prepared a bill, apart from its principles, as I have ever seen. It is not calculated to carry out the object they have in view, and this fact may be made known to these gentlemen if you appear before them. Again, look at its operation upon the jury box, but more particularly upon the militia. It proposes to discharge the whole body of the firemen of the City of New York, if they think best, after they have served but three months, from military service in New York during their lifetime. There is another thing to which I wish to call your attention. Suppose that the firemen of New York, feeling the insult that is put upon them, should say to gentlemen, 'We'll resign to-day; we cannot submit to these charges and slanders upon us,' what would be the feeling of the insurance companies? What would be the feeling of the owners of property in this great city? These appeals ought to be made to them; and so far as concerns the character of the department, I, for one, should be ready to compare the department with the police, taking it from the head down. I would not for a moment stand in the halls of the legislature and hear a man say what was said by Mr. Acton, without bringing the thing home to himself. As an old fireman, I have a good deal of feeling upon this subject, and am quite stirred up about this matter. I desire that we should all stand by our integrity, and show to these gentlemen at Albany that the Fire Department of this city has a character, has integrity, and is equally entitled to honorable mention as any public organization of the kind in this city or elsewhere."

Richmond had fallen, and New York and the entire country were excited over the death struggle of the Confederacy, but the news of the final passage of the bill renewed interest in the fate of the "fire laddies." Much that was harsh and foolish was said and printed. A few hot-headed Volunteers said they would not run to fires, but second thought and the proverbial adaptability of the citizens of the metropolis to circumstances prevailed over rash utterances. It was seen that "de masheen" was no more, and the "Mose" element had gone with it. There was much gathering in company quarters and debating, but the sentiment in favor of the new system, provided it was declared constitutional, was overwhelming, and Chief Engineer John Decker, in a communication to the Common Council, asked for instructions. Mayor Gunther sided with law and order in spite of his preferences, and urged the Volunteers to turn a deaf ear to "suggestions which may be made by ill-advised or designing individuals, but faithfully to obey the laws of the land and the direction of the officers of the department and others in authority."

The Board of Aldermen passed the following:

Whereas, The Legislature of this State has just passed an act which substitutes the Paid system in place of the present Volunteer organization of the Fire Department in this city; and

Whereas, Some time must necessarily elapse ere this new system can be properly or efficiently placed in a position to meet all that would be required therefrom, in respect to the full protection of the lives and property of the citizens; and

Whereas, In the interregnum that must exist between the present time and the arranging of said system, in such a way as to be at all equal in efficiency to the present Volunteer organization, much suffering, and, it may be, loss of life, would ensue in case of a disastrous conflagration, nine-tenths of the community living and having their little all in places peculiarly subject thereto, unless the present Volunteer organization still continues in active service; therefore,

Resolved, That the Common Council of the City of New York would most earnestly urge upon the officers and members of the New York Fire Department the public necessity of their still continuing their former energetic and humane efforts in arresting on all occasions, as heretofore, the progress of the devouring element, thereby not only preventing thousands of helpless women and children from being rendered homeless and destitute, but wreathing around the memory of the Volunteer organization of the New York Fire Department a record of fame and usefulness, of which both themselves and their children in after time may well be proud.

John Decker strenuously urged the firemen to continue to do duty, and although some company quarters were sarcastically placarded and decorated, a revulsion in feeling occurred so quickly that companies which had been represented to have shown signs of insubordination or resentment, contradicted the reports so that the newspapers began to praise the conduct of the Volunteers, and one of them in a laudatory editorial says, very justly:

"This action proves—what we have always believed to be true—that the Fire Department proper was composed of a gallant, fearless, and honorable body of our citizens, and that whatever may have been alleged against the body was the result of the disturbing element which hung upon its flanks in the shape of rowdies and disturbers of the peace, who were to this gallant army of brave, self-sacrificing men, what camp followers and plunderers are to a regular army. The course which the members of the department are now pursuing entitles them to the highest praise which is due to the law-abiding citizens, and although the Volunteer Firemen's organization is no longer to comprise one of our local institutions, to have been a member of it will be a lasting honor."

A newspaper, sketching the social features of the Volunteer organization, said :

"What now shall we have in the city to supply the annual balls given by the various companies so numerously that they occupy nearly every dancing night of the winter ? What will take the place of the jovial surprise parties continually occurring during the winter at the fire-houses, where the sisters and sweethearts and wives of the laddies enjoyed themselves so genially and hospitably, as there was no opportunity in all other social assemblies of our working classes, and which were to our most aristocratic, richest, and best educated young men an absolute relief from the stately balls and stiff-backed parties of the upper ten ? What will become of the excursions, the clam-bakes, the country jaunts, with music and dancing, that the fun-loving firemen indulged in all the summer long ? Mayhap there were rough fellows among the fire boys ; but they were generous and honest, anyhow, they claimed ; and though they had once and awhile a little fight among each other, they were always orderly as a body, they always subserved the good of the city, they were the pride of all great parades, they were the pet institution of the metropolis. The city can never cease to gratefully remember that the draft riots were rendered abortive because of their efforts ; that by their exertions, hand in hand with the police, New

York was saved from desolation and utter horror, and the mobs were finally quelled. It was certainly not inappropriate to re-member these things last night, even though it should be hinted that they might be written in the same spirit as the epitaphs of dead men, in which their faults are con-signed to the dust and forgotten for all time.

"Probably the social organiza-tion of many of our fire companies will be continued for a long time. There are old companionships, not of the "bunk" and the "run" alone, but of the family, of the ball room, of the festive circle, of the summer excursion company, of the young folks' associations, that can-not be broken up. Most of the com-panies have on hand private funds of their own, the disposition of which has not been decided, but which it has been proposed to adopt as the fund of social clubs to be es-tablished, which may possibly in time—who can tell—rival the "Cen-tury" or the "Athenæum." Some of the companies, indeed, have now

C. C. PINCKNEY.

social organizations comprising their members, though under distinct and separate rules, and these will probably be continued."

Perhaps the best refutation of many charges made against the Volunteers is the fact that nearly all the members of the Paid Department were selected from those who were legislated out of honorary, arduous, and unpaid office on March 30, 1865.

While the Volunteers acquiesced in the act of the Legislature, Democratic New York in a certain sense took up the cudgels for them, and grumbled at legislative amendment. The manner of appointment of the commissioners was especially offensive to many. "Why not," asked some, "appoint the mayor and Common Council in Albany ?" Friends of the Volunteers regretted its demise mainly on account of its social features, its balls, enthu-siasm, *esprit du corps*, romance, surprise parties, picnics, and what not.

They also remembered how they stemmed the tide of anarchy in the riots of 1863, and were not yet prepared to make room for "a staid, slow-horse, methodical, paid concern." Chief Decker, in a circular, urged all to do their duty *"until such time as the Board of Engineers and Foremen shall determine upon certain matters of interest to the Department in its present condition."*

Governor Fenton acted promptly on the fifth of April, four days before General Lee surrendered. He sent the names of Charles C. Pinckney, Martin B. Brown, Samuel Sloan, and Thomas W. Booth to the Senate for confirmation. Horace Greeley was disappointed in not securing a nomination for his candidate, Harry W. Genet, afterwards known as "Prince Hal."

Mr. Pinckney, a Republican, who is yet in business, and appears to be but little older than he was a score of years ago, was ex-president of the Board of Councilmen, and in the insurance and real estate business. He was a member of the Union League Club, and had done active duty in Phœnix Hose Company No. 22. He was active and adapted to executive business.

MARTIN B. BROWN.

Martin B. Brown, also a Republican, the well-known printer, is of course active and rejuvenated, as all good anglers and sportsmen are. He had been a member of United States Engine Company No. 23.

Samuel Sloan, then ex-state senator and president of the Hudson River Railroad, is the present head of the Delaware, Lackawanna, and Western Railroad. At the time of his nomination he had no leaning towards any political faction, but was claimed as a Democrat.

James W. Booth, a Republican, whose death occurred several years ago, was a dyer and contractor. He afterwards was elected state senator.

Clamor was raised in Albany and New York when the names were published, because of the alleged partisan complexion of the board, and on April 11 the New York delegation refused to report on the confirmation of the commissioners. The commissioners were, however, confirmed, but on the thirteenth of April, through trouble between certain senators and Governor Fenton, the Senate rejected the nominations by the following vote:

AYES—Allen, Angel, Bailey, Cole, Cook, Dutcher, Folger, Hastings, Hoyt, Jaliand, Laimbeer, Low, Munger, Strong, Williams—15.

NAYS—Allaben, Ames, Andrews, Beach, Bell, Chrystie, Cornell, Cozans, Fields, Hawes, Hobbs, Humphrey, Murphy, Shafer, Smith, White, Woodruff —17. To confirm them, a week later, May 3, 1865, Commissioners Pinckney, Brown, Engs, and Booth were sworn in at Albany by Secretary of State Depew, Samuel Sloan having declined to serve, and drew by lot the following terms of office: Pinckney, two years; Booth, four years; Engs, six years; and Brown eight years. Mr. Engs, in drawing his lot, said he was aged, and would not live to serve out the term. The commissioners who were sworn in came to New York with the Secretary of State by the Albany boat, on which they had an informal meeting, and on the afternoon of Thursday, May 4, 1865, held the first meeting of the Metropolitan Fire Department, in the office of the Hanover Fire Insurance Company, of which Mr. Engs was vice-president, at No. 45 Wall Street, after a second informal meeting at Mr. Pinckney's office, No. 8 Pine Street.

Mr. Engs, a Democrat, who was a wine merchant and a member of an old firm, still in business, was a member of Volunteer Engine Company No. 21, Fulton Engine Company in 1813, and assistant engineer of the Old Department from 1824 to 1833. He was an officer in various corporations, and a member of the Legislature, and president of the Association of Exempt Firemen. He died on the nineteenth of May, 1875, widely regretted.

Charles E. Gildersleve was born in New York city in 1827, and was a lover of fire duty from his earliest remembrance. As

CHARLES E. GILDERSLEVE.

soon as his years would permit he became a member of Oceanus Engine Company No. 11 in 1846; served four years with the old machine, during which time he was secretary and assistant foreman. He resigned in 1850 and joined Mutual Hook and Ladder Company No. 1. This company was in a poor condition, from a fireman's point of view, when Mr. Gildersleve joined. There was no life, no enthusiasm, no push; but in a short time all this was changed, new blood was infused, the roll was filled, and No. 1 became one of the quickest and best truck companies in the city, and an indispensable addition to the down-town working force. Mr. Gildersleve served faithfully with No. 1 as member and officer. When Zophar Mills was foreman of the Exempt Engine, Mr. Gildersleve thought he would try a little more fire duty, and, although he had already passed through sixteen years of service, he joined under the old veteran, and was shortly afterwards made secretary, and then promoted to assistant foreman. At the organization of the new Department Mr. Gildersleve was made clerk to the commissioners, and remained with the Metropolitans from

1865 until 1875. He is still in good condition, looking as if he could stand twenty years more of fire duty.

Commissioners Pinckney, Engs, Booth, and Brown knew that—although the Volunteers acquiesced in the public sentiment that nothing illegal should be done—the law would be invoked and the constitutionality of the act of March 30, 1865, would be tested. So, at the meeting of the fourth of May, they perfected their organization. Mr. Booth presided, Mr. Brown was secretary *pro tem.*, and after two ballots, Mr. Pinckney was elected president, and Mr. Engs treasurer. On a second ballot for secretary, Mr. Charles E. Gildersleve was elected. Then a resolution that Messrs. Pinckney and Brown call on Comptroller Matthew T. Brennan and Street Commissioner Charles G. Cornell, state their views, and, if necessary, make a demand for the property of the city belonging to the Fire Department, was adopted. The Volunteers

JAMES W. BOOTH.

had since the fourth of April been conferring with the members of the Common Council on the proper steps to be taken in reference to the "Metropolitan Fire Act." The Common Council was composed as follows:

ALDERMEN.—Morgan Jones, president; John Moore, Michael Norton, Ignatius Flynn, Joseph Shannon, William H. Gedney, Peter McKnight, Lewis R. Ryers George A. Jeremiah, John Brice, Bernard Kelly, Peter Masterson, John D. Ottiwell, James O'Brien, Terence Farley, B. W. Van Voorhis.

COUNCILMEN.—James Hayes, president; Patrick H. Keenan, Isaac Robinson, John Stacom, Edwin M. Hagerty, John Healy, Charles Koster, Bernard Kenny, James G. Brinckman, Thomas Brady, Samuel P. Patterson, William A. Taylor, John Houghtalin, Thomas Leavy, George McGrath, J. Wilson Green, Abraham Lent, Michael Smith, Thomas O'Callaghan, Patrick Russell, William Joyce, Hugh Reilly, David Fitzgerald, Valentine Cook.

Next day the commissioners were served with notice of two legal actions taken by John Cochrane, state attorney general. One was an injunction in the name of the mayor, aldermen, and Commonalty, and Chief Decker, restraining the commissioners from taking possession of any real estate then used by the Fire Department. The other was in the form of *quo warranto* proceedings to compel the commissioners to show by what warrant they held office. Waldo Hutchins and Judge Allen were engaged as counsel by the commissioners, and it was argued that the proceedings before them should be friendly, and on the twelfth of May judgment against the commissioners was taken *pro forma* before Judge Foster, and on the twenty-fifth of May Judges

Ingraham, Clerke, and Barnard decided "that the New Department is merely local, and confined to the City of New York, and in substitution of the former one, and is hence unconstitutional." On this the case was taken to the Court of Appeals.

On the third of May a special meeting of the Board of Engineers and Foremen of the Volunteer Department was held at Firemen's Hall. Chief Decker was in the chair, and Alexander V. Davidson was secretary. The chair announced the news from Albany, and said that in his opinion the old officers were the only legal ones, and Commissioners John J. Gorman, president, William M. Tweed, Thomas Lawrence, Edward Bonnell, and Thomas Flender would go on as if nothing had been done. The appropriations for the Department had been cut down one-half to cripple it, but the new fire ordinances of the Common Council would be carried out. It was time that some action was taken, as there were signs of insubordination in the Department. On a vote, the following companies voted to support the Old Department:

Engine Companies 1, 2, 3, 4, 7, 8, 9, 11, 13, 14, 16, 17, 19, 20, 21, 22, 23, 24, 25, 26, 27, 29, 30, 31, 32, 36, 39, 42, 44, 46, 47, 48.

Hose Companies 1, 2, 4, 5, 6, 7, 8, 9, 11, 13, 14, 16, 17, 19, 24, 27, 28, 32, 33, 37, 38, 41, 42, 47, 50, 55, 56, 59, 60, 61.

Hook and Ladder Companies 2, 3, 5, 6, 11, 12, 13, 14.

Hose Company No. 21 recorded a vote in favor of the New Department. Cries of "Put him out," "Disband the company" were raised, and Chief Decker is reported as saying that if he found any company going back on the Old Department he would disband it, and lock up its quarters and apparatus. Others favored allowing any company to vote as it thought fit. A notice was sent to companies not represented to report their choice.

ANSWERING AN ALARM.

CHAPTER XLVII.

WORK OF THE NEW COMMISSIONERS.

Enforcing Order and Discipline.—The Metropolitans Getting into Harness.—Active Co-operation of the Old Companies.—Chief Decker Required to Continue in the Performance of his Duty.—The Chief Relieved at his own Request from further Service.—Volunteer Companies Mustered Out.—Retirement of Engineers.—Introduction of a Uniform.—Regulations for the Guidance of Firemen.—The Board Acknowledges the Services of the Volunteers.—Fire, Academy of Music ; Tragic Death of Two Brave Firemen.

THE new commissioners, after securing counsel, decided to go on arranging for the organization of the department, but to keep their proceedings secret. The committee appointed to see Comptroller Brennan reported that he " wanted time for reflection." Street Commissioner Cornell could not comply because of the injunction. Chief Decker, to check an ugly spirit that had manifested itself, issued a circular, in which he said that in his opinion the bill for a Paid Department was unconstitutional, but if the courts decided otherwise the Volunteers should and would acquiesce quietly, and surrender their quarters and apparatus. He ordered the force to continue to perform duty under the ordinance of December 31, 1864, and threatened to disband any company guilty of a breach of peace, disobedience of orders, or neglect of duty. The new commissioners requested the clerk of the Common Council, David T. Valentine, to comply with Section 21 of the Metropolitan Act, requiring him to register and return all firemen. Chief Decker was requested to make legal returns to Mr. Valentine. The engineers in charge in Brooklyn reported their force organized and ready for instruction and communication. May 10, at a meeting of Volunteer delegates at Firemen's Hall, Engine Companies Nos. 10, 15, 35, 38, 42, and 53 ; Hose Companies Nos. 21, 25, 36, and 39 ; and Hook and Ladder Companies Nos. 7 and 8 were recorded as in favor of the New Department. The new commissioners met the same day. There were six or seven hundred applications for appointment as paid firemen, many of them from Volunteers, and the following blank was issued :

To the Board of Commissioners of the Metropolitan Fire Department :
The undersigned respectfully solicits an appointment as .... in the Metropolitan Fire Department. Has served as a fireman in the city of .... for the period of .. years in .... Company No. ..

    Age.............. ....
    Occupation...
    Married or single..
    Residence..
                                        (SIGNATURE.)
    References..

This settled all doubt of the intention of the new board to appoint Volunteers, and had a good effect. The new commissioners were desirous of having the best advice obtainable, and they invited the following gentlemen, who were regarded as thoroughly *au fait* in fire matters, to meet them : Zophar Mills, James M. McLean, Thomas Boese, Peter N. Cornwell, George T. Hope, John A. Cregier, Carlisle Norwood, and James M. McGregor. Messrs. McLean, Hope, Cregier, and McGregor, and J. B. Leverich and James Pinckney met the commissioners a couple of days later and gave their views, and on the nineteenth of May the following estimate of the expenses of the Department for 1865 was prepared, and Mayor Gunther and Comptroller Brennan were invited to meet the board as a Board of Estimate.

FINANCIAL ESTIMATE FOR 1865.

Basis.—30 steamers with tenders attached, 17 hook and ladder trucks with appurtenances complete, 2 hand engines and tenders.

5 new first-class steamers with tenders complete, $25,000; repairing and altering apparatus, viz.: hook and ladder trucks, engines and furnishing tenders, $40,900; building stables, and altering houses, $60,000; horses, 39,000; harness, $99,100; feed for horses, $15,600 ; horseshoeing, $1,100; new hose, $40,000; fuel, oil, and other supplies, $50,000; repairing apparatus, $30,000; gas and gas fixtures, $7,000. Contingencies —office furniture, stationery, etc., $20,000; telegraph supplies, $9,500. Salaries. —Commissioners, $10,-328.80 ; secretary, clerks, messengers, and yard men, $10,000; telegraph operators, $3,000; bellringers, $9,600; chief engineer, $1,500; 12 assistant e gineers, $7,200; 30 engineers for steam ers, $13,500; 40 foremen of companies, $16,000; 40 astista t foremen, $15,000; 40 drivers, $14,000; 30 stokers, $10,500; 10 tillermen, $3,500; 280 hose and truckmen, $98,000; 100 men for hand apparatus, $5,000. Total, $564,228.80.

BROADWAY, SOUTH OF VESEY STREET.

May 22, Messrs. Engs and Booth were appointed a committee " to examine reports of operations of fire departments of other cities, and collect therefrom such items as may be of interest to the Board, and present a report, with such rules and regulations for the Department as may be necessary," and Commissioner Engs moved " that the subject of communication by telegraph for fires be referred to a special committee of two to report what will be required to be done in addition to the present arrangements in order to secure its entire advantages, and enable the city to dispense with bellringing." The motion was carried, and Messrs. Pinckney and Brown were appointed. Badges, a seal, and uniforms were discussed at this meeting. On the twenty-seventh of May, Edwin Estes, foreman of Hook and Ladder Company No. 7, tendered the services of his company to the new commissioners. June 20 the Court of Appeals reversed the decision of the General Term of the Supreme Court. The opinion was given by Judge Henry E. Davis, and was concurred in by all except Judge John W. Brown.

The commissioners met next day at No. 156 Broadway, and Treasurer Engs presented the draft of an address to the firemen of the City of New York, which was adopted, and ordered to be published, as follows:

New York, June 21, 1865.

To the Firemen of the City of New York:

The Act entitled "An Act to create a Metropolitan Fire Department and establish a Fire Department therein," having been decided by the Court of Appeals to be constitutional, the commissioners under said Act deem it to be their duty to apprise you of the fact and to declare their purpose of organizing, without unnecessary delay, the Metropolitan Fire Department

This incipient step in our official capacity is in advance of all other action in order that your attention may be called to the following extracts from the law under which we act.

Section 5.—The Metropolitan Fire Department is empowered and directed to possess and exercise fully and exclusively all the powers, and to perform all the duties for the government, management, maintenance, and direction of the Fire Department of the City of New York.

Section 19.—All members of the present Fire Department, regularly enrolled at the time of the passage of this Act, shall be retained by the present Chief Engineer under oath to the Clerk of the Common Council of said City of New York, who shall faithfully perform their duties until regularly discharged by said Commissioners, and not otherwise; shall be entitled to all the privileges and exemptions to which exempt firemen are entitled by the laws of this State.

Section 20.—Immediately on the organization of said Department, all persons who shall be firemen in the City of New York shall be under the control and government of said Metropolitan Fire Department, and if they shall so remain until they are discharged by said Department, shall be entitled to all the privileges and exemptions allowed by the laws of the State of New York, the same as if they served out the full term as prescribed by the laws of the State of New York, and the said Department shall have full power to discharge by resolution said firemen or any portion of them whenever they may deem proper.

The Act requires that in selecting the appointees of the Metropolitan Fire Department preference shall be given to those applicants who have served in the Volunteer Department, and this shall be most cheerfully complied with, the Board being now ready to receive applications from such of them as may feel disposed to serve in the new organization.

The expressed determination of many of the officers and members of the Volunteer Department to continue their aid until the New Department is in operation demands from us an acknowledgment of this manifestation of public spirit and regard for law and order, and assures our fellow-citizens that the changes which are to take place will be made in a manner to secure public safety.

The commissioners enter upon their duties with some practical knowledge of the various labors which are imposed upon them, but encouraged on their way by the belief that the entire success which has attended the establishment of a Paid Department in other cities cannot fail to be realized here, and that our brother firemen, with whom it has been our happiness to act in the Volunteer Department will, in the end, agree with us that the system, now about to be introduced, is adapted to the best interests of our fellow-citizens In relation to the Charity Fund of our Old Volunteer Department, it will be both our duty and our pleasure to sustain it by every means in our power, and to give any support to the Trustees of that Fund in continuance of its noble benefits.

C. C. Pinckney, P. W. Engs, James W. Booth, M. B. Brown.

The old companies began to fall into line. G. B. Tunison, foreman of Engine Company No. 52, reported it ready for service, as did Hose Company No. 33. On the twenty-second of June the Fire Commissioners were informed by the Police Commissioners that, if they chose, they could be accommodated at Police Headquarters. D. T. Valentine, clerk of the Common Council, sent in a list of all regularly enrolled firemen on March 30, 1865, and Chief Decker was invited to meet the commissioners. June 23, Hook and Ladder Company No. 8 and Hose Company No. 3 reported for duty. That day the following was sent to Chief Decker :

"JOHN DECKER, Esq., Chief Engineer, etc., etc.

"SIR : The Metropolitan Fire Department desires you to continue in the performance of your duties as chief engineer in the City of New York until further orders. You will therefore require obedience to your authority, and report to this Department any violation thereof.

"By order of the Board,

"C. C. PINCKNEY, *President.*

"CHARLES E. GILDERSLEVE, *Secretary.*"

The commissioners had had an interview with him, and had learned his intention to do his full duty. He was by resolution authorized to procure necessary supplies, if they could not be obtained from the Street Commissioners. June 24, the commissioners first met in Firemen's Hall, and, after selecting the old trustee room for meetings, resolved that it be the headquarters of the board. It was announced at this meeting that the day before the Board of Estimates had resolved, despite the negative votes of Mayor Gunther and Comptroller Brennan, to apply to the Board of Supervisors for six hundred thousand dollars for 1865, and seven hundred and fifty thousand dollars for 1866. Many old companies announced themselves " ready for duty." Dr. J. H. Griscom, through Henry A. Oakley, Esq., secretary of the Howard Insurance Company, set forth the necessity of creating a surgical staff for the department to bar the admission of incompetent persons, and prevent deception by firemen who wanted to get excused from duty on the ground of sickness. The use of Firemen's Hall was given to the Exempt Firemen and Board of Trustees of the Fire Department. The comptroller recognized the new commissioners in the following order :

"CITY OF NEW YORK, DEPARTMENT OF FINANCE, COMPTROLLER'S OFFICE, June 24, 1865.

"To all persons having charge of the real estate and personal property of the City of New York, now in use and occupation by the Fire Department:

"Permission is hereby granted to the commissioners of the Metropolitan Fire Department, established under an Act passed March 30, 1865, to take possession of the real estate and other property of the city, now occupied and used for the Fire Department, and over which I have any authority or control.

"MATTHEW T. BRENNAN, *Comptroller.*"

Messrs. Pinckney and Brown were, on the twenty-sixth of June, authorized to visit cities where fire engines were constructed, to get information as to the cost and construction of the highest class. June 27, Chief Decker sent in the following communication :

" OFFICE CHIEF ENGINEER, FIRE DEPARTMENT, NEW YORK, June 27, 1865.

" CHARLES C. PINCKNEY, Esq., President Board of Metropolitan Fire Commissioners.

"SIR : To your note of the twenty-third instant, desiring me to continue in performance of my duties as chief engineer until further notice, I respectfully reply that in accordance with my own feelings I desire to retire from active duty. As I am not an applicant for the position, but in order to act consistently, and to carry out the spirit of the resolution adopted by the Board of Engineers and Foremen of the Volunteer Fire Department, while the controversy relative to the constitutionality of the bill was pending, and while the public mind was fearful that the Old Department would refuse to perform duty, I volunteer my services to the new organization until a reasonable time shall have elapsed sufficient for the new Board of Fire Commissioners to take charge of all matters appertaining to the Department. Very respectfully,

"JOHN DECKER, *Chief Engineer.*"

The same day, on the application of ex-Commissioners William M. Tweed, Edward Bonnoll, Thomas Lawrence, Thomas Flender, and John J. Gorman, Hose Company No. 26 was restored to duty. The pay of bellringers was fixed at eight hundred dollars per annum, and that of engineers at nine hundred dollars per annum. June 30 the engineers and foremen met at Firemen's Hall, and on motion of Assistant Engineer John Hamill, the following resolution was adopted:

Whereas, it was stated at Albany, before the committee, the Volunteer firemen were anxious to get positions in the Paid Department, *Resolved*, that a committee be sent to the new Commissioners that they will perform duty up to the first of August, if the Commissioners will honorably discharge all members of the Volunteer Fire Department. If not, they will cease to perform duty July 10.

This was carried by twenty-nine to twenty-four, but a number of disqualified companies did not vote. July 3 the commissioners tabled the communication, and on the eighth of July notified the firemen and engineers that they were not at present able to comply with the demand. July 17, Assistant Engineers Alexander V. Davidson, William Lamb, John Hamill, Bernard Kenny, and Bartley Donohue gave notice that they ceased to perform duty as assistant engineers on the eleventh of July. That day the Bank of the Manhattan Company was designated as the bank for keeping the funds of the Department, and the following was sent to Chief Decker:

"To JOHN DECKER, Esq., Chief Engineer.

"SIR: This Board feels that it is due to you and in accordance with your expressed wish, to have a period fixed when we shall be prepared to relieve you from your voluntary servi es as Chief Engineer of the Metropolitan Fire Department. They would therefore now respectfully inform you that arrangements are in progress by which this can be accomplished on the first day of August next. "

The organization of the New Department was watched by the New York Board of Fire Underwriters, and so important was the selection of the chief engineer of the department considered, that a special committee was appointed to place the matter before the Underwriters in the form of a report, of which the following are extracts:

*　*　* It is expected of us that we will make such suggestions to the Metropolitan Fire Commissioners as our experience as insurers qualifies us to make, and our deep interest in the efficiency of the Department justifies. Our policies embrace and protect hundreds of millions of property in this city, and we are, therefore, deeply concerned in having the most thoroughly efficient Department possible. *　*　*

The undersigned believe that the realization of the benefits expected to be derived from the new system about to be inaugurated will mainly depend upon the selection of the first executive officer of the Department—the chief engineer. *　*　*

The head of this important arm of the public service is required now to be something more than a "practical fireman," and an expert in extinguishing burning buildings; and we believe the commissioners will make a grave mistake if they do not secure talent and qualifications of a different kind from those which have hitherto been thought to be sufficient for that officer to possess. *　*　*

To place this great emporium in the best state possible with reference to security against fire, is a task requiring the exercise of the highest ability; and the superintendent of the Fire Department, or chief engineer (as the law designates him), being the person whose business it is to take cognizance of existing defects and abuses, to discern danger, to anticipate calamities, and to recommend to the commissioners for their approval such measures as the public interest requires, should be a man of rare acquirements and endowments, and if the office is held by one who will *fill* it, we believe that it will be second to none under the city government in dignity, influence, and usefulness.

The Fire Department of this city should be the most perfect on the Continent. It should be a model not only in the perfectness of its apparatus and the wisdom of its regulations, but the influence of the Department should be felt in elevating the standard of security in warehouses, hotels, places of public assemblage and tenements, and in the buildings of the city generally. * * * The work cannot be divided. It naturally devolves on the chief engineer, and if he proves himself capable, he will not lack for fame and reward. Such a man would not only be the first executive officer of our Fire Department, but he would be in effect the controller and regulator of all the Fire Departments in the country. * * *

The assistant engineers should and doubtless will be selected from the most experienced and best qualified firemen of the Old Department. The senior member of the assistants should perform similar duties to those heretofore performed by the chief, and the presence of the superintendent or chief under the New Department would only be necessary when unusual measures are demanded or when circumstances arise calling for the exercise of unusual responsibility.

We do not suppose that it now is or hereafter will be the intention of this board to suggest to the Fire Commissioners the appointment of any particular person to the office of chief engineer, unless they are solicited to do so; but it may not be inappropriate, in view of the difficulty which will probably be encountered in obtaining the services of one possessing the qualifications which the undersigned think indispensable, to suggest to the commissioners (provided the views herein expressed are concurred in by the board), that the proper person could probably be found among the eminent generals of our army, and especially among those whose education as military and civil engineers would qualify them for the important position of chief engineer of the New York Fire Department.

All of which is respectfully submitted,
GEORGE W. SAVAGE, A. B. McDONALD,
HENRY A. OAKLEY.

NEW YORK, July 11, 1865.

ONE OF OUR FIREMEN.

This was approved, and a correspondence with the Fire Commissioners resulted, on the fourteenth of July, 1865, in an interview with them, when the report was left with them, it being understood that the commissioners were favorably impressed with the views embraced in it.

The first ballot for a successor to Chief Decker was taken July 19, and resulted as follows: Alfred Carson, 1; T. L. West, 1; J. L. Perley, 1; and John Baulch, 1. The subsequent two ballots on that day were: Baulch, 1; West, 2; M. Shannessey, 1; West, 1; Carson, 1; and R. C. Brown, 2. The balloting was resumed June 21, as follows: Fourth—Brown, 2; West, 1; Carson, 1. Fifth—Carson, 2; Brown, 2. Sixth—Carson, 2; Brown, 1; William Haw, Jr., 1. Seventh—Brown, 1; Haw, 1; E. Bates, 1; Carson, 1. Eighth—Haw, 2; Miller, 1; John J. Gorman, 1. Ninth—Haw, 2; Carson, 2. Tenth—West, 2; Haw, 1; M. Halloran, 1. Eleventh—Halloran, 2; Carson, 1; Elisha Kingsland, 1. Twelfth—Carson, 1; Gorman, 1; Halloran, 1; Kingsland, 1. Thirteenth—Cregier, 1; Brown, 1; Carson, 1; Perley, 1. Fourteenth —Cregier, 2; Perley, 2. Fifteenth—Cregier, 2; Perley, 2. Sixteenth—Cregier, 2; Kingsland, 1; Perley, 1. Seventeenth—Brown, 2; Carson, 2. Eighteenth —Brown, 2; West, 2. Nineteenth—H. Curry, 1; Brown, 2; West, 1. Twentieth—Carson, 2; Brown, 1; West, 1. Twenty-first—West, 2; Brown, 1; Haw, 1. Twenty-second—West, 2; Brown, 1; Kingsland, 1. Twenty-third —West, 2; Brown, 2. Twenty-fourth—West, 2; Brown, 1; Perley, 1. Twenty-fifth—Carson, 2; Perley, 2. The balloting was suspended until the twenty-seventh of July, when the twenty-sixth ballot gave—West, 2; Perley 1; and John B. Leverich, 1. The next ballot was—Perley, 2; West, 1; and Kingsland, 1. On the twenty-eighth ballot Elisha Kingsland was elected by three votes to one for Perley.

ELISHA KINGSLAND was a member of Hose Company No. 32, afterwards Engine Company No. 26, of which his brother, Oliver H. Kingsland, was the last foreman. Mr. Kingsland became foreman of his company, and afterwards was assistant engineer for over eleven years. He was the first chief of the Paid Fire Department, and is now an employee of the Board of Underwriters. Mr. Kingsland had an accident at a fire in Forsyth Street in 1854, and narrowly escaped serious injury.

July 28, the comptroller was requested to place fifty thousand dollars to the credit of the Fire Department with the city chamberlain, and the "sinews of war" were provided for. The commissioners had been feeling their way to the

ELISHA KINGSLAND.

appointment of the first engine company. A first-class engine, that had been ordered of the Amoskeag Manufacturing Company, to cost four thousand five hundred dollars, and, after several quarters for it had been selected and rejected, it was decided to house it in the building occupied by the Exempt Engine Company, in the northeast corner of the City Hall Park. Commissioner Engs rode on it to its first destination. Foreman John J. Gorman readily complied with a request that the members of the Exempt Engine Company aid the company of the new engine when it was formed. Messrs. Engs and Brown then selected officers and men, and on then thirty-first of July the company was formed. The commissioners appreciated the action of the officers and members of Exempt Engine Company, and on the ninth of August, on a communication from John J. Gorman, foreman of Exempt Engine Company, requesting that the company may be relieved from active duty in connection with Metropolitan Steam Fire Engine Company No. 1, as the Paid company had been appointed, Commissioner Brown offered the following resolutions, which were adopted:

Resolved, That at their own request, the Exempt Fire Engine Company be relieved from further active duty with Metropolitan Steam Fire Engine Company No. 1.

Resolved, That the readiness with which Exempt Engine Company came forward and volunteered to take charge of the new steamer, and the promptness and zeal manifested by that company in the discharge of duty with said steamer, is deserving of special mention and commendation.

Resolved, That the thanks of this Board be, and they are hereby, tendered to the Exempt Engine Company for the valuable assistance rendered by them to this Department.

Resolved, That the secretary furnish the Exempt Engine Company with a copy of these resolutions.

Exempt Engine Company's status, when it was disbanded, was as follows: Stationed in Centre Street, near the Park. Had a steam engine and tender. Members: John J. Gorman, foreman; J. Y. Watkins, Jr., first assistant; E. F. Lasak, second assistant; George R. Connor, third assistant; John M. Harned, secretary; Joshua Isaacs, assistant secretary; James Cholwell, James Gilmore, Howard E. Coates, John Rush, Jr., John W. Farmer, Hugh Curry, Theodore E. Kemp, James Tucker, Joseph D. Costa, George Duroche, James B. Terhune, Joseph Lawrence, H. H. Carpenter, Charles L. Maurer, John K. Lyon, Dennis Hayes, Samuel Lawrence, C. P. Currie, Charles M. Johnston, William Symes, Thomas S. Weeks, Matthew Ellis, Leonard Warner, James H. Finch, Aaron J. Quimby, David Roberts, James Moran, John R. Gridley, Daniel Ward, C. Sandford, John E. Flagler, John A. Pinckney, Joseph H. Edgerley. Its furniture, etc., was purchased for Metropolitan Engine

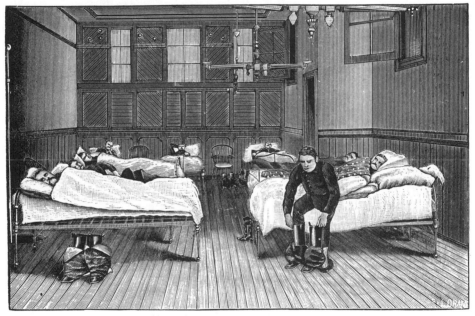

BUNK ROOM OF NO. 33 ENGINE COMPANY.

Company No. 1 for one hundred and fifty dollars. The first Metropolitan Company started the work of forming other companies, went on quickly, and by December 1 the city was protected by Paid companies except in the upper districts, where the companies were on a semi-Volunteer basis.

The Volunteer Companies went out of service as follows:

"Hudson" Engine No. 1; house ordered locked up July 13. "Excelsior" Engine No. 2; disbanded October 25. "Forrest" Engine No. 3; disbanded November 1. "Niagara" Engine No. 4; disbanded November 20. "Protection" Engine No. 5; disbanded September 20. "Americus" Engine No. 6; disbanded August 28. "Lexington" Engine No. 7; disbanded October 25. "Manhattan" Engine No. 8; disbanded October 25. "Marion" Engine No. 9; disbanded October 25. "Water Witch" Engine No. 10; disbanded November 1. "Oceanus" Engine No. 11; disbanded October 25. "Knickerbocker" Engine No. 12; disbanded November 1. "Eagle" Engine No. 13; disbanded November 1. "Columbian" Engine No. 14; disbanded November 1. "Hibernia" Engine No. 15; disbanded November 10. "Mohawk" Engine No. 16; disbanded November 20. "East River" Engine No. 17; disbanded November

20. "Union" Engine No. 18; disbanded November 10. "Lafayette" Engine No. 19; disbanded November 1. "Washington" Engine No. 20; disbanded September 20. "Fulton" Engine No. 21; disbanded November 1. "Protector" Engine No. 22; discharged September 20. "United States" Engine No. 23; disbanded October 25. "Jackson" Engine No. 24; disbanded October 25. "Cataract" Engine No. 25; disbanded November 1. "Jefferson" Engine No. 26; disbanded November 1. "Fort Washington" Engine No. 27; disbanded November 10. "Pacific" Engine No. 28; disbanded November 20. "Guardian" Engine No. 29; disbanded October 25. "North River" Engine No. 30; disbanded November 1. "Peterson" Engine No. 31; disbanded November 1. "Peter Masterson" Engine No. 32; disbanded November 10. "Black Joke" Engine No. 33; retired July 28. "Howard" Engine No. 34; disbanded November 1. "Columbus" Engine No. 35; disbanded November 10. "Equitable" Engine No. 36; disbanded November 1. "Tradesman" Engine No. 37; disbanded November 10. "Southwark" Engine No. 38; disbanded November 1. "Franklin" Engine No. 39; disbanded November 10. "Lady Washington" Engine No. 40; disbanded October 25. "Clinton" Engine No. 41; disbanded October 28. "Empire" Engine No. 43; disbanded November 1. "Manhattan" Engine No. 43; disbanded November 10. "Live Oak" Engine No. 44; disbanded November 1. "Aurora" Engine No. 45; disbanded November 1. "Valley Forge" Engine No. 46; disbanded November 1. "Croton" Engine No. 47; disbanded November 20. "Mazeppa" Engine No. 48; disbanded October 25. "Pocahontas" Engine No. 49; disbanded November 1. "Mutual" Engine No. 51; disbanded November 1. "Undine" Engine No. 52; disbanded November 1. "Hudson River" Engine No. 53; disbanded November 1.

"Eagle" Hose No. 1; disbanded November 20. "Niagara" Hose No. 2; disbanded November 1. "Independent" Hose No. 3; disbanded November 1. "Marion" Hose No. 4; disbanded November 1. "Edwin Forrest" Hose No. 5; disbanded November 1. "Croton" Hose No. 6; disbanded November 1. "Ringgold" Hose No. 7; disbanded November 1. ' City" Hose No. 8; disbanded September 20. "Columbian" Hose No. 9; disbanded November 1. "Liberty" Hose No. 10; disbanded November 1. "Gulick" Hose No. 11; disbanded November 20. "Washington" Hose No. 12; disbanded November 20. "Jackson" Hose No. 13; disbanded November 1. "Excelsior" Hose No. 14; disbanded November 20. "Atlantic" Hose No. 15; disbanded November 1. "Tompkins" Hose No. 16; disbanded November 1. "Clinton" Hose No. 17; disbanded November 1. "Franklin" Hose No. 18; disbanded September 20. "American" Hose No. 19; disbanded November 1. "Humane" Hose No. 20; disbanded November 1. "Hudson" Hose No. 21; disbanded November 1. "Phoenix" Hose No. 22; disbanded November 1. "Perry" Hose No. 23; disbanded November 1. "National" Hose No. 24; disbanded November 10. "United States" Hose No. 25; disbanded November 1. "Rutgers" Hose No. 26; disbanded November 20. "Neptune" Hose No. 27; disbanded November 1. "Pearl" Hose No. 28; disbanded September 20. "Metamora" Hose No. 29; disbanded November 1. "George B. McClellan" Hose No. 30; disbanded November 1. "Putnam" Hose No. 31; disbanded November 1. "Index" Hose No. 32; disbanded November 20. "Warren" Hose No. 33; disbanded November 20. "Crystal" Hose No. 35; disbanded November 1. "Oceana" Hose No. 36; disbanded November 1. "Madison" Hose No. 37; disbanded November 1. "Amity" Hose No. 38; disbanded November 20. "Mohawk" Hose No. 39; disbanded November 1. "Empire" Hose No. 40; disbanded November 10. "Alert" Hose No. 41; disbanded November 1. "Mazeppa" Hose No. 42; disbanded November 10. "Pioneer" Hose No. 43; disbanded November 10. "Washington Irving" Hose No. 44; disbanded November 10. "C. Godfrey Gunther" Hose No. 45; disbanded November 1. "Mechanics" Hose No. 47; disbanded November 10. "American" Hose No. 48; disbanded November 1. "Lady Washington" Hose No. 49; disbanded November 1. "Hope" Hose No. 50; disbanded November 1. "Relief" Hose No. 51; disbanded September 20. "Harry Howard" Hose No. 55; disbanded November 10. "Nassau" Hose No. 56: dispensed with July 19. "Manhattan" Hose No. 59; disbanded November 10. "M. T. Brennan" Hose No. 60; disbanded November 1. "Zephyr" Hose No. 61; disbanded November 1.

"Mutual" Hook and Ladder No. 1; disbanded September 20. "Chelsea" Hook and Ladder No. 2; disbanded November 1. "Phoenix" Hook and Ladder No. 3; disbanded November 20. "George B. McClellan" Hook and Ladder No. 4; disbanded November 1. "Union" Hook and Ladder No. 5; disbanded November 1. "Lafayette" Hook and Ladder No. 6;

disbanded November 11. "Mechanics" Hook and Ladder No. 7; disbanded November 1. "Empire" Hook and Ladder No. 8; disbanded October 25. "Washington" Hook and Ladder No. 9; disbanded November 1. "Cornelius V. Anderson" Hook and Ladder No. 10; disbanded November 1. "Harry Howard" Hook and Ladder No. 11; disbanded October 25. "Friendship" Hook and Ladder No. 12; disbanded September 20. "Marion" Hook and Ladder No. 13; disbanded November 10. "Columbian" Hook and Ladder No. 14; disbanded October 25. "Baxter" Hook and Ladder No. 15; disbanded November 1. "Liberty" Hook and Ladder No. 16; disbanded September 20. "John Decker" Hook and Ladder No. 17; disbanded November 10. "Hibernia" Hook and Ladder No. 18; disbanded November 1.

The following is an exact record of the first membership of the Metropolitan Companies, with their formation in chronological, not numerical, order:

METROPOLITAN STEAM FIRE ENGINE COMPANIES.

Company No. 1 organized July 31, 1865, at No. 4 Centre Street, in quarters of Exempt

HOOK AND LADDER NO. 3.

Engine Company. Had an Amoskeag steamer, built in 1865, and tender drawn by horses.

Foreman, William Corgan; assistant foreman, Walter T. Furlong; engineer, James H. Ward; stoker, James Leavy; driver, Joseph Douglass; firemen, William A. Kipp, Alexander McDonald, David Conner, James Rooney, Charles B. Angevine, William F. Hayes, Robert L. Wintringham (first member killed on duty).

Company No. 2 organized September 1, 1865, at No. 304 West Forty-seventh Street, in quarters of Hudson Engine Company No. 1, Had a steamer built in 1864 by William H. Van Ness, and tender drawn by horses.

Foreman, Robert Roberts; assistant foreman, Theodore A. Webb; engineer, Louis A. Lallemont; stoker, J. D. Fisher; driver, Benjamin F. Kocks; firemen, John Newman, Michael Glennon, John Canavan, James Flay, Arthur Dougherty, Samuel Griffiths, Henry Schuck.

Company No. 4 organized September 8, 1865, at No. 39 Liberty Street, in quarters of City Hose No. 8. Had an Amoskeag steamer, built in 1861, and tender drawn by horses.

Foreman, Thomas Macauley; assistant foreman, William F. Flock; engineer, William Matthews; stoker, Thomas P. Powers; driver, Michael C. Deiter; firemen, Dominick Sicot, Martin McEvoy, Thomas Irwin, Thomas T. Campbell, John Scanlan, Patrick Corrigan, Francis P. Murray.

Company No. 6 organized September 8, 1865, at No. 100 Cedar Street, in quarters of Washington Engine No. 20. Had an Amoskeag steamer, built in 1865, and a tender drawn by horses.

Foreman, Joseph J. Mallen; assistant foreman, James Whelan; engineer, Timothy Flynn; stoker, Edward Steadman; driver, John W. Regan; firemen, Louis Flock, Joseph Derry, Theodore Dakin, John McKowen, Peter Byrnes, John Nolan, George Jacobs.

Company No. 10 organized September 8, 1865, at No. 28 Beaver Street, in quarters of Franklin Hose No. 18. Did first duty with a hand engine while an Amoskeag steamer was making.

Foreman, John Batterbury; assistant foreman, J. A. Lewis; engineer, E. Mansfield Clark; stoker, M. J. Cullan; driver, Patrick Boyle; firemen, John H. Griffen, Martin Cherry, Patrick Folger, Henry Holtje, Richard F. Scully, Timothy Leary, Thomas Cammon, Martin Goss.

Company No. 7 organized September 8, 1865, at No. 26 Chambers Street, in quarters of Protector Engine No. 22. Had an Amoskeag engine, built in 1865, and tender drawn by horses.

Foreman, Joseph Boynton; assistant foreman, James I. Costa; engineer, Thomas Coady; stoker, Edward Hogan; driver, Richard W. Ash; firemen, William Keane, Jules Malloy, Thomas Killey, William Conlin, William Campbell, John Conry, William H. Plunkett.

Company No. 8 organized September 11, 1865, at No. 106 East Fiftieth Street, in quarters of Relief Hose No. 51. Had an Amoskeag steamer, built in 1860, and tender drawn by horses.

Foreman, John H. Van Tassell; assistant foreman, William Frost; engineer, Hiram S. Williams; stoker, George Jarvis; driver, Albert Homer; firemen, John Pye, John H. Grooves, Thomas Harrison, Charles H. Smith, John I. Eagan, George W. Bell.

Company No. 3 organized September 14, 1865, at No. 279 West Seventeenth Street, in quarters of Jackson Engine No. 24. Had a steamer, built by James Smith in 1864, and tender drawn by horses.

Foreman, John H. McNeil; assistant foreman, John A. Corvie; engineer, Charles Chambers; stoker, John Ritchie; driver, Thomas Clark; firemen, Alexander Ritchie, Alfred F. Lewis, Asa J. Henderson, Joseph Burns, John Fray, James Moran, P. W. Black.

Company No. 18 organized September 14, 1865, at No. 26 West Tenth Street, in quarters of Guardian Engine No. 29. Had a steamer, built by Lee & Larned in 1859, and tender drawn by horses.

Foreman, William H. Housner; assistant foreman, Clinton McDonald; engineer, William A. Elliott; stoker, William M. Gordon; driver, Robert Beattie; firemen, James Roland, Oscar A. Pesoa, John Lee, Thomas Leonard, John H. Bush, James G. Gerau, Robert Beattie.

Company No. 15 organized September 18, 1865, at No. 269 Henry Street, in quarters of Americus Engine No. 6. Had a steamer, built by Silsby Mynderse & Co. in 1861, and tender drawn by horses.

Foreman, James Little; assistant foreman, Thomas Henry; engineer, Thomas Mulligan; stoker, James Riley; driver, George W. Erb; firemen, Thomas Lahey, Albert Shick, David Peffers, William Hyland, Daniel McCauley, Edward Quinn, Thomas Bannan.

Company No. 16 organized September 18, 1865, at No. 109 East Twenty-fifth Street, in quarters of Lexington Engine No. 7. Had a steamer, built by Silsby Mynderse & Co. in 1860, and tender drawn by horses.

Foreman, William E. Sanbeg; assistant foreman, Thomas W. Wilson; engineer, James P. Teller; stoker, William F. Wilson; driver, Thomas A. Rogers; firemen, William F. Baker, William E. Arnold, Patrick Murray, William O'Brien, John O. Roberts, Charles F. Waterbury, Samuel Davis.

Company No. 19 organized September 18, 1865, at No. 227 West Twenty-fifth Street, in quarters of Mazeppa Engine No. 48. Had a steamer, built by James Smith in 1862, and tender drawn by horses.

Foreman, Stephen Mitchell; assistant foreman, William Shaw; engineer, Thomas Abbott; stoker, Thomas Pyne; driver, James McCutcheon; firemen, William Bullough, Thomas McDonough, John Rennie, Edward H. Slocum, Robert Mitchell, Owen O'Rourke, Henry Burnett.

Company No. 20 organized September 18, 1865, at No. 47 Marion Street, in quarters of Marion Engine No. 9. Had a steamer, built by James Smith, and tender drawn by horses.

Foreman, Hugh Bonner; assistant foreman, Charles Bathman; engineer, Edward A. Willoughby; stoker, James Hogan; driver, Michael Brennan; firemen, George Wilson, James Bush, Jacob Hickman, Peter A. Meeks, Philip Herrlick, John McCarrick, James A. Campbell.

Company No. 5 organized September 25, 1865, at No. 186 East Fourteenth Street, in the quarters of United States Engine No. 23. Had a steamer, built by James Smith in 1863, and tender drawn by horses.

Foreman, David B. Waters; assistant foreman, Patrick McKeever; engineer, William J. Hamilton; stoker, Charles H. Riley; driver, Alonzo A. Smith; firemen, James F. Butler, Peter H. Walsh, John J. Corley, Michael J. Stapleton, William H. Farrell, Francis Reilly, Patrick J. Burns.

Company No. 13 organized September 25, 1865, at No. 99 Wooster Street, in quarters of Oceanus Engine No. 11. Had a steamer, built by James Smith in 1863, and tender drawn by horses.

Foreman, John F. Gerau; assistant foreman, Cornelius Bloodgood (first appointed a fireman, and promoted on the resignation of W. F. Earle, who did not serve at all); engineer, John R. Day; stoker, John McLoughlin; driver, Robert Pollock; firemen, Frederick Wemmell, Edward Price, Jacob Regus, Hugh Kittson, George F. Rice, Charles Clarke, Patrick Gough.

Company No. 17 organized September 29, 1865, at No. 91 Ludlow Street, in quarters of Manhattan Engine No. 8. Had a steamer, built in 1861 by the Portland Company, and tender drawn by horses.

Foreman, Robert V. Mackey; assistant foreman, Noah L. Chamberlain; engineer, James Hamilton; stoker, William H. St. John; driver, Thomas H. Griffith; firemen, James Neville, William Wood, David Closey, William Long, William Sheehan, Henry Brengel, William H. Ranson, Thomas Harrington.

Company No. 9 organized September 29 at No. 55 East Broadway, in quarters of Excelsior Engine No. 2. Had an Amoskeag engine, built in 1865, and tender drawn by horses.

Foreman, Stewart Carson; assistant foreman, Patrick H. Stewart; engineer, Thomas Haley; stoker, Daniel O'Keefe; driver, John I. Herrick; firemen, Elisha Van Brunt, John Knapp, Edward McArdle, Edward Roche, John Conway, William E. Hogan, Andrew Lennon.

Company No. 11 organized October 2 at No. 437 East Houston Street, in quarters of Live Oak Engine No. 44. Had an Amoskeag engine, built in 1861, and tender drawn by horses.

Foreman, Julian C. Harrison; assistant foreman, John W. Miller; engineer, Alfred Hoyt; stoker, Joseph Gorman; driver, William H. Young; firemen, Thomas A. Carroll, George T. Florence, Hugh McGinley, George Wyman, John O'Neil, Charles Travis, Michael Knapp.

Company No. 21 organized October 4, 1865, at No. 142 East Fortieth Street, in quarters of Naiad Hose Company No. 53. Had a steamer built by James Smith, and tender drawn by horses.

Foreman, James B. Hunt; assistant foreman, John A. Biglin; engineer, Stephen O'Brien; stoker, Edward O'Donnell; driver, John Carr; firemen, Albert Stone, Victor D. Mahoney, William Barber, Joseph O. Davis, John Morgan, Cornelius McNally, Henry Bennett.

Company No. 22 organized October 4, 1865, at Third Avenue and Eighty-fifth Street, in quarters of Americus Hose No. 48. Had a steamer built by Joseph Banks, and tender drawn by horses.

Foreman, John B. Dinham; assistant foreman, Nicholas Smith; engineer (after delay), William Beaman; stoker, John W. Kennedy; driver, Joseph Lutz; firemen, William L. Meeks, H. J. Clark, John C. Post, William Quinn, John McMenomy, Thomas Haines, Schuyler Topping.

Company No. 14 organized October 6, 1865, at No. 15 East Eighteenth Street, in quarters of Metamora Hose No. 29. Had an Amoskeag engine, built in 1865, and tender drawn by horses.

Foreman, William H. Wilson; assistant foreman, George B. Nicholson; engineer, Thomas Cowan; stoker, Charles F. Golden; driver, John Barden; firemen, George W. Hall, Thomas P. Stephenson, Daniel J. Meagher, Thomas W. Gillett, Terence P. Brennen, E. S. Rhodes, William P. Daniels.

Company No. 23 organized October 6, 1865, in Sixty-eighth Street, near Tenth Avenue, in quarters of Harry Howard Engine No. 36. Had at first a hand engine and a steam engine drawn by hand.

Foreman, Henry A. Linden; assistant foreman, George McLoughlin; engineer, John Slattery; stoker, Adam Feit; driver, James A. McCormack; firemen, William Bennett, John Cotton, Christopher C. Flick, Bartley Monahan, William H. Van Houton, Charles H. Reed, Lafayette Sharp.

Suburban Company No. 36 organized partly on a volunteer basis—the company being paid a lump sum per annum, and the members following their usual avocations—October 11, 1865, in Fourth Avenue, between One Hundred and Twenty-sixth and One Hundred and Twenty-seventh Streets, in quarters of Pocahontas Engine No. 49. Had two hand engines.

Foreman, Robert C. Brown; assistant foreman, William Seaman; firemen, James Crowley, John D. Lee, H. S. McDowell; George J. Stouter, William A. Waterbury, C. W. Ridley, James P. Bremer, William Taylor, Philip Northrup, Robert J. Post, William Healey, Samuel Christie, Andrew Van Varren, Matthew Table, John W. Brown, Edward Huntington, R. A. Mawbey, John Hempstead, Henry Watervelt. George H. Eagleton, Charles B. Jones, Charles A. Wilkins, Samuel T. Allaire, W. R. Pettigrew, Frederick Alonzo, Henry L. Niven, David Hanson, R. G. Rudd, Theodore Fink, Jacob R. Wilkins, William R. Gilleland, John W. Church, Edward J. Keech, Jonathan Hanson.

Suburban Company No. 37 organized partly on a volunteer basis—the company being paid a lump sum per annum, and the members following their usual avocations—October 11, 1865, at One Hundred and Twenty-second Street, between Second and Third Avenues, in quarters of Undine Engine No. 52. Had two hand engines.

Foreman, G. B. Tunison; assistant foreman, E. Doughty; firemen, R. M. Christie, E. B. Tunison, P. Traphagen, William H. Johnson, James E. Watson, William F. Haradon, James H. Searles, George Keller, Frank Straub, L. B. Tupper, J. A. McCosker, F. A. Steele, N. W. Moulton, H. H. Cook, F. McL. Wallace, James Doughty, Oloff Peterson, George H. E. Lynch, G. B. Conkling, J. E. Demarest, S. W. Tompkins, Henry C. Mount, John Becker, William Robins, James P. Bremner, Charles L. Tupper, Adam Jacobi.

Suburban Company No. 38 organized partly on a volunteer basis—the company being paid a lump sum per annum, and the members following their usual avocations—October 11, 1865, in Eighty-fifth Street, between Third and Fourth Avenues, in quarters of Americus Hose No. 48. Had two hand engines.

Foreman, John Hay; assistant foreman, William H. Marshal; firemen, William J. Kelley, Andrew Dunning, Charles M. Piper, William Sanderson, Hugh Conaghan, Henry Schaffer, Weston Higbie, John H. Bradley, D. Bartley, Edward Cobussier, F. C. M. Moore, Theodore E. Dye, George W. Johnson, Peter Wooley, Lewis Anderson, Louis Lewis, William Baldwin, William H. McCarty, P. H. McNally, James Bridge, John R. Vail, William H. Thomas, David Opdike, Geo. W. T. Thomas, Patrick Murtha, Alonzo Brown, Joseph Johnson, John Coady.

Company No. 24, organized October 11, 1865, at No. 78 Morton Street, in quarters of Howard Engine No. 34. Did first duty with a hand engine, afterwards with an Amoskeag.

Foreman, William H. Wood; assistant foreman, Patrick Fitzsimmons; engineer, James Rogers; stoker, John N. Connell; driver, Patrick Trainor; firemen, Albert Tier, James Kelley, William H. Hardy, Thomas Walker, William Cavanagh, William Harrison, Patrick Trainor, James Greenwood.

Company No. 25 organized October 13, 1865, at No. 148 Fifth Street, in quarters of Jefferson Engine No. 26. Had a steamer built by the Portland Company in 1861, and tender drawn by horses.

Foreman, John Alden; assistant foreman, Silas Lyng; engineer, Charles E. Struck; stoker, William Peto; driver, George W. Evans; firemen, Schuyler Livingstone, Benjamin A. Gicquel, Charles Lynch, Henry A. Burger, Charles Willert, William Cahill.

Company No. 12 organized October 13, 1865, at No. 261 William Street, in quarters of Eagle Engine No. 13. Had a steamer built by James Smith in 1863, and tender drawn by horses.

Foreman, James Oates; assistant foreman, Joseph Williams; engineer, Joseph Shaw;

HOOK AND LADDER NO 3, WITH LADDER EXTENDED.

driver, William P. Allen; stoker, James O'Neil; fireman, Joseph W. Moran, Henry Murray, William Hern, Washington Montange, Malachi Haley, John Pettit.

Company No. 26 organized October 16, 1865, at No. 138 West Thirty-seventh Street, in quarters of Valley Forge Engine No. 46. Had a steamer built by Lee & Larned in 1859, and tender drawn by horses.

Foreman, William M. Mitchell; assistant foreman, Alexander McNeil; engineer, Wm. A.

Brickell; stoker, A. D. Keifer; driver, Benjamin Johnson; firemen, Samuel C. Campbell, Archibald Stewart, Oliver Hawkins, Robert Wray, Jacob Tooker, John McCreadle, Gideon L. Tooker.

Company No. 27 organized October 16, 1865, at No. 173 Franklin Street, in quarters of North River Engine No. 30. Had a steamer built by Joseph Banks in 1863, and tender drawn by horses.

Foreman, Luke A. Murphy; assistant foreman, David H. Beardsley; engineer, George Brown; stoker, James Davis; driver, Charles H. Tucker; firemen, Edward Kelley, William Stoker, John Stanley, John Murphy, William Mason, Francis Walls, Patrick Kennie.

Company No. 28 organized October 20, 1865, at No. 211 East Eleventh Street, in quarters of Forrest Engine No. 3. Did first duty with a hand engine.

Foreman, William Donnelly; assistant foreman, Hugh Lindsey; engineer, Edward Minton; stoker, Henry Peters; driver, Charles Shardon; firemen, Joseph F. Malloy, John B. Carpenter, James Flood, Patrick Kennedy, Patrick Costello, Patrick Flynn, Richard Delaney.

Company No. 29 organized October 20, at No. 304 Washington Street, the quarters of Hudson River Engine No. 53. Had a steamer built by James Smith in 1859, and tender drawn by horses.

Foreman, Arnot Spence; assistant foreman, William E. Smith; engineer, John Slattery; stoker, Anthony McCaffrey; driver, Edward Carpenan; firemen, John Grimes, James Hunter, Thomas McGrath, John B. Wilson, Richard Norris, Luke Kavanagh, James McKay.

Company No. 30 organized October 20, 1865, at No. 18 Renwick Street, in quarters of Alert Hose No. 41. Did first duty with a hand engine.

Foreman, William Simpson; assistant foreman, William Harrison; engineer, George Henderson; stoker, Robert A. McFarland; driver, William H. Scott; firemen, Samuel G. Jackson, Richard Nodine, Isaac Wiltsie, Richard D. Hall, William Mahony, James Meehan.

Company No. 31 organized October 20, 1865, at No. 116 Leonard Street, in quarters of Fulton Engine No. 21. Had a steamer built by A. B. Taylor, Son & Co. in 1862, and tender drawn by horses.

Foreman, Peter Weir; assistant foreman, Patrick Gavagan; engineer, Robert Mullen; stoker, J. D. Ferris; driver, John Casey; firemen, Michael Hart, John R. Scoble, John F. Murphy, James McNamee, John H. Kehoe, James Collins, John J. Bresnan.

Company No. 32 organized October 20, 1865, at No. 18 Burling Slip, in quarters of Edwin Forrest Hose No. 5. Had a steamer built by Joseph Banks in 1864, and tender drawn by horses.

Foreman, William Buckley; assistant foreman, John Pettit; engineer, D. T. Mullin; stoker, James Burke; driver, William Wilson; firemen, John F. Horan, John Hewitt, Patrick H. Downey, Thomas H. Downs, John Walker, James Burke, William Cotter, Benjamin Dunlop.

Suburban Company No. 39 organized partly on a volunteer basis—the company being paid a lump sum per annum, and the members following their usual avocations—October 27, 1865, in Lawrence Street, Manhattanville, in quarters of Manhattan Hose No. 59. Had a hand engine.

Foreman, James E. Poole; assistant foreman, Nicholas Kuntz; firemen, William Cowen, Thomas Schneider, Patrick Sullivan, John Mead, John S. Poole, James Pettit, John Moore, Aaron Meyer, Terence Gray, A. W. M. Hume, George Kintz, George Craft, Thomas McIntyre, John McClenahan, John Higgins, Andrew Geraty, Patrick Guilfoyle, George W. Smith, William Kehoe, Elias Garrahant, John Meyer, Alfred Lyon, Jeremiah Butler, Casper Miller, George O. Roberts.

Company No. 34 organized October 30, 1865, at No. 286 West Thirty-third Street, in quarters of Mazeppa Hose No. 42. Had a steamer built by William H. Van Ness in 1854, and tender drawn by horses.

Foreman, William P. Daniell; assistant foreman, John Coyle; engineer, Lewis A. Lallemont; stoker, William Wray; driver, Daniel Kash; firemen, George A. Campell, Eugene A. Pettigrew; Charles E. Mackey; Peter Funcke, William E. Looker, John Lynch, James Lavelle.

Suburban Company No. 40 organized partly on a volunteer basis—the company being paid a lump sum per annum, and the members following their usual avocations—October 30, 1865, at Carmansville, in quarters of Fort Washington Engine No. 27.   Had a hand engine.

Foreman, William Harris, Jr. ; assistant foreman, George Kirkland ; firemen, Charles H. Robinson, John Short, James Buckridge, Edward Scallon, Resolved Gardner, James O'Rourke, Charles C. Townley, Erhardt Maixner, John Cooper, M. I. Quigg, Philip Schule, Mortimer Ward, John Scallon, Munson W. Smith, Thomas H. Gegan, Bernard Murray, William Depperman, Mathias Sinndinger, Thomas Fulton, George Briggs, William Barry, James B. Archer, M. I. Corley, Thomas Coffrey, William H. Porter, James Houston, James Robertson, Bernard Gardner, John Watson, Robert Dazell, I. Hamilton Cathill, Christian Santer, George Finn.

Company No. 33 organized November 1, 1865, at No. 220 Mercer Street, the quarters of

INTERIOR OF ENGINE HOUSE.

Niagara Engine No. 34.   Had a steamer built by Joseph Banks in 1863, and tender drawn by horses.

Foreman, Henry M. Van Wart ; assistant foreman, James Gilmartin ; engineer, George Shaw ; stoker, James Newman ; driver, James Tucker ; firemen, John Larkin, Christopher Iles, Thomas F. Gibney, Christian Van Rensselaer, Thomas F. Sculley, John Mullen, John Courtney.

HOOK AND LADDER COMPANIES.

Company No. 1 organized September 8, 1865, at No. 28 Chambers Street, in quarters of Mutual Hook and Ladder No. 1.   Had a truck built by C. E. Hartshorn, drawn by horses.

Foreman, William Brandon ; assistant foreman, John Moore ; driver, Patrick Honigan ; firemen, Thomas J. Cortisos, William F. Craft, Charles Verry, Patrick Spillane, George Hanley, James J. Gilfeather, Thomas J. Hart, James McAlpin, William McKenzie.

Company No. 2 organized September 11, 1865, at Lexington Avenue and Fiftieth Street, in quarters of Liberty Hook and Ladder No. 16.   Had a truck built by C. E. Hartshorn in 1862, drawn by horses.

Foreman, Andrew J. Brady ; assistant foreman, John Rourke ; driver, Ernest Keyser, Jr.;

firemen, Henry Holdsworth, Edward Story, Jr., Robert Amos, Roger B. Hamblett, Edward S. Smith, Minthorne D. Tompkins, Jr., Thomas Hutchingson, Samuel Hunt, Philip Ramee.

Company No. 3 organized September 11, 1865, at No. 78 East Thirteenth Street, in quarters of Friendship Hook and Ladder No. 12. Had a truck built by C. E. Hartshorn in 1862, drawn by horses.

Foreman, James Timoney; assistant foreman, John McCue; driver, John Hearn; firemen, William J. Mullin, James Horn, John Haley, John Hearn, James McGee, John R. Hennessey, John A. Thompson, Michael Kelly, John W. White.

Company No. 4 organized September 18, 1865, at Forty-eighth Street and Eight Avenue, in quarters of Empire Hook and Ladder No. 8. Had a truck built by C. E. Hartshorn in 1859, drawn by horses.

Foreman, Michael Snyder; assistant foreman, George H. Cornell; tillerman, Henry Schuck; driver, Christopher Siebert; firemen, Mathias Hines, Frederick Peyer, John McClave, John Brown, John Frederick, Francis Frank, Charles Metz.

Company No. 5 organized September 25, 1865, at No. 96 Chambers Street, the quarters of Columbian Hook and Ladder No. 14. Had a truck built by Pine & Hartshorn in 1856, drawn by horses.

Foreman, Charles Oscar Shay; assistant foreman, William Wood; driver, Phillip Voris; firemen, William E. Lawrence, Charles S. Pardee, John Babcock, John L. Gulick, John Ward, Jacob Van Orden, John Fulton, Theodore Ertz, James Wright.

Company No. 6 organized September 27, 1865, at No. 180 Clinton Street, the quarters of Harry Howard Hook and Ladder Company No. 11. Had a truck built by C. E. Hartshorn in 1862, drawn by horses.

Foreman, Abram C. Hull; assistant foreman, Henry M. Jones; driver, Peter H. Benjamin; firemen, Francis I. Reilly, Charles L. Kelly, Edward McPhelan, Edward Bradburn, John Brown, James H. Balentine, John F. McLoughlin, Patrick Donohue.

Company No. 7 organized October 11, 1865, at 119 East Twenty-eighth Street, in quarters of Washington Hook and Ladder No. 9. Had a truck built by William Williams in 1859.

Foreman, Robert King; assistant foreman, William H. Pine; driver, James Martin; firemen, John I. Kelly, William T. Crane, Charles N. Hammond, John Welsh, James J. Evans, Patrick Wren, Edward Gorman, Dennis F. Sullivan, Samuel W. Hutchings.

Suburban Company No. 13 organized partly on a volunteer basis—the company being paid a lump sum per annum, and the members following their usual avocations—October 11, 1865, in Eighty-seventh Street, between Third and Fourth Avenues, in quarters of Cornelius V. Anderson Hook and Ladder No. 10. Had a hand truck.

Foreman, Cyrus T. Frost; assistant foreman, James Martin; firemen, Erastus Lent, P. M. Dwight, A. H. Payne, John Hanson, William H. Keller, David Brown, Jesse C. Boughton, George S. Rockwell, Jacob Brower, John S. Bosworth, John McClymont, Henry L. Dexter, Andrew Morrow, James Gerton, Nicholas Geiger, Joseph C. Totton, John R. Higbie, Albert Cox, George I. Gregory, John Warre, George W. Frost, William Morgan, Edward Wright, James M. Goodenough, James I. Marshal, Jr., James Wallace, William Gerton, William G. Mollan.

Company No. 8 organized October 16, 1865, at No. 153 Franklin Street, in quarters of Baxter Hook and Ladder No. 15. Had a truck built by C. E. Hartshorn in 1863, drawn by horses.

Foreman, George W. Quackenbush; assistant foreman, Edward S. Moore; driver, John E. Willerts; firemen, Joseph Johnson, James J. Pettit, James H. Monroe, John F. Burke, John Steene, Milton J. C. Mangan, John Brackett, Edward McPhelan, John Green.

Suburban Company No. 14 organized partly on a volunteer basis—the company being paid a lump sum per annum, and the members following their usual avocations—October 20, 1865, in One Hundred and Twenty-fifth Street, between Third and Fourth Avenues, in quarters of Mechanics' Hook and Ladder No. 7. Had a hand truck.

Foreman, John S. Anderson; assistant foreman, James M. Randell; firemen, William H. H. Bingham, Morris D. Meyers, Simeon Simmons, Thomas E. B. Hawks, John Magill, N. N. Thompson, George Rogers, Charles W. Kile, W. S. Stewart, William Thompson, John D. Angus, John D. Thees, George W. Van Wagner, Jr., Charles H. Schultz, James A. Reading,

James E. Braine, William Thompson, Christopher Wray, James Brown, G. Sackett, C. W. Ridley, R. J. Post, Robert Blair, Fletcher Place, W. S. Barnes, William McClellan, A. E. Cutter, John Thompson.

Company No. 9 organized October 20, 1865, at No. 195 Elizabeth Street, in quarters of Hibernia Hook and Ladder No. 18. Had a truck built by W. H. Vanness, drawn by horses.

Foreman, William Rowe; assistant foreman, John McCauley; driver, Patrick Conaghan; firemen, Thomas C. Lee, Patrick Fagan, Timothy McDonald, Timothy Donovan, Daniel Scully, John Carroll, James Heaney, John Sattler, Peter Steffern.

Company No. 10 organized October 20, 1865, at No. 28 Ann Street, in quarters of Lady Washington Hose No. 40. Had a truck built by William Williams in 1861.

Foreman, William W. Bowles; assistant foreman, William Bingham; driver, Peter Mulvehill; firemen, Garrett Murphy, Michael Nagle, Daniel King, William Gardner, Henry Schultz, John McNamara, John McKenzie, Francis Lynch, Thomas L. Jacobus.

Company No. 11 organized October 27, 1865, at No. 548 Fifth Street, in quarters of Mechanics' Hose No. 47. Had a truck built by C. E. Hartshorn in 1860, drawn by horses.

Foreman, Christopher H. Reynolds; assistant foreman, Morris W. Roberts; driver, Thomas H. Beebe; firemen, Timothy Dillon, Thomas F. Rielly, Alfred Hendrickson, Edward J. Russell, Peter Vetter Jr., William Quigg, John Anckner, Thomas E. Schiell.

Suburban Company No. 15 organized partly on a volunteer basis—the company being paid a lump sum per annum, and the members following their usual avocations—October 30, 1865, at Tenth Avenue and One Hundred and Fifty-ninth Street, the quarters of John Decker Hook and Ladder No. 17. Had a hand truck.

Foreman, Michael McDermott; assistant foreman, William Mackey; firemen, Robert Reinhart, John McLoughlin, John Joyce, Thomas Armstrong, Peter Appen, Charles Bruhl, John McCauley, John Duff, William Farmer, Robert Barrell, Henry Brecht, Christopher Harden, M. T. Branagan, William Quinn, Augustus Ilse, James Reed, Martin Cummings.

Company No. 12 organized December 1, 1865, at No. 165 West Twentieth Street, in quarters of Liberty Engine No. 50.

Foreman, James Walton; assistant foreman, William Terhune; driver, Charles Nodine; firemen, David Gilles, Theodore Hendricks, Robert Williams, Thomas William Geary, James C. Orton, Isaac S. Parsons, John Hopper, George Daniells, James McDowell.

The organization of the new companies, and the retirement of the Volunteers, was effected under the critical observation of the public, who were divided into friends of the Old system and the New and the Volunteers. It is not necessary to enter into complete details of the action of certain Volunteer companies, who, under bad advisement, chose to oppose in various ways the organization of the New Department. There was some exhibition of bad feeling between the Volunteers and the new companies. Their allies, the "runners," were responsible for the mischief that was done. Hose were cut at fires, apparatus were retarded in their way to them. The "Mets" were greeted with cries of "Man found dead," etc., and the members of the Fire Insurance Patrol, which was considered to represent the obnoxious insurance interest, fared ill for many months. "Throw the red caps out" was often the cry of "Metropolitans" when, at fires, the insurance patrolmen entered a building to put waterproof covers on property. The detrimental alacrity that distinguished some of the Volunteer companies at fires, where slap-dash and reckless activity were very often considered the acme of fire duty, was for a long time continued in the Paid Department. This resulted in unnecessary damage to apparatus and property. Water was used recklessly when a pail or two would have sufficed. Hose costing $1.55 to $1.65 a foot, and which was then of riveted leather— the first step toward better hose was taken a couple of years later—was dashed around or neglected until it became as dry, brittle and unserviceable as bark, and had to be taken to the "yard" to be "slushed" or soaked in vats of grease and other implements of fire fighting. Notably, "butts" were "banged around," to be broken, dented, and in other ways rendered unserviceable. The worst act attributed to the Volunteers while the New Department was organizing was the burning of the quarters of Black Joke Engine No. 33, in Fifty-eighth Street, near Broadway, on the twenty-second of November, 1865. The company was then under disability, and its apparatus was removed, and public opinion was divided as to the guilt of a member or members of the company or zealous "runners." The Metropolitans, once under discipline, rarely noticed insult or worse. It was not rare, when paid men came at a fire, for some one to step out of a crowd and vent his displeasure in a blow ; but the encounters that took place were petty in comparison with the less serious of the Volunteer scrimmages.

John Decker turned over to the new commissioners the following property :

Thirty-four steam fire engines, thirty-six engine tenders, twenty-five hand engines, forty-nine hose carriages, thirty-nine jumpers, twenty-one crabs, eighteen hook and ladder trucks, one thousand one hundred and ninety-seven lengths of leather hose (59,850 feet), one hundred and fifty-two and a half lengths of rubber hose (7,625 feet), four hundred and twenty-four feet of Croton Hose, eighty-five and a half lengths of suction, ninety-nine brass pipes, two copper pipes, one hundred and fifty-six leather pipes, two thousand two hundred and forty-seven chairs in good order, two hundred and eighteen broken chairs, two hundred and eighty-six lanterns, three hundred pails, two hundred and twenty-six brooms, one hundred and forty-five scrub-brushes, ninety-three Chamois, one hundred and thirty-six axes, two hundred and six hooks in good order, forty broken hooks, forty-two picks, one hundred and twelve ladders, one hundred and fourteen sponges, two hundred and thirty-eight mops, three hundred cans, one hundred and twenty-eight hoisting apparatus, seventy-nine tables, five hundred and fourteen wrenches, fifty-six screw wrenches, eighty-seven loads of wood, twenty-eight and a half tons of coal, two hundred and sixty chandeliers, eight hundred and six brackets, one hundred and thirty-six burners, six hundred and twenty-three globes, thirty-two stoves and pipes, ninety-four hose washers, one hundred and eight jacks, one hundred and twenty-four signals, twenty-seven coal scuttles, eleven monkey wrenches, nineteen crowbars, eight gallons of oil, fifty-one pitchforks, five pipe-holders, two hundred and six straps, two hundred and seventeen ropes, one hundred and ninety-five and a half pendants, fifteen desks, seven hub wrenches, six cap wrenches, one poker, seventy-two side lamps, twelve nozzles, seven reducers, four extra tongues, twenty-four shovels, fourteen benches, five oil feeders, two extra sets of wheels, one length hemp hose, two extra valves, alarm bells, ten striking apparatus, five wash basins, one iron safe, ten field glasses, eleven spy glasses, twelve pounds of cotton waste, one hammer, seven spittoons, one gas stand, seven closets, fifteen dust brushes, twelve clocks, five slates, one book, ten water coolers, one extra lever, eight tool wrenches, five dust pans, fifteen mats, eight tin boilers, three carpets, one lounge, one large closet with pigeon holes, one letter press, two screw chairs, one eyelet puncher, three oilcloths, one mirror slab, three shoemakers' seats, four hundred feet of condemned hose, two hose benches, one platform scale, ten bars of soap, sixteen pairs of hose butts, one windlass and fall, two work tubs.

On the sixth of September, 1865, the organization of the New Department had so far progressed that the commissioners were able to dispense with the services of the assistant engineers of the Volunteer Department. They recognized their services in the following resolution :

Resolved, that the Metropolitan Fire Commissioners are deeply impressed with the obligations they are under to those of the assistant engineers of the Old Volunteer Department who have up to the present time rendered to them and to the city valuable services since the passage of the law creating a New Department, and they respectfully tender to those gentlemen their most sincere thanks for their aid.

The engineers thus retired were Timothy L. West, William Lamb, Joseph

L. Perley, Eli Bates, James Long, Bernard Kenny, Bartley Donohue, Thomas Duffy, John Hamill, Michael Shannessy, Alexander V. Davidson, Timothy Sullivan, Peter Weir, Gilbert J. Orr, Thomas Cleary, Michael Halloran, Abram Horn, George H. E. Lynch. Several of these had already retired.

The same day the commissioners elected eleven assistant engineers, whose pay was fixed at one thousand two hundred dollars per annum, viz. : Joseph L. Perley, Gilbert J. Orr, Eli Bates, Thomas Sullivan, and Michael Shannessy of Chief Decker's staff, and William Banham, Jr., W. W. Rhodes, John Conley, Joseph D. Costa, Bernard Sheridan, and Peter Y. Everett. Joseph L. Perley was made first assistant engineer, at a salary of two thousand dollars per annum. Two days after, William Lamb, foreman of the Corporation Yard, and Alexander V. Davidson, chief clerk to the chief engineer, were retired. Garrett B. Tunison succeeded Mr. Davidson at a salary of one thousand dollars a year.

Several of the engineers resigned or in other ways left the Department, so that the first official list was as follows :

Engineer Eli Bates, Engine Companies Nos. 3, 14, 18, 33. Engineer Gilbert J. Orr, Engine Companies Nos. 1, 7, 9, 12, 31, and Hook and Ladder Company No. 1. Engineer Thomas Sullivan, Engine Companies Nos. 11, 15, and Hook and Ladder Companies 6, 11. Engineer Michael Shannessy, Engine Companies Nos. 2, 19, 23, 34, Hook and Ladder Companies 4, 12. Engineer John Conley, Engine Companies Nos. 4, 6, 10, 29, 32, Hook and Ladder Company 10. Engineer B. Sheridan, Engine Companies Nos. 5, 25, 28, Hook and Ladder Companies 3, 9. Engineer William W. Rhodes, Engine Companies Nos. 16, 21, 26, Hook and Ladder Company 7. Engineer William Banham, Jr., Engine Companies Nos. 8, 22, Hook and Laddder Company 2. Engineer Robert V. Mackey, Engine Companies Nos. 17, 20, 24, Hook and Ladder Company 5. Engineer William Brandon, Engine Companies Nos. 13, 17, 30, Hook and Ladder Company 8.

The pay of the force was fixed under a construction of the law which created the department as follows :

Chief engineer, $3,000 per annum; assistant to chief, $2,000 per annum; district engineers, $1,200 per annum; foremen, $800 per annum; assistant foremen, $750 per annum; engineers, $900 per annum; ordinary firemen, $700 per annum; suburban engineers, $400 per annum; each suburban company, $1,000 per annum.

The embarrassments of the commissioners were not confined to delay in procuring funds. The resigning of members of all grades when companies were thought to be on an active footing, and the active or passive opposition of the element that at last wrecked the Volunteer system. For many weeks the fire companies that were appointed under the act of the thirtieth of March, 1865, wore such uniforms as they chose. When regular uniforms were discussed in September, 1865, there was instantly opposition from some of the best men in the New Department and a number of like desirable members. At one time it appeared as if a majority of the force would resign rather than wear "livery." The commissioners set a good example by choosing for themselves and wearing the following uniform :

"A blue cloth cap (navy style) a frock-coat made of navy-blue cloth, double-breasted, made to button up close to the neck, with seven department regulation buttons of bronze metal on each breast, three on each skirt behind, and four on each sleeve at the cuff. A single-breasted vest made of the same material as coat, without collar, and eight regulation buttons. Pantaloons made of the same material as coat. Surtout overcoats made of navy-blue pilot cloth, double-breasted, made to button up close to the neck, with seven regulation buttons on each breast, three on each skirt behind, and four on each sleeve at the cuff."

This had the best effect, but many resignations were sent in when the regulations prescribing a uniform for the firemen were promulgated.

The first regulations for the guidance of the Paid Firemen, gotten up in September, 1865, were as strict as the times permitted. The following were the general rules :

SECTION 13.—The members shall keep the houses and bedding clean and in good order. They shall accompany their apparatus going to or returning from a fire, and when on duty at a fire, when not otherwise directed by the officer in command, shall remain by their apparatus. The foreman shall cause to be kept by the officers and members of the force (serving in rotation as they stand on the roll) a proper and efficient watch day and night, so that at all times two men shall be on patrol in the neighborhood of the engine or hook and ladder house, and one on watch in the house. Members doing such patrol duty shall report at the house hourly until relieved.

SECTION 14.—Racing to or from fires is prohibited ; and if the apparatus of the several companies proceed on the same street or avenue to or from a fire, they shall do so in single file.

SECTION 15.—Crossing a line of hose when in use by a steam fire engine is, unless in cases of the most absolute necessity, strictly prohibited.

SECTION 16.—Drivers will be held responsible for any damage caused by them, or carelessness displayed in conveying their apparatus to or from a fire.

SECTION 17.—The officer in command shall precede his apparatus in going to or from a fire.

SECTION 18.—No officer or member of the force shall appear on duty except he be properly clothed in the uniform prescribed for the department ; nor shall any officer or member of a fire company appear at a fire without his fire-cap.

SECTION 19.—No spirituous or intoxicating liquors shall be allowed on the premises of any Metropolitan Fire Company, nor shall any game of chance be permitted thereon.

SECTION 20.—No officer or member shall use profane, immoral or indecent language in or about any engine or hook and ladder house, or while at, going to, or returning from a fire ; nor shall any officer or member visit places where intoxicating liquors are sold while in the uniform of this department.

SECTION 21.—Officers of companies, after a fire, having hose which do not belong to them, shall return the same to the company to whom it belongs.

SECTION 22.—The driver, engineer and stoker may ride on the engine, and the driver and one man on the tender, in going to or returning from fires, and no more ; and the officer in command will be held responsible for a violation of this rule.

As soon as possible after the organization of the Metropolitan Board, a committee was appointed to devise badges, etc., not only for the members of the force, but insurance officers, members of the Fire Patrol, and others having business within the fire lines, to keep out the element that had done so much to bring the Volunteers into disrepute. The following rules in regard to badges were adopted :

INSIGNIA AND BADGES

The fire marshal was required to have a fire-cap with " Fire Marshal " on the front or a black patent leather band with same. The superintendent of buildings and his inspectors were required to have on their caps a patent leather band with their title. Reporters were required to wear a badge with the word " Reporter " and the name of their paper. Officers of insurance companies wore an oval silver badge with the name of their company on it. The superintendent of the Fire Insurance Patrol had a badge with his title on it. The other members of Insurance Patrol had a red fire-cap with their number and initials on it, or a red leather band with " I. P." and number on it in white or gilt letters, or a badge.

The following were the fire insurance officers first named by the Metropolitan Commissioners as having badges to give them admission through the fire lines, in February, 1866:

INSURANCE COMPANY.	PRESIDENT.	SECRETARY.
Ætna, ...	Frederick A. Conkling,	H. C. Beach.
Arctic, . . .	S. Milton Smith,	Vincent Tellyon.
Astor, ...	Robert D. Hart,	James H. Reilly.
Atlantic, . . .		Horatio Dover.
American, . . .	James M. Halstead,	Thomas L. Thomas.
American Exchange, .	Henry Butler,	William Raynor.
Adriatic, . . .	William A. Sears,	Frank W. Lewis.
Brevoort, . . .	James C. Harriott,	John C. Haviland.
Broadway, . . .	Hiram M. Forrester,	
Brooklyn, . . .	T. P. Furnald,	J. W. Cheney.
Baltic, ...	William S. Corwin,	W. H. Kipp.
Citizens', . . .		Edward A. Walton.
City, ...	R. A. Reading,	Samuel Townsend.
Clinton, . . .		James B. Ames, Jr.
Columbia, . . .	Alfred Douglas,	John B. Arthur.
Commercial, . .	Joseph Petit,	
Commercial Mutual, .	Daniel Drake Smith,	
Continental, . .		Cyrus Peck.
Corn Exchange, . .		W. H. Windsor.
Commerce, . .	Benjamin Babcock,	W. E. Hoxie.
Croton, ...	Thomas Stillwell,	John M. Tompkins.
Central Park, . .	Ramsen Appleby,	J. L. Townsend.
Eagle, ...		Alexander J. Clinton.
Excelsior, . . .	M. F. Hodges,	S. M. Craft.
Exchange, . . .	James Van Noden,	Richard C. Canbes.
Empire City, . .		William A. Burtis, Jr.
Firemen's, . . .	J. V. Harriott,	Abner Hayward.
Firemen's Fund, . .	Nathan B. Graham,	Henry Buchman.
Fireman's Trust, . .		P. W. Burrell.
Fulton, ...	W. A. Cobb,	James M. Rankin.
Greenwich, . . .	S. C. Harriott,	James Harrison.
Grocers', . . .	Sampson Moore,	James G. Platt.
Germania, . . .	Randolph Garrigue,	John E. Kahl.
Globe, . . .	Leonard Kirby,	Alfred A. Reeves.
Guardian, . . .		Walter H. Paye.
Harmony, . . .	R. O. Gleven,	Daniel D. Gassner.
Hamilton, . . .	J. C. Winans,	James Gilmore.
Hanover, . . .	D. L. Stone,	B. S. Walcott.
Home, ...		John McGee.
Howard, . . .	Samuel T. Skidmore,	H. A. Oakley.
Humboldt, . . .	William Mulligan,	Alexander Wiley, Jr.
Hoffman, . . .		Joseph W. Wildey.
Indemnity, . . .		Emmons Clark.
Irving, ...	Mason Thomson,	Martin L. Crowell.

INSURANCE COMPANY.	PRESIDENT.	SECRETARY.
Importers' and Traders',		F. W. Ballard.
International,	Charles Taylor,	C. C. Hine.
Jefferson,		Samuel E. Belcher.
Knickerbocker,		B. D. Skidmore.
Lamar,	E. A. Anthony,	Isaac R. St. John.
Lenox,	George A. Jarvis,	Walter M. Franklin.
Lorillard,	Carlisle Norwood,	John C. Mills.
Lafayette,		James B. Thompson.
Manhattan,		George B. Hodgsden.
Mechanics',	Daniel Chambers,	
Mercantile,	W. A. Thomson,	W. A. Anderson.
Merchants',	C. V. B. Ostrander,	J. L. Douglass.
Metropolitan,	James L. Graham,	Henry H. Porter.
Market,	Ashen Taylor,	Henry P. Freeman.
Montauk,		John C. Philip.
Morris,	Edward A. Stansbury,	Abraham M. Kirby.
National,		Henry C. Drowne.
Nassau,	W. M. Harris,	Thomas B. Jones.
New York Bowery,	William Hibbard,	G. G. Taylor.
New York Equitable,	Richard J. Thorn,	John Miller.
New York Fire,	Daniel Underhill,	A. Colsen, Jr.
New Amsterdam,	David S. Manners,	Isaac D. Cole, Jr.
Niagara,	J. D. Steele,	
North American,	James W. Otis,	R. W. Bleecker.
North River,		John Hegeman.
North Western,	William Lecount,	
Pacific,	Amos F. Hatfield,	Thomas F. Jeremiah.
Park,	William Jaffray,	Stephen M. Long.
People's,		William Martin.
Relief,	Joseph Pinckney,	W. E. Crary.
Republic,	Robert S. Hine,	D. F. Curry.
Resolute,	J. Euhlthorn,	W. M. Randell.
Royal,	A. B. McDonald,	
Rutgers',	Isaac O. Barker,	
Stuyvesant,	Samuel P. Patterson,	William F. Leggett.
Standard,		W. M. St. John.
Sterling,	Payson Ogden,	A. L. Soulard.
St. Nicholas,	William Winslow,	John J. Searing.
Star,	George W. Savage,	N. C. Miller.
United States,	Abraham S. Underhill,	W. W. Underhill.
Union Mutual,	F. S. Lathrop,	Ferdinand Stagg.
Washington,	George C. Satterlee,	W. H. Lathrop.
Williamsburg City,		H. Giraux.
Yonkers of New York,		John W. Murray.
Ætna of Hartford,	J. A. Alexander,	
Charter Oak,	Charles M. Peck.	
Sun Mutual.		Isaac H. Walker.

FIRE INSURANCE SURVEYORS.

Merchants',	Michael Hynard.
Brooklyn,	T. C. Bergen.
Lafayette,	W. Blain.
Resolute,	Hiram Funk.

FIRE INSURANCE PATROL, Alfred Carson, Superintendent.

PATROL No. 1.—Captain, John Cornwell; first assistant, Thomas E. Howe; second assistant, Andrew A. Burrows; patrolmen, Edmund Lister, James Franklin, Charles Doxey,

George Bostman, John Haight, Samuel White, Stephen Hallich, Sidney Spellman, Charles Atkinson, Joseph Walsh, Henry Jones, John Cairns, Jeremiah Twomey, Benjamin Smith, John Hartman, John Kimmons, William Bassett, Edward Butler, James McCann, Edward Adams, Francis Raymond, Jacob Van Winkle, John S. Craft, Henry Hempsted, John Slowey, James Guest, Samuel Barnes, Joseph Bellows, John Lake, John Farnwell, Lewis Sinn.

Captain, John Mackey ; first assistant, John Keegan ; second assistant, John H. Warren ; patrolmen, Stephen Hallich, Thomas Foley, James Craft, Thomas Kipp, Michael Noll, John Plunkett, John Walsh, George Stuyvesant, Philip Butler, William Mawley, Henry Wetzel, Theodore Arnold, David Clute, David Adams, John Reed, Andrew Glore, Joseph Contie, Geo. Daniels, George Reed, Peter Schields, Joseph Ruchman, Charles Holder, Thomas Boerum, Thomas Gray, Peter Rose, William Minard, Henry Schoble, William H. Pook, William Reamon, Anderson Woods, George Heckadorn, Joseph Hunter.

PATROL No. 2.—Captain, John P. Lacour ; assistant, George Shannon ; patrolmen, Henry Allaman, George Van Benschoten, Dennis McCarthy, George Wright, Aaron Watson, Joseph W. Sandford, William Symes, James E. Colgrove, John Hannon, James McKenzie, Gardiner Van Brunt, George Frazier, John Lee, W. H. Johne, Edgar Smith, Edgar E. Laing.

Captain, John Crossin ; assistant, Joseph Gerrodett ; patrolmen, John Rafferty, Bernard Clements, Charles Chamberlain, Francis Jackson, Elias Van Benschoten, John Neigengost, William Hubert, Martin Kraus, T. B. Book, M. Robertson, John Brower, Thomas Mitchell, Thomas Rettenfield, William Henderson, F. Brimmer.

Although the commissioners showed no favors to, and disciplined all, rebellious companies and members, both of the Volunteer and Paid Departments, whenever an opportunity occurred to oblige or advantage the retiring force, it was done. In this way the furniture and necessary outfits of many Volunteer companies were purchased for the Paid force, which took possession of their quarters, and Volunteer companies were allowed to take away as relics portions of the apparatus. A pleasant feature of the period between the decision of the Court of Appeals on the constitutionality of the Metropolitan Act and the putting of the Paid force into active service, was the readiness which men like John J. Gorman, James Hayes, and many others, who fought the Paid system to the end, gave the benefit of their experience, aid and advice, to the New regime. As an illustration of this, take the meeting of engineers and foremen at Fireman's Hall on the first of July, 1865, when Martin J. Keese said in substance that he was going to do his duty as long as the new commissioners desired. He did not care if it was Thomas C. Acton's house that was on fire ; he would be one of the first to go and put it out, and when certain organs shortly after announced a terrible riot in the Fifth District between certain companies, Hugh Bonner, W. F. Squires and W. H. Pierpoint lost no time in denouncing the statement as a falsehood gotten up to injure the Volunteers. The last meeting of the representatives was held in Firemen's Hall July 24, 1865, and they were addressed by Treasurer John S. Giles.

The appointment of employees on the clerical staff and in the fire telegraph bureau proceeded slowly. Charles L. Chapin was appointed superintendent of telegraph August 4, 1865, vice Charles Robinson, contractor ; and John W. Smith, lineman, and S. S. Parker, battery boy, were appointed a few days later. Patrick Dailey, Isaac G. Seixas and Abraham D. Carlock were the first operators. The Paid force was then below Eighty-seventh Street, and at first there were only sixty-three signal stations established, and district alarms were sent out above Fourteenth Street. There were no shut boxes, and their establishment was retarded by patent right claims. At one of the first meetings of the Metropolitan Fire Commissioners a plan to stop the ringing of the alarm bells was discussed, but the nuisance was not abated until many years later. August 30, the board received notice from Governor Fenton of the resignation of James W. Booth, and next day Mr. Joshua G. Abbe was appointed commissioner by Messrs. Pinckney, Engs and Brown.

Four days after Mr. Abbe's appointment, a meeting of the board which had been secret was opened to the press and public September 8 ; Alexander V. Davidson was retired as chief clerk to the chief engineer, and Garrett B. Tunison was appointed in his stead.

The committees as then appointed were : Appointments and Discipline— Commissioner Abbe. Buildings and Supplies—Commissioner Brown. Apparatus and Hose—Commissioner Engs. Finance and Telegraph—Commissioner Pinckney. Mr. Abbe was able and conscientious, and did his duty as a commissioner as well as circumstances permitted, but the composition of the

JOSHUA GROSVENOR ABBE.

board was such that the tie votes often thwarted measures of reform, discipline, and improvement, and the result was a lack of efficiency, the rank and file not being slow to take sides indicated by the votes of the commissioners. In spite of this and an increase in the number of fires and losses—which was basely charged to the Volunteers—the Paid Department compared favorably with the Old system. The records of the mustering out of the Volunteers show the number returned as active firemen by the clerk of the Common Council as three thousand eight hundred and ten, but the records of the fire commissioners indicate a less number. These records are known as being far from complete. Several companies did not send in returns, and many firemen did not claim their discharge, while the resolution that no discharge should be granted unless the firemen had done fifty per cent. of duty, has since been upset by a decision of the courts. About one hundred and sixty firemen appointed by the Old commissioners in April, May, and June were not recognized by the Metropolitan commissioners. Such Volunteers as did the duty prescribed were recognized on the sixth of November, 1865, in the following resolution offered by Commissioner Engs :

Resolved, That the Board hereby acknowledges the public services of those members of the Volunteer Fire Department who continued until relieved by resolution, to perform their duty as firemen at the sacrifice of long cherished attachments, thereby exhibiting a striking example of respect for the dignity of Constitutional Law.

Resolved, That we tender them individually and officially our sincere thanks for the services thus rendered, and the assurance of our continued regard.

The first step towards creating a fund for the relief of firemen and their families was taken on the twenty-seventh of November, 1865, when Commissioner Engs offered the following:

Resolved, that the Committee on Appointments and Discipline be requested to present to this Board at its next regular meeting a plan for establishing a fund for the care and relief of those members of the Metropolitan Fire Department force who may be injured or become sick in the performance of their duties, and for the families of those who may die in consequence.

This was legalized by Chapter 756 of the Laws of 1866, creating the Metropolitan Fire Department Relief Fund. Its revenue was derived from all fines and penalties collected by the attorney, fees for permits, etc., all fines of members of the force, donations, and an assessment not to exceed twenty dollars per annum on all persons entitled to its benefits. Section 3 provided that:

"Said fund, as·soon as the same shall amount to the sum of ten thousand dollars, shall be liable for the payment of the recipients of relief severally entitled thereto, the sums as follows: To each person permanently disabled while in actual performance of any duty assigned him by said department, the sum of twenty dollars per month for the term of his natural life; to each person who shall become superannuated after a service of ten years in the employment of said department, annually thereafter an annuity of two hundred and fifty dollars, payable quarter-yearly, during the term of his natural life; to the family or relatives of any deceased person who shall be killed while actually engaged in the performance of any duty assigned by said department, or who shall die from any injuries received resulting from the performance of said duties, the sum of two thousand dollars, to be paid in the order following: first to his widow, if any him surviving; second, to his children under fifteen years, if any him surviving, equally, share and share alike; third, to a father living with and dependent on his support for a living; fourth, to a mother living with and dependent on his support for a living.

The first trustees were C. C. Pinckney, president, and P. W. Engs, treasurer, with Mayor John T. Hoffman and James M. McLean, president of the Board of Fire Underwriters, *ex officio* trustees.

The first victims of fire service under the Metropolitan commissioners were Robert Wintringham, of Engine Company No. 1, and George Bell, of Engine Company No. 8. Both died in 1865, the former being run over, and the latter was brought to his grave by exposure.

On the first of November, 1865, the commissioners recognized in complimentary resolutions the services of Assistant Engineers George H. E. Lynch, Michael Halloran, and Abraham Horn; and Halloran, Horn, and John Hart were appointed district engineers in Harlem, Yorkville, Manhattanville, Bloomingdale, and Carmansville. On the same date outrages by the followers of the Volunteers had become so frequent that a reward of five hundred dollars was offered by the commissioners for the detection and conviction of any person cutting hose and disabling or impeding engines and firemen.

With the advent of 1866 the commissioners prepared to combat the difficulties which beset them in spite of attacks by the press and a public sentiment that the Metropolitan Department had fallen short of what was expected of it. Early in January Superintendent Chapin had established forty-one special signal stations and one hundred and eighteen ordinary signal stations which were designated, as fires occurred, on the eleven alarm bells. At the end of the year there were one hundred and eighty-seven signal stations. The city above One Hundred and Sixth Street was divided into eight fire districts, viz.:

District No. 1, Ward's Island; District No. 2, Randall's Island; District No. 3, One Hundred and Sixth to One Hundred and Sixteenth Street and Sixth Avenue to the East River; District No. 4, One Hundred and Sixth to One Hundred and Sixteenth Street and Sixth Avenue to the North River; District No. 5, One Hundred and Sixteenth to One Hundred and Twenty-fifth Street and Sixth Avenue to the East River; District No. 6, One Hundred and Sixteenth to One Hundred and Twenty-fifth Street and Sixth Avenue to the North River; District No. 7, north of One Hundred and Twenty-fifth Street and Sixth Avenue to the Harlem River; District No. 8, north of One Hundred and Twenty-fifth Street and Sixth Avenue and from Harlem River to the North River.

The carrying of speaking trumpets, except on parades, was abolished. The care of the one hundred and twenty-four horses in the various quarters necessitated the employment of a superintendent, and William Burns was chosen on the seventeenth of January, 1866. The first hitching-up drill system was ordered at the same time by a resolution offered by Commissioner Abbe.

The public were not backward in recognizing the efficiency of the New Department when its members did good duty, and testimony to this effect was from time to time sent to the commissioners. There was no lack of material wherewith to make firemen; in fact, the applications for appointment accumulated to such an extent that in April a resolution was adopted at the instance of Commissioner Abbe which gave exempt firemen preference over all other applicants, of whom two thousand four hundred had sent in their names. The Legislature at this time slightly increased the salaries of the force. Much anxiety and annoyance were caused by fires which were believed to be incendiary, and that at the Academy of Music, May 21, 1866, led the commissioners to offer a reward for the discovery of the person who set it on fire, and a standing reward of a like sum for six months for any conviction of an incendiary. In June the commissioners required every engine to be supplied with apparatus to keep the water at boiling point, or as near it as possible. Under an act relating to the storage of combustibles, Charles T. Polhemus was appointed attorney to the board at a salary of one thousand two hundred dollars per annum, June 15, 1866.

The cost of the department for 1866 was nine hundred and thirty-six thousand dollars (December 1, 1865, to December 1, 1866), and one hundred and ninety-eight alarms of fire—forty-six of which were for serious outbreaks—were responded to. There were forty-five arrests for incendiarism during the year, and fourteen convictions for arson. Sixteen new first and second-class Amoskeag engines replaced apparatus manned by volunteers. Private Thomas Irwin and Dominick Scott, of Engine Company No. 4, and foreman D. B. Waters and Private P. H. Welsh, of Engine Company No. 5, were killed in the discharge of duty, and their families received each one thousand dollars on policies donated to the members of the force by the New York Accidental Insurance Company.

In their statutory reports to Governor Fenton, the commissioners and chief engineer took occasion to make some laudatory and strong comments. The latter said:

"It cannot be denied that the first attempts to establish this department as an active, reliable force, met with antagonism, not more from the avowed hatred of those who opposed and stood aloof from belonging to it, than from the covert, unsuspected malignity of some who joined its ranks, and, for a while, pretending to be on the side of right, were really plotting its destruction. That day has, however, gone by, and with pleasure do I look upon the body of men now under my command; from time to time there may indeed be causes for the exercise of strict discipline, but they generally will be found to arise more from error of judgment than of heart."

The commissioners' comments were :

"Noise and confusion in our streets on the occasions of alarms of fire have ceased; the sick and dying are no longer disturbed by the yelling of 'runners,' the machinery is drawn quietly to the scene of duty, the inhabitants are left to enjoy their needed rest, and vehicles may pass on unmolested.

"Racing and fighting between companies is unknown, and the city police are relieved from

ACADEMY OF MUSIC FIRE, 1866.

the disagreeable duties which they were formerly called upon to perform by arrests; disputes between companies no more hinder operations at a fire.

"Thieves cannot fully get within the police lines; only the few citizens who have the badge of privilege are permitted to enter. 'Runners' no longer meddle with the duties of our firemen. The loss by theft so commonly added to claims upon insurance companies are rarely alluded to, consequently the saving of property counts by thousands. Beyond these advantages resulting from our present system of fire duty, comes to us the inestimable blessings resulting from the breaking up of the 'runners' organization, and the consequent release of our youth from one of the ways that lead to ruin. We may estimate the loss of wealth, but who can measure the loss of character which befalls the youth so misled, the loss of his services in the walks of life, and an end that puts him beyond the pale of hope. That we have been instrumental in rescuing such from the jaws of destruction, it is to us a gratifying reflection."

Only a few days after this was written the commissioners passed resolutions continuing the reward of one thousand dollars for the conviction of every incendiary, asking the mayor to call the attention of the municipal authorities to the matter, and requesting the co-operation of the Board of Fire Under-writers. The last request led to the appointment of a committee consisting of Messrs. Rankin, Hope and Norwood, by the underwriters, to confer with the fire commissioners. In 1866 the first Paid fire-boat, the '*John Fuller*,' was hired. Blackwell's Island was protected by hand apparatus.

The Academy of Music was destroyed by fire on Monday, May 21, 1866. This fire broke out shortly before midnight; the curtain had scarcely fallen upon the last act of " La Juive "; the audience had just departed, and the artistes had only left their dressing-rooms, when the alarm was given that the Academy of Music was on fire. The gas was not yet extinguished in a portion of the building, and the doors on Fourteenth Street were still open. The first indications were observed in light wreaths of smoke issuing from the upper windows immediately under the roof. The firemen soon arrived and carried their hose into the building, and, as soon as water could be supplied, they poured a stream on the portions of the house where the fire was visible. When the fire first broke out, it was supposed that it could be extinguished by the hydrant streams within the building. Three small lines were promptly attached, but did not reach the flames. On the arrival of Hook and Ladder Company No. 3, lying in East Nineteenth Street and running a tender, they stretched it from a hydrant under direction of Engineer Sullivan, who was in the immediate neighborhood at the time of the occurrence, but the force being insufficient they could accomplish but little. Soon after, Engine Company No. 3 came on the ground, and got a line in on the rear—while Engine Companies 13 and 14 were on duty at the front or main entrance; 13's pipe was stretched nearly to the middle of the parquet, and was manned by John F. Denin and Hugh Kitson, when the gas exploded. Denin was so seriously injured that he had to be conveyed to the New York Hospital for treatment. He was seriously burned, but not fatally so, and finally recovered. Engine No 16, which stood at the corner of Fourteenth Street and Third Avenue, was surrounded by flames, and the members were compelled to abandon it for a time. It was finally drawn away badly injured. Engine Company No. 36, of Harlem, of which Robert C. Brown was foreman, came all the way down to the fire, and worked two hours and a half to save Worcester's piano factory from destruction.

The progress of the fire was checked at daybreak, and immediately after-wards the firemen began the search for their missing brethren. About half-past ten the body of Peter H. Walsh, private of Engine Company No. 5, was discovered below the central portion of the stage, the legs and arms being completely burned off. The remains of David B. Waters, foreman of Engine Company No. 5, were not recovered until about half-past two in the afternoon. They were found lying over one of the heaters near the stage entrance. They were badly burned like his companions. Waters had been a member of 23 Engine in the Old Department. Waters and Walsh had started in the build-ing to find their pipe and relieve the men at it, when they unfortunately missed their way and were lost in the smoke and flames. The funerals of the unfortun-ate men were largely attended, the officers and members of the department acting as a body guard and as pall bearers.

CHAPTER XLIX.

THE NEW DEPARTMENT SEVERELY CRITICISED.

Resignation of Commissioner Brown.—Appointment of General Shaler, M. B. Wilson, T. B. Myers and James Galway.—The Board Exclusively Republican.—A Manifesto of Much Interest.—Bureau of Combustibles.—A Reward for the Conviction of Incendiaries.—A Board to Pass on the Competency of Officers.

IN the year 1867 it was seen that something was amiss with the New Department. In spite of honest endeavors to do better than the Volunteers, the Metropolitans were not fortunate at great fires, and insurance rates became higher. Citizens and the press grumbled, and at the assembling of the Legislature it was evident that action would be taken by it. A plea of scarcity of hydrants was ridiculed by some who said that the Volunteers did better with fewer, and the insinuation that the ousted Volunteers were responsible for some of the fires was denounced as infamous. Some of the grumbling was odd. Persons wrote to the papers to complain that the horses attached to the apparatus were driven too fast, and Mr. Henry Bergh addressed a communication to the commissioners on the subject, in which he denounced such driving as reckless, and protested against it. The commissioners tried to stem the tide of public opinion by ordering an investigation of the condition of many of the buildings and warehouses of the city for evidences of their unsafe and improper condition. Steps were taken to organize the suburban companies as paid companies, and the complaint that the discipline of the force was bad was met by a resolution to make trials of delinquents public in order to "contribute largely toward disciplining" them.

But a disastrous fire in Broadway, known as the Chittenden fire, provoked a fresh outbreak of public comment. It was charged that the Metropolitans had there proved their inability to cope with a disaster, and an investigation was ordered by the commissioners, which ended in Messrs. Pinckney, Brown and Engs exonerating the Department, on the twenty-fifth of March. Mr. Abbe dissented. Meanwhile, on the twenty-first of February, 1867, the Assembly insurance committee met at the Metropolitan Hotel "to take into consideration the large loss of property by fire, and inquire into the means of extinguishment." The members were: Messrs. Younglove, Penfield, Frear, Lefevre and Blauvelt. Mr. George W. Savage, of a committee appointed by the National Board of Fire Underwriters, then in session, first testified. He ascribed the losses, which were unusually heavy, to incendiarism, slowness of firemen to get to work, failure to enforce laws, want of proper inspection of buildings, and accumulation of cumbustible matter in buildings. He charged that Chief Kingsland was incompetent, and was in favor of a department organized with military precision, with a man of West Point training for engineer. Other witnesses were equally condemnatory. The committee made a report which resulted in several bills being passed with a view of ousting the commissioners. The newspapers which had lauded the new Commission turned against it, and one which had spoken very badly of the Volunteers had severe things to say of their successors.

Commissioner Brown resigned on the thirtieth of March, 1867, because of the serious illness of his wife, who died shortly after. His act was the subject of unfeeling comment, but Governor Fenton subsequently appointed him Port Warden to emphasize his contradiction of the malicious reports. On the twelfth of April the Assembly passed Chapter 408 of the Laws of 1867, and the Senate passed it five days later. It required the Governor to nominate a fifth fire commissioner within a few days of the act becoming a law, said commissioner to hold office for ten years, and the successors of the present commissioners to hold office for ten years. Commissioner Pinck-

ALEXANDER SHALER.

ney's term had about expired, and Messrs. Engs and Abbe sent in their resignations. On the eighteenth of April Governor Fenton nominated, and the Senate confirmed, Monmouth B. Wilson, captain of the Thirty-first Precinct, as the fifth commissioner, General Alexander Shaler in place of Mr. Pinckney, Colonel Theodorus Bailey Myers in place of Mr. Engs, James Galway in place of Mr. Brown (who would have been succeeded by Colonel Emmons Clark had he chosen to accept the position), and Mr. Abbe, whose resignation was virtually not accepted.

In 1867, two years after the substitution of the Paid Department system for the Volunteer, General Shaler was put at the head of the Fire Department. For three years

he remained as president, and until 1873 as a commissioner. The results of the reforms and improvements made under that management were practically manifested by the steady reduction of the losses by fire, from $6,428,000 in 1866 to $2,120,212 in 1870. It was during these three years— 1867–'70—that the Department was converted into a well-organized, disciplined, and successful institution, and it is conceded that General Shaler was the controling master spirit of the commission, and that to him was due the establishment of orderly and systematic methods, as well as the thorough disciplining of the force. During this period the Fire Commissioners had unlimited power over their subordinates, and could dismiss or reduce in grade at will, without the semblance of a trial. This power was, however, not arbitrarily exercised. During this period boards of officers were organized in the department for the examination of candidates for promotion, and promotions were made for merit only. Candidates for appointment to the corps of firemen were also required to pass a rigid physical examination and to possess the rudiments, at least, of a common school education. These improvements, also suggested by General Shaler, not only stood the test of time, but the principles of good administration underlying the systems thus voluntarily introduced in an important branch of the public service, have since been made the basis of laws for the reform of the entire civil service, national, state and municipal.

General Shaler and his colleagues in the Board of Fire Commissioners during that period also had practically unlimited power in the matter of fixing the amount of the annual appropriations for the department, the Board of Estimate and Apportionment having then only nominally the authority to determine the amount of the appropriation for the Fire Department. This great power, it is easy to see, could have been much abused by unscrupulous officials. But the expenditures for this period show that no less attention was paid to economy than to the efficiency of the department. During the period of his presidency, General Shaler organized and taught classes composed of the officers and engineers in their respective duties. His next effort was to rid the department of the officers who unfortunately could or would not learn. The power of summary dismissal vested in the commissioners was even then not exercised, but all who were deficient were given the further opportunity of passing a board of examination composed of their own officers, which finally decided upon the question of their fitness to remain. To General Shaler is also due the inauguration in 1867 of the admirable property accountability system in the Fire Department so frequently commended then and since in the public press and by public officials.

Until May, 1873, General Shaler remained as one of the commissioners of the Fire Department, continuing, though

THEODORUS BAILEY MYERS.

no longer president, to give all his energies to the performance of his duties.

THEODORUS BAILEY MYERS, when the Metropolitan Fire Department was created by the Legislature, was appointed by the governor as a member of the Board of Commissioners. Not soliciting the position, and having no claims as an active politician, this was probably due to his successful administration of the affairs of the Sixth Avenue Railway, of which he had been first executive officer, and subsequently president, and aided to restore it to its present prosperity. On the twenty-first of April, 1861, he had left it, on a leave of absence, in the 'Baltic,' with the Twelfth Regiment, one of the first that started for the capitol, accepting, without compensation, the temporary position of quartermaster, and in charge of the supplies which had been intended to be thrown into Fort Sumter. After visiting Fortress Monroe, the day after the burning of Norfolk—the Potomac being closed—they proceeded to Annapolis. Finding General Butler, already arrived, in command, on reporting to him and turning over the needed stores, he was, although personally unknown to the general, selected as an *aide de camp,* and assigned to the duty of quartermaster. He visited New York soon after, and raised, under a department order, two hundred and fifty men, without any expense to the government beyond their rations, the use of the Park barracks, and their transportation. With these he proceeded to Baltimore with Colonel Kilpatrick, with the same number of volunteers for his mounted rifles.

When General Wool relieved General Butler, Mr. Myers was placed on his staff—a selection probably due to the circumstance that the general and his father, who had been crippled at Chrystler's Fields, in the Canada campaign, had been captains together in the Thirteenth Regular Infantry in the war of 1812. After much detail duty and some service in reconnoisances, but no regular engagement, he was, in the fall, imperatively recalled to his railroad by a sudden difficulty, which terminated his military service, with less regret because the country had become fully aroused and the material to supply official posts was abundant.

When he became Fire Commissioner, his military experience was found to be invaluable, and he had an able co-laborer in General Shaler. Each company was placed on a basis of efficiency equal to that of a regular section of field artillery. Each man had his place and duty, which he was expected to perform. Rapidity in getting under way on an alarm, and progress to the points of service, system in conveying signals, and all the details for concerted action, first from the nearest post, the putting of an immediate cordon around the burning building to protect property from depredation and exclude unauthorized access; all these were rapidly formulated or improved and enforced. The bill for the storage of combustible materials suggested by the underwriters was one of the measures to which he gave particular attention. He prepared and furthered its passage at Albany. The act giving a half portion of the tax on foreign insurance companies, then held by the old organization, to the department, was also a subject for his attention. He afterwards represented the board as its volunteer counsel, for which his profession fitted him, often saving expense.

The board authorized a lyceum, and devoted to its use the large upper hall, in which he collected, by their authority as commissioner in charge, a collection of several thousand volumes, issued to the members as a circulating library, to occupy leisure time at their quarters. In this he also collected examples of old apparatus, emblems, trophies, and curious documents connected with the early history of New York. The librarian was the clerk allowed to him, the first being John R. Thompson, once editor of the *Southern Literary Messenger,* a poet of ability and a gentleman of admirable modesty, who, after serving as a secretary of the Confederate Legation in London and Paris, returned to New York.

Commissioner Myers continued for a time to act as counsel to the Board after his duties had terminated; subsequently he declined a reappointment by Mayor Havemeyer, and has since devoted himself to study and literary pursuits.

This made a republican Board of able, pushing men, fully aware that to succeed they must, from the start, do away with the causes that made the first commission less efficient and popular than it was expected to be. May 1 they met, and after electing General Shaler president and Mr. Abbe treasurer, provided for the reorganization of the committees, and the revision of the rules and regulations of the force, and the rules of the Board. May 8 the committees were formed as follows: Appointments, Discipline, Supplies, Apparatus, Finance, Telegraph, Buildings and Hose. The clerical force was placed under the direction of the secretary; appointments and promotions were to be under civil service regulations, and foremen, assistant foremen and engineers were to be promoted from the ranks and on grounds of meritorious conduct and qualifications. The system of appointments was first attacked, and a new and better form of application was adopted.

Commissioner Wilson's first act was to condemn the inadequate protection given Blackwell's Island; to suggest better protection for its six thousand inhabitants; to designate it by a fire signal, and to arrange for transportation of fire apparatus to it.

On the first of June the Commissioners "declared their intentions" in the following circular to the force. Its ringing tenor drew a line between the present and the past, and no good member of the department misconstrued it:

OFFICE BOARD OF COMMISSIONERS METROPOLITAN FIRE DEPART-MENT, FIREMEN'S HALL,

NEW YORK, June 1, 1867.

To the Officers, Members and Employees of the Metropolitan Fire Department:

It has already been the duty of the Board of Commissioners (sitting as the Committee on Appointments), to pass upon several cases of violation of the rules. These complaints

JAMES GALWAY.

have been disposed of as leniently as possible, in consideration of the fact that the discipline of the Department had been heretofore less vigorously enforced than it will be in future, and that an impression may have resulted that the rules were prepared without an intention to enforce them. This will not, in future, be the case. Members of this Department possess privileges, and receive a compensation from the authorities, far superior to those engaged by any other branch of the public service. * * *

For the act of every member the Commissioners are responsible to the public, and it is their duty, when its rules are disregarded, to relieve themselves by promptly bringing the offender to justice. Neglect to do this, from sympathy or any other consideration, would be criminal in them. There can be no middle condition in any organization like this, whether civil or military. * * *

There is no lack of material, where a man fails in his duty, to supply his position. Over twenty-three hundred applications already on file, and a daily importunity at Headquarters for appointments, strongly urged by parties whom the Commissioners would be glad to oblige, proves that those who are in the enjoyment of the privilege of membership should do their utmost, by a zealous performance of their duty, to justify the Commissioners, to whom most of them are personally unknown, in adhering to a rule to make no removals except for incompetency or fault. Some of the friends of the old system are hostile to the new organization, have magnified its defects and predicted its failure. This is simply impossible if we do our duty to the public and to each other.

In furtherance of these views, and in anticipation of the publication of all the rules, now in the hands of a committee, the Commissioners consider it proper to call the attention of the officers and employees of this Department to a few general Regulations, which they will expect to see enforced :

1st. That the Assistant Engineers shall be strict and energetic in the performance of the duties laid down for them. That they shall be untiring in their vigilance, as well in the extinguishment of fires as in improving the efficiency and discipline of their several divisions. In case they find any fireman, or other officer or member of the Department, incompetent or unwilling to perform his duties, they shall, without hesitation or favor, see that charges are preferred.

2d. That the foreman or other officer in command of a company shall remember that he occupies a position of great trust, and that upon him the men of his company will naturally look as a model. He should bear in mind that, as an officer, he is not to allow his personal feelings to interfere with the discharge of his duty. All violations of the rules, or factious opposition to their enforcement, must be reported at once. Blank charges for this purpose will be furnished. The omission to make a complaint will be considered as an offense on the part of the officer. While it is desired that the best feeling should exist between officers and men in this Department, it is to be remembered that, to command the respect and obedience of others, self-respect is essential. Too much familiarity between officers and men is not compatible with discipline, nor with the duties that office imposes. When a man occupies a position of rank he acts for the Department, and not for himself. * * * No absence will be allowed, even on leave or lay off, unless reported to the officer in command, and his permission granted.

3d. The quarters of the different companies were left in bad condition by their former occupants, by the removal of their private property, the suspension of repairs, and by changes to accommodate horses. The more pressing emergency to provide for the active usefulness of the Department has caused some delay in repairs, which will be attended with large expense. The Department will place them in condition as rapidly as possible. Every man is naturally attached to his home. To many members of this Department, who are unmarried, their quarters are their only homes, and there is no reason why the same interest in their embellishment and neatness should not be taken by all the members, so far as in their power, as in the case of their own houses. A small company fund, to be voluntarily contributed, would aid much, added to such details as the Department is confined to. The neatness and taste displayed by Hook and Ladder Company No. 5 entitles them to be mentioned in orders, as well as cited as an illustration of what is meant by this suggestion. It is not doubted that a similar spirit will soon be developed by other companies. It has been a matter of surprise to the Commissioners that men should congregate and sit about their apparatus or horses, when they can, in most cases, easily arrange a comfortable sitting-room up-stairs, away from the dampness and fumes of the stable. Lounging about the doors of the house, or congregating on the walk, is constantly complained of by the neighbors and passers-by, and has a very bad appearance. The front doors should be kept open in fine weather, when the company is not absent, as much as practicable, to admit light and air, and in order to allow the public to look in and see the neatness and order prevailing. At least one man should always be on duty on the first floor to guard against trespass or depredation. No visitor not connected with the Department, or having some special business with it, can be allowed to remain for any length of time, beyond an ordinary opportunity to gratify his curiosity, in any of the houses, without a report to the officer in charge, and his consent obtained. Engine houses are places for business, and not for lounging.

4th. The waste of gas, fuel, feed and fodder, is to be avoided. It is to be borne in mind that the expenses of this Department fall upon the people, and the commissioners are responsible for their application. The waste of gas has become a serious evil. The bill presented each month shows at a glance the waste and economy of each company. Some of the companies who are most extravagant have received notices, which will be followed by a system of personal liability for the waste, if continued. No man is expected to use the property of the Department more economically than he would his own.   *   *   *

5th. The officers and men should be neat and cleanly in their appearance. When on duty at a fire it is not expected that this rule will be enforced, for their first business is to extinguish the fire, without regard to clothing, or even to person, if the emergency require; but after the fire is over, there are no damages which their equipments can suffer, which the use of benzine or French soap on their clothing, of whiting on their buttons and plates, and of blacking on their boots, will not restore. There is an abundance of time for this in the large amount of leisure on their hands. Each company should likewise be *uniformly* clothed on each day (except in case of an alarm, when all considerations of dress, except the fire-cap and overcoat, are to be disregarded); and it is not the meaning of uniform that one man in the same company should be in his shirt, another in his sack, and a third in his overcoat, or one in slippers, another in shoes, another with his boots over his trousers, and yet another with his trousers over his boots. Work to be done about the quarters will call for working dress; when the work is over the regulation dress will be resumed. It is unbecoming the credit of the Department that a few slovenly men should throw it in disrepute, when the means are afforded by their now liberal pay for every member to appear at all times decently and well clad. The accumulation of old and worn citizen's clothing is to be avoided, one serviceable citizen's suit being all that is required to have. It is suggested to the various companies that they purchase new uniforms and caps at the same time of the same cloth, and that if they are furnished by the same person no doubt a saving will be made. This, with the system required as to wearing them, will prevent the variety of color and condition of clothing which is otherwise inevitable. The closets afford ample room for the disposal of clothes not in use, other than the overalls drawn over the fire-boots for instant use. The bathing tubs should be freely used, not only as a sanitary measure, but because cleanliness is essential to public respect. The beds of the companies are to be kept cleanly, and in such condition as to be at all times presentable to visitors without reflecting on their owners or the officers. Want of cleanliness in this will be a subject for charges. It is the intention of the Board to supply each bed with a pillow-case and spread, to be used in the daytime and removed at night, and placed in the closet of its owner, in order

GEN. ALEX. SHALER'S BADGE.
[As Fire Commissioner.]

to insure uniformity and neatness. In future, as in other branches of the public service, each man will provide his bed-clothes.

6th. When a superior officer, or a visitor accompanied by a superior officer, visits their quarters, it will be apparent that both politeness and discipline require that the officers and men should rise and salute them, showing that degree of discipline and respect for the position which they in turn will require should they attain, as they may if deserving, such promotion as is open to every man in this Department.

7th. The Commissioners have noticed with pleasure the general good condition of the apparatus and of the horses of the Department, and the pride taken by the men in these important elements of usefulness. They desire to encourage this, and also the spirit of honorable emulation. The condition of their brasses, and the sleekness of their horses' coats, strike at once a practiced eye, and give evidence of the good working condition of both. On everything connected with keeping these on an efficient footing, and their prompt use when required in the protection of property and life, too much attention cannot be bestowed. They are like tools of the skillful workman; and the citizens judge from what they see of the condition of the officers and men, and of the cleanliness and order of their apparatus, as to the efficiency of the Department. The reputation of the Department depends on its efficiency, and its perpetuation on its reputation. In both every member has a personal interest.

8th. At a fire each officer and fireman is to remember that his first duty is to extinguish the fire and protect property and life from the flames, and only second to that to prevent the *slightest* pillage or depredation.   *   *   *

9th. Some critical member of the Department who seeks to draw his pay without performing his duty, and takes no pride in the service or the buttons he wears, may say to his comrades, in reading the suggestions contained herein, that they dwell on trifles unworthy the attention of the Commissioners or the observance of the men. To such the commissioners would say that the history of the world shows that everywhere, in every service and in every business, an aggregate of trifles is the basis of discipline ; and discipline the guarantee of success. *   *   *

This order will be read to each company in the Department, and placed on file for reference.   By order of the Board,

ALEXANDER SHALER, *President.*

CHARLES E. GILDERSLEVE, *Secretary.*

Chief Kingsland supplemented this by an order calling the attention of the district engineers to their responsibility for the general condition, in all respects, of the companies under their charge, insisting on proper deportment and order, and requiring cognizance and reports of violation of rules.

The aim and intent of this circular was readily understood by all to whom it was addressed. It drew a line between the past and the present, and its date was that of the beginning of the Paid Fire Department on a business basis. The commission was well received by the public and the press. One reform rapidly succeeded another, and the reorganization of the department was proceeded with briskly and systematically. One of the first measures of importance was the division of the companies among the engineers, as follows, on the tenth of May :

Eli Bates,	Engine Co.'s Nos.	3, 14, 18, 33.	H. & L. Co.'s Nos.		12.
G. J. Orr,	" "	1, 7, 31.	" "		1.
Thomas Sullivan,	" "	5, 35, 28.	" "		3.
M. Shannessy,	" "	2, 19, 23, 34.	" "		4.
John Conley,	" "	4, 6, 10, 29, 32.	" "		10.
B. Sheridan,	" "	9, 12, 15.	" "		6.
W. W. Rhodes,	" "	16, 21, 26.	" "		7.
W. Banham, Jr.,	" "	8, 22.	" "		2.
R. V. Mackey,	" "	11, 17, 20.	" "		9, 11.
W. Brandon,	" "	13, 24, 27, 30.	" "		5, 8.

A system of preferment of charges against delinquent members was adopted, and that of to-day is almost the same, and the results of trials were transmitted to the force with instructive and pertinent comments. The tendency to carelessness and extravagance in the receipt and disposition of supplies was checked by the appointment of Carl Jussen, the present secretary of the board, as storekeeper or property clerk. The Volunteers who desired to be honorably discharged had been hurt by an illiberal construction of the law of March 30, 1865, and the following resolution, passed June 5, 1867, on motion of General Shaler, pleased them :

Resolved, That all members of the former Volunteer Department who have faithfully performed their duty, as appears from the records of the company to which they were attached up to the date of being relieved, or who were from good or sufficient reasons prevented from so doing, shall be entitled to receive an honorable discharge from the department.

Civil service reform was recognized on June 19, 1867, in the following, offered by Commissioner Wilson :

Resolved, That the district engineers be, and are hereby, directed to report to the chief engineer the names of privates in their department who have performed meritorious acts since its organization, for the purpose of selecting from the ranks suitable persons to fill vacancies for offices now existing in the different companies.

Commissioner Myers offered the following as a substitute :

Resolved, That the district engineers be directed to report to the chief engineer, for competitive examination, the names of two men from each company possessing, in their opinion, the best qualifications for promotion as assistant foremen. That in making such selection consideration to be given to meritorious conduct in the performance of duty and such characteristics as will command the respect of their subordinates, and without favoritism or personal preference, but solely with a view to the benefit of the department.

The Bureau of Combustibles was organized June 22, 1867, under Chapter 873 of the Laws of 1866, with Commissioner Wilson at its head. Its personnel were : John H. Wilson, clerk, at one thousand five hundred dollars a year; and the following inspectors at five hundred dollars per annum, John A.

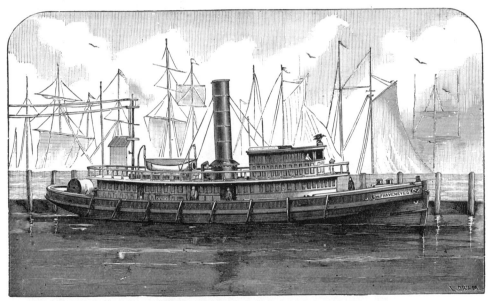

FIRE-BOAT WILLIAM F. HAVEMEYER.

Cregier, Surveyor Mercantile Fire Insurance Company; A. P. Moore, Surveyor Manhattan Fire Insurance Company; Theodore Keeler, Surveyor of the Lorillard Fire Insurance Company; and John H. Forman, Surveyor of the International Fire Insurance Company. Operations against persons who illegally stored dangerously inflammable articles and explosives were begun immediately. A step toward grading the force was made in the middle of July, when Commissioners Myers and Shaler, in reporting to their colleagues on the estimates for 1868, the increase in expenditures and the necessity of economy, presented the following resolution :

Resolved, That the appointment of firemen hereafter made shall be of acting firemen, at a rate of compensation not exceeding seven hundred dollars per annum, such active firemen to be in the line of promotion, and to have precedence, as candidates for appointments as firemen, whenever the means at the control of the commissioners justify the further increase of that grade, provided that the number of acting firemen shall not at any time exceed six in any company.

Then plans were discussed for the placing in commission of a boat to be used for fires on the river front, and the rules for ringing the alarm bells were amended so that the post-office bell rang for all fires south of Seventy-ninth Street, and the other bells rang five rounds for the first alarm, and seven rounds for a second alarm for signals in the various districts. Rewards were offered for the arrest and conviction of incendiaries, and the public were invited to note suspicious circumstances at fires and communicate information. Violations of law, especially in regard to the proper protection of openings in roofs, having resulted in the death of firemen, and fires having rapidly become uncontrollable because of hatchways being left open, the attorney was directed to frame amendments to existing laws. Stringent regulations for the storage of fireworks were adopted.

On the eighteenth of September a resolution was adopted to improve the intelligence and moral tone of the department by establishing libraries in the several quarters of companies. The scheme resulted, three months later, in the formation of the Firemen's Lyceum at Fire Headquarters under Commissioner Myers. Charles E. Gildersleve was treasurer, and Charles De F. Burns, now secretary of the Board of Park Commissioners, librarian. The lyceum is now scattered among the battalion headquarters and in several company quarters. The first donations were : American Fire Insurance Company, $100 ; R. J. Livingston, $50 ; Spott & Hawk, $25 ; John Jay, $25 ; Phelps, Dodge & Co., $25 ; the Fire Underwriters, $250 ; Vestry of Trinity Church, $200 ; William Tilden & Nephew, $50. The library soon had two thousand five hundred volumes. The Metropolitan Fire Department Mutual Aid Association was started in October, 1867.

A breeze was created in the Board the same month, by a resolution which was offered by Commissioner Wilson, and which was adopted, to the effect that no member of the department be permitted to be a delegate or representative to any political or nominating convention ; and later the Citizens' Association, through Peter Cooper, attacked Mr. Abbe's right to act as a commissioner because he had been nominated for sheriff on the republican ticket. John H. Martindale, the attorney-general, advised the fire commissioners to appoint another commissioner ; but Mr. Abbe, in a communication to his colleagues, denied receiving notice of his nomination, and asserted that he had declined it, so that the other commissioners accepted his statement and declined to act. The first department surgeon, Dr. Charles B. McMillan, was designated at the end of November, 1867. Assistant Chief Engineer Perley was appointed chief of the repair yard in Elizabeth Street, and H. A. Gilbertson, superintendent. Hitherto so little had the Volunteer system been changed that few members of companies rode on the apparatus, but ran with the horses. On the fourth of December, 1867, alterations were ordered on all apparatus to enable officers and men to ride. New York, on the first of January, 1868, had no longer companies on a semi-volunteer basis. On the twenty-eighth of December, 1867, the eight suburban engines and hook and ladder companies, Engine Companies Nos. 36, 37, 38 and 39, and Hook and Ladder Companies Nos. 13, 14 and 15, were ordered to be disbanded, and the following Paid companies were established :

Metropolitan Engine Company No. 35, located on One Hundred and

Nineteenth Street, between Second and Third Avenues; steamer third size, built by James Smith, New York City, and four-wheeled tender.

Assistant foreman (in command), William Frost; engineer of steamer, Albert Stone; firemen, Phillip Ramee, John C. Post; hosemen, Rufus E. Russell, William H. Taylor, Oscar A. Stowe, John J. Wilson, Robert H. Black, John J. Murphy.

Metropolitan Engine Company No. 36, located on Fourth Avenue, between One Hundred and Twenty-sixth and One Hundred and Twenty-seventh Streets; steamer third size, built by James Smith, New York City, and four-wheeled tender.

Assistant foreman (in command), John A. Cowie; engineer of steamer, George Jarvis; firemen, Adam Jacoby, George A. Campbell; hosemen, James Crowley, Henry C. Mount, Thomas B. Morris, Michael Daily, John Brodie, William O. Seaman, William Johnson, Henry L. Nunns.

Metropolitan Engine Company No. 37, located at Manhattanville; steamer third size, built by Lee and Larned, New York City, and four-wheeled tender.

Foreman, William H. Young; engineer of steamer, Henry Blessing; firemen, James B. Pettit, Michael Herity; hosemen, John Murray, Samuel H. Waugh, John McKibbin, John Ferris, Patrick Sullivan, George Graff, Valentine Smith, Patrick Casey.

Metropolitan Engine Company No. 38, located on Tenth Avenue, between One Hundred and Fifty-fourth and One Hundred and Fifty-fifth Streets; steamer third size, built by R. M. Clapp, New York City, and four-wheeled tender.

Foreman, William Simpson; engineer of steamer, John A. Munger; firemen, James Dunn, Henry M. Ahrens; hosemen, John Watson, Abram Cornish, Edward Clearwater, James Hueston, Richard Van Varick, Peter H. Hunt, Gardner Conklin.

Metropolitan Hook and Ladder Company No. 13, located on Eighty-seventh Street, between Third and Fourth Avenues; truck built in 1865 by Charles E. Hartshorn, New York City.

Foreman, Jacob Van Orden; firemen, Charles M. Moore, John H. Van Tassel; ladderman, Alvin Buckbee.

Metropolitan Hook and Ladder Company No. 14, located on One Hundred and Twenty-fifth Street, between Third and Fourth Avenues; truck built in 1856 by John H. Sickles, New York City; rebuilt in 1862 by James P. Conk, New York City.

Assistant foreman (in command), Henry M. Jones; firemen, Samuel Hunt, Jeremiah Kelly; laddermen, Joseph Saxe, Mathias Schweppenhauser, William Hahn, Frederick Newbauer, Peter Hoffman, John Paul, Harry Graham, Joseph Murray, George W. Bush.

Metropolitan Hook and Ladder Company No. 15, located on Tenth Avenue, between One Hundred and Fifty-fourth and One Hundred and Fifty-fifth Streets; truck built in 1859 by William Williams, New York City.

Assistant foreman (in command), John Coyle; firemen, Thomas H. Brannigan, Patrick Conaghan; laddermen, J. Wallace Stickney, James Veitch, Isaac O. Woodruff, John F. Cunningham, Robert M. Hutchinson, Joseph McEvoy, Michael Howe, Peter Brady.

The new companies' hosemen were paid three hundred dollars a year each, and the laddermen a like sum. Both were under the rules of the department, but could follow their avocations when not on fire duty. The changes necessitated others in the assignment of the engineers. Assistant Engineer Perley commanded all the fire organizations north of Twenty-third Street; District Engineer Banham, all the companies above Eightieth Street; Rhodes, all between Twenty-third and Eightieth Streets, east of Sixth Avenue; and Shannessy, all west of Sixth Avenue, between these streets.

The commissioners were eager to acquire knowledge from those who had had experience with Paid and partially Paid Fire Departments, and an examination of the systems in operation; and in November, Messrs. Shaler and Myers visited Boston, Cleveland, Detroit, Chicago, Fort Wayne, Cincinnati, and Baltimore, and made useful and interesting reports. These advocated a semi-paid system for the upper part of the city, and prudence in adopting a new telegraph system. One of the results of offering rewards for the conviction of incendiaries was the sending to prison of two incendiaries, Gaetano Castagnetto and Thomas A. Lambert, and the payment of the rewards offered. Fire Marshal Baker and Policeman Charles Van Duzer, who was pensioned in 1885, shared one reward of one thousand dollars.

The year 1868 saw the commissioners surrounded with interference from Albany, and embarrassed by the gradual increase in the pay of the force. By Chapter 408 of the Laws of 1867, the salaries were: chief engineer, $4,500; assistant engineer, $2,500; district engineers, $1,800; foremen, $1,300; assistant foremen, $1,100; engineers, $1,200; privates, $1,000. The estimate of the year was $893,600, of which sum $716,770 was for salaries. The citizens' association took the department in hand, and after a conference with the commissioners, and a searching investigation, reported that its workings were marked by the greatest efficiency. The report was signed by William Wood, chairman; William Bloodgood, S. S. Constant, Nathaniel Sands, R. M. Henry and T. J. Powers. But the opponents of the commission, the Paid Department system, and innovations, continued their attacks in the press. One of the organs said:

"At Albany, in the Assembly, after sweeping resolutions of censure and broad charges of corruption and inefficiency, the following committee was appointed to "investigate" the Fire Department: Alexander Frear, chairman; G. J. Bamler, of Erie; M. C. Murphy, of New York; W. C. Jones, of Kings; Christopher Johnson, of New York; William Bristol, of Wyoming; and Jacob Worth, of Kings. The committee held four sessions, and the testimony adduced was such as to call for the following sarcastic resolutions, which were offered at a meeting of the commissioners by Mr. Myers:

Resolved, That the Board feels gratified for the recent searching investigation by a committee of the Honorable House of Assembly into the system on which its business is conducted, into the efficiency of this Department under their control, into the economy and fidelity with which the public money is disbursed, and into the benefits derived therefrom, directly or indirectly, by individual commissioners, beyond the amount of their salary.

Resolved, That without anticipating the report of the said committee, it is matter of pride for this Board to know that this evidence has established the fact that this Department has been so managed as to prove upon such investigation an exception to the theory of many citizens, that to hold public office in New York is necessarily to be incompetent, dishonest, and corrupt.

The committee only reported the testimony taken. The investigation was generally regarded as a political scheme, and the evidence upset the charges of inefficiency, political "dickering," favoritism, extravagance, and corruption. But a bill was sent to the Democratic Assembly to increase the force and its pay, and the Republican Senate asked the commissioners if such were necessary or proper. The commissioners replied in the negative, and Messrs. Galway and Myers went to Albany and fought the bill, which Mr. Abbe favored, and it failed to become a law. Its defeat saved the department an aggregate of expense amounting to eight hundred and eighty-three thousand eight hundred and sixty dollars and twenty-four cents. Senators Crowley, Palmer, Banks, and Kennedy were largely instrumental in defeating the bill, which contained several "ring" schemes, among them a "back pay grab" in the interest of Thomas C. Fields.

In June, 1868, through the stupidity, or worse, of Engineer P. W. Hand, who was punished by dismissal from the department, the Amoskeag engine of Company No. 1 exploded at a fire at No. 53 Bowery with fatal results. The disaster was caused by the strapping down of the safety valve, which leaked.

On the thirtieth of July, 1868, Assistant Engineer Perley, a district engineer, the medical officer, and a foreman were constituted a board to pass on the competency of officers of the department, and in August the president of the commission was authorized to take command at fires as the highest officer of the department. Nothing in this action was intended to deprive Chief Kingsland of his power and authority.

Commissioner JOSHUA GROSVENOR ABBE died of pulmonary disease at Windham, Ct., on the twenty-first of September, 1868. His memory was honored in suitable resolutions offered by his associates, and his funeral was attended by District Engineers William Brandon and Robert V. Mackey; and Foremen John H. McNeil, Metropolitan Engine Company No. 3; William H. Wilson, Metropolitan Engine Company No. 14; George A. Erlacher, Metropolitan Engine Company No. 13; N. L. Chamberlain, Metropolitan Engine Company No. 17; Samuel Yates, Metropolitan Engine Company No. 27; George McLoughlin, Metropolitan Engine Company No. 32; John Moore, Metropolitan Hook and Ladder Company No. 1; Charles O. Shay, Metropolitan Hook and Ladder Company No. 5; Robert King, Metropolitan Hook and Ladder Company No. 7; James H. Monroe, Metropolitan Hook and Ladder Company No. 8; Wm. Rowe, Metropolitan Hook and Ladder Company No. 9; and Christopher H. Reynolds, Metropolitan Hook and Ladder Company No. 11.

Mr. Galway succeeded Mr. Abbe as treasurer of the department, and a code of telegraphic fire signals from Station 2 to Station 727 was adopted. The engineers were redistricted, the rules for sending out alarms were amended, the telegraph system was brought near to that of the present day, and the first inspection of the companies was made in October.

On the twenty-second of October the sign "Firemen's Hall" was taken down at the Mercer Street headquarters, and one bearing "Headquarters Metropolitan Fire Department" put up. November 12, Mr. James M. McLean was appointed to succeed Mr. Abbe.

An order of December 26, 1868, defined the boundaries of the engine districts, organized the battalions and brigades, military fashion, assigned commanding officers, and established the following ranking grades:

Title of Position.	Assimilated Rank.
Chief Engineer	Colonel.
Assistant Engineer	Lieut. Colonel.
District Engineer	Major.
Foreman	Captain.
Assistant Foreman	Lieutenant.

Engineers of Steamers..........................Sergeant.

Firemen..Private.

Hosemen and Laddermen........................Cadet.

In January, 1869, the Committees of the Board were reorganized as follows: Appointments, all the Commissioners; Supplies, Galway and Wilson; Finance, Myers and McLean; Buildings, Galway and Myers; Telegraph, McLean and Wilson; Apparatus, Wilson and Galway; Combustibles, Wilson and McLean.

In March the various companies were organized for patrol beats in three brigades and eight battalions, and strict rules were made in regard to patrol service and the keeping of the journals of companies.

Chief Kingsland, a democrat, was not chary of criticism, and some remarks of his in regard to an order of the commissioners which related to the school

JAMES M. McLEAN.

of instruction, having been reported at headquarters, an inquiry was ordered, which, in the end, brought about his retirement from the service. The investigation was begun in April, and he resigned December 14, 1869. Shortly after, steps were taken to revolutionize the telegraph system. May 12, 1869, Mr. James M. McLean was appointed commissioner, to succeed himself, by his colleagues. It that month fire extinguishers were introduced. May 31 the force was notified of the promotion of C. O. Shay and Christopher H. Reynolds to the rank of district engineers. Preparations to have a well equipped telegraph system went on, and, in June, the treasurer was directed to include in his estimates for 1870 "a sum not exceeding four hundred thousand dollars" for a complete fire alarm telegraph, and on the eleventh of August, C. T. & J. N. Chester's proposal for its construction was accepted.

Captain EYRE M. SHAW, Chief Officer of the Metropolitan Fire Brigade of London, England, visited the United States in July, 1870, and when he was about to start on a tour through the principal cities, he penned a letter to General Alexander Shaler, in which he said: "Before taking my tour through the United States I must trouble you with this short letter, offering my most sincere and heartfelt thanks for all the kindness and attention which I have received from you and your colleagues, and the department generally over which you so ably preside."

This was sixteen years ago, and London is, to-day, almost as antiquated in its methods of fire extinguishing as was New York in 1865, in comparison with the system of 1869.

Captain Eyre Massey Shaw, C. B., is the head of the London Fire Brigade.

He was born at Monkstown, County Cork, Ireland, in 1830, being the third son of B. R. Shaw, Esq., of Monkstown and Belvelly, and a cousin of Sir Robert Shaw, Bart., of Bushey Park. He was educated at Dr. Coghlan's well-known academy, Queenstown, and afterwards went to Trinity College, Dublin, where he greatly distinguished himself, taking his B. A. and M. A. degrees. He went to sea for two years, and was a member subsequently of the North Cork Rifles, and for two years was on the staff. After retiring from the army in 1860 he

CAPTAIN EYRE MASSEY SHAW.
[Chief of the London Fire Department.]

became superintendent of the Borough forces of Belfast, including Police and Fire Brigade, and on the death of Mr. Braidwood, at the great fire in Tooley Street, in 1861 (which burned for a fortnight), was appointed to his present post. He is a deputy-lieutenant in Middlesex, and now a Companion of the Bath. In 1875 he drilled a force in Egypt for the Khedive.

Captain Shaw has been wounded twice very severely in the performance of his duty, and several times less so. In 1865 he visited America for the purpose of inspecting the principal Fire Departments in the country. Originally the London Fire Brigade was appointed by the fire insurance companies, but about twelve years ago the Metropolitan Board of Works took it in hand, and placed Captain Shaw at its head. There are, in the four districts into which he has divided London, fifty fire engine stations, one hundred and nine fire-escape stations, four floating stations, fifty-six telegraph lines, one hundred and four miles of telegraph lines, three floating steam fire engines, one iron barge to carry a land steam fire engine, three large land steam fire engines, twenty-six small land steam fire engines, twelve seven-inch manual fire engines, sixty six-inch manual fire engines, thirty-six under six-inch manual fire engines, seventeen hose carts, one hundred and twenty-five fire-escapes and long scaling ladders, and four hundred and twenty firemen, including the chief officer, the four superintendents, and all ranks.

The Avondale mine disaster, in the autumn of 1869, resulted in an appeal for aid for the families of the sufferers to the members of the department, and Mr. C. E. Gildersleve, as treasurer of the fund, sent one thousand and twenty-two dollars and twenty-five cents to H. Gaylord, of Plymouth, Pa. On the twenty-fifth of October, 1869, the large death rate having increased the burdens of the Mutual Aid Society, the treasurer was authorized to donate two thousand dollars to it. November 1 a Bureau of Statistics was created, and a few days later, a complete Manual of Instruction for Commanding Officers of Engine and Hook and Ladder Companies in the care and use of their apparatus was issued. November 11 classes of instruction were formed for the instruction of officers of the department in their duties under the direction of the president. There were three classes—the First, of the engineer officers; the Second, of the company commanders; and the Third, of company officers not in command. The chief engineer, when able, was required to attend the meetings of each class. Chief Kingsland's resignation was accepted, and complimentary resolutions on his administration were passed, when Joseph L. Perley was made his successor. His salary was four thousand five hundred dollars per annum, and that of the "Chiefs of Brigade," two thousand four hundred dollars per annum.

R. D. HATCH.

The title of chief engineer was changed to "Chief of the Department," and the assistant engineers were made "Chiefs of Battalion," except R. V. Mackey, "Department Inspector," and William Brandon, Eli Bates and W. W. Rhodes, designated respectively as Chiefs of the First, Second and Third Brigades.

The year 1870 found the Legislature at Albany prepared and able to do the bidding of the ring, and it was evident the Fire Department would not be neglected. The commissioners, however, ignored the inevitable, and continued to perfect the system. January 13 an Examining Board was substituted for the Board of Officers. It was composed of the Chief of the Department, the Chiefs of Brigades, the Department Inspector, and the Medical Officer, who were to pass on the conduct and qualifications of the officers of the department. Chief Orr and Lieutenant Eyner, of Engine Company No. 34, were designated as Examiners of Engineers. February 14 two hundred thousand dollars was paid on account of the new telegraph to Chester & Co. In March the ringing of second and third alarms on the tower bells was discontinued, and only three rounds of first alarms was struck on them. March 16 the new telegraph system, with alarm signal boxes, as at present, was completed below Fourteenth Street, for signals 2 to 346, and on the thirty-first of March arrangements were made to connect Blackwell's, Ward's and Randall's Islands with the city by submarine telegraphy. The tower bells were then at the Postoffice, Spring Street, Marion Street, Essex Market, Union Market, Jefferson

Market, Twenty-fifth Street, Thirty-third Street, Fifty-first Street, Yorkville and Mount Morris.

The "Tweed Charter"—Chapter 137 of the Laws of 1870—was passed April 5, 1870. John T. Hoffman was Governor; Allen C. Beach, Lieutenant Governor, and William Hitchman, Speaker of the Assembly. In New York, A. Oakey Hall was Mayor; Richard B. Connolly, Comptroller; William M. Tweed, Commissioner of Public Works; Alexander Frear, Commissioner of Charities and Correction; Peter B. Sweeny and Thomas C. Fields, Commissioners of Public Parks; when Mr. Hall appointed, as Fire Commissioners of the City of New York, General Shaler, Speaker William Hitchman, and Messrs. James S. Hennessy, James Galway and John J. Blair.

JAMES S. HENNESSY was born in London, England, in 1828. He came to this country with his parents when he was seven months' old. Until 1865 he resided in Philadelphia, and for several years was prominently connected with the Quaker City Fire Department, and in the Fire Association represented Vigilant Fire Company. For many years he was paying teller of the Bank of North America. Coming to New York, he engaged in the notion business with his brother. In April, 1870, he was appointed fire commissioner by Mayor Oakey Hall for a term of five years, but in 1873 was legislated out of office with the rest of the Board; while in office he was treasurer of the Board. Mr. Hennessy was trustee of the Emigrant Industrial Savings Bank, and at the time of his death was chairman of the Finance Committee of the Irish Emigrant Society. He died on May 6, 1874.

JAMES S. HENNESSY.

New York was fortunate at this juncture that other men were not appointed. The new commissioners met at Fireman's Hall on April 11, and Mr. Hitchman was made president and Mr. Hennessy treasurer. All the rules, regulations, and general and special orders of the Metropolitan Fire Department were affirmed and continued in force. May 6 Colonel T. Bailey Myers was appointed attorney and counsel to the Board, at a salary of five thousand dollars per annum. Two weeks later the Metropolitan sign at Fireman's Hall was taken down, and the sign "Headquarters Fire Department City of New York" was put up, and wherever, on apparatus, quarters or insignia, "M. F. D." had been, "F. D. N. Y." was placed.

May 30, William Lamb, formerly assistant engineer under the Volunteer system, was appointed inspector of fire apparatus; Joseph L. Perley was made chief of the bureau of the chief engineers at a salary of four thousand five hundred dollars, and Robert V. Mackey was designated as assistant to him at a salary of two thousand four hundred dollars; Henry Close was appointed superintendent of the repair yard, which was moved to Amity Street, now West Third Street, in the place of H. A. Gilbertson, at a salary of two thousand five hundred dollars.   July 6, Foreman John L. Cregier, Engine Company No. 12, G. L. Tooker, Engine Company No. 34, A. C. Hull, Hook and Ladder Company No. 6, resigned to follow the fortunes of Commissioner Wilson, who had succeeded John Cornwell as superintendent of the fire insurance patrol. December 15, the committee on telegraph reported in favor of accepting C. T. & J. N. Chester's telegraph line above Fourteenth Street.   On the first of January, 1871, alarm-signal boxes 351 to 919 went into service, as well as a complete system of "patrol beats."   In March the bell at the Post-office tower ceased to strike, but the tower was used as a lookout station. Charles L. Chapin resigned as superintendent of telegraph, and C. Kinney Smith succeeded him.   The office of assistant engineer of steamer, at eleven hundred dollars per annum, was created, and the complement of engine companies south of Twenty-third Street was fixed at one foreman or captain, one assistant foreman or lieutenant, one engineer or sergeant, one assistant engineer or corporal, and eight firemen or privates.   North of Twenty-third Street each engine company had six firemen.   In other respects the organization was the same.   June 7, Charles E. Gildersleve resigned as secretary, and was appointed chief clerk of the Bureau of Combustibles, at a salary of two thousand five hundred dollars, and W. B. White was appointed secretary at the same salary.   Dr. Charles McMillan had tendered his resignation, and was succeeded by Dr. Christopher Prince, whose salary was fixed at five thousand dollars per annum.   June 28, Foreman Benjamin A. Gicquel, Engine Company No. 5, James H. Monroe, Hook and Ladder Company No. 8, and Walter T. Furlong, Engine Company No. 6, were promoted to the rank of chief of battalion.

The Fall of the year 1871 saw the commissioners much embarrassed for want of funds.   They had to go around, hat in hand, to procure a loan to pay their men.   November 2, the board met, to learn that the Board of Fire Underwriters had set apart one hundred and eighty-seven thousand dollars to meet the pay-rolls.   Andrew H. Green, Deputy Comptroller, had deposited in the department bank twenty-seven thousand one hundred and eighty-three dollars and thirty-four cents, the balance of the appropriation for 1871.   Thomas F. Jeremiah was instrumental in getting the advance from the underwriters.

The firemen did full and satisfactory duty, nevertheless, and twenty-seven members of it, including Assistant Engineer Rhodes, were in the early morning of the eighth of November, injured to a greater or less degree, by the falling of a wall at No. 479 Sixth Avenue.   November 22, at the suggestion of Chief Perley, a system of special telegraph calls and signals was adopted.   His Imperial Highness, Alexis, Grand Duke of Russia, on the twenty-eighth of November, witnessed a parade of the department, composed of three battalions under Chiefs Orr, Shay and Sullivan, and his praise at the appearance and organization of the apparatus and men was as warm as it was unstinted. When news of the condition of the firemen of Chicago, after the great fire there, was received, a subscription was raised for them by the department, and two thousand six hundred and thirty dollars were collected and sent to Mayor Mason.

On December 20 the title of superintendent of telegraph was changed to chief of telegraph bureau, and the salary was made three thousand five hundred dollars. A week later, on motion of Commissioner Hennessy, the number of assistant engineers was increased to twelve. Foreman William H. Nash, of Engine Company No. 8, and George A. Erlacher, of Engine Company No. 13, were promoted. Poor Erlacher was fatally injured at a fire at No. 183 Water Street on the seventeenth of January, 1873.

The first days of 1872 saw the fire commissioners yet embarrassed for lack of funds to pay the members of the department and meet obligations. Comptroller Andrew H. Green announced three hundred and fifty-two thousand two hundred and sixty-six dollars and seventeen cents appropriated for the Fire Department from January 1 to April 30, 1872. June 5 Inspectors Moore, Cregier, Forman and Keeler, of the bureau of combustibles, were discontinued, and John A. McCosker was appointed inspector at a salary of two thousand dollars per annum. June 22, by an explosion at No. 18 Liberty Street, twenty firemen were injured, and Edward Burke, of Engine Company No. 4, was killed. James Sutton & Co., of *The Aldine*, No. 23 Liberty Street, got up a subscription for the sufferers. The following is a report on the injured and the disposition of the fund:

Edward Burke, fireman, Engine Company 4; residence, 96 Henry Street; single; died of injuries. William Kline, fireman, Engine Company 4; residence, 441 Pearl Street; married, four children; seriously. Francis Murray, fireman, Hook and Ladder Company 6; at time of fire performing duty with Engine Company 4; residence, 38 Washington Street; wife dead, two children living; seriously. Thomas Flynn, fireman, Engine Company 4; residence, 16 Broome Street; married, two children; seriously. John McNamara, fireman, Hook and Ladder Company 10; residence, 30 Roosevelt Street; married, one child; seriously. John Harris, assistant foreman Engine Company 4; residence, 430 West Twenty-seventh Street; married, two children; seriously. John Regan, fireman, Engine Company 6; residence, 12 Greenwich Street; married, no children; seriously. Thomas J. Cortissos, fireman, Engine Company 6; residence, 24 Watts Street; married, two children; seriously. Louis Schlamp, fireman, Hook and Ladder Company 10; residence, ————; married, two children; seriously. James H. Monroe, assistant engineer; residence, — Franklin Street; married, four children; severely. Patrick Donohue, foreman, Engine Company 4; residence, — Grand Street; married, three children; severely. James Heany, assistant foreman, Hook and Ladder Company 9; residence, 161 Elizabeth Street; married, one child; severely. John Schwab, fireman, Hook and Ladder Company 10; residence, 39 Hester Street; single; slightly. John Batterberry, foreman, Engine Company 6; residence, 48 Broad Street; married, two children; slightly. John Hillis, fireman, Engine Company 4; injuries very trifling. James Hunter, fireman, Hook and Ladder Company 8; injuries very trifling. John Finn, fireman, Hook and Ladder Company 1; injuries very trifling. Dennis Reagan, fireman, Engine Company 6; injuries very trifling. Patrick O'Callaghan, fireman, Hook and Ladder Company 10; injuries very trifling. James Donovan, fireman, Engine Company 6; injuries very trifling. George Smith, fireman, Engine Company 4; injuries very trifling.

The fund was distributed as follows, in check, to order of each: To the nine seriously injured, $70.44 each, $634.00; to the three severely injured, $56.67 each, $170.00; to the two slightly injured, $32.50 each, $65.00; to the seven triflingly injured, $20.00 each, $140.00. Total amount subscribed, $1,009.00.

July 17 Assistant Engineer Eli Bates was appointed assistant to Chief Perley. The Post-office tower was finally abandoned September 24, 1872. The commissioners, during the month, again locked horns with the comptroller on a requisition from them for one hundred and twenty-five thousand dollars. Mr. Green held that, under the amended charter of 1870, the Fire Department had no right to a separate treasury and disbursing officer. Proceedings by mandamus were taken against the comptroller by the commissioners, but the

Supreme Court denied the motion. The salaries were paid by the comptroller *pendente lite*. In October a system of ambulance calls over the fire wires was adopted.

On the twenty-first of November the commissioners estimated the expenses of the department for 1873 at one million three hundred and sixty-four thousand nine hundred dollars, of which nine hundred and forty-four thousand four hundred dollars were for salaries; and asked for one hundred thousand dollars more for new buildings.

A detail of firemen of all grades attended the funeral of the Hon. Horace Greeley, on the fourth of December, 1872. On the last day of this year Mr. Alexander T. Stewart sent a contribution of one thousand dollars to the relief fund.

One of the first important acts of the year 1873 was the inspection of theaters and other buildings, with a view of discovering their weak points. January

JOSEPH L. PERLEY.

31, Dr. Charles McMillan came back to the department as associate medical officer. April 30, 1873, the Legislature passed the charter of the committee of seventy, known as Chapter 335 of the Laws of 1873. It provided that the Mayor—William F. Havemeyer—should nominate, and, by and with the consent of the Board of Aldermen, appoint three fire commissioners—one for two, another for four, and the third for six years, from the first of May, 1873, at a salary of five thousand dollars, except the president, whose salary was fixed at seven thousand dollars.

Although General Shaler framed that part of the act which related to the Fire Department, he was not destined to be a member of the Fire Department of the City of New York.

Mayor Havemeyer, without solicitation, sent for Chief Perley, announced his intention of nominating him for commissioner, and he, Mr. Cornelius Van Cott, and Ex-Judge Roswell D. Hatch, were nominated and confirmed, Perley for six years, Hatch for four years, and Van Cott for two years. The Board organized on the nineteenth of May, 1873, by selecting Mr. Perley as president, and Mr. Hatch as treasurer; and the same day Eli Bates was appointed chief of the department, and Charles Oscar Shay assistant chief. The same day General Shaler issued an address, in which he exhorted the officers and men to be obedient and do their duty under all circumstances.

JOSEPH L. PERLEY, born in New York, 1835, was a mechanical engineer. He went to public school (in those days called common school) old No. 5, at Stanton and Sheriff Streets. He learned his trade at Eckfort Iron Works, corner of Cannon and Stanton Streets. Mr. Perley joined the Department in 1856, about the time he came of age, having run as a volunteer for five years previously. He joined Live Oak Engine Company No. 44 in 1856. He was elected an assistant foreman in 1860, and almost immediately after assistant engineer. He served in the latter capacity until 1865. He was appointed under the Paid Department as first assistant engineer, and was assigned to duty in the lower section of the city, south of Canal Street, and at the same time placed in charge of the machinery of the Department and superintendent of the repair shops, all the engines having to be altered to the new system. In 1868 he was relieved from duty in the repair shop and was placed in command of that portion of the city north of Twenty-third Street, for the purpose of organizing the Department in that section. While so serving, in 1869, he was promoted to be chief of the Department, and so served until May, 1873, when Mayor Havemeyer requested him to accept the appointment of commissioner for six years. He was made president, serving for four years, and relieved in 1879.

When Chief ELI BATES retired from the new Department May 1, 1884, he ended a fireman's career which had lasted thirty-eight years and one day. A carpenter by trade, he had not passed his twenty-first birthday, on April 29, 1846, when he received his certificate, and joined Guardian Engine Company No. 29, located at Jefferson Market. His connection with the company lasted until 1862. In 1852 he became assistant foreman, and three years later was promoted to foreman. From 1862 until the Volunteer organization was dissolved Mr. Bates

CHIEF ELI BATES.

performed the duties of assistant engineer, and he joined the Paid Department as district engineer, a rank now designated as chief of battalion. His district lay on the west side of the city, south of Forty-second Street. Later he was transferred to the east side, with Fourteenth Street as the north boundary of his district. In June, 1871, Mr. Bates was made assistant to Chief Perley, whom he succeeded in command of the Department May 19, 1873. For the next eleven years Chief Bates' gray horse and plain buggy were familiar to New Yorkers as they dashed through the streets in answer to alarms. The chief's quarters were with No. 9 Truck in Elizabeth Street, and he attended all fires south of Twenty-third Street. During his term of office there were several fires which caused immense property losses, but none where there was appalling loss of life. Three theaters—the Park, Windsor, and Standard—were burned within a short time, but the first and the last took fire before the time for the performance, while the Windsor began to blaze at midnight on Thanksgiving, 1883. Chief Bates was twice injured in the performance of duty. There was a fire at West and Murray Streets, January 4, 1867, when the ladder on which he was standing slipped, and his right knee was severely injured. Five years ago he entered a burning flour store in South Street, and fell while coming down-stairs. His chest struck heavily upon an iron girder, and his body was bruised over the ribs. In 1869 he was instrumental in saving a family on the fifth story of a house at Cherry and Montgomery Streets.

With other officers of the new Department in 1865 Chief Bates had many difficulties to fight. For the Volunteer service—four thousand strong—were substituted five hundred men. The engines were feeble compared with those of the present day, and much of the hose was bad. Friends of the Old and enemies of the New organization were ready to spy out defects and errors. There was practically no fire alarm telegraph, but signals were sent by bells and the police wires—two slow and uncertain methods. Except Engine 22, at Third Avenue and Eighty-fifth Street, the "full pay" companies were all south of Fifty-ninth Street. The upper part of the city was defended by Volunteer companies, which each received one thousand dollars from the city per year for expenses. "Hosemen" and "laddermen" were paid for work at fires, but went on duty only when alarms sounded. To-day firemen ride to the spot where they are needed; then the machines were too light to carry them, and they had to run. The work was harder and the danger greater than now.

Efforts were made to turn the Robinson system of alarms to account, but they failed. On March 28, 1870, the present telegraph arrangement was ready for service below Fourteenth Street, but the poles were like angels' visits, "few and far between," and often the wires came down, so that there were long delays in getting apparatus at work. Chief Bates attached great importance to a perfect system of alarms. He claimed credit for the invention of the simultaneous call. There had been first, second, and third alarms, and special calls for particular companies, but no signal to bring a large force immediately to grapple with an immense fire. The chief's idea was approved by the commissioners, and an order announcing the new signal to the Department had been drawn up. Before it was officially promulgated, the big fire at No. 444 Broadway broke out, February 8, 1876. Chief Bates sounded his new call, but the telegraph operator at headquarters refused to recognize it. A second alarm was then sent out from Broadway and Eleventh Street, and as fast as the companies arrived they were sent down to the fire. The order was promulgated without further delay. Although the simultaneous call is rarely heard, it has been used on several occasions when its usefulness was proven beyond question. One other reform Chief Bates instituted. Originally no matter how threatening the fire was, the first, second, and third alarms were sent out in regular order. Now an officer, believing that the circumstances demand it, may send out a third alarm when the fire is discovered.

On two occasions Chief Bates performed fire duty beyond the city limits. Both times the fire was in the Export Lumber Company's yard at Long Island City. The second, and more severe fire, was in the autumn of 1880, when Chief Bates went to the rescue with the fireboat 'Havemeyer.' He pushed up the pellucid waters of Newtown Creek, and had to fight the fire from the leeward side. Smoke was blown npon the boat in clouds, and sparks fell upon her in showers. The men demurred, but the chief refused to give up the fight, and held his position until the flames were subdued. Mayor-elect Grace, who had watched the struggle, congratulated the chief upon the success of his pluck. Since his retirement ex-Chief Bates has lived in a pleasant cottage in Harlem.

WILLIAM B. WHITE.

Mr. WILLIAM B. WHITE, ex-secretary of the Paid Fire Department, was born in Baltimore, December 15, 1835. His parents were New Englanders. His widowed mother took him to New York when he was four years old, and educated him. A Republican, he twice represented the Ninth Ward in the Common Council of this city, and in 1866 he was elected councilman of the Sixth District. At the end of this time he was elected member of the Board of Aldermen, and served from 1867 to 1870. In this year he was defeated for State Senator. While alderman, General Grant nominated him collector of Internal Revenues of the Sixth District, and he was confirmed by the Senate, and received his commission December 29, 1869. June 15, 1871, he was appointed secretary of the Paid Fire Department, and was removed July 15, 1875.

EDWARD W. SAVAGE.

EDWARD W. SAVAGE, chief book-keeper of the Fire Department, is a man qualified by experience and probity of character to discharge the duties of his position. He is known and respected for his intelligence and courtesy. For a number of years he has held his present office, to the satisfaction of his superior officers.

NOZZLE.

CHAPTER L.

THE DEPARTMENT GAINS IN EFFICIENCY.

Appointment of a Fire Marshal.—A Corps of Sappers and Miners.—Steamboats Havemeyer and Mills.—Business Rules and Regulations.—Superintendent of Buildings.—English and American Fire Services.—Instructions in Life Saving.—Several Destructive Fires.—The Dry Goods District.—President Purroy's Water Tank.

The new Board speedily availed themselves of the sweeping provisions of the law which legislated out of office all but the Foremen and members of Engine and Hook and Ladder Companies. On the 19th of May, Commissioner Hatch resigned as Treasurer, and Mr. Van Cott was chosen. Wm. B. White was appointed Secretary, Eli Bates, Chief of the Department, and Charles Oscar Shay, Assistant Chief. By direction, Chief Bates nominated the following corps of assistants—Chiefs of Battalions—and they were confirmed : James H. Monroe, William H. Nash, Gilbert J. Orr, Benjamin A. Gicquel, William W. Rhodes ; Foreman Hugh Bonner, Engine Company No. 20 ; Foreman William Rowe, Hook and Ladder Company No. 9 ; Foreman John W. Miller, Engine Company No. 17 ; Foreman Robert King, Hook and Ladder Company No. 1 ; Foreman John S. Fisher, Hook and Ladder Company No. 2.

Next day George H. Sheldon was appointed Fire Marshal at $3,000 a year, in spite of influence invoked by Mr. Thomas McSpedon, who was legislated out of office which he held under the Police Commissioners ; and Alexander V.

GEO. H. SHELDON, FIRE MARSHAL.

Davidson, Storekeeper, at $2,000 a year. Dr. Christopher Prince, Medical Officer, made way on the 27th for Dr. Charles McMillan at $2,500 a year, and Dr. A. J. Minor was appointed vice Medical Officer at $2,000 a year. C. K. Smith was made Superintendent of Telegraph at $2,500 per annum ; William Terhune, Inspector of Combustibles, at $2,500 ; Charles E. Gildersleve, Chief Clerk in this bureau at the same salary, and Jacob Springsteed, Superintendent of Horses. June 4th, Charles F. Hill was appointed Assistant Fire Marshal, vice James S. Burnton, who declined the office, and ex-Assistant Engineer Walter T. Furlong, Surveyor of Combustibles, an office he held until his death in February, 1874. At about this time peculiar influences which, later on, led to a fearful accident and well-grounded accusations of jobbery and corruption, introduced to the Commissioners and Secretary White, Mrs. Mary Belle Scott Uda, a fascinating woman, who procured a patent right for a life-saving and hose-carrying apparatus, known as an aerial ladder, and she was favored in June with tests of her apparatus. William Matthews was made Foreman of the machine shops, under Chief of Battalion Orr. Edward Savage was made Chief Book-keeper at a salary of $2,500 per annum.

The estimate of expenses for 1874 was made at $1,455,011. September 10, the Bureau of Combustibles was moved to Firemen's Hall. Hook and Ladder Company No. 16 was organized on the old Bloomingdale road, between Ninety-seventh and Ninety-eighth streets, on the 23d of October, 1873.

Under the Act of May 23d, 1873 (afterward amended to Chapter 329 of the Laws of 1873), "to provide for the annexation of the towns of Morrisania, West Farms and Kings Bridge, in the County of Westchester, to the City and County of New York," the Board, on the 21st of November, instructed Superintendent Smith to inspect the territory and report on telegraphic facilities, and Chief Bates was directed to estimate the number of men and apparatus necessary to cover the new district.

Under the Act of the 12th of June, 1873, the corps of sappers and miners was organized. Chief Shay had command of it, and, on the 10th of December, 1873, Julius H. Striedinger was, on the recommendation of Brevet Major General John Newton, United States Engineers, appointed Instructor of the Corps of Sappers and Miners at $2,000 a year. December 24th, J. Elliott Smith, the present Superintendent of Telegraph, was appointed Assistant Telegraph Operator at a salary of $1,200. The force of the Department in the Twenty-third and Twenty-fourth wards was established at two steam engine companies, four chemical engine companies, and two hook and ladder companies, to be known as the Tenth Battalion, and Engine Companies Nos. 41 and 42, Chemical Engine Companies Nos. 1, 2, 3 and 4, and Hook and Ladder Companies Nos. 17 and 18.

The regulations for these companies provided, among other rules, as follows:

The hosemen and laddermen herein provided for shall receive pay at the rate of three hundred dollars per annum, sleep in the engine and truck houses, attend all fires, conform to the rules and regulations that are now, or may hereafter be prescribed, attend at the houses of their respective companies on two afternoons in each month, to be designated by the Battalion Commander, for inspection or practice, assist in cleaning the apparatuses and horses after each fire alarm, and in policing the houses when required by the Company Commander, and shall have the privilege of pursuing their avocations at points convenient to the houses of their respective companies. They will also be required to provide themselves with the uniform, which shall consist of a uniform-coat, shirt, fire-cap and fatigue-cap, as prescribed by General Order No. 1, series 1868, office Chief Engineer, and, in addition thereto, dark blue or black cloth trowsers will be worn when on duty.

In December, $1,274 were subscribed by the firemen for the firemen of Memphis, Tenn., who suffered from the scourge of yellow fever.

The first noteworthy event of 1874 was a resolution to propose plans and specifications for a first-class Department Fire-boat. At the end of January Assistant Chief Engineer Shay planned the organization of the Corps of Sappers and Miners, and his scheme was approved.

In February certain company quarters were turned into soup kitchens to enable Lorenzo Delmonico to properly dispense the bounty of Mr. James Gordon Bennett, of the *Herald*.

May 15th the revised estimate of expenses of the Fire Department for 1874 was $1,608,654.33. June 24th, Superintendent of Telegraph C. K. Smith resigned, and John H. Emerich succeeded him. William H. Sawyer, Commissioner Hatch's candidate for Superintendent, was made Chief Operator, but he failed to qualify, and, two months later, J. Elliott Smith was given the position. In August, Sharmon Ross rebuilt the Amity Street repair shops, and Wood, Dialogue & Co., of Philadelphia, were awarded the contract for the new Steam Fire-boat, their bid being $23,800. In September the estimate of expenses for the Department for 1875 was $1,436,932. In October self-propelling engines were given to Companies 8, 11, 24 and 32. The Police boat Seneca was equipped for use as a fire-boat. Suitable resolutions were passed December 2d on the death of Mayor William F. Havemeyer, and his memory was officially honored.

During 1874 the Bureau of Combustibles waged war on the dealers in dangerous vinorem, and secured convictions which resulted in driving the stuff out of the market and lessening the number of fires and accidents by it.

In January, 1875, the final estimates of the year were fixed by the Board of Apportionment at $1,316,000. The Committee on Discipline was discontinued, so the Fire Board tried delinquents. January 27, to oust a Chief of Battalion, a resolution was passed directing the Chief Engineer to select ten persons as Chiefs of Battalion from the uniformed force, and he named Chiefs Orr, Bonner, Nash, Gicquel, Fisher, Monroe, Rowe, Miller, King and Rhodes, the existing Chiefs. Monroe was a week later reduced to the rank of Foreman, and sent to Hook and Ladder Company, No. 9, against the wish of President Perley, and E. W. Wilhelm was made Chief of Battalion.

The new steam fire-boat was, on motion of Commissioner Van Cott, named the William F. Havemeyer.

Engine Company, No. 39, was organized in March in Sixty-seventh Street, between Third and Lexington Avenues, with Martin Walsh Foreman, William Duane Assistant Foreman, C. E. Bensel Assistant Engineer, and Privates John O'Connor, John Shaller, Daniel Mannix, E. J. Carney, E. Hogan and August Levi. In April preparations were made to man the Havemeyer. Its complement was arranged as follows : One Foreman, one Assistant Foreman, one Engineer, One Pilot and five firemen. Chemical Engine Companies, Nos. 5 and 6, were organized, the former at No. 304 West Forty-seventh Street, and the latter at No. 77 Canal Street, April 17th.

April 28th the Havemeyer was reported finished, and she was manned as follows: Foreman, Thomas H. Griffiths ; Assistant Foreman, James H. Ford ; Engineer, Charles B. Seaver ; Assistant Engineer, Patrick Hughes ; Pilot, Peter Van Orden ; Firemen, A. H. Wright, Matthew D. Conry, James Buckley, John Stapleton and Dennis J. Leary. She was berthed at Pier No. 1, North River. May 5th, Mayor William H. Wickham's nominee, Vincent C. King, succeeded Mr. Van Cott as Commissioner.

VINCENT C. KING was foreman of Hose Company No. 23 from 1853 to 1858. He was also, for four years Commissioner of the Board of Appeal in the Volunteer Fire Department from 1860 to 1864. In 1875 he was appointed Commissioner by Mayor Wickham in the new Paid Fire Department and remained in that position for six years. He was President of the Board for four years when the salary was $7,500 a year, the other Commissioners receiving $5,000 a year. The original commissioners of the new Fire Department were Philip W. Engs, Martin B. Brown, James W. Booth and William Hitchman. They had $10,000 a year. But this was cut down subsequently to $5,000 and made the uniform salary for all the Commissioners as it is to-day. Altogether in the old and new Fire Departments Mr. King spent over twenty years.

"What was the difference," Mr. King was asked by the writer, "between the old and the new Fire Department?"

"Well," he replied, "they have better engines in the present department men and they have the use of steam to pump and work their supply of water, and they may be able to send a stream of water to a much higher altitude than could be done by the

VINCENT C. KING.

old engines, but the old engines had but one advantage that the present ones have not. There was then a strong and abundant flow of Croton water and it was half the battle in a big fire as it came with a rush from the hydrants. Under the circumstances of the city at the time the department was equal to every emergency of fire because there were no big buildings then, few higher than three stories and the firemen were able to control them. But there were engines in those days that could throw a stream of water over Reilly's liberty pole, down near Franklin street and West Broadway, 175 feet high. Reilly (I guess he was the original one) kept a hotel and the boys used to bring their engines down just for the fun of seeing which of them could make the biggest shoot of water. It used to stir up the greatest excitement."

Ex-Commissioner Philip W. Engs died May 19, 1875, and the Commissioners honored his memory in appropriate resolutions and attended his funeral.

On the 7th of July Charles E. Gildersleve and W. B. White left the service of the Department, and Carl Jussen became Acting Secretary. "Siamese" connections and 1½-inch nozzles were applied to all Hook and Ladder Companies below Fifty-ninth Street.

Brave and able Peter Weir, Foreman of Engine Company, No. 23, died in August, 1875, and he was buried on the 14th of August from No. 38 Elm Street, with suitable departmental honors, Foreman John H. Kehoe, Engine 5; Joseph Poynton, Engine 20; Arnot Spence, Engine 27; John J. Bresnan, Engine 33; George Quackenbush, Hook and Ladder 10, and James Walton. Hook and Ladder 12, being the pall-bearers.

PETER WEIR was born in the Sixth Ward about 1840. He joined Fulton Engine Company No. 21 and was elected successively representative, assistant foreman and foreman. In 1865 he was elected Assistant Engineer and served as such until the Paid Department was organized. He was appointed foreman of Engine Company No. 31. He commanded this company until 1871 when he was transferred to Engine Company No. 25, located in the house formerly occupied by Black Joke Engine Company No. 33. He continued in command of this until his death. Chief Gicquel said: "Peter Weir was a genial, whole-souled man, beloved by everybody. He was one of the hardest worked men in the department. His name was placed on the roll of merit for gallantry. In appearance he was anything but a dude, but he was every inch a fireman. A better one I don't believe the department has ever seen. He rarely wore a fire cap at a fire. He seemed to be utterly oblivious of everything, except the fire, when on duty. His death was brought about by over-exertion and exposure."

PETER WEIR.

The collapse of the aerial ladder scheme occurred on the 14th of September, 1875, on the Tweed Plaza, at Canal Street and East Broadway. Several public trials of the invention had been given, and the dangerous character of the apparatus had been commented on. On one occasion, when one of the ladders appeared to be about to topple over, Chief Bates prevented it by slashing a line, which was carried to the top of the ladder. The final experiment was made on the Plaza, in the presence of a vast crowd of spectators and many firemen and others interested in such matters. The ladder was raised in eight sections to a height of ninety-seven feet, and Chief William H. Nash, of the Fourth Battalion, ascended, followed by Fireman Philip J. Maus, of Hook and Ladder Company No. 6; Fireman William Hughes, of Engine Company No. 6, four other firemen and an Assistant Engineer. Chief Nash had reached the summit of the ladder, when it snapped far below him and dashed Nash, Maus and Hughes, who were above the fracture, to the cobble-stones of the square. Nash and Maus were instantly killed, and Hughes died within an hour. No one else was injured. The accident revived gossip, which charged a corrupt understanding with Mrs. Uda, and the payment of a large portion of the $25,000 she received from the city for her rights, and public indignation ran to an intense pitch. The Fire Commissioners promptly sat down on the aerial business.

September 15th Commissioner King offered a resolution, which was adopted, prohibiting the further use of ladders, as it had been demonstrated that they were useless, and there was good reason to believe that the invention was foisted on the Department at an enormous expense and by corrupt means.

CHIEF NASH was, during the war, a member of Berdan's Corps of Sharpshooters, and attained the rank of Assistant Adjutant General. He was buried from 149 Clinton Street, and his funeral was attended by six companies formed of details from the various battalions, and commanded by Chief William Rowe, and the pall-bearers were: Foreman George W. Erb, Engine 9; Thomas

Judge, Engine 11; J. A. Patten, Engine 15; John Farlow, Engine 17; Thos. Leonard, Hook and Ladder 6, and J. H. Monroe, Hook and Ladder 9. Maus was buried from No. 159½ Essex Street, and Hughes from No. 10 Monroe Street.

The Board had been for six months without a Treasurer, when, on the 8th of November, Mr. King having signified his declination of the office, and Mr. Hatch refusing to serve, President Perley took the position. In December the Automatic Signal Company were authorized to make connections for the transmission of fire signals. At midnight, December 31, 1875, the fire bells rang out: "1-7-7-6—1-8-7-6," amid the clang of other bells, firework detonations, cheers and the discharge of fire-arms.

February 8, 1876, saw one of the most destructive fires New York had ever had. It broke out at 6:25 P. M., at No. 444 Broadway, destroyed, or partly destroyed and damaged 22 buildings, occupied by 37 firms, and the loss on an insurance of $3,418,099.97 was $1,750,000. While firemen were keeping a safe in the ruins of No. 444 Broadway cool with a line of hose, a wall fell and killed Foreman David Clute and David Muldrew, of Engine Company No. 30, and so injured Assistant Foreman John H. Bush, of the same company, that he died. Thomas J. Cortissos, also of the same company, was laid up for several months with injuries received.

In May new and complete regulations for the government of the Fire Alarm Telegraph, a revised code of signal stations, and new assignments to duty at them were promulgated, bringing the system up to that of the present day.

June 7, Medical Officer Dr. McMillan resigned, and was succeeded by Dr. A. J. Minor, the vice medical officer. Dr. Frank L. Ives was made vice medical officer. In September the estimate for the expenses of 1877 was made at $1,249,386. On the 22d of December Col. Carl Jussen was made Secretary of the Board.

COLONEL CARL JUSSEN, Secretary to the Board of Fire Commissioners, was born January 2d, 1843, in Julich, Rhenish Prussia. His family emigrated to this country in 1848, and after a sojourn of six months, settled in Columbus, Wisconsin, where his father engaged in business, and five years later removed to Watertown, Wisconsin. He received a common-school education in both places, and was also taught German by his mother, who superintended his education. In 1858 he went to Chicago, and served a two years, apprenticeship to an architect, returning to Watertown in 1860. He read law for a few months in the office of his brother in Madison, Wisconsin, and at the age of nineteen, in 1862, enlisted in the 23d Regiment, Wisconsin Volunteers (Infantry). He was made sergeant of Co. D before leaving the camp of instruction and rendezvous, and was promoted Sergeant-Major in May, 1863, and Adjutant in August, 1863. He was detailed as acting Assistant Adjutant General of the Third Brigade, Second Division, 10th Army Corps, and subsequently as Aide-de-Camp to Brigdier-General Alexander Shaler, then commanding first a brigade of the Reserve Corps of the Mississippi, and last the Third Division Seventh Army Corps, and the geographical district of the White River, Arkansas. He participated in a bloodless campaign in Kentncky to the Fall of 1862, then in the attack on Vicksburg from the north at the close of that year, the division resulting in the capture of Arkansas Post on the Arkansas River; the Vicksburg campaign under General Grant in 1863; the Bayou Teche campaign later in the same year; an expedition to Matagorda Bay, Texas, early in 1864;

the disastrous Red River campaign in the Spring of the same year; the expedition to Mobile Bay in the same year, and numerous small expeditions and raids. When Colonel Jussen was mustered out of service and honorably discharged on July 4th, 1865, he returned to Watertown, Wis., and engaged in business, remaining there until September, 1866, when he removed to this city. He was employed as draughtsman in the office of Renwick & Sands, architects, and was appointed clerk in the Fire Department in 1867. In 1875, was detailed as acting Secretary, and appointed Secretary on January 1, 1877.

CARL JUSSEN.

Colonel Jussen was married on October 14, 1868, to Camilla J. Shaler, oldest daughter of General Shaler, and has four children. At the same time he was appointed Aide-de Camp by General Shaler, Quartermaster on January 1, 1873, and Division Inspector on October 5, 1874, which latter position he still holds, having also served almost continuously as Acting Assistant Attorney General of the First Division N. G. S. N. Y. in charge of the Headquarters records.

The fire at the Brooklyn Theatre, on the night of the 5th of December, 1876, by which from 250 to 290 persons lost their lives — the number of victims could only be computed, after positive identification of the majority of them, from stray limbs and ashes, and reports of those who met them on the night of the disaster, never to be seen again—awakened a live and earnest interest in the condition of places of assembly in New York. On the 2d of January, 1877, an order was issued directing proper and complete examinations of theatres to discover how the public were protected, and to secure reports of what was needed to prevent such a disaster in this city.

LOCK ON DOOR, FOOT OF STAIRS OF THE BURNT BROOKLYN THEATRE.

Dr. A. J. Minor, medical officer, resigned in January, 1877, and was succeeded by Vice Medical Officer L. F. Ives, whose position was accepted by Dr. Pierre C. F. Des Landes. The cutting down of the estimates necessitated the creation of the rank of private, at $800 a year for new appointees. March 28th, Mr. C. De F. Burns, Librarian of the Lyceum, was appointed Assistant

Secretary. The recommendations to managers of places of public amusement not having been generally complied with, the Board directed the delinquents to procure proper means for extinguishing and preventing fires without delay, by virtue of the power given them in Section 5, Chapter 742, of the Laws of 1871, and persisted until they were obeyed.

JOHN J. GORMAN, nominated by Mayor Smith Ely, Jr., was confirmed January 3d to succeed Judge Hatch. Mr. King was elected President, and Gorman Treasurer. Mr. John J. Gorman is a native type of the self-made New Yorker. He was born in this city October 5, 1828, and educated in Public School No. 3, corner of Grove and Hudson Streets. At the age of eighteen he became a member of the Volunteer Fire Department (May 12, 1846), and from that date was a prominent member in several companies. At the disbandment of the Volunteer Fire Department he was foreman of Exempt Fire Engine Company.

JOHN J. GORMAN.

Few men now living can point to a record of greater activity and usefulness in Fire Department matters than Mr. Gorman. The highest offices and honors in the Department have been successively bestowed upon him in recognition of his services. He was elected Fire Commissioner in the Old Department, May 12, 1859, and held that position until 1862; during the last two years of that period he was President of the Board. In 1865 he was elected a Trustee of the Widows' and Orphans' Fund and elected Secretary thereof, which position he held successively for nineteen years; on the twentieth year he was chosen President of the Fund, which office he still holds. In May, 1877, Mr. Gorman was appointed Fire Commissioner of the Department as now organized, and continued in the Board until November 15, 1883, at which date he resigned, and was appointed one of the Police Magistrates of the city, which position he now occupies. During his terms of Fire Commissioner he introduced numerous improvements, and while President of said Board prepared and introduced a series of invaluable rules and regulations, one of which, regarding the mode for prevention of fire or panic in theatres, was favorably received.

On the organization of the widely known "Free Masons' Club," of this city, he was chosen President, and during its existence devoted considerable time and attention to its interests. In fact, no institution or society has ever been neglected where he was placed in a position of trust and confidence.

Jacob Springsteed, Superintendent of Horses, resigned June 13th, 1877. In

July the question of moving the telegraph operators from the first floor of Firemen's Hall to the third floor was considered, and preparations were made to fit up the new quarters. In August, William Terhune, Inspector of Combustibles, was removed and succeeded by Peter Seery, and James Cummings, Property-clerk, was succeeded by Samuel T. Keese. Commissioner Perley voted against these changes as against the removal of several clerks. The estimates for 1878 were made at $1,234,870. September 19th, Dr. Pierre F. C. Des Landes, medical officer, was removed, and Dr. Marion S. Butler was appointed. September 21st, Theodore Elliott, Foreman of Stables, was made Superintendent of Horses. October 23d, arrangements were made to have the gate-house of the Reservoir at Central Park connected with Firemen's Hall by telegraph, to enable the operators to signal for increased pressure of water when a large fire occurred. Pearce & Jones' bids of $7,300 for apparatus for the new telegraph plant, and one of $2,874 for the cabinet and wood-work were accepted in October.

Early in January interest in the cases of several clerks who had been removed, and who sought reinstatement in the courts, centered on the proceedings in Supreme Court, General Term. Ex-Commissioner Roswell D. Hatch appeared for the clerks, and Assistant Corporation Counsel Dean for the Commissioners. The clerks who undertook the proceedings were Joseph H. Munday, Michael F. Cummings and David Graham. The clerks removed were called up to say why they should not be ousted because their duties could be better performed by some one else. Judges Davis and Daniels concurred in Judge Brady's decision in favor of the clerks, who were reinstated.

The problem arising from the tendency to high·buildings, and an unsatisfactory water supply which prevented operations on the upper floors, was the subject of serious consideration, and on the 28th of January, 1878, John Ericsson, Charles H. Haswell and Julius H. Striedinger, Civil Engineer and Assistant Chief of the Department, C. O. Shay, were created a Board of Survey to test the aerial ladders in the possession of the Department, and report on their safety and efficiency. Mr. Ericsson did not serve. Mr. Haswell simply reported plans to improve the aerial ladders, but they were never carried out. The aerial ladders were never again used, and the one which broke on the Tweed Plaza was broken up at the repair shops. The three others were sold in 1885.

In February, were drawn up and promulgated business-like rules and regulations for the guidance and direction of heads of department superintendents, clerks and employees. March 13th, William Terhune, the reinstated Inspector of Combustibles, was removed, and Peter Seery was appointed. The same month Chief Orr, of the repair shop, was busy with several sets of swinging harness—a California invention now in general use here—which accelerated hitching up in an extraordinary degree. The new telegraph office was ready for occupation on the 26th of March, 1878. In April, in order that the means of communicating alarms of fire be less restricted, the Commissioners sanctioned the delivery of keys for street boxes to responsible citizens. The spring and summer of the year were uneventful so far as the history of the growth and progress of the Department are concerned. In August the estimates of the expenses for 1879 were made at $1,291,842.50, which were subsequently cut down to $1,254,970, including $30,000 for three new quarters for apparatus. In October, President Gorman reported his visit to the National Firemen's Tournament at Chicago, under resolution of the Board of August 7th, and submitted specifications and drawings of the Corps of Pompiers of St. Louis. November 26th, Assistant Fire Marshal Orr was removed for violating rules and causing false reports of official doings to be published, and ex-Trustee William Dodge succeeded him. Early in the autumn a subscription was started in the Department in aid of the Firemen's Charitable Association of New Orleans, to assist those who suffered from the yellow-fever epidemic. Nearly $2,160 was collected, of which $500 went to Memphis ; and the firemen of this city sold 1,160 tickets for a concert given at Gilmore's Garden, in aid of the sufferers, by the Firemen's Ball Committee of the Old Volunteer Fire Department. In December, the Firemen's Lyceum was divided into two equal parts, one of which was placed in each of the battalions of the Department as a Battalion Library, and the Assistant Foreman of the battalion quarters was designated as Librarian, and Assistant Secretary Charles De F. Burns was appointed General Librarian. The ringing of the tower bells south of 59th Street was discontinued on the 21st of December.

January, 1879, tested the resources of the Fire Department, and many persons were injured. On the 7th, J. W. Irving of Engine 29 was killed at No. 75 Vesey Street. January 14th, 23 engines and 7 hook and ladder companies were called to a fire which extended from No. 458 to No. 472 Broadway and No. 134 to 136 Grand Street, and caused a loss of $1,321,973.05. Fireman John Reilly, of Engine 17, was killed. January 17th, a fire started at No. 62 and 64 Worth Street, destroyed 4 buildings and damaged 13 others in Worth, Thomas, Duane, Church and Leonard Streets, and 48 firms lost $1,976,735. January 30th, Fireman Edward McGaffney, of Engine 33, had his sight destroyed at a fire at No. 483 and 485 Broadway. The families of the killed and the injured men were relieved by generous subscriptions and the proceeds of an entertainment at Niblo's Garden.

When the Legislature of 1879 met, various schemes to upset the Board of Fire Commissioners were started. Matters went so far that the candidates for four commissionerships to be created were named, but, on May 6th, Mayor Edward Cooper nominated Cornelius Van Cott to succeed Commissioner Perley, whose term of office had expired, and he was confirmed on the 20th of May. Two days later he again sat in the Board as Commissioner.

CORNELIUS VAN COTT, who succeeded Commissioner Perley in the Board of Fire Commissioners, was born in the City of New York, in the Fifteenth Ward, on President Lincoln's birthday, February 12, 1838. He was educated in Public School No. 16, in Thirteenth Street, of which David Patterson was the distinguished principal. He had an early love for books, and chose first the printer's trade, entering the establishment of the old American Tract Society. Subsequently he was apprenticed to Messrs. Dusenbury & Van Dusen, and learned the trade of carriage building. Mr. Van Dusen was foreman of Southwark Engine 38, then located in Ann Street. Young Van Cott quickly got a liking for the fireman's life, and in 1858, when twenty years old, joined Hose Company No. 7. From the very first he was in favor of a paid department. Mr. Van Cott was appointed an Inspector of Customs, a post which he surrendered to engage in the fire insurance business. After he had been elected a director of Ætna Fire Insurance Company (of which Colonel F. A. Conkling was president) he held for several years the office of vice-president of that corporation. He developed into a sound and capable financier, and in time became known as a first-class underwriter. He was also connected with the Hanover Insurance Company, and for a number of years has been a trustee of the West Side Savings Bank.

His education and his training peculiarly fitted him for the office of Fire Commissioner, and in 1873 Mayor Havemeyer appointed him to a seat in the Board. Mr. Van Cott served for six years and was finally elected treasurer. His services were recognized by a graceful testimonial from members of New York's best known merchants and business men. When Mayor Cooper came

CORNELIUS VAN COTT.

into power, 1879, Mr. Van Cott was reappointed by him, and his fellow commissioners elected him President of the Board, May 9, 1881. Shortly after he resigned the post of President. It was a great tribute to his integrity and ability that he (a Republican) should have been appointed by a Democratic Mayor and confirmed by a Democratic Board of Aldermen. Subsequently he was re-elected treasurer and again elected President in 1883. His term of office expired in 1885.

Among the acts which distinguished Mr. Van Cott while a Fire Commissioner were the abolition of bell-ringing (which latterly had become a nuisance), the repeal of the law passed for the removal of the Forty-second Street reservoir, the enlarging of the mains in the lower part of the city, the construction of floating steam fire engines, and the appointment of a municipal fire marshal independent of the insurance companies. He was in charge of the repair shops, and his mechanical knowledge was here eminently useful.

Ever punctual, strict as a disciplinarian, having a thorough knowledge of the minutest details of everything connected with the Department, always ready to listen to suggestions for the advancement of the interests of the service and every member connected with it, he had rendered himself by those means one of the most popular of Fire Commissioners.

June 16th, Foreman John McCabe, of Engine Company No. 14, took charge of the repair shops, and Chief Orr was sent to the Tenth Battalion. Serious charges were made against him, but he defeated them, and entirely vindicated himself. At this time Abner Greenleaf's Portable Water-Tower had been tested and put into service with a view of buying it. The first public test was in Washington Square, and the advantages of the apparatus were mmediately recognized. In July the position of Chief Operator was abolished, and J. Elliott Smith was appointed Assistant Superintendent of Telegraph. In August the Fire-boat Havemeyer was sent to her new berth at Pier No. 1, North River. The estimate of expenses for 1880 was made at $1,333,860, including $30,000 for three new company quarters, and $1,307,670 were appropriated. In November Fireman Henry C. Mount was fatally injured at a fire at the Eighth Avenue car stables, Forty-ninth Street and Eighth Avenue, and his family were placed beyond the reach of poverty by subscriptions collected by General Lloyd Aspinwall, General Martin T. McMahon, General C. K. Graham, Thurlow Weed, William Remsen, Henry G. Chapman, Jenkins Van Schaick, Lispenard Stewart, T. Searl Barclay, John D. Lawson, and Charles T. Ulrich.

January 28, 1880, Foreman John J. Bresnan, of Engine Company No. 33, and Francis J. Reilly, of Hook and Ladder Company No. 1, were made chiefs of battalion. Preparations were made to give the Blackwell's Island institutions and their inmates additional protection against fire by the construction of quarters for an engine. January 31st J. H. Emerich, Superintendent of Telegraph, was removed, and J. Elliott Smith was promoted to fill the vacancy. A. W. Parmelee was made Assistant Superintendent, and resigned ; but two days later the office of Superintendent and Assistant Superintendent were abolished, and those of Chief Operator and Assistant Chief Operator were created for Foreman Thomas Hutchinson and J. Elliott Smith, respectively. In February the officers and men of the Department were permitted to collect subscriptions for the *Herald* Irish Famine Fund, and paid in $3,062.77. February 30th a fierce and uncontrollable fire broke out in the sub-cellar of Nos. 384 and 386 Broadway, spread to and damaged seven other Broadway buildings, and two in White Street, did $750,000 damage, and called into service 23 engines and 10 hook and ladder companies. By the collapse of the building, due to improper foundations, Firemen Thomas J. Dougherty and John L. Cassidy, of Hook and Ladder Company No. 1, went down with the roof to their death. Subscriptions for their families realized $2,955, Dieckerhoff, Raffloer & Co. subscribing $250. Tefft, Griswold & Co. and other firms were equally generous. The Fire Commissioners ordered an investigation, and, on March 3d, Mr. Van Cott reported that the falling of the floors and roof of Nos. 384 and 386 Broadway were due to the supports of the central girder granite piers in the sub-cellar and iron columns in the basement, and Chief Bates was directed to report on all buildings similarly perilous in case of fire.

Under the Consolidation Act (Chapter 551 of the Laws of 1880) the Fire Commissioners, on the 3d of June, called on Henry J. Dudley, late Superintendent of Buildings, to turn over to the Board all papers, etc., in his custody, and to give his consent in writing to the transfer of the unexpended balance of the appropriation for the Department of Buildings for 1880 to the Fire Department, and the Board of Estimate and Apportionment was asked for such balance, amounting to $29,315.76. Mr. Dudley got out a writ of prohibition from Judge Joseph Potter, of the Supreme Court, against the Fire Commissioners. William L. Findley was, on the 4th of June, appointed Attorney to the Fire Department under the Consolidation Act, and on July 1st the position of Chief Operator and Assistant Chief Operator of Fire Alarm Telegraph were abolished, and that of Superintendent of Fire Alarm Telegraph created, and J. Elliott Smith was made Superintendent. At this time Abner Greenleaf introduced the water tower to the notice of the Commissioners. It seemed to meet a want of an apparatus to throw a strong stream into the upper floors of buildings, and was taken on test. July 27th, Mr. Dudley submitted gracefully to an adverse decision of Justice Potter, and surrendered his office and records. Assistant Fire Marshal William Dodge was placed in charge of them, at No. 2 Fourth Avenue, and on the 29th of July William P. Esterbrook was made

WILLIAM P. ESTERBROOK.

Inspector of Buildings, with a salary of $4,000 per annum, by the votes of Commissioners Van Cott and Gorman. Commissioner King voted for T. H. McAvoy. Edward G. Dumahaut was made Chief Clerk under Mr. Esterbrook, and in a short time the Bureau was further organized, as follows: Wm. H. Clare, Record Clerk; John J. Tindale, Plan Clerk; J. J. Carroll, Charles M. Seibert and Jas J. Giblin, clerks; Charles K. Hyde, Chief Examiner; Andrew Owens, Assistant Chief Examiner, and E. C. Maloy, William Winterbottom, P. B. McGivin, Henry La-Forge, John Hughes, Patrick Tallon, John Riley, Robert V.

MacKay and John H. Hyatt, Examiners. The Bureau speedily settled down to work. August 9th the Chief of the Department ordered an inspection of buildings to ascertain deficiencies in fire escapes, whether by absence, faulty construction or obstruction, and the Board directed Chief Bates and Assistant Chief Shay to examine all buildings in course of erection, construction or alteration, and report any violation or evasion of law, and officers and members of the Department were required to see that laws in relation to camp-stools and other obstructions in aisles, lobbies and other passages in places of amusement were strictly enforced. In September the estimate of the expenses of the Department were made at $1,568,959, including $60,000 for "a new floating engine," and $36,000 for the Bureau of Inspection of Buildings. In October Theodore Elliot, Superintendent of Horses, was succeeded by Frederick G. Gale.

In November and December Charles Oscar Shay, Assistant Chief of the Department, made, by order of the Board, the most exhaustive tests of the different capacities of several steam fire engines that have ever been made by any Fire Department officer. His reports are regarded to-day as texts for all engineers. They were with the Ahrens Manufacturing Company's engine, from Company 13; the Clapp & Jones engine, from Company 33, and the

Manchester Locomotive Works' (Amoskeag) engine, from Company 20. The final results were as follows:

GENERAL AVERAGES.

ENGINES.	STEAM PRESSURE.	WATER PRESSURE.	PRESSURE AT PIPES.
No. 13..............................	120.33	166.70	88.38
No. 20..............................	101.64	143.14	74.54
No. 33..............................	110.83	173.55	93.03

DISTANCE THROWING.

Distance in feet water was thrown, each engine tested three minutes each hour. The last two hours of trial distance not taken.

TIME.	7 to 8	8 to 9	9 to 10	10 to 11	11 to 12	12 to 1	1 to 2	2 to 3
Engine No. 13........	205	220	190	240	225	185	210	210
Engine No. 20........	...	...	...	205	200	220	180	...
Engine No. 33........	230	235	230	230	230	235	220	215

AMOUNT OF COAL CONSUMED.

All Engines................................ ....17,028 lbs.
Of which Engine No. 13 consumed................................4,960 lbs. 6 hours' work
Of which Engine No. 20 consumed................................5,692 lbs. 5½ hours' work
Of which Engine No. 33 consumed................................6,694 lbs. 8½ hours' work

AVERAGE PER HOUR.

Engine No. 13 consumed...496 lbs. per hour
Engine No. 20 consumed...993½ lbs. per hour
Engine No. 33 consumed...776⅞ lbs. per hour

During the year "four-way" connections for concentrating water from one to four engines were applied to Hook and Ladder Companies 1, 3, 5, 6, 8, 9, 10 and 12, to reach the tops of high buildings with powerful streams.

In January, 1881, Dr. Samuel M. Johnson was appointed Vice Medical Officer. Charles H. Haswell was directed to prepare plans and specifications for a new floating engine. In March Chief Bates and Assistant Chief Shay were created engineers by the Board for the purposes of Section 3, of Chapter 726, Laws of 1873, giving the "Engineers in command" at a fire authority to raze by explosion any building, or buildings, to arrest the progress of a fire. The city was divided into two medical districts, divided by Broadway, Twenty-third Street and Fourth Avenue to Fordham. March 30th the tests of the water-tower had been so satisfactory that the Commissioners recommended its purchase for $4,000 to the Common Council. May 9th Cornelius Van Cott was elected President of the Board, and a week after Captain McCabe was made Chief of Battalion. In August Mr. Van Cott resigned as President, and became Treasurer, Mr. John J. Gorman taking the vacant position. September 13th Henry D. Purroy was confirmed as Commissioner, vice Vincent C. King, on a nomination of Mayor William R. Grace, made on the 10th of May, 1880, and laid on the table.

HENRY D. PURROY was born in this city on August 27th, 1848. He was the son of the late John B. Purroy, a prominent lawyer many years ago in this

city.   He was educated in St. John's College, Fordham, and admitted to the
bar November, 1869.   He was the first representative for the annexed district
in the Board of Aldermen, and was President of the Board.   Mr. Purroy is
a Democrat in politics, and until 1881 was connected with Tammany Hall,
having been one of the thirteen Sachems in 1879, 1880 and 1881, and chairman
of its Executive Committee during 1880.   He joined the County Democracy in
1884, and is now Chairman of its Executive Committee.   He was appointed
Fire Commissioner in 1881—elected President of the Fire Department in

HENRY D. PURROY.

1885.   He introduced many improvements into the Department, among them
being the establishment (two years prior to the Civil Service Act) of a School
of Probation of applicants for appointment as firemen, the organization of the
Life Saving Corps the remodelling of the Department houses, the building of
the Fire Boat, etc., etc.

On the 29th of September the estimate for 1882 was made at $1,498,850,
including $134,000 for new quarters.   The amount of $1,464,200 was appropriated.   October 8th the Examining Board and Examining Board of Engineers were consolidated with Chiefs Shay, Bonner, Rowe, Denman and Reilly
as its members.   October 10th seventeen engines and six hook and ladder
companies battled for 18 hours with a fire that destroyed and damaged the
stables of the Fourth Avenue Railroad Company and other of their property, the Morrell storage warehouse and dwellings, and caused a loss estimated at $2,392,691. Foreman D. J. Meagher and Fireman Thos. Carney,

of Hook and Ladder Company No. 3, and Private John Flanagan, of Engine Company No. 1, were slightly injured while at work. October 14th Chief of Battalion Gilbert J. Orr was relieved from active service, but retained as a member of the uniformed force at a salary of $1,250 per annum, and Chief of Battalion W. W. Rhodes was retired on a similar pension. Next day Foreman Michael F. Reeves and Francis Mahedy were made Chiefs of Battalion. In November the Board accepted an offer of the Standard Oil Company of the service at fire in New York of the company's boats Standard, F. W. De Voe, Daylight, Brilliant and C. R. Stone. November 9th the ricketty buildings, Nos. 53 and 55 Grand street, condemned by the Department fell, killing 9 persons and injuring 5. The Commissioners instituted a searching investigation and passed resolutions to take such action official and legislative to prevent such calamities in the future. An investigation resulted in the removal of Chief Examiner Charles K. Hyde, of the Bureau of Inspection of Buildings, for neglect of duty.

In November, Commissioner Purroy reported $2,371.75 collected from the members and employees of the Department for the relief of the sufferers by the forest fires in Michigan.

December 12th, the frightful calamity of the Ring Theatre, at Vienna, prompted the following resolution and subsequent satisfactory action:

Resolved, That an immediate inspection be made of all theatres and places of amusement wherein machinery and scenery are used in the city of New York by the Chiefs of Battalions in their respective districts, with directions to make a detailed report of such inspection in writing to this Board, with an accurate description of each structure, the material of which it is constructed, its size and seating capacity, the location of the dressing-rooms, carpenter and paint shops, the facilities for egress in case of fire or other alarm, stating width of entrances and exits, the method of sending out an alarm, and the exact distance from stage to alarm box, and whether a more direct communication cannot be established between such theatres or places of amusement and the headquarters of this Department; also the location of gas jets or lights of any other description used around the stage or other parts of the building, the protection from ignition, with recommendations, where necessary, from further protection from fire; also the fire appliances on hand and ready for use in case of fire, and whether proper care is taken of each appliances; also any violation of the Combustible or Building Laws; also of what material the proscenium arch is made, its height from the stage, and whether it extends to the roof of the building; the openings that are in it above the stage, and if there are any openings in the roof of the building, with such recommendations as may be deemed necessary for the further protection of life and property in all such places of amusement in the city of New York.

December 24th, all but 6 engines and 2 hook and ladder companies below Thirty-fourth Street were called out to fight four fires that were burning at the same time. One at No. 61 East Twelfth Street did $500 damage; another at No. 359 Broadway—a dry goods warehouse—$195,000 damage; a third at No. 140 Centre Street, slight damage, and the other a tea warehouse, Nos. 71 and 72 South Street, $1,025,800 damage.

One of the last acts of the Board in 1881 was to require the Inspector of Buildings to report within fifteen days all modifications of or additions to the laws relating to buildings or the rules governing the Bureau of Inspection of Buildings, which, in his opinion, might be necessary to insure the better protection of life and property. Early in February the medical force of the Department was made one Medical Officer and two Vice Medical Officers; and Dr. Robert A. Joyce was appointed to the latter position. January 28th, on the report of Battalion Chief Bresnan, the Commissioners adopted a resolution recommending the use of asbestos cloth or other non-inflammable material for stage costumes, and that they be daily inspected.

January 31st, 1882, at 10:12 P. M. a destructive and fatal fire broke out in the Potter or *World* Building, which faced on Park Row, Beekman

BURNING OF THE WORLD BUILDING.

Street and Nassau Street. It did more than $400,000 damage, and twelve persons were in various ways killed. The fire directed attention to a source of peril to life and property which had before created apprehension, and on the 3d of February Commissioner Purroy offered the following resolution, which was adopted :

Whereas : there have recently been constructed in this city a great number of large flats and business houses, reaching in many cases to a height exceeding one hundred feet; and whereas the extreme height to which it is possible to stretch and manage extension ladders have been probably reached, and does not exceed seventy feet, thus making futile the best efforts of this Department toward rescuing the occupants of the upper stories of the buildings above mentioned whenever such occupants are cut off from escape from below ; therefore be it

Resolved, That the Chief of Department be and is hereby instructed (keeping in view the increased height of the buildings above mentioned) to report to this Board in writing his views in regard to what improvement in the appliances and complements of the Department, what changes in regard to the erection and construction of fire-escapes, and what regulation as to the construction and maintenance of fire-proof shutters are necessary, together with any suggestions in regard to the better protection of life and property he may deem advisable.

Chief Bates' report favored the providing of each Hook and Ladder Company with scaling-ladders, one of fifteen feet and one of twenty feet, and a life-line, and the principal companies were thus equipped. Commissioner Purroy's foresight was displayed in the resolution which resulted in the " doubling up " of the most important companies.

March 15th Engine Company No. 49 was organized on Blackwell's Island. In the spring a malicious fellow, discharged from the service of the Department, put the Department and the police to much trouble and expense by sending out false alarms. In May Pusey & Jones, of Wilmington, Del., was given the contract for a new floating fire engine, their bid being $45,000, and Clapp & Jones contracted to construct the engines for $11,800. Later on the boat was named the Zophar Mills (Engine 51), in honor of an old and distinguished volunteer fireman, and stationed at Pier No. 42, North River. July 14th three fierce fires were burning at the same time in the lower part of the city, namely, in a cotton storage at Nos. 15 to 25 Whitehall Street; the Empire Paint Works, at Nos. 243 and 245 Pearl Street, and at the soap manufactory at Nos. 418 to 424 Washington Street. More than $170,000 damage was done, but the loss was insignificant when the prevention of a conflagration in each case is considered. To these three fires 42 of the 67 fire extinguishing companies in the city were called, with 417 officers and men. July 31st 17 engines and 5 hook and ladder companies were on duty at a fire which started in Hecker's Mills and burned to Water, Monroe and Cherry Streets and Pike Street and Slip, doing $202,000 damage. In September the estimate for 1883 was made at $1,671,905 and $1,551,345 were appropriated. D. G. Gale, Superintendent of Horses, was removed, and James Shea was appointed.

The training stables for the green horses of the Department were established at the vacated quarters of Engine Company No. 37, at No. 58 Lawrence Street.

Commissioner Purroy made a report favoring the appointment of an instructor in life-saving, and on January 24th Chris Hoell, of the St. Louis Pompier Corps, was engaged to instruct the Life-Saving Corps, a branch of the School of Instruction, which was located in the quarters of Engine Company No. 47, in their duties. The Corps were instructed and trained in the use of scaling and ordinary ladders and life-lines and other life-saving appliances, at the Old Sugar House, at the foot of West 158th Street. Chief Bonner was at the head of the School and instructor in the practical duties of a fireman, and candidates for appointment had to pass the School, and get a report on the degree of proficiency exhibited and the branch of the service for which they were best qualified.

February 5th Police Inspector Byrnes was thanked for the arrest of the "fire-alarm fiends" and the breaking up of an organized plan of systematic and malicious

CHRIS HOELL.

annoyance to the active members of the Department by sending out false alarms.

During the month, Water Tower No. 1 was placed on test service in the quarters of Engine Company No. 7. In March the District Messenger Companies were required to connect their offices with Fire Headquarters, as several serious fires, and the death of at least one person, were found to be due to a popular belief that the companies had direct communication with the Fire Department.

January 3d, Chief of Battalion Hugh Bonner was made Second Assistant Chief of the Department, and on the 11th Foreman Thomas Gooderson, of Engine Company No. 35, was promoted to the rank of Chief of Battalion. The peril to the city in the event of the destruction of the telegraph apparatus at Headquarters had been considered for several years, and Commissioner Purroy's suggestion that a duplicate set of apparatus be made and put in a fire-proof building is about to be carried out.

STEAMBOAT ZOPHAR MILLS.

The new fire-boat, the Zophar Mills, was at this time the subject of much comment and the object of much attention, as it was intended to be the most powerful and useful fire extinguishing auxiliary in the world and worthy of the name of the veteran and famous fireman which had been given it. The boat was known as Engine No. 51, and the tests of her pumps, which were made by the Clapp & Jones Manufacturing Company, of Hudson, N. Y., were made at Pier No. 52, East River, on the 27th of March, 1883. Of it the *Fireman's Journal* said:

"She was taken to the dock at the foot of Montgomery street and subjected to an eight hours' test, throwing water in a variety of ways. The first test was with eight 1 1-2 inch streams, then the lines were Siamesed into four larger streams, and in every way the most satisfactory results were obtained. With a 3 1-4 inch hose and a 2 1-2 inch nozzle, a stream was thrown some 280 feet, and but for a cross wind a much greater distance would have been obtained. It was a wet, disagreeable day, with a keen, cutting wind blowing, so that the distance record did not do justice to the work, but the pumps proved satisfactory in every particular."

The official report of Charles Oscar Shay, Assistant Chief, was that the tests were entirely satisfactory. The capacity of the pumps was found to be, with the four pistons, traveling in the aggregate 1,200 feet per minute, and, with the usual percentage deducted for friction, etc., the actual discharge would be about 2,200 U. S. gallons per minute.

An exceedingly favorable report was made afterward by B. F. Isherwood, Chief Engineer, U. S. N.; Theo. Zeller, Chief Engineer, U. S. N., and Robert Domby, Chief Engineer, U. S. N., of the Bureau of Steam Engineering, Navy Department, April 23, 1883. Robert R. Farrell, Foreman of the Fire-boat Havemeyer, was made Foreman, of the Zophar Mills, and the first firemen were : Henry Albright, William J. de l'Armitage, John Brady, John Stenson and Alfred Lewis, privates ; P. J. McEntee, Andrew Gaffney, and Wm. M. Gordon, firemen. The temporary organization of this company, on December 31, 1882, was : C. D. Purroy, Foreman; John Barber, Assistant Foreman; Patrick Riley, Thomas Tallman, and John Iles, Engineers ; Patrick Barker and Thomas Friston, Pilots ; and A. J. Cook, John J. McNamee, John E. Boyle, P. J. McEntee, W. M. Gordon, Andrew Gaffney, Thomas O'Halloran and Abraham Walton, firemen.

May 9th, 1883, Mayor Franklin Edson reappointed the Hon. John J. Gorman, and, on motion of Henry D. Purroy, the Board was reorganized with Cornelius Van Cott, President, and Henry D. Purroy, Treasurer. Christopher Hoell, of the St. Louis Fire Department, who had instructed classes in life-saving with various appliances of his invention, severed his connection with the Department in May, and a complimentary and well-deserved eulogy was passed by the Board.

In June, keyless street boxes for the transmission of fire-alarms were put up. The first step toward underground telegraphic communication was on the

RICHARD CROKER.

3d of August, when the Attorney asked what power the Department had to put fire telegraph wires underground, and, if none, what action was necessary to acquire it. Later on, Superintendent J. Elliott Smith was directed to visit Washington and report on a system of underground telegraphic communication there. In September the estimate for the cost of the Department for 1884 was fixed at $1,685,129.20. On the 21st of November Richard Croker, a practical and experienced fireman and engineer, was appointed Commissioner by Mayor Edson, vice John J. Gorman appointed Police Justice.

The question of protecting what is termed the "dry goods district," which may be said to cover the territory bounded by West Broadway, Spring Street, Crosby and Elm Streets and Chambers Street, had become a burning one. Mr. Purroy made a comprehensive and able report which favored a system by which water could be pumped into portable tanks from the rivers to points of vantage by the fire-boats, and taken from the tanks by the land engines. In 1883 double companies were established in the quarters of Engine Companies 12, 13, 16, 31 and 33, and Hook and Ladder Companies 6 and 9. The prominent fires of the year were the Inman Pier fire, February 1; loss, $391,000; and mercantile property, at Nos. 537 and 539 Broadway, September 18th; loss, $435,721.

FIRE.—INMAN PIER.

The "dry goods district" is the richest in the city. In one block of it, bounded by Worth, Thomas, Church Streets and Broadway, the property (including buildings and contents) is worth $25,000,000. From 1877 to 1882 the total losses by fire in the dry-goods districts amounted to $6,490,496; the fire insurance premiums received (less expenses) were $2,345,000; losses over receipts, $4,145,496. No wonder the companies declined to insure fully, and the merchants tried Europe in vain. More water was wanted to induce the insurance men to accept more risks. Chief Bates instanced Ridley's store from Orchard to Allen Streets, and also Lord & Taylor's, each taking in a large space, that were in danger of destruction by fire from a lack of water. "If ever a fire gets hold of these places," said he, "it will burn pretty smartly. In that neighborhood all the pipes are small, and the water pressure is very light. For ordinary uses, it runs well enough, but not for extraordinary fires."

In 1882 there were 2,001 fires in this city, which damaged or destroyed 942 buildings.

Loss on buildings and vessels...$	978,132
Loss on contents...	3,217,828
Total loss...	4,195,900
Estimated insurance on buildings and vessels...................................	9,880,656
Estimated insurance on contents...	11,471,745
Total estimated insurance..$	21,352,401

"Take the line of Church Street," said Mr. Pollak, then of the North British Mercantile, now of the Niagara; "and you will see buildings from 60 to 100 feet in height full of inflammable material. They contain costly silks, averaging in value in single buildings a million of dollars. Church Street is not over forty feet in width, but there is hardly a warehouse on that line from Vesey Street up that has an iron shutter above the first floor. There is nothing to protect one building from its neighbor opposite in case of fire. In Leonard Street, near Church Street, there is a high building containing enormous wealth. Though it is what we call a brick and stone structure, yet a fire opposite would reach it and cause it to burn down in a very short time. If the wind blew that way, everything would be against the Fire Department. The water in that district is at the very lowest pressure."

"For the better protection of the vast property in the dry goods district," said President Van Cott, of the Fire Commission, "the question of the water supply is a very important one. There is no doubt that it is entirely inadequate on the line of West Broadway. The Fire Commissioners think that stationery cisterns should be placed at all important points in the district, and direct connections made with the Croton water mains. These cisterns could be placed under the sidewalks and properly covered. Then, in the event of a great fire, we could raise the cover and turn on the water to the cistern, into which the suction-pipes of half a dozen engines could be placed at once. Then we would have an abundance of water which cannot be obtained from the hydrants."

WATER TANK.

"Tanks would be required," said Chief Bates, "at such places as Ridley's in Grand Street, Claflin's, and in Nassau Street. At these points there is danger of a very serious fire. The main water pipes are laid four feet from the surface of the ground, and if the cisterns were put five feet under, they could easily be filled with water   There could be stopcocks to shut off the water from the cistern when full.   When an engine has a solid body of water to draw from, she can throw a stream of enormous height and force."

On this subject Lieutenant Kensehan, of Engine No. 31, said: "Some years ago, at the big fire on Grand Street and Broadway, where two of our men were killed, we had about twelve lines on the roof.   But there was a fatal lack of water.   It would just spurt out and then go back.   That was a $3,000,000 fire, destroying five buildings.   Some companies get into a main when there is enough water; there are other pipes which won't give any. When these companies get into a main, the best engine gets all the water.

Mr. F. C. Moore, Second Vice-President of the Continental Fire Insurance Company, said : "There are two things which tend to keep alive the apprehension of a great fire in that district which will extend from river to river. One is the fault of the construction of the buildings, many of them being above the height which the Fire Department can reach with their steamers.   The other is the lack of water.   The great fire in Worth Street in 1876 proved that there were faults in the division walls not known to the underwriters."

The proposed tank system has obtained great favor in all quarters, and may be carried out.   When the aqueduct is finished, the Fire Department will have all the water necessary for coping with the greatest of conflagrations.

Mr. Purroy's suggestion in regard to a portable water tank to protect the dry goods district had not been forgotten.   Chief John McCabe, in charge of the repair shops carried out the idea, and in February had built a tank on Mr. Purroy's design, on the 25th of February the Board ordered a test of it.

The test was entirely satisfactory, and the tank was put in service on the 15th of March, 1884, under the following general order :

"A portable water-tank to furnish water from the rivers to the land engines, after being supplied therewith by the fire-boats and a four-wheel hose-tender with 600 feet of new rubber 3¼-inch hose, will be put in service on the 17th instant, and pending the preparation of the quarters of Engine Company No. 20, where they are to be permanently located, they will be temporarily placed in the quarters of Engine Company No. 27.   The following rules will govern their use :

1. At any fire occurring within the distance of a half mile from the river-fronts where there is either a failure or scarcity of water, the officer will, if in his discretion he deem it advisable, call for the tank, the tender and a fire-boat by means of the special call 18-1, followed first by the number of the station at which the tank is required to be placed, and second, by the number of the station on the river-front nearest to which the fire-boat is required to report as for example ; the fire being at Worth Street and West Broadway, the call will be 18-1 (the preliminary signal or notice that the tank, tender and fire-boat will be required), 82 (the station at Washington and Jay streets, where the tank is to be placed), and 81 (the station at West and Harrison streets, where the fire-boat is to report).

2. When the special call is sent, the officer in command will at once dispatch a disengaged team of horses from among those at the fire, or elsewhere available, with a detail of two men, to bring the tank to the point designated.

3. Upon the receipt of the special call, the tender designated to co-operate will immediately proceed in advance of the tank to the point indicated for the latter, and stretch its hose by the nearest and best route towards the point on the river-front where the fire-boat lands.

4. The fire-boat at the time designated to respond to alarms from the last station indi-

cated in the call shall at once proceed to the nearest available landing place thereto, and immediately stretch sufficient hose to connect with the hose from the tank.

5. When the officer in command determines upon sending the call he shall at once make all necessary arrangements by detailing officers and men, obtaining additional hose and making such other dispositions as will secure prompt connections between the fire-boat, tank and hand engines, and guard against interference with and damage to the lines of hose.

6. Nothing contained in Section 1 of this order shall be construed to prevent the use of the tank, tender and fire-boat at a greater distance than a half mile from either line or in any other that may be deemed proper by the officer in command at the fire."

In March, Commissioner Purroy studied, under the authorization of the Board, fire extinguishing methods at Milwaukee, Detroit and other cities, and made a report thereon. On the 9th of April, the Board recognized the bravery of Fireman John Binns, Thomas F. Barrett and Michael E. C. Graham, who rescued Louis Castaign at the fire at the St. George's flats, Nos. 223 and 225 East Seventeenth Street.

April 23d, 1884, Chief of Battalion, John W. Miller, was retired on a pension of $1,250 a year, and on the 29th came the retirement of Eli Bates, Chief of the Department on $2,350 a year on the report of the medical officers of disability caused or induced by the actual performance of the duties of his position. Their retirements led to the following promotions and changes: Charles Oscar Shay, Assistant Chief to be Chief of the Department; Hugh Bonner, Second Assistant Chief, Assistant Chief; John McCabe, Chief of Battalion in charge of the repair shops; Second Assistant Chief, Foreman Charles D. Purroy, Engine Company No. 1, and Foreman Thomas Lally, of Hook and Ladder Company No. 1, Chief of Battalion, and Foreman John Castles, of Engine Company No. 18, in charge of repair shops. Up to this time Christopher Hoell, who had instructed the classes in life saving had furnished scaling ladders and belts to the Department under the contract, but Foreman Castles began to make them on models prepared by Chief McCabe. In May, the office of Superintendent of horses was abolished, and Superintendent Joseph Shay was appointed a foreman with supervision of the Training and Hospital Stables and the selection of horses for the Department. June 10, 1884, the Board offered advancement to any member of the force below the rank of Foreman, and suitable recognition if above that rank, or to a uniformed member who should invent a proper means of casting a life line to the top of a building from a distance of not less than 300 feet within thirty days. October 10th, the estimate of the expenses for 1885 was fixed at $1,774,773. During the year resolutions were adopted that applicants for promotion must have passed through the classes of the school of instruction, and that promotion to the grade of Engineers and Assistant Engineers must be made from men who had attended the repair shops thirty days. It was also provided that men once detailed to one branch of the service should not be transferred to another except in cases of emergency.

In May, the improper and unlooked for uses which persons holding badges put them to caused their recall, and for the use of citizens and the press, officers and members of the uniformed force and the ununiformed officials and subordinates of the Department three badges were designed.

February 4, the Board received the resignation of Mr. William P. Esterbrook, Inspector of Buildings. Mr. Esterbrook's integrity, energy and zeal were conspicuous, but he was independent of office and the severity of his connection with the Department was due to a controversy about the putting of fire escapes on the the flats of John H. Sherwood at Forty-fourth Street and Fifth Avenue. The act of resignation was considered hasty and unnecessary. The same month a plan of lightening the labors of the horses and men of the Department by having alarms sent so as to pass by a number of company quarters remote from the fire signalled was suggested, but so far it has not ripened.

February 16th, 1885, Mr. Esterbrook was succeeded as Inspector of Buildings by Mr. Albert F. D'Oench, a practical builder and architect.

ALBERT FREDERICK D'OENCH, Superintendent of Buildings, was born at St. Louis, Mo., on Christmas Day, 1852. His father, William D'Oench, one of the most prominent of St. Louis' citizens, was of Flemish origin and was born in Silesia, and his mother, whose family were Alsatians, was born in Hamburg. They came to America in 1838 and grew up with St. Louis. Mr. D'Oench studied at Washington University and received the degree of M. E. in 1872 when he went to Stuttgart and took the three years course of architecture. After traveling in Germany, Austria, Switzerland, France and England he returned to America in the Fall of 1875 to become a draughtsman in the office of Mr. Lopold Eidlitz the well known archi-

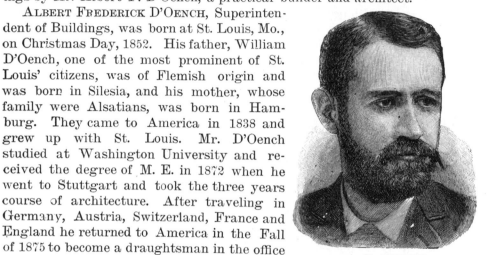

A. F. D'OENCH,
Superintendent of Buildings.

tect and once principally engaged on drawings for the new Capitol at Albany. Afterwards he worked in the office of Messrs. Richard M. Hunt and Edward E. Raht, finishing his course of training in 1881. He established himself as an architect in 1882 and in 1885 on the strongest and most flattering recommendations was appointed Inspector of Buildings to succeed Mr. W. P. Esterbrook by Commissioners Van Cott, Purroy and Croker and under the law was made Superintendent, January 12, 1886. His administration of the affairs of the Bureau of Inspection of Buildings has caused neither his friends nor the public to regret his selection which it is fair to state that in transacting business he departed little from the course laid down by his predecessor.

Belts and snaps were provided for members of the Life Saving Corps to enable them to attach themselves to use their hands and arms freely when secured by the snaps to ladders. Gilbert T. Orr, Chief of Battalion, relieved from duty at fires, died on the 9th of March. March 23d, the following important resolutions were adopted :

Whereas, frequent and sometimes very serious delays occur in sending alarms after the discovery of fires, notwithstanding the means afforded for that purpose ; and

Whereas, The first minutes after the outbreak of fires, if the alarm is properly sent, are of greater value to the householders and owners in the saving of loss, and to the firemen, than subsequent hours of labor and effort to extinguish fires ; and

Whereas, the delay in sending alarms for fires generally results from want of information as to the location of the nearest fire-alarm box ; therefore

Resolved, That the cards prepared under the direction of this Board, showing the location of the fire-alarm box nearest to each building in this city, giving directions as to the sending of alarms, and suggesting precautions to be taken against fires resulting from some of the most prolific causes, be turned over to the Chief of Department for distribution through the companies in their respective districts, with directions to have one or more carefully and neatly tacked up in each building, above the reach of children, in as conspicuous a position as practicable, and preferably in the various classes of buildings, as follows :

    In dwellings of all kinds and office buildings, in the main hallways;

    In hotels, factories, warehouses, stables, etc., in the offices or near the front doors ;

    In schools, churches, etc., in the vestibules or lobbies;

    In places of amusement, in or near the ticket office and upon the stages ;

    In mercantile establishments, etc., in the offices or near the desks ; and

Resolved, That the owners and occupants of buildings be requested, by the representatives of this Department detailed to distribute the cards, to permit them to be as conspicuously placed as possible, and that the names and addresses of all persons refusing to receive such cards be reported to the Board.

April 6th, 1884.—The General Term of the Supreme Court having reversed the decision of the Board which dismissed private Robert L. Kent for drunkenness while on duty, and substituted a punishment of suspension from pay and duty for six months, thereby establishing the guilt of the officer and the correctness of the Board's decision, the attorney was directed to appeal the case.

ELWARD SMITH.

Mr. ELWARD SMITH, a veteran fireman appointed by Mayor Grace to succeed Mr. Cornelius Van Cott, whose term of office had expired, took his seat in the Board on the 9th of May, and Mr. Henry D. Purroy was elected President and Mr. Richard Croker Treasurer.

In April structures put up on the south side of Sixty-second Street, west of Tenth Avenue. fell, killing several persons. They were erected by the "jerry" builder Buddensiek, and on the 15th of this month two neglectful examiners of the Bureau of Buildings were removed.

In order to more thoroughly equip the members of the Department for life-saving emergencies, the following resolution was adopted on May 20th:

Whereas, The records of this Department show that since the extension of the life-saving service to all the Hook and Ladder Companies, in August, 1883, the lives of the following persons, viz.: John Hurley, at fire No. 332 East Thirtieth Street, on September 25th, 1883; Louis Castaign, at fire St. George's Flats, on April 7, 1884; Kate Leary, at fire Nos. 16 and 18 South William Street, on February 21st, 1885; a man, woman and boy, named Koernich, and an unknown woman, at fire No. 672 First Avenue, on May 3, 1885, have been saved by means of the scaling-laders and other appliances in the hands of the members of the Life-Saving Corps; and

Whereas, It is believed that the above list of persons saved might have been increased if it had been feasible to extend the life-saving service to the Engine Companies of the Department, for the reason that life is usually lost at fires in the first few moments immediately preceding the alarms, and the Engine Companies, as a rule, arrive ahead of the Hook and Ladder Companies; therefore,

Resolved, That the Foreman in charge of Repair Shops be instructed to fit up, with promptness, the four-wheeled tenders of the Department; in accordance with the suggestions made by the Assistant Chief of Department, so that they will each safely carry at least two of the scaling-ladders and other appliances needed for life saving at fires; and further

Resolved, That with a view of affording some hope to persons who may be forced, as a last chance, to jump from burning buildings, the Assistant Chief of Department be authorized to have made the safest possible jumping-sheet, so that, if adopted, the firemen may be instructed in the use of such sheets, and they may be placed on each Hook and Ladder truck and four-wheeled tender in the Department.

Resolved, That while the air-gun invented by Otto Rigl, and approved by the Assistant Chief, is being approved and perfected, the Board authorize the Chairman of the Committee on Apparatus and Telegraph to purchase six Travis guns with all their attachments, at a cost of $55 each, to be used in firing a life-line to persons in danger on the roofs or in the windows of burning houses.

All these life-saving services are now carried by the truck companies.

June 12th, under the provisions of Chapter 456 of the Laws of 1885, Mr. A. F. D'Oench, Inspector of Buildings, was made Superintendent of Buildings. July 1st, Mr. Charles De F. Burns, Assistant Secretary, resigned to become Secretary of the Department of Public Parks, and the Board recognized his services in very complimentary resolutions. Mr. Enoch Vreeland, Jr., succeeded Mr. Burns as Assistant Secretary on the 19th of August.

In September Chief Charles O. Shay reported the distribution of cards showing the location of alarm boxes, as provided in the resolution of March 22d, as completed. Superintendent D'Oench submitted regulations for the inspection of passenger elevators, and on October 10th they were approved, and Mr. William H. Class was promoted to the supervision of passenger elevators, with M. T. Gaughan and John Crossen as assistants. This action led to a tempest in a teapot. The Board of Examiners, created by the act which reorganized the Bureau of Buildings, who held that the assistants, or "inspectors" or "supervisors," must pass an examination before them, and that they had a right to make rules not only for their government, but for the Commissioners. Mr. W. L. Findley, Attorney for the Department; George W. Van Sicklen, the Examiner's lawyer, and others, spoiled much paper on opinions, and Corporation Counsel Lacombe ended the matter by deciding that the examination was not necessary.

The Departmental estimate for 1886 was approved at $1,904,156.10.

In November, 1885, the following rules fixed the stations of Hook and Ladder men at fires:

I.—Commanding officers of Hook and Ladder companies shall have exclusive control and direction in the raising and placing of all ladders, and shall not permit their use by anyone before they are in proper and safe position; they shall not be used at any time thereafter by any person not a regular or probationary member of the Department, or persons rescued, and by them only under the following restrictions:

1. The number of persons permitted on the various sized ladders simultaneously shall not exeeed—

To each 10 to 15 feet ladder, one.

To each 20, 25 or 30 feet ladder, two.

To each ladder more than 30 feet, three.

2. When used for pipe-lines, the pipeman only will be permitted at the pipe, and he will fasten the line to an iron round if conveniently near, or if not, he will hitch it on two wooden rounds, in such manner as to prevent the kinking of the pipe.

3. If it be a 35-feet ladder, the second man shall take position just below the point at which the pressure bends the ladder, where the line will also be fastened, preferably to an iron round, or in lieu thereof, two wooden rounds. With all other ladders, the second man shall take position with feet resting upon the first round above the point where the poles support the ladder, where the line shall be fastened in the manner above prescribed.

4. If a third man is required, he shall take position on the ladder near the butt.

5. While their services are not needed in shifting the line, the second and third man will not be required to maintain the prescribed position.

6. After shifting the line, the second and third man will resume the position prescribed, and fasten it as before indicated.

7. Before shifting a line from a ladder over 25 feet long, it must be cleared of water.

8. Officers and reliefs may use the ladders at any time, but must not pass the second man except at the point above designated for fastening the line.

February, 1886, apprehension was felt along the line of the new aqueduct because of the storage of large quantities of high explosives near the shafts. An explosion at Fordham Landing made decisive action necessary, and Mr. Peter Seery, Inspector of Combustibles, made such seizures, reports and regulations as to reduce danger to a minimum. March 12th, 1886, Chief Francis Mahedy lost his life from injuries received in a collision while going to a fire.

April 23d Mr. Elward Smith offered a resolution that "Henry D. Purroy be and hereby is appointed a committee to visit England and France for the purpose of examining into the fire departments of London, Paris and other large cities, with reference to their method of appointment, tenure of office, organization, discipline, apparatus and water-supply for fire extinguishing purposes."

Under this Mr. Purroy made a memorable and satisfactory visit to Europe. While he derived but little information or few hints from foreign fire extinguishing methods, his reception everywhere was of the most cordial and gratifying nature. On his return Mr. Purroy published the following:

" A charming and painstaking host in his native country is Colonel A. C. Couston, Chief of the Paris Fire Department or *Regiment des Sapeurs Pompiers de Paris*. This gallant and handsome officer was born in 1834 and en-

tered the French Army when 18.   Three years later he was promoted to a
Sub-Lieutenancy in the 5th Infantry.   He first smelled powder in the Crimean

COL. A. C. COUSTON.

War and was present
at the burning of
Varna, the battles of
Balaclava and Inker-
man and in the attack
of the Lex on the 2d of
May was wounded and
was mentioned for
conspicuous courage
in the orders of the
day.   He was also at
the battle of Tractir,
and at the taking of
Sebastopol he was
again noticed for val-
or and was made
Lieutenant on the
30th of August, 1826.
In 1857 he distin-
guished himself by
saving an army cap-
tain who was in im-
minent danger of
drowning in the
Rhone at Arles and
was commissioned as
Doctor of Schools and
Instructor in Rifle
Practice.   At the
breaking out of the
Italian war in 1859

he was assigned as Lieutenant of Voltigeurs and for his conduct on
the field was decorated with the ribbon of the order of Military Valor of
Sardinia.   In 1862 and 1863 he was Staff officer to General de Valazè.   Then
came the Mexican campaign.   He received his commission as captain on the
20th of January, 1864, and was with the Foreign Legion in the expeditionary
columns sent to Queretaro, Verde-san-Luis, Tamanlipas, Valle Purissimà
and Calorcè.   At Rio Feio he was appointed commandant.   When in Africa
he distinguished himself at the cholera outbreak at Gèryville, with the Ar-
baouat Column and in the Rasoul and Figuig expeditions.   At the outbreak
of the Franco-Prussian war he was at South Ovan in Africa.   He was registered for active service and went to the field chief of the 7th Battalion.   At
Coulmiers his first serious encounter with the advancing legions of the Prus-
sians took place.   At Juranville he had a horse killed under him and was made
an officer of the Legion of Honor of which he became a member in 1855.   As
commander of the Forty-Second Regiment de marche he was present at the
battles of Villersexel, Hèricourt and Cluse and was wounded at the latter

engagement, February 1st, 1871. In 1873 he took part in the military manœuvres at St. Quentin as major of the Forty-Fifth, and in 1877 he was promoted Lieutenant Colonel of the Forty-Second Regiment and commanded it at the manœuvres of the Tenth Corps. July 10th, 1881, he was commissioned Colonel of the Eighty-eighth Regiment of Line Infantry. His next service was with the Nineteenth Army Corps at South Ovan and then with the Seventeenth Corps in which he directed the Brigade manœuvres with non-commissioned officers. August 22d, 1881, he was called to the command of the Paris Fire Department. His administration has been a signal success and his fitness has been recognized in very flattering official orders. He traveled in Europe and America to study fire extinguishing service and used the information he acquired in reorganizing that of Paris so that in four years all that was advanced in the systems in vogue in the principal cities of the world and which was possible to apply to the Paris service was adopted even to acquiring engines used in Foreign Departments. Colonel Couston has been an officer of Public Instruction since 1879, and his military and technical knowledge was perfected in travels in Austria, Italy, England, Holland, Belgium and this country. America has no better friend than the accomplished, modest and able Chief of the Sapeurs-Pompiers of the capital of France. Colonel Couston's headquarters are on the Boulevard du Palais. His corps is in the War Department, but the Minister of the Interior has supervision of the expenses and the service at fires is under the Chief of Police."

During his trip he met Chief Benjamin A. Gicquel, of the Seventh Battalion, on leave of absence, who was also the recipient of much appreciated courtesies.

Mr. Purroy returned to New York just in time to act on a painful and embarrassing matter. Ample preparations to protect life and property on the 5th of July, which was on Monday, had been made by Chief Shay. In the evening a fire broke out at No. 2293 Third Avenue, from the ignition of fireworks on a stand, and an alarm was sent out, and Chief of Battalion Francis J. Reilly sent out second and third alarms and special calls for six engines. When Second Assistant Chief John McCabe arrived and took command he found a large fire, but in the judgment of the best men in the Department the engines on the ground were amply sufficient to cope with it, and this opinion is sustained by the fact that they did extinguish it. Chief McCabe was, however, impelled to send out the call known as the "Three Sixes," thus: 6, 6, 6—12—5, 1, 8—767, so that all the companies due on a third alarm at Seventh Avenue and Forty-ninth Street were brought to Third Avenue and 126th Street, so that the city north of Fourteenth Street was entirely unprotected. The engines and trucks summoned by the "Three Sixes" were sent back as they arrived by Chief Shay, but the greater portion of the city was in peril for nearly an hour, despite the prompt action of Assistant Chief Hugh Bonner, who sent apparatus to the district that was deprived of protection by McCabe's action. He was tried by Commissioners Purroy and Smith, after suspension from pay and duty, and was defended by Roswell D. Hatch, E. S. Clark and George B. McClusky. On July 21st the decision of Messrs. Purroy and Smith dismissed Chief McCabe. The General Term of the Supreme Court ordered his reinstatement, March 2, 1887.

CHAPTER LI.

FIRE DEPARTMENT TELEGRAPH SYSTEM.

Its Construction and Development.—Records of the several Superintendents and their Efforts to Perfect the System.—Superintendent Smith.—A Man with a Creditable Record.—Vigilant, Enterprising, Scientific.—Central Office of the Fire-Alarm Telegraph.

THE telegraph in connection with the fire service has become an indispensable adjunct, and as much a necessity in communicating the existence and locality of a fire as the steam and other improved apparatus for extinguishing. Indeed, successful management of fires depends so much upon early and instantaneous information that the telegraphic system is now considered as important as any branch of the department. The old-time method of detecting fires by the aid of look-outs upon high towers situated in different parts of the city, and communicating their existence to the public, and approximating to the locality by striking the tower bells, was kept up until the Fire Alarm Telegraph System was put in operation.

At this time a system of telegraph was in use connecting the various bell towers with each other, which was continued, and the look-outs were maintained at Union Market, Essex Market, Marion Street, Spring Street, Jefferson Market, Twenty-sixth Street, Thirty-third Street, Yorkville and Mount Morris for some time, but they have gradually been abandoned, and the old towers removed, with the exception of the one at Mount Morris and at Morrisania.

The Fire Alarm telegraph was constructed under the old Gamewell patent, and was put in operation in January, 1871, by the contractors, Messrs. Charles T. and J. N. Chester, and Mr. Charles T. Chapin was appointed Superintendent. The Central Office was located on the second floor of Fireman's Hall, in the room lately occupied by the President of the Board. This system embraced the territory of Manhattan Island, including that of the East River islands, and consisted in its equipment of 2780 poles, 612 miles of wire, divided into 56 circuits, viz., 41 box signal circuits, 3 key and bell circuits, 2 tower circuits, 2 dial circuits, and 1 police circuit, 548 alarm boxes, with 54 alarm gongs and 42 key and bell magnets in the houses of the fire companies, and 16 dial instruments in the quarters of the district engineers or battalion commanders, and the necessary receiving and transmitting apparatus in the Central Office, the alarms from the street boxes and bell towers on receipt at the Central Office being repeated and transmitted to the several companies over the gong circuits, which was the only one source upon which companies depended for receiving alarms. Each company was provided with a key and bell instrument, connected with a talking circuit, for the purpose of informing the

Central Office by signal when about to leave quarters, and on their return to quarters after an absence.

Mr. Chapin was succeeded as Superintendent in March, 1871, by Mr. C. K. Smith. The annexation of the Westchester District to the city on January 1st, 1874, made necessary the extension of the lines beyond the Harlem River, and in the early part of that year this was accomplished by cabling the river at Third Avenue and at Macomb's Dam. In this district were located six companies, which were equipped with the regular apparatus as in use throughout the department. In 1874 the position of Superintendent was vacated by Mr. C. K. Smith, and Chief Operator John H. Emerick was placed in charge until the September following, when Mr. Emerick was made Superintendent and Mr. J. Elliot Smith was made Chief Operator and subsequently appointed Assistant Superintendent. In January, 1880, the position of Superintendent being vacated by Mr. Emerick, Mr. Smith was appointed Superintendent.

J. Elliot Smith, the present head of the Fire Alarm Telegraph System, has been connected with the department since 1873, at which time he entered the department as Assistant Operator, was promoted as Operator the following July, and made Chief Operator in September of the same year. In July, 1879, he was promoted to be Assistant Superintendent, the office of Chief Operator being at the same time abolished, and on February 1st, 1880, was appointed Superintendent.

Superintendent Smith was born in Northfield, Vermont, in 1834, received his education in the Select School of the town and at the Vermont Seminary at Newbury.

On the opening of the Boston and Montreal telegraph line under the old Bain system, he learned the art of telegraphy, and was placed in charge of

J. ELLIOT SMITH.

the office at Northfield, then the headquarters of the Vermont Central Railroad, at the age of sixteen, his superintendent being Professor Moses G. Farmer, the original inventor of the Fire Alarm Telegraph System. In this occupation he continued some three or four years, with the exception of an interval of two or three school terms. Engaging then in the transportation office of the Company, going thence to the cashiership of the transportation department of the Boston and Lowell Railroad, which position he left at the breaking out of the war. He joined General Butler's New Orleans expedition. On the arrival of the Federal Army at New Orleans, and the occupation of the city, he was appointed by General Butler Military Superintendent of Telegraph in the Department of the Gulf, with instructions to take possession and management of all telegraph lines, including those of the Police and Fire Alarm.

As the different lines connecting into New Orleans had been almost completely destroyed by the Confederate authorities as they left the city on the approach of the Union forces, the work of reconstruction was extremely difficult, the more so from lack of the necessary material, and to supply operators it became expedient to draw from the rank and file and establish a school for instruction.

By this method and with the aid of reinforcements imported from the North, the requisite force was provided with which 350 miles of lines were put in operation as fast as reconstructed.

The officials in charge of the Fire Alarm and Police Telegraphs were required by the Commanding General to take the oath of allegiance to the Government as necessary to their retention in office. This they refused to do, believing themselves indispensible to the service of the city, consequently secure in their position. Not so, however, with the General, who ordered Superintendent Smith to dispossess the entire force as soon as he could do it with safety. This was done within a few weeks as soon as a relieving force could be organized, and these systems remained under Mr. Smith's management until May, 1864, when they were restored to the civil government. During the twelve years of Mr. Smith's connection with the New York Department, his constant aim and study has been to add every improvement to the telegraph system which would tend to benefit the service. When first entering the department he saw the importance of reducing the time occupied in the transmission of the alarm signals from the street boxes to the companies, and on his appointment as chief operator he at once directed his energies to the perfecting of the device by which the several companies were enabled to receive alarms from the street boxes direct, and at the same time they are received at the Central Office. For want of space in the operating room at that time the improvement could only be attached to a single circuit, enough, however, to show the immense benefit in gaining of time, and the

FIRE ALARM BOX.

advantage of an additional means for the transmission of the signals. The importance of this and other suggested improvements so favorably impressed the Commissioners, that they provided a liberal appropriation for the purpose, and Mr. Smith was charged with the carrying out of the improvements, the details of which he carefully devised, and which were thoroughly carried to completion under his personal supervision ; and at the hour of nine o'clock and twenty minutes P.M., the 25th of March, 1878, the electric life was in a moment transfused from the veins and apparatus of the old office to the new room in the upper story of Fireman's Hall, and to the magnificent and multitudinous paraphernalia prepared for it, and constituting the equipment of the finest arrangement of its kind in existence, and now known as the New York system.

A curious incident connected with the operation was the fact that the first fire signal received and transmitted through the new office was the Headquarter's station, which was received within a few minutes after the transfer had been made, and found to be occasioned by a fire on the same block. On the arrival of the midnight relief force at the old office their astonishment was great to find their former office abandoned and in a state of chaos. The transfer had been a perfect success, not a hitch occurring.

The wires of the New York Fire Alarm Telegraph are carried exclusively on poles, no housetops being used for the purpose. There are now nearly 7,000 poles and 1,050 miles of wire, divided into 78 circuits, all of which are metallic, with two or three exceptions; there are 53 box signal circuits, five of which connect with the public schools, and three connect with theatres, manufactories, hotels and other buildings, and known as special building circuits.

There are four combination circuits connecting with the various company houses throughout the department which receive the signals at the Central Office from the fire alarm boxes, and convey them direct to the companies.

CARD OF INSTRUCTION TO HOUSEHOLDERS IN CASE OF FIRE.

Eight gong circuits carry the alarms to the large gongs in each company's quarters as transmitted upon the repeating instruments, twelve telephone circuits connect with each company, the quarters of the principal officials of the department, the Gate House in Central Park, the head-quarters of the Police Department, and a watchman's circuit connects with the department repair shops and the hospital stable.

There are 972 signal boxes, 654 of which are attached to poles, 26 are located in city institutions, the property of the city, 131 are located within the public-school buildings, also the property of the city, and 161 are connected with the theatres, hotels, manufactories, and other private buildings.

There are in use in the department 83 large electro mechanical gongs, 74 combination, alarm, and talking instruments, 92 sets of telephones, forming the equipment of the quarters of the respective companies and the principal officials of the department.

THE FIRST RUNNING CARD OF THE PAID DEPARTMENT. ONLY SIXTY-THREE STATIONS IN 1865 FOR THE ENTIRE CITY!

METROPOLITAN FIRE DEPARTMENT.

NEW YORK, November 6th, 1865.

To the Officers and Members of the Metropolitan Fire Department:

Below will be found a list of Alarm and Signal Stations below Fourteenth Street, adopted by the Board of Metropolitan Fire Commissioners, together with a list of Engine and Hook and Ladder Companies, which are to do duty as designated.

Fire Companies lying above Fourteenth Street will do duty by Bell Alarms in the 1st, 2d, 3d, 4th, 5th and 6th Districts, as heretofore.

All Bell-ringing below Fourteenth Street will be discontinued from and after   except, in case the Telegraph at the Bell Towers should not be in working order, in which case of emergency, the Bells will ring the Signal Station Number. For instance, should the Fire be in the vicinity of Old Slip and Water Street, the Bell will ring 1 (interval) 2 (interval) 3, or such other number as may designate the station or locality.

☞ Officers and Members of the several Companies in the Department are particularly enjoined to become familiar with the Numbers of the Alarm and Signal Stations in which they are designated to do duty. A slate will be provided for the purpose of recording the Number of the Station from which the Alarm was received, and on which the Officers of the Company will cause the same to be noted before the house is closed after the apparatus has left for a fire.

To give an Alarm of Fire, unlock and open the Side-box, pull down the Bell-handle as far as it will come, then release it, close and lock the Box. Should no ticking be heard in the Telegraph-box after pulling the Bell handle down, you will then send notice of the fire to the nearest Bell Tower or Police Station.

Keys to open the Telegraph-box will be furnished to the Foreman of each Company, who will be held responsible for all Alarms sent from the Station.

Signal.	Location of Alarm Station.	Alarm.	Engine Company.	Hook and Ladder Co.
1	Firemen's Hall	First	3 5 14 18 20 24 25 33 13 30	3 5 9
		Second	11 17 27	6 8
2	Chamber, near Centre	First	1 4 6 7 9 10 12 27 29 31 32	1 6 8 10
		Second	13 15 17 20 30	5 9
3	Centre, near Chamber	First	1 4 6 7 9 10 12 27 29 31 32	1 6 8 10
		Second	13 15 17 20 30	5 9
4	Cedar, near Broadway	First	1 4 6 7 9 10 12 27 29 31 32	1 8 10
		Second	13 15 17 20	6 9
5	Beaver, near Broad	First	1 4 6 7 9 10 12 27 29 31 32	1 8 10
		Second	13 15 17 20	6 9
6	Liberty, near Nassau	First	1 4 6 7 9 10 12 27 29 31 32	1 8 10
		Second	13 15 17 20	6 9
12	Burling Slip, near Water	First	1 4 6 7 9 10 12 27 29 31 32	1 8 10
		Second	13 15 17 20	6 9
13	William, near Pearl	First	1 4 6 7 9 10 12 15 29 31 32	1 6 10
		Second	13 17 20 27	8 9
14	East Broadway, near Catherine	First	1 7 9 11 12 15 17 20 25 31	1 6 9
		Second	4 6 29 32	8 10
15	Franklin, near Hudson	First	1 4 6 7 12 27 29 30 31 32	1 8 10
		Second	9 10 13 24	5 9
16	Franklin, near Varick	First	1 4 6 7 12 27 30 31 32 29	1 8 10
		Second	9 10 13 24	5 9
21	Clinton, near Division	First	9 11 12 15 17 20 25 28	6 9 11
		Second	1 5 13	1 3
23	Henry, near Gouverneur	First	9 11 12 15 17 20 25 28	6 9 11
		Second	1 5 13	1 3
24	Eleventh, near Av. B	First	5 11 15 16 17 25 28 33	3 7 9
		Second	9 13 20	5 6
25	Ludlow, near Delancey	First	9 11 12 15 17 20 25 28	6 9 11
		Second	1 5 13	1 3
26	Houston, near Columbia	First	5 9 11 15 17 25 28	3 6 11
		Second	12 20 33	7 9
31	Elizabeth, near Bayard	First	5 9 11 12 15 17 20 25 31	6 9 11
		Second	7 13 32 33	1 3
32	Elizabeth, near Prince	First	5 11 13 15 17 20 25 33	6 9 11
		Second	9 18 24	3 5
34	Marion, near Prince	First	5 11 13 15 17 20 25 33	6 9 11
		Second	9 18 24	3 5
35	Wooster, near Spring	First	13 14 15 17 18 20 24 26 33 30	3 5 9
		Second	3 5 11	6 11

Signal.	Location of Alarm Station.	Alarm.	Engine Company.	H. & L. Cos.		
36	Mercer, near Fourth St............	First......	3 5 13 14 17 18 20 24 33	3	5	9
		Second....	11 15 25	6	11	
41	Fifth St., near 1st av.......... ...	First.......	5 11 14 16 17 25 28 33	3	9	11
		Second....	13 15 18	6	7	
42	Fourteenth St., near 1st Av.	First......	5 11 14 16 17 18 25 28 35	3	7	11
		Second....	9 13 15	5	6	
43	Thirteenth St., near 4th Av......	First.......	5 13 14 16 18 25 28 33	3	7	11
		Second....	3 11 24	5	9	
45	West 10th St., near Greenwich Av	First..	3 5 14 18 24 25 30 33	3	5	9
		Second. ..	13 16 28	8		
46	Charles, near Bleecker...........	First......	3 13 14 18 24 25 30 33	3	5	9
		Second....	5 27 28	8		
51	Morton, near Hudson.......... ...	First.......	3 13 14 18 20 24 25 30 33	5	8	9
		Second....	5 27 28	3		
52	New, near Exchange Place.......	First......	1 4 6 7 9 10 12 27 29 31 32	1	8	10
		Second....	13 15 17 20	6	9	
53	Beekman, near William..........	First......	1 4 6 7 9 10 12 27 29 31 32	1	8	10
		Second....	13 15 17 20	6	9	
54	Grand, corner Ludlow......	First......	9 11 12 15 17 20 25 28	6	9	11
		Second....	1 5 13	1	3	
56	Madison, near Clinton....	First......	9 11 12 15 17 20 25 28	6	9	11
		Second....	1 5 13	1	3	
61	Franklin, near Baxter...........	First......	1 4 6 7 9 12 20 27 29 31 32	1	6	8
		Second......	10 13 15 17 30	5	9	
62	Attorney, near Delancey........	First......	9 11 12 15 17 20 25 28	6	9	11
		Second....	1 5 13	1	3	
63	Eighteenth, near Broadway......	First......	3 5 13 14 16 18 25 33	3	5	7
		Second....	11 28 24	9	11	
64	Seventeenth, near 9th Av........	First.......	3 5 13 14 18 24 25 33	3	5	7
		Second.....	28 30	9		
65	Elm, near Broome...............	First......	5 11 13 15 17 20 25 33	6	9	11
		Second....	9 18 24 31	3	5	
71	Spring, near Varick.......	First......	6 13 18 24 27 30 31 33	5	8	9
		Second....	1 7 20 12	1	10	
72	Leonard, near Elm..............	First......	1 4 6 7 9 12 20 27 29 31 32	1	8	10
		Second....	10 13 15 17 30	5	9	
73	Fifth, near Av. D...............	First......	5 9 11 15 17 25 28 33	3	6	11
		Second....	12 20	7	9	
123	Old Slip, corner Water..........	First......	1 4 6 7 9 10 12 27 29 31 32	1	8	10
		Second....	13 15 17 20	6	9	
124	Custom House.................	First... ..	1 4 6 7 9 10 12 27 29 31 32	1	8	10
		Second....	13 15 17 26	6	9	
125	Foot of Wall, near East River....	First......	1 4 6 7 9 10 12 27 29 31 32	1	8	10
		Second....	13 15 17 20	6	9	
126	Harpers' Building...............	First......	1 4 6 7 9 12 27 29 31 32	1	8	10
		Second....	13 15 17 20	6	9	
131	Morris, corner Washington........	First......	1 4 6 7 9 10 12 27 29 31 32	1	8	10
		Second....	13 15 17 20	6	9	
132	Cortlandt, corner Washington....	First......	1 4 6 7 9 10 12 27 29 31 32	1	8	10
		Second....	13 15 17 20	6	9	
134	St. Paul's Church.	First......	1 4 6 7 9 10 12 27 29 31 32	1	8	10
		Second....	13 15 17 20	6	9	
135	Greenwich St., corner Barclay....	First......	1 4 6 7 12 27 29 30 31 32	1	8	10
		Second.....	9 10 13 24	5	9	
136	Police, Chamber, near Greenwich	First.......	1 4 6 7 12 27 29 30 31 32	1	8	10
		Second....	9 10 13 24	5	9	
141	City Hospital..................	First......	1 4 6 7 9 12 20 27 29 31 32	1	8	10
		Second....	10 13 15 17 30	5	9	
142	Broadway, corner Canal.........	First... ..	1 7 9 12 13 17 20 29 30 31	6	8	9
		Second.....	11 15 25	1	10	
143	Bowery, corner Grand....	First.....	5 9 11 12 13 17 20 25	6	9	11
		Second.....	18 31 32	3	5	
145	Canal, corner Hudson..	First.....	6 12 13 18 20 24 27 30 31	5	8	9
		Second.....	1 4 7	1	10	
146	Hudson, corner King...........	First......	3 13 18 20 27 30 33 24	5	8	9
		Second....	1 5 14	3		
151	Houston, corner Thompson.......	First......	13 14 17 18 20 24 25 33 30	3	5	9
		Second.....	3 5 11	11	8	
152	Washington, corner Bank........	First... ...	3 13 14 18 20 24 25 30 33	3	5	9
		Second....	5 27 28	8		
153	Twelfth St., corner 9th Av........	First......	3 13 14 18 20 24 30 33	3	5	
		Second.....	5 25	8	9	
154	Fifth Av., corner 9th St..........	First.	3 5 13 14 18 20 25 28 33	3	5	9
		Second.....	11 17	11		
156	Cooper Institute........	First......	5 11 13 14 18 20 25 28 33	3	9	11
		Second.....	15 17	6		
161	Eighth St., corner Av. D.	First......	5 9 11 15 17 25 28	3	6	11
		Second.....	18 20 33	9		
162	Third St., corner Av. B...........	First......	5 9 11 15 17 25 28	3	6	11
		Second.....	18 20 33	9		
163	Houston St., corner 2d Av........	First......	5 11 15 17 20 25 28 33	3	9	11
		Second.....	9 13 18	5	6	
164	Foot of Grand St., East River....	First......	5 9 11 15 17 20 25 28	6	9	11
		Second....	1 12 13	1	3	
165	Cherry, near Pike................	First......	5 9 11 12 15 17 20 25 28	6	9	11
		Second.....	7 13	1	3	

ELISHA KINGSLAND, Chief Engineer.

Among more recent and valuable improvements made is that of placing all the wires centering into head-quarters underground in its immediate vicinity, and the introduction of a safety device to prevent damage to the valuable apparatus from the excessive currents from the electrical illuminating wires, which formerly had occasioned much trouble and damage to the apparatus, and on one or more occasions nearly destroying the entire system.

This was caused by the wires of the department and those of the illuminating companies becoming crossed, whereby the terrific currents of the latter were conducted to the more delicate instruments in the Central Office, burning them up and setting fire to the combustible surroundings. Experiments have been made in the department with underground wires dating back to September, 1884, at which time two six-wire leaden-covered Waring cables were connected along Eighth Avenue, between Seventy-second and Seventy-third Streets, and the overhead wires removed. Since that time the same kind of cables has been put in service in different parts of the department, and with such good results as to induce Superintendent Smith to recommend that all the wires extending from the Central Office be placed underground for a limited distance, as in case of a serious fire in the immediate locality the entire overhead system would be imperiled The recommendation was approved, and the work of trenching and laying was commenced on Saturday, the 24th of October, 1885, and as far as the underground work was concerned, was completed the following Tuesday. It is hoped that the success of this initial departure from the hazardous overhead system will result in the speedy placing of every fire alarm wire under ground.

Superintendent Smith's report, made some two months after the completion of this work, is as follows:

" All the wires connecting the Central Office of this department start from the office switch-board in Waring anti-induction cables, and pass to the basement of the building, where they enter a distributing switch for the greater convenience of the circuits in the different streets. From this point the cables, thirty-four in number, and containing one hundred and ninety (190) wires, with an aggregate length of about twenty-eight (28) miles, enter the ground and pass under the streets in different directions to the junction poles. These poles are situated at a distance from one to four blocks away. Here the cables are carried up the poles in wood and iron boxing, where they are joined to the overhead wires through lightning arresters placed in boxes upon the poles. Thirty of the cables contain six conductors each, three have three conductors each, all of the corrugated pattern, and one independent or single wire cables. One of the six-wire cables connects direct to the head-quarters of the Police department and the newspaper press offices in Mulberry Street, and one connects with the conduit of the Western Union Telegraph Company under Broadway. The conduit here mentioned extends south under Broadway to Dey Street and north as far as Fourteenth Street, thence to and up Fifth Avenue to Twenty-third Street. Along this route there are ten street boxes attached to lamp-posts, from each of which extends a Waring cable under the pavement, entering the conduit at a neighboring flush-box or man-hole, and there connecting with the department circuits provided by the Western Union Company, and running the entire length of the conduit, making a circuit of seven miles.

" The work of trenching and laying was begun on Saturday, the 24th of

October, 1885, and was practically completed the following Tuesday morning, having caused no interference nor inconvenience to street traffic, although car tracks were crossed at five different points, and one mass of six cables (thirty-three wires) were laid across Broadway, the most crowded thoroughfare in the city. Upon the completion of the work and connecting in this underground system with the aerial lines, not a fault had developod in any of the cables, and all remain perfect up to the present time. In addition to the cables here spoken of are several Waring cables placed in different parts of the city, which were laid in 1884, and all as perfect in their service as when laid.

"While in constant dread of serious disturbances, to which we are liable, from storms, etc., especially in the winter season, it is a satisfaction to feel

TELEGRAPH APPARATUS, OLD FIRE HEADQUARTERS, MERCER STREET.

that, though limited, we have some portion of the system not within its reach, and with a continuance of successful working, a strengthening of the belief that the proper place for the wires of this department, as a measure of economy as well as safety, is under the streets."

The Central Office of the Fire Alarm Telegraph is on the third floor of the Headquarters Building, and located at the east end of a room whose dimensions are 70 by 40 feet. Commencing at the front end of the room is a raised flooring or platform occupying twenty-two feet in width, and extending into the room the same distance, with an extension of three and a half feet, with broad steps leading to it from the main floor. On the two sides of this elevated portion, and the end where it joins the side of the building, elegant and artistic cabinet work of solid mahogany, beautifully carved, and divided into pilasters and paneling to accommodate the electrical apparatus rises ten feet above the platform, the end portion being placed three feet distant from the front wall of Headquarters to permit a passage between it and the wall, and leave an opening in the centre six feet in width to correspond to a window directly opposite, the two wings of the cabinet work joining overhead.

On the sides of the windows, within recesses in the wall of the building, are located annunciators connected with lightning arresters and automatic protectors, one hundred upon each side, to which the outside circuits (which here terminate, as before related, in the underground or sub-way cables) are connected. From this apparatus the wires enter the cabinet work at the top and connect at the rheostat switch-board mounted upon an upright marbleized-slate base, and occupying a position in one of the wings, the uses of which are to connect a delicate apparatus for discriminating by a system of measurements the locality of faults on the circuits, etc.

From here the wires extend to the main switches which occupy the central portion of the cabinet on one side of the office, and are mounted upon marbleized-slate bases three feet wide, the aggregate length of which is twenty feet, containing some nine hundred switches, and from which wires radiate to every part of the office, and which have their uses for testing in a variety of ways. Each circuit connecting at the switch-board is provided with a small needle galvanometer, similar to a watch face, and arranged upon a projecting shelf under the switches, and mounted upon marble bases with glass dials. These little instruments show at all times the exact electrical condition of the circuits to which they belong, and are used in connection with the switches to detect the existence upon the circuits of crosses or leakages, and where such faults are indicated the operator switches in the measuring apparatus at the rheostat switches, and determines the exact locality of the fault. They are also used for determining the condition of the electro-motive force. This consists of a battery of nearly two thousand jars, situated in the basement of the building about two hundred feet distant from the telegraph office.

Two hundred and twenty-five wires, aggregating in length about nine miles, are required to make the connections between the battery-room and the switch-board.

Above the switch-board are placed electric annunciators corresponding in numbers to the engine and hook and ladder companies for informing the operators at a glance the situation of the force—that is what companies are in or out of quarters. This is controlled by a key-board on the desk, in the body of the platform.

When a company leaves its quarters on a still alarm, or for any purpose is temporarily out of service, it signals the Central Office upon the combination circuits, and the annunciator is made to show that such company is out. Likewise on its return to quarters the proper signal is given, and the annunciator is set to show the company "in service." Thus the operators are always informed, when a fire signal is received, just what companies can be depended upon to respond.

The cabinets on the opposite side, facing the switch-board, contain the apparatus for receiving and recording the signals and the system of transmitting to the department simultaneously with their receipt from the street boxes. All the wires entering here are through the main switch-board passing beneath

the floor and up into the cabinet. Here under a glass case is a large registering instrument with a capacity of fifty circuits, with an independent ink-
recording pen for each box circuit. This instrument is provided with paper
ten inches in width, on which the signals are recorded, and which is fed from a
roll beneath the instrument passing through and under a glass plate in the
counter shelf for a distance of four feet, so that the last signal received is in
view, and entering the cabinet is again reeled up. Directly over the register
and in the same case is placed the combination switch, consisting of a hard
rubber bar about two feet long, sliding in a strip of mahogany placed horizontally and inlaid with numerous metal bearings. Upon each side of the slide,
upon the wood are mounted a multitude of flat springs, their ends overlapping
and terminating upon the metal bearings in the rubber, by which two or more
springs are in electrical contact. To these springs are attached wires connecting with the combination circuits extending to all the department quarters in
the city, and to the telephone circuits and local apparatus to which it is desired
to give instantaneous connection with a street box circuit. Connected to and
extending in a line from the Combination Switch eight feet, on either side, with
a covering of plate glass, is a polished steel bar two inches wide and one-fourth
of an inch thick, supported on its edge by steel rollers. In the face of this bar
at intervals of three inches a slot one-fourth of an inch wide is cut on an angle.
Under the bars at corresponding intervals are the circuit switches to work in
unison with the combination. They consist of pieces of hard rubber six inches
long, three-fourths of an inch wide, inlaid with metal bearings, and slide in
perpendicular grooves at right angles to the steel bar. At each side of the
slides flat german silver springs having wire connections to the various circuits, etc., are screwed to the wood, and their ends terminating on the metal
bearings in the slides. The top end of the slide, which extends above the steel
bar, has a friction roller fitting the diagonal slot in the bar. The lower end is
connected to a lever with a handle extending outward. By pulling down this
handle the bearings of the slide of the circuit switch on which the springs rest
are taken from their normal position and placed in contact with others of the
springs. The downward movement carrying the friction roller within the slot
in the steel bar causes it to move and to carry with it the slide of the Combination Switch, thereby effecting a large number of changes in the circuits by the
simple movement of the handle.

All the different pieces of apparatus pertaining to a given circuit connecting
with the receiving and automatic transmission are arranged in a line vertically.
First the lever switch, etc., then the key, above that the shunt switch, pulling
out similarly to an organ stop, for placing in the circuit an increased electro-
motive force at will, and shunting the relay to obviate change in its adjustment. Above that, under a glass plate, is the relay, which is connected directly
on the circuit, then the local peg switch, which makes connection with the Register and the Annunciator over it or with the duplicates in another part of the
office, above that being the list of stations on the circuit and the Annunciator
showing the number of the circuit.

Beside the fifty circuit recording instrument there is a sixteen circuit
recorder recently added for the accommodation of new circuits, and a duplicating instrument with fifty-six pieces, whereby in the event of accident
any of the circuits can be transferred to the duplicating instrument. There is

also an instrument for recording the outgoing alarm signals with an independent pen connecting with each gong circuit through the repeaters, making its records in red ink, and with the combination circuits recording those signals in blue ink, and attached to which is a multipled repeating relay to which the several telephone circuits are connected, and on which all fire signals are repeated; the repeating transmitters through which the alarms are sent on the gong circuits, consist of three, and are located upon pedestals in the middle of the platform. The principal and most important of these is a marvel of mechanism and ingenuity. Two sets of double cylinders connected with a powerful battery, arranged to revolve in unison, and making contact with springs having their connections with the gong circuits so that a single revolution of the cylinder gives one electric pulsation to each circuit. The motive power is a train of numerous wheels, etc., moved by weights. Connecting with this main train or movement is a series of four auxiliary movements, each being independent of the other, and which are brought into action in connection with the main train at the will of the operators. These auxiliary movements consists each of three dials or circular discs, indexed upon their rims with plain figures, the first having 1 to 25, and the other two having 1 to 9, each set moving on one axis. The discs here described control the battery current to the cylinders, and the different figures to which the indices may be set, indicate such number of strokes as are to be transmitted to the instruments in connection with the circuits. If the signal is to be a continuous number of blows with an equal interval of time between them, say a test signal of eleven, the first disc of the series in use will be set to the "11" on the index. The effect will be to supply battery to the cylinder just while eleven revolutions are made, the mechanical arrangement or relationship being such as to

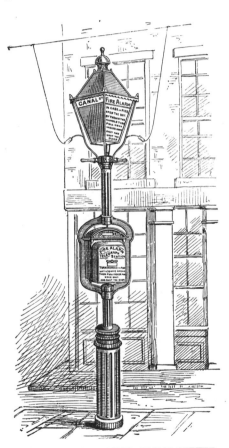

NEW FIRE ALARM BOX, CANAL STREET
AND BROADWAY.

cut off the battery supply as soon as the desired number of pulsations have been given, thus feeding to the circuits the eleven pulsations, each of which gives a blow upon the gongs and makes a record on the registers. The capacity for transmitting by any one of the auxiliaries is twenty-five continuous blows or any less number, or any combination up to 999, so that with the four series it is possible to transmit with one setting of the index a continuation of twelve distinct numbers of blows. The available numerals embraced within three digits, or up to 999, having been absorbed, it has become necessary to add the fourth digit for numbering signal stations. If the signal be composed of two numbers in combination like 2–3 the two discs of the same series are used, one being set to 2 and the other at 3, and if another number is to be added to the combination, say 4, then the third disc is set to 4. As soon as the 2 has been given the first disc cuts off the current for an extra interval, then follows the 3, and again an extra interval and the 4 is given, thus the breaking up of the continuity in the nine blows drive them into the combination 2–3–4. To transmit a signal of this class an additional disc of another auxiliary is required, and the full capacity of the two is six numbers or up to 999 999. It is doubtful if the demands of the city, created through its very rapid growth, will ever exceed the possibilities of this instrument for meeting its requirements. Another of the repeaters is provided with contact cylinders, etc., and a case of wheels, one for each station, and to transmit a signal the wheel corresponding to it in number is placed in its position upon a shaft and the machinery is started, the wheel performs the same duty in controlling the battery current as the indexed discs in the other instrument, but its capacity is limited to the regular station signals. The third repeater is much smaller and has but a single dial. It is used for testing and other purposes.

Telephones are affixed to the cabinet-work of the office, and connection is thus maintained with every company house and the principal officials for department business solely. The different apparatus used in the receiving and transmitting of a fire signal having been described, it is only necessary to explain that when a signal box is pulled for a fire the operators on duty are first apprised of it by the dropping of the annunciators, showing the number of the circuit on which the box is located, followed by the number of the box. The handle of the switch and combination is pulled down by the operator, allowing the succeeding signals to be automatically transferred to the companies. Every horse in service is unhitched at the first tap of the instrument. The full signal is struck all through the city upon the instruments of the combination, as well as on the telephone bells, and recorded upon the paper of the register. The assistant operator has meanwhile prepared the transmitting repeater by setting it to the signal number, and the signal then follows over the gong circuits working in the same houses, but over other wires and on different gongs. Except that an imperfection may exist in the Combination circuit, such of the force as are assigned to duty at the station indicated rarely ever wait long enough to hear the latter signal, and within thirty seconds from the start of the signal from the box—except, perhaps, in the case of a high number—the companies assigned have left their quarters in response.

The signal boxes which are distributed throughout the city are connected with the Central Office by special circuits—that is, no other use is made of the circuits except for signalling fire alarms. The number of boxes on each circuit is from fifteen to twenty-five, and the arrangement of circuits is such that no two boxes in the same neighborhood are on the same circuit, so that in the event of one of the wires being out of order, there is still a chance for connection by means of the other circuits. Keys for the boxes are placed convenient for access, generally in drug stores and similar public places, and a sign on each box informs the public where the keys are to be found. Every policeman and fireman has keys. They are also provided to reputable citizens who ask for them, it being stipulated that they shall be carried upon their person. A couple of years ago Superintendent Smith began to put the Tooker keyless door, which can be opened by any one by turning a handle, on street boxes. The turning of the handle sounds a bell on the inside of the door, and the sound is continued during the time required to effect the opening and the transmission of an alarm—about a quarter of a minute—ample to attract the attention of the police or other persons in the vicinity, thus rendering it unsafe for persons to tamper with them. Much time is thus saved in important districts in transmitting an alarm, which under other circumstances would necessitate the procuring and use of a key. They proved to be so popular that whenever an opportunity occurs keyless doors are put to boxes, and in the near future few boxes will be closed, and these will be in districts where the funny or malicious adult or child would be able to tamper with a keyless box without great danger of detection. The boxes are arranged with clock-work, and springs furnish power. They are provided with circuit breakers, wheels which are notched, and contact springs which have their ends bearing upon the wheel. On opening the box a hook is seen and a sign "Pull the hook once." The pull operates on the clock-work, and the notches on the wheel passing under the springs *break the circuit once for each notch*, and sending to the tape or record in the Central Office an indication corresponding to the notches on the wheel. The numbers and combination being different in each box, the operators know instantly from what box a signal comes.

SENDING THE ALARM.

The usual method of attaching the boxes to poles has been greatly improved by adopting an invention of Superintendent Smith, whereby iron gas lamp posts are altered into combination lamp and signal posts. The posts are cut off as they stand five feet from their bases, and an ornamental frame-work of iron attached. This has a receptacle for the signal box. The column of the post is connected again at the top of the frame, and on its top is placed the lamp with a red display globe, indicating that a fire signal box is below. The gas supply is through the column and frame. There have been nearly two-score of these combination posts established and connected with the underground cables, for which they were specially designed. They are both practical and ornamental. Another invention of Superintendent Smith recently put in use was the special signal box. They were destined for the school-houses of the city, and 130 are now in use. They transmit calls for fire, police, and ambulance service by simply manipulating "pointers" on the boxes and pulling a hook. Then the desired signal is received at the Central Office twice, and the location once. The normal condition of the box is for a fire signal, but when the pointer is used, other boxes are in service which by the use of a key can be made to send four other special signals, among them second and third alarms.

The regular force employed in the operating of the telegraph bureau consists of a superintendent, a chief operator, three operators, five assistant operators, one clerk, two battery men, five linemen, two box inspectors, one instrument-maker, one machinist, and a floating force of climbers and laborers at day's wages. The Central Office force is: George Farrell, Chief Operator; Edward Sellew, Christopher Jones, Edward S. Sims, Operators; Daniel W. Hernon, Frank D. Collis, Frank W. Lord, John H. Kavanagh, Francis Fitzpatrick, Assistant Operators, and Gabriel Van Cott, Jr., Clerk.

So far this chapter has referred only to the telegraph system and appliances as they existed in the old Headquarters in Mercer Street. Arrangements at the present writing are being made to transfer the entire telegraphic paraphernalia to the sixth floor of the new Fire Headquarters, 67th street, between Third and Lexington Aveues. What changes, if any, this will bring about in the system remains to be seen. It is hardly possible that any considerable improvement can be effected. But the advances in elecctrical sciences are so rapid and numerous, that it is impossible to prophesy what the near future may bring forth, to revolutionize in a great measure the existing state of affairs.

FIREMEN FIGHTING FIRE.

CHAPTER LII.

THE ROLL OF MERIT.

Deeds of Self-sacrifice and Heroism Which Prove that the Age of Chivalry is not of the Past.—Names
that will Live in History and in the Hearts of an Appreciative Community.—The Bennett and
Stephenson Medallists.—A Chapter on Life Saving.

A SYSTEM of recording conspicuously meritorious acts by officers and
members of the Paid Fire Department was begun in 1868 under the
following resolution in the Committee of Appointments, dated November
22, 1868:

Resolved, That the secretary be instructed to open and keep under his personal supervision, a book of record, which shall be called "The Roll of Merit M. F. D.," in which shall
be entered the names of such officers and members of the department as may have, in the
judgment of the board of commissioners, distinguished themselves in the discharge of their
duties, with a full record of the act by which they have become entitled to the honor of
being there enrolled. Opposite to each name shall be stated the action taken by this Board
in making rewards in each case.

The roll of merit is as follows.

MINTHORNE D. TOMPKINS, assistant foreman Hook and Ladder Company No.
1, on the fourteenth of November, 1868, at the Stewart House, Nos. 476 and 480
Broadway, where the tenants, fourteen in number, were cut off from escape,
at great personal risk, and in spite of injuries sustained, rescued six persons,
one of whom, a woman, he carried from the fourth floor to the street.

PATRICK DONOHUE, assistant foreman of Hook and Ladder Company No.
9, aided Tompkins in the rescue of some of the imperiled persons.

JAMES HEANEY, foreman Hook and Ladder Company No. 9, saved the lives
of two persons at the Stewart Building fire.

JOHN KAVANAGH and CHRISTOPHER C. FLICK, firemen Engine Company
No. 20, rescued at the Stewart Building fire a woman and child who were in
the direst peril on the second floor. Flick's intrepidity nearly cost him his
life.

MICHAEL BRENNAN, fireman Engine Company No. 20, on the twentieth of
January, 1869, at No. 80 Prince Street, rescued John Miller, who was surrounded by flames, and who dared not brave them and the dense smoke by
which he was cut off.

RICHARD D. HALL, fireman Engine Company No. 30, on the sixteenth of
March, 1869, at No. 437 Canal Street, learning that an old woman was perishing in the attic, struggled through the dense smoke, and rescued her by
carrying her down a ladder.

JOSEPH WEIDMAN, foreman Hook and Ladder Company No. 2, was placed
on the roll for arresting two men who had committed a burglary at Mrs.
Thomas Cochrane's, No. 48 East Forty-ninth Street.

MATTHEW HICKS, foreman Engine Company No. 5, at No. 615 East Fourteenth Street, on the thirtieth of March, 1869, forced his way to the third floor, through smoke which came from a fierce fire in the cellar, and rescued two half suffocated boys.

WILLIAM H. NASH, foreman Engine Company No. 28. At the above fire this gallant and ill-fated officer, after calming and advising the members of twenty families, first rescued an old and helpless woman on the second floor, and then, standing on the top rung of a ladder, passed down five persons who were at the window of the fifth floor.

JAMES H. MONROE, foreman Hook and Ladder Company No. 8, on the thirteenth of April, 1870, at No. 88 Bayard Street, discovered on arriving at the fire that the inmates were unconscious of their peril. Arousing them, he went to the top floor, and found two men, two women and a child unconscious from the smoke, and, calling for aid, handed them to firemen who had run up ladders.

WILLIAM F. HAYES, assistant foreman of the same company, was conspicuous in aiding his commanding officer at this fire.

ANDREW LYNAR, fireman of Engine Company No. 15, at No. 564 Grand Street, on the sixth of April, 1870, forced his way up-stairs and rescued a little child who was imploring aid at a window of the upper floor. Lynar was burned in returning to the street, but the child was not hurt.

ELI BATES, chief of the Fourth Battalion, at No. 73 Montgomery Street, on the twenty-sixth of September, 1870, found twenty families in danger and imploring help from the windows. On one of the first ladders which were raised, Bates ascended to a mother who stood at a fifth story window with a babe in her arms crying, " Save my child ! oh, do save my child ! " and brought them to the street.

BENJAMIN A. GICQUEL, foreman of Engine Company No. 9, at this fire, was, with other officers and firemen, driven to the street by the flames. Ladders were raised, and after many had been passed down them there was a rumor that two widows and their two children had perished on one of the upper floors. Gicquel carried his life in his hand when he entered the building by a ladder, but he found and rescued all four, who were partly suffocated, and for his gallantry was promoted to be a battalion chief.

WILLIAM F. HAYES, foreman of Hook and Ladder Company No. 6, rescued four persons at this fire at personal risk.

JUSTIN A. PATTEN, foreman Engine Company No. 11, at this fire, rescued three persons from the roof.

DENTON E. HEMSWORTH, fireman of Hook and Ladder Company No. 6, was Foreman Gicquel's chief aid in rescuing the four persons at the same fire.

WILLIAM F. CRAFT, fireman of Hook and Ladder Company No. 6, rendered like service here.

JOHN MCDERMOTT, fireman of Hook and Ladder Company No. 6, was equally brave and efficient.

GILBERT J. ORR, chief of the Tenth Battalion, at No. 23 Seventh Avenue, on the sixteenth of June, 1870, entered the building in spite of smoke, which was suffocating, and rescued from the fourth floor Patrick Dyer, his wife and six children.

JACOB VAN ORDEN, foreman of Hook and Ladder Company No. 5, at this fire, rescued Mrs. Burns, a visitor, and a servant girl who were suffocated. Van Orden first went down-stairs, with Mrs. Burns and the servant hanging from each arm. Afterwards saved other lives.

THOMAS L. JACOBUS, fireman in Van Orden's company at this fire, rescued a helpless old woman and aided in saving three other persons.

JACOB VAN ORDEN, foreman of Hook and Ladder Company No. 5, at the Phoenix Plaster Mills, Nos. 426 to 430 West Thirteenth Street, on the nineteenth of December, 1870, rescued, at great personal risk, two women who were in tenement houses in front of the mills, and which had taken fire.

JOHN D. SULLIVAN, fireman of Van Orden's company, saved two lives at this fire.

CHARLES McNAMEE, fireman of Engine Company No. 13, at No. 75 Grand Street, on the fourteenth of January, 1871, in fierce flames and dense smoke from burning jute, entered the attic by a ladder and rescued a girl who had lost her presence of mind and was in most serious peril.

THOMAS J. DOUGHERTY, fireman Hook and Ladder Company No. 1, at No. 450 Pearl Street, on the seventeenth of January, 1871, rescued an old and feeble woman from a room in the rear of the third floor.

EDWARD W. WILHELM, assistant foreman of Engine Company No. 13, on the tenth of January, 1871, rendered incalculable service by extinguishing, without an alarm, a fire which broke out on the fifth floor of the Prescott House.

CHAS. L. KELLY, assistant foreman Engine Company No. 9, on the ninth of February, 1871, at a fire in a liquor store on the northeast corner of Division and Forsyth Streets, climbed the front of the adjoining building by the shutters and awnings, and, entering the building on fire, dragged three suffocated persons to a window and passed them to men on ladders.

DENTON E. HEMSWORTH, fireman Hook and Ladder Company No. 6, at No. 37 East Broadway, on the second of March, 1871, rescued a husband, wife and child, who were cut off from escape on the upper floor of the building.

WILLIAM F. CRAFT, fireman Hook and Ladder Company No. 6, aided in this rescue, with

WILLIAM McKENZIE, fireman of Hook and Ladder Company No. 1, and

THOMAS FARRELL, foreman of the same company.

AMBROSE L. AUSTIN, fireman Engine Company No. 15, was, on the twenty-fourth of April, 1871, attending to duty at the Repair Yard in Elizabeth Street when an alarm of fire came for an outbreak at No. 33 Bowery. Going there, he saw a woman fall from the basement steps into what appeared to be a furnace. Austin, in rescuing her, was burned about the face.

PETER WEIR, foreman Engine Company No. 25, on the seventeenth of August, 1871, at No. 15 Forsyth Street, went through smoke and flames to the sixth floor, rescued a woman and child, and, getting through the roof scuttle, carried them to a place of safety.

ROBERT A. McFARLAND, assistant foreman Hook and Ladder Company No. 4, on the twenty-third of December, 1871, at No. 479 Tenth Avenue and No. 502 West Fifty-first Street, rescued two children from a room on the second story.

JOHN BROWN, fireman of the same company, did similar service at this fire.

THOMAS HENRY, assistant foreman Hook and Ladder Company No. 6, at No. 23 Suffolk Street, on the fifteenth of February, 1872, saved eight lives, those of Mr. and Mrs. Metz, Mary Walsh, Mrs. Greenwald and four children. They were cut off on the second floor, and Henry passed them all out to comrades.

GEORGE MCLAUGHLIN, assistant foreman Engine Company No. 31, at No. 161 Leonard Street, on the seventh of April, 1872, rescued, at great personal risk, a colored woman, who, while tipsy, had set fire to her apartment.

THOMAS HUTCHINSON, foreman Hook and Ladder Company No 1, at No. 63 Baxter Street, on the twentieth of December, 1872, was compelled by fire and smoke to retreat to a rear fire escape on the second floor. Hanging to the fire escape of the third floor was a boy, who, at Hutchinson's bidding, let go, and Hutchinson caught him and saved him.

WILLIAM ROWE, foreman Hook and Ladder Company No. 9. Maillard's confectionery store, restaurant and hotel, Nos. 619 and 621 Broadway, were on fire on the twenty-seventh of December, 1872. The majority of the guests, aroused in the dead of a bitter cold night, escaped in their night clothes, but a few were surprised and cut off. Foreman Rowe risked his life in entering the building, and was instrumental in saving Julia Mulhearn, Benjamin Fitch, Rosanna Daly, August Clause, Mary Fox and a Mr. Gordon.

JAMES HEANY, assistant foreman of Rowe's company,

JAMES MCGIVNEY, fireman, and

THOMAS D. REILLY, fireman, shared the honors of the rescue with their commanding officer.

WILLIAM H. NASH, chief of the Fourth Battalion, on the thirtieth of December, 1872, at No. 223 Division Street, hearing from Widow Rends that her children, Matilda and Abbie, were cut off from escape in a room on the first floor, braved death to rescue them, and, going through fire and smoke to the room, caught up the children and saved them.

THOMAS HENRY, assistant foreman Hook and Ladder Company No. 6, at this fire, at personal risk, rescued Lewis Levy and his son Charles.

JOHN J. O'BRIEN, fireman of Henry's company, at this fire, rescued Mary Rosenthal, aged twenty.

GEORGE W. ERB, foreman of the same company, rescued Charles Cohn, who was partly suffocated on the second floor, by going up the new fire escape.

JOHN F. DU FLON, fireman of the same company, rescued a sick and bed-ridden lad from the second floor.

JOSEPH F. MCGILL, foreman Hook and Ladder Company No. 11, on the third of March, 1873, was at the fierce fire which broke out at Nos. 35 and 37 Vesey Street. The fire seized on the upper part of the building, and when Harriet Colgan, from one of the top windows, shrieked for aid, McGill went up a ladder and rescued her shortly before the floors fell in.

THEODORE DAKIN, fireman Engine Company No. 13, on the eighteenth of March, 1873, at No. 94 Greene Street, was severely burned in rescuing a boy, Henry Marschoff, who was cut off from escape, and was abandoned by his parents.

AMBROSE L. AUSTIN, and

FRANCIS CAREY, foreman Engine Company No. 3, on the twenty-seventh of

March, 1873, at No. 119 Ninth Avenue, in arousing the inmates, found Elizabeth and Sarah Early, Sarah Murray and Josephine Welch insensible in a room on the top floor. The firemen were cut off from escape by the stairs, but they took all the rescued persons to the street by getting out of a window and climbing to an awning, and thence to the street.

TERRENCE P. BRENNAN, assistant foreman Hook and Ladder Company No. 3, on the second of April, 1873, was at No. 126 Fourth Avenue when escape for four persons on the upper floor was cut off. Brennan rescued them from a ladder when they were half suffocated and were resigned to their fate.

JOHN P. FLOOD, fireman of this company, at this fire, rescued Stella and Louisa Lauri at great personal risk.

MICHAEL MCAVOY, fireman of this company, in aiding in their rescue, was seriously burned.

ALFRED CONNORS, foreman Hook and Ladder Company No. 10, on the twentieth of July, 1873, was on his way to a fire in Fulton Street, when Mary Brady, at Cortlandt Street and Broadway, attempted to run across the path of the truck. Connor, who was ahead of the apparatus, seized the woman and both were drawn down by the horses. The woman was killed and Connor was seriously injured.

WILLIAM W. RHODES, assistant engineer Hook and Ladder Company No. 2, and

JOHN SATTLER, foreman of Hook and Ladder Company No. 2, on the first of May, 1873, at No. 334 East Twenty-sixth Street, the stairs of which could not be used because of fire and smoke, rescued eight persons who were in peril on the third story.

JOHN MCPARLEN, fireman Hook and Ladder Company No. 7, on the first of May, 1873, at No. 334 East Twenty-sixth Street, was severely burned in extinguishing fire in the clothing of Mrs. Mary McGinniss, in whose apartment a kerosene lamp had exploded.

WILLIAM H. NASH, chief of the Fourth Battalion, on the twenty-third of August, 1873, at No. 13 Forsyth Street, mounted a ladder, and, standing on the top rung of it, rescued Nathan Urvinez, his wife, and three children. The woman, when taken in Chief Nash's arms, fainted, and she, her babe and her rescuer would have fallen but for timely aid from members of Hook and Ladder Company No. 9. At this fire Betsy Goldberg, Minnie Urvinez, Michael, Benjamin and Mont Wolf were rescued by

WILLIAM D. CLENDENNING,

TIMOTHY MCDONALD and

GEORGE BUTLER, firemen Hook and Ladder Company No. 9. McDonald, in spite of warnings that he would not come out alive, entered the burning structure and saved the father of the Wolf family and one of his children.

HENRY SCHRICKS, assistant foreman Engine Company No. 34, at No. 423 West Thirty-second Street, in response to heartrending appeals from a woman whose child had been left in the house, broke away from his comrades, who thought him foolhardy, rescued the child, who was insensible, and was burned slightly in groping his way back to the street.

THOMAS LALLY, assistant foreman Hook and Ladder Company No. 6, on the twentieth of May, 1874, at No. 18 Clinton Street, where a number of persons were cut off from escape by the stairs, saved the lives of two children on the fourth floor.

WILLIAM H. NASH, chief of the Fourth Battalion, at this fire, gallantly saved the lives of a man, his wife, and five children, from a ladder.

THOMAS F. FARMAN,

WILLIAM WOGAN,

WILLIAM H. GUY, and

GEORGE W. TOWN, firemen Hook and Ladder Company No. 6,

THOMAS HARRISON and

ALBERT HENDRICKSON, helped in the above rescue.

JOHN McCLANE, foreman of Hook and Ladder Company No. 11, saved Rica and Isidore Garlish and Herman Lands at the same fire.

JOSEPH MOSE, fireman Engine Company No. 28, on the twenty-third of July, 1874, at No. 194 Avenue C, aided

EDWARD O'BRIEN, assistant foreman of his company, in most gallantly rescuing from an upper room Ellen McGuire and her grandchildren, Hannah and Ellen, who were huddled together and partly suffocated.

WILLIAM MITCHELL, foreman Engine Company No. 10, at No. 13 Cherry Street, on the twenty-fifth of June, 1874, when a drunkard, James Gill, had set fire to a gunny bag manufactory, saw through a window a man crawling in fire and smoke. With the aid of

THOMAS BATTERBERRY, assistant engineer of the company, Mitchell battered down red-hot iron doors and shutters and rescued the man, whose name was not ascertained.

ANTHONY STEPHENSON,

JOHN WRIGHT and

JOHN HERN, firemen Hook and Ladder Company No. 3, on October 18, 1874, at No. 156 Third Avenue, rescued four women and a man who were cut off from escape and unconscious.

JUSTIN A. PATTEN, foreman,

JAMES HORN, assistant foreman, and

CHARLES W. SMITH, fireman of Engine Company No. 11, on the twentieth of December, 1874, at No. 88 Lewis Street, took Amanda Clarkson and her children, Elizabeth and George, from the attic to the roof and saved them at personal risk.

JAMES McCUTCHEN, assistant foreman, and

JOHN H. GRIFFIN, foreman Hook and Ladder Company No. 12, on the twenty-fourth of January, 1875, at No. 189 Eighth Avenue, when the inmates were cut off from escape by a blazing staircase, rescued three children, Raphael, Martha and Dora Harris.

JAMES HORN, assistant foreman Engine Company No. 11, on the twenty-sixth of March, 1875, at Nos. 353 and 355 Rivington Street, at midnight, found Anthony Paul imprisoned on the fourth floor and about to throw his children, Josephine, Joseph C. and Catherine, into the street, and jump after them with Adeline D. Paul, his wife. Horn burst into the room, picked up two of the children, and, followed by the others, went to the roof and saved all.

JOHN CARNEY, fireman Engine Company No. 3, on the second of October, 1875, at No. 517 East Sixteenth Street, heard that Julia Nichols, a bedridden

WM B. KIRCHNER (1883)

P. H. SHORT (1885)

JOHN LEVINS (1880)

J. L. ROONEY (1882)

DANIEL J. MEAGHER (1878)

JOS. McGOWAN (1876)

T. J. DOUGHERTY (1877)

M. COMMERFORD (1881)

JOHN BINNS (1884)

PAUL BAUER (1879)

sexagenarian, was left on the second floor. At great personal risk he broke down the door of her room and saved her.

JOHN P. FLOOD and

JACOB REITER, firemen Hook and Ladder Company No. 3, at this fire, found Bridget Kelly and Isabella Dennigan partly suffocated on the fifth floor, and saved them.

Members of Hook and Ladder Company No. 11, on the thirteenth of April, 1875, at No. 138½ Pitt Street, at 12.25 A. M., rescued Charles Kuhne, his wife Hannah, and their six children, whose escape by the stairs and back piazza was cut off by a fierce fire. Particular mention was made in the roll of meri of the conduct of firemen

JOHN McCLANE,

THOMAS LARKIN and

MICHAEL McAVOY.

JOSEPH McGOWEN, fireman Engine Company No. 6, on the fourteenth of April, 1876, at No. 15 Thomas Street, and his comrade, fireman

THOMAS KEENAN, learned on arriving at the fire that Mary Molony, Julia Roach and four children were cut off on the third floor. McGowen entered the building, and through an attic window passed three of the children to Keenan, who was on the cornice of an adjoining building. The others were taken to the roof. All were nearly exhausted by terror and inhaling smoke.

JAMES LEVINS, fireman Engine Company No. 8,

JOHN ROBERTSON and

JACOB LAMBRECHT, firemen, Hook and Ladder Company No. 2, at No. 743 Third Avenue, on the thirtieth of April, 1876, rescued Catherine Shea and her children, James and Anna, who were cut off from escape on the third floor and were screaming at the window.

DANIEL BRADLEY, assistant foreman Hook and Ladder Company No. 1, at No. 60 Mulberry Street, on the eighth of December, 1876, rescued Harris Levy, fourteen months old, who had been forgotten and was unconscious.

NICHOLAS P. LOESCH, a fireman in Bradley's company, nearly lost his life in saving, at the same fire, from the fifth floor, Abraham Amer, four years old.

Officers and members of Hook and Ladder Company No. 4, on the tenth of December, 1876, at No. 482 Ninth Avenue, most gallantly rescued seven members of the Dettmar family, Miss Lena Minsi, and Margaret and Mary Ann Early, who were in great peril and cut off from escape.

DENNIS MURPHY, fireman Engine Company No. 43, the 'William F. Havemeyer,' was put on the roll of merit for having, on the twenty-fourth of March, 1876, rescued Mrs. Nelly Mullen, chambermaid on the boat, from drowning.

JAMES A. GALLAGHER, fireman Engine Company No. 19, at No. 509 Eighth Avenue, on the nineteenth of November, 1876, forced his way through fire and smoke to the second floor landing, and picked up and carried safely to the street Mrs. Sarah Ferrir, mother of Mrs. S. Sumner, who was insensible.

HUGH J. GOLDEN, assistant foreman Engine Company No. 20, at No. 47 Elizabeth Street, on the twenty-seventh of February, 1877, aided by

JOHN RIELLY, fireman of his command, rescued Mrs. Mary Harkins and her son John at great personal risk.

JOHN MILLER, chief of battalion; THOMAS LALLY, assistant foreman; and WILLIAM H. GREY. TIMOTHY DWYER, THOMAS O'HEARN, PATRICK FOHY,

JOHN CAVANAGH, and GEORGE MURPHY, firemen, Hook and Ladder Company No. 6, were, on the eleventh of March, 1877, at No. 24 Ludlow Street, when the bursting of a kerosene lamp caused a fire that spread rapidly from the second floor. The inhabitants were panic stricken, but by ladders and from the roofs of adjoining houses, the officers and firemen named took out Abraham Lavin, a child who was dead, and rescued David Lavin aged six, Hattie Manson aged ten, Louis Frank aged five, Bernard Frank aged three, Mark Frank aged three, Annie Weisburg aged eight, Rosanna Weisburg aged thirty, and Herman Frank aged five.

THOMAS J. DOUGHERTY, fireman, Hook and Ladder Company No. 1, on the thirty-first of March, 1877, at No. 29 North William Street, learned that Julius Frank and Elizabeth Stevens were perishing in the sub-basement. Dougherty, with an axe, descended, and cutting down two doors, found them unconscious in dense smoke. He carried them under the front stoop and passed them up to members of his company, having to raise each person about eight feet. Only his great endurance and strength enabled him to withstand the heat and smoke, and raise and pass out the sufferers.

DENNIS J. DORAN, fireman, Engine Company No. 17, on the twenty-eighth of August, 1877, at No. 188 Eldridge Street, braved heat and smoke, and after three attempts, rescued Lena Zeigler, a child, from a bedroom on the third floor, when she was almost suffocated.

WILLIAM H. REYNOLDS, fireman, Engine Company No. 14, at the Park Theater, on the twenty-fourth of October, 1877, so quickly extinguished canvas scenery that had been fired by a gas bracket, as to prevent a panic and frightful loss of life. The terror of the audience was allayed, and the fireman was loudly applauded.

LUKE GLEESON, fireman, Engine Company No. 12, on the fourteenth of December, 1877, at No. 112 Chatham Street, found Charles Roeder and Louis Stanboeck partly insensible on the third floor. Carrying one and followed by the other he took them to the first floor, when they recovered and were able to go to the street unaided.

PATRICK HEALY, fireman, Engine Company No. 14, on the seventh of January, 1878, at the New York Dental College, saved the life of Mrs. James Gracie, of No. 200 East Fortieth Street, by extinguishing a fire on her dress, which was caused by an alcohol lamp falling on her.

MICHAEL F. REEVES, foreman, Hook and Ladder Company No. 8, on the fourth of January, 1878, and

JOHN HOPE, a fireman of his company, at No. 132 West Broadway, found sixteen persons calling for help at the windows, they being unable to escape by the stairs. Calming them and raising ladders, they, with other members of the company, rescued James A. Hart, his wife, and three children; Thomas Kent, his wife and child; Michael Shiels, W. C. Wilkins, a man whose name was not ascertained, two brothers named Laing, P. Smith, F. Zebro, and Charles Hoff.

WILLIAM KLINE,

CHARLES HOPPER, and

JOHN MCKEON, firemen, of Reeves' company, and

JOHN J. MCMANUS, fireman, of Engine Company No. 27, shared in the honor of these rescues.

Officers and members of Hook and Ladder Company No. 6, on the second of April, 1878, at No. 5 Hester Street, gallantly rescued Sarah Goldberg, her children, David, Mary, and Solomon, and Jacob, Samuel, Abraham, and Mary Leszinsky, children.

DANIEL J. MEAGHER, foreman, Hook and Ladder Company No. 3, on the second of May, 1878, at No. 28 East Fourteenth Street, acted promptly on seeing Mrs. Sarah Freeman hanging out of a fourth story window. A ladder raised was found to be too short, although held by hooks and stood on the stoop. Ordering the ladder to be raised quite erect, and away from the building, Meagher went up, stood on the top rung, told her to be calm and hold her limbs rigid, and then to drop. As she fell he caught her, and passed her safely to

JOHN P. FLOOD, fireman of his company, who, despite a sprained foot, aided in the rescue.

THOMAS O'HALLORAN and

JAMES H. CAMPBELL, firemen, Hook and Ladder Company No. 8, on the sixteenth of September, 1878, at No. 149 West Broadway, at great personal risk, rescued Thomas Denham and Mary A. Young.

PATRICK KENNEDY, fireman, Hook and Ladder Company No. 14, at No. 358 East One Hundred and Twenty-third Street, on the thirteenth of March, 1879, rescued Charles E. Quinn, who was overcome by smoke in bed in a hall room on the third floor.

MICHAEL CONNORS, fireman, Engine Company No. 14, at No. 190 Sixth Avenue, on the tenth of April, 1879, before the ladders arrived climbed up the front of the building, and found, partly suffocated by intensely hot smoke, Marie Oxley and her children, Marie, John, and Alice, and rescued them.

Officers and members of Hook and Ladder Company No. 4, on the twenty-second of April, 1879, at No. 619 Sixth Avenue, rescued from fire and suffocation Mrs. E. X. Monstery, Miss M. Monstery, and Consuela Monstery, members of the family of Colonel T. H. Monstery. The following members of the company were particularly mentioned in the reports:

ROBERT WILLIAMS, foreman; JOHN BROWN and TIMOTHY McAULIFFE, firemen.

LAWRENCE P. FARLEY, fireman, Engine Company No. 20, on the twenty-third of April, 1879, at No. 52 Prince Street, prevented Josephine Lash, aged sixteen, from jumping to the yard from the second floor, and going up-stairs, carried her to an adjoining house.

GEORGE GILLIES, foreman, Engine Company No. 26, on the twenty-fourth of May, 1879, at No. 221 West Forty-third Street, was unable to go up-stairs to the rescue of a number of persons imprisoned on the third floor because of the heat and smoke. But a painter's scaffold was in front of the house, and, drawing himself up to it from the stoops of a house next door, he rescued Miss Nellie Fitzgerald, Miss Belle Shaffer, William Hammond, Emil Sultan, and Alexander Bofil.

ALEXANDER McDONALD, assistant foreman, Hook and Ladder Company No. 8, at No. 528 Broome Street, on the fourteenth of July, 1879, found Maria Brine and her children, Edward and Carrie, asking for help from a window of the third floor. McDonald went up a ladder, calmed them, and took them to the street by the stairs.

WILLIAM J. COLBY, assistant foreman, Hook and Ladder Company No. 4, and firemen WILLIAM T. LEAR, JOHN BROWN, BERNARD J. REILLY, and WILLIAM JACKSON, at No. 402 West Fortieth Street, on the twenty-fifth of September, 1879, rescued Henrietta Schwab, who was unconscious, and her son, who was partly overcome by smoke. Both were carried down a ladder to the street, the stairs being impassable.

PATRICK J. LYNCH, private, Engine Company No. 11, on the fourteenth of November, 1879, at No. 80 Cannon Street, where many lives were lost, saw Maria Barbisher, who was at a third story window, drop her son John into the arms of a citizen. Then Lynch caught her daughter Mary, ten years old, but was thrown to the ground by her weight. Lynch told the mother to be calm, and he would save her. While he was making his way through fire that burned him seriously, the woman jumped out of the window, and was killed. Lynch narrowly escaped being killed in reaching a place of safety. For his courage and humanity he was promoted to the grade of fireman.

PATRICK MCCARTHY, assistant foreman, Engine Company No. 20, at No. 301 Mulberry Street, rear, on the twenty-fifth of December, 1879, rescued Patrick Houston, aged sixty, who was insensible from smoke on the third floor.

PAUL BAUER, fireman, Hook and Ladder Company No. 4, at Nos. 405 and 407 West Fiftieth Street, on the twenty-seventh of December, 1879, before any companies had arrived, rescued Mrs. Avilla Staniford from a third story window by a ladder raised on the shoulders of citizens.

BERNARD MCALLISTER, private, Engine Company No. 11, at No. 54 Sheriff Street, on the fifteenth of January, 1880, rescued, at great personal risk, Henrietta Cohn, a child, who was nearly suffocated on the third floor at the same fire.

JOHN W. MILLER, chief of battalion, rescued Willie Cohen, another child, at equal risk to himself.

M. D. CONRY, assistant foreman, Engine Company No. 21, with his subordinate firemen,

JOHN SCULLY,

CHARLES CALLAHAN and

JAMES LEVINS, at No. 99 Park Avenue, on the second of May, 1880, jumped twelve feet from a roof, and rescued, insensible, Bridget Murray, a servant, who had been driven there by fire.

FRANCIS MAHEDY, foreman, with

JAMES BYRNES, assistant foreman, and firemen

SYLVESTER BENNETT,

JAMES A. MCGINN,

E. H. TOBIN and

THOMAS MCCARTHY, of Engine Company No. 1, on the twenty-sixth of July, 1880, at No. 253 West Twenty-ninth Street, saved from suffocation and jumping from windows, Mrs. Agnes Brady and her five children, Mrs. Emma Martin and three children, and Mrs. Eva Feltner and nine members of her family.

THOMAS LARKIN and

JACOB REITER, firemen, Hook and Ladder Company No. 11, at No. 328 East Houston Street, rescued, on the same day, from the third floor, Teresa Long and her daughter Jenny, who were in imminent danger of suffocation.

J. T. HANLON, private, Engine Company No. 23, and

GEORGE W. GREER, private, Hook and Ladder Company No. 2, on the sixteenth of August, 1880, at No. 1618 Broadway, rescued Lucy Flouert, aged seventeen, who was imprisoned and insensible in a vault.

JOHN LEVINS, fireman, Hook and Ladder Company No. 2, at No. 112 East Fifty-fifth Street, on the ninth of October, 1880, found Mary L. Frey cut off from escape in a rear room on the third floor, by passing in from a window of a building next door. He saved her with a rope passed him by his comrades.

DANIEL SHERLIN, fireman, Hook and Ladder Company No. 9, at No. 223 East Broadway, on the same day, rescued, in the attic, Mary Jackson, thirty years old.

C. W. SMITH, fireman, Hook and Ladder Company No. 9, on the fourth of November, 1880, at No. 76 Elizabeth Street, rescued Frank Jeher, who, in attempting to save papers in B. F. Graley's horseshoeing shop, which was on fire, had fallen insensible.

Officers and members of Hook and Ladder Company No. 6 and Engine Company No. 9 distinguished themselves on the eighth of November, 1880, at No. 11 Market Street, by their quick and safe rescue of Delia Schwab and Rachel Allen, and two children, Rachel and David Fine.

LUKE KAVANAGH, fireman, Engine Company No. 6, on the ninth of February, 1881, at No. 68 New Church Street, the factory of the Western Electric Manufacturing Company, saw a man leaning out of a fifth-story window and in great peril. Going to No. 70, he lowered himself over a cornice to a projection fifteen inches wide, and a short ladder being passed to him, he held it on the projection until the man, Julius Ehrlich, who was aged and weighed over two hundred pounds, descended, and he aided him to reach the roof of the house next door. The act called forth the following praise:

WESTERN ELECTRIC MANUFACTURING COMPANY,
62 AND 68 NEW CHURCH STREET,
CHICAGO, 220–232 KINZIE STREET.   NEW YORK, February 17, 1881.

To the Board of Fire Commissioners, New York:

GENTLEMEN: We desire to express our cordial appreciation of the services of the Fire Department in extinguishing the fire at our factory on February 9. The efficiency and skill displayed by the first battalion, under the direction of Chief Rowe, as well as by all other members of the department present, were all that stood between us and the total destruction of our factory. It was a well-fought fire. We desire especially to mention the very noble conduct of Fireman Luke Kavanagh, who, at great peril to himself, rescued our workman, Julius Ehrlich, from his dangerous position in the fifth story. The excellence of the service of the department on the occasion of our fire, and the devotion and courage of Luke Kavanagh in risking his life for a stranger, are only repetitions of many similar experiences in this city—experiences that have justly given the Fire Department of this city its splendid reputation.

Yours respectfully,

THE WESTERN ELECTRIC MANUFACTURING COMPANY,

GEORGE M. PHELPS, JR., Superintendent.

WILLIAM H. FLEMING, foreman, Engine Company No. 12, on the fourth of January, 1881, at No. 35 Madison Street, found the stairway on fire and escape to the street cut off. A child, Minnie Egan, was hanging from a fire escape, and, with the aid of a citizen, he broke her fall by holding out a coat. Then going to No. 33 Madison Street, he got on a rear fire escape and saw the child's mother, Margaret, at the window of the burning building.   An alley separated the houses, and fireman Fleming, with the aid of

MICHAEL COMMERFORD, fireman, of his company, made a bridge over the alley, found the woman and saved her. Then he attempted to rescue three more of her children, but was driven back by heat and smoke. Commerford then made the attempt, and, lying down on the ladder and groping in the room, found William and John, who were insensible, and passed them out to his commander. Nelly Egan was afterwards found dead.

TERENCE P. BRENNAN, assistant foreman, and

ANTHONY STEPHENSON, fireman, Hook and Ladder Company No. 3, on New Year's Day, 1881, at No. 110 East Fourteenth Street, found in danger of suffocation, on the third floor, and rescued, Albert Rossy, Albert Klaus and Ernest Kailber.

ABRAHAM STORM, private, Engine Company No. 46, on the fourteenth of May, 1881, in Third Avenue, between Eighty-third and Eighty-fourth Streets, at great personal risk, stopped the runaway team of Louis Bauer, thus saving many persons from serious injury or worse.

Officers and members of Hook and Ladder Company No. 4, on the sixteenth of June, 1881, at No. 317 West Forty-sixth Street, rescued Julius M. Samter and Adolph Arh, whose escape from the fourth floor had been cut off.

JAMES HAMILTON,

JOSEPH F. FLOCK, and

WILLIAM MOCLAIR, firemen, Engine Company No. 43, on the twenty-sixth of July, 1881, rescued at Pier No. 1, North River, Charles Reinhardt, a drunkard, who was drowning.

WILLIAM MOCLAIR, fireman, and

THOMAS P. LEONARD, stoker, Engine Company No. 43, on the fourteenth of August, 1881, at Pier No. 1, North River, rescued Lizzie Miller, who attempted to drown herself.

JAMES HAMILTON, fireman, Engine Company No. 43, on the eighteenth of September, 1881, at Pier No. 1, North River, rescued from drowning Norman Auerham, of No. 8 Lewis Street.

JOHN FLANAGAN, private, Engine Company No. 1, on the fourteenth of October, 1881, at No. 447 West Sixteenth Street, while suffering from injuries sustained at a fire, rescued from the upper part of the house Joseph Eagan, a child, who was almost suffocated.

WILLIAM J. COLBY, foreman Hook and Ladder Company No. 8, on the fifteenth of November, 1881, at No. 499 Canal Street, rescued three persons. A ladder could not be put against the building on fire because of an awning, so it was raised to the next building. Colby went to the roof, and in the attic of the burning structure found Lizzie Pfeiffer, her child Hannah, and Harriet Brown. When he was about to pass out with the child the woman seized him, and but for

LOUIS S. HOAGLAND, fireman, and

JOHN J. KENNY, private of his company, he would have fallen. All the persons in danger—who were burned—so near were they to destruction, were conveyed to the street.

JOSHUA WALLACE, private, Engine Company No. 31, on the twenty-second of November, 1881, at No. 38 East Broadway, found Rachel Harris, fifty-eight years old, insensible from smoke on the top floor, and carried her to the street.

JOHN L. ROONEY, fireman, Hook and Ladder Company No. 10,

HENRY MURRAY, assistant foreman,

JOHN SCHWAB, fireman,

JOHN J. HORAN and

JAMES E. NOLAN, private, in same company, at the Potter Building Fire, on the thirty-first of January, 1882, especially distinguished themselves. Rooney, standing on a ladder raised five feet from Beekman Street, saved Miss Ida Small. Murray and Horan saved Alexander Roberts with a ladder resting on the sill of a third story window. Two men were caught as they dropped from a signboard on the fourth story by Nolan, who was on the top of a ladder, and Schwab joined in peril and piloted to the street five men.

MICHAEL MCAVOY, fireman, Hook and Ladder Company No. 3, on the twenty-eighth of May, 1882, at No. 519 East Eleventh Street, in clearing the smoke-charged tenement of its inmates, was caught on the third floor, and had to take to the rear fire escape. Going by this to the fourth floor, moans guided him to Mrs. Anne Haven, who was fifty years old and bedridden. McAvoy took her to a rear window, and comrades hoisted her to the roof, and succeeded in getting her to the street.

FRANK LEONARD, fireman, Engine Company No. 15, and

THOMAS O. HEARN, fireman, Hook and Ladder Company No. 6, at No. 43 Suffolk Street, on the twenty-ninth of May, 1882, in dense smoke, rescued Samuel and Sarah Franks and Rene Solaar.

THOMAS MCCARTHY, fireman, Engine Company No. 1, at No. 225 West Twenty-seventh Street, on the twenty-seventh of June, 1882, hearing that William Price, a negro child, had been forgotten, went up the fire escape and saved him. Both McCarthy and the child were slightly burned.

THOMAS LALLY, foreman,

JAMES MCTAGGART, fireman, and

J. C. O'SHAUGHNESSY, private, Hook and Ladder Company No. 1, at No. 103 Washington Street, on the twenty-first of July, 1882, rescued Emma Vorgen, Mary Fetteral, Augusta Berghold and Annie Alms, who were cut off from escape and were screaming at windows of the third floor.

JOHN W. MILLER, chief of battalion,

JOHN H. KEHOE, foreman,

JOHN RIORDAN, assistant foreman,

JOHN FROBOESE and

WILLIAM MCGLONE, firemen, of Hook and Ladder Company No. 6, at No. 290 Grand Street, on the tenth of November, 1882, rescued Pauline Cohen, aged fifty-three, Abraham Cohen, aged sixty-eight, and Annie Nessnor, aged forty-eight, who were cut off from escape by the stairway by smoke and fire.

JOHN J. HORAN, private, Hook and Ladder Company No. 1, on the sixth of January, 1883, at Nos. 307 and 309 Broadway, discovered Emily and Marianna Devine cut off by smoke, and rescued them.

PATRICK H. DOWNEY, assistant engineer, Engine Company No. 29, at Pier No. 36, North River, on the first of February, 1883, took an icy bath and risked his life, but saved private Peter Smith, of Engine Company No. 7, who was drowning.

WILLIAM J. COOK, fireman, Engine Company No. 39, at the Cambridge Flats, No. 48 East Sixty-fourth Street, on the seventh of March, 1883, groped about the burning building in dense smoke and saved first an old lady whose name was not ascertained, and then carried out Harriet Perkins and Ann Smith, who were partly asphyxiated

WILLIAM LANSAR, private, Engine Company No. 13, on the seventeenth of March, 1883, learned of a fire at Prince and Greene Streets, and, going there, heard that three women were in peril on the third floor. Driven out of the house by smoke and fire, he climbed up the front of the building by projections, and took out and passed them in peril to firemen who had put up a ladder too short to reach the third floor.

WILLIAM B. KIRCHNER, private, Engine Company No. 17, on the twenty-ninth of March, 1883, at No. 138 Eldridge Street, heard people crying for help within. All the ladders brought by citizens were too short, and the department ladder had not arrived. Kirchner went to the roof of the next house, and on that of the building on fire found John McCabe helpless from fright and smoke inhalation. Placing him where he was safe, Kirchner rescued McCabe's wife, who was crippled by rheumatism, by dragging her out of an attic window. In carrying her away he jumped an alley three feet wide between 136 and 134.

JAMES McTAGGART, fireman, and

GEORGE McGRATH, private, Hook and Ladder Company No. 1, at No. 338 Pearl Street, on the same day, by means of ladders to the rear of the fourth floor, rescued Miss Pinkey Broadwell, partly insensible, her mother, Lucy, and her sister, Maggie, who were unconscious from smoke.

JOHN H. MERTENS, assistant engineer, Engine Company No. 42, on the twenty-eighth of May, 1883, at Third Avenue and One Hundred and Sixty-sixth Street, rescued Mamie Sherwood, a child, whose clothes had caught fire, and saved her life by wrapping his coat around her.

CHARLES KNOEPFEL, private, Engine Company No. 19, on the thirty-first of August, 1883, at the Methodist Episcopal Church, No. 359 West Twenty-fourth Street. When in the rear, a scaffold rope had broken so that William Horner fell and was fatally injured. Knoepfel saw William F. Smith, Horner's companion, clinging to the rope, which had not parted. He scaled a fence, went to the roof, and pulled up Smith, who fainted when safe.

TIMOTHY SULLIVAN, private, Hook and Ladder Company No. 6, on the twenty-eighth of January, 1884, at No. 81 Thomas Street, put out fire in the clothes of Frances Houck, the victim of a kerosene accident, and ran with her to the Chambers Street Hospital.

JAMES HEANY, assistant foreman, Hook and Ladder Company No. 1, at No. 4 Dover Street, on the twelfth of February, 1884, took to the fire escape Patrick Cronin, his wife, and their five half-suffocated children.

FRANCIS MAHEDY, chief of battalion, and

JOHN BANKS, fireman, Engine Company No. 7, at the Erie Building, No. 214 Duane Street, on the nineteenth of February, 1884, when escape by the stairs had been cut off, rescued the janitor, Arnold Keift, his wife, and their four children, from the fifth story.

HENRY W. McADAMS, foreman, Hook and Ladder Company No. 7, at No. 36 East Twelfth Street, on the twenty-fourth of March, 1884, rescued Mrs. C.

M. Maxwell from a third story window, and carried her by a ladder to the street.

THOMAS F. FREEL, private, Engine Company No. 43, at the foot of West Eighteenth Street, on the fourth of April, 1884, jumped into the North River, and saved a boy, Henry J. Whittaker.

JOHN BINNS,

WILLIAM J. MULHARE,

E. C. GRAHAM, and

THOMAS F. BARRETT, privates, Hook and Ladder Company No. 3, and

THOMAS J. MOONEY, private, Engine Company No. 5, at the St. George flats, Nos. 223 and 225 East Seventeenth Street, on April 7, 1884, distinguished themselves conspicuously. The official record relates that " Upon arriving at the scene of the fire, Louis Castaigne, the elevator boy, was discovered at one of the seventh story windows calling for help, the fire having extended so rapidly as to make it impossible for him to come down the stairway. Being ordered by the company commander to scale the front of the building to rescue the imperiled boy, Binns at once proceeded to do so, followed by Graham and Barrett, and while they were ascending from story to story by means of the scaling ladders, the long extension ladder of the company was raised to its full height, reaching to the sill of the sixth story windows. Private Binns, having reached the fifth story by means of the scaling ladder, stepped from thence to the extension ladder, carrying his scaling ladder with him, which he then hooked into the window of the seventh story, and ascending it, found the boy in an exhausted and excited condition ; he reassured and quieted him, and passed him down safely to his comrades below. Binns then made as thorough a search as practicable of the upper part of the building ; descended to the fifth floor, where he was joined by Private Mulhare, of Hook and Ladder Company No. 3, and found Robert W. Lockwood cut off from means of escape, who was aided to the street by way of the extension ladder. In recognition of the courage, agility, and good judgment so prominently displayed by Private Binns on this occasion, as well as of his other good qualities, he was successively promoted assistant foreman and foreman. In the meantime it was learned that other occupants, who were seen at the upper windows on the side of the building, were in danger, and private Mooney succeeded in rescuing Mrs. J. L. Lockwood, an invalid son, Louis Lockwood, aged nine years, and Jennie Wilson, a servant, from their perilous situation."

SAMUEL BANTA, private, Hook and Ladder Company No. 9, at 20 and 22 Pell Street, on the twenty-fourth of April, 1884, proved himself a true hero. Walls had fallen, and fireman David H. Soden, of Engine Company No. 11, was buried. At first only his cries could be heard. Presently he could be seen in danger of roasting alive from burning debris, and held down by wood, iron, and bricks. Banta volunteered to cut his way to Soden and save him, and while comrades propped and held up the truck, Banta, with a saw, crow-bar, and axe, worked two hours before an ambulance surgeon could get near Soden to give him aid, stimulants having after the first hour been administered with a sponge.

CHARLES FROST, private, Engine Company No. 24, at No. 233 Bleecker Street, on the thirteenth of July, 1884, to rescue Mary E. Lane, who was appealing for aid from a third story window, climbed to a second story window

THE BENNETT MEDALISTS.

from a booth, and then, by a projection. to where the woman was. He tranquilized the woman until a ladder was raised, and carried her to the street. The smoke was so dense that they could not be seen from below.

PATRICK MEAD, fireman, Hook and Ladder Company No. 8, at No. 374 Second Avenue, on the seventeenth of May, 1884, endangered his life by dense smoke and intense heat to save an infant, Mary McDonald, who had been left in a room on the second story, and was insensible.

HENRY W. MCADAMS, foreman, Hook and Ladder Company No. 2,

MICHAEL SALMON, fireman, and

JOSEPH ARCENEAU, private, same company,

RICHARD GORMAN, private, Hook and Ladder Company No. 4, and

DEWITT C. BOGGOTT, fireman, Engine Company No. 50, at No. 931 Third Avenue, in the early morning of July 13, 1884, found persons hanging from the windows of the second, third, and fourth floors, calling for help. By the fire escape, stairs, and ladders, they rescued Lottie Nelson, Lizzie Ingalls, P. Madison, Mrs. P. Young and her daughter Susan, Mr. Eidman, Mr. and Mrs. Lowe, and W. Wyman and his five children.

Officers and members of Hook and Ladder Company No. 2 were afterwards honorably mentioned as a body in connection with this fire.

WILLIAM REILLY, private, Engine Company No. 24, on the fourth of August, 1884, at 170 Varick Street, found Mrs. McGloin hanging from a third story window and nearly exhausted. Climbing up an awning and standing on the sash of the second story window, he told the woman to drop, and caught her and took her to the street.

JOHN T. NEEDHAM, assistant foreman, and

THOMAS F. REYNOLDS, private, Hook and Ladder Company No. 8, at No. 54 Charlton Street, on the fourth of August, 1884, found Caroline Pesks, sixty years old, and her daughter Mary, twenty-five years old, cut off by fire, and carried them down a ladder to the street.

WILLIAM D. FRAZER, assistant foreman, and

JOSEPH A. COTTRELL, private, Hook and Ladder Company No. 1, at No. 42 Baxter Street, on the twenty-ninth of September, 1884, with JOSEPH F. MC-GILL, chief of battalion, and officers and members of Hook and Ladder Company No. 6, rescued nine bewildered persons, and then, on searching the building, found Jeremiah Griffin and Abraham Delinski, a child, who were partly suffocated, and at no inconsiderable risk got them safe to the street.

THOMAS F. FREEL, private, Engine Company No. 43, at pier No. 48 East River, on the fourth of November, 1884, rescued from drowning William Rapp, of Greenwich, Ct.

WILLIAM D. FRAZER, assistant foreman, Hook and Ladder Company No. 1, at No. 70 Baxter Street, on the fourteenth of December, 1884, climbed an awning, entered the second floor, which was full of dense smoke, and guided by cries and moans, found Mrs. Betsey Butterick and her three children exhausted. A ladder had been raised, and he passed them one by one to comrades.

TIMOTHY FITZPATRICK, JAMES MONAGHAN, SAMUEL MCQUIGLEY and PETER LORRM, firemen, Hook and Ladder Company No. 7, on the fourth of February, 1885, rescued, at No. 203 East Thirty-first Street, Mrs. E. F. Roberts and her three children, by ladders, from the second floor, their escape being cut off by smoke and fire.

PETER H. SHORT, foreman, and JOHN O. FURMAN, JOHN O. KING and JOSEPH A. COTTRELL, firemen, of Hook and Ladder Company No. 1; SAMUEL P. LYNCH and JOHN CLARKE, firemen, of Hook and Ladder Company No. 10; and DANIEL LYONS, fireman, of Engine Company No. 10, on the twenty-first of February, 1885, at Nos. 16 and 18 William Street, and Nos. 57, 59 and 61 Beaver Street, at great personal risk, rescued Mr. and Mrs. Ernest Jaede, their daughter Mina, Josephine Kraft and Mary Leavy. Six persons lost their lives at this fire, and one person was injured. The rescues were made with a chain of scaling ladders and ordinary ladders, and had the firemen been properly informed of the presence in the building of those who were lost, they would have been saved.

WILLIAM REILLY and CHARLES FROST, firemen, Engine Company No. 24, on the twenty-first of February, 1885, at No. 368 Greenwich Street, at no small personal risk, rescued Julia Welsh, Catharine Kennedy and Patrick McCarthy, all aged people, the latter being an octogenarian. The woman Welsh was in the basement, which was full of fire and smoke, and her clothes were ablaze. Fireman Reilly, in his first attempt at rescue, was badly burned, but he renewed the effort, and took her to the street. The others were rescued from the attic by Frost, who carried them to the street in spite of thick smoke.

JOHN T. NEEDHAM, assistant foreman, and JAMES H. SHUTE, SAMUEL ROSEBURY and MOSES RYER, firemen, of Hook and Ladder Company No. 8, on the sixteenth of February, 1885, at No. 164 Franklin Street, rescued by ladders, the building being charged with smoke, Henry Lussing, his wife and child, and Michael Lynch, his wife and child.

ROBERT C. MANNING and JAMES M. NUGENT, firemen, Hook and Ladder Company No. 3, at No. 337 East Fourteenth Street, on the twenty-second of February, 1885, rescued, at personal risk, Mrs. Carlstone and baby, Miss Schwartz, Henry Stern, wife and two children, Mrs. Mary Kennedy and her two daughters, Mrs. McLaughlin and her daughter.

Members of Hook and Ladder Companies Nos. 3, 4 and 7, and Engine Companies Nos. 8, 5, 14, 16 and 39, are honorably mentioned for services at a fire which broke out in the rear of the first floor of the five-story tenement, No. 672 First Avenue, at the dead of night on the third of May, 1885, and cut off all escape by the stairs. Eight persons were suffocated, killed or died. Ida Roebrick, Paul Kroner, Sophia Kroner, Rosalie Humphreys, Martha Kretschmar, Alfred Kretschmar, Kate Limbacher and daughter, George Hurley, wife and daughter, William Flannagan and H. Lehnpult were rescued in an exhausted condition, and sent to Bellevue Hospital. The alarm was tardily given; apparatus which should have responded were at another fire, and all the persons who lost their lives perished before the firemen could aid them. The many who were saved went to the windows, and were taken down by scaling ladders, ladders, life lines and the fire escapes.

FRANCIS J. REILLY, chief of Eleventh Battalion, and Assistant Foreman JOHN LEONARD, Engine Company No. 36, and Assistant Foreman LAWRENCE MURPHY, Engine Company No. 37, on the sixth of May, 1885, at No. 228 West One Hundred and Twenty-sixth Street, at great personal risk, the building being full of fire and charged with smoke, rescued Edward Hellenkamp, his wife, son and daughter.

GUSTAVE FUHRMANN, fireman, Hook and Ladder Company No. 6. On the twelfth of May, 1885, Maria Sullivan was driven by fire to the windows of the third story of No. 82 Mulberry Street, and her plight was so desperate that she got out of one of them and hung by the sill. She was nearly exhausted when Fuhrmann climbed up the front of the building, by projections, until he was able to support the woman, who was eventually taken down by a ladder.

JOHN J. EAGAN, foreman, and EDWARD J. LEAVY, fireman, of Engine Company No. 21, were burned and partially suffocated on the twenty-seventh of May, at No. 250 East Fortieth Street, in rescuing a child, Henry Dumar, from a room which was a sheet of flame, and in seeking for persons supposed to be in peril.

DIXON McQUEEN, fireman, Engine Company No. 51, was entered on the roll of honor for having, on the fifth of June, 1885, gallantly rescued from drowning Ellsworth Barry, aged nineteen, an employee of the Delamater Iron Works.

THOMAS AHEARN, assistant foreman of Hook and Ladder Company No. 11, on the seventh of June, 1885, at No. 312 East Houston Street, at personal risk, and by climbing up the front of the building, rescued a boy, Isidore Schnieber, who was cut off from escape. The same day, Ahearn, with Gustave Fuhrmann, of Hook and Ladder Company No. 6, went to an alarm of fire at No. 49 Pitt Street; Joseph and Annie Granger, children, were imprisoned in a room on the fourth floor, and ascent by the stairs was impossible. Ahearn and Fuhrmann mounted the fire escape and saved them.

JOHN R. KROWL, fireman, Hook and Ladder Company No. 2, was off duty on the third of September, 1885, but he assisted to raise ladders at a fire at No. 236 West Nineteenth Street, and rescued a Mrs. Spring from the second story of the building. At this fire the members of Hook and Ladder Company No. 12 distinguished themselves by rescuing Mrs. Carlyle, an unknown woman, Mr. and Mrs. Harrigan, Mrs. Wallace, and William Reinmuth. Simon Murray, of this command, rescued Mrs. Carlyle and the unknown woman from a window of the fourth floor, which was four feet above the top of the ladder on which he stood, and Luke Clayton, another member, rescued Reinmuth by going to the fifth floor of an adjoining building and dragging him into a window from the burning house while a citizen held him by the legs.

THOMAS F. FREEL, fireman, Engine Company No. 34, at great personal risk, rescued Robert E. Morrison, a boy, of No. 33 Cherry Street, from drowning at Pier No. 48, East River, on the fourth of September, 1885.

DIXON McQUEEN, fireman, Engine Company No. 51, on the third of October, 1885, risked his life to save that of Leo Barto, aged eighty-nine, No. 270 West Twelfth Street, who had fallen into the North River at Thirteenth Street.

LAWRENCE MURPHY, assistant foreman of Engine Company No. 37, was, on the eleventh of November, 1885, placed on the roll of merit, for having, on the sixth of May of that year, saved the life of E. Hellenkamp, a broker, of No. 56 Wall Street, at the fire at No. 228 West One Hundred and Twenty-sixth Street. Murphy had been placed on the roll of merit with Chief Reilly and Assistant Foreman John Leonard, but was put on it again on a communication from Mr. Hellenkamp.

W. E. McDONALD, fireman, Engine Company No. 44, was put on the roll of merit for having, on the twenty-third of November, 1885, at a fire at No.

404 East Sixty-fourth Street, after deterring four persons, Bohemians, from jumping into the street, saved them by taking them down a ladder.

CHARLES FORBACH, JOHN T. WHELAN, and GEORGE MOORE, firemen of Engine Company No. 53, on the thirtieth of December, 1885, at No. 1627 Lexington Avenue, put their lives in peril to rescue Sophie Altman and Richard Altman, children, and Mrs. Davis and her child Sadie. The building was so full of fire and smoke that the stairs could not be used. By the rear fire escape they found the Altman children insensible and passed them out. Then they aided Mrs. Davis to reach the next house. When they attempted to escape with the child they found themselves cut off on all sides, and had to remain at a fourth story window until rescued by a ladder.

WILLIAM BRAISTED, assistant foreman, JOHN E. NICKERSON and JOHN J. KENNY, of Hook and Ladder No. 5, and ANDREW GAFFNEY, assistant foreman of Engine Company No. 30, for rescuing Mary Cuneo, aged eleven; Charles Cuneo, aged nine; Rosie Cuneo, aged seven; Joseph Cuneo, aged five; John Cuneo, aged three; Angelo Cuneo, aged thirty-nine; and Teresa Cuneo, aged forty; and Louis Cuneo, aged eleven months old, at fire No. 17 Carmine Street, on January 4, 1886.

PHILIP PITZER, fireman, of Engine Company No. 13, while on leave of absence for twenty-four hours, rendered voluntary services at fire No. 13 Spruce Street, March 7, 1886. He was injured about the head.

T. HEAD, assistant foreman, and second grade fireman J. A. FISHER, and H. T. HEINZ, of Engine Company No. 5, for rescuing Peter Grady at fire No. 528 East Thirteenth Street, on March 26, 1886.

EDWARD MEEHAN assistant foreman, of Engine Company No. 12, at great personal risk, rescued Charles Eberhardt, aged nine years, from drowning at Staten Island, at 12.30 P. M., on August 19, 1886.

JOHN D. DALRYMPLE, fireman, of Hook and Ladder Company No. 4, at great personal risk, rescued from roof of a third story extension in rear of burning dwelling, Edmund O. Breinage, aged twenty-five years, who was unable to escape, on September 28, 1886.

THOMAS F. BARRETT and ANTHONY STEPHENSON, firemen of the first grade, and ANTHONY MALLOY, fireman of the second grade, of Hook and Ladder Company No. 3, rescuers of Mrs. Mary Cummings, at fire No. 63 East Twelfth Street, on October 20, 1886.

JOHN BARBER, assistant foreman of Engine Company No. 51, rescued Robert Cobane, aged seventy-four years, from drowning at foot of Thirteenth Street, N. R., on October 30, 1886.

WASHINGTON RYER, fireman, of Engine Company No. 12, at great personal risk, rescued Jessie and Bessie Whittle, aged eleven and thirteen years, respectively, at fire at 2149 Third Avenue, on November 22, 1886. The girls were in an unconscious condition on the third floor. Ryer covered them with a bed quilt, and had considerable difficulty in fighting his way down-stairs.

J. NIMPHIUS, fireman, of Hook and Ladder Company No. 14, at the same fire, rescued, at great personal risk, Mary Adams, aged fifty years. She was found unconscious in bed on the fourth floor, with a broken leg.

This completes the record of the heroic men whose names comprise the Roll of Merit. Is it not a chapter of brave deeds, such as cannot be found chronicled in any other branch of public service the wide world over?

THE BENNETT MEDALISTS.

The Bennett Medal was originated in April, 1869, when the following correspondence was had :

NEW YORK, April 13, 1869.

GENTLEMEN : My father being desirous of adding an additional competition to the members of the Metropolitan Fire Department in the discipline, courage and honesty with which their duties are now performed, and which were particularly called to his notice at the fire at his country residence during last September, has directed me to enclose the sum of fifteen hundred dollars, and requests that you will pay five hundred dollars to Messrs. Tiffany & Co. for the die of a medal they are preparing, and use the income of the balance in procuring, annually, a gold medal to be struck from the same, and to be conferred by you and your successors in this trust, upon such members of the Department as you may, in your judgment, consider best entitled to the reward.

Very truly yours,

JAMES GORDON BENNETT, JR.

To Messrs. T. Bailey Myers, James M. McLean and Robert S. Hone, Esquires.

NEW YORK, April 16, 1869.

DEAR SIR :—We have received your note of the thirteenth instant enclosing your check for fifteen hundred dollars, with the request that we should use five hundred dollars of the amount in payment for the die of a medal which you have ordered, and the income of the balance in annually preparing and conferring a gold medal, in the name of your father, on the members of the Fire Department whom we consider to be the most meritorious.

Although it will be difficult to make the selection from so much individual merit, as the Department is developing, we accept the trust with a full appreciation of the compliment conferred in our selection as trustees of your father's generous endowment, and will cause to be prepared a formal acceptance insuring its perpetuity.

We are, very truly, yours,

T. BAILEY MYERS,
JAMES McLEAN,
ROBERT S. HONE.

J. Gordon Bennett, Jr., Esq.

The following were, and are, the holders of a medal, endowed by the late James Gordon Bennett, proprietor of the New York *Herald*, whose attention was directed to the discipline, courage, and honesty of the officers and members of the Department on the occasion of a fire at his country residence at Washington Heights. The heroic acts for which the medals were given are detailed in the Roll of Merit :

1868.—MINTHORNE D. TOMPKINS, assistant foreman, Hook and Ladder Company No. 1, for act of November 14, 1868.

1869.—BENJAMIN A. GICQUEL, foreman, Engine Company No. 9, for act of September 26, 1869.

1871.—CHARLES L. KELLY, assistant foreman, Engine Company No. 9, for act of February 9, 1871.

AMBROSE L. AUSTIN, fireman, Engine Company No. 15, for act of April 24, 1871.

1872.—THOMAS HENRY, assistant foreman, Hook and Ladder Company No. 6, for act of February 15, 1872.

THOMAS HUTCHINSON, fireman, Hook and Ladder Company No. 1, for act of December 20, 1872.

1873.—WILLIAM H. NASH, chief of battalion, for act of December 30, 1872.

1873.—ALFRED CONNOR, fireman, Hook and Ladder Company No. 10, for act of July 20, 1873.

1873.—HENRY SCHUCK, assistant foreman, Engine Company No. 34, for act of December 7, 1873.

1874.—WILLIAM MITCHELL, foreman, Engine Company No. 10, for act of June 25, 1874.

1875.—JAMES HORN, assistant foreman, Engine Company No. 11, for act of March 26, 1875.

1876.—JOSEPH McGOWAN, fireman, Engine Company No. 6, for act of April 14, 1876.

1877.—THOMAS J. DOUGHERTY, fireman, Hook and Ladder Company No. 1, for act of March 31, 1877.

1878.—DANIEL J. MEAGHER, foreman, Hook and Ladder Company No. 3, for act of May 2, 1878.

1879.—PAUL BAUER, fireman, Hook and Ladder Company No. 4, for act of December 27, 1879.

1880.—JOHN LEVINS, fireman, Hook and Ladder Company No. 2, for act of October 9, 1880.

1881.—MICHAEL CONNERFORD, fireman, Engine Company No. 12, for act of January 4, 1881.

1882.—JOHN L. ROONEY, fireman, Hook and Ladder Company No. 10, for act of June 31, 1882.

1883.—WILLIAM B. KIRCHNER, private, Engine Company No. 17, for act of March 29, 1883.

1884.—JOHN BINNS, private, Hook and Ladder Company No. 3, for act of April 7, 1884.

1886.—PETER H. SHORT, foreman, Hook and Ladder Company No. 1, for act of April 18, 1886.

THE STEPHENSON MEDALISTS.

The Stephenson medal was started in July, 1867, in the following correspondence:

NEW YORK, July 18, 1867.

Alexander Shaler, Esq., President Board of Commissioners Metropolitan Fire Department :

DEAR SIR: We are pleased to express our admiration of the efficiency of the Fire Department as exhibited last night at the fire which consumed the bonded warehouse and distillery in East Twenty-sixth Street. We were present for four hours during the fire, and in a position to see the working of men and apparatus. The order, quietness, sobriety, obedience, intelligence and efficient effort surpassed our experience or conception. While we are thankful that these (under Providence) saved our lumber depot from destruction, we are exultant that this strong arm of our city's service is so well directed.

Respectfully, etc.,

JOHN STEPHENSON & Co.

P. S.—Inclosed please find check for two hundred and fifty dollars, which please appropriate to the interest of your department. The efficiency of your department saved us from much loss at the recent fire in East Twenty-sixth Street. We congratulate you on the good condition of your command.

Respectfully, etc.,

JOHN STEPHENSON & Co.

The medal is a recognition of the attainment of the highest standard of efficiency and discipline in a command, given to foremen.

1883.—ARNOT SPENCE, foreman, Engine Company No. 27.
1884.—DAVID CONNOR, foreman, Engine Company No. 23.
1885.—JOSEPH SHAW, foreman, Hook and Ladder No. 13.

NOBLE RESCUE BY A BOY.

About eight o'clock on the morning of January 4, 1881, a disastrous fire broke out in the five-story brick building, No. 35 Madison Street. The lower floor was unoccupied except by a liquor saloon in the front. Eight families

lived on the four upper floors, one on either side of the stairway on each story. The stairs ran directly through the center of the house, and in order to econo- mize space, many sharp angles were made, so that the stairs might almost be called spiral. They were so narrow that two persons could scarcely pass each other, and when the flames had once started, they shot upward.. The bartender in the saloon ran out into the street and summoned a policeman, who sent out the alarm. The firemen responded promptly. Engine Companies Nos. 7, 12, and 9, with Chief Bonner, of the Second Battalion, were the first to arrive. A second alarm was sent out, and this brought five additional engines and four hook and ladder trucks to the scene. The police had considerable trouble in keeping back the crowd. The men of the house had nearly all gone to their day's work, but thirty-one women and children were imprisoned in the burning building, and entirely cut off from all retreat by the door-way. The fire escape was practically useless, as it was directly opposite the burning stairway, and the platforms—being of wood—caught fire very soon, and the iron ladder was heated so that it could not be used. On the third floor, rear, the McKenna family had their home. The family consisted of Mr. McKenna, his wife, and four children. The father had gone to his work, and his wife had just gone down the street a little way, leaving the younger children behind in the care of the eldest, Charles, a lad of fourteen years, but as brave and with as strong a nerve as most men of double his age and experi-ence. On the mother's return she found the smoke belching from the door-way, making it impossible for her to enter. Charles, hearing the agonizing cries of his terrified mother, opened the door leading to the landing; he found all retreat that way cut off. Below was a sheet of flame, and the stairs were crackling and ready to fall. Be-hind him a dense cloud of smoke threat-ened suffocation if he attempted escape by the roof. His own apartments were rapidly filling with smoke, and the flames were approaching the door. Shutting it hastily, he rushed to the window, and opening it, looked out. The fire was blazing out all around him. His decision was made in an instant. Seizing the baby, which was lying on the bed, he threw it out of the window, clear over the fence of the next yard, where it fell unharmed in a pile of snow. He next grasped Hugh and dropped him to some men, who were standing on a shed in the rear of the house. He then attempted to throw his brother James, nine years

CHARLES F. McKENNA.
[The young hero of the Madison street fire.]

old, out in the same way, but he refused to leave the room. He got him to the window, but the boy would not jump, telling his brother that he would cer-tainly be killed. Charles finally went to the back of the room, ran towards him unexpectedly, lifted him in his arms, and dropped him to the crowd below. He was not in the least hurt. Charles then got on the fire escape, around which the flames were flying, and lowered himself to the lowest balcony, from which he jumped into the yard, landing on his feet uninjured, save for scorched hands. He told the story afterward as calmly as though relating a boyish adventure. Fireman Commerford received the Bennett medal for his services at this fire. The fire started through the carelessness of a plumber, who was thawing out the pipes in the cellar with a gasoline lamp. Ten persons lost their lives at this fire, and six were badly injured.

CHAPTER LIII.

OFFICERS AND THEIR COMMANDS.

Chief Shay.—Assistant Chiefs.—Chiefs of Battalion.—Foremen and Assistant Foremen.—Their Duties and Responsibilities.—Boundaries of Fire Districts.—Location of Engine Companies.

THE Bureau of the Chief of Department consists of the uniformed force of the Department, and is charged by law "with the duty of preventing and extinguishing fires, and of protecting property from water used at fires." A number of rules specify the duties of the uniformed force; rules which are enforced with all the power of rigid discipline. Summarized, these rules are as follows:

The force are required to devote their entire time to the service of the

ENGINE COMPANY NO. 6.

Department; to attend all fires or alarms at stations to which they are assigned; to exert their greatest energy and best ability to do their full duty under any and all circumstances. Obedience must be prompt, implicit, unqualified, and unequivocal. Each member of the force is held responsible for any want of judgment, skill, neglect, or failure on his part which may cause unnecessary loss of life, limb, or property; to remove all persons in danger in the burning or adjoining premises; to endeavor to detect incendiaries; obtain evidence to convict persons bringing or sending false alarms. The use of obscene, immoral, disrespectful, impudent, or other improper language, is prohibited, while it is required that each and every member of the Department must always be respectful and gentlemanly to his superiors, equals, and citizens, and courteous to subordinates. The rules prohibit the use of spirituous, malt, or intoxicating beverages. Conduct unbecoming an officer or gentleman, or in any manner prejudicial to the good reputation, order, or discipline of the Department, will not be tolerated.

The Chief of the Department has control and direction of his bureau and of all clerks assigned to duty therein. He is held responsible to the Board of Fire Commissioners for the conduct and management of his bureau, and of the uniformed force. The chief is likewise required to see that all laws, ordinances, rules and regulations, orders and directions for the government of his bureau, are promptly enforced.

Assistant Chief of Department, under the Chief of Department, has command of the First, Second, Third, Fourth, and Sixth Battalions. The commanding officers of these battalions send their company, fire, and consolidated morning reports, and all other papers, heretofore sent to the Chief of Department direct, to the Assistant Chief of Department, so as to have them in his possession at or before 10 o'clock A. M.; forwards such papers, with

SAMUEL. M. JOHNSON. M.D.   FRANK. L. IVES. M.D.   ROBERT. A. JOYCE. M.D.

BOARD OF MEDICAL OFEICERS.

proper endorsement and recommendations noted thereon, to the Chief of Department not later than 12 o'clock M., each day, unless actual duty at fires, or fatigue caused thereby, should prevent.

Second Assistant Chief of Department, under the Chief or Acting Chief of Department, has command of the Fifth, Seventh, Eighth, Ninth, Tenth, and Eleventh Battalions. The commanding officers of these battalions send their company, fire, and consolidated morning reports, and all other papers heretofore sent to the Chief of Department direct, to the Second Assistant Chief of Department, so as to have them in his possession at or before 10 o'clock A. M., and are forwarded, with proper endorsements and recommendations noted thereon, to the Chief of Department, not later than 12 o'clock M., each day, unless actual duty at fires, or fatigue caused thereby, should prevent.

Chiefs of Battalion, under his command, are responsible for promptness in the discharge of their duty, and that of the companies under them; also for the condition of their companies in or out of quarters, and for any neglect in carrying out fully and minutely the "bill of dress" order, and each and every order, rule, law, or ordinance governing the uniformed force; and when he may learn of any violation or direliction, he shall report or cause to be reported to the Board, through the regular channels, by proper and well-sustained charges, any and all delinquencies.

The Chiefs of Battalion are required to be on duty day and night at their respective headquarters, except when necessarily called elsewhere on Department business, or on leave of absence; to attend all fires at stations to which they may be assigned, and promptly report their arrival at fires to the officer in command; the first at a fire assumes command, and has full control until the command is assumed by the Chief or Assistant Chief.

Foremen of companies have absolute command and control of their respective companies, the house watchmen, engineer and assistant engineer of steamers, drivers, and tillermen, who shall obey orders implicitly.

The Assistant Foreman, in the absence of the Foreman, assumes all the

CHARLES O. SHAY.
[Chief N. Y. F. D.]

latter's functions and responsibilities. When the Foreman is present the Assistant obeys his commands promptly and cheerfully.

Any officer or member of the uniformed force, or any employee of the Department, found guilty of transgressing any law, ordinance, rule, resolution, regulation, circular, orders—general, special, or verbal—may be reprimanded, fined, reduced in grade and pay, suspended from pay and duty, or be dismissed from the service of the Department, as the Board of Commissioners may determine, and any person so dismissed shall not, under any circumstances, have his case reopened, or again be a member of the Department.

CHARLES O. SHAY, chief of the New York Fire Department, was born on October 22, 1834, in the Eighth Ward of New York City. By trade he was a carpenter. He entered the Volunteer Department. In 1858 was a member of Hook and Ladder Company No. 14, remaining an active member until the Paid Department came into existence. Under the New system he was appointed foreman of Hook and Ladder Company No. 5. On June 1, 1869, he was promoted to the position of district engineer. He commanded the Sixth, Third and Fifth Districts respectively. May 19, 1873, he was appointed assistant chief of the Department, and on May 1, 1848, to his present office.

HUGH BONNER was born in Ireland on June 14, 1839. He arrived in this country when he was eight years old. His connection with the Volunteers dates from the night the Columbia Foundry was destroyed by fire, December, 1853. He joined Lady Washington Engine Company No. 40. He was elected assistant foreman of his company in April, 1861, and was foreman in 1863, 1864, and 1865. While foreman of Lady Washington Company he was notified of his appointment to the same post in the Metropolitan Fire Department, and assigned to the command of Engine Company No. 20.

While in command of this company Foreman Bonner was given charge of and operated the first self-propelling steam fire engine and chemical engine ever introduced in the New Department. Bonner was promoted to be chief of battalion on May 21, 1873, and was assigned to the command of the Second Battalion, remaining in this command during the next ten years. During this period he operated successfully the first water tower ever introduced in any department.

In 1875, at a fire in a dwelling on Bayard Street, on approaching the building, Chief Bonner saw a woman hanging from the gutter of the roof. He ascended through the building to

HUGH BONNER.
[Assistant Chief.]

the attic floor, which was found densely charged with heat and smoke. Passing through the room he found the window near which the woman was hanging. He reached out, caught her, and carried her to a place of safety. At the fire in the Frankfort House in 1874 he effected another rescue. The fire originated in a store room, and extended to the hallway on the sixth floor, cutting off all means of escape. Six or eight lodgers were imprisoned in these rooms. By the greatest effort, and with the aid of several men, he finally reached the poor people, all of whom were partially suffocated, and placed them in safety.

He was promoted second assistant chief January 4, 1883, and assigned to the district north of Fourteenth Street. While in this position he was directed to recommend a plan of organization for a school of instruction, which, on being presented to the Board of Commissioners, was adopted by them, and he was assigned as instructor to the school. He was promoted assistant chief of the Department May 1, 1884, and assigned to the duty of generally supervising the several apparatus with life saving appliances. He was appointed by the mayor civil service examiner for the Fire, Police, and Park Departments of this city. He is the designer and inventor of several of the most useful and important implements at present in use by the Department for opening buildings.

FRANCIS J. REILLY was appointed a member of the Fire Department in September, 1865; promoted assistant foreman in October, 1870; foreman on July 1, 1871; chief of battalion February 1, 1880. On the dismissal of John McCabe, second assistant chief, for incompetency, in July, 1886, the Board of Fire Commissioners ordered the chief and assistant chief to present the name of the chief of battalion who in their judgment was most competent to fill the vacancy; a few days later they presented the name of Francis J. Reilly. He was confirmed,

FRANCIS J. REILLY.
[Second Assistant Chief.]

and is now the incumbent of that office, with his headquarters in the house of Engine Company No. 1, No. 165 West Twenty-ninth Street.

BENJAMIN A. GICQUEL, Chief of the Seventh Battalion, was born in New York, February 1, 1842. After attending the public schools, he followed the trade of a jeweler for a time. He began to take an interest in fire matters very early, and finally joined Clinton Hose Company No. 17, a prominent organization of the Volunteer Department. He was secretary of the company. Chief Gicquel was appointed a member of the Paid Department in 1865. Three months later he was made assistant foreman of his company. On the third of May, 1866, he was promoted to foreman, and assigned to Engine Company No. 5, and subsequently served in Engine Companies Nos. 9 and 25. In 1871 he was advanced to the post of chief of battalion, and was placed in command of the Sixth, and two years later transferred to the Fifth, now the Seventh, where he is at present stationed. The construction of buildings, the origin and nature of fires, and the ways and means to subdue them, have all been studied in detail by him.

BENJAMIN A. GICQUEL.

He was the second recipient of the Bennett Medal. The act for which the medal was presented was the saving the lives of two women and two children at a fire in Montgomery Street on the morning of September 26, 1869. In 1880 he made a thorough inspection of all the theaters in New York. At a

JOHN S. FISHER.

fire on the corner of Cherry and Montgomery Streets, on July 20, 1882, which broke out about midnight, Chief Gicquel mounted a ladder to climb to the roof, and when he had reached the third story, lost his footing and fell to the ground. He was in the hospital for three months after this accident.

On May 1, 1886, Chief Gicquel left for Europe to study the Fire Departments of the chief cities. While in Paris he met Henry D. Purroy, President of the Fire Commissioners, and both were royally entertained by Col. A. C. Couston, Chief of the Paris Fire Department.

JOHN S. FISHER, chief of battalion, New York Fire Department, joined Hook and Ladder Company No. 15 in 1856, at that time located on Third Street, near Avenue D, and subsequently became connected with Engine 35 and Hook and Ladder 16. In the latter company he was an active member on the disbandment of the Volunteer Department. During his service as a volunteer

fireman, he secured the experience in fighting fire which has distinguished him in the present Department as a cool, intrepid and valuable officer. For several years after the organization of the Paid Department he was a bellringer on the lookout towers. On February 8, 1868, he was appointed a fireman, and assigned to Hook and Ladder 2. On May 30, 1868, he was promoted to be assistant foreman of Hook and Ladder 7, and on July 15, 1869, he was advanced to the rank of foreman, and assigned to the same company. He was subsequently transferred to Hook and Ladder 2, and while in that company was severely burned by an explosion at a fire in a dyeing establishment at Sixth Avenue and Forty-third Street. The injuries

WILLIAM ROWE.

sustained laid him up for two months. On May 21, 1873, his merit as a foreman was again recognized, and he was promoted to the rank of chief of battalion, and assigned to the Fifth Battalion, in command of which he remained only a few months, when he was transferred to the Eighth Battalion.

WILLIAM ROWE, Chief of Battalion, New York Fire Department, was born December 24, 1842. He joined Hook and Ladder Company No. 18 on June 8, 1864. On the organization of the present department he was appointed foreman of Hook and Ladder Company No. 9, October 20, 1865. He was promoted to the rank of chief of battalion May 21, 1873, and assigned to the Third Battalion, and transferred to the First Battalion February 15, 1875, and afterwards to the Twelfth Battalion, where he is at present stationed.

SAMUEL CAMPBELL, chief of battalion of the New York Fire Department, entered the Volunteer service when he was twenty-one years old. He joined Washington Irving Hose Company No. 44 on October 8, 1863. He became treasurer of the company,

SAMUEL CAMPBELL.

and remained with it until the organization of the New Department, when he was appointed to Engine Company No. 26, October 16, 1865. In that company he served in turn as driver, stoker, and assistant engineer, and was finally promoted to be assistant foreman to Engine Company No. 23, September 1, 1869. He was made foreman on February 1, 1873, and assigned to Engine Company No. 32. Two years later, on September 25, he was promoted to chief of battalion, and assigned to the Sixth.

JOHN J. BRESNAN, chief of the Sixth Battalion, was a member of Fulton Engine Company No. 21 in the Volunteer Department. He was appointed a member of the Metropolitan Fire Department on October 20, 1865, and assigned to Engine No. 31. Promoted to be assistant engineer of Engine No. 12 on February 1, 1870. On July 1, 1870, he was promoted to the rank of assistant foreman, and transferred to Engine Company No. 6. He also

JOHN J. BRESNAN.

served for a short time in Engine Companies Nos. 13 and 20. March 1, 1873, he was appointed foreman of Engine Company No. 33. He commanded this company until February 1, 1880, when he was appointed chief of the Sixth Battalion, with headquarters in the house of Hook and Ladder No. 3.

MICHAEL F. REEVES, chief of the Tenth Battalion, New York Fire Department, was born in Ireland, December 27, 1843. He came to the United States with his parents when four years old. From New York the family went to

Albany, returning to New York in the course of a few years. Michael has lived in New York since he was seven years old, and so has a thorough knowledge of the city. On the sixteenth of April, 1867, two years after the organization of the present department, he was appointed a fireman. He was first assigned to Hook and Ladder Company No. 10, in Fulton Street, where he saw plenty of hard service. On the fifteenth of October, 1870, his efficiency was recognized by promotion to assistant foreman of Hook and Ladder Company No. 1. He remained with this company only until August, 1, 1871, when he was further promoted to foreman of Hook and Ladder Company No. 8. Here he distinguished himself by most faithful and heroic services for a period of nearly ten years. He secured for the company the highest possible reputation, which it still retains, and was himself placed on the Merit roll of the department for heroic conduct. On the first of November, 1881, he was promoted chief of the Third Battalion.

MICHAEL F. REEVES.

Once he was very severely injured, and was laid up for three months; indeed, not fully recovering for eighteen months. The accident happened on the seventh of January, 1879, at a fire at No. 75 Vesey Street. A portion of the building fell, and Reeves was buried beneath the ruins. His coolness and skill were remarkable at a fire at No. 132 West Broadway on January 4, 1874, when he was instrumental in saving the lives of many tenants. For this his name was placed on the roll of Merit.

In the Old Department Reeves was a member of Hose Company No. 45, when it was in Avenue A and Nineteenth Street.

JOSEPH F. McGILL.

JOSEPH F. McGILL, chief of the Third Battalion, was born November 14, 1843. He joined Hudson River Engine Company No. 53 on February 18, 1864, and served until the Old Department was legislated out of existence. Chief McGill was appointed a fireman in the Metropolitan Fire Department on March 21, 1866, and assigned to Engine Company No. 12, in Wooster Street.

Promoted assistant foreman in April, 1870, and transferred to Engine Company No. 27; was appointed foreman of Engine Company No. 33 in 1872. He commanded Hook and Ladder No. 10; Engine Companies Nos. 7 and 30 until the introduction of self-propelling steamers, when he was sent to command the one assigned to Engine Company No. 32 in Burling Slip. He was promoted to be chief of batallion on August 12, 1883, and assigned to the Third Battalion, which he has successfully commanded until the present. Chief McGill's name was placed on the roll of Merit while in command of Hook and Ladder 10, for the rescue of Harriet Colgan from the upper part of the burning buildings, Nos. 35 and 37 Vesey Street, on March 3, 1873. On November 22, 1879, Mr. Edward W. Tapp presented Chief McGill with a handsome gold watch and chain, on behalf of the merchants in the district of Engine Company No. 32, of which Chief McGill was then foreman.

THOMAS GOODERSON.

THOMAS GOODERSON was appointed a fireman on February 1, 1874, and assigned to Engine Company No. 35. He was promoted assistant foreman of Engine Company No. 22 on December 20, 1875; transferred to Engine Company No. 36, January 4, 1876; and on April 11, of the same year, was appointed foreman of Engine 37; transferred to Engine 35 on June 1, 1879. On January 15, 1884, he was appointed a chief of battalion, and sent to command the Twelfth Battalion. Chief Gooderson was transferred to the Ninth Battalion on May 1, 1886, where he is now stationed. His record as a fireman is first-class.

THOMAS LALLY.

THOMAS LALLY, chief of the Fifth Battalion, was born in the west of Ireland, on November 16, 1850. His family emigrated to this country when he was very young, and settled on the east side of this city. He was appointed a member of the Fire Department August 15, 1870, and assigned to Engine Company No. 25; was transferred to Hook and Ladder No. 9 September 1 of the same year; promoted assistant foreman of Hook and Ladder No. 6, April 21, 1873; transferred to Hook and Ladder No. 10 on April 4, 1879. On November 1, 1881, he was promoted foreman of Hook and Ladder No. 1. He was appointed chief of the Third Battalion (now the Fifth) on May 1, 1884. Chief Lally's name may be found on the roll of Merit more than once, for the rescue of imperilled persons. On the twentieth of May, 1874, he rescued two children from the fourth floor of the burning building, No. 18 Clinton Street. He assisted in the rescue of eight persons on March 11, 1877, at No. 24 Ludlow

CHAS. D. PURROY.

Street. He again figures as assisting in the rescue of four persons on July 21, 1882.

CHARLES D. PURROY, chief of Second Battalion, was appointed a fireman on January 22, 1880; promoted assistant foreman, April 5, 1881. December 31, 1882, he was promoted foreman; and on May 1, 1884, he went a grade higher, chief of the Second Battalion.

JOHN J. CASHMAN, chief of battalion, New York Fire Department, was born on September 25, 1845. When twenty-one years old he was appointed a fireman on October 19, 1866, and assigned to Engine Company No. 13. He was transferred to Engine Company No. 29 soon after, and on the fifteenth of February, 1872, was promoted to the rank of assistant foreman, and assigned to Engine Company No. 6. He was transferred to Engine 27 in October, 1873, and promoted to the rank of foreman from that company on April 29, 1879, and assigned to Engine Company No. 29. He was transferred to Hook and Ladder Company No. 5, in September, 1883, and to Hook and Ladder Company No. 8, November, 1883. He was made chief of the First Battalion on September 12, 1884.

PETER H. SHORT was a member of the Albany Fire Department from 1872 to 1874. He came to this city in 1875, and was appointed a member of this Department on May 1, 1875; he was promoted assistant foreman on June 1, 1880, and foreman April 18, 1883, and chief of batallion on August 1, 1886. Chief Short has a record of which he might well be proud. On February 21, 1885, at a fire in Nos. 16 and 18 William Street, and Nos. 57, 59 and 61 Beaver Street, Chief Short, then foreman of Hook and Ladder No. 1, with the assistance of firemen Furman, King, Cottrell, Lynch, Clarke and Lyons, rescued at great personal risk, Mr. and Mrs. Jaede, their daughter, and Josephine Kraft and Mary Leary. Six persons lost their lives at this fire, and one person was injured. For this act he was presented with the Bennett Medal, and a resolution was presented to the Board of Fire Commissioners asking for his promotion. This resolution was signed by the leading insurance and business

JOHN J. CASHMAN.

men of this city. On April 18, 1886, with the assistance of firemen Larkin and Tompkins, Chief Short rescued, at great personal risk, Mrs. Hannah Riley and her three children, from the fourth floor of the burning building, No. 89 Mulberry Street.

The late FRANCIS MAHEDY was born in this city in 1839. He joined the Volunteer Fire Department in 1859, and afterwards became foreman of Engine Company No. 31, and served until the breaking out of the war, when he enlisted in the army. On his return Mr. Mahedy again resumed command of No. 31. He served with this company until the disbandment of the Department.

He was appointed a member of the Paid Department in 1870, and assigned to Engine Company No. 27; he was promoted assistant foreman, and transferred to Engine Company No. 12. While assistant foreman of this company, he was buried for four hours at a fire which occurred in Duane Street.

PETER H. SHORT.

Later on he became attached to Engine Company No. 28, where he was advanced to the position of foreman, and transferred to Engine Company No. 1. In 1881 he was appointed chief, and assigned to the command of the Second Batallion, where he served for nearly three years, and was then transferred to the Fourth Batallion. It was while in command of this batallion that he met his tragic death, which is still fresh in the memory of all. While driving to a fire his wagon collided with an engine, throwing him out; he died two hours later. His funeral was a grand sight; his batallion marched to the ferry, as did Veteran and Volunteer Firemen's Association. His wagon was covered with a black pall, and his fire-hat upon the seat, with a bouquet lying by the side of it. The horse, covered with a black netting, was led by the driver who was in the wagon when the collision took place. The funeral procession was under the supervision of Chief Gicquel.

THE LATE FRANCIS MAHEDY.

His tragic death was mourned by a host of friends, outside as well as inside the department, as his manly nature and gallant conduct in official life had endeared him to all.

FIRE DISTRICTS.

The city is subdivided into thirteen districts, bounded as follows:

First District—Battery, North River, Chambers Street, and East River.

Second District—Chambers Street, North River, Houston Street, South Fifth Avenue, and West Broadway.

Third District—Chambers Street, West Broadway, South Fifth Avenue, Houston Street, Crosby to Howard, to Elm, to Reade, to Centre, and Chambers Streets.

Fourth District—Chambers Street, Centre to Reade, to Elm, to Howard, to Crosby Streets, Houston Street, and East River.

Fifth District—Houston Street, North River, Twenty-third Street, and East River.

Sixth District—Twenty-third Street, North River, Fifty-ninth Street, and East River.

Seventh District—Fifty-ninth Street, North River, One Hundred and Tenth Street, and Fifth Avenue.

Eighth District—Fifty-ninth Street, Fifth Avenue, One Hundred and Tenth Street, and East River.

Ninth District—One Hundred and Tenth Street, North River, Spuyten Duyvil Creek, Harlem River, and Eighth Avenue.

Tenth District—One Hundred and Tenth Street, Eighth Avenue, Harlem and East Rivers.

Eleventh District—East and Harlem Rivers, Kingsbridge and Fordham Roads, and Pelham Avenue, and Bronx River.

Twelfth District—Pelham Avenue, Fordham and Kingsbridge Roads, and Spuyten Duyvil Creek, North River, Westchester County, and Bronx River.

Thirteenth District—Governor's, Bedloe's, and Ellis' Islands in the bay, used and controlled by the United States Government for military purposes; Blackwell's, Ward's, Randall's, and North Brothers' Islands in the East River, used for charitable, correctional, and sanitary purposes by the city.

LOCATION OF ENGINE COMPANIES.

Engine Company No. 1, 165 West Twenty-ninth Street.
Engine Company No. 2, 530 West Forty-third Street.
Engine Company No. 3, 417 West Seventeenth Street.
Engine Company No. 4, 39 Liberty Street.
Engine Company No. 5, 340 East Fourteenth Street.
Engine Company No. 6, 100 Cedar Street.
Engine Company No. 7, 22 Chambers Street.
Engine Company No. 8, 165 East Fifty-first Street.
Engine Company No. 9, 55 East Broadway.
Engine Company No. 10, 8 Stone Street.
Engine Company No. 11, 437 East Houston Street.
Engine Company No. 12, 261 William Street.
Engine Company No. 13, 99 Wooster Street.
Engine Company No. 14, 14 East Eighteenth Street.
Engine Company No. 15, 269 Henry Street.
Engine Company No. 16, 223 East Twenty-fifth Street.

Engine Company No. 17, 91 Ludlow Street.
Engine Company No. 18, 132 West Tenth Street.   (Fuel Depot No. 4.)
Engine Company No. 19, 355 West Twenty-fifth Street.   (Fuel Depot No. 12.)
Engine Company No. 20, 47 Marion Street.
Engine Company No. 21, 216 East Fortieth Street.
Engine Company No. 22, 159 East Eighty-fifth Street. (Fuel Depot No. 14.)
Engine Company No. 23, 235 West Fifty-eighth Street.
Engine Company No. 24, 78 Morton Street.   (Fuel Depot No. 14.)

WATER TOWER EXTENDED.

Engine Company No. 25, 342 Fifth Street.
Engine Company No. 26, 220 West Thirty-seventh Street.
Engine Company No. 27, 173 Franklin Street.
Engine Company No. 28, 604 East Eleventh Street.
Engine Company No. 29, 193 Fulton Street.
Engine Company No. 30, 253 Spring Street.
Engine Company No. 31, 116 Leonard Street.
Engine Company No. 32, 108 John Street.
Engine Company No. 33, 15 Great Jones Street.
Engine Company No. 34, 440 West Thirty-third Street.
Engine Company No. 35, 223 East One Hundred and Nineteenth Street.

Engine Company No. 36, 2333 Fourth Avenue.

Engine Company No. 37, 83 Lawrence Street.

Engine Company No. 38, Tenth Avenue, between One Hundred and Fifty-fourth and One Hundred and Fifty-fifth Streets.

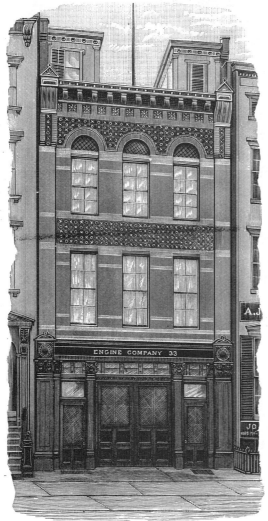

HOUSE OF ENGINE 33.

[No. 15 Great Jones Street.]

Engine Company No. 39, 159 East Sixty-seventh Street.

Engine Comapny No. 40, Sixty-eighth Street, between Tenth Avenue and Boulevard.

Engine Company No. 41, 501 North Third Avenue.

Engine Company No. 42, Fulton Avenue, between One Hundred and Sixty-seventh and One Hundred and Sixty-eighth Streets.

Engine Company No. 43 (Floating engine), Pier 1 (new), North River.

Engine Company No. 44, 221 East Seventy-fifth Street.

Engine Company No. 45, Division Street, near Boston Road.

Engine Company No. 46, Morris Street, between Madison and Washington Avenues.

Engine Company No. 47, Tenth Avenue, between Ninety seventh and Ninety-eighth Streets.

Engine Company No. 48, Thomas Avenue, near Kingsbridge Road.

Engine Company No. 49, Blackwell's Island.

Engine Company No. 50, One Hundred and Sixty-sixth Street, between Washington and Third Avenues.

Engine Company No. 51 (Floating engine), Pier 42, North River.

Hook and Ladder Company No. 1, 26 Chambers Street.

Hook and Ladder Company No. 2, 126 East Fiftieth Street. (Fuel Depot No. 13.)

Hook and Ladder Company No. 3, 108 East Thirteenth Street.

Hook and Ladder Company No. 4, 788 Eighth Avenue.

Hook and Ladder Company No. 5, 96 Charles Street.

Hook and Ladder Company No. 6, 77 Canal Street.

Hook and Ladder Company No. 7, 217 East Twenty-eighth Street.

Hook and Ladder Company No. 8, 7 North Moore Street.

Hook and Ladder Company No. 9, 209 Elizabeth Street.

Hook and Ladder Company No. 10, 191 Fulton Street.

Hook and Ladder Company No. 11, 742 Fifth Street.

Hook and Ladder Company No. 12, 243 West Twentieth Street.

Hook and Ladder Company No. 13, 159 East Eighty-seventh Street.

Hook and Ladder Company No. 14, 120 East One Hundred and Twenty-fifth Street.

Hook and Ladder Company No. 15, Old Slip, between Water and Front Streets.

Hook and Ladder Company No. 17, One Hundred and Forty-third Street, near Third Avenue.

Hook and Ladder Company No. 19, Ogden Avenue, between Birch and Union Streets.

Fuel Depot No. 1, 5 Duane Street.

Fuel Depot No. 2, 10 East Thirty-third Street.

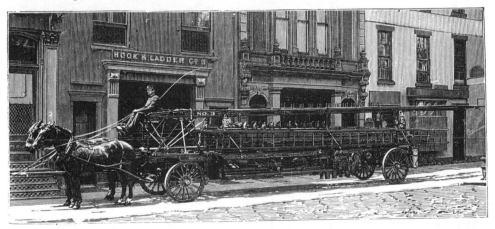

HOOK AND LADDER NO. 3.—WITH EXTENSION LADDER CLOSED.

Fuel Depot No. 3, 106 East Thirteenth Street.

Fuel Depot No. 4, (see Engine Company No. 18.)

Fuel Depot No. 5, 304 West Forty-seventh Street.

Fuel Depot No. 6, 84 Attorney Street.

Fuel Depot No. 7, 28 Beaver Street.

Fuel Depot No. 8, 209 East One Hundred and Twenty-second Street.

Fuel Depot No. 9, (see Engine Company No. 24).

Fuel Depot No. 10, 304 Washington Street.

Fuel Depot No. 11, 173 Elm Street (and storehouse).

Fuel Depot No, 12, (see Engine Company No. 19).

Fuel Depot No. 13, (see Hook and Ladder Company No. 2).

Fuel Depot No. 14, (see Engine Company No. 22).

Storehouse, 20 Eldridge Street.

Storehouse, 180 Clinton Street.

Storehouse, 199 Christie Street; also occupied by second section of Hook and Ladder Company No. 9.

First Battalion.—Headquarters at the quarters of Engine Company No. 29, No. 193 Fulton Street.

Engine Companies Nos. 4, 6, 10, 29, and 32, and Hook and Ladder Companies Nos. 10 and 15.

Second Battalion.—Headquarters at the quarters of Engine Company No. 7, No. 22 Chambers Street.

Engine Companies Nos. 7, 12, 27, and 31, and Hook and Ladder Companies Nos. 1 and 8.

Third Battalion.—Headquarters at the quarters of Engine Company No. 30, No. 253 Spring Street.

Engine Companies Nos. 13, 18, 24, 30, and 51, and Hook and Ladder Company No. 5

Fourth Battalion.—Headquarters at the quarters of Engine Company No. 17, No. 91 Ludlow Street.

Engine Companies Nos. 9, 11, 15, 17, and 43, and Hook and Ladder Companies Nos. 6 and 11.

HOOK AND LADDER NO. 1.

Fifth Battalion.—Headquarters at the quarters of Engine Company No. 14, No. 14 East Eighteenth Street.

Engine Companies Nos. 1, 3, 14, 19, 26, and 34, and Hook and Ladder Company No. 12.

Sixth Battalion.—Headquarters at the quarters of Engine Company No. 33, No. 15 Great Jones Street.

Engine Companies Nos. 5, 20, 25, 28, and 33, and Hook and Ladder Companies Nos. 3 and 9.

Seventh Battalion.—Headquarters at Fuel Depot No. 5, No. 304 West Forty-seventh Street.

Engine Companies Nos. 2, 23, 40, and 47, and Hook and Ladder Company No. 4.

Eighth Battalion.—Headquarters at Fuel Depot No. 2, No. 160 East Thirty-third Street.

Engine Companies 8, 16, 21, and 39, and Hook and Ladder Companies Nos. 2 and 7.

Ninth Battalion.—Headquarters at Fuel Depot No. 8, No. 209 East One Hundred and Twenty-second Street.

Engine Companies Nos. 22, 35, 36, 44, and 49, and Hook and Ladder Companies Nos. 13 and 14.

Tenth Battalion.—Headquarters at the quarters of Engine Company No. 50, One Hundred and Sixty-sixth Street, between Washington and Third Aves.

Engine Companies Nos. 41, 42, 45, 46, 48, and 50, and Hook and Ladder Company No. 17.

Eleventh Battalion.—Headquarters at the quarters of Engine Company No. 37, No. 83 Lawrence Street.

Engine Companies Nos. 37, 38, and 52, and Hook and Ladder Company No. 19.

The following are designated as the Company Districts of the Department in which the respective company commanders shall take cognizance of all violations of law relating to the erection, alterations, and repair of buildings,

CHIEF BRESNAN ANSWERING AN ALARM.

and the storage, handling, transportation, and sale of combustibles, fireworks, and explosives, the encumbrance of hydrants, etc., and in which they shall also be responsible for the care of the fire alarm telegraph and other property of the Department.

BOUNDARIES OF COMPANY DISTRICTS.

Engine No. 1.—Twenty-third Street, Fifth Avenue, Thirty-first Street, and Eighth Avenue.

Engine No. 2.—Forty-second Street, Eighth Avenue, Fifty-third Street, and North River.

Engine No. 3.—Gansevoort and Thirteenth Streets, Eighth Avenue, Twenty-first Street, and North River.

Engine No. 4.—Exchange Place, Broadway, Fulton and Gold Streets, Maiden Lane, and William Street.

Engine No. 5.—East Tenth Street, Second Avenue, Twenty-first Street, and Avenue A.

Engine No. 6.—Battery Place, Broadway, Liberty Street, and North River.

Engine No. 7.—Broadway, Chambers, Duane, Rose, Frankfort, Gold, and Fulton Streets.

Engine No. 8.—Fiftieth Street, Sixth Avenue, Fifty-ninth Street, and East River.

Engine No. 9.—Catharine Street, Bowery, Canal Street, East Broadway. Jefferson Street, and East River.

Engine No. 10.—Battery Place, Broadway, Exchange Place, William Street, Pearl Street, Coenties Slip, and East River.

Engine No. 11.—Grand, Clinton, Houston Streets, and East River.

ENGINE NO. 14.

[Charles Shay, Foreman.]

Engine No. 12.—Dover, Frankfort, Rose, Duane, Chatham, Catharine Streets, and East River.

Engine No. 13.—Canal Street, Broadway, Houston and Sullivan Streets.

Engine No. 14.—Fourteenth Street, Sixth Avenue, Twenty-third Street, and Fourth Avenue.

Engine No. 15.—Jefferson Street, East Broadway, Clinton, Grand Streets, and East River.

Engine No. 16.—Twenty-first Street, Fourth Avenue, Twenty-third Street, Fifth Avenue, Twenty-seventh Street, and East River.

Engine No. 17.—Grand, Eldridge, Houston, and Clinton Streets.

Engine No. 18.—Fourth and Thirteenth Streets, Eighth Avenue, Fourteenth Street, and Fifth Avenue.

Engine No. 19.—Twenty-first Street, Eighth Avenue, Thirty-first Street, and North River.

Engine No. 20.—Broadway, Houston, Mott, and Canal Streets.

Engine No. 21.—Thirty-fourth Street, Fifth Avenue, Fortieth Street, Sixth Avenue, Forty-second Street, and East River.

Engine No. 22.—Seventieth Street, Fifth Avenue, Ninety-eighth Street, Lexington Avenue, Eighty-sixth Street, and Third Avenue.

Engine No. 23.—Fifty-third Street, Sixth Avenue, Fifty-ninth Street, and North River.

Engine No. 24.—Houston, Thompson, Fourth, and Christopher Streets, and North River.

Engine No. 25.—Houston Street, Bowery, Fourth Avenue, Stuyvesant, Tenth Streets, and Avenue B.

Engine No. 26.—Thirty-first Street, Eighth Avenue, Fortieth Street, and Fifth Avenue.

Engine No. 27.—Chambers, Hudson, Desbrosses Streets, and North River.

Engine No. 28.—Tenth Street, Avenue A, Twenty-first Street, and East River.

Engine No. 29.—Liberty Street, Broadway, Fulton, Greenwich Streets, Park Place, and North River.

Engine No. 30.—Desbrosses, Hudson, Canal, Sullivan, Houston Streets, and North River.

Engine No. 31.—Broadway, Canal Street, Bowery, Chatham, Baxter, and Worth Streets.

Engine No. 32.—Maiden Lane, Gold, Frankfort, and Dover Streets, and East River.

Engine No. 33.—Houston and Thompson Streets, Fifth Avenue, Eighth Street, Fourth Avenue, and Bowery.

Engine No. 34.—Thirty-first Street, Eighth Avenue, Forty-second Street, and North River.

Engine No. 35.—One Hundred and Tenth Street, Eighth Avenue, One Hundred and Twentieth Street, and East River.

Engine No. 36.—Harlem Bridge, Third Avenue, One Hundred and Twenty-sixth Street, Eighth Avenue, One Hundred and Fortieth Street, and Harlem River.

Engine No. 37.—One Hundred and Tenth Street, Eighth Avenue, One Hundred and Fortieth Street, and North River.

Engine No. 38.—One Hundred and Fortieth Street, Harlem River, Spuyten Duyvil Creek, and North River.

Engine No. 39.—Fifty-ninth Street, Fifth Avenue, Seventieth Street, and East River.

Engine No. 40.—Fifty-ninth Street, Eighth Avenue, Eighty-second Street, and North River.

Engine No. 41.—Harlem River, One Hundred and Forty-fourth Street, St. Ann's Avenue, One Hundred and Sixty-first Street, Jerome Avenue, McComb's Dam Bridge.

Engine No. 42.—Bungay Street, One Hundred and Forty-ninth Street, St. Ann's and Fordham Avenues, One Hundred and Seventieth Street, Boston Road, Union Avenue, Home Street, Westchester Avenue, Bronx River, Long Island Sound.

Engine No. 44.—Seventieth Street, Third Avenue, Eighty-sixth Street, East River.

Engine No. 45.—Westchester Avenue, Home Street, Union Avenue, Boston Road, One Hundred and Seventieth Street, Fordham Avenue, Lorillard Street, Pelham Avenue, Bronx River.

Engine No. 46.—One Hundred and Seventy-fourth Street, Walnut Street, One Hundred and Seventy-third Street, Fordham Avenue, Lorillard Street, One Hundred and Eighty-eighth Street, Thomas Avenue, Kingsbridge Road, and Jerome Avenue.

Engine No. 47.—Eighty-second Street, Eighth Avenue, One Hundred and Tenth Street, and North River.

Engine No. 48.—Pelham Avenue, Lorillard Street, One Hundred and Eighty-ninth or Powell Street, Thomas Avenue, Kingsbridge Road, line of New York City and Northern Railroad, northern boundary of City and Bronx River.

PETER SEERY.
[Superintendent of Bureau of Combustibles.]

Engine No. 49.—Blackwell's, Ward's and Randall's Islands.

Engine No. 50.—One Hundred and Sixty-first Street, Fordham Avenue, One Hundred and Seventy-third Street, Walnut Street, One Hundred and Seventy-fourth Street, and Jerome Avenue.

Engine No. 52.—Spuyten Duyvil Creek, Harlem River, Kingsbridge Road, line of New York City and Northern Railroad, northern boundary of City, North River.

Hook and Ladder No. 1.—Chambers Street, Broadway, Worth, Baxter, and Chatham Streets.

Hook and Ladder No. 2.—Forty-second Street, Sixth Avenue, Fiftieth Street, and East River.

Hook and Ladder No. 3.—Eighth Street, Fifth Avenue, Fourteenth Street, Fourth Avenue, Twenty-first Street, Second Avenue, and Stuyvesant Street.

Hook and Ladder No. 4.—Fortieth Street, Eighth Avenue, Fifty-third Street, and Sixth Avenue.

Hook and Ladder No. 5.—Christopher, West Fourth, Gansevoort Streets, and North River.

Hook and Ladder No. 6.—Canal, Mott, Grand, Clinton Streets and East Broadway.

Hook and Ladder No. 7.—Twenty-seventh Street, Fifth Avenue, Thirty-fourth Street and East River.

Hook and Ladder No. 8.—Chambers Street, Broadway, Canal and Hudson Streets.

Hook and Ladder No. 9.—Grand, Mott, Houston, and Eldridge Streets.

Hook and Ladder No. 10.—Park Place, Greenwich and Fulton Streets, Broadway, Chambers Street, and North River.

Hook and Ladder No. 11.—Houston Street, Avenue B, Tenth Street, and East River.

Hook and Ladder No. 12.—Fourteenth Street, Eighth Avenue, Twenty-third Street, and Sixth Avenue.

Hook and Ladder No. 13.—Eighty-sixth Street, Lexington Avenue, Ninety-eighth Street, Fifth Avenue, One Hundred and Tenth Street, and East River.

Hook and Ladder No. 14.— One Hundred and Twentieth Street, Eighth Avenue, One Hundred and Twenty-sixth St., Third Ave., and Harlem River.

Hook and Ladder No. 15.—Coenties Slip, Pearl and William Streets, Maiden Lane, and East River.

Hook and Ladder No. 17.—Harlem River, One Hundred and Forty-fourth Street, St. Ann's Avenue, One Hundred and Forty-ninth Street, Bungay Street, Long Island Sound.

Hook and Ladder No. 19.—McComb's Dam Bridge, Jerome Avenue, Kingsbridge Road, Harlem River.

Report of the Bureau of Combustibles for the year ending December 31, 1885 :

| COMPLAINTS OF VIOLATIONS, ETC. | Pending last report. | Received since. | Total to be Disposed of. | DISPOSITION. | | | | | | Now Pending. |
				Complied on Notice.	Unfounded.	Penalties Collected.	Penalties Remitted.	Prosecution Recommended.	Total.	
Selling kerosene oil below test..............	3	5	8	..	..	3	5	..	8	..
Selling kerosene oil without license.........	..	2	2	..	2	..	..	..	2	..
Chimney fires................................	31	219	250	..	..	87	124	27	238	12
Hoistways found open after conclusion of business.............................	9	24	33	..	1	6	21	4	32	1
Fire hydrants obstructed....................	3	53	56	50	6	.·.	..	..	56	..
Lights unprotected...........................	..	2	2	..	2	..	..	..	2	..
Want of fire extinguishing appliances........	13	5	18	3	2	..	..	..	5	13
Want of telegraphic communication.........	5	..	5	1	4	..	..	..	5	..
Kerosene or naphtha, etc., in excessive quantity.	..	16	16	7	9	..	..	..	16	..
Fireworks, chemicals, matches, etc., kept without permit........................	..	3	3	1	2	..	..	..	3	..
Powder, etc., improperly stored, transported, etc............................	..	3	3	..	3	..	..	..	3	..
Chimneys, flues, heating apparatus, etc., unsafe......................	4	29	33	18	12	..	..	..	30	3
Ashes in wooden boxes, etc..................	..	8	8	4	1	..	..	..	5	3
Hay, straw, cotton, rags, and other vegetable fibre stored in excessive quantity.	12	16	28	10	18	..	..	..	28	..
Lime, spirits, varnish, etc., stored in excessive quantity.....................	1	7	8	7	1	..	..	..	8	..
Total........................	31	392	473	101	63	96	150	31	441	32

Special surveys made to determine the fitness of premises for the storage of combustibles or explosive materials....................... 547

Special surveys of places of amusement............................. 5

Samples of kerosene oil collected and tested........................ 8,965

CHAPTER LIV.

FIRE INSURANCE : ITS BENEFICENCE AND IMPORTANCE.

The Great Benevolent Society.—Blest Offspring of Modern Civilization.—The Friend of the Poor, the Guardian of the Helpless, the Protector of Home, the Safeguard of Honorable Competence.

MANY volumes each the size of this work would be required to give the history of Fire Insurance and the Board of Fire Underwriters. The united companies virtually control, as mentors and censors, not only the Fire Department of New York, but in a certain sense the men and methods connected with Fire Extinguishing in the United States, and they are to be regarded as managers of business concerns which profit by the efficiency of a municipal department in the pay of the tax payers. It is not within the scope of this work to present anything like a full history of the Board, but a brief sketch will be necessary and interesting.

One of the best retrospects of combined insurance interests was in an address made in this city on the 26th of April, 1876, to the National Board of Fire Underwiters of the United States, by Henry A. Oakley, Esq., of the Howard Insurance Company, President of the Board. Mr. Oakley regretted that a proposition to erect in the Centennial Grounds, in Philadelphia, a building wherein insurance men could meet, and another building wherein the statistics of fire insurance business in this country during the century should be collected were not carried out. " Fire insurance," he went on to say, " can scarcely claim to have been known in the early part of our nation's history. Philadelphia is entitled to the honor of having established the first fire insurance company in America, for in 1752 the Philadelphia Contributionship, or, as it is sometimes styled, ' Hand in Hand,' was founded, a company still in prosperous existence, and whose chief promoter, and one of whose original directors was Benjamin Franklin. This company celebrated its Centennial nearly a quarter of a century ago, and shows evidence to-day of the wise management which characterized its early career. Differences, however, seem to have arisen among its trustees as to the exposure of property by the trees which at that early date must have been a feature in the City of Brotherly Love, and from the attraction they presented to lightning, the company ceased to insure property which had trees in front of it. The result was a new organization in 1784, by some of the promoters of the first and other prominent citizens, called the Mutual Insurance Company, which adopted as its seal or mark, a tree in leaf which gave to it the name of the ' Green Tree,' by which it is familiarly known, and its plate bearing this badge is still affixed to houses. In the year 1787 another company bearing the same name—Mutual

Assurance Company—was founded in New York, and it still exists with the very appropriate title of the 'Knickerbocker Fire Insurance Company.'

"The next organization was the Insurance Company of North America, of Philadelphia, founded in 1794 on the stock plan, whose representatives are among us to-day as active, earnest promoters of this Board. In 1797 the Massachusetts Fire Company was chartered in Boston, but it long since passed out of existence, and in 1798, in the same city, the Massachusetts Mutual was organized, and after having weathered many storms ceased to exist in 1872, as a result of the great fire. There was established in the town of Boston, in 1724, 'The Sun Fire Office in Boston,' by Joseph Marion, and also about the same period 'The North American Insurance Company,' whose exact date it appears impossible to obtain. Both of these companies are supposed to have been individual enterprises, as no record of their incorporation can be found.

DRAWING FROM AN OLD INSURANCE CERTIFICATE.

New York in 1806 organized the Eagle Fire, still extant, and in 1810 Hartford organized its pioneer company, 'The Hartford Fire Insurance Company,' whose importance to us and the public generally we all feel disposed to recognize. Mr. Cornelius Walford, of London, in a paper which I had the pleasure of hearing him read before the Middlesex Archæological Society, made known the fact of the existence of mutual fire associations for two centuries or more before the great fire in London of 1666, while on the continent of Europe individual underwriting was known as far back as the twelfth century. In his curious and interesting article in the Insurance Cyclopædia on 'Fire Insurance,' he has gathered the early history of fire underwriting into a compact form. He states that the first company really formed in England was in 1680, called the Fire Office, afterward the Phœnix; this was followed in 1683 by another, which seems to have been a formidable rival, and was called the Friendly Society. These companies were only organized for the insurance of buildings. The first company chartered to insure merchandise and other personal property was the Lombard in 1704. In 1710 the Sun Fire Office was established, followed in 1714 by the Union, in 1711 by the Hand in Hand, in 1717 by the Westminster, in 1720 by the London Assurance Corporation, and in 1721 by the Royal Exchange. * * * The system of association in boards is as old as the business itself. I was told in London that such an association existed in the latter half of the last century, which has been continued down in various forms to the present day, many of the companies which originated it still being members. As early as 1819 such an association was formed in the city of New York, when only eight companies were in existence, and it continued to make additions to its members until 1827, when it was merged into a regular Board of Underwriters. To show that it was to be proof against disaster either from within or without, it took the euphonious name of the 'Salamander Society.' Its records still exist and are in my possession."

On the 20th of April, 1858, at the First Annual Dinner of the New York Board of Fire Insurance Companies, A. B. McDonald, Esq., of the Royal Insurance Company of Liverpool, in responding to a toast, said that the early history of the Old Association of Fire Insurance Companies was involved in some obscurity, its records having perished in the fire of 1835. Of its original members not one survived, and of those who were members in 1829, when Mr. McDonald joined it, but few survived. "The rapidly increasing population and commerce of this city after the peace of 1815," continued the speaker, "led to the formation of this association about the year 1825 or 1826." Among the companies originally represented in the association, he said, were the Mutual, the first Fire Insurance Company established in this State after the Revolution, a company whose records afford a curious and interesting history of the rise of fire insurance in this city, which has paid in full all just claims upon it since 1787, and still maintains a vigorous existence under its present name of Knickerbocker, the Globe, with a capital of a million dollars, the Eagle, the Washington, the Merchants, with capitals of four hundred thousand dollars each, and many others.

"The rules and regulations of the association," he continued, "were founded on two leading principles, viz.: Uniformity of Rates and Non-payment of Commissions for procuring business. The operation of these principles, which were adhered to with fidelity, elevated the Associated companies to a high position in public estimation; so great was the confidence felt in their stability that, prior to 1835, investments in their shares were made by executors to estates and other trustees in preference to bank stocks. These principles survived the destructive conflagrations of 1835 and 1845, and on the reorganization of the companies after both these calamities they were adopted as the basis of the revived Association. One period in the history of Fire Insurance in this city is so full of instruction and warning as to deserve a notice. About 1843 a large increase of companies, of which a number did not connect themselves with the Association, and were not governed by its rules and regulations, led to a strenuous competition for business. Several members withdrew from the Association and reduced their rates of premium. A reduction of the associated rates followed. and was succeeded by reduction after reduction to rates far below a compensation for the losses. The ruin which the companies were thus inflicting on each other was completed by the conflagration of 1845. It may be remarked that the companies which commenced this unfortunate course were hopelessly insolvent, and were never resuscitated."

Other authorities differ with Mr. Oakley. Some writers trace insurance back to the second Punic war, but it appears well established that the first fire insurance was contemplated in 1696, when the "Amicable" Company was established in England.

In 1858, when the "Salamanders," or Old Association of Fire Insurance Companies of the City of New York, was merged in the New York Board of Fire Insurance Companies, interesting majority and minority reports were presented to the Association. In one of the reports it was stated that there were at that time doing the business of fire insurance in this city seventy-nine companies which were incorporated by the State of New York, and one incorporated by the State of New Jersey, making a total of eighty companies, employing an aggregate cash capital of sixteen millions one hundred and fifty-six thousand dollars; that there were also several mutual companies engaged largely in the same business, but the committee regarded those having cash capitals only, as being more closely allied in interest, and as having a more direct bearing upon the questions under consideration. Of the eighty companies there were forty-three with an aggregate capital of nine millions four hundred and four thousand dollars, which were associated for objects of mutual benefit, each company being subject to certain rules and restrictions adopted by such association, the remainder comprising thirty-seven companies, with an aggregate capital of six millions seven hundred and fifty-two thousand dollars, had no association in common, but a large majority of them having been organized within the past eight years deemed it necessary, to ensure their success, to act independently of the association, or, in other words, to place their capital in direct competition with that represented in the board. Among other things it was resolved that the agreement to adhere to a standard of rates as signed by the companies not members of the association, be also signed by the members of the Board of Underwriters, that a committee be appointed for the purpose of calling a convention of all the fire insurance companies of New York, Brooklyn, and Jersey City, to devise means for the adoption of a standard of rates, and that to such convention be referred also the subject of paying commission, or modifying the then system of brokerage, or of abolishing the system altogether. The majority report was signed by W. F. Underhill, Robert D. Hart, Horatio Dorr, and John Baker.

In the majority report it was said: "One important fact must not be lost sight of, viz.: that the present standard rates are much higher in this city, taking all things in consideration, than is charged in most, if not all, of the principal cities in the Union. The rates charged in the city of Boston on warehouse risks are from $\frac{3}{8}$ to $\frac{3}{4}$ per cent. In Philadelphia, from 50 to 65 cts. In Baltimore, from 60 to 75 cts; while in this city they range from 65 to 112 cts., averaging about 85 cts. This enhanced rate in New York over the rates prevailing in other cities named, and in cities too that have a large number of home companies, has induced the establishment of numerous agencies in this city, many of the agents being authorized to take risks from

10 to 15 cts. less than the rates charged by this association." Edward Anthony was the signer of this report.

Mr. Underhill was Secretary of the Peoples; Mr. Hart, Secretary of the Astor; Mr. Dorr, Secretary of the Atlantic, of Brooklyn; Mr. Baker, Secretary of the Mercantile, and Mr. Anthony, President of the Lamar.

The Salamander Society, an organization of fire underwriters, which existed between 1819 and 1826, had for several years no standing officers, but at the meeting a president and secretary were elected. At the time of its organization there existed eight Fire Insurance Companies, viz.: Globe, Eagle, Mutual, Franklin, Fulton, Washington, Merchants and Mechanics, and when it ceased to exist, there were in addition the Ætna, Chatham, Contributionship, Equitable, Firemen's, Farmer's, Greenwich, Howard, Jefferson, Lafayette, Manhattan, North River, Phœnix, Protection, Sun, Trader's,

SECRETARY'S BADGE.

Orange, Tradesmens' and United States. Of the Presidents were Gabriel Furman, Mutual; Swords, Washington; Jackson, Globe; Edward Laight, Eagle, and Henry Rankin, father of James M. Rankin, Globe; of the companies which belonged to the association, the Ætna, Eagle, Equitable, Howard, Manhattan and Mutual, Knickerbocker, survive. At the first meeting held January 29, 1819, it was resolved, on motion of Mr. Henderson, President of the Globe, that buildings of brick or stone covered with slate, tile or metals, and having solid iron doors and window shutters in the rear, and no building in front within 100 feet, be insured as of the first class; by Mr. Henderson, that the risks on ship chandlery be insured at the same premium as groceries.

In May, 1819, rates appeared to have stirred up the Salamanders, for the following was adopted on motion of Mr. Printard, of the Globe: "That a committee of five be appointed to revise the present rates of premium, and the regulations of the Fire Insurance Companies with a view to have the same printed, and the said committee report at the next meeting." The committee consisted of Messrs. Laight, Eagle; Pintard, Mutual; Underhill, Fulton; Harris, Washington; and Lawrence, Merchants'. August 6th, a report on rates and long term policies was made. In it was the following:

Say the premium for one year is $100,

A present payment of 93.45 = $100 payable 1 year hence
A present payment of 87.34 = $100 payable 2 years hence.
A present payment of 81.62 = $100 payable 3 years hence.
A present payment of 76.28 = $100 payable 4 years hence.
A present payment of 71.29 = $100 payable 5 years hence.
A present payment of 66.33 = $100 payable 6 years hence.

By this calculation a person insuring for 7 years, $100 yearly premium, would pay $576.75, whereas by the present rate he pays $600.

The committee therefore recommend that the following discounts should be allowed, which are, fractions excluded, in conformity with the above principle, viz.: for two years,

3½ per cent. ; three years, 7 per cent. ; four years, 9½ per cent. ; five years, 12½ per cent. ; six years, 15 per cent. ; 7 years, 17½ per cent.

Insurances made for a shorter term than one year will be charged as follows :

For nine months ⅞ of the annual premium.
For six months ¾ of the annual premium.
For five months ⅔ of the annual premium.
For three months ½ of the annual premium.
For two months ⅖ of the annual premium.
For one month ⅓ of the annual premium.

The classes of hazards and rates of insurance were :

	Addition to rate of house.	Special premium.
Apothecaries	25	
Bakers	37½	
Boat Builders	25	
Booksellers (stocks only)	12½	
Bookbinders	37½	
Brick kilns		75
Brownstone works	25	
Cabinet makers	25	
Carpenters	12½	
Chair makers	12½	
Confectioners	12½	
Chinaware (stock unpacked)	25	
Chocolate makers, with stove	12½	
Colormen (stock only)	12½	
Coopers	25	
Couch makers	25	
Chip and straw hats	12½	
Corn in stock		50
Druggists	25	
Dyers	25	
Flax	12½	
Founders	25	
Farmers, viz. :		
Dwelling houses		50
Stables		75
Dead stock therein		75
Live stock therein		50
Stock in stacks		50
Glass, unpacked	25	
Glass, in packages	12½	
Grocers	12½	
Hay in stacks		50
Hemp	12½	
Houses, building or repairing	25	
Looking-glass, in packages	12½	
Looking-glass, unpacked	25	
Malt houses with kiln	50	
Mills, viz. :		
Bark mills		75
Corn and grist mills, no kiln		87½
Corn and grist mills, with kiln		125
Cotton mills		
Flour mills		
Fulling mills		100
Metal mills	12½	
Oil mills, with stove		150
Paper mills, with stove		150
Paper mills, no stove		75
Saw mills		75
Snuff mills		150
Woolen mills		150

N. B.—Distinct sums are to be specified in the insurance of mills under the following heads, viz. :

	Addition to rate of house.	Special premium.
Machinery.		
Movable utensils and stocks.		
Musical instrument sellers (stock only)............	12½	
Musical instrument makers......................	25	
Oil..	12½	
Pictures and prints (stock only).................	12½	
Pitch...	12½	
Sail-makers...................................	12½	
Saltpetre.....................................	12½	
Ship chandlers................................	12½	
Ships and cargoes on board one year...........		70
Ships and cargoes on board eleven months......		65
Ships and cargoes on board ten months.........		60
Ships and cargoes on board nine months........		55
Ships and cargoes on board eight months.......		50
Ships and cargoes on board seven months.......		45
Ships and cargoes on board six months.........		40
Ships and cargoes on board five months........		35
Ships and cargoes on board four months........		30
Ships and cargoes on board three months.......		25
Ships and cargoes on board two months.........		20
Ships and cargoes on board one month.........		12½
Ship builders.................................	25	
Soap makers..................................	25	
Spirits..	12½	
Stables.......................................	25	
Stationery (stock only)........................	12½	
Straw in ricks................................		50
Sugar refiners................................	75	
Tallow melters................................	25	
Tar...	12½	
Tavern keepers...............................	12½	
Tile kilns.....................................		75
Timber yards, if isolated......................	50	
Turpentine...................................	12½	
Turpentine manufactories.....................		50

In the case of chocolate makers the policy specified that the company was not responsible for loss of stock in drying. In that of corn in stacks, stock in

INSURANCE BADGE.

BADGE: BOARD OF FIRE UNDERWRITERS.

stacks and hay in stacks the clause was "not responsible for damage in natural heating." Country stores were privileged to keep gunpowder. In the case of mills the several insurance companies were at liberty to fix their own rate of premium. These rates were more or less strictly adhered to, thanks to the prodding of those who were disposed to "cut" by conservative companies. Matters of this sort appear to have been harmonized in February, 1820, by a resolution appointing Messrs. Tibbits, Henderson and Laight a committee "to consider and report at the next meeting of the representatives of the Fire Insurance Companies what penalty ought to be incurred for any willful deviation from the rates of insurance agreed upon by the respective fire insurance offices, which penalty if agreed to shall be referred to the several companies for concurrence, and when concurred in shall be binding on all companies," thus in fact establishing a Tariff Association.

A step similar to that legalized in 1886 was taken in April, 1821, under the following resolution: "That a committee be appointed to examine the policies of the different companies for the purpose of having them uniform." A uniform "Form of Policy" was agreed upon on the 19th of June. It was so clear and distinct in setting forth the interests of the insurer and insured that it was used until recent years as was the "Rent Policy" and "Form of Application" approved of at the same time.

The classes of hazards and rates of annual premiums were set forth in the following table:

CLASSES OF HAZARDS AND RATES OF ANNUAL PREMIUMS.

1st.	2d.	3d.	4th.
Buildings of brick or stone covered with tile, slate, or metal, the doors and windows of solid iron, 22 cents per $100.	Buildings of brick or stone covered with tile, slate, or metal, 25 cents per $100.	Buildings of brick or stone, roofs three-fifths of tile, slate, or metal, the rest shingled, 30 cents per $100.	Buildings of brick or stone covered with wood, $37\frac{1}{2}$ cents per $100.

5th.	6th.	7th.	8th.
Buildings of frame filled in with brick, the front entirely of brick, 50 cents per $100.	Frame buildings filled in with brick, $62\frac{1}{2}$ cents per $100.	Frame buildings, hollow walls with brick front, 70 cents per $100.	Buildings entirely of wood, 75 to 100 cents per $100.

Not Hazardous.—Goods not hazardous are to be insured at the same rates as the buildings in which they are contained, and are such as are usually kept in Dry Goods stores, including also Household Furniture and Linen, Cotton in Bales, Coffee, Flour, Indigo, Potash, Rice, Sugars, Teas, Spices, Paints ground in Oil, and Threshed Grain.

Hazardous.—The following Trades, Goods, Wares, and Merchandise are considered *hazardous*, and are charged with $12\frac{1}{2}$ cents per $100 in addition to the premium above named for each class, viz.: Booksellers' stock, Chair makers, Chocolate makers, Confectioners, China, Glass and Earthenware in Packages, Flax, Hemp, Printers' stock, Milliners, Musical Instrument Sellers' stock, Oil, Pitch, Pictures and Prints, Sail makers, Ship chandlers, Spiritous Liquors, Saltpetre, Tin, Turpentine, Tavern keepers, Tobacco manufacturers, and Watch makers' stock.

Extra Hazardous.—The following Trades and Occupations, Goods, Wares, and Merchandise are deemed *extra hazardous*, and will be charged 25 cents and upward per $100 in addition to the premium above specified for each class, viz.: Aqua fortis, Apothecaries or Druggists, Boat Builders, Coach Makers, Cabinet Makers, Carpenters in their own shops or buildings erecting or repairing, Chemists, China, Glass and Earthenware unpacked and buildings in which the same are packed, Coopers, Dyers, Ether, Founders, Fodder and Grain unthreshed, Hay, Musical Instrument makers, Spirits of Turpentine, Straw, Soap Boilers and

Tallow Chandlers, and all manufactories requiring the use of fire heat. Gunpowder is not insurable except by special agreement.

Special.—Mem. Bakeries, Breweries, Bookbinderies, Distilleries, Fulling Mills, Grist Mills, Malt Houses, Paper Mills, Printing Offices, Sugar Refineries, and Saw Mills may be insured at special rates of premium.

Country Houses.—N. B. Country houses standing detached from other buildings, though of the 6th, 7th, and 8th class, will be insured at 50 cents per $100. Barns and stables in the country 75 cents per $100.

☞ Ships in port or their Cargoes, and Ships building or repairing may be insured against fire.

The first standing officers of the Salamanders were elected September 8, 1823, when Mr. Jackson of the Globe was chosen Chairman and O. H. Hicks of the Fulton, Secretary. In October Messrs. Tibbitts, Lord, Champlin and Mercein were appointed a committee to draft by-laws for the guidance of the Board. A set was approved of in December. In January, 1826, a new organization, a revision of rates and the consolidation of interests were considered, and among other things it was resolved that a deposit of $500 be made by each company to insure adherence to rules and regulations and that "the funds so deposited by the several companies be placed in charge of a committee of the officers of the same, who are to loan out said funds on the hypothecation of any funded debt of the United States or of this State, or the hypothecation of the stock of any banking institution in this city the value of which said stock when so hypothecated shall be above par, the interest so accruing on said loans to be paid over annually or semi-annually to the respective companies." A meeting was held and the resolutions were agreed to except by the United States, Firemen's and Greenwich Companies, and the outcome was a new association of companies known as the Fire Insurance Association under the presidency of Mr. Jackson. This organization established new tariff rates in 1835, when there was a reorganization due to collapse, in 1842, again in 1844 after the second great fire, and afterward in 1848. The most stable of the associations, the Board of Fire Insurance Companies, was organized in 1850.

We find that prior to 1850 Mr. Edward W. Laight was President of the New York Board of Fire Insurance Companies, and was succeeded in 1850, 1851 and 1852 by Nathaniel Richards, Mr. George T. Hope being secretary. The first call for statements from insurance companies was made from the Comptroller's office, Albany, on Jan. 7, 1829, by Wm. L. Marcy. The Revised Statutes provided that only corporations *thereafter* created should file annual statements, so that it was not until 1864 that all insurance companies, compelled by the new law to do so, sent in their reports. The first New York Fire Insurance Company to file a statement was the New York in 1833, the year after its creation. It was as follows:

The following balance-sheet exhibits a statement of the property and funds of this company January 9, 1833 :

Amount of Capital paid in December 18, 1832	$200,000.00
Amount of Premiums secured up to January 7–9, 1833	397.11
Total	$200,397.11
By amount of loans on bank stock	$156,625.00
By amount of loans in public stocks	15,000.00
By amount of loans on bond and mortgage on real estate	7,750.00

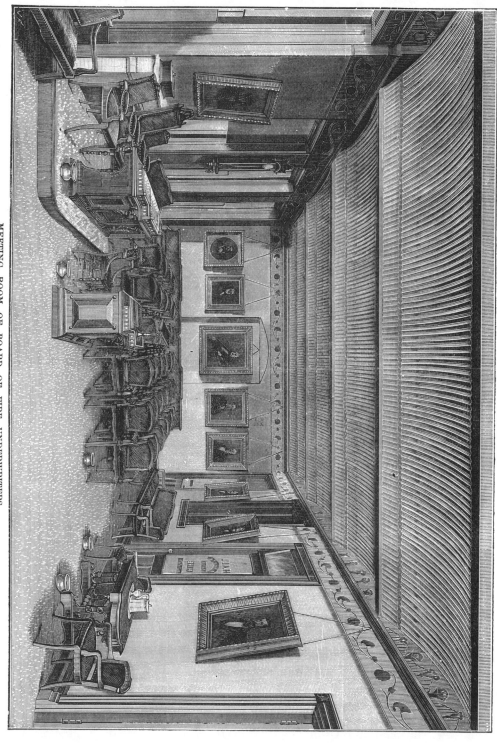

MEETING ROOM OF BOARD OF FIRE UNDERWRITERS.

By amount of expenses, viz., furniture, books, etc.......................... 771.74
By amount of loans on cash in Merchant's and Trader's Bank............. 20,177.57
By amount of cash in iron chest on hand........ .... 72.80

Total..$200,397.11

In 1833 Comptroller A. C. Flagg rapped the following New York Stock Fire Insurance Companies over the knuckles, reminding them not only of the financial penalty, but that a failure to report within a month of the receipt of the circular, laid them open to dissolution as insolvent corporations (I. R. S., § 22, p. 594): American, Bowery, Clinton, City, Firemen's, Guardian, Jefferson, Long Island, Mechanics', New York, National, Phœnix, Sun and Union.

The reports to Comptroller Flagg for 1835 had black eyes. "Losses by the late fire in the First Ward of this city" played havoc with the capital. The Stock Companies which made reports from the city were the City, loss, $156,000; Greenwich, $35,182.73; Guardian, $300,000; Bowery, New York, $100,000. In the reports for 1836 we find the City, among its assets, giving a claim for property blown up with gunpowder, $24,244.95. The East River reported its capital swept away by the fire, etc., the commencement of new business with $250,000 of new capital. The Jefferson included in claims against it that of Evans & Carman, whose store was blown up by order of the Corporation of the City amounting to $6,650, and acknowledged the impairment of its capital. The Merchants' took advantage of "An Act for the benefit of certain Insurance Companies in the City of New York" passed 12th of February, 1836. The New York, in its assets, $8000 due from the United States Bank surplus on an assignment of a bond and mortgage as collateral security for money borrowed to pay wages. The North American speaks of bonds and mortgages coming to it as receivers of the late Phœnix Insurance Company. In the reports for 1845, the great fire of that year is alluded to. In December, 1848, Comptroller Millard Fillmore suggested to the Legislature the taxation of Mutual Insurance Companies. He also addressed a circular to the Mutual Fire Insurance Companies of the State requiring reports, and received a few from suburban companies, one of which was as follows:

Farmers' Mutual Insurance Company of Sherburne, Chenango County. Only loss since the Company was chartered is eleven dollars. N. B.—This company has stopped business in consequence of Mutual Companies having become of late rather unpopular. Most of the policies run out in 1850.—December 29, 1848. B. H. Marks, Secretary.

The Act of April 10, 1849, placed Fire Insurance Companies incorporated in other States, and doing business in the State of New York, virtually on an equality with the companies of the State, and subjected them to the same restrictions. They were required, if they did business in New York or King's County, to have a capital of $150,000. Under the law the following Joint-Stock Fire Insurance Companies filed reports for 1849: Ætna of Hartford, American of Philadelphia, Columbia of Philadelphia, Columbus of Ohio, Deleware Mutual Safety of Philadelphia, Franklin of Philadelphia, Franklin of Boston, Hartford of Connecticut, State of Pennsylvania, Merchants' of Kentucky, Lexington of Kentucky, Manufacturers' of Boston, Merchants' of Boston, Nashville of Tennessee, National of Boston, Neptune of Boston, Norwich of Connecticut, North American of Philadelphia, Protection of Hartford, Protection of New

EDGAR. W. CROWELL. HENRY A. OAKLEY.

JOSEPH WALKER.

JONATHAN J. THORNE. NATHANIEL. RICHARDS.

REPRESENTATIVE INSURANCE MEN.

Jersey, Providence Washington of Rhode Island, and Tennessee of Nashville.

The President and Secretary of the New York Board of Fire Insurance Companies from 1850 to 1858, when the "Salamanders" became the "New Association," and to 1865, when the Paid Department "came in," were:

1850, 1851 and 1852. Nathaniel Richards, President; George T. Hope, Secretary.

1853. Joshua S. Underhill, President; George T. Hope, Secretary.

1854. Mr. J. S. Underhill, President. Mr. Hope resigned on account of sickness, and was succeeded by Milton J. Smith, who continued in office until 1859.

1855, 1856, Mr. J. S. Underhill, President.

1857, Richard J. Thorne, President.

1858, year of reorganization, the officers and committeemen were.

President—Joseph Walker, of the Security Insurance Co.

Vice-President—George C. Satterlee, of the Washington.

Secretary—J. Milton Smith, of the Home.

Treasurer— Charles H. Birney, of the East River.

STANDING COMMITTEES.

Executive Committee.—George T. Hope, of the Continental Insurance Company; C. V. B. Ostrander, of the Merchants'; Jonathan D. Steele, of the Niagara; Richard J. Thorne, of the New York Equitable; Joseph Hoxie, of the Commonwealth; Stephen Crowell, of the Phœnix; Benjamin W. Benson, of the Beekman.

Committee on Rates.—Edward A. Stansbury, of the Metropolitan Insurance Company; J. Milton Smith, of the Home; George W. Savage, of the Jersey City; Wm. F. Underhill, of the People's'; Wm. Mulligan, of the Humboldt; Wm. W. Henshaw, of the Long Island; Thomas Greenleaf, of the Hope.

Committee on Deviations.—Horatio Dorr, of the Atlantic Insurance Company; Walter Underhill, of the Merchants' and Traders'; Richard Ten Eyck, of the Williamsburgh; J. V. Harriott, of the Firemens'; Doras L. Stone, of the Hanover; E. B. Fellows, of the Rutgers; Wm. Jaffray, of the Park.

Committee on Fire Patrol.—C. V. Anderson, of the Lorillard Insurance Company; Daniel Underhill, of the New York Fire and Marine; Frederick R. Lee, of the Stuyvesant; Thomas F. Jeremiah, of the Pacific; H. M. Forrester, of the Broadway; John G. Storm, of the Lenox; James M. Rankin, of the Fulton.

Committee on Heating of Buildings.—Henry A. Oakley, of the Howard Insurance Company; A. B. McDonald, of the Royal; Ed Anthony, of the Lamar; John H. Funk, of the LayFayette; John S. Tappan, of the Union Mutual; James H. Pinckney, of the Relief; Wm. Callender, of the Harmony.

Committee on Applications for Membership.—James M. Halstead, of the American Insurance Company; Thomas W. Thorne, of the National; Joseph Ketchum, of the Corn Exchange; Jacob Brouer, of the Ætna; R. W. Bleecker, of the North American; Thomas A. Emmet, of the New World; John C. Bergh, of the Columbia.

1859—Mr. Walker, President; Mr. W. F. Underhill, became Secretary, and held the office until 1864.

1860—Mr. G. S. Fox was elected President, but declined to serve, and Mr. Richard J. Thorne was elected and served in 1861 and 1862.

1863—Mr. John D. Steele, President.

1864, 1865—Mr. George T. Hope, President, and Mr. Robert D. Hart, Secretary.

These years marked important events. In them the system of watching for incendiaries and prosecuting them was perfected by the appointment of a Fire Marshall, Mr. Alfred Baker. October 15, 1857, it was resolved to in future call the Association the Board of Fire Underwriters, and this preceded the reorganization of April 15, 1868. June 24, 1858, the following resolution in regard to cutting rates was passed:

That in case of a deviation from the rates of premium by writing below the established rates it shall be the duty of the company making such deviation to pay the amount of premium named on each policy into the treasury for the benefit of the Fire Patrol Fund, subject to the decision of the Executive Committee.

Anxiety was felt about the water supply at this time, for on the 26th of October a committee of three was appointed to inquire into the matter.

In December, 1861, on a report of a Special Committee on unrefined petroleum, it was declared " positively uninsurable in all buildings in compact portions of the city, and in all public warehouses, privileged for storage of hazardous, and extra hazardous merchandise, and such oils are considered insurable only when in detached and properly ventilated sheds and warehouses, specially adopted by their construction for that purpose, and devoted exclusively to the storage of such oils or substances of a similar character, and then only at a special rate, not less than three per cent." The storage of benzine, benzole, naptha, and refined petroleum was also restricted.

March 17, 1864, the creation of a paid fire department was foreshadowed by the passing of the following resolution :

Resolved, That the subject of promoting the greater efficiency of the Fire Department be referred to a special committee to inquire into the same, and report to a subsequent meeting of this Board.

The committee appointed by President Hope consisted of James M. McLean, President of the Citizens' Fire Insurance Co.; Carlisle Norwood, President of the Lorillard ; James M. Rankin, Secretary of the Fulton ; Rudolph Garrigue, Richard A. Reading, T. J. Glover and T. G. Churchill. A month later the committee were discharged and the matter was referred to the executive committee. November 28th plans had so far advanced that each company was assessed one-tenth of one per cent. of the amount of its capital for the advancement of the scheme, one-half to be handed over to the Citizens' Association and the remainder to the Committee on Fire Department. The same day the Board offered a reward of $3,000 for the conviction of any and all incendiaries in New York, Brooklyn, Jersey City and Hoboken. This was because of the attempt to burn the city by Southern sympathizers, and the Mayor had offered a reward of $2,000 for their arrest. The early days of 1865 were passed in discussing the Paid Fire Department Bill presented at Albany. The chief opposition was to including Brooklyn in its operations. February 14th a communication from Mr. Peter Cooper embodied a suggestion which was not carried out until President Henry D. Purroy had his portable tank constructed. Said Mr. Cooper : " In order to stimulate these men and preserve the greatest degree of purity in their body and devotion to the interests of the city I propose that it should be made their pecuniary interest to faithfully perform their duty." He urged the placing of tanks of elevated water held at convenient places in the city so high that the force of water will make all the hydrants equal to fire engines for the purpose of extinguishing fires by simply hoisting a gate so as to let the water press on the mains of the city.

The officers of the Board from the establishment of a Paid Fire Department to the present were : 1865—President, George T. Hope ; Secretary, Robert D. Hart. 1866—President, James M. McLean ; Secretary, Frank W. Ballard. 1867—President, James M. McLean ; Secretary, W. W. Henshaw. 1868—President, James M. McLean ; Secretary, W. W. Henshaw. 1869—President, Henry A. Oakley ; Secretary, W. W. Henshaw. 1870—President, Henry A. Oakley ; Secretary, W. W. Henshaw. 1871—President, George W. Savage ;

REPRESENTATIVE INSURANCE MEN.

Secretary, W. W. Henshaw. 1872—President George W. Savage; Secretary, W. W. Henshaw. 1873—President, Rudolph Garrigue; Secretary, W. W. Henshaw. 1874—President, E. W. Crowell; Secretary, W. W. Henshaw. 1875—President, E. W. Crowell; Secretary, W. W. Henshaw. 1876—President, D. A. Heald; Secretary, W.W. Henshaw. 1877—President, D. A. Heald; Secretary, W. W. Henshaw. 1878—President, E. A. Walton; Secretary, W. W. Henshaw. 1879—President, E. A. Walton; Secretary, W. W. Henshaw. 1880—President, Thomas F. Jeremiah; Secretary, W. W. Henshaw. 1881— President, Thomas F. Jeremiah; Secretary, W. W. Henshaw. 1882—President, Peter Notman; Secretary, W. W. Henshaw. 1883—President, Peter Notman; Secretary, W. W. Henshaw. 1884—President, N. C. Miller; Secretary, W. W. Henshaw. 1885—President, N. C. Miller; Secretary, W. W. Henshaw. 1886—President, Henry H. Hall; Secretary, W. W. Henshaw.

When in April, 1865, the affairs of the Committee on Paid Fire Department were settled it was found that they had spent $21,836.50, more than half of the assessment on the companies, and an additional assessment of one-tenth of one per cent. was ordered. Appropriate action was taken in regard to the victories which marked the close of the war and the death of President Lincoln. On the 17th of April, 1865, the members of the Board met at the Insurance Rooms, No. 156 Broadway, and Messrs. Edward A. Stansbury, Robert O. Glover and James M. McLean, and passed resolutions regarding the assassination of President Lincoln. One of the resolutions read:

Resolved, That the members of this Board join with the nation and the whole civilized world in execration of the spirit which has prompted this deed, and in profound and personal sorrow for the bereavement which it has inflicted on us.

On January 30th, 1866, a special committee reported a proposed act for the incorporation of the Board. The draft of the bill was not presented until March 5th, 1867, and the Act of Incorporation was passed May 9th, 1867. The first meeting of the new Board was on the 15th of May, when measures were taken to dissolve the association and transfer its property. May 20th Mr. McLean and Mr. Henshaw were re-elected. Shortly after the alarming frequency of fires and the unusual losses therefrom caused an inquiry by the Assembly Committee on Insurance Companies, who met a Committee of the Board. Afterward the Board's Committee made suggestions before a joint meeting of the Senate and Assembly Committees on Insurance. Out of the conference came a bill which created another Fire Commissioner, an act regulating the Storage of Combustible Materials, an act to create a Superintendent of Buildings, and an act to create a Fire Marshal. In November incendiarism had became so common that the Board appropriated $50,000 to be offered in rewards for convictions, not exceeding $5000 in any one case. The act creating a Fire Marshal was not passed until the spring of 1868, and Captain Charles N. Brackett was appointed.

A leap from 1868 to 1886 is necessitated by want of space to chronicle the minor events of this period against the important events of the last-named year, one of the most important in the annals of underwriting. The only digression permissible is to refer to the important discussions and action of various committees in the Dry Goods District in 1882 and 1883. The district was understood to be that bounded by Chambers, Elm, Crosby, and Spring

Streets, South Fifth Avenue, and West Broadway, and the value of the stocks held is estimated at $200,000,000. Among those who actively participated in the inquiry were James Harrison, Superintendent of Rates and Survey, an office created in 1872, and Messrs. Washburn, Adee, Hollinshead, Hope, Jeremiah, Kennedy, Beddall, Kahl, Bacon, Douglass, and the following merchants: Charles S. Smith, of George C. Richardson & Co.; William E. Tefft, of Tefft, Weller & Co.; J. H. Dunham, of Dunham, Buckley & Co.; John R. Waters, of Megroz, Portier, Grose & Co.; C. N. Bliss, of Bliss, Fabyan & Co.; J. H. Reed, of Bates, Reed & Cooley; John Claflin, of H. B. Claflin & Co.; Jacob Wendell, of Wendell, Fay & Co.; William L. Strong, of William L. Strong & Co.; John Gibb, of Mills & Gibb; Elkan Naumburg, of Naumburg, Kraus, Lauer & Co.; Charles Sternbach, of H. Herrmann, Sternbach & Co.; James O. Carpenter, of William H. Lyon & Co.; E. F. Browning, of William C. Browning & Co.; Charles T. Smith, of William H. Smith & Co.

The main work of 1886 was the adoption of the standard Fire Insurance Policy of the State of New York, which went into effect on the 20th of October, 1886, under chapter 488 of the Laws.

There was also established the Metropolitan Association of Fire Underwriters under section 19 of the by-laws, who adopted a schedule of minimum rates which with the rates of the New York Tariff Association constituted the rates in the Metropolitan District of the 7th of October, 1886. This was under a compact reported by the following committee: Edw. A. Walton, Rud. Garrigue, George M. Coit, W. E. Horwill, J. E. Leffingwell, M. A. Stone, J. Q. Underhill, W. B. Ogden, T. F. Jeremiah, P. B. Armstrong, E. F. Beddall, N. W. Meserole, Thomas Gaines, A. A. Reeves, J. A. Silvey, Henry H. Hall (*ex-officio*). The preamble of the compact was as follows:

1. That all risks of every description in the Metropolitan District be equally rated.
2. That no commission be paid in excess of 10 per centum of the premium.
3. That no rebate to the assured be made by the companies from established rates, and that rules be prepared under which the rebating of commissions by brokers shall be effectually prevented.
4. That penalties be fixed for the infraction of any of the rates and rules that may be adopted by the Association.

The officers first elected for the Association were, E. A. Walton, President of the Citizens', President; Edward Gaines, Secretary of the Eagle, Vice-President; David L. Kirby, of Mills, Ford & Co., Secretary, and W. M. St. John, President of the Standard, Treasurer.

The New York Board of Fire Underwriters of to-day, whose offices at the Boreel Building, No. 115 Broadway, were first occupied in 1878, is a great institution. The companies having in various ways representation in it have $185,415,352.00 of assets against $10,586,175,402.00 of risks. Its officers and committees are:

President.—Henry H. Hall, Manager of the Northern, of London.
Vice-President.—George M. Coit, Agent of Hartford companies.
Secretary.—William W. Henshaw, Assistant Manager of the Royal, of London.
Assistant Secretary.—David L. Kirby, of Mills & Ford, Agents.
Treasurer.—William A. Anderson, President of the Mercantile.
Executive Committee.—William M. St. John, Chairman; Samuel P. Blagden, Vice-Chairman; J. F. Halsted, Stephen Crowell, Edmund Driggs, D. Underhill, J. E. Pulsford, S. E.

Belcher, J. S. Hollinshead, James A. Silvey, Henry E. Bowers, A. M. Kirby, Chas. M. Peck, Samuel Townsend, George T. Patterson, Jr., Charles Sewall, E. R. Kennedy, James A. Alexander, Peter Notman, J. M. Hare, C. A. Hull, T. Y. Brown, F. O. Affeld, James Yereance, J. Jay Nestell, William B. Ogden, T. F. Jeremiah, David Adee, Charles L. Gunn, D. F. Fernald, E. Litchfield, Thomas Clark, Jr., T. B. Jones, E. Dwight, Jr., William DeL. Boughton, Walter K. Paye, D. A. Heald, Henry A. Oakley, E. A. Walton, N. C. Miller.

Ex-officio Members.—Henry H. Hall, George M. Coit, William W. Henshaw, David L. Kirby, William A. Anderson.

STANDING COMMITTEES.

Finance.—J. F. Halsted, Chairman; Stephen Crowell, Vice-Chairman; Edmund Driggs, Daniel Underhill, S. E. Belcher, J. E. Pulsford, J. S. Hollinshead.

Fire Patrol.—George T. Patterson, Jr., Chairman; A. M. Kirby, Vice-Chairman; James A. Silvey, Charles M. Peck, Samuel Townsend, Henry E. Bowers, Samuel P. Blagden.

Laws and Legislation.—E. R. Kennedy, Chairman; C. A. Hull, Vice-Chairman; Charles Sewall, William M. St. John, Peter Notman, James A. Alexander, J. M. Hare.

Surveys.—James Yereance, Chairman; Charles L. Gunn, Vice-Chairman; T. Y. Brown, J. Jay Nestell, William B. Ogden, F. O. Affeld, David Adee.

Police and Origin of Fires.—William DeL. Boughton, Chairman; Walter K. Paye, Vice-Chairman; D. F. Fernald, Thomas Clark, Jr., T. B. Jones, E. Litchfield, E. Dwight, Jr.

Arbitration.—Peter Notman, Chairman; Henry A. Oakley, E. A. Walton, T. F. Jeremiah, D. A. Heald, N. C. Miller.

Patents.—S. E. Belcher, Chairman; James A. Alexander, Samuel Townsend, T. B. Jones, F. O. Affeld.

Membership.—James Yereance, Chairman; J. F. Halsted, E. R. Kennedy, George T. Patterson, Jr., William DeL. Boughton.

Water Supply.—J. H. Washburn, Chairman; J. Jay Nestell, A. M. Kirby, Chas. Sewall, Chas. L. Gunn.

Adjustment of Losses.—Wm. M. St. John, Chairman; Peter Notman, Edmund Driggs, Chas. H. Ford, J. F. Halsted, Chas. M. Peck, J. M. Hare, E. F. Beddall.

Delegate to Board of Examiners of Building Department.—Wm. M. St. John.

The Companies represented and their representatives, members of the Board, are as follows:

American.—James M. Halsted, President; David Adee, Secretary; W. H. Crobies, Assistant Secretary.

American Exchange.—William Raynor, President; Thomas Clarke, Secretary; Robert L. Young, Assistant Secretary.

Broadway.—Hiram M. Forrester, President; E. B. Magnus, Secretary.

Brooklyn.—F. P. Furnald, President; B. T. Rhode, Jr., Secretary.

Citizens.—James M. McLean, President; E. A. Walton, Vice-President; Frank M. Parke, Secretary.

City.—Samuel Townsend, President; D. J. Blauvelt, Secretary: A. L. Hyde, Assistant Secretary.

Clinton.—George T. Patterson, Jr., President; C. E. W. Chambers, Secretary.

Continental.—H. H. Lamport, President; F. C. Moore, Vice-President; Cyrus Peck, Vice-President and Secretary; A. M. Kirby, Secretary Local Department; C. H. Dutcher, Secretary Brooklyn Department.

Eagle.—A. J. Clinton, President; Thomas J. Gaines, Secretary.

Empire City.—Lindley Murray, Jr., President; David J. Burtis, Secretary.

Exchange.—Richard C. Combes, President; G. W. Montgomery, Secretary.

Fireman's.—J. F. Halsted, President; Samuel Darbee, Secretary.

German-American.—John W. Murray, Vice-President; James A. Silvey, Secretary.

Germania.—Rudolph Garrigue, President; Hugo Schuman, Secretary.

Globe.—Alfred A. Reeves, President; E. A. Holley, Secretary.

Guardian.—William C. Thompson, President; Walton K. Paye, Secretary.

Hamilton.—D. D. Whitney, President; D. D. Leeds, Secretary.

Hanover.--B. S. Walcott, President; J. R. Lane, Vice-President and Secretary; C. L. Roe, Assistant Secretary.

Home.—Charles J. Martin, President; D. A. Heald, Vice-President; J. H. Washburn, Vice-President and Secretary; T. B. Green and W. L. Bigelow, Assistant Secretaries.

Howard.—Henry A. Oakley, President; Charles A. Hall, Vice-President and Secretary; George H. Allen, Assistant Secretary.

Jefferson.—Samuel E. Belcher, President; William B. Flowery, Secretary.

King's County.—William E. Horwill, President; E. S. Terhune, Secretary; C. J. Wolf, Assistant Secretary.

Knickerbocker.—Edmund W. Albro, President; S. D. Leverich, Vice-President; William B. Hodson, Secretary.

Long Island. – Jonathan Ogden, President; Henry Blatchford, Secretary.

Manufacturers' and Builders'.—Edward V. Low, President; J. J. Nestell, Secretary.

Mechanics'.—William H. Hale, Vice-President; Walter Nichols, Secretary.

Mercantile.—William A. Anderson, President; C. W. Parmelee, Secretary.

Merchants'.—J. H. Morris, President; Isaac S. Mettler, Secretary.

Montauk.—D. F. Fernald, President; George F. Malby, Secretary; George Gill, Assistant Secretary.

Mutual.—Edward A. Moen, President; P. B. Armstrong, Secretary.

Nassau.—Thomas B. Jones, President; W. T. Lane, Secretary.

National.—Henry T. Drowne, President; F. J. Walton, Secretary.

New York..—David J. Underhill, President; A. Colson, Secretary.

New York Bowery.—J. A. Delanoy, Jr., President; Charles A. Blauvelt, Secretary.

New York Equitable.—John Miller, President; Charles L. Gunn, Secretary.

Niagara.—Peter Notman, President; Thomas F. Goodrich, Vice-President; West Pollack, Secretary.

Pacific.—T. F. Jeremiah, President; Frank T. Stinson, Secretary.

Park.—Willim Jaffray, President; William Valentine, Secretary.

Peoples'.—Frederick V. Price, President; A. C. Milne, Secretary.

Peter Cooper.—Nathan C. Ely, President; William H. Riblet, Secretary.

Phœnix.—Stephen Crowell, President; W. R. Crowell, Vice-President; Philander Shaw, Secretary.

Rutgers'.—E. B. Fellows, President; Joseph Hanford, Secretary.

Standard.—William M. St John, President; Robert H. Meyers, Secretary.

Star.—N. C. Miller, President; J. R. Smith, Vice-President; James M. Hodges, Secretary.

Stuyvesant.—S. P. Patterson, President; G. B. Rhodes, Secretary.

United States.--W. W. Underhill, President; Samuel Craft, Vice-President; George E. Cook, Secretary.

Westchester.—G. R. Crawford, President; John O. Underhill, Secretary.

Williamsburg City.--Edward Driggs, President; N. W. Mesrole, Secretary; F. H. Way, Assistant Secretary.

FOREIGN COMPANIES.

Royal.—E. F. Beddall, Manager; William W. Henshaw, Assistant Manager.

Guardian.—H. E. Bowers, Manager.

Norwich Union.—Charles P. Frame and J. M. Hare, Managers.

Transatlantic.—E. Harbers, Manager.

Phœnix of London.—A. D. Irving, Manager; E. B. Clark, Assistant Manager.

London Assurance.—B. Lockwood, Manager.

Liverpool and London and Globe.--J. E. Pilsford, Manager; H. W. Eaton, Deputy Manager.

Commercial Union—Alfed Pell, Manager; Charles Sewall, Assistant Manager.

Lancashire.—E. Litchfield, Manager; George Pitchard, Assistant Manager.

Queen.—J. A. Macdonald, Manager.

London and Lancashire. —James Yerance and J. Beavan, Joint Managers.

North British and Mercantile.—Samuel P. Bladgen and Charles E. White, Managers.

Fire Association of London.—A. B. M. Roome and Frank Lock, Joint Managers.

Hamburg-Bremen.—F. O. Affeld, Manager.
Sun of London.—R. C. Rathbone, Agent.
Northern of London.—H. H. Hall, Manager.

AGENTS.

Ætna of Hartford.—James A. Alexander.
Equitable and Merchants', of Providence.—David Adee.
Hartford of Hartford, Springfield, and Franklin, of Philadelphia.—George M. Coit.
Mercantile and American, of Boston.—R. O. Glover.
Insurance Co. of State of Pennsylvania and Insurance Co. of North America, of Philadelphia.—J. S. Hollinshead.
American and Firemen's, of Newark.—David L. Kirby.
American Central and Citizen's, of St. Louis, Detroit and Michigan, of Detroit, and Farmer's Mutual, of York, Pa.—John Mulville.
Merchant's and Newark, of Newark, N. J.—William B. Ogden.
Imperial and City of London, London, Firemen's, of San Francisco, Reliance, Fire Association, and United Firemen's, of Philadelphia.—Charles M. Peck.
New Hampshire, of Manchester, Citizen's, of Pittsburg, and Buffalo German.—T. J. Temple.
Albany, of Albany.—E. A. Walton.
St. Paul, of St. Paul.—John M. Whiton.
California, of San Francisco, Various Boston Underwriters, County and Spring Garden, of Philadelphia, and Marine, of St. Louis.—E. R. Kennedy and Samuel R. Weed.
Firemen's, of Baltimore, and People's and Boatmen's, of Pittsburg.—George H. Pell and E. Dwight, Jr.
Commercial, of San Francisco, and Traders', of Chicago.—John C. Mills and Charles H. Ford.
Commerce, of Albany, Union, of San Francisco, Security, of New Haven, Firemen's, of Dayton, Ohio, and Atlantic, of Providence.—N. L. Roosevelt and William DeL. Boughton.
Sun, of San Francisco.—Edmund Driggs and F. H. Way.
Orient, of Hartford, and British America, of Toronto.—Edward Rowell and R. G. Hone.
Concordia, of Milwaukee.—George T. Patterson, Jr.
Gerard, of Philadelphia.—Henry Honig.
Washington and Prescott, of Boston.—Charles H. Post and J. T. McCurdy.
Lion and Scottish Union and National, of England, Providence, Washington, of Rhode Island, and Connecticut, of Hartford.—W. K. Lathrop and W. A. Scott.
Pennsylvania, of Pittsburg, and Citizen's, of Dayton.—Peter Deyo.
Pennsylvania and American, of Philadelphia, Manufacturers' and Merchants' and Western, of Pittsburg.—Frame & Hare.
Falls City, Kentucky and Jersey City of Newark.—A. C. Quackenbush.

President Hall's address to the Board on his election in May, 1886, contained some important statements and figures. The following table gave the assessed valuation of real estate in this city each year since 1866:

1867,	. .	$555,442,062.00
1868,	. . .	623,235,305.00
1869,	. .	684,183,918.00
1870,	. . .	742,105,675.00
1871,	. .	769,306,410.00
1872,	. . .	797,125,115.00
1873,	. .	836,691,980.00
1874,	. . .	881,547,995.00
1875,	. .	883,643,545.00
1876,	. . .	892,428,165.00
1877,	. .	$895,063,933.00
1878,	. . .	900,855,700.00
1879,	. .	918,134,380.00
1880,	. . .	942,571,690.00
1881,	. .	976,735,199.00
1882,	. .	1,035,203,816.00
1883,	. . .	1,079,130,669.00
1884,	. .	1,119,761,597.00
1885,	. .	1,168,443,137.00

The following table showed the premiums reported for fire patrol assessment in the same years, less brokerage :

1867,	. . .	$8,222,845.00
1868,	. . .	7,369,061.00
1869,	. . .	6,872,885.00
1870,	. . .	6,085,281.00
1871,	. . .	6,606,352.00
1872,	. . .	7,001,802.00
1873,	. . .	8,281,508.00
1874,	. . .	7,879,622.00
1875,	. . .	6,802,331.00
1876,	. . .	5,838,013.00
1877,	. . .	$5,032,669.00
1878,	. . .	4,008,789.00
1879,	. . .	4,612,948.00
1880,	. . .	4,990,966.00
1881,	. . .	5,103,749.00
1882,	. . .	5,539,049.00
1883,	. . .	5,874,008.00
1884,	. . .	6,089,621.00
1885,	. . .	5,887,577.00

He submitted a brief analysis of the business of this city since 1873, selecting this date as it follows the Chicago and Boston fires. The following table gives a comparison of the premiums and their distribution in 1873 and 1885 :

		COMPANIES (1873.)		PER CENT.	COMPANIES (1885.)		PER CENT.
Locals,	.	(85)	$5,583,124.00	67	(55)	$2,895,550.00	49
Agency,	.	(77)	1,511,269.00	18	(69)	1,181,224.00	20
Foreign,	.	(11)	1,187,114.00	15	(22)	1,810,803.00	31
			$8,281,507.00	100		$5,887,577.00	100

In the course of his address Mr. Hall said :

"The local companies having decreased in number from fifty-nine to fifty-five, and the foreign companies from twenty-five to twenty-two, the agency companies have increased from fifty-nine to sixty-two, showing that the efforts to secure reform have been, in a measure, thwarted not only by the tariff companies themselves, but by the companies which have ignored the rules of the Tariff Association, many of the latter having most to fear from a failure to correct present abuses."

WILLIAM PITT PALMER.

A history of Fire Insurance and underwriting in New York would be incomplete without a more than passing reference to the friend of Washington Irving, Lewis Gaylord Clark, and many other *literati*, William Pitt Palmer, "the Laureate of the Salamanders." This gentleman, who was the President of the Manhattan Fire Insurance Company, was a native of Massachusetts, and was graduated from Williams College. He came to New York to study law, but he abandoned this profession to study medicine, and just as he had completed his studies he became a clerk in the Manhattan Fire Insurance Company's office. This was in 1834, and he continued in its service until its dissolution. Mr. Palmer had a facile pen in many branches of literature, but it was at the social board that he was conspicuous by his wit and genial conviviality. He was a poet of no mean order, but his forte lay in *jeux de mots,* and some of his rhymes applied to his profession were exceedingly humorous.

TABULATED STATEMENT OF INSURANCE AND LOSS IN THE CITY OF NEW YORK FOR THIRTY YEARS, ENDING APRIL 30, 1886.

COMPILED AND ARRANGED BY WILLIAM M. RANDELL, ESQ., SECRETATY OF THE NEW YORK BOARD OF FIRE UNDERWRITERS.

[Compiled from the report of the Committee on Fire Patrol to the New York Board of Fire Underwriters.]

Years.	Insurance.	Loss.	Years.	Insurance.	Loss.
1855....	2,699,484.00	887,439.00	1873....	14,399,034.55	3,456,057.62
1856....	2,755,300.00	563,906.00	1874....	9,201,589,53	1,500,508.00
1857....	5,009,823.00	1,408,327.00	1875....	12,814,175.02	1,971,962.41
1858....	2,294,637.00	686,255.00	1876....	13,041,846.94	3,194,229.46
1859....	2,353,600.00	457,623.00	1877....	12,630,026,43	2,016,064.75
1860....	4,609,930.00	1,576,563.00	1878....	13,626,619.94	2,211,569.04
1861....	6,192,285.00	1,394,689.00	1879....	23,036,302.34	4,884,495.50
1862....	5,115,561.00	1,220,439.00	1880....	13,545,654.93	2,621,930.12
1863....	4,640,751.00	1,245,211.00	1881....	16,816,493.05	2,246,864.50
1864....	8,094,800.00	2,113,454.00	1882....	18,532,901.54	4,198,417.34
1865....	11,896,502.00	4,323,998.00	1883....	22,725,864.91	3,647,909.67
1866....	12,330,787.00	5,806,592.00	1884....	23,932,740.38	3,674,402.41
1869....	8,340,448.00	2,918,673.00	1885....	27,802,956.17	4,147,443.49
1870....	11,590,574.00	2,582,573.00	1886....	26,278,862.49	3,064,276.38
1871....	11,765,127.00	2,302,355.00			
1872....	11,072,755.68	1,637,324.99	Total.	$360,147,432.90	$73,961,552.68

INSURANCE AND LOSS FOR THIRTY YEARS ENDING APRIL 30, 1886.
BUILDINGS AND CONTENTS SOUTH OF CANAL STREET.

PATROL NO. 1.

Years.	Insurance.	Loss	Years.	Insurance.	Loss.
1855....	1,621,720.00	540,522.00	1873....	6,192,074.26	1,431,237.18
1856....	1,851,200.00	390,547.00	1874....	5,665,400.39	851,169.99
1857....	3,869,150.00	1,034,396.00	1875....	7,854,420.00	1,207,404.74
1858....	2,072,500.00	455,314.00	1876....	4,625,857.43	652,089.56
1859....	1,098,065.00	206,481.00	1877....	5,111,778.32	602,084.67
1860....	2,974,830.00	1,108,949.00	1878....	6,773,843.94	973,169.83
1861....	4,942,050.00	1,096,577.00	1879....	13,331,683.01	2,855,792.18
1862....	3,828,516.00	936,018.00	1880....	6,373,180.37	1,396,671.29
1863....	2,447,170.00	630,013.00	1881....	8,687,089.77	1,123,017.79
1864....	5,201,320.00	1,471,384.00	1882....	8,869,520.42	2,059,028.97
1865....	5,972,512.00	1,920,157.00	1883....	9,694,426.12	1,534,663.96
1866....	7,581,920.00	3,147,966.00	1884....	10,936,730.85	1,466,104.41
1869....	4,710,207.00	1,195,462.00	1885....	12,313,406.68	1,938,148.92
1870....	7,037,500.00	1,123,861.00	1886....	9,253,092.37	1,068,902.59
1871....	6,880,245.00	1,435,827.00			
1872....	6,150,350.00	683,563.47	Total,	$183,921,758.93	$36,536,460.55.

INSURANCE AND LOSS FOR THIRTY YEARS ENDING APRIL 30, 1886.
BUILDINGS AND CONTENTS NORTH OF CANAL AND SOUTH OF FOURTEENTH STREETS.

PATROL NO. 2.

Years	Insurance.	Loss.	Years	Insurance.	Loss.
1855....	799,950.00	211,907.00	1873....	4,968,271.94	1,325,179.87
1856....	560,605.00	70,432.00	1874....	2,140,209.14	418,853.87
1857....	693,643.00	213,779.00	1875....	3,142,343.34	456,228.73
1858....	888,575.00	143,709.00	1876....	6,337,299.97	2,317,108.04
1859....	970,910.00	132,383.00	1877....	4,549 022.37	1,215,392.77
1860....	821,470.00	188,193.00	1878....	3,457,921.00	508,411.66
1861....	790,375.00	166,512.00	1879....	5,345,527.66	1,611,943.26
1862....	953,795.00	171,712.00	1880....	3,498,687.33	462,180.91
1863....	1,445,670.00	500,774.00	1881....	3,782,564.35	456,223.97
1864....	1,156,375.00	360,464.00	1882....	4,338,205.00	769,037.53
1865....	5,265,560.00	2,257,222.00	1883....	7,543,640.00	1,333,715.60
1866....	4,117,692.00	2,359,917.00	1884....	7,631,254.63	1,404,410.08
1869....	2,012,549.00	836,872.00	1885....	9,262,731.23	1,223,295.92
1870....	3,142,224.00	921,585.00	1886....	9,719,941.20	1,441,642.61
1871....	2,972,482.00	528,742.00			
1872....	2,580,286.68	348,068.81	Total.	$104,889,780.84	$24,354,617.29

INSURANCE AND LOSS FOR THIRTY YEARS ENDING APRIL 30, 1886. BUILDINGS AND CONTENTS NORTH OF FOURTEENTH AND SOUTH OF FIFTY-NINTH STREETS.

PATROL NO. 3.

Years.	Insurance.	Loss.	Years.	Insurance.	Loss.
1855....	253,214.00	116,395.00	1873....	3,238,688.35	699,640.57
1856....	342,895.00	102,727.00	1874....	1,323,630.00	226,233.48
1857....	382,380.00	118,172.00	1875....	1,675,711.68	271,145.50
1858....	329,662.00	86,320.00	1876....	1,815,339 54	193,142.54
1859....	268,075.00	114,134.00	1877....	2,604,175.74	151,826.75
1860....	661,430.00	166,480.00	1878....	3,106,530.00	698,211.24
1861....	441,260.00	118,711.00	1879....	3,955,441.67	362,618.71
1862....	232,500.00	55,174.00	1880....	3,117,222.23	652,859.97
1863....	741,166.00	111,664.00	1881....	3,609,108.93	504,118.25
1864....	1,722,505.00	272,986.00	1882....	4,433,141.12	1,244,334.45
1865....	647,930.00	141,145.00	1883....	4,546,722.69	655,178.50
1866....	623,025.00	293,109.00	1884....	4,171,579.00	677,851.56
1869....	1,344,992.00	688,804.00	1885....	4,241,105.76	682,210.69
1870....	1,146,000.00	330,932.00	1886....	5,316,565.92	304,028.63
1871....	1,744,550.00	297,266.00			
1872....	2,342,119.00	605,692.71	Total.	$60,378,665.63	$10,943,112.55

INSURANCE AND LOSS TWENTY-EIGHT YEARS ENDING APRIL 30, 1886.
BUILDINGS AND CONTENTS NORTH OF FIFTY-NINTH STREET.

PATROL NO. 4.

Years.	Insurance.	Loss.	Years.	Insurance.	Loss.
1855....	24,600.00	18,615.00	1874....	72,350.00	4,250.00
1856....	600.00	200.00	1875....	141,700.00	37,183.44
1857....	64,650.00	41,980.00	1876....	263,350.00	31,889.32
1858....	3,900.00	912.00	1877....	365,050.00	46,760.56
1859....	16,550.00	4,625.00	1878....	288,325.00	31,776.31
1860....	152,200.00	112,941.00	1879....	403,650.00	54,204.35
1861....	18,600.00	13,289.00	1880....	556,565.00	110,217.95
1862....	100,750.00	57,535.00	1881....	737,730.00	163,504.49
1863....	6,745.00	2,760.00	1882....	892,035.00	126,016.39
1864....	14,600.00	8,620.00	1883....	941,076.10	124,331.61
1865....	10,500.00	5,474.00	1884....	1,193,175.90	126,036.36
1866....	8,150.00	6,500.00	1885....	1,985,712.50	303,787.96
1869....	272,700.00	197,535.00	1886....	1,989,263.00	249,702.55
1870....	264,850.00	206,195.00			
1771....	161,850.00	40,520.00	Total,	$10,957,227.50.	$2,127,362.29.

[No. 2141]

Dwelling House
Tenth Rate
Dollars — 625

Premium — 6.25
Deposit — 25
Dollars — 31. 25

By the Mutual Assurance Company
Of the City of New-York.

This POLICY of ASSURANCE Witnesseth, That

Mangle Minthorne

having become, and by these Presents becoming a Member of *The Mutual Assurance Company of the City of New York,* agreeably to the Charter thereof, bearing Date the Twenty-third Day of March, in the Year one thousand seven hundred and ninety eight. And for and in Consideration of the Sum of *Thirty one Dollars and twenty five Cents* —————————— in Hand paid by the said *Mangle Minthorne* ————— to the Treasurer of the said Company, being the Amount of Premium and Deposit for Insuring the Sum of *Six hundred and twenty five Dollars* ——————————————— unto the said *Mangle Minthorne* ————— Executors, Administrators and Assign, upon

His Dwelling House Situated No 79 on the South side of Vesey Street, Bounded East by M Minthornes 2 Story frame House No 77 — West, by, M. Minthornes 2 Story Store No 183 and South by Yard and other Yards; as described in the Surveyors Report — No 2326 Book E Folio 292 and is classed in the Tenth Rate of Insurance —

during the Term of *Seven* — Years, from and after the Date hereof: Part of which said Sum of *Thirty one Dollars and twenty five Cents* to wit, the Sum of *Twenty five Dollars* —————————— is hereby declared to be deposited by the said *Mangle Minthorne* ————— as a Pledge or Caution for the Performance of the Duties and Obligations of the said *Mangle Minthorne* ————— as a Member of the said Corporation, according to the Bye-laws thereof.

NOW WE, *The Mutual Assurance Company of the City of New-York,* for and in Consideration of the Premises, do hereby certify, that the said *Mangle Minthorne* has ————— come insured, and by these Presents *is* insured by us the said Company, upon the said *Dwelling House* ————— in the said Sum of *Six hundred and twenty five Dollars* ——————— from and against all Loss or Damage by Fire during the Term aforesaid, according and subject to the Conditions, Regulations and Provisions contained and specified in the Bye-laws and Ordinances of the Corporation aforesaid. IN TESTIMONY WHEREOF, We, the said *Mutual Assurance Company of the City of New York,* have caused our Seal to be affixed to these Presents, and the same to be signed by our President, and counter-signed by our Secretary, on the *eighteenth* — Day of *March* — in the Year of our Lord one thousand *eight* — hundred. —————

Rob. Lenox President

Saml Boyd Secy

NEW YORK MUTUAL ASSURANCE COMPANY

POLICY OF ASSURANCE, MUTUAL ASSURANCE COMPANY.

In a sketch necessarily so incomplete, the writer can only give but brief notices of a few of the many well-known insurance men of this city, who, by their energy and experience, have earned a national reputation, and built up the present admirable system, by which they have made their names honorable household words. As many leading insurance officials have been prominently identified with the Fire Department at some period of their lives (mostly with the Volunteer), sketches and portraits of quite a number of them will be found among the biographies of old firemen. It is not always an easy matter to discriminate who shall appear upon the list where all are, in a sense, equally deserving. "Some are born great, while others have greatness thrust upon them."

DANIEL A. HEALD, Vice-President of the Home Insurance Company, of New York, is the leading fire underwriter of the United States. Mr. Heald's services to the profession, gratuitously rendered and not properly appreciated, have justified the assertion that has been made that no other fire underwriter of late years has done so much to uplift the profession or advance the real

DANIEL A. HEALD.

interests of fire insurance as he. His position as President of the National Board of Fire Underwriters has given Mr. Heald prominence and influence. But this official prominence came to him unsought and naturally and of right. He was a central figure in the Convention which, in 1866, created the National Board of Fire Underwriters, and ever since he has been an important factor in sustaining that organization. His consistent action and his energetic and eloquent arguments have greatly tended to keep that body in existence. Mr. Heald was born at Chester, Vermont, on the 4th of May, 1818. He lived on a farm in that vicinity until he was sixteen years old.

But he had aspirations beyond mere farm life, and cultivating his mind and talents, with such meagre opportunities as were within his reach, he fitted himself for college, and entering Yale, he pursued the regular course of study, and was graduated, with honor, from that venerable seat of learning in the year 1841, at the age of twenty-three. Thereafter he read law in the office of Judge Daggett, of New Haven, and subsequently, in May, 1843, was admitted to the bar in Vermont, where he practiced successfully until 1856. In connection with his law practice in Vermont he served as agent for the Ætna and other Hartford insurance companies for thirteen years, and in 1856 he accepted the position of General Agent of the Home Insurance Company, of New York, and removed to that city. In April, 1868, after twelve years of service, equally useful to his company and to insurance interests generally, he was elected Second Vice-President of the Home Insurance Company, and in January,

1883, was made Vice-President of the company—the position he now occupies.

Meanwhile Mr. Heald has filled an important position at all times in both the New York Board of Fire Underwriters and the National Board of Fire Underwriters. Of both these organizations he has been a prominent member during the past twenty-five years or more. Of the National Board he was not only a constituent member, but one of the organizing factors. He had more to do, possibly, than any other single individual in making it evident to insurance men in 1866 that something must be done to save the companies from ruin, and thereby conserve the true interests of property owners, by a common union. The creation of the National Board of Fire Underwriters was the result; and Mr. Heald's active endeavors and his impressive presentation of facts and figures were largely instrumental in bringing about this result. This was as long ago as July, 1866. And, ever since, Mr. Heald has stood squarely by the doctrines he then laid down. From that time until now he has continuously labored for the building up of fire insurance interests, and has represented in his own person and as an insurance officer, as well as President of the National Board, whatever was sound and safe and of good report in fire underwriting.

His addresses as President of the National Board and before other insurance conventions, have become standard authorities in fire insurance circles, and have been so quoted all over the world. The address delivered at Chicago several years ago on "Fire Underwriting as a Profession," has never been equalled. And his speech at the twentieth anniversary of the organization of

MARTIN L. CROWELL.

the National Board of Fire Underwriters, in July, 1886, at New York, is confessed to be one of the best presentations of fire insurance history and suggestions in all the records of fire insurance.

As an insurance expert he is *facile princeps* the leading mind of the profession. Among underwriters he is known as "Judge Heald," so clear-headed and judicial are his opinions held to be upon subjects connected with fire insurance in all its ramifications. Had he not chosen the profession of fire underwriting, he would have made an equally prominent mark as a lawyer or a judge.

MARTIN L. CROWELL was well known among insurance men, more especially for his labors in connection with fire protection. He was appointed on the Patrol Committee to fill a vacancy in the Fall of 1867, and in the Spring of 1868 was elected Chairman of the Committee, retaining that position by subsequent annual elections until the Spring of 1882, when he was elected Treasurer of the New York Board of Fire Underwriters, and by virtue thereof an *ex-officio* member of the Committee. The honored trust of Treasurership was held by him until his removal by death on April 1, 1884.

GEORGE T. PATTERSON, JR.

Mr. Crowell held the position of chief executive officer of the Fire Patrol for fifteen consecutive years. This is an eventful length of time devoted to active service in a common interest without compensation, especially as this burden of responsibility was increased at times by murmurings of complaint from associates in the business, when well-ordered plans of protection failed to accomplish the good intended. The Fire Patrol Committee said of him: "Mr. Crowell was a man endowed by nature with a character to win the respect of the brotherhood of man, quiet, unobtrusive, honest, faithful, firm in his convictions of right and wrong, with great respect for the opinion of others; honest to a fault, and faithful in the discharge of every duty."

GEO. T. PATTERSON, JR., was born in New York City September 15, 1850, Entered the office of the Pacific Insurance Company in March, 1865. In June, 1869, he transferred his business talents to the North British and Mercantile Insurance Company. In June, 1874, he was elected Secretary of the Clinton Fire Insurance Company, and was elected President of the Clinton in February, 1881, when he was thirty-one years of age, the youngest man that was ever chosen to fill such a position. Mr. Patterson is alert on fire department matters, is a stirring member of the New York Board of Fire Underwriters and Chairman of the Fire Patrol Committee.

NICHOLAS C. MILLER was connected with the Star Fire Insurance Company in 1864; was made the Secretary of the company, and held the position until 1868, when he was

NICHOLAS C. MILLER.

chosen as its President; remained at the head of affairs until 1886, when the company decided to relinquish business. He is now engaged in settling up the affairs of the company. Mr. Miller has been a member of the New York Board of Fire Underwriters for twenty-three years; was chairman of the Committee of Surveys during 1880-1882; chairman of the Executive Committee of the Board for two years; was the vice-president, and has been the president of the Board during the past year.

WILLIAM P. HENSHAW was born in Brooklyn, N. Y. His first appearance in fire insurance methods was in 1853, as a clerk with the Long Island Insurance Company, in 1857; the company recognizing his valuable services, promoted him to the responsible position of secretary, which office he held until 1879, when he became connected with the Royal Insurance Company, of Liverpool, as one of its managers, and is still actively engaged in furthering the interests of this extensive corporation. Mr. Henshaw is closely identified with the New York Board of Fire Underwriters, and has been the secretary of the Board for twenty consecutive years.

WILLIAM M. RANDELL. — In a handsomely furnished office adjoining the meeting room of the New York Board of Fire Underwriters, no one is more readily or frequently found than a genial, quick-witted, well-informed gentleman. The gentleman is Mr. William M. Randell, and he is best known as the secretary of the Committee on Fire Patrol of the New York Board of Fire Underwriters. His history and that of his ancestors is interesting.

The Randell family on the paternal side traces its origin back to Adolph Myer, who settled in Harlem in 1661, and was one of the original patentees under the Dongan Patent in 1667. The grandfather of the subject of this

WILLIAM P. HENSHAW.

sketch married in the Myer family in 1770, and at the close of the Revolutionary War purchased the island since known as Randell's Island, where he lived for a period of fifty years. His son David, the father of William M. Randell, was a lawyer by profession and a veteran of the war of 1812. In 1836 and 1837 he was an alderman of the city, at a time when such city officials possessed judicial powers and were associate judges in trials for criminal offenses. Several years after he was appointed by Governor William H. Seward a judge of the Marine Court. Judges in those days were appointed, not elected.

The Randell family have been more or less identified with fire history for many years. An uncle, three cousins and two brothers served their time as members of the Volunteer Fire Department. William M. Randell joined the Department in 1847; he was then under age. The formula of swearing to the application for appointment was not then required. His first company, Hose 10, was located on Dover near Pearl Street, and performed duty in the lower portion of the city, in what was then known as the seventh and eighth fire disricts. The company was under the command of George A. Buckingham, who was an importer and jobber of woolens. After a service of five years, one as private, three as secretary, and one as assistant foreman, he resigned and joined some acquaintances in the formation of Hose Company No. 53, which secured a location in Church near Franklin Street. This was also a down-town company. He remained here as an active and honorary member until the company threw up the organization, owing to its inability to increase or retain the roll of membership to the proper standard.

The organization of Hose Company 53 was the beginning of a new order of things in Fire Department circles. The house was expensively furnished— paintings, pianoforte, library, and in fact, all the luxuries and comforts of a home, with kitchen and dining-room, where they received their friends and associates, and many were the entertainments given. This outlay was at the expense of the individual members, and the example thus set was followed by other companies, and a moral influence was thrown around the life of a fireman who before this had experienced but hard work by day and by night in the discharge of his duty. Mr. Randell subsequently became a member of the Exempt Engine Company.

WILLIAM M. RANDELL.

In 1855 he was appointed chief clerk of the Board of Fire Commissioners, a commission which had been created by the Legislature for the purpose of correcting many evils and abuses which had crept into the Fire Department. The power of appointing and dismissing, the investigation of complaints against companies and individuals, the formation and disbandment of companies, were among the duties assigned the commissioners by the law. The office was not a sinecure; many evils existed, and the time of the Board, and consequently that of the clerk, was occupied night after night in carrying out the law. Several years were devoted to this service, when he resigned, owing to other business engagements.

A few years later Mr. Randell was elected a member of the Firemen's Ball Committee, an organization of many years' standing, whose object was to aid in increasing the Benevolent Fund of the Department. What that committee has done in the cause of charity is best shown in the statement that during a part of its existence, say from 1848 to 1873, it placed in the coffers of the fund the sum of one hundred thousand dollars. One of the most interesting events connected with that committee was on the occasion of their fiftieth anniversary, when a concert, vocal and instrumental, was gotten up and held at Madison Square Garden for the benefit of the yellow fever sufferers at New Orleans, from which was realized the sum of five thousand four hundred dollars. The committee still retains its organization, and Mr. Randell his membership. In 1864 he was one of the committee chosen to represent the Fire Department at the Metropolitan Fair given in aid of the United States Sanitary Commission. The amount realized from the Fire Department donations and sales exceeded the sum of thirty thousand dollars. In 1870 he became a member of the Exempt Fireman's Association, and is now a life member of the organization. In 1880 he was elected a trustee of the Benevolent Fund of the Department, from which he resigned after some two years of service.

Mr. Randell's business as a fire underwriter and an officer of the Fire Patrol has given him much experience and knowledge respecting fire matters. Entering the insurance business in 1852, as senior clerk in the Lorillard Fire Insurance Company, which had just been organized under the management of two prominent ex-fire officials, Cornelius V. Anderson and Carlisle Norwood, he remained until appointed, in 1857, secretary of the Resolute Fire Insurance Company, and was its secretary twenty-one years, or until it retired from business. In 1865 he was elected one of the Committee on Fire Patrol of the Board of Fire Underwriters, and at the same time appointed its secretary, which latter position he still retains, attending to its increasing labors and responsibilities with the same earnestness that he gave to it in years gone by. The annual reports of the Fire Patrol, which have been compiled by him since 1866, will show the great changes and improvements in the fire service, especially in the Fire Patrol. Not only has Mr. Randell been identified with legislative, administrative

ELDRIDGE G. SNOW, JR.

and benevolent objects in fire matters, but he was up to quite a recent period an attendant at all fires of magnitude which occurred in this city.

Many interesting books and papers relative to fires and individuals can be found in Mr. Randell's library, and he is in himself a walking directory of facts and figures, and is often appealed to for information, and is quoted as authority on matters connected with fires and losses. He is also secretary of the Committee on Arbitration, Finance, Laws and Legislation, Police, and Origin of Fires, and Patents and Useful Devices of the New York Board of Fire Underwriters.

ELDRIDGE G. SNOW, JR., was born in Waterbury, Conn., in January, 1841. His early education fitted him to follow the profession of his father, who was a physician. But the young man, not finding it congenial, entered the office of the Home Insurance Company, of New York, in 1863, and in 1873 was appointed by the company State agent for Massachusetts, and in consequence took up his residence in Boston. There he remained until July, 1885, when he was called to the office of the company in New York, having been elected

JOHN H. WASHBURN.

assistant secretary, and in this capacity is now more immediately connected with the extended agency department of the company. Mr. Snow was also an honorary member of the Veteran Firemen's Association of New York.

JOHN H. WASHBURN, vice-president and secretary of the Home Insurance Company, of New York, the largest company in the State of New York, was born in Massachusetts in 1828, and graduated from Amherst College. He entered the office of the Home Insurance Company in 1859, was appointed assistant secretary in 1865, and elected secretary in 1867. In 1884 he was elected vice-president. His rapid promotion speaks loudly for his business qualifications and general ability. Mr. Washburn is also a member of the Tariff Association of the New York Board of Fire Underwriters, and is anhonorary member of the Veteran Firemen's Association of this city.

THE FIRE PATROL may be said to have originated at the fire at Smith's tea warehouse in Water street, between Dover and Roosevelt Streets, in 1839. In February, 1853, the first superintendent was appointed, namely, S. J. Willis. His salary was one hundred and twenty-five dollars per annum. Alfred Carson was the first superintendent of salvage under the charter of 1867. He was succeeded, in November, 1867, by John Cornwell. In May, 1883, the rules and regulations governing the Patrol were revised and promulgated in general orders. The Patrols were designated 1, 2, 3 and 4, instead of Lower, Central, Upper and Eastside, and captains were dubbed lieutenants.

The Patrol Committee for 1884–85 were: James A. Silvey, chairman; R. D. Alliger, vice-chairman; C. M. Peck,

ABRAM C. HULL.

S. P. Blagden, G. M. Colt, W. A. Burtis and W. M. St. John. Mr. W. A. Burtis died in January, 1885, and he was succeeded by Mr. George T. Patterson, Jr. The present superintendent is Abram C. Hull.

ABRAM C. HULL, the Superintendent of the Fire Patrol of New York City, was born in the Seventh Ward of this city in the year 1835. His father, John G. Hull, was many years in the hardware business on the east side of the city and sent the lad to the old Henry and Fifth Street Grammar Schools. He began work at the ship carpenter business, and built one or two famous yachts. His love of adventure took him to the Pacific coast in the employ of the Peruvian Steamship Company, and upon his return he remained a short time at home, then went to New Orleans for the Star Navigation Company, and upon returning home again, began running to fires, and at the age of twenty-one joined Mechanics' Hose Company No. 47, and twelve months later became a member of Marion Hook and Ladder Company No. 13. He was soon elected assistant foreman and foreman of his company, and continued as such until the organization of the Paid Department. He was appointed foreman of Hook and Ladder Company No. 6, September 27, 1865—one of the most popular truck companies in the Department under his administration. Many times he was detailed by Chief Kingsland as acting district engineer. He remained with Hook and Ladder Company No. 6 until July, 1870, when he was appointed by the Fire Underwriters as captain of No. 1 Fire Insurance Patrol; remained until March, 1886, when he was promoted to his present position of superintendent. He has now performed nearly thirty

CAPTAINS OF FIRE PATROL.

years' continuous fire service in this city. Superintendent Hull has an aversion for idle words; a conviction that a man never arrives at an age when he has no need of adding to his knowledge; fine sympathy for subordinates, coupled with the strictest discipline, and a perfect knowledge of matters pertaining to his office.

F. S. Groves, John Kimmens, John Rafferty and J. M. Sandford, captains.

The following resolution marked the adoption of a life-saving medal by the committee:

The New York Board of Fire Underwriters enter upon their record, their approbation of the self-sacrificing services of Insurance Patrolman Thomas McCann, of the Lower Patrol, who, at the risk of his own life, rescued five children from the third floor of a burning tenement building, No. 103 Washington Street, on the afternoon of July 21, 1882, and in consideration of which this Board authorizes the Fire Patrol Committee to have prepared a gold medal of honor, the same to be presented to Patrolman McCann, as a token of the appreciation of this Board for his heroic services in the cause of humanity.

The committee are constantly in receipt of communications praising the members of the Patrol for good and gallant services.

FIRST WAGON FOR CARRYING COVERS.

CHAPTER LV.

THE HAND AND STEAM FIRE ENGINES.

Their Origin, Growth and Development.—Fire Apparatus in Use Before the Christian Era.—The Force Pump.
—The Invention of Fire Engines.—Application of the Air Chamber.—Introduction of Leather Hose.—
Newsham's and Simpkins's Inventions.—Ericsson's Portable Steam Engine, Etc., Etc.

THE invention of the fire-engine is of great antiquity and involved somewhat in obscurity. In chronicles relating to the destruction of cities by
fire about the commencement of the Christian Era, and particularly concerning the burning of the town of Nicomedia in Bythania, the lack of machines or apparatus proper for extinguishing the flames was mentioned. The
word *sipho,* used in said chronicles, being translated and so understood generally as meaning fire engines. Hesychius and Isidorus, who lived in the beginning of the seventh century, prove that in the fourth century at least a
fire engine, properly so-called, was understood under the term *sipho.* The
question still remains at what time this apparatus for extinguishing fires was
introduced at Rome. From the numerous ordinances for preventing accidents
by fire, and in regard to extinguishing fire, which occur in the Roman laws,
there is reason to conjecture that that capital was not unprovided with those
useful implements and machines, of the want of which in a provincial town
the historian Pliny complained. In the East engines were employed not only
to extinguish but to produce fires. The Greek fire, invented by Callinicus,
an architect of Heliopolis, a city afterward named Balbec, in the year 678, the
use of which was continued in the East until 1291, and which was certainly
liquid, was employed in many different ways ; but chiefly on board ship, being
thrown from large fire engines on the ships of the enemy. Sometimes this
fire was kindled in particular vessels, which might be called fire-ships, and
which were introduced among a hostile fleet; sometimes it was put into jars
and other vessels which were thrown at the enemy by means of projectile machines, and sometimes it was squirted by the soldiers from hand engines ; or,
as appears, blown through pipes. But the machines with which this fire was
discharged from the fore-part of ships could not have been either hand
engines or such blow pipes. They were constructed of copper and iron, and
the extremity of them sometimes resembled the open jaws and mouth of a lion
or other animal. They were painted and even gilded, and it appears that
they were capable of projecting the fire to a great distance. These machines
by ancient writers were expressly called spouting-engines. John Cameniata,
speaking of the siege of his native city, Thessalonica, which was taken by the
Saracens in the year 904, says that the enemy threw fire into the wooden works
of the beseiged, which was blown into them by means of tubes and thrown from
other vessels. That statement proves that the Greeks in the beginning of the

tenth century were no longer the only people acquainted with the art of preparing that fire, the precursor of gunpowder. The emperor Leo (tenth century), in his treatise on the art of war, recommended such engines with a metal covering to be constructed in the fore-part of ships. There is no doubt the use of a force pump for extinguishing fires was long known before the invention of Greek fire. It is uncertain at what time the towns in Germany were first furnished with fire-engines. It is believed that they had regulations in regard to fires much earlier than engines, and the former are not older than the first half of the sixteenth century. The oldest respecting the city of Frankfort-on-the-Main is of the year 1460. The first general ordinance respecting fires in Saxony was issued by Duke George in 1521. The first for the city of Dresden, which extended also to the whole country, was dated 1529. At Augsburg an express regulation in regard to building was drawn up and made publicly known as early as 1447. In turning over old chronicles we find it remarked

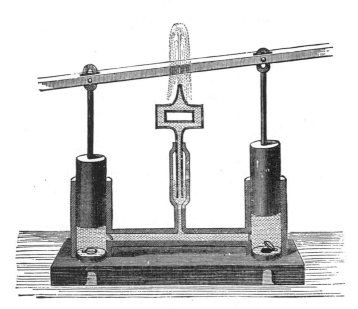

EGYPTIAN FIRE ENGINE, 200 B. C.

that great fires began to occur less frequently in the sixteenth century; and this was undoubtedly to be ascribed to the improved mode of building, the precautions enjoined to prevent fires and the introduction of apparatus for extinguishing them. Thus, in the year 1466, straw, thatch, and in 1474, the use of shingles were forbidden at Frankfort.

But by the invention of fire-engines everything in those respects became so much changed that a complete revision of the regulations in regard to the extinguishing of fires was rendered necessary, and therefore the first mention of town fire-engines is to be found in the new fire ordinances of the sixteenth and following century. In the building accounts of the city of Augsburg fire-engines are first mentioned in the year 1518. They are called in those accounts "instrument for fires," "water syringes," useful at fires—which would imply that the machine was then in its infancy. At that time they were made by a goldsmith at Friedberg, named Anthony Blatner, who the same year became a citizen of Augsburg. From the account given as to the construction of the wheels and levers, and the greatness of the expense, there is reason to conclude that these were not small, simple, hand-engines, but large and complex machines.

In the year 1657 the well-known Jesuit father, Casper Schott, was struck with admiration on seeing at Nuremburg a fire-engine which had been made there by John Hautsch. It stood on a sledge, ten feet long and four feet broad. The water cistern was eight feet in length, four feet in height, and two in width. It was moved by twenty-eight men, and forced a stream of water an inch in diameter to the height of eighty feet. The machine was drawn by two horses. Hautsch refused to show the internal construction of it to Schott, who, however, readily conjectured it; and from what Schott has handed down it is easily perceived that the cylinders did not stand in a per-

SYRINGE OF SIXTEENTH CENTURY.

pendicular direction, but lay horizontally in a box, so that the pistons moved horizontally and not vertically. Upright cylinders, therefore, belong to the more modern improvements. Schott added that it was not a new invention, as there were such engines in other towns, and he himself forty years before, and consequently in 1617, had seen one, but much smaller, in his native city. Schott was born in 1608 at Königshofen, not far from Würzburg.

The first regulations at Paris respecting fires, as far as is known, were made to restrain incendiaries, who in the fourteenth century, under the name of *Boutefoux*, occasioned great devastation not only in the capital but in the provinces. That city appears to have obtained fire-engines for the first time in the year 1699; at any rate, the king at that period gave an exclusive right to Dumourier Duperrier to construct those machines called *pompes portatives;*

PRIMITIVE FIRE ENGINE. THE FIRST MAN-
UFACTURED IN THE UNITED STATES.

and he was engaged at a certain salary to keep in repair seventeen of them purchased for Paris, and to procure and pay the necessary workmen. In the year 1722 the number of these engines was increased to thirty, which were distributed in different quarters of the city. The city, however, besides these thirty royal engines, had a great many others which belonged to the Hotel de Ville, and with which Duperrier had nothing to do.

In the middle of the seventeenth century fire-engines were very imperfect. They had neither an air-chamber nor buckets, and required a great many men to work them. They consisted merely of a sucking-pump and forcing-pump united, which projected the water only in spurts and with continual interruption.

Such machines on each movement of the lever experienced a stoppage, during which no water was thrown out; and because the pipe was fixed it could not convey water to remote places, though it might reach a fire at no great distance where there were convenient doors and windows to afford it a passage. At the same time the workmen were exposed to danger from the falling of the houses on fire. Hautsch adapted to his engine a flexible pipe which could be turned to any side; but certainly not an air-chamber, as Schott would have mentioned it. In the time of Belidor there were no other engines in France, and the same kind alone were used in England in 1760. At least that conclusion is induced by the account given by Ferguson, who called Newsham's engine, which threw the water out in a continual stream, a new invention. In Germany the oldest engines were of that kind.

Who first conceived the idea of applying to the fire-engine an air cham-

HIBERNIA FIRE ENGINE. (PHILADELPHIA, 1752).

ber, in which the included air, by compressing the water, forces it out in a continued stream, is not known.

According to a conjecture of Perrault, Vitruvius seems to speak of a similar construction. But the obscure passage in question might be explained in another way. There can be found no older fire-engine constructed with an air-chamber than that of which Perrault has given a figure and description. He says it was kept in the king's library at Paris, and during fires could project water to a great height; that it had only one cylinder and yet threw out the water in one continued jet. He mentions neither its age nor the inventor; and it can only be added that Perrault's book was printed in 1684. The principle of this machine, however, seems to have been mentioned before by Mariotte, who on this account is by some considered as the inventor.

It is certain that the air-chamber, at least in Germany, came into common use after it was applied by Leupold to fire-engines, a great number of which he manufactured and sold. He gave an account of it in a small work which was published in 1720; but at first he kept the construction a secret. The engines which he sold consisted of a strong copper box closely shut and well soldered. They weighed no more than 16 pounds, occupied little room, had only one cylinder, and a man with one of them could force up the water without interruption to the height of from twenty to thirty feet. About 1725, Du Fay saw one of Leupold's engines at Strasburg, and discovered by conjecture the construction of it, which he made known in the Transactions of the Academy of Sciences at Paris for that year. It is singular that on this occasion Du Fay says nothing of Mariotte or of the engine in the king's library.

Another improvement, no less useful, is the leather hose added to the engine and to which the fire pipe is applied, so that the person who directs the jet of water can approach the fire with less danger. This invention belongs to two Dutchmen named Jan and Nicholas van der Heide, who were inspectors

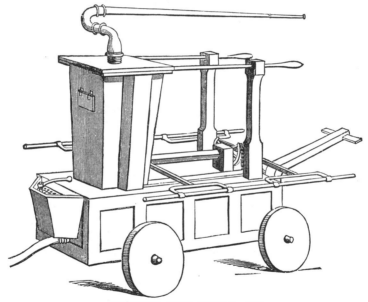

AMERICAN FIRE ENGINE, 1789.

of the apparatus for extinguishing fires at Amsterdam. The first public experiments made with it took place in 1672, and were attended with so much success that at a fire next year the old fire engines were used for the last time, and the new ones introduced in their stead. In 1677 the inventor obtained an exclusive privilege to make these engines during a period of twenty-five years. In 1682 engines on this construction were distributed in sufficient numbers throughout the whole city, and the old ones were entirely laid aside. In 1695 there were in Amsterdam sixty of these engines, the nearest six of which were to be employed at every fire. In the course of a few years they were common throughout all the towns in the Netherlands.

The employment of flexible hose strong enough to bear a good pressure of water has in no small degree increased the facility and effect with which fires can be controlled by means of water forced through it. The invention of the

Van der Heides, after its introduction into Holland, became common in other parts of the continent, but it did not find its way into England until nearly a hundred years later. The great difficulty with the leather hose was to make it water tight. The seams were sewn like the leg of a boot, and the pressure caused them to open and leak badly, so that much of the water was lost where the hose was carried too far. Notwithstanding this defect, leather was found to be the best material for the purpose on account of its strength and durability, substitutes, such as canvas and seamless woven hose, invariably giving way after short usage. Some sorts of hose were made of canvas covered with a cement or paint to make them water tight; another sort was the seamless hose woven in a tubular form by machines such as has been introduced at a very recent period as a new invention; but leather still continued to be used with such satisfactory results as to prove the truth of the old proverb, that "there is nothing like leather." Until the year 1808 the defective character of the hose seriously impaired its usefulness at fires. In that year Messrs. Sellers & Pennock, of Philadelphia, furnished a most valuable contribution to the means in use for extinguishing fire, by the invention of riveted hose. The substitution of copper rivets for fastening seams removed the last obstacle to its employment, and leather hose has since played a conspicuous part among the instruments for extinguishing fires in America.

Riveted hose, by greatly increasing the effectiveness of engines at a distance from the fire, produced a radical change in the extinguishment of conflagrations. Formerly suction hose was made of short metallic cylinders, placed end in end and covered with canvas or leather. They were easily crushed, however, because they were not sufficiently elastic. Afterward stout spiral wire was substituted and found to answer the purpose. The objections urged against leather hose were the liability to defects—the leather, its tendency to crack, and the constant care necessary to keep it flexible, by the application of grease or oil. Some other materials were invented, among them, besides canvas and linen, india rubber. The india rubber, whether used alone or as a lining for canvas or linen, was held to be superior. This material was first brought out in England in 1827. So well did it stand the severe tests to which it was subjected, that it was soon adopted by the most of the insurance companies. One test was the plugging up the nozzle of a length of india rubber and a length of leather hose attached to a powerful engine well worked. The leather hose blew out or burst in the solid part of the leather, and the india rubber was uninjured and broke down the engine. Many makers preferred this hose when trying engines for range and height, because of the smoothness and evenness of its interior. Moreover, after use and before being rolled up, it was only necessary to dry it. At fires it was found necessary to keep hose of this kind away from the heated ruins, and it was recommended that care should be taken in laying out to avoid those parts where damage might arise to it from this cause.

In 1720 hose woven without a seam was made of hemp at Leipsic by Beck, a lace weaver. After this it was made by Erke, a linen weaver of Weimar, and at a later period it was made of linen at Dresden and also in Silesia. In England, Hegner & Ehrliholzer had a manufactory at Bethnal Green, near London, where they made water-tight hose without seams.

All the circumstances relating to the Vander Heide invention have been related by the inventor in a particular work which, on account of the excellent engravings it contains, is exceedingly valuable. Of these the first seven represent dangerous conflagrations at which the old engines were used but produced very little effect. One of them is the fire which took place at the Stadt-house of Amsterdam in the year 1652. The twelve following plates represent fires which were extinguished by means of the new engines, and exhibit at the same time the various ways in which the engines may be employed with advantage. According to an announced calculation the city of Amsterdam lost by ten fires, when the old apparatus was in use, 1,024,130 florins; but in the following five years after the introduction of the new engines, the loss occasioned by forty fires amounted only to 18,355 florins; so that the yearly saving was ninety-eight per cent. Of the internal construction of these engines no description or plates have been given; nor is there anything to show that they were furnished with an air-chamber, though in the patents they were always called "spouting engines," which threw up one continued jet of water. The account given even of the nature of the pipe or hose is short and defective, probably

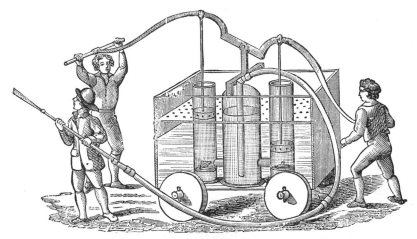

LONDON FIRE ENGINE, 1765.

with a view to render it more difficult to be imitated. It is only said that it was made of leather in a particular manner; and that besides being thick it was capable of resisting the force of the water.

The conveyer or bringer was invented also about the same time by these two Dutchmen. This name was also given at a later period to a box which had on one side a sucking-pump and on the other a forcing pump. The former served to raise the water from a stream, well, or other reservoir, by means of a stiff leathern pipe screwed to the engine, the end of which widened into a bag, supported near the reservoir, and kept open by means of a frame, while the laborers poured water into it from buckets. A pump, however, to answer this purpose was soon constructed by the Van der Heides, who named it a snake pump. By its means they were able to convey the water from the distance of 1,000 feet, but there is no account of the manner in which it was made. From the figure it is conjectured that they used only one cylinder with a lever. Sometimes also they placed a portable pump in the water, which was thus drawn into a leathern hose connected with it and conveyed to the engine. Every pipe or hose for conveying water in this manner they called a *wasserschlange*, water-snake, and this was not made of leather, like the hose furnished with a force pipe, but of sail cloth. They announced, however, that it required a particular preparation, which consisted in making it water tight by means of a proper cement. The pipe, also, through which the water was drawn up, was stiffened and distended by means of metal rings; otherwise the external air on the first stroke of the pump would compress the pipe so that it could admit no water. Thus it is seen that pipes made of sail-cloth are not so new an invention as many have supposed.

From these facts one may readily believe that engines with leathern hose were certainly not invented by Gottfried Fuchs, director of the fire apparatus at Copenhagen in 1697, as was publicly announced in 1717, with the addition that this invention was soon employed both in Holland and at Hamburg. Fuchs seems only to have made known the Dutch invention in Denmark, on the occasion of the great fire which took place on the 19th of April, 1689, at the Opera House at Amalienburg, when the beautiful palace of that name and more than three hundred and fifty persons were consumed. At any rate, in consequence of that calamity an improvement was made in the fire establishment by new regulations issued on July 23, 1689, and that engines on the Dutch construction which had been used more than twelve years at Amsterdam were introduced.

Hose or pipes of this kind for conveying water were, however, not entirely unknown to the ancients. At least the architect Apollodorus says that to convey water to high places, exposed to fiery darts, the gut of an ox having a bag filled with water attached to it might be employed, for on compressing the bag the water would be forced up through the gut to the place of its destination. This was surely a conveyor of the simplest kind.

Newsham's fire-engine was a side-brake, double-cylinder engine, mounted on four wheels, and with an air-chamber, goose-neck and suction pipe. The work on the brakes was assisted by men on the box who threw their weight upon treadles on the pump-levers. Pumps were single-action force-pumps, worked by chains passing over segments on the pump-levers. The engine was perhaps the first successful fire-engine.

The engine which eventually superseded Newsham's was invented by Simpkin, and patented in 1792. The main improvement was in compactness and adaptation to traveling with speed to the spot where its services were needed. The valves were contained in separate chambers, instead of being placed in the cylinders and air-chamber. By this means they were easily reached without the disconnection of the main portions of the pump.

Another form of fire-engine was invented by Bramah in 1793, improved by Rowntree, and eventually by Barton, whose engine was on the vibrating principle.

Steam-power for extinguishing fires was in use in manufacturing establishments many years before it was employed on portable machines. Every factory of any pretensions had its steam-driven pump with hose and other attachments calculated to reach every portion of the establishment.

The manufacture of steam fire-engines in England, as a regular branch of industry, is of recent origin. The first steam fire-engine was constructed in 1829 in London by Messrs. Braithwaite & Ericsson. Later on four more were

made, and all were eminently successful. So strong, however, was the preju_
dice against them that from 1832 to 1852 no more were made in that country,
and public attention seemed to wane. After a lapse of twenty years, and
about twelve years after steam fire-engines had been in use in the United
States, the London Fire Engine Establishment altered one of the hand-worked
floating engines on the Thames into a steam fire-engine. Until 1860 no further
progress was made in the way of encouraging their manufacture. The strongest opponent of the fire-engine in England was Mr. James Braidwood, Superintendent of the London Fire Engine Establishment. In time, however, he
changed his opinion. The great objection, strange to say, urged against the
new engines from 1829 to 1856 was that they threw too much water. The
application of steam-power to work a force pump, arranging the engine,
boiler, pumps, etc., on wheels, so as to be easily portable, and thus enable it

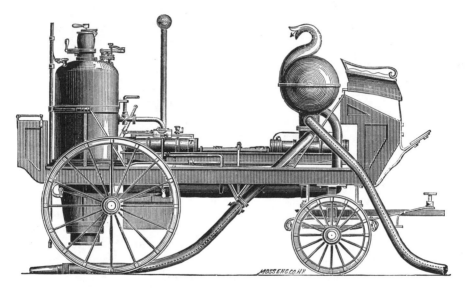

FIRST STEAM FIRE ENGINE EVER BUILT (LONDON, 1829).

to be readily employed as a fire-engine, was due to Mr. John Braithwaite,
civil engineer. In conjunction with Captain Ericsson he constructed an engine
of ten horse power, with two horizontal cylinders and pumps, each steam piston and that of the pump being both attached to one rod. The waste steam
from the cylinders was conveyed through the tank containing the feed water
by means of two coiled pipes, thus giving the feed water a good temperature
previous to its being pumped into the boiler. Its weight complete was 45 cwts.,
and it threw from 30 to 40 tons of water per hour to a height of 90 feet, having
thrown well over a pole that height. In five hours it consumed three bushels
of coke. This engine gratuitously rendered signal service at many important
fires, saved thousands of pounds' worth of property, and in return the insurance companies presented Mr. Braithwaithe's men with £1 ($5)! The London
Fire Brigade antagonized him in every way. In 1831 Mr. Braithwaite constructed his second steam fire-engine, of five horse power. It had a steam

cylinder 7 in. by 18 in., with a pump of 6½ in. by 18 in., giving a proportion of steam cylinder to pump of 1.16 to 1. When working with a steam pressure of 50 lbs. on the inch, and making 40 strokes per minute, it threw 27 cubic feet of water per minute = 15 cwts., through a one-inch nozzle, to a height of 109 feet, and gave 5.6 horse power. When working with 60 lbs. steam pressure, and making 35 strokes per minute, it threw 23.6 cubic feet of water per minute = 13 cwts. 19 lbs., through a ⅞-inch nozzle, to a height of 108 feet. This engine was worked in France at several towns, with great success, and afterward taken to Russia with similar results.

The third engine built by Mr. Braithwaite had two cylinders, but three pumps, placed horizontally and driven by gearing from the crank shape of the engine, so as to reduce the speed of the pump pistons. The fourth steam fire-engine was the "Comet," of 15 horse power, built in 1832 for the King of

CAPT. ERICSSON.

Prussia. Its boiler was similar to the others, and it had two horizontal cylinders, each 12 in. diameter by 14 in. stroke, making 18 strokes per minute, and the two pumps were each 10½ in. diameter by 14 in. stroke. The engine was arranged to work with four sets of hose, together or separately. The total weight was four tons. In from 13 to 20 minutes from lighting the fire the engine was started with 70 lbs. of steam, and with a single nozzle of 1¼ in. diameter the water was thrown from 115 to 120 feet vertically, the engine making 18 strokes per minute, and at this rate the weight of water thrown amounted to 1 ton, 7 cwts. and 13 lbs. per minute. At an angle of 45 to 50 degrees the water was thrown to a distance horizontally of 164 feet. The engine was equal to at least 90 tons of water per hour at the average working rate. The consumption of fuel was about three bushels of coke per hour. The fifth engine was an experimental one, built in 1833.

In 1835 Mr. Braithwaite designed a floating steam fire-engine capable of throwing 187.5 cubic feet of water per minute. In 1850 Mr. P. Clark, the assistant engineer of the West India Docks, arranged one of Downton's pumps in one of their tugs, so that it could be driven by gearing from the engine and the steam engine used in propelling the vessel. This was the first steam-floating fire-engine on the Thames, and it threw 600 gallons of water per minute, 20 feet higher than the highest warehouse in the docks, and with a nozzle of 1½ inch diameter, threw to a distance of from 160 to 180 feet. Until the year 1852 the two most powerful engines of the London Fire Engine Establishment were the two floating engines worked by hand, one stationed at Southwark Bridge and the other, or lower float, at Rotherlithe. Two years later a boat was built and fitted up expressly in a floating steam fire-engine. It was 130 feet long, built of iron, and cost $15,000. The engines were 80 horse-power. It was said that this engine had thrown 2,000 gallons of water per minute through four separate nozzles at the same time to a distance of 180 feet.

Messrs. G. Rennie & Son in 1836 constructed a portable disc engine and disc pump mounted on wheels for use in the Woolwich Dockyard, either as a steam fire-engine or as a pump for emptying the caissons. The engine had a cylinder 13 inches in diameter and the pump was 9 inches in diameter. It is said that when making 320 revolutions a minute, with 45 lbs. of steam, lifting the water 10 feet and with a pressure of 62 lbs. in the discharge pipe, the water was thrown through a three-inch diameter hose and a nozzle of 13-16 inch diameter to a total height of from 140 to 150 feet.

Messrs. Shand and Mason, the most famous builders in England, constructed their first land steam fire-engine in 1856, and the machine was sent to Russia. The steam cylinder which actuated the pump was inverted and situated near the air vessel of the pump, which was made double-acting, one barrel being placed over the other, and a double-throw crank was placed between them. One or both of the pistons or plungers of the pump was fitted with a valve, and the piston-rod of the steam cylinder was connected directly with the p ston of the upper pump barrel, which latter served as a guide to the piston-rod of the steam cylinder. Beneath the seat was placed the hose-reel or a box for containing the hose and implements. In 1859 one of Messrs. Shand and Mason's steamers, with an 8½ inch cylinder and 6 inch stroke, was tried at Waterloo Bridge, and in six minutes from lighting, the fire was stated to have had 10 lbs. on the square inch, and in 10½ minutes 30 lbs. with a ¾ inch nozzle; the height reached was estimated to be 140 feet, and the horizontal distance 161 feet.

Mr. James Shekleton, a Dundalk engineer, constructed in 1860 the first steam fire-engine in Ireland. It weighed 22 cwts., and had a vertical tubular boiler with internal circulating tubes, on the plan of Silsby, Myndorse & Company, of the United States, dry smoke box and an effective heating surface of 40 square feet, the water space around the fire-box being fitted with a circulating plate. The working pressure was 80 lbs. on the square inch, with the engine making 120 strokes per minute.

In July, 1860, a land steam fire-engine was for the first time used by the London Fire Engine Establishment in one of the back streets of Doctor's Commons. The weight of the machine with men, ovals and water, ready to rnn out, was 84 cwts., and it took three horses to draw it. In the same year a steam floating fire-engine was constructed by the Messrs. Merryweather from the designs of Mr. E. Field, civil engineer, to be placed in a steam tug and used for protecting the warehouses in the Tyne Docks. The water supply, however, was inadequate to the needs of the engine. In 1861 Messrs. Merryweather & Sons constructed, also from the designs of Mr. Field, their first land steam fire engine, the "Deluge," which was quite a success. It was of 30 horse-power, and threw water through a nozzle 1½ inches in diameter 10 feet over a chimney 140 feet in height, altogether 180 feet, through a 1⅜ inch nozzle to a distance of 202 feet horizontally, and through a 1¼ inch nozzle 215 feet horizontally.

In 1861 Messrs. Shand & Mason manufactured three steam fire engines on wheels to run on the rails for the London and Northwestern Railway. They had double horizontal cylinders and pumps, and slotted cross heads and fly-wheels. One of them with a nozzle of one and one-quarter inch diameter threw a stream vertically to a height of 170 feet, and horizontally 225 feet. In the next year the firm constructed a steam fire engine for the town of Sothenbury. In 1861 Messrs. Merryweather & Sons constructed a famous steamer called the "Forrest," which did good service at numerous London fires.

Mr. William Roberts, of Millwall, in 1861, built the first self-propelled steam fire engine ever made in England or Europe. It was supported on three wheels, one in front being the steering wheel, and arranged so as to be employed in driving machinery. The extreme length was 12 feet 6 inches, extreme breadth 6 feet 4 inches, and its gross weight with ovals, water, hose, ladders and tools complete was a little above 7½ tons. The engine was suspended on springs. The engine power consisted of two vertical cylinders, 6 inch diameter and 12 inch stroke, working the crank shaft, etc., by means of cross heads and side rods. The engine was driven along the public roads at 18 miles per hour. With a nozzle of 1⅜ inches diameter, the stream was thrown over a chimney (140 feet high,) and a horizontal distance of 182 feet, exclusive of broken water

OLD PHILADELPHIA FIREMAN AND ENGINE, 1840.

and spray. The steam pressure varied from 50 lbs. to 160 lbs., with 100 revolutions per minute. On one occasion the engine with 170 lbs. of steam and 112 revolutions per minute, using 1½ inch nozzle, delivered 450 gallons of water per minute. In the same year Mr. William Roberts constructed his second land steam fire engine, the "Princess of Wales." On the 31st of July, 1863, in twelve minutes from lighting the fire the engine got to work. It accommodated 18 men, with a great quantity of appliances, ladders, etc.

In 1863 Mr. James Shand obtained a patent for improvements in steam fire engines, in which patent the vertical engines made by Messrs. Shand, Mason & Co., were subsequently substituted. In the same year the change engine "Sutherland," which gained the first prize of $1,250 at the Crystal Palace trials, with six other engines, English and American, in 1863, was built by Messrs. Merryweather & Sons. The "Sutherland" discharged ten gallons of water at each revolution or stroke, and delivered water through nozzles at the rate of between 800 and 1,000 gallons per minute. It has thrown water through a 1½ inch nozzle to a horizontal distance of 235 measured feet. It was purchased by the Government and placed for service in the Royal Dockyards at Devonport.

In the same year a steam fire engine for the Imperial Library at St. Petersburgh, was designed and constructed by Mr. T. W. Cowan, engineer, of Greenwich. The boiler, engines and pumps were carried on a wrought iron framing, 7 inches deep and ¼ inch thick, strengthened with angle iron and mounted on springs, the whole being carried on four wheels. The weight of the engine was four tons, and it was drawn by three horses, when using delivery hose of 2½ inch diameter with a nozzle of 1¼ inches and a steam pressure of 120 lbs., a height of 170 feet and a distance of 210 feet were obtained.

In 1863 Mr. Egestorff, of Hanover, constructed a steam fire engine for the fire engine establishment of that city. The cylinder was 8½ inches by 9 inches

NEW YORK FIREMAN AND ENGINE.

and the pumps 7 inches; the valves metal of the description known in Hanover as Carretts. In the same year Messrs. Merryweather & Sons constructed a small steam fire engine for the Alton Volunteer Fire Brigade. The machine had a single steam cylinder and pump, the cylinder being 6⅜ inches by 18 inches stroke, and the pumps 4¾ inches diameter and 18 inches stroke. The weight was 25 cwts. One of these 25 cwt. single cylinder engines was found to have exerted a power equal to 32½ horses, or 1⅓ horse power for each cwt. of engine. In this year Messrs. Shand, Mason & Co., constructed 17 steam fire engines, two for the London Fire Brigade, two for Lisbon, three for the Bombay and Barsoda Railway Company, four for Russia, two for New Zealand, one for Austria, one for Poland, one for Denmark and one for Dublin.

In 1865 Mr. William Roberts constructed his third steam fire engine, the "Excelsior," which was made to order for the Arsenal Rio de Janeiro. With a one inch nozzle the engine threw a stream over a pole 80 feet high and 120 feet from the branch pipe, or a total of 144 feet from the branch to the top of the mast. The vertical lift of the suction at starting was 6 feet and 10 feet when the tide left. In the same year Messrs. Moltrecht, of Hanbury, constructed a small steam fire engine with a single horizontal cylinder and two horizontal pumps, which was not successful. Also in 1865 Mr. Fland, of Paris, built a steam fire engine.

In 1865 Messrs. Merryweather & Sons constructed eleven engines: two medium sized cylinder engines for the Spanish Government; one large sized double cylinder for her Majesty's Government for use at Portsmouth Dockyard; one medium sized double cylinder for the Liverpool Corporation; one similar size for the French Government, for Brest Dockyard; one medium single cylinder for the Dutch Government, for the Amsterdam Dockyard; one small sized cylinder for Dublin; one similar size for Manilla: one similar size for Redruth, and one medium sized single cylinder floating engine for the Northeastern Railway, for use at Newcastle. Mr. William Roberts constructed a steam fire engine for Hong Kong, which was an exact duplicate of the "Excelsior" in all respects, except that brass tubes were used in the boiler in place of iron. In this engine in 45 seconds, the guage started, in 3 minutes and 5 seconds, 5 lbs. of steam, and in 9 minutes and thirty-two seconds the engine was at work with 100 lbs. of steam, throwing through a 1¼ inch nozzle water to the height of full 160 feet.

The following table gives the date when the English firms commenced to build land steam fire engines, to be drawn by horses, and the total number of such engines made by them in England and Ireland up to 1866:

	Date.	No. Built.
Braithwaite & Ericsson	1829	5
G. Rennie & Sons	1856	1
Shand, Mason & Co.	1858	60 of all kinds.
J. Shekleton	1860	1, the first Irish steam fire engine.
Merryweather & Sons	1861	17 and three floating engines.
Wm. Roberts	1862	5, one self-propelled and one floating.
T. W. Cowan	1863	1
J. W. Gray & Son	1863	1

The Button steam fire engine has upright tubular boilers, with submerged smoke-box and combustion-chamber. The crane neck frame is employed in the construction of these engines. The pumps are of the best bronze metal, and are so arranged that the water connot come in contact with any iron, thus preventing the liability to rust, however long they may be out of use.

The Gould steam fire engine, manufactured by B. S. Nichols & Company, Burlington, Vt., has a vertical tubular boiler with submerged smoke-flues and tapering fire-box. The feedwater is heated by passing through the fire-box, a circulating valve being placed on the outside between the boiler and heater, so that when the feed-pump is stopped a perfect circulation can be established between the heater and the boiler. The boilers have an uncommonly large heating surface and steam-room in proportion to the work to be done by the engine, consequently they steam very freely, being capable of raising sufficient steam from cold water in from three or four minutes' time, to play through a hundred feet of hose. The engines are vertical, reciprocating; the steam cylinders resting on columns which are attached to the crane-neck frame and to the boiler.

The Jeffer's engine has an upright boiler, steel tubular of peculiar construction, with inverted smoke-box and furnace and copper tubes, which generate steam very rapidly. Steam can be raised in from four and a half to five minutes. The engines are vertical, with steam cylinders resting on independent columns attached to the frame, and have patent cylindrical steam-valves. A straight, wrought-iron frame is employed in the construction of those engines, which is attached to logs on each side of the boiler; the front end sustains the pump, air-vessel and steam-cylinder, while the rear sustains the coal bunker. The discharge-gate is located in front; and in consequence of a patent relief-valve in connection with the pump, and an ingenious cut-off nozzle attached to the hose, the water can be cut off at any time without in any way interfering with the working of the engine, as when the steam is cut off the relief-valve is automatically opened between the discharge and the suction pipes.

The Neafie & Levy engines are horizontal, and stand quite still when working, with the exception of that vibratory motion which is peculiar to all horizontal machines. They are powerful, durable and efficient.

In the Ives' engine the boiler is an upright tubular with conical smoke-box, submerged combustion-chamber, and contracted waist. The feed-water is heated before entering the boiler by being passed through a copper coil inside of the smoke-stack. The engines are horizontal, with the base of their cylinders so formed as to saddle the cylindrical frame to which they are attached by a row of bolts on each side. The valves are so conveniently arranged as to be capable of being cleaned, renewed or repaired at very short notice. Printz's automatic discharge valves are used, by means of which the water can be shut off at the nozzle at any time without stopping the engine.

The firm of Lee & Larnard built one or two large self-propelling engines which were very unwieldy and necessarily slow to be brought into service. One of them, the John G. Storms, was placed in charge of the Exempt Fire Company, and located at No. 4 Centre Street, a building which stood in the rear of the Hall of Records. The same firm built a rotary engine of much lighter pattern, weighing about six thousand pounds, and arranged so as to be drawn by hand power. The engine was purchased by the Fire Insurance interests, and presented to Manhattan Engine Company No. 8, and through the exertion of the late Robert C. Brown, proved a success, notwithstanding the great opposition from other companies in the Department. The same year Guardian Engine Company No. 29 received an engine of the same pattern from the same manufacturer, only one size smaller; ex-Chief Eli Bates was foreman. The same year James Smith, builders of fire apparatus in West Broadway, built a piston engine of small size, to be drawn by hand power, and was placed in service and used with great success by Hudson Hose Company No. 21 (after Engine 53). Mr. James Dale, now assistant engineer in the Brooklyn Fire Department, was the engineer of No. 21, who managed to make this style of engine very popular. The company was located in the Erie Building, 304 Washington Street. Dale was mentioned by Mayor Whitney among those deserving honor in 1887 for saving human life. The same year Valley Forge Engine Company No. 46 received from Lee & Larnard a rotary engine, same as Engines 8 and 29, and the following year, 1860, New York Engine Company 47 (formerly Hose 5), and Southwark Engine 38, received from same firm a similar engine to that of No. 46.

The Amoskeag Manufacturing Company of Manchester, N. H., in 1860 brought to this city a piston engine which was placed in charge of Paulding Hose Company No. 57, located at 162 West 18th Street, by the authorities, which was afterward bought, and proved to be a valuable auxiliary to the fire service. In the year 1861 Americus Engine 6 and Lexington 7 applied to the Common Council for steam engines and were furnished with rotary engines built by the Silsby, Mynderse & Company, Seneca Falls, N. Y. The same year the Portland Manufacturing Company sold to the city two piston engines. One was placed in charge of Empire Engine Company 42, the other in charge of Jefferson Engine Company 26, and the same year Black Joke Engine 33 and Jackson Engine Company 24 received each one of the Smith pattern. In 1862 Engine Company 9 and 58 received an engine built by A. B. Taylor & Son, of this city, and Engine Company 11, James Smith's pattern. In 1863 Engine Company 4, 30 and 51, received engines built by Jos. Banks of this city, and Engine Companies 12, 13, 28 and 31 engines built by Jas. Smith of New York ; Engine Company 22 one built by Mr. Jeffers. In 1864 Engine Companies 1, 15 and 37 received engines built by A. Van Ness of this city, and Engine Companies 10 and 20 machines built by Jos. Banks. All these were *Piston Engines.*

In the year 1865 the Metropolitan Fire Department was organized, and many of the engines above numerated were altered to be drawn by horses, and were used until larger and more powerful ones were substituted in their places.

The Metropolitan Commissioners in 1865 contracted with the Amoskeag Manufacturing Company, of New Hampshire, to build at once for use twenty (second size engines) of what are called U Tank Single Pump, weight, about seven thousand pounds when equipped for service, with 8-inch steam cylinder, 12-inch stroke and 4½ inch water cylinder, and most of them were in service in January, 1887, being the same style as that used by Paulding Hose Company 57 of the Volunteer Department, an engine which was built in 1860, and at this time still in service.

The engines of more modern pattern are what are called Double Pump Engines, nearly the same as above, only that they are double acting, having two steam and water cylinders with 8-inch stroke. The first engine placed in service under the new system was a large double engine, and known as "Metropolitan No. 1," of which William Corgan was foreman, and was located in the house formerly occupied by Exempt Company No. 4, Centre Street, facing the entrance to the Brooklyn Bridge, at City Hall Park.

During the year 1871, when the horse disease known as the " Epizootic " was raging all over the country, the commission caused to be built five self-propelling engines of large size and placed in service, and assigned to the following companies : Engine Company 20, Foreman, Hugh Bonner, now Assistant Chief ; Engine 32, Foreman, Jos. F. McGill, now Batallion Chief ; Engine Company 8, Foreman, John Welsh ; Engine Company 11, Foreman, Isaac Fisher, and Engine No. 24, Wm. McLaughlin, Foreman. These engines are still in service, and under the able management of the above-mentioned officers rendered good service to the city.

It will be remembered that the large fire in Boston, Mass., occurred at this time, and the want of horses to draw the apparatus was one of the probable causes of delay which gave the fire such a start, which would not have occurred otherwise.

The following clear and interesting explanation of the steam fire engine is furnished by ex-Chief Engineer Joseph L. Perley :

" The steam fire engine is simple and compact. The engine is attached to the boiler and both are carried on what are called shears. In some cases the water tanks act as such. In large cities the running gear differs according to condition and character of the streets. The boilers differ somewhat as to the interior, the main object being strength and lightness; the outer shell being steel, and the flues or tubes being made of composition, and many of them seamless brass. Some boilers have as many as the space will allow for the purpose of obtaining as much heating surface as possible. The engine is attached to the boiler on one side, so that the steam chest may be as near the steam dome as possible, the cylinder having steam ports at either end, leading directly to the steam chest. The steam before entering, flows from the boiler into the steam chest, then into the cylinder, where it acts upon the piston and produces motion. The steam is admitted from the steam chest to the cylinder through a valve, and when the steam so admitted has performed its work of driving the piston either up or down, another valve opens and permits this steam to escape from the cylinder into a passage for the exhaust. Steam which is used in the dome of the boiler, after performing its functions in the steam cylinder to create what is called artificial draft, which adds to the intensity of the fire in the furnace of the boiler, The main water pump is also attached to the boiler, below the steam cylinder, and is connected with the steam cylinder by means of a piston, in the centre of which is what is called a link, which connects with the crank shaft by a link block or journal. The balance wheels are also attached to the shaft, and near the crank is an eccentric which connected by an eccentric rod or strap made of brass, occasions the valves to work the engine when in operation, and to continue so without the aid of any agency other than the revolutions of the engine when in motion. The steam cylinders as a rule are always larger than the water cylinders, sometimes one-half again larger. The stroke generally is from 8 to 12 inches, so that the water pressure can be increased to double that of the steam if necessary. The pumps differ somewhat in form of construction, but perform similar to each other, being double acting receiving and discharging its water at every stroke or revolution. Each pump has a partition separating the water from the receiving and discharging chambers. In that partition there is a valve called a relief valve, which acts to relieve the discharging chamber of the pump, as would the safety valve upon the boiler, and can be adjusted the same so that an overpressure of water can be relieved or returned back to the receiving chamber of the pump. Engines have a steam and water guage placed so the engineer can always see when the engine is in motion. What water is required to feed the boiler and resupply that which has passed out of it in steam, is taken from the main pump when the engine is in motion.

Should the boiler require water when the engine is not in motion it can be taken from a tank, which is placed upon the engine for that purpose, which can be done by using the relief valve and allowing the water to circulate in the main

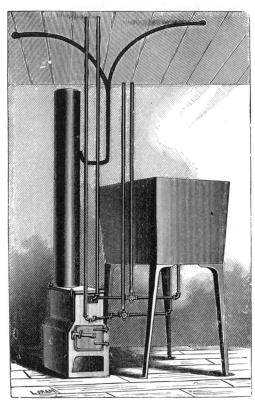

FIRST STEAM COIL FOR STEAM FIRE ENGINE
BOILER.

pump, without discharging water through the hose. Tanks are connected by supply pipes leading to main pump also to the feed pumps which can be used to inject water into the boiler, on which a check valve is located near the bottom to prevent a greater pressure of steam from forcing it back. These pipes are also protected from frost by a system of small steam pipes which are used to inject steam into, and prevent freezing in extreme cold weather. Engines generally are used to handle the water from hydrants, and to force it to distant points where most required to extinguish fires, also the river water when fires are adjacent to it, for that purpose. Each engine has two large 4½ inch suction pipes, when connected can reach the water from docks or piers. A fuel pan is also arranged in the rear of the boiler and near the furnace door to carry fuel capable of lasting until fuel wagons are brought to the fire. Foreman and engineers of company usually ride on fuel pan in going to and returning from fires. While engine is standing in quarters the boiler is connected to a heating apparatus, which is used in keeping the water in the boiler at the boiling point, that steam may be generated in a short time upon leaving quarters, and the engine be placed in service as soon as proper connections can be made and hose laid to the place where water is required.

Each boiler has a tram pipe attached, with steam whistle and four guage cocks, to ascertain the quantity of water in the boiler that the engineer may keep it well supplied."

In 1884, at the Annual Convention of the National Association of Fire Engineers held at Chicago, Chief Engineer G. C. Hale, of Kansas, Mo., read a paper on the desirable points of mechanism in steam fire engines. "A steam fire engine," said Chief Hale, "to meet the requirements of present engineers, should contain first, a quick-steaming boiler, as time is an element of great importance in combating fires, a delay of a few minutes in a critical case may result in a large conflagration. Especially is this true of fires in large manufacturing establishments filled with combustible material. Delays are dangerous, is an old maxim, and is nowhere more truly demonstrated than in getting up steam in the boiler of a steam fire-engine after an alarm is tapped—other things equal, that engine in which a working steam power is most quickly required is to be preferred. Second, the construction and mounting of the boiler on the engine frame should permit of a satisfactory working on an even ground. It is not always possible to locate a steam fire-engine over the cisterns or other source of supply in such a manner that it will be substantially level from aft and crosswise, and if it was possible, no time can be consumed in levelling it up without serious risk to the burning property. A steam fire-engine boiler should, therefore, be adapted to work equally well whether level or considerably out of plumb. Third, a steam fire-engine, as a whole, should be constructed in such a manner that no reasonable possibility exists of headage or derangement while going to or in use at a fire, and yet it should be provided with facilities for quick and positive repair. Fourth, the general construction of the engine, as a whole, should be especially adapted to rapid and sometimes rough handling in making ready in answering an alarm, and to the severest strains in transit over rough and uneven roads. Fifth, the boiler of a steam fire-engine should be absolutely exempt from the possibility of explosions either while steaming up or at work during a fire. The pumps of a steam fire engine should be adapted to work without injury with turbid or gritty water, if occasion should require, as it is not always possible to obtain water for fire-engines from clear sources of supply, and engines are frequently compelled to derive water from rivers or other natural water ways, the streams of which carry large quantities of sand or silt in mechanical suspension. Of course such matter must pass through the pumps, and excepting the valves and pistons, are constructed with especial reference to the use of this character of water, they will deteriorate very rapidly, diminishing the efficiency of the engine and demanding frequent repairs."

During the past eighteen or twenty years the improvements in England in steam fire-engines have not been very important. The changes have been improvements in various parts of the working gear.

So far we have touched upon the history of the steam fire-engine in Europe. The first steam fire-engine constructed in the United States was designed and built by Mr. Paul Rapsey Hodge, C. E., in this city in 1840-41. It was a self-propelled engine, the first of the kind ever constructed, with horizontal cylinders and pumps, a locomotive boiler, in some respects like the style introduced by Edward Bury for locomotives; the slab or plate framing to which the cylinder and pumps were attached, afterward used in locomotives, and wrought iron wheels, which were manufactured by the Matteawan Company for Mr. Hodge. It was arranged to be drawn by horses, if required, as well as by hand and its own steam power. The engine was begun on December 12, 1840, and completed April 25, 1841.

Mr. Hodge had induced the several insurance companies to give him a conditional order for a steam fire engine, his contract being that the engine should be capable of forcing 6,000 lbs. of water per minute to a height of 120 feet. In 1865 Mr. Hodge wrote a letter to an English author stating that he had begun the construction of his engine many months before Captain John Ericsson landed in New York. It had been claimed that Captain Ericsson had built the first American steam fire engine. Mr. Hodge showed that Captain Ericsson had made a design for one, a copy of which was published in

Ewbank's "Hydraulics," but it was never made. It was said to be precisely the same as that built by Mr. John Braithwaite in London in 1829. In the year 1840 Captain Ericsson had obtained the gold medal which was offered by the Mechanics' Institute of New York for the best plan of steam fire-engine. The difference in the design and in the engine built by Mr. Braithwaite was in the boiler.

The construction of Mr. Hodge's engine was very simple. The surface of the boiler was very great for a boiler of its weight, being only (without water) 1,600 lbs. net. There were two continuous wrought frames on each side of the boiler, on to which the two steam cylinders and two double-acting water pumps were attached. The steam cylinders were 9½ inch diameter and 14 inch stroke. The two pumps were 8¼ inch diameter and 14 inch stroke, the same piston rod working both through engines and pumps direct. In front of the bed plate was an arrangement for a four, three, two or one jet. The larger single jet was through a 2¼ inch nozzle; if two, each through a 1½ inch; if four, each through a 1⅛ inch nozzle. The quantity of water thrown was very much greater than that contracted for. The height of the stream attained 166 feet, and the quantity thrown to that height through a 2¼ inch nozzle was 10,824 lbs. The engine was drawing the water through four lengths of suction from a depth of 12 feet.

In 1851 Mr. W. L. Lay designed a self-propelled steam fire-engine at Philadelphia, with a rotary pump, and provided with a plan by which carbonic acid gas could be used to propel the engine to the fire whilst steam was being raised. The fire was to be urged by a fan or blower, and when at work the engine was to be raised off the ground so as to allow the driving wheels to act as fly wheels when the engine was pumping, as was done in Mr. Hodge's engine. It was to throw three or four hundred gallons of water per minute, was provided with a hose-reel, steering apparatus and the usual accompaniments, and was estimated to weigh 1½ tons.

In 1853 Mr. A. B. Latta, of Cincinnati, constructed a steam fire-engine, a self-propeller, which ran on three wheels. The cylinders were two in number, placed on each side, the pumps being in front of the cylinders, the piston-rods of the steam cylinders were continued to form the rods of the pumps, and the engines were so arranged as to couple to the driving-wheels when required when driving-wheels placed behind the fire-box. The leading wheel could turn in any direction so as to admit of the easy steering of the engine. It could throw one to six streams of water, and was fitted with a 6½ inch suction hose 24 feet long, and was reckoned to throw 2,000 barrels of water per hour. It would get to work in five minutes, and it required four men and four horses to work it and run it out. On one occasion it threw a stream 291 feet to where the spray fell, the nozzle being 1¾ inch diameter.

In 1855 Abel Shawk, of Cincinnati, built an engine with the following results: Steam was formed in 5 minutes and 15 seconds after the torch was applied, the water being quite cold; in one minute afterward the guage showed 15 lbs., and in 7 minutes 20 seconds after lighting, 50 lbs., and in 8 minutes from lighting the engine was started, the steam quickly rising to 180 lbs. When raising water by the suction from the Delaware against a moderate breeze with a 1¼ inch nozzle, a horizontal distance, excluding spray, 176 feet was reached; with 325 feet of hose and a 1⅛ inch nozzle it threw 120 feet against the wind; with 925 feet of hose and a ¾ inch nozzle the engine threw to a height of 40 feet at 70 feet horizontal distance from the engine, the steam pressure being 96 lbs. on the square inch.

The firm of Messrs. Poole & Hunt, of Baltimore, Md., began building steam fire engines in 1858, and in 8 years completed seven—one of the first class, four of the second class and two of the third class. Their engines had no screw, bolt or handle, or any other appurtenance more than was necessary. The boilers were upright multitubular, with a square fire-box and enlarged steam space. They were fed by a feed or force-pump, and were arranged to take a supply by a connection with the main air vessel. These engines raised sufficient steam for starting in from five to six minutes from the time the fire was lighted, the water being cold in the boiler. The first class engines, with a 1⅜ inch nozzle, threw to a horizontal distance of 257 feet; the second class, with a 1⅛ inch nozzle, to a horizontal distance of 240 feet; the third class, with a 1 inch nozzle, to a horizontal distance of 235 feet.

Messrs. Ettenger & Edmond, engineers and steam fire engine builders, of Richmond, Va., began the construction of steam fire engines in 1859. The boilers were vertical with 165 iron tubes of 1½ inches diameter; steam cylinders 9 inches by 15 inches, one in each engine, with two pumps to each placed horizontally, each pump 3½ inches by 15 inches, the contents being equal to the 5 inch pumps. The suction hose was 4½ inches in diameter, and the delivery hose 2½ inches in diameter. The weight of the engine complete, with wood and water ready to run out was 6,600 lbs. These engines would throw water to a horizontal height of 240 feet with a 1⅛ inch nozzle, and to a vertical height of 160 to 180 feet. The average steam pressure used when working at a fire was 60 lbs. on the square inch in 7 minutes from lighting the fire. Two of the first engines were sent to the Fire Department of Richmond Va., the third to St. Petersburg to the order of Messrs. Winans & Harrison.

Towards the close of 1859 trials of steam fire engines were made at Philadelphia, the engines having been on exhibition at the Fair of the Agricultural Society. The following machines contested:

"Good Intent" built by Reany & Neapie, of Philadelphia—steam cylinder, 8 inches diameter and 12 inches stroke; pump, 4¾ inches and 12 inches stroke; weight, 5,400 lbs.; 1 inch nozzle, horizontal distance, 169 feet; vertical height, 140 feet.

"Weccacoe," built by Merrick & Sons, Philadelphia—steam cylinder, 8½ inches diameter and 14 inches stroke; pump, 6 inches diameter and 14 inches stroke; 1¼ inch nozzle, horizontal distance, 109 feet, vertical height, 83 feet.

No. 7, "Baltimore," built by Poole & Hunt, Baltimore—steam cylinder, 14 inches diameter and 12 inches stroke; pumps, 6 inches diameter and 12 inches stroke; weight, 5,456 lbs.; 1 inch nozzle, horizontal distance, 196 feet; vertical height, 166 feet.

"Independence," built by Hunsworth, Eakins & Co., at People's Works, Philadelphia—steam cylinder, 10½ inches diameter and 14 inches stroke; pumps, 5½ inches diameter and 14 inches stroke; nozzle, 1¼ inch, horizontal distance, 193 feet; vertical height, 143 feet.

"Washington," built by Poole & Hunt, Baltimore—steam cylinder, 12½ inches diameter and 12 inches stroke; pump, 6⅜ inches diameter and 12 inches stroke; weight, 3,582 lbs; nozzle, 1¼ inches, horizontal distance, 239 feet; **vertical** height, 178 feet.

"Mechanic," built by Reaney & Neapie, of Philadelphia—steam cylinder, 8 inches diameter and 12 inches stroke; pump, 4⅝ inches diameter and 16 inches stroke; weight, 5,760 lbs.; nozzle 1 inch, horizontal distance, 203 feet; vertical height, 167 feet.

"Hibernia," built by Reaney & Neapie, Philadelphia—steam cylinder 1¼ inches diameter and 14 inches stroke; pump, 6½ inches diameter and 14 inches stroke; weight, 8,000 lbs.; nozzle, 1⅚ inches; horizontal distance, 254 feet; vertical height, 181 feet.

"Southwark," built by Lee & Larned, New York—steam cylinder. A self-propelling engine; 2 steam cylinders, each 7½ inches diameter and 14 inches stroke; one rotary pump, 17 inches diameter and 10 inches wide; weight, 9,000 lbs.

"Citizen," of Harrisburg (first-class) fully manned, using 10 feet of hose

FIRST STEAM FIRE ENGINE BUILT IN AMERICA, 1840.

and a nozzle 1 inch in diameter, worked for 2 minutes, reached a horizontal distance of 196 feet.

"Assistance," of Philadelphia (first class), length of hose and diameter of nozzle the same, reached a horizontal distance of 182 feet, 4½ inches.

"Washington" (second class) 50 feet of hose and a ⅞ inch nozzle, reached a horizontal distance of 154 feet.

"Philadelphia" (second class) under the same circumstances, reached a horizontal distance of 188 feet, 3 inches.

"Weccacoe" (second class) as above, a horizontal distance of 154 feet.

"Globe" (second class) as above, a horizontal distance of 150 feet and 5 feet allowance.

'Franklin" (second class) of Frankford, as above, a horizontal distance of 158 feet and 5 feet allowance.

In 1860, Messrs. Ettinger & Edmond, of Richmond, Va., built a steam fire engine for St. Petersburgh, the machine was placed low down on straight axles, and could not turn over whilst going around corners; complete, the weight was 5,000 pounds. It was the design of Mr. A. M'Causland. It threw a $1\frac{1}{8}$ inch stream 220 feet, a $1\frac{1}{2}$ inch stream 143 feet, and a $1\frac{1}{4}$ inch stream 183 feet. At a trial in Philadelphia it threw a $1\frac{1}{2}$ inch stream 250 feet. In the same year an engine built by Neapie & Levy, for San Francisco, with a cylinder 8 inches by 12 inches, and pump $4\frac{1}{2}$ inches by 12 inches, threw a $1\frac{1}{4}$ inch stream at Philadelphia 253 feet horizontally.

In 1860, a small steam fire engine or model, exhibited at the county fair, Rensselaer, Troy, weighing $2\frac{1}{2}$ lbs., threw a stream about the size of a pin, to a distance of 4 feet 6 inches; the steam cylinder was horizontal, $\frac{1}{2}$ inch diameter, and $\frac{3}{4}$ inch stroke. At the California State Fair, Henry Rice exhibited a model made by himself; the steam cylinder was $\frac{3}{16}$ inches diameter, with $\frac{7}{16}$ inch stroke, and ran at the rate of 2,000 revolutions per minute.

Pittsburgh, Pa., had an engine weighing between 4,000 and 5,000 lbs., on the model of the "Southwark," of Philadelphia, which raised steam in 6 minutes and threw a $\frac{3}{4}$ inch stream over a six-story building.

In September, 1860, the "Huron," a first class double cylinder engine with plunger pumps, at a competition in Troy, threw water in 7 minutes from the lighting of the fire, in 8 minutes reaching 100 feet, in 14 minutes 200 feet, and so on reached 223 feet 9 inches, pumping through 50 feet of 3 inch hose, and using $1\frac{3}{8}$ inch nozzle. The "Michigonne," a first class double cylinder engine with rotary pump, played two powerful streams for 4 hours continuously through 1,600 feet of hose, to which two 150 feet lengths with a separate branch on each were attached, making 1,750 altogether, the engine being 75 feet lower than the branches.

In 1860, the "Arba Read," steam fire engine, a first class single cylinder engine, with double acting plunger pump, threw a single stream through 450 feet of hose, and a $1\frac{1}{4}$ inch nozzle to a distance of 200 feet horizontally; a $1\frac{1}{8}$ inch stream was thrown to a distance of 275 feet through 50 feet of hose. The highest steam pressure used was 240 lbs. on the square inch.

The "Fire-King," a first class double cylinder engine with plunger pumps, belonging to the Fire Department of Manchester, on one occasion reached a distance of 207 feet horizontally with a $\frac{7}{8}$ inch jet; then it threw a stream 292 feet with a $1\frac{1}{4}$ inch nozzle. Another machine that attracted attention was the "J. C. Cary." Its cylinders were $7\frac{1}{2}$ inches diameter with 14 inch stroke, driving a rotary pump. The boiler consisted of 114 pairs of double tubes, each $2\frac{1}{2}$ inches diameter, containing one of $1\frac{1}{2}$ inch diameter inside it, the annular space between the two being occupied by water, whilst the fire is circulated among the larger and within the smaller tubes. The engine weighed $5\frac{1}{2}$ tons, and at a public trial threw 1,100 gallons of water per minute. The height attained with a $1\frac{3}{8}$ inch nozzle was 267 feet horizontally; a 2 inch stream reached 232 feet; and a $2\frac{1}{4}$ inch stream through an open butt 196 feet.

In 1862, Messrs. Lee & Larned, of New York, sent to the International Exhibition at London, one of their small sized rotary pump engines, called 5 horse power, which elicited the greatest approbations from all the engineers

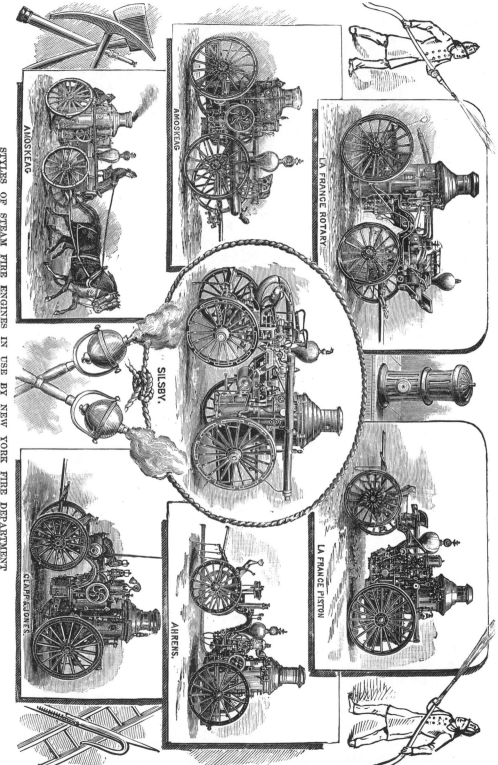

STYLES OF STEAM FIRE ENGINES IN USE BY NEW YORK FIRE DEPARTMENT

AMOSKEAG

AMOSKEAG

LA FRANCE ROTARY

SILSBY.

CLAPP & JONES.

AHRENS.

LA FRANCE PISTON

who inspected it, both for its beautiful workmanship and satisfactory working. The engine itself, which had neither water tank nor coal bunkers, weighed 1 ton 12 cwt. The cylinder was 7 inches diameter with $8\frac{1}{2}$ inch stroke, and had a pair of light balance wheels to carry it over the centres; the piston rod was $1\frac{1}{4}$ inch diameter, the crank shaft $1\frac{3}{4}$ inch bearing, the boiler 4 feet high by 26 inches, outside diameter at steam chest. The boiler had 125 feet of heating surface. A tender at will was attached behind to carry the hose, coals, etc. In the same year the firm built a steam fire engine in England, weighing 3 tons $2\frac{1}{2}$ cwts; carrying a moderate quantity of coal, several hundred feet of hose, a tool chest and six men.

Many of the engines now in use in this country have conical India rubber disc-valves, held in position by spiral springs, giving sufficient area of opening with very limited lift. Crane neck frames have superseded the straight or parallel, as they admit of the boiler and machinery being placed lower down on the frame, and afford great facilities for turning around in narrow streets or contracted situations. The blower pipe, that was at one time so extensively used in the smoke stacks of fire engines for the purpose of increasing the draught, is now nearly, if not entirely, superseded by the variable exhaust, and nearly if not all fire engine houses have stationery steam boilers, generally located in the cellar, on which steam is kept up steadily for the purpose of keeping the water in the boiler hot. Steam can now be raised in from 10 to 12 minutes while running to a fire. Now the simplest kind of engine is considered the most durable and efficient. The vertical form of cylinder is held to be the best, as vertical pumps can be attached directly to the boiler, thereby making the working of the engine smoother in consequence of the weight being against the lift. Moreover loss is avoided by carrying steam from the boiler to the cylinder through pipes exposed to the atmosphere. The wear on the rubbing surfaces of vertical engines is also less than horizontal or inclined engines suffer.

The water pistons of steam fire engines, like those of steam pumps, are almost exclusively made of leather, as that material possesses superior advantages over any other for that purpose, they are either made solid or in the shape of a disc. The difficulty which so materially interfered with the usefulness of the steam fire engine for many years after its introduction, that of being manufactured at a distance from the place where it was used, is now successfully overcome by the establishment of machine shops in connection with nearly all the Fire Departments of the country, and repairs can be quickly made. Under the Paid Fire Department system all the worn out, complicated or inefficient engines were allowed to fall into disuse, or were sold to country towns and none were retained but those that had a good reputation for efficiency, durability and economy.

Steam engines should be so designed as to be capable of working at either slow or fast speed and to discharge an amount of water proportionate to the speed at which they are worked. The reason why, it has been said, the American system of quick running engines has given more satisfactory results than those of English make, has been that the proportion employed in this country approach very nearly to those used in locomotives, where the suction pipe into the pump is as large as the barrel of the pump itself. This has been considered a common sense proceeding because time, however short, is necessary to enable any operations to be carried out, more especially when its material to be worked on is water, and that as in the steam fire engine, through all kinds of difficulties in the shape of friction, contracted and awkward passages, small holes or entrances into large spaces, &c. On comparison it has been noted that the engines by American makers have the best proportions: next to these the long-stroked, steady-running English engines; whilst the worst proportions of any are those of the quick-running engines where the direction of motion is changed oftenest in the shortest times, and the area of suction opening is least when compared with the area of pump piston, so that the largest space has to be filled through the smallest hole, and that, too, in the smallest amount of time, the stroke being so short and the direction of motion so rapidly changed in the short period during which the piston moves in any given direction.

The names of the principal manufacturers of steam fire engines in this country are as follows: Neapie & Levy, Philadelphia, Pa.; Knowlton & Co., Philadelphia, Pa.; Clapp & Jones, Hudson, N. Y.; Button & Son, Waterford, N. Y.; Silsby Manufacturing Co., Seneca Falls, N. Y.; C. Ahrens & Co., Cincinnati, O.; Amoskeag Manufacturing Co., Manchester, N. H.; Ives & Bro., Baltimore, Md.; Wm. Jeffers, Pawtucket, R. I.; B. S. Nichols & Co., Burlington, Vt.

The Ahrens' engine is upright and double acting; the steam cylinder resting on columns which are attached to the frame and to the boiler, and forms supports for the crank-shaft bearing. The air-pump is a new and important feature, and is used for keeping the air vessels constantly supplied with air which has the effect of rendering the hose quite steady when the engine is working. These engines are in very general use in the Western States.

The Clapp & Jones engine has a vertical boiler with fire and water tubes. The fire tubes extend from the crown sheet of the fire up through the top of the shell. The safety and throttle valves are combined in one piece. The draught can be so regulated by means of variable exhaust nozzles as to maintain a uniform pressure in the boiler. The engines are horizontal, and are known as "piston" engines, and the pumps are double acting. The suction hose is always attached and ready for use. Steam can be raised from cold water in from four to six minutes from the time of lighting the fire.

The Silsby Rotary Engine has a vertical boiler with water tubes passing directly through the fire, which are closed at the bottom, and often at the top, where they pass through a water tight plate and communicate with the water in the boiler. Steam can be generated in from four to six minutes. Salt or sea water can be used without inconvenience. There is an attachment to the boilers by which a portion of the exhaust steam may be turned into the supply tank, for the purpose of heating the water, thus, it is claimed, effecting a great saving in fuel, and relieving the boiler of the evils resulting from unequal expansion and contraction induced by cold feed-water.

The Amoskeag engines are vertical, with steam cylinder and pumps attached to an upright tubular boiler, with inverted smoke box. The pumps are double acting, with receiving screws on each side, and are surrounded by a circular chamber which forms the suction and discharge openings. The discharge and suction chambers of the pumps are connected by a relief valve.

The engines are built either single or double self-propelling, or to be drawn by horses, with either straight or crane-neck frames. They can be turned with great ease, within very narrow limits, by means of a set of compound gearing so arranged on the axle that in turning the engine, the two rear wheels are driven at varying speeds.

In General Orders of the New York Fire Department, instructions have been given for the benefit of engineers who have not had much experience in running engines. They are purely technical, and therefore of interest only to professional men. The following are the supplies with which every engine in the Department is furnished:

Twenty feet of suction hose, a suitable brass strained for suction hose, a brass hydrant connection for suction hose, a brass signal whistle, two plated guages, one to indicate the pressure of water upon the boiler, and the other the pressure of water at the pumps or leading hose, two discharge pipes for leading hose, with a complete set of changeable nozzles from $7\frac{1}{2}$ inch diameter

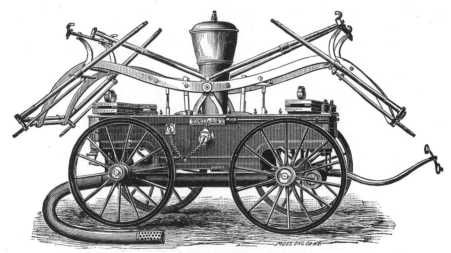

AMERICAN FIRE ENGINE, 1857.

to $1\frac{1}{4}$ inch diameter inclusive, two brass-bound fireman's hand lanterns, a large brass oil can, a jack-screw for convenience in oiling the axles, an oval shovel and fire poker. A small tool-box furnished with such small tools as may be required about the engine in use, such as hammers, wrenches, and the like.

Dimensions of a second-class, double plunge engine, crane-neck frame: Height from floor to top of smoke-stack, 8 feet 8 inches; length over all, including tongue, 23 feet 2 inches; diameter of boiler, 2 feet 7 inches; diameter of pumps, $4\frac{1}{2}$ inches; stroke of pump, 8 inches; diameter of steam cylinders, $6\frac{7}{8}$ inches; number of discharge gates, 2; capacity in gallons per minute, 700; weight, about 5,400 lbs. Second-class double pump crane-neck engine: Diameter of grate surface, 32 inches; size of door, 8 by 12 inches; number of tubes, 258; diameter of tubes (internal), $1\frac{1}{8}$ inch; bottom of boiler to bottom of pressure pipe, 20 inches; bottom of pressure pipe to first guage cock, 12 inches; distance between guage cocks, 5 inches; number of gallons to third guage cock, 40 cubic feet; steam room, 3 feet.

CHAPTER LVI.

THE ARCHITECTURAL GROWTH OF THE CITY.

First Habitations Occupied by White Settlers on Manhattan Island.—Primitive Structures.—Dutch Architecture.—Some Important Buildings Erected About the Beginning of the Present Century.— More Recent Improvements.—The Great Expansion of the City.—Fire-Proof Buildings.—Churches, Public Edifices, Flats and Private Dwellings.

THE HISTORY of New York City from an architectural point of view is simply unique. The growth of the city and its rapid extension, while being thoroughly remarkable, are not without their parallel in other cities throughout the United States. But for magnitude, practicability and grandeur of its buildings it is simply unequalled. Among these are to be found some of the finest of any throughout the world—finest not only from their exterior appearance and general arrangement, but finest in the eminently deft manner in which the whole work has been carried out ; from the skillful way in which advantage has been taken of modern scientific appliances, and from the near approach which has been obtained to what is one of the fundamental laws of the art—the exact requirements of the occupier.

The American architect differs from those of other countries in an important particular—he is more of an engineer. He has at his disposal means and appliances unknown a few years back, and he takes advantage of them, and in the design of his buildings combines together science and art. It has been said, and with a good deal of truth, that what really amounts to a new school of architecture identified with and being peculiar to the country, has sprung up during the past few years.

American architecture, and particularly that of New York City, has received in the past very severe criticism. It has been affirmed that every style and almost every combination of styles under the sun are to be found within its limits. Probably this is so, but at the same time it is open to question whether the practical adaptibility of the various styles could be equalled.

Some account of the history of the architecture of the city will be interesting, although it is doubtful whether it can be properly termed a history, comprised, as it chiefly is, within the past thirty or forty years.

Further back than that, however, we must go to trace the progress of the city to its remarkable condition as at present existing. On the discovery of the island by Henry Hudson in 1609, the Indians who were then the inhabitants occupied what may be looked upon as the first houses upon it. It was the habit of these Indians to live in villages containing up to several hundred inhabitants. Frequently their houses would be as much as five hundred feet long, varying to shorter lengths according to the number of separate families it was intended they should accommodate. The breadth of the buildings was always uniform, being about twenty feet, and were constructed by a series of framing formed by placing saplings at intervals, and bending them to meet at the top. The exterior of the dwelling was completed by a covering of the boughs of trees, while the interior was carefully covered with bark. There was no description of floors to these buildings, nor any chimney, the smoke from the fires escaping through a hole in the roof.

Henry Hudson, who, although an Englishman, was in the employ of the

POST OFFICE.

Dutch Government, sailed back to Holland with great news of his discovery, and not long afterward settlers began to arrive in small numbers. In 1624 there were about 200 persons on Manhattan Island.

In 1626 was constructed what really formed the first permanent structure upon the island, consisting of a block house of some considerable extent. The dwellings of the greater part of the inhabitants were at this time not, as many imagine, log cabins. As a fact, most of them were even more simple, and consisted of what really formed little better than mere cellars, comprising simple excavations in the ground roofed in, and forming a very rude description of habitation. Other dwellings were small buildings of two rooms on a floor with a thatched roof.

During the years 1633-35 we have records showing of considerable work being done in building. Van Twiller, a Governor appointed by the Dutch West India Company, built a fort some 300 feet by 250 feet at a cost of $1,688, and a house for himself which was certainly the most elaborate erection which up to that time had been attempted in America. These were both erected of bricks which were imported from Amsterdam, and numerous other small buildings were put up about the same time. During 1633 was also erected a church which probably formed the first place of public worship. This was a plain and unpretentious building of moderate size constructed of wood, and was located on Pearl Street on the East River shore.

In the year 1660 De Graaf and Hogboom established a brick-yard, and some time previously the introduction of a saw-mill to the city was the means of providing facilities for the erection of a number of frame dwellings, which sprang up rapidly.

These erections were for the most part of the plainest description, and even fifty years later were but little better. They consisted, as a rule, of two rooms, built over one another, with a fire-place of stone, and single door and a window in each room. The roof was not shingled, but was most generally covered in by thatching with straw.

With the advent of William Kieft, the third Governor, in 1638, various improvements in the structures of the city were made, and chief among them the erection inside the fort of a new church, the old wooden one having by this time fallen into decay. This building was of stone and cost $1000, in those days not an inconsiderable sum.

In 1656 the inhabitants of the city numbered about one thousand persons, occupying some one hundred and thirty houses, while in 1664, when the Duke of York acquired the city, it had increased to probably five or six times that number. The description of the dwellings at this time was distinctly modest and unpretentious but comfortable and convenient. Invariably they were erected on the plan of the Dutch in the Old World, with a surrounding garden large enough to accommodate a cow, a horse, and, perhaps, a few other animals, and with the interior fitted with the cheerful and capacious fireplaces, sometimes built in a corner but more often occupying the most prominent of the walls of the apartment.

From a description of the city in 1708 we learn that most of the houses were of timber, while a number were of brick and others of stone. The extent of the city at that time can be gathered from the fact that there were nine places devoted to the exclusive use of public worship.

The style of building in the more important brick structures was frequently to form a gable on the front wall, with stepped or turreted sides in the old Dutch style. The roofs of these buildings were very highly pitched, and were often formed on the inside into two or more floors, which were lighted by a series of dormers.

It was a peculiarity that the brick buildings were often checkered or ornamented on the face by patterns of darker bricks than the remainder of the wall. This arose from the fact that these early brick makers wasted none of their bricks, those burning black being utilized in the manner described for forming ornaments. An old Dutch house of the kind built in 1626 and rebuilt 1697, stood on Pearl Street until 1828, when it was demolished.

And so the growth of the city went on, increasing rapidly year by year, finer and better buildings being erected as time past. In 1742 was erected the Washington Hotel, a fine building at the foot of Broadway, which formed the residence of Sir William Howe and other eminent men connected with the history of the city. The first theater was opened in 1761, and in 1764 Sandy Hook was first provided with a lighthouse.

We can now pass over the intervening years, during which the growth of the city steadily increased, until we come to the period of the beginning of

SEVENTH REGIMENT ARMORY.

the present century. Certainly the most important building erected during that decade was the present existing City Hall, of which a fine engraving will be found on page 343. This building was commenced in the year 1803 and completed 1812. It was originally placed in a fine and extensive park, well planted with trees. This has now been considerably diminished in size. It is two hundred and sixteen feet in length, one hundred and five feet in breadth, and fifty-one feet high. It cost five hundred and fifty thousand dollars, and undoubtedly reflects great credit upon its originators. The building consists of two stories, in addition to basement and attic floors, and contains the Mayor's office, the City Library, the chamber of the Common Council, and various other offices of the city authorities.

The style of architecture is the Italian in one of its purest forms; the classical Ionic and Corinthian orders being employed with much good judg-

UNITED BANK BUILDING. BROADWAY AND WALL STREET.

ment. On the exterior the building has an imposing appearance, notwithstanding the number of lofty and important erections by which it is surrounded, and which would tend, in a building less perfectly designed, to considerably impair its beauty. The walls on three sides are erected entirely of white marble, brought from the quarries in Stockbridge, Mass., and on the remaining side of brown stone. A cupola, containing a four-dial clock, surmounts the building, and adds much to its appearance.

The first edifice answering the purpose of a City Hall was erected in 1642. It was built of bricks imported from Holland, and had a high pitched roof, studded with small dormer windows, and covered in with heavy flat tiles. The second town hall was completed about 1700. The location of this hall was on the northern end of Broad Street, at that time quite a central position.

The great fire of 1776 greatly damaged the structure, and a new roof and other reparations had to be carried out. The covering for the roof was slate, and this is probably the first building in the city on which that material was used for the purpose.

The extent of the city increased rapidly, and we now make a halt at the year 1832, and look around and take a glance at the city at that day. Broadway was built upon up to about Union Square, with some few residential edifices above it. In it were St. Paul's, Grace and Trinity Churches, and the old Masonic Hall, then recently erected near Duane Street. This building was of granite and occupied an area of fifty-seven feet by ninety feet. The large hall was exclusively used for the purpose of meetings, and was the most expansive in the city.

Nearly opposite this building was the New York Hospital, bounded by Broadway, Church Street and Duane Street. It was set back from the main thoroughfare, and had in front an avenue planted with trees. The extent of the building was four hundred and fifty feet by four hundred and forty feet in breadth; and the main structure, erected in light brown stone, was one hundred and thirty-six feet by fifty feet.

On Wall Street the most important buildings was the Merchants' Exchange, now used for the Custom House, and a number of banks and insurance offices, comparatively few of which remain. There were also to be found several shops mostly two stories high, painted in light tints and very cheerful in appearance. On Beekman Street was the important Clinton Hall, an edifice comprising a large mercantile library, reading room, and an apartment for the exhibition of works of art. This was erected in 1829.

There were five theaters in the city, of which the principal were the Park, located close to the City Hall, and erected in 1820, and the American Theater. Of the favorite open spaces were the Battery, Washington Square, Union Place (now Union Square), Clinton Square, and others. The material used in building was even at this late date largely of brick, although with the increased facilities for the transportation of material, stone was becoming more extensively employed. The architecture generally, was, as a rule, solid and substantial, if somewhat plain. Brick fronts with semi-circular or segmental arches over the doors and windows, and perhaps a brick pediment on the main entrance, comprised the extent of the greater portion of the residences, although in the more extensive erections stone was largely used.

Coming now to the year 1866, we find that several very important and handsome buildings had been erected during that interval. Among these a few of the principal ones may be mentioned. Foremost among them was the

Astor Library on Lafayette Place, a building of sufficient excellence in design to be a conspicuous ornament to the city at this day. The library was erected in the Romanesque style of architecture in brick, with a brown stone front up to the top of the first story, and brown stone trimmings above. During the past few years an addition has been made of an extra wing sixty-five feet by one hundred feet. Through the generosity of the Astor family, this library is now one of the finest in the world, comprising some two hundred thousand volumes, many of them of great value.

The familiar Mercantile Library building, on Astor Place and Eighth Street, was erected previous to this period. The style cannot be looked upon as indicating the general architecture then prevalent. Another of the familiar buildings erected about this time was the edifice occupied by the institution founded by Peter Cooper. It covers an entire block on Seventh Street and Fourth Avenue, and was erected at a cost of six hundred and fifty thousand dollars. The building is of a massive, if somewhat plain exterior, and has recently undergone extensive alterations and structural additions. The institution provides for the free education of the working classes in sciences and arts, and includes an extensive library and reading room. The founder has added a sum of one hundred and fifty thousand dollars to the amount originally expended upon the building,

NEW JEFFERSON MARKET COURT HOUSE.

and has devoted by a deed of trust the complete institution, with all its income derived from rents, issues and profits, to the public.

The present new Produce Exchange has been declared to be one of the finest buildings of its class in the world. The building stands in Whitehall Street, facing Bowling Green, and was built on the site of some old brown stone houses which it was at first endeavored to convert into a suitable building. The walls are constructed of red brick, ornamented and embellished with terra cotta trimmings, and are erected upon a series of wooden piles, necessitated by the weak nature of the soil. The style of architecture adopted is the Italian Renaissance, and the building, which is three hundred and seven feet long, and one hundred and fifty broad, has a handsome clock tower two hundred feet high. In the interior is a fine hall, used for the purposes of the assocition, which measures two hundred and fifteen feet long, and one hundred and thirty-four feet wide. Of important buildings erected at later periods, we have a large number of great interest.

Foremost among the buildings devoted to ecclesiastical purposes in the city is that of St. Patrick's Cathedral. It is in the decorated or geometrical style of Gothic architecture, and is being erected—for it will probably be several years to come before it is finished— from the designs and under the superintendance of James Renwick, architect. This building, which was commenced in 1858, is one of the finest erections in America, and presents a magnificent appearance. Its cost when finished is calculated will amount to about $2,500,000.

POTTER BUILDING. PARK ROW AND BEEKMAN STREET.

Trinity Church on Broadway, nearly facing Wall Street, was completed in 1846. It stands upon the site of a church erected in 1697 and of others completed afterward. It is admirably located, with an open space surrounding it, and is a very handsome structure. The walls are built of brown stone, and there are fine stained-glass windows and a reredos of considerable artistic beauty. In the churchyard is a monument erected in brown stone by the Trinity Corporation in connection with the war of the Revolution.

MILLS BUILDING. EXCHANGE PLACE AND BROAD STREET.

Another familiar church to the New Yorker is Grace Church on Broadway and Tenth Street. This is a very fine building, erected in 1842 in the Gothic style in white granite and freestone. Various additions have been made to it in the shape of minor buildings in connection from time to time, and lastly, a new stone spire has been placed upon it. The interior is elaborately and beautifully carved work. The position of the church is an excellent one, making it conspicuous for some miles down Broadway.

The Fifth Avenue Presbyterian Church, or as it is sometimes termed, Dr. John Hall's Church, is a fine building, measuring 200 feet by 100 feet, and 60 feet high. Two towers, each 100 feet in height, form striking features, and are utilized for the purposes of ventilation. M. Carl Pfeiffer was the architect of the church, which it has been stated is the most perfectly ventilated building in the city. This is effected by admitting the fresh air into the basement and passing it over pipes attached to the ceiling. It is then admitted to each pew in the church as required, being regulated by the occupant. In the tower are revolved large fans which assist in expelling the vitiated air. In the warm weather ice is substituted for the coil of pipes, and thus the air is admitted into the church at any degree of heat required.

St. Paul's Church, built in 1766, is of great interest, as being the oldest church in the city. Among the modern buildings of this description may be mentioned St. Thomas's, on the corner of Fifth Avenue and Fifty-third Street and the Presbyterian Church-on the same avenue on the corner of Fifty-fifth Street.

If any person familiar with New York was asked to name the best-known and most conspicuous building in the city, he would have little difficulty in deciding upon the new buildings of the Post-Office. Located immediately opposite the City Hall, and in the very center of the commercial portion of the city, it is now familiar to the sight of thousands as a beautiful and convenient edifice.

This building was completed in 1875, and certainly forms a magnificent pile, of which New Yorkers may well be proud. It stands upon a quadrangular piece of land, which has a frontage of 340 feet on Broadway, and of 290 feet on the North side. In its construction no wood whatever has been employed, iron, stone, brick and cement chiefly composing it. The style is Renaissance based upon the Doric order, and the manner in which the general design has been worked out is very pleasing, as giving the appearance of exceptional solidity, with a grace and well-considered effect that is to be much commended.

The Grand Central Depot, on Forty-second Street and Madison Avenue, was built by the New York and Harlem and the New Haven Roads at a cost of $2,250,000. It measures 695 feet long, and is 240 feet broad, and covers 61 city lots. It admits 150 cars, and includes waiting rooms and the company's offices. The building is erected in red brick, with trimmings of a light-brown stone.

The Masonic Building, on the corner of Twenty-third Street and Sixth Avenue, was erected by the designs of Architect Le Brun. It is five stories high, and has a large Mansard roof rising 155 feet above the sidewalk. The style of the architecture is classical, somewhat severely treated, but the building is essentially a beautiful one of a solid and massive appearance.

It is probable that the present Custom House, located on Wall Street, will not be much longer used for that purpose. With the commercial growth of the city it has become quite inadequate in size, so that it is very probable that a new building will soon be erected. It was formerly the Merchant's Exchange, and consists of a massive pile, chiefly of Quincy granite. A portico runs the whole length of the front, supported by eighteen columns, each of which is 38 feet in height and 4½ feet in diameter. A flat roof and rotunda cover in the building, the latter being borne by a number of fine pillars of solid Italian variegated marble.

On the block bounded by Centre, Elm, Franklin and Leonard Streets, and occupying a space of 200 feet by 253 feet, is the City Prison, or as it is generally termed, "The Tombs." This building is a most striking one from the unfamiliar style of its architecture, which is a pure example of the Egyptian style of the most severe type. As a building it is of great interest, but, although it has from time to time been much praised from the purity of design, it is doubtful whether the style, rigid, stiff and severe as it is, could be carried out again with advantage, or whether it accords with the prevailing idea of the fitness of things.

One of the most conspicuous features of the architecture of the city are the numerous large blocks of offices erected in the lower portion of the city. Illustrations of several of the most important of these are included in these pages. As a typical example, the block known as Mill's Building on Wall Street may be taken. This building was

STEWART MANSION. 5TH AVENUE AND 34TH STREET.

completed in 1882 from the designs of Architect George B. Post. It is nine stories in height, exclusive of the basement, which is used as a cellarage. On the first story is a large entrance-hall, lighted from the roof, which also lights a single staircase constructed of wrought iron, with slate treads and landings.

It is characteristic of this purely modern description of construction, that the staircase should be very small, compared to the size of the building and the number of occupants. The reason of this is that nearly the whole of the traffic is conducted by elevators, which are kept running throughout the day. Here, in Mill's Building, there are kept four elevators running at the same time, so that persons wishing to ascend or descend are at the most only kept waiting a few moments.

Columbia College was founded in 1752, and occupied a building erected in

1756 on the block now occupied within Murray, Church and Barclay Streets. The present building on Forty-ninth Street was originally erected for an institution for the deaf and dumb, and was fitted up for the purposes of the college in 1857. Previously the buildings were located on the west side of Park Place, quite near to the City Hall.

Since the year 1866 the real architectural history of the city has commenced; but as the period is so recent, most of the buildings erected stand to-day, so that a description of the principal of them, with the dates of their erection, will prove of interest, and will indicate the extent of the development.

The magnificent mansion erected by the late A. T. Stewart, on the corner of Thirty-fourth Street and Fifth Avenue, is one of the most complete and beautiful residences of the city. Its style of architecture and general concep-

RESIDENCE OF MR. GEORGE VANDERBILT. 5TH AVENUE AND 50TH STREET.

tion in design is exceedingly striking, carried out as it is, entirely in white marble. The interior is beautifully decorated, and the whole residence, which is said to have cost no less than two million dollars, is one the finest in America. Since the death of Mrs. Stewart it has been proposed by the authorities to purchase this building for the purposes of a headquarters for the municipal government.

On other pages we give engravings of the residences of the Vanderbilt family on Fifth Avenue. Of these fine residences there are four, that on the corner of Fifty-first Street being built of brown stone, elaborately treated.

The Lenox Library is a fine building, located near Fifth Avenue on Seventieth Street, and cost to build and furnish nearly one million dollars. The main portion is set back from the road, and there is an extending wing on each side enclosing a space in front. The material used in its construction is white marble, and the style of architecture is classical, treated somewhat freely. The building was first opened in 1877, and contains a unique collection of valuable literature, including a large number of Shakesperian works.

Perhaps the most important structure devoted to educational purposes in the city is the fine Gothic building of the Normal College on Sixty-ninth

MR. CORNELIUS VANDERBILT'S RESIDENCE. 5TH AVENUE AND 57TH STREET.

Street. It is three hundred feet long and one hundred and twenty-five wide, and contains accommodation for fifteen hundred pupils.

The present New York Hospital is located on Fifteenth Street, between Fifth and Sixth Avenues, and was opened in 1876. It forms a most striking erection, six stories high, with a large projecting portion in the center, and a prominent high pitched roof. The whole building is admirably conceived to admit light, air and sunshine, and the ventilation and heating of the building are as nearly perfect as may be. Twenty large windows are placed on each of the upper floors, without counting those in the central projection. The approach to the building is through the main entrance hall in the center, which is one of an imposing size and appearance.

Perhaps the most marked feature of the new architecture, as compared to the old, is in the erection of the apartment houses throughout the city. Broadly

HOUSE OF MR. WILLIAM K. VANDERBILT. 5TH AVENUE AND 51ST STREET.

speaking, they may be said to have been erected on about the same lines. There is generally a large main entrance-hall, with a courtyard at the back, which, in the better class of them, is covered in with glass.

This description of house is rented off in suites of apartments, and the rents paid are often extremely high, being not unfrequently placed at auction, they become so valuable. The Osborne Flats, illustrated on another page, is a typical example of a building of this character. The building is twelve stories high, and ranks among the highest of its class in the world.

Among others of these remarkable structures, which so characterize the residential part of the city, are the "Spanish Flats," located in a fine position opposite Central Park on Fifty-ninth Street and Seventh Avenue. These consist of three enormous buildings built in one block, each being nine stories in height. The architect has dealt with the difficult problem which high buildings present in the elevation in a remarkably successful manner, and has produced a pile of much beauty and attractiveness. This has been effected by breaking up the front with recessed and arched spaces, in forming balconies, bays and oriel windows, and in placing bold turrets on the opposite corners of the building.

The Gramercy, on Gramercy Park, the Chelsea, on Twenty-third Street, and the "Dakota," on Eighth Avenue and Seventy-second Street, are other fine buildings of the same class.

But beyond these examples of the more spacious erections of the apartment house description of dwelling, there are a number of other very fine buildings of the same class distributed throughout the city, and although space will not permit of more particular mention here, they form prominent and notable features in the architecture of New York city.

Then we have other forms of the same order of dwelling, comprised and included in the terse phrase of "flats." It was in the year 1878 that the first dwelling of this description was erected in New York city. The notion of this manner of living was probably borrowed to a great extent from the French, many of whom have lived in houses or flats for the past two or three centuries. At the time of its introduction, the idea was quickly caught on, and what amounted almost to a craze for building flats became apparent, as may be witnessed by the large number of such buildings at the present time existing, and all of which have been erected during the past few years.

Many arguments have been presented, pro and con, as to the advantages of such buildings, but it is probable that the scheme has reached its culmination, for it is more generally understood now what serious disadvantages there are attending such a system of living.

Not the least among the ... s that of the danger attending a conflagration, and although happily the actual loss of life in such buildings in past years has not been large, it cannot be denied that the fact is almost entirely due to efficiency of our fire and hook and ladder companies.

Taking cases where loss of life has been occasioned, a single case may be mentioned which occurred in March, 1883. This was a fire in which two lives were lost. It was one of the description of buildings generally known as a tenement house, and the usual fire escapes fixed to the building were provided.

The law on the subject of fire escapes, as amended by the Act passed June 5, 1885, in all dwellings, says:

"All dwelling houses now erected, or that may hereafter be erected, more than two stories in height, occupied or to be occupied by two or more families, on any floor above the first, and all buildings already erected more than three stories in height, occupied or used as a hotel, boarding or lodging house, or any factory, mill, offices, manufactory or workshop, shall be provided with such good and sufficient fire-escapes, or other means of egress in case of fire, as shall be directed by the Superintendent of Buildings, and said Superintendent shall direct such means of egress to be provided in all cases."

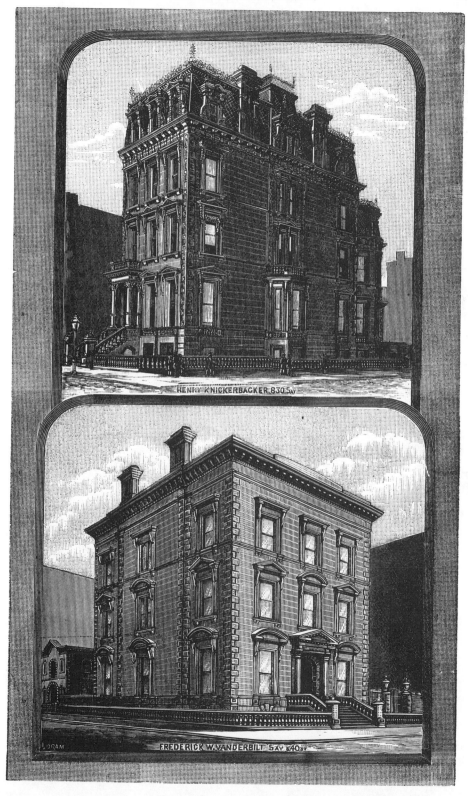

HENRY KNICKERBACKER, 830 5ᴬᵛ

FREDERICK W. VANDERBILT, 5ᴬᵛ & 40ˢᵀ

In the building referred to, fire-escapes were duly provided, and yet two lives were lost. It should not be forgotten that such means of escape being special, are to a very great extent unfamiliar to the persons who have to use them, so that on a fire occurring, they are often little better than useless. There is a provision in the same Act, as that from which the above extract was taken, to the effect that all these fire-escapes shall be kept clear and free from obstructions. Among the lower class of tenants the custom is largely prevalent of using them as convenient store places, and unless the

MR. OGDEN GOELET'S HOUSE; NO. 608 5TH AVENUE.

janitor or other person in charge is very vigilant, they soon become crowded and therefore wholly unfit for use. The danger of such habits is sufficiently obvious, and is well illustrated by the case above mentioned.

Since the years 1879-80 the construction of all apartment houses has been regulated by the Board of Health, and although many of them as at present erected leave much to be desired, the improvement upon the style at first adopted is considerable and undoubted.

As showing the height of perfection which some of the dwellings of these days have reached, the subject of electric lighting may be referred to in connection with the illumination of streets and for domestic purposes. Previous to the year 1761, the lighting of the public streets of New York was not attempted at all in any systematic manner, although lanterns were fixed at a few of the more important points in the city. It was the custom for some of the generous-hearted inhabitants to place lights in their windows for the purpose of enabling pedestrians to find their way.

RESIDENCE OF MR. A. M. HOYT 934 5TH AVENUE.

The house of Mr. A. M. Hoyt, which was erected by Mr. Hoyt in 1882—1883, is thoroughly fire-proof, built of brick, and with iron beams and partitions all through with brick. The style is old Colonial and finished in hard wood.

In about the year 1761 provision was made by the authorities to light the streets by means of oil lamps at the public expense. These were usually fixed on iron or wooden brackets projecting from the walls. The appearance of the streets at that day must have been peculiar in the extreme. The low-framed dwellings with their overhanging gables, and the more important brick structures with the characteristic feature of the Dutch style in the turreted or stepped gables, dimly lighted by the oil-lamps placed few and far between, forms a striking contrast with their present condition.

In the year 1825 gas was first employed in the city, when the house No. 7 Cherry Street, then a fashionable locality, was fitted with it at a cost of $10

DR. WHITE'S HOUSE: S. E. CORNER 66TH STREET AND 5TH AVENUE.

per 1,000 feet. A few years afterward it became generally employed for street illumination, and gas mains were laid down in some of the principal streets. This steadily progressed, as required by the growth of the city, until a special provision was made by the Board of Aldermen for lighting the whole of the upper portion of the city up to and including the extensive district to Yorkville, Manhattanville, Harlem and Washington Heights.

But of recent years the science of electricity has made a very rapid advance, and the electric lights have become to be used in preference to any other. The beautiful clear, white light in all sections of the city is now one of the most striking sights which meet the eye of a stranger entering New York for the first time.

Electric lights for street illumination in the city are so far all of the " arc " description, or those in which candles of carbon are employed, in contradiction to the lamps in which the light emanates from an incandescent wire. Almost without exception the power from which the light is obtained is derived from engines turning enormous dynamos located at various convenient stations throughout the city. The plan of sub-letting lights by the company to stores, factories, dwelling-houses and other buildings on the route is very successfully worked, a shunt wire being taken from the main cable as required. Other of the large factories and stores have their own electric plant upon the premises.

It has already been pointed out how largely the efficiency of the fire department, as at present constituted, depends upon electricity to aid it. The systems of signalling the fire alarms, and the other important adjuncts, depend almost wholly for their efficiency upon electricity, while for lighting purposes it is becoming more generally employed day by day.

In private dwellings the electric system of lighting by incandescent lamps has become very popular, although, of course, the cost of fitting and maintaining the apparatus precludes its general employment.

There is certainly one private dwelling-house which has a complete set of electric plant upon the premises, and this is in East Thirty-sixth Street at the house No. 139. There electricity is employed not only for producing the light for illuminating purposes, but for various labor-saving appliances, for assisting in the decoration and as a protection to the house, in providing safeguards against burglars, and in other ways. The owner and occupier of the house is himself a practical electrician, and the apparatus are exceedingly ingenious and probably unique in their way.

For lighting purposes, specially designed chandeliers are provided, fitted with small incandescent lamps, which have a remarkably pretty appearance and answer admirably the purpose of illumination. The arms of the chandeliers are formed to represent flowers, and the globes are tinted. In the hall is fitted a lamp of a somewhat similar kind, and an apparatus is provided by which this lamp is automatically lighted late at night when the remainder of the house is in darkness. This is effected by opening the hall-door. On an upper floor is provided a switch to turn off the light, so that on a person coming home late after the people in the house have retired for the night, he is enabled to light the hall lamp by opening the front door, and to turn it out when he gets up-stairs.

In every room of this house is fitted an automatic fire alarm, by which an alarm-bell is caused to ring when the temperature rises above 110°, so that the risk of the building being burned down is very slight. Burglar alarms are fitted to every window, and are of a peculiar kind. They consist of simple mechanism, on the adjustment of which every electric lamp in the house is lighted when a window is opened.

Most of the larger buildings throughout the city are protected in the same way by automatic fire alarms being placed in positions where a high temperature will operate on the mechanism, and making electrical contact will send an alarm to the station. Other apparatus of the kind are provided in which there is, in addition to the mechanism for sending the alarm, an ap-

CHAS. CROCKER. Nº 4 W. 58. ST.

ELLIOTT. F. SHEPARD Nº 2 W. 52. ST.

pliance whereby a stream of water is turned on at the same time. For the most part all these fire alarms are exceedingly effective for they send the signal at the most important time, when the fire is only in its incipient stage, and when efforts to subdue and extinguish are of much more value than when it has once obtained a fair hold on the building.

The subject of the construction of the buildings of New York city to resist the action of fire, is an interesting and important one. As it has already been shown, the city has suffered from at least three great conflagrations, the ex-

HOUSE OF H. H. COOK. 5TH AVENUE, BETWEEN 78TH AND 79TH STREETS.

tent of which was sufficient to destroy property valued in the aggregate at $36,000,000. Then, in addition, there are the innumerable smaller fires, of more or less extent, which bring the value of property destroyed up to a very high total.

Many of the larger buildings are specially designed and constructed to render them fire-proof; but it must be remembered that no material can be absolutely fire-proof, and hence such buildings are at the best only safeguards of a desperate description.

As a rule, iron and brick play the most important part in the construction of this description of fabric. It is well understood, however, by firemen how little reliance is to be placed upon iron during a burning of a building, and it has often been remarked that they will go into a wooden building at such a time without hesitation, while in the case of an iron construction, they will show far greater reluctance.

Wood, then, although appearing at the first flush to be essentially a combustible material, really forms, under some circumstances, a good material to prevent the spread of fire. A system of this kind, patented a few years back, may be here referred to as being substantially what is required in the erection of the less important of our structures. The objection to the use of fire-proof floors, as ordinarily built is, that the iron which usually forms the framework of the construction bends or breaks when subjected to an intense heat.

In this system, instead of building in joists or beams, twelve or sixteen inches apart in the ordinary way, they are placed close together side by side, and are firmly connected by iron spikes. This forms what is practically a solid piece of timber, some nine inches deep, according to the depth of the floor, and is finished underneath with a plastered ceiling in the ordinary manner. As the inventor points out, it would take longer and require a greater heat to burn through a solid piece of timber of this depth, than it would to completely injure, if not destroy, many of the floors constructed in the ordinary way of iron.

The objection to placing the floor joists and the timbers of flat roofs apart, is that it gives rise to a current of air between them, and to prevent such a draft, sheet iron is in some systems of building fixed between them.

Of course the wood construction is a special one, and only applicable and useful in the smaller description of buildings. Brick or burnt clay is probably the best description of fire-proof material in existence. Stone is not to be relied upon, with few exceptions. If it be granite it will freely crack and splinter under the influence of extreme heat, while if it be limestone, either in the form of marble or in the softer varieties, it will be quickly changed to lime.

The most successful forms of fire-proof floors are those which consist of iron joists or beams supporting arches of brick between them. The iron is protected by a thick covering of fire-clay or concrete, and the supporting iron columns are shielded in the same manner. Where this is done, and the party or divisional walls are of sufficient width and are constructed of brick, a building is rendered as nearly fire-proof as may be.

Among the special aids for the prevention of fire are the use of abestos, fire-proof paint and other materials. In the case of theaters the law compels the owner to saturate with some approved non-combustible material all the stage scenery, curtains, decoration and woodwork on or about the stage.

It has been pointed out with reason that comparing New York to a city like London, there are many more great fires in the former than the latter. In a paper printed in the *Forum*, Commissioner Henry D. Purroy shows very clearly to what this is due. The principal reason is the humidity of the atmosphere in London, which is very uniform, and on the average lacks only 18 per cent. of complete saturation. This wetness, naturally, prevents wood from easily catching light, and is a most important aid in the prevention of fire. In New York the atmosphere is on the average considerably less moist, and the woodwork correspondingly drier. Then a second cause is the difference in temperature in the two cities during the winter months. When the thermometer lowers, the number of domestic fires and extent of artificial heating is greater and the liability of fire increased. London is 6.68 degrees warmer in the winter than New York, and it will be seen how far that lessens the liability of conflagrations.

A further important cause is the density of population, which is about 40 per cent. higher in New York than in the most crowded parts of England's metropolis. The style of the buildings, the great extent and height of them, and the large quantity of timber employed in their construction, added to the many old timber dwellings still standing, render the fact of the liability of a fire taking place here much more likely than in London.

RESIDENCE OF C. A. POSTLEY. CORNER 63D STREET AND 5TH AVENUE.

The splendid system and organization of the Fire Department, however, ensures that, notwithstanding these facts, the loss of property by fire is undoubtedly and emphatically kept at a minimum.

The various appliances in use for preventing the spread of fires are many. In large buildings the danger of fire increasing is very great, chiefly from the great impetus they attain by the extent of combustible material. To lessen this danger a special provision is made in the local building laws, which provides that iron doors of a suitable thickness shall be placed in proper positions to divide a building up into sections. Such doors are closed every night, and are so constructed that on a fire occurring during the day they may be readily shut. In this way is the fire confined to the portion of a large building where it broke out.

One of the most fruitful sources of the rapid spread of fire is the modern method of building in this city, which gives rise to a considerable number of large or smaller vertical shafts. A fire occurring at the bottom of such a shaft may very quickly reach the top of the building, as the shaft promotes a draught. In the enormous number of apartment houses built throughout the city this danger is perhaps the greatest of any. The peculiar arrangement of the rooms necessitated by the high price of land and the consequent desire to get as much as possible on to it gives rise to air shafts from top to bottom of the building. Sometimes there are two, but oftener several, and, as pointed out, the danger is great. Then there are the numerous shafts for dumb waiters and elevators, which increase the danger from the same source.

In the larger buildings, as those numerous ones found in the lower portions of the city, special construction is provided to lessen this danger. These usually consist of iron or other screens, which may be readily drawn across the shaft at night, and any other time when necessary.

The City of New York now comprises an area of forty-one and one-half

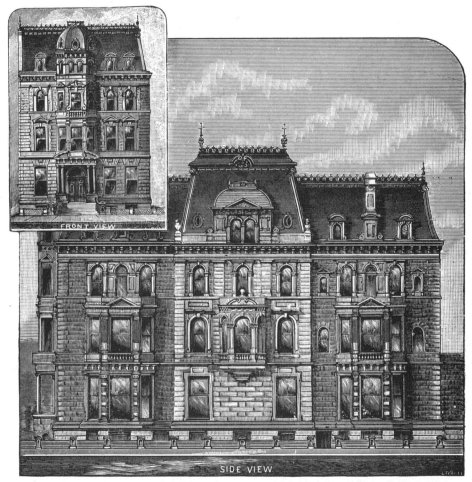

HOME OF MRS. ROBERT L. STUART. NO. 871 5TH AVENUE.

square miles, or twenty-six thousand acres, and includes the whole of Manhattan Island, and various of the smaller islands, in the East River and in the Bay. Its northern limit is Yonkers, and on the remaining three sides it is bounded by water—the East and the Hudson Rivers; and on the south the grand New York Bay, to which is to a great extent probably due its great and rapid growth.

The lower portion of the city is very densely populated, and the whole of the island, from the Battery up to High Bridge—a distance of nearly fifteen miles—is well covered with habitations. Building operations are being carried on to a very considerable extent, and especially in that portion of the city above Fifty-ninth Street.

Comparing its population and extent of dwellings with the greatest Metropolis of the world—London—it will be found that in the portion of the city south of Fortieth Street it is more thickly populated. Thus, taking the last census in 1880, we find that in New York there was a population of eight

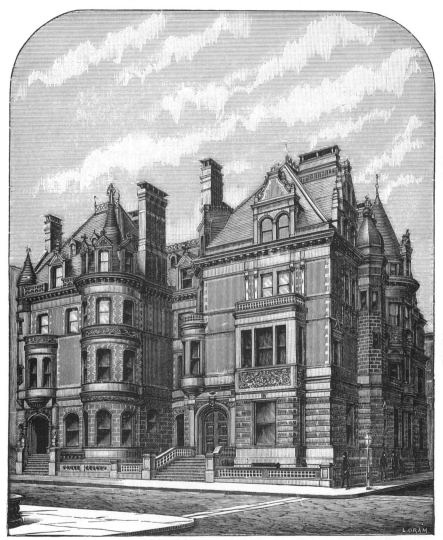

DR. S. W. WEBB.
NO. 680 5TH AVENUE.

MR. H. McK. TWOMBLY.
NO. 684 5TH AVENUE.

hundred and thirteen thousand and seventy-six persons, and seventy-three thousand six hundred and eighty-four dwellings, in the district bounded by Fortieth Street and the East and Hudson Rivers, or 16.37 persons on the average to each building.

Taking London as being comprised within the district measuring one hundred and twenty-two square miles, that is, excluding the more suburban districts, we have a population of three million eight hundred and fourteen thousand five hundred and seventy-four persons, and five hundred and twenty-eight thousand seven hundred and ninety-four houses, or 7.21 per dwelling, against 16.37 in this city.

Of course, the American style of living to a great extent in flats and apartment houses, gives rise to these figures, but the bearing they have upon the likelihood of conflagrations is important. It is probable, too, that if a smaller section of the city were taken, comprised in the smaller tenement-house districts, the figures given above would be much higher.

Within the past few years was made an innovation of great importance to

MR. C. L. TIFFANY. MADISON AVENUE AND 72ND STREET.

New York City in the shape of the four lines of elevated railroads. The system is admirable in its practical usefulness to the traveling public, although its effect upon the architectural beauty of the city, and upon the fine avenues it overshadows, is very serious. It is safe to say that in no country in the world outside of America would personal rights to property, and the artistic beauty of a city, be allowed to be so largely interfered with as they are by these railways. Still it is now an accomplished fact, and of inestimable advantage in traveling. The only pity was that some other and better system—such as an underground railway, for instance—was not found to accomplish the same result.

The road is purely and entirely a work of the engineer, and no attempt whatever has been made to render the road ornamental or pleasing to the eye beyond the most meagre description at the stations. Considering the harm it did to the appearance of the city, the buildings it hid, and the conspicuous position of it, one would have thought that a graceful and ornamental appearance would have been aimed at. This would not have been difficult. A series of interlaced arches, spaced up and forming arcades, would have made the structure much less an eyesore than it is at present. Still it is useful, eminently so, and there the matter ends.

The first of the elevated roads erected was a small experimental piece, commenced in 1868, on Greenwich Street. This was about half a mile long, and remained until 1873, when it was carried on up to Thirtieth Street. In 1876 it was extended to Sixty-first Street and to the Battery. The Sixth Avenue line was built up to Fifty-ninth Street in 1878, and was afterward extended to One Hundred and Fifty-fifth Street. During 1878 the railroad along Third Avenue was erected, and in the following year the Second Avenue.

This bold and original engineering scheme represents an investment of over $43,000,000. The height above the roadway is 14 feet at the lowest parts, but in many portions considerably exceeds that height. The high viaduct above Central Park is 45 feet high, and at Eighth Avenue and One Hundred and Tenth Street the road is 59 feet above the sidewalk. The foundations used for the upright pillars upon which the whole structure is erected, extend in some cases to the great depth of 36 feet below the surface. Thus, the total depth from top to bottom of the structure at these points is 95 feet.

The extent of the materials required in its erection can be gathered from the fact that in the West Side extension from Eighty-third Street to the Harlem River, and having a length of about four miles, there were 16,200 tons of iron required. The cost of the foundations for the high pillars reached the high sum of $200,000 a mile, so that it can be easily understood that the erection of the railroad was a very costly undertaking.

The elevated roads, although of so considerable an advantage, do not meet the growing requirements of the traffic. With the enormous increase in the size of the city, a quicker system is needed, and various schemes have been put forth to solve the problem which has arisen. Among these is a system of underground railroads, and this will be the one which will most probably prove most acceptable to the public in general.

An improvement in the same direction will probably take place in the system of traffic outside the elevated roads.

Within the next ten to twenty years it is not improbable that tunnels will be found beneath the North and East Rivers, connecting all the railroads at one central depot underneath the ground. Goods could then be forwarded by being placed directly on to the tracks by means of shafts and elevators placed upon the line of tracks at suitable intervals, and the saving of time and advantage is obviously great.

An account of New York City would be incomplete without some mention of the great bridge connecting New York with Brooklyn, a piece of work which is without doubt unequaled anywhere throughout the world.

For a number of years the idea of building a bridge across the East River to connect the two cities was entertained by the more enthusiastic of our engineers, but for a long time it was thought to be impracticable. In the year 1867, however, a scheme became matured and was made of practical effect by being incorporated by the New York Legislature as a company. Various surveys were made and data and opinions collected as to the best site, and

OSBORNE FLATS. 57TH STREET AND 7TH AVENUE.

eventually in 1869 the Brooklyn tower was located, and the complete plans of the work settled and approved by the Secretary of War.

On January 3rd, 1870, work was commenced on the foundations of the tower, and progressed quickly to a completion on May 24th, 1883, when the bridge was opened to the public.

The extent of the structure may be fairly appreciated from the following figures : From anchorage to anchorage it is 2,325 feet long, with an approach 900 feet in length on the Brooklyn side and 1,546 feet on the New York side. The height of the roadway is 119¼ feet above mean high tide, while from the top of the ridge of stone on the Brooklyn tower to the bottom above the foundation is 316 feet. Measuring between corresponding points on the New York tower, the height is 349½ feet. The extent and solidity of these towers are very great. One measures 141 feet by 59 feet, and the other 141 feet by 57 feet. The weight of the Brooklyn tower is 93,079 tons.

The bridge, being a suspension one, the support really depends upon a number of cables, each of which is 15¾ inches in diameter and contains 3,515 miles of wire. A number of other minor wire ropes are extended to form a description of network beneath the cables to assist in the support of the structure.

There are roads for vehicles and a wide footway for passengers, and, in addition, a service of cars operated by moving cables.

The total cost of the structure was $15,337,057, and of this two-thirds were paid by the city of Brooklyn and one-third by the city of New York.

As indicating the extent to which the bridge is used, it may be mentioned that during the year 1886 27,436,707 persons crossed from side to side, of whom 2,965,400 walked.

The style and description of the architecture of a city, will obviously depend largely upon the materials at the command of the builder, and not the least among the reasons to which the fine architecture of the city has reached may be attributed the fact of the facility with which he can get materials of the best kinds.

New York is happily situated for architecture in this respect, as it is by reason of its clear sky and absence of smoke Brick is largely employed for the less important description of buildings, but stone of different varieties— white and variegated marble, brown and blue freestone—are used, often with granite, for a great number of the buildings.

The abundance of timber has had the effect of producing a very excellent system generally in construction. Not only are the roof and floor timbers of the buildings, as a rule, of ample dimensions, but the interior of the houses, even of those making no pretensions to elegance, are generally finished in a very complete manner, and are frequently fitted up in polished walnut or other hard wood. In many of the plain brick houses the stone sills and trimmings are of marble, as suitable and enduring a material as could be obtained.

It is much to be regretted that the general standard of substantiality in construction and materials of the buildings of the city should have been so greatly lowered by the reprehensible practices of forming many of the cornices of sheet-iron, and painting them in imitation of stone. The custom is of comparatively recent date, and considering the abundance of material, and the decided lowering in merit and architectural value of a building, it is surprising that builders should continue to spoil their buildings with such shams.

But as a whole, the architecture of the city is extraordinary in its completeness and elegance, growing at so rapid a pace year by year, that one is lost in wonderment as to where it will end.

CHAPTER LVII.

MISCELLANEOUS FIRE MATTERS.

Improved new Engine Houses.—Description of the New Headquarters' Building.—A Fine Edifice.—The Fire Marshal.—Knowing Horses and Dogs.—Life in the Engine House.—Getting Quickly to a Fire.—Running Risks.—St. George's Flats.

THERE are many interesting things about the New Fire Department which yet remain to be told. Some of them we group together in this chapter under appropriate headings.

RECENT IMPROVEMENTS IN THE ENGINE HOUSES.

It is interesting to note the various steps by which the houses of the old-time Volunteer Fire Department have been developed into the typical house of the present Department. The old-time company partook largely of the nature of a club, and this was evident throughout the building. The front was often of brown stone, richly decorated, the first story always nicely finished, and the second story generally divided into parlors, having woodwork, mantels, and plaster ornaments, such as were to be found in the parlors of the most fashionable dwellings in the city. The present house is more substantially built than the old, but all the glitter is rigidly excluded, and perhaps nothing remains of the old plan but the fact that each must contain a room in the first story for the apparatus.

There were two types of houses in use at the beginning of the present Department, regulated by the size of the lot on which they were built. In the smaller buildings, not having room for the horses outside, they were placed in stalls at the rear of the house and facing the side wall. The larger ones had a separate stable built at the rear of the lot and with an open space or yard intervening between it and the front building. When an alarm came, two sets of wide double doors had to be opened, and the horses crossed this yard before reaching the apparatus. As the value of seconds in reaching a fire began to be appreciated, the horses were gradually removed from the separate stables and located at the rear of the apparatus room, as in the smaller houses above noted.

In 1877 the development of the present house may be said to have begun. The experiment was then tried of extending the first story of one of these old houses to the rear of the lot. In this extension stalls were built along the walls on each side. They were open at each end, and the horses faced towards the front, and when an alarm of fire arrived, no time was, therefore, lost, as formerly, in the horses backing from their stalls and turning around to get to their places. This change was no sooner made than a further improvement suggested itself. Why not put the stalls forward, near the apparatus? This was immediately done, and as the horses would thereby reach the engine quicker than the men could from the story above, the extension was used as a bunk room. Some little time before this the Department commenced substituting sliding front doors for the old folding ones.

The new buildings erected at this time were generally on the same plan, but the stories were made much higher than formerly, and the window area was greatly increased. The second story was used as a sitting room, and in the third story, rear, was placed a drying room and the wardrobes for the men. At the front was a hay and feed room, connecting with the first story by a hay shute, and galvanized iron leaders for the feed, stored in metallic feed boxes. Over the roof were placed a hose tower and a tank room. The fronts were

INCIDENTS IN THE LIFE OF A FIREMAN.

quite simple, built of iron in the first story, and brick and brown stone above, the whole being surmounted by a galvanized iron cornice. Above the roof the towers were unornamented.

On the introduction, a few years ago, of sliding poles between the stories, the first story rear bunk room was no longer required, and this space was made available for apparatus and spare horses. The bunk room was then placed in the second story, and the third story remained as before. Under this arrangement, the upper stories were made longer than previously, and wherever the lot admitted of it, a small rear yard was left. The towers above the roof were also made decorative in galvanized iron, and the fronts elaborated by terra-cotta diaper work over the windows and in the cornice.

When the bunk room was moved to the second story, the desirability of removing the hay and feed room from the third story and throwing it open as a sitting room, became apparent. In the houses, therefore, subsequently built, a shallow fourth story at the front was added, to contain the tank and the hay and feed, and it also supplanted the towers. The drying room was removed to the cellar, thus leaving the third story entirely unencumbered. The addition of this fourth story also improved the external appearance of the houses at an insignificant additional expense. In one of the houses, where space was valuable, it was economized by the introduction of a spiral iron staircase, and this was found to be such an improvement that spiral stairs are now built in the rear of all the new houses.

This is substantially the evolution in the planning of the houses within the last nine years, and further improvements, suggested by the president of the

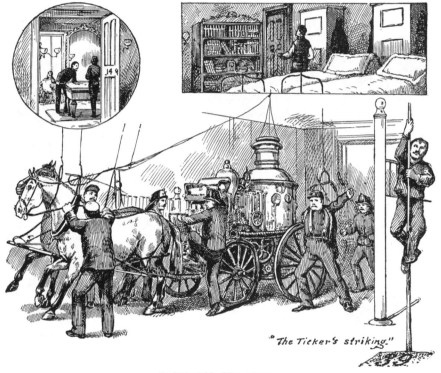

"The Ticker's striking."

EAGER FOR THE FRAY.

department, and greatly increasing the capacity of the houses, is about being made, by introducing a powerful hydraulic elevator at the rear, connecting the cellar with the first story, by which additional reserve engines may be ready for use when required.

In regard to minor details, the change is not less striking. In the interior, the elaborate ornamentation of the old houses has entirely disappeared, and for it has been substituted work of a simple and substantial character far more appropriate. The first story is now, after a series of experiments, entirely lined with wood. The flooring of this story is made like a ship's deck of 3″ × 3″ Georgia pine, all laid edge grain and tightly caulked. The second and third stories are wainscoted, and the fourth story is lined similar to the first. All the woodwork throughout the buildings is varnished. No plaster cornices or ornamented work of any kind is used. In fact, the health and comfort of the men and horses, and the ability to answer an alarm in the shortest possible time, alone governs the planning of the present buildings.

The New Fire Department headquarters, just completed, is situated on the north side of Sixty-seventh Street, west of Third Avenue, and covers a plot of ground fifty by one hundred feet. Before entering the building to see the conveniently arranged offices, we will glance at the front. Although simple in its design, it expresses that dignity and solidity in its construction befitting the home of such an important Municipal Department. The first story is divided into three large openings. The two western ones give access to the quarters of Engine No. 39 and Hook and Ladder No. 16 ; they are framed with iron, the lintels over them being of singular design, decorated with salamander heads. The third opening gives access to the elevator and stairs leading to the general offices of the department. This door is quite elaborate in treatment. On either side are two red Scotch granite columns supporting large carved capitals carrying a decorated arch and pediment. The bases of the columns are decorated with grotesque heads of animals ; on the lintel of the door is a "ribbon moulding," which may stand as an architectural representation of some of the apparatus of the Life Saving Corps, while over the pediment is a flaming torch in stone. The wall surface of this story, as well as the story above, is boldly rusticated. The windows of the stories above all center over these openings. The line of single windows over the eastern door prepares the eye for the tower which soars above the roof, while the continuing of a solid pier over the iron column separating the engine room from that of the truck company, preserves an appearance of solidity of support which might easily have been destroyed by these necessarily large openings. The second story is also divided into three openings; the two western ones having each two heavy stone mullions separating them into three windows. The piers of this story being quite large, the monotony which might otherwise have existed in the simple rustication is avoided by two polished black granite tablets, containing the date of erection, names of the commissioners, the architects, and purposes of the building.

Above this story the building is constructed of brick with stone trimmings, and although the third story is thus constructed of the inferior material—brick—it is here, nevertheless, that the main effect of the front is concentrated, and the passer-by would at once recognize—by the two large windows, each fifteen by eight feet, with their noble stone balconies, enriched with carving and polished black granite balustrades, by the superior enrichment of the third window of this story, and the greater attention paid to carved detail throughout—that here are the apartments of the commissioners. The fourth story is divided into five arched windows, four of them being in pairs. Carving is used sparingly in this story. The story above is divided into seven openings, six of them in two groups of three windows each, with polished black granite columns between them. This story is decidedly more ornate than the one below, which serves as a foil to the rest of the front, and by the increased depth of the jambs, gives shadow to the upper part of the building, and aids the effect of the stone cornice above. This cornice does not run entirely across the front, but stops some thirteen feet from the eastern side, thus marking the tower which starts at the sixth story. Above the cornice is a Mansard roof slated with black slate, and containing two large stone Mansard windows, each of two arched openings, united by a gable containing some

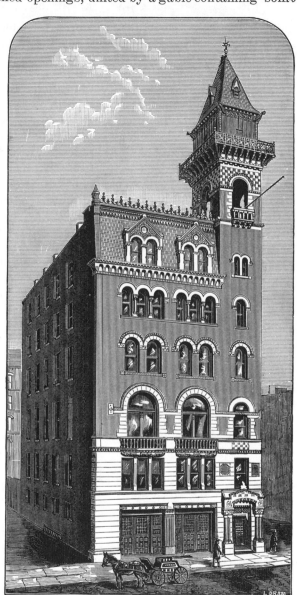

NEW FIRE HEADQUARTERS.
[Otis Brothers' Elevator.]

simple but effective carving. The roof is terminated by a deck-moulding of copper of ornamental design, and having a row of flaming torches. The tower in this story contains two small windows. Above thereof is the belfry story of tower, having a large arched window on each side, through which the bell may be seen from the street below. The front window has a stone balcony, giving an extended view of the city, but the view is not to be compared to the one to be had from the broad iron balcony of the story above, and which runs around the tower and forms the cornice of the belfry story. From here is a noble view of the city and all the surrounding country. Between the brackets of the balcony are boldly projecting stone shields on the four sides of the tower. The lookout story itself is of iron, treated as such, with no attempt to imitate a more valuable material, and surmounted by a slated spire, terminated by a copper finial.

The dimensions of the front are: width, 50 feet; heighth to cresting of Mansard, 101 feet; and to top of spire, 160 feet above the curb. The materials are granite, brown sand stone from Kocher's quarry, Philadelphia brick and iron.

The distribution of the various floors is as follows: in the cellar are placed the boilers, dynamo engines, etc., necessary for heating and lighting the building, etc. The first story is occupied by Engine No. 39 and Hook and Ladder No. 16. The fittings of these quarters are certainly as fine as are to be found anywhere. The walls are wainscotted to a heighth of seven feet with yellow pine, and above are faced with glazed brick. The ceiling is of corrugated iron, with concrete arches above. The floors of the stalls are of artificial stone, and the balance of floors are laid of edge grain Georgia pine, as is usual in the New York fire-houses. The second story is used as bunk rooms for the men, and is finished in ash.

On the third floor the commissioners rooms occupy the entire front. The sliding doors which separate these rooms are so arranged that when desired they can be thrown into one large Board room. The artition dividing them from the large room, for the clerical force, is of oak, paneled to a heighth of seven feet six inches, and glazed with plate glass to the ceiling. On the east side, beyond the staircase and elevator, is a vault for the safe keeping of the records of the department, and still further back the toilet rooms.

The Building Bureau occupies the fourth story; the rooms for the Superintendent and the Attorney being in front, and the rest of the space, with the exception of the portion set apart for toilet rooms, is devoted to the clerks. inspectors, etc., belonging to this branch of the department.

The fifth story front is given to the Bureau of Combustibles, and the balance of the floor to the School of the Life-saving Corps and the Medical Examiner of the department. Spray and other baths are provided here for the use of the life-savers. The rear wall of the building has been built with especial reference to these men, and the rear yard, 50 × 100 feet, is devoted to their use. The larger part of the sixth story is used by the Telegraph Department; the battery room to the rear, and the instrument room and private room of the superintendent to the front. The remainder of this story is used by the Fire Marshal.

The building is constructed of fire-proof materials throughout. The floors are of iron beams, with terra-cotta or brick arches between, and filled up solid with concrete to the under side of the flooring boards. The partitions (with the exception of a few made in cabinet work), are of porous terra-cotta; the two staircases are of iron; even the window frames and sashes are either of iron, or iron coated, to prevent the communication of fire from a conflagration in the neighborhood. The roof is of brick, and the endeavor has been throughout to make a building which, for its purposes, shall be fire-proof.

The building is heated by steam, lit by either gas or electricity, and has a large hydraulic elevator. It was erected from plans and under the superintendence of N. Le Brun & Son, architects for the Department.

NAPOLEON LE BRUN, the well-known architect, was born in Philadelphia, Pennsylvania, in which city at the early age of fifteen he began his professional studies in the office of the distinguished architect of the National Capitol at Washington, Thomas U. Walter.

Mr. Le Brun was barely in his twenty-second year, when, with characteristic energy and industry, he had established a practice of his own, and before two decades had elapsed, had designed and erected under his personal supervision many prominent public and private buildings in his native city and State.

Among the most noted of these public edifices may be mentioned the Cathedral of Philadelphia, the American Academy of Music, the Seventh Presbyterian Church, the Girard Estate Buildings, and several prisons in the interior of Pennsylvania.

About twenty years ago Mr. Le Brun decided to make New York his permanent home. In this city he has erected the Masonic Temple, the New York Foundling Asylum, several large and elegant churches, many of the latest improved engine houses, and the Headquarters of the Fire Department in Sixty-seventh Street, recently finished. He is a Fellow of the American Institute of Architects, and an active member of the New York Chapter of the said Institute, whose representative he is in the Board of Examiners of the Building Bureau of the New York Fire Department.

Mr. Le Brun's long, varied, and practical experience have made his opinion sought for and valued as an expert and adviser in many building enterprises throughout the country.

His strict integrity and conscientious treatment of any subject which he undertakes, are characteristic

SURROGATE DANIEL G. ROLLINS.

traits which distinguish him in a high degree. His two sons inherit these traits as well as his talents, and are following the same profession with honor and success.

ALFRED E. BAKER.

THE FIRE MARSHALS.

The office of Fire Marshal was due to a suggestion of Mr. Alfred E. Baker. In the spring of 1854, while a reporter on the New York *Herald*, he was struck by the number of peculiar fires of doubtful origin, and noticed that the authorities made no efforts to find the cause of them. Mr. Baker had the endorsement of Chief Engineer Carson. The police justices, at the instance of Police Justice Stuart, took the matter in hand, and the Board appointed Mr. Baker their clerk, to investigate the cause of fires, but without pay. The fire insurances raised a fund out of which to remunerate him for his services, and he assumed, and was recognized, by the title of Fire Marshal—a title now used in every city of the United States. One of his first acts was to bring to justice, for the crime of arson, Charles A. Peverilly, for attempting to fire the storage warehouse, No. 147 Front Street.

At the expiration of the first year a meeting was called of insurance companies, and on motion of Mr. George J. Hope, president of the Continental Insurance Company, an increase of subscription was made, creating a fund sufficient to give a better salary to Mr. Baker, and also to employ an assistant, thereby approving the necessity and usefulness of the office. In order to make his investigations as complete as possible, Mr. Baker obtained permission from Chief Carson and the Board of Engineers to wear the uniform of a fireman—red shirt, fire-cap, and fire-coat. The Board of Police Commissioners conferred upon him a sergeant's shield, on which was engraved "Fire Marshal, New York." Mr. Baker continued his successful investigations up to 1868. Legislative action was then taken, instituting a fire marshal, adopting Mr. Baker's title, investing the appointing power in the Board of Police Commissioners.

Police Captain Brackett was made Mr. Baker's successor. Captain Brackett held the office for about two years, but a change of the Police Board caused his removal, and ex-Alderman Thomas McSpeden received the appointment, and while McSpeden was in office the Legislature again took action, placing the appointing power of a fire marshal in the hands of the Board of Fire Commissioners. McSpeden was superseded by Mr. George H. Sheldon.

FRITZ ANDREE.
[Fire Bug.]

The office of Metropolitan Fire Marshal was created by Chapter 563 of the Laws of 1868, and was made part of the police system, the police commissioners having the power of appointment, and the powers and duties of the incumbent extended over the entire Metropolitan District. The title was changed by Chapter 584 of the Laws of 1871—when the Metropolitan District was abolished —to City Fire Marshal, and the duties of the office were confined to the city's limits. The office was abolished by the reform charter of 1873 (Chapter 335, Laws of 1873, Section 117), and the Bureau of the Fire Marshal was created in the Fire Department by Section 769, Chapter 335 of the Laws of 1873, and the power of appointment was vested in the fire commissioners. George H. Sheldon, who succeeded Mr. McSpeden, was appointed fire marshal by Commissioners Perley, Hatch, and Van Cott, on the twenty-first of May, 1873. He still holds the position, and has done the following work:

ARRESTS FOR ARSON, MAY 21, 1873, TO FEBRUARY 1, 1886.

Total number	142	Discharged by magistrates	9
Indicted	130	Cases dismissed by Grand Jury	3

THE INDICTED CASES.

Tried and convicted	61	Tried and used as witnesses	3
Tried and acquitted	11	Died before trial	2

THE SENTENCES.

CAUSES CÉLÉBRES.

On the thirty-first of July, 1873, a fire started in the cellar of No. 2349 Third Avenue, occupied by Rudolph and Fritz Andree, brothers, Andree's wife, a servant girl, and two journeymen barbers. Rudolph and the wife of Fritz were abroad at the time. The journeymen and the servant had narrow escapes, one of the men having to cling to a window sill by his fingers until rescued. Evidences of incendiarism

RUDOLPH ANDREE.
[Fire Bug.]

were found in different parts of the cellar and kitchen, and next day the brothers were arrested and held for examination by the fire marshal by Justice

WIFE OF FRITZ ANDREE.
[Fire Bug.]

McQuade, bail being fixed at two thousand dollars. They found bondsmen and submitted to examination, but were so frightened by the fire marshal's interrogatories that they absconded. A reward of two hundred dollars was offered for their arrest, and postal cards on which were their portraits, were sent to all the cities of the United States. Letters which were intercepted showed that they had fled to London, England, and that they were about to return to Prussia, their native land. The Berlin police was warned, and they arrested the fugitives on the sixth of February, 1874. The State Department learned that, as they were Prussian subjects, they could not be extradited, but that they were amenable under an admirable German law for offenses committed beyond Prussian territory, and the evidence against them was asked for by the German government. In December Marshal Sheldon gave the German Consul General, Hirkel, in New York, exemplified copies of all the testimony, with diagrams of the premises that were fired, and oil cans and other evidences of arson. In October, 1875, the prisoners were brought to trial in the City Court of Berlin. Fritz Andree was convicted, and sent to prison for two years. Rudolph was placed under police surveillance. After conviction, Fritz confessed that he committed the crime to obtain money by his insurance to send his homesick wife back to Germany.

Fire broke out on the twenty-ninth of December, 1873, in the cap manufactory of Julius Sarner, who was heavily insured. Sarner rated as a "suspect" on account of previous settlements of fire losses which were unsatisfactory to the underwriters. They endeavored to probe his operations, but no satisfactory evidence was obtained against him. Marshal Sheldon, after a patient investigation, laid the case before the Grand Jury, and in March, 1874, Sarner was indicted for perjury in a sworn statement in regard to the value of his stock on hand, and the quantity and value of the goods which were burnt. Sarner's trial lasted from the fourteenth to the twenty-ninth of May, 1874. He was prosecuted by Daniel G. Rollins, assistant district attorney, and now surrogate of this county, and defended by Mr. James M. Smith. He was found guilty, and remanded for sentence. On the thirtieth of May he committed suicide in the Tombs by taking Paris green.

On the tenth of September, 1877, Ellen Carey, to gratify a hatred of Thomas Donnelly and his wife, who lived in a shanty near that of her husband, a blaster, at One Hundred and Fortieth Street and Tenth Avenue, made a clumsy attempt to burn them alive by kindling a fire outside the door of their hut, the only means of exit. She used blasting powder, kerosene, paper, and kindling wood. The powder blew the bonfire "every which way," and saved the lives of Donnelly and his wife. The evidence against the woman was complete. She was seen near the shanty of the Donnellys shortly before the fire occurred, and among the rubbish was a piece of wall paper which contained powder such as her husband used. The paper fitted into a tear in a piece on a shelf in Mrs. Carey's shanty. Mrs. Carey was sentenced to end her days in prison.

A large double tenement house at No. 11 Ludlow Street was on fire on the tenth of November, 1878. The flames originated in the apartment of Joseph Levy. The fire was typical of many which had occurred shortly before on the east side of the city, and the origin of them was pronounced incendiary, but the criminal or criminals could not be detected or traced. It was evident that an organized gang were at work to make money out of insurance companies, without any thought of the lives or property that were imperilled, and Charles H. Perley, of the fire marshal's office, and Foreman Dempsey, of Engine Company No. 9, had been detailed to watch certain suspected persons, among whom were Isaac Perlstein, Charles Bernstein, and Abraham D. Freeman. They were found to have a rendezvous in a beer saloon in East Broadway, near Engine 9's quarters, and it was finally discovered that they worked for a clique of fire speculators, setting fire to such premises as were pointed out by those interested in the insurance. Evidences of their criminality were laid before the Assistant District Attorney Rollins, but he was not willing to risk the escape of such villains on secondary proof, and he urged the fire marshal to be patient, and instruct those who were watching the "fire bugs" to extreme but cautious vigilance. Then it happened that Dempsey and Perley followed them from their rendezvous, saw them enter No. 11 Ludlow Street, and Perley saw them enter Levy's room, and come out. A little later Levy's place was ablaze, and Perley, breaking into the room, helped to put out the fire. Later in the night, Perlstein, Bernstein, Freeman, and Levy met at the beer saloon to curse the activity of the Fire Department, which had thwarted their plan. Two days after they were in jail on indictments, cursing their greed of gain. Judge Cowing sentenced Perlstein for life on the twenty-fifth of January, 1879, and Levy to the same living death on the tenth of June of that year. Judge Barrett passed like sentences on Freeman and Bernstein on the twenty-sixth of February, 1879. Cohen Davis, a lying witness, to prove an alibi for Freeman, was convicted of perjury, and on the eighteenth of March, 1879, was sent to state prison for seven years by Judge Gildersleeve. Mr. Daniel G. Rollins conducted the prosecution in each case. Many persons who should have shared the fate of the convicts fled to escape arrest. In the succeeding year the fires in the district in which the fire bugs, Perlstein, Bernstein & Co. operated, were one hundred less than the previous year, when they were at large, in spite of a general increase in fires throughout the city.

Late at night on the twenty-third of November, 1885, the seventy inmates of the double tenement house, No. 404 East Sixty-fourth Street, were aroused by a fast spreading fire, which had its origin in rooms on the second floor, occupied by Henry Kohout, his wife, and Edward Kohout. The fire went to the roof, destroying the two upper floors, and in the wreck were found the calcined bodies of Mary Fialla, a Bohemian widow, and her two children; many others in the house came near sharing their fate. The Kohouts were arrested on very direct evidence that liquid substance of an inflammable nature was used to favor the spread of the flames in their rooms and on the stairs. The motive for arson was discovered in policies of insurance for nine hundred dollars on property worth seventy-five dollars. The prisoners were indicted for murder and arson, and the intricate case, made doubly so by the language of the principal witnesses—Bohemians—was conducted by Assistant District Attorney Fitzgerald in a masterly manner. The woman was not pursued. The men were convicted and sentenced for life by Recorder Smyth. They would have been hanged had any one been able to swear that the masses of charred flesh found in the ruins were the bodies of Mary Fialla and her children. The evidence which secured the conviction of the Kohouts was obtained by Captain John Gunner and Detective Campbell of the Twenty-eighth Precinct.

On March 25, 1886, fire was discovered in the basement of the tenement house, No. 528 West Thirty-ninth Street, occupied by John McGrath and wife Mary, as a grocery and dwelling. The fire was discovered at 3:35 P. M.; the place was securely locked at the time, McGrath and his wife having left home early in the morning, previously announcing that they were going to Jersey. When the doors were broken open, fires were found burning in different rooms, and evidences of incendiarism were discovered, consisting of kindling wood soaked with kerosene, and pieces of candle placed upon it. The contents were insured for one thousand dollars. The stock, upon examination, was found worth less than two hundred dollars.

McGrath and his wife returned that evening; were arrested; indicted on April 26 for arson in the second degree; tried and convicted before Judge

Gildersleeve on July 15, 1886. McGrath was sentenced to ten years in states prison, and his wife to seven years in the penitentiary.

SAGACIOUS FIRE DOGS AND HORSES.

MECHANICS, No. 47, (which was also called Old Red Gal or Poultice Hose), had a famous fire dog—a big Newfoundland called Major. Major was said to have as much common sense as half a dozen bipeds. When the old bell used to ring for a fire the dog was as alert as any of the company. If, however, the bell did not strike exactly five or six (showing the alarm was in the district) he would not budge. His manner would say as plain as words "Not this fire, some other fire." But when the exact strokes were heard Major was wild with impatience to be off with the boys. Once a member, a little the worse for liquor, fell asleep on the carriage. The gong pealed out six; every man was ready except the sleeper. Major seized him with his teeth as if to carry him off, but got no response. Then the intelligent animal gave the man a good shake, and rousing him to a sense of his duty, darted off with the company. Alas! poor Major at last died of too much water. He had left No. 47 to take service with some one else, got caught in the mud somewhere out in New Jersey, the tide came in, and he was drowned before his friends could reach him. He is now stuffed and in a glass case.

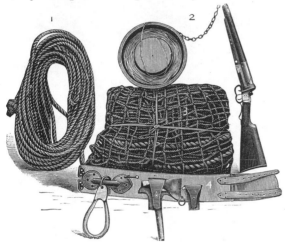

1, LIFE ROPE; 2, LIFE RIFLE LINE; AND 3, JUMPING NET; 4. BELT WITH SNAP AND TOOLS.

There are many interesting stories told about fire horses. Chief Bresnan had a horse auctioned off because of old age. After passing through several hands the old nag finally became the property of a "refuse" cartman. One day the cartman came to an engine house to take away the garbage, and had backed up to the pit in the rear. Suddenly the gong sounded an alarm. The old fire horse pricked up his ears. The spirit of former days was awakened, his youth seemed to have returned, and he bounded away carrying with him part of the stairway and almost smashing the engine, which he encountered.

Another superannuated department horse was bought by a Williamsburg milkman. One day the man of milk and water was serving his customers at the corner of Houston Street and the Bowery, and the old horse was standing quietly, and perhaps sadly awaiting the "git up" of his new master. Presently a hubbub, a clatter and rattle, was heard in the neighborhood. Along the Bowery rushed a fire engine. The first glimpse the old horse got of the machine new life seemed to have been inspired into his bony carcass, and off he darted after the engine, with the milk cans clattering behind him. His master was breathless and perspiring freely when at last he caught up with the enthusiastic brute. The superannuated fire horse was standing contentedly in the full glare of the fire, seemingly under the impression that he had done his whole duty.

Engine Company No. 8, located in North Moore Street, had a remarkable horse, and wonderful stories are told of him. For instance, when he was thirsty and wanted a drink he would back out of his stall, go to the hydrant, turn the faucet with his mouth, and, after drinking, would turn the water off and return to his stall. He would catch in his mouth a handkerchief thrown into the air as it descended, and put it into the pocket of one of the member's coats. He would lift any leg called out to him, and go down on his knees as in the act of saying his prayers at the word of command.

"JIM" OF ENGINE 33.

That animal, it must be conceded, was pretty intelligent, but what will be said of the horse that Engine Company No. 17 rejoiced in the possession of. Here are some of the marvelous things he knew and would do: He knew the stations on which the company performs duty. He showed it in this way, it is said: whenever the gong sounded an alarm he ran to his place and snapped his pole-snap to a ring in a strap for that purpose. Upon the sounding of the gong for other stations striking more than two blows, if the man on house patrol did not stop him, he would pull the bunk-room gong, and as the men came tumbling down-stairs he would neigh with satisfaction at having turned them out of their beds. On returning from the house to the stable, if he could get a broom he would sweep his stall or break the broom handle and throw it over the fence into the next yard. When he wanted a drink of water, he, too, knew how to get it; he went to the watering trough, turned the faucet, and drank his fill; then, it is asserted, he would fill a pail with water and take it to the other horse, and after having finished, if not detected before, he would neigh to let his friends know what he had been up to. Smart horse, that.

A FIREMAN'S LIFE.

An engine house now is a very quiet place, except just when an alarm is received and when the company has returned from a fire. When everything has been made clean and trim, the firemen sit around the station house quietly reading, smoking, or chatting. At night the place is still more tranquil. Arranged at equal distances along the sides of a narrow dormitory up-stairs, are ten or a dozen cribs. It is midnight and the cribs are occupied. At the side of each bed is placed a pair of high boots, into which a pair of trousers have been carefully tucked. Everything is in apple-pie order, and the boots and trousers have evidently been arranged with an eye to an emergency.

Below on the ground floor stands a large fire engine of modern pattern, multiplying the surrounding objects upon its shiny surface. The wheels are painted vermilion, and the paint is without flaw. Every part susceptible of polish is polished. Indeed, the whole thing looks highly ornamental, and the spectator feels that it would be a pity to soil it by a drop of water. When it returns from a fire it is less gay. The furnace is filled with fuel, and a brand soaked in petroleum is ready for lighting; but the steam is already up to a pressure of five pounds, as the tremulous little guage shows the necessary heat passing into the boiler through a pipe from a stationary furnace in the cellar of the building. The hose carriage, or tender, occupies a place behind the engine, and farther in the rear are three stalls in possession of three fine, large, glossy horses, whose pet names are inscribed in gilt letters over the manger, and whose sleek condition betokens unusual care.

Suddenly the electric current causes a bell to sound, the measured strokes being given in quick and startling succession. The men spring from their beds simultaneously, as if they had been lying awake waiting for this summons. Ten or twelve pairs of legs are at one and the same time thrust into the trousers and boots, and are pulled on with two hitches. The trousers close upon the hips, so that no time is lost with suspenders or belts. There is a terrific racket below. The bell is still sounding, repeating the signal five times over. Down a brass rod in one corner of the room slide the firemen in rapid succession. On the ground floor they find the horses already hitched to the engine, the driver on the box, and the furnace lighted. Each man jumps to his place on the tender, the doors are flung open, and in one minute from the first sound of the alarm the company is on its way to the fire. In fact, it is not unusual for an engine to be out of the house and on its way to a fire within forty seconds of the moment when the bell first strikes. During the first visit of the Grand Duke Alexis to New York, an alarm of fire was sounded at the Clarendon Hotel, in Fourth Avenue near Seventeenth Street, and a stream of water was turned upon the building by an engine within two minutes and thirty-five seconds, the engine having been manned and brought four blocks in the meantime.

The location of the fire is known instantly. Behind the captain's desk is a placard exhibiting the number of every alarm box in town, with the spot where it is placed. While the men are getting ready, the captain glances at the card, and the moment the last stroke of the bell is heard, shouts to the driver the location of the fire. The wild gallops through the streets, the vehe-

ment blazing of the furnace, the bright line of sparks following in its wake, the shouts of the spectators, the scurrying of vehicles out of the way, all produce a thrilling effect, even upon the men who have had years of experience. Although an alarm of fire may prove not to have resulted in a dollar's worth of damage, yet the same zeal and celerity are shown as if millions were known to be involved. When the men return to the station, no matter how tired they may be, the engine is restored to its original brilliancy, the horses are groomed, the harness is washed with castile soap, the hose is readjusted on the tender, and soon the company is prepared for another alarm.

Each man has his own place on the tender, where he leaves his hat and coat, donning these articles on the way to the fire. The horses are almost as well trained and as zealous as the men. The moment the alarm sounds they spring out of their stalls and put themselves into the shafts without a word of direction. Up to that moment they have been haltered, but the stroke of the bell releases them by an automatic arrangement of weights, pulleys and shafts. So, too, the pipes connecting the boiler of the engine with a boiler in

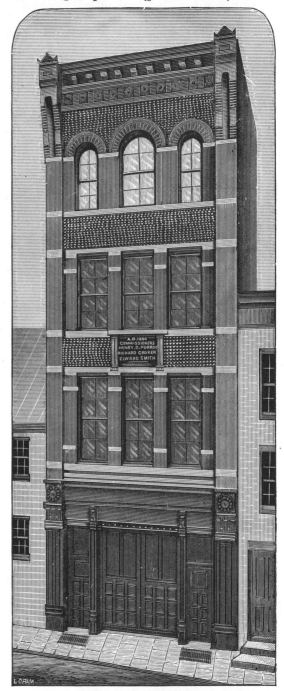

NEW ENGINE HOUSE IN ELM STREET,
[Between Spring and Broome Streets.]

the cellar of the building, and thus maintaining several pounds of steam in the former, though its furnace is not lighted, are automatic. As the engine leaves the station for a fire, the pipes close themselves, and do not require a moment's attention from the engineer, who has simply to leap with his assistant, on to the platform, and to hold on for dear life. The driver secures himself on the box by straps, without which he could not keep his seat. Alarm or no alarm, the men are always ready and in habitual suspense. The constant watching and waiting take the edge off their capacity for surprise. They are mechanically responsive to the stroke as the weight which releases the halters of the horses. No matter in which quarter of the city a fire is, the alarm is sent to every station house, and at the first stroke of the bell every company is required to prepare for action. The completion of the signal may show that only about one-tenth of the companies in the city are required, but the rest are ready to dash out of the station while the gong is still hammering and vibrating the last note of the signal.

It is because the horses see so little of outdoor life that they display so much activity when an alarm is sounded, and put all their strength into their gait. A foreman of a company was once asked why it was necessary to halter them at all when

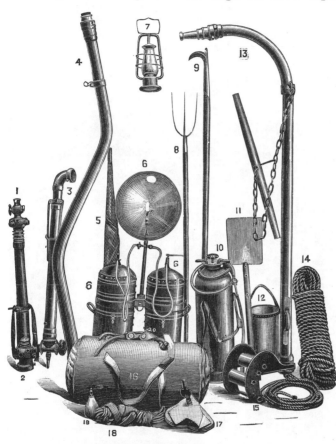

EXTINGUISHING TOOLS.

[1, Combination distributor and controlling nozzle on pipe; 2, Distributor for cellars, roofs and shipping; 3, Distributor with extension pipe; 4, Basement pipe; 5, Danger flag for Elevated R. R.; 6, Calcium light with tanks and appliances; 7, Danger lamp for Elevated R. R.; 8, Hay fork; 9, Ordinary hook; 10, Extinguisher; 11, Shovel; 12, Bucket; 13, Cellar and subcellar pipe with attachments; 14, Roof rope; 15, Hose and ladder hoister for roofs, window sills, wells, etc.; 16, Respirator bag; 17, Bellows for charging; 18, Life line; 19, Danger whistle; 20, Eye protectors.

they were so intelligent in the performance of their duties. "Bless you," he answered, "they'd play tricks on us if we didn't tie 'em up. There's a fellow," he added, pointing to a powerful gray in superb condition that snapped at a visitor who attempted to rub its nose, "that has been steadily at work in the department for over eleven years; knows his business like a man, that horse does; but he's up to many a little game, and would raise brimstone if he'd the chance."

The sitting rooms of the stations are comfortably furnished, decorated with portraits of the past and present worthies of the department, and supplied with books, dominoes, cards, chess, and other games. In the old days of the Volunteers the presence of cards and dominoes would have subjected the owners thereof to fines. The playing of any games of chance would have been considered a dire offense. The following extract from the minutes of Hose Company No. 36 will show how great the difference is between the Old and the New Departments on this subject :

November 5, 1851.—*Resolved*, That any member of this company found playing cards or any game of hazard in the house, for the first offense shall be fined one dollar, and for the second offense he shall be expelled from the company, and if not a member of the company, he shall be refused admittance in the house for the future.

Of course, this is not desirable now, as the conditions of the men are changed,

ENGINE COMPANY NO. 33.

and our firemen must have some relaxation, and very little time they get for it. Now, as in olden times, the discussion of politics and the use of profanity are strictly forbidden. "Gentlemen," said a prominent official, once addressing some new appointees, "you have been chosen from among eight hundred applicants, and I expect you all to be sober, industrious, and honest; and I also expect that you will obey all orders with alacrity and willingness. Avoid all discussions with your fellow laborers, and do all your work without grumbling. Politics and religion are subjects which I positively forbid being discussed. Ignore them absolutely. Vote for whom you please, go to any church you choose, but you must not engage in electioneering. Should you become involved in a misunderstanding with a fellow member of the department, come to me and I will arbitrate your difference at once. Be sober, for if you are drunk your brains are out, and you are no longer fit for duty. Drunkenness will certainly not be tolerated. In your whole deportment show yourselves to be gentlemen. I consider you such, and there is no reason why you should not act as gentlemen at all times. Profanity is uncalled for. It is a vile habit, and one which I have always got along without. I never practice it, and hope that you will follow my example. Be polite ; and now report at your posts."

The life of a fireman, now as ever, is as adventurous as that of a soldier; nay, it is not too much to say that the former runs far more risk than the latter. The fireman is on duty night and day, facing the enemy that never runs away, but stays to conquer or be conquered. When the alarm rings in the station house no man knows but that it may be the summons to his death. The vehicle that whirls to a fire may be swiftly conveying him to an agonizing end. But of this he never stops to think. The greater the peril the more eager is he to face it. Many and many a time have those soldiers of fire placed themselves in imminent danger and been warned by onlookers to retire. But again and again have these warnings been reiterated ere these gallant men thought of flinching from their posts while a chance remained to check, even in the slightest degree, the ravages of the flames. They mount to the loftiest buildings, from every window of which streams of fire are pouring.

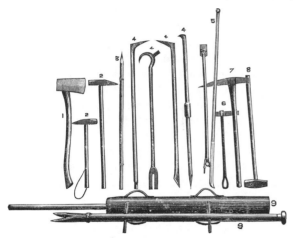

KIT OF BURGLARS' TOOLS CARRIED BY HOOK AND LADDER NO. 3.

[1, Working axe; 2, Iron shutter and door openers; 3, Crowbar; 4, Set of forcible entrance tools; 5, Door opener; 6, Swedging tool, 7, Pick axe; 8, Mawl; 9, Rams.]

Down into suffocating cellars they will go with their hose, while, mayhaps, rivers of molten lead, or avalanches of burning timber are falling around them. Underneath façades swaying to and fro, or tottering walls, half-blinded with smoke, they will toil and toil, while spectators are fearing that every moment will be their last. Into the very jaws of death—a room aflame or filled with volumes of suffocating smoke—they will unhesitatingly rush to rescue women and children.

Acts of heroism, materials for the pages of thrilling romances, are plentiful in the records of the department. We could fill a volume larger than this with the details of such daring deeds. We can give only a few :

Ten or a dozen years ago, during a fire in Trinity Building on Broadway, a heavy beam fell from the roof on eight firemen in such a way that it prostrated them without crushing them. The wood was on fire from end to end, and did not leave them space to rise in. They lay close to the floor which was smoking and covered with sparks, and the beam continued to burn over them within a few feet of their heads, threatening to roast them to death. One of the pipes had been buried with them, and when they discovered it they turned it against the flames. Steaming to death now threatened them, as the water vaporized in the heat, and filled their crib with scalding white clouds. But the circumstance saved them, by enabling them to abate the fire below until their comrades outside had lifted the beam from over them.

Another building on Broadway was burning in 1877. It was agreed between three hose men, who were stationed on the roof, and one of the officers stationed below, that as soon as the fall of the roof appeared imminent to him he should call to them, and they should leap to the next building, over an intervening alley five or six feet wide. In the meantime they did not distress themselves, but worked steadily with their streams, which were poured down the scuttles. The hiss and lapping of the flames, the fierce pulsations of the engines, the trumpeted orders of the chiefs, and the crash of falling iron and timber were so loud and confusing that a voice might have easily been lost in them. Notwithstanding this fact, the men held to their insecure ground until a gentle rattling indicated that the roof was about to collapse, and they heard the officer below cry, " Leap!" It was a fearful moment. There were hundreds of people watching them. Every spectator held his breath. Then, almost simultaneously, the bold hose men sprang from one parapet to another, and they had barely done so when a dense volume of smoke and sparks shot into the air, and a pit of flame remained where the men had stood before. The pent-up feelings of the crowd were let loose, and a roaring cheer drowned the roaring of the fire and the loud laboring of the engines.

There are many, too many, sad episodes, also to record. A man has been killed by being knocked from a ladder by a misdirected stream of water, or wandering over the roofs of houses, falls down an open scuttle, and is either crippled for life or killed. He runs the risk of his engine or truck colliding with a vehicle, with all the dreadful consequences, and there are a thousand and one other accidents to which he is liable in the service of his calling. Some of these we record in other chapters. The chapter devoted to the Roll of Merit will give an idea of the heroism and dangers of a fireman's life.

There is likewise to be enumerated among the risks run by firemen the probability of coming in contact with contagious diseases. Here is an amusing story from the Old Department : " In 1857 a fire occurred in a humble tenement in Baxter Street. Several of the inmates were sick and unable to escape. The men of Hose Company No. 14 dashed in among the flames to the rescue. The last man was carried out by James R. Mount, Cooley, Lyons, and Evans, of No. 14. They were conveying the patient still farther up the street out of the way of the engines, when a woman rushed up and cried, " Thank God, he is saved ! But oh ! my husband will die, for he has the small-pox bad ! " As if their burden was red-hot iron, the affrighted firemen dropped it, and started back aghast. There was a place called Begg's saloon, at No. 71 Mulberry Street, and the firemen made a rush for this to disinfect themselves with as much whiskey as they could carry. They did not care for the fire and the crumbling building, but the small-pox—oh ! That was worse than death.

THE HOOK AND LADDER TRUCK.

The long hook and ladder trucks are objects of wonder to the stranger visiting the station, and he cannot understand how these seemingly unwieldy machines can get quickly to a fire. But they do, and quite as quickly as the engines. It is a marvelous sight to see one of these machines manned, dashing through the street, and turning the sharp corner of a street with as much ease as a hand-cart. The driver in front has, without a doubt, a perilous task; also the brakeman in the rear. But driver and brakeman manage the machine with as much dexterity as the sailing master of a yacht, and rarely cause a collision. In the winter time, when the car companies pile up the snow in little mountains in the gutters, trucks have come to grief from this cause, and, being upset, many men have thus been injured. In the densely populated districts hook and ladder companies go out on a first alarm with four engines. Should people be cut off in an upper story, in the twinkling of an eye the long ladders are against the walls, and the men climbing rapidly to the rescue.

Should the fire have eaten the partition, the hooks are plied to tear down the walls.

GETTING QUICKLY TO A FIRE.

The men have been constantly on the lookout for improvements that would reduce the time in getting out to a fire. The sliding pole has an immense advantage over the old-fashioned pell-mell rush down the stairs, saving nearly a minute of preparation, and every second tells nowadays. Captain Rafferty's Fire Patrol No. 3, in West Thirtieth Street, was the first to have a contrivance superior to another invention—a trap door. The device, working smoothly

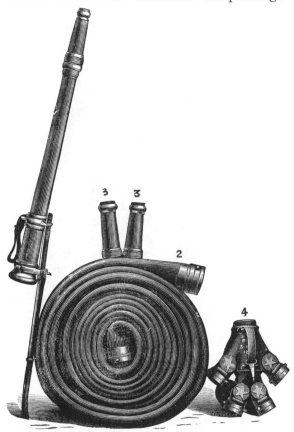

[1, Large play pipe; 2, Three and a quarter hose; 3, Three nozzle stick; 4, Siamese for long connection.]

and quickly, saved some seconds of time lost in sliding down the brass poles and clambering to the seat on the engines. In exhibition drills Drivers Lyell and Root have been able to drop to their seats and start the truck in less than two seconds, which is away ahead of anything done in the patrol truck manning. The trap is cut in the ceiling immediately over the driver's seat on the heavy truck. It is surrounded on the floor above by a polished brass railing four feet high that shines like a mirror. The drivers' beds are right beside this railing. When an alarm sounds at night they spring from their beds together, seize the railing, and let their bodies drop horizontally through the trap. The instant the door opens they let go and catch a second brass bar fitted into the ceiling, like an acrobat dropping from one trapeze to another. This second bar balances them and prevents them from falling forward in their five-foot drop to the truck seat. A weight attached to a pulley rope shuts the trap door with a bang the moment they disappear through the trap.

The time in hitching is wonderfully quick, and it would seem that it cannot possibly be made less, notwithstanding the hopes of those who are constantly on the lookout for further improvements in this direction. At present, with the exception of two acts, everything is automatic. These two acts are the movement of the horses from the stalls to their places beside the engine shaft, and the snapping of the collars over their necks by the watchman. And both these are done in such a perfect way that they are as good as automatic any-how. Automatic machinery does all of the rest of the work quick enough to make your head swim if you try to time the details. The instant the operator at Fire Headquarters opens the circuit to send an alarm, the current drops a metal ball right beside the gong. The ball strikes, presses down a bar of brass, and pulls a steel wire that automatically un-hitches the springs at the sides of the stalls that hold the halters of the horses. The hammer of the gong, simultaneously with the first alarm stroke, stops the little "record" clock that is perched on a shelf beside the gong, and thus automatically keeps a record of the time consumed in go-ing to a fire, putting it out, and returning. By comparing the little clock with the big clock on the wall, that is kept going all the time, the captain of the company can tell at a glance just how long it took to do

THOS S. BRENNAN.
[Com. of Charities and Corrections.]

any given piece of work. The harness is always suspended over the shaft by an automatic iron "hanger." It is held in position there by springs. When the driver grabs the reins the tension loosens the springs, the harnesses drop down upon the horses, the watchman snaps the collars around the horses' necks, and automatic weights attached to little pulleys in the ceiling carry the framework of the "hanger" up overhead out of the way. Improvements are steadily being made in the collars that the fire horses wear. They are made in two sections, fastened with a hinge at the top, and snap together at the bottom with an automatic steel spring lock. Collars made of cast-iron were introduced in some of the engine houses. They are sixteen pounds lighter than the leather collars, which weigh thirty-six pounds each, and they are considered more durable and serviceable. These collars can be fastened around the horses' necks in a fraction of a second.

A new automatic special alarm has been introduced, by which time is saved in transmitting an alarm from a regular street box, and is made use of by many big buildings. This alarm consists of an electric contrivance hitched on to the ceiling of each floor of the building and attached to a very sensitive wire. A certain dangerous degree of heat in any particular floor, no matter how generated, will cause the wire to expand and start a current that drops a disk in the engine houses of the district in which the building is located, and on this disk is inscribed not only the exact location of the building, but also the exact part of the building in which the fire, or the heat that is great enough to produce fire, if not checked, has broken out.

RESCUED FROM TOP WINDOWS.

On April 7, 1884, the building known as the St. George Flats, Nos. 223 and 225 East Seventeenth Street, was the scene of a conflagration. The building, in an architectural sense, was a striking feature of the east side. There are few buildings used for domestic purposes that exceed it in height. It was seven stories high from the sidewalk (exclusive of the basement), and was eight stories in the rear.

It was of a composite style of architecture, was built of blue stone, with Nova Scotia and terra cotta trimmings, and presented an imposing appearance exteriorly.

Placards were hung just inside the entrance, giving the tenants to understand that "these flats are absolutely fireproof." When once the fire started this so-called "fireproof" structure burnt with the fierceness and rapidity of a tinder box, and defied all the ex-

BURNING OF ST. GEORGE FLATS.

ertions of the ample force of firemen that was on hand to stay the fury of the flames until they had consumed every perishable thing in the building, and left nothing but the walls standing. The building was arranged to accommodate two families on each floor, one family on either side of the main hallway. There were seven rooms to each flat, and an extra room on the top floor, to be used as a storage or a servant's room, to suit the occupants. The main door was in the center of the building and almost on a level with the sidewalk.

The person who gave warning of the fire was Louis Castaing, the elevator boy. He was about sixteen years old. He proved to be the hero of the hour, and almost sacrificed his life to save the lives of others.

The firemen who assisted in the rescue of the imperilled inmates were Binns, Barrett, and Graham, of No. 3 truck. Mrs. Lockwood, and her child and her maid, were rescued from a rear window. Four men held a ladder on their shoulders standing on the roof of an adjoining building, while policemen Kelly and Gilbride went up and rescued them.

Four men of the Insurance Patrol No. 3 were cut off from escape on the fifth floor. They escaped through a side window by letting themselves drop a distance of two stories to the roof of an adjoining building. They escaped unhurt. They were Lieutenant Locour, Sergeant Moore, and Patrolmen Price and Fry.

The assistant engineer, Fredrick Kimmelberger, is the man who was coachman for Judge Van Brunt, of Bay Ridge, L. I, when the house was attacked by midnight burglars, on which occasion two noted cracksmen—Mosher and Douglass—lost their lives. He claims the credit of shooting them. He was in the cellar showing the firemen where he thought the fire was. The dumbwaiter fell upon him, the rope having been burned. He was badly crushed. Two firemen of Engine No. 5, James Rape and T. J. Mooney, and James Campbell of Engine No. 14, were also hurt.

Seven women, finding their way cut off by the front passageway, flew for safety to the fire-escapes in the rear. These they descended until they reached the second story. To reach the ground from thence they had to creep down a thirty-foot iron ladder, and by that means reach the yard. This in their hurry and alarm they were unable to do. Neither could they force open the trap door. Their position was rendered still more perilous by the risk of being brained by all kinds of household utensils that came flying out of the back windows. Two of the women were preparing to spring from the fire-escapes when the inmates of the opposite house called on them to stay where they were, and then took a ladder and helped them down.

Theirs was a most perilous position. Never did the firemen work harder or exhibit more gallantry. The building was, by reason of its great height and general construction, a hard one to handle from a fireman's standard. Here the water tower came into operation with good effect. The modern appliances and appurtenances of a fireman's life were here of signal service. But for these the building would have been totally destroyed in short order. The so-called fire-proof structure burned like a tinder-box. But the force of firemen were equal to the occasion. It was, in fact, a battle for life against the mad, devouring flames. These were not subdued, however, until they had gutted the premises, and left the building in a ruined condition.

HOW TO BECOME A FIREMAN.

To become a fireman a person must be twenty-one years of age and of good moral character. He goes first to the secretary, and procures from him a blank, which he fills out, and gets four reliable men to sign, certifying that they have known him never to have been indicted or convicted of any crime; that they have known him for a certain number of years. The candidate then returns it to the secretary. He is then sent before the Medical Board and examined as to his physical condition. He is measured, weighed, and the circumference of his chest taken, which must come within the following :

Minimum circumference of chest tolerable in applicants.

HEIGHT.		CIRCUMFERENCE OF CHEST.
Feet.	Inches.	Inches.
5	7	33
5	8	34
5	9	34½
5	10	35
5	11	35½
6	—	36
6	1	36½
6	2	37
6	3	37½
6	4	38

STATURE AND WEIGHT.—The stature shall not be below 5 feet 7 inches, nor the weight below that marked as its minimum accompaniment in the subjoined table : * *

HEIGHT.		MINIMUM WEIGHT.
Feet.	Inches.	Pounds.
5	7	140
5	8	145
5	9	150
5	10	155
5	11	160
6	—	165
6	1	170
6	2	175
6	3	180
6	4	185

He must state whether he is subject to fits, piles, and whether his father or mother are dead ? If either or both, what they died of ? Whether he has any brothers or sisters dead ? What they died of ? If this examination is satisfactory, he goes to the gymnasium and his powers of endurance are tested. From there he goes before the Board of Civil Service Examiners. He must have a fair knowledge of the three R's. In the meantime his application has been sent to the Chief of Battalion in whose district he lives, who investigates what he has sworn to in the application. His references are seen and examined. If this is all right, the chief returns it with his approval, presuming that he has passed all the examinations. He is appointed for fifteen days on probation, without pay. Then comes the course of instruction. He reports at the foot of West One Hundred and Fifty-eighth Street every morning at ten o'clock (Sundays and legal holidays excepted); here he is instructed in the use of all the ladders and implements of the life-saving corps. He is taught to hold a pipe, and in fact, everything pertaining to a fireman's career. In the afternoon he goes to the headquarters in Sixty-seventh Street, near Third Avenue. Here a verbal course of instruction is given; when this is over, he is assigned to an engine or truck company, where he sleeps and answers all alarms, and does duty as a fireman. This is the routine which a candidate follows day after day, until his half month of probation has ended. If his company and Batallion commanders report favorably on him, he is appointed, and receives one thousand dollars for the first year, one thousand one hundred dollars for the second, and then becomes a fireman of the first grade with a salary of one thousand two hundred dollars.

THE LIFE SAVING CORPS.

General orders No. 4; issued on June 7, 1883. *Resolved,*

I. The establishment of a school of instruction, and the rules governing it, are hereby announced to the Department.

II. Second Assistant Chief of Department Bonner is designated as instructor of the school, with power to select two assistants from the uniformed force, to be detailed at his request by the Chief of Department.

III. Until further orders the school will he located in the quarters of Engine Company No. 47, the third floor of which will be suitably arranged and fitted up with all the necessary appliances for the purpose.

IV. The school will be divided into two classes : The first, or "Life Saving Corps," will be devoted to instruction and training in handling and using scaling and ordinary ladders, life lines, etc., and all other life saving appliances now in use or hereafter introduced. The second class to be devoted to general instruction in the practical duties of a fireman in quarters and at fires, and particularly in the handling, care, and use of all implements, tools, etc., employed in extinguishing fires.

V. After passing a satisfactory examination by the medical officer, a candidate applying for appointment to the uniformed force, and volunteering to go to the school of instruction for a term of ten days, on probation and without pay, shall, if appointment is contemplated, be referred to the instructor, by endorsement on his application for appointment, on the direction of either of the commissioners, to determine his qualifications under a course of training in the first class. At the expiration of the term of probation the instructor shall r e t u r n the application, with his report endorsed thereon, stating the candidate's qualifications. Inability to learn the proper handling of the life saving implements, or indifference to the instruction given, shall be regarded as disqualifying the candidate for membership; and if the instructor shall report a c a n d i d a t e incompetent, from any cause, to become proficient in the first class, he shall be ineligible for appointment. If a candidate is reported suitable and able to become proficient in the first class, and is appointed, he shall at once be assigned to a company, in which he shall perform duty at night, and at other times when his presence is not required in the school of instruction, to which he shall be ordered by the company

HOELL LIFE SAVING APPARATUS.

commander to complete the course of instruction and training, reporting for that purpose to the instructor at the foot of West One Hundred and Fifty-eighth Street, at 10 A. M., on the day after his appointment takes effect, Sundays and legal holidays excepted, and thereafter at such times and places as the instructor may direct. At the close of the training and instruction, the instructor shall return the copy of the order of appointment (transmitted to him at the time of his appointment), with his report endorsed therein, in which shall be stated the degree of proficiency attained, and the branch of the service for which the appointee is best qualified.

VI. Members of the uniformed force volunteering for instruction in the first class, shall be ordered by the Chief of Department to report to the instructor at 10 A. M. on the day after the receipt by him of their application, Sundays and holidays excepted, at the foot of West One Hundred and Fifty-eighth Street, and upon the completion of the course of instruction, he shall be reported by the instructor as to the degree of proficiency attained.

VII. The instructor shall keep a book of the name, age, height, weight, address or company number, date of entry, and degree of proficiency.

VIII. Each Hook and Ladder Company in the Department shall carry three ladders, three belts, three life lines, and all life saving appliances as may be found necessary.

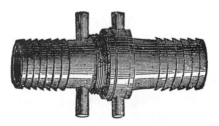

HOSE COUPLING.

CHAPTER LVIII.

SOME WELL KNOWN CHIEFS OF FIRE DEPARTMENTS.

Heads of Fire Departments Throughout the Country.—Big Cities With Distinguished Fire Chiefs.—Men who Have Risen Through Merit.—Their Experiences and Responsibilities.—The National Association of Fire Engineers.

S. E. COMBS, Chief of Fire Department, Worcester, Mass., was born in the town of Holden, Mass., May 10, 1826. He joined the Worcester Fire Department in 1848, since which time he has been in continual fire service. An act to establish a Fire Department in the town of Worcester, Mass., passed the Legislature of this Commonwealth February 25, 1835. The first Board of Engineers were Lewis Bigelow, John F. Clark, Isaac Davis, Francis F. Merrick, George T. Rice, General Nathan Heard, Lewis Thayer, Samuel Ward, and Ichabod Washburn. At the first meeting of the Board, May 2, 1835, Isaac Davis was elected chief engineer; Lewis Bigelow, assistant chief; and Ichabod Washburn, clerk.

The following table shows the chief engineers since 1835:

Isaac Davis, 1835 to 1836; General Nathan Heard, 1837 to 1839; Henry W. Miller, 1840 to 1844; Joel Wilder, 1845 to 1849; Erastus N. Holmes, 1850 to 1854; L. W. Sturtevents, 1855 to 1859; S. A. Porter, 1859 to 1860; L. N. Hudson, 1860 to 1861; Alyirus Brown, 1861 to 1865; A. B. Lovell, 1866 to 1868; R. M. Gould, 1869 to 1872; S. E. Combs, 1872 to 1887.

WILLIAM KAESS, chief engineer of the Poughkeepsie Fire Department, was born in New York city on August 26, 1842. He moved to Poughkeepsie in February, 1866. He has held the office of chief engineer of the Poughkeepsie Fire Department longer than anyone ever held it before. He is a member of the Veteran Firemen's Association of this city, and also a life member of the Firemen's Association of the State of New York.

M. E. HIGGINS, chief of Fire Department, Albany, N. Y., on January 16, 1865, was elected a member of Niagara Engine Company No. 6; served as such until December 17, 1866, when transferred to Hook and Ladder Company No. 2 as a member; served as such until the organization of the steam Department in 1867, when he was reappointed by the board of fire commissioners as a ladderman, attached to the same company; served until May 14, 1869, when he was promoted to the position of relief engineer, and on December 22, of the same year, was placed in charge of steamer No. 6 as the regular engineer; served until August 1, 1878, when he resigned as engineer and was appointed a hoseman of the same company; served as such until December 27, 1880, when he was promoted to the position of foreman of the same company; served until June 1, 1885, when he was promoted to an assistant engineer, and at the death of the late Chief James McQuade, July 25, 1886, was placed in charge of the department; served as acting chief until August 3, 1886, when he was promoted to chief.

HUGH F. SWEENEY, chief engineer of the Wilmington, Del., Fire Department, was born in that city on the twenty-fourth day of July, 1850; has been a fireman from boyhood, and a member of Fame Hose Company No. 1 for eighteen years. The department has flourished under his management, and is reported to be equal to any Volunteer Department in the country. Chief Sweeney is considered by citizens and firemen to be one of the best chiefs the city has ever had.

W. R. JOYNER, chief of the Fire Department, Atlanta, Ga., was born in Cobb County, Ga., June 30, 1854, and moved to Atlanta when quite young. At the age of fifteen he was appointed torch bearer of Hook and Ladder Company No. 1 (volunteers); at sixteen was elected a regular member of the same company. In November, 1872, when just past the age of eighteen, he was elected second assistant foreman; November, 1873, was elected first assistant foreman; November, 1874, was elected foreman (each time without opposition), and held that position until January, 1877, when he was elected chief of the Volunteer Fire Department, also without opposition, being only twenty-two and a half years old, and holding the record at that time of being the youngest chief in the United States. January, 1878, he was re-elected without opposition. Was again nominated for 1879, but declined to run. He was then put back as foreman of Hook and Ladder Company, and remained in that position until the Paid Department took charge, which was in July, 1882. The general council elected him chief of the paid service, but he declined to take it, as he was then city marshal, and that place was worth more money. In July, 1885, he was elected chief by the general council, and the salary was raised to two thousand five hundred dollars per annum to induce him to accept, as he was still city marshal, and would not change places, as the chief's salary was only one thousand three hundred and fifty dollars per annum. So the change as above stated was made. When he took charge the department was in bad shape, and insurance was high. Now the department is willing to show up with any, and claims to be as well equipped as the best. The insurance has been reduced, and the department is the pride of Atlanta.

JOHN LINDSAY, Chief of Fire Department, St. Louis, Mo., was appointed a member of the Fire Department June 1, 1867, and was connected with Hook and Ladder No. 1 for seven years; was appointed assistant chief in 1874, and first assistant in 1881, and chief in April, 1885, on the retirement of Chief H. C. Sexton.

HENRY E. FARRIER, chief of the Jersey City Fire Department, was a volunteer of Diligent Hose Company No. 3, Jersey City Fire Department. Upon the breaking out of the war he enlisted in the Twenty-first New Jersey Volunteers. After the war he became a member of his old love, Diligent 3, and remained as such until 1871, when he was appointed the first chief of the Paid Fire Department. He held this office until 1877. The political complexion of the Board was then changed, and he was dismissed, but was reinstated in 1881 as chief, and continues to discharge the duties of that office to the present day.

JOHN T. DENMEAD, assistant chief engineer of the Jersey City Fire Department, was in his early days a member of Peterson Engine Company

FIRE DEPARTMENT CHIEFS.

No. 15 (Old Maid), of this city. He moved to Jersey City, and became a member of the Fire Department of that city. In 1861 he enlisted in the Second New Jersey Volunteers. On the return of the regiment he re-enlisted in the Thirteenth New Jersey Volunteers. When the war ended he became a member and assistant foreman of 2 Truck; he held this position until June 6, 1871, when he was made clerk to the new Board of Fire Commissioners. In 1877 he was dismissed for political reasons. He was reinstated in 1881 as assistant chief, and occupies that responsible position to the present day.

J. LOUIS MEYER, chief engineer, Hoboken Fire Department, New Jersey, is thirty-one years of age. He commenced doing fire duty as a runner with Washington Hook and Ladder Company No. 1, of Hoboken, at the age of sixteen; continued until the age of twenty-one, and joined as a member of Washington Hook and Ladder Company No. 1 on March 2, 1877, and since has served the company and Fire Department in the following capacities:

May 3, 1878, elected trustee of Washington Hook and Ladder Company 1, for three years.

June 7, 1878, elected trustee to the Widows' and Orphans' Fund of the Hoboken Fire Department, for two years.

March 21, 1879, elected secretary of the Widows' and Orphans' Fund of the Hoboken Fire Department.

March 5, 1880, re-elected trustee to the Widows' and Orphans' Fund, for two years.

March 18, 1880, re-elected secretary of the Widows' and Orphans' Fund.

May 7, 1880, elected assistant foreman of Washington Hook and Ladder Company 1.

May 6, 1881, elected foreman of Washington Hook and Ladder Company 1.

March 18, 1881, re-elected secretary of the Widows' and Orphans' Fund.

March 3, 1882, re-elected trustee from Washington Hook and Ladder Company No. 1 to the Board of Trustees of the Widows' and Orphans' Fund, for two years.

May 5, 1882, re-elected foreman of Washington Hook and Ladder Company No. 1.

March 9, 1881, elected secretary of the Board of Officers of the Hoboken Fire Department.

April 15, 1882, re-elected secretary of the Board of Officers.

March 23, 1883, re-elected secretary of the Board of Trustees of the Widows' and Orphans' Fund.

May 4, 1883, elected treasurer of Washington Hook and Ladder Company No. 1.

May 9, 1885, elected assistant engineer of the Hoboken Fire Department.

May 10, 1886, elected chief engineer of the Department.

September 29, 1886, elected vice-president of the New Jersey State Firemen's Association, at the convention held in Phillipsburg, N. J., on the above date.

The foregoing offices have all been filled by him for their full terms.

The Hoboken Fire Department has seven companies, composed as follows: Hoboken Engine Company No. 1. Washington Hook and Ladder Company No. 1. Excelsior Engine Company No. 2. Oceana Hose Company No. 1. Liberty Hose Company No. 2. Empire Hook and Ladder Company No. 2. Meadow Engine Company No. 3.

Total number of active members, two hundred and twenty-five.

After a great number of troubles and difficulties the fire telegraph system has been introduced and adopted.

R. H. WALKER, chief engineer, Elmira, N. Y., is thirty-nine years old, and has been a fireman from a mere boy. He joined the old Volunteer Fire Department in 1864, but had served as torch boy three years previously. He was a member of Neptune Engine Company, a hand engine, until 1867, when he was transferred to Independent Hose Company No. 3, which was an incorporated body. He served as foreman in this company for seven years, and was a member of the Board of Trustees of the Elmira Fire Department. He was elected chief of the Volunteer Department in 1875; served one year. The Department was disbanded in May, 1878. The city organized a partial Paid Fire Department. He was appointed chief engineer in 1881, and has held the office since then, the fifth year. The Department is governed by a Board of Fire Commissioners. John B. Stanchfield, mayor of the city, is president. The commissioners are Charles Hazzard and Geo. M. Robinson. They have four steam fire engines, three hose carts, one Hays truck, and one double tank chemical engine, forty-one fire alarm boxes, and a thorough system of the Gamewell Telegraph. The Department has one chief engineer, one assistant, who is superintendent of telegraph, three foremen of companies, and seven permanent men; the rest, thirty-three in all, are call men, making twenty-six call men.

WILL Y. ELLETT, Elmira, N. Y., was born on July 12, 1852. He joined the Volunteer Department as torch boy of Steamer Company No. 1 in 1865. The Department was divided in 1869, and he went with one of the new companies known as Goodell No. 5; became foreman of the company in 1873, and continued as such until the Department disbanded in 1878. He was appointed in the present Paid Department on March 12, 1883, as assistant chief, and as superintendent of fire alarm telegraph in September of 1884.

JULIUS PEARSE, chief engineer of Denver Fire Department, was born in Germany, March 25, 1847. His parents removed to United States, settling in Chicago, Ill., about 1852, where he resided until September, 1868, when he took Horace Greeley's advice and moved out west and settled in Denver, Col., early in October, 1868. In the summer of 1872, when the Holly Water Works were completed, he interested himself in the organization of the Denver Fire Department under Chief Trounstine, and in the following fall assisted in organizing the Woodie Fisher Hose Company No. 1, being appointed first pipeman. This office he held until May, 1873, when he was elected first assistant foreman. At the annual election of the company in August, 1873, he was elected foreman, which he filled until he was elected chief of the department in April, 1875. He was re-elected in 1876, and served with distinction until April, 1877, when he was succeeded by Thomas Clayton.

In March, 1882, when the Denver Paid Fire Department was organized, he was appointed assistant chief and superintendent of fire alarms, and in the following November, 1882, he became chief engineer of the department, which position he has filled to the satisfaction of the citizens of Denver ever since.

Mr. Pearse is also one of the organizers of the Colorado State Firemen's Association, having served as president of said association the first and second year of its existence, 1876 and 1877.

FIRE DEPARTMENT CHIEFS.

FRED. E. WINDSOR, Warren, Warren County, Pa., was elected foreman on July 3, 1883; re-elected twice; and in April, 1886 elected chief from an unexpired term of foreman and given the honor of being the youngest chief in Pennsylvania. He is now a member of the National Association of Fire Engineers, and undoubtedly its youngest member. He has charge of one hundred and ninety-three men, three hose, one truck, one steamer and hydrant system. He is twenty-six years of age.

GEORGE C. FAGER, SR., is the oldest fireman in the State of Pennsylvania in active service. He was born in Harrisburg in 1814, and is now nearly seventy-two years of age, but as a fireman in the brave and energetic discharge of a fireman's duty, he has no equal; and he displays a zeal and an activity that might well be envied by young men not half his age. He first joined the Harrisburg Fire Department in 1828, becoming a member of the Friendship Fire Company. It was then, as now, an active, strong, fire company, albeit the fire laddies of those days did duty with buckets in quenching fire, and had none of the effective and powerful steam fire engines now in use. In 1835 the present Citizen Fire Company was organized, and Mr. Fager became one of its charter members. He is now the only original member of the Citizen Fire Company belonging to the company, as an active member. A few of the original members are still living, but they long ago ceased to do fire duty. When the Citizen Fire Company was organized, a hand suction fire engine was purchased, the first ever in use in Harrisburg; it was manufactured by Bates, of Philadelphia, and was run by Mr. Fager, who was selected engineer by his company. He continued in charge of the machine until it was discarded for a steam fire engine. In the early days of Mr. Fager's service as a fireman there was no hose in use, buckets being the only means of carrying water. Mr. Fager has been frequently honored by Harrisburg firemen. He is now and has been for many years the treasurer of the Citizen Fire Company, and during the years 1878, 1879 and 1880, was the chief engineer of the entire city fire department. He is a a well preserved old gentleman, popular with the firemen, and a good citizen. He himself knows of no fireman in the State of the same age in active service.

M. J. SULLIVAN, Chief Engineer Long Island City Fire Department, was born in South Boston, Mass., in 1826, and by force of circumstances was compelled to earn a living before he had completed his education. On July 28, 1862, he enlisted in the Second New York Fire Zouaves, served three years, was wounded twice, and was honorably discharged in 1865. In 1870 was instrumental in organizing Friendship Hook and Ladder Company No. 3, of Long Island City, in which company he served as foreman for the first three years, and two years after he was elected chief. In 1876 he was elected assistant engineer, and in April, 1886, chief engineer.

SAMUEL BEMISH, Chief Engineer of Rochester, N. Y., was born in Rochester in 1843. He very early showed a predilection for a fireman's life, and when still almost a youth joined the volunteers. When the civil war broke out, young Bemish, full of patriotic ardor, enlisted in the Thirteenth Regiment, New York Volunteers. After being a short time with his regiment he caught typhus fever and was invalided home. Upon his recovery, nothing daunted by his first experience of soldiering, the gallant young fellow joined the One Hundred and Fortieth Regiment, New York Volunteers, and served with his colors until the close of the war. When mustered out of the military service he rejoined his original one. He served as hoseman for three years, and was then promoted foreman. After holding the latter position for three years, Mr. Bemish was elected in 1871 to be assistant chief engineer, which office he retained with credit to himself and advantage to the department for nine years, when the department became a paid one. Under the new regime he was a foreman, and acted as assistant for three years. Then he was elected assistant chief, and on March 5, 1886, was promoted to be chief engineer. The office is an elective one by the Executive of the Common Council. Mr. Bemish distinguished himself on many occasions, and rendered excellent service at the great brewery and lumber yard fires.

The Rochester Fire Department is well favored with a supply of water. It has one extinguisher, four steamers to fall back on if needed, three hook and ladder trucks, and seven hose carriages, each having twelve hundred feet of hose. There are besides, three volunteer fire companies attached to the paid department, and a fire patrol. Last year the fire losses were about one hundred thousand dollars. The department has one of the very best of reputations. Its steamers were introduced shortly after the war.

G. H. CLOYES, Chief Engineer of the Portland, Me., Fire Department, was born in Framingham, Middlesex County, Mass., on November 22, 1837. He served in the fire department of his native town for three years, and then joined the Portland organization on June 22, 1856. His energy, courage, and skill were in due time recognized by promotions, and in 1880 he was made chief of the department.

FRED. HORNUNG, Chief Engineer of the Buffalo Fire Department, is one of the finest-looking firemen in the United States. He is six feet two inches tall, and powerfully built. His father, who settled in Buffalo over fifty years ago, was a yet bigger and a more powerful man, and is still (1886) alive. Fred. Hornung was born in 1848. Before he was twenty-one years old he joined Hook and Ladder Company No. 2. In 1876 and 1877 he was in charge of the supply stores; then for three years he was assistant chief. In 1883 the Board of Fire Commissioners, recognizing his merit and his services, appointed him chief engineer. Since his appointment as chief, Mr. Hornung has increased the efficiency of the department.

The reputation of the Buffalo Fire Department is known all over the country. It possesses seventeen steam engines, one hose cart attached to each steam engine, four chemical engines, and one hose tower. The salary of the chief engineer is two thousand four hundred dollars a year; there are seventeen engineers at $840; twenty-five foremen at $720; twenty-five assistant foremen at $600; fifty drivers at $600; seventeen stokers at $600; and seventy-one firemen at $600. Another company is to be added before the close of the year (1886), as soon as a house is built; an appropriation has also been made for a fireboat. Last year the fire losses were three hundred and seventy-five thousand dollars. At the Gilbert Starch Works, the Music Hall, and three big fires, the department was conspicuous for its efficiency. The small diameter of the water mains, however, has embarrassed the gallant Buffalo firemen to some extent, but gradually bigger pipes are being laid.

LEWIS P. WEBBER, chief engineer of the Boston Fire Department, is a native of the Empire State, and was born November 18, 1843. At the age of twenty

he made his *debut* as a fully fledged fireman, when he became a member of
Tremont Engine Company No. 7, of the Roxbury Fire Department. When
steam took the place of hand engines, in 1864, he was appointed a hoseman on Dearborn Steamer No. 1. On annexation of Roxbury to Boston, this
company became Company No. 14. In 1868 he was elected assistant foreman,

FIRE DEPARTMENT CHIEFS.

and in 1870 foreman. When the department was reorganized, in 1874, the fire
commissioners made him permanent foreman of this command. His qualities
as a fireman advanced with his good record, for on May 13, 1880, he was called
to more responsible fields of labor, and transferred to Engine Company No. 3,
which is located in what is known as the lumber district. Here he made his
mark, for he always had the respect and confidence of the command, as well
as others he came in contact with. The commissioners, in introducing

the rules and regulations to the department, say: "Something must necessarily be left to the intelligence and discretion of individuals; and, according to the degree in which they show themselves possessed of these qualities, and to their zeal, activity and judgment on all occasions, will be their claims to future promotion and reward." If ever there was an officer who lived up to these instructions, it was Captain Webber. This was a noticeable fact which the commissioners could not be blind to, and it was the expression from every mouth that faithful service had been rewarded when Captain Webber was promoted and assigned as district engineer of the Eighth Fire District, September 8, 1884.

Captain Webber was hardly settled among what promised to be his future surroundings, when the seat in the Board of Fire Commissioners left vacant by the retirement of Ed. A. White was filled by the election of Chief Engineer Green. Then came the perplexing question of who would be chief engineer. There were four candidates in the field from the board of engineers, and all pushed forward by their friends in no uncertain terms. It seemed to the commissioners that they must overcome the ill feeling that must come from the selection of either of the applicants. They held several consultations, when, at one of these consultations, Commissioner Fitzgerald made the remark: "I wish Captain Webber was a member of the board a little longer than he has been; he has every qualification, and would make an excellent executive head." The opinion of Commissioner Fitzgerald met with the approval of his associates, and Captain Webber was at once elected chief engineer by the unanimous vote of the board. The appointment gave entire satisfaction. Chief Webber entered upon his duties October 23, 1884. From his advent to the chiefship Chief Webber has had many disastrous fires to cope with, and has thus far proved an able and successful fire engineer.

MAJOR EDWARD HUGHES is Chief of the Louisville Fire Department. Nearly every one knows jolly Major Edward Hughes, the veteran Chief of the Department. He was born for his position, and no one has ever thought of disturbing him for the sake of putting another man in his place. He has held his position under three administrations. He was born and reared in Louisville, Kentucky. He entered the Volunteer fire service when but a stripling, becoming a member of Union No. 2 Company.

From pipeman he was elected chief director of his company, though but nineteen years old, which position he held until 1858, when the pay department was organized. Young Hughes joined the new organization as pipeman, but was soon promoted to captain for his many brave and daring acts. As there was but one position in the department the young man had not filled—that of engineer—and being anxious to learn all about the department, he took charge of Engine No. 5, and was considered the best engineer in the department. He was afterwards elected assistant chief of the department. In 1879 Major Hughes was elected by a unanimous vote of the General Council to the position of chief, was re-elected four times successively, the last time in 1885. For four years he never had any opposition for the place, and it is presumed that he never will. He has been chief longer than any other man. The men under him are well treated, and take delight in showing the gallant chief that they appreciate him when duty calls.

A. P. LESHURE, Chief Engineer of the Springfield, Mass., Fire Department, was born on October 15, 1828, at Woodstock, Conn. In 1852 he went to Springfield, and two years later joined the fire department. He was foreman of Engine Company No. 2 in 1856, assistant engineer from 1862 to 1866, chief engineer in 1870, and re-elected in 1874. Chief Leshure is considered to be one of the most capable firemen in the country.

HENRY REILLY, Chief Engineer of Syracuse, N. Y., was born in Albany in 1845. In early life he came to Syracuse and joined the volunteer department. In 1871 he was appointed foreman of one of the companies, and when the department became a paid one continued in the service. In 1881 Mr. Reilly was promoted to be clerk in the board of fire commissioners. Chief Engineer Eckel was killed about this time, and two months after being appointed clerk, Mr. Reilly was appointed chief engineer. His excellent record, coolness in danger, and thorough acquaintance with the duties of a fireman, were his strongest recommendations. The office is held during the pleasure of the fire commissioners. The Syracuse Fire Department is a very excellent one, small as it is, but considering the increase in the population, at least two engines and one hook and ladder company additional are needed.

At present the department possesses four engines, one chemical engine, and one hook and ladder truck. The loss by fires average yearly from one hundred and twelve thousand to one hundred and twenty-five thousand dollars. In the first five and a half months of 1886 there were eighty-five calls. The fire department has no sort of control over the erection of houses, except within a very confined limit, and there it can forbid only the erection of wooden dwellings.

D. J. SWENIE, Fire Marshal and Chief of Brigade of Chicago, Ill., has seen one of the biggest fires the world has ever witnessed. He was captain of 13 Engine Company, when the city was burned to the ground in the memorable year of 1871. He was born in 1834, in Glasgow, Scotland. When quite a youth he came to America, settled in Chicago, and joined the Volunteers (No. 3 Engine) in 1849. He was seen to be a clever and indefatigable fireman, and all through his connection with the department he proved to be full of resources, reliable in times of peril, alert, and thoroughly imbued with the spirit of a true fireman. Mr. Swenie has been chief and fire marshal since 1879, and was assistant chief seven years before that. There are no politics in the Chicago Department; the chief has full control, there being no commissioners to hamper him. His assistant passes on fires, and reports to him. There are ten chiefs of battalion. There are thirty-eight engines in commission, eleven hook and ladder trucks, eight chemical engines, and five hundred and eleven men. The department has been a paid one since 1858. In the year 1885 there were over one thousand seven hundred and seventy calls, and the losses amounted to two million seven hundred thousand dollars. There is now an ample water supply in Chicago, and its system of fire boxes is far ahead of anything of the kind elsewhere. A fire box is put into the house of any citizen who asks for it, and a record kept of it. Through this, the police, the fire patrol, and so on, can be called, according to the emergency. No finer department can be found anywhere than that which Chicago possesses under its zealous chief, D. J. Swenie.

THOMAS L. WORTHLEY, president of the National Association of Fire

FIRE DEPARTMENT CHIEFS.

Engineers, was the first fireman of Long Branch, N. J. He organized that department in 1872. He has attended every one of the National Association conventions since 1879. He left his home in Little Silver, Monmouth County, N. J., when he was sixteen years of age, to earn his own living. For eight years he was a carman. Twenty years ago Worthley left New York for Long Branch, where he established a sale and exchange stable, and soon had a flourishing business. Several times he held the office of street commissioner, and from foreman became chief of the Long Branch Fire Department. Mr. Worthley was born in 1837.

MAJOR HORACE N. RUMSEY is Chief of the Department at Seneca Falls, N. Y. In the Empire State there are now few chief engineers more widely known than Chief Rumsey of Seneca Falls. During the past year Chief Tom Scott, of Little Falls; Chief Edder, of Syracuse; and other brave firemen, have gone to their reward. Although younger in the calendar, Major Rumsey was the compeer of them and their associates, and at the State conventions none were more genial than Tom Scott and Major Rumsey, who were the warmest of friends. Chief Rumsey comes from a family distinguished in fire annals. The name is synonymous with Fire Department work throughout the United States. Major Rumsey's father was for many years chief of the Seneca Falls Fire Department, until he was succeeded by the son four years ago. Chief Rumsey, excepting the time he was serving in the army, has been connected with the Seneca Falls Fire Brigade since he was fourteen years old, a period of more than thirty years. In his department he has two Silsby steamers, one Rumsey hook and ladder truck, a Silsby chemical extinguisher, a Rumsey protective wagon, and a hand engine, with a fire patrol. The chief has the credit of being a model fireman—always at the front when there is a necessity, equally as sure to be cool and collected in emergencies. His presence is familiar to firemen throughout the United States, as he is an extensive traveler in the interests of Rumsey & Company, limited, manufacturers of fire apparatus at Seneca Falls.

Chief Rumsey is a member of the National Association of Fire Engineers, and was elected to the Executive Board at Providence in August, 1886.

ALBERT C. HENDRICK joined Franklin Hose Company No. 4, New Haven Fire Department, in July, 1850, at the age of seventeen. He was elected treasurer January 15, 1851; secretary, September 8, 1852; assistant foreman, March 15, 1852; a member of Franklin Engine Company No. 4 same year, remaining a member until the company was disbanded in 1854. He was elected assistant foreman of Mutual Hook and Ladder Company No. 1 in 1857, foreman in 1858, serving until the war broke out in 1861, when, being first sergeant of the New Haven Grays, he went with the company in the Second Regiment Connecticut Volunteers; was afterwards first lieutenant and captain in the Twelfth Connecticut Volunteers. He was wounded at Winchester, Va., September 19, 1864, and was honorably discharged at the termination of the war. On returning from the war he again joined Mutual Hook and Ladder Company No. 1 as a private. He was appointed chief July 24, 1865, serving six terms of three years each, when the charter of the city was so altered as to make the position of chief of the New Haven Fire Department a life position. He was president of the National Association of Fire Engineers 1875 and 1876; elected treasurer of same in 1877, and still holds that responsible position.

W. EDWARD PLATT, Chief of Augusta, Ga., Fire Department, was born in that city January 21, 1852. He was torch boy, and then tillerman, of the Pioneer Hook and Ladder Company in 1867 and 1868; since then he has been foreman of the said company, and has been chief for several years. He is a cool and clearheaded, brave fireman. His grandfather, Charles Platt, was foreman of Company No. 9, in New York city, in 1826. His father, Charles A. Platt, has been an active fireman in Augusta for thirty-five years, and his uncle Jacob was chief for twelve years, both being sons of Charles Platt, foreman No. 9.

HARRY C. MILLER, Chief of the Hudson (N. Y.) Fire Department, was born in Hudson, September 25, 1856. He attended the public schools until 1871; then entered Williston Seminary at Easthampton, Mass., and finished the course with the class of '75. He returned to Hudson, June, 1875, and went into the hotel business, which he still continues. He joined Evans Hook and Ladder Company, September, 1875; was elected second assistant in 1876, first assistant in 1877, and captain in 1879. Mr. Miller was elected chief of the department December 15, 1884, and took the office January 1, 1885, and was no doubt the youngest chief in New York State at that time. The Hudson Department is composed of six hose and one truck company, consisting of two hundred and sixty-five men. The chief is elected by the department for a term of two years, and appoints two assistants under him. The city has fine water works, and has from eighty to one hundred and twenty-three pounds pressure, according to location of hydrant.

CHIEF GEORGE W. TAYLOR, Richmond, Va., was born in Richmond, Va., in 1846; entered the Fire Department as runner in 1866; soon after was promoted to foreman, and afterwards promoted to first assistant chief; in 1878 elected to chief; was president of the National Association of Fire Engineers in 1883, serving with credit to himself and the association.

THOMAS WILKINSON, born in Alexandria, Va., May 25, 1836, was a member of Independent No. 6, Volunteer Fire Department of Baltimore, Md., when Thomas Buckley was lost at the Lombard Street fire, and carried the last message to him he ever received. He was a member of No. 6 for two years, and had been a member of the Fire Department at Cumberland, Maryland, for twelve years.

Also a member of the Fire Department at Dallas, Texas, for seven years, four years of which time he served as foreman.

Since October, 1885, he has been assistant chief of the Dallas Paid Fire Department. He has also been president of the Firemen's Relief Association of the Dallas Fire Department since its organization.

JAMES W. DICKINSON, Chief of Cleveland, Ohio, was born in Saxon River Village, Windsor County, in the State of Vermont, on December 25, 1836. In his youth he attended the common schools of his native town, of Lowell, Springfield, Mass., and Wheeling, W. Va. At the age of eight years his attendance at the public school located on the Commons, in a building also occupied by Mazeppa Engine Company No. 10, in Lowell, awakened in him at that early age instincts and desires so strong as to shape and control his future course in life.

He removed to Cleveland, Ohio, in 1851, arriving there on the day of the memorable college riot. In 1853 he joined Cataract Engine Company No. 5

as a torch boy, and on September 5, 1855, he was elected a member of that company. In the following year he was made second assistant foreman, and in 1857 was advanced to the position of first assistant. When in 1859 he was elected foreman of that company he was the proudest man in the Volunteer Fire Department of that city.

Chief Dickinson is a born musician, and when in 1861 the war of the Rebellion broke out, he was among the first to respond to President Lincoln's call for three months' men, joining Leland's Band, which was attached to the Nineteenth Ohio Volunteer Infantry Regiment, Colonel Samuel Beattie commanding.

After his honorable discharge at the end of his enlistment, he re-enlisted, and was assigned to the Forty-first Ohio Regiment, under the command of Colonel W. B. Hazen, and was present at, and witnessed, several of the historic battles of the late war. He remained with that regiment until all regimental bands were discharged in the fall of 1862. Upon his return to Cleveland he agitated the question of a Paid Fire Department, and notwithstanding the strong opposition to the project on the part of the Volunteer forces, he succeeded in having it established, and tendered to the city the services of Cataract Company No. 5. The city authorities then gave him the privilege of selecting the men for his company for the Paid Fire Department, which he did from the members of the Volunteer Company, placing four stationary and two minute men to that company.

On January 23, 1863, Mr. Dickinson was placed in charge of Engine Company No. 2, in which place he remained eleven years.

In May, 1864, the patriotic spirit of this veteran was again aroused, and again he re-enlisted, joining Company E, of Cleveland's local regiment, known as the One Hundred and Fiftieth Regiment, O. V. I., commanded by Colonel W. H. Haywood, and was subsequently detailed for service in the then famous Leland Band.

In 1873 he attended the World's Fair, Vienna, Austria, as engineer in charge of the American exhibit of rotary steam fire engines, and on his return, in February, 1874, succeeded John McMahon as second assistant chief. In 1875 he was advanced to the rank of first assistant chief, and, on December 22, 1880, reached the topmost rung in the fireman's ladder of promotion by his election as chief of the Cleveland Fire Department. During his career as a fireman he organized the Fireman's Relief Association, and was mainly instrumental in having the present comprehensive pension law passed for the benefit of firemen, their widows, orphan children, and dependent parents. The new fireboat exists only through his persistent efforts in its behalf. The chief is in the prime of life, of portly size, a big-hearted, good-natured man, with an inexhaustible fund of anecdote, wit, and humor.

He has had several most miraculous escapes from death while in the performance of duty, but he never falters in the discharge of the obligations of his high calling.

He is kind towards every member of the force under him, watchful over their lives at fires, and has the unbounded confidence of Cleveland's best business men in his ability to handle and extinguish fire.

NATIONAL ASSOCIATION OF FIRE ENGINEERS.

A convention of chief engineers and chief officers of the Fire Departments of the United States was held at Raine's Hall, Baltimore, Md., on October 20, 1873, and a permanent organization was there formed. This organization has since become a large and powerful body. Its first president was Chief John S. Damrell, of Boston, Mass.; recording secretary, Chief Raymond, of Cambridge, Mass.; corresponding secretary, Chief Hills, of Rome, Ga.; assistant secretaries, Chiefs Hall, of Vicksburg, Miss., Saltzman, of St. Joseph, Md., and Cozzens, of Newport, R. I.; treasurer, Chief Nevins, of Brooklyn, N. Y. Chief Engineer Hill, of Cleveland, O., proposed the following :

Whereas, Experience has shown that the Fire Departments of the country should be provided with a universal or standard coupling for hose and fire hydrants, so that when a city or town calls for aid, in case of large fires or conflagrations from another city or town, that each department can act in unison with the other. Therefore, be it

Resolved, That a committee be appointed by this convention to take under consideration, and report back to this convention, the practicability of adopting a standard coupling of some kind, to be used by all Fire Departments throughout the United States.

From this it will be seen that the object of the organization was to benefit the various departments in the country. Interesting subjects bearing on fire matters were proposed for discussion at the annual convention, and proved to be productive of much good.

The second annual convention was held at St. Louis, Mo., on October 5, 6, 7, and 8, 1874. The members met in the Mercantile Library Hall, and Chief H. Clay Sexton, of St. Louis, was appointed president.

The third annual convention was held at Firemen's Hall, Mercer Street, New York, on October 4, 5, 6, 7, and 8, 1875. Chief Eli Bates, of the New York Fire Department, was unanimously elected president, but Mr. Bates declined the honor, owing to a pressure of business. Chief A. C. Hendrick, of New Haven, Conn., was then unanimously elected president.

The fourth annual convention was held in the City Armory Building, Philadelphia, Pa., on September 4, 5, 6, and 7, 1876. Chief William H. Johnson, of Philadelphia, was elected president.

The fifth annual convention was held in the Senate Chamber of the Capitol Building of Nashville, Tenn., on September 4, 5, and 6, 1877. Chief William Stockwell, of Nashville, was elected president.

The sixth annual convention was held in the Council Chamber, Cleveland, O., on September 10, 11, and 12, 1878. Chief John A. Bennett, of Cleveland, was elected president.

The seventh annual convention was held in the Masonic Temple, in the City of Washington, D. C., on September 9, 10, 11, and 12, 1879. Chief Martin Cronin, of Washington, was elected president.

The eighth annual convention was held in Lancer's Hall, Boston, Mass., on September 14, 15, and 16, 1880. Chief William A. Green, of Boston, was elected president. Mayor Prince welcomed the members of the association to the hospitalities of Boston, and invited them to participate in the celebration of the two hundred and fiftieth anniversary of the settlement of the city. At this convention a committee that had been appointed at the previous meeting in Washington to prepare a constitution and by-laws for a National Relief Association, reported, and a committee of four, consisting of Chiefs Stockwell, of Nashville, Tenn., Hills, of Rome, Ga., Hendrick, of New Haven, Conn., and McCool, of Pottsville, were designated to carry out the suggestions offered. These gentlemen reported that it was more advisable to establish a National Fireman's Life Association, but the report was laid on the table, and the subject dropped.

The ninth annual convention was held in the hall of the House of Delegates at the State Capitol, Richmond, Va., on September 13, 14, and 15, 1881. Chief G. Watt Taylor, of Richmond, was elected president. Mayor Carrington made an address of welcome.

The tenth annual convention was held in Melodeon Hall, Cincinnati, O., on September 12, 13, 14, and 15, 1882. Chief Joseph Bunker, of Cincinnati, was elected president. Mayor Means addressed the convention. One of the features of the session was an interesting address made by Mr. S. F. Covington, president of the Globe Insurance Company, of Cincinnati, who said that the annual destruction of property by fire in the United States was one hundred million dollars, and to replace it would require the surplus production of one hundred thousand men at two dollars per day for twenty years, or that of two million men, which was one-fifth of the male adult population of the country, as shown by the census of 1880, at the same compensation, for one year.

The eleventh annual convention was held in the Washington Artillery Armory, New Orleans, La., on October 24, 25, 26, and 27, 1883. Chief Thomas O'Connor, of New Orleans, was elected president. Mayor Behan extended a hearty welcome to the members.

The twelfth annual convention was held in the Grand Pacific Hotel, Chicago, Ill., on September 9, 10, 11, 12, and 13, 1884. Chief D. J. Swenie, of Chicago, was elected president, and in the unavoidable absence of Mayor Harrison, Comptroller T. J. Gurney made the address of welcome on behalf of the city.

The thirteenth annual convention was held at the Ocean Hotel, Long Branch, N. J., on September 8, 9, 10, 11, and 12, 1885. Chief Thomas L. Worthley, of Long Branch, was elected president. An address of welcome was made by Mr. William H. Bennett, of Long Branch, and, on behalf of the New Jersey State Firemen's Association, Mr. Weeks delivered an address.

The fourteenth annual convention was held at the Masonic Hall, Providence, R. I., on August 24, 25, 26, and 27, 1886. Chief George A. Steere, of Providence, was elected president. The meeting was opened with prayer by the Rev. Augustus Woodbury, and Mayor Gilbert F. Robbins delivered an address. Chief Leshure read an interesting paper on the " Flow of Water through Iron Pipes."

Captain HENRY A. HILLS, secretary of the National Association of Fire Engineers, was born on June 7, 1838, in Boston, Mass. His father was a Boston merchant, at one time a member of the State Legislature, and served in the Fire Department. Young Henry was a real chip of the old block, and began to run with the "machine" when he was only sixteen years old. When eighteen he became a full-fledged firemen, joining Niagara Engine Company No. 3, of Cambridge, his family having removed from Boston in the meantime. Three years after, when the Cambridge chief engineer organized a fire police, Mr. Hills was among the first selected. In 1860 he joined Washington Engine Company No. 9, an independent organization owned by the Lowell Railroad

Company. Within a year the young man was elected a clerk of the company.

In 1863 Mr. Hills was offered an agency of the American Alarm Telegraph owned by John F. Kennard & Co., and represented the company first in Washington and later in Chicago. While in this position he supervised the building of fire alarm telegraphs in some of the most important cities in

this country and Canada. It was in 1868, having left the American Company to go into business with his brother, at Rome, Ga., that Mr. Hills took it upon himself to organize the Citizens' Hook and Ladder Company No. 1, and his public spiritedness in this respect was rewarded with the foremanship of the new company. He soon came to be recognized as one of the best firemen in Rome, and when the election for chief engineer drew near in 1872 his popularity brought his name forward as a candidate for that office. He was elected and held the office honorably for six years, with good results to the city, for, with the exception of a single fire, the fire loss during his terms of office did not exceed ten thousand dollars all told. He was also chosen super-

HENRY A. HILLS.

intendent of the city waterworks. Mr. Hills' reputation as a scientific fire engineer was made. In 1876, Atlanta, Ga., called on him to equip and start a Salvage Corps, as also did Nashville, Tenn. He also gave an estimate, at special request, for equipping a Fire Department for the city of Cairo, Egypt. Mr. Hills held his position as superintendent of waterworks in Rome until 1878. In 1878 Mr. Hills accepted the superintendency of the Dallas, Texas, waterworks, where he remained for some time. While in Dallas he became president of the East Dallas Steam Fire Engine Company No. 2. Mr. Hills' health did not agree with the Southern clime where duty had called him, and he was not slow in accepting, two years ago, a lucrative position as live stock agent of the C. C. C. and I. Railway at Cincinnati, where he still continues. Mr. Hills is still a fireman, however, taking a warm interest in fire matters, and, as secretary of the National Association, contributes his quota of effort in benefiting the fire cause.

INDEX.

VOLUNTEER DEPARTMENT.

PAID DEPARTMENT.